M000026683

UNITED STATES
HISTORY

Modern Times

Daina Ramey Berry, Ph.D.

Albert S. Broussard, Ph.D.

Lorri Glover, Ph.D.

James M. McPherson, Ph.D.

Donald A. Ritchie, Ph.D.

Mc
Graw
Hill

About the Cover

This image shows current United States Supreme Court Justice Sonia Sotomayor (1954–) during her Senate confirmation hearings. Justice Sotomayor is the first Latina justice on the Supreme Court.

This photo shows the Newark Eagles, a team in one of the two segregated professional Negro baseball leagues that operated in the United States between the 1880s and 1958.

A scene from the March on Washington for Jobs and Freedom on August 28, 1963, at the height of the civil rights movement. Lasting from 1954 to 1968, the civil rights movement combated racial discrimination, civic disenfranchisement, and segregation.

The Ford Model T was the first widely affordable automobile in the United States. Its lower cost was made possible by innovations in mass production techniques.

The Silver Star medal is the United States military's third highest decoration for valor in combat. It can be awarded more than once to an individual in the military who display acts of gallantry in battle.

The dome of the United States Capitol building is an unmistakable landmark in Washington, D.C. The Capitol is where the House of Representatives and the Senate convene to make laws for the United States. President Abraham Lincoln oversaw the dome's construction during the Civil War.

Ronald Reagan (1911–2004) was the 40th president of the United States. He was from the state of California and as president he prioritized a strong diplomatic stance against the Soviet Union.

The obverse (front-facing) side of the Great Seal of the United States. This seal, a symbol of authority, is used on all official government documents, such as passports, and was created in 1782.

Cover Credits: (t to b, l to r): Pierre Barlier/Abaca Press/ Alamy Stock Photo; Laura Young/E+/Getty Images; uschools/ E+/ Getty Images; FatCamera/E+/Getty Images; Everett Collection Inc / Alamy Stock Photo; National Archives and Records Administration (NLS-WHPO-A-C584(12); Source: Warren K. Leffler/Library of Congress Prints and Photographs Division [LC-DIG-ppmsca-03128]; Peter Mah/iStockphoto/ Getty Images; Andrew B. Graham/Library of Congress Prints and Photographs Division [LC-USZC4-2108]

mheducation.com/prek-12

Copyright © 2023 McGraw Hill

All rights reserved. No part of this publication may be reproduced or distributed in any form or by any means, or stored in a database or retrieval system, without the prior written consent of McGraw Hill, including, but not limited to, network storage or transmission, or broadcast for distance learning.

Send all inquiries to:
McGraw Hill
8787 Orion Place
Columbus, OH 43240

ISBN: 978-1-26-494955-7
MHID: 1-26-494955-3

Printed in the United States of America.

3 4 5 6 7 8 9 LWI 26 25 24 23 22

Authors

Daina Ramey Berry, Ph.D., is the Oliver H. Radkey Regents Professor and Chair of the History Department at the University of Texas at Austin. She is the author and editor of several books, including *The Price for Their Pound of Flesh*, which won three book awards, and co-author of *A Black Women's History of the United States* which was a finalist for an NAACP Image Award in Literary Non-Fiction. Dr. Berry is an Associate Editor for the *Journal of African American History* and a Distinguished Lecturer for the Organization of American Historians.

Albert S. Broussard, Ph.D., is professor of History at Texas A&M University, where he has taught since 1985. Professor Broussard has published three books, *Expectations of Equality: A History of Black Westerners* (2012); *Black San Francisco: The Struggle for Racial Equality in the West, 1900-1954* (1993); and *African American Odyssey: The Stewarts, 1853-1963* (1998). He is a former president of the Oral History Association and a former chair of the Nominating Committee of the Organization of American Historians. Dr. Broussard was the recipient of a distinguished teaching award from Texas A&M University in 1997 and presented the University Distinguished Faculty Lecture in 2000. In the spring of 2005, he was the Langston Hughes Professor of American Studies at the University of Kansas. Dr. Broussard also served three terms on the board of directors of Humanities Texas and as a consultant to the Texas Education Agency. He is a past president of the Society for Historians of the Gilded Age and Progressive Era.

Lorri Glover, Ph.D., is the Bannon Endowed Chair in the History Department at Saint Louis University. She is the author or editor of ten books, including *Founders as Fathers: The Private Lives and Politics of the American Revolutionaries*; *The Fate of the Revolution: Virginians Debate the Constitution*; and *Eliza Lucas Pinckney: An Independent Woman in the Age of Revolution*. Dr. Glover has served as president of the Southern Association for Women Historians, a Distinguished Lecturer with the Organization of American Historians, and on the Executive Council of the Southern Historical Association.

James M. McPherson, Ph.D., is George Henry Davis Professor Emeritus of American History at Princeton University. Dr. McPherson is the author of 11 books about the Civil War era, including *Tried by War: Abraham Lincoln as Commander in Chief,* for which he won the 2009 Lincoln Prize. Dr. McPherson is a member of many professional historical associations, including the American Battlefield Trust.

Donald A. Ritchie, Ph.D., is Historian Emeritus of the United States Senate. Dr. Ritchie received his doctorate in American history from the University of Maryland after service in the U.S. Marine Corps. He has taught American history at various levels, from high school to university, and is the author of several books, including *The U.S. Congress: A Very Short Introduction*; *Reporting from Washington: A History of the Washington Press Corps*; and *Press Gallery: Congress and the Washington Correspondents,* which received the Organization of American Historians' Richard W. Leopold Prize. Dr. Ritchie has served as president of the Oral History Association and as a council member of the American Historical Association.

Academic Consultants

Davarian Baldwin, Ph.D.
Professor of American Studies
Trinity College
Hartford, Connecticut

Miroslava Chavez-Garcia, Ph.D.
Professor of History
University of California, Santa Barbara
Santa Barbara, California

Mark Cheathem, Ph.D.
Professor of History
Cumberland University
Lebanon, Tennessee

C. Joseph Genetin-Pilawa, Ph.D.
Associate Professor of United States History
George Mason University
Fairfax, Virginia

Michelle Nickerson, Ph.D.
Associate Professor of History
Loyola University
Chicago, Illinois

Jason Smith, Ph.D.
Professor of History
University of New Mexico
Albuquerque, New Mexico

Jon White, Ph.D.
Associate Professor of History
Christopher Newport University
Newport News, Virginia

Amy Wood, Ph.D.
Professor of History
Illinois State University
Normal, Illinois

Program Consultants

Timothy M. Dove, M.A.
Secondary Social Studies Educator
Founding staff member of Phoenix Middle School
Worthington, Ohio

Douglas Fisher, Ph.D.
Professor and Chair of Educational Leadership
San Diego State University
San Diego, California

Linda Keane, M.Ed.
Special Education Resource Teacher
Merrimack Middle School
Merrimack, New Hampshire

Nicole Law, Ph.D.
Professional Learning Author/Consultant
Culturally Responsive and Fortifying Practices
Corwin Professional Learning
Indianapolis, Indiana

Peter Levine, Ph.D.
Lincoln Filene Professor of Citizenship & Public Affairs
Tisch College of Civic Life
Tufts University
Medford, Massachusetts

Emily M. Schell, Ed.D.
Executive Director, California Global Education Project
University of San Diego
San Diego, California

Meena Srinivasan, MA, NBCT
Executive Director, Transformative Educational
  Leadership (TEL)

Table of Contents

Historian's Toolkit

INTRODUCTION LESSON

01 Introducing the Historian's Toolkit   HT2

LEARN THE SKILLS LESSONS

02 What is History?   HT5

03 How Does a Historian Work?   HT9

04 How Does a Historian Interpret History?   HT13

05 History and Related Fields   HT17

06 Geographer's Handbook   HT21

Apply What You Have Learned   HT33

TOPIC 1
Creating a New Nation
PREHISTORY TO 1877

INTRODUCTION LESSON

01 Introducing Creating a New Nation   2

LEARN THE EVENTS LESSONS

02 The American Revolution   7

Primary Source: The Declaration of Independence   13

03 The Constitutional Convention   19

04 The Constitution Handbook   25

The Constitution of the United States   35

INQUIRY ACTIVITY LESSON

05 Analyzing Sources: The Bill of Rights   55

TAKE INFORMED ACTION   60

LEARN THE EVENTS LESSON

06 American Expansion and Growing Tensions   61

INQUIRY ACTIVITY LESSON

07 Analyzing Sources: Reforming Society   67

TAKE INFORMED ACTION   72

LEARN THE EVENTS LESSON

08 The Civil War and Reconstruction   73

INQUIRY ACTIVITY LESSON

09 Turning Point: The Compromise of 1877   79

TAKE INFORMED ACTION   82

REVIEW AND APPLY LESSON

10 Reviewing Creating a New Nation   83

(l)IMBI/Alamy Stock Photo; (r)Everett Collection/Shutterstock

TOPIC 2
Migration, Industry, and Urban Society

`1865–1914`

INTRODUCTION LESSON

01 Introducing Migration, Industry, and Urban Society   88

LEARN THE EVENTS LESSONS

02 Miners, Ranchers, and Farmers Change the West   93

03 Western Pioneers and Native Americans   97

INQUIRY ACTIVITY LESSON

04 Analyzing Sources: Americanizing Native Americans   103

TAKE INFORMED ACTION   108

LEARN THE EVENTS LESSONS

05 Industrialization   109

06 Big Business and Unions   115

07 Immigration   121

INQUIRY ACTIVITY LESSON

08 Understanding Multiple Perspectives on Immigration and Nativism   125

TAKE INFORMED ACTION   130

LEARN THE EVENTS LESSONS

09 Urbanization and Social Reform   131

10 Populism and Racism   137

INQUIRY ACTIVITY LESSON

11 Turning Point: *Plessy* v. *Ferguson*   143

TAKE INFORMED ACTION   146

REVIEW AND APPLY LESSON

12 Reviewing Migration, Industry, and Urban Society   147

TOPIC 3
American Expansion and World War I

`1870–1920`

INTRODUCTION LESSON

01 Introducing American Expansion and World War I   152

LEARN THE EVENTS LESSONS

02 Imperial Tensions   157

03 New Latin American Diplomacy   163

04 The U.S. Enters World War I   167

05 World War I Impacts America   173

INQUIRY ACTIVITY LESSONS

06 Turning Point: Ending World War I   179

TAKE INFORMED ACTION   182

07 Analyzing Sources: The Red Scare   183

TAKE INFORMED ACTION   186

REVIEW AND APPLY LESSON

08 Reviewing American Expansion and World War I   187

(l)Library of Congress, Prints & Photographs Division, Detroit Publishing Company Collection; (r)Library of Congress Prints and Photographs Division [LC-DIG-ppmsca-40036].

TOPIC 4
Progressivism and the Jazz Age

1890–1929

INTRODUCTION LESSON

01 Introducing Progressivism and
the Jazz Age   192

LEARN THE EVENTS LESSON

02 Progressive Era Reforms   197

INQUIRY ACTIVITY LESSON

03 Understanding Multiple
Perspectives of the Progressives   203

    TAKE INFORMED ACTION   206

LEARN THE EVENTS LESSONS

04 A Growing Economy   207

05 African American Culture
and Politics   213

INQUIRY ACTIVITY LESSON

06 Analyzing Sources: The Harlem
Renaissance   217

    TAKE INFORMED ACTION   222

LEARN THE EVENTS LESSON

07 A Clash of Values   223

REVIEW AND APPLY LESSON

08 Reviewing Progressivism and
the Jazz Age   229

TOPIC 5
The Great Depression and the New Deal

1929–1941

INTRODUCTION LESSON

01 Introducing the Great Depression
and the New Deal   234

LEARN THE EVENTS LESSON

02 Hoover's Response to
the Depression   239

INQUIRY ACTIVITY LESSON

03 Turning Point: The Stock Market
and the New Deal   245

    TAKE INFORMED ACTION   248

LEARN THE EVENTS LESSONS

04 Life During the Great Depression   249

05 The First New Deal   253

06 The Second New Deal   259

INQUIRY ACTIVITY LESSON

07 Analyzing Sources: Roosevelt's
Political Critics   265

    TAKE INFORMED ACTION   270

REVIEW AND APPLY LESSON

08 Reviewing the Great Depression
and the New Deal   271

(l)Hulton Archive/Getty Images; (r)National Archive/Hulton Archive/Getty Images.

TOPIC 6
World War II

1933–1945

INTRODUCTION LESSON

01 Introducing World War II   276

LEARN THE EVENTS LESSONS

02 The Origins of World War II   281

03 The Holocaust   287

INQUIRY ACTIVITY LESSON

04 Understanding Multiple Perspectives About American Neutrality   293

     TAKE INFORMED ACTION   298

LEARN THE EVENTS LESSONS

05 The United States Mobilizes for War   299

06 World War II in Europe   305

07 World War II in the Pacific   311

INQUIRY ACTIVITY LESSON

08 Turning Point: The D-Day Invasion   319

     TAKE INFORMED ACTION   322

REVIEW AND APPLY LESSON

09 Reviewing World War II   323

TOPIC 7
Cold War Foreign Policy

1945–1991

INTRODUCTION LESSON

01 Introducing Cold War Foreign Policy   328

LEARN THE EVENTS LESSONS

02 The Early Cold War Years   333

03 Foreign Policy in the 1950s and 1960s   339

INQUIRY ACTIVITY LESSON

04 Analyzing Sources: The Cold War in Space   345

     TAKE INFORMED ACTION   350

LEARN THE EVENTS LESSONS

05 Foreign Policy in the 1970s and 1980s   351

06 Ending the Cold War   355

INQUIRY ACTIVITY LESSON

07 Turning Point: The Soviet Union Collapses   359

     TAKE INFORMED ACTION   362

REVIEW AND APPLY LESSON

08 Reviewing Cold War Foreign Policy   363

(l)Galerie Bilderwelt/Hulton Archive/Getty Images; (r)Thomas Imo/Photothek/Getty Images

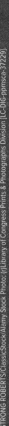

(l)H. ARMSTRONG ROBERTS/ClassicStock/Alamy Stock Photo; (r)Library of Congress Prints & Photographs Division [LC-DIG-ppmsca-37229].

TOPIC 8
Postwar Domestic Issues

1945–1980

INTRODUCTION LESSON

01 Introducing Postwar
Domestic Issues 368

LEARN THE EVENTS LESSONS

02 Cold War Fears at Home 373

03 Truman and Eisenhower 377

04 Postwar American Society 383

INQUIRY ACTIVITY LESSONS

05 Turning Point: The Warren Court 391

    TAKE INFORMED ACTION 394

06 Analyzing Sources:
The Great Society 395

    TAKE INFORMED ACTION 400

REVIEW AND APPLY LESSON

07 Reviewing Postwar Domestic Issues ... 401

TOPIC 9
The Civil Rights Movement

1954–1978

INTRODUCTION LESSON

01 Introducing the Civil Rights
Movement 406

INQUIRY ACTIVITY LESSON

02 Understanding Multiple
Perspectives About Discrimination
and Segregation 411

    TAKE INFORMED ACTION 416

LEARN THE EVENTS LESSONS

03 The Civil Rights Movement Begins ... 417

04 Challenging Segregation 423

INQUIRY ACTIVITY LESSON

05 Analyzing Sources: Civil Rights
Movement Activists 429

    TAKE INFORMED ACTION 434

LEARN THE EVENTS LESSON

06 The Civil Rights Movement
Continues 435

REVIEW AND APPLY LESSON

07 Reviewing the Civil Rights
Movement 441

TOPIC 10
The Vietnam War
1954–1975

INTRODUCTION LESSON

01 Introducing the Vietnam War   446

LEARN THE EVENTS LESSONS

02 American Involvement in
Vietnam Begins   451

03 The Antiwar Movement   457

INQUIRY ACTIVITY LESSON

04 Turning Point: The Pivotal
Year of 1968   463

  TAKE INFORMED ACTION   466

LEARN THE EVENTS LESSON

05 The Vietnam War Ends   467

REVIEW AND APPLY LESSON

06 Reviewing the Vietnam War   473

TOPIC 11
More Civil Rights Voices
1968–PRESENT

INTRODUCTION LESSON

01 Introducing More Civil Rights Voices   478

LEARN THE EVENTS LESSONS

02 The Modern Feminist Movement   483

03 Organizing for Latino Rights   489

04 The Civil Rights Movement Expands   495

INQUIRY ACTIVITY LESSONS

05 Turning Point: The Americans
with Disabilities Act   501

  TAKE INFORMED ACTION   504

06 Analyzing Sources: Building
New Freedom Movements   505

  TAKE INFORMED ACTION   510

REVIEW AND APPLY LESSON

07 Reviewing More Civil Rights Voices   511

(l)SAUER Jean-Claude/Paris Match/Getty Images; (r)Wally McNamee/Corbis Historical/Getty Images

(l)National Archives and Records Administration; (r)US Navy Photo/Alamy Stock Photo.

TOPIC 12

Political Divisions

1970–2000

INTRODUCTION LESSON

01 Introducing Political Divisions — 516

LEARN THE EVENTS LESSON

02 The 1970s and Watergate — 521

INQUIRY ACTIVITY LESSON

03 Analyzing Sources: The Senate Watergate Committee Hearings — 525

TAKE INFORMED ACTION — 530

LEARN THE EVENTS LESSONS

04 The Reagan Revolution — 531

05 The New World Order — 537

INQUIRY ACTIVITY LESSON

06 Turning Point: The Computer Changes Society — 543

TAKE INFORMED ACTION — 546

LEARN THE EVENTS LESSON

07 The Clinton Administration — 547

REVIEW AND APPLY LESSON

08 Reviewing Political Divisions — 553

TOPIC 13

The New Millennium

2000–PRESENT

INTRODUCTION LESSON

01 Introducing the New Millennium — 558

LEARN THE EVENTS LESSONS

02 The Election of 2000 — 563

03 The War on Terrorism — 567

04 Bush's Domestic Challenges — 573

05 The Modern Environmental Debate — 577

06 Obama's Presidency — 581

INQUIRY ACTIVITY LESSON

07 Understanding Multiple Perspectives on Immigration — 589

TAKE INFORMED ACTION — 594

LEARN THE EVENTS LESSON

08 Trump Takes Office — 595

09 Resistance and Protest During the Trump Years — 603

10 The 2020s Begin — 609

INQUIRY ACTIVITY LESSON

11 Analyzing Sources: The 2020 Campaign — 617

TAKE INFORMED ACTION — 622

REVIEW AND APPLY LESSON

12 Reviewing the New Millennium — 623

Reference

Reference Atlas   627

Geographic Dictionary   640

Glossary/Glosario   642

Index   661

Primary and Secondary Sources

TOPIC 1

Chief Justice William Cushing, Massachusetts court ruling, 1783 12

Letter from George Washington to Congress, September 17, 1787 34

Maryland Toleration Act, 1649 56

Thomas Jefferson, letter to James Madison, December 20, 1787 57

Linda R. Monk, "Why We the People? Citizens as Agents of Constitutional Change," *History Now*, Fall 2007 59

The English Bill of Rights, 1689 60

Henry Clay, speech to Congress, January 29, 1850 63

Dorothea Dix, Memorial to the Legislature of Massachusetts, 1843 68

Alexis de Tocqueville, *Democracy in America*, 1832 69

The Doctrines and Discipline of the African Methodist Episcopal Church, 1817 70

Horace Mann, *Reply to the "Remarks" of Thirty-one Boston Schoolmasters on the Seventh Annual Report of the Secretary of the Massachusetts Board of Education*, 1844 71

American Tract Society, "One Glass More," 1826 . . 72

President Abraham Lincoln, The Gettysburg Address, 1863 75

Representative Eppa Hunton, proceedings of the 1877 Electoral Commission, February 26, 1877 . . 81

National Republican, February 12, 1877 81

TOPIC 2

Merrill Gates, Board of Indian Commissioners, 1907 104

National Indian Defense Association, *The Council Fire and Arbitrator*, June 1883 105

Reverend Myron Eells, *Ten Years of Missionary Work Among the Indians of Skokomish, Washington Territory, 1874-1884*, 1886 105

Ely S. Parker, letter to Cousin Gayaneshaoh, c. 1885 106

Dawes General Allotment Act, February 1887 107

Department of the Interior, *The Problem of Indian Administration*, 1928 107

Luana Mangold, oral history transcript, January 19, 1981 108

Justice Oliver Wendell Holmes, *Northern Securities* v. *United States*, 1904 117

Chinese Exclusion Act, May 6, 1882 127

Governor Edward Stevenson, poster, April 27, 1886 127

A. Cahan, *Yekl: A Tale of the New York Ghetto*, 1896 128

Marie Prisland, *From Slovenia to America*, 1968 129

Hilda Satt Polacheck, *I Came a Stranger: The Story of a Hull House Girl* 130

Zalmen Yoffeh, "The Passing of the East Side," *Menorah Journal*, 1929 132

Andrew Carnegie, *The Gospel of Wealth and Other Timely Essays*, 1886 134

Booker T. Washington, *Up From Slavery*, 1901 142

W.E.B. Du Bois, "Address of the Niagara Movement, to the Country," 1906 142

Justice Henry Billings Brown, *Plessy* v. *Ferguson*, May 18, 1896 144

Justice Marshall Harlan, *Plessy* v. *Ferguson*, May 18, 1896 144

W.E.B. Du Bois, *The Souls of Black Folk*, 1903 . . . 145

Mary Church Terrell, "The Progress of Colored Women," 1898 145

National Negro Committee, charter, 1909 146

TOPIC 3

President Theodore Roosevelt, Fourth Annual Message to Congress, December 6, 1904 165

Charles Evans Hughes, *The Official Report of the Proceedings of the Sixteenth Republican National Convention*, June 1916 169

President Woodrow Wilson, *Congressional Record*, 1917 171

American soldier, *The American Spirit*, November 3, 1918 172

Christopher B. Daly, "How Woodrow Wilson's Propaganda Machine Changed American Journalism," April 28, 2017 180

President Woodrow Wilson, The Fourteen Points, January 8, 1918 181

The Covenant of the League of Nations, January 20, 1920 181

"Resolution of Ratification as Voted on by the Senate," *New York Tribune*, March 20, 1920 . . . 182

American Socialist Party, "Long Live the
Constitution of the United States," 1917 184

"3,000 Arrested in Nation-Wide Round-Up of
Reds," *New York Tribune*, January 3, 1920 185

A. Mitchell Palmer, The *Forum*, 1920 186

TOPIC 4

President Theodore Roosevelt, Annual
Message to Congress, 1907 202

Lincoln Steffens, *The Shame of the Cities*,
1904 204

"The Man Who Is Leading the Fight for Pure
Food," *Washington Times*,
November 20, 1901 205

Florence Kelley, *Some Ethical Gains Through
Legislation*, 1905 206

Samuel Strauss, "Things Are in the Saddle,"
Atlantic Monthly, November 1924 210

Alain Locke, *The New Negro*, 1925 218

Nicholas L. Gaffney, *The Journal of African
American History*, Summer 2013 218

Bessie Smith, "Tain't Nobody's Business
If I Do," 1923 219

Langston Hughes, "The Negro Artist and the
Racial Mountain," 1926 220

Claude McKay, "America," *Harlem Shadows:
The Poems of Claude McKay*, 1922 221

W.E.B. Du Bois, "Criteria of Negro Art," 1926 222

Alice Roosevelt, *Crowded Hours*, 1933 223

President Calvin Coolidge, quoted in
the *New York Times*, January 18, 1925 224

TOPIC 5

President Herbert Hoover, speech on
October 22, 1928 241

Franklin Roosevelt, speech at the Democratic
National Convention, July 2, 1932 244

President Franklin Roosevelt, First Inaugural
Address, March 4, 1933 247

California state legislature, "Apology Act
for the 1930s Mexican Repatriation
Program," 2005 250

Harry Hopkins, *Spending to Save: The Complete
Story of Relief*, 1936 257

Ervin E. Lewis, *A Primer of the New Deal*, 1933 . . 258

Bruce Bliven, "Sitting Down in Flint," *New Republic*,
January 27, 1937 261

President Franklin Roosevelt, "Memorandum on
Conference with FDR Concerning Social
Security Taxation," 1941 261

Merlo J. Pusey, *The Supreme
Court Crisis*, 1937 263

President Franklin Roosevelt, Second Inaugural
Address, 1937 263

Herbert Hoover, "The Challenge to Liberty,"
Saturday Evening Post,
September 8, 1934 266

Huey Long, *Congressional Record*,
May 23, 1935 267

Reverend Charles E. Coughlin, *A Series of
Lectures on Social Justice*, November 11, 1934 . . 268

Frank E. Gannett, "Regarding President Franklin
D. Roosevelt's Attempt to Pack the Supreme
Court," February 23, 1937 269

Robert M. La Follette, "In Support of FDR's Court-
Packing Plan," February 13, 1937 269

Henry Gill, No. 3, Federal Writers'
Project, 1938 270

President Herbert Hoover, *The Challenge to
Liberty*, 1934 273

TOPIC 6

President Franklin Roosevelt, "Statement on
Neutrality Legislation," 1937 285

Lend-Lease Act, 1941 286

Frederic Morton, *Facing History and
Ourselves*, 1938 288

Captain Luther D. Fletcher, *World War II: From
the Battle Front to the Home Front*, 1945 291

Elie Wiesel, *Night*, 1960 291

Nye Committee, The Nye Report,
February 24, 1936 294

President Franklin Roosevelt, "Quarantine
speech," October 5, 1937 295

Cordell Hull, communication to the Marquess of
Lothian, September 2, 1940 296

President Franklin Roosevelt, "Four Freedoms
speech," January 6, 1941 296

America First Committee flyer, 1941 297

Evelyn Peyton-Gordon, *Washington Daily
News*, December 12, 1940 297

L.B. Nichols, FBI memorandum on the America First
Committee, December 16, 1940 298

King Victor Emmanuel, to Mussolini,
July 25, 1943 307

Tehran Declaration, December 1, 1943 308

Rose Meier, describing conditions at
Bataan, 1942 311

Robert Sherrod, *Tarawa: The Story of a
Battle*, 1944 315

General Douglas MacArthur, radio broadcast,
October 20, 1944 316

President Harry Truman, "Swearing in of Harry Truman," April 12–13, 1945 316

General Dwight D. Eisenhower, speech to soldiers, June 6, 1944 320

Rep. G.V. Montgomery, Committee on Veterans Affairs, October 24, 1994 321

President Bill Clinton, D-Day National Remembrance Day, June 6, 1994 321

Lt. Col. Thomas D. Morgan (ret.), Army History, Winter 1996 322

President Harry Truman, August 9, 1945 325

William Leahy, I Was There, 1950 325

Robert H. Jackson, during Nuremberg Trials, 1945. . .326

TOPIC 7

Declaration of Liberated Europe, 1945 334

Eleanor Roosevelt, "The Struggle for Human Rights," September 28, 1948 335

President Harry Truman, address to Congress, March 12, 1947 .337

President Harry Truman, address to the Civil Defense Conference, May 7, 1951 340

President Dwight Eisenhower, farewell address, January 1961 343

President Dwight Eisenhower, "Reaction to the Soviet Satellite: A Preliminary Evaluation," October 16, 1957 346

O.M. Gale, Office of the Secretary of Defense memo, April 14, 1958 346

President John F. Kennedy, Address to Joint Session of Congress, May 25, 1961 347

President John F. Kennedy, Address at Rice University, September 12, 1962 347

President John F. Kennedy, transcript, November 21, 1962 348

NASA press release commemorating the moon landing's 50th anniversary, 2019 349

NASA web site, NASA Technologies Benefit Our Lives 350

Mikhail Gorbachev, Address to the Politburo of the Central Committee of the Socialist United Party of Germany, October 7, 1989 360

Ronald Reagan, Remarks at Brandenburg Gate, June 12, 1987 360

Brent Scowcroft, Memorandum for the President, September 5, 1991 361

Boris Yeltsin, Memorandum of Telephone Conversation with George H.W. Bush, December 8, 1991 361

Mikhail Gorbachev, Memorandum of Telephone Conversation with George H.W. Bush, December 25, 1991 362

TOPIC 8

Senator Joseph McCarthy, Wheeling Intelligencer, 1950 375

Joseph Welch, during the Army-McCarthy hearings, 1954 376

President Harry Truman, message to the U.S. House of Representatives, June 20, 1947 378

President Harry Truman, State of the Union address, January 5, 1949 379

President Dwight Eisenhower, speech before the United Nations, December 8, 1953 380

President Jimmy Carter, "Crisis of Confidence" speech, July 15, 1979 390

Justice Hugo Black, Engel v. Vitale ruling, June 25, 1962 392

Justice Earl Warren, Miranda v. Arizona ruling, October 1965 392

Geoffrey R. Stone and David A. Strauss, American Heritage, Winter 2020 393

Joe B. Frantz and Earl Warren, interview transcript, September 21, 1971 394

President Lyndon Johnson, State of the Union Address, January 4, 1965 396

United States Office of Education, federal report, 1966 397

Student Nonviolent Coordinating Committee, report, January 22, 1965 398

President Lyndon Johnson, signing Economic Opportunity Act, August 20, 1964 398

U.S. General Accounting Office, report, 1969 399

President Lyndon Johnson, State of the Union Address, January 14, 1969 400

Senator Joseph McCarthy, telegram to Truman, February 11, 1950 403

President Harry Truman, reply to McCarthy, March 31, 1950 403

TOPIC 9

Lucy Overton, Lower Tidewater in Black and White, 1982 412

Cpl. Rupert Trimmingham, Yank: The Army Weekly, April 28, 1944 413

Charles Gratton, Remembering Jim Crow: African Americans Tell About Their Life in the Segregated South 414

Jackie Robinson, letter to President Eisenhower, May 13, 1958 414

John A. Stokes, interview for Voices of Freedom 415

Negro Motorist Green Book, 1948 416

Dr. Martin Luther King, Jr., quoted in *Parting the Waters: America in the King Years,* 1989 419

President John F. Kennedy, speech on civil rights, June 11, 1963 424

Dr. Martin Luther King, Jr., from the "Address in Washington," August 28, 1963 425

Senator Richard Russell, *Congressional Record,* August 1963 426

Reverend C.T. Vivian, Civil Rights History Project, 2011 430

Ella J. Baker, letter to the Democratic National Committee, July 20, 1964 430

Diane Nash and John Seigenthaler, in *Freedom Riders,* 2011 431

Black Panther Party leaflet, Federal Bureau of Investigation online records 432

Gloria Hayes Richardson and Joseph Mosnier, Southern Oral History Program, Smithsonian Institute's National Museum of African American History & Culture, July 19, 2011 432

Fannie Lou Hamer, interview, 1966 433

Julian Bond, The *Student Voice,* July 5, 1965 434

Stokely Carmichael, "What We Want," *New York Review of Books,* September 1966 437

Ruth Batson, *Voices of Freedom,* 1990 439

TOPIC 10

McGeorge Bundy, *The Best and the Brightest,* 1972 454

Ronald J. Glasser, *Vietnam: A History,* 1997 454

Jerry D. Coffin, "Clergy and Laity Concerned About Vietnam," from FBI Records 458

Tom Hayden, *Port Huron Statement,* 1962 459

Dr. Benjamin Spock, press conference, October 2, 1967 460

Douglas Brinkley, from "The Sage of Black Rock," *American Heritage,* Spring 2012 464

President Lyndon Johnson, televised address, March 31, 1968 465

National Mobilization Committee to End the War in Vietnam, letter, August 1968 466

President Richard Nixon, Address to the Nation on the War in Vietnam, November 3, 1969 467

Jan Barry, "Why Veterans March Against the War," *New York Times,* April 23, 1971 468

Lorrie Accettola, personal narrative, Kent State University Special Collections and Archives .. 468

Doug Johnson, *Touched by the Dragon,* 1998 471

TOPIC 11

Betty Friedan, interview with Voice of America, 1984 484

NOW Statement of Purpose, 1966 484

Gloria Steinem, testimony before a Senate subcommittee in support of the ERA, May 1970 485

Representative Shirley Chisholm, August 10, 1970 486

Phyllis Schlafly, February 1972 487

Ernesto Galarza, *Barrio Boy,* 1971 489

Representative Phillip Burton, speech before Congress, August 25, 1965 491

Hernández v. *Texas* ruling, 1954 492

Marc Grossman, "By Giving Our Lives, We Find Life," from *Stone Soup for the World* 493

American Indian Movement (AIM) testimony before Congress, 1972 496

Judith Heumann, statement before Congress, September 27, 1988 502

President George H.W. Bush, statement on signing the ADA, July 26, 1990 503

"ADA Fact Sheet," July 26, 1990 504

Andrew L. Aoki and Don T. Nakanishi, in *PS: Political Science and Politics,* September 2001 506

bell hooks, *Ain't I a Woman: Black Women and Feminism,* 1981 506

Robert Kennedy, speech supporting farmworkers, March 10, 1968 507

The White House, "Establishing a National Commission on the Observance of International Women's Year," January 9, 1975 508

Troy Johnson, *The Occupation of Alcatraz Island: Indian Self-Determination and the Rise of Indian Activism* 509

Gwenn Craig, testimony before the Subcommittee on Employment Opportunities of the Committee on Education and Labor, October 10, 1980 510

TOPIC 12

Chief Justice Warren Burger, *United States* v. *Nixon,* 1974 524

George H.W. Bush, diary entry, August 9, 1974 524

"The Watergate Committee," U.S. Senate Select Committee on Presidential Campaign Activities 526

"Gavel-to-Gavel: The Watergate Scandal and Public Television," American Archive of Public Broadcasting website 526

Senator Daniel Inouye, opening statement, May 17, 1973...............................527

President Richard Nixon, letter to Senator Sam Ervin, Jr., July 1973.........................527

Rufus Edmisten, interview transcript, September 8, 2011....................................528

Carl Feldbaum, Justice Department memo to Leon Jaworski, August 9, 1974 528

"Gavel-to-Gavel: The Watergate Scandal and Public Television," American Archive of Public Broadcasting website 529

Senate Select Committee on Presidential Campaign Activities, final report, June 1974.................................530

Midge Decter, "Looting and Liberal Racism," *Commentary,* September 1977 531

President Bill Clinton, from an address at Vietnam National University, November 17, 2000 541

National Research Council, *Funding a Revolution: Government Support for Computing Research,* 1999 544

Eric Jaffe, "How the Computer Revolution Changed U.S. Cities," *Bloomberg,* December 28, 2015.........................545

S.V. Ravichandran, "Mobile phones and teenagers: Impact, consequences, and concerns—parents/caregivers perspectives," Unitec Institute of Technology, 2009.........546

President Bill Clinton, "Remarks on Signing the National and Community Service Trust Act of 1993," September 21, 1993..................549

Representative Newt Gingrich, Contract with America, 1994 551

President Bill Clinton, commencement address at Carleton College, June 10, 2000 552

TOPIC 13

Justice John Paul Stevens, *Bush* v. *Gore,* December 12, 2000.......................566

President George W. Bush, Address to Joint Session of Congress, September 20, 2001 ... 568

President George W. Bush, press conference, November 4, 2004 574

Representative Nancy Pelosi, speech to the House of Representatives, January 4, 2007 ...576

Lois Gibbs, *Love Canal: The Story Grows . . .,* 1998 579

President Barack Obama, Address at Grant Park, November 4, 2008 582

U.S. Citizenship and Immigration Services, DACA Guidelines, 2012....................... 591

Obama Administration, "Taking Action on Immigration," November 20, 2014 591

Pia Orrenius, George W. Bush Institute, Spring 2016...............................592

Commissioner on U.S. Customs and Border Protection Mark Morgan, June 23, 2020......593

Attorney General Jeff Sessions, to Acting Secretary Duke, September 4, 2017..........594

President Donald Trump, Inaugural Address, January 20, 2017 596

Hillary Clinton, discussing the 2016 election.... 604

President Donald Trump, describing protests in Charlottesville, Virginia....................607

President Donald Trump, January 6, 2021 Rally 614

Senator Mitch McConnell, speaking about President Trump............................ 615

President Joe Biden, Inaugural Address, January 20, 2021............................ 615

President Joe Biden, Inaugural Address, January 20, 2021............................ 616

Pew Research Center, Important Issues in the 2020 Election, August 13, 2020 618

Representative Lauren Underwood, *Congressional Record,* June 25, 2020 619

The White House, "President Trump: We Have Rejected Globalism and Embraced Patriotism," August 7, 2020............................ 619

Senator Charles Schumer, *Congressional Record,* September 29, 2020 620

Senator John Cornyn, *Congressional Record,* October 24, 2020 620

President-elect Joe Biden, acceptance speech, November 7, 2020......................... 622

Senator Charles Schumer, defending the USA PATRIOT Act..............................625

Senator Russ Feingold, criticizing the USA PATRIOT Act..............................625

Biographies

Juan José Herrera (c. 1840s–1902?) 95

Mary Fields (c. 1832–1914) 98

Madam C.J. Walker (1867–1919) 116

Jane Addams (1860–1935) 136

Ida B. Wells (1862–1931) 141

Queen Liliuokalani (1838–1917) 159

Alvin York (1887–1964) 171

Ernest Hemingway (1899–1961) 211

Aaron Douglas (1899–1979) 215

Eleanor Roosevelt (1884–1962) 243

1st Filipino Regiment (1942–1946) 312

Henry Kissinger (1923–) 352

Mikhail Gorbachev (1931–) 356

Esther Brunauer (1901–1959) 375

Emmett Till (1941–1955) .420

James Farmer (1920–1999) 425

Ho Chi Minh (1890–1969) 453

Gloria Jean Watkins (1952–2021) 485

César Chávez (1927–1993) & Dolores Huerta
    (1930–) 493

Greta Thunberg (2003–) 580

Analyzing Supreme Court Cases

Dred Scott v. Sandford, 1857 64

Plessy v. Ferguson, 1896 143

Korematsu v. United States, 1944 304

Engel v. Vitale, 1962 392

Miranda v. Arizona, 1965 .392

Brown v. Board of Education, 1954 418

Heart of Atlanta Motel, Inc. v.
    United States, 1964 436

Tinker v. Des Moines, 1969 459

New York Times v. United States, 1971 469

Loving v. Virginia, 1967 497

Kelo v. City of New London, 2005 575

Maps

TOPIC 1

European Exploration 5

Northwest Ordinance of 1787. 20

Overland Trails West, 1840–1860 62

Seceding States, 1860–1861. 66

The Disputed Election of 1876 80

Growth of the United States to 1853. 86

TOPIC 2

Railroads and Universities. 91

Mining Helps Build a Nation, 1848–1890 94

Native American Battles and Reservations,
    1860–1890 101

Natural Resource Sites of the United States 110

Federal Land Grants to Railroads 113

Strikes and Labor Unrest, 1870–1900. 120

Immigration Settlement Patterns, Late 1800s 124

TOPIC 3

Major Imperial Powers, 1900 155

The Roosevelt Corollary and Dollar
    Diplomacy, 1903–1934 164

The War in the Trenches 170

TOPIC 4

U.S. Industrialization. 195

Woman Suffrage, 1869–1920 199

The Great Migration, 1917–1930. 214

TOPIC 5

Fleeing the Effects of the Dust Bowl. 237

The TVA, 1940. 256

TOPIC 6

Global Scale of World War II. 279

The Voyage of the SS *St. Louis*,
    May 13–June 17, 1939 289

The Holocaust, 1939–1945. 290

The War in Europe, 1942–1945. 306

The Battle of Midway. 314

Island Hopping in the Pacific, 1942–1945 315

D-Day 324

TOPIC 7

Global Cold War, 1947–1989. 331

The Division of Germany, 1945. 334

The Iron Curtain in Europe, 1948 336

The Cuban Missile Crisis, October 1962 344

TOPIC 8

The Interstate Highway System 371

The Presidential Election, 1960 385

TOPIC 9

Segregation in the United States, Mid-Twentieth
    Century 409

Percentage Change of Southern African
    Americans Registered to Vote. 428

TOPIC 10

Why did Vietnam matter to the United States? 449

The Ho Chi Minh Trail. 456

The Election of 1968. 462

TOPIC 11

Estimated Unauthorized Resident Population,
    2000. 481

ERA Ratification, 1972–1982 486

TOPIC 12

The Rise of the Sunbelt, 1950–1980. 519

The Persian Gulf War, 1991 538

World Trading Blocs. 541

TOPIC 13

COVID-19 in the United States, 2020 561

Presidential Election, 2000. 565

Presidential Election of 2016 604

U.S. Early Voting Options 618

2020 Presidential Election Results 621

REFERENCE ATLAS

United States Political 628

United States Physical 630

Middle America Physical/Political 632

Canada Physical/Political 634

Middle East Physical/Political. 636

World Political 638

Charts and Graphs

TOPIC 1

Townshend Acts, 1767 8

The Revolutionary War 11

Checks and Balances. 26

How a Bill Becomes a Law 28

The Federal Court System 30

Resources of the Union and the Confederacy 73

Casualties of the Civil War 76

TOPIC 2

Immigration to the United States, 1865–1914 121

Immigration to the United States, 1890–1910 122

Factors in Western Migration and Change 147

Geographical Distribution of Population in
    the United States, 1870–1890 149

Native American Population, 1870–1890 149

Vertical Integration and Horizontal Integration. . . . 150

TOPIC 3

Paying for World War I 174

American Imperialism 187

The War's Impact 188

TOPIC 4

A Growing Economy. 230

Clashing Values. 230

TOPIC 5

Cyclical Effect 236

Stock Prices, 1920–1932 246

Number of Bank Failures, 1920–1938. 247

Social Welfare Expenditures Under Public
    Programs, 1929–1940 248

Hoover's Response to the Depression. 271

TOPIC 6

U.S. Armed Forces, 1939-1946. 300

Mobilizing Industry. 302

Time Line of the Events Leading up to
    World War II. 323

The Industry and Troops of World War II 326

TOPIC 7

Marshall Plan Aid, 1948–1951 337

TOPIC 8

The Birthrate, 1940–1970 382

Inflation and Unemployment Rates. 390

Aspects of the 1950s Second Red Scare. 401

The Other America. 402

Number of People Age 65 and Older. 404

TOPIC 9

Challenging Segregation 441

African American Voter Registration in Selected
    Southern States, 1964 and 1967 442

African American Poverty Rates and
    Education Status 442

TOPIC 10

Number of U.S. Military Advisors in Vietnam. 452

Opposition to the Vietnam War 460

The U.S. Military Presence in Vietnam 470

Refugees Arriving in the United States
    of America by Year, 1975–1989. 472

Going to War in Vietnam 473

TOPIC 11

Women in the Workplace 488

Growth of Latino Population in the
    United States 490

The Feminist Movement 511

TOPIC 12

The Budget Deficit 535

The Watergate Scandal. 553

TOPIC 13

Hate Crimes Against Muslims, 1996–2014. 569

Home Foreclosures 583

Confirmed COVID-19 Cases in the United
    States, 2020–2021. 610

Focusing on Afghanistan and Iraq. 623

Topic Activities

Making Connections to Today

Analyze Points of View 86
Create a Chart 150
Creating a Comparison Chart 190
Compare and Contrast Issues Over Time 232
Create a Venn Diagram 274
Analyze a Current Event 325
Write a News Story 366
Interpreting Statistical Data 404
Podcast Presentation 444
Write a Biographical Summary 476
Write an Architectural Analysis 514
Conduct an Interview 556
Evaluate Web Sources 626

Understanding Multiple Perspectives

Debate Your Points 85
Compare Chart Data 149
Comparing Political Cartoons 189
Make a Game 231
Draw a Conclusion 273
Write an Editorial 325
Draw Conclusions 365
Connecting Historical Events 403
Write an Informative/Explanatory Essay 443
Compare and Contrast Points of View 475
Complete a Table 513
Draw Political Cartoons 555
Write an Editorial 625

Analyzing Change

Write a Monologue 232

Analyzing Graphs

Interpret Historical Data 475

Analyzing Primary Sources

Interpreting an Advertisement 403

Building Citizenship

Create a Venn Diagram 85
Present a Biography 149
Creating a Public Announcement 190
Establish International Principles 326
Write an Informative Essay 513

Geographic Reasoning

Write to Compare 86
Write an Environmental Study 274
Compare Maps 366
Draw an Environmental Map 476
Label a Map 556

Making Connections to Art

Create a Playlist 231
Describing a Mural 273
Create Protest Art 514

Making Connections to Economics

Make a Prediction 150
Compare Data 625

Making Connections to Music

Interpreting Music 404
Evaluate Evidence 443

Making Connections to Science

Create a Blueprint 85
Sketch an Invention 365
Create a Graph 555
Write a Scientific Summary 626

Understanding Chronology

Creating an Annotated Time Line 189
Create a Group Time Line 443

Understanding Data

Explain Visual Information 326

Scavenger Hunt

United States History Modern Times contains a wealth of useful information throughout the program. This scavenger hunt exercise will help you know where to look to access all of this information.

ACTIVITY Complete these questions with your teacher or with your parents. You will grow familiar with how the textbook is organized and how to get the most out of your reading and study time. Let's get started!

1. How many lessons are in Topic 4?

2. Which lesson type provided gives you an overview of the content found in each Topic?

3. Where can you find the Compelling Questions for the Inquiry Lessons?

4. How do you know which words are vocabulary terms?

5. Where do you find the graphic organizers in your textbook?

6. You want to quickly find a map in the book about the Tennessee Valley Authority. Where do you look?

7. Where would you find an explanation for the meaning of the terms *latitude* and *longitude*?

8. If you need to know the Spanish term for *gross domestic product*, where would you look?

9. Where can you find a list of all the maps in a Topic?

10. Where are two places that you can look to find information on Mary Fields?

1960

96%

Library of Congress, Prints and Photographs Division [LC-USZ62-100382].

Historian's Toolkit

By studying history in places such as classrooms, libraries, and museums, we can learn what was important to people from an earlier time.

INTRODUCTION LESSON

01	Introducing the Historian's Toolkit	HT2

LEARN THE SKILLS LESSONS

02	What is History?	HT5
03	How Does a Historian Work?	HT9
04	How Does a Historian Interpret History?	HT13
05	History and Related Fields	HT17
06	Geographer's Handbook	HT21
	Apply What You Have Learned	HT33

Nick Brundle Photography/Moment/Getty Images

Introducing the Historian's Toolkit

Perspectives on History

❝ One cannot and must not try to erase the past merely because it does not fit the present . . .❞

— Golda Meir; Israeli Prime Minister, 1969–1974

❝ We do not just risk repeating history if we sweep it under the carpet, we also risk being myopic [shortsighted] about our present.❞

— Chimamanda Ngozi Adichie, Nigerian author

❝ Study the past if you would define the future.❞

— Confucius; Chinese philosopher, political theorist

❝ History is not just the relation of events. History is also the search for what remains after the passage of events.❞

— Jorge Basadre, Peruvian historian

PHOTO: (tl)U.S. News & World Report Magazine Photograph Collection, Library of Congress, LC-DIG-ppmsc-03265; (cr)ev radin/Alamy Stock Photo; (bl)Historica Graphica Collection/Heritage Images/Hulton Archive/Getty Images; (bc)Zuri Swimmer/Alamy Stock Photo; TEXT: (tr)Meir, Golda. My Life. New York: G.P. Putnam's Sons, 1975; (cr)Adichie, Chimamanda Ngozi. In Adewale-Gabril, Toyin. "In the Footsteps of Chinua Achebe." Interview by Ike Anya. Sentinel Poetry - Online Magazine Monthly, Issue # 12 (November 2003). ISSN 1479-425X. http://www.sentinelpoetry.org.uk/magazine1103/page14.html; (c)Confucius. Quoted by Zhang Haihua and Geoff Baker. Think Like Chinese. Sydney: The Federation Press, 2008; (br)Basadre, Jorge. "Jorge Basadre's 'Peruvian History of Peru,' Or the Poetic Aporia of Historicism." Hispanic American Historical Review 88, no. 2 (May 2008), 247-283. https://doi.org/10.1215/00182168-2007-120.

" . . . [H]istory has shown us that courage can be contagious, and hope can take on a life of its own. "

— Michelle Obama; Lawyer, writer, first African American First Lady of the United States

" If understanding is impossible, knowing is imperative [necessary], because what happened could happen again . . .
For this reason, it is everyone's duty to reflect on what happened. "

— Primo Levi; Italian-Jewish author, Holocaust survivor

" Still, I am convinced that, in good times or bad, critical [serious] ones, transitional [changing] ones, or normal ones, history can help human beings think better, live more richly, and act more wisely. "

— Joyce Appleby, American historian

" We are not merely passive pawns of historical forces; nor are we victims of the past. We can shape and direct history. "

— Daisaku Ikeda;
Japanese author,
Buddhist philosopher,
educator

" . . . [I]deas, cultures, and histories cannot seriously be understood or studied without their force, or more precisely their configurations [arrangements] of power, also being studied. "

— Edward Said; American professor, political activist, literary critic

PHOTO: (tl)Chip Somodevilla/Getty Images News/Getty Images; (crl)Agence Opale/Alamy Stock Photo; (cl)courtesy of Joyce Appleby; (br)Leonardo Cendamo/Hulton Archive/Getty Images; TEXT: (tr)Obama, Michelle. "Remarks by The First Lady During Keynote Address at Young African Women Leaders Forum." Speech. Regina Mundi Church, Soweto, South Africa, June 22, 2011. Washington, D.C.: The White House - Office of the First Lady; (c)Levi, Primo. "Auschwitz and Survival." In The Voice of Memory: Interviews 1961-1987. Edited by Marco Belpoliti and Robert Gordon. Translated by Robert Gordon. New York: The New Press, 2001; (cl)Ikeda, Daisaku. "'People's Diplomacy': A Power to Resist the Currents of History." The Japan Times (Tokyo), May 11, 2006. https://www.japantimes.co.jp/opinion/2006/05/11/commentary/world-commentary/a-power-to-resist-the-currents-of-history/; (cr)Appleby, Joyce. "The Power of History." The American Historical Review 103, no. 1 (1998): 1-14. Accessed January 26, 2021. doi:10.2307/2650771; (b)Said, Edward W. Orientalism. New York: Random House, Inc., 1979.

Looking Ahead

Throughout the next lessons, you will learn about the nature of history, historical thinking skills, and the processes that historians use to carefully examine the past. You will also learn how other fields of study, such as civics and geography, connect to historical inquiry.

Later in the course, you will examine Compelling Questions in the Inquiry Lessons and develop your own questions about the history of the United States. Review the time line to preview some of the key events that you will learn about as you explore American history.

What Will You Learn

In these lessons that provide an overview of the process of studying history, you will learn:

- the goals historians have for studying the past.
- how history is commonly organized into eras and other time periods.
- the ways that historians examine past events.
- how history connects to other fields of study.
- how to interpret historical and geographic representations such as time lines and maps.

UNITED STATES HISTORICAL ERAS

900

C. 950–1350 Cahokia civilization flourishes

1492 Christopher Columbus reaches the Americas

1607 The English settle Jamestown, Virginia

1619 Enslaved Africans are brought to Virginia by European traders

1776

JULY 4, 1776 Declaration of Independence signed

SEPTEMBER 1787 The U.S. Constitution is drafted

APRIL 12, 1861 Fort Sumter is attacked (right)

JANUARY 1, 1863 Emancipation Proclamation goes into effect

1889 Oklahoma Land Rush

1900

AUGUST 18, 1920 Nineteenth Amendment gives women voting rights

1940 First Social Security checks mailed

DECEMBER 7, 1941 Japan attacks Pearl Harbor

AUGUST 1945 United States uses atomic bombs on Japan; World War II ends

JULY 1964 The Civil Rights Act of 1964 passes

1987 INF Treaty signed between United States and Soviet Union

SEPTEMBER 11, 2001 Terrorists attack the United States

2020

Sequencing Time Based on this time line, about how many years of history can you expect to study throughout the course? How can you tell?

National Park Service.

What Is History?

National Park Service.

READING STRATEGY

Understanding Craft and Structure Each section of text deals with an aspect of history. Use the chart below to record details about the study of history—what it is, who does it, why, and how.

History	
What?	
Who?	
Why?	
How?	

Why Study History?

GUIDING QUESTION

What types of things can history reveal about the past?

People study history to gain a clearer understanding of human society. We examine past events to see how decisions are made and how solutions to problems are considered. History explores the way that society and nations change or why they stay the same. History tells the story of the ways that cultures develop over time. Learning about the past helps us understand the present. Why is a war being fought in a certain area? Why does one country separate into two? Why do people migrate, or move, from one place to another? Understanding the events that people experienced in the past can help us make sense of the current events that take place today. Understanding history can aid our ability to predict what might happen in the future. This ability can enable us to make better decisions about today and tomorrow.

Think about the choices you and your household make in your daily life. What goods does your household buy? What places do you want to visit? What groups, activities, or causes do you support or are you involved in? What type of future are you working toward? To answer these questions, you consider what you already know about your options. Maybe you research to find out more about a place, an organization, or a job. You take what you know, learn more, and then make an informed decision.

People use a similar process to connect their knowledge about history to the political, economic, and social issues of their world. A better understanding of the past enables citizens to make more informed decisions about issues, policies, and elections in the modern world. Suppose that people did not know that early American revolutionaries had fought for independence and the right

These people are learning about history from a park ranger at a Grand Canyon archaeological site. Such talks are opportunities to study history in more ways than reading books.

Historian Barbara Bair looks at presidential campaign documents housed in the Library of Congress. Access to these types of materials provides important avenues into understanding the past.

to form their own government—one in which they could participate. Knowledge of the past helps citizens make sense of the present and protect basic rights.

History, or the record of past people and events, offers insight into how people have lived, how complex societies have formed and collapsed, and the reasons why human cooperation and conflict have occurred throughout the past. History helps us understand why our community, nation, and world are the way they are. The more people know about the past, the better they can understand the present and make informed decisions.

Who Studies History?

Those who study the people and events of the past are called historians. Historians are like detectives of the past; they study how events are connected. They use clues to find the reasons that something happened. Historians also look for the effects, or results, of an event. They ask questions, such as "What happened?" and "Why did it happen?" They inquire, "How did things change?" and "How has it influenced today?" They consider, "How are these events related?" Sometimes they wonder, "What might have happened if . . . ?"

Historians start out as students with an interest in the past. They spend years building up their knowledge to gain a broad understanding of history through formal studies through undergraduate and graduate studies in college. They read secondary sources, which are other historians' interpretations of past events. They also read, and often translate, primary sources—documents written by people who experienced or observed the events while they occurred. Other primary sources include artifacts and artwork created by people in the past. Historians study

and interpret a wide variety of materials and look for connections. These may involve oral histories or interviews of participants who experience significant events in history. Historians make comparisons and trace connections between events and people. They learn how to understand contrasting points of view. They can identify causes and effects, sequences, as well as patterns of behavior and decisions that help explain human choices. Historians synthesize information from these many sources to form their own conclusions and generate their own explanations about past events, conditions, and peoples.

To formulate credible conclusions, historians take care to use reliable sources from varying perspectives. A primary source document tends to offer only one point of view. A history told from one point of view is incomplete. That is why historians study, interpret, and combine information from multiple sources to present a fuller historical account. Historians have biases based on personal experiences and the times in which they live, but they must strive for objectivity as much as possible in their work.

Historians study the recent past as well as the distant past. Training may begin with a broad study of history, but no one person can examine all the historical information in existence. So, historians also specialize in, or focus on, one period, topic, or region. For example, one scholar might specialize in U.S. history while others might focus on the history of China, women's history, religion, ancient civilization, or modern times. Scholars in these areas likely have even more specific fields of research, such as the U.S. Civil War, Islamic empires in the Middle Ages, apartheid in South Africa, or the social impacts of the Industrial Revolution. Studying history helps us understand how we fit into the human story. Some clues to our place in that story are the languages we speak, the technologies we use, and the pastimes we enjoy. These result from events that happened in the past. Studying history also helps us develop the knowledge and skills we need to participate in public life as informed citizens. It helps us understand that certain events brought us to the present, and the choices we and others make today will shape the future.

Time and Place

Historians look at people and events of history in the setting of time and space. To better understand the past, historians often work with specialists in other fields of study. For example, history is typically studied alongside geography, a practice that better reveals spatial relationships essential to understanding the dynamics of political relationships. Historians also develop a number of skills to research, organize, and

Chris Maddaloni/CQ Roll Call/Getty Images.

write about history. You will learn about these skills and practice them throughout your study of United States history. Let's start with time.

✓ CHECK FOR UNDERSTANDING

Identifying What questions does history help people answer?

Measuring and Organizing Time

GUIDING QUESTION

What tools do we use when measuring time?

To study the past, historians must have a way to identify and describe when events happened. They do that by measuring and labeling time in different ways.

Periods of History

Historians divide history into blocks of time known as **eras**, or periods. A period of 10 years, for example, is called a decade, while a period of 100 years is known as a century. Centuries are grouped into even longer time periods, which are given unique names to represent that specific period.

To be a historical era, a period of time has to have a common set of major characteristics, typically based on a combination of the politics, economics, technology, and social and cultural issues of that time. Some of the things common in one era might continue to the next era, but usually several major events occur, leading historians to identify it as a new era.

For example, the decades since the end of World War II have been a time of great change, and historians disagree over how best to divide it. Many historians see 1945 to 1991 as one historical era, because 1945 marks the start of the Cold War and 1991 marks the end of the Cold War. Others focus on events within the United States. Still other historians like to divide the post-war era into decades, "the 50s," "the 60s," "the 70s," because of the dramatic cultural changes that took place during each decade. Other historians prefer to divide the post-war years into eras based on major political, economic, or technological changes. Whatever method is used, historians understand a time period by focusing on the major characteristics that differentiate it from other times in history.

Because the history of the United States is so short, the historical eras people use tend to be only a few decades long at most. Historians focus on the major characteristics that make one period of time different from other times in history.

Calendars

A calendar is a system for breaking time into units. It allows us to measure how much time has passed between events. Cultures have developed different calendars based on important events in their history. Some cultures developed calendars based on the cycle of the moon. The Chinese and Jewish calendars, for example, base their months on the appearance of the new moon. The most commonly used "Western" calendar was originally Christian; it begins with the year in which Jesus was thought to have been born. The Jewish calendar begins about 3,760 years before the Western calendar, at the time when Jewish tradition says the world was created. Muslims date their calendar from the time at which their prophet, Muhammad, left the city of Makkah for Madinah. This was year 622 C.E. in the Western calendar.

Dating Events

The dates in this book are based on the Western calendar, which uses a year of 365 days. The years before the birth of Jesus are known as B.C.E. ("before common era"). The years after are called C.E. ("common era"). To date events that took place before the birth of Jesus, or B.C.E., historians count backwards from 1 C.E. There is no year "0." The year before 1 C.E. is 1 B.C.E. To date events after B.C.E., historians count forward. The year after 1 C.E. is 2 C.E.

This Aztec sun stone helped this civilization measure time more accurately. Artifacts such as this help historians and archaeologists understand civilizations that no longer exist as they once did.

Shutterstock/buteo.

era time period

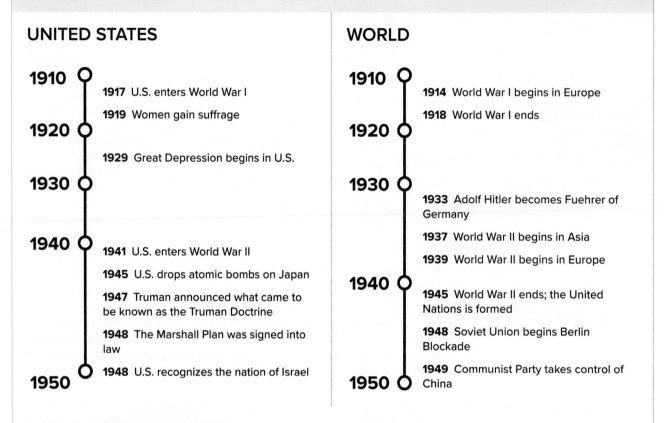

Key Events in U.S. and World History, 1910–1950

Time lines can show events related to one or more categories, such as regions or societies, that took place during the same time period. Pay close attention to titles and labels to fully understand what information a time line presents.

UNITED STATES

1910
1917 U.S. enters World War I
1919 Women gain suffrage

1920
1929 Great Depression begins in U.S.

1930

1940
1941 U.S. enters World War II
1945 U.S. drops atomic bombs on Japan
1947 Truman announced what came to be known as the Truman Doctrine
1948 The Marshall Plan was signed into law
1948 U.S. recognizes the nation of Israel

1950

WORLD

1910
1914 World War I begins in Europe
1918 World War I ends

1920

1930
1933 Adolf Hitler becomes Fuehrer of Germany
1937 World War II begins in Asia
1939 World War II begins in Europe

1940
1945 World War II ends; the United Nations is formed
1948 Soviet Union begins Berlin Blockade
1949 Communist Party takes control of China

1950

1. **Understanding Chronology** How much time passed between the first and last events on each time line?

2. **Sequencing** What event in Europe preceded the start of World War II?

Using Time Lines

In studying the past, historians focus on **chronology,** or the order of dates in which events happened. An easy way to make sense of the flow of dates and events is to use or make a **time line**—a diagram that shows the order of events within a period of time. Time lines also show the length of time between events. Most time lines are divided into regular segments of time, with events placed on the time line at the date when the event occurred. A horizontal time line is read from left to right. Vertical time lines are read from top to bottom.

Usually, the dates on a time line are evenly spaced. Sometimes, however, a time line covers events that occur over too many years to show on one page. In this case, a slanted or jagged line might be placed on the time line to show that a certain period is omitted from the time line. A time line can be a single line, or it can be two or more lines stacked on top of each other, called multilevel time lines.

✓ **CHECK FOR UNDERSTANDING**

1. **Determining Central Ideas** Why do historians organize history into eras?

2. **Explaining** Why does knowing the calendar and dating system used for this text matter?

LESSON ACTIVITIES

1. **Explanatory Writing** Why do people study history? Write a short letter to a friend in which you explain the importance of learning about past people and events to their present lives.

2. **Using Multimedia** Think about an event, era, or group of people you would like to learn about. Locate five different kinds of sources from different perspectives that tell you about that subject. Prepare a slideshow in which you identify the significance as well as assess the reliability of each source.

---

chronology order of dates in which events happened

time line diagram that shows the order of events within a period of time

03

How Does a Historian Work?

READING STRATEGY

Analyzing Key Ideas and Details Read the descriptions of the professional practices of historians. Use a graphic organizer like the one below to record how and why a historian works.

Practices of Historians	Reasons for Practice

Asking Questions

GUIDING QUESTION
Why is it important to distinguish fact from historical writing?

Compelling Questions

Historians use many of the same skills as detectives. They ask questions about the information they find from the past. For example, they might ask:

- Why did a disagreement lead to war and what was the effect?
- How did events of the past change people's lives?

Such questions help us focus on historical problems. Inquiry is an important step in any investigation. By asking questions, historians can better identify key issues. They can also determine how and why events happened and the effects of events. Compelling questions are posed at the beginning of sections throughout this text to help you better understand the past.

Changing Interpretations

How people view history changes over time. Sometimes an event happens in the present that reveals that a past event is significant enough to be studied. Historical interpretations change as more information becomes available. For example, a country that previously kept information from the public may open its archives.

Another reason interpretations change over time is because historians emphasize different types of evidence. Some historians may focus on political leaders and their evidence to interpret the past. Others may emphasize how the rules and structures of a society shape the choices and decisions people have. Or historians may put their emphasis on understanding how the ideas and culture of a society best describes their time of history.

How Is It Relevant?

Historians evaluate a lot of information to find what they need and whether each piece of evidence is relevant. This means selecting the data that helps answer their research questions and filtering out all of the other evidence and setting it aside.

For example, if you want to learn more about family life in colonial America, you should spend your research and evaluation time focusing on information about marriage and the number of children in families. This type of information is relevant to the question that you are trying to answer. A description of the procedures and actions of colonial government would not be as relevant. That is because that type of research on government does not explain the types of families who lived during the period.

✓ **CHECK FOR UNDERSTANDING**

1. **Analyzing** How are historians similar to detectives?
2. **Explaining** Why do historians need to evaluate the relevance of evidence?

Examining the Evidence

GUIDING QUESTION

What types of evidence do historians use to understand the past?

One important question a historian must ask: "Is there supporting evidence?" Another important task of the historian is to determine whether information in a source is verifiable. This means the historian must check if the information can be proven by other evidence. Evidence is something that shows proof or an indication that something is true. Evidence could be in the form of material objects, such as a soldier's uniform or artifacts from an archaeological dig.

Other evidence may appear in documents or written materials that were created during a historical event. Historians use the evidence in historical sources to interpret what happened in the past.

Primary and Secondary Sources

Historians look for clues about the past in primary and secondary sources. **Primary sources** are first-hand pieces of evidence from people who saw or experienced the events described. Primary sources include written documents, such as letters, diaries, and official records. Literature or artwork from a particular time and place is a primary source. Spoken interviews and objects such as photos, tools, and clothing are also primary sources.

Secondary sources are created after the event. They are created by people who were not part of the historical event. The information in secondary sources is partially based on primary sources.

Some common examples of secondary sources that you have likely used include biographies that describe people's lives, history books that provide overviews of events, and other textbooks. Historians study secondary sources for background information and for a broader understanding of an event. A historian must use primary sources, however, to find new evidence about a subject.

Analyzing Sources

Like a historian, when you read primary or secondary sources, you should ask yourself these questions.

1. Who created the source?
2. Why was the source created—what was its purpose and for whom was it written?
3. What is the source about?
4. When was the source created?
5. How was the source created?
6. Is the source a primary or secondary source?

Once historians identify this basic information, they evaluate the sources to determine if they are credible, or truthful. This is because each source reflects a point of view.

Comparing Types of Sources

A historian uses a variety of source material to create the most complete picture possible of the past society or time period being studied.

TYPES OF PRIMARY SOURCES
Printed publications include newspapers, magazines, and books. Web sites and e-mails are considered printed publications even though they are in electronic format.
Songs and poems describe events and people's reactions to the events.
Visual materials include original paintings, drawings, photographs, films, and maps. Political cartoons and other types of cartoons can also be visual primary sources.
Oral histories are interviews that are recorded to collect people's memories and observations about their lives and experiences.
Personal records include autobiographies, journals, and letters.
Artifacts, such as tools, are objects that were used by people in the past.

Making Connections What can an artifact tell you about the past that a newspaper cannot?

---

primary sources first-hand pieces of evidence such as written records from people who saw or experienced the events described

secondary sources written documents or media about an event the authors did not experience first-hand

Evaluate the Credibility of Sources

The more times you can answer "yes" to the following questions about a source, the more credible and reliable you may consider the source:

- Are facts presented in the source supported with evidence?
- Is the language used in the source objective and not emotional?
- Can the same information be found in another source?
- Is the source's creator trustworthy? Does he or she have **credentials** (kreh • DEN • shulz), or qualifications that establishes an expert understanding of the subject matter?
- Does the author or speaker acknowledge and consider other viewpoints?

Identifying Point of View

A **point of view** is a general attitude about people and life. The creator of a source has a point of view that selects which events to focus on, who the key players are, and which details are worth recording. A point of view is the particular focus a person takes when considering a problem or situation.

Frame of Reference

When interpreting a writer's words or a historical person's actions, one should also consider **frame of reference.** This refers to the experiences and historical and cultural factors that influence a person or a group at a specific time. Historical influences are especially important when analyzing past events or writings. For example, we might find early peoples' fears of events, like solar eclipses, amusing. At that time, however, there was no proven scientific explanation for that event.

Considering Bias

Sometimes a writer's point of view is expressed as a **bias,** or an unreasoned judgment about people and events. A bias is a one-sided, unexamined view. A person who is biased has made a judgment about an event, a person, or a group without really considering the many parts of the situation.

Biased speakers and writers can be detected in various ways. Their statements use opinions or emotional words such as *ignorant, impossible, great,* and *wonderful.* They also tend to use words that allow no exception, such as *all, always,* and *never.* It is important to be aware of point of view, bias, and frame of reference in your own study of history.

Multiple Perspectives

Historians seek to uncover point of view and bias in historical documents and articles. They look for the ideas and facts that the author of the source emphasizes. They also think about what ideas and facts the author might be leaving out.

To make sense of the past, historians must weigh the known evidence and try to figure out what the facts are. Then they need to bring the facts together to answer the questions that interest them. In doing this, they must use their judgment. This means that their own viewpoints come into play.

Historians try to be aware of point of view and bias both in their sources and in themselves. Therefore, they check new sources and their own ideas against sources already known to be trustworthy. To get a balanced picture, historians study documents with other points of view. It is important to consider multiple perspectives, or different views, of a historical event. Not all people or groups of people experience the same event in the same way. Good students of history piece together different perspectives to help them interpret history. In this way, we can get a clearer, more well-rounded view of events that occurred.

✓ **CHECK FOR UNDERSTANDING**

1. **Describing** How do historians evaluate the credibility of a source?
2. **Summarizing** Why is it important to identify point of view and frame of reference when evaluating a source?

Researching and Writing About History

GUIDING QUESTION

How do historians determine if information is worth using for research?

Researching

Global communication systems have transformed the study of history. People are connected and online throughout the world as they have never been before. Some archives, or collections of historical documents, have become more accessible for research. This happens as archives are digitized, or reproduced, and made available to the public over the Internet.

Looking for information on the Internet is part of historical research today. It can be a challenge to

---

credential a degree or association with an institution, agency, or business in a specialized field of study that qualifies someone as an expert

point of view a general attitude about people and life

frame of reference experiences and historical and cultural factors that influence a person or a group at a specific time

bias a personal and sometimes unreasoned judgment about people and events

Today, historians must be familiar with the variety of online materials and be skilled at effective research on the Internet.
Explaining Why is it important to know the different meanings of URL address endings?

determine if the information you located is credible. Good historians follow a few important guidelines as they gather information to determine its credibility.

Authorship

Many articles on the Internet are unsigned. A reader has no way of knowing who wrote the content and whether the author is an expert on the subject. However, reliable articles will be signed by well-known experts on the subject. The authors will include details about their credentials, or evidence that they are experts.

Web URLs

A uniform resource locator, or URL, is the address of an online resource. A URL that ends in .gov should be a government entity. This site probably contains accurate data. This data is usually as up-to-date as possible. A URL that ends in .edu is usually a site for an educational institution, such as a college or university. Most .edu sites pride themselves on accuracy. It is possible that documents on these sites may contain opinions in addition to facts. Nonprofit organizations usually use .org at the end of their URLs. These sites may contain much reliable data but nonprofit organizations usually have a goal to achieve and may prioritize the information that supports its cause. So you should look for opinion-based statements and be wary of any bias. You must carefully review all URLs when conducting research to ensure that your sources are factual and are free of bias.

Plagiarism

To **plagiarize** (PLAY • juh • RYZ) is to present the ideas or words of another person as your own without offering credit to the source. Plagiarism is similar to forgery, or copying something that is not yours. It also violates or breaks **copyright laws.** These laws prevent the unauthorized use of a writer's work. If you copy a written text word-for-word, or repeat an idea as your own without identifying your source, that is plagiarism. Some scholars have ruined their careers through

plagiarism. They used content from books or the Internet without citing the source or giving credit.

To avoid plagiarism, follow these rules:

- Put information in your own words.
- When you restate an opinion from something you read, include a reference to the author: "According to Smith and Jones, . . . "
- Always include a footnote when you use a direct quotation from one of your sources.

Interpreting History

When studying history, it is important to take a balanced approach. Balance is necessary to interpret history in a way that takes into account social and political context. For example, the writers and supporters of the Constitution did not believe women needed the right to vote or much independent say in society and government operations. Today, however, women use and expect these political and social rights. Your evaluations of history should be based on the context and evidence. While it is important to apply contemporary ideas and attitudes to the study of history to identify mistakes, evaluations of history must also try to explain historical context and evidence.

✓ **CHECK FOR UNDERSTANDING**

1. **Identifying** How and why should you avoid plagiarism when writing about history?
2. **Making Connections** Why is determining credibility especially important when conducting research using the Internet?

LESSON ACTIVITIES

1. **Narrative Writing** Explain how you would begin research on a historical topic. What would be your initial steps based on what you have learned in this lesson?
2. **Collaborative Writing** With a partner, discuss the thinking skills that historians must use when studying the past.

plagiarism to present the ideas or words of another person as your own without offering credit to the source

copyright laws laws that prevent the unauthorized use of a writer's work

IJGil C/Shutterstock; Shutterstock; (r)Ill.studio/Shutterstock.

04
How Does a Historian Interpret History?

READING STRATEGY

Integrating Knowledge and Ideas As you read the lesson, use a graphic organizer like this to record different ways in which historians approach explaining and interpreting the past.

Ways to Explain the Past

Interpreting History

GUIDING QUESTION

Why do historians draw different conclusions about events of the past?

More Than Facts

Historians do not think that facts alone explain history. Like pieces of a puzzle, the evidence is put together by people using their reason to explain events.

In the same way, historians must use their knowledge to give factual evidence (names, dates, places, and events) meaning and put them in an order that people can easily understand. Historians piece together the credible evidence and draw conclusions. They use their own knowledge of the past to interpret, or explain, the meaning of events. Then, they present their findings in a clear, readable, and convincing form. In doing so, a historian is intentionally shaping an understanding of evidence in their own understanding of the past. A good historian must be prepared to explain that interpretation and understand that the story will be compared to the interpretation of other historians so that the most accurate interpretations is eventually agreed upon.

Understanding Time and Place

Historians study people and events within a historical context, or a specific time and place in the past. They connect historical people and events to the central issues of the time. These central issues are the main ideas, or patterns, that we see in human societies, including war and peace, the rise of scientific and technological inventions, and the forms of government and societies. Through these issues, historians can form a more complete understanding of the past.

Historians also sequence events, or place events in the order in which they occurred. Certain key words—such as *first, next, last, then, before,* and *after*—can help you understand the sequence of events. Sequencing helps historians organize information. From the pattern of the data, they can determine how events are related to each other. The relationship among these events can help historians identify historical importance and cause and effect.

Understanding Cause and Effect

Historical events are linked by cause and effect. A **cause** is what makes an event happen. The result of a cause is known as an **effect.** Historians look for cause-and-effect links to explain why events happened.

Usually, one event is produced by many causes. Similarly, one event often produces several different effects. These relationships explain why things happen. The diagram below shows a simple cause-and-effect relationship.

British Parliament applies new taxes on the English colonies in America		The American colonies unite and revolt against Great Britain

Diagrams showing cause-and-effect relationships often use arrows to show the connection between events.

cause what makes an event happen   **effect** the result of a cause

Because many historical events are related, cause-and-effect relationships can extend over a long period of time. To trace these relationships as they grow more complex, look for clue words that alert you to a cause-and-effect relationship, such as *because, led to, brought about, produced,* and *therefore.* Historians ask questions about the information they find from the past to help them better identify cause-and-effect relationships. Some examples of these types of questions include: *Why did people migrate to new continents? How did this affect the people who lived there?* Such questions help us focus on complex historical issues. Given this complexity, historians must weigh and consider multiple causes and effects at the same time to gain further insight into the past. Only after considering the full range of causes and effects will a historian begin to understand the repercussions and connections between past events.

Continuity and Change

History is a story of change, and historians look at the differences and similarities of events. Therefore, historians study how events greatly differ from each other. Some historical changes have occurred quickly. For example, over the course of a decade, the British colonies in North America declared, revolted, and fought to achieve independence from Great Britain. Unlike other governments at the time, this nation defined itself within new ideas from the Enlightenment that valued representative democracy, individual rights, and the consent of the governed. A historian can identify the sequence of changes that occurred in the relationship between Great Britain and its American colonies and then identify the cause-and-effect relationships that explain why those changes occurred.

While looking at historical changes, historians also search for **continuity,** or the unbroken patterns in history. They study how traditions and concerns link people across time and place. For example, life in India today is affected by the Hindu religion, which is more than 3,000 years old. Even though life in India is very different today than in the past, the continuity of the Hindu religion is key to understanding India's history.

Error and Chance in History

History has often been made by chance, oversight, or error. For example, Christopher Columbus believed that his voyage in 1492 led him to the East Indies, the islands off the coast of Asia. Today the Caribbean islands where he landed are often called the West Indies. Also, the Native Americans whom he met were called Indians because of this misunderstanding.

Explorations after Columbus, however, revealed that Columbus did not reach Asia at all. He had found a part of the world unknown to Europeans, Asians, and Africans. In the following years, the Spanish explored most of the Caribbean region. In time their voyages led to the rise of the Spanish Empire in the Americas.

Mistakes have not only shaped historical events. They have also influenced peoples' understanding of the past. For example, Portuguese traders in the 1500s were the first Europeans to see the stone ruins of Great Zimbabwe in south central Africa. They believed they had found the fabled capital of the Queen of Sheba mentioned in the Christian Bible. Later travelers came to the conclusion that the ruins were the work of Egyptians or Phoenicians. These incorrect views were held for nearly 400 years. Then, British archaeologists studying the ruins in the early 1900s proved that the ruins were built by a powerful African civilization. The people of this civilization were the ancestors of the Shona, a group that lives in Zimbabwe today.

Different Interpretations

History is often called an ongoing discussion about the past. Historians discuss what the facts are. They also argue about how to interpret the facts. What causes these differences?

Despite the efforts of the best minds, some facts are **ambiguous,** or not always clear to interpret. What the facts mean often depends on the historian's judgment. In addition, historians come to the evidence with different points of view. As a result, historians often arrive at different interpretations of the same event. For example, in the past many historians identified Columbus as a skilled leader who brought order to the lands he explored. Today, however, historians analyze Columbus's actions while also taking into account the disease impacts and population devastation that resulted from such exploration. Which conclusion about Columbus is correct? A historian must rely on evidence to support his or her position.

The discussion also changes as historians find new evidence that leads them to question old interpretations. Sometimes historians take a new look at existing evidence and see things others may have ignored. As they do so, they may explain events differently on the basis of more evidence.

The questions that historians ask reflect the issues of the times in which they live. As a result, there is never a final, complete version of history that satisfies everyone. There will always be new questions to ask of the past.

✓ **CHECK FOR UNDERSTANDING**

1. **Identifying Cause and Effect** Why might historians need to study multiple causes and effects of a historical event?

2. **Describing** Why is the study of continuity and change important to historians?

---

continuity continuous or unbroken patterns of occurrence in history

ambiguous not clear; interpretations may vary

Analyzing Information

GUIDING QUESTION

What types of skills are needed to analyze information?

Social studies skills help you understand and use information. You use some skills to gather information. You use other skills to analyze the information or to generate new information.

Sequencing Events

In reading or writing for social studies, it is important to know how ideas, events, or people come before or follow each other. When we list events, ideas, and objects in a logical order, we are sequencing.

You might not realize it, but you sequence tasks or events every day. You arrange your time so that the most important tasks get done first. For example, you might plan to do your homework before you play tennis. We also make sense of events by placing them in the order in which they happened. When you tell a story to your friends, you describe events in order. Above all, sequencing is used to clearly tell a story from the beginning, through the middle, and to the end.

Certain key words—such as *first, next, last, then, before,* and *after*—can help you understand the sequence of a story or a time line of events.

Finding Main Ideas

Throughout your study of this program, you will read about ideas, people, and events. These details are easier to understand when they are connected to one main idea. The main idea is the principal concept the other ideas depend on for meaning. Understanding the main idea allows you to grasp the whole picture or story. Follow these steps to find the main idea.

- Before reading the material, determine the setting of the document: the time, the place, and the author.
- Read the material and ask, "What is the purpose of this information?"
- Read the first sentence of the first paragraph. The main idea of a paragraph is often found in the topic sentence. The main idea of a large section of text is often found in a topic paragraph.
- Identify details that support the main idea.

These same basic steps can be followed to find the main idea that a speaker is conveying. Start by identifying the speaker's purpose. Speakers usually present the main idea at the beginning of their verbal communication and then provide supporting details and examples. Repeating the main idea throughout the speech keeps the audience focused on it.

Sometimes you might be asked to summarize information. A **summary** is a shortened version of a passage. Summarizing involves using your own words and style to express another writer's ideas. It presents only the most important ideas but not the minor details of the passage. Look at the graphic organizer below that explains how to summarize text.

Categorizing

Understanding large quantities of information can be frustrating. It is easier, however, if you are able to organize the information into **categories,** or groups.

When we categorize, we group together items that share characteristics. For example, department stores categorize items based on their uses. Shoes and boots are located in the footwear department, while music players and DVDs are found in electronics. Use these tips to help you categorize information.

- As you study a topic, identify items that have similar characteristics. List items in separate columns.
- Label these categories with appropriate headings.
- Add facts to the categories as you continue reading.
- Review the categories. If necessary, divide the categories into additional categories or combine categories that are too similar.

Once you have categorized the material, look for patterns and relationships.

Comparing and Contrasting

To make a comparison, look for similarities among ideas or objects. You can also examine contrasts—qualities that make each of the ideas or objects unique. When you know how to compare and contrast, you can make better choices. To compare and contrast, examine the text, images, or other items and follow these steps.

1. Select the items to compare or contrast.
2. Determine what you are comparing or contrasting.
3. Look for similarities between the categories.
4. Look for differences that set the categories apart from each other.

 1. Identify the main ideas of the passage. → 2. Organize and present these main ideas using your own words. → 3. Check that you stated the meaning of the original passage correctly.

This graphic organizer identifies the steps for summarizing a text.

summary a shortened version of a passage that presents its key ideas or findings

categories groups of information

Comparing and Contrasting What similarities and differences can you see regarding the changes in rail technology that has occurred in the United States?

Generalizing and Predicting

If you say, "We have a good soccer team," you are making a generalization, or overall statement that applies to the entire group, about your team. If you say that the team has not lost a game this season, you are providing evidence to support your generalization.

When studying social studies, it is often necessary to put together supporting statements to make a generalization. In some cases, authors provide only supporting statements, and you will need to make generalizations on your own. To make generalizations, follow these steps.

- Identify the subject matter, and gather facts and examples related to it.
- Identify similarities or patterns among these facts.
- Use these similarities or patterns to create general ideas about the subject.

In order to make a prediction, you first must review what you already know about a situation by listing facts, events, and people's responses. The list will help you recall events and how they affected people. Next, analyze patterns that you have observed. Try to determine what the patterns show. Then use your knowledge and observations of similar situations. Ask yourself, *What were the consequences of a similar decision or action that occurred in the past?* Analyze each of the potential consequences by asking, *How might this occur?* Then try to make a prediction about what might happen next. Then, predict how these breakthroughs might affect future daily life in areas such as social life, the economy, politics, culture, and the environment.

For practice in predicting, research online about possible future scientific discoveries and technological innovations (such as a cure for cancer, the driverless car, and artificial intelligence). Then, predict how these breakthroughs might affect future daily life in areas such as social life, the economy, politics, culture, and the environment.

Making Inferences and Drawing Conclusions

When you make an **inference,** you "read between the lines" to figure out something that is not stated directly. A **conclusion** is an understanding based on details or facts that you read or hear. In order to make inferences and draw conclusions as you read, summarize the key facts and ideas. Think about what you already know about the topic. Use this knowledge to make an inference and draw a conclusion.

✓ **CHECK FOR UNDERSTANDING**

1. **Identifying** What is the difference between and inference and a conclusion?
2. **Describing** What skills help historians understand and use information?

LESSON ACTIVITIES

1. **Informative Writing** Identify key ways in which historians present information about the past. In a paragraph, explain why historians consider continuity, change, and historical context when presenting history.
2. **Collaborating** With a partner, pick a major topic related to American history, such as the American Revolution. Research how 2–3 different credible sources explain the topic of history you selected, noting any differences in interpretation.

---

inference to identify a message that is not directly stated in a communication by inferring meaning, often based on context

conclusion an understanding based on details or facts

(l)Library of Congress Prints and Photographs Division [LC-DIG-ppmsca-18100]; (r)Mark Williamson/Stockbyte/Getty Images.

05
History and Related Fields

READING STRATEGY

Integrating Knowledge and Ideas As you read, complete a graphic organizer similar to the one here by noting examples of how the subjects discussed all fit under the category of social studies.

Social Studies	
Geography	
Economics	
Civics	
Science	

The Social Studies

GUIDING QUESTION

What do you learn about when you study social studies?

Geography is the study of Earth's physical features and the living things—humans, animals, and plants—that inhabit it. People who study geography are called geographers. They examine where all the Earth's physical features are located and how they relate to one another and to people who live there. Geography, however, is only one subject area you will learn about in your social studies classes. A person who studies social studies must learn about different subject areas in order to understand events or concepts more thoroughly.

When you combine the different subject areas of social studies together, you begin to see how they relate to each other. For example, a region's physical geography can influence the type of economy it has. If a region has access to numerous waterways, its economy might be based on trade or fishing. Another example might be that if a region has historically been ruled by one person, then its government today might be less democratic. People who study the social studies use many tools to analyze, or examine, this information. As you develop these skills you will also understand the social studies more thoroughly.

✓ **CHECK FOR UNDERSTANDING**

Making Connections How might an understanding of a region's geography help someone understand that same region's political leanings?

History and Economics

GUIDING QUESTION

How are history and economics related?

Charts, graphs, and diagrams are important tools for historians who investigate economies, or the ways societies produce, sell, and buy goods. Statistics, or mathematical data, are scarce for the economies of long ago.

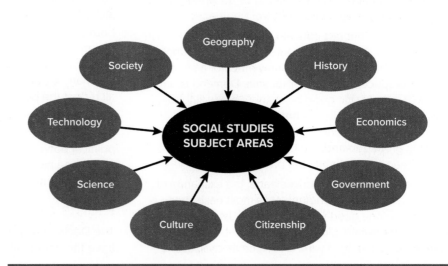

History, geography, economics, and civics are just some of the subject areas that are part of social studies.

However, statistics for modern economies are abundant and provide historians with much information. Economists, or scientists who study economies, have developed economic indicators to measure a modern economy's performance.

Economic indicators are statistics that tell how well an economy is doing and how well the economy is going to do in the future. They include:

- the number of jobless,
- the rate at which prices rise over time, and
- the amount of goods and services that are made and sold.

Historians also analyze the costs and benefits of economic and political issues. This analysis requires figuring out the costs of any historical action and comparing it with the benefits of that action. To do so, they must understand the basic concepts of economics and how they affect human thought and action.

One of the most basic concepts in economics—and one that underlies almost every economic cause and effect in history—is **scarcity.** A condition of scarcity exists when there are not enough resources to provide for what people need or want. For example, a severe drought can dry up fertile farmlands, causing a scarcity in crops. Without enough water, livestock will die of thirst. There will not be enough food, and people may starve. We can think of many examples of scarcity that can be caused by drought conditions.

When people face scarcity, they are forced to make decisions. For example, when the Dust Bowl hit the southern Great Plains in the 1930s, as many as 2.5 million people migrated in hopes of finding a better life in areas unaffected by the drought. How did they make such a decision? They weighed the **opportunity cost** of leaving against waiting for conditions to improve and decided it was better to leave. Opportunity cost is the value of the next-best option when considering several alternatives. It is what you give up when you decide on one course of action over another.

Another economic concept that stems from scarcity and can affect the course of history is supply and demand. Supply refers to how much of a specific good a producer has to offer for sale. Demand is how many of the specific good consumers are willing to buy at the price producers are asking for it. If the supply is large, the price often goes down, because it is not in great demand. If there is a demand for more goods than are available, the price often rises.

Supply and demand drives trade, the exchange of one thing of value for another. At its most basic, trade is exchanging one good for another of equal value. A knitter, for example, may barter a sweater with a yarn spinner for a supply of yarn. Over time as civilizations developed, trade became driven by wealth and money, which directly represents wealth. Today, we are more likely to pay for goods with money than we are to barter one good for another. But the concept is the same: resources are exchanged for other resources. And a scarcity of resources can lead to conflicts and wars as easily as it can lead to migration or to the formation of international alliances and trade agreements. That is why it's important for historians to understand how economic concepts affect both individuals and nations.

A solid understanding of basic economic concepts is also important in our personal lives. We have to make financial decisions by weighing opportunity costs every time we consider making a purchase. We can use our knowledge of supply and demand to help us decide to buy something now or to wait until demand (and prices) drop. Personal financial literacy is also an important aspect of economic education.

☑ **CHECK FOR UNDERSTANDING**

Analyzing What role might the analysis of opportunity cost play in a nation's decision to negotiate a trade alliance to obtain necessary resources instead of waging war?

History and Civics

GUIDING QUESTION

How are history and civics related?

History helps us understand where we came from and who we are today. We see role models of the past who can influence how we may choose to live our lives today. Civics can help us do that.

Civics is the study of governments and how they function. The role of a government is to enact and enforce laws, negotiate and honor treaties with other nations, and assure the well-being of its citizens. The United States is a republic, which means it is governed by representatives of the citizens who live here. It is also a democracy, because the citizens vote to select both their representatives and their leaders. There are two major political parties in the United States—the Democratic Party and the Republican Party. But there are many other smaller political parties as well. They all reflect the political views of their members.

A democratic republic is much different from a monarchy, in which one individual holds hereditary political power, or an authoritarian dictatorship, in which one individual or a group of unelected leaders holds absolute power over citizens.

Rights of Citizenship

The Declaration of Independence says that Americans have the right to life, liberty, and the pursuit of

---

scarcity a situation where there is not enough of a resource to provide what people need or want

opportunity cost the value of the next-best option when considering several alternatives

happiness. The U.S. Constitution protects the rights and freedoms of every American citizen. All Americans have the right to freedom of expression. This means that they can speak and write openly. They can attend peaceful gatherings. They can worship as they choose. They have a right to receive a fair trial. They have a right to vote for public officials and to serve in public office.

Duties and Responsibilities

By law, citizens must carry out some duties. Obeying all federal, state, and local laws is one of the first duties of citizenship. Citizens have a duty to pay taxes, which pay for the services they receive from the government. Citizens must serve on a jury if the government asks them to. Citizens must be ready to defend the United States and the Constitution.

Citizens also have responsibilities. We should stay informed about important issues to help us make wise choices when we vote. These choices will affect our everyday lives. Voting is a way to guide the priorities of our government.

Citizens should respect the rights and views of other people. The United States has welcomed people of many different backgrounds. They all share the same freedoms. Before you deny a right to someone else, put yourself in that person's place. Think how you would feel if someone tried to take away your rights.

Finally, citizens should take part in their local community. By working with together, we help make our neighborhoods and towns better. There are different ways to keep our communities strong. We can volunteer our time. We can join neighborhood groups, and we can serve in public office.

Being a Globally Competent Citizen

Today the world faces many global problems. When people travel, disease can spread quickly. Many countries have close economic ties to other nations. Because of this, economic problems in one country affect other countries. In addition, as the world becomes increasingly interconnected, it is clearer than ever that sometimes nations must work together for shared goals. World leaders must often work together to deal with these complicated international issues.

Being a globally competent citizen does not mean giving up your duties and responsibilities as a citizen of the United States. It means thinking about how you can make the world a better place by your actions. Making the effort to stay informed and to respect the views of others helps all Americans and the rest of the world.

Voting is a key right of citizenship. But to take on that role of voter, you must first register yourself to vote.

Making Connections What responsibility must each citizen fulfill before exercising the right to vote?

✓ CHECK FOR UNDERSTANDING

Making Connections Why do you think freedom of expression is important in a republic such as the United States?

History and Science

GUIDING QUESTION

How are history and science related?

Historians use science to study prehistory. As scientists, they study physical evidence to learn about our ancestors. Historians who are not scientists often work with those who are, or use the information scientists have found.

Digging Up the Past

Since the invention of writing, people have recorded important events. These written records give historians a window to the past. Students of prehistory look into an even deeper past, one without writing. They must find a different kind of window.

Archaeology (ahr•kee•AHL•luh•jee) is the study of the past by looking at what people left behind. Archaeologists dig in the earth or search underwater for remains of the past. They often discover **artifacts** (AHR•tih•FAKTS)—objects made by people. Common artifacts include tools, pottery, weapons, and jewelry. Archaeologists also study human and animal bones, seeds, trees, mounds, pits, and ancient canals.

Paleontology (PAY•lee•AHN•TAH•luh•jee) also looks at prehistoric times. Paleontologists study fossils

---

archaeology the study of past human life by scientifically studying material remains

artifact an object made by humans, often from the past

paleontology a science that relies on the excavation and study of plant and animal remains from previous geological periods

LM Otero/Associated Press.

Many historians focus their study on materials that individuals leave behind on purpose, such as diaries or videos. Archaeologists often study the material that is left behind on accident.

Interpreting How has science become a key part of an archaeologist's job?

to learn what the world was like long ago. **Fossils** are the remains of plant and animal life that have been preserved as rock from a much earlier time.

Anthropology (AN•thruh•PAH•luh•jee) is the study of human culture and how it develops over time. Anthropologists focus their study on human artifacts and human fossils so that they can better explain human society before the existence of written records.

Archaeology and Artifacts

One of the most important and difficult jobs for archaeologists is dating the artifacts that they find. The earliest artifacts are pieces of hard rock that were chipped into cutting or digging tools or into weapons. How do archaeologists determine the age of these artifacts? Early scientists correctly assumed that artifacts buried deeper in the ground are older than those found closer to the surface. In most cases, that is still true.

Archaeologists also use trees to date artifacts. A tree forms a new growth ring every year. Scientists count the number of rings in a wooden object, such as a house beam, and compare the pattern with the rings of a tree whose age they know. In that way, they can identify dates as far back as 3,000 years.

In 1946 Willard Frank Libby, an American scientist, discovered that all living things contain a radioactive element called carbon-14. After plants and animals die, the carbon-14 within them gradually disappears. Scientist can measure how much carbon-14 a skeleton or the remains of a wooden boat contain to estimate how old the object is. This is called radiocarbon dating.

Radiocarbon dating, however, is only accurate for dating objects that are no more than about 5,000 years old. Another method—thermoluminescence (THUHR•moh•LOO•muh•NEH•suhns) dating—allows scientists to make more precise measurements back

to 200,000 years. This method dates an object by measuring the light given off by particles trapped in the soil surrounding the artifact or fossil.

Scientists have also discovered that blood molecules can survive millions of years. When found on rocks, tools, or weapons, these molecules can tell us how the artifacts were used. DNA is also providing new data. By analyzing the remains of plants on stone tools, scientists can find out more about early farming.

Although scientists have developed many methods to measure the age of artifacts, what we know about the past will continue to change as new information is discovered and new scientific methods of dating are developed. What is certain is that by analyzing the artifacts and other clues, archaeologists work with historians to develop hypotheses and construct interpretations of prehistorical and ancient civilizations.

✓ **CHECK FOR UNDERSTANDING**

Understanding Supporting Details How do archaeology, paleontology, and anthropology work together to give researchers a picture of culture thousands of years ago?

LESSON ACTIVITIES

1. **Explanatory Writing** Research an event in the history of the United States and write an informative essay explaining the role of economics and civics in the cause and the outcome of the event.

2. **Interpreting Information** With four or five class members, research to find a current archaeological dig within the United States. Create a presentation that explains archaeology, paleontology, and anthropology work together to build our understanding about people and culture.

---

fossil remains, impression, or trace of past plant or animal life from a previous geological period that has been preserved in Earth's crust

anthropology the scientific study of human beings through analysis of past cultures, physical characteristics, social relationships, and environmental pressures

National Archives and Records Administration.

06

Geographer's Handbook

READING STRATEGY

Analyzing Key Ideas and Details As you read the lesson, use a graphic organizer like this to distinguish between map projections and globes. How accurately does each represent Earth?

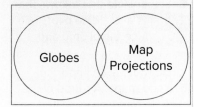

History and Geography

GUIDING QUESTION

How do geographers use the Five Themes and Six Essential Elements of Geography?

When studying history, you will discover how geography has shaped the course of events in history. Landforms, waterways, climate, and natural resources all have helped or hindered human activities. Usually people have learned either to adapt to their environments or to transform them to meet their needs. Having a better understanding of the types of geography resources available to you will help you comprehend and analyze the history you study.

Five Themes of Geography

Geographers have tried to understand the best way to teach and learn about geography. In order to do this, geographers created the *Five Themes of Geography*. The themes act as a guide for teaching the basic ideas about geography to students like you. Here is a description of the five themes:

1. Location describes where something is. Absolute location describes a place's exact position on the Earth's surface. Relative location expresses where a place is in relation to another place.
2. Place describes the physical and human characteristics that make a location unique.
3. Regions are areas that share common characteristics.
4. Movement explains how and why people and things move and are connected.
5. Human-Environment Interaction describes the relationship between people and their environment.

THE SIX ESSENTIAL ELEMENTS

These elements help geographers and students perform basic evaluations of geographic data and material.

Element	Definition
The World in Spatial Terms	Geography is the study of the location and spatial relationships among people, places, and environments. Maps reveal the complex spatial interactions.
Places and Regions	The identities of individuals and peoples are rooted in places and regions. Distinctive combinations of human and physical characteristics define places and regions.
Physical Systems	Physical processes, like wind and ocean currents, plate tectonics, and the water cycle, shape the Earth's surface and change ecosystems.
Human Systems	Human systems are things like language, religion, and ways of life. They also include how groups of people govern themselves and how they make and trade products and ideas.
Environment and Society	Geography studies how the environment of a place helps shape people's lives. Geography also looks at how people affect the environment in positive and negative ways.
The Uses of Geography	Understanding geography and knowing how to use its tools and technologies helps people make good decisions about the world and prepares people for rewarding careers.

The Six Essential Elements

People who teach and study geography thought that the Five Themes were too broad. In 1994 geographers created 18 national geography standards. These standards were more detailed about what should be taught and learned. The Six Essential Elements act as a bridge connecting the Five Themes with the standards.

✓ **CHECK FOR UNDERSTANDING**

Identifying What are the six essential elements of geography?

Using Maps and Globes

GUIDING QUESTION

How do maps and globes present information?

A **globe** is a scale model of the Earth. Because planet Earth is round, a globe presents the most accurate depiction of geographic information such as area, distance, and direction. However, globes show little close-up detail. A printed **map** is a symbolic representation of all or part of the planet. Unlike globes, maps can show small areas in great detail.

From 3-D to 2-D

Think about the surface of the Earth as the peel of an orange. To flatten the peel, you have to cut it into segments that are still connected as one piece. To create maps that are not interrupted, mapmakers, or **cartographers,** use mathematical formulas to transfer information from the three-dimensional globe to the two-dimensional map. However, when the curves of a globe become straight lines on a map, distortion of size, shape, distance, or area occurs.

Great Circle Routes

A straight line of true direction—one that runs directly from west to east, for example—is not always the shortest distance between two points. This is due to the curvature of the Earth. To find the shortest distance, stretch a piece of string around the globe from one point to the other. The string will form part of a **great circle route,** an imaginary line that follows the curve of the Earth. Ship captains and airline pilots use these great circle routes to reduce travel time and conserve fuel.

The idea of a great circle route is an important difference between globes and maps. A round globe accurately shows a great circle route, as indicated on the map. However, the flat map shows the great circle distance (dotted line) between Tokyo and Los Angeles to be far longer than the true direction distance (solid line). In fact, the great circle distance is about 314 miles (505 km) shorter.

Great Circle Route
The Great Circle Route is an imaginary line that follows the curve of Earth.

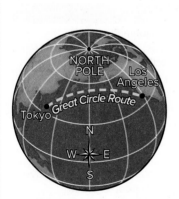

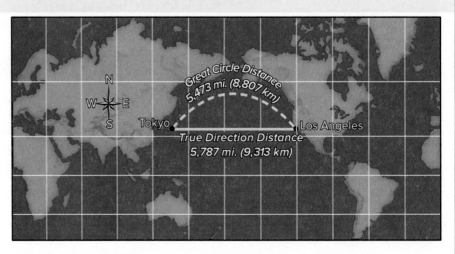

Describing What are the problems that arise when the curves of a globe become straight lines on a map?

---

globe a scale model of Earth

map a symbolic representation of all or part of the planet

cartographer a mapmaker

great circle route a straight line of true direction on a globe

Projections

To create maps, cartographers project the round Earth onto a flat surface—making a **map projection.** Distance, shape, direction, or size may be distorted by a projection. As a result, the purpose of the map usually dictates which projection is used. There are many kinds of map projections, some with general names and some named for the cartographers who developed them. Three basic categories of map projections are shown here: planar, cylindrical, and conic.

Planar Projection

A **planar projection** shows the Earth centered in such a way that a straight line coming from the center to any point represents the shortest distance. Also known as an azimuthal projection, it is most accurate at its center. As a result, it is often used for maps of the Poles.

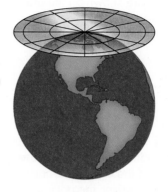

Cylindrical Projection

A **cylindrical projection** is based on the projection of the globe onto a cylinder. This projection is most accurate near the Equator, but shapes and distances are distorted near the Poles.

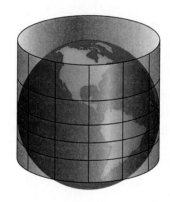

Conic Projection

A **conic projection** comes from placing a cone over part of the globe. Conic projections are best suited for showing limited east-west areas that are not far from the Equator. For these uses, a conic projection can indicate distances and directions fairly accurately.

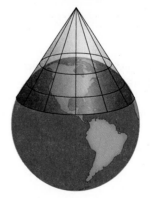

map projection placing the round Earth onto a flat surface, which will alter how the shape and size of land forms and other geographic features appear

planar projection a map projection that presents the Earth centered, resulting in the most accurate projection of the Poles; also called azimuthal projection

cylindrical projection a map projection based on the projection of the globe onto a cylinder shape

conic projection a map projection based on placing a cone over part of the globe; it accurately shows east-to-west distances near the Equator

Common Projections

Each type of map projection has advantages and some degree of inaccuracy. Four of the most common projections are shown here.

Winkel Tripel Projection

Most general reference world maps are the Winkel Tripel projection. It provides a good balance between the size and shape of land areas as they are shown on the map. Even the polar areas are depicted with little distortion of size and shape.

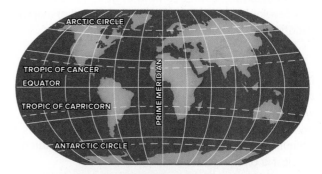

Robinson Projection

The Robinson projection has minor distortions. The sizes and shapes near the eastern and western edges of the map are accurate, and outlines of the continents appear much as they do on the globe. However, the polar areas are flattened.

Goode's Interrupted Equal-Area Projection

An interrupted projection looks something like a globe that has been cut apart and laid flat. Goode's Interrupted Equal-Area projection shows the true size and shape of Earth's landmasses, but distances are generally distorted.

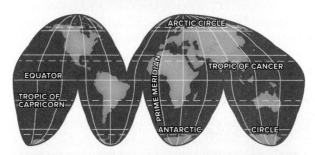

Mercator Projection

The Mercator projection increasingly distorts size and distance as it moves away from the Equator. However, Mercator projections do accurately show true directions and the shapes of landmasses, making these maps useful for sea travel.

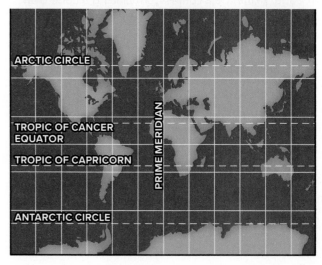

Determining Location

Geography is often said to begin with the question: Where? The basic tool for answering the question is location. Lines on globes and maps provide information that can help you locate places. These lines cross one another forming a pattern called a **grid system,** which helps you find exact places on the Earth's surface.

A **hemisphere** is one of the halves into which the Earth is divided. Geographers divide the Earth into hemispheres to help them classify and describe places on Earth. Most places are located in two of the four hemispheres.

Latitude and Longitude

Lines of **latitude,** or parallels, circle the Earth parallel to the Equator and measure the distance north or south of the Equator in degrees. The Equator is measured at 0° latitude, while the Poles lie at latitudes 90°N (north) and 90°S (south). Parallels north of the Equator are called north latitude. Parallels south of the Equator are called south latitude.

Lines of **longitude**, or meridians, circle the Earth from Pole to Pole. These lines measure distance east or west of the **Prime Meridian** at 0° longitude. Meridians east of the Prime Meridian are known as east longitude. Meridians west of the Prime Meridian are known as west longitude. The 180° meridian on the opposite side of the Earth is called the International Date Line.

The Global Grid

Every place has a global address, or **absolute location.** You can identify the absolute location of a place by naming the latitude and longitude lines that cross exactly at that place. For example, Tokyo, Japan is located at 36°N latitude and 140°E longitude. For more precise readings, each degree is further divided into 60 units called minutes.

grid system a pattern of intersecting lines on a map or globe that determines exact location on Earth's surface

hemisphere one of the halves geographers divide the Earth into

latitude lines that circle the Earth parallel to the Equator

longitude lines that circle the Earth from Pole to Pole

Prime Meridian the line of longitude set at 0°

absolute location a global address determined by the intersection of longitude and latitude lines

Latitude

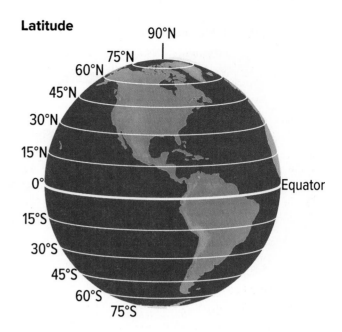

Longitude

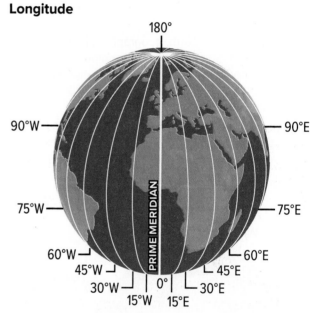

Global Grid

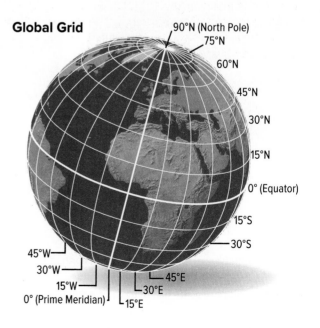

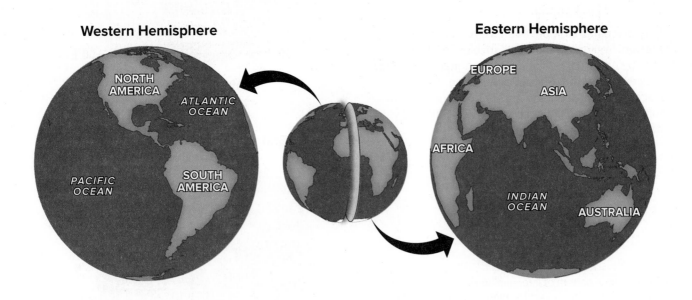

Northern Hemisphere

- ASIA
- AFRICA
- EUROPE
- North Pole
- PACIFIC OCEAN
- ATLANTIC OCEAN
- NORTH AMERICA

Southern Hemisphere

- INDIAN OCEAN
- AUSTRALIA
- AFRICA
- South Pole
- ATLANTIC OCEAN
- ANTARCTICA
- SOUTH AMERICA
- PACIFIC OCEAN

Hemispheres

To locate a place on Earth, geographers use a system of imaginary lines that crisscross the globe. You have already learned about the latitude and longitude lines that help to form the global grid which can be used to identify a place's absolute location.

The Equator (ih•KWAY•tuhr) is one of those lines. It circles the middle of Earth like a belt and divides Earth into "half-spheres" or hemispheres (HEH•muh•sfihrz).

Everything north of the Equator is in the **Northern Hemisphere**. Everything south of the Equator is in the **Southern Hemisphere**.

The Prime Meridian and the International Date Line divide the Earth into the Eastern and Western Hemispheres. Everything east of the Prime Meridian for 180° is in the **Eastern Hemisphere.** Everything west of the Prime Meridian for 180° is in the **Western Hemisphere.**

Western Hemisphere

- NORTH AMERICA
- ATLANTIC OCEAN
- PACIFIC OCEAN
- SOUTH AMERICA

Eastern Hemisphere

- EUROPE
- ASIA
- AFRICA
- INDIAN OCEAN
- AUSTRALIA

Northern Hemisphere the half of the globe north of the Equator

Southern Hemisphere the half of the globe south of the Equator

Eastern Hemisphere the half of the globe east of the Prime Meridian for 180°

Western Hemisphere the half of the globe west of the Prime Meridian for 180°

Reading a Map

In addition to latitude and longitude, maps feature other important tools to help you interpret the information they contain. Learning to use these map tools will help you read the symbolic language of maps more easily.

An important step in reading a map is to study the map key. It explains the lines and symbols used on a map and the tools provided. The map scale provides a measuring line that tells you the distances represented on the map.

A symbol called a compass rose tells you the position of the four cardinal directions. These directions help you explain the relative location of any place on Earth. Most maps use different colors to make clear the different information on the map. This could be the different countries or states that make up the subject area of the map.

Northern Europe

A map key, title, boundary lines, compass rose, and scale bar reveal important information about maps.

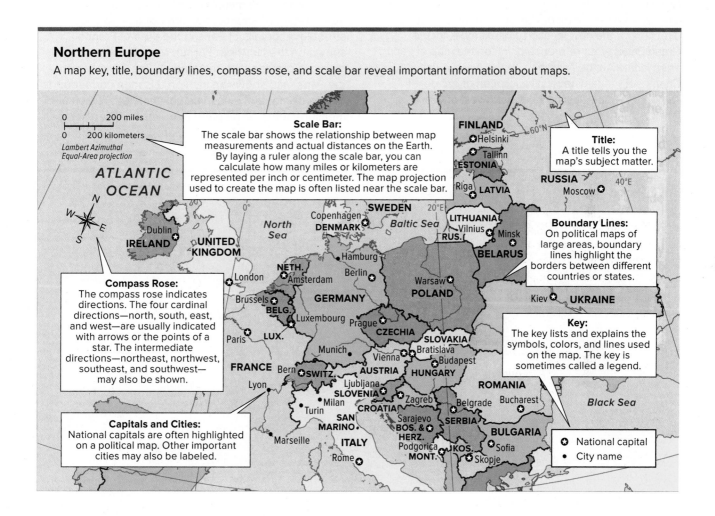

Scale Bar:
The scale bar shows the relationship between map measurements and actual distances on the Earth. By laying a ruler along the scale bar, you can calculate how many miles or kilometers are represented per inch or centimeter. The map projection used to create the map is often listed near the scale bar.

Title:
A title tells you the map's subject matter.

Boundary Lines:
On political maps of large areas, boundary lines highlight the borders between different countries or states.

Key:
The key lists and explains the symbols, colors, and lines used on the map. The key is sometimes called a legend.

Compass Rose:
The compass rose indicates directions. The four cardinal directions—north, south, east, and west—are usually indicated with arrows or the points of a star. The intermediate directions—northeast, northwest, southeast, and southwest—may also be shown.

Capitals and Cities:
National capitals are often highlighted on a political map. Other important cities may also be labeled.

- ✪ National capital
- • City name

Using Scale

All maps are drawn to a certain scale. **Scale** is a consistent, proportional relationship between the measurements shown on the map and the measurement of the Earth's surface.

Absolute and Relative Location

As you have learned, absolute location is the exact point where a line of latitude crosses a line of longitude. Another way to indicate location is by **relative location,** or the location of one place in relation to another. To find relative location, find a reference point—a location you already know—on a map. Then look in the appropriate direction for the new location. For example, locate Grand Palais (your reference point) on the map of Paris. Then locate Arc de Triomphe on the Avenue des Champs-Élysées. The relative location of Arc de Triomphe can be described as northwest of Grand Palais.

Maps of Differing Scale

A small-scale map can show a large area but little detail. Most of the maps shown in this lesson are small-scale maps that display large geographic areas.

For example, the map of Northern Europe shows the many countries of that continent in a single image. In order to do this, the scale of the map must be small to show all of the land area and the nations of Europe all together. On the Northern Europe map, the scale bar shows you that an inch on the map corresponds to approximately 200 miles in actual distance.

A large-scale map, like the map of Paris, provides more details of an area. You are not able to see street-level details of Paris in the area of France shown on the Northern Europe map. But a large-scale map can provide that information. The scale bar on the Paris map shows an inch on this map corresponds to approximately 1 mile in actual distance. The small measurements correspond to much smaller distances than on the map of Northern Europe.

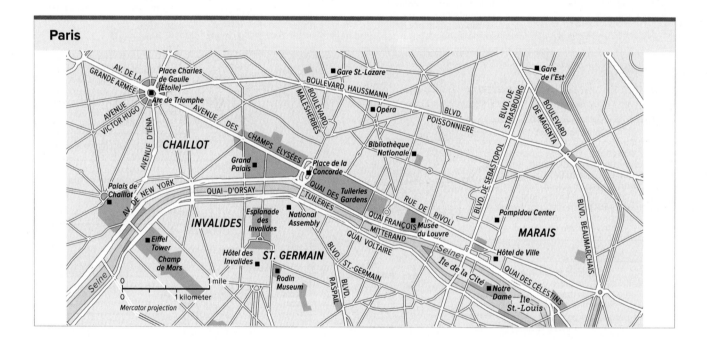

Paris

---

scale a consistent, proportional relationship between the measurements shown on a map and the measurements of Earth's surface

relative location the location of one place in relation to another

Physical and Political Maps

Physical maps and political maps are the two main types of maps in this book. A **physical map** shows the location and the topography, or shape, of the Earth's physical features. A study of an area's physical features often helps explain its historical development. A **political map** shows the boundaries and locations of political units, such as countries, states, and cities. Non-subject area is usually shown in a different color to set it apart from the main area of the map. This non-subject area gives you a context for the region you are studying.

Physical maps use shading and texture to show general relief—the differences in elevation, or height, of landforms. Landforms are physical features such as plains, mountains, plateaus, and valleys. Physical maps show rivers, streams, lakes, and other water features.

Many features on a political map are human-made, or determined by humans rather than by nature. Some human-made features are boundaries, capital cities, and roads. Political maps may also show physical features such as mountains and rivers.

Thematic Maps

Maps that emphasize a particular kind of information or a single idea are called **thematic maps.** This textbook includes thematic maps that show civilizations, migrations, natural resources, war, trade, and exploration.

Maps that use colors, symbols, lines, or dots to show information related to a specific idea are called qualitative maps.

✓ **CHECK FOR UNDERSTANDING**

1. **Explain** What is the best use for each of the following types of maps: physical map, political map, thematic map, qualitative map?

2. **Describe** What elements of a map help you interpret the information the map displays?

---

physical map a map that shows the location and shape of the Earth's physical features

political map a map that shows the boundaries and location of political units such as counties, states, and cities

thematic maps maps focused on a specific kind of information or a single idea

Physical Map

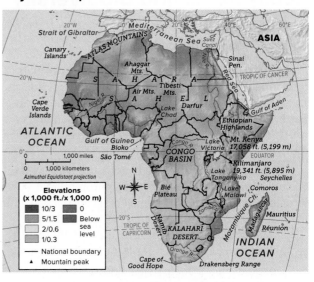

Political Map

Thematic Map

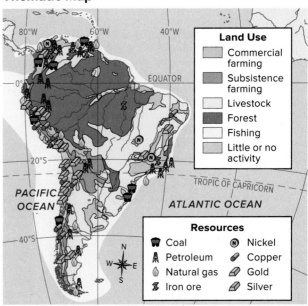

Ecosystems and Biodiversity

GUIDING QUESTION

What are ecosystems and biodiversity?

An **ecosystem** is a community of plants and animals that depend upon one another and their surroundings for survival. There are many different ecosystems on Earth. Plants, animals, and micro-organisms interact within an ecosystem. **Biodiversity** is the variation of life forms within an ecosystem.

Rain forests are one type of ecosystem. Nowhere is biodiversity more apparent than in tropical rain forests, which harbor at least half of all animal and plant species on Earth. Although the world's largest remaining tropical rain forests are in Brazil, there are temperate rain forests from North America to Australia.

Desert climates occur in just under one-third of the Earth's total land area. The natural vegetation of a desert ecosystem consists of scrub and cactus, plants that tolerate low and unreliable precipitation, low humidity, and wide temperature ranges. This arid landscape is in the Sahara Desert.

As the human communities expand, they threaten natural ecosystems. Because Earth's land, air, and water are interrelated, what affects one part of the system affects all the other parts—including humans and other living things. The photograph shows deforestation, in this case clear-cutting of the Brazilian rain forest.

✓ **CHECK FOR UNDERSTANDING**

Identifying Why do scientists pay attention to ecosystems and biodiversity?

Rain forest

Desert

Clear-cutting deforestation in Brazil

ecosystem a community of plants and animals that depend upon one another and their surroundings for survival

biodiversity the variations of life-forms within an ecosystem

(t)pxhidalgo/123RF.com; (c)Oliver Marquardt/Westend61/Image Source; (b)LeoFFreitas/Moment/Getty Images.

Geographic Information Systems

How do cartographers use geographic information systems to represent Earth?

Modern technology has changed the way maps are made. Most cartographers use computers with software programs called **geographic information systems** (GIS). A GIS is designed to accept data from different sources—maps, satellite images, printed text, and statistics. The GIS converts the data into a digital code, which arranges it in a database. Cartographers then program the GIS to process the data and produce maps. With GIS, each kind of information on a map is saved as a separate electronic layer.

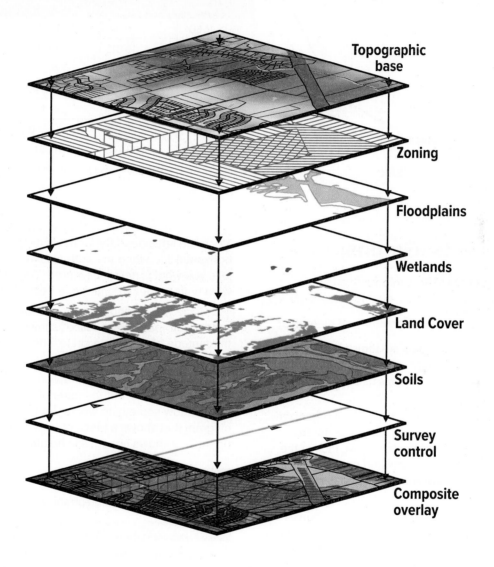

Topographic base

Zoning

Floodplains

Wetlands

Land Cover

Soils

Survey control

Composite overlay

✓ **CHECK FOR UNDERSTANDING**

Describing How does GIS allow cartographers to create maps and make changes to maps quickly and easily?

---

geographic information systems a software program that arranges a variety of data in a database and uses those data layers to produce maps

Growth of Immigrant American Colonial Population

The immigrant (non-native) population grew rapidly during the Colonial Period. In England's Southern colonies, enslaved people accounted for much of this growth, representing a majority of the population in some places.

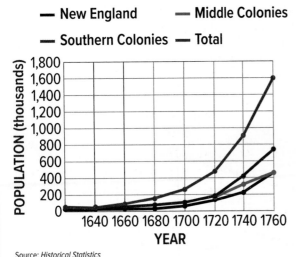

- New England
- Middle Colonies
- Southern Colonies
- Total

Source: *Historical Statistics of the United States*

Slave Trade to North America and British Caribbean			
	Mainland North America	British Caribbean	TOTALS
1601–1650	141	34,726	34,867
1651–1700	19,815	370,391	390,206
1701–1750	178,100	771,972	950,072
1751–1800	180,745	1,367,848	1,548,593
1801–1850	93,105	218,475	311,580
1851–1866	476	0	476
TOTALS	388,746	2,763,412	3,235,794

Source: Slave Voyages; slavevoyages.org/assessment/estimates

Using Charts, Graphs, and Diagrams

GUIDING QUESTION

What are the uses of charts, graphs, and diagrams?

Charts, graphs, and diagrams are tools for showing information. The first step to understanding these visual aids is to read the title. This tells you the subject.

Charts show facts and numbers in an organized way. They arrange data in rows and columns. To interpret a chart, first read the title. Next, look at the labels at the top of each column and on the left side of the chart. The labels explain what the data is measuring.

Graphs summarize and present information visually. Bar graphs use thick, wide lines to compare data. They are useful for comparing amounts. Line graphs show changes over a particular period of time. A climate graph, or climograph (KLY • muh • graf), combines a line graph and a bar graph. It shows the long-term weather patterns in a place.

To read a bar graph, line graph, or climograph, first look at the title to find out the subject. Then look at the labels along the side and bottom. The vertical line along the left side of the graph is the *y*-axis. The horizontal line along the bottom is the *x*-axis. One axis tells you what is being measured. The other axis tells what units of measurement are being used.

Circle graphs show how the whole of something is divided into parts. Each "slice" shows a part or percentage of the whole circle. The entire circle totals 100 percent.

Diagrams are special drawings. They show steps in a process, point out the parts of an object, or explain how something works. An elevation profile is a diagram that shows a piece of land as if it were sliced open. This shows changes in height.

✓ CHECK FOR UNDERSTANDING

Identifying What type of graph shows change over time?

LESSON ACTIVITIES

1. **Explanatory Writing** What is the purpose of the five themes of geography? Write a paragraph where you explain why geographers created the five themes.

2. **Collaboration** Working with a partner, locate examples of political and thematic maps in the text. Compare and contrast political and thematic maps.

---

chart a way to show facts and numbers arranged in rows and columns in an organized way

graph a means of summarizing and presenting information visually

diagram special drawing that shows steps in a process, points out the parts of an object, or explains how something works

Apply What You Have Learned

A Understanding History

ACTIVITY **Writing to Describe** Review what you have learned about how historians conduct their job and why they engage in this work. Then write a short 3–4 paragraph essay describing what you have learned. In your essay, be sure to include details about how historians study the past, what outcomes they wish to achieve, and why it is useful for students and professional historians to study history today.

B Understanding Time and Place

ACTIVITY **Making a Personal and Historical Time Line** Using the skills that you have learned, make a time line of major personal milestone events that have occurred throughout your own life. Some examples may include your birth, the start of school, and so on. Then, use an almanac or other historical source to add significant national and world events that took place around the time of the personal events you noted on your time line. Working in pairs, compare time lines with another student and discuss how you think your own personal history might influence your view of national or world events in history.

C Understanding Cartography

ACTIVITY **Making Maps** Cartographers are mapmakers. To become more familiar with the work of cartographers, use the Geography Handbook to make a map of your community, town, city, or state. Considering the five themes of geography, determine what location you will describe and its unique physical and human characteristics. Next decide whether you want to create a physical or political map. Include important details on your map such as a title, boundary lines, cities or important buildings, a scale bar, and a key or legend explaining the symbols you use. Remember that both political and physical maps may show key physical features such as mountains and rivers. Once you finish the map, evaluate how well it represents characteristics of the place you mapped. Consider how a professional cartographer might map the same area.

D Identifying Sources

ACTIVITY **Organizing Primary and Secondary Sources** Write a list of at least ten possible types of sources, such as textbooks or newspapers, you can think of that someone might consult to find information about historical events. You may refer back to lessons in this Topic for ideas. When you are done, exchange lists with another student and identify whether you think each item on the list would be considered a primary or secondary source. Explain your reasoning. You may use a graphic organizer like the one below to organize your information.

Item listed	Primary or Secondary?	Explanation?
1.		
2.		
3.		
4.		
5.		
6.		
7.		
8.		
9.		
10.		

E Understanding Multiple Perspectives

ACTIVITY **Identifying Missing Narratives** When analyzing historical information, historians must keep in mind that sources may only provide a limited picture of what was really happening in a particular place and time. In most societies, history was recorded by and about those with the most power. In some societies, the lack of a written language means that historians have no written records to rely on. Historians must often seek out alternative sources or make inferences from the evidence of artifacts to determine what life was like for others in society whose stories were not included in traditional historical records.

By 1820 the Cherokee were one of the last groups of Native Americans in the southeastern part of the United States. Many of the Cherokee attempted to assimilate, or adapt, to aspects of American culture. Some dressed in clothing similar to what white Americans wore. Other Cherokee became Christian. Some even became owners of large farms worked by enslaved people. Cherokee leaders reorganized the life of the Cherokee people to attempt to coexist with white settlers. Sequoyah, a Cherokee leader, invented a Cherokee alphabet, which led to the development of a Cherokee written language. Historians know this led to the creation of the first Cherokee newspaper, known as the *Cherokee Phoenix,* which printed articles in both English and Cherokee. However, until recently, historians did not know the Cherokee also left inscriptions in the Cherokee language on the walls of caves in what is today northeastern Alabama. "I never thought I would be looking at documents in caves," said Julie Reed, a Native American historian who is also Cherokee. The inscriptions offer historians a previously missing narrative.

Archaeologist Jan Simek said, "The writing was important because it suggested some continuity with a tradition that we knew went very far back in the past, so we started to record this stuff. It was a writing system that we couldn't read or write so we asked Cherokee scholars to come help us do it." Through the help of Cherokee scholars, they translated the messages. They believe the texts are records of rituals associated with a stickball game played by the Cherokee. Consider the importance of identifying this missing narrative: How does this evidence shed light on the Cherokee mindset in a time of assimilation? How does knowledge of this missing narrative affect our understanding of the forced removal of the Cherokee during the 1830s?

Gannon, Megan. "Cave Markings Tell of Cherokee Life in the Years Before Indian Removal." Smithsonian Magazine, April 10, 2019. https://www.smithsonianmag.com/history/cave-markings-tell-cherokee-life-years-indian-removal-180971928/.

F Making Connections to Today

ACTIVITY **Identifying Bias** People often think of history simply as something that happened in the past, but interpretations of past events often change over time. Sometimes these changes take place because historians uncover new sources of information or because later events change understanding of prior events. Interpretations can also change because of the historians themselves, whose points of view may be shaped by their own biases and in the times during which they live. Think about your own perspective. Make a list of all the factors about yourself and the times you live in that might influence your view of past events. Write a paragraph explaining what you might try to do to overcome any biases you might have.

G Evaluating Sources

ACTIVITY **Bias in Sources** Historians rely upon sources other than personal experience to ascertain the importance of key events of the past. The expectation is that history is based on the recording of facts with a degree of objectivity rather than reliance on personal opinion. However, history is often relayed through sources with biased views. Some bias may be detected by paying attention to the identity and political interests of the speaker. At times, a speaker may present a highly selective view of history without necessarily deviating from the facts. This often happens in the case of the political representation of facts involving current events and statistics. A source's bias might be revealed through the obvious omission of contrary views or relevant facts. Hyperbole, or exaggerated pronouncements that incite an emotional response, is also a characteristic of bias.

Review a reputable source of news. Identify a news article about a current event. Now identify an opinion piece in a reputable newspaper about the same or similar topic. Look for bias in both the news article and the opinion piece. It is usually expected for opinion pieces to promote a particular point of view or opinion. However, some opinion pieces may present a point of view using biased speech. Note any obvious examples of bias in the news article and the opinion piece. The bias should be clear without additional research into the topic from the kind of language featured in the article. Now compare the biases between the news article and the opinion piece. How are the degrees of objectivity similar or different? How much bias is present in each article, and what does this reveal?

H Practicing Research Techniques

ACTIVITY **Evaluating the Reliability of Internet Sources** Good historians try to utilize reliable sources in their research. They also practice high standards that include avoiding plagiarizing the work of others, unlike the student in this cartoon:

"I didn't write the book report. I downloaded and printed it directly from the Internet, but I did collate and staple it myself."

» Cartoons can make plagiarism seem humorous, but it is illegal and can lead to serious consequences.

Historians may now access millions of documents online that were once only available in person from rare archives. A lot of incorrect information can also be found online. Make a list of all the clues to look for when identifying reliable Internet sources. Prepare to keep this list in an easily accessible location for reference as you conduct research during this course.

Aaron Bacall/Cartoon Stock.

Understanding Map Scale

Maps You have learned how maps of different scales illustrate different information. A small-scale map, like the political map below of the country of France, can show a large area but little detail. Note that the scale bar on this map indicates that about 1 inch is equal to 200 miles. A large-scale map, like the map of Paris, can show a small area with a great amount of detail. Study the scale bar. Note that the map measurements correspond to much smaller distances than on the map of France.

Copy the Venn diagram here and use it to identify the similarities and differences of small-scale maps and large-scale maps.

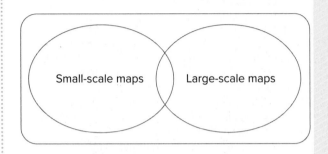

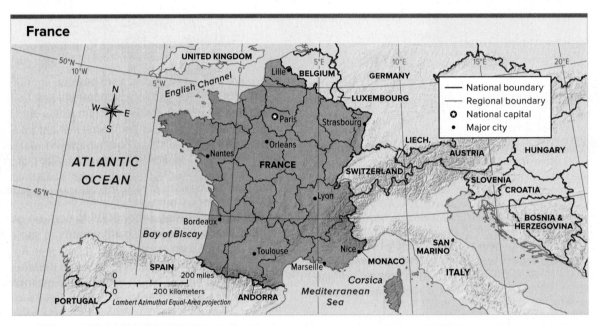

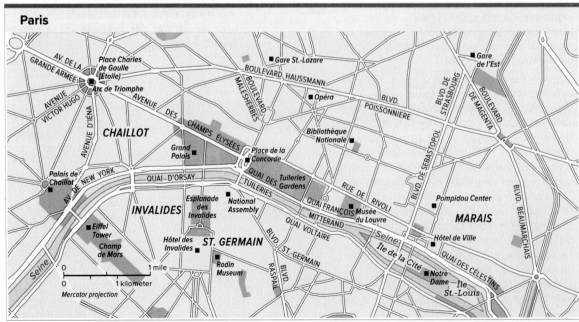

Creating a New Nation PREHISTORY TO 1877

This modern watercolor of an 1829 drawing depicts boats using the Erie Canal. The construction of the Erie Canal took eight years, and its opening in 1825 eased trade and migration to Lake Erie and nearby regions.

INTRODUCTION LESSON

01 Introducing Creating a New Nation   2

LEARN THE EVENTS LESSONS

02 The American Revolution   7

03 The Constitutional Convention   19

04 The Constitution Handbook   25

06 American Expansion and
     Growing Tensions   61

08 The Civil War and Reconstruction   73

INQUIRY ACTIVITY LESSONS

Primary Source: The Declaration
of Independence   13

The Constitution of the United States   35

05 Analyzing Sources: The Bill of Rights   55

07 Analyzing Sources: Reforming Society   67

09 Turning Point: The Compromise of 1877   79

REVIEW AND APPLY LESSON

10 Reviewing Creating a New Nation   83

Everett Collection/Shutterstock.

THE IROQUOIS CONFEDERACY

Iroquois tradition holds that before the arrival of Europeans in North America, three Native Americans joined forces to spread peace among five warring Haudenosaunee, or Iroquois, nations and unite them into a **confederacy,** an alliance for mutual support or common actions. Today that confederacy is viewed by some scholars as one of the world's earliest examples of a democracy.

This story, known as the "Peacemaker" story, features Deganawida, the Peacemaker; Onondaga chief Hiawatha; and Iroquois head clan mother Jigonsaseh. They convinced the five Iroquois nations to form the Iroquois Confederacy sometime between the late 1300s and the late 1500s. The confederacy was known by several names, including the Iroquois League and the Five Nations.

In the beginning, the Iroquois Confederacy consisted of the Mohawk, Oneida, Onondaga, Cayuga, and Seneca nations. These nations were connected by similar languages, cultures, and common goals. The members of the Confederacy resided in what is today upper New York state and southeastern Canada. Around 1722, a sixth nation, the Tuscarora, joined, and the confederacy became the Six Nations. Today, the Great Council of the Six Nations—Mohawk, Oneida, Onondaga, Cayuga, Seneca, and Tuscarora—still meets to discuss policy.

Members of the Confederacy lived according to the Great Law of Peace (Gayaneshagowa). This collection of more than 100 laws outlined complex systems for checks on authority, consensus for decisions, clan organization, the rights of the people, religious ceremonies, war, treason, and secession of nations.

> **" Our wise Forefathers established union and amity between the Five Nations. This has made us formidable. "**

The ideas of the Great Law of Peace fostered cooperation, free will, and social equality.

The Confederacy was already powerful when European explorers arrived in North America. Some Native Americans began trading beaver pelts for European firearms. This led to a scarcity of beavers and to warring between the Iroquois Confederacy and other Native American tribes. By allying with other Native American groups, French armies overcame the Confederacy between 1666 and 1696. However, the newly-formed Six Nations joined with the British against the French during the 1700s.

Some American leaders, including Benjamin Franklin, admired the Confederacy's structure and laws. In 1744 a leader of the confederacy, Canassatego, urged the thirteen American colonies to unite in the same way the Iroquois had:

> **"** Our wise Forefathers established union and amity [friendship] between the Five Nations. This has made us formidable. This has given us great weights and authority with our neighboring nations. We are a powerful Confederacy, and by your observing the same methods our wise Forefathers have taken, you will acquire fresh strength and power; therefore whatever befalls you, do not fall out with one another. **"**

—Canassatego, leader of Onondaga Nation, 1744

The Great Law of Peace may have provided one model for the U.S. Constitution. The 100th Congress of the United States recognized the Confederacy for its contributions in 1988.

Canassatego. 1744. Quoted in Indian treaties printed by Benjamin Franklin, 1736-1762. Philadelphia: Historical Society of Pennsylvania, 1938.

confederacy an alliance for mutual support or common actions

GO ONLINE Explore the Student Edition eBook and find interactive maps, time lines, and tools.

Fototeca Storica Nazionale/Hulton Archive/Getty Images

This 1921 illustration depicts the Onondaga chief Hiawatha speaking to Iroquois leaders during the formative years of the Iroquois Confederacy. Although this artist depiction represents a speculative version of events, Iroquois tradition holds that Hiawatha was one leader critical to the creation of the Five Nations.

Understanding the Time and Place:
The American Continent, Prehistory to 1754

People have been living on the land that is now the United States for thousands of years. Complex civilizations existed in North America, Central America, and South America long before European explorers sailed into the New World.

Mesoamerican Cultures

Scientists are uncertain about when the first people arrived in the Americas, but evidence suggests that humans came to these regions between 15,000 and 30,000 years ago. These early Americans were hunters and gatherers. They gathered edible plants and fruits and hunted animals such as fish, antelope, caribou, and woolly mammoths. They moved from place to place, following seasonal patterns, to find enough food to eat and to follow migratory animals. This lifestyle started to change between 7,500 and 9,500 years ago, when some early Americans learned to plant crops. The **agricultural revolution** began in Mesoamerica, the region that today includes central and southern Mexico and Central America. The agricultural revolution gave rise to Mesoamerica's first civilizations.

Scientists believe the first people to develop a civilization in Mesoamerica were the Olmec. Near what is now Veracruz, Mexico, Olmec culture emerged between 1500 B.C.E. and 1200 B.C.E. The Olmec developed a sophisticated society with large villages, temples, and pyramids.

The Maya created one of Mesoamerica's mightiest civilizations, which began around 200 C.E. in the Yucatán Peninsula and expanded into what is now Central America and southern Mexico. The Maya developed complex calendars and built large cities with pyramids at the center. These pyramids were feats of engineering; some were 200 feet (61 m) high and are still standing today. Atop each pyramid stood a temple where priests performed ceremonies dedicated to the many Maya gods. Maya civilization thrived until the 900s, when—for reasons that remain a mystery—they began abandoning their Yucatán cities. Maya cities in what is today Guatemala flourished for several more centuries, although they began to decline around the 1500s.

North of the Maya were the Toltec people. The Toltec built Tula, an extensive city with large pyramids and palaces. They were among the first American peoples to use gold and copper in art and jewelry. Around 1150 C.E., the Tula fell to the Chichimec. The Mexica, a group of Chichimec, founded the city of Tenochtitlán around 1325 in the area that is now Mexico City. Eventually, the Mexica called themselves the Aztec. The Aztec were another mighty Mesoamerican civilization that created a vast empire by conquering neighboring cities. They developed a military that controlled trade in the region. By 1500, an estimated 5 million people were living under Aztec rule.

Southwestern Cultures

People in what is now the Southwestern United States developed their own cultures, and many anthropologists believe agricultural techniques spread north from Mesoamerica. By 700 C.E., the Hohokam thrived in what is now south-central Arizona by using a large system of irrigation canals. This enabled them to use water from the Gila and Salt Rivers to grow crops such as corn, beans, squash, and cotton. The Hohokam also made decorative pottery and turquoise pendants. Their culture thrived for more than 1,000 years, but it began to decline in the 1300s and had disappeared by the 1500s.

Between 700 C.E. and 900 C.E., the Anasazi emerged in the region where Utah, Colorado, Arizona, and New Mexico meet. The term "Anasazi," or "ancient ones," is how the Navajo referred to this culture. The Anasazi built a network of basins and ditches to collect enough water to survive in the harsh desert. The Anasazi living in Chaco Canyon in what is now northwest New Mexico, built multistory buildings, later called **pueblos** by Spanish explorers, out of adobe and cut stone. These pueblos could be very large and complex. Pueblo Bonito, for example, had more than 600 rooms and probably housed at least 1,000 people.

Mississippian Cultures

The fertile soil of the Mississippi River valley supported a culture that emerged between 700 B.C.E. and 900 B.C.E. The Mississippians built great cities with flat-topped pyramids and mounds, such as the city of Cahokia in what is today Illinois. The largest of these groups were the Cherokee, who formed their distinct culture after Cahokia's decline around 1400 C.E. The Cherokee settled in North Carolina, eastern Tennessee, and northeastern Georgia. Most people lived in towns with buildings organized around a central plaza. Men hunted and women did most of

---

agricultural revolution period when early peoples learned how to plant and raise crops

pueblo Spanish for "village"; term used by early Spanish explorers to denote large housing structures built by the Anasazi

European Exploration

Beginning in the late 1400s, European nations sought to explore the globe. Once European explorers arrived in the Americas, the lives of indigenous peoples forever changed.

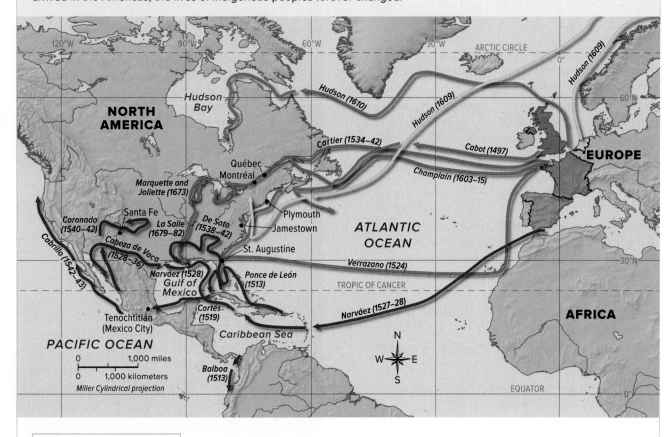

GEOGRAPHY CONNECTION

1. **Global Interconnections** Which country had the most explorers in the Americas?
2. **Patterns and Movement** Which explorer was sponsored by two different European nations? Which two nations sponsored the explorer's activities?

the farming. Mississippian culture also spread into the Great Plains. However, around 1500, many Plains people abandoned their farming villages, possibly because of war or drought, and became nomadic. They survived by following the migration of bison herds.

Northeastern Cultures

In the Northeast, Algonquian-speaking peoples lived throughout the region now known as New England. Algonquian-speaking peoples in modern-day Virginia formed the Powhatan Confederacy. Native Americans in New England and Virginia were among the first to encounter English settlers. Iroquoian-speaking peoples also lived in the Northeastern United States and Canada. Kinship groups lived in longhouses in large towns that were protected by **stockades.** Similar to other Native American groups, Iroquois men hunted and women farmed.

European Exploration

Beginning in the late 1400s and continuing throughout the next several centuries, European powers, particularly Spain, France, the Netherlands, and England, explored the globe looking for new land to acquire as colonies. Spain was the first to arrive in the Americas. In 1521, for example, a Spaniard named Hernán Cortés and his troops destroyed the Aztec city of Tenochtitlán. French and Dutch settlers set up colonies and permanent settlements in Canada and as far south as the Gulf of Mexico. The French and Dutch relied heavily on the fur trade. England began setting up colonies in the Northeast at the beginning of the seventeenth century. Competition between European nations steadily increased and more land in the Americas was divided up among them as more colonies were established.

---

stockades a line of posts set firmly to form a defense

Looking Ahead

In these next lessons, you will learn about the events leading to the United States becoming a country. While studying this time period, you will understand the American Revolution and the creation of the U.S. Constitution. You will learn about America's westward expansion and the role of slavery in the new nation. And you will understand the causes and effects of the Civil War and Reconstruction.

You will examine Compelling Questions in the Inquiry Lessons and develop your own questions about creating a new nation. Review the time line to preview some of the key events that you will learn about.

What Will You Learn

In these lessons that provide a prologue to the history of the United States from prehistory through the Civil War and Reconstruction period, you will learn:

- the different civilizations of Native American cultures in North America.
- about the different colonies established by European nations.
- how growing disagreements between the North American colonies and Great Britain led to revolution.
- the impact of the American Revolution.
- about the challenges faced by the government under the Articles of Confederation.
- the major principles of democracy outlined in the Constitution.
- how new states caused sectional arguments in the government.
- what compromises were created to balance the number of free and slave states.
- the significance of the *Dred Scott* Supreme Court ruling.
- how the election of 1860 led to a divided Union.
- the key events and individuals in the Civil War.
- the consequences of Radical Republicans taking control of Congress.

? COMPELLING QUESTIONS

- **What ideas of the Revolution are reflected in the Bill of Rights?**
- **How did reformers change nineteenth-century America?**
- **How was the Compromise of 1877 a turning point?**

KEY EVENTS OF
CREATING A NEW NATION

1763

OCTOBER 1763 King George III issues Proclamation of 1763

MARCH 22, 1765 British Parliament passes Stamp Act

APRIL 19, 1775 Battles of Lexington and Concord start Revolutionary War

JULY 4, 1776 Declaration of Independence signed (right)

MARCH 1781 Articles of Confederation ratified by the states

SEPTEMBER 3, 1783 Treaty of Paris signed, officially recognizing United States independence

1787

SEPTEMBER 1787 U.S. Constitution drafted

DECEMBER 1791 10 of the 12 proposed amendments pass as the Bill of Rights

1836

MARCH 1836 Texas declares independence from Mexico; key battle at Alamo mission

MARCH 1857 U.S. Supreme Court issues decision in *Dred Scott* v. *Sandford*

JANUARY 1, 1863 President Lincoln issues Emancipation Proclamation

DECEMBER 6, 1865 Thirteenth Amendment ratified, abolishing slavery

1877

1877 Compromise of 1877 ends Reconstruction

DNY59/E+/Getty Images

Sequencing Time Identify the events that reveal legal decisions regarding slavery and explain the importance of each.

02

The American Revolution

READING STRATEGY

Analyzing Key Ideas and Details As you read, use a graphic organizer like the one below to take notes about each event that led to the American Revolution.

Event	Details
Gaspee Affair	
Boston Tea Party	
Intolerable Acts	
Lexington and Concord	
Bunker Hill	
Common Sense	
Declaration of Independence	

Prelude to Conflict

GUIDING QUESTION

How did Great Britain's actions anger the American colonists after the French and Indian War?

In the 1740s, the British and French both tried to control the Ohio River valley. The French wanted to use the Ohio and Mississippi Rivers to travel from the St. Lawrence River valley to Louisiana. British fur traders and land speculators, who bought or claimed land from the Native American nations in the region, were also interested in the valley's economic possibilities.

Britain asked its colonies to prepare for war with the French and to negotiate an alliance with the Iroquois. The Iroquois controlled western New York—land the French passed through to reach the Ohio River—which made them useful allies of the British. In 1754 colonial delegates met with Iroquois leaders in Albany, New York, to seek an alliance.

At the Albany Conference, the Iroquois only offered limited aid to Britain. The conference also issued the Albany Plan of Union, a proposal developed by Benjamin Franklin. The Plan of Union argued that the colonies should form a centralized union to defend their shared interests. Although the colonies rejected the plan, some colonial leaders were thinking about joining together.

In 1755 French and Native American forces ambushed British troops and killed British general Edward Braddock. His aide, Lieutenant Colonel George Washington, organized a retreat. Convinced that the British were weak, the Delaware and Shawnee peoples sided with the French and began attacking British settlers in western Pennsylvania. For the next two years, the conflict raged along the frontier, and the British fleet gradually cut off supplies and reinforcements from France. The war ended in 1763 with the Treaty of Paris, which virtually eliminated French power in North America.

Growing Colonial Anger

Great Britain's victory in 1763 left the country deeply in debt. The nation needed to not only pay down the cost of the French and Indian War but it also faced the new costs of governing and defending new territory. The policies adopted to solve these financial problems enraged the America colonists.

In the spring of 1763, Pontiac, chief of the Ottawa people, went to war against the British. Native American groups burned towns where settlers had defied a treaty that prevented them from settling on Native American lands west of the Appalachian Mountains. King George III responded by issuing the Proclamation of 1763, which drew a north-south line along the Appalachian Mountains, west of which the colonists could not settle without permission. This angered colonial farmers and land speculators. That same year, George Grenville became prime minister and first lord of the British Treasury. Grenville knew that merchants were smuggling many goods into and out of the colonies without paying **customs duties.** Parliament passed a law allowing smugglers to be tried at a new vice-admiralty court in Nova Scotia. Colonists argued that these vice-admiralty courts denied their rights as British citizens. Grenville also introduced the Sugar Act, which imposed taxes on imports of raw sugar, molasses, and other goods. Under the act, the property of merchants accused of smuggling was presumed illegal until its legality was proven. The Currency

---

customs duty a tax on imports and exports

Townshend Acts, 1767

Charles Townshend believed that custom duties, which were indirect taxes, would meet with less colonial resistance than the direct taxes imposed by the Stamp Act.

Name of Act	What It Did
Suspending Act	Banned the New York legislature from meeting until it complied with the 1765 Quartering Act, which required colonial authorities to provide housing, food, fuel, and transportation for British troops.
Revenue Act	Put new customs duties on imported glass, lead, paper, paint, and tea. Violators faced trial in vice-admiralty courts, and their private property could be seized without due process. The act also legalized writs of assistance, allowing customs officers to enter any location.
Commissioners of Customs Act	Established an American Customs Board in Boston to enforce strict trade and shipping regulations. The act was meant to reduce smuggling and raise money by collecting taxes on imported goods.
Indemnity Act	Reduced duties on tea imported to England by the British East India Company and refunded export duties. It aimed to help the failing company export tea to the colonies that was cheap enough to compete with smuggled Dutch tea.

ECONOMICS CONNECTION

1. **Interpreting** How would these acts have alleviated Britain's financial problems?
2. **Analyzing Points of View** Why might the colonists have viewed the acts as coercive?

Act of 1764, which banned the use of paper money in the colonies in an effort to slow **inflation,** further angered the colonists.

Parliament then passed the Stamp Act in 1765. This act taxed most printed materials and was the first direct tax levied on the colonists. In response the Virginia House of Burgesses passed resolutions declaring that Virginians could be taxed only by their own representatives. Other colonial assemblies passed similar resolutions. By summer, a group called the Sons of Liberty was organizing demonstrations and intimidating stamp distributors. In October 1765 representatives from nine colonies gathered for what became known as the Stamp Act Congress. They issued a declaration that taxation depended upon representation, so only the colonists' political representatives—not Parliament—could tax them.

When the Stamp Act went into effect soon after, the colonists ignored it and began boycotting all British goods. Rather than supporting British manufacturing, the Daughters of Liberty organized spinning bees, where women spun thread to make their own cloth. In New York, 200 merchants signed a **nonimportation agreement,** pledging not to buy any British goods until Parliament repealed the Stamp Act. Parliament repealed the act in 1766 but also affirmed its authority to make laws for the colonies.

During the Stamp Act crisis, Britain's financial problems worsened. Protests in Britain forced Parliament to lower property taxes there, yet the government still had to pay for its troops in America. In 1767 Charles Townshend, the Crown's chief financial officer, introduced new regulations and taxes, which came to be called the Townshend Acts. The Townshend Acts infuriated many colonists. The Massachusetts assembly began organizing resistance against Britain. In February 1768 Samuel Adams and the Massachusetts assembly drafted a "circular letter" criticizing the acts to send to other colonies. When British officials ordered the Massachusetts assembly to withdraw the letter, the assembly refused, and the British then ordered the assembly dissolved. In August 1768 the merchants of Boston and New York responded by signing nonimportation agreements. Philadelphia's merchants joined the boycott in March 1769.

In May 1769 Virginia's House of Burgesses passed the Virginia Resolves, stating that only it could tax Virginians. Under orders from Britain, Virginia's governor dissolved the House of Burgesses. In response, the leaders of the House of Burgesses—including George Washington, Patrick Henry, and Thomas Jefferson—called the members to a convention, which passed a nonimportation law blocking the sale of British goods in Virginia.

---

inflation the loss of value of money

nonimportation agreement a pledge by merchants not to buy imported goods from a particular source

Tensions Turn Violent

In Boston riots sparked by the Townshend Acts led the British to send more troops to manage tensions. On March 5, 1770, a crowd of colonists began taunting and throwing snowballs at a British soldier guarding a customs house. Captain Thomas Preston and a squad of soldiers responded. The troops fired into the crowd, ultimately killing five people and wounding six. The shootings became known as the Boston Massacre. Despite the media sensationalism of the event, the soldiers were not convicted. Before the situation could worsen, news arrived that the British had repealed almost all of the Townshend Acts, and peace and stability temporally returned to the colonies.

Colonial Turmoil

After Britain repealed the Townshend Acts, trade and smuggling resumed. To intercept smugglers, the British sent customs ships, such as the Gaspee, to patrol North American waters. In June 1772, when the Gaspee ran aground, some 150 Rhode Island colonists seized and burned the ship. The British sent a commission to investigate and gave its members the power to take suspects to Britain for trial. Colonists believed this violated their right to a trial by a jury of their peers. In response, Thomas Jefferson suggested that each colony create a **committee of correspondence** to communicate with the other colonies about British activities.

In May 1773 Britain's Parliament tried to help the British East India Company out of debt by passing the Tea Act of 1773, which reduced the tax on tea that the company shipped to the colonies. The act angered some colonists, who did not want to pay the tax. In October 1773 the company shipped 1,253 chests of tea to Boston, New York, Philadelphia, and Charles Town. The committees of correspondence decided that the tea must not be unloaded. On December 16, 1773, about 150 men disguised as Native Americans dumped 342 chests of tea into Boston Harbor in what came to be called the Boston Tea Party.

The Boston Tea Party was the last straw for the British. In the spring of 1774 Parliament passed four new laws that came to be known as the Coercive Acts, which were intended to punish Massachusetts and put an end to colonial challenges to British authority. That summer, the British also introduced the Quebec Act, which would ultimately result in colonists living in territories with no elected assembly. The Coercive Acts and the Quebec Act together became known as the Intolerable Acts.

On September 5, 1774, 55 colonial delegates from 12 of Britain's North American colonies met in Philadelphia for what became the First Continental Congress. The Congress issued a Declaration of Rights and Grievances, which expressed loyalty to the king, but also condemned the Intolerable Acts. The delegates agreed to hold a second Continental Congress in May 1775 if the crisis had not resolved. When the Second Continental Congress met, the delegates voted to "adopt" the militia army surrounding Boston, which they named the Continental Army, and placed it under the command of George Washington. Still, many colonists were unwilling to break away from Great Britain. In July 1775, the Second Continental Congress sent a document known as the Olive Branch Petition to King George III, which declared the colonies' loyalty and asked him to call off hostilities until the situation could be negotiated peacefully. When the Olive Branch Petition arrived in London in August 1775, the king refused to look at it. Instead he issued the Proclamation for Suppressing Rebellion and Sedition, declaring that the colonists were now in "open and avowed rebellion."

✓ **CHECK FOR UNDERSTANDING**

1. **Describing** How did British actions anger the American colonists after the French and Indian War?
2. **Making Connections** Why do you think King George III's actions in 1775 might have provoked the colonists?

The Revolution Begins

GUIDING QUESTION

What were the key turning points for the colonial forces during the war?

As the Patriots' protests grew stronger and more vocal, the British government saw a rapid military victory as the best way to overcome the rebellion in the colonies. Government officials believed their forces were stronger and better organized than were the colonists, but this belief would prove untrue as the battles raged on and Britain's position worsened throughout the conflict.

In April 1775 the British government risked armed conflict by ordering General Gage to arrest the Massachusetts Provincial Congress. Not knowing where the Congress was sitting, Gage decided to seize the militia's supply depot at Concord instead. After clashing with colonial **minutemen** in Lexington, the British troops arrived in Concord only to discover that the colonial militia had already removed most of the military supplies. Once again clashing with the colonial militia, the British retreated to Boston.

By May 1775, the militia had surrounded Boston, trapping the British. Determined to gain control of the

---

committee of correspondence committee organized in each colony to communicate with and unify the colonies

minutemen companies of civilian soldiers who boasted they were ready to fight at a minute's notice

Edward Percy Moran's 1909 painting shows British troops retreating from colonial military at the Battle of Bunker Hill.

city, the British decided to seize the hills north of the city. Warned in advance, the Massachusetts militia acted first, and on June 16, 1775, they dug in on Breed's Hill near Bunker Hill and stopped two British attacks before running out of ammunition and retreating. The Battle of Bunker Hill, as it came to be called, helped build American confidence because it showed that the colonial militia could stand up to the British. Shortly afterward, General Gage resigned and was replaced by General William Howe. The situation became a stalemate with the British surrounded by colonial militia.

Declaring Independence

By 1776, American sentiment had moved away from negotiation. Frustrated by Britain's refusal to compromise, many Patriot leaders began to call for independence. The Second Continental Congress started acting as an independent government, negotiating with the Native Americans and establishing a postal system, a Continental Navy, and a Marine Corps.

As the Revolution began, Governor Dunmore of Virginia organized two Loyalist armies to assist British troops in Virginia, one composed of white Loyalists, the other of enslaved Africans. In December 1775 the Patriot troops attacked and defeated Dunmore's forces near Norfolk, Virginia. Months later the British pulled their soldiers out of Virginia, leaving the Patriots in control. While fighting raged in the South, Washington ordered his troops to capture the hills south of Boston. After the Americans seized the hills by surprise and surrounded Boston, the British navy evacuated the British troops, leaving the area under Patriot control. Despite their defeats, it was clear that the British were not backing down.

As the war dragged on, more Patriots began to think it was time to declare independence, although they feared that most colonists were still loyal to the

king. In January 1776 public opinion changed when Thomas Paine published a persuasive pamphlet called *Common Sense*, which attacked King George III. In early July a Committee of Five submitted a document that Thomas Jefferson of Virginia had drafted on independence. On July 4, 1776, the Continental Congress issued this Declaration of Independence. Drawing on the new political theories of the Enlightenment, it stated that people are endowed with unalienable rights not granted by the government and that the only reason people created government was to protect their rights. The only legitimate powers a government had were the powers it got from the "consent of the governed." The Declaration of Independence marks the birth of the United States, the first modern democratic republic.

Key Battles and Leaders

The British had sent a huge force to seize New York City, and the Continental Congress asked General George Washington to defend it. Nonetheless, the British captured the city, using it as their headquarters for the rest of the war, and Washington moved most of his troops to White Plains, New York. Rather than confronting Washington's forces in White Plains, the British headed toward Philadelphia—where the Continental Congress was meeting—in October 1776. Washington quickly moved his troops to arrive there first, but the British stopped the advance and dispersed into winter camps in New Jersey. On December 25, 1776, Washington responded with a daring winter attack on the British at Trenton.

After losing Philadelphia to British general William Howe in 1777, Washington set up winter camp at Valley Forge, where two European military officers, the Marquis de Lafayette from France and Baron Friedrich von Steuben from Prussia, helped train the troops in important military techniques. Meanwhile, General Benedict Arnold's American troops drove back British and Iroquois forces under the command of British general John Burgoyne at Fort Ticonderoga in New York. Burgoyne was then defeated by General Horatio Gates's American forces at the Battle of Saratoga, surrendering on October 17, 1777. The victory greatly boosted American morale.

The British turned their attention to the South, where they believed they had the strongest Loyalist support. In December 1778 British troops captured Savannah, Georgia. Then British general Henry Clinton surrounded Charles Town, South Carolina, trapping the American forces inside. On May 12, 1780, the Americans surrendered, and about 5,500 were taken prisoner, the greatest American defeat in the war. In the spring of 1781 British general Charles Cornwallis marched into Virginia to conquer it, joining forces with Benedict Arnold, a former American general who had changed sides to fight for the British. When a large American force led by General Anthony Wayne, Baron

Library of Congress, Prints and Photographs Division [LC-USZC4-4970]

The Revolutionary War

While the Revolutionary War involved many battles, those at Trenton, Saratoga, and Yorktown were significant because they led to American victories. The location of each battle aided the Continental Army in meeting its goals.

Key Battles	Importance of Geography	Significance of Outcome
Trenton December 1776	• General Washington made use of poor weather conditions, leading 2,400 men across the Delaware River to launch a surprise attack on the British.	• Hessian mercenaries were defeated. • Continental Army gained supply of weapons. • Morale of Washington's troops improved.
Saratoga October 1777	• General Gates's men fortified high ground near Saratoga that overlooked the Hudson River and built a line of defense between the hills and river.	• The French were convinced that the Americans had a chance of victory against Britain. • America and France signed two treaties in which France recognized American independence and became an official ally.
Yorktown September-October 1781	• Cornwallis retreated to the coastal town of Yorktown after being outnumbered in Virginia. The Continental Army blocked Cornwallis by land, while French troops prevented an escape by sea.	• Cornwallis surrendered to George Washington. • The Revolutionary War officially ended with a negotiated peace treaty in 1783.

GEOGRAPHY CONNECTION

1. **Identifying Cause and Effect** How did geography negatively affect the British military at Trenton, Saratoga, and Yorktown?

2. **Making Connections** How did the victory of the Continental Army at Trenton aid the Patriot forces?

Friedrich von Steuben, and the Marquis de Lafayette arrived, Cornwallis, outnumbered and too far inland, retreated to the coastal town of Yorktown to protect his supplies and to maintain communications by sea.

On September 28, 1781, American and French forces began bombarding Yorktown. On October 14, Washington's aide, Alexander Hamilton, led an attack that captured key British defenses. Three days later, Cornwallis began negotiations to surrender, and on October 19, 1781, some 8,000 British soldiers laid down their weapons.

The Treaty of Paris

In March 1782 Parliament voted to begin peace negotiations. The Americans relied on the skills of John Adams, Benjamin Franklin, and John Jay, who conducted most of the negotiations for the United States. On September 3, 1783, treaties were signed—between Britain and the United States and between Britain and France and Spain. In the final set of agreements, known as the Treaty of Paris, Britain recognized the United States of America as an independent nation, with the Mississippi River as its western border, even though this was land under Native American control. Britain gave Florida back to Spain, and France received colonies in Africa and the Caribbean. On November 24, 1783, the last British

troops left New York City. The American Revolution was over, and a new nation was born.

CHECK FOR UNDERSTANDING

1. **Analyzing** How did Thomas Paine help persuade colonists to declare independence?

2. **Explaining** Why was the American victory at Saratoga a key turning point in the war?

The War's Impact

GUIDING QUESTION

How did the Revolutionary War affect people?

While the American ideals of equality and liberty were not equally applied to all people after the war's end, women had participated in the Revolutionary effort. Before the war, women organized boycotts and protest actions. Women contributed on both the home front and the battlefront. With their male family members at war, some women took over running family farms. Women traveled with the army and helped keep the soldiers ready for fighting by cooking, washing, and nursing the wounded. Some worked on the edge of battle by serving as spies and couriers; a few even joined the fighting.

DINAH MORRIS'S CERTIFICATE OF FREEDOM.

This nineteenth century engraving shows Dinah Morris, who was one of the first enslaved people in the North granted her freedom during the American Revolution.

Analyzing Visuals How did African Americans react to emancipation according to this illustration?

The Revolution did not help most Native Americans. The American Revolution caused a civil war among the Iroquois Confederacy, and the Confederacy was weakened as member groups fought against each other. Few Native Americans on either side of the conflict received recognition for their contributions. Even more damaging than wartime casualties, Native American contact with both Patriot and British soldiers caused another smallpox epidemic between 1775 and 1782.

Both the British and the Patriots offered freedom to enslaved African Americans for fighting, and many African Americans seized the chance for freedom by running to the British forces. On the Patriot side, state militias enlisted African Americans, and an estimated 5,000 African American soldiers fought in the Continental Army during the Revolution.

After the Revolution, some Americans realized that enslaving people did not fit in with the new ideals of liberty and equality and acted to change the new nation's laws. The Pennsylvania legislature passed a gradual **emancipation** act in 1780. But even though some desired to free enslaved people, even in states that passed emancipation acts, freedom was not instant. Despite the contradictions between the stated ideals of liberty and independence, people's economic interests often held strong sway. Over the next few decades, other Northern states passed laws that freed enslaved people when they reached a certain age.

Some African Americans sued to win their freedom when Massachusetts's new constitution said that all people were free and equal. Quock Walker, an enslaved person, believed that the law was on his side. Massachusetts chief justice William Cushing agreed and found in Walker's favor:

emancipation the act or process of freeing enslaved persons

> Our [state] Constitution . . . sets out with declaring that all men are born free and equal—and that every subject is entitled to liberty and to have it guarded by the laws, as well as life and property—and in short is totally repugnant to the idea of [people] being born slaves. This being the case, I think the idea of slavery is inconsistent with our own conduct and Constitution.

—Chief Justice William Cushing, Massachusetts court ruling, 1783

Discrimination against African Americans did not disappear when a few were freed. African Americans could often only get low-level manual labor jobs. Free African Americans in the North also faced voting restrictions, segregation, or kidnapping and transportation to the South, where they would again be enslaved.

Some of those enslaved in the South who were lucky enough to gain freedom moved to Northern cities to find jobs, even though slavery still existed in the North as late as 1827. Some found new life in previously barred occupations, such as artists and ministers. Some formerly enslaved people fled to other parts of the British empire for freedom, including 5,000 who were evacuated with the British in 1782.

The South, however, still relied on the labor of enslaved people to sustain its agricultural economy, and Southern leaders showed little interest in ending slavery. Only Virginia took steps toward ending the institution by passing a law in 1782 that encouraged freeing enslaved people, especially those who had fought in the Revolution. But only about 10,000 enslaved people obtained their freedom this way, and the vast majority of African Americans in the state and throughout the region remained in bondage.

✓ **CHECK FOR UNDERSTANDING**

Determining Central Ideas What was the main reason that slavery took longer to eradicate in the South than in the North after the Revolution?

LESSON ACTIVITIES

1. **Argumentative Writing** Suppose that you are a colonial leader during the American Revolution. Write a letter to convince the ruler of a European nation to support the Americans in the war.

2. **Using Multimedia** Conduct research with a partner to learn more about the role of African Americans, Native Americans, or women of various ethnic backgrounds during the American Revolution. Work together to create a multimedia report about their contributions to the war and how they affected its outcome. Share your report with the class.

PHOTO: Classic Collection 2/Alamy Stock Photo; TEXT: Cushing, William. The Case of Nathaniel Jennison. Boston: John Wilson and Son, 1874.

The writers of the Declaration of Independence included Benjamin Franklin, John Adams, and Thomas Jefferson.

The Declaration of Independence

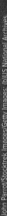

(t)John Parrot/Stocktrek Images/Getty Images; (b)US National Archives.

When the Declaration of Independence was written in 1776, with very few exceptions, the people of the world were governed by monarchs, emperors, and absolute rulers. Since Roman times, there had been very little development in political ideas regarding the relationship between the individual and the government. By the time of the Enlightenment in the eighteenth century, many new ideas had emerged. Those ideas culminated in the American Declaration of Independence.

JULY 4, 1776.

PRIMARY SOURCE : DECLARATION OF INDEPENDENCE

In Congress, July 4, 1776. The unanimous Declaration of the thirteen united States of America,

[Preamble]

PREAMBLE

The Declaration of Independence has four parts. The Preamble explains why the Continental Congress drew up the Declaration.

When in the Course of human events, it becomes necessary for one people to dissolve the political bands which have connected them with another, and to assume among the powers of the earth, the separate and equal station to which the Laws of Nature and of Nature's God entitle them, a decent respect to the opinions of mankind requires that they should declare the causes which **impel** them to the separation.

[Declaration of Natural Rights]

DECLARATION OF NATURAL RIGHTS

The second part, the Declaration of Natural Rights, states that people have certain basic rights and that government should protect those rights. John Locke's ideas strongly influenced this part. In 1690 Locke wrote that government was based on the consent of the people and that people had the right to rebel if the government did not uphold their right to life, liberty, and property.

We hold these truths to be self-evident, that all men are created equal, that they are **endowed** by their Creator with certain unalienable Rights, that among these are Life, Liberty, and the pursuit of Happiness.

That to secure these rights, Governments are instituted among Men, deriving their just powers from the consent of the governed,

That whenever any Form of Government becomes destructive of these ends, it is the Right of the People to alter or to abolish it, and to institute new Government, laying its foundation on such principles and organizing its powers in such form, as to them shall seem most likely to effect their Safety and Happiness. Prudence, indeed, will dictate that Governments long established should not be changed for light and transient causes; and accordingly all experience hath shewn, that mankind are more disposed to suffer, while evils are sufferable, than to right themselves by abolishing the forms to which they are accustomed. But when a long train of abuses and **usurpations,** pursuing invariably the same Object evinces a design to reduce them under absolute **Despotism,** it is their right, it is their duty, to throw off such Government, and to provide new Guards for their future security.

impel force

endowed provided

usurpations unjust uses of power

despotism unlimited power

Engrossed copy of the Declaration of Independence, August 2, 1776; Miscellaneous Papers of the Continental Congress, 1774–1789; Records of the Continental and Confederation Congresses and the Constitutional Convention, 1774–1789, Record Group 360; National Archives.

[List of Grievances]

Such has been the patient sufferance of these Colonies; and such is now the necessity which constrains them to alter their former Systems of Government. The history of the present King of Great Britain is a history of repeated injuries and usurpations, all having in direct object the establishment of an absolute Tyranny over these States. To prove this, let Facts be submitted to a candid world.

He has refused his Assent to Laws, the most wholesome and necessary for the public good.

He has forbidden his Governors to pass Laws of immediate and pressing importance, unless suspended in their operation till his Assent should be obtained; and when so suspended, he has utterly neglected to attend to them.

He has refused to pass other Laws for the accommodation of large districts of people, unless those people would **relinquish** the right of Representation in the Legislature, a right **inestimable** to them and formidable to tyrants only.

He has called together legislative bodies at places unusual, uncomfortable, and distant from the depository of their Public Records, for the sole purpose of fatiguing them into compliance with his measures.

LIST OF GRIEVANCES

The third part of the Declaration is a list of the colonists' complaints against the British government. Notice that King George III is singled out for blame.

Declaration of Independence by John Trumbull depicts the presentation of the Declaration of Independence to John Hancock (seated right), president of the Continental Congress.

John Parrot/Stocktrek Images/Getty Images

---

relinquish give up   **inestimable** priceless

He has dissolved Representative Houses repeatedly, for opposing with manly firmness his invasions on the rights of the people.

He has refused for a long time, after such dissolutions, to cause others to be elected; whereby the Legislative Powers, incapable of **Annihilation,** have returned to the People at large for their exercise; the State remaining in the mean time exposed to all the dangers of invasion from without, and **convulsions** within.

He has endeavoured to prevent the population of these States; for that purpose obstructing the Laws for **Naturalization of Foreigners**; refusing to pass others to encourage their migrations hither, and raising the conditions of new Appropriations of Lands.

He has obstructed the Administration of Justice, by refusing his Assent to Laws for establishing Judiciary Powers.

He has made Judges dependent on his Will alone, for the **tenure** of their offices, and the amount and payment of their salaries.

He has erected a multitude of New Offices, and sent hither swarms of Officers to harass our people, and eat out their substance.

He has kept among us, in times of peace, Standing Armies without the Consent of our legislature.

He has affected to render the Military independent of and superior to the Civil Power.

He has combined with others to subject us to a jurisdiction foreign to our constitution, and unacknowledged by our laws; giving his Assent to their Acts of pretended legislation:

For **quartering** large bodies of troops among us:

For protecting them, by a mock Trial, from punishment for any Murders which they should commit on the Inhabitants of these States:

For cutting off our Trade with all parts of the world:

For imposing Taxes on us without our Consent:

For depriving us in many cases, of the benefits of Trial by Jury:

For transporting us beyond Seas to be tried for pretended offences:

For abolishing the free System of English Laws in a neighbouring Province, establishing therein an Arbitrary government, and enlarging its Boundaries so as to **render** it at once an example and fit instrument for introducing the same absolute rule into these Colonies:

For taking away our Charters, abolishing our most valuable Laws, and altering fundamentally the Forms of our Governments:

---

annihilation destruction

convulsions violent disturbances

Naturalization of Foreigners process by which foreign-born persons become citizens

tenure term

quartering lodging

render make

For suspending our own Legislatures, and declaring themselves invested with power to legislate for us in all cases whatsoever.

He has **abdicated** Government here, by declaring us out of his Protection and waging War against us.

He has plundered our seas, ravaged our Coasts, burnt our towns, and destroyed the lives of our people.

He is at this time transporting large Armies of foreign mercenaries to compleat the works of death, desolation and tyranny, already begun with circumstances of Cruelty & **perfidy** scarcely paralleled in the most barbarous ages, and totally unworthy the Head of a civilized nation.

He has constrained our fellow Citizens taken Captive on the high Seas to bear Arms against their Country, to become the executioners of their friends and Brethren, or to fall themselves by their Hands.

He has excited domestic **insurrections** amongst us, and has endeavoured to bring on the inhabitants of our frontiers, the merciless Indian Savages, whose known rule of warfare, is an undistinguished destruction of all ages, sexes and conditions.

In every stage of these Oppressions We have **Petitioned for Redress** in the most humble terms: Our repeated Petitions have been answered only by repeated injury. A Prince, whose character is thus marked by every act which may define a Tyrant, is unfit to be the ruler of a free People.

Nor have We been wanting in attention to our British brethren. We have warned them from time to time of attempts by their legislature to extend an **unwarrantable jurisdiction** over us. We have reminded them of the circumstances of our emigration and settlement here. We have appealed to their native justice and magnanimity, and we have conjured them by the ties of our common kindred to disavow these usurpations, which, would inevitably interrupt our connections and correspondence. They too have been deaf to the voice of justice and of **consanguinity.** We must, therefore, acquiesce in the necessity, which denounces our Separation, and hold them, as we hold the rest of mankind, Enemies in War, in Peace Friends.

John Hancock's signature on the Declaration of Independence.

---

abdicated given up

perfidy violation of trust

insurrections rebellions

petitioned for redress asked formally for a correction of wrongs

unwarrantable jurisdiction unjustified authority

consanguinity originating from the same ancestor

DNY59/E+/Getty Images

RESOLUTION OF INDEPENDENCE

The final section declares that the colonies are "Free and Independent States" with the full power to make war, to form alliances, and to trade with other countries.

SIGNERS OF THE DECLARATION

The signers, as representatives of the American people, declared the colonies independent from Great Britain. Most members signed the document on August 2, 1776.

[Resolution of Independence by the United States]

We, therefore, the Representatives of the united States of America, in General Congress, Assembled, appealing to the Supreme Judge of the world for the **rectitude** of our intentions, do, in the Name, and by Authority of the good People of these Colonies, solemnly publish and declare, That these United Colonies are, and of Right ought to be Free and Independent States; that they are Absolved from all Allegiance to the British Crown, and that all political connection between them and the State of Great Britain, is and ought to be totally dissolved; and that as Free and Independent States, they have full Power to levy War, conclude Peace, contract Alliances, establish Commerce, and to do all other Acts and Things which Independent States may of right do.

And for the support of this Declaration, with a firm reliance on the Protection of Divine Providence, we mutually pledge to each other our Lives, our Fortunes and our sacred Honor.

John Hancock
President from Massachusetts

Georgia
Button Gwinnett
Lyman Hall
George Walton

North Carolina
William Hooper
Joseph Hewes
John Penn

South Carolina
Edward Rutledge
Thomas Heyward, Jr.
Thomas Lynch, Jr.
Arthur Middleton

Maryland
Samuel Chase
William Paca
Thomas Stone
Charles Carroll of Carrollton

Virginia
George Wythe
Richard Henry Lee
Thomas Jefferson
Benjamin Harrison
Thomas Nelson, Jr.
Francis Lightfoot Lee
Carter Braxton

Pennsylvania
Robert Morris
Benjamin Rush
Benjamin Franklin
John Morton
George Clymer
James Smith
George Taylor
James Wilson
George Ross

Delaware
Caesar Rodney
George Read
Thomas McKean

New York
William Floyd
Philip Livingston
Francis Lewis
Lewis Morris

New Jersey
Richard Stockton
John Witherspoon
Francis Hopkinson
John Hart
Abraham Clark

New Hampshire
Josiah Bartlett
William Whipple
Matthew Thornton

Massachusetts
Samuel Adams
John Adams
Robert Treat Paine
Elbridge Gerry

Rhode Island
Stephen Hopkins
William Ellery

Connecticut
Samuel Huntington
William Williams
Oliver Wolcott
Roger Sherman

rectitude rightness

03

The Constitutional Convention

READING STRATEGY

Analyzing Key Ideas and Details As you read, complete a graphic organizer like the one below to take notes.

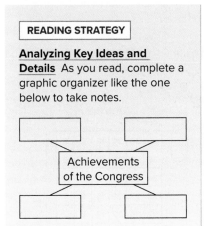

The Articles of Confederation

GUIDING QUESTION

What challenges did the new government face?

On July 4, 1776, the 13 colonies declared themselves to be free and independent states, united in their separation from Great Britain. But that declaration did not mean the states viewed themselves as a united country. Instead, each state considered itself a separate, **sovereign** entity with its own constitution, customs, and priorities. At the same time, Americans realized that waging war against the British required coordination and cooperation among the states. American success depended on raising an army and speaking with a single voice when establishing alliances in Europe and negotiating with Native Americans at home. The states knew they needed a way to settle disputes between themselves and protect their boundaries from outside encroachment.

As a result the Continental Congress set out to develop a plan for a central government—one strong enough to accomplish these goals but still weak enough to prevent it from interfering in the operation of the states. Because Americans had just rebelled against a strong, centralized British government, they sought a government with a more decentralized power.

In November 1777 the Continental Congress adopted the Articles of Confederation, a plan for a loose union of the states under the authority of a governing body called Congress. Under the Articles of Confederation each state would select a delegation to send to the capital city once a year. This group, generally referred to as Congress, was the entire government; there were no executive and judicial branches. The Confederation Congress had the right to declare war and sign treaties, but it did not have the power to impose taxes. It was also explicitly denied the power to regulate the economy. Instead, the states retained those powers and remained sovereign under the Articles.

Congressional Successes

Without the power to tax or regulate trade, the government depended on state contributions for funding. The Congress also raised money by selling land west of the Appalachian Mountains, even though Native Americans possessed and lived on that land.

To make it easier for American settlers to buy land, the Congress passed the Land Ordinance of 1785, which arranged the territory into townships that were further divided into 36 sections. In each township, one section was set aside for creating and maintaining public education.

In 1787 the Congress passed the Northwest Ordinance, which created the Northwest Territory, the area north of the Ohio River and east of the Mississippi River. This area was eventually divided into several territories. When the population of a territory reached 60,000, the territory could apply for admission as a state. The Northwest Ordinance also protected civil liberties and banned slavery in the new territory. This meant that as the nation expanded, it would be divided between Southern slave-holding states and Northern free states. The Congress tried to promote trade with other nations

---

sovereign possessing supreme authority

Northwest Ordinance of 1787

The Northwest Ordinance established a process for creating new states and admitting them to the Union "on an equal footing with the original States in all respects."

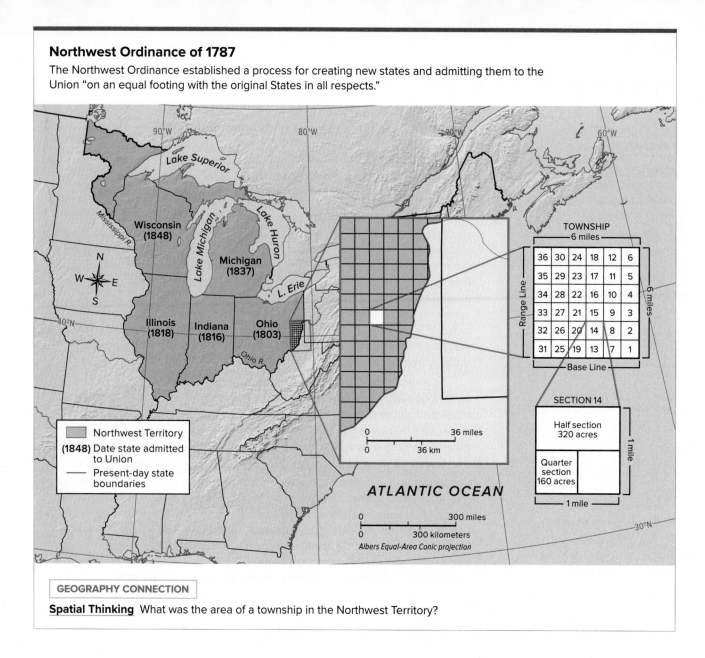

GEOGRAPHY CONNECTION

Spatial Thinking What was the area of a township in the Northwest Territory?

such as Holland, Prussia, and Sweden through new treaties. The U.S. also traded with French colonies in the Caribbean.

Weaknesses in the Articles

The western land ordinances and trade treaties were important achievements. However, the lack of power to regulate trade and impose taxes weakened the Congress, making it difficult to solve other problems.

During the boycotts of the 1760s and the Revolutionary War, American artisans and manufacturers had prospered by making goods that people had previously bought from the British. After the war, British merchants flooded the United States with inexpensive British goods, driving many American artisans out of business. Several states restricted

British imports, but they did not all impose the same **duties,** or taxes, on foreign goods. The British took their goods to the states with the lowest taxes and then moved those products to the other states. The states tried to prevent the British from exploiting the different trade laws by levying tariffs on British goods that crossed state lines. Each state was beginning to act independently, which threatened the unity of the new nation.

The Congress also faced diplomatic problems. Many American merchants and planters had borrowed money from British lenders before the war.

As part of the 1783 Treaty of Paris, which ended the Revolutionary War, the United States had agreed that the states would let the British lenders sue in American courts to recover their debts. However, some

duty a tax on imports

states made this process difficult or refused to return to Loyalists their property confiscated during the war.

In retaliation, British forces continued to occupy frontier posts despite a provision in the treaty calling for them to leave American soil. The Confederation Congress had no power to impose taxes to raise the money for a financial settlement with Britain, or to compel the states to send troops to enforce the treaty. The Confederation Congress's limited power also prevented a diplomatic solution when Spain forbade Americans from depositing their goods on Spanish territory at the mouth of the Mississippi River, effectively closing the Mississippi to frontier farmers, who used the river to ship their goods to market.

To make matters worse, the country was experiencing a severe economic **recession,** and farmers were particularly affected. Farm prices had fallen, and many farmers were deeply in debt with mortgages to pay. At the same time, debt-ridden states needed to repay the bonds they had issued to borrow money from wealthy merchants and planters during the war. With the war over, their creditors wanted the bonds to be redeemed for gold or silver.

The states could raise taxes to pay their debts, but farmers and other debtors urged the states to issue paper money instead. Paper money was not backed by gold and silver, so inflation—a decline in the value of money—began. Debtors could pay their debts more easily with money that was losing value, but lenders would not receive the true value of the amount originally borrowed.

Seven states issued paper money between 1785 and 1787. In Rhode Island paper money became so worthless that merchants refused to accept it. After a mob rioted against the merchants, the state assembly passed a law forcing merchants to accept the paper money or be arrested and fined. This demonstrated to wealthier Americans that under the Articles of Confederation the people could exploit the weakness of this government against them.

Shays's Rebellion

The property owners' fears seemed justified when an uprising known as Shays's Rebellion erupted in Massachusetts in 1786, triggered by the state's decision to raise taxes instead of issuing paper money to pay off its debts. Since the wealthy in Massachusetts from the eastern part of the state controlled the legislature, taxes fell most heavily on poor farmers, particularly those in western Massachusetts. As the recession grew worse, many found it impossible to pay their taxes as well as their mortgages and other debts, causing them to lose their farms.

Angry at the state legislature's indifference to their plight, in late August 1786 farmers in western Massachusetts rebelled. They closed down several county courthouses to block farm foreclosures and then marched to the state supreme court. The rebelling farmers argued that they were being unfairly taxed and were being ignored by their state government—echoing the language and the arguments of the Revolutionary War. Daniel Shays, a bankrupt farmer and veteran of the Continental Army, emerged as one of the leaders of the rebellion.

In January 1787 Shays and about 1,200 farmers headed to a state arsenal intending to seize weapons before marching on Boston. In response the governor sent a force under General Benjamin Lincoln to defend the arsenal. Before Lincoln arrived, Shays attacked, and the militia defending the arsenal opened fire, killing four farmers. The next day Lincoln's troops arrived and ended the rebellion, but the emotions and the issues the rebellion had raised were harder to disperse.

People with greater income and social status saw Shays's Rebellion, as well as inflation and an unstable currency, as signs that the republic was at risk. They feared that as states became more responsive to poor people, the states would take property from the wealthy and weaken property rights. People began to argue for a stronger central government. The Confederation Congress's failure to deal with these issues, as well as the problems with trade and diplomacy, only added fuel to their argument.

✓ CHECK FOR UNDERSTANDING

1. **Explaining** Why did the Congress need to enact the Land Ordinance of 1785?

2. **Summarizing** What economic concerns of the people did the government face after Shays's Rebellion?

Understanding the Constitutional Convention

GUIDING QUESTION

What problems did the delegates face during the Constitutional Convention?

The political and economic problems facing the United States in 1787 led many American leaders to two conclusions: the nation would not survive without a strong central government, and the Articles of Confederation had to be revised or replaced. People who supported a stronger central government became known as "nationalists." Influential nationalists included Benjamin Franklin, George Washington, John Adams, James Madison, and the financier Robert Morris.

One of these nationalists was James Madison, a member of the Virginia legislature. Madison was well

recession an economic slowdown

aware of Virginia's trade problems with the other American states and with Great Britain. He believed that a stronger national government was needed.

In 1786 Madison convinced Virginia's legislature to call for a convention of all the states to discuss trade and taxation problems. Representatives from the states were to meet in Annapolis, Maryland. Yet delegates from only five states attended, too few to reach a final decision. The delegates did discuss the weakness of the Articles of Confederation and expressed interest in modifying them.

Another important nationalist, New York delegate Alexander Hamilton, recommended that the Confederation Congress itself call for a convention. Members of the Congress were initially reluctant to do so, but news of Shays's Rebellion changed many minds. In February 1787 Congress called for a convention of the states "for the sole and express purpose of revising the Articles of Confederation." Every state except Rhode Island sent delegates to what became known as the Constitutional Convention.

In May 1787 the delegates took their places in the Pennsylvania State House in Philadelphia. They knew they faced a daunting task: to balance the rights of the states with the need for a stronger national government. The 55 delegates who attended the convention included some of the most distinguished leaders in the country. The majority were trained in law, and most of the others were planters and merchants. Most had experience in colonial, state, or national government. Seven had served as governors. Thirty-nine had been members of the Congress. Six had signed the Declaration of Independence.

The delegates chose George Washington of Virginia, hero of the American Revolution, as presiding officer. At 81, Benjamin Franklin of Pennsylvania was the oldest delegate. Other notable delegates included Alexander Hamilton, Connecticut's Roger Sherman, and the scholarly James Madison, who became the

principal architect of the Constitution and took careful notes on the debates. They closed the meetings to the public to help ensure honest and open discussion free from outside political pressures.

Plans and Compromises

The Virginia delegation brought a detailed plan—mostly the work of James Madison—for a new national government. The Virginia Plan recommended scrapping the Articles of Confederation and creating a new national government with the power to make laws binding upon the states and to raise money through taxes. The plan also proposed that the government be divided into legislative, executive, and judicial branches, and that the legislature, or Congress, be divided into two houses. The voters in each state would elect members of the first house. Members of the second house would be nominated by the state governments but actually elected by the first house. In both houses the number of representatives for each state would reflect that state's population, giving states with large populations like Virginia, New York, and Massachusetts more votes than states with smaller populations.

Madison's Virginia Plan drew sharp reactions. The delegates accepted the idea of dividing the government into three branches, but the smaller states strongly opposed any changes that would base representation on population because they feared that the larger states would always outvote them. William Paterson, a New Jersey delegate, offered a counterproposal that came to be called the New Jersey Plan. His plan modified the Articles of Confederation instead of abandoning that government entirely. It called for Congress to have a single house in which each state was equally represented and gave Congress the power to raise taxes and regulate trade. The delegates had to choose only one plan for further negotiation. After debating on June 19, the convention voted to proceed with the Virginia Plan. Thus, the convention delegates decided to go beyond their original purpose of revising the Articles of Confederation and instead create a new structure for government.

After the convention voted for the Virginia Plan, tempers flared as delegates from the small states insisted that each state have equal representation. In July 1787 the convention appointed a committee to find a compromise. The alternative that the committee worked out was based on a proposal from Roger Sherman of Connecticut. Called the Connecticut Compromise, or the Great Compromise, it proposed that membership in one house of Congress—the House of Representatives—would be based on population. Voters would elect the representatives, while the state legislatures would choose the senators.

The Constitution, beginning with the words "We the People," serves as a written framework for the government.

Interpreting What do the words "We the People" suggest about the government formed by the Constitution?

doublediamondphoto/E+/Getty Images

The Three-Fifths Compromise

The committee also proposed that each state could elect one member to the House of Representatives for every 40,000 people. This led to another clash between the delegates centered on slavery and pitted Northern states and Southern states against one another. Enslaved people accounted for about 40 percent of the population in the Southern states compared to less than 4 percent in the Northern states.

Southern delegates wanted enslaved people to count toward their total since this would help slaveholding states maintain a balance of power with the more heavily-populated Northern states—and protect the institution of slavery. The Northern delegates objected because enslaved people could not vote or exercise other rights as citizens. They also suggested that if enslaved people were counted for representation, they should be counted for taxation too—something the Southern delegates opposed. In the end, a solution referred to as the Three-Fifths Compromise was agreed upon. Every five enslaved persons would count as three free persons to determine both representation and taxes.

The dispute over how to count enslaved people was not the only issue dividing the North and the South. Southerners feared that a strong national government might impose taxes on the export of farm products or ban the continued importation of new enslaved laborers, which would threaten their social control and their wealth. Protecting the international slave trade was particularly important to delegates from Georgia and the Carolinas, where planters hoped to expand the plantation system. Planters in the Upper South, on the other hand, had a higher population of enslaved people, so they were less dependent on the international slave trade. When delegates from the Upper South wavered on their support for protecting the slave trade, delegates from the Lower South made it clear that they were willing to leave the Union rather than give in. To gain the support of Northern delegates, Southern delegates agreed to make it easier for Congress to regulate trade, something that Northern merchants and artisans desired.

Afraid that the Union would fall apart without a deal, convention delegates decided that Congress could not end the slave trade until 1808 nor could it impose high taxes on the importation of enslaved people. They also agreed that the new Congress could not tax exports. In addition the Southern delegates successfully pushed for one more protection of slavery—the Fugitive Slave Clause—which required free states to return runaways to bondage in the South.

On September 20, 39 of the delegates signed the new Constitution and sent it to the Confederation Congress. Eight days later, Congress sent the Constitution to the states for deliberation. Nine of the thirteen states had to ratify the Constitution for it to take effect.

Amending the Constitution

The delegates in Philadelphia recognized that the Constitution might need to be amended, or changed, over time. But to prevent constant changes, the delegates made the process difficult. An amendment could be proposed by a vote of two-thirds of the members of both houses of Congress. Alternatively, two-thirds of the states could call a constitutional convention to propose new amendments. To become effective, the proposed amendment then had to be ratified by three-fourths of the state legislatures or by conventions in three-fourths of the states.

✓ **CHECK FOR UNDERSTANDING**

1. **Describing** What compromises were made in the process of creating the new government? What concerns did they address?
2. **Explaining** Why did the convention delegates make it difficult to amend the Constitution?

The New Government's Powers

GUIDING QUESTION

How did the new Constitution reflect a republican government?

The debates and compromises at the Constitutional Convention created a federal constitution that differed from the Articles of Confederation in fundamental ways. The new Constitution increased the number of houses in the legislature from one—the Congress—to two—the House of Representatives and the Senate. It also changed the way delegates were chosen. Under the Articles of Confederation, members of Congress were appointed annually by state legislatures. Under the Constitution, representatives were elected every two years by voters and senators were chosen by state legislatures for a six-year term.

Two of the biggest structural changes involved the exercise of executive and judicial power. The government under the Articles of Confederation lacked a separate executive branch. Members of Congress elected a president every year and government departments were run by committees created by the Congress. There was also no separate judicial branch. Legal disputes were left to the states and local courts, while the Congress acted as a court for conflicts between the states. The Constitution created two new branches of government—the executive branch and the judicial branch. Executive

This print shows the House of Representatives wing in the Capitol. The Framers of the Constitution sought to balance power among the states in part through the House of Representatives.

power rested with a president, elected every four years by the Electoral College. The president would have the power to conduct foreign policy, select officers to run government departments, and appoint foreign ambassadors and judges. The judicial branch included the Supreme Court as well as additional lower courts that Congress would create. The president would appoint judges and the Senate would confirm or reject them.

Finally, the Constitution addressed two of the weaknesses that had plagued the Articles of Confederation Congress: the ability to levy taxes and to regulate trade. Under the Articles, only states could levy taxes, and the Congress could regulate only foreign trade but not trade between the states. The new Constitution, however, allowed the federal government to levy taxes and regulate both foreign and interstate trade. States lost the sovereignty they had under the Articles of Confederation in favor of a stronger federal government.

The Constitution did more than simply correct the weaknesses of the Articles of Confederation; it also created a new federal system of government in the form of a democratic republic. The Framers purposely began the Constitution with the words, "We the People" to emphasize the idea that political power came from the people.

As a democratic republic, the United States allowed citizens to elect representatives to govern for them. This was a radical idea at the time, even though during this period only white male property owners had the right to vote. The structure differed greatly from that of the European monarchies of the day, which bestowed governmental power upon kings and queens.

The success of the Constitutional Convention in creating a government that reflected the country's many different viewpoints was, in George Washington's words, "little short of a miracle." John Adams called the convention "the single greatest effort of national deliberation that the world has ever seen." Nonetheless, it would be a long time before all populations—not just white, male property owners— would benefit from all of the rights it bestowed.

✓ CHECK FOR UNDERSTANDING

Explaining Why is the U.S. government considered a democratic republic?

LESSON ACTIVITIES

1. **Informative/Explanatory Writing** Consider what you have learned about the varying opinions of delegates at the Constitutional Convention. Write a paragraph or two describing the different arguments that were presented during the discussion over a key point of debate. Explain why viewpoints varied over this point.

2. **Presenting** Act out some of the debates that took place at the Constitutional Convention, such as the debate about the Virginia Plan versus the New Jersey Plan. Choose a side to represent and then form teams. Argue on behalf of the side you are representing by using details from the text along with any additional information you have found in other sources.

Hum Images/Alamy Stock Photo

04

The Constitution Handbook

READING STRATEGY

Analyzing Key Ideas and Details As you read about the Constitution, use the major headings of the handbook to fill in an outline like the one shown.

I. Major Principles

  A.

  B.

  C.

  D.

  E.

Major Principles

GUIDING QUESTION

How does the Constitution lay the framework for individual rights and a balanced representative government?

The principles outlined in the Constitution were the Framers' solution to the complex problems of a representative government. The Constitution rests on seven major principles of government: (1) **popular sovereignty,** (2) republicanism, (3) limited government, (4) **federalism,** (5) separation of powers, (6) checks and balances, and (7) individual rights.

Popular Sovereignty and Republicanism

The opening words of the Constitution, "We the people," reinforce the idea of popular sovereignty, or "authority of the people." In the Constitution, the people consent to be governed and specify the powers and rules by which they shall be governed.

The Articles of Confederation's government had few powers, and it was unable to cope with the many challenges facing the nation. The new federal government had greater powers, but it also had specific limitations. A system of interlocking responsibilities kept any one branch of government from becoming too powerful.

Voters are sovereign; that is, they have ultimate authority in a republican system. They elect representatives and give them the responsibility to make laws and run the government. For most Americans today, the terms republic and representative democracy mean the same thing: a system of limited government in which the people are the final source of authority.

Limited Government

Although the Framers agreed that the nation needed a stronger central authority, they feared misuse of power. They wanted to prevent the government from using its power to give one group special advantages or to deprive another group of its rights. By creating a limited government, they restricted the government's authority to specific powers granted by the people.

The delegates to the Constitutional Convention were very specific about the powers granted to the new government. Their written outline of the government's structure also shows what they intended. Articles I, II, and III of the Constitution describe the powers of the federal government and the limits on those powers. Other limits are set forth in the Bill of Rights.

Federalism

In establishing a strong central government, the Framers did not deprive states of all authority. The states gave up some powers to the national government but retained others. This principle of shared power is called federalism. The federal system allows each state to deal with its needs in its own way. But at the same time it lets the states act together to deal with matters that affect all Americans.

popular sovereignty authority of the people

federalism political system in which power is divided between the national and state governments

The Constitution defines three types of government powers. Certain powers belong only to the federal government. These **enumerated powers** include the power to coin money, regulate interstate and foreign trade, maintain the armed forces, and create federal courts (Article I, Section 8). Congress is also given the right to make all laws "necessary and proper," often called the "elastic clause."

The second kind of powers are known as **reserved powers,** including the power to establish schools, set marriage and divorce laws, and regulate trade within the state. Although reserved powers are not specifically listed in the Constitution, the Tenth Amendment says that all powers not granted to the federal government "are reserved to the States, or to the people."

The third set of powers defined by the Constitution is **concurrent powers**—powers the state and federal governments share. They include the right to raise taxes, borrow money, provide for public welfare, and administer criminal justice. Conflicts between state law and federal law must be settled in a federal court. The Constitution declares that it is "the supreme Law of the Land."

Separation of Powers

To prevent any single group or institution in government from gaining too much power, the Framers divided the federal government into three branches: legislative, executive, and judicial. Each branch has its own functions. The legislative branch, Congress, makes the laws. The executive branch, led by the president, carries out the laws. The judicial branch, consisting of the Supreme Court and other federal courts, interprets and applies the laws, and the Supreme Court can rule laws unconstitutional.

In addition to separate responsibilities, the members of each branch are chosen in different ways. The president nominates federal judges, and the Senate confirms or rejects these appointments. People vote for members of Congress. Voters cast ballots for

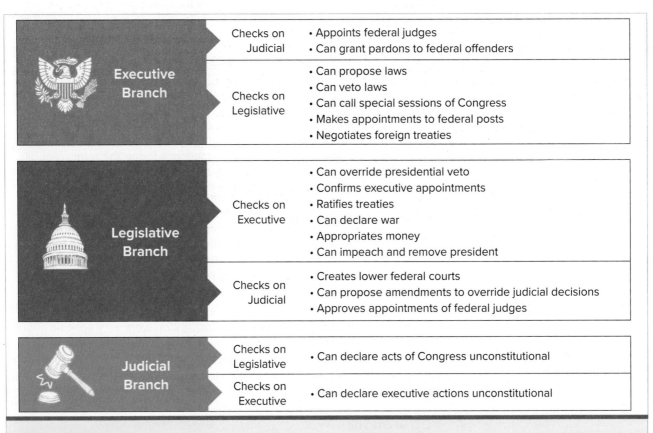

Executive Branch	Checks on Judicial	• Appoints federal judges • Can grant pardons to federal offenders
	Checks on Legislative	• Can propose laws • Can veto laws • Can call special sessions of Congress • Makes appointments to federal posts • Negotiates foreign treaties
Legislative Branch	Checks on Executive	• Can override presidential veto • Confirms executive appointments • Ratifies treaties • Can declare war • Appropriates money • Can impeach and remove president
	Checks on Judicial	• Creates lower federal courts • Can propose amendments to override judicial decisions • Approves appointments of federal judges
Judicial Branch	Checks on Legislative	• Can declare acts of Congress unconstitutional
	Checks on Executive	• Can declare executive actions unconstitutional

Checks and Balances

This system of checks and balances limits the power of each branch of government.

1. **Identifying** Why is it important for the legislature to override an executive veto?

2. **Interpreting Visuals** Based on the information in the chart, which of the branches appears to be the weakest?

---

enumerated powers powers listed in the Constitution as belonging to the federal government
reserved powers powers retained by the states

concurrent powers powers shared by the state and federal governments

president, but the method of election is indirect. In most states, the candidate who receives the majority receives that state's electoral votes, which total the number of senators and representatives the state has in Congress, while some states award their electoral votes proportionally. Electors meet to formally elect a president. A candidate must win a majority of votes in the Electoral College to win.

Checks and Balances

The Framers deliberately created a system of checks and balances in which each branch can check, or limit, the power of the other branches. This system prevents any one branch from becoming too powerful. For example, imagine Congress passes a law. The president can reject the law by veto. Congress can override the president's veto if two-thirds of the members of both the Senate and the House of Representatives vote again to approve the law. The Supreme Court could then rule that law unconstitutional.

Individual Rights

In 1791 the states ratified 10 amendments to the Constitution to protect basic rights, including freedom of speech and religion and the right to a trial by jury. Congress approved these amendments, called the Bill of Rights. Over the years, 17 more amendments have been added to the Constitution. Some give additional rights to American citizens and some modify how the government works. Included among them are amendments that abolish slavery, guarantee voting rights, authorize an income tax, and set a two-term limit on the presidency.

✓ **CHECK FOR UNDERSTANDING**

1. **Identifying Connections** How does the Constitution protect individual rights and balance representation?
2. **Describing** Why did the Framers choose to list the powers of the federal government?

The Legislative Branch

GUIDING QUESTION

How is the legislative branch organized and what are its functions?

The legislative branch includes the two houses of Congress: the Senate and the House of Representatives. Congress's two primary roles are to make the nation's laws and to decide how to spend federal funds. The government cannot spend any money unless Congress appropriates, or sets aside, funds. All tax and spending bills must originate in the House of Representatives and be approved in both the House and the Senate before moving to the president to be signed.

Congress also monitors the executive branch and investigates possible abuses of power. The House of Representatives can **impeach,** or bring formal charges against, any federal official it suspects of wrongdoing or misconduct. If an official is impeached, the Senate acts as a court and tries the accused official. Officials who are found guilty are removed from office.

The Senate has additional powers. Two-thirds of the Senate must approve treaties made by the president. The Senate also confirms or rejects presidential appointments of federal officials, such as department heads, ambassadors, and federal judges.

All members of Congress represent their constituents, the people of their home states and districts. As a constituent, you can expect your senators and representative to promote national and state interests. Senators and representatives introduce thousands of **bills**—proposed laws—every year, although presidential leadership can influence what bills are introduced. Because individual members of Congress cannot possibly study all these bills carefully, both chambers form committees of selected members to evaluate proposed legislation.

Standing committees are permanent committees in both the House and the Senate that specialize in a particular topic, such as agriculture, commerce, or veterans' affairs. These committees are usually divided into subcommittees that focus on a particular aspect of an issue. The House and the Senate also form temporary select committees to deal with issues requiring special attention.

Occasionally the House and the Senate form joint committees to consider specific issues. One type of joint committee, a conference committee, has a special function. If the House and the Senate pass different versions of the same bill, a conference committee meets to work out a compromise acceptable to both.

Once a committee in either house of Congress approves a bill, it is sent to the full Senate or House for debate. After debate, the bill may be passed, rejected, or returned to the committee for further changes. When both houses pass a bill, it goes to the president. If the president approves the bill and signs it, the bill becomes law. If the president vetoes the bill, it does not become law unless Congress takes it up again and votes to override the veto.

✓ **CHECK FOR UNDERSTANDING**

1. **Summarizing** How is the legislative branch organized, and what are its functions?
2. **Explaining Cause and Effect** What happens when a president vetoes a bill?

---

impeach to bring formal charges against a federal official

bill a proposed law

How a Bill Becomes a Law

The legislative process begins when a member of Congress introduces a bill. Both chambers of Congress must review and approve a bill before requesting the president's signature.

Summarizing What is the role of a conference committee?

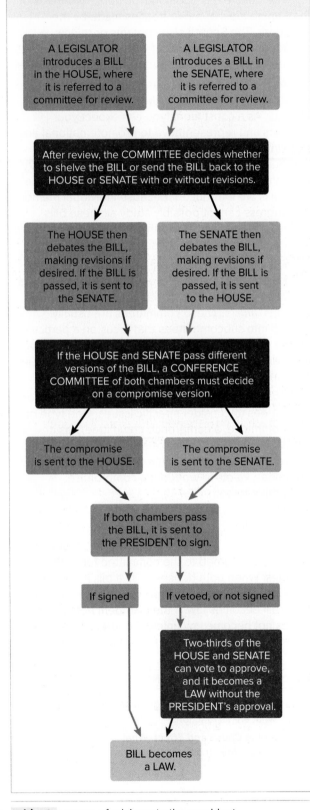

A LEGISLATOR introduces a BILL in the HOUSE, where it is referred to a committee for review.

A LEGISLATOR introduces a BILL in the SENATE, where it is referred to a committee for review.

After review, the COMMITTEE decides whether to shelve the BILL or send the BILL back to the HOUSE or SENATE with or without revisions.

The HOUSE then debates the BILL, making revisions if desired. If the BILL is passed, it is sent to the SENATE.

The SENATE then debates the BILL, making revisions if desired. If the BILL is passed, it is sent to the HOUSE.

If the HOUSE and SENATE pass different versions of the BILL, a CONFERENCE COMMITTEE of both chambers must decide on a compromise version.

The compromise is sent to the HOUSE.

The compromise is sent to the SENATE.

If both chambers pass the BILL, it is sent to the PRESIDENT to sign.

If signed

If vetoed, or not signed

Two-thirds of the HOUSE and SENATE can vote to approve, and it becomes a LAW without the PRESIDENT's approval.

BILL becomes a LAW.

cabinet a group of advisors to the president

The Executive Branch

GUIDING QUESTION

How does the president carry out laws that Congress passes?

The executive branch of government includes the president, the vice president, and executive offices, departments, and agencies. The executive branch executes, or carries out, the laws that Congress passes.

The President's Roles

The president plays a number of different roles in government. These roles include serving as the nation's chief executive, chief diplomat, commander in chief of the military, chief of state, and legislative leader. As chief executive, the president is responsible for carrying out the nation's laws. As chief diplomat, the president directs foreign policy, appoints ambassadors, and negotiates treaties with other nations.

As commander in chief of the armed forces, the president can give orders to the military and direct its operations. The president cannot declare war; only Congress holds this power. The president can send troops to other parts of the world for up to 60 days but must notify Congress when doing so. The troops may remain longer only if Congress gives its approval or declares war.

As chief of state, the president is symbolically the representative of all Americans. The president fulfills this role when receiving foreign ambassadors or heads of state, visiting foreign nations, or honoring Americans. The president serves as a legislative leader by proposing laws to Congress and working to see that they are passed. In the annual State of the Union address to the American people, the president presents his goals for legislation in the upcoming year.

The Executive at Work

Many executive offices, departments, and independent agencies help the president carry out and enforce the nation's laws. The Executive Office of the President (EOP) consists of individuals and agencies that directly assist the president. Presidents rely on the EOP for advice and for gathering information needed for decision making.

The executive branch has 15 executive departments, each responsible for a different area of government. For example, the Department of State carries out foreign policy, and the Department of the Treasury manages the nation's finances. The department heads have the title of secretary, and are members of the president's **cabinet.** The cabinet helps the president set policies and make decisions. The president nominates members of the cabinet with the consent of the Senate.

The Qualities of an Effective Leader

The president must take on multiple challenging roles. Throughout American history, presidents have been both praised and criticized for their leadership. Being an effective leader in a federal constitutional republic requires a number of important qualities.

As chief of state and chief diplomat, the president represents the nation to the American people and to the world. To be effective, a president must demonstrate principles and conviction, yet be optimistic and friendly, open to others, and able to communicate clearly and effectively. Great leaders can inspire their people to greatness with their words, their confidence, and their determination.

As a legislative leader, the president must be able to compromise, to understand different points of view, and to work with many different personalities in Congress, while at the same time understanding clearly what principles and goals should be upheld. A president who bows to political pressures too often will be seen as weak or vacillating, but a president who refuses to negotiate and compromise with Congress will be seen as stubborn, aloof, or ineffective.

As commander-in-chief, the president has to be decisive and willing to make difficult decisions. At the same time, presidents must be willing to listen to advice and the expertise of those serving under them. The president is the final decision maker when the nation is at war, and his or her decisions can impact the lives of hundreds of millions of people. A president who refuses to act when necessary will be seen as timid and indecisive, which can embolden the nation's enemies. But if the president moves too quickly, it will be seen as reckless or dangerous.

As the head of an enormous and complex bureaucracy, the president must resist the temptation to go into too much detail on every little issue—there is not enough time. Instead, an effective chief executive must choose good people who can be trusted to implement the president's goals within the executive departments. The president must support the team he or she has chosen and be loyal to them. An effective president will set high expectations, have clear goals, and lead by example. At the same time, presidents have to hold their people and themselves accountable for any failures, and be willing to learn from mistakes.

As the chief executive responsible for carrying out the nation's laws and upholding the Constitution, the president, above all, needs integrity. Presidents have to implement laws they disagree with; they cannot allow personal feelings to interfere with their decisions or distort their judgment. They cannot give in to corruption and use their office for personal gain.

Nor should they make decisions purely on the basis of what will get them re-elected. The president, as the leader of a democratic republic, should listen to the people. But presidents must also reconcile competing demands and goals, and lead the nation in a way that upholds the Constitution and the nation's founding ideals and principles.

✓ CHECK FOR UNDERSTANDING

1. **Summarizing** How does the president carry out laws that Congress passes?
2. **Explaining Cause and Effect** Why must presidents be decisive?

The Judicial Branch

GUIDING QUESTION

How does the judicial branch function to review and evaluate laws and interpret the Constitution?

Article III of the Constitution calls for the creation of a Supreme Court and "such inferior [lower] courts as Congress may from time to time ordain and establish." The federal courts of the judicial branch review and evaluate laws and interpret the Constitution in making their decisions.

District and Appellate Courts

United States district courts are the lowest level of the federal court system. These courts consider criminal and civil cases that come under federal authority, such as kidnapping, federal tax evasion, claims against the federal government, and cases involving constitutional rights, such as free speech. There are 94 district courts, with at least one in every state.

The appellate courts, or courts of appeal, consider district court decisions in which the losing side has asked for a review of the verdict. If an appeals court disagrees with the lower court's decision, it can overturn the verdict or order a retrial. There are 14 appeals courts: one for each of 12 federal districts, one military appeals court, and an appellate court for the federal circuit.

The Supreme Court

The Supreme Court is the final authority in the federal court system. It consists of a chief justice and eight associate justices, however, Congress has the power to change that number by law. Most of the Court's cases come from appeals of lower court decisions. Only cases involving foreign diplomats or disputes between states can begin in the Supreme Court.

The president appoints the Court's justices for life, and the Senate confirms or rejects the appointments. The public has no direct input in selecting these justices. The Framers hoped that by appointing judges, they would be free to evaluate the law with no concern for pleasing voters.

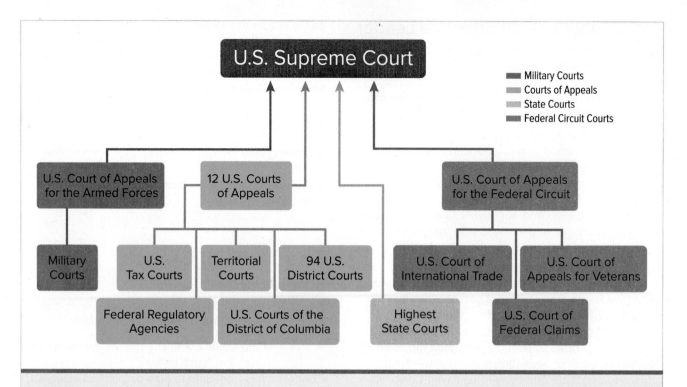

The Federal Court System

There are layers of federal courts to handle a variety of legal disputes.

Integrating Information How many appeals routes are there to the Supreme Court?

The president nominates members of the cabinet with the consent of the Senate. In 1803 Chief Justice John Marshall expanded the power of the Supreme Court by striking down an act of Congress in the case of *Marbury* v. *Madison*. Although not mentioned in the Constitution, judicial review has become a major power of the judicial branch. **Judicial review** gives the Supreme Court the ultimate authority to interpret the meaning of the Constitution.

✓ **CHECK FOR UNDERSTANDING**

1. **Identifying Effects** What are the advantages of appointing Supreme Court justices for life?
2. **Identifying Effects** What happened after Chief Justice John Marshall established the principle of judicial review?

Rights and Responsibilities

GUIDING QUESTION

What are the protections and freedoms the Constitution and the Bill of Rights provide Americans?

All citizens of the United States have certain basic rights, but they also have specific responsibilities. Living in a system of self-government means ultimately that every citizen is partly responsible for how society is governed and for the actions the government takes on his or her behalf.

The Rights of Americans

The rights of Americans fall into three broad categories: to be protected from unfair actions of the government, to receive equal treatment under the law, and to retain certain basic freedoms.

Parts of the Constitution and the Bill of Rights protect all Americans from unfair treatment by the government or the law, including the right to a lawyer when accused of a crime and the right to a trial by jury when charged with a crime. In addition the Fourth Amendment protects us from unreasonable searches and seizures. This provision requires police to have a court order before searching a person's home for criminal evidence. To obtain this, the police must have a very strong reason to suspect someone of a crime.

All Americans, regardless of race, religion, or political beliefs, have the right to be treated the same under the law. The Fifth Amendment states that no person shall "be deprived of life, liberty, or property, without due process of law." **Due process** means that the government must follow procedures established by law and guaranteed by the Constitution. The

judicial review the process by which the Supreme Court has the final authority to interpret the Constitution

due process the following of procedures established by law

Fourteenth Amendment requires every state to grant its citizens "equal protection of the laws."

The First Amendment describes our basic freedoms—freedom of speech, freedom of religion, freedom of the press, freedom of assembly, and the right to petition. In a democracy, power rests in the hands of the people. Therefore citizens in a democratic society must be able to exchange ideas freely. The First Amendment allows citizens to criticize the government, in speech or in the press, without fear of punishment. In addition, the Ninth Amendment states that the rights of Americans are not limited to those in the Constitution. Over the years, this has allowed Americans to assert other basic rights that have been upheld in court or assured by amending the Constitution.

The rights of Americans are not absolute. They are limited based on the principle of respecting everyone's rights equally. For example, many cities and towns require groups to obtain a permit to march on city streets. Such laws do limit free speech, but they also protect the community by ensuring that the march will not endanger other people.

In this and other cases, the government balances an individual's rights, the rights of others, and the community's health and safety. Most Americans are willing to accept some limitations on their rights to gain these protections as long as the restrictions are reasonable and apply equally to all. A law banning all marches would violate the First Amendment rights of free speech and assembly and be unacceptable. Similarly, a law preventing only certain groups from marching would be unfair because it would not apply equally to everyone.

Citizens' Responsibilities

Citizens in a democratic society have both duties and responsibilities. Duties are actions required by law. Responsibilities are voluntary actions. Fulfilling duties and responsibilities ensures good government and protects rights.

One basic duty of all Americans is to obey the law. Laws serve three important functions. They help maintain order; they protect the health, safety, and property of all citizens; and they make it possible for people to live together peacefully. If you believe a law is wrong, you can work through your representatives to change it.

Americans also have a duty to pay taxes. The government uses tax money to defend the nation, to build roads and bridges, and to assist people in need. Americans often benefit from services provided by the government. Another duty of citizens is to defend the nation. All males aged 18 and older must register with the government in case the nation needs to call on them for military service. Military service is not automatic, but a war could make it necessary.

The Constitution guarantees all Americans the right to a trial by a jury of their equals. For this reason, you may be called to jury duty when you reach the age of 18. Having a large group of jurors on hand is necessary to guarantee the right to a fair and speedy trial. You also have a duty to serve as a trial witness if called to do so.

Most states require you to attend school until a certain age. School is where you gain the knowledge and skills needed to be a good citizen. In school you learn to think more clearly, to express your opinions more accurately, and to analyze the ideas of others. These skills will help you make informed choices when you vote.

The responsibilities of citizens are not as clear-cut as their duties, but they are as important because they help maintain the quality of government and society. One important responsibility is to be well informed. Knowing what your government is doing and expressing your thoughts about its actions helps to keep it responsive to the wishes of the people. You also need to be informed about your rights and to assert them when necessary. Knowing your rights helps preserve them. Other responsibilities include accepting responsibility for your actions and supporting your family.

To enjoy your rights to the fullest, you must be prepared to respect the rights of others. Respecting the rights of others also means respecting the rights of people with whom you disagree. Respecting and accepting others regardless of race, religion, beliefs, or other differences is essential in a democracy.

Perhaps the most important civic responsibility of American citizens, beginning when they reach the age of 18, is to vote. Voting allows you to participate in the democratic process and to guide its direction. When you vote, you will be exercising your right of

The First Amendment guarantees freedom of assembly, among other rights.

Summarizing Why are basic freedoms as important today as they were when the Constitution was written?

Halfpoint/iStock/Getty Images Plus/Getty Images

self-government. If you disapprove of the job your representatives are doing, it will be your responsibility to help elect other people in the next election.

In addition to voting, there are other ways you can participate in the democratic process. You can let your representatives know what you think about issues through email, letters, telephone calls, petitions, and by taking part in public meetings or political rallies. You can join a political party and help campaign for a candidate that you support. Political parties are always looking for volunteers to help. In addition, membership in a party will let you play a role in choosing who runs as candidates for election. And the time may come when you too may want to participate by running for office. Participating in the democratic process reflects our patriotism. We live in a constitutional democratic republic. The national ethos—the beliefs and ideas Americans all share as a community—includes the belief that the best and most effective government is government of, for, and by the people. The only way to live up to those beliefs is to embrace them by participating in the democratic process.

The Constitution's preamble states that the goal of the people of the United States is "to form a more perfect union." Because the United States is a government of the people and a democratic republic, it becomes "more perfect" and moves closer to its goals when all of its people, in all of their variation and diversity, participate. If someone does not participate, the union does not have their input and is less likely to reflect a balance of all of the needs, concerns, and goals of the people. This makes it harder to achieve justice, peace, security, and liberty or to promote the general welfare.

If we truly love the country, then we want it to succeed, and if there are aspects that we do not like, the best way to change them is by getting involved in politics and working to bring about the changes we think are needed. Patriotism is not standing by while others act; patriots take action to help make their country better.

The United States is made up of a multitude of people. Many have come from all over the world— some to escape violence, poverty, or oppression and some seeking employment, education, and more opportunity. Whatever their reasons, each immigrant who becomes a citizen promises in their oath of allegiance that "I will support and defend the Constitution and laws of the United States of America against all enemies, foreign and domestic; that I will bear true faith and allegiance to the same, . . ." As citizens of a self-governing democratic republic, all American citizens share a common bond in that they stand for certain self-evident truths: "that all men are created equal, that they are endowed by their Creator with certain unalienable rights, that among these are life, liberty, and the pursuit of happiness."

✓ CHECK FOR UNDERSTANDING

1. **Summarizing** What are the protections and freedoms the Constitution and the Bill of Rights provide Americans?
2. **Explaining Effects** What is the consequence of people choosing not to vote?

Symbols and Mottos

GUIDING QUESTION

How do the symbols and mottos of the United States help to define American society?

All nations make use of symbols. A symbol is something that stands for something else. It is a short-hand way of remembering all the qualities and ideas embodied in something. Nations use symbols to remind people what the nation represents. They are also a statement of sovereignty. When a nation's flag is flown over something, it symbolizes that something belongs to the nation. Similarly, when a national seal is put on a document, it is saying that the document is an official statement of the nation. Symbols remind people of their nation's history, values, and goals. They evoke patriotism and pride. Perhaps most importantly, they remind people that, despite their differences, they are all united in one national community.

The American Flag

The best known and most visible symbol of the United States is the flag, sometimes nicknamed the Stars and Stripes; the Star-Spangled Banner; the Red, White, and Blue; or Old Glory. The Continental Congress approved the design of the flag in June 1777. The 13 alternating stripes on the flag represent the original 13 colonies that founded the United States. Each star in the blue field represents one state.

The stars were a metaphor for the new nation. Stars in the night sky are grouped into constellations, or patterns. The stars on the flag represent that the United States is a new constellation, a new arrangement in the world. The colors used on the flag have been said to have at least two meanings. They are the same colors as used on the British flag, and so remind the United States of its origins as British colonies. They are also the same colors used on the Great Seal of the United States, which was designed before the flag and have specific meanings: red for strength and courage; white for purity and innocence; and blue for perseverance, vigilance, and justice.

(bl)Oath of Allegiance for Naturalized Citizens. U.S. Department of Homeland Security: Citizenship and Immigration Services. (tr)The Declaration of Independence, Preamble, July 4, 1776. The National Archives and Records Administration.

E Pluribus Unum

On July 4, 1776, near a year before the Continental Congress decided on the design for a flag, it began work on the Great Seal of the United States. A seal is a type of signature. Most nations have an official symbol that they use to "seal," or sign, official documents and treaties with other nations. Seals date to the days when letters and documents would be signed and sealed by melting wax onto them and then pressing a symbol into the wax, "sealing" the envelope closed. They are also commonly put on coins and currency to show that the money has been officially issued by a particular country.

The Great Seal has two sides. On the one side is an eagle holding a banner with the Latin motto "E Pluribus Unum," which means "Out of Many, One." This motto refers to the creation of a nation from 13 separate colonies. Today it also is used to describe the United States as a country of many peoples from many different cultures, races, and backgrounds united into one nation. The motto was never made the official motto of the United States, but it has been used on American coins since the late 1700s.

On the same side of the seal, the eagle also clutches an olive branch with 13 leaves in one claw and 13 arrows in the other claw, symbolizing the nation's power in war and peace. The eagle also carries a shield with red and white stripes and a blue field. Thirteen stars, symbolizing the original 13 colonies, fly above the eagle.

On the opposite side of the seal are symbols that often puzzle people. There is an unfinished pyramid with 13 levels and the date 1776 in Roman numerals at its base. It represents the 13 colonies and the idea that the United States is a work in progress and not yet finished. A pyramid was chosen because it represents strength and duration, like the pyramids of Egypt that have lasted for thousands of years. Hovering over the pyramid is an eye in a triangle. The triangle looks like the capstone, or top of the pyramid, and the eye is intended to represent God watching over the nation. Above the eye are the Latin words "Annuit Coeptis," which mean "He approves the undertaking," indicating God approves of the new nation. Below the pyramid are the Latin words "Novus Ordo Seclorum," meaning "new order of the ages," referring to the idea that the United States, as a democratic republic, was a new way of organizing society in the world.

"The Star-Spangled Banner"

"The Star-Spangled Banner" is the national anthem of the United States. Its lyrics were first written down as a poem in 1814 by Francis Scott Key after he watched the British attack Fort McHenry during the War of 1812. The poem describes Key watching anxiously in the early morning dawn to see if the flag is again raised over "the land of the free and home of the brave." The song became popular in the 1800s and was played regularly on July 4th. In 1889 Secretary of the Navy

carterdayne/E+/Getty Images

People waving American flags at Barack Obama's 2009 inauguration. The flag is a key symbol of the United States.

Determining Central Ideas How would the flag change if more states joined the Union?

Benjamin Tracy ordered that it be played whenever the Navy raised the American flag, but the song did not become the official national anthem of the United States until 1931.

In God We Trust

The official motto of the United States is "In God We Trust." The origin of the phrase probably dates to the national anthem. In the fourth verse of "The Star-Spangled Banner" is the phrase: "And this be our motto: 'In God is our Trust.'" But the motto was not approved by Congress at the time, and for much of its history, the United States did not have an official motto.

The phrase was used as a battle cry by some units in the Union army, and after the Civil War in the late 1800s, Congress approved the phrase "In God We Trust" for use on American coins. Since 1938 all United States coins have had this phrase inscribed on them. In 1956 with the United States in the midst of the Cold War with the Soviet Union, Congress declared the national motto to be "In God We Trust." The motto was meant to assert the general American belief in God and to contrast it with the communist belief in atheism. In 1957 the phrase began to be used on American paper currency as well.

In recent years the motto has become controversial. Some people argue that it violates the First Amendment's ban on government establishing a religion. Lower courts, as well as the Supreme Court, have repeatedly ruled that the motto and its use on coins and currency is not a violation of the First Amendment because it serves a ceremonial, not a religious, purpose and does not constitute the creation of a state church.

» This one cent coin displays the national motto "In God We Trust."

A Living Document

Creating the United States Constitution was no easy task. Delegates to the Constitutional Convention argued and debated. They drafted and redrafted early versions of the document. Finally, after months of hard work, they agreed upon a final draft that would establish the framework for the government we still have today. President George Washington proudly presented the Convention's hard work to Congress and, ultimately to the nation.

66 In all our deliberations on this subject, we kept steadily in our view that which appears to us the greatest interest of every true American, the consolidation of our Union, in which is involved our prosperity, felicity, safety—perhaps our national existence. This important consideration, seriously and deeply impressed on our minds, led each State in the Convention to be less rigid on points of inferior magnitude than might have been otherwise expected; and thus, the Constitution which we now present is the result of a spirit of amity, and of that mutual deference and concession, which the particularity of our political situation rendered indispensable. 99

—Letter from George Washington to Congress, September 17, 1787

The success of the Constitutional Convention in Philadelphia was in creating a government structure that reflected the country's different viewpoints—at least as they understood those viewpoints in the eighteenth century. The government created did not secure liberty for everyone living in the United States. But the document that they agreed upon allowed flexibility and change to be built into it.

Because of the spirit of independence that existed in the United States, the Constitution has endured while also being significantly changed and reinterpreted over time as the nation that it supports has also changed. The Constitution was not a perfect document. When written, it reflected some of the narrow views of the eighteenth century. It denied full citizenship to women. It protected the use of enslaved labor. It said nothing about Native Americans living within the nation. But the citizens of the United States have used the power within the Constitution to make the government better. The Constitution allowed for the changes necessary to guide a nation that the Philadelphia delegates could not possibly have envisioned.

✓ CHECK FOR UNDERSTANDING

1. **Describing** How do the symbols and mottos of the United States help to define American society?

2. **Explaining Causes** Why was the Great Seal of the United States the first symbol created by Congress?

LESSON ACTIVITIES

1. **Argumentative Writing** Write a short paragraph taking a pro or con position on the following question: Should communities permit rallies by unpopular groups, such as the Ku Klux Klan, even though such rallies may upset some members of the community or could possibly incite violence?

2. **Collaborating** In small groups, research and make a presentation about the presidential seal, and explain the meaning and historical significance of each part of the seal. Focus on the motto above the eagle's head that reads "E Pluribus Unum," Latin for "Out of Many, One."

PHOTO: Ken Cavanagh/McGraw-Hill Education; TEXT: Washington, George. 1787. Letter to Congress, Sept. 17, 1787 in The Debates and Proceedings in the Congress of the United States with An Appendix. Vol. I, compiled 1834 by Joseph Gales. Washington: Gales and Seaton.

This painting shows delegates at the Constitutional Convention in Philadelphia, 1787.

The Constitution of the United States

The Constitution of the United States is a truly remarkable document. It was one of the first written constitutions in modern history. The entire text of the Constitution and its amendments follow. For easier study, those passages that have been set aside or changed by the adoption of amendments are printed in blue. Also included are explanatory notes that will help clarify the meaning of important ideas presented in the Constitution.

(t)WDC Photos/Alamy Stock Photo; (b)larry1235/Shutterstock

PREAMBLE

The **Preamble** introduces the Constitution and sets forth the general purposes for which the government was established. The Preamble also declares that the power of the government comes from the people. The Constitution contains seven divisions called articles. Articles I, II, and III create the three branches of the national government.

The printed text of the document shows the spelling and punctuation of the parchment original.

ARTICLE I.
THE LEGISLATIVE BRANCH

Article 1 is the longest segment of the Constitution, describing the structure and functional powers of the legislative branch.

SECTION 1

Congressional Structure The power to make laws is given to a Congress made up of two chambers to represent different interests: the Senate to represent the states and the House to be more responsive to the people's will.

SECTION 2, CLAUSE 3

The Three-Fifths Compromise The "three fifths of all other Persons" phrasing represents an agreement to end a debate between the states. It allowed slave-holding states to count a portion of their enslaved population (who were not allowed to be citizens and could not vote) when determining their membership in the lower house of Congress.

Preamble

We the People of the United States, in Order to form a more perfect Union, establish Justice, insure domestic Tranquility, provide for the common defence, promote the general Welfare, and secure the Blessings of Liberty to ourselves and our Posterity, do ordain and establish this **Constitution** for the United States of America.

Article I

Section 1

All legislative Powers herein granted shall be vested in a Congress of the United States, which shall consist of a Senate and House of Representatives.

Section 2

[1.] The House of Representatives shall be composed of Members chosen every second Year by the People of the several States, and the Electors in each State shall have the Qualifications requisite for Electors of the most numerous Branch of the State Legislature.

[2.] No person shall be a Representative who shall not have attained the Age of twenty five Years, and been seven Years a Citizen of the United States, and who shall not, when elected, be an Inhabitant of that State in which he shall be chosen.

[3.] Representatives and direct Taxes shall be apportioned among the several States which may be included within this Union, according to their respective Numbers, which shall be determined by adding to the whole Number of free Persons, including those bound to Service for a Term of Years, and excluding Indians not taxed, three fifths of all other Persons. The actual **Enumeration** shall be made within three Years after the first Meeting of the Congress of the United States, and within every subsequent Term of ten Years, in such Manner as they shall by Law direct. The Number of Representatives shall not exceed one for every thirty Thousand, but each State shall have at Least one Representative; and until such enumeration shall be made, the State of New Hampshire shall be entitled to chuse three; Massachusetts eight, Rhode-Island and Providence Plantations one, Connecticut five, New-York six, New Jersey four, Pennsylvania eight, Delaware one, Maryland six, Virginia ten, North Carolina five, South Carolina five, and Georgia three.

---

preamble introduction

constitution principles and laws of a nation

enumeration census or population count

United States Constitution, 1787.

[4.] When vacancies happen in the Representation from any State, the Executive Authority thereof shall issue Writs of Election to fill such Vacancies.

[5.] The House of Representatives shall chuse their Speaker and other Officers; and shall have the sole Power of **Impeachment.**

Section 3

[1.] The Senate of the United States shall be composed of two Senators from each State, chosen by the Legislature thereof, for six Years; and each Senator shall have one Vote.

[2.] Immediately after they shall be assembled in Consequence of the first Election, they shall be divided as equally as may be into three Classes. The Seats of the Senators of the first Class shall be vacated at the Expiration of the second Year, of the second Class at the Expiration of the fourth Year, and of the third Class at the Expiration of the sixth Year, so that one third may be chosen every second Year; and if Vacancies happen by Resignation, or otherwise, during the Recess of the Legislature of any State, the Executive thereof may make temporary Appointments until the next Meeting of the Legislature, which shall then fill such Vacancies.

[3.] No Person shall be a Senator who shall not have attained to the Age of thirty Years, and been nine Years a Citizen of the United States, and who shall not, when elected, be an Inhabitant of that State for which he shall be chosen.

[4.] The Vice President of the United States shall be President of the Senate, but shall have no Vote, unless they be equally divided.

[5.] The Senate shall chuse their other Officers, and also a **President pro tempore,** in the Absence of the Vice President, or when he shall exercise the Office of the President of the United States.

[6.] The Senate shall have the sole Power to try all Impeachments. When sitting for that Purpose, they shall be on Oath or Affirmation. When the President of the United States is tried, the Chief Justice shall preside: And no Person shall be convicted without the Concurrence of two thirds of the Members present.

[7.] Judgment in Cases of Impeachment shall not extend further than to removal from Office, and disqualification to hold and enjoy any Office of honor, Trust or Profit under the United States: but the Party convicted shall nevertheless be liable and subject to Indictment, Trial, Judgment and Punishment, according to Law.

Section 4

[1.] The Times, Places and Manner of holding Elections for Senators and Representatives, shall be prescribed in each State by the Legislature thereof; but the Congress may at any time by Law make or alter such Regulations, except as to the Places of chusing Senators.

---

impeachment bring charges against an official

president pro tempore presiding officer of the Senate who serves when the vice president is absent

---

SECTION 3, CLAUSE 1

Voting Procedure Originally, senators were chosen by the legislators of their own states. The Seventeenth Amendment changed this, so that senators are now elected by their state's people. There are 100 senators, 2 from each state.

WHAT MIGHT HAVE BEEN

Electing Senators South Carolina delegate Charles Pinckney suggested during the Convention that the members of the Senate come from four equally proportioned districts within the United States and that the legislature elect the executive every seven years.

SECTION 3, CLAUSE 6

Trial of Impeachments One of Congress's powers is the power to impeach—to accuse government officials of wrongdoing, put them on trial, and, if necessary, remove them from office. The House decides if the offense is impeachable. The Senate acts as a jury, and when the president is impeached, the Chief Justice of the United States serves as the judge. A two-thirds vote of the members present is needed to convict impeached officials. *What punishment can the Senate give if an impeached official is convicted?*

[2.] The Congress shall assemble at least once in every Year, and such Meeting shall be on the first Monday in December, unless they shall by Law appoint a different Day.

Section 5

[1.] Each House shall be the Judge of the Elections, Returns and Qualifications of its own Members, and a Majority of each shall constitute a **Quorum** to do Business; but a smaller Number may **adjourn** from day to day, and may be authorized to compel the Attendance of absent Members, in such Manner, and under such Penalties as each House may provide.

[2.] Each House may determine the Rules of its Proceedings, punish its Members for disorderly Behaviour, and, with the **Concurrence** of two thirds, expel a Member.

[3.] Each House shall keep a Journal of its Proceedings, and from time to time publish the same, excepting such Parts as may in their Judgment require Secrecy; and the Yeas and Nays of the Members of either House on any question shall, at the Desire of one fifth of those Present, be entered on the Journal.

[4.] Neither House, during the Session of Congress, shall, without the Consent of the other, adjourn for more than three days, nor to any other Place than that in which the two Houses shall be sitting.

Section 6

[1.] The Senators and Representatives shall receive a Compensation for their Services, to be ascertained by Law, and paid out of the Treasury of the United States. They shall in all Cases, except Treason, Felony and Breach of the Peace, be privileged from Arrest during their Attendance at the Session of their respective Houses, and in going to and returning from the same; and for any Speech or Debate in either House, they shall not be questioned in any other Place.

[2.] No Senator or Representative shall, during the Time for which he was elected, be appointed to any civil Office under the Authority of the United States, which shall have been created, or the **Emoluments** whereof shall have been encreased during such time; and no Person holding any Office under the United States, shall be a Member of either House during his Continuance in Office.

Section 7

[1.] All Bills for raising **Revenue** shall originate in the House of Representatives; but the Senate may propose or concur with Amendments as on other **Bills.**

[2.] Every Bill which shall have passed the House of Representatives and the Senate, shall, before it become a Law, be presented to the

SECTION 6, CLAUSE 1

Pay and Privileges To strengthen the federal government, the Founders set congressional salaries to be paid by the United States Treasury rather than by members' respective states.

Originally, members were paid $6 per day. In 2015 all members of Congress received a base salary of $174,000.

SECTION 7, CLAUSE 1

Revenue Bills All tax laws must originate in the House of Representatives. This ensures that the branch of Congress that is elected by the people every two years has the major role in determining taxes.

quorum minimum number of members that must be present to conduct sessions

adjourn to suspend a session

concurrence agreement

emoluments salaries

revenue income raised by government

bill draft of a proposed law

President of the United States; If he approve he shall sign it, but if not he shall return it, with his Objections to that House in which it shall have originated, who shall enter the Objections at large on their Journal, and proceed to reconsider it. If after such Reconsideration two thirds of that House shall agree to pass the Bill, it shall be sent, together with the Objections, to the other House, by which it shall likewise be reconsidered, and if approved by two thirds of that House, it shall become a Law. But in all such Cases the Votes of both Houses shall be determined by yeas and Nays, and the Names of the Persons voting for and against the Bill shall be entered on the Journal of each House respectively. If any Bill shall not be returned by the President within ten Days (Sundays excepted) after it shall have been presented to him, the Same shall be a Law, in like Manner as if he had signed it, unless the Congress by their Adjournment prevent its Return, in which Case it shall not be a Law.

[3.] Every Order, **Resolution,** or Vote to which the Concurrence of the Senate and House of Representatives may be necessary (except on a question of Adjournment) shall be presented to the President of the United States; and before the Same shall take Effect, shall be approved by him, or being disapproved by him, shall be repassed by two thirds of the Senate and House of Representatives, according to the Rules and Limitations prescribed in the Case of a Bill.

Section 8

[1.] The Congress shall have the Power to lay and collect Taxes, Duties, Imposts and Excises, to pay the Debts and provide for the common Defence and general Welfare of the United States; but all Duties, Imposts and Excises shall be uniform throughout the United States;

[2.] To borrow Money on the credit of the United States;

[3.] To regulate Commerce with foreign Nations, and among the several States, and with the Indian Tribes;

[4.] To establish an uniform Rule of **Naturalization,** and uniform Laws on the subject of Bankruptcies throughout the United States;

[5.] To coin Money, regulate the Value thereof, and of foreign Coin, and fix the Standard of Weights and Measures;

[6.] To provide for the Punishment of counterfeiting the Securities and current Coin of the United States;

[7.] To establish Post Offices and post Roads;

[8.] To promote the Progress of Science and useful Arts, by securing for limited Times to Authors and Inventors the exclusive Right to their respective Writings and Discoveries;

[9.] To constitute Tribunals inferior to the supreme Court;

SECTION 7, CLAUSE 3
How Bills Become Laws A bill may become a law only by passing both houses of Congress and being signed by the president. The president can check Congress by rejecting—vetoing—its legislation. *How can Congress override the president's veto?*

SECTION 8
Powers of Congress
Expressed powers are those powers directly stated in the Constitution. Most of the expressed powers of Congress are listed in Article I, Section 8. These powers are also called enumerated powers because they are numbered 1–18. *Which clause gives Congress the power to declare war?*

---

resolution legislature's formal expression of opinion

naturalization procedure by which a citizen of a foreign nation becomes a citizen of the United States

SECTION 8, CLAUSE 18

Elastic Clause The final enumerated power is often called the "elastic clause." It gives Congress the right to make all laws "necessary and proper" to carry out the powers expressed in the other clauses of Article I. It is called the elastic clause because it lets Congress "stretch" its powers to meet future unknown situations.

The limits of this elasticity was first addressed in *McCulloch* v. *Maryland,* when the Supreme Court favored a broad interpretation. The Court ruled that the elastic clause let Congress use its powers in any way not specifically prohibited by the Constitution. *What does the phrase "necessary and proper" in the elastic clause mean?*

WHAT MIGHT HAVE BEEN

The Slave Trade Section 9, Clause 1 mentions that the United States will not end its participation in the international slave trade until 1808. This was another compromise to get southern states to support the Constitution. The clause was set aside by the ratification of the Thirteenth Amendment.

SECTION 9, CLAUSES 2 & 3

Denied Federal Powers A writ of habeas corpus issued by a judge requires a law official to bring a prisoner to court and show cause for holding the prisoner. A bill of attainder is a bill that punishes a person without a jury trial. An "ex post facto" law is one that makes an act a crime after the act has been committed. *What does the Constitution say about bills of attainder?*

[10.] To define and punish Piracies and Felonies committed on the high Seas, and Offences against the Law of Nations;

[11.] To declare War, grant Letters of Marque and Reprisal, and make Rules concerning Captures on Land and Water;

[12.] To raise and support Armies, but no Appropriation of Money to that Use shall be for a longer Term than two Years;

[13.] To provide and maintain a Navy;

[14.] To make Rules for the Government and Regulation of the land and naval Forces;

[15.] To provide for calling forth the Militia to execute the Laws of the Union, suppress Insurrections and repel Invasions;

[16.] To provide for organizing, arming, and disciplining, the Militia, and for governing such Part of them as may be employed in the Service of the United States, reserving to the States respectively, the Appointment of the Officers, and the Authority of training the Militia according to the discipline prescribed by Congress;

[17.] To exercise exclusive Legislation in all Cases whatsoever, over such District (not exceeding ten Miles square) as may, by Cession of particular States, and the Acceptance of Congress, become the Seat of Government of the United States, and to exercise like Authority over all Places purchased by the Consent of the Legislature of the State in which the Same shall be, for the Erection of Forts, Magazines, Arsenals, dock-Yards, and other needful Buildings; And

[18.] To make all Laws which shall be necessary and proper for carrying into Execution the foregoing Powers, and all other Powers vested by this Constitution in the Government of the United States, or in any Department or Officer thereof.

Section 9

[1.] The Migration or Importation of such Persons as any of the States now existing shall think proper to admit, shall not be prohibited by the Congress prior to the Year one thousand eight hundred and eight, but a Tax or duty may be imposed on such Importation, not exceeding ten dollars for each Person.

[2.] The Privilege of the Writ of Habeas Corpus shall not be suspended, unless when in Cases of Rebellion or Invasion the public Safety may require it.

[3.] No Bill of Attainder or ex post facto Law shall be passed.

[4.] No Capitation, or other direct, Tax shall be laid, unless in Proportion to the Census or Enumeration herein before directed to be taken.

[5.] No Tax or Duty shall be laid on Articles exported from any State.

[6.] No Preference shall be given by any Regulation of Commerce or Revenue to the Ports of one State over those of another: nor shall Vessels bound to, or from, one State, be obliged to enter, clear, or pay Duties in another.

[7.] No Money shall be drawn from the Treasury, but in Consequence of Appropriations made by Law; and a regular Statement and Account of the Receipts and Expenditures of all public Money shall be published from time to time.

[8.] No Title of Nobility shall be granted by the United States: And no Person holding any Office of Profit or Trust under them, shall, without the Consent of the Congress, accept of any present, Emolument, Office, or Title, of any kind whatever, from any King, Prince, or foreign State.

Section 10

[1.] No State shall enter into any Treaty, Alliance, or Confederation; grant Letters of Marque and Reprisal; coin Money; emit Bills of Credit; make any Thing but gold and silver Coin a Tender in Payment of Debts; pass any Bill of Attainder, ex post facto Law, or Law impairing the Obligation of Contracts, or grant any Title of Nobility.

[2.] No State shall, without the Consent of the Congress, lay any Imposts or Duties on Imports or Exports, except what may be absolutely necessary for executing its inspection Laws: and the net Produce of all Duties and Imposts, laid by any State on Imports and Exports, shall be for the Use of the Treasury of the United States; and all such Laws shall be subject to the Revision and Controul of the Congress.

[3.] No State shall, without the Consent of Congress, lay any Duty of Tonnage, keep Troops, or Ships of War in time of Peace, enter into any Agreement or Compact with another State, or with a foreign Power, or engage in War, unless actually invaded, or in such imminent Danger as will not admit of delay.

Article II

Section 1

[1.] The executive Power shall be vested in a President of the United States of America. He shall hold his Office during the Term of four Years, and, together with the Vice President, chosen for the same Term, be elected, as follows.

[2.] Each State shall appoint, in such Manner as the Legislature thereof may direct, a Number of Electors, equal to the whole Number of Senators and Representatives to which the State may be entitled in the Congress: but no Senator or Representative, or Person holding an Office of Trust or Profit under the United States, shall be appointed an Elector.

[3.] The Electors shall meet in their respective States, and vote by Ballot for two Persons, of whom one at least shall not be an Inhabitant of the same State with themselves. And they shall make a List of all the Persons voted for, and of the Number of Votes for each; which List they shall sign and certify, and transmit sealed to the Seat of the Government of the United States, directed to the President of the Senate. The President of the Senate shall, in the Presence of the Senate and House of Representatives, open all the Certificates, and the Votes shall then be counted. The Person having the greatest Number of Votes shall be the President, if such Number be a Majority of the whole Number of Electors appointed; and if there be more than one who have such Majority, and have an equal Number

SECTION 10, CLAUSES 1-3

Denied State Powers The clauses in Section 10 list limits on the states. These restrictions were designed, in part, to prevent an overlapping in functions and authority with the federal government.

ARTICLE II.
THE EXECUTIVE BRANCH

Article II creates an executive branch to carry out laws passed by Congress. Article II lists the powers and duties of the president, describes qualifications for office and procedures for electing the president, and provides for a vice president.

WHAT MIGHT HAVE BEEN

Term of Office Alexander Hamilton also provided his own governmental outline at the Constitutional Convention. Some of its most distinctive elements were that both the executive and the members of the Senate were "elected to serve during good behaviour," meaning there was no specified limit on their time in office.

SECTION 1, CLAUSE 3

Former Method of Election In the election of 1800, the top two candidates received the same number of electoral votes, making it necessary for the House of Representatives to decide the election. To eliminate this problem, the Twelfth Amendment, added in 1804, changed the method of electing the president stated in Article II, Section 1, Clause 3. The Twelfth Amendment requires that the electors cast separate ballots for president and vice president.

WHAT MIGHT HAVE BEEN

Qualifications The New Jersey Amendments, sponsored by the smaller states, raised the possibility of making the executive a committee of people rather than a single individual. Also, executives were not allowed to run for a second term of office under this plan.

SECTION 1, CLAUSE 5

Presidential Qualifications The president must be a citizen of the United States by birth, at least 35 years of age, and a resident of the United States for 14 years.

SECTION 1, CLAUSE 6

Vacancies If the president dies, resigns, is removed from office by impeachment, or is unable to carry out the duties of the office, the vice president becomes president. (see Amendment XXV)

SECTION 1, CLAUSE 7

Salary Originally, the president's salary was $25,000 per year. The president's current salary is $400,000 plus a $50,000 nontaxable expense account per year. The president also receives living accommodations in two residences—the White House and Camp David.

SECTION 2, CLAUSE 1

Cabinet Mention of "the principal officer in each of the executive departments" is the only suggestion of the president's cabinet to be found in the Constitution. The cabinet is an advisory body, and its power depends on the president. Section 2, Clause 1 also makes the president the head of the armed forces. This established the principle of civilian control of the military.

of Votes, then the House of Representatives shall immediately chuse by Ballot one of them for President; and if no person have a Majority, then from the five highest on the List the said House shall in like Manner chuse the President. But in chusing the President, the Votes shall be taken by States, the Representation from each State having one Vote; A quorum for this Purpose shall consist of a Member or Members from two thirds of the States, and a Majority of all the States shall be necessary to a Choice. In every Case, after the Choice of the President, the Person having the greatest Number of Votes of the Electors shall be the Vice President. But if there should remain two or more who have equal Votes, the Senate shall chuse from them by Ballot the Vice President.

[4.] The Congress may determine the Time of chusing the Electors, and the Day on which they shall give their Votes; which Day shall be the same throughout the United States.

[5.] No Person except a natural born Citizen, or a Citizen of the United States, at the time of the Adoption of this Constitution, shall be eligible to the Office of President; neither shall any Person be eligible to that Office who shall not have attained to the Age of thirty five Years, and been fourteen Years a Resident within the United States.

[6.] In Case of the Removal of the President from Office, or of his Death, Resignation, or Inability to discharge the Powers and Duties of t he said Office, the Same shall devolve on the Vice President, and the Congress may by Law provide for the Case of Removal, Death, Resignation or Inability, both of the President and Vice President, declaring what Officer shall then act as President, and such Officer shall act accordingly, until the Disability be removed, or a President shall be elected.

[7.] The President shall, at stated Times, receive for his Services, a Compensation, which shall neither be encreased nor diminished during the Period for which he shall have been elected, and he shall not receive within that Period any other Emolument from the United States, or any of them.

[8.] Before he enter on the Execution of his Office, he shall take the following Oath or Affirmation:—"I do solemnly swear (or affirm) that I will faithfully execute the Office of President of the United States, and will to the best of my Ability, preserve, protect and defend the Constitution of the United States."

Section 2

[1.] The President shall be Commander in Chief of the Army and Navy of the United States, and of the Militia of the several States, when called into the actual Service of the United States; he may require the Opinion, in writing, of the principal Officer in each of the executive Departments, upon any Subject relating to the Duties of their respective Offices, and he shall have Power to grant Reprieves and Pardons for Offences against the United States, except in Cases of Impeachment.

[2.] He shall have Power, by and with the Advice and Consent of the Senate, to make Treaties, provided two thirds of the Senators present concur; and he shall nominate, and by and with the Advice and Consent of the Senate, shall appoint Ambassadors, other public Ministers and Consuls, Judges of the supreme Court, and all other Officers of the United States, whose Appointments are not herein otherwise provided for, and which shall be established by Law: but the Congress may by Law vest the Appointment of such inferior Officers, as they think proper, in the President alone, in the Courts of Law, or in the Heads of Departments.

[3.] The President shall have Power to fill up all Vacancies that may happen during the Recess of the Senate, by granting Commissions which shall expire at the End of their next Session.

Section 3

He shall from time to time give to the Congress Information of the State of the Union, and recommend to their Consideration such Measures as he shall judge necessary and expedient; he may, on extraordinary Occasions, convene both Houses, or either of them, and in Case of Disagreement between them, with Respect to the Time of Adjournment, he may adjourn them to such Time as he shall think proper; he shall receive Ambassadors and other public Ministers; he shall take Care that the Laws be faithfully executed, and shall Commission all the Officers of the United States.

Section 4

The President, Vice President and all civil Officers of the United States, shall be removed from Office on Impeachment for, and Conviction of, Treason, Bribery, or other high Crimes and Misdemeanors.

Article III

Section 1

The judicial Power of the United States, shall be vested in one supreme Court, and in such inferior Courts as the Congress may from time to time ordain and establish. The Judges, both of the supreme and inferior Courts, shall hold their Offices during good Behaviour, and shall, at stated Times, receive for their Services, a Compensation, which shall not be diminished during their Continuance in Office.

Section 2

[1.] The judicial Power shall extend to all Cases, in Law and Equity, arising under this Constitution, the Laws of the United States, and Treaties made, or which shall be made, under their Authority;—to all Cases affecting Ambassadors, other public Ministers and Consuls;—to all Cases of admiralty and maritime Jurisdiction;—to Controversies to which the United States shall be a Party;—to Controversies between two or more States;—between a State and Citizens of another State;—between Citizens of different States,—between Citizens of the same State claiming Lands under Grants of different States, and between a State, or the Citizens thereof, and foreign States, Citizens or Subjects.

SECTION 2, CLAUSE 2

Treaties The president is responsible for the conduct of relations with foreign countries. *What role does the Senate have in approving treaties?*

SECTION 4

Reasons for Removal From Office This section states the reasons for which the president and vice president may be impeached and removed from office. Andrew Johnson, Bill Clinton, and Donald Trump have been impeached by the House. Richard Nixon resigned before the House could vote on possible impeachment.

ARTICLE III.
THE JUDICIAL BRANCH

The Constitution only describes the Supreme Court but provided for other federal courts. The judiciary of the United States has two different systems of courts. One system consists of the federal courts, whose powers derive from the Constitution and federal laws. The other includes the courts of each of the 50 states, whose powers derive from state constitutions and laws.

SECTION 2, CLAUSE 1

General Jurisdiction Federal courts deal mostly with "statute law," or laws passed by Congress, treaties, and cases involving the Constitution itself.

SECTION 2, CLAUSE 2

The Supreme Court A court with "original jurisdiction" has the authority to be the first court to hear a case. The Supreme Court generally has "appellate jurisdiction" in that it mostly hears cases appealed from lower courts.

SECTION 2, CLAUSE 3

Jury Trial Except in cases of impeachment, anyone accused of a crime has the right to a trial by jury. The trial must be held in the state where the crime was committed. Jury trial guarantees were strengthened in the Sixth, Seventh, Eighth, and Ninth Amendments.

ARTICLE IV.
RELATIONS AMONG THE STATES

Article IV explains the relationship of the states to one another and to the national government. This article requires each state to give citizens of other states the same rights as its own citizens, addresses the admission of new states, and guarantees that the national government will protect the states.

WHAT MIGHT HAVE BEEN

Fugitive Slaves Article IV, Section 2, Clause 3 legally prevented escaped slaves who were captured in free territory from demanding their freedom. They were supposed to be returned to their slaveholder. The clause was set aside by the ratification of the Thirteenth Amendment.

[2.] In all Cases affecting Ambassadors, other public Ministers and Consuls, and those in which a State shall be Party, the supreme Court shall have **original Jurisdiction.** In all the other Cases before mentioned, the supreme Court shall have **appellate Jurisdiction,** both as to Law and Fact, with such Exceptions, and under such Regulations as the Congress shall make.

[3.] The Trial of all Crimes, except in Cases of Impeachment, shall be by Jury; and such Trial shall be held in the State where the said Crimes shall have been committed; but when not committed within any State, the Trial shall be at such Place or Places as the Congress may by Law have directed.

Section 3

[1.] Treason against the United States, shall consist only in levying War against them, or in adhering to their Enemies, giving them Aid and Comfort. No Person shall be convicted of Treason unless on the Testimony of two Witnesses to the same overt Act, or on Confession in open Court.

[2.] The Congress shall have Power to declare the Punishment of Treason, but no Attainder of Treason shall work Corruption of Blood, or Forfeiture except during the Life of the Person attainted.

Article IV

Section 1

Full Faith and Credit shall be given in each State to the public Acts, Records, and judicial Proceedings of every other State. And the Congress may by general Laws prescribe the Manner in which such Acts, Records and Proceedings shall be proved, and the Effect thereof.

Section 2

[1.] The Citizens of each State shall be entitled to all Privileges and Immunities of Citizens in the several States.

[2.] A Person charged in any State with **Treason,** Felony, or other Crime, who shall flee from Justice, and be found in another State, shall on Demand of the executive Authority of the State from which he fled, be delivered up, to be removed to the State having Jurisdiction of the Crime.

[3.] No Person held to Service of Labour in one State, under the Laws thereof, escaping into another, shall, in Consequence of any Law or Regulation therein, be discharged from such Service or Labour, but shall be delivered up on Claim of the Party to whom such Service or Labour may be due.

---

original jurisdiction authority to be the first court to hear a case

appellate jurisdiction authority to hear cases appealed from lower courts

treason violation of the allegiance owed by a person to his or her own country, for example, by aiding an enemy

Section 3

[1.] New States may be admitted by the Congress into this Union; but no new State shall be formed or erected within the Jurisdiction of any other State; nor any State be formed by the Junction of two or more States, or Parts of States, without the Consent of the Legislatures of the States concerned as well as of the Congress.

[2.] The Congress shall have Power to dispose of and make all needful Rules and Regulations respecting the Territory or other Property belonging to the United States; and nothing in this Constitution shall be so construed as to Prejudice any Claims of the United States, or of any particular State.

Section 4

The United States shall guarantee to every State in this Union a Republican Form of Government, and shall protect each of them against Invasion; and on Application of the Legislature, or of the Executive (when the Legislature cannot be convened) against domestic Violence.

Article V

The Congress, whenever two thirds of both Houses shall deem it necessary, shall propose **Amendments** to this Constitution, or, on the Application of the Legislatures of two thirds of the several States, shall call a Convention for proposing Amendments, which, in either Case, shall be valid to all Intents and Purposes, as Part of this Constitution, when ratified by the Legislatures of three fourths of the several States, or by Conventions in three fourths thereof, as the one or the other Mode of **Ratification** may be proposed by the Congress; Provided that no Amendment which may be made prior to the Year One thousand eight hundred and eight shall in any Manner affect the first and fourth Clauses in the Ninth Section of the first Article; and that no State, without its Consent, shall be deprived of its equal Suffrage in the Senate.

Article VI

[1.] All Debts contracted and Engagements entered into, before the Adoption of this Constitution, shall be as valid against the United States under this Constitution, as under the Confederation.

[2.] This Constitution, and the Laws of the United States which shall be made in Pursuance thereof; and all Treaties made, or which shall be made, under the Authority of the United States, shall be the supreme Law of the Land; and the Judges in every State shall be bound thereby, any Thing in the Constitution or Laws of any State to the Contrary notwithstanding.

[3.] The Senators and Representatives before mentioned, and the Members of the several State Legislatures, and all executive and judicial Officers, both of the United States and of the several States, shall be bound by Oath or Affirmation, to support this Constitution; but no religious Test shall ever be required as a Qualification to any Office or public Trust under the United States.

---

amendment a change to the Constitution

ratification process by which an amendment is approved

SECTION 3, CLAUSE 1

New States Congress determines the basic guidelines for applying for statehood. Maine and West Virginia were created within the boundaries of another state. President Lincoln recognized the West Virginia government as the legal government of Virginia during the Civil War. This allowed West Virginia to secede from Virginia without obtaining approval from the Virginia legislature.

ARTICLE V.
THE AMENDMENT PROCESS

Article V explains how the Constitution can be changed. All 27 amendments were proposed by a two-thirds vote of both houses of Congress. Only the Twenty-first Amendment was ratified by constitutional conventions of the states. The other amendments were ratified by state legislatures. *What is an amendment?*

ARTICLE VI.
CONSTITUTIONAL SUPREMACY

Article VI contains the "supremacy clause." This clause establishes that the Constitution, laws passed by Congress, and treaties of the United States "shall be the supreme Law of the Land." The "supremacy clause" recognizes the Constitution and federal laws as supreme when in conflict with those of the states.

ARTICLE VII.
RATIFICATION

Article VII addresses ratification and states that, unlike the Articles of Confederation, which required approval of all thirteen states for adoption, the Constitution would take effect after it was ratified by nine states.

Article VII

The Ratification of the Conventions of nine States, shall be sufficient for the Establishment of this Constitution between the States so ratifying the Same. Done in Convention by the Unanimous Consent of the States present the Seventeenth Day of September in the Year of our Lord one thousand seven hundred and Eighty seven and of the Independence of the United States of America the Twelfth. In witness whereof We have hereunto subscribed our Names,

Signers

George Washington,
President and Deputy from Virginia

New Hampshire
John Langdon
Nicholas Gilman

Massachusetts
Nathaniel Gorham
Rufus King

Connecticut
William Samuel Johnson
Roger Sherman

New York
Alexander Hamilton

New Jersey
William Livingston
David Brearley
William Paterson
Jonathan Dayton

Pennsylvania
Benjamin Franklin
Thomas Mifflin
Robert Morris
George Clymer
Thomas FitzSimons
Jared Ingersoll
James Wilson
Gouverneur Morris

Delaware
George Read
Gunning Bedford, Jr.
John Dickinson
Richard Bassett
Jacob Broom

Maryland
James McHenry
Daniel of St. Thomas Jenifer
Daniel Carroll

Virginia
John Blair
James Madison, Jr.

North Carolina
William Blount
Richard Dobbs Spaight
Hugh Williamson

South Carolina
John Rutledge
Charles Cotesworth Pinckney
Charles Pinckney
Pierce Butler

Georgia
William Few
Abraham Baldwin

Attest: William Jackson, Secretary

THE AMENDMENTS

This part of the Constitution consists of changes and additions. The Constitution has been amended 27 times throughout the nation's history.

THE BILL OF RIGHTS

The first 10 amendments are known as the Bill of Rights (1791). These amendments limit the powers of the federal government. The First Amendment protects the civil liberties of individuals in the United States. Yet, the amendment's freedoms are not absolute. They are limited by the rights of other individuals. *What freedoms does the First Amendment protect?*

Amendment I

Congress shall make no law respecting an establishment of religion, or prohibiting the free exercise thereof; or abridging the freedom of speech, or of the press; or the right of the people peaceably to assemble, and to petition the Government for a redress of grievances.

Amendment II

A well regulated Militia, being necessary to the security of a free State, the right of the people to keep and bear Arms, shall not be infringed.

Amendment III

No Soldier shall, in time of peace be **quartered** in any house, without the consent of the Owner, nor in time of war, but in a manner to be prescribed by law.

quarter to provide living accommodations

Amendment IV

The right of the people to be secure in their persons, houses, papers, and effects, against unreasonable searches and seizures, shall not be violated, and no **Warrants** shall issue, but upon probable cause, supported by Oath or affirmation, and particularly describing the place, to be searched, and the persons or things to be seized.

Amendment V

No person shall be held to answer for a capital, or otherwise infamous crime, unless on a presentment or indictment of a Grand Jury, except in cases arising in the land or naval forces, or in the Militia, when in actual service in time of War or public danger; nor shall any person be subject for the same offence to be twice put in jeopardy of life or limb; nor shall be compelled in any criminal case to be a witness against himself, nor be deprived of life, liberty, or property, without due process of law; nor shall private property be taken for public use without just compensation.

Amendment VI

In all criminal prosecutions, the accused shall enjoy the right to a speedy and public trial, by an impartial jury of the State and district wherein the crime shall have been committed, which district shall have been previously ascertained by law, and to be informed of the nature and cause of the accusation; to be confronted with the witnesses against him; to have compulsory process for obtaining Witnesses in his favor, and to have the assistance of counsel for his defence.

Amendment VII

In Suits at common law, where the value in controversy shall exceed twenty dollars, the right of trial by jury shall be preserved, and no fact tried by a jury, shall be otherwise reexamined in any Court of the United States, than according to the rules of **common law.**

Amendment VIII

Excessive **bail** shall not be required, nor excessive fines imposed, nor cruel and unusual punishments inflicted.

Amendment IX

The enumeration in the Constitution, of certain rights, shall not be construed to deny or disparage others retained by the people.

AMENDMENT 5

Rights of the Accused This amendment contains protections for people accused of crimes. One of the protections is that government may not deprive any person of life, liberty, or property without due process of law. This means that the government must follow proper constitutional procedures in trials and in other actions it takes against individuals. *According to Amendment V, what is the function of a grand jury?*

AMENDMENT 6

Right to Speedy and Fair Trial A basic protection is the right to a speedy, public trial. The jury must hear witnesses and evidence on both sides before deciding the guilt or innocence of a person charged with a crime. This amendment also provides that legal counsel must be provided to a defendant. In 1963, in *Gideon v. Wainwright*, the Supreme Court ruled that if a defendant cannot afford a lawyer, the government must provide one to defend him or her. *Why is the right to a "speedy" trial important?*

AMENDMENT 9

Powers Reserved to the People This amendment prevents government from claiming that the only rights people have are those listed in the Bill of Rights.

---

warrant document that gives police particular rights or powers

common law law established by previous court decisions

bail money that an accused person provides to the court as a guarantee that he or she will be present for a trial

AMENDMENT 10

Powers Reserved to the States This amendment protects the states and the people from the federal government. It establishes that powers not given to the national government and not denied to the states by the Constitution belong to the states or to the people. These are checks on the "necessary and proper" power of the federal government, which is provided for in Article I, Section 8, Clause 18.

AMENDMENT 11

Suits Against the States The Eleventh Amendment (1795) provides that a lawsuit brought by a citizen of the United States or a foreign nation against a state must be tried in a state court, not in a federal court. The Supreme Court had ruled in *Chisholm* v. *Georgia* (1793) that a federal court could try a lawsuit brought by citizens of South Carolina against a citizen of Georgia.

AMENDMENT 12

Election of President and Vice President The Twelfth Amendment (1804) corrects a problem that had arisen in the method of electing the president and vice president, which is described in Article II, Section 1, Clause 3. This amendment provides for the Electoral College to use separate ballots in voting for president and vice president. *If no candidate receives a majority of the electoral votes, who elects the president?*

Amendment X

The powers not delegated to the United States by the Constitution, nor prohibited by it to the States, are reserved to the States respectively, or to the people.

Amendment XI

The Judicial power of the United States shall not be construed to extend to any suit in law or equity, commenced or prosecuted against one of the United States by Citizens of another State, or by Citizens or Subjects of any Foreign State.

Amendment XII

The electors shall meet in their respective states and vote by ballot for President and Vice-President, one of whom, at least, shall not be an inhabitant of the same state with themselves; they shall name in their ballots the person voted for as President, and in distinct ballots the person voted for as Vice-President, and they shall make distinct lists of all persons voted for as President, and of all persons voted for as Vice-President, and of the number of votes for each, which lists they shall sign and certify, and transmit sealed to the seat of the government of the United States, directed to the President of the Senate;—The President of the Senate shall, in the presence of the Senate and House of Representatives, open all the certificates and the votes shall then be counted;—The person having the greatest number of votes for President, shall be the President, if such number be a **majority** of the whole number of Electors appointed; and if no person have such majority, then from the persons having the highest numbers not exceeding three on the list of those voted for as President, the House of Representatives shall choose immediately, by ballot, the President. But in choosing the President, the votes shall be taken by states, the representation from each state having one vote; a quorum for this purpose shall consist of a member or members from two-thirds of the states, and a majority of all the states shall be necessary to a choice. And if the House of Representatives shall not choose a President whenever the right of choice shall devolve upon them, before the fourth day of March next following, then the Vice-President shall act as President, as in the case of the death or other constitutional disability of the President. The person having the greatest number of votes as Vice-President, shall be the Vice-President, if such number be a majority of the whole number of Electors appointed, and if no person have a majority, then from the two highest numbers on the list, the Senate shall choose the Vice-President; a quorum for the purpose shall consist of two-thirds of the whole number of Senators, and a majority of the whole number shall be necessary to a choice. But no person constitutionally ineligible to the office of President shall be eligible to that of Vice-President of the United States.

majority more than half

Amendment XIII

Section 1

Neither slavery nor involuntary servitude, except as a punishment for crime whereof the party shall have been duly convicted, shall exist within the United States, or any place subject to their jurisdiction.

Section 2

Congress shall have power to enforce this article by appropriate legislation.

Amendment XIV

Section 1

All persons born or naturalized in the United States, and subject to the jurisdiction thereof, are citizens of the United States and of the State wherein they reside. No State shall make or enforce any law which shall **abridge** the privileges or immunities of citizens of the United States; nor shall any State deprive any person of life, liberty, or property, without due process of law; nor deny to any person within its jurisdiction the equal protection of the laws.

Section 2

Representatives shall be apportioned among the several States according to their respective numbers, counting the whole number of persons in each State, excluding Indians not taxed. But when the right to vote at any election for the choice of electors for President and Vice President of the United States, Representatives in Congress, the Executive and Judicial officers of a State, or the members of the Legislature thereof, is denied to any of the male inhabitants of such State, being twenty-one years of age, and citizens of the United States, or in any way abridged, except for participation in rebellion, or other crime, the basis of representation therein shall be reduced in the proportion which the number of such male citizens shall bear to the whole number of male citizens twenty-one years of age in such State.

Section 3

No person shall be a Senator or Representative in Congress, or elector of President and Vice President, or hold any office, civil or military, under the United States, or under any State, who, having previously taken an oath, as a member of Congress, or as an officer of the United States, or as a member of any State legislature, or as an executive or judicial officer of any State, to support the Constitution of the United States, shall have engaged in insurrection or rebellion against the same, or given aid or comfort to the enemies thereof. But Congress may by a vote of two-thirds of each House, remove such disability.

Section 4

The validity of the public debt of the United States, authorized by law, including debts incurred for payment of pensions and bounties for

---

abridge to reduce

Abolition of Slavery Amendments Thirteen (1865), Fourteen, and Fifteen often are called the Civil War or Reconstruction amendments. The Thirteenth Amendment outlaws slavery.

AMENDMENT 14

Rights of Citizens The Fourteenth Amendment (1868) originally was intended to protect the legal rights of the freed enslaved people, although there have been periods when it was not enforced. Its interpretation has been extended to protect the rights of citizenship in general by prohibiting a state from depriving any person of life, liberty, or property without "due process of law." It also states that all citizens have the right to equal protection of the laws.

AMENDMENT 14, SECTION 2

Representation in Congress This section reduced the number of members a state had in the House of Representatives if it denied its citizens the right to vote. Later civil rights laws and the Twenty-fourth Amendment guaranteed the vote to African Americans.

AMENDMENT 14, SECTION 3

Penalty for Engaging in Insurrection The leaders of the Confederacy were barred from state or federal offices unless Congress agreed to remove this ban. By the end of Reconstruction, all but a few Confederate leaders were allowed to return to public service.

AMENDMENT 14, SECTION 4

Public Debt The public debt acquired by the federal government during the Civil War was valid and could not be questioned by the South. The debts of the Confederacy, however, were declared to be illegal. *Could former slaveholders collect payment for the loss of enslaved labor?*

AMENDMENT 15

Voting Rights The Fifteenth Amendment (1870) prohibits the government from denying a person's right to vote on the basis of race. Despite the law, many states denied African Americans the right to vote by such means as poll taxes, literacy tests, and white primaries.

AMENDMENT 16

Income Tax The origins of the Sixteenth Amendment (1913) date back to 1895, when the Supreme Court declared a federal income tax unconstitutional. To overturn this decision, this amendment authorizes an income tax that is levied on a direct basis.

AMENDMENT 17

Direct Election of Senators
The Seventeenth Amendment (1913) states that the people, instead of state legislatures, elect United States senators. *How many years are in a Senate term?*

service in suppressing **insurrection** or rebellion, shall not be questioned. But neither the United States nor any State shall assume or pay any debt or obligation incurred in aid of insurrection or rebellion against the United States, or any claim for the loss or emancipation of any slave; but all such debts, obligations and claims shall be held illegal and void.

Section 5

The Congress shall have power to enforce, by appropriate legislation, the provisions of this article.

Amendment XV

Section 1

The right of citizens of the United States to vote shall not be denied or abridged by the United States or by any State on account of race, color, or previous condition of servitude.

Section 2

The Congress shall have power to enforce this article by appropriate legislation.

Amendment XVI

The Congress shall have power to lay and collect taxes on incomes, from whatever source derived, without **apportionment** among the several States and without regard to any census or enumeration.

Amendment XVII

Section 1

The Senate of the United States shall be composed of two Senators from each State, elected by the people thereof, for six years; and each Senator shall have one vote. The electors in each State shall have the qualifications requisite for electors of the most numerous branch of the State legislatures.

Section 2

When **vacancies** happen in the representation of any State in the Senate, the executive authority of such State shall issue writs of election to fill such vacancies: Provided, That the legislature of any State may empower the executive thereof to make temporary appointments until the people fill the vacancies by election as the legislature may direct.

Section 3

This amendment shall not be so construed as to affect the election or term of any Senator chosen before it becomes valid as part of the Constitution.

---

insurrection rebellion against the government

apportionment distribution of seats in House based on population

vacancy an office or position that is unfilled or unoccupied

Amendment XVIII

Section 1

After one year from ratification of this article, the manufacture, sale, or transportation of intoxicating liquors within, the importation thereof into, or the exportation thereof from the United States and all territory subject to the jurisdiction thereof for beverage purposes is hereby prohibited.

Section 2

The Congress and the several States shall have concurrent power to enforce this article by appropriate legislation.

Section 3

This article shall be inoperative unless it shall have been ratified as an amendment to the Constitution by the legislatures of the several States, as provided in the Constitution, within seven years from the date of the submission hereof to the States by the Congress.

Amendment XIX

Section 1

The right of citizens of the United States to vote shall not be denied or abridged by the United States or by any State on account of sex.

Section 2

Congress shall have power by appropriate legislation to enforce the provisions of this article.

Amendment XX

Section 1

The terms of the President and Vice President shall end at noon on the 20th day of January, and the terms of the Senators and Representatives at noon on the 3d day of January, of the years in which such terms would have ended if this article had not been ratified; and the terms of their successors shall then begin.

Section 2

The Congress shall assemble at least once in every year, and such meeting shall begin at noon on the 3rd day of January, unless they shall by law appoint a different day.

Section 3

If, at the time fixed for the beginning of the term of the President, the President elect shall have died, the Vice President elect shall become President. If a President shall not have been chosen before the time fixed for the beginning of his term, or if the President elect shall have failed to qualify, then the Vice President elect shall act as President until a President shall have qualified; and the Congress may by law provide

---

AMENDMENT 18

Prohibition The Eighteenth Amendment (1919) prohibited the production, sale, or transportation of alcoholic beverages in the United States. Prohibition proved to be difficult to enforce. This amendment was later repealed by the Twenty-first Amendment.

AMENDMENT 19

Woman Suffrage The Nineteenth Amendment (1920) guaranteed women the right to vote. By then women had already won the right to vote in many state elections, but the amendment made their right to vote in all state and national elections constitutional.

AMENDMENT 20

"Lame-Duck" The Twentieth Amendment (1933) sets new dates for Congress to begin its term and for the inauguration of the president and vice president. Under the original Constitution, elected officials who retired or who had been defeated remained in office for several months. For the outgoing president, this period ran from November until March. Such outgoing officials, referred to as "lame ducks," could accomplish little. *What date was chosen as Inauguration Day?*

AMENDMENT 20, SECTION 3

Succession of President and Vice President This section provides that if the president elect dies before taking office, the vice president elect becomes president.

for the case wherein neither a President elect nor a Vice **President elect** shall have qualified, declaring who shall then act as President, or the manner in which one who is to act shall be selected, and such person shall act accordingly until a President or Vice President shall have qualified.

Section 4

The Congress may by law provide for the case of the death of any of the persons from whom the House of Representatives may choose a President whenever the right of choice shall have devolved upon them, and for the case of the death of any of the persons from whom the Senate may choose a Vice President whenever the right of choice shall have devolved upon them.

Section 5

Section 1 and 2 shall take effect on the 15th day of October following the ratification of this article.

Section 6

This article shall be inoperative unless it shall have been ratified as an amendment to the Constitution by the legislatures of three-fourths of the several States within seven years from the date of its submission.

Amendment XXI

Section 1

The eighteenth article of amendment to the Constitution of the United States is hereby repealed.

Section 2

The transportation or importation into any State, Territory, or possession of the United States for delivery or use therein of intoxicating liquors, in violation of the laws thereof, is hereby prohibited.

Section 3

This article shall be inoperative unless it shall have been ratified as an amendment to the Constitution by conventions in the several States, as provided in the Constitution, within seven years from the date of the submission hereof to the States by the Congress.

Amendment XXII

Section 1

No person shall be elected to the office of the President more than twice, and no person who had held the office of President, or acted as President, for more than two years of a term to which some other person was elected President shall be elected to the office of the President more than once. But this Article shall not apply to any person holding the office of President when this Article was proposed by the Congress, and

---

president elect individual who is elected president but has not yet begun serving his or her term

---

AMENDMENT 21

Repeal of Prohibition The Twenty-first Amendment (1933) repeals the Eighteenth Amendment. It is the only amendment ever passed to overturn an earlier amendment. It is also the only amendment ratified by special state conventions instead of state legislatures.

AMENDMENT 22

Presidential Term Limit The Twenty-second Amendment (1951) limits presidents to a maximum of two elected terms. The amendment wrote into the Constitution a custom started by George Washington. It was passed largely as a reaction to Franklin D. Roosevelt's election to four terms between 1933 and 1945. It also provides that anyone who succeeds to the presidency and serves for more than two years of the term may not be elected more than one more time.

shall not prevent any person who may be holding the office of President, or acting as President, during the term within which this Article becomes operative from holding the office of President or acting as President during the remainder of such term.

Section 2

This article shall be inoperative unless it shall have been ratified as an amendment to the Constitution by the legislatures of three-fourths of the several States within seven years from the date of its submission to the States by the Congress.

Amendment XXIII

Section 1

The District constituting the seat of Government of the United States shall appoint in such manner as the Congress may direct:

A number of electors of President and Vice President equal to the whole number of Senators and Representatives in Congress to which the District would be entitled if it were a State, but in no event more than the least populous State; they shall be in addition to those appointed by the States, but they shall be considered, for the purposes of the election of President and Vice President, to be electors appointed by a State; and they shall meet in the District and perform such duties as provided by the twelfth article of amendment.

Section 2

The Congress shall have power to enforce this article by appropriate legislation.

Amendment XXIV

Section 1

The right of citizens of the United States to vote in any primary or other election for President or Vice President, for electors for President or Vice President, or for Senator or Representative in Congress, shall not be denied or abridged by the United States or any State by reason of failure to pay any poll tax or other tax.

Section 2

The Congress shall have power to enforce this article by appropriate legislation.

Amendment XXV

Section 1

In case of the removal of the President from Office or his death or resignation, the Vice President shall become President.

Section 2

Whenever there is a vacancy in the office of the Vice President, the President shall nominate a Vice President who shall take the office upon confirmation by a majority vote of both Houses of Congress.

AMENDMENT 23

D.C. Electors The Twenty-third Amendment (1961) allows citizens living in Washington, D.C., to vote for president and vice president, a right previously denied residents of the nation's capital.

The District of Columbia now has three presidential electors, the number to which it would be entitled if it were a state.

AMENDMENT 24

Abolition of the Poll Tax The Twenty-fourth Amendment (1964) prohibits poll taxes in federal elections. Prior to the passage of this amendment, some states had used such taxes to keep low-income African Americans from voting. In 1966, the Supreme Court banned poll taxes in state elections as well.

AMENDMENT 25

Presidential Disability and Succession The Twenty-fifth Amendment (1967) established a process for the vice president to take over leadership of the nation when a president is disabled. It also set procedures for filling a vacancy in the office of vice president.

This amendment was used in 1973, when Vice President Spiro Agnew resigned after being charged with accepting bribes. President Nixon appointed Gerald R. Ford as vice president in accordance with the Twenty-fifth Amendment. A year later, President Nixon resigned and Ford became president. President Ford then filled the vice presidential vacancy with Nelson A. Rockefeller. Thus, individuals who had not been elected held both the presidency and the vice presidency. *Whom does the president inform if he or she cannot carry out the duties of the office?*

AMENDMENT 26

Voting Age of 18 The Twenty-sixth Amendment (1971) lowered the voting age in both federal and state elections to 18.

AMENDMENT 27

Congressional Salary Restraints The Twenty-seventh Amendment (1992) was initially proposed by James Madison in 1789, but it was never adopted. In 1982, Gregory Watson, then a student at the University of Texas, discovered the amendment while doing research for a school paper. Watson made the amendment's passage his crusade.

Section 3

Whenever the President transmits to the President pro tempore of the Senate and the Speaker of the House of Representatives his written declaration that he is unable to discharge the powers and duties of his office, and until he transmits to them a written declaration to the contrary, such powers and duties shall be discharged by the Vice President as Acting President.

Section 4

Whenever the Vice President and a majority of either the principal officers of the executive departments or of such other body as Congress may by law provide, transmit to the President pro tempore of the Senate and the Speaker of the House of Representatives their written declaration that the President is unable to discharge the powers and duties of his office, the Vice President shall immediately assume the power and duties of the office of Acting President.

Thereafter, when the President transmits to the President pro tempore of the Senate and the Speaker of the House of Representatives his written declaration that no inability exists, he shall resume the powers and duties of his office unless the Vice President and a majority of either the principal officers of the executive department or of such other body as Congress may by law provide, transmit within four days to the President pro tempore of the Senate and the Speaker of the House of Representatives their written declaration that the President is unable to discharge the powers and duties of his office. Thereupon Congress shall decide the issue, assembling within forty-eight hours for that purpose if not in session. If the Congress, within twenty-one days after receipt of the latter written declaration, or, if Congress is not in session, within twenty-one days after Congress is required to assemble, determines by two-thirds vote of both Houses that the President is unable to discharge the powers and duties of his office, the Vice President shall continue to discharge the same as Acting President; otherwise, the President shall resume the power and duties of his office.

Amendment XXVI

Section 1

The right of citizens of the United States, who are eighteen years of age or older, to vote shall not be denied or abridged by the United States or by any State on account of age.

Section 2

The Congress shall have power to enforce this article by appropriate legislation.

Amendment XXVII

No law, varying the compensation for the services of Senators and Representatives, shall take effect, until an election of representatives shall have intervened.

05

Analyzing Sources: The Bill of Rights

 COMPELLING QUESTION

What ideas of the Revolution are reflected in the Bill of Rights?

Plan Your Inquiry

In this lesson, you will investigate some of the protections that many Americans believed should be incorporated into the new Constitution through the addition of a bill of rights.

DEVELOP QUESTIONS

Developing Questions About Civil Liberties and Civil Rights Think about some of the founding principles of the American colonies and how these principles were incorporated into American constitutional government. Then read the Compelling Question for this lesson.

Develop a list of three Supporting Questions that would help you answer the Compelling Question for the lesson. Write these in a graphic organizer like the one below.

APPLY HISTORICAL TOOLS

Analyzing Primary and Secondary Sources You will work with a variety of primary sources and one secondary source in this lesson. These sources focus on important principles of American government that were eventually incorporated into the Bill of Rights. Use a graphic organizer like the one below to record and organize information about the sources. Note ways in which each source helps you answer the supporting questions you created. Not all sources will help you answer each of your supporting questions. Only include relevant sources in your graphic organizer.

Supporting Questions	Source	How this source helps me answer the Supporting Question
Question 1:		
Question 2:		
Question 3:		

After you analyze the sources, you will:

- use the evidence from the sources
- communicate your conclusions
- take informed action

Background Information

Many Americans, including some supporters of the new U.S. Constitution, believed that the document should include a bill of rights in order to explicitly protect people's fundamental liberties and freedoms from being violated by government. Federalists argued that the Constitution already protected people's rights and freedoms because it specifically laid out the powers of government. Anti-Federalists argued that the document contained no guarantee of religious freedom, no restriction against keeping armies in peacetime, no protection of the right to bear arms or freedom of the press, and no guarantee of the right to trial by jury. The early English colonists had brought many of these ideas to America. The states eventually ratified the U.S. Constitution with the promise to add these changes. Even though these amendments officially protected fundamental liberties and freedoms, not all Americans originally enjoyed the rights of "the people" as stated in the Constitution.

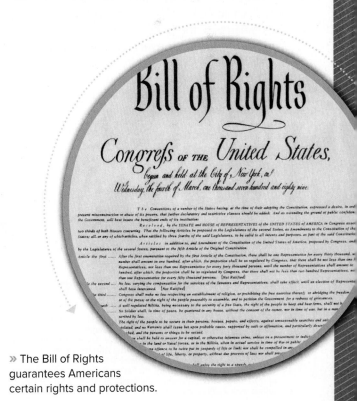

» The Bill of Rights guarantees Americans certain rights and protections.

©leezsnow/iStockphoto.com

Maryland Toleration Act: An Act Concerning Religion

The Maryland Toleration Act was passed by Maryland Colony in 1649. Maryland was initially created as a home for persecuted Catholics, though people of other religious denominations also lived there. Experience with religious persecution led Maryland's colonists to ensure that their religious freedom was officially protected. This focus on religious freedom from early colonial times made it unsurprising that the authors of the new Constitution's Bill of Rights would put a focus on protecting religious freedom within this new government.

PRIMARY SOURCE : GOVERNMENT DOCUMENT

" . . . Be it Therefore. . . **Ordeyned** and enacted . . . that noe person or persons whatsoever within this Province, or the Islands, Ports, Harbors, Creekes, or havens thereunto belonging professing to beleive in Jesus Christ, shall from henceforth bee any waies troubled, Molested or **discountenanced** for or in respect of his or her religion nor in the free exercise thereof within this Province or the Islands thereunto belonging nor any way compelled to the beleife or exercise of any other Religion against his or her consent, soe as they be not unfaithfull to the Lord Proprietary, or molest or conspire against the civill Governement established or to bee established in this Province under him or his heires. And that all and every person and persons that shall presume Contrary to this Act and the true intent and meaning thereof directly or indirectly either in person or estate . . . shalbe compelled to pay **trebble** damages to the party soe wronged or molested, and for every such offence shall also forfeit 20s sterling in money or the value thereof, half thereof for the use of the Lord Proprietary, and his heires Lords and Proprietaries of this Province, and the other half for the use of the party soe wronged or molested as aforesaid, Or if the partie soe offending as aforesaid shall refuse or bee unable to recompense the party soe wronged, or to satisfy such fyne or forfeiture, then such Offender shalbe severely punished by publick whipping and imprisonment during the pleasure of the Lord Proprietary, or his Lieutenant or cheife Governor of this Province for the tyme being without baile or **maineprise.** "

–September 21, 1649

ordeyned established by law

discountenanced looked at with disfavor

trebble [treble] triple; three times the amount

maineprise requirement to appear in court

EXAMINE THE SOURCE

1. **Analyzing** Based on the excerpt, what were the consequences of violating someone's religious freedom in Maryland?

2. **Inferring** Based on the excerpt, what limit on religious freedom continued to exist in Maryland after this act was passed?

A LAW OF MARYLAND Concerning RELIGION.

Oraſ much as in a well-governed and Chriſtian Commonwealth, Matters concerning Religion and the Honour of God ought to be in the firſt place to be taken into ſerious conſideration, and endeavoured to be ſettled. Be it therefore Ordained and Enacted by the Right Honourable CÆCILIUS Lord Baron of Baltemore, abſolute Lord and Proprietary of this Province, with the Advice and Conſent of the Upper and Lower Houſe of this General Aſſembly, That whatſoever perſon or perſons within this Province and the Iſlands thereunto belonging, ſhall from henceforth blaſpheme GOD, that is curſe him; or ſhall deny our Saviour JESUS CHRIST to be the Son of God; or ſhall deny the Holy Trinity, the Father, Son, & Holy Ghoſt; or the Godhead of any of the ſaid Three Perſons of the Trinity, or the Unity of the Godhead, or ſhall uſe or utter any reproachful ſpeeches, words, or language, concerning the Holy Trinity, or any of the ſaid three Perſons thereof, ſhall be puniſhed with death, and confiſcation or forfeiture of all his or her Lands and Goods to the Lord Proprietary and his Heirs.

PHOTO: Historic Collection/Alamy Stock Photo; TEXT: Maryland Toleration Act, September 21, 1649.

Jefferson Champions a Bill of Rights

When the Constitution was passed Thomas Jefferson was serving as U.S. minister to France. Jefferson wrote letters home after the drafting of the document in which he expressed his thoughts about the new government's structure. In this letter to James Madison, Jefferson lists several things he likes about the Constitution but then highlights some areas that he believes are insufficient.

PRIMARY SOURCE : LETTER

66 . . . I like the organization of the government into Legislative, Judiciary, & Executive. I like the power given the Legislature to levy taxes, and for that reason solely approve of the greater house being chosen by the people directly. For tho' I think a house chosen by them will by very illy qualified to legislate for the Union, for foreign nations &c. yet this evil does not weigh against the good of preserving inviolate the fundamental principle that the people are not to be taxed but by representatives chosen immediately by themselves. I am captivated by the compromise of the opposite claims of the great & little states, of the latter to equal, and the former to proportional influence. I am much pleased too with the substitution of the method of voting by persons, instead of that of voting by states; and I like the negative given to the Executive with a third of either house, though I should have liked it better had the Judiciary been associated for that purpose, or invested with a similar and separate power. . . . I will now add what I do not like. First the omission of a bill of rights providing clearly & without the aid of **sophisms** for freedom of religion, freedom of the press, protection against standing armies, restriction against monopolies, the eternal & **unremitting** force of the habeas corpus laws, and trials by jury in all matters of fact triable by the laws of the land & not by the law of Nations. To say, as mr. Wilson does, that a bill of rights was not necessary because all is reserved in the case of the general government which is not given, while in the particular ones all is given which is not reserved, might do for the Audience to whom it was addressed, but is surely a **gratis dictum,** opposed by strong inferences from the body of the instrument, as well as from the omission of the clause of our present confederation which had declared that in express terms. . . . Let me add that a bill of rights is what the people are entitled to against every government on earth, general or particular, & what no just government should refuse or rest on inference. 99

–Thomas Jefferson to James Madison, December 20, 1787

---

sophisms invalid arguments

unremitting constant

gratis dictum a statement made but not intended to be acted on

---

EXAMINE THE SOURCE

1. **Analyzing** What does Jefferson mean by the final phrase of the excerpt: "no just government should . . . rest on inference"?

2. **Explaining** According to Jefferson, who is entitled to a written protection of rights?

Jefferson, Thomas. 1787. From Thomas Jefferson to James Madison, 20 December 1787, Jefferson Papers.

Senate Edits to Initial Amendments

The initial version of the Constitutional amendments passed by the House of Representatives and then sent to the Senate included 17 amendments. This source shows Senate revisions to the document passed by the House. The Senate passed a resolution containing 12 amendments. The House and the Senate then sent the 12 amendments to the states, which ratified 10 at the time. These 10 amendments are now known as the Bill of Rights.

PRIMARY SOURCE : DOCUMENT

CONGRESS OF THE UNITED STATES.

In the House of Representatives,

Monday, 24th August, 1789,

RESOLVED, BY THE SENATE AND HOUSE OF REPRESENTATIVES OF THE UNITED STATES OF AMERICA IN CONGRESS ASSEMBLED, two thirds of both Houses deeming it necessary, That the following Articles be proposed to the Legislatures of the several States, as Amendments to the Constitution of the United States, all or any of which Articles, when ratified by three fourths of the said Legislatures, to be valid to all intents and purposes as part of the said Constitution—Viz.

concurring

ARTICLES in addition to, and amendment of, the Constitution of the United States of America, proposed by Congress, and ratified by the Legislatures of the several States, pursuant to the fifth Article of the original Constitution.

ARTICLE THE FIRST.

After the first enumeration, required by the first Article of the Constitution, there shall be one Representative for every thirty thousand, until the number shall amount to one hundred, after which the proportion shall be so regulated by Congress, that there shall be not less than one hundred Representatives, nor less than one Representative for every forty thousand persons, until the number of Representatives shall amount to two hundred, after which the proportion shall be so regulated by Congress, that there shall not be less than two hundred Representatives, nor less than one Representative for every fifty thousand persons.

amendment

ARTICLE THE SECOND.

for the services of the Senators & Representatives

No law varying the compensation ~~to the members of Congress~~, shall take effect, until an election of Representatives shall have intervened.

a

ARTICLE THE THIRD.

one religious sect or society in preference

Congress shall make no law establishing ~~religion, or prohibiting~~ ~~the free exercise thereof, nor shall the rights of Conscience be infringed.~~ *Articles of Faith or a mode of Worship, or prohibiting the free exercise of Religion,*

EXAMINE THE SOURCE

Analyzing In this draft of the Bill of Rights, Article the Third is the most heavily edited. In the final Bill of Rights, this language is found in the first Amendment and states, "Congress shall make no law respecting an establishment of religion, or prohibiting the free exercise thereof; or abridging the freedom of speech, or of the press; or the right of the people peaceably to assemble, and to petition the Government for a redress of grievances." Why do you think the Senate made this article more explicit?

Tango Images/Alamy Stock Photo

Who Are "We the People"?

The protection of citizens' rights and liberties was of utmost importance to the Framers of the Constitution, yet these leaders failed to include a bill of rights in 1787. Many states' ratification of the Constitution was contingent upon promises Federalists made to later pass these amendments. Even after the ratification of the Bill of Rights, however, not everyone benefited from its guarantees. As author Linda R. Monk points out, the foundations of the Constitution provide for an active citizenry. Ultimately, "we the people" would apply to many more Americans because of excluded groups' civic efforts.

SECONDARY SOURCE : ARTICLE

❝ 'We the People?' asked Patrick Henry at the Virginia convention to ratify the new Constitution in 1788. 'Who authorized them to speak the language of "We the People," instead of "We the States"?' Looking back, we can be grateful that Henry did not attend the Constitutional Convention in Philadelphia—and not just because of his views on federalism. Without a government based on the power of the *people* to effect change, the US Constitution would not have endured for the past 220 years.

. . . Who are 'We the People'? This question troubled the nation for centuries. As legendary orator Lucy Stone, one of America's first advocates for women's rights, asked in 1853: '"We the People"? Which "We the People"? The women were not included.' Neither were white males who did not own property, American Indians, or African Americans—slave or free. Yet, one by one, these groups were eventually brought within the Constitution's definition of 'We the People' through civic movements dedicated to that purpose.

White men without property sought the right to vote after the Constitution was adopted. . . . This question was ultimately answered by state governments, which faced the democratic tides of the Jacksonian era. But another group of people lost their constitutional rights as a result. During the 1830s, the Cherokee Nation argued that American Indians were protected under the Constitution. . . . Only in 1924 were Native Americans finally given full citizenship under the Constitution, by act of Congress.

African Americans also sought to be included in the Constitution's definition of 'We the People.' . . . [After the Civil War] came the Fourteenth Amendment, which made African Americans full citizens—at least on paper. Yet it would be another century before African

Americans would begin to enjoy anything approaching 'equal protection of the law.'

Women were active in the abolitionist movement from the very beginning, and many abolitionists . . . supported equal rights for women. . . . Litigation to apply the Fourteenth Amendment's protections to women failed. It was direct action against the White House during World War I that finally turned the tide for women's suffrage.

Through the amendment process, and the civic movements that demanded such amendments, more Americans were eventually included in the Constitution's definition of 'We the People.' . . .

The modern Civil Rights Movement proved that monumental change, while difficult, could be achieved by a group of determined citizens—even when the Congress, the president, and the Supreme Court could not guarantee the outcome. Government institutions, in the end, are limited or empowered by the people upon whose authority they rest. . . .

George Washington echoed this reality when he wrote Patrick Henry to persuade him to support the new Constitution. Washington admitted that the Constitution was not perfect, but rather perfectible through the amendment process. 'I wish the Constitution which is offered had been made more perfect, but I sincerely believe it is the best that could be obtained at this time; and . . . a constitutional door is opened for amendment hereafter.' ❞

—Linda R. Monk, "Why We the People? Citizens as Agents of Constitutional Change." *History Now*, Fall 2007

EXAMINE THE SOURCE

Analyzing Ideas Why does the author say that Americans are lucky that Patrick Henry did not attend the Constitutional Convention?

Monk, Linda R. "Why We the People? Citizens as Agents of Constitutional Change." History Now. Fall 2007

The English Bill of Rights

The English Bill of Rights is a key component of British government. It was passed in 1689 to ensure the rule of law, the power of Parliament, and to guarantee certain rights and privileges to citizens.

PRIMARY SOURCE : GOVERNMENT DOCUMENT

❝ [W]hereas . . . his Highness . . did . . . cause letters to be written to the Lords . . . for the choosing of such persons to represent them . . . to be sent to Parliament . . . in order to such an establishment as that their religion, laws and liberties might not again be in danger of being **subverted**. . . .

And thereupon the said Lords . . . being now assembled in a full and free representative of this nation, . . . declare

That the pretended power of suspending the laws or the execution of laws by regal authority without consent of Parliament is illegal;

That the pretended power of dispensing with laws or the execution of laws by regal authority, as it hath been assumed and exercised of late, is illegal;

That levying money for or to the use of the Crown by pretence of prerogative, without grant of Parliament, for longer time, or in other manner than the same is or shall be granted, is illegal; . . .

That election of members of Parliament ought to be free;

That the freedom of speech and debates or proceedings in Parliament ought not to be impeached or questioned in any court or place out of Parliament;

That excessive bail ought not to be required, nor excessive fines imposed, nor cruel and unusual punishments inflicted; . . .

And that for redress of all grievances, and for the amending, strengthening and preserving of the laws, Parliaments ought to be held frequently. . . .❞

subverted overthrown

EXAMINE THE SOURCE

Analyzing Text What are some of the protections in the English Bill of Rights that were also included in the Bill of Rights?

Your Inquiry Analysis

EVALUATE SOURCES AND USE EVIDENCE

Refer to the Compelling Question and the Supporting Questions you developed at the beginning of this lesson.

1. **Gathering Sources** Think back to the Compelling Question at the beginning of the lesson. Did the sources fully answer this question? Which sources helped you most directly answer the Compelling Question? What other information might you want to find in order to fully answer the question?

2. **Evaluating Sources** Looking at the sources that helped you answer the Compelling Question, evaluate the sources as evidence. What details from each provided the most evidence for answering the Compelling Question? How does the included secondary source challenge the idea of the Compelling Question and your Supporting Questions?

3. **Synthesizing** Review the sources in this lesson more closely. How do the older sources written during colonial times inform the writing of the Bill of Rights? Explain.

COMMUNICATE CONCLUSIONS

Identifying Arguments Work with a partner to identify which rights and freedoms were included in the Bill of Rights. Then brainstorm a list of protections that were left out of the Bill of Rights. Work with a partner to prepare a multimedia presentation on what might have been included in the final document but was not. Be sure to provide an explanation of why your ideas should have been included. Present your conclusions to your classmates.

TAKE INFORMED ACTION

Creating a Poster on the Constitution Think about the following question: Did the U.S. Constitution achieve all of its goals? Construct an answer to this question in the form of an educational poster. Be sure to use both historical and modern-day examples to support your response. When you are constructing your poster, ensure that you have evaluated various perspectives.

The Statutes, Revised Edition, Vol. 2. London. Eyre and Spottiswoode. 1871.

American Expansion and Growing Tensions

READING STRATEGY

Analyzing Key Ideas and Details As you read, use a graphic organizer like the one below to take notes.

Cause	Event	Effect
	Westward Journey	
	Gold Rush	
	War with Mexico	
	Compromise of 1850	
	Fugitive slave Act	
	Kansas-Nebraska Act	
	Southern Secession	

Settling the West

GUIDING QUESTION

What events caused Americans to go to war with Mexico?

In 1800 about 387,000 white settlers lived west of the Appalachian Mountains. By 1820 that population had risen to more than 2.4 million, and continued to grow rapidly. By the Civil War, more Americans lived west of the Appalachians than lived along the Atlantic Coast. Some Americans headed west for religious reasons, while others wanted to own their own farms and start a new life.

As American settlers carried their possessions, hopes, and dreams to their new homes on the frontier, some also brought enslaved African Americans. The great expanse of newly acquired farmlands and the search for natural resources, such as gold, required an ever-increasing number of workers in the fields and in the mines. Even though slavery was prohibited in the Northwest Territory, it was still allowed in the rest of the new territories. Thus, the opening of the West to settlement also opened new territories in the southwest to slavery. As the number of enslaved people increased throughout the country in the first half of the 1800s, the areas in which slavery existed increased as well.

The Westward Journey and Building a New Life

Emigrants made the journey in groups of covered wagons called wagon trains. Before starting out, they assembled outside a frontier town. Early wagon trains hired mountain men to guide them. Later, most of the **overlanders**—people who traveled west over the land as opposed to those who traveled by sea—used guidebooks to find their own way.

The typical trip west took five to six months, with wagon trains progressing about 15 miles (24 km) per day. Generally, men drove the wagons, hunted game, and cared for the animals, while women looked after the children, cooked meals, cleaned the camp, and washed clothes.

The geographic and physical challenges were great on these journeys west. But pioneers also had to navigate through lands populated by Native Americans. Although travelers feared attacks by Native Americans, these attacks were rare. By one estimate, 362 emigrants died in conflicts with Native Americans between 1840 and 1860, while emigrants killed 462 Native Americans in the same period. Native Americans often gave emigrants food and helpful information about routes, edible plants, and sources of water. Overlanders also renewed their provisions by trading other goods with Native Americans, sometimes using horses as currency.

As overland traffic increased, Native Americans on the Great Plains became concerned and angry over the threat pioneers posed to their way of life. The Lakota, Cheyenne, Arapaho, and other groups relied on buffalo for food, shelter, clothing, tools, and countless other necessities of everyday life. Now they feared that the age-old migrations of the buffalo herds would be disrupted.

Settling the Far West

As more American pioneers pushed farther west, beyond the Rocky Mountains and into the Pacific Coast regions, disputes with other nations over who controlled these lands were renewed. President James K. Polk took a strong stance regarding what came to be known as the Oregon Question. The United

overlander someone who travels over the land to the West

States, Britain, and Native Americans all laid claim to Oregon Country, which included present-day Oregon, Washington, and British Columbia, Canada. In 1818 Britain and the United States had agreed to occupy the land jointly. In the 1830s, American missionaries began arriving in Oregon with the goal of converting Native Americans to Christianity. These missionaries spread the word about Oregon and persuaded others to come to the lush Willamette Valley.

In June 1846, the United States and Great Britain negotiated the Oregon Treaty. In this agreement, the United States received all of Oregon south of latitude 49°N and west of the Rocky Mountains except for the southern tip of Vancouver Island. In exchange, the British were guaranteed navigation rights on the Columbia River.

Two years later, thousands of Americans began flooding the foothills of the Sierra Nevada in California, south of the new Oregon Territory, after gold was discovered in the region. By the end of 1849, more than 80,000 "Forty-Niners" had arrived to look for gold. The increase in California's population enabled it to apply for statehood. Congress had to decide whether it would be a free state or a slave state. Although President Zachary Taylor, Polk's successor, was a slaveholder, he did not think slavery's survival depended on its expansion westward. He believed that the way to avoid a fight in Congress was to have Californians make their own decision about slavery. With Taylor's encouragement, California applied for admission as a free state in late 1849.

Texas and the War with Mexico

In the 1820s, after Mexico passed several colonization laws, **empresarios,** or colonization agents,

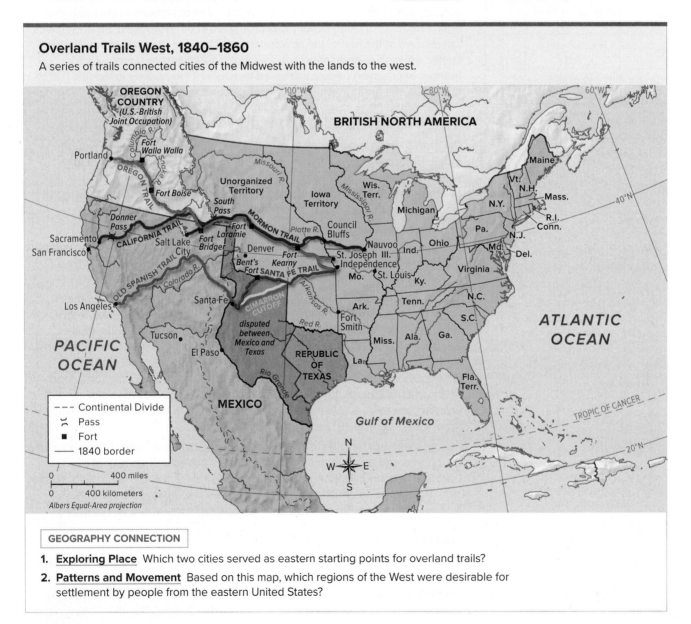

Overland Trails West, 1840–1860
A series of trails connected cities of the Midwest with the lands to the west.

GEOGRAPHY CONNECTION

1. **Exploring Place** Which two cities served as eastern starting points for overland trails?
2. **Patterns and Movement** Based on this map, which regions of the West were desirable for settlement by people from the eastern United States?

empresario a person who arranged for the settlement of Texas land grants in the early 1800s encouraged Americans to settle the Mexican region of Texas. Open rebellion developed when settlers wished to create their own government. The people of Texas experienced early losses to the Mexican army at the Alamo and Goliad. Eventually Texans defeated Mexican forces at the Battle of San Jacinto in April 1836.

The citizens of the new Republic of Texas quickly voted in favor of joining the United States. Texas wished to be admitted to the Union as a slave state, which antislavery leaders in Congress opposed. The annexation of Texas became a key issue in the presidential race of 1844. Democratic candidate James K. Polk promised to annex Texas, which he accomplished after winning the election. Texas's entry into the Union in 1845 outraged Mexico. President Polk's plans to acquire California added to the conflict. In November 1845 the president tried to buy California, but Mexico's president refused to meet with the U.S. envoy, sparking war between Mexico and the United States. Polk subsequently ordered U.S. troops to what Mexico considered its territory.

Before war with Mexico was officially declared, settlers in northern California began an uprising of their own. These settlers quickly overcame the weak official Mexican presence in the territory. On June 14, 1846, they declared independence and proclaimed California the Bear Flag Republic. The war cost Mexico California and the country suffered several major defeats, but Mexico refused to surrender. President Polk sent General Winfield Scott to seize Mexico City. After a six-month campaign beginning in the Gulf Coast city of Veracruz, Scott's forces captured Mexico's capital city in September 1847.

On February 2, 1848, Mexico's leaders signed the Treaty of Guadalupe Hidalgo, ending the war. Mexico gave the United States more than 500,000 square miles (1,295,000 sq. km) of territory, which included the present states of California, Nevada, and Utah, as well as most of Arizona and parts of New Mexico, Colorado, and Wyoming. Mexico accepted the Rio Grande as the southern border of Texas. In return, the United States paid Mexico $15 million and took over $3.25 million in debts that Mexican government owed to U.S. citizens.

✓ CHECK FOR UNDERSTANDING

1. **Identifying** What issue prevented the quick annexation of Texas as a state after Texans won independence from Mexico?

2. **Explaining** Based on the terms of the Treaty of Guadalupe Hidalgo, why was the U.S. annexation of Texas met with such outrage in Mexico?

Slavery and Western Expansion

GUIDING QUESTION

How did the political system attempt to resolve the issues of sectionalism and slavery?

When California applied for statehood, attempts by Congress to find a compromise on slavery further heightened opposing viewpoints. Senator Lewis Cass of Michigan suggested that the citizens of each new territory should be allowed to decide for themselves if they wanted to permit slavery. This idea came to be called **popular sovereignty.** However, both the North and the South worried that the addition of new states could tip the balance of free and slave states and give more power to the opposing side.

As the 1848 presidential election approached, both major candidates—Democrat Lewis Cass and Whig General Zachary Taylor—remained vague on the issues. On Election Day, Taylor won a narrow popular victory and more than half of the electoral vote.

Compromise of 1850 and the Fugitive Slave Act

After the January 1848 discovery of gold in the Sierra Nevada, news of the find swept the nation and around the globe. The California Gold Rush was on. To maintain order, Californians decided to seek statehood and applied to enter the Union as a free state in December 1849. At the time, the Union consisted of 15 free states and 15 slave states. If California tipped the balance, the slaveholding states would become a minority in the Senate. A few Southern politicians began to talk of secession. In early 1850 Senator Henry Clay of Kentucky proposed allowing a compromise measure:

66 California, with suitable boundaries, ought, upon her application, to be admitted as one of the States of this Union, without the imposition by Congress of any restriction in respect to the exclusion or introduction of slavery within those boundaries. 99

—from a speech to Congress, January 29, 1850

Clay also proposed that the rest of the newly acquired land be organized without restrictions on slavery. He called for Congress to be prohibited from interfering with the domestic slave trade and to pass the Fugitive Slave Act to help Southerners recover enslaved African Americans who had fled to the North.

At first, Congress did not pass Clay's bill, in part because President Taylor opposed it. Then, Taylor died unexpectedly in July. Vice President Millard

Clay, Henry. January 29, 1850. In Congressional Globe. 31st Congress 1st Session. Washington: Government Printing Office, 1850.

---

popular sovereignty the idea that people living in a territory had the right to decide by voting whether to allow slavery or not

DRED SCOTT V. *SANDFORD*, 1857

BACKGROUND OF THE CASE Between 1833 and 1843, enslaved African American Dred Scott and his wife Harriet had lived in the free state of Illinois and in the part of the Louisiana Territory that was considered free under the Missouri Compromise. After the Scotts returned to Missouri, both Dred and Harriet filed individual lawsuits in 1846 in the Missouri state court seeking freedom. They argued that, because they had lived in free areas, they were also free. Harriet's case was dismissed, but Dred's case advanced with the understanding that the result would apply to Harriet as well. Dred Scott won his case in 1850, but the decision was reversed by the Missouri Supreme Court in 1852. Scott's attorneys then took the case to the federal courts in 1854 because, by this time, the legal holder of Dred Scott lived in New York and not Missouri, as Scott did. After losing at the federal district level, Scott appealed to the U.S. Supreme Court.

HOW THE COURT RULED The 7–2 decision against Scott enraged many Northerners and delighted many in the South. In his lengthy opinion for the Court, Chief Justice Roger B. Taney ruled that African Americans—enslaved or free—were not citizens of the United States. Thus, Scott had no rights under the Constitution and no right to sue in federal court. Further, Taney decreed that Congress did not have the authority to ban slavery in the territories. Thus, the Missouri Compromise was unconstitutional.

» Dred Scott and Harriet Robinson Scott

1. **Determining Central Ideas** Why was the Missouri Compromise declared unconstitutional?
2. **Explaining** Why was the decision in *Dred Scott* v. *Sandford* so significant?

Fillmore succeeded him and quickly threw his support behind the measure, which had been divided into several smaller bills. By September, Congress had passed all parts of the Compromise of 1850.

Henry Clay had conceived the Fugitive Slave Act as a measure to benefit slaveholders. However, it created hostility toward slavery among many Northerners. Under this law, a slaveholder or slave catcher had only to point out alleged runaways to have them taken into custody. The accused then would be brought before a federal commissioner. African Americans had no way to prove their cases. Either an affidavit asserting that the captive had escaped from a slaveholder or testimony by a white witness was all a court needed to order the person sent to the South.

The Underground Railroad helped thousands of enslaved persons flee to the North. "Conductors" transported freedom seekers in secret. The most famous conductor was Harriet Tubman, who had escaped slavery. Cincinnati, Ohio, where author Harriet Beecher Stowe lived, was one stop in this network. She was inspired to "write something that would make this whole nation feel what an accursed thing slavery is." Her book, *Uncle Tom's Cabin,* changed Northern perceptions of slavery and angered Southerners.

The Crisis Over Kansas

The opening of the Oregon Territory and the admission of California made the need for a transcontinental railroad to unite the country obvious. However, the location of the railroad's eastern starting point was in dispute. Southerners favored a route from New Orleans to San Diego. Democratic senator Stephen A. Douglas wanted the eastern starting point to be Chicago. Knowing this route would run through unsettled lands west of Missouri and Iowa, he prepared a bill to organize the region into a new Nebraska territory. Southern senators delayed this bill and made it clear that before Nebraska could be organized, Congress had to repeal part of the Missouri Compromise and allow slavery in the new territory.

Douglas agreed to repeal the antislavery provision of the Missouri Compromise and divided the new region into two territories: Nebraska to the north and Kansas to the south. Under the Kansas-Nebraska Act, Nebraska was intended to be free territory, while Kansas was intended for slavery. Warned that the South might secede without such concessions, President Franklin Pierce finally gave his support to the bill. Congress passed the Kansas-Nebraska Act in May 1854.

PHOTO: Library of Congress, Prints & Photographs Division (LC-USZ62-79305); TEXT: Life of Harriet Beecher Stowe. Copyright © 1890 by Harriet Beecher Stowe. Compiled from her Letters and Journals by her son, Charles Edward Stowe, published by Houghton, Mifflin and Company, Boston and New York.

Hordes of Northerners hurried into Kansas to create an antislavery majority. They were led in part by John Brown, who would later be involved in the raid on Harpers Ferry. Before the March elections of 1855, however, thousands of armed Missourians crossed the border to vote illegally, helping to elect a proslavery legislature. Furious antislavery settlers countered by drafting their own constitution that banned slavery.

By January 1856, Kansas had two territorial governments, one opposed to slavery and the other supporting it. As more Northern settlers arrived, border ruffians began attacks. "Bleeding Kansas," as newspapers dubbed the territory, had become the scene of a territorial civil war.

Politics and Sectional Divisions

The repeal of the Missouri Compromise had a dramatic effect. Proslavery Southern Whigs and antislavery Northern Whigs began to split the party. During the congressional elections of 1854, many former Northern Whigs joined forces with a few antislavery Democrats and the Free-Soil Party. This coalition was officially organized as the Republican Party in 1856. Republicans wished to prevent Southern planters from gaining control of the federal government. Republicans did not agree on abolishing slavery, but they did agree that it had to be kept out of the territories.

At the same time, the American Party, also known as the Know-Nothings, was gaining political momentum. This anti-Catholic, nativist party opposed immigration. The party began to come apart, however, when members from the Upper South and the North split over the Kansas-Nebraska Act. Most Northern Know-Nothings were absorbed into the Republican Party.

In the 1856 presidential election, three candidates mounted a serious challenge. Democrat James Buchanan of Pennsylvania, who had campaigned on the idea that only he could save the Union, won the election.

Just two days after Buchanan's inauguration, the Supreme Court ruled in a landmark case involving slavery, *Dred Scott* v. *Sandford*. Dred Scott was an enslaved Missouri man who had been taken north to work in free territory for several years. After he returned with his slaveholder to Missouri, Scott sued for his freedom, arguing that living in free territory had made him a free man. Dred Scott's case went all the way to the Supreme Court, which ruled against him. While Southerners celebrated the *Dred Scott* decision, Republicans called it a "willful perversion" of the Constitution. After the *Dred Scott* decision, the conflict in "Bleeding Kansas" intensified.

North Wind Picture Archives/Alamy Stock Photo

✓ **CHECK FOR UNDERSTANDING**

1. **Explaining** What was an unintended consequence of the Fugitive Slave Act?
2. **Making Connections** What was the effect of the *Dred Scott* decision on the growing sectional crisis?

The Union Dissolves

GUIDING QUESTION

What events led to the secession of the Southern states?

In 1859 abolitionist John Brown seized an arsenal in Harpers Ferry, Virginia, in an attempt to begin an insurrection, or rebellion, against slaveholders. His arrest and execution caused him to be viewed as a martyr in a noble cause by some, while others viewed him as a Northern aggressor.

The 1860 Election

John Brown's raid became a turning point for the South. In April 1860, Democrats from across the nation gathered in Charleston, South Carolina, to choose their nominee for president. When Northerners rebuffed the idea of a federal slave code in the territories, 50 Southern delegates stormed out of the convention.

In June 1860, the Democrats reconvened in Baltimore. Again, Southern delegates walked out. The remaining Democrats then chose Stephen Douglas as their candidate. The Southern Democrats nominated their own candidate, John C. Breckinridge. John Bell, from the Constitutional Union party, also ran.

This hand-colored woodcut depicts a raid by Confederate sympathizer William Clarke Quantrill on Lawrence, Kansas, in 1863. Quantrill and his band of about 300 men destroyed more than 200 homes and left 150 men dead or dying in their raid.

Drawing Conclusions Why do you think Quantrill's raids in Kansas were so destructive?

Seceding States 1860–1861

The North, led by President Lincoln, was determined to preserve the Union. The South, on the other hand, was determined to start a new nation to preserve the institution of slavery.

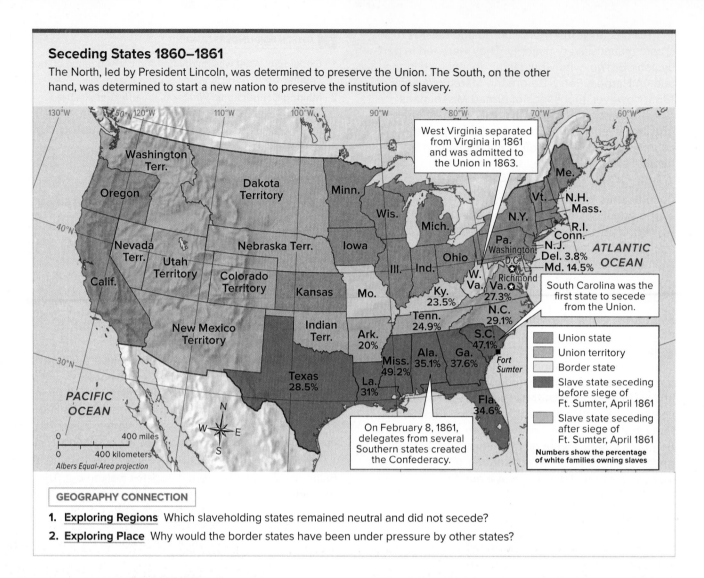

West Virginia separated from Virginia in 1861 and was admitted to the Union in 1863.

South Carolina was the first state to secede from the Union.

On February 8, 1861, delegates from several Southern states created the Confederacy.

Ky. 23.5%
W. Va. 27.3%
Tenn. 24.9%
N.C. 29.1%
S.C. 47.1%
Ala. 35.1%
Ga. 37.6%
Miss. 49.2%
La. 31%
Ark. 20%
Texas 28.5%
Fla. 34.6%
Del. 3.8%
Md. 14.5%

Legend:
- Union state
- Union territory
- Border state
- Slave state seceding before siege of Ft. Sumter, April 1861
- Slave state seceding after siege of Ft. Sumter, April 1861

Numbers show the percentage of white families owning slaves

0 400 miles
0 400 kilometers
Albers Equal-Area projection

GEOGRAPHY CONNECTION

1. **Exploring Regions** Which slaveholding states remained neutral and did not secede?
2. **Exploring Place** Why would the border states have been under pressure by other states?

Republicans, realizing they stood no chance in the South, needed a candidate who could sweep most of the North. They nominated Abraham Lincoln, who had gained a national reputation through a series of debates with Douglas in 1858. Lincoln believed that slavery was morally wrong and opposed its spread into the territories. With the Democrats divided, Lincoln won the election.

The South Secedes

Many Southerners viewed Lincoln's election as a threat to their slave-based economy and culture. They saw no choice but to secede. Shortly after Lincoln's election, the South Carolina legislature called for a convention. On December 20, 1860, amid marching bands, fireworks, and militia drills, the convention voted unanimously to repeal the state's ratification of the Constitution and dissolve its ties to the Union.

By February 1, 1861, Mississippi, Florida, Alabama, Georgia, Louisiana, and Texas had also voted to secede and declared themselves to be a new nation: the Confederate States of America, or the Confederacy. Arkansas, Tennessee, North Carolina, and Virginia

seceded in April 1861. A minority in these states did not want to leave the Union, but the majority of Southerners viewed secession as similar to the Revolution—an action taken to uphold their political rights, including their political right to protect the institution of slavery.

✓ **CHECK FOR UNDERSTANDING**

1. **Making Connections** How did events connected with "Bleeding Kansas" correspond to the political unrest that led to secession?

2. **Summarizing** What political decisions leading up to the 1860 election enabled Lincoln to win the presidency?

LESSON ACTIVITIES

1. **Informative/Explanatory Writing** Write a short essay tracing the growth of tensions caused by the issue of slavery from the nation's westward expansion to secession.

2. **Using Multimedia** Conduct research with a partner to learn more about John Brown's raid on Harpers Ferry and the role it played in the growing division between the North and South. Share your report.

07

Analyzing Sources: Reforming Society

 COMPELLING QUESTION

How did reformers change nineteenth-century America?

Plan Your Inquiry

In this lesson, you will investigate the motivations and efforts of reformers in the United States during the 1800s.

DEVELOP QUESTIONS

Developing Questions About Reform Think about what causes people to demand reform. What problems spur citizens to action? How do citizens go about making changes? What problems are they trying to solve? Read the Compelling Question for this lesson and then develop a list of three Supporting Questions that would help you answer the Compelling Question for the lesson. Write these in a graphic organizer like the one below.

APPLY HISTORICAL TOOLS

Analyzing Primary Sources You will work with a variety of primary sources in this lesson. These sources focus on the identities and goals of American reformers during this period of history. Use a graphic organizer like the one below to record and organize information about the sources. Note ways in which the sources help you answer the Supporting Questions you created. Not all sources will help you answer each of your supporting questions. Only include relevant sources in your graphic organizer.

Supporting Questions	Primary Source	What this source tells me about reform in nineteenth-century America	Questions the source leaves unanswered
	A		
	B		
	C		
	D		
	E		
	F		
	G		

After you analyze the sources, you will:
- use the evidence from the sources.
- communicate your conclusions.
- take informed action.

Background Information

During the early to mid-1800s, a revival of religious fervor swept across the nation. Known as the Second Great Awakening, this era of religious intensity defined a movement to revive people's commitment to religion.

Spurred on by this religious revival, as well as a heightened belief in the power of individuals to improve society, reform movements arose. The reformers selected here embraced efforts to expand and improve care for people with mental illness, aid the poor, improve education, stop the abuses caused by excessive alcohol consumption, and achieve greater racial equality.

» The spirit of reform swept the United States in the early 1800s, encouraging the development of social institutions such as public schools. This illustration depicts a teacher and her students in a one-room school from the mid-1800s.

North Wind Picture Archives/Alamy Stock Photo

Memorial to the Legislature of Massachusetts

Dorothea Dix visited a Massachusetts prison as a Sunday School teacher and was appalled by the treatment of the mentally ill. She reported her findings to the state legislature in 1843. Her efforts resulted in changes to the treatment of the mentally ill around the United States. Note that the use of the words *idiot* and *insane* reflect the terminology of the time period and were not considered derogatory. These words are no longer used in this manner and are now considered personal insults.

PRIMARY SOURCE : ARTICLE

" About two years since leisure afforded opportunity, and duty prompted me to visit several prisons and **alms-houses** . . . I found, near Boston, in the Jails and **Asylums** for the poor, a numerous class brought into unsuitable connexion with criminals and the general mass of Paupers. I refer to Idiots and Insane persons, dwelling in circumstances not only adverse to their own physical and moral improvement, but productive of extreme disadvantages to all other persons brought into association with them. . . . *I tell what I have seen*—painful and as shocking as the details often are—that from them you may feel more deeply the imperative obligation which lies upon you to prevent the . . . continuance of such outrages upon humanity.

. . . I proceed, Gentlemen, briefly to call your attention to the *present* state of Insane Persons confined within this Commonwealth, in *cages, closets, cellars, stalls, pens! Chained,*

naked, beaten with rods, and *lashed* into obedience.

. . . [P]ut away the cold, calculating spirit of selfishness and self-seeking; . . . come up to these halls and consecrate them with one heart and one mind to works of righteousness and just judgment. . . . Raise up the fallen; succor the desolate; restore the outcast; defend the helpless. . . . "

—Dorothea Dix, *Memorial to the Legislature of Massachusetts*, 1843

alms-house shelter for the poor

asylum shelter

EXAMINE THE SOURCE

1. **Describing** Describe why Dix is writing the letter.
2. **Inferring** Why does Dix feel she needs to speak for the people she describes in her letter?

Benevolent Societies and Tract Literature

Benevolent societies that used the religiously faithful to fight social problems grew during this period. This image shows the efforts of the American Tract Society. The Society handed out tracts—religious pamphlets—to promote its Christian beliefs.

EXAMINE THE SOURCE

1. **Analyzing** Why do you think the artist shows children in the illustration?
2. **Inferring** Based on the image, what kinds of people were members of the American Tract Society?

PRIMARY SOURCE : IMAGE

» from *The American Tract Magazine*, August 1825

PHOTO: HathiTrust; TEXT: Dix, Dorothea Lynde. Memorial. To the Legislature of Massachusetts. [protesting Against the Confinement of Insane Persons and Idiots in Almshouses and Prisons]. Boston: Munroe & Francis, 1843.

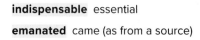

Tocqueville's Views on American Religion and Politics

Alexis de Tocqueville visited the United States between 1831 and 1832 in order to closely study American culture, government, and society. He wrote about what he had learned in *Democracy in America*. Tocqueville described the key features of American government and society. One observation focused on the importance of religion in the United States. Tocqueville was traveling during the religious fervor of the Second Great Awakening, which most likely impacted his observations.

PRIMARY SOURCE : BOOK

66 Religion in America takes no direct part in the government of society, but it must nevertheless be regarded as the foremost of the political institutions of that country; . . . it is in this same point of view that the inhabitants of the United States themselves look upon religious belief. I do not know whether all the Americans have a sincere faith in their religion, for who can search the human heart? but I am certain that they hold it to be **indispensable** to the maintenance of republican institutions. . . .

. . . I have known of societies formed by the Americans to send out ministers of the Gospel into the new Western States to found schools and churches there, lest religion should be suffered to die away in those remote settlements, and the rising States be less fitted to enjoy free institutions than the people from which they **emanated**. . . . Thus religious zeal is perpetually stimulated in the United States by the duties of patriotism. . . . [I]f you converse with these missionaries of Christian civilization, you will be surprised to find how much value they set upon the goods of this world, and that you meet with a politician where you expected to find a priest. They will tell you that 'all the American republics are collectively involved with each other; if the republics of the West were to fall into anarchy, or to be mastered by a despot, the republican institutions which now flourish upon the shores of the Atlantic Ocean would be in great peril. It is, therefore, our interest that the new States should be religious, in order to maintain our liberties.' 99

indispensable essential

emanated came (as from a source)

» Alexis de Tocqueville

EXAMINE THE SOURCE

1. **Analyzing** With what does Tocqueville associate "free institutions" in the United States?
2. **Inferring** What historical development may have contributed to Tocqueville's impression of the relationship between religion and politics in the United States during this period?

PHOTO: Heritage Images/Hulton Fine Art Collection/Getty Images; TEXT: Tocqueville, Alexis de, Democracy in America, v. 1. Reeve, Henry, trans. London: Saunders and Otley, 1835.

The Beecher Family

Lyman Beecher (center, front) was a nationally known Presbyterian minister. He cofounded the American Temperance Society. Catharine Beecher (second from left, front) was a teacher and education reformer. She started female seminaries to improve education opportunities for some women. Edward Beecher (center, back) organized the first antislavery society in Illinois. Harriet Beecher Stowe (far right, front) was also involved in antislavery groups and published *Uncle Tom's Cabin* in 1851. Henry Ward Beecher (far right, back) and Charles Beecher (second from right, back) were also pastors. Isabella Beecher Hooker (far left, front) advocated in Connecticut for equal property rights for husbands and wives and also cofounded the Connecticut Woman Suffrage Association.

PRIMARY SOURCE : PHOTOGRAPH

» The Beecher family, c. 1860

EXAMINE THE SOURCE

Speculating Based on the image, what can be deduced about the social and economic status of the Beecher family? How might this have affected their reform efforts?

Forming the African Methodist Episcopal Church

In 1787 a group of black Methodists withdrew from St. George's Methodist Episcopal Church in Philadelphia after being forced into segregated seating. In 1816 the group formally established the African Methodist Episcopal (AME) Church.

PRIMARY SOURCE : BOOK

66 We deem it necessary to **annex** to our book of discipline, a brief statement of our rise and progress. . . . In November, 1787, the coloured people belonging to the Methodist Society in Philadelphia, convened together, in order to take into consideration the evils under which they laboured, arising from the unkind treatment of their white brethren, who considered them a nuisance in the house of worship, and even pulled them off their knees while in the act of prayer, and ordered them to the back seats. From these, and various other acts of unchristian conduct, we considered it our duty to devise a plan in order to build a house of our own . . . in this undertaking, we met with great opposition from an elder of the Methodist church . . . who threatened, that if we did not give up the building, erase our names from the subscription paper, and make acknowledgments for having attempted such a thing, that in three months we should all be publicly expelled from the Methodist society. Not considering ourselves bound to obey this injunction, and being fully satisfied we should be treated without mercy, we sent in our resignations. 99

—*The Doctrines and Discipline of the African Methodist Episcopal Church*, 1817

annex to attach as a condition

EXAMINE THE SOURCE

1. **Identifying the Main Idea** Describe why the African Methodist Episcopal Church was formed.

2. **Interpreting** How did the African American members of the church view white members' actions?

PHOTO: Historical/Corbis/Getty Images; TEXT: The Doctrines and Discipline of the African Methodist Episcopal Church. Philadelphia: Richard Allen and Jacob Tapisco, 1817

Educational Reform in Massachusetts

Horace Mann was a Massachusetts lawyer, educator, and politician during the 1800s who advocated for excellence in public education. By the mid-1800s, Massachusetts public schools, which had been established in the mid-1600s, had declined. Reformers created a state board of education to work on improvements, and Mann served as its first secretary. Mann believed that public education provided by well-trained teachers was essential to the maintenance of a free republic.

PRIMARY SOURCE : BOOK

> 66 The spirit of inquiry which, within the last forty years, has done so much to improve the useful arts and sciences, has entered the field of education also. It would be strange indeed, if the doctrines and practices of the seventeenth and eighteenth centuries in regard to the training of children, should need no modification in the nineteenth. New questions will arise, and discussions upon them should be welcomed rather than discouraged. . . .
>
> . . . In my Circular to the committees, in 1838, I put the following question, in regard to the most important branch of secular knowledge taught in our schools:
>
> *'Are there defects in teaching scholars to read? This inquiry is not made in regard to the pronunciation of words, and the **modulation** of the voice. But do the scholars fail to understand the meaning of the words they read? Do they fail to master the sense of the reading lessons? Is there a presence in the minds of the scholars, when reading, of the ideas and feelings intended to be conveyed and excited by the author?'*
>
> When the several answers to this question were set down and the average computed, it appeared that 'eleven twelfths' of all the children in the reading classes of the public schools, did not understand the meaning of the words they read,—did not master the sense of the reading lessons,—and that the ideas and feelings intended by the author to be conveyed and excited in the readers' minds, still rested in the author's intention, never having reached the place of their destination.
>
> . . . Indeed, no one who has not read the school committees' reports, from 1838 up to 1841, can form any conception of the earnestness and energy of lamentation with which they bemoaned the condition into which the public schools had fallen. The following [citation] from the very able report of the town of Springfield, for 1839–1840, drawn up, I believe, by the Rev. Doros Clark, are a specimen of hundreds of others: 'In closing their report, the committee cannot avoid expressing the conviction, that the work of perfecting our Common School system is truly **Herculean.**' 99

—Horace Mann, *Reply to the "Remarks" of Thirty-one Boston Schoolmasters on the Seventh Annual Report of the Secretary of the Massachusetts Board of Education*, 1844

modulation the use of tone or pitch to show meaning

Herculean extraordinarily difficult

EXAMINE THE SOURCE

1. **Identifying the Main Idea** In your own words, what is the committees' main concern?
2. **Analyzing Points of View** For what reason does Mann believe the Common School system may be failing to educate students properly?

Mann, Horace. Reply to the "Remarks" of Thirty-one Boston Schoolmasters on the Seventh Annual Report of the Secretary of the Massachusetts Board of Education. Boston: Wm. B. Fowle and Nahum Capen, 1844.

"One Glass More."

The American Tract Society, founded in 1825, published more than 5 million pages of religious literature a year by the late 1820s. Below is a poem published by the American Tract Society in 1826 as part of its goal to support the temperance society.

PRIMARY SOURCE : POEM

❝ Stay, mortal, stay! nor heedless thus
Thy sure destruction seal;
Within that cup there lurks a curse,
Which all who drink shall feel.

Disease and death, for ever nigh,
Stand ready at the door,
And eager wait to hear the cry
Of—'*Give me one glass more.*'

Go, view the prisoners' gloomy cells;
Their sins and misery scan;
Gaze, gaze upon these earthly hells—
In drink their woes began.

Of yonder children, bathed in tears,
Ask, Why is mother poor?
They'll whisper in thy startled ears,
'Twas father's *One glass more.*'

Stay, mortal, stay! repent, return,
Reflect upon they fate:
The poisonous **draught** for ever **spurn**—
Spurn, spurn it, ere too late.

Oh, fly the horrid grogshop then,
Nor linger at the door,
Lest thou perchance should'st sip again
The treacherous '*One glass more.*'

Trust not to thy deceitful heart,
The Saviour's grace implore;
Through him from every sin depart,
And touch that glass no more. ❞

—American Tract Society, "One glass more." 1826

draught [British spelling of *draft*] a portion consumed while drinking

spurn reject with disdain

EXAMINE THE SOURCE

1. **Analyzing Text** What has caused the prisoners' misfortune, according to the poem?
2. **Inferring** To what does the American Tract Society link the consumption of alcohol?

Your Inquiry Analysis

EVALUATE SOURCES AND USE EVIDENCE

Reflect back to the Compelling Question and the Supporting Questions you developed at the beginning of this lesson.

1. **Gathering Sources** Which sources helped you answer the Compelling Question most directly? Which sources helped you answer your Supporting Questions? Are you still lacking information about the reform movements that took place as a result of the Second Great Awakening? Make a list of further questions about these reform movements, and identify where you might find information to answer them.

2. **Evaluating Sources** Looking at the sources, evaluate the identities of the reformers. Who were these people? Where did they live? What Americans are not represented in these sources, and why?

3. **Comparing and Contrasting** Compare and contrast two of the written sources in this lesson more closely. What issue does each source examine? What tone is expressed by each writer or speaker? Is the person concerned, outraged, or merely conveying information? Explain.

COMMUNICATE CONCLUSIONS

Identifying Arguments Work with a partner to choose two of the written sources that make a case for reform. Are the sources appealing to logic or to emotion? Select phrases from each that best reveal the arguments being made. Prepare a poster on how each of the sources makes its case. Your poster should identify each source, its primary arguments, and phrases that reflect the arguments. Share your poster with the class.

TAKE INFORMED ACTION

Constructing a Reform Plan Consider an issue that you are highly concerned about. What are the conditions of the issue that are causing concern? What should be done to resolve the issue? How could showing the conditions of your issue of concern, such as the sources in this lesson have done, help spur improvements? Put together a plan of reforms to address your issue of concern and present your plan to the class. Then, after you have received feedback and revised your plan, write a letter to a relevant official with details of your reform plan.

American Tract Society, "One glass more." (1826). Alcohol, Temperance & Prohibition. Brown Digital Repository, Brown University Library. https://repository.library.brown.edu/studio/item/bdr:30122/

08

The Civil War and Reconstruction

Understanding Craft and Structure As you read, use a graphic organizer like the one below to list the major events leading from the beginning of the Civil War through Reconstruction.

I. The Early Stages

   A.

   B.

II.

   A.

The Early Stages

GUIDING QUESTION

How did the war shift from preserving the Union to ending slavery?

All attempts at compromise between the North and the South over slavery failed. The outcome of the 1860 election accelerated the start of the Civil War.

Although the South had many experienced officers to lead its troops in battle, the North had several economic advantages. In 1860 the population of the North was about 22 million, while the South had about 9 million people, more than one-third of whom were enslaved. Not all southerners agreed with the decision to secede, and approximately 100,000 southerners served in the Union Army. In 1860 almost 90 percent of the nation's factories were in the Northern states, which could provide troops with ammunition and other supplies more easily. The South had only half as many miles of railroad track as the North. Northern troops could more easily disrupt the Southern rail system and prevent the movement of supplies and troops. The Union also controlled the national treasury and could expect continued revenue from tariffs. Many Northern banks held large reserves of cash, which they lent the government by purchasing bonds.

In contrast to the Union, the Confederacy's financial situation was poor, and became worse over time. Most Southern planters were in debt and

Resources of the Union and the Confederacy

	Union	Confederacy
Total Population	23,300,000	9,100,000 (over 3,000,000 enslaved)
White male population (18–45 years)	4,600,000	1,100,000
Bank deposits	$207,000,000	$47,000,000
Value of manufactured goods	$1,730,000,000	$156,000,000
Railroad mileage	22,000	9,000
Value of firearms produced	$2,290,000	$73,000
Pig iron production	951,000 tons	37,000 tons
Coal production	13,680,000 tons	650,000 tons
Corn and wheat production	698,000,000 bushels	314,000,000 bushels
Draft animals	5,800,000	2,900,000
Cotton production	43,000 bales	5,344,000 bales

Source: U.S. Bureau of the Census, *Historical Statistics of the United States: Colonial Times to 1970, Bicentennial Edition, Part 1 and Part 2*, Washington, D.C., 1975.

ECONOMICS CONNECTION

Interpreting What was the one area in which the Confederacy had greater resources than the Union? Explain the likely reason for it.

unable to buy bonds. Southern banks were small and had few cash reserves, so they could not buy many bonds, either. The best hope for the South to raise money was by taxing trade. But the Union Navy quickly blockaded Southern ports, reducing trade. The Confederacy enacted direct taxation of its people, but many Southerners refused to pay. The Confederacy was forced to print paper money, causing rapid inflation in the South.

The Civil War was, in many respects, the first modern war. It was fought with large, civilian armies and required vast amounts of supplies. Cone-shaped bullets allowed accuracy at much greater distances. Instead of standing in a line, troops defending positions began to use trenches and barricades for protection. Attrition—the wearing down of one side through exhaustion of soldiers and resources—also played a critical role. President Lincoln and the Northern states had rejected the assertion that states could secede from the Union. The Civil War began in April 1861 when Confederate forces fired upon federal troops in Fort Sumter in Charleston Harbor as Northern forces attempted to resupply the fort. Confederate president Jefferson Davis claimed that the seceding states were fighting for the same "sacred right of self-government" that had inspired the American Revolution and that the Confederacy would "seek no conquest . . . all we ask is to be let alone."

First Battle of Bull Run

Soon after the war began, Lincoln approved an assault on Confederate troops gathered near Manassas

African American servicemen, such as the members of the band of 107th U.S. Colored Infantry at Fort Corcoran, Virginia, made up about eight percent of the Union army.

Drawing Conclusions Why did so many African Americans enlist in Union forces?

Junction, Virginia. The First Battle of Bull Run started well for the Union, but the tide turned when reinforcements helped the Confederates defeat the Union forces. The outcome made it clear that the North would need a large, well-trained army to prevail against the South.

The War in the West

The Union blockaded Southern ports along the Atlantic, but the South used small, fast ships to smuggle goods past the blockades. In April 1862, Union forces seized New Orleans, the South's largest city, and gained control of the lower Mississippi River. In early 1862, Union general Ulysses S. Grant began a campaign on the Cumberland and Tennessee Rivers. Control of these rivers would split Tennessee and provide the Union with a route into Confederate territory. All of Kentucky and most of western Tennessee eventually fell to Union control.

The War in the East

While Grant fought in the West, Union general George B. McClellan's forces set out to capture Richmond, Virginia, the Confederate capital. In late June 1862, Confederate general Robert E. Lee began a series of attacks on McClellan's forces. Together the two sides suffered more than 30,000 casualties. On September 17, 1862, Lee's forces met McClellan's in Maryland at Antietam (an·TEE·tuhm) Creek. The fight was the bloodiest one-day battle in American history, ending with nearly 6,000 soldiers killed and another 17,000 wounded. McClellan did not break Lee's lines, but he inflicted so many casualties that Lee decided to retreat to Virginia. The Battle of Antietam was a crucial victory for the Union. The British had been ready to intervene as a mediator if Lee's invasion had succeeded because the British wanted to protect their supply of Southern cotton. The events of Antietam made the British wait to see how the war progressed. The South's defeat at Antietam also convinced President Lincoln that the time had come to end slavery in the South.

The Emancipation Proclamation

In the North, most Democrats had opposed ending slavery while Republicans were divided. With Union casualties rising, however, many Northerners began to agree that slavery had to end, both to punish the South and to make the Union soldiers' sacrifices worthwhile. On September 22, 1862, Lincoln publicly announced that he would issue the Emancipation Proclamation—a decree freeing all enslaved persons in states still in rebellion after January 1, 1863. Because the Proclamation only freed the enslaved in states at war with the Union, it did not address slavery in the border states. By its very existence, however, the Proclamation

The Protected Art Archive/Alamy Stock Photo

transformed the conflict over preserving the Union into a war of liberation.

✓ **CHECK FOR UNDERSTANDING**

1. **Analyzing** Why was it necessary for the Union to send troops to the West?

2. **Explaining** Why do you think the Battle of Antietam inspired Abraham Lincoln to issue the Emancipation Proclamation?

The Turning Points and Final Battles

GUIDING QUESTION

Why were Vicksburg and Gettysburg turning points in the war?

As 1863 began, more than two years of battle still lay ahead, and the casualties continued to increase. New military technology produced a huge number of casualties, and doctors, who had little understanding of infections and germs, struggled to tend to the wounded. Disease was one of the greatest threats facing soldiers as more soldiers died from disease than from battle wounds. Smallpox, dysentery, typhoid, and pneumonia killed thousands. Battlefield physicians often had to amputate arms and legs to prevent gangrene and other infections from spreading.

It was in this field of battlefield medicine that the only woman ever to win the Medal of Honor made her contribution. Mary Edwards Walker was one of the few women before the Civil War to earn a medical degree. When the Civil War erupted, she volunteered to help the Union Army and worked as a surgeon near the front lines. She frequently crossed enemy lines to treat civilians, and on one such mission in 1864, she was arrested as a spy and imprisoned for four months. For her contributions to the war effort, Walker was awarded the Medal of Honor in 1865.

Vicksburg

Gaining control of the Mississippi River was a vital element of the Union strategy for winning the Civil War. If the Union could capture Vicksburg, Mississippi, the last major Confederate stronghold on the river, then the North could cut the South in two. In May 1863, Grant launched two assaults, but the city's defenders repulsed both attacks and inflicted high casualties. Grant decided to put Vicksburg under **siege** by cutting off its food and supplies and bombarding it until its defenders gave up. On July 4, 1863, with his troops starving, Vicksburg's Confederate commander surrendered.

Gettysburg

Meanwhile in Virginia, Lee had defeated Union forces at Fredericksburg and Chancellorsville. Emboldened by these victories, Lee launched another invasion of the North in June 1863. As Lee's army foraged in the Pennsylvania countryside, some of his troops headed into Gettysburg, hoping to seize a supply of shoes.

When they arrived near the town, the Confederate soldiers discovered two brigades of Union cavalry. On July 1, 1863, as Confederates pushed the Union troops out of the town, the main forces of both armies hurried to the scene of the fighting. On July 2, Lee attacked, but the Union troops held their ground. The following day Lee ordered nearly 15,000 men under the command of General George E. Pickett and General A. P. Hill to make a massive assault. The attack, known as Pickett's Charge, resulted in 7,000 casualties in less than half an hour but failed to break the Union lines. Lee's troops retreated back into Virginia.

At Gettysburg, the Union suffered 23,000 casualties and the South an estimated 28,000—more than one-third of Lee's entire force. The battle proved to be the turning point of the war in the East. The Union's victory strengthened the Republicans politically and ensured once again that the British would not recognize the Confederacy. The battlefield was also the site of one of President Lincoln's most stirring speeches, in which he tried to turn the destruction of the battle into a moment of inspiration:

66 Four score and seven years ago our fathers brought forth on this continent, a new nation, conceived in Liberty, and dedicated to the proposition that all men are created equal. Now we are engaged in a great civil war, testing whether that nation, or any nation so conceived and so dedicated, can long endure. . . . It is rather for us to be here dedicated to the great task remaining before us—that from these honored dead we take increased devotion to that cause for which they gave the last full measure of devotion—that we here highly resolve that these dead shall not have died in vain—that this nation, under God, shall have a new birth of freedom—and that government of the people, by the people, for the people, shall not perish from the earth. 99

—President Lincoln, from The Gettysburg Address, November 19, 1863

For the remainder of the war, Lee's forces remained on the defensive, slowly giving ground to the advancing Union Army.

The Thirteenth Amendment

More Union successes followed. General Grant secured control of the Mississippi River, and Lincoln rewarded

---

siege a military blockade of a city or fortified place to force it to surrender

Abraham Lincoln. 1863. Nicolay Copy of the Gettysburg Address. Holograph manuscript. Manuscript Division, Library of Congress.

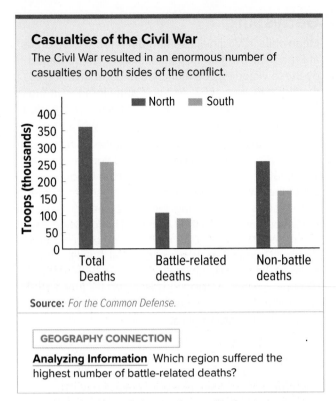

Casualties of the Civil War

The Civil War resulted in an enormous number of casualties on both sides of the conflict.

Troops (thousands) — North ■ South ■

Total Deaths · Battle-related deaths · Non-battle deaths

Source: *For the Common Defense.*

GEOGRAPHY CONNECTION

Analyzing Information Which region suffered the highest number of battle-related deaths?

him by appointing him general in chief of the Union forces. Grant then began a relentless series of attacks against Lee's forces, slowly pushing deeper into Virginia. In June 1864 Grant's troops reached the fortifications outside the city of Petersburg. After the failure of initial attacks, he put the city under siege. As the siege dragged on, support for the war declined, and Lincoln expected to lose the 1864 presidential election. In September 1864, however, General William T. Sherman captured Atlanta and then began a march to the sea, **pillaging** and destroying railroads, warehouses, mills, and factories. Sherman's troops weakened Southern support for the war even as the march's success revitalized the North's support. Lincoln was reelected in a landslide victory.

The president interpreted his reelection as a mandate from the voters to end slavery permanently by amending the Constitution. The Senate had passed an amendment the previous spring, but Lincoln and Congressional Republicans needed a coalition of antislavery Democrats to get that amendment passed in the House of Representatives.

On January 31, 1865, the Thirteenth Amendment, which banned slavery in the United States, narrowly passed the House of Representatives and went to the states for ratification. By December 1865, enough states had ratified the amendment for it to go into effect. The Amendment marked a culmination of the abolitionist movement that had begun after the American Revolution. It also finally applied the self-evident truths of the Declaration of Independence

"that all men are created equal" and had an unalienable right to liberty.

The War Ends

By the spring of 1865, Lee knew that time was running out. On April 2, 1865, Union troops cut the last rail line into Petersburg, Virginia. Lee's troops attempted to escape Grant's forces in the area, but Union cavalry blocked the road. With his battered troops surrounded, outnumbered, and starving, Lee surrendered to Grant at Appomattox Court House on April 9, 1865.

With the war over, Lincoln delivered a speech describing his plan to restore the Southern states to the Union. Lincoln mentioned including African Americans in Southern state governments. One listener, actor John Wilkes Booth, sneered to a friend, "That is the last speech he will ever make." Although his advisers had repeatedly warned him not to appear unescorted in public, Lincoln went to Ford's Theatre with his wife to see a play on April 14, 1865. During the third act, Booth slipped quietly behind the president and shot him in the back of the head. Lincoln died the next morning.

The North's victory saved the Union and strengthened the power of the federal government over the states. It transformed American society by ending slavery, but it also left the South devastated and many questions unresolved. Americans tried to answer these questions in the years following the Civil War—an era known as Reconstruction.

✓ **CHECK FOR UNDERSTANDING**

1. **Explaining** What was the significance of the Union victory at Vicksburg?
2. **Summarizing** How did the Battle of Gettysburg affect Confederate forces?

Reconstruction

GUIDING QUESTION

What important decisions had to be made concerning the fate of the seceded states and the rights of those freed from slavery?

At the end of the Civil War, the president and Congress grappled with the difficult tasks needed to bring the country back together while making necessary legal and political changes to end slavery and racial discrimination.

Opposing Plans for Reconstruction

In December 1863 President Lincoln had offered a general amnesty, or pardon, to Southerners who took an oath of loyalty to the United States and accepted the

---

pillage to loot or plunder

Booth, John Wilkes. In Impeachment Investigation: Testimony Taken Before the Judiciary Committee of the House of Representative in the Investigation of the Charges Against Andrew Johnson. Copyright © 1867 by U.S. Government Printing Office.

Union's requirements concerning slavery. However, certain Confederate officials and military officers were not included in the offer. In his Second Inaugural Address in March 1865 Lincoln spoke of ending the war "with malice toward none, with charity for all."

Resistance to Lincoln's plan surfaced among a group of Republicans in Congress known as Radical Republicans. They had three main goals. First, they wanted to prevent the leaders of the Confederacy from returning to power after the war. Second, they wanted the Republican Party to become a powerful political force in the South. Third, they wanted the federal government to help African Americans achieve political equality by guaranteeing their right to vote in the South. Many of the Radical Republicans had been abolitionists before the Civil War and had pushed Lincoln to make emancipation a goal of the war. They knew that securing voting rights for African American men in the South would help their party win elections. Most believed in a right to political equality for all men, regardless of race.

Vice President Andrew Johnson, a Democrat from Tennessee, assumed the presidency after Lincoln's assassination. Like Lincoln, Johnson believed that a moderate policy was best to bring the seceded states back into the Union and to win Southern loyalty. Unlike Lincoln, he did not believe in protecting the political rights of African Americans.

Johnson had been selected as Lincoln's running mate in the 1864 presidential election to gain the support of other War Democrats. Throughout the war, Johnson had remained a staunch Unionist, and his pro-Union stance had led Lincoln to install him as the military governor of Tennessee in 1862. In that role, he had dealt harshly with Confederate planters. However, Johnson's past treatment of Southern planters had stemmed from his dislike of the planter class rather than from support for African Americans.

In the summer of 1865 Johnson initiated what he called his restoration program. He offered to pardon and to return the property of all former citizens of the Confederacy who took an oath of loyalty to the Union. He excluded former Confederate officers and officials from the pardon, as well as any Confederate citizen with property worth more than $20,000. Under another program, each former Confederate state had to call a constitutional convention to revoke its decree of secession, ratify the Thirteenth Amendment, and reject all Civil War debts. Under these provisions, Johnson began granting pardons to thousands of Southerners.

Many congressional Republicans were angered when Southern voters elected a number of former Confederate officials to Congress. They were further outraged when Southern state legislatures passed a series of laws known as **black codes** that limited African Americans' rights. While black codes varied somewhat between states, they all intended to keep African Americans in a condition similar to slavery. The laws outlined a variety of crimes that African Americans could be charged with, including vagrancy, or homelessness; making insulting gestures; and creating mischief. Other laws prevented African Americans from voting, serving on juries, giving evidence in court, traveling freely, choosing their own occupations, or marrying a white partner.

The Fourteenth Amendment

In June 1866, to permanently block states from imposing black codes and other restrictions on African American rights, Congress passed the Fourteenth Amendment to the Constitution. This amendment granted citizenship to all persons born or naturalized in the United States and prevented states from denying people freedom or property "without due process of law." It also declared that no state could deny any person "equal protection of the laws."

In March 1867 the Radical Republicans—congressional Republicans who felt Johnson's reconstruction plan was too lenient—passed the Military Reconstruction Act dividing the former

In 1867 African Americans in Virginia voted for the first time, as shown in this hand-colored woodcut. More than 93,000 African Americans voted in this election in Virginia.

Speculating Why do you think this woodcut documented African Americans voting in this election in 1867?

---

black codes laws passed in the South just after the Civil War aimed at controlling freedmen and enabling plantation owners to exploit African American workers

PHOTO: North Wind Picture Archives/Alamy Stock Photo; TEXT: Lincoln, Abraham. "Second Inaugural Address." Washington, D.C., March 4, 1865. Library of Congress, Manuscript Division, Abraham Lincoln Papers: Series 3.

Confederacy—except for Tennessee, which had ratified the Fourteenth Amendment in 1866—into five military districts. For the former Confederate states to regain control of their state governments and be allowed to elect members to Congress, state leaders had to give the right to vote to all adult male citizens regardless of race and ratify the Fourteenth Amendment.

The Fourteenth Amendment was a turning point in American political and legal history. Since its ratification in 1868, it has been used to expand federal power over the states and to extend civil rights through its equal protection clause. It also led to the doctrine of incorporation, the idea that the Bill of Rights applies to state governments not just the federal government.

Although Southern states continued to discriminate against African Americans in the late nineteenth century and well into the twentieth century, the Fourteenth Amendment empowered the African American civil rights movement and helped to ensure its success in the 1950s and 1960s.

The Fifteenth Amendment

In the meantime, tensions between Radical Republicans and President Johnson increased. After Johnson purposely broke a law called the Tenure of Office Act, the House of Representatives voted to impeach the president. The impeachment trial in the Senate ended one vote short of convicting Johnson. Although Johnson remained in office, he did not run for reelection in 1868. That year the Republicans nominated General Grant to be their presidential candidate. Grant won easily, and Republicans kept control of Congress.

Recognizing the importance of African American suffrage, Congress passed the Fifteenth Amendment to the Constitution. This amendment declared that the right to vote "shall not be denied . . . on account of race, color, or previous condition of servitude." By March 1870, enough states had ratified the amendment to make it part of the Constitution. Radical Reconstruction changed Southern politics by bringing hundreds of thousands of African Americans into the political process for the first time. But it angered many white Southerners, who fought back against the federal government's policies, through Democratic Party politics and the formation of terrorist organizations such as the Ku Klux Klan, whose members carried out organized violence against African Americans and white Republicans.

The South During Reconstruction

By the autumn of 1870, all former Confederate states had rejoined the Union. The Freedmen's Bureau worked to feed and clothe war refugees and help formerly enslaved people. Many Northerners traveled to the South, where many were elected or appointed to positions in the new state governments. Southerners called these newcomers **carpetbaggers** because some arrived with their belongings in suitcases made of carpet fabric. Some white Southerners, called **scalawags** by other white Southerners, did work with the Republicans and supported Reconstruction. Having gained the right to vote, African American men entered politics with great enthusiasm. They served as legislators and administrators in nearly all levels of government. Republicans built a coalition of poor Southern-born white farmers, African Americans, and Northern carpetbaggers to elect Republican candidates.

Compromise of 1877

After Ulysses S. Grant became president in 1869, scandals and economic pressures damaged his administration. In the 1870s, Democrats began to regain power in the South. The 1876 presidential election pitted Republican Rutherford B. Hayes against Democrat Samuel Tilden. On Election Day, 20 electoral votes were disputed, including 19 in the three Southern states controlled by Republicans. The outcome of this election has been called the Compromise of 1877.

The compromise reportedly included a promise to pull federal troops out of the South in return for a Republican victory. While historians are not sure if a deal really took place, Union troops did leave the South within a month of Hayes taking office. However, it is also true that the nation and Republican leaders were ready to end Reconstruction.

✓ **CHECK FOR UNDERSTANDING**

1. **Explaining** Why did the Radical Republicans oppose Johnson's Reconstruction plan?
2. **Making Connections** How did the Fourteenth and Fifteenth Amendments work together to promote civil rights in the United States?

LESSON ACTIVITIES

1. **Narrative Writing** Suppose that you are a soldier at Appomattox Court House who witnessed Lee's surrender to Grant. Write a letter or a journal entry describing the scene and your thoughts about it.

2. **Presenting** Work with a partner to create an informative presentation about the Freedman's Bureau. Explain what its mission was and who was responsible for its creation. List its successes and failures. Present your findings to the class.

---

carpetbagger name given to any Northerner who moved to the South after the Civil War and supported the Republicans

scalawag name given to any Southerner who supported the Republicans and Reconstruction of the South

Turning Point: The Compromise of 1877

 COMPELLING QUESTION

How was the Compromise of 1877 a turning point?

Plan Your Inquiry

In this lesson, you will investigate how disputed election results in the presidential contest of 1876 led to a compromise that would become a significant turning point in American history.

DEVELOP QUESTIONS

Developing Questions About Disputed Elections Think about typical American presidential elections. Usually, Americans can expect that citizens will cast their ballots, and the winner will be easily determined. The results may even be predictable before the election takes place. For a few elections in American history, however, this has this not been the case. Review the Compelling Question for this lesson, and then write three Supporting Questions that might help you answer the Compelling Question for the lesson. Write these in a graphic organizer like the one below.

APPLY HISTORICAL TOOLS

Analyzing Primary and Secondary Sources You will work with several primary sources and one secondary source—a map of the 1876 presidential election results—in this lesson. These sources focus on reactions to and results from the election. Use a graphic organizer like the one below to record and organize information about each source. Note ways in which each source helps you answer the supporting questions you created.

Source	Author/ Creator	Description/ Notes	Which Supporting Questions does this source help me answer?
A			
B			
C			
D			

After you analyze the sources, you will:
- use the evidence from the sources
- communicate your conclusions
- take informed action

Background Information

The outcome of the 1876 presidential election between Republican Rutherford B. Hayes and Democrat Samuel Tilden remained in dispute for months after the November 7 election. Though Tilden had clearly won 184 electoral votes and Hayes 165, the legality of 20 electoral votes were in question. Nineteen were in Louisiana, South Carolina, and Florida, and the twentieth was in Oregon. Congress appointed a 15-person commission to review and certify the contested votes. The Commission released its final recommendation to the House of Representatives on February 23.

After much debate, several Southern Democrats joined with House Republicans and voted to accept the commission's findings. On March 1, 1877, the House of Representatives gathered to officially count the votes. The results were announced in the early morning hours of March 2. Hayes was declared the winner. He was inaugurated three days later.

Some people believed Hayes would not have won without the support of Southern Democrats. They thought that a deal had been made. For this reason, the outcome of the election has been called the Compromise of 1877.

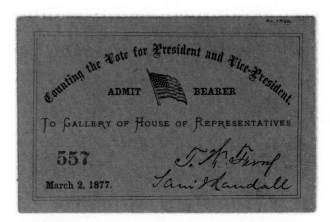

Counting the Vote for President and Vice-President.
ADMIT [flag] BEARER
To Gallery of House of Representatives.
557
March 2, 1877.

» Members of the House gathered to officially count the Electoral votes to determine a winner for the 1876 election. This ticket gave the bearer access to view the decision. The inauguration of Rutherford Hayes was held three days later on March 5, 1877.

Library of Congress, Rare Book and Special Collections Division, Printed Ephemera Collection

The Disputed Election of 1876

This map shows the results of the disputed election of 1876 between Samuel Tilden and Rutherford Hayes. Twenty of the electoral votes cast were disputed by the government and the results were unclear. Nineteen of those twenty disputed electoral votes came from three southern states—Florida, Louisiana, and South Carolina. All three of these states were still under the control of the Republican Party. It took a special commission of Congressmen to resolve the election, though voters unhappy with Hayes's eventual victory questioned the honesty of the political decision.

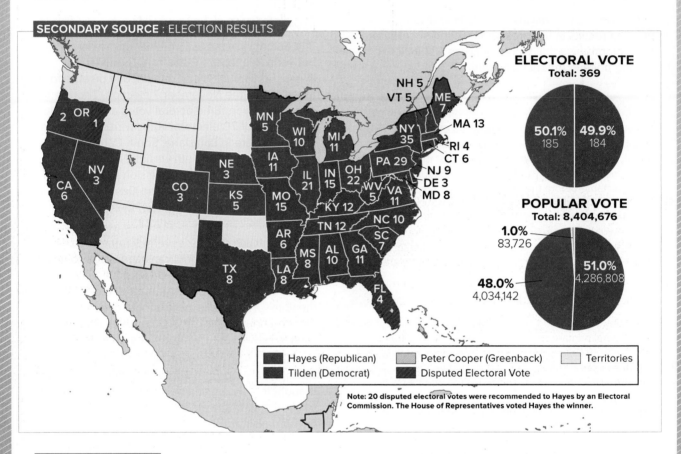

SECONDARY SOURCE : ELECTION RESULTS

ELECTORAL VOTE
Total: 369

50.1% 185 | 49.9% 184

POPULAR VOTE
Total: 8,404,676

1.0% 83,726
51.0% 4,286,808
48.0% 4,034,142

Legend:
- Hayes (Republican)
- Tilden (Democrat)
- Peter Cooper (Greenback)
- Disputed Electoral Vote
- Territories

State electoral votes: OR 2/1, NV 3, CA 6, NE 3, CO 3, KS 5, MN 5, WI 10, MI 11, IA 11, IL 21, IN 15, OH 22, MO 15, KY 12, TN 12, AR 6, MS 8, AL 10, GA 11, TX 8, LA 8, FL 4, NC 10, SC 7, WV 5, VA 11, PA 29, NY 35, NH 5, VT 5, ME 7, MA 13, RI 4, CT 6, NJ 9, DE 3, MD 8

Note: 20 disputed electoral votes were recommended to Hayes by an Electoral Commission. The House of Representatives voted Hayes the winner.

EXAMINE THE SOURCE

1. **Spatial Thinking** Which candidate was most popular with voters in the Western states?

2. **Human Population** How does the map show that a divide still existed in the United States?

(l)Electoral Commission: "South Carolina." Congressional Record: Containing the Proceedings of the Electoral Commission Appointed Under the Act of Congress Approved January 29, 1877, Entitled "An Act to Provide for and Regulate the Counting of Votes for President and Vice President, and the Decisions of Questions Arising Thereon, For the Term Commencing March 4, A.D. 1877, Part IV, Volume V. Washington: Government Printing Office, 1877; (tr)"About National Republican." 1860. Chronicling America, Library of Congress; (br)"The Battle for Power." National Republican. February 12, 1877.

B

The 1877 Electoral Commission

On February 8, the Electoral Commission voted to accept Florida's disputed electoral votes for Hayes. This excerpt is from Virginia Representative Eppa Hunton, who served as a brigadier general in the Confederate Army and as a delegate to the Virginia Secession Convention in 1861.

PRIMARY SOURCE : COMMITTEE PROCEEDINGS

❝ . . . By a vote of eight to seven this Commission has decided on purely technical grounds that Florida and Louisiana voted for Hayes . . . I say this Commission has disappointed public expectation, because the country expected of it that it would decide who had been elected President and Vice-President by the people. They did not expect of us that we would merely confirm the judgment of corrupt and illegal returning boards, who were ready to put the Presidency up to the highest bidder in the public market.

. . . [O]n the day of election and for several weeks preceding . . . [Federal] troops were sent into the State not for the purpose, as avowed, of preserving the peace and quelling insurrection, but to overawe the voters. The troops were stationed near the polls on the day of election and did obstruct the free expression of the popular will.

. . . That all this and much more was done by the public authorities and protected by the troops of the Federal Government with the design to deter men, and especially colored men, from voting the democratic ticket.

If the half of this is true . . . can it be said there was a free election in that State? . . . Can we say their votes are the votes provided by the Constitution? ❞

—Representative Eppa Hunton, February 26, 1877

EXAMINE THE SOURCE

1. **Identifying Bias** What is Hunton's opinion of the commission's report? Why do you think this is the case?

2. **Drawing Conclusions** What role does Hunton assert the federal government played in the outcome of the election?

C

The Battle for Power

The excerpt below comes from a February 12, 1877, issue of the *National Republican*, a daily newspaper published in Washington, D.C. Its publishers and writers claimed they were not partisan. However, an early mission statement, to "advocate and defend the principles of the Republican Party," seems to indicate otherwise.

PRIMARY SOURCE : NEWSPAPER

❝ The scheme of the rebel Democracy now delay, and the first act in that drama of delay was on Saturday played. . . . As soon as the fact was **ascertained** on Friday that the Electoral Tribunal had decided in favor of the HAYES and WHEELER electors from Florida, a conference of prominent Democrats was held, and it was decided to defeat the will of the people by indirection. . . .

There are rumors very generally credited that the . . . policy of delay will be adopted and every obstacle possible thrown in the way of the count with a view to protract it beyond the fourth of March, when this Congress expires, and the power to count will cease when the law (and not the Constitution, as erroneously stated) requires the Secretary of State to call a new election, the President of the Senate meantime discharging the duties of the Executive office. The precedent established on Saturday of a recess immediately after an objection is entered, gives the Democrats in the House the power to force a new election . . . When the decision of the tribunal is announced, if it is adverse to the Democrats, they threaten to adopt the recess plan, urging against the assurance of popular condemnation the plea that they have nothing to lose and everything to gain by the venture . . . ❞

—*National Republican*, February 12, 1877, p. 1

---

ascertained made sure of

EXAMINE THE SOURCE

1. **Identifying Bias** Identify three phrases in this piece that show its political bias. Indicate the most important parts of each of the phrases.

2. **Explaining** According to the excerpt, what sparked the "policy of delay"?

The New Policy Train

The Compromise of 1877 reportedly included a promise by Republicans to pull federal troops out of the South if Hayes were elected. In April 1877 Hayes did indeed pull federal troops out of the South. Without soldiers to support them, the last Republican governments in South Carolina and Louisiana collapsed, bringing an end to Reconstruction. This cartoon reinforces the shifting political actions that resulted from Hayes's decisions. Leaving the former Confederacy to make its own political and social choices without the influence of Northern enforcement brought an end to Reconstruction reform efforts and caused the creation of a segregated South for many decades to come.

PRIMARY SOURCE : LITHOGRAPH

THE NEW POLICY TRAIN.
CONDUCTOR HAYES—"All aboard, Mr. Packard! We want to take all you Carpetbaggers in one trip!"

» The man holding the bag labeled "S.B. Packard Maine" is Maine-born Republican Stephen B. Packard, who lived in Louisiana after the war. He was elected as governor in a disputed election in which the Democratic candidate also claimed victory. Each side set up rival governments. When Hayes declined to use federal troops to support Packard's government, Packard was forced to yield and leave Louisiana.

EXAMINE THE SOURCE

1. **Analyzing Perspectives** Do you think this cartoon was drawn by a Northern cartoonist or a Southern one? Explain your answer.

2. **Identifying Themes** Why does the artist show Rutherford B. Hayes as the conductor?

Your Inquiry Analysis

EVALUATE SOURCES AND USE EVIDENCE

Reflect back to the Compelling Question and the Supporting Questions you developed at the beginning of this lesson.

1. **Gathering Sources** Review your graphic organizer. Which sources helped you answer your Supporting Questions most directly? Which sources, if any, best help you answer the Compelling Question? Explain your answers.

2. **Evaluating Sources** Looking at the sources that helped you answer your Supporting Questions, evaluate the reliability of each source. What details made that source a particularly useful source to answer your question? How does bias factor into the reliability of each source?

3. **Comparing and Contrasting** Compare and contrast the two sources in this lesson that critique the work of the commission. What tone is expressed by each writer? Is the person angry or merely conveying information? Is the information trustworthy? Explain.

COMMUNICATE CONCLUSIONS

Analyzing Information Prepare a short presentation on why the Compromise of 1877 is considered a turning point in U.S. history. Use details from the sources to show the viewpoints of each side and to explain why this event is known as the Compromise of 1877. Consider how best to communicate your conclusions to your classmates, such as through an essay or a multimedia presentation.

TAKE INFORMED ACTION

Creating a Plan for Compromise Think about an issue on school campuses that requires compromise, such as cell phone usage at school. There are typically two sides to this argument: students' belief that they should be able to use their phones, and administration policies against cell phone usage in the classroom. Determine the benefits and drawbacks of each side's position. Create a plan that balances the needs of both the administration and the students and share it with students and administration officials.

"The New Policy train." Frank Leslie's Illustrated Newspaper, April 21, 1877, p. 128. HathiTrust

Reviewing Creating a New Nation

Summary

The Earliest Peoples

The earliest peoples who inhabited the Americas originally migrated from Asia. Over thousands of years, they established thriving cultures. Europeans transformed the Americas through colonization and the African slave trade. Eventually Britain controlled the original colonies that would form the United States.

A Revolutionary Spirit

After the French and Indian War, Parliament increased taxes and the British military in the colonies, angering colonists. The Continental Congress was organized to negotiate with British authorities, and colonies organized boycotts of British goods. Incidents such as the Boston Massacre, the *Gaspee* Affair, and the Boston Tea Party increased tensions. When British forces attempted to seize weapons held by the Massachusetts militia, the American Revolution began.

In 1776 members of the Continental Congress wrote the Declaration of Independence, proclaiming their intention to found a new nation called the United States of America. Under the leadership of General George Washington and with help from key allies such as France and Spain, the Patriots began to win victories in battles such as Trenton and Saratoga. The British surrender at Yorktown in 1781 ended major fighting, and the Treaty of Paris of 1783 settled the terms of the war.

Creating a Constitution

Leaders created a system of government under the Articles of Confederation, which granted most political authority to the states and diminished the powers of the national government. The Articles reflected colonial distrust of a centralized government and monarchy. After the Revolution ended, weaknesses in the Articles led to the Constitutional Convention. The U.S. Constitution established a federalist system that divided power between the states and national government. It also established a strong federal government with three branches—executive, judicial, and legislative—and powers shared through a series of checks and balances.

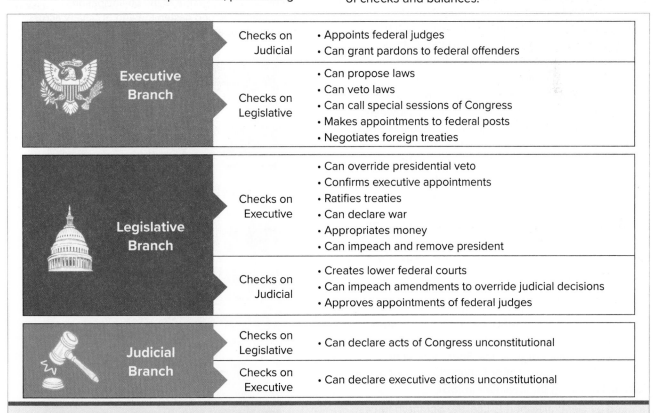

Executive Branch	Checks on Judicial	• Appoints federal judges • Can grant pardons to federal offenders
	Checks on Legislative	• Can propose laws • Can veto laws • Can call special sessions of Congress • Makes appointments to federal posts • Negotiates foreign treaties
Legislative Branch	Checks on Executive	• Can override presidential veto • Confirms executive appointments • Ratifies treaties • Can declare war • Appropriates money • Can impeach and remove president
	Checks on Judicial	• Creates lower federal courts • Can impeach amendments to override judicial decisions • Approves appointments of federal judges
Judicial Branch	Checks on Legislative	• Can declare acts of Congress unconstitutional
	Checks on Executive	• Can declare executive actions unconstitutional

Checks and Balances

The Constitution is designed to limit each government branch's power with the other two.

The American Nation Grows

After the American Revolution, the United States slowly gained more lands. The early Industrial Revolution brought new opportunities and new challenges. The population of the new nation was growing rapidly, and many Americans began to settle west of the Appalachian Mountains. By the 1840s, the concept of "Manifest Destiny" encouraged many to expand all the way to the Pacific Ocean. Westward settlement often brought American settlers and military into conflict with Native Americans, who were pushed off the lands their societies had inhabited for centuries.

Westward expansion also brought the United States into conflict with other nations. A treaty between the United States and Great Britain established the border between the United States and Canada. American settlers in the Mexican province of Texas waged a successful war for independence several years before joining the United States. War with Mexico gave the United States control of all the lands west of Texas to California by 1848.

Conflicts Over Slavery

Conflicts over slavery increased. By the early 1800s, slavery had been abolished in Northern states. Reformers, called abolitionists, wanted to outlaw slavery throughout the country. Federal leaders tried to maintain a balance between slave and free states, but as new territories opened up in the West, many fought to keep them free from slavery. Southern leaders wanted to protect the expansion of slavery and the power of slaveholding states in Congress. Others advocated for popular sovereignty, which would allow the local white male population to vote on the issue.

The Compromise of 1850 sought to resolve conflicts between the slave and free states. However, tensions only intensified. Northerners strongly opposed the Fugitive Slave Act, which required returning runaway enslaved people to their owners. The Underground Railroad helped many enslaved people escape to freedom. Conflicts over the future of slavery in Kansas led to the nickname Bleeding Kansas. The *Dred Scott* decision and John Brown's attack on Harpers Ferry further divided North and South. By the election of 1860, the country was on the verge of war.

The Civil War

After Republican Abraham Lincoln won the presidential election of 1860, seven Southern states seceded from the Union and formed the proslavery Confederate States of America. Four more states joined the Confederacy after fighting broke out at Fort Sumter, launching the Civil War in 1861.

Led by General Robert E. Lee, the Southern forces won several notable battles early in the conflict. The Northern armies struggled to find a strong leader until Lincoln placed General Ulysses Grant in charge. With the North's advantage in economic, industrial, and human resources, Grant's forces could outlast the enemy, even if it meant high casualties on both sides. Lincoln issued the Emancipation Proclamation, declaring enslaved people in the rebelling states to be free. This changed the goal of the war from preserving the Union to ending slavery. Soon after, Lee's forces lost their last attempt to invade the North at the bloody Battle of Gettysburg. After four long years of fighting, the war ended when Lee surrendered to Grant at Appomattox Court House in 1865. The Civil War had been the deadliest conflict in the history of the United States.

Reconstructing the Nation

After Lincoln was assassinated in 1865, the task of reconstructing the nation divided Congress and the new president, Andrew Johnson. The ensuing division resulted in Johnson becoming the first president to be impeached, although he was not convicted. During Congressional Reconstruction, U.S. military forces occupied the South in order to protect African Americans' civil rights. The Thirteenth, Fourteenth, and Fifteenth Amendments were added to the Constitution. Reconstruction ended in 1877, when it is believed Republicans agreed to remove troops from the South to end Democratic opposition in a contested presidential election.

The Emancipation Proclamation

Lincoln's announcement of the Emancipation Proclamation helped hasten the end of slavery across the United States.

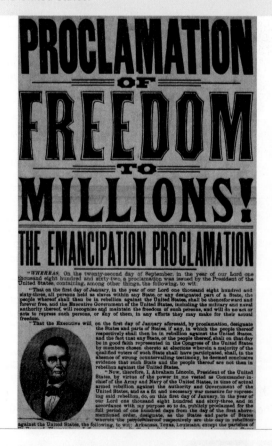

Library of Congress, Rare Book and Special Collections Division, Alfred Whital Stern Collection of Lincolniana.

Apply What You Have Learned

 ## Understanding Multiple Perspectives

Today most Americans looking back at the American Revolution would probably consider themselves Patriots. When fighting broke out, however, many colonists sided with Great Britain. Some thought that the colonies would be safer under British control. Others believed that the rebels were disloyal to the king and country that had provided for them.

ACTIVITY **Debate Your Points** With a partner, use your textbook and other sources to review arguments made for and against the war by Loyalists and Patriots. Then prepare for a debate. One partner in your pair will represent a Loyalist, and the other partner will represent a Patriot. Engage in a debate from your respective points of view. Then switch roles and debate the other side using different supporting evidence. Work together to write a summary of what you learned about different perspectives on the war.

 ## Building Citizenship

During the American Revolution, Patriot leaders wanted to build a new nation of citizens who considered themselves American rather than British. After the Revolution, many Americans strongly identified as citizens of their state rather than of their nation. The Constitution sought to strengthen an American sense of shared ideals.

ACTIVITY **Create a Venn Diagram** Using your textbook, Internet materials, and other resources, examine how the U.S. government under the Articles of Confederation and the Constitution differed from the government of England during the same period. Use the diagram below to compare and contrast life as a citizen of England and the United States during the post-Revolutionary period.

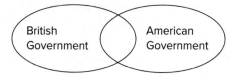

 ## Making Connections to Science

The Industrial Revolution not only changed many aspects of life in early America but also laid the groundwork for technology still in use today. While some manufacturing technology has become more dependent upon computerization, many of the basic engineering principles of the machines and technologies first created during the Industrial Revolution are still in use in modern factories.

ACTIVITY **Create a Blueprint** Using Internet resources, find an image of a machine used in a modern textile factory and research information about its history and design. Using this information, create a blueprint or 3-D model of the machine, adding call-out boxes that note the elements of the machine that have been in use since the earliest days of textile mills.

Geographic Reasoning

When the United States first declared its independence from Great Britain, it included just 13 states along the East Coast, bordering on the Atlantic Ocean. By the end of the war with Mexico, the United States controlled lands spanning from the Atlantic to the Pacific, or "from sea to shining sea." This expansion had significant cultural and political implications for the still young nation.

ACTIVITY **Write to Compare** Examine the map below, which shows the expansion of lands controlled by the United States up until 1853. Identify one area where control changed from 1776 to 1853. Using your textbook and other resources, research what life was like in that location in 1776 compared with 1853. Write a brief description of how life changed for people in that area as the United States gained control.

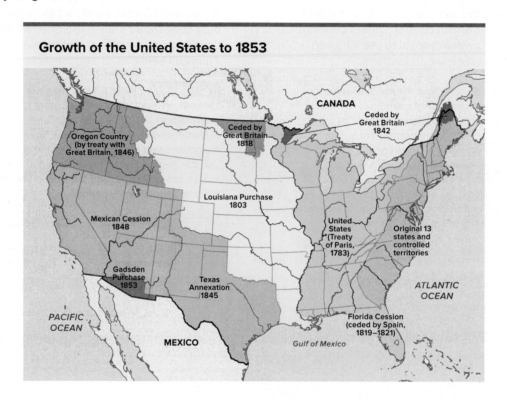

Growth of the United States to 1853

CANADA

Ceded by Great Britain 1842

Ceded by Great Britain 1818

Oregon Country (by treaty with Great Britain, 1846)

Louisiana Purchase 1803

Mexican Cession 1848

United States (Treaty of Paris, 1783)

Original 13 states and controlled territories

Gadsden Purchase 1853

Texas Annexation 1845

ATLANTIC OCEAN

PACIFIC OCEAN

MEXICO

Florida Cession (ceded by Spain, 1819–1821)

Gulf of Mexico

 Making Connections to Today

Some activists today believe that the U.S. government should pay reparations to the descendants of enslaved people because of the failed promises of Reconstruction and the years of discrimination that followed. Reparations are payments made to make amends to people for wrongdoing against them. The U.S. government has only paid reparations in very rare cases. Still, some believe that reparations to the descendants of enslaved people would balance the scales of justice.

ACTIVITY **Analyze Points of View** Research points of view on the issue of reparations for African American enslavement. Write an essay in which you explain the various positions, the court cases that have been filed, and the outcomes of the cases. You might also want to consider other instances of compensation for historical injustices, such as those involving Native Americans and seized lands.

TOPIC 2

Migration, Industry, and Urban Society 1865–1914

Taken around the turn of the twentieth century by photographer Jacob Riis, this color-adjusted photograph shows Mulberry Street, a bustling thoroughfare in the heart of an immigrant neighborhood in New York City.

INTRODUCTION LESSON

01 Introducing Migration, Industry, and Urban Society   88

LEARN THE EVENTS LESSONS

02 Miners, Ranchers, and Farmers
Change the West   93

03 Western Pioneers and
Native Americans   97

05 Industrialization   109

06 Big Business and Unions   115

07 Immigration   121

09 Urbanization and Social Reform   131

10 Populism and Racism   137

INQUIRY ACTIVITY LESSONS

04 Analyzing Sources: Americanizing
Native Americans   103

08 Understanding Multiple Perspectives on
Immigration and Nativism   125

11 Turning Point: *Plessy* v. *Ferguson*   143

REVIEW AND APPLY LESSON

12 Reviewing Migration, Industry, and Urban Society   147

Library of Congress, Prints & Photographs Division, Detroit Publishing Company Collection.

ANSWERING THE KLONDIKE'S CALL

In August 1896 three men—Skookum Jim Mason, Dawson Charlie, and George Washington Carmack—discovered gold in Canada's Yukon Territory, a remote mountainous region bordering Alaska. Rumors of riches ripe for the plucking quickly spread, and hordes of hopeful, desperate people made the trek to Alaska.

But getting to the gold was no easy task. In fact, the 600-mile journey from Alaska to the Yukon gold fields was so difficult that the Canadian government required prospectors entering the region to have at least a year's worth of supplies. Skagway and Dyea quickly became boomtowns because they were near trails that prospectors used to travel into Canada. To call the Chilkoot Trail (out of Dyea) and the White Pass Trail (out of Skagway) dangerous would be a gross understatement. People were murdered, others died from avalanches, diseases, malnutrition, or hypothermia. The Chilkoot Trail was too steep to use pack animals, so prospectors carried supplies on their backs, until tramways were built late in 1897. Pack animals, mainly horses, were used on White Pass Trail, but more than 3,000 animals died from being overburdened and pushed too hard. White Pass Trail was often called by the alternative name Dead Horse Trail.

People looking to make money in Alaska and Canada did not always go to find gold. The boomtowns near the trails sold supplies and gave the prospectors places to live while they prepared for the journey. Although the prospecting world was dominated by men, women seeking adventure, independence, and fortune also traveled to Alaska and the Klondike. Harriet Pullen, for example, worked as a cook for a wealthy man in Skagway and baked and sold apple pies as a side venture. She also used her horses to carry prospectors' gear over White Pass Trail. She made enough to support herself and her three children. Eventually, she bought a house from the man she used to cook for and turned it into one of Alaska's most luxurious hotels. Of her arrival in Skagway, Pullen said, "I only had seven dollars to my name. I didn't know a soul in Alaska. I had no place to go. So I stood on the beach in the rain, while tented Skagway of 1897 shouted, cursed, shot and surged about me."

Nellie Cashman, another adventurous woman, had been a prospector throughout the West, supporting her enterprises with steady work managing boarding houses and restaurants. By the time she arrived in Dawson, a city in Canada near the Klondike mining district, in February 1898 she was too late to stake a claim, so she opened a store. She was eventually able to buy claims from other prospectors, but she never made money mining gold. She was a popular, active member of the community, helping to raise money for the local hospital and donating generously to her church. In 1900, the *Klondike Nugget* wrote that she "knows more about mining in all branches than many a man who poses as an expert."

The Klondike Gold Rush lasted only three years—from 1896 to 1899. More than 100,000 people traveled to the region during that time. The town of Dawson City became known as the "Paris of the North." The city boasted a population of nearly 30,000 people during its gold rush height. But very few people were successful in the Klondike. Most hopeful prospectors left broke, having spent all their money on supplies without ever striking it rich. The Dyea boomtown disappeared, but the cities of Dawson and Skagway remain, relics of the past's golden dreams and reminders of the wild frontier spirit.

> " I only had seven dollars to my name. I didn't know a soul in Alaska. I had no place to go. "

(tr)Pullen, Harriet. Quoted in "Harriet Pullen." Klondike Gold Rush National Historical Park. October 29, 2019; (br)Quote about Nellie Cashman. Klondike Nugget. In "Women Who Went To The Klondike." Klondike Gold Rush National Historical Park. February 10, 2020.

History and Art Collection/Alamy Stock Photo

Men and women rushed northward to seek gold during the Klondike Gold Rush of the late 1890s. This photograph, likely taken in the Yukon Territory, shows miners at work.

Understanding the Time and Place: United States, 1860–1890

Westward expansion occurred throughout the Civil War and increased in the years after the war's end. The Morrill Land-Grant Act of 1862 helped establish new colleges and universities throughout the United States. In addition, immigration steadily increased the population, and new railroads were built to better connect North and South and East and West. These developments, among others, brought floods of people westward, expanding the United States with enough people for the territories to apply for statehood.

Westward Expansion

Many people moved West with the idea of striking it rich. The California Gold Rush of 1848, the Comstock Lode in Nevada in 1859, and the discoveries of other deposits of gold, silver, and copper made mining a central part of life in the West. But mining was not easy nor was it safe. Mining operations destroyed the land, and the mineral deposits did not last.

Mining towns would spring up and exist as long as the mines paid off; once the mines were depleted of their minerals, the mining towns became ghost towns. Despite the "boom-and-bust" nature of mining, enough people moved West to allow several territories—such as California, Nevada, Montana, Colorado, Wyoming, and the Dakotas—to qualify for statehood before the turn of the century.

Others moved West because of the opportunities the area provided for cattle ranching. The federal government owned vast areas of land called the **open range**, and ranchers could use these areas to feed their herds free of charge. Railroad expansion also helped cattle ranchers. After the Civil War, beef was needed along the East Coast, and ranchers used the railroads to ship their cattle. Although the open ranges would become fenced-in ranches by the late 1880s, cattle ranching remained an important part of the West.

The federal government also passed legislation that encouraged westward expansion. For example, the Land-Grant College Act—often called the Morrill Act after Justin Smith Morrill, the Vermont congressman who sponsored it—gave each state 30,000 acres for each of its congressional seats. Some states used this land to create new colleges; others sold the land grants and used the proceeds to turn existing state and private colleges into A&M colleges, which specialized in agriculture and the mechanic arts.

Business and Industry

Improved technologies, expanding industries, and increased production of goods helped support a growing economy and an increasingly powerful business class. Legislation in the 1830s supported the creation of corporations, which became larger and more central to the economy as the nineteenth century turned into the twentieth.

In the late 1800s, America had a **laissez-faire** economic policy, which meant federal and state governments tried to avoid interfering with the economy. Competition, with little regulation, drove businesses. This economic attitude helped the United States become an economic power through innovation and industrialization, and it increased the standard of living for many, including immigrants. But industrial jobs, such as working in a factory or a mine, were dangerous and unhealthy, and little was done to

Industry grew rapidly in the United States during the late 1800s and early 1900s. However, laborers, like these Pennsylvania steel workers, sometimes faced difficult and even dangerous working conditions.

Making Connections How did the development of a complex industry like steel manufacturing impact the role of government during this time?

open range vast areas of grassland owned by the federal government

laissez-faire economic philosophy that government should interfere as little as possible in a nation's economy

The Keasbury-Gordon Photograph Archive/KGPA Ltd/Alamy Stock Photo.

Railroads and Universities

The Land-Grant College Act of 1862 helped fund and establish colleges throughout the United States. These colleges created centers of learning with a particular focus on agriculture, ensuring future generations of Americans could grow the crops needed to feed the expanding nation and its growing economy.

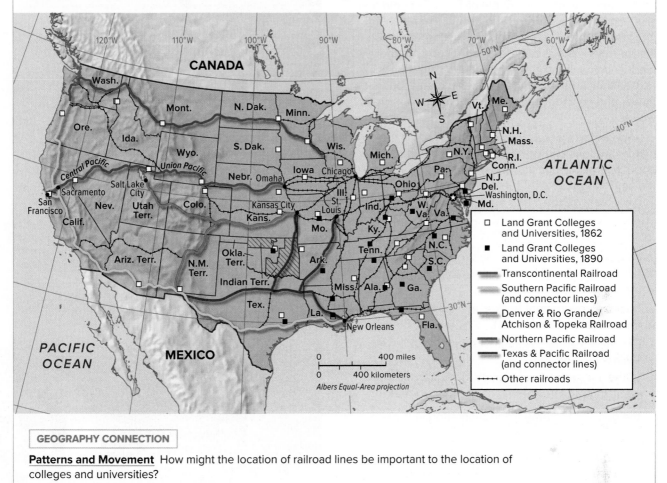

GEOGRAPHY CONNECTION

Patterns and Movement How might the location of railroad lines be important to the location of colleges and universities?

protect workers. The bottom line of business—making profit—created an increasing income and social gap between owners and the workers they employed.

Native Americans

The expansion of the United States did not benefit everyone. As more settlers moved west, more land was used or destroyed for mining, farming, and ranching. This land was not uninhabited. Native Americans had been living on it for thousands of years, and violence often broke out as they sought to protect themselves and their way of life. New settlers and the government forced Native Americans to relocate, either through violence, or through treaties, or a combination of the two. These agreements

outlining reservation land and support were, more often than not, never fulfilled. Some believed the best solution for Native Americans was through **Americanization**.

Native Americans were encouraged to **assimilate** into American society rather than preserving their language, culture, traditions, and way of life. In the 1880s the federal government created boarding schools that were separate from the reservations. Native American children were sent to these schools, sometimes against their and their parents' wishes. The schools required them to only speak English, to choose an English name, and they were required to dress in American-style clothes.

Americanization the process of acquiring or causing a person to acquire American traits and characteristics

assimilate to absorb a group into the culture of another population

Looking Ahead

In these next lessons, you will learn about the causes and effects of the westward expansion of the United States. While studying this time period, you will understand the influence of the discovery of gold and silver and the expansion of the mining and ranching industries. You will learn about the lasting effects on Native Americans as new settlers moved onto their land. And you will examine how industrialization helped transform the United States into an economic power and how the new economy affected the lives of workers.

You will examine Compelling Questions in the Inquiry Lessons and develop your own questions about Migration, Industry, and Urban Society. Review the time line to preview some of the key events that you will learn about.

What Will You Learn?

In these lessons focused on the growth and development of the United States after the Civil War, you will learn:

- how the government backed western expansion through economic support.
- how new technology improved farming in the Great Plains.
- the key conflicts between Native Americans and the U.S. Army.
- the goals of the Americanization effort in the late nineteenth century.
- the factors and circumstances that fostered the development of an industrial economy.
- why forming unions was difficult.
- how immigration and the growth of cities affected the United States's society and politics.
- to identify the key individuals leading reform movements during this period of American history.
- how to describe the African American struggle for civil rights at the turn of the twentieth century.

? COMPELLING QUESTIONS

- **How were Native Americans affected by Americanization?**
- **How did Americans react to immigration?**
- **How did African Americans experience and resist segregation in the late nineteenth century?**

KEY EVENTS OF

MIGRATION, INDUSTRY, AND URBAN SOCIETY

1862
MAY AND JULY 1862 Homestead Acts and Morrill Land-Grant Act passes

NOVEMBER 29, 1864 Sand Creek Massacre

MAY 10, 1869 Transcontinental Railroad completed in Promontory Point, Utah

1875
JUNE 1876 Battle of Little Bighorn

1882 Standard Oil trust forms

MAY 4, 1886 Haymarket Riot

OCTOBER 28, 1886 Statue of Liberty dedicated in New York Harbor

1887 Congress passes the Dawes Act, affecting Native Americans across the nation, including Lakota leader Sitting Bull (right)

1889 Oklahoma Land Rush

JULY 1892 Homestead Strike

1894 Pullman Railroad Strike

1900
1900 AFL becomes the nation's largest union

1901 J. P. Morgan forms U.S. Steel

1912
1912 IWW leads strike of textile workers in Lawrence, Massachusetts

Everett Historical/Shutterstock.

Sequencing Time Identify the events that reveal workers' dissatisfaction and explain how these events reveal that dissatisfaction.

02

Miners, Ranchers, and Farmers Change the West

READING STRATEGY

Analyzing Key Ideas and Details As you read, use a graphic organizer like the one below to list the effects of mining and ranching on settlement, land, and people in the American West.

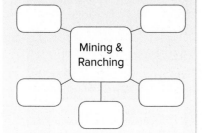

The Economic Lure of Mining

GUIDING QUESTION

How did mineral discoveries shape the settlement of the West?

Mining played an important role in the settling of the American West. Demand for minerals rose dramatically after the Civil War as the United States changed from a farming nation to an industrial nation. Mining also led to the building of railroads to connect the mines to factories in the east.

Boomtowns

In 1859 a prospector named Henry Comstock staked a claim near Virginia City, Nevada. When others found a rich source of minerals nearby, Comstock claimed he owned the land and quickly struck a deal to share the fortune. He later sold his claim for thousands of dollars, not realizing that the sticky, blue-gray clay that made mining in the area difficult was nearly pure silver ore worth millions. News of the Comstock Lode, as the strike came to be called, brought a flood of prospectors to Virginia City. The town grew from a few hundred people to nearly 30,000 in just a few months. So many people arrived that Nevada was admitted as the thirty-sixth state in the Union in 1864.

Quickly growing towns like Virginia City were called boomtowns. The term *boom* refers to a time of rapid economic growth. But as mines were used up, many boomtowns went "bust"—a term borrowed from card games in which players lost all their money. In Virginia City, for example, the silver mines were exhausted by the 1880s, and most residents moved on, leaving just a few hundred people behind. Other towns were completely abandoned and became ghost towns.

Mining Leads to Statehood

After gold was discovered in 1858 in Colorado near Pikes Peak, miners rushed to the area, declaring "Pikes Peak or Bust." The unsuccessful headed home, complaining of a "Pikes Peak hoax," but in truth, the Colorado mountains contained plenty of gold and silver hidden beneath the surface. Deep deposits of lead mixed with silver were found at Leadville in the 1870s, making Leadville one of the West's most famous boomtowns. This bonanza spurred the building of railroads through the Rocky Mountains and transformed Denver (the supply point for the mining areas) into the second-largest city in the West after San Francisco. Colorado became a state on August 1, 1876.

The discovery of gold in the Black Hills of the Dakota Territory and copper in Montana drew miners to the region in the 1870s, and when the railroads were completed, many farmers and ranchers settled the area. In 1889 Congress admitted three new states: North Dakota, South Dakota, and Montana. In the Southwest, the Arizona Territory followed a similar pattern. Miners had already begun moving to Arizona in the 1860s and 1870s to work one of the nation's largest copper deposits. When silver was found at the town of Tombstone in 1877, it set off a boom that lasted about 30 years. Arizona had enough people to apply for statehood by 1912, as did the neighboring territory of New Mexico.

Mining Helps Build a Nation 1848–1890

The discovery of gold and silver led to the growth of western territories.

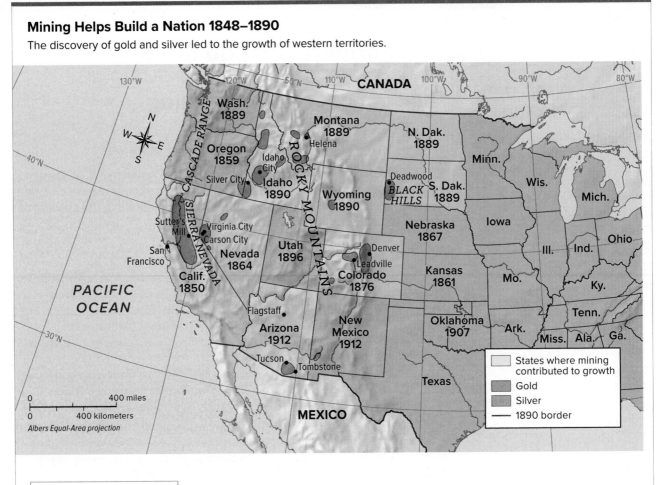

GEOGRAPHY CONNECTION

1. **Spatial Thinking** What is a likely reason Nevada and California were two of the first western territories to become states?

2. **Exploring Regions** Which two territories were the last to enter as states? Why might this have been the case?

Environmental Impacts of Mining

Early prospectors extracted shallow deposits of ore in a process called placer mining, using simple tools like picks, shovels, and pans. Other prospectors used a sluice to divert the current of a river into trenches, where the water was directed to a box with metal "riffle" bars that caused heavier minerals to settle to the bottom of the box. A screen at the end kept the minerals from escaping with the water and sediment.

When deposits near the surface ran out, miners began **hydraulic mining** to remove large quantities of earth and process it for minerals. Miners sprayed water at very high pressure against the hill or mountain they were mining. The water pressure washed away the dirt, gravel, and rock and exposed the minerals beneath the surface.

Hydraulic mining began in the Sierra Nevada mountains in California, generating millions of dollars in gold. However, it also devastated the local environment. Millions of tons of silt, sand, and gravel were washed into local rivers, raising the riverbed and causing rivers to overflow their banks. Flooding wrecked fences, destroyed orchards, and deposited rocks and gravel on what had been good farm soil, destroying thousands of acres of rich farmland.

In the 1880s, farmers fought back by suing the mining companies. In 1884 federal judge Lorenzo Sawyer ruled in favor of the farmers, declaring hydraulic mining a "public and private nuisance" and issuing an injunction stopping the practice. Congress eventually passed a law in 1893 allowing hydraulic mining if the mining company created a place to store the sediment. By then, most mining companies had moved to quartz

---

hydraulic mining method of mining by which water is sprayed at a very high pressure against a hill or mountain, washing away large quantities of dirt, gravel, and rock and exposing the minerals beneath the surface

mining, in which deep mine shafts are dug, and miners go underground to extract the minerals.

✓ CHECK FOR UNDERSTANDING

1. **Explaining** What role did mining play in the development of the American West?
2. **Identifying Cause and Effect** In what ways did hydraulic mining affect the western environment?

Cattle Drives and Southwest Settlement

GUIDING QUESTION

Why was cattle ranching an important business for the Great Plains?

The lure of the Great Plains brought other Americans west to herd cattle. The Texas longhorn, a cattle breed descended from Spanish cattle introduced two centuries earlier, was well adapted to this region and flourished on scarce water and tough prairie grasses. By 1865, some 5 million roamed the Texas grasslands. Another boon to cattle ranching was the open range, a vast area of grassland that the federal government owned. Here, ranchers could graze their herds free of charge and without breaching another's private property.

The Long Drive and the End of the Open Range

Prior to the Civil War, ranchers had little incentive to move cattle to market because beef prices were low and transporting to eastern markets was not practical. But during the war, cattle had been slaughtered in huge numbers to feed the armies of the Union and the Confederacy, causing beef prices to soar. Also, by this time, railroads had reached the Great Plains, heading to towns in Kansas and Missouri. Ranchers and livestock dealers realized that if they could move their cattle to the railroad, the longhorns could be sold for a huge profit and shipped east to market.

In 1866 ranchers rounded up about 260,000 longhorns and drove them to Sedalia, Missouri—the first "long drive." Other cattle trails soon opened, including the route to Abilene, Kansas, as the railroads expanded in the West. Cowboys from major ranches went north with the herds, which could number anywhere from 2,000 to 5,000 cattle.

Before long, sheep herders moved their flocks onto the range and farmers came in, breaking up the land for their crops. With the invention of barbed wire, hundreds of square miles of fields were eventually fenced cheaply and easily, thereby blocking the cattle trails. The cattle industry faced other struggles as prices plunged in the mid-1880s and many ranchers went bankrupt. In addition the harsh winter of 1886–1887

Stringo, Charles. *A Cowboy Detective.* Chicago: M.B. Conkey Company, 1912.

BIOGRAPHY

JUAN JOSÉ HERRERA (c. 1840s–1902?)

In New Mexico, residents of the town of Las Vegas were outraged when English-speaking ranchers tried to fence in land that had long been used by the community to graze livestock. In 1889 Juan José Herrera and two of his brothers organized a large group of Hispanos to fight back. Calling themselves *Las Gorras Blancas* ("The White Caps"), the secret organization raided ranches owned by English speakers, tore down their fences, and burned their barns and houses. Attempts were made to call in federal troops to stop the raids, but the president refused to send them. The raids finally ended in 1891.

"EL CAPITÁN" Herrera's followers called him "El Capitán" after his service as a captain in the Union Army during the Civil War. After the war, Herrera spent time working for the government as an Indian agent in several Western states. By the time he returned to New Mexico, Herrera spoke French, English, and several Native American languages. He entered politics in New Mexico and quickly gained a reputation as a labor organizer. Herrera never admitted his participation in Las Gorras Blancas, and though he was arrested, the charges were dropped.

Determining Central Ideas Why did Herrera help organize Las Gorras Blancas?

buried the Plains in deep snow, causing many cattle to freeze or starve to death. Although the cattle industry survived, it was changed forever. The era of the open range ended, and cowboys became ranch hands. From then on, herds were raised on fenced-in ranches.

New Southwestern Settlers

For centuries much of what is today the American Southwest belonged to Spain's empire. After Mexico won its independence, the region became the northern territories of the Republic of Mexico. When the United States defeated Mexico in 1848, it acquired this vast region. According to Articles VIII and IX of the Treaty of Guadalupe Hidalgo, which ended the war, the region's Hispanos, or descendants of Spanish settlers, retained their property and civil rights and could become American citizens. However, the promise of property protection was never fulfilled. Congress struck down Article X of the treaty, which guaranteed protection of Mexican land grants, and many states did not honor the spirit of the treaty.

This is what occurred in California. As the Spanish mission system collapsed in the early 1800s, the Mexican government issued land grants to distribute the mission lands to elite Hispano families. These land grants took the form of ranchos—ranches that covered large tracts of land. The Mexican government roughly marked the boundaries of each rancho on maps, but this lack of clear legal documentation created issues when California became a U.S. territory and then a state. In an effort to sort out Hispano land claims, Congress passed the California Land Act of 1851, which established a land claims commission. However the commission's proof-of-property requirements and high legal fees worked against the Hispanos. As the legal process dragged on for years, Hispanos were forced to sell off more and more of their land to pay legal fees, so that by the time their cases were settled, many had no land to claim.

Prior to this time, the Hispanos had a rich and vibrant culture that centered around the ranchos. Some elite families had hundreds of thousands of acres for raising cattle. They produced meat, hides, and tallow for making candles and soap. Both Native Americans and landless Hispanos worked the ranchos.

Then in 1849 a heavy influx of California gold rush "Forty-Niners" changed this society dramatically. California's population grew from about 14,000 to 100,000 in less than two years and its demographic pattern changed significantly. Suddenly, Hispanos were vastly outnumbered. Though Hispanos served in many state and local offices, when California achieved statehood in 1850 they found their status diminished and were often relegated to lower-paying jobs.

The cattle boom of the 1870s and 1880s also had a tremendous impact on Hispanos in the Southwest, where many had long worked as vaqueros (the Spanish word for "cowboys"). While they were called "Spanish," many vaqueros had both Spanish and Native American heritage or were Native American, African American, or multiracial. Spanish vaqueros had a long history of sharing their techniques for managing cattle. They shared methods of branding with Florida cattlemen as far back in history as when Florida was a Spanish colony. This interaction with American cowboys enriched the English language with such Spanish words as *lariat*, *lasso*, and *stampede*. The vaqueros also introduced Americans to foods such as barbacoa, or barbecue. But with the increasing demand for beef in the eastern United States, English-speaking ranchers wanted to expand their herds and claimed large tracts of land of Mexican origin.

Despite the influx of these English-speaking settlers, Hispanos in New Mexico remained more influential in public affairs than did their counterparts in California and Texas. Hispanos remained the majority, both in population and in the territorial legislature, and frequently served as New Mexico's territorial delegates to Congress.

As more railroads were built in the 1880s and 1890s the population of the Southwest continued to swell. The region attracted not only Americans and European immigrants from the East, but also immigrants from Mexico. Mexican immigrants worked mainly in agriculture and on the railroads. In the growing cities of the Southwest—such as El Paso, Albuquerque, and Los Angeles—many Hispanos settled in neighborhoods called **barrios**. These neighborhoods had Spanish-speaking businesses and Spanish-language newspapers, and they helped keep their cultural and religious traditions alive.

✓ CHECK FOR UNDERSTANDING

Summarizing Why was cattle ranching an important business for the Great Plains?

LESSON ACTIVITIES

1. **Argumentative Writing** Suppose that you are a farmer near Nevada City, California, in the 1880s. Write a letter explaining why hydraulic mining endangers your livelihood and should be banned.

2. **Using Multimedia** Work with a partner to create a multimedia presentation that shows how an influx of English-speaking settlers affected the lives of Hispanos in the Southwest during the mid- to late 1800s. You may include such features as photos, maps, music, or audio clips in your presentation.

barrio Spanish-speaking neighborhoods in a town

03

Western Pioneers and Native Americans

READING STRATEGY

Analyzing Key Ideas and Details As you read, use a graphic organizer like the one below to list the ways the government encouraged settlement in the Great Plains.

Assistance in Settling Great Plains

Adjusting to Life on the Plains

GUIDING QUESTION

What encouraged settlers to move west to the Great Plains?

The Great Plains and western prairies is a vast region located between the Mississippi River and east of the Rocky Mountains in the United States and Canada. Summer temperatures could top 100°F, and prairie fires were a frequent danger. Swarms of grasshoppers destroyed crops, and winter brought terrible blizzards and extreme cold. To get water, settlers had to drill wells more than 100 feet deep and operate the pump by hand.

Major Stephen Long, who explored the region with an army expedition in 1819, called the it the "Great American Desert." Long considered the Plains unfit for agriculture and said that the lack of wood and water would make it impossible for people to settle there.

During the late 1800s, railroad construction and development stimulated growth. Railroad companies sold land along the rail lines at low prices and provided credit to settlers. Pamphlets spread the news across Europe and America that cheap land could be claimed by anyone willing to move. Republicans and congressional representatives in the North viewed the settlement of the West as key to developing the new territories and driving economic growth.

In 1862 the government encouraged settlement on the Great Plains by passing the Homestead Act. For a small registration fee, an individual could file for a **homestead**—a tract of public land available for settlement. A homesteader could claim up to 160 acres of land and receive the title to it, which granted them full legal ownership, after living there for five years. For white and free African American settlers, the Act provided a legal method to acquire a clear title to property on the frontier. With property rights assured and railroads providing lumber and supplies, settlers began moving to the Plains in large numbers. By 1890, the federal government had granted 373,000 homesteads. In total the Homestead Act provided more than 270 million acres of land to claimants. Most claims, however, were granted to railroads, speculators, and those in the mining, lumber, and cattle industries.

Native Americans had a very different perspective on the Homestead Act. The legal aids to white and African American homesteaders did not apply to Native Americans. In fact, the act was designed to dispossess Native Americans of their lands. Congress chose to open reservation lands throughout the region, from the Indian Territory in present-day Oklahoma to the large Sioux and Chippewa lands in South Dakota and Minnesota, leaving Native Americans with no legal recourse to protect their lands. The Indian Wars of the late 1800s were, in large part, due to the influx of white settlers.

✓ **CHECK FOR UNDERSTANDING**

Analyzing What developments of the late 1800s attracted settlers to endure the hardships of the Great Plains?

---

homestead a piece of U.S. public land acquired by living on it and cultivating it

BIOGRAPHY

MARY FIELDS
(c. 1832–1914)

Mary Fields was an American postal worker who encouraged others to move to Montana in the late 1800s. She later became one of the most charismatic figures of the American West. Fields was born into slavery around 1832 in Tennessee. After the end of the Civil War, she moved to Toledo, Ohio, and began a lengthy friendship with Mother Amadeus and the Ursuline Convent.

ARRIVAL IN MONTANA In 1887 Fields moved to an area just outside Cascade, Montana, to work for Mother Amadeus, who had founded St. Peter's Catholic Mission School several years earlier. At about six feet in height, Fields was able to provide protection, chop firewood, drive supply wagons, and handle other maintenance work at the mission. Fields later opened several small businesses in the town of Cascade, including a restaurant and laundry service, but both ventures failed. Fields nonetheless earned the respect of the all-white town due to her generosity, determination, and work ethic.

THE STAR ROUTE In 1895 Fields was awarded a Star Route contract to deliver mail for the U.S. Postal Service between Cascade and the surrounding areas. Although not technically an employee of the U.S. Postal Service, Fields was the first African American woman ever to deliver mail. Dependable mail delivery was crucial both to the settlement and economic growth of the West and to the effective processing of land claims. In addition, the presence of the U.S. Postal Service in pioneer communities in the West established a direct link to the rest of the nation. Fields's reliability in delivering the mail, even in dangerous weather and terrain, earned her the nickname "Stagecoach Mary." She continued her work as a postal carrier into her 70s.

> **Identifying** What qualities did Mary Fields possess that made her a successful Star Route postal carrier?

New Farming Technology

GUIDING QUESTION

What new technology revolutionized agriculture and made it practical to cultivate the Plains?

The harsh, dry climate and densely packed soil of the Great Plains required new farming methods and technological innovations. One new method, called **dry farming,** was to plant seeds deep in the ground where there was enough moisture for them to grow. By the 1860s, Plains farmers were using steel plows, threshing machines, seed drills, and reapers, which made dry farming possible. Still, soil on the Plains could blow away during a dry season. As the population grew, the impact of the **sodbusters,** as those who plowed the Plains were called, changed the environment. Many farmers eventually lost their homesteads through the combined effects of drought, overuse of the land, and wind erosion of the soil.

Large landholders could buy mechanical reapers and steam tractors that made it easier to harvest a large crop. Threshing machines knocked kernels loose from the stalks, and mechanical binders tied the stalks into bundles for collection. These innovations were well suited for harvesting wheat, a crop that could endure the dry conditions of the Plains.

During the 1880s many farmers from the old Northwest Territory moved to the Great Plains to take advantage of the inexpensive land and the new technology. The Wheat Belt began at the eastern edge of the Great Plains and covered much of the Dakotas and parts of Nebraska and Kansas. The new machines allowed a family to bring in a substantial harvest on a wheat farm of several hundred acres. Some wheat farms covered up to 65,000 acres and were called **bonanza farms** because of the big profits they yielded. Like mine owners, bonanza farmers formed companies, invested in property and equipment, and hired laborers as needed.

Farmers Fall on Hard Times

Bountiful harvests in the Wheat Belt helped the United States become the world's leading exporter of wheat by the 1880s. But a severe drought struck the Plains in the late 1880s, destroying crops and ruining the soil. Competition from other wheat-producing nations increased at the same time. By the 1890s, a glut of wheat on the world market caused prices to drop.

Crop losses and degraded soil were partly due to weather and partly to farming methods. Plowing the soil year after year had depleted the nutrients needed

---

dry farming a way of farming dry land in which seeds are planted deep in the ground where there is some moisture

sodbuster a name given to Great Plains farmers

bonanza farm a large, highly profitable wheat farm

GRANGER.

PHOTO: Library of Congress Prints and Photographs Division [LC-USZ62-33975]; TEXT: Turner, Frederick J. 1921. The Frontier in American History. New York: Henry Holt and Company.

Farmers in South Dakota use steam to plow and seed a field in this 1907 photograph.

Drawing Conclusions How might this seed drill have changed the lives of these farmers?

for plant growth, resulting in a loss of native grasses necessary for maintaining the prairie ecosystems. These same agricultural practices would eventually bring about the Dust Bowl of the late 1920s and 1930s.

Some farmers tried to make it through these difficult times by mortgaging their land—borrowing money from a bank based on the value of their land. If they failed to meet their mortgage payments, they forfeited the land to the bank. Some who lost their land continued to work it as tenant farmers, renting the land from its new owners. By 1900, tenants cultivated about one-third of the farms on the Plains.

Closing the Frontier

On April 22, 1889, the government opened one of the last large territories for settlement. Within hours, thousands of people raced to stake claims in an event known as the Oklahoma Land Rush. The next year, the Census Bureau reported that there was no longer a true frontier left in America. In reality, the Homestead Act continued to encourage new settlement into the 1900s, but the "closing of the frontier" marked the end of an era. It worried many people, including historian Frederick Jackson Turner, who believed that the frontier had provided a "safety-valve of social discontent." It was a place where Americans could always make a fresh start. In the decades to follow, many Americans continued to go West to seek opportunities.

Most settlers did indeed make a fresh start, adapting to the difficult environment of the Plains. Water from their deep wells enabled them to plant trees and gardens. Railroads brought lumber and brick to replace sod as a building material, coal for fuel, and

manufactured goods from the East, such as clothes and household goods. Small-scale farmers rarely became wealthy but they could be self-sufficient. Typical homesteaders raised cattle, chickens, and a few crops. The real story of the West was about ordinary people who settled down and built homes and communities through great effort.

✓ **CHECK FOR UNDERSTANDING**

Identifying How did new technologies help improve settlers' ability to cultivate larger, more profitable farms?

The Struggle on the Plains

GUIDING QUESTION

Why did westward migration change the Native Americans' way of life?

For centuries the Great Plains were home to many groups of Native Americans. Some lived in farming and hunting communities, while others practiced a migration cycle following the seasonal movement of their animal herds and flora growth. The Native American nations on the Plains were divided into bands, ranging from a few dozen to several hundred people, who lived in extended family groups. Settlers who migrated to the Plains deprived these groups of their hunting grounds, broke treaties that had guaranteed Native Americans their own land, and often forced them to relocate. Native Americans resisted by attacking settlers' property and occasionally going to war with them.

The Dakota Uprising

In 1862 the Dakota people had a conflict with the settlers in Minnesota. The Dakota had agreed to live on a reservation in exchange for **annuities,** but the annuities frequently never reached them. At the time, many Dakota lived in poverty and faced starvation. When local traders refused to provide food on credit, the Dakota protested by launching a five-week-long rebellion that killed hundreds of settlers. A military tribunal sentenced more than 300 Dakota to death after the uprising. President Lincoln, after reviewing the evidence, reduced the number condemned to death to 38. Others fled the reservation when federal troops arrived and became exiles in a region bearing their name—the Dakota Territory. The military execution carried out on December 26, 1862, remains the largest mass execution in the history of the U.S. military and the largest mass execution of indigenous people in American history.

Red Cloud's War

The Dakota Territory was also home to the Lakota who had won control of their hunting grounds from other

annuity money paid by contract at regular intervals

Native Americans. Lakota leaders included Red Cloud, Crazy Horse, and Sitting Bull. In December 1866 the U.S. army was building forts along the Bozeman Trail, the path to the Montana gold mines. Crazy Horse tricked the fort's commander into sending Captain William Fetterman and about 80 soldiers to pursue what they thought was a small raiding party. Hundreds of waiting warriors wiped out Fetterman's troops, an event that became known as Fetterman's Massacre and marked the start of "Red Cloud's War." The Lakota continued to resist military presence in the region, and in 1868 the army abandoned its posts along the trail.

Sand Creek Massacre

In the 1860s, tensions rose between miners entering the Colorado territory in search of silver and gold and the Cheyenne and Arapaho who lived there. In the 1861 Treaty of Fort Wise, the Cheyenne and Arapaho gave up most of their land to the U.S. government in exchange for a smaller area to live on in southeastern Colorado, which bordered the waters of Sand Creek. Some Cheyenne and Arapaho refused to recognize this treaty.

As the number of settlers increased and encroached on Native American lands, renegade bands of Cheyenne and Arapaho raided wagon trains and ranches. By the summer of 1864, dozens of homes had been burned and an estimated 200 settlers killed. The governor gave an ultimatum that Native Americans either surrender at Fort Lyon or be subject to attack.

In November 1864, Cheyenne Chief Black Kettle brought several hundred Cheyenne to Fort Lyon to negotiate a peace deal. The fort's commander, Major Scott Anthony, allowed Black Kettle to make camp at nearby Sand Creek. Shortly afterward, Colonel John Chivington of the Colorado Volunteers attacked Black Kettle's camp.

Witnesses reported that the Cheyenne flew a white flag of truce at Black Kettle's camp to signal negotiations and that Chivington ignored the flag and attacked the unsuspecting Native Americans. Fourteen U.S. soldiers died during the two-day struggle. Estimates of the Native American warriors, women, and children slain vary from 69 to 600.

A Doomed Plan for Peace

As conflicts escalated, in 1867 Congress formed the Indian Peace Commission that proposed creating two large reservations on the Plains, one for the Lakota and Dakota and another for Native Americans of the southern Plains. Federal agents would run the reservations, and the army would deal with groups that refused to report or remain there. Although negotiators pressured Native American leaders into signing treaties, they could not ensure that leaders or their followers would abide by them. The Native Americans who did move to reservations faced many of the same conditions that drove the Dakota to violence—poverty, despair, and the corrupt practices of American traders.

✓ CHECK FOR UNDERSTANDING

1. **Explaining** How did the arrival of new settlers affect the Native American groups on the Great Plains?
2. **Summarizing** Why was the Indian Peace Commission's plan unsuccessful?

The Last Native American Wars

GUIDING QUESTION

Why did some Native Americans choose to leave the reservations?

By the 1870s, many Native Americans had left the reservations in disgust, frustrated by the restrictive treatment they received there. They wanted to return to the tradition of hunting buffalo on the open plains. The buffalo were rapidly disappearing, however, as professional buffalo hunters sought hides for markets in the East and other hunters killed for sport. When buffalo blocked rail traffic, the railroads killed them and fed the meat to workers. The army, determined to force Native Americans onto reservations, encouraged buffalo killing. By 1889, very few buffalo remained.

Battle of the Little Bighorn

In 1876 prospectors overran the Lakota reservation in the Dakota Territory to mine gold in the Black Hills—an area the Lakota considered the most sacred place on earth. They saw no reason to abide by a treaty that settlers were violating, so many left the reservation to hunt near the Bighorn Mountains in Montana. The government responded by sending an expedition accompanied by Lieutenant Colonel George A. Custer and the 7th Cavalry. Custer underestimated the fighting abilities of the Lakota and the Cheyenne. On June 25, 1876, he launched a three-pronged attack on one of the largest groups of Native American soldiers ever assembled on the Great Plains. The Native American forces rapidly defeated Custer's force of more than 200 soldiers, killing them all. Newspaper accounts that portrayed Custer as a victim of a massacre caused public outcry in the East, and the army stepped up its campaign on the Plains. Sitting Bull and his followers fled to Canada, but the other Lakota were forced to return to the reservation and give up the Black Hills.

Flight of the Nez Perce

Farther west, the Nez Perce people led by Chief Joseph refused to be moved to a smaller reservation in Idaho in 1877. When the army came to relocate them, they fled their homes and embarked on a journey of

Native American Battles and Reservations, 1860–1890

After military defeats, many Native Americans moved to reservations in different areas of the country.

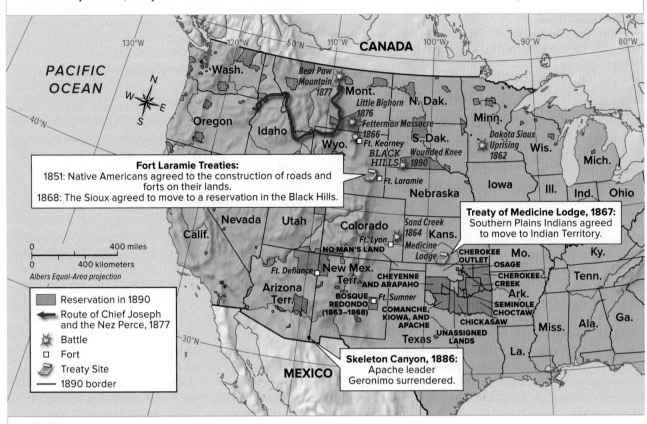

GEOGRAPHY CONNECTION

1. **Exploring Regions** In what region of the United States did a majority of battles occur between the settlers and the Native Americans during this time period?

2. **Human-Environment Interaction** From which state to which state did the Nez Perce travel in 1877? Through what other states did they pass?

---

more than 1,300 miles. In October 1877, Chief Joseph acknowledged that the struggle was over. He and his followers were then exiled to Oklahoma.

Tragedy at Wounded Knee

Native American resistance on the Lakota reservation came to a tragic end in 1890. Defying government orders, the Lakota continued to perform the Ghost Dance. The Ghost Dance was a ritual that provided a source of hope for many Lakota, who had suffered through decades of conquest, dispossession, and the loss of their culture and way of life. They believed that by acting out the ceremonies and songs, settlers would disappear, buffalo would return, and Native Americans would be reunited with their dead ancestors. In essence the Lakota would return to their traditional way of life before the American conquest.

Federal authorities had banned the ceremony, fearing it would lead to violence. They blamed the latest defiance on Sitting Bull, who had returned from Canada. The government sent police to arrest him. Sitting Bull's supporters tried to stop the arrest. In the exchange of gunfire that followed, Sitting Bull was killed and a group of Ghost Dancers fled the reservation. On December 29, 1890, as the U.S. 7th Cavalry was trying to disarm a large group of fleeing Lakota, fighting broke out at Wounded Knee Creek in South Dakota. Between 200 and 300 Lakota men, women, and children were slain by the 7th Cavalry troops, who employed the use of rapid-firing cannons. In addition, about 25 U.S. soldiers died in the conflict.

✓ **CHECK FOR UNDERSTANDING**

1. **Identifying Cause and Effect** What were the main reasons for Custer's defeat at the Battle of Little Bighorn?

2. **Determining Central Ideas** Why was the Ghost Dance so significant to the Lakota?

Americanization and the Dawes Act

GUIDING QUESTION

How did the effort to Americanize Native Americans hurt their connection to their cultural past?

Some Americans had long opposed the mistreatment of Native Americans. In her 1881 book *A Century of Dishonor*, Helen Hunt Jackson detailed the years of broken promises and injustices. Other Americans thought that Native Americans should be encouraged to abandon their traditional tribal culture and **assimilate** into American society by learning English, adopting American culture and values, and eventually becoming American citizens.

Beginning in the 1880s, the Bureau of Indian Affairs sponsored the creation of Indian boarding schools. In 1879 Richard Henry Pratt established the first Native American boarding school in Carlisle, Pennsylvania. By 1902, some 25 similar schools were open. Officials pressured Native American parents to send children to these schools, where they were required to speak English, choose an English name, cut their hair to match American styles, attend church, and learn vocational skills. Many believed this "Americanization" would save Native Americans from extinction. However, these schools were controversial. They were often underfunded, poorly maintained, and discipline was strict—including forcing students to give up their native language and names. The schools were often repressive, and cases of abuse were reported.

A second Americanization strategy encouraged Native Americans to abandon reservations and become independent landowners. In 1887 Congress passed the Dawes Act, altering the reservation system by dividing land into **allotments** for farming or ranching. Under the act, 160 acres were allotted to each head of household, 80 acres to each single adult, and 40 acres to each child. Any land remaining would be sold to American settlers, with the proceeds going into a trust for Native Americans. Citizenship would be granted to Native Americans who stayed on their allotments for 25 years.

While some Native Americans succeeded as farmers or ranchers, many had little training or enthusiasm for either. Finding their allotments too small to be profitable, they leased them. Many found themselves swindled out of land by federal agents, land speculators, and others. Some Native American groups had grown attached to their reservations and did not want to see them divided into homesteads. Few stayed long enough to qualify for citizenship.

The idea of Native American citizenship had been a goal of President Ulysses S. Grant. During his first term Grant appointed his friend Ely S. Parker, a member of the Seneca nation, as Commissioner of Indian Affairs. Grant and Parker set out to reform the federal government's harsh treatment of Native Americans and to work toward Native American assimilation. The Grant and Parker "Peace Policy," however, was undermined by Congress and others who disagreed with its policies.

Some American reformers disagreed with Dawes Act policies and supported Native American efforts to retain their autonomy and tribal-held lands. Thomas Bland helped found the National Indian Defense Association in the 1880s, arguing that allotments would hurt, rather than help, Native Americans.

The assimilation policy proved a dismal failure. Native American culture on the Plains depended on buffalo for food, clothing, fuel, and shelter. When the buffalo herds were wiped out, there was no way to sustain the traditional way of life. Although the Dawes Act failed in its goals, American reformers continued to advocate for assimilation. In the early 1900s, groups such as the Friends of the Indians and the Indian Rights Association began to push for citizenship for all Native Americans, believing it would encourage greater assimilation. Finally, in 1924 Congress passed the Citizenship Act, granting all Native Americans citizenship—though this was not something all Native Americans wanted, since it represented a violation of tribal sovereignty. In 1934 the Indian Reorganization Act reversed the Dawes Act's policy of assimilation. It restored some reservation lands to the control of Native Americans and allowed them to elect their own governments.

✓ CHECK FOR UNDERSTANDING

Cause and Effect What effect did Helen Hunt Jackson's book *A Century of Dishonor* have?

LESSON ACTIVITIES

1. **Argumentative Writing** Write an essay expressing your opinion about whether the "closing of the frontier" described by historian Frederick Jackson Turner was good or bad for the country.

2. **Presenting** Use the Internet or print resources and work with a partner to research a major conflict that took place between the U.S. government and Native American groups between the 1860s and 1900. Present an oral report to the class, describing the conflict and its impact on Native Americans.

---

assimilate to absorb a group into the culture of another population

allotment a plot of land assigned to an individual or a family for a specified use

04

Analyzing Primary Sources:
Americanizing Native Americans

 COMPELLING QUESTION

How were Native Americans affected by Americanization?

Plan Your Inquiry

In this lesson, you will investigate the effects of the policies that the U.S. government used to assimilate Native Americans into U.S. society.

DEVELOP QUESTIONS

Developing Questions About Assimilation Think about the definition of the word *assimilate*: to absorb a group into the culture of another population. What might happen to the groups that are absorbed? What elements of their own cultures might they be required to give up? Read the Compelling Question for this lesson. Then develop three Supporting Questions that could help you answer the Compelling Question for the lesson. Write these in a graphic organizer like the one below.

APPLY HISTORICAL TOOLS

Analyzing Primary Sources You will work with a variety of primary sources in this lesson. These sources focus on the treatment of Native Americans in the United States and the effects of Americanization. Use a graphic organizer like the one below to record and organize information about each source. Note the sources that answer each of your Supporting Questions and give details about each source.

Source	Supporting Questions	What does this source tell me about . . .	Questions the source leaves unanswered
A			
B			
C			
D			
E			
F			
G			
H			

After you analyze the sources, you will:
- use the evidence from the sources
- communicate your conclusions
- take informed action

patronizing treating people with an attitude of superiority

Background Information

Government programs to "civilize" Native Americans began in the early 1800s. In 1819 Congress passed the Civilization Fund Act, with the stated goals of teaching Native Americans "good moral character" through Christianity and providing basic education and vocational training.

In the late 1800s some Americans began to argue that the solution to the injustices experienced by Native Americans was "Americanization." They encouraged Native Americans to abandon their traditional culture and assimilate into American society. This belief resulted in boarding schools opening across the country designed to Americanize native children. Laws stipulated that children were to be enrolled by their parents voluntarily; however, many Native American children were forcibly removed from their homes.

Some of the efforts of the late 1800s were genuinely intended to improve conditions for Native Americans. However, white Americans tended to be **patronizing** toward Native Americans. While white Americans claimed to advocate on behalf of Native Americans, they believed it was their duty to help native peoples improve their culture. Much of the language in the following historical sources reflects a dismissive attitude toward Native Americans' ability to make wise choices. From a modern perspective, some of the language used is controversial.

» Three Lakota boys are "Americanized," 1883

(l)History and Art Collection/Alamy Stock Photo; (r)The Reading Room/Alamy Stock Photo.

A

The Goal of Americanization

By 1900, there were many boarding schools for Native American children across the United States. The purpose of the schools was to strip Native American children of their cultural identities and "Americanize" them. The schools offered vocational and other kinds of training, and required students to stop using their given names and drop their native languages and traditions. Most schools were modeled on the U.S. Training and Industrial School, founded in 1879 at Carlisle Barracks in Carlisle, Pennsylvania. The Carlisle School was created by Richard H. Pratt. His first students were 50 Cheyenne, Kiowa, and Pawnee children.

PRIMARY SOURCE: SPEECH

66 All who are interested in the Indian should honor the heroic work and the rugged eloquence of General Richard H. Pratt, better known as Captain Pratt, the founder and for a generation the honored head of the Carlisle Indian School, who, from East to West at meetings which were gathered to see and to listen to a group of the students from the Carlisle Industrial School proclaimed this doctrine: It has been said, 'There is no good Indian but a dead Indian;' I say to my students, 'Let us accept that statement. Let us kill the savage Indian in every tribesman, but save and develop the man that is in every Indian. By education and Christianization let us kill the old Indian and save the true man.' 99

—Merrill Gates, Board of Indian Commissioners, 1907

EXAMINE THE SOURCE

1. **Analyzing Text Presentation** Which phrases in the excerpt suggest that Americanization aimed to eliminate all elements of Native American culture?

2. **Inferring** What does the speaker see as the "true man" that resides within every Indian? Do you agree with this idea? Why or why not?

B

"Robinson Crusoe Making a Man of His Friday"

Robinson Crusoe is a novel written in 1719 by English novelist Daniel Defoe. The story is about Robinson Crusoe, a fictional sailor who is shipwrecked on an island for 28 years. While on the island, Crusoe rescues a native person who was captured by a group of cannibals. He names the man Friday because he saved him on a Friday. Crusoe vows to turn Friday into an English-speaking Christian. The cartoon below is a satirical usage of the novel's characters. Crusoe in the cartoon is President Ulysses S. Grant. Grant believed Native Americans should be U.S. citizens. Friday is a Native American. At the bottom right of the cartoon are a rake, a hoe, and a plow. Next to the plow is a book labeled "A B C." The quote on the wall says "By the sweat of thy brow shalt thou earn thy bread."

PRIMARY SOURCE: POLITICAL CARTOON

» *Harper's Weekly*, 1870, by Thomas Nast

EXAMINE THE SOURCE

1. **Determining Central Ideas** What do you think the rake, hoe, and plow in the cartoon are meant to symbolize? Why are the Native American weapons placed where they are?

2. **Inferring** Why does the cartoon portray the Native American as Friday?

PHOTO: Library of Congress Prints and Photographs Division (LC-USZ61-1912); TEXT: Gates, Merrill E. "Historical Address—Twenty-Five Years at the Lake Mohonk Indian Conference." *Proceedings of the Twenty-Fifth Annual Meeting of the Lake Mohonk Conference of Friends of the Indian and Other Dependent Peoples.* Lake Mohonk, NY: Lake Mohonk Conference, 1907.

(l)National Indian Association. "Some Infamous Facts Tersely Told." The Council Fire and Arbitrator 6:1, June 1883; (r)Eels, Myron: Ten Years of Missionary Work Among the Indians at Skokomish, Washington Territory, 1874-1884. Boston: Congregational Sunday-School and Publishing Society, 1886.

C

Pamphlet of the National Indian Defense Association

The *Council Fire and Arbitrator* was a monthly journal. According to the journal's masthead, it was "devoted to the civilization and rights of the American Indian, and the promotion of the principles of **arbitration** as a preventive of war between different nations." The June 1883 volume includes an excerpt from a pamphlet published by the National Indian Association.

PRIMARY SOURCE: JOURNAL

66 Among the following are some of the reasons why we should earnestly press the work of our association. Our national wrongs to Indians continue. Indians are still robbed. Still, as in the past, 'when the Indian's horses and cattle are big enough to be of service, they are driven off in herds by white renegades.' Indians are still 'removed.' Still, when their lands are coveted, they too are driven from home, though harvests are ready to garner, with the ruthless message that 'all the land in the State is required for its white settlers.' . . . Almost every **appropriation** made has been with the professed purpose of making the Indian self-supporting; yet he has been banished to wild reserves and required to farm where farming would be impossible even to white men, and still, though his arms and ammunition have been taken from him, so that he could not hunt, he has been forbidden to leave the reservation. If he would try lumbering he has been told, after the logs from his own land were ready for market, that the title to them remains in the Government. . . . 99

–*The Council Fire and Arbitrator*, Vol. VI, No. 6, June, 1883

arbitration the process of settling a dispute between two groups

appropriation the action of taking something for use without the owner's permission

EXAMINE THE SOURCE

1. **Analyzing** According to the source, what has the U.S. government forced Native Americans to do?
2. **Explaining** How does the author view the government's attempts at making Native Americans "self-supporting"?

D

A Missionary's View

Myron Eells's parents were missionaries who moved the family to Oregon in 1849. Eells graduated from seminary then led a church in Idaho before moving to the Skokomish Reservation in the state of Washington. He studied the languages and cultures of Native Americans in Washington and wrote many books.

PRIMARY SOURCE: BOOK

66 The Indians are in our midst. Different solutions of the problem have been proposed. It is evident that we must either kill them, move them away, or let them remain with us. . . .

One writer has proposed to move them to some good country . . . and leave it to them. We have been trying to find such a place for a century—have moved the Indians from one reservation to another, and from one State or Territory to another, but have failed to find the desired haven . . . It is more difficult to find it now than it ever has been, as Americans have settled in every part of the United States, and built railroads, telegraph lines and towns all over the country. . . .

Therefore the Indians are with us to remain. They are to be our neighbors. The remaining question is, Shall they be good or bad ones?

If we wish them to become good neighbors, something must be done. . . . People may call them savage, ignorant, superstitious and the like. . . . 'The remedy for ignorance is education;' . . . White people cannot *keep* the civilization which they already have without the school and the church; and Indians are not so much abler and better that they can be raised to become good neighbors without the same. 99

–Reverend Myron Eells, *Ten Years of Missionary Work Among the Indians at Skokomish, Washington Territory, 1874-1884*, 1886

EXAMINE THE SOURCE

1. **Analyzing** What is Eells's main argument?
2. **Understanding Perspectives** How does Eells's background reflect his point of view?

Ely Parker Letter

Ely S. Parker was a Seneca born on a Native American reservation in 1828. His name in the Seneca language was Do-ne-ho-ga-wa. Parker was well educated and successful in school. He wanted to be an attorney, but state law prevented noncitizens from practicing law. He became an engineer instead. He later served under General Ulysses S. Grant in the Civil War. When Grant became president, he appointed Parker as commissioner of Indian Affairs, a position he served in for two years.

» Ely S. Parker

PRIMARY SOURCE : LETTER

66 . . . To you though I will confess and you must not abuse or betray my confidence, that I have little or no faith in the American Christian civilization methods of [healing?] the Indians of this country. It has not been honest, pure or sincere. Black deception, damnable frauds and persistent oppression has been its characteristics, and its religion today is, that the only good Indian is a dead one. Guns stand, loaded to the muzzle, ready to prove this lie. Another creed under which the Indian is daily sinking deeper into the **quagmire** of oppression is, that 'might makes right,' and on it is based the **fallacy** transferred or transposed from the Negro to the Indian 'that the Indian has no rights which the white man is bound to respect.' . . . Misguided Indian philanthropists tell us that absorption of the aboriginal race into the great body politic is their only hope of salvation. I see nothing in the experiment but an accelerated motor for the absorption of the Indian race back into the bosom of Mother Earth. The only salvation for the Indians, and the only solution of the great Indian problem is to give them secular and industrial schools in abundance. This alone will perpetuate their life. There is land enough on this portion of God's footstool called America for the Indian and the white man to live upon side by side without jostling and exemplifying the Kilkenny cat game. The Indian wishes to be let alone in his wigwam. His good life is bound up and interwoven with his law, his women and his children.

Our wise legislators at Washington, the Indian Aid and the Indian Rights Associations are all advocating with a red hot zeal, the allotment and civilization schemes. Lastly come the Board of Indian Commissioners adding fuel to the existing fires, by telling us that the Indians are 'fast accepting the policy' that would make them responsible citizens. They say that 6000 Indians already hold allotments of lands in severalty and that not less than 75,000 more are asking for the same privilege. I do not believe in the sanctity or truth of the statement. The Indians, as a body, are deadly opposed to the scheme, for they see in it too plainly the certain and speedy dissolution of their tribal and national organizations. It is very evident to my mind that all schemes, to apparently serve the Indians, are only plausible pleas put out to hoodwink the civilized world that everything possible has been done to save this race from total annihilation, and to wipe out the stain on the American name for its treatment of the aboriginal population. . . . But I am writing an uncalled for thesis on Indian rights and wrongs, an almost inexhaustible theme, so I drop it since no good can result to continue it– Education to be made first above all. Other good things will follow. 99

—Ely S. Parker to Cousin Gayaneshaoh, c. 1885

quagmire a difficult position   **fallacy** mistaken idea

EXAMINE THE SOURCE

1. **Analyzing** What does Parker believe is the most important objective in addressing the plight of Native Americans in the United States?

2. **Contrasting** How does Parker's view of assimilation differ from that of the philanthropists?

PHOTO: War Department. Office of the Chief Signal Officer/U.S. National Archives and Records Administration; TEXT: Ely S. Parker Letter to Cousin Gayaneshaoh (Harriet Maxwell Converse), ca. 1885, MS 674, Folder 5, Ely Samuel Parker Papers, Newberry Library.

[(l)An Act to Provide for the Allotment of Lands in Severalty to Indians on the Various Reservations, and to Extend the Protection of the Laws of the United States and the Territories over the Indians, and for Other Purposes; Public Law 105, 49th Cong., 8 February, 1887; (r)Meriam, Lewis, et al. The Problem of Indian Administration: Report of a Survey Made at the Request of Honorable Hubert Work, Secretary of the Interior, and submitted to him, February 21, 1928. ERIC Document ED 087573. Baltimore: The Johns Hopkins Press, 1928.

F

Dawes Act

The Dawes General Allotment Act was enacted by Congress in February 1887. It designated some 138 million acres of land to be parceled out to select Native Americans to establish them as productive Native American farmers. Any remaining land after the distribution would be put up for sale to white Americans. Many of the act's supporters had good intentions, but the act had negative consequences. It weakened the social structure of native groups. Many native people lived in extreme poverty on the reservations. In addition, around two-thirds of the land set aside was eventually purchased by white Americans.

PRIMARY SOURCE : LAW

" **Sec. 6.** That upon the completion [of] said allotments and the patenting of the lands to said allottees, each and every [member] of the respective bands or tribes of Indians to whom allotments have been made shall have the benefit of and be subject to the laws, both civil and criminal, of the State or Territory in which they may reside; and no Territory shall pass or enforce any law denying any such Indian within its jurisdiction the equal protection of the law. And every Indian born within the territorial limits of the United States to whom allotments shall have been made under the provisions of this act, or under any law or treaty, and every Indian born within the territorial limits of the United States who has voluntarily taken up, within said limits, his residence separate and apart from any tribe of Indians therein, and has adopted the habits of civilized life, is hereby declared to be a citizen of the United States, and is entitled to all the rights, privileges, and immunities of such citizens, whether said Indian has been or not, by birth or otherwise, a member of any tribe of Indians within the territorial limits of the United States without in any manner affecting the right of any such Indian to tribal or other property. "

—Dawes General Allotment Act of 1877

EXAMINE THE SOURCE

Identifying the Main Idea What is the main purpose of Section 6 of the Dawes Act?

G

The Problem of Indian Administration

Authors of this report, issued in February 1928 at the request of the Secretary of the Interior, traveled for seven months and visited some 95 reservations, schools, and hospitals in Native American communities. The report details the economic, educational, and health conditions of Native American populations, and makes recommendations for addressing the issues.

PRIMARY SOURCE : GOVERNMENT REPORT

" The poverty of the Indians and their lack of adjustment to the dominant economic and social systems produce the vicious circle . . . The only course is to state briefly the conditions found that are part of this . . . cycle of poverty and maladjustment.

. . . Although accurate mortality and morbidity statistics are commonly lacking, the existing evidence warrants . . . that both the general death rate and the infant mortality rate are high.

. . . With . . . few exceptions the diet of the Indians is . . . generally insufficient in quantity, lacking in variety, and poorly prepared. The two great preventive elements in diet, milk, and fruits and green vegetables, are notably absent. Most tribes use fruit and vegetables in season, but even then the supply is . . . insufficient.

. . . In justice to the Indians it should be said that many . . . are living on lands from which a trained and experienced white man could scarcely wrest a reasonable living. . . . Often when individual allotments were made, they chose . . . the poorer parts, because those parts were near a domestic water supply or a source of firewood, or because they furnished some native product . . . Frequently the better sections of the land originally set apart for the Indians have fallen into the hands of the whites, and the Indians have retreated to the poorer lands remote from markets. "

—*The Problem of Indian Administration*, 1928

EXAMINE THE SOURCE

Analyzing Points of View According to the authors, what factors contributed to lack of success at farming among Native Americans?

Student Life at Carlisle School

The excerpt below was written by the daughter of a man who had been a student at the Carlisle School. Luana Mangold describes her father's experience at the school as positive and the skills he learned as beneficial to his later life and success. But the successes achieved by some came at a cost. This excerpt describes how the school administration often relied on punishment as a tool to discourage unwanted behavior, such as following cultural traditions.

PRIMARY SOURCE: ORAL HISTORY INTERVIEW

66 You had to speak English all the time. If you were caught speaking your other, you know, something else, you were punished. Because I can remember Dad saying that they used to—he'd have to sneak over to so-and-so's place to talk with him or cook up something, you know. But they kind of made it a point to not let any little cliques of different groups start. They'd really keep it down.

I know that some of the effect was to ridicule people that insisted on talking their own language at the school. . . .

But I know, especially in the beginning, you weren't allowed to be with anybody that you could just talk your own language to. They separated them out like that. . . .

Because these students were only going to be there, say three to five years, and you can imagine to accomplish a change that they wanted to accomplish, that really took a lot of work, you know, on the part of the teachers and the students to absorb all this. And the only way you can do it is pushing, pushing through, you know. You're not going to take each one and coddle them. 99

—Luana Mangold, January 19, 1981

EXAMINE THE SOURCE

1. **Analyzing Text** Do you think Mangold views the school as successful? Explain your answer.

2. **Inferring** What methods does the writer say were used in the school? How would those methods be viewed in an educational setting today?

Your Inquiry Analysis

EVALUATE SOURCES AND USE EVIDENCE

Reflect back to the Compelling Question and the Supporting Questions you developed at the beginning of this lesson.

1. **Gathering Sources** Which sources helped you answer the Compelling Question and your Supporting Questions most directly? What other perspectives might reveal more information about the subject of Americanization? Where might you look to find that information?

2. **Evaluating Sources** Looking at the sources that helped you answer your Supporting Questions, evaluate the viewpoints of each source. What details made each source useful for answering each question? How do the sources differ in the information provided?

3. **Comparing and Contrasting** Compare and contrast two of the sources in this lesson more closely. Choose two that present opposing perspectives on Americanization. What details show the source's point of view? Which arguments are most compelling? Explain your answer.

COMMUNICATE CONCLUSIONS

Presenting Work with a partner to compare the Supporting Questions each of you wrote at the beginning of the lesson. Choose three of these Supporting Questions to answer using the sources. Then, prepare a short multimedia presentation on how the sources helped you answer the Supporting Questions you chose. Consider including quotes from the sources in your presentation. Give your presentation in front of your classmates.

TAKE INFORMED ACTION

Creating a Slide Show Think about an issue today in which the United States is benefiting from something that is considered controversial by some people, such as maintaining trade relationships with countries that have human rights issues or violations. What are the opposing arguments for each side in the controversy? Put together an educational slide show that presents facts and arguments for both sides.

Mangold, Luana. "Interview with Helen Norton." Carlisle Indian School Oral Oral History Project. January 19, 1981.

05
Industrialization

READING STRATEGY

Analyzing Key Ideas and Details As you read about the changes industrialization brought to the United States, complete a graphic organizer like the one below, noting the causes of industrialization.

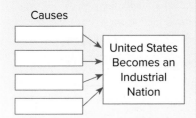

Industrial Advantages

GUIDING QUESTION

What conditions existed in the United States that helped industrialization?

Although the First Industrial Revolution reached the United States in the early 1800s, most Americans still lived on farms when the Civil War began. After the war, industry rapidly expanded into a Second Industrial Revolution, which was characterized by increased technology. Millions of Americans left their farms to work in mines and factories. By the early 1900s, the United States was the leading industrial nation. Its **gross national product** (GNP) was roughly three times what it had been in the late 1860s.

Natural Resources

The United States' industrial success was driven by its vast natural resources, including timber, coal, iron, and copper. This allowed American companies to obtain resources cheaply without importing them. Many of these resources were located in the American West, and Western settlement helped accelerate industrialization, as did the transcontinental railroad. Railroads took settlers and miners to the West and carried resources back to the East.

People also began using a new resource: petroleum. Even before the automotive age, petroleum was in high demand because it could be turned into kerosene, a fuel used in lanterns and stoves. The American oil industry began in western Pennsylvania, where residents had long noticed oil bubbling to the surface of area springs and streams. In 1859 Edwin Drake drilled the first oil well near Titusville, Pennsylvania, and by 1900, oil fields had been drilled from Pennsylvania to Texas. As oil production rose, it fueled economic expansion.

A Large Workforce

The work force available to American industry was just as important for industrialization. Between 1860 and 1910. the population of the United States nearly tripled. This population growth provided industry with a large workforce and created greater demand for consumer goods.

Population growth arose from three sources: a sharp increase in immigration, better living conditions, and longer lifespans. Better living conditions allowed more children to survive to adulthood and adults to live longer. At the same time, social and economic conditions in parts of Europe and China led to a sharp increase in immigrants to the United States searching for better lives. Between 1870 and 1910, more than 17 million immigrants arrived.

Electric Power

New inventions and technology increased the nation's productivity, improved transportation and communication, and led to new industries that produced more wealth and jobs. Thomas Alva Edison, a great innovator, and his company invented new products and improved existing inventions. Edison first achieved international fame in 1877 with the invention of the phonograph and later perfected the electric generator and the light bulb. His laboratory invented or improved many devices, including the battery and the motion

---

gross national product the total value of goods and services produced by a country during a year

Natural Resource Sites of the United States

A wealth of natural resources helped fuel U.S. industrialization.

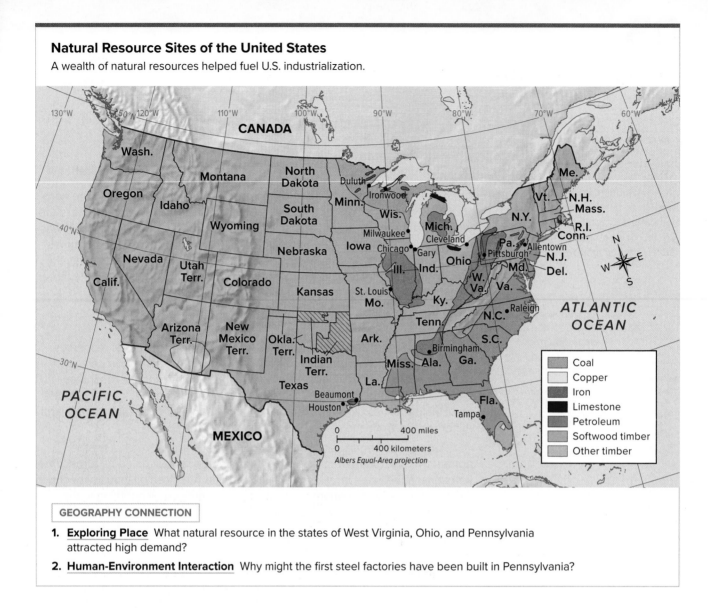

GEOGRAPHY CONNECTION

1. **Exploring Place** What natural resource in the states of West Virginia, Ohio, and Pennsylvania attracted high demand?
2. **Human-Environment Interaction** Why might the first steel factories have been built in Pennsylvania?

picture. In 1882 Lewis Latimer, who worked for Edison, invented a process for making cheap long-lasting carbon filaments for light bulbs. With this, electric lighting became increasingly affordable. In 1889 several Edison companies merged to form the Edison General Electric Company (known today as GE).

George Westinghouse developed an alternating current (AC) system to distribute electricity over long distances using transformers and generators. City streets became safer as streetlights were installed. Electric trolley cars improved commute times to work, and new electric devices made domestic chores easier. AC current and transformers are still used today. In 1866 Cyrus Field laid a telegraph cable across the Atlantic Ocean and enabled faster communication between the United States and Europe. In 1874 Alexander Graham Bell began experimenting with ways to transmit sound via an electric current. In 1876 he succeeded. A year later he founded the Bell Telephone Company, which eventually became the American Telephone and Telegraph Company (AT&T). The telephone transformed communications. Businesses

could place orders more quickly and receive news sooner that might shape their choices for better decision making.

Standard of Living Improvements

Technology improved the standard of living. Shortly after the Civil War, Thaddeus Lowe invented an ice-making machine, allowing low-cost ice year-round for ice boxes that kept food fresh. In the early 1870s, Gustavus Swift hired an engineer to develop a refrigerated railroad car. Swift shipped the first refrigerated load of fresh meat in 1877. The widespread use of refrigerated shipping containers enabled fresh food, especially meat, to be shipped long distances year round. As a result, the price of food began to drop, and the quality of food people could obtain improved dramatically.

The rapid pace of innovation continued through the late 1800s. In 1873 Christopher Scholes invented the typewriter. In 1886 Josephine Cochrane developed the automatic dishwasher. In 1888 George Eastman patented the first handheld camera. In 1893 Frank and Charles Duryea built the first gasoline powered carriage. Power-driven sewing machines and cloth cutters rapidly moved the clothing business from small tailor shops to large factories. Similar changes took place in shoemaking. Large factories began using new processes and inventions to mass-produce shoes efficiently and inexpensively and passed the savings on to their customers in the form of lower prices. By the early 1900s, tailors and cobblers had nearly disappeared. The prices of many products dropped as the United States industrialized.

✓ CHECK FOR UNDERSTANDING

1. **Analyzing** In addition to inventing things, how else did Edison and his company contribute to technological progress?

2. **Making Connections** What innovation greatly expanded the usefulness of electricity? How?

Creating Big Business

GUIDING QUESTION

What advantages did large corporations have during this industrialization period?

By 1900, big business operating vast complexes of factories dominated the economy. The **corporation,** which spread out risk among many stockholders, made big business possible. Corporations sold stock to finance the business. Few corporations existed before the 1830s because entrepreneurs had to sway state legislatures to issue them charters. In the 1830s states began allowing companies to become corporations and issue stock without a charter.

With the money raised from selling stock, corporations could invest in new technologies, hire large workforces, and purchase machines. They efficiently moved raw materials for production and achieved **economies of scale,** in which the cost of manufacturing is decreased by producing goods quickly in large quantities. Large-scale production of products had been increasing in the United States since the late 1790s, when Eli Whitney explored the idea of interchangeable parts to produce his cotton gin, and later, guns. The concept of interchangeable parts involves machines making large quantities of identical parts that could then be assembled to create a finished product. Whitney's ideas, and those of others,

moved the manufacturing process from individual skilled craft workers toward an automated process of unskilled workers performing repetitive construction with finely created identical components.

Big corporations had several advantages. They could produce more goods at a lower cost and could stay open in bad economic times by cutting prices to increase sales. Railroad rebates further lowered their operating costs. This led to one of the major costs of **laissez-faire** (leh•say•FAYR), economics: small businesses, many family-owned, that could not compete with large corporations were forced out of business. Laissez-faire is a French phrase meaning "let people do as they choose."

Consolidating Industry

Although a laissez-faire economy benefited **consumers** because the intense competition led to falling prices, business leaders did not like the competition. Cutting prices to beat the competition also cut into profits. However, with no regulations governing their competition, companies were free to make deals with each other to fix prices by organizing pools, or agreements to keep prices at a certain level. American courts and legislatures were suspicious of pools because they interfered with competition and property rights. As a result, even though companies could legally fix prices, they had no legal protection and could not enforce their pool agreements in court. Pools generally broke apart whenever one member cut prices to steal market share from another.

Carnegie and Rockefeller

Andrew Carnegie, a Scottish immigrant, started working in a textile factory at the age of 12. Working his way up through the ranks, he became the superintendent of the Pennsylvania Railroad. Carnegie bought shares in iron mills and factories that made sleeping cars and railroad locomotives, as well as a company that built railroad bridges. By his early 30s, he quit his job to concentrate on his investments. Through his business activities, he met Sir Henry Bessemer, who had invented a new process to make high quality steel efficiently and cheaply. After meeting Bessemer, Carnegie opened a steel mill in Pittsburgh in 1875 and began using the Bessemer process.

To make his company more efficient, Carnegie began the vertical integration of the steel industry. A vertically integrated company owns all of the different businesses on which it depends for its operation.

---

corporation an organization that is authorized by law to carry on an activity but treated as though it were a single person

economies of scale the reduction in the cost of a good brought about by increased production at a given facility

laissez-faire economic philosophy that government should interfere as little as possible in a nation's economy

consumer a person who buys what is produced by an economy

Instead of paying companies for coal, lime, and iron, Carnegie's steel company bought coal mines, limestone quarries, and iron ore fields. Vertical integration saved money and enabled many companies to expand.

Successful business leaders also frequently pushed for horizontal integration, which combined firms in the same type of business into one large corporation. When a company began to lose market share, it would often sell out to competitors to create a larger organization. John D. Rockefeller achieved an almost completely horizontal integration of the oil industry through a series of buyouts. By 1880, the company controlled about 90 percent of the oil refining industry in the United States. When a single company achieves control of an entire market, it becomes a **monopoly.**

✓ CHECK FOR UNDERSTANDING

Determining Central Ideas What factors give large corporations an advantage over small businesses?

New Business Organizations

GUIDING QUESTION

What new organizational methods were used at this time to help business success?

Many Americans feared monopolies because they believed that a monopoly could charge whatever it wanted for its products. They argued that one cost of laissez-faire economics was that it allowed the creation of large powerful corporations that could control prices and manipulate politicians and laws to ensure that they did not face any new competition.

Supporters of laissez-faire disagreed. They asserted that monopolies had to keep prices low because high prices could allow competitors to reappear with lower prices. In an effort to stop the rise of monopolies, many states made it illegal for one company to own stock in another company in the late 1800s. However companies formed trusts to get around these laws. A **trust** is a legal arrangement that allows one person to manage another person's property. The person who manages that property is called a trustee. Stockholders gave their stocks to a group of trustees, who awarded them with shares of the trust and a portion of the trust's profits. Trustees managed the stock but did not own it and could control a group of companies as if they were one merged company.

In 1889 New Jersey further accelerated the rise of big business with a new incorporation law. This allowed

corporations set up in New Jersey to own stock in other businesses. Many companies immediately used this to create holding companies. A **holding company** does not produce anything, but instead owns the stock of companies that do produce goods, effectively merging them into one large enterprise.

Investment bankers specialize in helping companies issue stock. Companies sell large blocks of stock to investment bankers at a discount, who would then find **investors** and sell the stock for a profit. Perhaps the most successful investment banker was J.P. Morgan. After years of trying to buy Carnegie Steel, J.P. Morgan bought out Andrew Carnegie in 1901 and renamed it U.S. Steel. Within a few years, U.S. Steel was the first billion-dollar business in the United States.

Selling the Product

The vast array of products led retailers to look for new ways to attract consumers. N. W. Ayer and Son, the first advertising company, pioneered the use of large illustrated ads, and by 1900, retailers were spending more than $90 million a year on advertising in newspapers and magazines. Advertising drew readers to the newest retail business: the department store. In 1877 advertisements billed John Wanamaker's new Philadelphia department store, the Grand Depot, as the "largest space in the world devoted to retail selling on a single floor." Soon many department stores offered a huge selection of products. Chain stores, a group of retail outlets owned by the same company, first appeared in the mid-1800s. Chains, such as Woolworth, focused on offering low prices.

To reach the millions who lived in rural areas, retailers began issuing mail-order catalogs. Two of the largest mail-order retailers were Montgomery Ward and Sears, Roebuck and Co. They used attractive illustrations and appealing descriptions to advertise thousands of items for sale.

 CHECK FOR UNDERSTANDING

Describing What is the purpose of a holding company?

The Railroads

GUIDING QUESTION

How did the transcontinental railroad help the country's economic development?

In 1865 the United States had about 35,000 miles of railroad track, almost all of it east of the Mississippi

---

monopoly total control of a type of industry by one person or one company

trust a combination of firms or corporations formed by a legal agreement, especially to reduce competition

holding company a company whose primary business is owning a controlling share of stock in other companies

investor one who puts money into a company in order to gain a future financial reward

Wanamaker, John. Quoted in Morris, Charles. The Tycoons. New York: Henry Holt and Company, 2005.

River. After the Civil War, railroad construction expanded dramatically. By 1900, the United States had more than 200,000 miles of track.

The Transcontinental Railroad

The railroad boom continued in 1862 with the Pacific Railway Act. This act gave two corporations—the Union Pacific and the Central Pacific—permission to build a transcontinental railroad. It also offered each company land along its right-of-way.

The Union Pacific Railroad began pushing westward from Omaha, Nebraska, in 1865. Railroad workers of the Union Pacific included miners and farmers, cooks, Civil War veterans, Irish immigrants, adventurers, and ex-convicts. At its project's height, the Union Pacific employed about 10,000 workers. The Central Pacific Railroad began as the dream of engineer Theodore Judah. He sold stock in his fledgling Central Pacific Railroad Company to four Sacramento merchants: Leland Stanford, Charley Crocker, Mark Hopkins, and Collis P. Huntington. These "Big Four" eventually made huge fortunes. Because of a shortage of labor in California, the Central Pacific Railroad hired about 10,000 workers from China. It paid them about $1 a day. All the equipment—rails, cars, locomotives, and machinery—was sent by ship from the eastern United States to San Francisco.

Workers completed the transcontinental railroad in only four years, despite many challenges. The Central Pacific laid a total of 688 miles of track. The Union Pacific laid 1,086 miles. On May 10, 1869, hundreds of spectators at Promontory Summit, Utah, watched as dignitaries hammered five gold and silver spikes into the rails that joined the Union Pacific and Central Pacific.

Railroads Spur Growth

The transcontinental railroad was the first of many lines built to connect the nation after the Civil War. Railroads increased the markets for many products, spurring industrial growth. Railroad companies stimulated the economy by spending huge amounts of money on steel, coal, timber, and other materials. Building railroad lines often required more money than private investors could raise on their own.

Federal Land Grants to Railroads

From 1870 to 1890, the railroads added more than 100,000 miles of track.

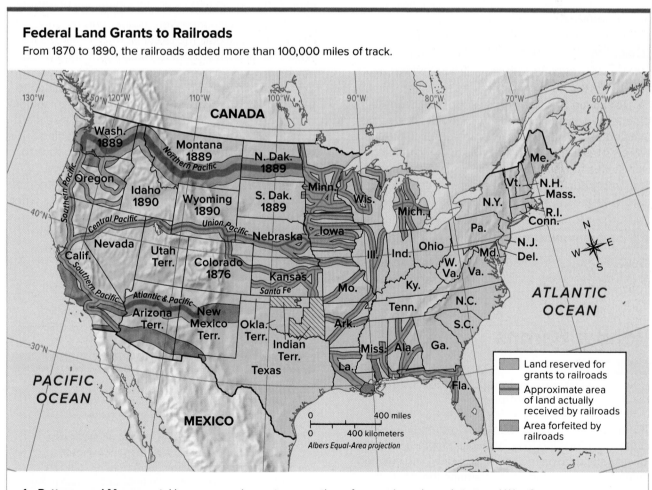

1. **Patterns and Movement** How many major routes were there for people and goods to travel West?

2. **Human-Environment Interaction** How did the locations of federal land grants to railroads influence the growth of the West?

To encourage railroad construction across the Great Plains, the federal government gave **land grants** to many railroad companies. The railroads then sold the land to settlers, real estate companies, and other businesses to raise money to build the railroad. During the 1850s and 1860s, the federal land grant system gave railroads more than 120 million acres of public land, an area larger than New England, New York, and Pennsylvania combined. Several railroads, including the Union Pacific and Central Pacific, received enough land to cover most of the cost of building their lines.

The expansion of railroad networks had an enormous economic impact, especially after the standardization of track gauge—the width of the tracks. During the Civil War, Union and Confederate forces discovered the difficulties of using lines with different track gauges as they tried to move their troops across different networks. Beginning in the 1860s, most railroads began shifting to a standard gauge, increasing efficiency and enabling businesses to ship goods to wider markets across the continent. Efficient transportation and increased mechanization created the conditions to produce and distribute goods on a mass scale cheaply and efficiently. To increase efficiency even more, in 1883 U.S. railroads began using four time zones to better coordinate scheduling: Eastern, Central, Mountain, and Pacific. The U.S. government would officially adopt the practice in 1918.

To reduce the risks of train accidents, Granville T. Woods, an African American inventor, developed the Synchronous Multiplex Railway Telegraph in the 1880s. Woods's telegraph enabled trains to communicate with stations along the lines and with other trains. Station conductors and train engineers could know exactly where trains were at all times.

✓ CHECK FOR UNDERSTANDING

Explaining Besides opening new markets, how did the construction of railroads stimulate the economy?

Robber Barons

GUIDING QUESTION

How did the government grants to build railroads result in large-scale corruption?

The great wealth many railroad entrepreneurs gained in the late 1800s led to accusations that they swindled investors and taxpayers, bribed officials, and cheated on their contracts and debts. Perhaps the most notoriously corrupt railroad owner was Jay Gould, who

practiced "insider trading" and manipulated stock prices. Bribery occurred because the government was so deeply entangled in funding the railroads. Railroad investors discovered they could make more money by selling free government land grants than by operating a railroad—some bribing political representatives to vote for more grants. Corruption in the industry became public in 1872 with the Crédit Mobilier scandal. Crédit Mobilier was a construction company set up by several stockholders of the Union Pacific Railroad, including Oakes Ames, a member of Congress. To convince Congress to give the railroad more grants, Ames sold other members of Congress shares at prices well below their market value.

During the election campaign of 1872, a letter appeared in the *New York Sun* listing members of Congress who had bought shares. The scandal caused widespread anger and led to the impression that railroad entrepreneurs were "robber barons." The term "robber baron" is from the Middle Ages. Like the robber barons of past, railroad robber barons of America's Gilded Age engaged in unethical business practices. Most tried to monopolize their industries through often corrupt methods. Robber barons often exploited workers and customers in pursuit of fortune.

Not all railroad men were robber barons. James J. Hill was not. Hill built the Great Northern Railroad from Wisconsin and Minnesota to Washington state without any federal land grants or subsidies. He acquired existing rail lines and planned railroad construction to pass by existing towns. He offered low fares to settlers who homesteaded along his route. He also identified products that were in demand in China, including cotton, textiles, and flour, and hauled those goods to Washington to ship to Asia. This way his railroad efficiently hauled goods both east and west instead of sending goods east and coming back empty like other railroads. The Great Northern became the most successful transcontinental railroad and one of the few that was not eventually forced into bankruptcy.

✓ CHECK FOR UNDERSTANDING

Summarizing Why did robber barons bribe people in Congress?

LESSON ACTIVITIES

1. **Informative/Explanatory Writing** Write several paragraphs explaining how the growth of the railroad influenced settlement patterns.

2. **Presenting** With a group, design and present a product that could have been manufactured, marketed, and sold from 1850 to 1900. Conduct research to ensure it could have been made using the technology of the time.

---

land grant a grant of land by the federal government especially for roads, railroads, or agricultural purposes

Big Business and Unions

READING STRATEGY

Analyzing Key Ideas and Details As you read about big business and unions, complete a graphic organizer like the one below to record key events in business regulation and union activities.

Business Regulation	Union Activities

Free Enterprise vs. Business Regulations

GUIDING QUESTION

What factors led to the United States industrializing?

One important reason the United States industrialized rapidly was the nation's free enterprise system. The profit motive attracted many ambitious people. **Entrepreneurs**—people who risk their capital in organizing and running a business—believed they could make money in industry. Foreign investors from Europe also saw great opportunities for profit in the United States.

Part of what attracted entrepreneurs was government's support for the idea of laissez-faire. Supporters of laissez-faire believe that the government should not interfere in the economy except to protect private property rights and maintain peace. They argue that government regulations increase costs.

In many ways, the United States practiced laissez-faire economics in the late 1800s. State and federal governments kept taxes and spending low and did not impose costly regulations or control wages and prices. The United States was also one of the largest free trade areas in the world, unlike Europe, which was divided into dozens of countries, each with tariffs. However, the government did not follow laissez-faire in everything.

Since the early 1800s, Northern leaders wanted high tariffs to protect manufacturers from foreign competition and supported federal subsidies for companies building roads, canals, and railroads. Southern leaders opposed subsidies and favored low tariffs to promote trade and to keep the cost of imported goods low. After the Southern states seceded, the Republican-controlled Congress passed the Morrill Tariff, nearly tripling tariff rates. In the early 1900s, business leaders began to push for free trade. They believed they could now compete internationally and win sales in foreign markets.

New Federal Government Laws

Some of the most visible and long-lasting efforts to regulate business were focused at the national level. Congress passed a number of proposals to regulate the economy under the presidential administrations of Theodore Roosevelt, William Howard Taft, and Woodrow Wilson. Many progressives agreed that big business needed regulation, and some believed the government should break up big companies to restore competition. This led to the passage of the Sherman Antitrust Act in 1890.

Others argued that big business was the most efficient way to organize the economy, but they pushed for government to regulate big companies and prevent them from abusing their power. The Interstate Commerce Commission (ICC), created in 1887 to regulate the railroads, was an early example of this kind of thinking. The ICC grew out of the concern that states did not have the power to regulate railroads, since railroads crossed state lines. This concern was based on the 1886 Supreme Court decision in *Wabash, St. Louis & Pacific Railroads* v. *Illinois*. The state of Illinois had taken the railroad to court, arguing that it violated Illinois state law by charging one shipper more than another to transport goods between Illinois and New York. The lower court ruled in the state's favor. The Supreme Court, however, ruled against Illinois, arguing that the railroad was transporting goods across state lines, which made it interstate

entrepreneur one who organizes, manages, and assumes the risks of a business or enterprise

PHOTO: GL Archive/Alamy Stock Photo; TEXT: U.S. Constitution. 1789. Washington, D.C.: National Archives and Records Administration.

MADAM C. J. WALKER (1867–1919)

Entrepreneur Madam C. J. Walker was one of the first African American women in the United States to become a millionaire. Walker was born Sarah Breedlove on December 23, 1867, on the Louisiana cotton plantation where her parents were enslaved before the Emancipation Proclamation. She was the first child in the family born into freedom. Orphaned at 7, married at 14, and widowed at 20, she moved to St. Louis, Missouri, with her young daughter to be close to her two older brothers, who were barbers.

BUSINESS While in St. Louis, Walker worked as a washerwoman and attended night school. She later became a sales agent for the Poro Company, an African American haircare company begun by Annie Turnbo. Plagued by a scalp condition that was causing her to lose her hair, Walker began working on a remedy of her own when available products proved ineffective. After moving to Denver, Colorado, she married Charles J. Walker and began selling her products directly to African American woman under her married name, Madam C. J. Walker. Madam Walker sold her products through agents she called "beauty culturists." Walker eventually headquartered her successful manufacturing company in Indianapolis, Indiana. Over time, she expanded her business, eventually employing thousands of beauty culturists and selling her products internationally.

PHILANTHROPY Walker was committed to providing jobs for African American women. She encouraged her employees to engage in philanthropic and educational efforts. Walker led by example, donating money to scholarship funds, orphanages, and other causes such as the African American Young Men's Christian Association in Indianapolis. Walker died at the age of 51, but her legacy lived on through her daughter and her philanthropic endeavors.

Analyzing How did Madam C. J. Walker show her entrepreneurial spirit?

commerce. Blocked at the state level, progressives turned to the federal government for regulation.

Some activists even went so far as to advocate socialism—the idea that the government should own and operate industry for the good of the community. They wanted the government to buy up large companies, especially industries that affected everyone, such as railroads and utilities. At its peak, socialism had some national support. Socialist Eugene V. Debs won nearly a million votes as the American Socialist Party candidate for president in 1912.

Roosevelt Takes on the Trusts

President Theodore Roosevelt thought that trusts and other large business organizations were efficient and part of the reason for American prosperity. Yet he also felt that the monopoly power of some trusts hurt the public interests. He wanted to ensure that trusts did not abuse their power.

His first target was J. P. Morgan's railroad holding company, Northern Securities. The company planned an exchange of stock that would merge existing railroad systems, creating a monopoly on railroad traffic in the Northwest. Farmers and business owners feared that without railroad competition, shipping rates would rise and reduce their profits. In 1902 Roosevelt ordered the attorney general to sue Northern Securities under the Sherman Antitrust Act, charging Northern Securities with restraint of trade. The suit puzzled J. P. Morgan, who asked what could be done to fix the problem. Unmoved, Roosevelt proceeded with the case. In 1904 the Supreme Court ruled in *Northern Securities* v. *United States* that Morgan's firm had violated the Sherman Antitrust Act. Roosevelt was hailed as a "trustbuster," and his popularity grew.

Northern Securities and the Commerce Clause

The Supreme Court's decision in the *Northern Securities* case marked yet another shift in the relationship between the federal government and private business. Article I, Section 8, of the Constitution states that "The Congress shall have Power . . . To regulate Commerce with foreign Nations, and among the several States. . . ." It was agreed that the Constitution gives the federal government the power to regulate commerce between the states, not within a state. But the definition of what constituted "interstate commerce" was open to interpretation. In the late 1800s the Court had applied a very strict interpretation of the commerce power. For example, when a sugar company gained control of 98 percent of the sugar industry, the Court ruled in *United States* v. *E.C. Knight* (1894) that the Sherman Antitrust Act could not be applied because the sugar was

A GLIMPSE INTO THE FUTURE.—FAST AND TIGHT

In this political cartoon, President Theodore Roosevelt is shown trying to contain the power of trusts.

Speculating What might the creator of this cartoon have been trying to suggest about trusts by illustrating them as a pig?

manufactured within a state. Manufacturing, the Court said, did not involve interstate commerce, even though the sugar was sold across state lines.

In the *Northern Securities* case, the Court began broadening its interpretation. Northern Securities was based in one state and was simply buying stock in other companies. However, the Court, in a narrow 5-4 decision, decided the Antitrust Act could still be applied. In his dissent, Justice Oliver Wendell Holmes warned that the decision had created a slippery slope: "If the act before us is to be carried out according to what seems to me the logic of the argument . . . I can see no part of the conduct of life with which, on similar principles, Congress might not interfere." Over time, his comment has proved accurate. It would take many decades and several Supreme Court decisions, but the interpretation of the commerce clause of the Constitution has gradually expanded to give the federal government more power to regulate private business.

The Coal Strike of 1902

As president, Roosevelt believed that it was his job to keep society operating efficiently by helping settle conflicts between different groups and their interests. In the fall of 1902, he put this belief into practice. He

worked to help resolve a coal strike between mine owners and nearly 150,000 members of the United Mine Workers (UMW). The UMW wanted increased pay, reduced hours, and union recognition. If the strike had dragged on, the nation would have faced a coal shortage that could have shut down factories and left many homes unheated in winter.

Roosevelt urged the UMW and the mine owners to accept arbitration—a settlement negotiated by an outside party. The union agreed to arbitration. However, the mine owners refused arbitration until Roosevelt threatened to order the army to run the mines. By intervening in the dispute, he took the first step toward establishing the federal government as an honest broker between powerful groups in society.

Regulating Big Business

Despite his lawsuit against Northern Securities and his role in the coal strike, Roosevelt believed that most trusts were good for the economy and that the costs of antitrust action outweighed its benefits. He agreed with the opponents of trust-busting who argued that companies generally formed trusts because it was the most efficient way to do business. Breaking up a trust would make an industry less efficient and drive up costs for the public. Moreover, by taking a company to court, the uncertainty in the industry until the case was resolved would distort the economy and make it less efficient.

Roosevelt generally accepted these arguments against antitrust action and was keenly aware that America's biggest companies were now competing globally against foreign companies. U.S. Steel had formed a trust in the United States, but was competing against huge European steel companies in Britain, France, and Germany. Standard Oil had formed a trust in the United States, but was competing globally against Burmah Oil in Britain (known now as BP), Royal Dutch Petroleum (known now as Shell Oil), and many other companies. Antitrust action against an American company might hinder its ability to compete globally.

As a progressive Roosevelt valued efficiency, and he believed that the United States had to be a world power, militarily and economically, in order to prosper. But as a progressive, he also distrusted large concentrations of power and the potential for corruption and harm to the public good. So instead of aggressively seeking to break up trusts, he proposed to create a federal agency to investigate corporations and publicize the findings. He believed the most effective way to prevent big business from abusing its power was to keep the public informed.

In 1903 Roosevelt convinced Congress to create the Department of Commerce and Labor. The following year, it investigated U.S. Steel, a huge holding company that had been created in 1901. Worried about a possible antitrust lawsuit, the company's leaders met

PHOTO: North Wind Picture Archives/Alamy Stock Photo; TEXT: Northern Securities Company, et al., Appts v. United States. 193 U.S. 197 (1904).

privately with Roosevelt and offered to open their files for examination. In exchange, the department would privately tell the company about any problems and allow them to fix the problems quietly. Roosevelt accepted this "gentlemen's agreement," as he called it, and soon made similar deals with other companies. These deals gave him the ability to regulate big business without having to sacrifice economic efficiency by breaking up the trusts.

Keeping with his belief in regulation, Roosevelt pushed the Hepburn Act through Congress in 1906. The act was intended to strengthen the ICC by giving it the power to set railroad rates. At first, railroad companies were suspicious of the ICC. However, they eventually saw they could work with the commission to set rates and regulations that limited competition and prevented new competitors from entering the industry. By 1920, the ICC had begun setting rates at levels intended to ensure the industry's profits.

✓ CHECK FOR UNDERSTANDING

1. **Determining Central Ideas** What specific concerns led Roosevelt to take on trusts such as railroad companies?
2. **Describing** How did the Northern Securities case broaden the interpretation of the interstate commerce clause of the Constitution?

Working in the United States

GUIDING QUESTION

Why did workers try to form unions during the late 1800s?

There were many benefits of laissez-faire economics in the late 1800s—including rapid industrialization, dramatic innovation, and an improving standard of living—but the idea that governments should avoid regulating the economy had costs. Working conditions in factories and mines were dangerous. Many workers performed dull, repetitive tasks in dangerous, unhealthy working conditions, often breathing in lint, dust, and toxic fumes. Heavy machines without safety devices led to injuries. With no regulations governing workplace safety or training requirements, workers had no recourse when they were poorly treated other than to quit and look for new jobs—something few could afford.

While the average worker's wages rose by 50 percent between 1860 and 1890, the uneven division of income between the wealthy and the working class caused resentment among workers. In 1900 the average industrial worker made 22¢ per

hour and worked 59 hours per week. Between 1865 and 1897, **deflation** caused prices to fall, which increased the buying power of workers' wages. Although companies cut wages regularly in the late 1800s, prices fell even faster, so that wages were actually still going up in buying power. Workers, however, resented getting less money. Eventually, many concluded that they needed a union to bargain for higher wages and better working conditions.

Early Unions Face Opposition

There were two basic types of industrial workers in the United States in the 1800s—craft workers and common laborers. Craft workers, such as machinists, iron molders, stonecutters, shoemakers, and printers, had special skills and training. They received higher wages and had more control over their time. Common laborers had few skills and received lower wages.

Employers had to negotiate with trade unions because unions represented the skilled workers that they needed. However, they generally viewed unions as conspiracies that interfered with rights. Business leaders particularly opposed **industrial unions,** which united all the workers in a particular industry. To stop union formation, companies required workers to take oaths or sign contracts promising not to join a union and hired detectives to identify union organizers. Workers who tried to organize a union or strike were fired and placed on a blacklist, a list of "troublemakers" so that no company would hire them. Companies also used "**lockouts**" to break up existing unions by locking workers out of the property and refusing to pay them. If the union called a strike, employers would hire strikebreakers. Government set policies that supported business owners and impeded the development of unions. Courts frequently ruled that strikes were "conspiracies in restraint of trade," and labor leaders were often fined or jailed. State militias and federal troops would be used to break up strikes.

One reason for anti-unionism was a belief they were "un-American." In the 1800s the ideas of Karl Marx became very influential in Europe. Marx argued that the basic force shaping capitalist society was the class struggle between workers and owners. He believed that workers would one day revolt, seize control of factories, and overthrow the government, and eventually a society without classes would develop.

While many labor supporters agreed with Marx, a few supported full out anarchism—the belief that society does not need any government. In the late 1800s anarchists assassinated government officials and set off bombs across Europe in an attempt to

---

deflation a decline in the volume of available money or credit that results in lower prices, and therefore increases the buying power of money

industrial union an organization of common laborers and craft workers in a particular industry

lockout a company strategy to fight union demands by refusing to allow employees to enter its facilities to work

begin a revolution. During the same period, tens of thousands of European immigrants headed to America. Anti-immigrant feelings were already strong in the United States. People began to associate immigrant workers and unions with radical ideas. These fears often led officials to use the courts, the police, and the army to end strikes and break unions.

✓ CHECK FOR UNDERSTANDING

Identifying How did working conditions encourage workers to form unions in the late 1800s?

The Struggles of Union Organization

GUIDING QUESTION

What factors made it harder for unions to successfully form at this time?

Although workers tried on many occasions to create large industrial unions, they rarely succeeded. The First Amendment's right to "peaceful assembly" did not extend to violent actions, and these clashes with owners often led to violence and bloodshed.

The Great Railroad Strike

The Panic of 1873 was a severe recession that forced many companies to cut wages. The economy had still not recovered when, in July 1877, the Baltimore and Ohio Railroad announced it was cutting wages for the third time. In Martinsburg, West Virginia, workers walked off the job and blocked the tracks. Some 80,000 railroad workers across the country joined the strike, affecting two-thirds of the nation's railways. President Rutherford B. Hayes ordered federal troops to restore order. Over $10 million in railroad property had been destroyed and over 100 people were killed. The violence alarmed many Americans.

The Knights of Labor

The Knights of Labor, founded in 1869, took a different approach to labor issues. Its leader, Terence Powderly, used boycotts and arbitration, in which a third party helps workers and employers reach an agreement. The Knights welcomed women and African Americans. They called for an eight-hour workday, equal pay for women, no child labor, and worker-owned factories.

Supporters of the eight-hour workday called for a nationwide strike on May 1, 1886. On May 3, Chicago police intervening in a fight on a picket line opened fire on the strikers, killing 4. The next day, about 3,000 people gathered in Chicago's Haymarket Square. Someone threw a bomb, police opened fire, and workers shot back. About 170 were injured and 10 policemen killed. Eight men were arrested and convicted for the bombing on weak evidence. Yet, public anger was high, and 4 were executed.

Homestead and Pullman Strikes

In the summer of 1892, Homestead steel mill workers protested a 20 percent wage cut. For 14 hours, they fought against Pinkerton Detectives and strikebreakers hired by Henry Clay Frick. It took the Pennsylvania militia four months to make the strike collapse.

In 1894 the Pullman Palace Car Company cut workers' wages. American Railway Union (ARU) workers caused railroads to all but halt. A federal court issued an **injunction**, or formal order, to end the disruption. The Supreme Court later upheld the right to issue such an injunction, giving business a powerful tool for dealing with labor unrest.

The Coal Creek War

The Coal Creek mining company in Tennessee began leasing convicts as a cost-cutting measure. Miners went on strike to prevent the convicts from entering the mines. The convicts were forced to return to prison. The miners released the next batch of convicts sent to break the strike, leading to the repeal of the convict lease laws, ending Tennessee's practice of using prisoners as a labor force.

New Unions Develop

The American Federation of Labor (AFL) was the dominant labor organization of the late 1800s. In 1886 leaders of several national trade unions created the AFL. It focused on promoting the interests of skilled workers and had three main goals. First, it tried to convince companies to recognize unions and agree to collective bargaining. Second, it pushed for **closed shops**, meaning that companies could hire only union members. Third, it promoted an eight-hour workday.

By 1900, the AFL was the biggest union in the U.S., but it represented less than 15 percent of all nonfarm workers. Most AFL members were white men because the unions discriminated against African Americans, and most excluded women. Samuel Gompers was the first president of the AFL.

In 1905 a group of labor radicals, many of them socialists, created the Industrial Workers of the World (IWW). The IWW wanted to organize all workers in "One Big Union" of skilled and unskilled workers. In 1912 the IWW led a successful strike of 25,000 textile workers in Lawrence, Massachusetts, to protest wage cuts. The companies reversed the wage cuts after 10

---

injunction a court order whereby one is required to do or to refrain from doing a specific act

Strikes and Labor Unrest 1870–1900

Strikes and labor unrest were felt in all regions of the United States.

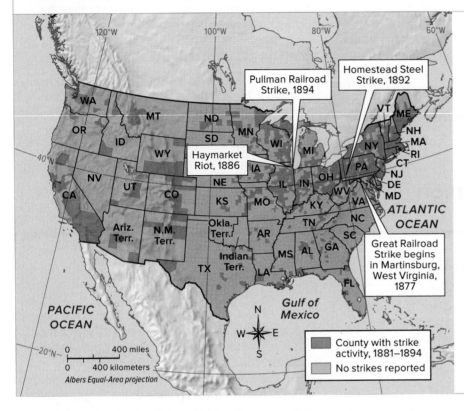

Pullman Railroad Strike, 1894

Homestead Steel Strike, 1892

Haymarket Riot, 1886

Great Railroad Strike begins in Martinsburg, West Virginia, 1877

PACIFIC OCEAN

Gulf of Mexico

ATLANTIC OCEAN

- County with strike activity, 1881–1894
- No strikes reported

400 miles
400 kilometers
Albers Equal-Area projection

Blizzard, Reese. Quoted in Ballard, Sandra L., and Hudson, Patricia L. Listen Here: Women Writing in Appalachia. Lexington: The University Press of Kentucky, 2013.

GEOGRAPHY CONNECTION

1. **Exploring Regions** What region of the country seems to have had the most strikes, and what region seems to have had the fewest strikes? Why do you think this was so?

2. **Interpreting** Based on what you have learned in this Topic, what types of industry experienced strikes in the counties shown in the western half of the United States?

weeks. Despite this victory the IWW never gained a large membership because of its radical philosophies.

Women and Organized Labor

By 1900, women made up more than 18 percent of the labor force but only one third were industrial workers, often in food-processing plants or the garment industry. Women were paid less than men even when they performed the same jobs.

One of the most famous labor leaders of the era was Mary Harris Jones, known as "Mother Jones." Jones worked as a labor organizer for the Knights of Labor before helping organize mine workers. Her public speaking abilities made her a very successful organizer, leading U.S. District Attorney Reese Blizzard to dub her "the most dangerous woman in America."

In 1900 Jewish and Italian immigrants who worked in the clothing business in New York City founded the International Ladies' Garment Workers Union (ILGWU), which represented female and male workers in the women's clothing industry. A 1909 strike of some 30,000 garment workers won the ILGWU recognition and better wages. In 1903 Mary Kenney O'Sullivan and Leonora O'Reilly decided to establish a separate union for women. With the help of Jane Addams and Lillian

Wald, they established the Women's Trade Union League (WTUL), which pushed for an eight-hour workday, a minimum wage, an end to evening work for women, and the abolition of child labor.

✓ **CHECK FOR UNDERSTANDING**

1. **Identifying Cause and Effect** What factors made it difficult for workers to form unions?

2. **Analyzing** Why did women need to form their own trade unions?

LESSON ACTIVITIES

1. **Informative/Explanatory Writing** What were Theodore Roosevelt's beliefs about big business, and how did he act on those beliefs during the early 1900s? Respond with a short essay.

2. **Presenting** Work in a small group to create a brief skit that dramatizes the early history of unions in the United States. The skit should include a scene with a union member reading aloud from a letter written to advocate changes in wages or other work policies.

---

closed shop an agreement in which a company agrees to hire only union members

READING STRATEGY

Analyzing Key Ideas and Details As you read, use a graphic organizer like the one below to take notes.

Reasons for Immigrating to U.S.	
Push Factors	Pull Factors

Immigrants in America

GUIDING QUESTION

How did immigrants of the late 1800s change American society?

Between 1865 and 1914, nearly 25 million people immigrated to the United States. Most, nearly 24 million, came from Europe, but more than 1.3 million Canadians moved south of the border, over 425,000 Latin Americans came north, and more than 450,000 Asians arrived during those years. Some **immigrants** were "pulled" to the United States by the promise of opportunities, while other immigrants were "pushed" from their home countries by hardships.

European Immigration

Europeans immigrated to the United States for many reasons. Many came because they were poor and American industries had plenty of jobs. However, Europe's industrial cities also offered plenty of jobs, so economic factors do not entirely explain why so many people immigrated. Many came to the United States to escape the restrictions of social class systems in Europe that kept them trapped at the bottom of society. Others left their homeland because of high rents, land shortages, and religious persecution.

Most immigrants passed through Ellis Island, a tiny island in New York Harbor. There, a huge, three-story building served as the processing center for

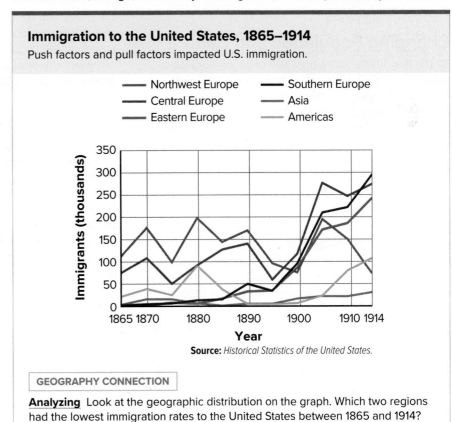

Immigration to the United States, 1865–1914
Push factors and pull factors impacted U.S. immigration.

— Northwest Europe — Southern Europe
— Central Europe — Asia
— Eastern Europe — Americas

Source: *Historical Statistics of the United States.*

GEOGRAPHY CONNECTION

Analyzing Look at the geographic distribution on the graph. Which two regions had the lowest immigration rates to the United States between 1865 and 1914?

immigrant a person who arrives in a foreign country with the intention of permanently living there

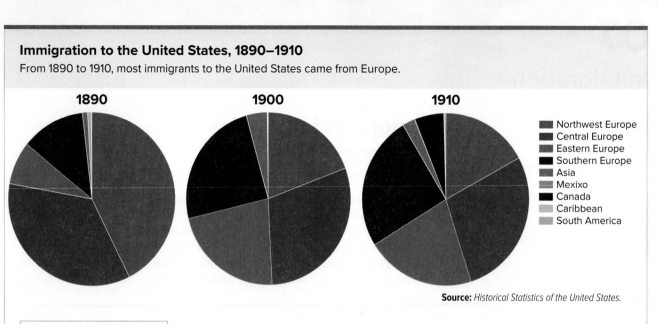

Immigration to the United States, 1890–1910

From 1890 to 1910, most immigrants to the United States came from Europe.

1890   **1900**   **1910**

- Northwest Europe
- Central Europe
- Eastern Europe
- Southern Europe
- Asia
- Mexixo
- Canada
- Caribbean
- South America

Source: *Historical Statistics of the United States.*

GEOGRAPHY CONNECTION

Comparing and Contrasting Compare European immigration in 1890 and 1910. What geographic pattern do you see on the graphs?

many of the immigrants arriving from Europe after 1892. Crowds filed past doctors for a health inspection, and those who failed the inspection might be separated from their families and returned to Europe. About 12 million immigrants passed through Ellis Island between 1892 and 1954.

Changing Population and Culture

By the late 1890s, more than half of all immigrants entering the United States were from eastern and southern Europe, including Italy, Greece, Austria-Hungary, Russia, and Serbia. This period of immigration is known as "new" immigration. The "old" immigration, which occurred before 1890, had been primarily of people from northern and western Europe.

Skilled Italian bricklayers and stonemasons contributed to the construction of many homes, churches, and buildings in American cities. Polish immigrants often became coal miners, meat-packers, and steel workers. Jewish immigrants often worked in the garment industry or became merchants. Members of all **ethnic** groups also headed west to settle the Great Plains as farmers and ranchers. By the 1890s, immigrants made up a large percentage of the population of major cities, including New York, Chicago, Milwaukee, and Detroit. Immigrants often lived in neighborhoods that were separated into ethnic groups, such as "Little Italy" or the Jewish "Lower East Side" in New York City. Italians, Russians, and Jews were likely to remain in New York City, while large numbers of Germans, Swedes, and Poles moved to Midwestern and mid-Atlantic cities such as Milwaukee, Pittsburgh,

and Chicago. Large numbers of Irish settled in the northeast and upper Midwest and became the largest ethnic group in Boston.

For many immigrants, living among those who spoke the same language and practiced similar traditions was comforting. Religion played a significant role in the development of these **enclaves,** or ethnic communities. Local churches, temples, and synagogues often became vital social centers. Businesses provided familiar products and services, while restaurants served traditional cuisines. Local newspapers featured articles in native languages. Although they provided a sense of security to the new immigrants, the enclaves often slowed assimilation into American culture by limiting interactions with people of different backgrounds. Many Americans viewed the ethnic enclaves as representing a reluctance to embrace "American" culture. In addition, the arrival of so many new immigrants stoked fears of job security and rapid cultural change. These fears led to hostility towards immigrants.

American culture had been overwhelmingly Protestant, but that began to change in the late 1800s as immigrants brought their religions with them. By the early 1900s, Catholics made up 17 percent of the population and had become the single largest religious denomination in the country. Orthodox Christians also became more common as large numbers of Greeks and Russians arrived. As persecution mounted in Russia, Poland, and Romania in the 1880s, a mass migration of East European Jews began. Most settled in New York City and on the east coast, but Jewish communities appeared across the

ethnic relating to large groups of people classed according to a common national or cultural background

enclave an area within a country or city that is comprised of people who share a nationality or culture

country. By the early 1920s, nearly two million Jews had settled in America.

Asian Immigration

In the mid-1800s China was suffering from severe unemployment, poverty, famine, and a civil war known as the Taiping Rebellion. These problems convinced tens of thousands of Chinese to head to the United States, as did news of the California Gold Rush. Between 1900 and 1908, large numbers of Japanese immigrated as Japan began building both an industrial economy and an empire, which disrupted Japan's economy and created hardships for its people.

Chinese immigrants settled mainly in west coast cities, especially San Francisco. Although many headed to the gold fields, most failed to make much money and took jobs as laborers and servants. Some became merchants or skilled at a trade. Many helped build the Central Pacific Railroad. Initially, Asian immigrants arriving in San Francisco were inspected at a two-story shed on the wharf. In 1910 California opened a barracks on Angel Island for Asian immigrants. Most of the immigrants were young men who nervously awaited the results of their immigration hearings in dormitories packed with double or triple tiers of bunks. This unpleasant delay could last for months.

✓ **CHECK FOR UNDERSTANDING**

1. **Describing** How did immigrants in the late 1800s change American society?
2. **Making Connections** What were some "push" and "pull" factors that prompted European and Asian immigration into the United States?

Many Chinese came to America to escape poverty and civil war. Some helped build railroads. Others set up small businesses. These children were photographed in San Francisco's Chinatown around 1900.

nativism hostility toward immigrants

Nativism and the Government Response

GUIDING QUESTION

Why did some people in the United States oppose immigration?

Eventually increasing immigration led to feelings of **nativism** for many Americans. Nativism is an extreme dislike of immigrants by native-born people. It surfaced due to Irish immigration in the 1840s and 1850s, but by the late 1800s, nativism was focused mainly on Asians, Jews, and Eastern Europeans. Some nativists feared that the influx of Catholics would swamp the mostly Protestant United States. The large influx of Jewish immigrants also added to this fear and led to a rise in antisemitism. Many labor unions argued that immigrants undermined American workers because they would work for low wages and accept jobs as strikebreakers.

Increased nativism led to the founding of two major anti-immigrant organizations. The American Protective Association, founded in 1887, was an anti-Catholic organization. Its members vowed not to hire or vote for Catholics and lobbied for restrictions of Catholic immigration to the United States. The APA built a large following in the Midwest and Northeast of the United States. On the West Coast, where sentiment against the Chinese was strong, violence erupted. Denis Kearney, an Irish immigrant, formed the Workingman's Party of California in 1877 to fight Chinese immigration. The party won seats in the California legislature and made opposition to Chinese immigration a national issue.

New Immigration Laws

Congress tried to pass several laws to limit the number of immigrants, but most of these were vetoed by presidents. However, President Chester Arthur signed two bills: the Chinese Exclusion Act of 1882 and the Immigration Act of 1882. The Chinese Exclusion Act barred Chinese immigration for 10 years and prevented those already in the United States from becoming citizens. The ban was renewed in 1892 and made permanent in 1902. It was not repealed until 1943.

The Immigration Act of 1882 imposed a head tax of 50 cents on each immigrant who arrived at a United States port. It gave immigration officials the authority to reject immigrants who had criminal records, were mentally disabled, or who were unable to take care of themselves "without becoming a public charge." The act also began federal oversight of immigration and gave responsibility to the Treasury Department to issue regulations, hire immigration agents, and build inspection stations. The law triggered a debate—which continues today—over how to regulate immigration.

The Picture Art Collection/Alamy Stock Photo

Immigration Settlement Patterns, Late 1800s

This map shows where different immigrant groups settled in the United States.

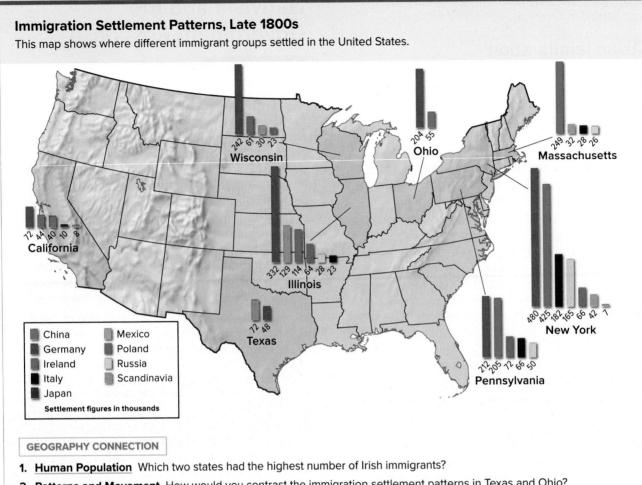

California
72 44 40 10 8

Wisconsin
242 61 30 23

Ohio
204 55

Massachusetts
249 32 28 26

Illinois
332 129 114 64 28 23

New York
480 425 182 165 66 42 7

Texas
72 48

Pennsylvania
212 205 72 66 50

Legend:
- China
- Germany
- Ireland
- Italy
- Japan
- Mexico
- Poland
- Russia
- Scandinavia

Settlement figures in thousands

GEOGRAPHY CONNECTION

1. **Human Population** Which two states had the highest number of Irish immigrants?
2. **Patterns and Movement** How would you contrast the immigration settlement patterns in Texas and Ohio?

Some western states continued targeting Asian immigrants with additional restrictions. California passed the Alien Land Act of 1913, prohibiting immigrants who could not attain citizenship from owning or leasing land. This act hit Japanese immigrants especially hard because many had built agricultural businesses in California.

The culmination of these early immigration laws was the Immigration Act of 1924, which limited the number of immigrants allowed into the United States through a national origins quota. Based on data from the 1890 census, the act limited new immigration to two percent of the nationalities already living in the United States. The law also banned immigration from all Asian countries except Japan and the Philippines and heavily favored immigration from Northern and Western Europe. Although these discriminatory laws mainly affected Asians, they limited immigration Southern and Eastern European countries as well.

Nonetheless, many immigrants remained optimistic—in part because of what they were fleeing and in part because of what they discovered upon arriving. No widespread famine, war, or rebellion existed in the United States during this period. The class system was not as rigid as in their countries of origin. Wages were comparatively high, jobs were plentiful if sometimes demeaning, and the Great Plains offered cheap land. There was an opportunity to be free that many immigrants had never experienced before.

✓ CHECK FOR UNDERSTANDING

Explaining Why did nativists oppose immigration?

LESSON ACTIVITIES

1. **Informative/Explanatory Writing** Write a short article describing the impact immigrants had on the United States during this period.

2. **Collaborating** Work in pairs to research one group of immigrants to the United States in the late 1800s. Then imagine that you are journalists interviewing an immigrant from the group you researched. Write an article describing how the interviewee's life in the United States compares to the person's home country. Read your article to the class and discuss.

08

Understanding Multiple Perspectives on Immigration and Nativism

? COMPELLING QUESTION

How did Americans react to immigration?

Plan Your Inquiry

In this lesson, you will investigate how Americans reacted to immigration and the growth of nativism from 1865 to 1914.

DEVELOP QUESTIONS

Developing Questions About Immigration and Nativism Think about how increasing immigration from different countries affected life across the United States, contributed to the rise of nativist sentiment, and led to specific policy changes at the state and national level. Then read the Compelling Question for this lesson. Develop a list of Supporting Questions that would help you answer the Compelling Question for the lesson. Write these in a graphic organizer like the one below.

APPLY HISTORICAL TOOLS

Analyzing Primary and Secondary Sources You will work with a variety of primary and secondary sources in this lesson. These sources focus on ways in which different groups of people responded to immigration as well as the rise of nativism. Use a graphic organizer like the one below to record and organize information about each source. Note the author or creator of each source as well as the perspective conveyed in each source. Then, identify which of your supporting questions the sources help answer. Not all sources will help you answer each Supporting Question. Only include relevant sources in your graphic organizer.

Source	Author/ Creator	Description/ Notes	Which Supporting Question does this source help me answer?
A			
B			
C			
D			
E			
F			
G			

After you analyze the sources, you will:
- use the evidence from the sources.
- communicate your conclusions.
- take informed action.

Background Information

In the late 1800s, millions of immigrants came to the United States. Some fled persecution, war, poverty and unemployment in their homelands, while others came to find jobs in the nation's growing industries and land for farming. During this time, most immigrants came from Europe, but sizable numbers also journeyed from Canada, Latin America, and Asia. This included many Chinese immigrants who had begun migrating to the Pacific Coast around 1849. At first they had come as part of the California Gold Rush; then, as gold mining petered out, many went to work building the western half of the first transcontinental railroad. Likewise, many Irish immigrants took jobs building the eastern half. Newly freed African Americans as well as Mexican Americans also helped build the railroad. For a while, railroad companies encouraged immigration to fill their labor demands. However, with the completion of the railroad in 1869, competition for jobs stoked racial and ethnic strife. At the same time, the United States was struggling to recover from the Civil War and to integrate newly freed African Americans into society. The nation's relentless efforts to develop the West provoked ongoing conflicts with Native Americans, too. These combined stresses sharply impacted reactions to ongoing immigration.

» This map shows the distribution of the foreign-born population in the United States in 1890. The darker the shading, the higher the foreign-born population density.

United States Census Office. 11Th Census, 1890, and Henry Gannett. Statistical atlas of the United States, based upon the results of the eleventh census. Washington, Govt. print. off, 1898. Map. https://www.loc.gov/item/07019233/.

Flow of European Immigration

Author and publisher William C. King produced a collection of historical data entitled *King's Illustrated Portfolio of Our Country* in 1906. In this self-styled "graphic atlas," the following chart lists annual immigration statistics from several European nations and regions as well as from China and Japan (in the middle row). The data reads from 1840 on the right to 1905 on the left. The data for 1870 begins beneath the middle of the title word *FROM*. Note the shifting trends in immigration from different countries and regions.

PRIMARY SOURCE: DATA CHART

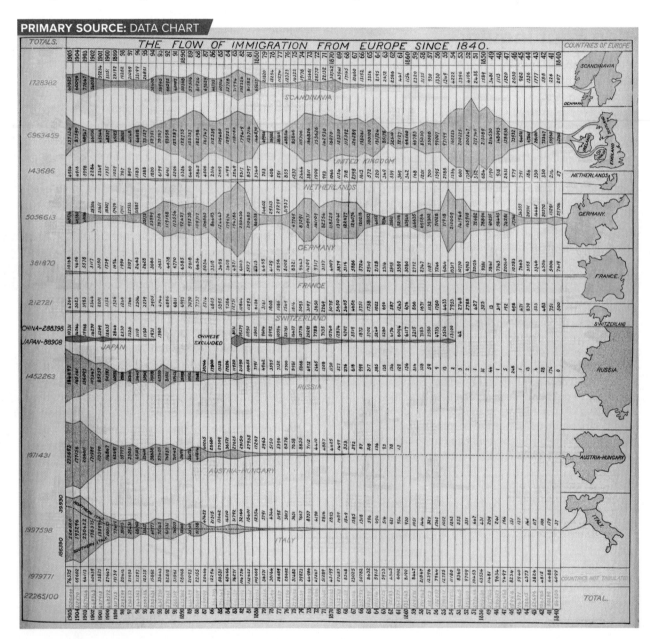

EXAMINE THE SOURCE

1. **Contrasting** Describe the different immigration trends from Western and Northern European nations and Southern and Eastern European nations from 1870 to 1905. How does the data from China and Japan differ from that of Europe in general?

2. **Drawing Conclusions** What does the data suggest about immigration from different regions? Consider the motivations of immigrants as well as U.S. policy.

King, William C. The Flow of Immigration From Europe Since 1840, 1906. Cornell University – PJ Mode Collection of Persuasive Cartography.

PHOTO: National Archives at Seattle, Records of United States District Courts; TEXT: (l)Chinese Exclusion Act, 1882; (r)Stevenson, Edward A. Territory of Idaho. Executive department. Proclamation [forbidding forcible expulsion of the Chinese after the first day of May 1886]. Boise City, April 27, 1886.

Chinese Exclusion Act of 1882

In 1882 a largely white Congress overwhelmingly passed the Chinese Exclusion Act, which President Arthur then signed. It was renewed in 1892 and made permanent in 1902. Congress did not repeal the exclusion laws until 1943.

PRIMARY SOURCE: LAW

66 Whereas in the opinion of the Government of the United States the coming of Chinese laborers to this country endangers the good order of certain localities within the territory thereof: Therefore,

Be it enacted by the Senate and House of Representatives of the United States of America in Congress assembled, That from and after the expiration of ninety days next after the passage of this act, and until the expiration of ten years next after the passage of this act, the coming of Chinese laborers to the United States be, and the same is hereby, suspended; and during such suspension it shall not be lawful for any Chinese laborer to come, or, having so come after the expiration of said ninety days, to remain within the United States. . . . 99

—Chinese Exclusion Act, May 6, 1882

EXAMINE THE SOURCE

1. **Analyzing** Describe the provisions of the law. What specific purpose does Congress express?

2. **Inferring** Why might Congress have set a limit on the terms of the law? What does its renewal imply about the public mood toward Chinese immigrants?

» Handbill from the Tacoma Anti-Chinese Committee, 1885

Idaho Supports Chinese Immigrants

Edward A. Stevenson served as governor of Idaho Territory from 1885 to 1889. Having moved West as part of the Gold Rush, Stevenson was keenly interested in developing the territory. He favored strong local rule and issued this statement to bar forced expulsion of Chinese immigrants from the territory.

PRIMARY SOURCE: POSTER TEXT

66 . . . Authentic statements and information from sources I deem reliable, have been received at this department from different localities in Idaho that numerous organizations have been formed and are now forming for the purpose of expelling, by force and violence, the Chinese who may be found in those localities on or after the FIRST DAY OF MAY, 1886, it is hoped that none of our citizens will join in which such a movement, nor **countenance** in any way such violations of law. The life and property of our citizens, and those of the Chinese as well, who are engaged in our midst in peaceful occupations, are entitled to and must receive the equal protection of the laws of our Territory.

I do, therefore, **admonish** the people in every portion of Idaho to oppose in every lawful way the institution of such riotous proceedings and mob violence. . . . 99

—Governor Edward Stevenson, April 27, 1886

countenance to approve or tolerate

admonish to warn

EXAMINE THE SOURCE

1. **Analyzing Points of View** What point of view does Stevenson express about Chinese residents of Idaho Territory?

2. **Making Generalizations** What does this excerpt suggest about the social and economic conditions within Idaho Territory at the time?

Yekl: A Tale of the New York Ghetto

Before coming to the United States, Jake lived in a town in northwestern Russia called Povodye. His given name then was Yekl or Yekelé. He left Russia to escape government discrimination against Jews and the resulting economic troubles faced by his father. Jake left his baby, his wife, and his parents to come to the United States. He first worked in a sweatshop in Boston and then moved to New York. As a young man, American Jewish author Abraham Cahan immigrated from Lithuania in 1882. He too settled in New York.

PRIMARY SOURCE : BOOK

❝ Three years had intervened since he had first set foot on American soil, and the thought of ever having been a Yekl would bring to Jake's lips a smile of patronizing commiseration for his former self. As to his Russian family name, which was Podkovnik, Jake's friends had such rare use for it that by mere negligence it had been left intact. . . .

He had to . . . nudge his way through dense swarms of bedraggled half-naked humanity; past garbage barrels rearing their overflowing contents in sickening piles . . . underneath tiers and tiers of fire escapes, barricaded and festooned with mattresses, pillows, and feather-beds not yet gathered in for the night. The pent-in sultry atmosphere was laden with nausea and pierced with a discordant and, as it were, plaintive buzz. Supper had been despatched in a hurry, and the teeming populations of the cyclopic **tenement houses** were out in full force 'for fresh air,' as even these people will say in mental quotation marks.

Suffolk Street is in the very thick of the battle for breath. For it lies in the heart of that part of the East Side which has within the last two or three decades become the **Ghetto** of the American metropolis, and, indeed, the metropolis of the Ghettos of the world. It is one of the most densely populated spots on the face of the earth—a seething human sea fed by streams, streamlets, and rills of immigration flowing from all the Yiddish-speaking centres of Europe. Hardly a block but shelters Jews from every nook and corner of Russia, Poland, Galicia, Hungary, Roumania . . . Jewish refugees from crying political and economical injustice; people torn from a hard-gained foothold in life and from deep-rooted attachments by the caprice of intolerance or the wiles of **demagoguery**—innocent scapegoats of a guilty Government for its outraged populace to misspend its blind fury upon; students shut out of the Russian universities, and come to these shores in quest of learning . . . Nor is there a tenement house but harbours in its bosom specimens of all the whimsical metamorphoses wrought upon the children of Israel of the great modern **exodus** by the vicissitudes of life in this their Promised Land of to-day. You find there Jews born to plenty, whom the new conditions have delivered up to the clutches of **penury**; Jews reared in the straits of need, who have here risen to prosperity; good people morally degraded in the struggle for success amid an unwonted environment; moral outcasts lifted from the mire, purified, and imbued with self-respect; . . . people with all sorts of antecedents, tastes, habits, inclinations, and speaking all sorts of subdialects of the same jargon, thrown pellmell into one social caldron—a human hodgepodge with its component parts changed but not yet fused into one **homogeneous** whole. ❞

—A. Cahan, *Yekl, A Tale of the New York Ghetto*, 1896

tenement house an urban apartment building with poor, unsafe and/or unsanitary living conditions

ghetto an isolated part of a city in which a marginalized group, such as the Jews, are made to live

demagoguery the use of prejudice and false claims to gain power

exodus a mass or large-scale departure

penury extreme poverty

homogenous similar in kind or nature

EXAMINE THE SOURCE

1. **Summarizing** Describe life in the Lower East Side of New York. What does the narrative say about the conditions that Jewish immigrants endured?

2. **Analyzing Perspectives** What were Jewish immigrants hoping to find in the United States? According to Cahan, did they find it?

Cahan, A. Yekl: A Tale of the New York Ghetto. New York: D. Appleton and Company, 1896.

Immigrants Getting Inspected

Ellis Island opened as a port of entry for immigrants on January 1, 1892. More than 450,000 passed through the station in its first year. In 1907, the year in which Edwin Levick took this photograph, a record 1.25 million immigrants passed through the inspection process, which included medical and mental evaluations. Inspectors also asked questions to verify the identities of immigrants, as well as to determine their origins, ethnicity, religion, and ability to work and take care of themselves. The process could take hours or days.

PHOTO: The Miriam and Ira D. Wallach Division of Art, Prints and Photographs: Photography Collection; The New York Public Library. "The pens at Ellis Island, Registry Room (or Great Hall). These people have passed the first mental inspection." New York Public Library Digital Collections. Accessed May 26, 2020. http://digitalcollections.nypl.org/items/510d47da-d778-a3d9-e040-e00a18064a99; TEXT: Prisland, Marie. From Slovenia to America: Recollections and Collections. Chicago: Slovenian Women's Union of America, 1968.

PRIMARY SOURCE : PHOTOGRAPH

» Immigrants wait in the "pens" at Ellis Island's Registry Room, also known as the Great Hall.

EXAMINE THE SOURCE

1. **Determining Context** Why do you think people in this photo were arranged in this manner?
2. **Analyzing Perspectives** How does the physical perspective of the photographer reflect the reality faced by the people sitting in the "pens"?

Arriving on Ellis Island

Marie Prisland immigrated to the United States from Slovenia, in Eastern Europe, in 1906 when she was fifteen years old. Prisland was one of more than 200,000 Slovenian immigrants to come to the United States between 1870 and 1924.

PRIMARY SOURCE : MEMOIR

66 A group of Slovenian immigrants, of which this writer was one, arrived in New York from . . . Austria. . . . we were transported to Ellis Island for landing and inspection. . . .

There were at least a hundred Slovenian immigrants. We separated ourselves, as was the custom at home—men on the right and women and children on the left. . . .

The day was warm and we were very thirsty. An English-speaking immigrant asked the nearby guard where we could get a drink of water. The guard withdrew and returned shortly with a pail of water, which he set before the group of women. Some men stepped forward quickly to have a drink, but the guard pushed them back saying: 'Ladies first!' When the women learned what the guard had said, they were dumbfounded, for in Slovenia . . . women always were second to men. . . . Happy at the sudden turn of events, one elderly lady stepped forward . . . and proposed this toast: 'Živijo Amerika, kjer so ženske prve!' (Long live America, where women are first!) 99

—Marie Prisland, *From Slovenia to America*, 1968

EXAMINE THE SOURCE

Analyzing How did the guards treat the women immigrants? How did the women interpret this gesture?

Ups and Downs in Chicago

Hilda Satt Polacheck immigrated with her parents from Poland to Chicago in 1892. They received help from Jane Addams and the other women of Hull House, an organization committed to helping immigrants. In this except, Polacheck describes some of her experiences as an immigrant.

PRIMARY SOURCE: BOOK

66 One evening, as my sister and I were leaving the factory, we saw a man at the entrance with his arms full of leaflets. . . . We were being asked to come to a meeting to help organize a union. My sister . . . was reluctant about going. She was always more cautious than I was. I however, decided to go to the meeting.

This was my introduction to trade unionism. About one hundred girls and a few men were gathered in a small smoky room. A man . . . told us of the advantages of an organized union. He urged us to organize a union.

. . . The next morning when I came to work I was called into the forelady's office and given whatever pay I had coming and was told that I was a troublemaker and that I had to get out and never come back. . . . And so ended my four-year career as a knitter.

. . . I was without work for about a week and Mother was beginning to worry about the rent, which was six dollars a month. . . . Not only did Mr. McCartney not ask for his rent, but he used to bring us gifts of candy and fruit. I will never forget when he came over just before Passover and without saying anything to Mother, he took my three small brothers to the neighborhood department store and brought each of them a complete outfit. . . . He did not come into the house, as he told us later he did not want to be thanked. When Mother finally did get the chance to thank him, he said: 'Shucks, I got so much pleasure doing it, it was cheap.' 99

—Hilda Satt Polacheck, *I Came a Stranger: The Story of a Hull-House Girl*

EXAMINE THE SOURCE

Contrasting How does the author's treatment at the factory contrast with her experience with the landlord, Mr. McCartney?

Your Inquiry Analysis

EVALUATE SOURCES AND USE EVIDENCE

Reflect back on the Compelling Question and the Supporting Questions you developed at the beginning of this lesson.

1. **Gathering Sources** Which sources helped you answer the Compelling Question and your Supporting Questions most directly? Which sources, if any, challenged the answers you thought you were going to arrive at when you created your supporting questions? Were there details you still need more information on, and where might you look to find that information?

2. **Evaluating Sources** Looking at the sources that helped you answer your supporting questions, evaluate the credibility of each source. What details made that source a particularly useful source to answer your question? Are there further details you may need in order to better evaluate the authority of these sources? How do you think the sources' backgrounds and experiences shaped their perspectives?

3. **Comparing and Contrasting** Compare and contrast two of the sources in this lesson more closely. Consider the subject, viewpoint, and tone of each source. How are they "alike and different"? How does the information provided by each source reinforce, complement, or counter the other? Explain.

COMMUNICATE CONCLUSIONS

Collaborating Discuss with one or two partners what the sources suggest about the reaction of the American public to immigrants between 1865 and 1914 and the rise of nativism. Together, formulate an argument regarding either social conditions or U.S. policy toward immigrants during that time. Be sure to cite at least two pieces of evidence from the sources to support your ideas. Then, change partners and take turns sharing and discussing your claims.

TAKE INFORMED ACTION

Brainstorming Social Actions and Policy Changes Think about the steps that people took to counter unjust treatment of immigrants or to help those who were struggling. Consider a population in your community or in the nation that faces similar challenges as the immigrants described in these sources. Brainstorm one individual action and one policy change that you could advocate to empower them to attain better or more equitable treatment and opportunities. Use reliable sources to describe the challenges faced by this population and explain your reasoning for each of your ideas.

Polacheck, Hilda Satt. I Came a Stranger: The Story of a Hull-House Girl. Epstein, Dena J. Polacheck, ed. Urbana: University of Illinois Press, 1991.

Urbanization and Social Reform

READING STRATEGY

Analyzing Key Ideas and Details As you read about urbanization and reform, complete a graphic organizer like the one below to identify problems the nation's cities faced.

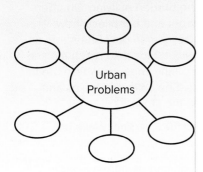

Urban Problems

Americans Migrate to the Cities

GUIDING QUESTION

How do you think life in big cities was different from life on farms and in small towns?

Most immigrants who arrived in the United States in the late 1800s settled in the nation's growing cities and took jobs in the rapidly expanding factories. At the same time, rural Americans began moving to the cities for better-paying jobs. Cities had much to offer—electric lights, running water, modern plumbing, plus attractions such as museums, libraries, and theaters. New York City, which had more than 800,000 inhabitants in 1860, grew to almost 3.5 million by 1900. Chicago swelled from some 109,000 residents to more than 1.6 million. By 1920, more Americans lived in urban areas than rural areas.

As cities grew, the rising value of land provided an incentive to build upward rather than outward. Aided by the invention of the safety elevator, tall, steel frame buildings called **skyscrapers** were built. Increasing population density led to the development of various kinds of mass transit. In 1890 horsecars, a railroad car pulled by horses, moved about 70 percent of urban traffic in the United States. Beginning with San Francisco in 1873, more than 20 cities installed cable cars. In 1887 engineer Frank J. Sprague developed the electric trolley car, and the following year, the country's first electric trolley line opened in Richmond, Virginia. In the largest cities, congestion became a severe problem. Chicago responded by building an elevated railroad, while Boston, followed by New York, built the first subway systems.

Separation by Class

In the growing cities the wealthy people, the middle class, and the working class lived in different parts of town. The boundaries between neighborhoods were well defined and can still be seen in some cities today. During the late 1800s, the wealthiest families established fashionable districts in the heart of the city. Americans with enough money could choose to construct homes in a variety of elaborate architectural styles. For example in Chicago real estate developer Potter Palmer chose to build something similar to a small English castle. In New York Cornelius Vanderbilt built a $3 million French château that had a two-story dining room, a gymnasium, and a marbled bathroom.

Upper-class men were usually business owners and their wives often did not work. Upper-class clothing was quite elaborate and expensive. As their homes grew larger, wealthy women increasingly relied on more servants, such as cooks, maids, butlers, nannies, and chauffeurs, and spent a great deal of money on social activities. Consequently, many of the women enjoyed a great deal of leisure time and hosted afternoon teas or cultural events. They also had more time to pursue activities outside the home, including "women's clubs." At first these clubs focused on social and educational activities, but over time "club women" became active in charitable and reform activities. For example the Women's Club in Chicago helped establish juvenile courts and exposed the terrible conditions at the Cook County Insane Asylum.

American industrialization expanded the middle class which included doctors, lawyers, engineers, managers, social workers, architects, and

skyscraper a very tall building

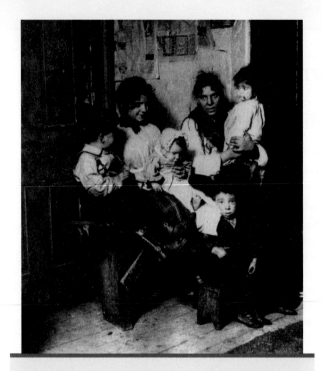

Near the turn of the century, crowded New York City tenements provided little space for large families.

"dumbbell" because the building was shaped like a dumbbell weight. The narrow part of the dumbbell was meant to create air shafts to provide ventilation, but in reality the shafts filled with foul-smelling air as residents filled them with garbage.

In New York City three out of four residents squeezed into dark and crowded tenements. Many families rented precious space to a boarder to earn extra money. Zalmen Yoffeh, a Jewish immigrant journalist, lived in a New York tenement as a child. He recalled his family's everyday struggle:

66 With . . . one dollar a day [our mother] fed and clothed an ever-growing family. She took in boarders. Sometimes this helped; at other times it added to the burden of living. Boarders were often out of work and penniless; how could one turn a hungry man out? She made all our clothes. She walked blocks to reach a place where meat was a penny cheaper, where bread was a half cent less. She collected boxes and old wood to burn in the stove. 99

–from "The Passing of the East Side," *Menorah Journal*, 1929

In 1890 Jacob Riis, an immigrant newspaper reporter who lived for a time in New York tenements, published *How the Other Half Lives*. The book, which included photographs showing the dire living conditions in tenements, brought the plight of the working poor to the public's attention. Riis and other reformers, including Lawrence Veiller who worked with Riis pushed for action. In 1900 Veiller put together an exhibition of photographs, charts, and maps to highlight the dangerous and unhealthy tenement conditions in New York City's Lower East Side. The exhibit prompted Theodore Roosevelt, the governor of New York, to form the Tenement House Commission, on which Veiller served. The commission's work led to passage of the Tenement House Act of 1901. In addition to other safeguards, the act required that new tenements be built on larger lots and that apartments have larger rooms, private bathrooms, and more light. The law also created the Tenement House Department to monitor compliance.

teachers. Many middle-class people moved away from the central city to escape crime and pollution and to afford larger homes. Some used new commuter rail lines to move to "streetcar suburbs." The middle class could, on average, afford their own homes, but the homes were more modest than the elaborate structures of the wealthy. Middle-class women did not often work at this time, and if they did it was because they wanted a specific career. The middle class could afford some luxuries and were developing the ability to purchase manufactured products in the industrial age.

Working-Class Living Conditions

Few families in the urban working class could hope to own or even rent a single-family home of their own. Most spent their lives in crowded **tenements,** or multifamily apartment buildings, where 12 adults might sleep in a room only about 13 feet wide. Tenements often lacked indoor plumbing or at best had communal toilets on each floor. Most interiors were dark and poorly ventilated. The space between buildings was tight—sometimes less than a foot— which blocked light from all but the front rooms. Some tenements were created by converting single-family homes once owned by wealthier urban residents into apartments and adding on floors or extensions. Other tenements were built new, often of inferior materials on lots that measured only 25 by 100 feet. One popular tenement design was called the

Even within the working class some people were better off than others. For example, white native-born men earned higher wages than African American men, immigrants, and women. In some cases the whole family worked, including the children. The dangerous working conditions faced by child workers, and the fact that they were not in school, alarmed many reformers.

More women took jobs outside the home. White native-born women often received better education than other women and this allowed them to find jobs

tenement multifamily apartments, usually dark, crowded, and barely meeting minimum living standards

PHOTO: General Photographic Agency/Hulton Archive/Getty Images; TEXT: Yoffeh, Zalmen. 1929. "The Passing of the East Side," in Schwarz, Leo, ed. The Menorah Treasury: Harvest of Half a Century. Philadelphia: The Jewish Publication Society of America, 1964.

as teachers, clerks, or secretaries. Many women, however, were domestic servants, with immigrant women often filling these jobs in the North and African American women doing such work in the South.

Urban Problems

The lure of industrial jobs and hopes of religious and political freedom brought waves of new immigrants to the cities, adding greatly to the urban population explosion. The vast majority of the immigrants were from Europe, and by the 1890s increasingly from Eastern and Southern Europe. Smaller numbers came from Canada, Latin America, and Asia. Many immigrants were poor and spoke little to no English when they arrived in the United States. Immigrant neighborhoods organized by a common language or country of origin grew in New York City, Chicago, and San Francisco. These neighborhoods provided some familiarity to immigrants as they grew accustomed to life in a new country. These neighborhoods also became a target for American nativists who had a strong dislike of the expanding immigrant population.

Crime was a growing problem in American cities. Minor criminals, such as pickpockets, swindlers, and thieves, thrived in crowded urban environments, and major crimes multiplied as well. From 1880 to 1900, the murder rate jumped sharply from 25 per million people to more than 100 per million people.

Disease and pollution posed even bigger threats. Improper sewage disposal contaminated drinking water and triggered epidemics of typhoid fever and cholera. Horse manure was left in the streets, chimneys belched smoke, and soot built up from coal and wood fires.

The **political machine,** an informal political group designed to gain and keep power, developed because cities had grown much faster than their governments. New city dwellers needed jobs, housing, food, heat for their homes, and police protection, and in exchange for votes, political machines and their party bosses eagerly provided these necessities. George Plunkitt, one of New York's most powerful bosses, explained the benefit of political machines: "I can always get a job for a deservin' man. . . . I know every big employer in the district and in the whole city, for that matter, and they ain't in the habit of sayin' no to me when I ask them for a job."

The **party bosses** also controlled the city's finances, enabling many to grow rich as the result of fraud or **graft,** gaining money or power illegally. Party bosses accepted bribes from contractors who were

supposed to compete fairly to win contracts to build streets, sewers, and buildings. Corrupt bosses also sold permits to their friends to operate public utilities. Tammany Hall, the New York City Democratic political machine, was the most infamous such organization. William "Boss" Tweed was its leader during the 1860s and 1870s, and his corruption led to a prison sentence in 1874. Opponents of political machines, such as cartoonist Thomas Nast, blasted corrupt bosses, while defenders argued that political machines provided necessary services and helped assimilate new city dwellers and respond to their needs.

✓ **CHECK FOR UNDERSTANDING**

1. **Describing** What were living conditions like for most of the urban working class?
2. **Making Connections** What types of problems developed due to the rapid growth of urban areas?

Social Darwinism and New Reforms

GUIDING QUESTIONS

What did different Americans believe were the causes of inequality? What was Social Darwinism, and how did it compare with the idea of individualism?

In 1873 Mark Twain and Charles Warner wrote the novel *The Gilded Age: A Tale of Today.* Historians later adopted the term for the era in American history that began about 1870 and ended around 1900. This period was a time of marvels in many ways. Amazing new inventions led to rapid industrial growth, cities grew in size, wealthy entrepreneurs built spectacular mansions, skyscrapers reached to the sky, and electric lights banished the darkness.

Twain and Warner's use of the term gilded age was a warning. A gilded item may be covered with gold on the outside, but it is made of cheap materials inside. A gilded age, then, might appear wonderful, but hides corruption, poverty, crime, and great inequality between the rich and the poor.

One of the strongest beliefs of the era—and one that remains strong today—was **individualism.** Many firmly believed that no matter how humble their origins, they could rise in society through their talents and commitment. No one expressed the idea of individualism better than Horatio Alger, who wrote

Plunkitt of Tammany Hall, George Washington Plunkitt, William L. Riordon. Copyright © 1905 by McClure, Phillips & Co.

political machine an organization linked to a political party that often controlled local government

party boss the person in control of a political machine

graft the acquisition of money in dishonest ways, as in bribing a politician

individualism the belief that no matter what a person's background is, he or she can still become successful through effort

more than 100 "rags-to-riches" novels. Alger's popular books convinced many young people that no matter how many obstacles they faced, success was possible.

Evolution and Human Society

Individualism was not the only powerful idea of the era. In 1859 Charles Darwin published *On the Origin of Species by Means of Natural Selection*. In the book, Darwin argued that plant and animal life had evolved over millions of years through a process he called natural selection. According to this theory, species that cannot adapt to their environment gradually die out, while those that do adapt thrive and pass on their advantageous traits to their descendants through inheritance. This process is biological and instinctual, not the result of conscious thought or action.

Many devout Christians found Darwin's conclusions offensive. They rejected the theory of evolution because they believed it contradicted the Bible's account of creation. Some clergy, however, concluded that evolution might have been God's way of creating the world. One of the most famous ministers of the era, Henry Ward Beecher, called himself a "Christian evolutionist."

Some social philosophers, such as Herbert Spencer of Great Britain, applied Darwin's biologically-based theory of evolution and natural selection to human society. Spencer argued that societies evolved through competition and natural selection. Darwin dismissed Spencer's theories and did not believe the evolutionary process had any relevance to human social institutions. Spencer coined the phrase "survival of the fittest" to explain why some societies grew in power and wealth while others did not. He believed that more advanced societies could benefit less advanced ones through trade and education, but he opposed Great Britain's imperialism. Spencer argued colonization impeded a weaker society's natural progress by interfering with competition. Similarly, he opposed government programs to help the poor because he believed they eroded the moral development of individuals, a trait he thought was inheritable. Spencer and others, such as American scholar William Graham Sumner, became known as Social Darwinists and their ideas as **Social Darwinism.** Some industrial leaders used these ideas to justify their support of laissez-faire capitalism. Social Darwinists were able to justify inequalities, while ignoring the role of racism, nativism, and prejudice in society.

Andrew Carnegie, the wealthy industrialist responsible for massive growth in U.S. steel, advocated a gentler version of Social Darwinism that he called the Gospel of Wealth. This philosophy held that wealthy Americans should engage in **philanthropy,** using their fortunes to help people help themselves. Building schools and hospitals, for example, was better than giving handouts to the poor. Carnegie funded the creation of public libraries because he believed they provided resources people needed to succeed. But Carnegie's aid also came with some assumptions about the needy.

> 66 Those worthy of assistance, except in rare cases, seldom require assistance. The really valuable men of the race never do, except in cases of accident or sudden change. . . . He is the only true reformer who is as careful and as anxious not to aid the unworthy as he is to aid the worthy, and, perhaps, even more so, for in almsgiving more injury is probably done by rewarding vice than by relieving virtue. . . . 99
>
> —Andrew Carnegie, from *The Gospel of Wealth and Other Timely Essays*, 1886

Carnegie's ideas were widely embraced by the nation's wealthy. The late 1800s was a time when many people made a great deal of money, but it was also an era of philanthropy. John D. Rockefeller founded the University of Chicago, and many universities, including Stanford, Vanderbilt, and Johns Hopkins, were named for the wealthy businessmen who helped found them. All across the nation, art museums, symphonies, and operas were funded by wealthy patrons.

The Rebirth of Reform

The tremendous changes of this era led to debates over how best to address society's problems. Some embraced individualism and Social Darwinism, others argued that society's problems could be fixed only if Americans and the government took a more active role in regulating the economy and helping those in need.

In 1879 journalist Henry George published *Progress and Poverty*, a discussion of the American economy that quickly became a best seller. George observed that the increase in wealth driven by industrialization should have eliminated poverty. But, he claimed, the "gulf between the employed and the employer is growing wider, social contrasts are becoming sharper." He believed that laissez-faire economics was making society worse. Most economists now argue that George's analysis was flawed. Industrialism did make some Americans very wealthy, but it also partially improved the standard of living for most others. At the time, however, Americans in the midst of poverty did not see improvement, and George's ideas led reformers to challenge Social Darwinism.

Social Darwinism a philosophy based on Charles Darwin's theories of evolution and natural selection, asserting that humans have developed through competition and natural selection with only the strongest surviving

philanthropy providing money to support humanitarian or social goals

Carnegie, Andrew. The Gospel of Wealth and Other Timely Essays. New York: The Century Co., 1900.

In 1883 Lester Frank Ward published *Dynamic Sociology*, in which he argued that humans were different from animals because they could make plans to produce the outcomes they desired. Ward's ideas came to be known as Reform Darwinism. Government, he argued, could regulate the economy, cure poverty, and promote education more efficiently than competition in the marketplace. Edward Bellamy published *Looking Backward*, a novel about a man who falls asleep in 1887 and awakens in the year 2000 to find that the nation has become a perfect society with no crime, poverty, or politics. In this fictional society, the government owns all industry and shares the wealth equally with all Americans. Bellamy's ideas were essentially a form of socialism.

A new style of writing known as naturalism also criticized industrial society. Naturalists challenged Social Darwinism by suggesting that people failed because they were caught up in circumstances they could not control. Stephen Crane, Jack London, and Theodore Dreiser were among the most prominent naturalist writers. Stephen Crane's novel *Maggie, A Girl of the Streets* (1893) told the story of Maggie, whose efforts to improve her life fail. Jack London's tales of the Alaskan wilderness demonstrated the power of nature over civilization. Theodore Dreiser's novels, such as *Sister Carrie* (1900), painted a world where people sinned without punishment and where the pursuit of wealth and power often destroyed their character.

Naturalist literature encouraged some people to become reformers to help the less fortunate, but it downplayed the ability of individuals to make a difference and encouraged resentment towards people in different social classes. This literature also implicitly asked readers to consider whether individualism and laissez-faire were leading to the best possible society, and readers often concluded that government intervention was the way to improve society.

Helping the Urban Poor

The Social Gospel movement worked to help the urban poor according to the biblical ideals of charity and justice. Advocates of the movement believed that God required them to not only save souls, but also to work to heal society. For example, Social Gospel advocates promoted literacy and campaigned for a shorter work week, higher wages, and an end to child labor. The movement was large and loosely organized with no central headquarters. Instead like-minded individuals, churches, and organizations worked to improve society. Unlike Social Darwinists, many Social Gospel advocates believed that the government had an important role in reforming society. Washington Gladden, a minister, was an early advocate who

Lester Frank Ward, scientist and sociologist, promoted universal education as the key to class, race, and gender equality.

Understanding Information How did Ward's theory in *Dynamic Socialism* separate humans from animals in terms of evolution?

popularized the movement in *Applied Christianity* in 1887. Walter Rauschenbusch, a Baptist minister from New York, became the leading voice in the Social Gospel movement. The movement inspired many churches to build gyms, provide social programs and childcare, and help the poor. The Salvation Army and the Young Men's Christian Association (YMCA) also combined faith and reform. The Salvation Army offered practical aid and religious counseling to the urban poor. The YMCA tried to help industrial workers and the urban poor by organizing Bible studies, citizenship training, and group activities and provided low-cost boarding houses for young men.

The **settlement house** movement began as an offshoot of the Social Gospel movement. In the late 1800s reformers—including many college-educated women—established settlement houses in poor neighborhoods that had large immigrant populations. The reformers lived in these settlement houses, which were community centers offering everything from medical care and English classes to kindergartens and recreational programs. These houses became communities that allowed the idea of family and feminine identity to expand. They provided a space to help these women advance their progressive ideals. Jane Addams, a Social Gospel advocate, opened Hull House in Chicago in 1889 with her romantic partner,

Alpha Stock/Alamy Stock Photo

settlement house an institution located in a poor neighborhood that provided numerous community services such as medical care, childcare, libraries, and English classes

JANE ADDAMS (1860–1935)

Jane Addams was born in Cedarville, Illinois, on September 6, 1860. After graduating from Rockville Female Seminary in 1881, she attempted to study medicine, but poor health got in her way. Unsure of what to do with her life, Addams traveled to Europe with Ellen Gates Starr. While in London, Addams and Starr visited Toynbee Hall, a settlement house that provided services to poor factory workers. The pair decided to open a settlement house in Chicago.

HULL HOUSE Upon their return to Chicago, Addams and Starr acquired a large house built by Charles Hull in a working-class neighborhood and opened it as a settlement in 1889. Over time, they added additional buildings, a playground, and a camp near Lake Geneva in Wisconsin. The Hull House complex eventually included a community kitchen, a swimming pool, a gymnasium, a daycare for working mothers, a kindergarten, an employment bureau, space for clubs and classes, an art gallery, a music school, an art studio, a library, and a labor museum. In addition to a place to gather, the settlement house offered college-level classes, English language classes, job training, bookbinding and craft classes, and a theater group.

REFORM EFFORTS Addams was active in other efforts to improve society. She helped establish the first juvenile court system; lobbied for sanitation, factory, and labor laws; and helped establish the School of Social Work at the University of Chicago. Addams was also active in the woman suffrage movement, the founding of the National Association for the Advancement of Colored People (NAACP), and the peace movement during World War I. Addams shared the Nobel Peace Prize in 1931 but was unable to attend the ceremony because of her health. She died on May 21, 1935.

> **Explaining** How did Jane Addams uphold the principles of the Social Gospel?

Ellen Starr. Jewish reformer Lillian Wald founded the Henry Street Settlement in New York City.

Industry needed more trained and educated workers, and between that pressure and reform efforts the number of children attending school rose from 7,562,000 in 1870 to 15,503,000 in 1900. Public schools were often crucial to the success of immigrant children. At school they were taught English and learned about American history and culture, a process known as **Americanization.** Schools also tried to instill discipline. Grammar schools divided students into grades and drilled them in punctuality, neatness, and efficiency—necessary habits for the workplace. Vocational education taught skills required for specific trades. Children in cities had greater access to education than those in rural areas. Since most African Americans were segregated into underfunded schools, some started their own schools, following the example of Booker T. Washington, who founded the Tuskegee Institute in 1881.

✓ **CHECK FOR UNDERSTANDING**

1. **Contrasting** How did Social Darwinism differ from individualism?

2. **Drawing Conclusions** How did advocates of the Social Gospel movement differ from Social Darwinists?

LESSON ACTIVITIES

1. **Argumentative Writing** Suppose that you are a newspaper editor in the late 1800s. Write an editorial in which you support or oppose government involvement in the economy. Draw on evidence from the lesson to support your argument.

2. **Using Multimedia** Work with a partner to create a photo and graphics exhibit showing the plight of the urban working class in the late 1800s. Be sure to caption your images. Share your exhibit with the class.

Americanization the process of acquiring or causing a person to acquire American traits and characteristics

The Library of Congress

READING STRATEGY

Understanding Craft and Structure As you read about the emergence of populism in the 1890s, use the major headings of the lesson to create an outline similar to this one.

Populism and Racism

I. Economic and Political Conflicts

  A.

  B.

Economic and Political Conflicts

GUIDING QUESTION

What kinds of problems did farmers face?

Up until the 1880s, when candidates won an election they replaced previous government workers with people who had supported their election in a practice known as patronage. Supporters of patronage claimed it ensured that government workers stayed loyal to elected representatives. But after the Civil War, many Americans believed patronage made the government inefficient and corrupt.

Civil Service Reforms

When Rutherford B. Hayes became president in 1877, he tried to end patronage. His actions divided the Republican Party into three groups: "Stalwarts" who supported patronage, "Halfbreeds" who backed some reform, and reformers. Despite Hayes's efforts, no reforms were passed.

In 1880, the Republicans nominated James Garfield, a "Halfbreed," for president and Chester A. Arthur, a "Stalwart," for vice president. Despite the feud over patronage, the Republicans managed to win the election. A few months later, President Garfield was assassinated by a man angry that he had not been given a government job.

This assassination changed public opinion. In 1883 Congress passed the Pendleton Act, requiring that some jobs be filled by means of competitive written exams instead of patronage. This began a professional civil service in which most government workers are hired based on qualifications.

In 1884 the Democrats nominated Grover Cleveland, the governor of New York, for president. Cleveland was a reformer with a reputation for honesty. The Republicans nominated James G. Blaine, a former Speaker of the House rumored to have accepted bribes. Some Republicans were so unhappy with Blaine that they supported Cleveland. Cleveland narrowly won the election. He then faced supporters who expected him to reward them with jobs. Reformers, on the other hand, expected him to increase the number of jobs under the civil service system. Cleveland chose a middle course and angered both sides.

Debating Economic Policy

Americans were concerned about large corporations, fearing that they were controlling prices and wages and corrupting the government. Small businesses and farmers were particularly angry at the railroads. While large corporations could negotiate lower rates because of the volume of goods they shipped, others were forced to pay higher rates. Eventually many states regulated railroad rates. In 1886 the Supreme Court ruled in the case of *Wabash, St. Louis, & Pacific Railway* v. *Illinois* that only the federal government could regulate interstate commerce.

Public pressure forced Congress to act, and in 1887 Cleveland signed the Interstate Commerce Act. This was the first federal law to regulate interstate commerce. The law limited railroad rates to what were "reasonable and just," outlawed rebates, and created the Interstate Commerce Commission (ICC), the nation's first independent regulatory agency. The ICC was not very effective in regulating the industry because it had to rely on courts to enforce its rulings.

This rare 1861 ten-dollar bill is an original "greenback".

While the ICC reduced pressure on farmers and small businesses, large companies passed on their increased shipping costs to the consumer.

Congress also faced pressure to ease burdens on American industry. Many Democrats thought that tariffs should be cut because they increased the price of imported goods and forced other nations to respond in kind, making it difficult for farmers to export surpluses. In 1890 Representative William McKinley pushed through a bill that cut some taxes and tariffs, but increased rates on other goods. The McKinley Tariff, intended to protect American industry, instead caused a steep rise in the price of all goods.

Debating the Money Supply

Populism was a movement to increase farmers' political power and work for economic justice. An economic crisis following the Civil War led farmers to join the Populist movement. New technology enabled farmers to produce more crops, but increased supply caused prices to fall. High tariffs also made it hard for farmers to sell their goods overseas. In addition, mortgages with large banks and rail shipping costs that continued to increase made the farmers' difficulties worse.

Some farmers thought adjusting the money supply would solve their problems. During the Civil War, the government had expanded the money supply by issuing millions of dollars in **greenbacks,** paper currency that could not be exchanged for gold or silver coins. The increased money supply without

an increase in goods for sale caused **inflation,** or a decline in the value of money. As the paper money lost value, the prices of goods soared.

After the Civil War, the government stopped printing greenbacks and began paying off its debts to manage inflation. Starting in 1873, Congress strictly limited the minting of silver coins. In 1876 Congress also announced that greenbacks would be redeemable for gold starting in 1879. These decisions meant that the money supply was insufficient for the growing economy. As the economy expanded, deflation—an increase in the value of money and a decrease in prices—began.

Deflation hit farmers especially hard. Falling prices meant that they sold their crops for less and then had to borrow money for seed and other supplies to plant their next crops. With money in short supply interest rates began to rise, increasing the amount farmers owed. Rising interest rates also made mortgages more expensive, and despite their lower income, farmers had to make the same mortgage payments to the banks. Farmers knew their problems were partly due to a shortage of currency. Some wanted the government to print more greenbacks. Others, especially those in the West where new silver mines had been found, wanted silver coins to be issued. Increasingly farmers realized that if they wanted the government to meet their demands, they had to organize.

The Grange and the Farmers' Alliance

In 1866 the Department of Agriculture sent Oliver H. Kelley to tour the rural South and report on farmers' conditions. Realizing that farmers were isolated, Kelley founded the first national farm organization, the Patrons of Husbandry, in 1867. It became known as the Grange.

In 1873 the nation plunged into a severe recession, and farm income fell sharply. Grangers responded by pressuring states to regulate railroad and warehouse rates. To reduce harmful competition among farmers, the Grangers also tried creating organizations called **cooperatives** in which member farmers worked together to increase prices and lower costs. None of the strategies improved farmers' economic conditions. As the Grange began to fall apart, a new organization, known as the Farmers' Alliance, formed. By 1890, the Alliance had more than 1 million members. The Alliance planned to create very large cooperatives called exchanges. The exchanges either failed because they overextended themselves, or because wholesalers, railroad owners, and bankers made it difficult for them

greenback a piece of U.S. paper money first issued by the North during the Civil War

inflation the loss of value of money

cooperative a store where farmers buy products from each other; an enterprise owned and operated by those who use its services

(both)B Christopher/Alamy Stock Photo

to stay in business. They also failed because they were still too small to affect world prices for farm products.

The Farmers' Alliance also denied membership to African American farmers, which limited the growth and power of the organization. In response, in 1886 African American farmers in Texas formed the Colored Farmers' Alliance and Cooperative Union. Like the Farmers' Alliance, the Colored Farmers' Alliance established cooperatives, held regular meetings, published newspapers, and worked to promote and protect the economic and political power of its members. Although both groups worked together and would eventually help found the People's Party, racial tensions weakened the relationship. The white members of the Farmers' Alliance who joined the People's Party remained opposed to full rights for African Americans, including their right to vote.

Populism

By 1890, many people in the Alliance were dissatisfied. They felt that they could only achieve their goals through politics. However, many Alliance members were distrustful of both the Republican and Democratic Parties and believed that both parties favored industry and banks over farmers. In July 1892 more than 1,000 delegates met in Omaha, Nebraska, to form the People's Party, also known as Populists. The party nominated James B. Weaver to run for president at its first national convention. They called for a return to unlimited coinage of silver. It also called for federal ownership of railroads and a **graduated income tax**.

In response to the labor strikes and violence that marked this era, Populists also adopted proposals that appealed to organized labor, such as an eight-hour workday and immigration restrictions. In the end, populism held little appeal to urban voters who continued their traditional party allegiances. Many workers continued to vote for the Democrats, whose candidate, Grover Cleveland, won the election.

Four years later, as the election of 1896 approached and with the economic upheaval of the Panic of 1893 still fresh in everyone's memory, the People's Party decided to make the free coinage of silver their campaign focus and to hold their convention after the Republican and Democratic conventions. They correctly believed that the Republicans would endorse a gold standard. They also expected the Democrats to nominate Grover Cleveland, even though Cleveland favored a gold standard. The People's Party hoped that when it endorsed silver, pro-silver Democrats would choose the Populists.

Their strategy failed. William Jennings Bryan made an impassioned pro-silver speech at the convention and won the Democratic nomination. The Populists faced a difficult choice: endorse Bryan and risk undermining their identity as a party, or nominate their own candidate and risk splitting the silver vote. They chose to support Bryan.

The Republicans appealed to workers with the promise that McKinley would provide a "full dinner pail." Most business leaders supported the Republicans, convinced that unlimited silver coinage would ruin the country. Many employers warned workers that if Bryan won, businesses would fail and unemployment would rise further. McKinley's reputation as a moderate on labor issues and as tolerant toward ethnic groups helped improve the Republican Party's image with urban workers and immigrants. When the votes were counted, McKinley had won.

The People's Party declined after 1896. The Populist goal of helping farmers with government intervention and regulating big business failed because they failed to appeal to urban workers in the northeast. Populist ideas, however, continued to influence the political debate. In the years ahead, many Populist ideas would be realized, including the eight-hour workday, restrictions on immigration, and a graduated income tax. Ironically, the key Populist goal of an increased money supply happened almost immediately after the election, as gold from the Klondike and new gold mines in South Africa flooded into the world's economy.

This gold rush poured millions of dollars into the nation's money supply without requiring a return to silver coins or paper currency. Mild inflation set in, credit became easier to obtain, and farmers and workers were less distressed. In 1900 the United States officially adopted a gold-based currency with the passage of the Gold Standard Act.

✓ CHECK FOR UNDERSTANDING

1. **Explaining** Why was civil service reform necessary?
2. **Identifying** What impact, if any, did the Populists have on American politics?

African American Response to Segregation

GUIDING QUESTION

How did African Americans resist racism and try to improve their way of life following Reconstruction?

Even before the end of Reconstruction, Southern states enacted laws that introduced **segregation,**

---

graduated income tax a tax based on the net income of an individual or business, and which taxes different income levels at different rates

segregation the separation or isolation of a race, class, or group

limiting African Americans' civil and voting rights. In addition, in 1896 the Supreme Court upheld in *Plessy v. Ferguson* the right of states to make laws that supported segregation. The ruling sustained the concept of "separate but equal" legal doctrine that enabled segregation.

Taking Away the Vote

The Fifteenth Amendment prohibits states from denying citizens the right to vote on the basis of "race, color, or previous condition of servitude." However, it does not bar states from denying the right to vote on other grounds. In the late 1800s, Southern states began imposing restrictions meant to make it hard or impossible for African Americans to vote.

In 1890 Mississippi began requiring all citizens registering to vote to pay a **poll tax** of $2, a sum beyond the means of most poor African Americans or poor whites. Mississippi also instituted a literacy test, which required voters to read and understand the state constitution. Few African Americans born after the Civil War had been able to attend school, and those who had grown up under slavery were largely illiterate. Even those who knew how to read often failed the test because officials deliberately picked difficult passages. Other Southern states adopted similar restrictions. The number of African Americans registered to vote in Southern states fell drastically between 1890 and 1900.

Election officials were far less strict in applying the poll tax and literacy requirements to whites, but the number of white voters also fell significantly. Louisiana introduced the "grandfather clause," which allowed any man to vote if he had an ancestor who could vote in 1867. Several Southern states adopted this provision, thus excluding African Americans from voting. This provision, adopted in several Southern states, exempted most whites from voting restrictions while excluding African Americans from the vote.

Legalizing Segregation

Racism and segregation existed in all parts of the country. However, Southern states passed laws that formalized segregation and rigidly enforced discrimination. African Americans in the North were often discriminated against, but segregation was different in the South. These laws became known as **Jim Crow laws.**

In 1883 the Supreme Court set the stage for legalized segregation when it overturned the Civil Rights Act of 1875. That law had prohibited keeping people out of public places on the basis of race and barred racial discrimination in selecting jurors. The Supreme Court, however, ruled that the Fourteenth Amendment did not prevent private organizations such as hotels, theaters, and railroads from practicing segregation.

Encouraged by the ruling and by the decline of congressional support for civil rights, Southern states passed Jim Crow laws that created racial segregation in virtually all public places. Southern whites and African Americans could no longer ride together in the same railroad cars or even drink from the same water fountains.

In 1892 an African American named Homer Plessy challenged a Louisiana law after he was arrested for riding in a "whites-only" railroad car. In *Plessy v. Ferguson*, the Court upheld the Louisiana law and the doctrine of "separate but equal" facilities for African Americans. The ruling established the legal basis for discrimination in the South for more than 50 years. While public facilities for African Americans in the South were always separate, they were far from equal.

The Anti-Lynching Crusade

Historian Rayford Logan characterized this time period as the nadir, or low point, of African American status in American society. The African American community responded to violence and discrimination in several ways.

In the late 1800s mob violence increased in the United States, particularly in the South. Between 1890 and 1899 an average of 154 people were lynched—executed, usually by hanging, without a legal trial—each year. In 1892 Ida B. Wells launched her crusade against lynching. After a mob drove Wells out of town, she settled in Chicago and continued her campaign, publishing a book in 1895 denouncing mob violence. Although Congress rejected an anti-lynching bill, the number of lynchings decreased significantly in the 1900s, due in part to the efforts of activists such as Wells.

Mary Church Terrell, a college-educated woman born during the Civil War, had lost a close friend to lynching. This death was the starting point of Terrell's lifelong battle against lynching, racism, and sexism. Terrell worked with woman suffrage workers such as Jane Addams and Susan B. Anthony and helped found the National Association for the Advancement of Colored People. She also formed the Women Wage Earner's Association, which assisted African American nurses, waitresses, and domestic workers. In addition, Terrell led a boycott against department stores in Washington, D.C., that refused to serve African Americans.

---

poll tax a tax of a fixed amount per person that had to be paid before the person could vote

Jim Crow laws statutes enacted to enforce segregation

The House Joint Resolution proposing the 15th amendment to the Constitution, February 3, 1870; Enrolled Acts and Resolutions of Congress, 1789-1999; General Records of the United States Government; Record Group 11; National Archives.

Alpha Historica/Alamy Stock Photo

» Ida B. Wells, investigative journalist and speaker, in 1893

BIOGRAPHY

IDA B. WELLS (1862–1931)

Born in Holly Springs, Mississippi, in 1862 to an enslaved family, Ida B. Wells is best known for her activism against lynching, which she called "our country's national crime." Wells's political and reform initiatives also included segregation and woman suffrage.

PROTEST ACTIVITIES Wells attended both Rust College and Fisk University and became a teacher in Memphis, Tennessee, around 1883. As she was teaching, she became a co-owner and an editor of a local African American newspaper, *Memphis Free Speech and Headlight*, and wrote editorials under a pseudonym condemning the disenfranchisement of and violence against African Americans.

In 1892 a store owner was lynched after defending his business against a white mob. Outraged, Wells wrote about the evils of lynching in her newspaper. In reaction to her speaking out against lynching, people threatened her life, and she eventually had to leave Memphis. Her anti-lynching activism did not stop, however.

In 1910 she formed the Negro Fellowship League, which helped African Americans who had newly migrated from the South and advocated criminal justice reform. She and her husband moved to an all-white Chicago neighborhood to challenge restrictive housing agreements. In 1913 she marched in Washington, D.C., in support of women's suffrage.

Citing Text Evidence How did Ida B. Wells try to stop the practice of lynching?

African American Middle Class

Despite the continued political and economic disadvantages they faced, many African Americans worked to improve their quality of life. Influential men like Booker T. Washington and W.E.B. Du Bois praised the growth of an emerging African American middle class in areas around the country.

In some places such as Durham, North Carolina, African American communities developed thriving manufacturing and service sectors independent of the white community. African Americans owned and operated a wide variety of businesses, including grocery stores, pharmacies, banks, clothing stores, and insurance companies.

Along with the formation of businesses, African American leaders realized the economic power of education and health care in improving lives. Before the Civil War, African Americans could not attend medical schools in the South, and only a few Northern schools would admit them. By 1904, seven medical schools for African Americans had been established, including Shaw University in North Carolina and Howard University in Washington, D.C.

Because African American patients could not receive treatment in white hospitals, new care facilities were needed. In Chicago in 1891, Dr. Daniel Hale Williams founded Provident Hospital and Training School for Nurses, the first African American-owned hospital in the country.

After the Civil War, many African Americans tried to improve their lives by moving from the South to more industrialized cities of the North. As they had done in the South, African Americans established their own communities. In the North, they still faced discrimination in hiring practices and business opportunities, even though it was not written into law. During and after World War I, when the nation's industries faced significant labor shortages, hundreds of thousands of African Americans migrated to the North to take advantage of new opportunities.

Competing Points of View

Influential educator Booker T. Washington proposed that African Americans concentrate on achieving economic goals rather than political ones. In 1895 Washington summed up his views in a speech called the Atlanta Compromise, which urged African Americans to postpone the fight for civil rights and instead concentrate on achieving equality through education and employment.

66 The wisest among my race understand that the agitation of questions of social equality is the extremest folly, and that progress in the enjoyment of all the privileges that will come to us must be the result of severe and constant struggle rather than of artificial forcing. . . . It is important and right that all privileges of the law be ours, but it is vastly more important that we be prepared for the exercises of these privileges. The opportunity to earn a dollar in a factory just now is worth infinitely more than the opportunity to spend a dollar in an opera-house. 99

–Booker T. Washington, from *Up from Slavery*, 1901

The Atlanta Compromise speech provoked a strong challenge from W.E.B. Du Bois, the leader of a new generation of African American activists. In his 1903 book, *The Souls of Black Folk*, Du Bois explained why he saw no advantage in giving up civil rights, even temporarily. He was particularly concerned with protecting and exercising voting rights. Du Bois felt that giving up ground on these issues in favor of economic equality was dangerous.

Du Bois helped create what became known as the Niagara Movement. In 1905 he and other African American leaders first met near Niagara Falls to demand complete political, civil, and social rights for African Americans, in contrast to Washington's views. At the Second Annual Convention of the Niagara Movement in 1906, Du Bois stated:

66 . . . We claim for ourselves every single right that belongs to a freeborn American, political, civil and social; and until we get these rights we will never cease to protest and assail the ears of America. The battle we wage is not for ourselves alone but for all true Americans. . . . We want discrimination in public accommodations to cease. . . . We want the laws enforced against rich as well as poor; against Capitalist as well as Laborer; against white as well as black. We are not more lawless than the white race [but] we are more often arrested, convicted, and mobbed. We want justice. . . . We want the Fourteenth amendment carried out to the letter. . . . We want the Fifteenth amendment enforced and no state allowed to base its franchise simply on color. . . . 99

–W.E.B. Du Bois "Address of the Niagara Movement, to the Country.

Delegates at the annual convention of the Niagara Movement in Boston, Massachusetts, 1907, worked toward guaranteeing political, civil, and social rights for African Americans.

Analyzing Visuals How might this photograph be evidence of an emerging African American middle class?

In the years that followed, many African Americans, including Washington and Du Bois, worked to win the vote and end discrimination. The struggle, however, would prove to be a long one.

✓ CHECK FOR UNDERSTANDING

1. **Identifying** What principle was held to be constitutional in the Supreme Court's 1896 *Plessy* v. *Ferguson* decision?

2. **Summarizing** How did African American community leaders respond to legalized segregation?

LESSON ACTIVITIES

1. **Argumentative Writing** Write a letter to the editor in the style of one that could have been written and printed in a local newspaper in the late 1800s expressing either support for or opposition to populist ideas and the goals of groups such as the Farmers' Alliance or the Colored Farmers' Alliance and Cooperative Union. Be sure to support your views with details from the lesson.

2. **Presenting** Work in small groups to prepare a series of short biographies of African American community leaders from the late 1800s and early 1900s. Do outside research to make each biography accurate. Choose one student to prepare a short introduction and conclusion. Present your work orally to the class.

PHOTO: History and Art Collection/Alamy Stock Photo; TEXT: (t)Washington, Booker T. Up from Slavery: An Autobiography. New York: Doubleday, Page & Co, 1907. (b)Du Bois, W.E.B. "Address of the Niagara Movement, to the Country. Issued by the Second Annual Convention of the "Niagara Movement" of American Negroes, in Session at Harper's Ferry, West Va., Aug. 16-19, 1906, in The Public, Volume 9, Sept. 1, 1906.

11

Turning Point: *Plessy* v. *Ferguson*

 COMPELLING QUESTION

How did African Americans experience and resist segregation in the late nineteenth century?

Plan Your Inquiry

In this lesson, you will investigate ways that African Americans experienced segregation in the late nineteenth century and how they resisted it.

DEVELOP QUESTIONS

Developing Questions About Segregation Think about the social and political changes that took place, especially in southern states, following the end of Reconstruction in 1877. Consider what happened when federal troops withdrew from the South, how conditions and policies like segregation affected African American citizens, and what steps African Americans took in response. Then read the Compelling Question for this lesson.

Develop a list of Supporting Questions that would help you answer the Compelling Question for the lesson. Write these in a graphic organizer like the one below.

APPLY HISTORICAL TOOLS

Analyzing Primary and Secondary Sources You will work with a variety of primary and secondary sources in this lesson. These sources focus on the context and significance of the U.S. Supreme Court ruling in *Plessy* v. *Ferguson* in 1896. Use a graphic organizer like the one below to record and organize information about each source. Note ways in which each source helps you answer the Supporting Questions you created. Not all sources will help you answer each of your Supporting Questions. Only include relevant sources in your graphic organizer.

Supporting Questions	Primary Source	How this source helps me answer the Supporting Question
Question 1:		
Question 2:		
Question 3:		

After you analyze the sources, you will:
- use the evidence from the sources.
- communicate your conclusions.
- take informed action.

Background Information

When federal troops withdrew from the South following the Compromise of 1877, Southern Democratic leaders began passing Jim Crow laws to restrict the rights of African American citizens. Among these were segregation laws. In 1887 Florida passed the first law segregating railroad cars, but others soon followed. In 1890 Louisiana passed the Separate Car Act, requiring railroads to provide separate cars for white and black passengers. Railroads presented a unique challenge because they crossed state lines. Segregation laws in one state thereby impacted not only citizens in that state but interstate travel. In 1891 a group of citizens decided to challenge the law. Homer Adolph Plessy, a man of mixed race, bought a railroad ticket and sat in the whites-only car. Following his arrest, he filed a case challenging the Separate Car Act on the grounds that it violated the equal protection clause of the Fourteenth Amendment. The case, *Plessy* v. *Ferguson*, went from a U.S. District Court to the Louisiana Supreme Court to the U.S. Supreme Court. The Supreme Court's ruling represented a turning point in U.S. policy toward African Americans as it established a legal precedent that would hold until 1954.

NEGRO EXPULSION FROM RAILWAY CAR, PHILADELPHIA.

» Engraved print from *The Illustrated London News*, 1856

Library of Congress Prints and Photographs Division [LC-USZ62-45698]

Equal but Separate Facilities

Below is the majority opinion in *Plessy* v. *Ferguson*. This landmark decision upheld segregation as legal—on one condition.

PRIMARY SOURCE : LEGAL RULING

❝ This case turns upon the constitutionality of an act of the . . . State of Louisiana, passed in 1890, providing for separate railway carriages for the white and colored races. . . . The first section of the statute enacts that all railway companies carrying passengers in their coaches in this State shall provide equal but separate accommodations for the white and colored races by providing two or more passenger coaches for each passenger train . . . No person or persons, shall be admitted to occupy seats in coaches other than the ones assigned to them on account of the race they belong to.

By the second section, it was enacted that the officers of such passenger trains shall have power and are hereby required to assign each passenger to the coach or compartment used for the race to which such passenger belongs; any passenger insisting on going into a coach or compartment to which by race he does not belong shall be liable to a fine of twenty-five dollars, or . . . imprisonment for . . . twenty days . . . and any officer of any railroad insisting on assigning a passenger to a coach or compartment other than the one set aside for the race to which said passenger belongs shall be liable to a fine of twenty-five dollars, or . . . imprisonment for a . . . twenty days . . . and should any passenger refuse to occupy the coach or compartment to which he or she is assigned by the officer of such railway, said officer shall have power to refuse to carry such passenger on his train . . . ❞

—Justice Henry Billings Brown, May 18, 1896

EXAMINE THE SOURCE

1. **Explaining** What does the law in question require?
2. **Determining Central Ideas** Why do you think the ruling included the phrase "equal but separate"?

Judge Marshall Harlan's Dissent

Justice John Marshall Harlan wrote the dissenting opinion in *Plessy* v. *Ferguson*, which explains his reasons for opposing the majority opinion. He was the only dissenting justice.

PRIMARY SOURCE : DISSENTING OPINION

❝ It was said in argument that the statute of Louisiana does not discriminate against either race but prescribes a rule applicable alike to white and colored citizens. . . . Everyone knows that the statutes in question had its origin in the purpose, not so much to exclude white persons from railroad cars occupied by blacks, as to exclude colored people from coaches occupied by or assigned to white persons. . . . The thing to accomplish was, under the guise of giving equal accommodations for whites and blacks, to compel the latter to keep to themselves while travelling in railroad passenger coaches. . . . If a white man and a black man choose to occupy the same public conveyance . . . it is their right to do so, and no government, proceeding alone on grounds of race, can prevent it without infringing the personal liberty of each. . . .

[I]n the view of the Constitution, . . . there is in this country no superior, dominant, ruling class of citizens. . . . The law regards man as man and takes no account of his surroundings or of his color when his civil rights as guaranteed by the supreme law of the land are involved. . . .

The arbitrary separation of citizens, on the basis of race, while they are on a public highway, is a badge of servitude wholly inconsistent with the civil freedom and the equality before the law established by the Constitution. It cannot be justified upon any legal grounds. ❞

—Justice Marshall Harlan, May 18, 1896

EXAMINE THE SOURCE

1. **Determining Context** To what part of the majority opinion does Justice Harlan most clearly respond?
2. **Analyzing** What evidence does Justice Harlan cite to support his argument that segregation "cannot be justified upon any legal grounds"?

(l)Plessy v. Ferguson, 163 U.S. 537 (1896); (r)Plessy v. Ferguson (dissent), 163 U.S. 537 (1896).

(l)Du Bois, W. E. B. The Souls of Black Folk. Chicago: A.C. McClurg, 1903; (l)Mary Church Terrell, The Progress of Colored Women; An address delivered before the National American Women's Suffrage Association at the Columbia Theater, Washington,D.C., February 18, 1898, on the occasion of its Fiftieth Anniversary (Washington, D.C.: Smith Brothers Printers, 1898); Daniel A.P. Murray Collection, Library of Congress.

C

W.E.B. Du Bois Describes Consequences of Segregation

A teacher, author, and activist, W.E.B. Du Bois, helped found the Niagara Movement and the National Association for the Advancement of Colored People. He wrote *The Souls of Black Folk* as a counterargument to Booker T. Washington's dual philosophy of self-help and accommodation.

PRIMARY SOURCE : BOOK

66 It is . . . possible to draw in nearly every Southern community a physical color-line on the map, on the one side of which whites dwell and on the other Negroes. The winding and intricacy of the geographical color-line varies . . . [I]n cities each street has its distinctive color, and only now and then do the colors meet in close proximity. . . .

To most libraries, lectures, concerts, and museums, Negroes are either not admitted at all, or on terms peculiarly galling to the pride of the very classes who might otherwise be attracted. . . . it is usually true that the very representatives of the two races . . are so far strangers that one side thinks all whites are narrow and prejudiced, and the other thinks educated Negroes dangerous and insolent. Moreover, in a land where the tyranny of public opinion and the intolerance of criticism is for obvious historical reasons so strong as in the South, such a situation is extremely difficult to correct. The white man, as well as the Negro, is bound and barred by the color-line, and many a scheme of friendliness and philanthropy, of broad-minded sympathy and generous fellowship between the two has dropped still-born because some busybody has forced the color-question to the front and brought the tremendous force of unwritten law against the innovators. 99

—W.E.B. Du Bois, from *The Souls of Black Folk*, 1903

EXAMINE THE SOURCE

1. **Identifying Cause and Effect** What examples of segregation does Du Bois give?
2. **Explaining** What does Du Bois mean by "tyranny of public opinion" and "intolerance of criticism"?

D

Mary Church Terrell Examines Segregation

Mary Church Terrell was born in the middle of the Civil War in Memphis, Tennessee. Her parents were formerly enslaved but later owned their own businesses, and Terrell received a college education. Terrell was active in the suffrage movement and served as the first president of the National Association of Colored Women. Terrell delivered this speech to the National American Woman's Suffrage Association in 1898.

PRIMARY SOURCE : SPEECH

66 . . . Questions affecting our legal status as a race are also constantly agitated by our women. In Louisiana and Tennessee, colored women have several times petitioned the legislatures of their respective States to repeal the obnoxious 'Jim Crow Car' laws, . . .nor will any stone be. . . left unturned until this **iniquitous** and unjust enactment against respectable American citizens be forever wiped from the statutes of the South.

. . . Make a tour of the settlements of colored people, who in many cities are relegated to the most noisome sections permitted by the municipal government, and behold the mites of humanity who infest them. Here are our little ones, the future representatives of the race, fairly drinking in the **pernicious** example of their elders, coming in contact with nothing but ignorance and vice, till at the age of six, evil habits are formed which no amount of civilizing or Christianizing can ever completely break. Listen to the cry of our children. 99

—Mary Church Terrell, from "The Progress of Colored Women," 1898

iniquitous wicked, sinful, grossly unjust

pernicious highly destructive or wicked

EXAMINE THE SOURCE

1. **Summarizing** What does Terrell say about the lives of African Americans in cities?
2. **Analyzing** How do these conditions serve as evidence of the harmful and unequal effects of segregation?

E

National Negro Committee

In August 1908 several thousand whites attacked members of a smaller black community in Springfield, Illinois. In response an interracial group of reformers met to form the National Negro Committee to plan out what would become the National Association for the Advancement of Colored People (NAACP). This charter outlines the founding goals of the group, including advocating for equal rights and justice and ending segregation.

PRIMARY SOURCE : GROUP CHARTER

66 We denounce the ever-growing oppression of our 10,000,000 colored fellow citizens as the greatest menace that threatens the country. Often plundered of their just share of the public funds, robbed of nearly all part in the government, segregated by common carriers, some murdered with **impunity,** and all treated with open contempt by officials, they are held in some States in practical slavery to the white community. The systematic persecution of law-abiding citizens and their **disfranchisement** on account of their race alone is a crime that will . . . drag down . . . any nation that allows it to be practiced . . .

. . . [W]e demand for the Negroes, as for all others, a free and complete education, whether by city, State or nation, a grammar school and industrial training for all and technical, professional, and academic education for the most gifted.

. . . We regard with grave concern the attempt manifest South and North to deny black men the right to work and to enforce this demand by violence and bloodshed. Such a question is too fundamental and clear even to be submitted to arbitration. 99

—The National Negro Committee, 1909

impunity freedom from legal punishment

disenfranchisement the loss of the right to vote

EXAMINE THE SOURCE

1. **Analyzing Point of View** What costs for African Americans does the platform attribute to segregation?

2. **Drawing Conclusions** How does this statement and the organization of the NAACP constitute "resistance" to segregation?

Your Inquiry Analysis

EVALUATE SOURCES AND USE EVIDENCE

Reflect back to the Compelling Question and the Supporting Question you developed at the beginning of this lesson.

1. **Gathering Sources** Which sources helped you answer the Compelling Question and your Supporting Questions most directly? Which sources, if any, challenged the answers you thought you were going to arrive at when you first created your Supporting Questions? What lingering questions do you have, and where might you look to find additional information?

2. **Evaluating Sources** Looking at the sources that helped you answer your Supporting Questions, evaluate the reliability of each source. What details made that source a particularly useful source to answer your question? What bias did it have? How might that bias have influenced the information in the source? Is the information still reliable as evidence? Why or why not?

3. **Comparing and Contrasting** Compare and contrast two of the sources in this lesson more closely. What goal does each source have, and how effective is the source in achieving that goal? How does each source add insight into *Plessy* v. *Ferguson* as a turning point in history? Explain.

COMMUNICATE CONCLUSIONS

Evaluating Claims Work in a small group to identify the main claim, or argument, of one source. On a note card record the claim and two pieces of supporting evidence provided by the source. Then reassign the groups to form new groups with at least one student for each source. Take turns sharing your note cards. As a group, use what you have learned to write a statement in response to the compelling question to share with the class.

TAKE INFORMED ACTION

Stating and Defending an Opinion The authors of these sources each stated and defended a specific opinion about the effects of segregation. Think about a social or economic policy that concerns you. State a clear position on that policy and identify two pieces of evidence—from personal experience, historical evidence (including legal precedent), or current events—to support your opinion. Use your ideas to write a paragraph in which you state and defend an opinion on the policy.

National Negro Committee. "Platform Adopted by the National Negro Committee, 1909.

12

Reviewing Migration, Industry, and Urban Society

Summary

Western Migration and Change

During the latter half of the 1800s numerous factors led to a rise in migration to lands between the Mississippi River and Pacific Ocean. In some areas discoveries of valuable metals led to mining booms as people flocked to mining areas hoping to strike it rich. The flood of miners led to rapid growth of towns and cities to serve their needs. Mining companies that could invest in equipment to search for ore soon dominated the landscape and hired many independent miners to work for them. These large-scale mining operations caused some environmental problems such as a build-up of silt that increased flooding in some areas. Eventually through government pressure the companies improved their techniques to better preserve the land.

Raising cattle was another business that thrived in the West, especially during the days of long-haul cattle drives and open range for grazing. As more farmers and sheepherders moved West, however, even the cattle industry had to make adjustments to survive.

Westward migration continued after the Civil War, as the U.S. government established more forts and people weary of war looked for a new start with the opportunity to own land. Immigrants also moved to the Western territories, helping make the West the most ethnically and racially diverse region in the nation. Westward migration often came at a price for Native Americans, who lost traditional hunting lands and were eventually forced onto reservations with fewer natural resources. U.S. military forces suppressed Native American resistance efforts. Government and charitable efforts to try to assist Native Americans often resulted in the loss of Native Americans' identities due to Americanization efforts.

Industrialization and Unionization

As more people were moving west, industrialization was starting to have a greater impact on American life and the economy. With its wealth of natural resources and large population, the United States was poised to take advantage of and improve upon the Industrial Revolution that had started in Europe. American industry brought jobs and new technology to cities and even to farmers in rural areas. It also gave rise to extremely wealthy industrial leaders like Andrew Carnegie and John D. Rockefeller, whose influence reached far beyond business. Industries such as the railroads gave rise to other businesses connecting markets and consumers.

Although industrialization created jobs, many workers faced dangerous working conditions with long hours and low pay. Concerns over the mistreatment of workers increased efforts to organize unions that advocated for change. Women, who were usually paid less than men and often worked under abusive conditions, were among the first to organize. Union efforts led to some collective actions such as strikes, but in most cases government officials supported industry leaders by breaking up strikes, sometimes violently.

Immigration and Urbanization

The availability of industrial jobs and land in North America, combined with numerous crises in European countries, gave rise to increased immigration to the United States in the late 1800s. Many of these immigrants were from poor backgrounds seeking to improve their stations in life. Industries sometimes recruited immigrants who were willing to work for low wages and in poor conditions because they needed the income. As the century wore on, the immigrant population became more diverse. Companies recruited Chinese workers to help build railroads. Many of these men later established businesses and

Factors in Western Migration and Change		
New Settlers and New Technology	Cheap land of Homestead Act encouraged settlement in the Great Plains	
	Farming technology made the Great Plains into the Wheat Belt	
	However, many farmers lost their homesteads due to drought, erosion, and overuse of the land	

sent for family members to join them. Northern industrial cities saw increasing numbers of immigrants fleeing poverty and persecution in Southern and Eastern Europe. Many immigrants came through Ellis Island on the East Coast and Angel Island on the West Coast. As the immigrant population became more diverse, some nativists pushed for limits on immigrants from certain countries, leading to a series of anti-immigration laws passed by Congress.

Job opportunities and immigration contributed to a rapid rise in the population of major U.S. cities. This population growth often outpaced housing and resources, placing great stresses on urban infrastructures. As the new economy gave rise to growing middle and wealthy classes, families with higher incomes began to move into outlying suburbs and neighborhoods, while poor families crowded into urban tenements. Overcrowding and poor resources led to problems such as increased crime, poor sanitation, disease, and fire hazards. Corrupt party bosses promised to fix such problems, but often used the system to gain wealth for themselves through corruption and bribery.

Reform, Populism, and Racism

Corruption and the growing divide between social classes led writers Mark Twain and Charles Dudley Warner to dub this era "the Gilded Age," a reference to the idea that the many underlying problems were being masked by the prosperity of the wealthy. Some believed the differences between the "haves" and "have-nots" was a sign of individual hard work or of one's natural superiority, a belief known as Social Darwinism. Some believers in Social Darwinism argued that the wealthy had a responsibility to help others through philanthropy. Some writers and philosophers challenged Social Darwinism, arguing that the wealthy would do more good by paying their workers higher wages than by contributing money to charities. These reformers ushered in a new era of movements that challenged some of the assumptions of the new economy. Some reformers tried to help poor individuals improve their prospects by teaching them new skills and helping them obtain an education. Through such efforts support for public education grew.

By the end of the century some reformers were pushing for new laws and policies to make the system fairer for all classes. At the same time, their efforts, combined with unrest among struggling farmers, led to the populist movement. This movement sought to give farmers and workers more political power and stabilize the economy, which had been prone to extreme ups and downs. Although populism never gained traction as a national political party, most of the policies the movement embraced would eventually become law.

One element that undermined both populism and the union movements was the deepening racial divide in the United States. Following the end of Reconstruction, segregation spread throughout the South and in most northern cities. Jim Crow laws and the increased dependence on sharecropping kept many African Americans mired in poverty with little political power. Racism often prevented poor and working-class white and African American people from working together for common causes. For example, unions and farming cooperatives were often segregated by race. As the passage of Jim Crow laws and lynchings increased, African American reformers like Ida B. Wells and W.E.B. Du Bois used the power of their writings to bring attention to these problems.

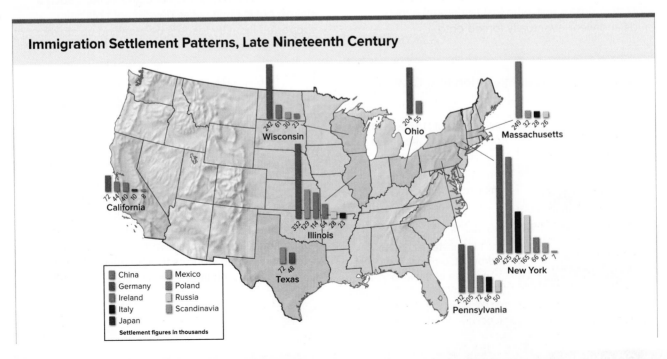

Immigration Settlement Patterns, Late Nineteenth Century

Wisconsin 242 61 30 23
Ohio 204 55
Massachusetts 249 32 28 26
California 72 44 40 10 8
Illinois 332 129 114 64 28 23
New York 480 425 182 165 66 42 7
Texas 72 48
Pennsylvania 212 205 72 66 50

China
Germany
Ireland
Italy
Japan
Mexico
Poland
Russia
Scandinavia

Settlement figures in thousands

Apply What You Have Learned

A Understanding Multiple Perspectives

Data includes factual information used for the purpose of reasoning, discussion, or calculation. Researchers rely on data to do their jobs, but good researchers take great care to understand how data is collected and presented to make sure they are drawing accurate conclusions from it. Many people use data to examine and support theories about events. They may also use data to support their own opinions on issues. When examining data, it is important to think about how it is presented and what data might be missing. Incomplete data may lead to a conclusion that might be different if further data was included. It is always important to think critically about any data you examine.

ACTIVITY **Compare Chart Data** Examine the two charts here, both of which present data about population trends within the United States between 1870 and 1890. Consider the following questions as you analyze these charts: What conclusions might one draw about population trends in the United States if they were only examining the chart labeled "Geographic Distribution of Population in the United States, 1870–1890"? What conclusions might one draw if they were only examining the chart labeled "Native American Population"? Write a paragraph explaining what conclusions you might draw from comparing both charts and how these conclusions might differ from those drawn from examining the data in each chart separately.

Geographic Distribution of Population in the United States, 1870-1890						
Year	Born in the West			Born in the East or abroad		
	Living in the West	Living in the East		Living in the East	Living in the West	
1870	3,324,048	135,769	3.9%	27,084,522	2,434,721	8.2%
1880	6,069,112	210,359	3.3%	33,685,290	3,510,737	9.4%
1890	9,416,035	282,359	2.9%	38,906,809	4,360,516	10.1%

Native American Population, 1870-1890		
	Total	On Reservations
1870	313,712	288,646
1880	306,543	256,127
1890	248,253	143,534

B Building Citizenship

In the late 1800s Jim Crow laws, discrimination, and poor working conditions were limiting the rights of African Americans, immigrants, women, and some working-class men. Yet many people from these groups found creative ways to use their skills and united with others to protest injustices they saw around them. Some did so through writing, founding organizations, or protesting.

ACTIVITY **Present a Biography** Review the names of some of the reformers mentioned in this lesson who are not featured in a separate biography. Choose one person about whom you would like to know more. Using library and Internet resources, research more information about this person's life and reform work. Create a brief presentation about this person that highlights how they tried to fight injustice during their lifetime. Present your research to a classmate or small group.

C Making Connections to Economics

The rise of industrialization brought with it many innovations, not just in technology, but also in the way business leaders structured their enterprises. Over time, some political leaders and reformers came to view a few of these new business practices as harmful to the economy and to consumers. They began to advocate for new laws to limit certain practices to make the free market fairer for all involved.

ACTIVITY **Make a Prediction** During the late 1800s corporations became much more complex. Some used organizational methods such as vertical integration and horizontal integration to maximize profits and weaken competition. Examine the chart below that shows how vertical integration and horizontal integration worked. Now consider what might happen if a steel company practiced both horizontal and vertical integration. Write down your prediction about what might happen to the price of steel in such a scenario and what impact this could have on other industries.

D Making Connections to Today

Labor unions are still around today, including some that were originally formed in the late 1800s. Membership in unions has ebbed and flowed over the years, along with their influence. Some business leaders and politicians argue that unions limit the free market and that many of the abuses that originally drove the formation of unions have been resolved. Others argue that unions are still necessary to protect workers from unfair or unsafe working conditions.

ACTIVITY **Create a Chart** Working in small groups, use your textbook, library, and Internet resources to research information to find out which unions in the United States had the highest membership in 1900. Then find out which unions have the highest membership today. Create a chart comparing union membership in 1900 to today. Note which industries had the highest union membership then and now.

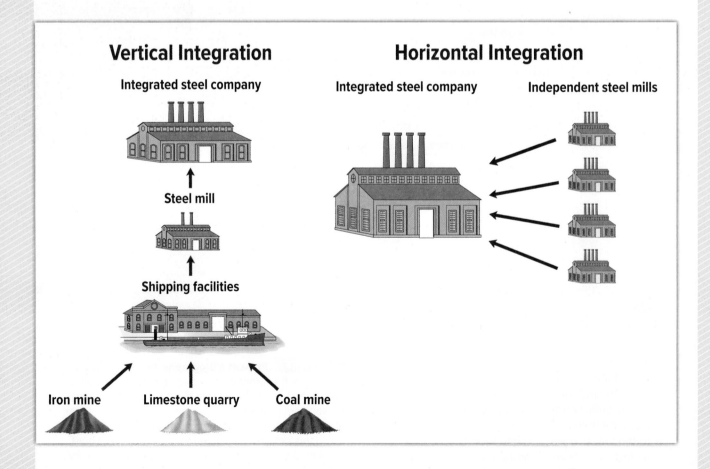

JOIN ME
THE FIRST TO FIGHT
ON LAND AND SEA
U·S·MARINES

Library of Congress Prints and Photographs Division [LC-DIG-ppmsca-40036]

TOPIC 3

American Expansion and World War I 1870–1920

World War I recruitment posters like this one from 1917 encouraged Americans to enlist in the armed forces.

INTRODUCTION LESSON

01 Introducing American Expansion and World War I   152

LEARN THE EVENTS LESSONS

02 Imperial Tensions   157

03 New Latin American Diplomacy   163

04 The U.S. Enters World War I   167

05 World War I Impacts America   173

INQUIRY ACTIVITY LESSONS

06 Turning Point: Ending World War I   179

07 Analyzing Sources: The Red Scare   183

REVIEW AND APPLY LESSON

08 Reviewing American Expansion and World War I   187

BUILDING A GLOBAL SHORTCUT

The Panama Canal is a forty-mile waterway that connects the Atlantic and Pacific Oceans. The canal's creation shortened the length of a trip between the American east and west coasts by about 8,000 nautical miles. The Canal created a simpler, swifter, and more inexpensive trade route. It is a feat of engineering that required fortitude, patience, and American intervention.

The United States controlled the Panama Canal from its completion in 1914 until 1979, but the building of the Canal began as a French project led by Ferdinand de Lesseps, who also built the Suez Canal. Lesseps planned to dig a sea-level canal along the path of the Panama Railroad, estimating 12 years and $132 million to complete the job. Digging began on January 20, 1882, after a coast-to-coast pathway had been created through the jungles of Panama. Workers used equipment such as tugboats, dredges, and steam-powered shovels. Lesseps had designed his plan to dam and divert the Chagres River after visiting the site only once, during the dry season. When the rains came, however, water and mudslides buried men and machines alike.

The rainy season also brought mosquitoes, leading to laborers dying of malaria and yellow fever. Disease caused 60 deaths in 1881, about 120 deaths in 1882, and 420 in 1883. The slow work continued until the end of 1888. French investors lost faith in Lesseps, and the Compagnie Universelle du Canal Interocéanique, which funded construction failed in 1889. The United States had paid the French about $40 million to dig eleven miles of channel. The cost in lives was also significant. It is estimated that about 20,000 French people died as a result of the Canal's construction.

Former **Rough Rider** and U.S. president Theodore Roosevelt had not given up on the Panama Canal,

> " No single great material work . . . is as of such consequence to the American people. "

however. In a speech to Congress shortly after becoming president, Roosevelt said, "No single great material work which remains to be undertaken on this continent is as of such consequence to the American people."

In 1902 the United States bought the rights to the French canal property and equipment. At the time, Panama was part of Colombia. However, since an independent Panama was beneficial to the United States' goals, the U.S. lent military support to the fight for Panamanian independence. Panama was able to declare its independence and was recognized by the United States in 1903. A 1904 treaty between Panama and the United States created the Panama Canal Zone, and work on the canal continued. The United States paid Panama $10 million dollars to take possession of the Panama Canal Zone. Initially, the United States incurred the same problems faced by the French: poor equipment and an insufficient workforce due to fear of yellow fever. With a change in leadership, however, came improvements—the project maintained American medical personnel on-site who understood the danger of mosquito-transmitted diseases. Even with more knowledge and precaution, just over 5,600 workers died during the America-led portion of the project.

Workers used heavy machinery, railroad cars, rock drills, and dynamite to remove millions of cubic yards of earth. Landslides, mudslides, and oppressive heat made the work slow and arduous. Nearly three decades after the initial project had begun, the Panama Canal officially opened to ship traffic on August 15, 1914. But Europe had more pressing matters to consider: the remarkable accomplishment was overshadowed by the beginning of World War I.

Rough Rider a volunteer cavalry unit during the Spanish-American War

The Annual Cyclopedia and Register of Important Events of the Year 1902. Copyright © 1903 by D. Appleton and Company.

President Theodore Roosevelt, at the controls of a steam shovel, inspects a Panama Canal construction site, 1906.

Determining Context Why do you think the Panama Canal would later become a symbol of American progress abroad?

Bettmann/Getty Images.

Understanding the Time and Place: The World, 1870–1920

The end of the nineteenth century and the beginning of the twentieth century marked an era of rapid change that transformed the world. Old empires expanded, and new ones emerged. An increase in technology, industrialization, trade, and imperialism made the world seem smaller and more interconnected than ever before.

The Rise of American Imperialism

European imperialism expanded in the last decades of the nineteenth century. Belgium, Germany, and Italy became new colonial powers, while France, Spain, Portugal, and Great Britain had been imperialist empires for years. Britain's navy had made it the world's dominant power for nearly a century. Many of Britain's colonies supplied it with the raw materials necessary to support its military and industrial economy. Imperialist empires sought to increase their colonies in order to find new markets, investment opportunities, and sources of raw materials.

The United States also moved toward a more imperialist foreign policy. After Reconstruction, many were uninterested in taking over new territories, but this began to change in the 1880s. This desire to annex new lands was fueled in part by Anglo-Saxonism, a theory that English-speaking nations were superior to other nations. Many Americans' desire to spread Christianity also bolstered the case for American imperialism. American imperialists were partially motivated by the notion that they had not only a right but also a duty to spread their particular ideas of civilization and democracy.

The United States began to **annex** nations for economic reasons, including access to better trade routes and materials. It purchased Alaska from Russia in 1867, giving it access to the northern rim of the Pacific. Hawaii was annexed in 1898 for new agricultural opportunities. Germany and the U.S. divided the Samoan Islands in 1899 so the U.S. gained an important harbor for trade with Asia. By the beginning of the twentieth century, the U.S. was a part of world affairs.

The United States was motivated by increasing competition with other nations; to this end, the U.S. government concentrated on building a large modern navy. The necessity of a strong navy and a network of naval bases was the focus of an 1890 book published by U.S. naval officer Captain Alfred T. Mahan. Mahan's book, *The Influence of Sea Power Upon History,* was supported by men in the highest levels of government.

A strong navy helped the U.S. win the Spanish-American War in 1898, giving Cuba its independence from Spain. However, the passage of the Platt Amendment in 1903 gave the U.S. control over Cuban affairs and the ability to buy certain lands in Cuba. Guam, Puerto Rico, and the Philippines also became part of America's empire.

Global Tensions

As more countries sought to increase their economic, military, and political strength, some colonial populations fought against foreigners trying to exert power over them. This increased global tension in many different places around the world.

For example, many countries wanted access to trade with China. In 1894 Japan and China fought a war over Korea, and the ease with which Japan won shocked many Western countries. Russia was also concerned about Japan's rising power. Russia, France, and Germany secured a diplomatic solution to the problem that forced Japan to return the land it had won from China. This guaranteed that none of these nations were excluded from Chinese trade. The 1899

Theodore Roosevelt became the first sitting president to travel officially outside the United States when he and First Lady Edith Roosevelt toured the Panama Canal Zone in 1906.

Library of Congress Prints and Photographs Division [LC-DIG-ppmsca-37588]

---

annex to incorporate a country or territory into the domain of another country or state

Major Imperial Powers, 1900

By 1900, the United States and much of Europe were involved in colonizing countries in Asia, Africa, and the Caribbean. This division of the world into colonizers and the colonized affected the lives of millions of people across the globe.

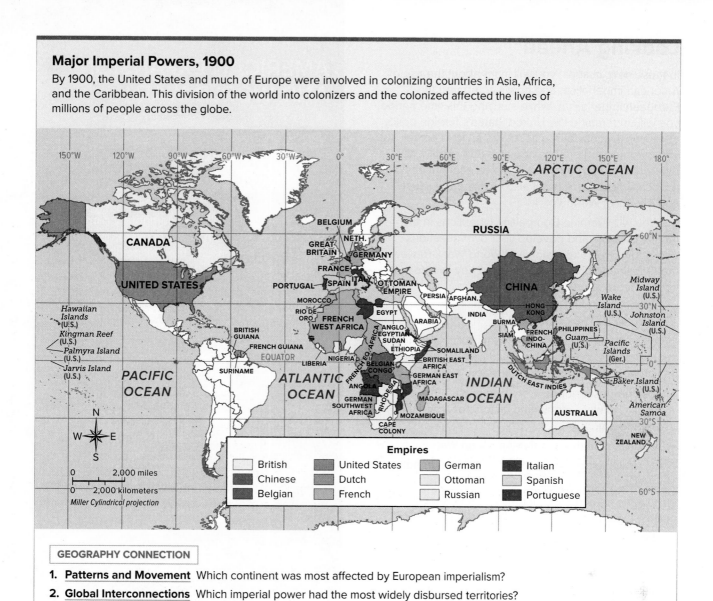

Empires

British	United States	German	Italian
Chinese	Dutch	Ottoman	Spanish
Belgian	French	Russian	Portuguese

GEOGRAPHY CONNECTION

1. **Patterns and Movement** Which continent was most affected by European imperialism?
2. **Global Interconnections** Which imperial power had the most widely disbursed territories?

Open Door Policy allowed countries to have equal access to trade with China; however, the Chinese resisted because they saw foreign influence changing their culture. Foreign embassies were attacked and more than 200 people were killed. What became known as the Boxer Rebellion ended when eight nations—Germany, Austria-Hungary, Great Britain, France, Italy, Japan, Russia, and the United States—intervened. The eruption into violence revealed the effects of foreign nations vying for power and influence in other countries.

The United States became involved in Central and South America to protect its economic interests and maintain stability and to ensure that European countries could not intervene there, a policy that originated in the 1823 Monroe Doctrine. President Theodore Roosevelt's 1904 corollary to the Monroe Doctrine stated that the United States could intervene when Latin American countries were engaged in significant wrongdoing. In

1913 President Woodrow Wilson ordered U.S. forces to intervene after dictator General Victoriano Huerta seized power in Mexico. Wilson assumed the Mexican people would welcome intervention because of Huerta's brutality, but anti-American riots broke out and the situation required international mediation. The United States sent Marines into Haiti in 1915 to put down a rebellion, and in 1916 Wilson sent American troops to replace the government in the Dominican Republic with one supported by the United States.

This global intervention was about competing to protect national interests and economies. By the late early twentieth century, the United States had become a global power intent on protecting its foreign interests and expanding its influence. In contrast, many Americans believed in isolationism, which favored staying out of foreign conflicts. Ultimately, U.S. interventionism drew the nation into the first World War.

Looking Ahead

In these next lessons, you will learn about the rise of American imperialism and how it compared to European imperialism. While studying this time period, you will understand the United States's foreign policy decisions as it navigated its role as a world power. You will learn about global competition and conflict as different empires sought to increase economic and political influence. You will also examine the causes and effects of World War I.

You will examine Compelling Questions in the Inquiry Lessons and develop your own questions about American Expansion and World War I. Review the time line to preview some of the key events that you will learn about.

What Will You Learn?

In these lessons focused on foreign policy and how the United States became a world power during the early twentieth century, you will learn:

- how the desire for new markets and the need for resources were motivating factors for American imperialism.
- the causes of the Spanish-American War.
- the developing history of American foreign policy in Asia.
- how the construction of the Panama Canal, the Roosevelt Corollary, and dollar diplomacy spread U.S. influence to other nations.
- the major causes of World War I, including militarism, alliances, imperialism, and nationalism.
- what American life was like on the home front during World War I.
- how the war affected the economy and the reasons for a Red Scare after the war.

❓ COMPELLING QUESTIONS

- **How did people seek to prevent another world war after 1919?**
- **How did fears about radical communism shape public policy?**

AMERICAN EXPANSION AND WORLD WAR I

1893 **1893** The United States overthrows Queen Liliuokalani of Hawaii

1898 USS *Maine* explodes in Havana Harbor; Treaty of Paris gives the United States temporary control of Cuba and control over Puerto Rico, Guam, and the Philippines

1904 **1904** Senate approves treaty leasing the Panama Canal

JUNE 28, 1914 Assassination of Archduke Franz Ferdinand

JULY 28, 1914 Austria-Hungary declares war on Serbia

MAY 5, 1915 German submarine sinks the *Lusitania* (right)

1917 **APRIL 6, 1917** United States declares war and joins World War I

APRIL 28, 1917 Selective Service Act passed

JUNE 15, 1917 Espionage Act passed

NOVEMBER 11, 1918 Armistice ends World War I

1918–1919 Deadly influenza pandemic spreads throughout world

1919 Race riots take place across the United States

1920 **1920** Red Scare and Palmer Raids occur

> **Sequencing Time** Identify the events that reveal the involvement of the United States in imperialism and explain how each event reveals this involvement.

Popperfoto/Getty Images.

02
Imperial Tensions

Dube, Musa W. Postcolonial Feminist Interpretation of the Bible. Nashville: Chalice Press, 2000.

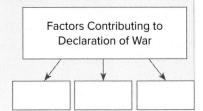

READING STRATEGY

Analyzing Key Ideas and Details As you read, use a graphic organizer like the one below to take notes about the imperial tensions that led to war.

Factors Contributing to Declaration of War

United States Imperialism

GUIDING QUESTION

Why did some people support the United States's increasing world influence?

Following the Civil War, most Americans focused on reconstructing the South, settling the West, and building up industry. But competition with Europe and a growing feeling of cultural superiority convinced many Americans in the 1880s that the United States should become a world power.

A Desire for New Markets

Many European nations were expanding overseas, a development called New Imperialism. **Imperialism** is the economic and political domination of a strong nation over a weaker one. European nations expanded their power overseas for many reasons. They needed to import raw materials for manufacturing. High tariffs in industrialized nations—intended to protect domestic industries—reduced trade, forcing companies to look for new markets overseas. Investment opportunities had also slowed in Western Europe, so Europeans began looking abroad for places to invest their capital. To protect these investments, European nations began exerting control over territories, turning some into colonies and others into **protectorates.** In a protectorate, the imperial power protected local rulers against rebellions and invasion and, in return, rulers usually had to accept Europeans' advice on how to govern their countries.

As the United States industrialized, many Americans noticed the expansion of European power overseas and took an interest in this new imperialism. Many concluded that the nation needed new overseas markets to keep its economy strong. The United States was becoming an industrial powerhouse, but overproduction threatened the economy in the late 1800s. Overseas markets offered an outlet for surplus American goods and a means of fostering economic growth and promoting stability. As a result, the country began investing in the sugar industry in Cuba and Hawaii and fruit in South America.

A Feeling of Superiority

Though economic considerations were important, they were not the only force behind expansion. Since the 1840s, the idea of Manifest Destiny had instilled in many Americans the belief that U.S. expansion was a God-given right and duty, and they looked beyond the nation's shores for places to extend their influence. In the late 1800s, many linked the idea of Anglo-Saxonism to Manifest Destiny. Historian John Fiske, for example, argued during this period that English-speaking nations had superior character, ideas, and systems of government. Americans who supported this argument believed the United States was destined to expand overseas and spread its civilization to others without recognizing that the places Americans often sought to "civilize" were established cultures that had deeply-rooted customs and beliefs.

An influential advocate of Anglo-Saxonism was Josiah Strong, a popular American minister in the late 1800s, who linked Anglo-Saxonism to Christian missionary ideas and swayed many Americans. "The Anglo-Saxon," Strong

imperialism the policy of a powerful nation exercising political and economic control over a weaker one

protectorate a nation that is under the control and protection of another nation

declared, "[is] divinely commissioned to be . . . his brother's keeper." By linking missionary work to Anglo-Saxonism, Strong convinced many to support an expansion of American power overseas.

Building a Modern Navy

As these ideas gained support, the United States became more assertive in foreign affairs. Some Americans came to believe that the United States would be shut out of foreign markets if it did not build up its navy and acquire bases overseas. U.S. naval officer Captain Alfred T. Mahan helped build public support for a navy when he published *The Influence of Sea Power Upon History* in 1890. Mahan wrote that many prosperous nations had a large fleet of merchant ships to trade with the world and a large navy to defend the nation's trade. The ideas in Mahan's book helped build public support for a big navy and for creating a network of naval bases to support it. It also tied several other ideas that increased support for imperialism. Anglo-Saxonism convinced many Americans they needed to expand into the world, while growing European imperialism threatened U.S. security. All of these ideas convinced Congress to authorize a large modern navy and expand American influence.

The United States sought to become the dominant power in the Western Hemisphere. The 1823 Monroe Doctrine had promoted the idea that any intervention by outside sources in the Americas could be interpreted as a hostile act against the United States itself. The expansion of the U.S. navy therefore represented a continuation of the Monroe Doctrine's goals of establishing the United States as a dominant power by creating a sphere of influence. Unlike European nations, the United States was more interested in establishing its political, economic, and moral influence around the globe than in establishing colonies.

Expansion in the Pacific

From the earliest days of the Republic, Americans expanded their nation by moving westward. When looking overseas for new markets, the United States looked farther west to the Pacific. As trade with Asia grew, the United States needed ports for its ships to refuel and resupply as they crossed the Pacific. In 1852 President Millard Fillmore ordered Commodore Matthew C. Perry to negotiate supplies trade with Japan. In 1853 warships under Perry's command entered Edo Bay (now Tokyo Bay). Japan's rulers, fearing the influence of Western ideas, had limited contact with the West. After seeing the warships, however, the Japanese realized they were not powerful enough to resist modern weapons. In 1854 Japan signed the Treaty of Kanagawa, giving the United States trading rights at two Japanese ports. In 1878 the United States negotiated permission to open a base at Pago Pago in the Samoan Islands, and an 1899 agreement divided Samoa between Germany

and the United States. In 1888 Germany had sought to take control of Samoa, underscoring the need for the United States to maintain a naval presence there.

Hawaii was the nation's biggest focus for Pacific expansion. Americans found that sugarcane grew well in Hawaii, and planters established sugar plantations there. In 1875 the United States signed a treaty exempting Hawaiian sugar from tariffs. This action was taken to aid Hawaii during an economic recession and to prevent Hawaii from turning to Britain or France for help. When the treaty was up for renewal, the United States insisted Hawaii grant it exclusive rights to a naval base at Pearl Harbor. In 1887 wealthy sugar planters led by Sanford Dole forced the Hawaiian king Kalākaua to accept a new constitution that limited the king's authority. The planters wanted to make Hawaii part of the United States. Tensions grew when Congress passed a new tariff in 1890 that gave subsidies to American sugar producers, making Hawaiian sugar more expensive. The planters knew that if Hawaii joined the United States, they too would get the subsidies. The next year, Queen Liliuokalani ascended the throne and tried to restore the monarchy's authority.

Backed by the American ambassador and U.S. Marines, the planters forced Liliuokalani to give up power and asked Dole to serve as president of the new Hawaiian Republic. Dole asked that the United States annex Hawaii but President Cleveland opposed imperialism, and tried to restore Queen Liliuokalani's power. Hawaii's new leaders decided to wait until a new president took office. In 1898 President McKinley allowed the United States to annex Hawaii and McKinley chose Dole to be the territory's first governor.

✓ **CHECK FOR UNDERSTANDING**

1. **Making Connections** Why did Americans' attitudes toward overseas expansion change?
2. **Identifying Cause and Effect** Why did the United States look to the Pacific for new markets?

War and Expansion

GUIDING QUESTION

How did the United States expand its power abroad during this period?

Cuba was one of Spain's oldest colonies in the Americas. Its sugarcane plantations generated considerable wealth for Spain and was a major producer of the world's sugar in the mid-1800s. Until Spain abolished slavery in 1886, about one-third of the Cuban population was enslaved and forced to work for wealthy landowners on the plantations. In 1868 Cuban rebels declared independence against Spanish authorities but the rebellion collapsed a decade later. Many Cuban rebels including their leader, José Martí, then fled to the United States.

» An undated portrait of Queen Liliuokalani

The History Collection/Alamy Stock Photo.

BIOGRAPHY

QUEEN LILIUOKALANI (1838–1917)

Queen Liliuokalani was born Lydia Kamakaeha in Honolulu on September 2, 1838, to a high-ranking Hawaiian family. Her mother served as an adviser to the Hawaiian king Kamehameha III. The young princess attended the Royal School, which was run by missionaries. At the school, she studied English and music and later traveled the Western world as part of her education. She joined the court of Kamehameha IV as a young girl, and in 1862 married John Owen Dominis, a government official who was the son of an American sea captain.

PATH TO THE THRONE Lydia's older brother, David Kalākaua, was named king in 1874. When her younger brother William Pitt Leleiohoku died in 1877, Lydia became the heir apparent. In line for the throne, she began using her royal name, Liliuokalani. While serving in King Kalākaua's court, Liliuokalani worked to establish schools for Hawaii's children and acted as regent when the king went on a world tour in 1881. Liliuokalani became the first queen of Hawaii in 1891 upon the death of her brother David, King Kalākaua.

A SHORT REIGN As queen, Liliuokalani strongly resisted U.S. influence. She sought to restore the full rights of the monarchy and expand rights for native Hawaiians. While many Hawaiians supported her efforts, Sanford Dole and other foreign business leaders removed her from the throne in 1893 and set up a provisional government. Her supporters waged a revolt in 1895 that led to Liliuokalani's arrest and temporary confinement in the palace. Liliuokalani never regained the throne, and Hawaii was annexed in 1898. Nevertheless, until her death in 1917, Liliuokalani remained in Honolulu as a proud Hawaiian citizen.

> **Explaining** How did Queen Liliuokalani become the first queen of Hawaii?

Supporting Cuba and Calls for War

By the early 1890s, the United States and Cuba had become closely linked economically. Cuba exported much of its sugar to the United States, and Americans had invested approximately $50 million in Cuba's sugar plantations, mines, and railroads. These economic ties created a crisis in 1894 when the United States imposed a new sugar tariff that devastated Cuba's economy. This caused Cuban rebels to launch a new rebellion in early 1895. Martí returned to lead the rebellion but died during the fighting. The rebels seized control of eastern Cuba and established the Republic of Cuba in September 1895. President Cleveland declared the United States neutral, but stories of Spanish atrocities in the *New York Journal* and the *New York World* swayed many in the rebels' favor. News reports, in which writers exaggerated or made up stories to attract readers, became known as **yellow journalism.** Although some stories were invented, Cubans indeed suffered horribly. The Spanish sent nearly 200,000 troops to put down the rebellion. To prevent villagers from helping the rebels, the Spanish herded hundreds of thousands of rural men, women, and children into "reconcentration camps," where tens of thousands died of starvation and disease.

In 1897 William McKinley became president of the United States. In September of that year, he asked Spain if the United States could help negotiate an end to the conflict so that the United States would not have to intervene in the war. Spain removed General Valeriano Weyler as governor general and offered the Cubans **autonomy** but only if Cuba remained part of the Spanish Empire. The rebels refused to negotiate.

Spain's concessions enraged many Spanish loyalists in Cuba, and in January 1898, they rioted in Havana. McKinley sent the battleship USS *Maine* to Havana to protect Americans living there, but on February 15, 1898, the *Maine* exploded in the Havana Harbor and 266 people died. Investigators in 1976 theorized that the explosion was likely due to a malfunction in the ship but, at the time, many Americans believed the Spanish did it. "Remember the *Maine*!" became the rallying cry for war against Spain.

yellow journalism sensational, exaggerated journalism

autonomy the right of self-government

McKinley faced tremendous pressure to go to war. **Jingoism**—aggressive nationalism—was strong within the Republican Party, but for most Americans concerns over the plight of the Cuban people played a greater role in pushing the United States toward war. On April 11, 1898, McKinley asked Congress to authorize the use of force, citing Spain's mistreatment of the Cuban people. On April 19, Congress proclaimed Cuba independent, demanded that Spain withdraw, and gave McKinley the authorization to deploy the armed forces if Spain did not comply. On April 24, Spain declared war on the United States.

A War on Two Fronts

The U.S. Navy blockaded Cuba, and the American naval squadron based in Hong Kong attacked Spain's fleet based in the Spanish colony of the Philippines. The U.S. Navy wanted to prevent the Spanish fleet from sailing east to attack the United States. On May 1, 1898, American ships entered Manila Bay in the Philippines and quickly destroyed the Spanish fleet. This victory caused the army to hastily assemble and sail 20,000 troops from San Francisco to the Philippines. On the way, the Americans seized the Spanish island of Guam.

While waiting for the American troops to arrive, U.S. Navy Commodore George Dewey contacted Emilio Aguinaldo, a Filipino revolutionary leader who had tried to overthrow the Spanish in 1896. Per Dewey's request, Aguinaldo and his rebels took control of most of the islands while American troops seized the Philippine capital of Manila.

The Spanish in Cuba were not prepared for war. Their soldiers were weak and sick, and their warships were old with untrained crews. Without the Spanish fleet, Spain struggled to supply its troops in Cuba. But the U.S. Army was also under-prepared. The army had recruited volunteers but lacked proper resources to train and equip them. One volunteer cavalry unit was a rough mix of cowboys, miners, and law officers known as the "Rough Riders" with Theodore Roosevelt second in command. Roosevelt had resigned as assistant secretary of the navy so that he could serve in Cuba.

Between June 22 and 24 in 1898, some 17,000 U.S. troops landed east of Santiago, Cuba. The Spanish fleet, protected by powerful shore-based guns, occupied Santiago Harbor. Americans wanted to capture those guns to drive the Spanish fleet out of the harbor and into battle with the American fleet waiting nearby. On July 1, Americans attacked Spanish positions near Santiago and the San Juan Heights. The Rough Riders and the 9th and 10th Cavalry Regiments—made up of African Americans nicknamed buffalo soldiers by the indigenous peoples they had fought in the West—attacked and held Kettle Hill. They then assisted in the capture of San Juan Hill. In Santiago the Spanish commander ordered the Spanish fleet to flee

the harbor, and on July 3, American warships attacked them, destroying every Spanish vessel. The Spanish in Santiago surrendered, leaving American troops to occupy nearby Puerto Rico.

Though the buffalo soldiers made valuable contributions while serving in Cuba, they had previously encountered resistance and conflict at home. Tampa, Florida, had served as a staging ground for soldiers headed to Cuba. There, the buffalo soldiers faced widespread discrimination from white businesses. On June 6, 1898, a group of drunken white soldiers shot at an African American child, narrowly missing him. The buffalo soldiers retaliated, and a riot between white and African American soldiers broke out. Many white businesses were destroyed in the process. In response, the military quickly loaded the soldiers on transports and sailed for Cuba, where these African American soldiers distinguished themselves in several battles.

Rebellion in the Philippines

Initially, Emilio Aguinaldo had welcomed the U.S. military, believing they would help the Philippines gain independence from Spain. He soon learned the United States had its own interests in mind. In 1899 Aguinaldo ordered his troops to attack the American soldiers who had been sent to the Philippines.

To fight the Filipino soldiers, the U.S. military established its own reconcentration camps to separate Filipino guerrillas from civilians. Hundreds of thousands died in military actions and from disease and starvation. More U.S. soldiers died fighting the Filipino guerrillas than died in combat during the Spanish-American War. In March 1901 American troops captured Aguinaldo, and on July 4, 1902, the United States declared the war over. However, fighting continued for years afterward. Gradually, the Filipinos gained more control over their government, and by the mid-1930s, they elected their own congress and president. The Philippines did not achieve full independence from the United States until 1946.

✓ **CHECK FOR UNDERSTANDING**

1. **Analyzing** Why was the United States willing to go to war with Spain over Cuba?

2. **Contrasting** How was the Spanish-American War different from earlier U.S. wars?

An American Empire

GUIDING QUESTION

What different points of view formed around the imperial debate?

American and Spanish leaders signed the Treaty of Paris on December 10, 1898. The United States

---

jingoism extreme nationalism marked by aggressive foreign policy

acquired Puerto Rico and Guam and paid Spain $20 million for the Philippines. After an intense debate, the Senate approved the treaty in February 1899. Americans debated what to do. Cuba received its independence but the United States grappled with what to do with the Philippines. The United States faced a difficult choice—remain true to its republican ideals or become an imperial power that ruled a foreign country without the consent of its people. The issue sparked intense political debate.

The Debate Over Annexation

Many people emphasized the benefits of taking the Philippines. It would provide another Pacific naval base, a stopover on the way to China, and a large market for American goods. Others believed America had a duty to help "less civilized" peoples. "Surely this Spanish war has not been a grab for the empire," commented one minister, "but a heroic effort [to] free the oppressed and to teach millions of ignorant, debased human beings thus freed how to live." While American troops had fought the guerrillas, the first U.S. civilian governor of the islands, William Howard Taft, had tried to win over the Filipinos by improving education, transportation, and health care. These reforms had slowly reduced Filipino hostility.

TAKE YOUR CHOICE.

Do you want a man who, having raised the stars and stripes on our new possession, will maintain them with dignity; or a man who will cut down "Old Glory" and make the laughing stock of the world?

Many people debated the decision to annex the Philippines, arguing over the costs and benefits of the new empire. In this 1896 campaign poster, President McKinley raises the American flag over the Philippines while William Jennings Bryan tries to chop it down.

Making Connections Based on the image, what do you think McKinley is trying to accomplish?

Not all Americans supported annexation. An anti-imperialist movement quickly formed, and many prominent Americans voiced their opposition to the United States becoming an imperial power. Andrew Carnegie argued that the cost of empire far outweighed the economic benefits. Samuel Gompers, head of the American Federation of Labor, worried that competition from cheap Filipino labor would drive down American wages. The social worker and reformer Jane Addams and the writer Mark Twain both believed imperialism violated American principles and traditions. Many people argued that it was inconsistent for a democratic republic founded on the idea of self-government to rule over others who would have no say in who was appointed to rule them. Presidential candidate William Jennings Bryan ran for the White House against President McKinley by arguing that there was no economic justification for imperialism. In the end, despite the objections of anti-imperialists, President McKinley decided to annex the islands. His thinking blended the ideas of many military and business leaders with those of Anglo-Saxonism.

A Turning Point

The year 1898 was a major turning point in American history. In just a few short months, the United States had defeated a European nation, demonstrated that its navy was one of the most powerful in the world, and had acquired its own empire. Increasingly the world's other great powers had to take American perspectives and policies into account, and in the years ahead the United States found itself drawn into issues and events thousands of miles from its own shores. The United States had become a world power.

Although the United States had promised to grant Cuba its independence, conditions were attached to the new Cuban constitution. The Platt Amendment, limited Cuba's ability to make treaties with other nations. Cuba had to allow the United States to buy or lease naval stations in its territory. The United States could also intervene in Cuba to keep order. The Platt Amendment effectively made Cuba an American protectorate and was not repealed until 1934.

In 1900 Congress passed the Foraker Act, establishing a civil government for Puerto Rico. The law provided for an elected legislature, and a governor and executive council that were appointed by the U.S. president. In 1917 Congress granted Puerto Ricans U.S. citizenship, and 30 years later, Puerto Ricans were allowed to elect their own governor. The debate over whether Puerto Rico should become a state, become independent, or continue as a self-governing commonwealth continues to this day.

Economic Effects of the War

By 1897, the year before the war, Americans had invested roughly $700 million in business ventures

PHOTO: Niday Picture Library/Alamy Stock Photo; TEXT: Weisberger, Bernard A. The Life History Of The United States, Vol 8. New York: Time, Inc., 1890.

overseas. By 1904, they had invested over $2.5 billion. American investment in Cuba's sugar plantations and mines surged. Hawaii was now an American territory, and companies there no longer had to pay tariffs to ship goods to the United States. The United States also invested in Puerto Rico's sugar industry and expanded its tobacco industry. Similar investments in the Philippines expanded its sugar industry and helped build railroads and open mines.

These developments cost both money and lives. Together, the war with Spain and the battle against the Filipino guerrillas had cost some $400 million. Including those who died in combat and as a result of disease, over 5,400 men had died in the war with Spain, and another 4,200 died fighting Filipino guerrillas.

American Diplomacy in Asia

In 1899 the United States was a major power in Asia, with naval bases all across the Pacific. Operating from those bases, the United States Navy—by then the world's third-largest navy—could exert power anywhere in East Asia. The nation's main interest in Asia, however, was not conquest but commerce. Between 1895 and 1900, U.S. exports to China quadrupled. Large Chinese markets excited U.S. business leaders, especially in the textile, oil, and steel industries.

In 1894 war erupted between China and Japan over Korea, which was a client state dependent upon China. Japan easily defeated China's massive military, demonstrating the extent of Japan's industrialization. In the peace treaty, China recognized Korea's independence and gave Japan territory in Manchuria.

Russians were concerned about Japan's rising power. They did not want Japan to acquire the Russia-bordered territory in Manchuria. Backed by France and Germany, Russia forced Japan to return the Manchurian territory it had acquired then demanded China lease the territory to Russia instead in 1898. Leasing meant the territory would still belong to China, even though a foreign government would maintain control. Soon Germany, France, and Britain demanded "leaseholds" in China. Each leasehold became the center of a country's **sphere of influence,** an area where a foreign nation controlled economic development.

U.S. politicians and businesspeople worried that China would be divided among the European powers and Americans would not be allowed to do business there. President McKinley and Secretary of State John Hay both supported an **Open Door policy** that would allow all countries to trade with China. In 1899 Hay asked countries with leaseholds in China not to discriminate against other nations that wanted to do business in their spheres of influence. Each nation responded by saying it accepted the Open Door policy

but would not follow it unless the others agreed. This policy helped the U.S. economy by ensuring that American companies could continue trade with China.

The Boxer Rebellion

While foreign countries debated access to China's market, secret Chinese societies organized to fight foreign control and influence. One group, the Society of Righteous and Harmonious Fists, was known to Westerners as the Boxers. In 1900 this group decided to destroy both the "foreign devils" and their Chinese Christian converts, whom they believed were corrupting Chinese society. The Boxers and some Chinese troops attacked foreign embassies in Peking (now Beijing) and Tientsin (now Tianjin), killing more than 200 foreigners. A large multinational force rescued those trapped and ended the rebellion.

During the crisis, Secretary of State John Hay convinced the participating powers to accept compensation from China for damages caused by the rebellion. The European powers agreed not to break up China into European-controlled colonies. The United States retained access to China's lucrative trade and gained a larger market for its own goods.

After McKinley's death in 1901, Vice President Theodore Roosevelt became president. Roosevelt supported the Open Door policy. He helped negotiate a 1905 resolution to a war between Japan and Russia. Roosevelt convinced Russia to recognize Japan's territorial gains and persuaded Japan to end the conflict. As the United States and Japan continued to compete for greater influence in Asia, they pledged to respect each other's territorial possessions, uphold the Open Door policy, and support China's independence.

✓ **CHECK FOR UNDERSTANDING**

1. **Contrasting** How did William Jennings Bryan and President McKinley differ in their views on annexation of the Philippines?

2. **Summarizing** Why did the United States want to eliminate spheres of influence in China?

LESSON ACTIVITIES

1. **Narrative Writing** Suppose that you are a Filipino living during the time of the U.S. annexation of the Philippine Islands. Write a journal entry in which you describe your feelings about American control of the islands. Conduct additional research to help you construct an effective narrative.

2. **Collaborating** Work in a small group to identify how the Spanish-American War altered America's foreign policy. As a group, design a poster or political cartoon illustrating America's foreign policy during the period directly following the Spanish-American War.

---

sphere of influence area of a country where a foreign nation enjoys special rights and powers

Open Door policy a policy that allowed all countries to trade freely with China

03

New Latin American Diplomacy

Theodore Roosevelt (1858-1919) to Henry L. Sprague, Albany, New York, January 26, 1900, Carbon copy letterbook, Gift of the heirs of Theodore Roosevelt, Jr., 1958-1965. Manuscript Division, Library of Congress.

READING STRATEGY

Analyzing Key Ideas and Details As you read, use a graphic organizer like the one below to take notes.

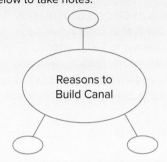

Reasons to Build Canal

U.S. Intervention in Latin America

GUIDING QUESTION

How did U.S. foreign policy in Latin America change during the Roosevelt, Taft, and Wilson administrations?

President McKinley was reelected in 1900, but his second term was cut short by an assassin's bullet. Vice President Theodore Roosevelt then assumed the presidency. As president, Roosevelt favored increasing U.S. power and believed that the United States had a duty to shape the "less civilized" corners of the Earth.

Roosevelt and Taft's Diplomacy

Roosevelt's point of view about what made a country more civilized carried with it many assumptions. He believed that displaying U.S. power to the world helped advance the success of the nation's foreign policy goals. Roosevelt expressed this belief with a West African saying, "Speak softly and carry a big stick."

In contrast, Roosevelt's successor, William Howard Taft, placed less emphasis on military force and more on economic development to ensure American influence and power around the world.

The Panama Canal

Roosevelt's "big stick" policy was evident in the American acquisition and construction of the Panama Canal. He and others believed that building a canal through Central America was vital to U.S. power in the world and would save time and money for commercial and military shipping. Instead of ships sailing 12,000 miles (19,312 km) around the treacherous tip of South America to get from New York to San Francisco, the Canal's route was only 4,900 miles (7,886 km) and took half the time.

In 1889 a French company abandoned its efforts to build a canal in Panama. In 1902 Congress authorized the U.S. purchase of the French company's assets and the construction of a canal. Panama was a province of Colombia at the time. In 1903 the United States offered Colombia a large sum of money and yearly rent for the right to build the artificial waterway and to control a narrow strip of land on either side of it. When Colombia refused, tension increased between Colombia and Panamanians who opposed Colombian rule. Worried that the United States might back out of its offer, the French company met with Panamanian officials and together they decided to make a deal with the United States.

In November 1903, with U.S. warships looming offshore, Panama revolted against Colombia. Within days, the United States recognized Panama's independence, and the two nations signed a treaty allowing the Panama Canal to be built. Roosevelt would be criticized on many fronts for the manner in which he "recognized" Panama's independence.

Panama's geography made building the Canal a challenge. The middle of the country is much higher than sea level. Engineers built a series of lakes and concrete locks to raise and lower ships as they traveled through the Canal.

Building the Canal was not just a daunting engineering and technological undertaking. It was also detrimental to workers' health and safety. During construction, malaria and yellow fever, transmitted by mosquitoes, sickened workers and slowed their progress. By inspecting and controlling all potential breeding places, Surgeon General of the U.S. Army William Crawford Gorgas helped minimize disease and allowed workers to continue building the canal.

Nonetheless, some 5,600 workers—many of them black West Indians—lost their lives as a result of accidents or disease between 1902 and 1914, when the Canal was completed. Despite the many significant challenges, the Panama Canal project both embodied the spirit of expansionism and served as an important tool. It became a symbol of American political power, domestic strength, and ingenuity in an international setting.

✓ CHECK FOR UNDERSTANDING

Analyzing How did completion of the Panama Canal help the United States compete internationally?

The Roosevelt Corollary

GUIDING QUESTION

Was President Roosevelt correct in his belief that a strong military presence improved U.S. global influence?

By the early 1900s, American officials had become concerned about large debts that Latin American nations owed European banks. In 1902, after Venezuela defaulted on its debts, Britain, Germany, and Italy blockaded Venezuelan ports. The crisis was resolved peacefully after the United States pressed

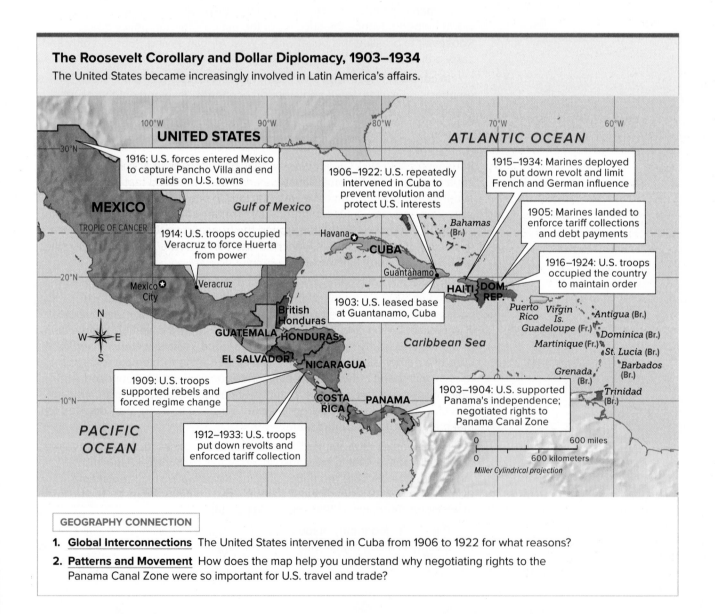

The Roosevelt Corollary and Dollar Diplomacy, 1903–1934
The United States became increasingly involved in Latin America's affairs.

1916: U.S. forces entered Mexico to capture Pancho Villa and end raids on U.S. towns

1906–1922: U.S. repeatedly intervened in Cuba to prevent revolution and protect U.S. interests

1915–1934: Marines deployed to put down revolt and limit French and German influence

1905: Marines landed to enforce tariff collections and debt payments

1914: U.S. troops occupied Veracruz to force Huerta from power

1916–1924: U.S. troops occupied the country to maintain order

1903: U.S. leased base at Guantanamo, Cuba

1909: U.S. troops supported rebels and forced regime change

1903–1904: U.S. supported Panama's independence; negotiated rights to Panama Canal Zone

1912–1933: U.S. troops put down revolts and enforced tariff collection

GEOGRAPHY CONNECTION

1. **Global Interconnections** The United States intervened in Cuba from 1906 to 1922 for what reasons?
2. **Patterns and Movement** How does the map help you understand why negotiating rights to the Panama Canal Zone were so important for U.S. travel and trade?

both sides to reach an agreement. Roosevelt then gave an address to Congress in which he stated what came to be known as the Roosevelt Corollary to the Monroe Doctrine. It stated that the United States would intervene in Latin American affairs when necessary to maintain economic and political stability in the Western Hemisphere.

> 66 Chronic wrongdoing . . . may, in America, as elsewhere, ultimately require intervention by some civilized nation, and in the Western Hemisphere the adherence of the United States to the Monroe Doctrine may force the United States, however reluctantly, in flagrant cases of such wrongdoing or impotence, to the exercise of an international police power. If every country washed by the Caribbean Sea would show the progress in stable and just civilization which with the aid of the Platt Amendment Cuba has shown since our troops left the island, and which so many of the republics in both Americas are constantly and brilliantly showing, all question of interference by this Nation with their affairs would be at an end. 99

> —Theodore Roosevelt, from his Fourth Annual Message to Congress, December 6, 1904

The goal of the Roosevelt Corollary was to prevent European powers from using the debt problems of Latin America to justify intervening in the region. The United States first applied the Roosevelt Corollary in the Dominican Republic, which had fallen behind on its debt payments to European nations. In 1905 the United States began collecting customs tariffs in the Dominican Republic, using the Marine Corps as its agent.

The Roosevelt Corollary effectively transformed the passive Monroe Doctrine into an effective policing tool to prevent nations Roosevelt deemed "less civilized" from drawing European powers into the region. Without entry, these European powers could not threaten the political power of the United States in the region.

Dollar Diplomacy

President Taft believed that supporting Latin American industry would increase trade and profits for American businesses, lift Latin America countries out of poverty, and increase American influence in the region. His policy came to be called **dollar diplomacy.**

To give Europeans fewer reasons to intervene in Latin American affairs, Taft's administration worked to replace European loans with loans from American banks. In 1911 American bankers began making loans to Nicaragua to support its shaky government. The next year, civil unrest forced Nicaragua's president to ask for greater assistance. U.S. marines entered Nicaragua, replaced the customs collector with an American agent, and formed a committee to control the customs commissions. U.S. troops supported the government and customs until 1933.

Woodrow Wilson's Diplomacy in Mexico

"It would be the irony of fate," said Woodrow Wilson just before he was inaugurated in 1913, "if my administration had to deal chiefly with foreign affairs." Wilson's experience and interest were in domestic policy. He was a university professor before entering politics and was a committed progressive, someone who applied new ideas to social reform. Foreign affairs, however, absorbed much of Wilson's time and energy as president.

Wilson opposed imperialism, believing that democracy was essential to a nation's stability and prosperity. He wanted the United States to promote democracy to create a world free of revolution and war. He hoped the United States would lead by moral example instead of force, but his first international crisis thwarted that hope. Even though Wilson was a proponent of democracy and self-determination, he also believed the United States had special rights and duties in Latin America. This belief led to U.S. intervention in Mexico.

For more than 30 years, Porfirio Díaz ruled Mexico as a dictator. During Díaz's reign, Mexico became much more industrialized, but foreign investors owned the new railroads and factories that were built. Most Mexican citizens remained poor and landless, causing discontent to erupt into revolution in 1910. Francisco Madero, a reformer who seemed to support democracy, constitutional government, and land reform, led the revolution. Madero, however, was an unskilled administrator. Worried about Madero's plans for land reform, landowners plotted against him. In 1913, General Victoriano Huerta seized power, and Madero was murdered.

Huerta's brutality repulsed Wilson, who refused to recognize the new government. Instead, Wilson announced a new policy. To win U.S. recognition, groups that seized power in Latin America would have to establish a government based on law, not on force. Wilson believed that U.S. support would encourage a less violent leader than Huerta to emerge. Meanwhile, Wilson ordered the navy to intercept arms shipments to Huerta's government and permitted Americans to arm Huerta's opponents. In April 1914 American sailors visiting the Mexican city of Tampico were arrested after entering a restricted area. After their release, their commander demanded an apology, but the

---

dollar diplomacy a policy of using financial power to reap international influence

(l)Theodore Roosevelt. Fourth Annual Message. December 6, 1904. John T. Woolley and Gerhard Peters, The American Presidency Project [online]. Santa Barbara, CA. Available from World Wide Web: http://www.presidency.ucsb.edu/ws/index.php?pid=29545#axzz1NCgvU Z78; (r)Brands, H. W. Woodrow Wilson. New York: Henry Holt and Company, 2003.

An American trooper stands guard over the burned remains of Columbus, New Mexico, a town raided by Pancho Villa and Mexican soldiers in 1916.

Speculating How might such a raid have influenced American sentiments about relations between the United States and Mexico?

Mexicans refused. Wilson saw the refusal as an opportunity to overthrow Huerta. Soon after Congress authorized the use of force, Wilson learned that a German ship was unloading weapons at the Mexican port of Veracruz. Wilson immediately ordered American warships to Veracruz, where U.S. Marines seized the city. Although the president expected the Mexican people to welcome his action, anti-American riots broke out. Wilson then accepted international mediation to settle the dispute. Venustiano Carranza, whose forces had acquired arms from the United States, became Mexico's president.

Mexican farmers who believed Carranza did not do enough to help the common people conducted raids into the United States, hoping to force Wilson to intervene. In March 1916, Francisco "Pancho" Villa (VEE•yuh) and a group of **guerrillas** burned the town of Columbus, New Mexico, killing 17 Americans. Wilson responded by sending about 5,800 troops under General John J. Pershing across the border to find and capture Villa, but the expedition ended without success.

Wilson's Mexican policy damaged U.S. foreign relations. The British ridiculed the president's attempt to "shoot" the Mexicans into self-government. Latin Americans regarded his "moral diplomacy" as no improvement over Theodore Roosevelt's "big stick" diplomacy. In fact, Wilson followed Roosevelt's example in the Caribbean. In 1914 he negotiated exclusive rights for naval bases and a canal with Nicaragua, and in 1915 he sent marines into Haiti to put down a rebellion. In 1916 he sent troops into the Dominican Republic to set up a government he hoped would be more stable and democratic than the current regime.

✓ **CHECK FOR UNDERSTANDING**

Explaining What did the Roosevelt Corollary state?

LESSON ACTIVITIES

1. **Narrative Writing** Suppose that you are a Mexican citizen during Wilson's presidency. Write a radio news broadcast expressing your feelings about American actions in Mexico. Consider how best to communicate your message with your audience.

2. **Presenting** You and a partner are members of President Taft's administration working to replace European loans with loans from American banks. What kind of research would you need to do in order to ensure a smooth transition with the loans and the banks? Work together to create a proposal to present to the class.

guerrilla armed fighters who carry out surprise attacks

Corbis Historical/Getty Images

04

The U.S. Enters World War I

READING STRATEGY

Analyzing Key Ideas and Details As you read, identify the factors that contributed to World War I by completing a graphic organizer similar to the one here.

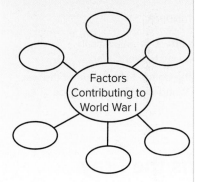

The War Begins

GUIDING QUESTION

What political circumstances in Europe led to World War I?

President Wilson wanted the United States, as a global power, to promote democracy to create a world free of revolution and war, but political conflicts in Europe prevented his vision from becoming a reality. Though there was resistance at home to U.S. involvement in a European war, eventually, the United States sent troops to fight in Europe.

Militarism and Alliances

In 1914 tensions were building among European nations, stemming from events that started in the previous century. As part of its plan to unify Germany in 1870, Prussia forced France to give up territory along the German border. To protect itself, Germany signed alliances with Italy and with the empire of Austria-Hungary, which controlled much of southeastern Europe. This became known as the Triple Alliance.

The new alliance alarmed Russian leaders, who feared that Germany intended to expand eastward. Russia and Austria-Hungary were also competing for influence in the Balkan region of southeastern Europe. Russia and France shared a common interest in opposing Germany and Austria-Hungary, which led to the Franco-Russian Alliance in 1894. The two nations promised to come to each other's aid in a war against the Triple Alliance.

Such alliances fostered **militarism**—the strong buildup of armed forces to intimidate and threaten other nations. Over time, German militarism pushed Britain to become involved in the alliance system. Britain's policy was to try to prevent one nation from controlling all of Europe. By the late 1800s, Germany had clearly become Europe's strongest nation. In 1898 Germany began building a large modern navy. The buildup threatened the British, who rushed to build warships. By the early 1900s, Britain and Germany were engaged in an arms race. The race convinced Britain to build closer ties with France and Russia, but the British refused to sign a formal alliance, so the relationship became known as an *entente cordiale*, or friendly understanding. Britain, France, and Russia became known as the Triple Entente.

For years the Ottoman Empire and the Austro-Hungarian Empire had ruled the Balkans. But, as **nationalism** spread in the late 1800s and early 1900s, national groups such as the South Slavs—Serbs, Bosnians, Croats, and Slovenes—began to press for independence. The Serbs, who were the first to gain independence, formed a nation called Serbia between the two empires. Serbia believed that its mission was to unite the South Slavs.

Russia supported the Serbs, but Austria-Hungary worked to limit Serbia's growth. In 1908 Austria-Hungary annexed Bosnia from the Ottoman Empire, outraging the Serbs. The annexation demonstrated that Austria-Hungary had no intention of letting the Slavic people in its empire become independent.

---

militarism a policy of aggressive military preparedness

nationalism loyalty or devotion to a nation

An Assassination Brings War

In June 1914 Archduke Franz Ferdinand, heir to the Austro-Hungarian throne, visited the Bosnian capital of Sarajevo. As he and his wife rode through the city, Bosnian revolutionary Gavrilo Princip rushed their car and shot them dead. The assassination occurred with the knowledge of Serbian officials who hoped to start a war that would damage Austria-Hungary.

Austria-Hungary decided they had to crush Serbia in order to prevent Slavic nationalism from undermining its empire. Knowing an attack on Serbia might trigger a war with Russia, the Austrians asked their German allies for support. Austria-Hungary then issued an ultimatum to the Serbian government. The Serbs counted on Russia to back them up, and the Russians, in turn, counted on France.

On July 28 Austria-Hungary declared war on Serbia. Russia immediately mobilized its army, including troops stationed on the German border. Within days, Germany declared war on Russia and France. World War I had begun. Germany immediately launched a massive invasion of France to secure the west before turning its attention east to Russia. German forces needed to advance through Belgium, but the British had signed a treaty with Belgium. When German forces crossed into Belgium, Britain declared war.

The assassination of Archduke Franz Ferdinand, heir to the Austro-Hungarian Empire, and his wife Sophie, ignited a war that tested European alliances.

Those fighting for the Triple Entente were called the Allies. Italy was initially part of the Triple Alliance but joined the Triple Entente in 1915 due to long-standing tensions with Austria-Hungary. Germany and Austria-Hungary joined with the Ottoman Empire and Bulgaria to form the Central Powers. Germany's plan was to defeat France before Russia could mobilize, but it failed. When Russia invaded Germany, the Germans were forced to move some troops eastward to thwart the attack. The Western Front became a bloody stalemate along hundreds of miles of trenches, with British and French forces on one side and German forces on the other.

✓ **CHECK FOR UNDERSTANDING**

1. **Identifying Cause and Effect** What political circumstances in Europe led to World War I?

2. **Summarizing** Before the United States entered the war, who were the Allies in World War I? Who were the Central Powers?

America Joins the Fray

GUIDING QUESTION

What motivated the United States to join the war?

When World War I began, President Wilson was determined to keep the United States out of a European conflict. He immediately declared the United States to be neutral and asked all Americans "to be impartial in thought as well as in action." Despite Wilson's hopes for neutrality, events gradually drew the United States into the war on the side of the Allies.

The Neutrality Debate

Despite the president's plea, most Americans supported one side or the other. Many German Americans supported their homeland, and many Irish Americans harbored hostility toward Britain, but, in general, public opinion favored the Allies. Many Americans valued the heritage, language, and political ideals they shared with Britain. Others treasured America's links with France, a great friend to America during the Revolutionary War.

For more than two years, the United States remained neutral. A debate began over whether the country should prepare for war. Supporters of the "preparedness" movement believed that preparing was the best way to ensure the United States was not forced into the conflict. The debate would be an issue in the 1916 presidential election. Wilson campaigned on keeping the United States out the war and the hope of staying disentangled from the European conflict. His opponent, Supreme Court Justice Charles Evans Hughes, questioned whether it was possible for any nation to remain neutral and uninvolved:

PHOTO: Bettmann/Getty Images; TEXT: Wilson, Woodrow. 1914. Message to Congress, 63rd Cong., 2d Sess., Senate Doc. No. 566. Washington.

Participants in a women's peace parade march down Fifth Avenue in New York City, August 29, 1914.

Analyzing Perspectives
Why do you think these women organized for peace in 1914 when the United States did not enter the war until 1917?

PHOTO: Universal History Archive/Universal Images Group/Getty Images; TEXT: Official Report of the Proceedings of the Sixteenth Republican National Convention, reported by George L. Hart. Copyright 1916 by Lafayette B. Gleason.

66 It is to be expected that nations will continue to arm in defense of their respective interests, as they are conceived, and nothing will avail to diminish this burden save some practical guaranty of international order. We, in this country, can, and should, maintain our fortunate freedom from entanglements with interests and policies, which do not concern us. But there is no national isolation in the world of the twentieth century. 99

—Charles Evans Hughes, quoted in *The Official Report of the Proceedings of the Sixteenth Republican National Convention*, June 1916

In 1915 Carrie Chapman Catt and Jane Addams—leaders of the women's suffrage movement—founded the Women's Peace Party. This organization, along with others such as the League to Limit Armament, worked to keep America out of the war.

One select group of Americans was decidedly pro-British: President Wilson's cabinet. Only Secretary of State William Jennings Bryan favored neutrality. The other cabinet members argued forcefully on behalf of Britain. Many U.S. military leaders also backed Britain, believing an Allied victory was the only way to preserve the world's balance of power.

British officials worked diligently to win American support. One method they used was **propaganda,** or information designed to influence opinion. The British cut Germany's transatlantic telegraph cable to the United States so most war news would be based on British reports. The American ambassador to Britain endorsed many of these reports, and American public opinion swayed in favor of the Allies. Companies in the United States also had strong ties to the Allies, and many American banks invested heavily in an Allied victory. By 1917, American loans to the Allies totaled over $2 billion. Although other banks—particularly in the Midwest where pro-German feelings were strongest—lent some $27 million to Germany, the country's prosperity was intertwined with the Allies. If the Allies won, the investments would be paid back; if not, the money might never be repaid.

New Imperialism also played a part in driving the country toward war. The United States had built up a modern navy to cement its position as a world power and to strengthen European trade. The United States's economy depended on expanding into new overseas markets. War, especially on the seas, threatened to entangle the United States.

Moving Toward War

A series of events gradually **eroded** American neutrality and drew the United States into the war. Shortly after the war began, the British blockaded German ports. They forced neutral merchant ships sailing to Europe to land at British ports to be inspected for **contraband**—goods prohibited from shipment to Germany and its allies. The U.S. government protested Britain's decision because it

---

propaganda the spreading of ideas about an institution or individual for the purpose of influencing opinion

eroded to wear away at something until it disappears

contraband goods whose importation, exportation, or possession is illegal

interfered with American economic interests, including trade with Germany. However, the German response angered Americans even more. In February 1915, the Germans announced that they would use submarines called U-boats to sink without warning any ship they found in the waters around Britain. This decision violated an international treaty signed by Germany that banned attacks on civilian ships without warning.

On May 7, 1915, a U-boat sank the British passenger ship *Lusitania*, killing over 1,000 passengers—including 128 Americans. German sympathizers in the United States justified the attack in public, but the attack gave credibility to British propaganda. Many Americans were very angered by the American deaths. Wilson and his administration limited the U.S. response to official protests to Germany. In March 1916 a German U-boat torpedoed a French passenger ship, the *Sussex*. Wilson then decided to issue one last warning demanding that the German government abandon its methods, known as "unrestricted submarine warfare," or risk war with the United States. Germany did not want to strengthen the Allies by drawing the United States into the war. It promised, with certain conditions, to stop sinking merchant ships.

The United States Declares War

In January 1917 German official Arthur Zimmermann sent a telegram to the German ambassador in Mexico promising Mexico the return of its "lost territory in Texas, New Mexico, and Arizona" if it allied with Germany. British intelligence intercepted the Zimmermann telegram, and it ran in American newspapers.

On February 1, 1917, Germany announced that it would resume unrestricted submarine warfare, which included attacks on civilian passenger vessels. German military leaders believed that they could starve Britain into submission if U-boats began sinking all ships on sight. They did not believe that the United States could raise an army and transport it to Europe in time if it decided to enter the war. A week later diplomatic relations broke down between the United States and Germany. Between February and early April, German U-boats sank ten U.S. merchant ships, including three on the same weekend, killing Americans.

Furious, many Americans concluded that war with Germany was necessary. The renewed U-boat attacks and the Zimmermann telegram also led to a surge of anti-German sentiment and violence against many German Americans.

The War in the Trenches

Troops on both sides of the conflict dug an extensive network of trenches to protect themselves from artillery fire and enemy attacks.

From Ypres on France's coast, down through Somme, Marne, and Verdun, Allied forces held off German advances.

GEOGRAPHY CONNECTION

1. **Spatial Thinking** Along which borders did the line of trench warfare stretch?

2. **Exploring Regions** How do you think the Central Powers' war efforts were affected by fighting the war in the west and in the east?

Zimmermann Telegram, 1917: Decimal File, 1910–1929, 862.20212/82A (1910–1929), and Decoded Zimmermann Telegram, 1917; Decimal File, 1910-1929, 862.20212/69, General Records of the Department of State; Record Group 59; National Archives.

PHOTO: PJF Military Collection/Alamy Stock Photo; TEXT: Congressional Record, Containing the Proceedings and Debates of the First Session of the Sixty-Fifth Congress, Volume LV. Copyright © 1917 by the Government Printing Office.

BIOGRAPHY

ALVIN YORK (1887–1964)

Alvin Cullum York grew up poor in the mountains of rural Tennessee. He spent much of his childhood working to help his father support the large York family. Consequently, he received only several years of education, but he still learned to read and write. In 1911 William York, Alvin's father, died leaving Alvin and his mother with the task of raising his younger siblings. As a young man, York earned a reputation in the area as a heavy drinker and fighter, though he remained committed to supporting his family by working as a farmer and blacksmith. He also was a skilled marksman and hunter, qualities he would soon need. In 1915 York gave up his rowdy ways and became deeply religious. After being drafted in 1917, he unsuccessfully tried to avoid military service as a conscientious objector due to his pacifist Christian beliefs. York later became convinced that he could fight if it were for a just cause.

HERO OF THE ARGONNE On October 8, 1918, during the Battle of the Argonne Forest, German machine guns on a fortified hill fired on York's platoon and killed 9 men. York took command and charged the machine guns. He went on to kill several Germans, capture the machine guns, and take 132 prisoners. For his actions, York received the Medal of Honor and the French Croix de Guerre.

STILL LEADING Following the war, York built a school for the children living in his area of rural Tennessee. In the 1920s, he opened the Alvin C. York Foundation to increase educational opportunities. During the 1930s and early 1940s, as military tensions mounted once again in Europe and Asia, York became a vocal supporter of interventionist policies. Although he had experienced the horrors of war, York recognized the dangers posed by Nazi Germany and Japan, and advocated for the United States to take action against them.

» An undated photo of Alvin C. York, who was awarded the Medal of Honor in March 1919

Explaining How did York contribute to the American victory at the Argonne?

President Wilson's success at keeping the United States neutral had played an important part in his attempts to win White House reelection in 1916. Wilson's campaign slogan was "He kept us out of war." American voters who were against the nation's involvement in the war helped Wilson secure a narrow victory that returned him to the White House. Even so, however, the nation was pushed to respond to Germany's aggressive actions and Wilson, asked Congress to declare war on Germany on April 2, 1917:

66 It is a fearful thing to lead this great peaceful people into war. . . . But the right is more precious than peace, and we shall fight for the things which we have always carried nearest to our hearts—for democracy, for the right of those who submit to authority to have a voice in their own governments, for the rights and liberties of small nations. . . . 99

–quoted in the *Congressional Record*, 1917

Within days, the Senate and the House had voted for the resolution, and Wilson signed it. The United States was at war.

✓ CHECK FOR UNDERSTANDING

1. **Identifying** What events motivated the United States to join the war?

2. **Predicting** How do you think the American entry into the war will affect the conflict in Europe?

The Realities of War

GUIDING QUESTION

How did new technologies increase the number of casualties compared with previous wars?

By the spring of 1917, World War I had devastated Europe. Old-fashioned strategies and new technologies resulted in terrible destruction. Many Americans believed, however, that their troops would make a difference and quickly bring the war to an end.

Trench Warfare

Early offensives demonstrated that warfare had changed. Powerful artillery guns placed far behind the front lines hurled huge explosive shells onto the battlefield. More soldiers on the battlefield were killed by artillery fire than by any other weapon. As one American noted in his diary:

> 66 Many dead Germans along the road. One heap on a manure pile. . . . Devastation everywhere. Our barrage has rooted up the entire territory like a plowed field. Dead horses galore, many of them have a hind quarter cut off—the [Germans] need food. Dead men here and there. 99

—quoted in *The American Spirit*, November 3, 1918

Troops began digging miles and miles of very elaborate trenches deep into the ground hoping to protect themselves from the barrages of artillery shelling. On the Western Front—where German troops fought French, British, and Belgian forces—the troops dug a weaving network of trenches that stretched and connected to one another all the way from the English Channel in the north to the Swiss border in the southeast. Both sides stretched tight nets of barbed wire in the battlefield areas between the two sides' trench networks. Both armies also used a new weapon, the machine gun, to guard against the enemy.

Attacks usually began with a massive artillery barrage. Soldiers then climbed out of the trenches and did their best to race quickly across the rough landscape, through the barbed wires, and into machine gun fire toward enemy trenches. Troops used any weapon available to kill the enemy. The new style of fighting, eventually used by both sides, resulted in the loss of hundreds of thousands of lives and a stalemate on the Western Front. Offensive and defensive moves by the Allies and the Germans failed to be particularly successful.

New Technology

Breaking through enemy lines required new technologies. The Germans first used poison gas in 1915, and the Allies soon followed. Gas caused vomiting, blindness, and suffocation. Both sides developed gas masks to try to counter the deadly fumes. In 1916 the British military introduced the armored tank, which could crush barbed wire and cross trenches, but there were still too few of the slow, unreliable machines to revolutionize warfare.

World War I also marked the first use of aircraft in war. Early in the war, the Germans used giant rigid balloons called zeppelins to drop bombs on British warships in the North Sea. At first, airplanes were used to spy on enemy troops and ships. Then the Allies equipped them with machine guns and rockets to attack the German zeppelin fleet. Other aircraft carried small bombs to drop on enemy lines. As technology advanced, airplanes shot down other airplanes in

Soldiers wear gas masks to protect themselves from a new weapon, poisonous chlorine gas, 1917

battles that were known as dogfights. But early military aircraft were difficult to fly and easy to destroy. A combat pilot had an average life expectancy of about two weeks.

✓ CHECK FOR UNDERSTANDING

Summarizing How did new technologies increase the number of casualties compared with previous wars?

LESSON ACTIVITIES

1. **Informative/Explanatory Writing** Write a brief essay that identifies the fundamental causes of World War I and explains why the United States entered the war.

2. **Presenting** Work together in a group to discuss the main arguments for and against the entry of the United States into World War I. Take turns to propose one argument each. Arguments should be derived from lesson material, and reasonable conclusions should be taken from that material. The other students should listen to and write down each argument. Once all students have shared two arguments each, work together to prepare a short presentation that summarizes your group's arguments for and against the United States joining the war, and present a conclusion giving your own judgment about whether the decision was right.

PHOTO: Hutton Archive/Getty Images; TEXT: Eugene Kennedy Collection, Hoover Institution Archives.

05

World War I Impacts America

READING STRATEGY

Understanding Craft and Structure As you read, use the major headings of this lesson to create an outline similar to the one here.

World War I Impacts America

I. Organizing the World War

   A.

   B.

   C.

Organizing the Home Front

GUIDING QUESTION

How did government efforts help organize the U.S. economy for war?

Once the United States entered World War I, the U.S. government redirected vast amounts of resources toward the war effort. At the start of the war in April 1917, progressives controlled the federal government. Their ideas about planning and management shaped how the government organized the war effort.

Organizing the Economy

As part of the war effort, Congress created new agencies staffed by business executives, managers, and government officials to coordinate mobilization and ensure the efficient use of national resources. These agencies emphasized cooperation between big business and government. The War Industries Board (WIB) coordinated the production of war materials. The WIB told manufacturers what they could produce, allocated raw materials, ordered new factory construction, and sometimes set prices. The Food Administration was responsible for increasing food production while reducing civilian consumption. The agency encouraged families to conserve food and grow their own vegetables in **victory gardens.** The Fuel Administration managed use of coal and oil. To conserve energy, it introduced the first usage of daylight saving time, shortened workweeks for civilian goods factories, and encouraged Heatless Mondays.

By the end of the war, the United States had spent about $32 billion. To fund the war effort, Congress raised income tax rates, placed new taxes on corporate profits, imposed an extra tax on the profits of arms factories, and borrowed over $20 billion through the sale of Liberty Bonds and Victory Bonds. Americans who bought bonds were lending money to the government to be repaid with interest within a specified number of years.

American Workers Step Up

The war effort also required the cooperation of workers. To prevent strikes from disrupting the war effort, the government established the National War Labor Board (NWLB) in April 1918. The NWLB often pressured industry to improve wages, adopt an eight-hour workday, and allow unions the right to organize and bargain collectively. Labor leaders agreed not to disrupt war production in exchange. As a result, membership in unions increased by more than one million between 1917 and 1919.

With so many men in the military, employers began to hire women for jobs traditionally held by men. Some 1 million women joined the workforce for the first time, and another 8 million switched to better industrial jobs. Women worked in factories, shipyards, and railroad yards, and served as police officers, mail carriers, and train engineers. When the war ended, however, most women returned to their previous jobs or stopped working. Yet it had demonstrated that women were capable of holding jobs that many had believed only men could do.

victory garden a garden planted by civilians during war to raise vegetables for home use, leaving more of other foods for the troops

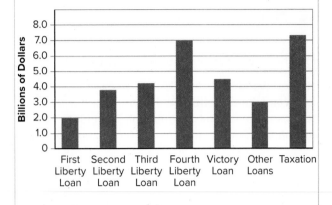

Paying for World War I
The U.S. government printed posters, organized parades, and asked celebrities to promote bond sales.

ECONOMICS CONNECTION

1. **Interpreting** What can you infer about government finances by comparing revenue raised through loans versus taxation?

2. **Inferring** What consequence might result from the way the war was paid for?

While African Americans had already started migrating north in the years before the war began, Henry Ford, desperate for workers, sent agents to the South to recruit African Americans for jobs at his plants. Other companies quickly followed suit. Promises of high wages and plentiful work convinced between 300,000 and 500,000 African Americans to move north. This massive population movement became known as the Great Migration. The racial makeup of such cities as Chicago, New York, Cleveland, and Detroit changed greatly, as did politics in the Northern cities, where African Americans were able to vote.

The war also encouraged other groups to migrate. Between 1917 and 1920, more than 100,000 Mexicans migrated to the Southwest, providing labor for farmers and ranchers. Mexican Americans also found new opportunities in factory jobs in many American cities. Like other immigrant groups before them, they faced hostility and discrimination and tended to settle in separate neighborhoods, called barrios, where they could support one another.

Building the Military

When the United States entered the war in 1917, the army and the National Guard together had only slightly more than 200,000 troops. Men quickly volunteered, but more were still needed. Many government leaders believed that forced military service was a violation of democratic and republican principles. Believing a **draft** was necessary, however, Congress, with Wilson's support, created a new system called selective service. All men between 21 and 30 were required to register for the draft. A lottery randomly determined the order in which they were called before a local draft board in charge of selecting or exempting people from military service. Eventually, about 2.8 million Americans were drafted. Others believed democracy was at stake and felt a duty to respond to their nation's call. Approximately 2 million additional men volunteered for military service.

World War I was the first war in which women officially served in the armed forces, although they were only allowed in non-combat positions. As the military prepared for war in 1917, it faced a severe shortage of clerical workers because so many men were assigned to active duty. Early in 1917, the navy authorized the enlistment of women to meet its clerical needs. More than 11,000 women served in the navy by the end of the war. While most performed clerical duties, others served as radio operators, electricians, pharmacists, chemists, and photographers. The army refused to enlist women. Instead, it began hiring women as temporary employees to fill clerical jobs. The only women to serve in the army were in the Army Nurse Corps. Women had served as nurses in both the army and the navy since the early 1900s but as auxiliaries. They were not assigned ranks and were not technically enlisted in the army or navy. More than 20,000 nurses served in the Army Nurse Corps during the war, including more than 10,000 overseas.

✓ **CHECK FOR UNDERSTANDING**

1. **Making Connections** How did the federal government mobilize the country for war?

2. **Identifying Cause and Effect** What long-term consequences do you think World War I had for women?

Controlling Free Speech

GUIDING QUESTION

How did the Espionage and Sedition Acts limit free speech during the war?

Soon after Congress declared war, President Wilson created the Committee on Public Information (CPI) to "sell" the war to the American people. Headed by journalist George Creel, the CPI distributed pamphlets and arranged for thousands of "four-minute speeches" to be delivered at movie theaters and other public places. Some 75,000 speakers, urged audiences to support the war in various ways, from buying war bonds to reporting draft dodgers to the authorities. Nongovernmental groups also helped raise awareness

draft to select a person at random for mandatory military service

and funds for the war. For example, the American Jewish Joint Distribution Committee raised $63 million in relief funds. The Jewish Welfare Board set up centers at home and abroad for Jewish servicemen.

In addition to using propaganda, the government passed legislation to limit opposition to the war and to fight **espionage,** or spying to acquire government information. The Espionage Act of 1917 made it illegal to aid the enemy, give false reports, or interfere with the war effort. The Sedition Act of 1918 made it illegal to speak against the war publicly. These acts allowed officials to prosecute anyone who criticized the government, leading to more than 2,000 convictions.

Despite protests, the Espionage and Sedition Acts were upheld by the Supreme Court. In *Schenck* v. *United States* (1919), the Court ruled that the government could restrict speech when the speech constituted a "clear and present danger."

 CHECK FOR UNDERSTANDING

Speculating Why do you think federal officials thought the Committee on Public Information was needed?

Ending the War

GUIDING QUESTION

Why was the arrival of U.S. forces so important to the war effort?

Nearly two million American troops marched into the Western Front stalemate in 1917. The American soldiers were inexperienced, but they were fresh and eager to fight. As the Americans began to arrive, many in Germany concluded that the war was lost.

Russia Leaves the War

In March 1917 riots broke out in Russia. Czar Nicholas II, the leader of the Russian Empire, abdicated his throne, and the Russian Revolution began. Leaders of the temporary government that took command were unable to deal adequately with the problems afflicting the nation. This led Vladimir Lenin's Bolshevik Party to seize power and establish a Communist government in November 1917.

Germany's military fortunes improved with the Bolshevik takeover. Lenin pulled Russia out of the war to concentrate on establishing a Communist state through a peace deal. Lenin agreed to the Treaty of Brest-Litovsk with Germany on March 3, 1918. Under this treaty, Russia gave up the Ukraine, its Polish and Baltic territories, and Finland. This allowed Germany to concentrate its forces on the western front.

Americans Enter Combat

General John J. Pershing, commander of the American Expeditionary Force (AEF), arrived in Paris on July 4, 1917. British and French commanders wanted to integrate American troops into their armies. Pershing refused, and eventually only one unit, the 93rd Infantry Division—an African American unit—was transferred to the French. On March 21, 1918, the Germans launched a massive gas attack and artillery bombardment along the Western Front. Strengthened by reinforcements from the Russian front, the Germans pushed deep into Allied lines. By early June, they were less than 40 miles (64 km) from Paris. In late May, as the offensive continued, the Americans launched their first major attack, quickly capturing the village of Cantigny. On June 1, American and French troops blocked the German drive on Paris at the town of Château-Thierry. On July 15, the Germans launched one last massive attack in an attempt to take Paris, but American and French troops held their ground.

With the German drive stalled, French marshal Ferdinand Foch, supreme commander of the Allied forces, ordered massive counterattacks. In mid-September, American troops drove back German forces at the battle of Saint-Mihiel. On September 26, 1918, the most massive offensive for the American Expeditionary Force was launched in the region between the Meuse River and the Argonne Forest. Although the Germans inflicted heavy casualties, their positions slowly fell to the advancing American troops. By early November, the Americans had opened a hole on the eastern flank of the German lines. All across the Western Front, the Germans began to retreat.

The Aftermath

Meanwhile, a revolution had engulfed Austria-Hungary. In October 1918 Poland, Hungary, and Czechoslovakia declared independence. By early November, the governments of the Austro-Hungarian Empire and the Ottoman Empire had surrendered to the Allies. In late October, sailors in Kiel, the main base of the German fleet, mutinied. Within days, groups of workers and soldiers seized power in other German towns. The German emperor stepped down, and on November 9, Germany became a republic. Two days later, the government signed an **armistice**—an agreement to stop fighting. On November 11, 1918, the fighting stopped.

More than 50,000 Americans died in combat, and over 200,000 were wounded. Another 60,000 soldiers died from disease, mostly from the influenza **pandemic** of 1918 and 1919. The flu pandemic was not

---

espionage spying, especially to gain government secrets

armistice a temporary agreement to end fighting
pandemic a disease that spreads worldwide

American Expansion and World War I   **175**

Theaters were among the businesses that closed in an effort to curb the flu epidemic.

Identifying Based on what you know about theaters, why were these closed to help fight the flu pandemic?

limited to the battlefield. It spread around the world and affected more than a quarter of all Americans. The disease killed an estimated 25 to 50 million people worldwide, including more than 675,000 Americans. This pandemic was especially lethal for young, healthy people. Because no vaccine existed, the only way people could combat this disease was by isolating, quarantining, disinfecting, practicing good hygiene, and limiting large gatherings.

A Flawed Peace

In January 1919 delegates from 27 countries traveled to the peace conference at the Palace of Versailles, near Paris. The treaty with Germany that resulted came to be called the Treaty of Versailles. Negotiations for the Treaty of Versailles lasted five months. President Wilson arrived in Paris in 1919 with a peace plan known as the Fourteen Points. It was based on "the principle of justice to all peoples and nationalities." In the first five points, Wilson proposed to eliminate the causes of the war through free trade, freedom of the seas, disarmament, negotiating colonial disagreements, and an end to secret alliances.

The next eight points addressed the right of **national self-determination,** the idea that the borders of countries should be based on ethnicity and national identity. Supporters of this idea believed that when borders are not based on national identity, nations are more likely to go to war to resolve border disputes. This principle also meant that no nation should keep territory taken from another nation. The fourteenth point called for the creation of a League of Nations. The League's members would help preserve peace by pledging to respect and protect each other's territory and political independence. Wilson was willing to give up his other goals in exchange for support for the League.

Not everyone was impressed by Wilson's idealism. In part because the United States had not suffered nearly as much as its European allies, Wilson was not interested in harsh punishments. But Premier Georges Clemenceau of France and British prime minister Lloyd George wanted to punish Germany for the suffering it inflicted on the rest of Europe. Additionally, Britain refused to give up its sizable naval advantage by agreeing to Wilson's call for freedom of the seas.

The Treaty of Versailles, reluctantly signed by Germany on June 28, 1919, included many terms designed to punish and weaken Germany. Germany's armed forces were greatly reduced, and its troops were not allowed west of the Rhine River. The treaty also specifically blamed "the aggression of Germany" for the war. This allowed the Allies to demand that Germany pay **reparations**—monetary compensation for all of the war damages it had caused. A commission decided that Germany owed the Allies about $33 billion. This sum far exceeded what Germany could pay all at once and was intended to keep its economy weak for a long time.

Wilson had somewhat better success in promoting national self-determination. The Austro-Hungarian Empire, the Russian Empire, and the German Empire were dismantled, and new nations created. In general, the majority of people in each new country were from one ethnic group. But both Poland and Czechoslovakia were given territory in which the majority of people were German, and Germany was divided in order to give Poland access to the Baltic Sea. This arrangement helped set the stage for a new series of crises in the 1930s.

The Treaty of Versailles ignored freedom of the seas, free trade, and Wilson's hope of negotiating colonial independence talks. France and Britain took over colonial areas in Africa and the Middle East, and they also gained ruling authority in the former Ottoman Empire. France received Syria and Lebanon, and Britain received Palestine including Transjordan and Iraq.

---

national self-determination the free choice by the people of a nation of their own future political status

reparations payment by the losing country in a war to the winner for the damages caused by the war

PHOTO: Vintage_Space/Alamy Stock Photo; TEXT: President Wilson's Message to Congress, January 8, 1918; Records of the United States Senate; Record Group 46; Records of the United States Senate; National Archives.

Opposition at Home

President Wilson was confident the American people would support the Treaty of Versailles, but he had badly underestimated opposition to the League of Nations in the Senate. One group of senators nicknamed "the Irreconcilables" refused to support the treaty under any circumstances. They assailed the League of Nations as the kind of "entangling alliance" that President George Washington and the other Founders had warned against. They believed that joining an international organization endangered American sovereignty.

A larger group of senators were led by the powerful chairman of the Foreign Relations Committee, Henry Cabot Lodge. This group pointed out that the Constitution requires Congress to declare war. Yet the League of Nations could require member states to aid any member that was attacked. These "reservationists" argued that this might force the United States into a war without Congressional approval. They agreed to ratify the treaty if it was amended to say that any military action by the United States required Congress's approval. Wilson refused, fearing the change would undermine the League's effectiveness.

Wilson decided to take his case directly to the American people. Starting in September 1919, he traveled some 8,000 miles and made more than 30 major speeches in three weeks. Soon afterward he suffered a stroke. The Senate voted in November 1919 and in March 1920, but both times it refused to give its consent to the treaty. After Wilson left office in 1921, the United States negotiated separate peace treaties with each of the Central Powers. The League of Nations took shape without the United States.

Postwar Economic Turmoil

After the war ended, government agencies removed their controls from the economy. A resulting inflation greatly increased the **cost of living**—the cost of food, clothing, shelter, and other essentials. With orders for war materials evaporating, factories laid off workers. Returning soldiers found that jobs were scarce. While workers wanted higher wages to keep up with inflation, companies resisted because inflation also drove up operating costs.

During the war, union membership had increased greatly. Business leaders, however, were determined to weaken unions after the war. By the end of 1919, more than 3,600 strikes involving more than four million workers had taken place. One of the most famous strikes of 1919 occurred in Boston, where roughly 75 percent of the police force walked off the job. Riots and looting forced Governor Calvin Coolidge to call in the National Guard. When the strikers tried to return to work, the police commissioner instead fired them.

Soon after the police strike, an estimated 350,000 steelworkers went on strike for higher pay, shorter hours, and recognition of their union. U.S. Steel refused to talk to union leaders and set out to break the union. It blamed the strike on foreign radicals and called for loyal Americans to return to work. In the interim, the company hired African American and Mexican workers as replacements. Clashes between company guards and strikers were frequent. In Gary, Indiana, a riot left 18 strikers dead. The strike collapsed in 1920, setting back the union cause in the steel industry for more than a decade.

Racial and Social Unrest

Postwar turmoil in the United States was also reflected in increased racial and social conflict. German Americans had been the target of discrimination during World War I and had their loyalties questioned even though most fully supported the U.S. war effort. Following the war, nativism and demands for social and cultural conformity swept the United States. German Americans were forced to assimilate into the English-speaking American culture or be branded outsiders. Many Americans and immigrants of German descent changed their personal and business names and hid their heritage.

The economic shift away from the wartime economy was also affected by the movement of many African Americans to the north during the war to work in factory jobs. Some returning soldiers blamed African Americans for taking their jobs during the war. Frustration and racism combined to produce violence. The height of this violence happened in the summer of 1919 when 25 race riots broke out across the nation.

The riots came to a head in July, when a mob of angry whites burned shops and homes in an African American neighborhood in Longview, Texas. A week later in Washington, D.C., groups of African Americans and whites fought each other for four days before troops got the riots under control. The worst violence occurred in Chicago in 1919. On a hot July day, an African American teenager—beaten for coming to shore on the whites-only side of the beach—drowned, resulting in a full-scale riot that lasted for almost two weeks until the government sent the National Guard to impose order.

A new generation of African Americans, however, grew determined to fight for democracy at home as they had in Europe. They began organizing a new fight for equality and civil rights at home. The NAACP experienced a surge in post-war membership during this period and launched a new campaign to pass a federal law against lynching.

---

cost of living the cost of purchasing goods and services essential for survival

This 1920 photo depicts a crowd gathering following an explosion on Wall Street in New York City.

Making Connections How did such bombings during the Red Scare contribute to growing fears about radical organizations?

The Red Scare

As early as the late 1800s, many Americans had accused immigrants of importing socialist and communist ideas and had blamed them for labor unrest and violence. Events in Russia seemed to justify fears of a Communist revolution. The strikes of 1919 fueled fears that Communists, or "reds," might seize power, leading to a nationwide panic known as the Red Scare. Many people were particularly concerned about workers using strikes to start a revolution.

In April 1919 the postal service intercepted more than thirty parcels containing homemade bombs addressed to prominent Americans. The next month, a parade in Cleveland to protest the jailing of American Socialist Party leader Eugene Debs turned into a series of riots. Two people were killed, and another forty were injured. In June, eight bombs in eight cities exploded within minutes of one another, suggesting a nationwide conspiracy. One of these bombs damaged the home of U.S. attorney general A. Mitchell Palmer.

Palmer established a special division within the Justice Department, the General Intelligence Division, that eventually became the Federal Bureau of Investigation (FBI). Although evidence pointed to no single group, Palmer's agents targeted the foreign-born. On November 7, 1919, Palmer ordered a series of raids on offices of the Union of Russian Workers in twelve cities. Less than seven weeks later, a transport ship left New York for Russia carrying 249 immigrants who had been **deported** from the country.

In January 1920 Palmer ordered another series of raids on the headquarters of various radical organizations. Nearly 6,000 people were arrested. Palmer's raids continued until the spring of 1920, and authorities detained thousands of suspects. Palmer's agents often ignored the civil liberties of suspects. Officers entered homes and offices without search warrants. Some suspects were jailed indefinitely and were not allowed to talk to their attorneys. Many of the nearly 600 immigrants who were deported never had a court hearing.

Although Palmer defended his actions, the raids failed to turn up any hard evidence of revolutionary conspiracy. The New York state legislature expelled five members of the Socialist Party in January 1920, and within a few months, nearly thirty states passed sedition laws making it illegal to join groups advocating revolution. Many linked radicalism with immigrants, which led to calls to limit immigration.

Economic problems, labor unrest, and racial tensions created a general sense of worry in the United States. During the 1920 campaign, Ohio governor James M. Cox and his running mate, Assistant Secretary of the Navy Franklin D. Roosevelt, ran on a platform of progressive ideals. President Wilson wanted to make the campaign a referendum on the Treaty of Versailles and the League of Nations. Republican Warren G. Harding, called for a return to "normalcy," saying the country needed to return to the days before the Progressive Era reforms. Harding won the election by a landslide. Many Americans hoped to put troubles behind them and build a prosperous and stable society.

✓ CHECK FOR UNDERSTANDING

1. **Determining Central Ideas** What was one lasting impact of World War I?
2. **Identifying Cause and Effect** What prompted Palmer to order a series of raids that led to thousands of arrests?

LESSON ACTIVITIES

1. **Informative/Explanatory Writing** Write a brief essay that explains the reasons why the U.S. Senate refused to give its consent to the Treaty of Versailles.

2. **Presenting** Do you think the League of Nations would have provided the effect Wilson desired? Why or why not? Write a short speech in which you argue for or against the League of Nations. You will deliver your speech to the class. As speeches are given, take notes on what you agree or disagree with so you can participate in a class discussion.

deport to expel an individual from the country

Library of Congress Prints and Photographs Division [LC-USZ62-132521].

06

Turning Point: Ending World War I

? COMPELLING QUESTION

How did people seek to prevent another world war after 1919?

Plan Your Inquiry

In this lesson, you will investigate how people sought to conclude World War I and make peace in a way that might prevent future conflicts.

DEVELOP QUESTIONS

Developing Questions About the End of World War I Think about how World War I ended, what steps Allied leaders took to secure peace, and how they hoped to prevent future global conflicts. Then read the Compelling Question for this lesson.

Develop a list of Supporting Questions that would help you answer the Compelling Question for the lesson. Write these in a graphic organizer like the one below.

APPLY HISTORICAL TOOLS

Analyzing Primary and Secondary Sources You will work with a variety of primary and secondary sources in this lesson. These sources focus on the conclusion of World War I, treaty making, and the formation of the League of Nations. Use a graphic organizer like the one below to record and organize information about each source. Note ways in which each source helps you answer the supporting questions you created. Not all sources will help you answer each of your Supporting Questions. Only include relevant sources in your graphic organizer.

Supporting Questions	Primary Source	How this source helps me answer the Supporting Question
Question 1:		
Question 2:		
Question 3:		

After you analyze the sources, you will:
- use the evidence from the sources
- communicate your conclusions
- take informed action

Background Information

In the summer of 1914 World War I erupted in Europe. At first, the United States tried to remain neutral. The public was divided over which side to support and whether to become involved at all. However, a series of troubling incidents, including German U-boat attacks, led President Woodrow Wilson to ask Congress to declare war in April 1917.

A year and a half later, on November 11, 1918, Germany signed an armistice that ended the fighting. Historians estimate that about 20 million people—military and civilian—died in the war. The United States lost more than 116,000 soldiers. Much of Europe was devastated, and the many nations involved still needed to negotiate peace. Representatives from 27 countries attended the Paris Peace Conference in January 1919. The negotiations—largely led by leaders of the United States, Britain, France, and Italy—took about five months. These individuals differed sharply in their approach to peace, and President Wilson faced the difficult task of persuading Congress and the American people to support his ideas and the outcome—the Treaty of Versailles.

» An American victory parade of returning U.S. soldiers passes through Victory Arch in Washington, D.C., 1919.

Library of Congress Prints and Photographs Division [LC-USZ62-78370]

The Committee on Public Information

Soon after Congress declared war, President Wilson issued an executive order forming the Committee on Public Information (CPI). This agency became the propaganda arm of the federal government, responsible for persuading the American public to support the war effort. Wilson appointed journalist George Creel as its chairman.

SECONDARY SOURCE : ARTICLE

66 At the time, most Americans got their news through newspapers, . . . In New York City, according to my research, nearly two dozen [English] papers were published every day . . . while dozens of weeklies served ethnic audiences.

. . . Creel organized the CPI into several divisions . . . The Speaking Division recruited 75,000 specialists who became known as 'Four-Minute Men' for their ability to lay out Wilson's war aims in short speeches. The Film Division produced **newsreels** intended to rally support . . . The Foreign Language Newspaper Division kept an eye on the hundreds of . . . U.S. newspapers published in languages other than English.

Another CPI unit secured free advertising space in American publications to promote campaigns aimed at selling war bonds, recruiting new soldiers, stimulating patriotism and reinforcing the message that the nation was involved in a great crusade against a bloodthirsty, antidemocratic enemy.

. . .The Division of Pictorial Publicity was led by a group of volunteer artists and illustrators. Their output included some of the most enduring images of this period, including the portrait by James Montgomery Flagg of a vigorous Uncle Sam, declaring, 'I WANT YOU FOR THE U.S. ARMY!' . . .

» The *Official Bulletin* was a daily newspaper published by the U.S. government.

Creel denied that his committee's work amounted to propaganda, but he acknowledged that he was engaged in a battle of perceptions. 'The war was not fought in France alone,' he wrote in 1920 . . . describing the CPI as 'a plain publicity proposition, a vast enterprise in salesmanship, the world's greatest adventure in advertising.' . . .

For most journalists, the bulk of their contact with the CPI was through its News Division, which became a veritable engine of propaganda on a par with . . . operations in Germany and England but . . . previously unknown in the United States. . . .

. . . [A]t the same time, the government was taking other steps to restrict reporters' access to soldiers, generals, munitions-makers and others involved in the struggle. So, after stimulating the demand for news while artificially restraining the supply, the government stepped into the resulting vacuum and provided a vast number of official stories that looked like news. . . .

The CPI News Division then went a step further, creating . . . a daily newspaper published by the government itself. Unlike the '**partisan** press' of the 19th century, the Wilson-era Official Bulletin was entirely a governmental publication, sent out each day . . . 99

–Christopher B. Daly, "*How Woodrow Wilson's Propaganda Machine Changed American Journalism*," April 28, 2017

---

newsreel a short film dealing with current events

partisan reflecting strong feelings toward one group, party, or side of an issue

EXAMINE THE SOURCE

1. **Analyzing Perspectives** According to Creel, what purpose did the CPI and its news bulletin have?
2. **Drawing Conclusions** How might the CPI and its news have shaped public opinion about the war and its aftermath?

PHOTO: National Archives and Records Administration; TEXT: Daly, Christopher B. "How Woodrow Wilson's Propaganda Machine Changed American Journalism," The Conversation, April 27, 2017.

(I)President Wilson's Message to Congress, January 8, 1918; Records of the United States Senate; Record Group 46: Records of the United States Senate, National Archives; (r)League of Nations, 1924. The Covenant of the League of Nations. Reproduced by The Avalon Project: Yale Law School - Lillian Goldman Law Library.

B

The Fourteen Points

In January 1918, President Wilson gave a speech to Congress in which he outlined his vision for peace. He proposed fourteen points that he believed should guide and shape any peace settlement with the Central Powers. First on the list was "open covenants of peace" in which nations conducted diplomacy "frankly and in the public view." Later, Germany agreed to open peace negotiations based on Wilson's Fourteen Points, but some leaders of Allied nations at the Paris Peace Conference had objections.

PRIMARY SOURCE : PEACE PLAN

" . . . We entered this war because violations of right had occurred which touched us to the quick and made the life of our own people impossible unless they were corrected and the world secure once for all against their recurrence. What we demand in this war, therefore, is nothing peculiar to ourselves. It is that the world be made fit and safe to live in; . . . The programme of the world's peace, therefore, is our programme; and that programme, the only possible programme, as we see it, is this: . . .

XIV. A general association of nations must be formed under specific **covenants** for the purpose of affording mutual guarantees of political independence and territorial integrity to great and small states alike. . . .

For such arrangements and covenants we are willing to fight and to continue to fight until they are achieved; but only because we wish the right to prevail and desire a just and stable peace such as can be secured only by removing the chief **provocations** to war, which this programme does remove. . . . "

–President Woodrow Wilson, January 8, 1918

covenant an agreement, especially a binding agreement

provocation an act that provokes or incites reaction

EXAMINE THE SOURCE

1. **Explaining** What purpose does President Wilson identify for the treaty negotiations?
2. **Summarizing** What solution does he suggest in order to achieve that purpose? How does he justify it?

C

The League of Nations

In January 1919, representatives from more than 30 countries signed the Treaty of Versailles. The treaty imposed harsh reparations on Germany. It also upheld a key provision of Wilson's Fourteen Points. In 1924 the newly established League of Nations adopted this Covenant.

PRIMARY SOURCE : INTERNATIONAL DOCUMENT

" THE HIGH CONTRACTING PARTIES,
In order to promote international co-operation and to achieve . . . peace and security by the acceptance of obligations not to resort to war, by the prescription of open . . . relations between nations, by the firm establishment of the understandings of international law as the . . . rule of conduct among Governments, and by the maintenance of justice and a . . . respect for all treaty obligations in the dealings of organised peoples with one another,

Agree to this Covenant of the League of Nations. . . .

ARTICLE 3. . . . The Assembly may deal at its meetings with any matter within the sphere of action of the League or affecting the peace of the world. At meetings of the Assembly each Member of the League shall have one vote, and may have not more than three Representatives. . . .

ARTICLE 10. The Members of the League undertake to respect and preserve as against external aggression the territorial integrity and . . . independence of all Members . . . In case of any such aggression . . . the Council shall advise upon the means by which this obligation shall be fulfilled.

ARTICLE 11. Any war or threat of war, whether . . . affecting any of the Members of the League or not, is hereby declared a matter of concern to the whole League, and the League shall take any action . . . to safeguard the peace of nations. . . . "

–The Covenant of the League of Nations, January 20, 1920

EXAMINE THE SOURCE

1. **Inferring** What does this document suggest many people view as the causes of World War I?
2. **Analyzing** How does the world envisioned by the League differ from pre–World War I conditions?

Senate Opposition

While participants at the Paris Peace Conference included the League of Nations in the treaty, not everyone liked it. Back home, President Wilson faced stiff opposition; many feared the treaty compromised U.S. sovereignty and would pull the nation to future disputes. Wilson traveled the country to promote the League. However, Congress did not ratify the treaty. The League began in 1920 with 48 members but without the United States.

PRIMARY SOURCE : NEWSPAPER

❝ That the Senate advise and consent to the **ratification** of the treaty of peace with Germany concluded at Versailles on the 28th day of June, 1919, subject to the following reservations and understandings, which are hereby made a part and condition of this resolution of ratification, . . .

Notice of Withdrawal

(1) The United States so understands and **construes** Article I that in case of notice of withdrawal from the league of nations . . . the United States shall be the sole judge as to whether all its international obligations and all its obligations under the said covenant have been fulfilled, . . .

(2) The United States assumes no obligation to preserve the territorial integrity or political independence of any other country by the employment of its military or naval forces, its resources, . . . or to interfere in any way in controversies between nations, . . . under any article of the treaty, for any purpose, unless . . . Congress, which, under the Constitution, has the sole power to declare war . . . shall, in the exercise of full liberty of action, by . . . joint resolution so provide. ❞

—"Resolution of Ratification as Voted on by the Senate," as printed in the *New York Tribune*, March 20, 1920

---

ratification formal approval

construe to interpret

EXAMINE THE SOURCE

1. **Interpreting** What does the Senate mean to accomplish with this document?
2. **Analyzing Points of View** Why do members of the Senate object to the League of Nations?

Your Inquiry Analysis

EVALUATE SOURCES AND USE EVIDENCE

Reflect on the Compelling Question and the Supporting Questions you developed at the beginning of this lesson.

1. **Gathering Sources** Which sources helped you answer the Compelling Question and your Supporting Questions most directly? Which sources, if any, challenged the preconceptions you had when you first wrote those questions? What additional information would you like to have, and where might you look to find that information?

2. **Evaluating Sources** Looking at the sources that helped you answer your Supporting Questions, evaluate the credibility of each source. Which details made that source a particularly useful source to answer your question? Are there further details you may need in order to better evaluate the authority of these sources? What bias do you detect in the sources, if any? Be sure to consider the background information about each source.

3. **Comparing and Contrasting** Compare and contrast two of the sources in this lesson more closely. Which source most clearly addresses the Compelling Question? Why? How do the two sources complement or contradict each other, if at all?

COMMUNICATE CONCLUSIONS

Identifying Arguments Write a letter to the Senate that blocked U.S. membership in the League of Nations. Using the sources—as well as your own ideas and knowledge of the history of World War I—explain whether you agree or disagree with its decision. Be sure to discuss the purpose and intention behind the League, its notable provisions, and any benefits or drawbacks that support your position. Include a quote from one or more of the primary sources you read.

TAKE INFORMED ACTION

Creating a Plan to Prevent Conflict Escalation With a partner or in a small group, brainstorm potential causes of conflict in the world today. Then, discuss steps that world leaders, businesses, and individual citizens can take to prevent escalation of conflict into war. Record your ideas as an official proposal, with an introduction, potential steps to take, and conclusion. Take turns reading aloud your proposal to the class, or record your team reading the proposal in audio or video to share as a podcast or webcast.

"Resolution of Ratification As Voted On by the Senate." New York Tribune. March 20, 1920.

Analyzing Sources: The Red Scare

 COMPELLING QUESTION

How did fears about radical communism shape public policy?

Plan Your Inquiry

In this lesson you will explore how conditions in the United States after World War I produced a wave of persecution known as the Red Scare.

DEVELOP QUESTIONS

Developing Questions About the Red Scare Think about social, economic, and political conditions in the United States before World War I. Consider how those conditions did and did not change during and after the war. Develop a list of Supporting Questions that would help you answer the Compelling Question for the lesson. Write these in a graphic organizer like the one below.

APPLY HISTORICAL TOOLS

Analyzing Primary Sources You will work with a variety of primary sources in this lesson. These sources focus on the rising fear of communism and immigrants, and distrust of organized labor that combined to produce the first Red Scare. Use a graphic organizer like the one below to record and organize information about each source. Note ways in which each source helps you answer the Supporting Questions you created. Not all sources will help you answer each of your Supporting Questions. Only include relevant sources in your graphic organizer.

Source	Author/ Creator	Description/ Notes	Which Supporting Question does this source help me answer?
A			
B			
C			
D			
E			

After you analyze the sources, you will:

- use the evidence from the sources
- communicate your conclusions
- take informed action

Background Information

The end of the nineteenth century saw widespread political corruption, new waves of immigration and anti-immigrant sentiment, Jim Crow laws, and the backlash to various progressive movements, including labor unions. Many people on the political left opposed fighting in World War I because they saw it as another way for the wealthy to exploit the labor and lives of the working class. Even as people united behind the war effort, the underlying strife remained.

These tensions reemerged with the war's end. The decline of war production led to a job shortage, and inflation increased the cost of goods. During the war, many women, African Americans, and immigrants had taken jobs they were now expected to give up. Labor unions, which had gained strength during the war, pressed for more reforms even as business leaders tried to quash whatever gains they had already made.

Meanwhile, the Bolsheviks had successfully seized control of Russia and launched a quasi-communist government. Many feared the influence of socialism and communism on the American working class. The resulting Red Scare lasted from 1919 into the 1920s.

» The Raleigh Hotel in Washington, D.C., locked out union employees rather than negotiate a labor contract with better wages and a ten-hour work day.

Library of Congress Prints and Photographs Division [LC-DIG-npcc-00380].

A

Assert Your Rights!

The text of this 1917 flyer, written by the American Socialist Party, argues against conscription—forcing people to serve in the military. This group, seen by many as dangerous and un-American, used patriotic language in the flyer to defend its stance.

PRIMARY SOURCE : FLYER

" The Constitution . . . is one of the greatest bulwarks of political liberty. It was born after a long, stubborn battle between king-rule and democracy. . . . In this battle the people of the United States established the principle that freedom of the individual and personal liberty are the most sacred things in life. . . .

The Thirteenth Amendment . . . embodies this sacred idea. The Socialist Party says this idea is violated by the Conscription Act. When you conscript a man and compel him to go abroad to fight against his will, you violate the most sacred right of personal liberty, . . .

In a democratic country each man must have the right to say whether he is willing to join the army. Only in countries where uncontrolled power rules can a **despot** force his subjects to fight. . . . This is tyrannical power in its worst form. . . .

Do you think [conscription] has a place in the United States? Do you want to see unlimited power handed over to Wall Street's chosen few in America? If you do not, join the Socialist Party in its campaign for the repeal of the Conscription Act. Write to your congressman and tell him you want the law repealed. . . . Come to the headquarters of the Socialist Party . . . and sign a petition for the repeal of the Conscription Act. Help us wipe out this stain upon the Constitution! "

—*"Long Live the Constitution of the United States,"* American Socialist Party, 1917

despot a ruler who holds absolute power

EXAMINE THE SOURCE

1. **Analyzing Perspectives** How does the flyer criticize the U.S. government? On what grounds?
2. **Contrasting** How does this excerpt contrast with popular perceptions of socialism?

B

"Now for a Round-Up"

The Espionage and Sedition Acts gave the government extraordinary powers to curtail criticism. This political cartoon by W. A. Rogers appeared in the *New York Herald* on May 9, 1918. It depicts Uncle Sam rounding up individuals labeled "Spy," "Traitor," "IWW," "Germ[an] money," and "Sinn Féin." The Industrial Workers of the World was both an anarchist and socialist labor organization. Sinn Féin was an Irish nationalist party seeking independence from Great Britain.

PRIMARY SOURCE : CARTOON

EXAMINE THE SOURCE

1. **Interpreting** What groups of people do the individuals gathered by Uncle Sam represent?
2. **Analyzing Points of View** Explain the main idea the artist wants to convey. What does Rogers suggest about the federal government's goals?

PHOTO: Library of Congress Prints and Photographs Division, Alfred Bendiner Memorial Collection, [LC-DIG-cai-2a14550]; TEXT: Socialist Party of America. "Assert Your Rights!" [flyer] In Charles T. Schenck v. United States, 249 U.S. 47 (1919).

Steel Company Advertisement

As World War I ended, and in the years after, many unions organized mass labor strikes while other groups of workers went on strike for the right to form unions. Millions of workers went on strike in 1918 and 1919. The Great Steel Strike began on September 22, 1919. More than 350,000 workers from cities across the nation walked out. They wanted higher wages, shorter workdays, and safer conditions. One steel company responded with this ad, which appeared in the *Pittsburgh Chronicle* on October 6, 1919. The bold headline presumed the workers would not succeed.

PRIMARY SOURCE : CARTOON

EXAMINE THE SOURCE

1. **Drawing Conclusions** Why do you think this ad includes its admonitions in eight languages? Who does that suggest is to blame for labor unrest?

2. **Analyzing Perspectives** Why is the character calling for strikers to resume work depicted as Uncle Sam? What attitude do you think the industrialists behind the ad wanted to convey to the American public?

"Reds" Round-Up

In 1919 dozens of bombs were sent to government officials—including A. Mitchell Palmer—and leading businesspeople. Palmer responded by organizing a special task force that raided homes, community centers, restaurants and other locations where suspected radicals, including many immigrants, were believed to gather. Many were held for months without trials.

PRIMARY SOURCE : NEWSPAPER ARTICLE

> 66 The Department of Justice, after three months of preparation, launched last night a nation-wide round-up of members of the Communist and Communist Labor parties.
>
> In New York City alone 880 warrants were issued for leaders among those who are attempting to introduce a soviet government in the United States. By 2 o'clock this morning 650 men and women had been taken from various parts of the greater city to Department of Justice headquarters at 21 Park Row.
>
> A. Mitchell Palmer, Attorney General, is in charge of this, the greatest offensive ever instituted by the government against radicals. Its scope extends from coast to coast. . . . More than three thousand **warrants** had been issued. . . .
>
> It is understood all aliens named in the warrants will be deported as soon as possible. Citizens arrested are to be turned over to the county prosecutors for trial. 99

—"3,000 Arrested in Nation-Wide Round-Up of 'Reds,'" *New York Tribune*, January 3, 1920

warrant an official document, signed by a judge, authorizing an arrest or a search of one's property

EXAMINE THE SOURCE

1. **Contrasting** Based on the article, how will officials treat citizens and foreigners differently?

2. **Identifying Bias** Identify types of information you might expect to see regarding the suspects that this article does not provide. What does this suggest about the potential bias of the media?

PHOTO: HathiTrust; TEXT: "3000 Arrested in Nation-Wide Round-Up of 'Reds'" New York Tribune, January 3, 1920.

The Case Against the "Reds"

Attorney General A. Mitchell Palmer responded to a wave of bombings with investigations and raids of suspected "radicals," which led to the deportation of many immigrants and labor organizers. In 1920 Palmer published this article in *The Forum* in response to critics of the Palmer raids.

PRIMARY SOURCE : MAGAZINE ARTICLE

> " In this brief review of the work which the Department of Justice has undertaken, to tear out the **radical** seeds that have entangled American ideas . . . I desire not merely to explain what the real menace of communism is, but also to tell how we have been compelled to clean up the country. . . .
>
> Like a prairie-fire, the blaze of revolution was sweeping over every American institution . . . a year ago. It was eating its way into the homes of the American workmen, . . . crawling into the sacred corners of American homes, . . . burning up the foundations of society. . . .
>
> How the Department of Justice discovered upwards of 60,000 of these organized agitators of the [Bolshevik] doctrine in the United States is the confidential information upon which the Government is now sweeping the nation clean of such alien filth. . . .
>
> I have been asked . . . to what extent deportation will check radicalism in this country. Why not ask what will become of the . . . Government if these alien radicals are permitted to carry out the principles of the Communist Party . . . .
>
> It is my belief that . . . while they have caused irritating strikes, and while they have infected our social ideas with . . . their unclean morals we can get rid of them and not until we have done so shall we have removed the menace of Bolshevism for good. "

— A. Mitchell Palmer, in *The Forum*, 1920

radical extreme; different from custom

EXAMINE THE SOURCE

1. **Explaining** How does the author describe communism, and to what purpose?
2. **Analyzing Points of View** What feelings does the author try to evoke, and how?

Your Inquiry Analysis

EVALUATE SOURCES AND USE EVIDENCE

Reflect on the Compelling Question and the Supporting Questions you developed at the beginning of this lesson.

1. **Gathering Sources** Which sources helped you answer the Compelling Question and your Supporting Questions most directly? Which sources, if any, provided unexpected information or raised further questions? What additional research might you do to clarify information or resolve questions?

2. **Evaluating Sources** Looking at the sources that helped you answer your supporting questions, evaluate the credibility of each source. Which source(s) clearly show evidence of bias? How does that bias potentially influence the information provided? What does that bias suggest about the source and its broader social and historical context?

3. **Comparing and Contrasting** Compare and contrast two of the sources in this lesson more closely. What message does each source seek to convey? What types of evidence, if any, does each source provide? Explain how the tone, facts, and opinions of each source provide insight into the era and help you answer the Compelling Question.

COMMUNICATE CONCLUSIONS

Collaborating With one or more partners, discuss what you learned from each source in response to your Supporting Questions. Then, work together to write a paragraph in response to the Compelling Question in which you cite evidence from at least three of the sources. Finally, draw a political cartoon or write an editorial to express one conclusion you and your partner(s) have drawn about the era. Share your work as part of a class newspaper or in a short presentation.

TAKE INFORMED ACTION

Investigating Policy Think about a government policy that relates to labor unions or workers' rights. Use appropriate resources to investigate the underlying motivations of the officials who propose and support that policy as well as the key positions of critics. Create an infographic to report your findings. Write a short paragraph explaining whether you support or oppose the policy and why. In your paragraph, discuss whether your opinion changed after you did additional research.

Palmer, A. Mitchell. The Case Against the "Reds". The Forum, v. 63. Feb. 1920, pp. 173–180.

08

Reviewing American Expansion and World War I

Summary

America's Expanding Global Role

During the late 1800s many European powers were expanding their empires throughout the world, especially by gaining new colonies in Asia and Africa. The Industrial Revolution relied upon natural resources these colonies could provide; thus, control of foreign lands became a symbol of power and a source of competitive pride among European nations. Even though Europe experienced relatively long periods of peace in the late 1800s, with few direct armed conflicts between the major powers, these nations were building up economic and military power, as well as pride in their own strength, through their empires. Meanwhile, the United States was also expanding its role in the world, focusing mainly on expanding markets for its industrial products and protecting its influence in the Western Hemisphere.

By the 1890s, some U.S. leaders were calling for expanding global power. As it expanded its navy, the United States needed bases in the Pacific to support military and trade ships. After U.S. naval forces played a role in the controversial American overthrow of Hawaii's Queen Liliuokalani, some prominent Americans warned U.S. leaders against trying to build colonial empires like the Europeans, noting that the United States had fought a revolution to free itself from British colonial authority. Others, however, argued that the United States had a moral duty to expand its "civilizing" culture to other lands.

The United States further expanded its global role when it offered support to Cubans trying to overthrow their Spanish colonizers. The Spanish-American War was a relatively short conflict that embroiled American forces in fighting not only in Cuba but also in the Spanish-controlled Philippines. After the war, the United States retained influence in Cuba and expanded its direct and indirect control of numerous former Spanish colonies. For the next several years and through various presidents, U.S. influence would grow throughout Latin America and parts of Asia, primarily through money, political pressure, and the presence of U.S. military forces.

World War I Begins

By the turn of the century, European powers were competing for global influence and tensions were increasing. Militarism led countries to increase the size and firepower of their armed forces. While secret alliances kept some countries from going to war with one another, these alliances based on promises of mutual support held the potential for drawing several countries into war at once. Along with increasing competition through imperialism and nationalism, militarism and these networks of alliances created a situation where one spark could set off a massive war.

That spark was the assassination of Austrian Archduke Franz Ferdinand by a Bosnian revolutionary. The assassination set off a chain reaction in which European Allies led by Britain, France, and Russia fought against the Central Powers led by Germany, Austria-Hungary, and the Ottoman Empire. Nearly all European countries and their colonies were drawn into the conflict.

Initially, President Wilson emphasized that the United States intended to remain neutral in the Great War (later known as World War I). Many Americans, insulated by the Atlantic Ocean, saw the conflicts as a European problem that should not concern the United States. Also, many Americans were divided in their sympathies, with some of British descent siding more with the Allies and those of German descent siding more with the Central Powers. Both sides used propaganda to muster support for their cause.

Increasingly, however, German U-boat activity threatened U.S. neutrality, placing American ships and citizens in harm's way. The German sinking of the *Lusitania* and the continued U-boat attacks began to shift American sympathies toward the Allies. Even though Wilson's pledge of neutrality helped him win a

---

American Imperialism
The vision of American imperialism rested on perceived economic, cultural, and political benefits.

A desire for new markets for industrial products
A belief in Manifest Destiny to spread American culture and democracy around the world
An emphasis on a powerful navy and controlling trade as key to global power

second term in 1916, his administration began to plan for the possibility of war. After the Zimmermann note revealed a German plan to try to forge an alliance with Mexico against the United States, Congress prepared for war. In April 1917, the United States officially entered the conflict on the side of the Allies.

The United States in World War I

Fighting in World War I was like nothing the world had ever experienced. Very early in the fighting, opposing forces became bogged down as they engaged in trench warfare. Little land exchanged hands as both sides amassed huge casualties, compounded by unsanitary conditions and ever deadlier weapons of the industrial age. Before it could help its Allies in the fighting, the United States needed to quickly recruit and train an army. Applying the same reform-minded spirit it had used to tackle social and political issues, Wilson's administration created new agencies to mobilize the war effort. The government also launched its own propaganda campaign to unify the country behind the war effort and quell dissent.

Opponents of the war, especially opponents of the draft used to raise troops, faced arrest and censorship. Some German Americans also found themselves under attack by neighbors who now questioned their loyalties. Americans with socialist and communist ideologies found themselves the targets of a Red Scare. Politicians warned that the United States could experience a communist revolution like that launched by the Bolsheviks in Russia. That revolution led Russia to withdraw from the war by the spring of 1918.

Russia's withdrawal from the war moved almost all the fighting to the Western Front. The Allies desperately needed American help. Although some American troops began arriving in the summer of 1917, they played a most crucial role in helping the Allies resist new German offensives in the spring of 1918.

As heavy fighting continued over the next several months, fresh American troops helped the war-weary Allies gain the upper hand over Central Power forces. Finally, an armistice was reached, leading to the end of fighting on November 11, 1918.

Aftermath of War

In the months after the cease fire, world leaders met in Versailles to work out details of a formal postwar treaty. President Wilson hoped others would follow his Fourteen Points, a plan for negotiating a lasting peace that would limit future armed conflicts. Many of the Allied leaders, whose countries had suffered significantly in the conflict, wanted to punish those they held most responsible for the Great War. The final Treaty of Versailles redrew the map of Europe, forcing Germany to accept most of the responsibility for the conflict and surrender its colonies and armies. Germany was also required to pay hefty reparations to the Allies for the destruction caused by the war.

Even though the final treaty included the creation of the League of Nations, a world organization Wilson hoped would help prevent future wars, political opposition to some of the terms prevented the U.S. Senate from ratifying the treaty or joining the League.

On the home front, the shift from a wartime to a peacetime economy brought with it a recession and new conflicts. Women and African Americans had played a huge role in providing labor in American wartime factories and increased their military presence. Prior to the war, many northern companies had recruited African American workers from the South. This Great Migration was accelerated by the war effort and continued for decades. Yet once the conflict was over, many veterans resented the competition for jobs in industries that were cutting back on labor just as they were returning home.

Union officials who had made gains for workers before the war found themselves weakened and under attack as part of the Red Scare. The year 1919 saw a record wave of racist and labor-related violence. The country ended the decade weary from years of upheaval and death.

The War's Impact
World War I and its aftermath changed American society.

SOCIAL AND CULTURAL EFFECTS OF WORLD WAR I				
African Americans migrate to factory jobs in North; standard of living and political influence improves	Women enter workforce in larger numbers because men are enlisted in the military	Hispanic Americans shift from field work to industrial work; more Mexicans migrate into the U.S.	Postwar economic transition is disrupted by worker strikes and race riots in several cities	Rise in anti-immigrant, anti-communist, and anti-union beliefs following the war

Apply What You Have Learned

Understanding Multiple Perspectives

The years between the Spanish-American War and the United States' entry into World War I saw dramatic changes in the role the U.S. took in world affairs. Although many Americans were critical of European imperialism and preferred a path of isolationism, every administration during this period took actions that increased U.S. involvement in other nations. Each president developed his own ideology for guiding foreign policy within his administration. Unique crises could still lead a president to break with his own guiding principles, as he deemed necessary.

ACTIVITY **Comparing Political Cartoons**
Political cartoonists of the time often addressed issues relating to world affairs in their published works. Working in small groups, choose one of the following subjects: Open Door policy, Panama Canal, Roosevelt Corollary, Dollar Diplomacy, or Wilson's efforts at moral diplomacy. Then, using your textbook, library, or Internet resources, locate two political cartoons of the time that express different points of view on the subject. Share your findings with the rest of the class, emphasizing the different points of view illustrated by the cartoons.

Understanding Chronology

World War I lasted slightly more than four-and-a-half years. During that time, it altered the history of the world, greatly shaping many events of the twentieth century in the decades that followed. Although the "fuel" for the war—including increasing imperialism, nationalism, militarism, and alliances—had been gradually building over many years, specific events sparked the outbreak of fighting, the developments during the conflict, and what happened afterward. Historians still analyze these events and debate how much the conflict and its aftermath were "inevitable" and how much could have been avoided.

ACTIVITY **Creating an Annotated Time Line** Review key dates between 1914 and 1919 mentioned in your textbook and assignments for this lesson. Using that material, create a time line of important dates related to the war, with annotations explaining the significance of each event. When you are finished, share your time line with another student to compare and review your work.

1914

1919

C Building Citizenship

Prior to entering the Great War, most Americans preferred to remain neutral in the conflict. Once Congress declared war on Germany, however, the U.S. government rallied the nation behind the war effort. Because many Americans had previously been skeptical about entering the war, it took special effort to rally public support for the efforts needed to raise and support an army on short notice.

ACTIVITY **Creating a Public Announcement**
World War I took place prior to the invention of television or computers. However, people often gathered in public places such as theaters, churches, or political rallies. The government enlisted the aid of "Four Minute Men" who gave short presentations at such gatherings, similar to a modern commercial, to rally support for the war. Organize into small groups. Then work together to develop a skit of less than four minutes promoting one of the U.S. government's civilian mobilization efforts during World War I, such as planting victory gardens or buying liberty bonds.

D Making Connections to Today

As deadly as combat proved to be during the Great War, few people were prepared for the devastation brought by the so-called "Spanish influenza" pandemic that spanned the globe starting in the spring of 1918. It affected almost one-fourth of the world's population and killed more people than direct fighting on the front lines. At the time, the flu pandemic seemed to start and end suddenly with much information about it shrouded in mystery due to wartime censorship and lack of scientific knowledge about pandemics. Historians now understand how the global movement of troops, malnutrition, and sanitation issues on the front contributed to the rapid spread of the disease.

ACTIVITY **Creating a Comparison Chart** Over the past century, many scientists have closely studied the 1918 Spanish flu outbreak to understand how pandemics begin and spread. Using library and Internet resources, look up information about the Spanish flu outbreak and the COVID-19 pandemic that began in late 2019 and impacted the U.S. in 2020. Then create a chart that compares information about the two outbreaks. Write a summary explaining how the study of the Spanish flu shaped responses to more recent pandemics.

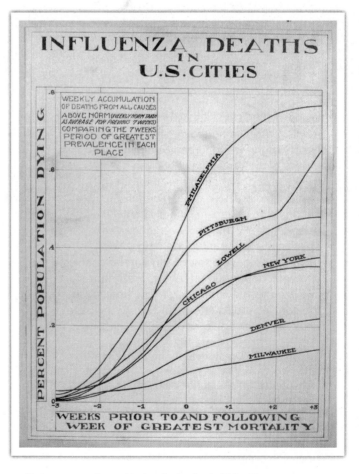

» Data were gathered to track deaths in U.S. cities during the Spanish flu epidemic.

Niday Picture Library/Alamy Stock Photo.

Progressivism and the Jazz Age 1890–1929

The early twentieth century featured many cultural and political changes. For example, women sought more social freedoms and financial independence. These women drove cross-country from Washington, D.C. to San Francisco in 1922.

INTRODUCTION LESSON

01 Introducing Progressivism and the Jazz Age   192

LEARN THE EVENTS LESSONS

02 Progressive Era Reforms   197

04 A Growing Economy   207

05 African American Politics and Culture   213

07 A Clash of Values   223

INQUIRY ACTIVITY LESSONS

03 Understanding Multiple Perspectives of the Progressives   203

06 Analyzing Sources: The Harlem Renaissance   217

REVIEW AND APPLY LESSON

08 Reviewing Progressivism and the Jazz Age   229

Hulton Archive/Getty Images

A GENIUS OF THE SOUTH

The 1920s and 1930s were a fruitful time for African American artists and writers. This period, called the **Harlem Renaissance,** was named for the New York City neighborhood where many African American artists lived. The emphasis on new expression during the Harlem Renaissance led to greater hope for change in the African American community.

Zora Neale Hurston was a pivotal writer and thinker of the Harlem Renaissance. Born in 1891, she spent her childhood in Eatonville, Florida, the first incorporated African American town in the country. Hurston's father was a successful carpenter and preacher and served as mayor of Eatonville. When Hurston's mother died in 1904 and her father remarried, life in Eatonville became too difficult for Hurston. She left to join a traveling theater company at age 16. Hurston attended Howard University from 1918 to 1924, and in 1925 she went to Barnard College to study anthropology. After graduating from Barnard in 1928, she completed two years of graduate study in anthropology at Columbia University with Franz Boas, the founder of the school of cultural anthropology in America.

Hurston specialized in **folklore,** particularly the folk traditions of African Americans in the South. She traveled widely, recording stories, songs, music, personalities, and ways of speaking to understand the local contexts in which people lived. Hurston also traveled to Haiti, and Haitian beliefs and cultural practices can be found throughout her work. Her scholarship influenced her literary pursuits and vice versa. Hurston often wrote dialogue in vernacular, which is the language or dialect native to a region. Her anthropological studies, such as *Mules and Men* (1935) and *Tell My Horse* (1938), captured vivid details of the people and cultures she examined.

Hurston became known as part of the Harlem Renaissance in 1925 after receiving a literary award from *Opportunity*, a magazine edited by Charles S. Johnson that focused on African American voices. Hurston was an active member of the Harlem circle in New York. She collaborated with Langston Hughes, another important writer of the era, on a play called *Mule Bone*, which they began in 1930 but never finished. Throughout the 1920s and 1930s, Hurston wrote plays, published novels, short stories, and essays, and supported herself by doing other work, such as teaching and serving as a writing assistant.

Despite her hard work and intelligence, she died in a welfare home in 1960 and was buried in an unmarked grave. The rediscovery of Hurston is attributed to the dedication of Alice Walker, a remarkable writer in her own right, who sought out Hurston's grave in 1973. Several previously unknown and unpublished plays were discovered in 1997 by a manuscript curator in the U.S. Copyright Office where Hurston had deposited them between the mid-1920s and mid-1940s.

Their Eyes Were Watching God (1937) is generally considered her most accomplished novel. Alice Walker remarked of it, "There is no book more important to me than this one." Walker's interest in Zora Neale Hurston brought about a resurgence of her work. Many of Hurston's texts, including her ten plays, were published in the late decades of the twentieth century. The attention of scholars and readers soon followed, finally restoring Hurston to a prominent place in American literary history.

> The emphasis on new expression during the Harlem Renaissance led to greater hope for change in the African American community.

Harlem Renaissance a cultural movement of African American artists and writers from about 1918 to 1937 with the Harlem district in New York City as the symbolic capital

folklore traditional customs, tales, sayings, dances, or art forms preserved among people, often of a particular time and place

Alice Walker.

GL Archive/Alamy Stock Photo.

In this portrait from 1937, Zora Neale Hurston beats a traditional percussion instrument. Hurston's skilled writing on culture and heritage made her a key artist during the Harlem Renaissance.

Understanding the Time and Place: The United States, 1890–1929

The end of the nineteenth century and the turn into the twentieth century marked an era of rapid and largely hopeful change in America. As the United States' economy strengthened and the country moved onto the global stage, social reformers began to fight against the societal transformations resulting from changes in industry, technology, and the wealth gap.

Progressive Politics

The Progressive Era was not a unified movement toward collective goals. Rather, it was a series of reform efforts that worked toward more equality for more people, facilitated in large part by the technological advances of the late nineteenth and early twentieth centuries. But not everyone benefited from these new technologies. Rural areas were often left behind, and an increasing number of people in urban areas—primarily immigrants—meant more job competition. African Americans were often intentionally excluded from reform movements.

Without regulations, employers could mistreat their employees without worry because replacements could easily be found. Progressive reformers sought social and political reforms because industrialization and urbanization had caused so many problems for working-class people. Journalists were among the earliest reformers. They sought to make the public aware of social ills, such as poverty and corrupt businesses and politicians. In 1890, for example, Jacob Riis's *How the Other Half Lives* exposed the crime and poverty experienced by many people in New York City.

Progressives wanted to improve government at the local, state, and national level by removing corrupt politicians who served themselves and not the voters who had elected them. Progressive reformers also wanted this new government to intervene in the economy to protect American workers and consumers. An early change was the Pendleton Act of 1883, which came about after President James Garfield's assassination by a disgruntled job seeker. The act required that jobs in the federal government be based on the merit of applicants, rather than relationships with political friends and allies of those in power.

Other important changes took place that gave citizens more influence in government. For example, Wisconsin introduced the **direct primary,** which soon spread to other states. Another reform is the initiative. After getting enough signatures to show voter support, **legislation** is introduced and the local or state legislative body can vote on it. A referendum allows citizens to vote on proposed laws directly. A recall gives voters the option to carry out a special election to remove someone from an elected office. Just as businesses became more streamlined with new technologies, progressives sought to improve government and social functioning by cleaning up corruption and allowing people to have a stronger voice in how things worked.

A Growing Economy

During the 1910s and 1920s, many Americans enjoyed an increased standard of living. Henry Ford's Model T, for example, came to market in 1908 for $850. Ford's assembly line a few years later quickened the process, and by 1925, a car was made every 10 seconds. This lowered the price of a car. In 1914 a car sold for $490, and it was only $295 by 1924.

Other car companies developed, creating competition, which only served to further reduce prices. More people could also commute longer distances, opening up new job opportunities. The airline, radio, and entertainment industries also developed during

This photograph by Jacob Riis in 1888 shows the conditions for immigrants in the Bayard Street tenement.

©Bettmann/Getty Images.

---

direct primary a primary, or election, where candidates are nominated for office by a direct vote

legislation the exercise of the power and function of making rules or laws

U.S. Industrialization

The industrialization of the late nineteenth century led to new inventions, technologies, and industries. An increasing population with more free time and more money to spend also increased consumerism and demand.

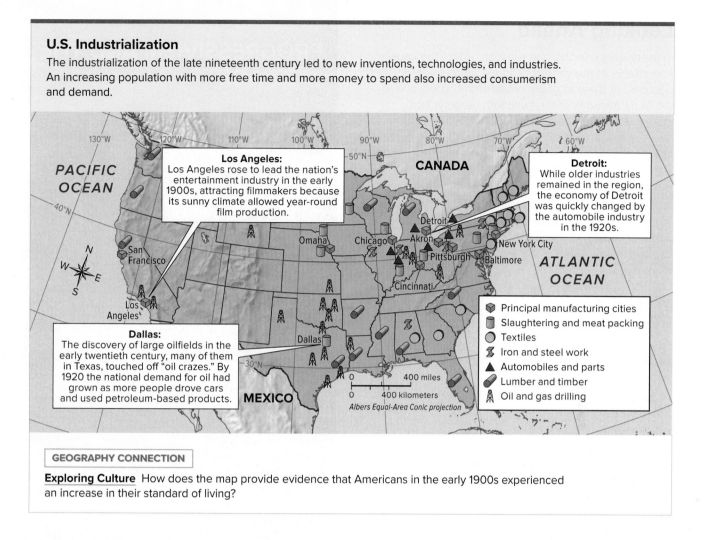

Los Angeles: Los Angeles rose to lead the nation's entertainment industry in the early 1900s, attracting filmmakers because its sunny climate allowed year-round film production.

Detroit: While older industries remained in the region, the economy of Detroit was quickly changed by the automobile industry in the 1920s.

Dallas: The discovery of large oilfields in the early twentieth century, many of them in Texas, touched off "oil crazes." By 1920 the national demand for oil had grown as more people drove cars and used petroleum-based products.

Legend:
- Principal manufacturing cities
- Slaughtering and meat packing
- Textiles
- Iron and steel work
- Automobiles and parts
- Lumber and timber
- Oil and gas drilling

Albers Equal-Area Conic projection

GEOGRAPHY CONNECTION

Exploring Culture How does the map provide evidence that Americans in the early 1900s experienced an increase in their standard of living?

---

this time. Many American families were making more money and new technologies, such as washing machines and refrigerators, gave them more free time.

Conflicts Between New and Old

An important voice that was heard during this era was that of women. Women were also influential leaders in the social welfare movement that sought to alleviate social ills such as crime, illiteracy, alcohol abuse, and child labor and protect the health and safety of Americans. Many women and religious leaders thought alcohol to be the root of social problems. The Eighteenth Amendment, which banned the production and sale of alcohol, was ratified the year before women won the vote. As women reformers became more involved in political change, their demands for a direct voice in politics grew more urgent. Women finally gained the right to vote after the Nineteenth Amendment was ratified in 1920.

Many people felt threatened by the changes of this era and fought against new, modern social values and the era's social disruptions. Immigrants and racial minorities were often blamed for this turmoil. Racial tensions in the Jim Crow South often erupted in

violence, and the Ku Klux Klan (KKK) reemerged as an active terrorist organization. This new KKK spread beyond the South by targeting any groups deemed "un-American," such as Roman Catholics, Jewish people, and immigrants, as well as continuing to target African Americans.

Between 1916 and 1970 in what was known as the "Great Migration," an estimated six million African Americans moved out of the South to large cities in the North, including Chicago, Detroit, Cleveland, and New York City. Rapid industrialization in Northern cities provided more jobs than the rural South, and many black southerners sought to escape racial oppression. Feeling ignored and often intentionally left out by the Progressive movement, African Americans sought their own reforms to fight racism and poor living conditions. Many great African American thinkers and reformers arose from this struggle, and the era saw an increase in African American artists and writers expressing their ideas, which led to both the Harlem Renaissance and the Jazz Age.

The political, cultural, and economic issues of this era continue to shape many of the questions that the United States still debates.

Looking Ahead

In these next lessons, you will learn about the causes and effects of the various progressive movements that occurred at the end of the nineteenth century and in the early decades of the twentieth century. While studying this time period, you will understand the social, political, and economic changes that took place in America. And you will examine how the clash between tradition and change forever altered American life.

You will examine Compelling Questions in the Inquiry Lessons and develop your own questions about progressivism and the Jazz Age. Study the time line to preview some of the key events that you will learn about.

What Will You Learn?

In these lessons focused on progressivism and the Jazz Age, you will learn:

- how the Progressive Era was expressed through political and economic actions.
- the different goals and groups involved in the woman suffrage movement.
- the importance of cultural and artistic contributions during these decades.
- the key artists and activists of the Harlem Renaissance and their work through primary and secondary sources.
- examples of social conflict that occurred during the 1920s.

? COMPELLING QUESTIONS

- **How did muckrakers seek to improve society?**
- **Why was the Harlem Renaissance a time of hope for African American artists and musicians?**

PROGRESSIVISM AND THE JAZZ AGE

1889 SEPTEMBER 18, 1889 Jane Addams opens Hull House in Chicago to aid immigrants (right)

1900 JUNE 20, 1906 Pure Food and Drug Act passes

1910 Mann-Elkins Act passes

FEBRUARY 3, 1913 Sixteenth Amendment gives Congress the power to collect income taxes

APRIL 8, 1913 Seventeenth Amendment allows for direct election of senators

OCTOBER 15, 1914 Clayton Antitrust Act is enacted

1915 1915 Resurrection of the Ku Klux Klan

1915 Start of the Great Migration

AUGUST 25, 1916 National Parks Service is created

1919 Eighteenth Amendment establishing Prohibition is ratified

1920 AUGUST 18, 1920 Nineteenth Amendment gives women voting rights

1920 Prohibition begins

1925 Scopes trial ignites debate over teaching of evolution

1922 McKay's *Harlem Shadows* is published

DECEMBER 30, 1927 The *Jazz Singer* is first "talking" motion picture

1930

Everett Collection/Shutterstock

Sequencing Time Identify the events that reflect changes made to the U.S. Constitution and explain what those changes revealed about American society during this period.

02
Progressive Era Reforms

READING STRATEGY

Analyzing Key Ideas and Details As you read, use a graphic organizer like the one below to summarize and categorize the central ideas of different groups during the fight for women's right to vote.

Group	Central Ideas
National Woman Suffrage Association	
American Woman Suffrage Association	
National Woman's Party	
Anti-Suffragists	

Understanding Progressive Reforms

GUIDING QUESTION

What reforms were used to make government more responsive to citizens?

Progressivism was a collection of different ideas, not a tightly organized political movement with one specific set of goals. Progressivism responded to problems in society that had emerged in part from the growth of industry, economic transformation, and increasing immigration and the resulting social tensions, but there were many different ideas about how to fix these problems. Some focused on social problems, such as crime, illiteracy, alcohol abuse, child labor, and health and safety. These social-welfare progressives created charities to help the poor and disadvantaged and pushed for new laws to fix social problems. Others focused on the economy and balancing the scales of power and wealth after rapid economic shifts and changes.

Women were prominent leaders of the social-welfare progressives. Most came from the middle or upper class and felt a responsibility toward working-class women, who faced issues related to poverty, safety, and abuse. Because the culture of the time generally expected fathers and husbands to work and provide for their families, women and children who lost their husbands and fathers were exceptionally vulnerable and more likely to be forced into poverty.

For progressives, the idea that poor women and children might be forced into dangerous working conditions was an important issue to be solved. For example, in two cases, *Lochner* v. *New York* (1905) and *Muller* v. *Oregon* (1908), the Supreme Court addressed the government's authority to regulate business to protect workers. In the *Lochner* case, the Court ruled that a New York law forbidding bakers to work more than 10 hours a day was unconstitutional because government could not interfere in the right of an employer and employee to make a contract. In the *Muller* case, which involved women working in laundries in Oregon, the Court upheld the state's right to limit hours, however. The Court stated in its ruling that healthy mothers were the state's concern and the limits on women's working hours did not violate their Fourteenth Amendment rights.

The government's role in regulating the workplace was rethought after a tragedy on March 25, 1911. A fire on the top floors of the Triangle Shirtwaist Company in New York City caused nearly 150 of the factory's 500 workers to lose their lives. Most of the factory's employees—and the fatalities—were young women. The disaster illustrated that fire precautions and inspections were inadequate. In response, New York created a Factory Investigating Commission and passed new laws to regulate workplace safety.

Child Labor Laws

The fight against child labor was an important issue for many reformers. Children had always worked on family farms, but mines and factories presented more dangerous working conditions. John Spargo's 1906 book *The Bitter Cry of the Children* presented detailed evidence of child labor conditions. It described coal mines that hired thousands of 9- or 10-year-old "breaker boys" to pick slag out of coal, paying them 60 cents for a 10-hour day. It described how the work bent their backs permanently and often crippled their hands.

Reports like these convinced states to pass laws limiting child labor, such as those that established a minimum age for employment and a maximum

Documentary photographers raised public awareness of child labor, which helped change the nation's labor laws.

Speculating How might working in this textile factory forever change the lives of these children?

number of hours children could work. Many states also began passing compulsory education laws, requiring young children to be in school instead of at work. Lillian Wald, Florence Kelley, and other progressives pushed the federal government to protect children's welfare. In 1912 President Taft signed a bill creating the United States Children's Bureau and named Julia Lathrop as the first director. The Bureau investigated issues like infant mortality, orphanages, and dangerous work conditions.

Political and Government Reforms

One group of progressives drew its ideas for increasing government efficiency from business. Such theories first became popular in the 1890s. Books such as Frederick W. Taylor's *The Principles of Scientific Management* (1911) described how a company increased efficiency by managing time, breaking tasks down into small parts, and using standardized tools—a scientific approach to business that some progressives wanted to extend to government.

Progressives hoped to make city government less corrupt and more efficient by ending the practice of hiring unqualified political supporters to run city departments. Progressives wanted experts to manage cities. For example, the commission plan divided city government into several departments with each one under an expert commissioner's control. The council-manager system employed a city manager who was hired by the city council.

Others focused on making government more democratic. Wisconsin's progressive governor Robert M. La Follette promoted his state's efforts to make elected officials more responsive and accountable to voters. These reformers wanted to end party bosses' control of convention delegates and the nomination of candidates. La Follette pressured the Wisconsin legislature to pass a law requiring parties to hold a direct primary in which all party members voted for a candidate to run in the general election. The direct primary soon spread to other states.

Additional government-based reforms included the initiative, the referendum, and the recall. The **initiative** permits citizens to introduce legislation and requires the legislature to vote on it. Typically, citizens need a certain number of petition signatures to make the initiative legally binding. A referendum allows citizens to vote on proposed laws directly. In some states, if the legislature passes certain laws, such as a change to taxes, the new law has to be approved by the public in a referendum. Referendums are also used to repeal existing laws. Both the referendum and the initiative gave reformers the power to bypass or overrule the legislature if it refused to support something the people wanted. The **recall** provides voters the option to demand a special election to remove an elected official from office before his or her term has expired.

Progressives targeted the Senate. The Constitution originally directed each state legislature to elect two senators, but political machines and business interests often influenced these elections. Once elected, some senators repaid their supporters with federal contracts and jobs. To counter corruption in the Senate, reformers called for the direct election of senators by voters. Congress passed a direct-election amendment in 1912, and in 1913 it was ratified as the Seventeenth Amendment to the Constitution. Although direct election was meant to end corruption, it also removed one of the state legislatures' checks on federal power.

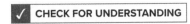 **CHECK FOR UNDERSTANDING**

Summarizing What types of reforms did the progressive movement make?

The Women's Suffrage Fight

GUIDING QUESTION

What competing approaches did women use to promote a constitutional amendment?

Even without the right to vote, women participated in politics. They held rallies and supported candidates. But

---

initiative the right of citizens to present legislation for approval by the legislature

recall the removal of an elected official from a government office through petitioning and voting

PhotoQuest/Archive Photos/Getty Images

GO ONLINE Explore the Student Edition eBook and find interactive maps, time lines, and tools.

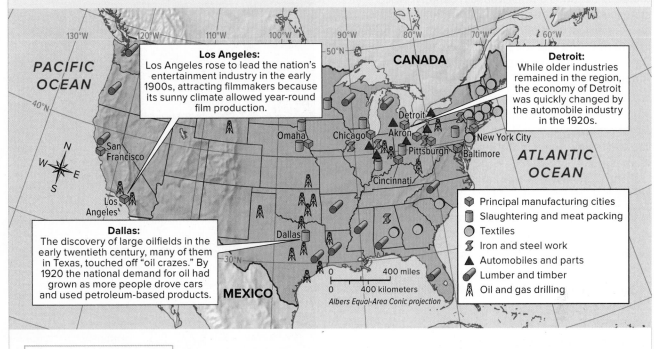

0 — 400 miles
0 — 400 kilometers
Albers Equal-Area Conic projection

women reformers wanted to use their voices to affect politics more directly, as men could. At the first women's rights convention in Seneca Falls, New York, in 1848 Elizabeth Cady Stanton convinced the delegates that winning suffrage—the right to vote—should be a priority. At the end of the convention, sixty-eight women and thirty-two men signed the Declaration of Sentiments, a document that echoed the Declaration of Independence.

Early Challenges

Many suffragists were also abolitionists, and in the years before the Civil War, ending slavery took priority over women's voting rights. After the Civil War, woman suffrage leaders wanted the Fourteenth and Fifteenth Amendments to be written to grant women the right to vote as well. The Fourteenth Amendment granted citizenship to "all persons born or naturalized in the United States" but did not specifically mention women or protections based on gender. The Fifteenth Amendment eliminated voting discrimination based on "race, color, or previous condition of servitude" but again left out women and specific gender-based protections. Though many suffragists were also abolitionists, some prioritized white woman suffrage over African American freedom.

In 1869 two groups formed with different approaches to achieving suffrage: the New York City-based National Woman Suffrage Association (NWSA), founded by Stanton and Susan B. Anthony, and the Boston-based American Woman Suffrage Association (AWSA), led by Lucy Stone and Julia Ward Howe. NWSA focused on a constitutional amendment, whereas AWSA focused on convincing state governments to grant women suffrage. In 1890 NWSA and AWSA united to form the National American Woman Suffrage Association (NAWSA). The state focus proved more effective, particularly in states in the Midwest and West. By 1900 Wyoming, Idaho, Utah, and Colorado had granted women full voting rights.

The movement did not include all women equally. While African American women played important roles in the foundation of the women suffrage movement, they were later excluded as white women saw their white racial identity as important to win the right to vote. African American women faced harassment, racism, and lack of access to education, jobs, and housing in ways that both African American men and white women did not. They formed clubs and organizations, such as the National Association of Colored Women's Clubs (NACWC), and they remained active in working for civil rights at the local and national level.

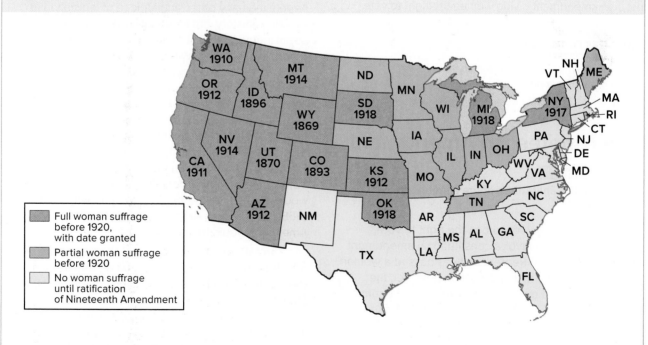

Woman Suffrage, 1869–1920

Woman suffrage gained strength after the Civil War.

Legend:
- Full woman suffrage before 1920, with date granted
- Partial woman suffrage before 1920
- No woman suffrage until ratification of Nineteenth Amendment

GEOGRAPHY CONNECTION

1. **Spatial Thinking** Which state or territory first granted women the right to vote?

2. **Patterns and Movement** In which direction did support for woman suffrage generally move throughout the country before 1920?

(1)US Const. Amend XIV, § 1., https://www.archives.gov/founding-docs/amendments-11-27; (2)The House Joint Resolution proposing the 15th amendment to the Constitution, February 3, 1870; Enrolled Acts and Resolutions of Congress, 1789-1999; General Records of the United States Government; Record Group 11; National Archives.

Building Support

As the progressive movement gained momentum, many women realized that they needed the vote to promote reforms and pass labor laws. Women began organizing events, handing out pamphlets, and delivering speeches. Many leaders of the suffrage movement were able to **lobby** state and federal legislators directly. To put more pressure on legislators, Quaker social worker and former NAWSA member Alice Paul founded the National Woman's Party (NWP). The NWP emphasized nonviolent protest to promote women's suffrage. Its members picketed, blocked sidewalks, and chained themselves to lampposts. Suffragist Rose Winslow and several other women, including Alice Paul, were arrested for picketing the White House in October 1917. After being sentenced to seven months in jail, Winslow, Paul, and other women prisoners went on a hunger strike. The hunger strikers were force-fed in prison, and the story garnered a lot of attention in the press, creating a national scandal.

NAWSA leader Carrie Chapman Catt made one final nationwide push for suffrage. She used NAWSA funds to support politicians who backed suffrage. She convinced the NAWSA to support President Wilson's reelection in 1916 and then supported the president when he took the country to war in 1917. News coverage of the NWP's protests put political pressure on government officials. President Wilson was trying to portray the United States as fighting for freedom and democracy in World War I. This context and the NAWSA's support motivated Wilson to ask Congress to pass an amendment giving women the right to vote.

☑ CHECK FOR UNDERSTANDING

Describing Why did women start pushing for voting rights during this time period?

The Nineteenth Amendment

GUIDING QUESTION

What were the limitations of the Nineteenth Amendment?

As more states granted women the right to vote, Congress began to favor a constitutional amendment. In 1918 the House of Representatives passed a woman suffrage amendment. In the Senate, however, the amendment failed by two votes. After the amendment failed to pass, the NWP successfully campaigned against the senators who had voted against it. The amendment came before Congress again in 1919. This time, it passed the House (304–89) and the Senate (56–25). However, the amendment still needed to be

lobby to conduct activities with the purpose of influencing public officials, particularly members of a legislative body

ratified by three-fourths of the forty-eight states. (Hawaii and Alaska were not states at the time.)

People opposed to a woman's right to vote believed that women were not capable or interested in participating in politics. Some thought giving women the vote would make them politically active and take them away from their roles as housewives and mothers. Opposition came from men as well as women. Many upper- and middle-class women, for example, thought politics would tarnish the moral and spiritual lives of women. Some women did not have the luxury of choosing whether to work, which connected suffrage to other social reforms aimed at improving the lives of working-class women.

Others believed that politics would interfere with social reform. Josephine Dodge, for example, had been advocating for day care for working mothers since the 1870s. In 1888 she founded a nursery that provided day care and education to immigrant children. She became increasingly active in opposing the suffrage movement because she believed political involvement would damage women's integrity.

After decades of work, protests, arrests, threats, and devotion to a single goal, the suffragists finally won the day. On August 18, 1920, Tennessee became the thirty-sixth state to ratify the amendment, by one vote. On August 26, the Nineteenth Amendment was certified as a part of the U.S. Constitution.

But the ratification of the Nineteenth Amendment proved to be only the first step in a long road toward equality for all. It did expand voting rights to more people than any other single piece of legislation in American history, but it did not correct the racial and social inequalities that continued to pervade America. Reformers like Ida B. Wells pushed for an end to lynching. African Americans continued to face voting barriers, and advocates like Mary Church Terrell continued to push for civil rights and voting rights. Federal law now prohibited discrimination based on race or sex but getting access to the voting booth was no easy task in many states, particularly in the Jim Crow South, where African American voters were prevented from voting by various legal barriers and brutal tactics. It would not be until the 1964 Civil Rights Act and the 1965 Voting Rights Act that the rights of African Americans would be truly protected.

The Nineteenth Amendment left many of the voting details to the states. Voter registration requirements were determined by state and local governments, who often used requirements to suppress minorities and immigrants. Some states prevented Native Americans from voting even after they were finally recognized as citizens by the 1924 Indian Citizenship Act.

Although women had run for political office before 1920, the Nineteenth Amendment helped more women successfully attain key positions at the local and state level. Between 1920 and 1923, at least 22 women were elected to mayoral positions in small towns. In 1928 Seattle became the first big city to elect a female mayor.

Women also had some success at the federal level. Ruth Hanna McCormick and Ruth Bryan Owen were elected to the U.S. House of Representatives in 1928. In 1920 President Wilson created the Women's Bureau in the U.S. Department of Labor and appointed Mary Anderson to lead it, which she did until 1944.

New organizations were also created that focused on improving public policies for women and children. One of the largest was the Women's Joint Congressional Committee (WJCC), a combined effort of 20 organizations that boasted more than 20 million members. The first great success of the WJCC was the Sheppard-Towner Maternity and Infancy Act, which gave states about $1 million a year to support maternity and child health clinics. The act was administered by the Children's Bureau. The state and federal partnerships created by the act provided a model that would be used to address the issues that arose a decade later during the Great Depression.

✓ CHECK FOR UNDERSTANDING

Explaining What effects did the Nineteenth Amendment have?

Roosevelt and Taft's Progressive Politics

GUIDING QUESTION

How did Roosevelt and Taft demonstrate a new role of government regulation in industry?

As the new progressivism led to sweeping changes in voting rights and social services, Presidents Theodore Roosevelt and William Howard Taft demonstrated a progressive attitude toward business regulation. Roosevelt's foreign policy promoted an aggressive government and expansionism. Domestically, however, he believed that government should balance the needs of competing groups on behalf of the public interest.

Roosevelt believed the most effective way to prevent big business from abusing its power was to keep the public informed and only attack a trust when necessary. The 1904 case, *Northern Securities* v. *United States*, had shifted the relationship between the federal government and private business. Before it had generally been agreed that Article I, Section 8, would of the Constitution gives Congress the power to regulate commerce with foreign nations and between states but not within a state. The *Northern Securities* ruling had broadened the legal understanding of commerce and, over time, the interpretation of the commerce clause expanded, allowing the federal government more and more power to regulate private business.

Roosevelt worked to make the federal government an honest broker between powerful groups. He intervened in the Coal Strike of 1902 by urging mine owners and the union to accept arbitration by a neutral third party. The union agreed but owners refused until Roosevelt threatened that the army would run the mines. He created the Department of Commerce and Labor that would oversee labor disputes in an impartial manner. Roosevelt also pushed the passage of the Hepburn Act in 1906, which strengthened the Interstate Commerce Commission (ICC) by giving it the power to set railroad rates. Roosevelt believed these reforms would create a balance between powerful groups and society and allow for a more efficient and fair economy.

Protecting the Consumer

By 1905, consumer protection had become a national issue. Americans increasingly felt that the costs of a laissez-faire approach to the economy outweighed the benefits. Journalist Samuel Hopkins Adams published several articles in *Collier's* magazine describing how unregulated companies patented and marketed medicinal potions they claimed would cure a variety of ills but were often little more than alcohol, colored water, and sugar. Some even contained dangerous compounds, such as opium and cocaine. Consumers could not know what they were taking or whether the medicines worked as claimed.

Many were equally concerned about the food they ate. Dr. W. H. Wiley, chief chemist at the United States Department of Agriculture, had issued reports documenting dangerous preservatives, including

The Meat Inspection Act of 1906 was one of many reforms that empowered the federal government to act on behalf of the public, protecting them from harmful substances.

Analyzing Visuals What evidence in this photograph shows the changes that the Meat Inspection Act may have had on the industry?

EverettCollection/Shutterstock

formaldehyde and borax, being used in what he called "embalmed meat." In 1906 Upton Sinclair published a novel, *The Jungle*, based on his observations of the slaughterhouses of Chicago. The appalling conditions in the meatpacking industry enraged consumers. Roosevelt and Congress responded with the 1906 Meat Inspection Act, which required federal inspection of meat sold through interstate commerce and allowed the Agriculture Department to set standards of cleanliness in meat packing plants. The Pure Food and Drug Act, passed on the same day in 1906, prohibited the manufacture, sale, or shipment of impure or falsely labeled food and drugs.

These two acts marked another change in the relationship between government and business. In both cases the U.S. Department of Agriculture (USDA) was given authority to inspect business operations and ensure that products were safe before they could be sold to the public. Consumers were less likely to become sick and could expect that products actually contained the ingredients listed on the labels. The costs of the law, as with other regulations of the economy, meant that companies had to charge more for their products. Putting labels on products cost money, and companies passed that on to consumers.

Environmentalism

Of all his progressive actions, Roosevelt may be best known for his efforts in environmental conservation. Roosevelt was an enthusiastic outdoorsman, and he valued the country's animals and rugged terrain. He cautioned against unregulated use of public lands and argued that conservation should be the guiding principle in managing the country's natural resources. In his 1907 annual message to Congress, Roosevelt said:

66 [T]o waste, to destroy our natural resources, instead of using it so as to increase its usefulness, will result in undermining in the days of our children the very prosperity which we ought by right to hand down to them amplified and developed. 99

In 1902 Roosevelt supported passage of the Newlands Reclamation Act that authorized the use of federal funds from public land sales to pay for irrigation and land development projects. The federal government thus began transforming the West's landscape and economy on a large scale. Roosevelt also supported careful management of the timber resources of the West. He appointed Gifford Pinchot to head the U.S. Forest Service, established in 1905. Roosevelt and Pinchot believed that trained experts in forestry and resource management should manage the nation's forests. Pinchot's department drew up regulations to control lumbering on federal lands. Roosevelt added more than 100 million acres to the protected national forests. He established five new national parks and 51 federal wildlife reservations.

Taft's Reforms

William Howard Taft, Roosevelt's secretary of war, won the election of 1908. Like many progressives, Taft believed high tariffs limited competition, hurt consumers, and protected trusts. Roosevelt had warned him that tariff reform would divide the Republican Party. Nevertheless, Taft called Congress into special session to lower tariff rates. The tariff debate did indeed divide the Republican Party into two groups: the progressives, who favored tariff reduction, and conservative Republicans, who wanted to maintain high tariffs to protect U.S. businesses. As negotiations dragged on, Taft's support for tariff reductions waned. Finally, he signed into law the Payne-Aldrich Tariff, which hardly cut tariffs at all and actually raised them on some goods, outraging progressives.

In 1909 Taft further angered progressives by replacing Roosevelt's secretary of the interior, James R. Garfield with Richard A. Ballinger. Gifford Pinchot accused Ballinger of planning to give valuable public lands in Alaska to a private business group for his own profit. Taft's attorney general investigated the charges and decided they were unfounded. A congressional investigation later cleared Ballinger. Taft removed Pinchot from his position when Pinchot made his opposition public. Roosevelt broke with Taft and this was one factor which cost Taft the election in 1912.

By the second half of Taft's term of office, many had become so frustrated with him that the congressional elections of 1910 resulted in a sweeping victory for Democrats and Progressive Republicans. Despite his political problems, Taft also had several successes. He brought twice as many antitrust cases in four years as Roosevelt had in seven. He also set up the Bureau of Mines to monitor the activities of mining companies, expand national forests, and protect waterpower sites from private development.

✓ **CHECK FOR UNDERSTANDING**

1. **Explaining** How did the government regulate business during the Roosevelt administration?

2. **Analyzing** How did Taft's decisions on tariffs split the Republican party?

LESSON ACTIVITIES

1. **Informative/Explanatory Writing** Write a paragraph about the effects of the Nineteenth Amendment on the voting rights of Americans.

2. **Collaborating** Work with a partner to write a script of a conversation between members of the NAWSA and the NWP. Create dialogue for two or more characters. Your script should demonstrate your understanding of the information in the lesson.

Roosevelt, Theodore. "Seventh Annual Message to Congress." Address, Washington, D.C., December 3, 1907.

03

Understanding Multiple Perspectives of the Progressives

 COMPELLING QUESTION

How did muckrakers seek to improve society?

Plan Your Inquiry

In this lesson, you will investigate the perspectives of progressive journalists known as "muckrakers."

DEVELOP QUESTIONS

Developing Questions About the Muckrakers Read the Compelling Question for this lesson. Think about the goals that individual muckrakers had and how their goals overlapped, complemented one another, and diverged. Consider, too, the methods they used in reporting. Then, develop a list of Supporting Questions to help you answer the Compelling Question in this lesson.

APPLY HISTORICAL TOOLS

Analyzing Primary Sources You will work with a variety of primary sources in this lesson. These sources focus on the perspectives and work of several progressive journalists known as "muckrakers." As you read, use a graphic organizer like the one below to record information about the sources that will help you examine them and check for historical understanding. Note ways in which each source helps you answer your Supporting Questions.

Supporting Questions	Primary Source	What this source tells me about....	Questions the source leaves unanswered
	A		
	B		
	C		
	D		

After you analyze the sources, you will:

- use the evidence from the sources.
- communicate your conclusions.
- take informed action.

Background Information

In the late 1800s and early 1900s several factors combined to produce a variety of economic, social, and political challenges. Industrialization spurred the rise of big business, urbanization, and dramatic shifts in the lives of workers. Increasing numbers of people left farm-centered rural life for cities to seek jobs in factories, mills, mines, ports, and other businesses.

Industrialization led to new forms of corruption. Some politicians granted favors to financial donors, placing the interests of large corporations and the wealthy over the needs of average workers. With little regulation, industries operated in ways that generated the most profit. A lack of regulation led to child labor, unsafe working conditions, and unwholesome food products. Muckrakers, such as investigative journalist Lincoln Steffens, highlighted corruption and other social ills and called for reform. Photographers such as Lewis Hine documented difficult conditions arising from industrialization.

» Children working in a New York City tenement earned $2.25 per week to help their families. Photograph by Lewis Hine, 1911.

Library of Congress

The Shame of the Cities

Lincoln Steffens worked as a newspaper reporter in New York City in the 1890s. During that time, he wrote about the effects of corrupt business and political practices. In 1901 he became managing editor of *McClure's Magazine*, a periodical that featured other progressive writers like Ida M. Tarbell, Upton Sinclair, Willa Cather, and Jack London. He reprinted many of his articles as a book, *The Shame of the Cities*, in 1904.

PRIMARY SOURCE : BOOK

❝ 'Let [a business man] introduce business methods into politics and government; then I shall be left alone to attend to my business.'

There is hardly an office from United States Senator down to **Alderman** in any part of the country to which the business man has not been elected; yet politics remains corrupt, government pretty bad, and the selfish citizen has to hold himself in readiness like the old volunteer firemen to rush forth at any hour, in any weather, to prevent the fire; . . . The business man has failed in politics as he has in citizenship. Why?

Because politics is business. That's what's the matter with it. That's what's the matter with everything,—art, literature, religion, journalism, law, medicine,—they're all business . . . .

No, the condemned methods of our despised politics are the master methods of our **braggart** business, and the corruption that shocks us in public affairs we practice ourselves in our private concerns. There is no essential difference between the pull that gets your wife into society or for your book a favorable review, and that which gets a **heeler** into office, a thief out of jail, and a rich man's son on the board of directors of a corporation; . . . none between a labor boss like Sam Parks, a boss of banks like John D. Rockefeller, a boss of railroads like J. P. Morgan, and a political boss like Matthew S. Quay. The boss is not a political, he is an American institution, the product of a freed people that have not the spirit to be free.

And it's all a moral weakness; a weakness right where we think we are strongest. Oh, we are good—on Sunday, and we are 'fearfully patriotic' on the Fourth of July. But the bribe we pay to the janitor to prefer our interests to the landlord's, is the little brother of the bribe passed to the alderman to sell a city street, and the father of the air-brake stock assigned to the president of a railroad to have this life-saving invention adopted on his road. . . . We are pathetically proud of our democratic institutions and our republican form of government, of our grand Constitution and our just laws. We are a free and sovereign people, we govern ourselves and the government is ours. But that is the point. We are responsible, not our leaders, since we follow them. We *let* them divert our loyalty from the United States to some 'party'; we *let* them boss the party and turn our municipal democracies into **autocracies** and our republican nation into a **plutocracy.** We cheat our government and we let our leaders loot it, and we let them wheedle and bribe our sovereignty from us. ❞

–Lincoln Steffens, *The Shame of the Cities*, 1904

alderman an elected member of a city legislative body

braggart a person who boasts loudly

heeler a henchman, or follower

autocracy a government in which one ruler holds absolute power

plutocracy a government controlled by the wealthy

EXAMINE THE SOURCE

1. **Drawing Conclusions** What effect does the author think that business has had on the nation?

2. **Interpreting** What reform(s) do you think the author would support to address the problem he describes? Explain.

Steffens, Lincoln. The Shame of the Cities. New York: McClure, Phillips & Co., 1904.

PHOTO: North Wind Picture Archives/Alamy Stock Photo; TEXT: "The Man Who Is Leading the Fight for Pure Food." Washington Times, November 20, 1901.

B

"The Man Who is Leading the Fight for Pure Food"

In the late nineteenth and early twentieth century, food production often involved unsanitary and unhealthy practices. Beginning in 1883, Dr. Harvey W. Wiley protested the use of fertilizers, dyes, and other substances in food. He called for laws to regulate food production and purity. The Meat Inspection Act and Pure Food and Drug Act were passed in 1906.

PRIMARY SOURCE : NEWS ARTICLE

" Once the manufacturers are compelled to label all their products truthfully, people will know exactly what they are getting. . . . The consumer is protected from the cheat and the manufacturer is prevented from cheating. . . .

The work on the pure foods has been along two separate lines—chemical experimentation and the determination of what were and what were not pure foods . . . .

Other [impure food manufacturing] practices which have been common are the introduction of **adulterants** to food stuffs and the sale thereof without any mention of the fact that these adulterants had been added, the substitution of foreign matter for valuable **constituents,** and the use of coloring matter. The law passed at the last term of Congress in regard to the inspection of imported foods has reduced such frauds to a minimum in imported foods and if the present bill goes through we will have the foods of this country well in hand. "

–"The Man Who Is Leading the Fight for Pure Food," *The Washington Times*, November 20, 1901

adulterant a corrupting substance added to something

constituent an essential part or ingredient

EXAMINE THE SOURCE

1. **Interpreting** What does the author mean by "pure" with regard to food and manufacturing practices?

2. **Analyzing Perspectives** What tone and position does the author take on the issue of food manufacturing and inspections?

C

"A Nauseating Job, but It Must Be Done"

In a speech on April 14, 1906, President Theodore Roosevelt discussed journalists who focused on exposing corruption, poverty, and other societal ills. He entitled the speech "The Man with a Muck Rake," alluding to an earlier novel—*The Pilgrim's Progress*—that referred to a man who never looked up from cleaning dirt and debris to see the good. Roosevelt believed that "muckrakers" focused too much on the bad. However, by that time, Upton Sinclair had written about the horrid conditions in meatpacking plants. Roosevelt had run on a progressive platform, so the publisher sent him an advanced copy of *The Jungle*, prompting him to take up the issue, too. Roosevelt commissioned a federal investigation into Sinclair's allegations and then pressured Congress to pass reforms.

PRIMARY SOURCE : CARTOON

A NAUSEATING JOB, BUT IT MUST BE DONE
President Roosevelt takes hold of the investigating muck-rake himself in the packing-house scandal.

» This cartoon from the *Utica Saturday Globe* is entitled "A Nauseating Job, but It Must Be Done" and shows Roosevelt using a muckrake.

EXAMINE THE SOURCE

1. **Analyzing Perspectives** What opinion does the cartoonist express about the meatpacking industry? What about on President Roosevelt? Explain.

2. **Inferring** What does the cartoon suggest about the influence of Upton Sinclair and muckrakers on public policy?

Some Ethical Gains Through Legislation

Florence Kelley grew up among abolitionists and women's rights reformers. In the 1880s she worked among Chicago's immigrant population at Jane Addams' Hull House. There, she learned about harsh working conditions in factories and the plight of child workers. From Chicago to New York City, Kelley made it her mission to improve working conditions and wages, as well as to end child labor.

PRIMARY SOURCE : BOOK

❝ [I]n the spring of 1903, a kindergartner in New York City, on missing from her class an Italian brother and sister aged four and five years, and visiting them in their homes, was told by their mother that they could not be spared from their work . . . They were engaged in wrapping colored paper around pieces of wire, to form the stems of artificial flowers which the family manufactured in their tenement home, the older sisters making the leaves and petals, and the other members of the group forming whole flowers and sprays.

The children were pointed out to the attendance agent who explained that, even under the statute of 1903, the **compulsory** attendance law exempted the younger child for three years and the older for two, assuming that each would then enter school on reaching the seventh birthday. The factory inspector, when the facts were brought to his attention, observed that the case did not appear to constitute a violation of the factory law, since the children were not receiving wages, and the group at work did not exceed the number authorized under the license to manufacture artificial flowers in their tenement home. ❞

–Florence Kelley, *Some Ethical Gains Through Legislation*, 1905

compulsory required (and enforced) by law

EXAMINE THE SOURCE

1. **Analyzing Perspectives** What problem does this source seek to address?

2. **Evaluating** What evidence does the author give to support the reforms that she seeks? How does she suggest that reforms to date have not done enough?

Your Inquiry Analysis

EVALUATE SOURCES AND USE EVIDENCE

Reflect back to the Compelling Question and the Supporting Questions you developed at the beginning of this lesson.

1. **Gathering Sources** Refer back to the Graphic Organizer you created as you read through the sources. How did each source help you answer the Supporting Questions you wrote? What additional information would you like to learn about or from each source to better answer your Supporting Questions?

2. **Evaluating Sources** Looking at the sources that help you answer the Supporting Questions, evaluate the credibility of each source. Consider whether each source reflects President Roosevelt's description of "muckrakers," and explain your reasoning. How does each source reflect bias, if any?

3. **Comparing and Contrasting** Compare and contrast two of the sources in this lesson more closely. Which does the best job of supporting his or her position? Why? Describe how each aims to improve society in some way, by what means, and how effectively it makes the point.

COMMUNICATE CONCLUSIONS

Collaborating Work with a partner to discuss how muckrakers use different media, such as investigative journalism, fiction, and political cartoons, to shine a light on public problems and help bring about change. Use your Supporting Questions and your graphic organizer to help you respond. Work together to craft a response to the Compelling Question, and share your response with the class.

TAKE INFORMED ACTION

Investigating and Reporting on an Issue Muckrakers identified problems in society that they felt needed to be solved. They investigated and wrote about these issues to raise awareness and encourage reforms. Identify a social, political, or economic problem in your community, state, or nation that concerns you. Put on your "muckraker" cap to find out more about the issue. Make a list of four to six questions that you have about the issue as well as possible resources where you might find answers. Follow up on one of those questions by researching one resource. Report on what you learned in a news brief. In that brief, note remaining questions that you have as well as additional research that needs to be done. Be sure to cite your source and write a headline.

Kelley, Florence. Some Ethical Gains Through Legislation. New York: Macmillan, 1910

04

A Growing Economy

READING STRATEGY

Analyzing Key Ideas and Details As you read, use a graphic organizer like the one below to take notes on the causes of growth and prosperity.

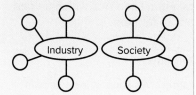

Woodrow Wilson's Progressive Changes

GUIDING QUESTION

What kind of reforms did President Wilson support during the progressive era?

After Theodore Roosevelt distanced himself from the political choices of President Taft, it was only a matter of time before progressives convinced Roosevelt to reenter politics. In late February 1912, Roosevelt announced he would enter the presidential campaign and attempt to replace Taft as the Republican presidential nominee. Roosevelt and Taft split the Republican voters, resulting in an Electoral College victory for their Democratic challenger, Woodrow Wilson. From Virginia, he was the first elected Southern-born president since the Civil War.

Wilson embarked on his own program of moderate progressive reform. Wilson tried to reform tariffs, the banking system, trusts, and workers' rights. He wanted to limit the power of the federal government in domestic economic matters and supported efforts to protect small businesses and farmers from corporate power. During that same period, he resegregated federal government offices. Wilson claimed that it was done to avoid friction.

The Sixteenth Amendment

One area of reform already under way involved taxes. Progressives had argued that the federal government's use of sales taxes, excise taxes, and tariffs to raise money was insufficient. They wanted to use an **income tax** to fund the government because it could be graduated, taxing wealthy people at a higher percentage than poor people. A graduated income tax is sometimes called a progressive tax. But the Supreme Court had denied this type of income tax because it included not only income but wealth from property or stock earnings. This type of direct taxation violated Article 1, Section 2, of the Constitution. Progressives wished to change the Constitution with an amendment that allowed the federal government to tax income no matter its source. Both Roosevelt and Taft had supported the amendment as did many political leaders in both parties. In February 1913, passage of the Sixteenth Amendment allowed for taxes on income.

A little over two months later, and only five weeks after taking office, President Wilson appeared before Congress to present his bill to reduce tariffs and introduce a federal income tax. Wilson actively lobbied members of Congress to achieve these goals. In 1913 Congress passed the Revenue Act of 1913, also known as the Underwood-Simmons Act. This law reduced the average tariff on imported goods to about 30 percent of the value of the goods and provided for levying a federal graduated income tax. The income tax was intended to replace the revenue lost by the tariff reductions.

The Federal Reserve and the FTC

Wilson next focused on modernizing the nation's banking system and ended up creating one of the most important tools of government economic regulation. The United States had not had a central bank since the 1830s. Periodic economic depressions had destroyed many small banks, wiping out much of their customers' life savings. To restore public confidence in the banking system, Wilson supported a federal reserve system. The Federal Reserve Act of

income tax a tax levied by the government directly on income

1913 created the regional reserve banks supervised by a Board of Governors appointed by the president. The Board could set the interest rates the reserve banks charged other banks, indirectly controlling the nation's interest rates and the amount of money in circulation.

The Federal Reserve Act became one of the most significant pieces of legislation in American history. It created an independent agency that began to use monetary policy to manage the nation's economy and shifted the country away from an inflexible gold or silver standard. Monetary policy refers to policies that adjust a nation's money supply to regulate the economy. If the Federal Reserve sets interest rates low, businesses and individuals will generally borrow more money. This increases the amount of money in circulation and causes the economy to grow. If interest rates are raised, people borrow less, which slows the economy but also reduces inflation. The goal of monetary policy is to contract the money supply if inflation is too high and expand the money supply if the economy is in a recession and unemployment is too high.

Wilson had campaigned on restoring economic competition by breaking up monopolies. In office he realized that big businesses were more efficient and unlikely to be replaced by smaller, more competitive firms. But congressional progressives demanded action against big business. In 1914 Congress created the Federal Trade Commission (FTC) to monitor business. The FTC had the power to investigate and issue "cease and desist" orders against companies it found to be engaging in **unfair trade practices,** or practices that hurt competition. If a business disagreed with the ruling, it could take the FTC to court. Wilson did not want the FTC to break up big business, but instead it was to work toward limiting unfair trade practices. He deliberately appointed conservative business leaders as the FTC's first commissioners.

Antitrust Actions and Child Labor

Dissatisfied by Wilson's approach, progressives in Congress responded by passing the Clayton Antitrust Act in 1914, which outlawed certain practices that restricted competition, such as price discrimination, or charging different customers different prices. The Clayton Antitrust Act corrected deficiencies in the Sherman Antitrust Act of 1890.

Before the law passed, labor unions lobbied Congress to exempt unions. As a result, the Clayton Antitrust Act stated that its provisions did not apply to labor organizations or agricultural organizations. When the bill became law, Samuel Gompers, the head of the American Federation of Labor, called the act the

workers' "Magna Carta" because it gave unions the right to exist.

Within a couple of years of the act's passage, President Wilson sought to address the problem of child labor. In 1916 Wilson signed the Keating-Owen Child Labor Act, the first federal law regulating child labor. The act prohibited the employment of children under the age of 14 in factories producing goods for interstate commerce. Although the Supreme Court declared the law unconstitutional in 1918, Wilson's effort helped his reputation among progressives.

He also supported the Adamson Act, which established the eight-hour workday for railroad workers, and the Federal Farm Loan Act, which helped provide low-interest loans to farmers.

✓ **CHECK FOR UNDERSTANDING**

1. **Explaining** Why did progressives support instituting an income tax?
2. **Contrasting** How did Wilson's approach to big business differ from that of progressives?

Economic Innovations

GUIDING QUESTION

What effects did mass production and rising incomes have on Americans' lives in the 1920s?

By the 1920s, the automobile had become part of American life. A 1925 survey conducted in Muncie, Indiana, found that 21 out of 26 families who owned cars did not have bathtubs with running water. As one farm wife explained, "You can't ride to town in a bathtub." Increased automobile ownership was just one example of Americans' rising standard of living. Real per capita earnings soared 22 percent between 1923 and 1929 even as work hours decreased. In 1923 U.S. Steel cut its daily work shift from 12 hours to 8 hours. In 1926 Henry Ford cut the workweek for his employees from six days to five, and farm machinery company International Harvester instituted an annual two-week paid vacation for employees. **Mass production,** or large-scale manufacturing done with machinery, made these changes possible by increasing supply and reducing costs. Workers made more, and the goods they bought cost less.

Assembly Lines and the Model T

The moving **assembly line** divided operations into simple tasks and cut unnecessary motion to a minimum, though there would be later arguments that this

---

unfair trade practices trading practices that derive a gain at the expense of competition

mass production the production of large quantities of goods by way of an automated process

assembly line a production system featuring machines and workers in a progressive arrangement of assembly

Berger, Michael L. "Farmers, Flivvers, and Family Life: The Impact of Motoring on Rural Women and Their Kin." U.S. Department of Transportation, Federal Highway Administration. Women's Travel Issues: Proceedings from the Second National Conference, Baltimore, MD. October 1996.

segmentation alienated people from their work. In 1913 automaker Henry Ford installed the first moving assembly line at a plant in Highland Park, Michigan. By the following year, workers were building an automobile every 93 minutes, and by 1925, a Ford car was rolling off the line every 10 seconds.

Ford's product, the **Model T,** demonstrated how sensitive product demand is to price. In 1908, the Model T's first year, the car sold for $850. In 1914 mass production reduced the price to $490. Ford also increased his workers' wages in 1914 to $5 a day—doubling their pay—and reduced the workday to eight hours. These steps were meant to win workers' loyalty and to undercut union organizers. By 1924, Model Ts were selling for $295, and Ford sold millions of them.

Ford's mass-production methods opened the door for new companies to manufacture cars, and by the mid-1920s, General Motors and Chrysler competed successfully with Ford. The auto industry also spurred growth in the production of steel, petroleum, rubber, plate glass, nickel, and lead. Cars revolutionized American life by easing the isolation of rural families and letting more people live farther from work. A new kind of worker, the auto commuter, appeared. Other forms of urban transportation, such as the trolley, became less popular.

New Products and Industries

In the 1920s some people began to earn enough money to meet their needs with some money left over. In response to this rising disposable income, many other new goods came on the market. Americans bought such innovations as electric razors, facial tissues, frozen foods, and home hair color. Mouthwash, deodorants, cosmetics, and perfumes became popular products. Companies created many new products for the home. As indoor plumbing became more common, Americans' concern for hygiene led to the development of various household cleaning products. New appliances advertised as labor-savers—such as electric irons, vacuum cleaners, washing machines, and refrigerators—changed the way people cleaned their homes and clothing and prepared meals. Often the increased standards of cleanliness of this time meant that although devices saved time, other household tasks took up that time.

New industries also began developing during this time period, including the young aviation industry, which began developing after the Wright brothers' first successful flight in 1903. American inventor Glenn Curtiss improved upon the Wright's early plane models with ailerons—surfaces attached to wings that could be tilted to steer the plane. Ailerons made it possible to build rigid wings and much larger aircraft. The federal government began to support the airline

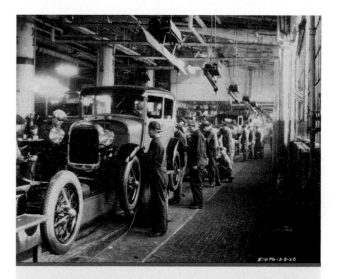

Workers assembled vehicles at factories like this one owned by the Ford Motor Company in Dearborn, Michigan, shown in this 1928 photo.

Explaining How does this photograph illustrate the use of an assembly line to manufacture cars?

industry. In 1918 the postmaster general introduced the world's first airmail service, and in 1925 Congress passed the Kelly Act, which authorized postal officials to hire private airplane operators to carry mail. The Air Commerce Act of 1926 provided federal aid to build airports, and in 1927 the transatlantic solo flight of former airmail pilot Charles Lindbergh banished doubt about the potential of aircraft. By 1928, 48 airlines were serving 355 American cities.

In 1913 American engineer Edwin Armstrong invented a special circuit that made it practical to transmit sound via long-range radio. The radio industry began a few years later. In November 1920, the Westinghouse Company broadcast the news of Harding's landslide election victory from station KDKA in Pittsburgh—one of the first public broadcasts in history. That success persuaded Westinghouse to open other stations. In 1926 the National Broadcasting Company (NBC) set up a network of stations to broadcast daily radio programs and, by 1927, almost 700 stations dotted the country. Sales of radio equipment grew from $10.6 million in 1921 to $411 million in 1929, by which time more than 12 million radios were in use across the country.

In 1928 the Columbia Broadcasting System (CBS) assembled a coast-to-coast network of stations to rival NBC. The two networks sold advertising time and hired musicians, actors, and comedians from vaudeville, movies, and the nightclub circuit to appear on their shows and bolster the impact of the advertisements. Americans experienced the first presidential election campaign to use radio in 1928, when the radio

Hulton Archive/Getty Images

Model T car produced from 1908 until 1927 by the Ford Motor Company

networks sold more than $1 million in advertising time to the Republican and Democratic Parties.

The America that a growing middle class of people were experiencing in the 1920s had come from many years of growth over the preceding decades. Writer Samuel Strauss wrote an article that measured this economic growth in the forms of convenience goods and new leisure. It was not an accurate description of life for all Americans, but it did paint a picture of new and exciting changes happening in a decade full of changes.

> 66 This is our proudest boast: 'The American citizen has more comforts and conveniences than kings had two hundred years ago.' It is a fact, and this fact is the outward evidence of the new force which has crossed the path of American democracy. This increasing stream of automobiles and radios, buildings and bathrooms, furs and furniture, liners, hotels, bridges, vacuum cleaners, cameras, bus lines, electric toasters, moving pictures, railway cars, package foods, telephones, pianos, novels, comic supplements—these are the signs. 99

> –"Things Are in the Saddle," *Atlantic Monthly*, November 1924

Easy Credit and Mass Advertising

One notable aspect of the economic boom was the growth of individual borrowing. Credit had been available before the 1920s, but most Americans had considered debt shameful. Now attitudes toward debt started changing, as people began believing in their ability to pay their debts over time. Many listened to the sales pitch "Buy now and pay in easy installments," and began to accumulate debt. Americans bought 75 percent of their radios and 60 percent of their automobiles on the installment plan. Some started buying on credit at a rate exceeding their income.

To attract consumers, manufacturers relied on new models of advertising that became standard in the 1920s. Advertisers linked products with qualities associated with the modern era, such as progress, convenience, leisure, success, and style, making purchasing the product a way for individuals to establish themselves as possessing those qualities. Advertisers also preyed on consumers' fears and anxieties, especially about one's status or weight.

Uneven Prosperity

Not all Americans shared in the economic boom of this decade. Thousands of African Americans who held factory jobs during World War I were replaced by returning servicemen. Native Americans, though granted citizenship in 1924, were often isolated on reservations where there was little productive work. Many immigrants also had trouble finding work. Most were farmers or factory workers making very low wages. Scores of people living in the Deep South also were left out of the economic boom as the agricultural economy eroded after World War I.

On average American farmers earned less than one-third of the income of other workers. Technological advances in fertilizers, seed varieties, and farm machinery allowed them to produce more, but higher yields without an increase in demand meant selling at lower prices. Between 1920 and 1921, corn and wheat prices declined considerably. Costs for improved farming technology continued to increase.

Many factors contributed to this "quiet depression" in American agriculture. During World War I, the government had urged farmers to produce more to meet the great need for food in Europe. Many farmers borrowed heavily to buy new land and new machinery to raise more crops. Sales were strong, prices were high, and farmers prospered. After the war, however, European farm output rose, and the debt-ridden countries of Europe had little money to spend on American farm products. In addition, Congress passed the Fordney-McCumber Act in 1922, making matters worse by raising tariffs dramatically. This dampened the American market for foreign goods and sparked a reaction in foreign markets against buying American agricultural products. The agricultural economy remained in recession throughout the 1920s.

✓ **CHECK FOR UNDERSTANDING**

1. **Identifying Cause and Effect** How did the automobile industry revolutionize transportation?

2. **Citing Text Evidence** What details in the text support the idea that the agricultural industry faced especially difficult challenges during the 1920s?

1920s American Culture

GUIDING QUESTION

How did artists and writers of the time describe the 1920s?

During the 1920s, American artists and writers challenged traditional ideas as they searched for meaning in the modern world. Many artists, writers, and intellectuals flocked to Manhattan's Greenwich Village and Chicago's South Side. The artistic and unconventional, or **bohemian,** lifestyle of these places permitted artists, musicians, and writers greater freedom of expression. They also allowed people to explore a wider array of lifestyles and identities.

---

bohemian unconventional; not bound by rules of society

Strauss, Samuel. 1924. "Things Are in the Saddle," in The Atlantic Monthly, November 1924, Vol. 134, No. 5.

Sueddeutsche Zeitung Photo/Alamy Stock Photo

ERNEST HEMINGWAY (1899–1961)

Born in a suburb of Chicago, Illinois, in 1899, Ernest Hemingway became one of the most important writers of the twentieth century. He wrote short stories and fiction in a simple and direct style that he learned while working as a journalist. James Joyce, Gertrude Stein, and other Modernist writers and artists in Paris also influenced Hemingway's writing. In turn, his spare and understated style inspired generations of American writers.

A NEW STYLE OF WRITING A decorated war hero, foreign correspondent, and expatriate, Hemingway's writing reflected his global experiences. His characters are often Americans abroad engaged in war, adventure, hunting, or bullfighting. His main characters often displayed strong personal codes of courage, professionalism, or skill. His writing rarely explained meaning to readers. He used this silence to build tension and allow for interpretation. Hemingway's first novel, *The Sun Also Rises*, published in 1926, chronicled expatriate life in Paris. In the 1950s, Hemingway won the Pulitzer Prize and the Nobel Prize in Literature for *The Old Man and the Sea*.

INTERNATIONAL FAME Hemingway became a celebrity during his life. He was often featured in national magazine photo spreads as he participated in vigorous sporting activities. His active life became a symbol of American masculine culture, similar to President Theodore Roosevelt. Hemingway spent much of his later life in Cuba. He also settled in Key West, Florida, where he fostered a colony of six-toed cats that is famous to this day.

> **Explaining** How did Hemingway's writing affect the style and subject matter of American literature?

Modern American Art

European art movements greatly influenced American modernists. There were a diverse range of artistic styles in this era, each attempting to express the modern experience. Modern art in the 1920s focused on trying to portray people's inner moods and feelings. As a result, much of the art was surreal or expressionist, using color, shape, and lines to portray the inner world of people's emotions. Surrealistic works, such as the painting *The Persistence of Memory* painted in 1931 by Salvador Dalí, and expressionistic works, such as *The Scream* by Edvard Munch in 1893, were often difficult for the general public to appreciate. These pieces could be discouraging in their depiction of society as fragmented and individuals as isolated.

Painter John Marin drew on the urban dynamics of New York City for inspiration. Painter Charles Sheeler applied the influences of photography and the geometric forms of Cubism to urban and rural American landscapes. Edward Hopper revived the visual accuracy of realism to convey a modern sense of disenchantment and isolation in haunting scenes. Georgia O'Keeffe's abstract landscapes and flowers were admired in many museums throughout her long life and are still cherished today. Henry Ossawa Tanner was the first African American painter to earn international recognition with paintings like *The Banjo Lesson*.

Poets and Writers

Writers of the 1920s varied greatly in their styles and subject matters. Common speech was used by Illinois poet and writer Carl Sandburg and in the novels of Pulitzer Prize winner Willa Cather, as in *The Song of the Lark,* to glorify the Midwest. Sinclair Lewis poked fun at small-town life in *Main Street*, while Edith Wharton criticized upper-class ignorance and pretensions in her Pulitzer Prize–winning novel *The Age of Innocence*. In Greenwich Village, another Pulitzer Prize winner, Edna St. Vincent Millay, wrote about women's inner lives.

Poetic styles also varied. Amy Lowell, Ezra Pound, and William Carlos Williams used clear, concise images to express moments in time. Others, such as T. S. Eliot, criticized what they saw as a loss of spirituality in modern life. Among playwrights, Eugene O'Neill was probably the most innovative. His plays, such as *Long Day's Journey Into Night*, were filled with bold artistry, modern themes, realistic characters and situations, and offered a modern vision of life that often touched on the tragic.

Some American writers, disillusioned by World War I and the emerging consumer society, moved to Paris, a center of artistic activity. American experimental writer Gertrude Stein dubbed these expatriates the "Lost Generation." Among these writers was Ernest Hemingway, who wrote moving novels about war and its aftermath, such as *A Farewell to Arms*. Another writer was F. Scott Fitzgerald, who criticized society's superficiality in *The Great Gatsby*, in which colorful characters chased futile dreams.

The literature of the 1920s had a far-reaching impact on readers. By criticizing class pretensions, consumerism, and the pursuit of material goods, the literature of the era encouraged people to think seriously about and consider how modern life was changing things and what value these changes brought. Many artists and writers of the 1920s attempted to portray the sense that modern life was meaningless, moral progress was impossible, and that people were losing their relationships and connections, which left little reason to try to achieve anything.

Popular Culture

The **mass media**—radio, movies, newspapers, and magazines aimed at a broad audience—did more than just entertain; it fostered a sense of shared experience that unified the nation. During the era of silent films, theaters hired piano players to provide music during the feature while subtitles explained the plot. Audiences gathered to see such stars as Mary Pickford, Charlie Chaplin, Douglas Fairbanks, Sr., and Rudolph Valentino. Unfortunately, many of these early silent films depicted harmful racial stereotypes such as blackface.

In 1927 the golden age of Hollywood began with the first "talking" picture, *The Jazz Singer,* launching new stars whose voices appealed to audiences.

Films of the 1920s reflected the issues and characteristics of the era in many ways. Some told stories of World War I and its aftermath and were often blunt about the impact of the war on people's lives. Many told stories of complicated relationships between men and women and reflected the new morality and changing nature of relationships and identity of the 1920s.

Film stars such as Clara Bow illustrated the energy and independence of the flapper. Because Bow was so popular and was seen in many ads of this period, she was nicknamed the "It girl." Many films also focused on Christian themes, dramatizing stories from the Bible and the values and beliefs of Protestantism.

Famous songwriter Irving Berlin worked in New York City's Tin Pan Alley, where composers wrote popular music heavily influenced by African American musical stars such as Aida Overton Walker and James

Reese Europe. The African American influence can be heard in many of Berlin's famous songs, including "Puttin' on the Ritz." Radio broadcasts offered everything from classical music to comedy. In the show *Amos 'n' Andy*, the troubles of two African American characters (portrayed by white actors) captured the nation's attention; however, the show was criticized for using crude racial stereotypes and blackface.

Sports such as baseball and boxing reached new heights of popularity in the 1920s thanks to motion pictures and radio even though sports were often highly segregated. Baseball star Babe Ruth became a national hero famous for hitting hundreds of home runs. African American baseball player Andrew "Rube" Foster helped create the first Negro National League. Fans also idolized boxer Jack Dempsey, who was world heavyweight champion from 1919 until 1926. When Dempsey attempted to win back the title in 1927, one store sold $90,000 worth of radios in the two weeks before the event.

Newspaper coverage helped build enthusiasm for college football. One famous player of the 1920s was Red Grange of the University of Illinois, who was known as the "Galloping Ghost" because of his speed and ability to evade the opposing team. Another famous football player was Jim Thorpe, a Native American athlete who played many sports, including football, and was the first Native American to win a gold medal at the Olympics in 1912. Fritz Pollard was one of the first two African American players in the NFL in 1920 and went on to become the first African American head coach. The triumphs of Bobby Jones, the best golfer of the decade, and tennis players Bill Tilden and Helen Wills also thrilled sports fans.

✓ **CHECK FOR UNDERSTANDING**

1. **Describing** How did many artists and writers of the time describe the 1920s?

2. **Identifying Cause and Effect** How did events in the 1920s affect the themes that came across in media?

LESSON ACTIVITIES

1. **Argumentative Writing** Think about the new products and industries that arose during the 1910s and 1920s. Choose a product or an industry that you think made the most significant impact. Write an argument detailing the reasons for your opinion.

2. **Collaborating** Work in a small group to create a new radio show set in the 1920s. As a group, design a poster advertising your radio show, come up with a name for it, and write a script for the first episode. Be prepared to talk about your new radio show and provide a premise for the first season.

---

mass media communication media, such as television and radio, intended to reach a wide audience

05

African American Culture and Politics

READING STRATEGY

Analyzing Key Ideas and Details As you read, use a graphic organizer like the one below to take notes.

Causes — Harlem Renaissance — Effects

Racial Tensions

GUIDING QUESTION

How did African Americans leaders and organizations fight for justice during the 1920s and 1930s?

As more African Americans moved to northern and western states, predominantly African American neighborhoods, similar to Harlem in New York City, emerged in cities across the country. Expanding job opportunities drew thousands of African Americans to Tulsa, Oklahoma, in the early 1900s. Tulsa's Greenwood District was one of the most prosperous African American communities in the United States, earning it the nickname "Black Wall Street." Development of successful African American communities such as the one in Tulsa was resented by white citizens in Tulsa and elsewhere. Distrustful and racist whites viewed African Americans as cultural and economic threats to their white-dominated towns.

In late May 1921, following published allegations that an African American man assaulted a white female elevator operator, a white mob surrounded the Tulsa courthouse where the accused was being held. African Americans who feared a lynching arrived armed with guns. A two-day rampage driven by whites demolished more than 1,400 homes and businesses, left nearly 10,000 people homeless, and burned the Greenwood District. The official number of deaths is unknown and still debated; historians place it anywhere between thirty and 300. The Tulsa race massacre remains one of the deadliest and most destructive racial incidents in American history.

The racial tensions that turned so deadly in Tulsa were also growing in other parts of the nation. An example of this was the renewed public presence of the Ku Klux Klan (KKK). The KKK originated in the South after the Civil War and used threats and violence to intimidate newly freed African Americans before disbanding in the 1870s. After waves of new immigrants arrived in the United States during the late nineteenth and early twentieth centuries, however, a second Klan formed to target not only African Americans but also Roman Catholics, Jews, and other groups said to be "un-American." William J. Simmons founded the new Ku Klux Klan in 1915 with a pledge to preserve America's white, Protestant civilization. With the help of professional promoters to sell Klan memberships, more and more people joined. By 1924, membership was close to 4 million as it spread beyond the South into the North and West.

The NAACP Battles Injustice

The National Association for the Advancement of Colored People (NAACP) battled against segregation and discrimination against African Americans. Its efforts focused primarily on lobbying public officials and working through the court system. The NAACP's persistent protests against lynching led to the passage of antilynching legislation in the House of Representatives in 1922. The Senate defeated the bill, but the NAACP's ongoing protests kept the issue in the news. Lynching statistics began decreasing after these legislative efforts failed, but the decrease resulted in part from the attention the NAACP and activists like Ida B. Wells brought to lynching.

In 1930 the NAACP joined with labor unions to launch a highly organized national campaign against the nomination of Judge John J. Parker to the U.S. Supreme Court. Parker's support for African American disenfranchisement and anti-union contracts moved the NAACP and labor leaders to campaign against

The Great Migration, 1917–1930

Thousands of African Americans migrated from the South to industrial cities of the North during this decade.

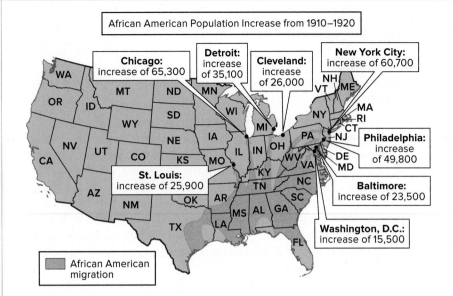

African American Population Increase from 1910–1920

Chicago: increase of 65,300

Detroit: increase of 35,100

Cleveland: increase of 26,000

New York City: increase of 60,700

Philadelphia: increase of 49,800

St. Louis: increase of 25,900

Baltimore: increase of 23,500

Washington, D.C.: increase of 15,500

African American migration

GEOGRAPHY CONNECTION

1. **Patterns and Movement** To what three Midwestern cities did many African Americans from the South migrate?

2. **Exploring Regions** In which cities did the greatest growth in the African American population occur?

---

him. Walter White, the secretary of the NAACP, testified against Parker when appearing before the Senate Judiciary Committee. White also organized the NAACP strategy of contacting senators and urging them to oppose Parker's nomination or lose support in the coming elections. By a narrow margin, the Senate refused to confirm Parker's nomination. This proved that African Americans had become a significant political force.

Black Nationalism

While the NAACP fought for integration and improvement in the economic and political position of African Americans, other groups began to emphasize black nationalism. Some began calling for African Americans to separate from white society, believing that separation was necessary for African Americans to achieve self-determination.

Jamaican-born Marcus Garvey was one promoter of Black Nationalism and black self-determination. He captured the imagination of millions of African Americans with his "Negro Nationalism." Garvey had founded the Universal Negro Improvement Association (UNIA) in the previous decade, aimed at promoting black pride and unity. He was inspired by Booker T. Washington's call for self-reliance but included an emphasis on self-defense in his philosophy. The central message of Garvey's Harlem-based movement focused on African American efforts to gain economic and political power. Garvey also advocated community control and cultural independence from whites. Garvey proposed leading them to Africa. Garvey incorporated the Black Star

Line shipping company to foster Black trade and aid with migration. Many of Garvey's followers did not want to leave the country for Africa. Despite that his philosophy of self-reliance remained appealing.

Garvey and the UNIA were part of a larger black nationalist immigrant community in Harlem that advocated radical politics. The African Blood Brotherhood (ABB), also based in Harlem, had a significant Caribbean-immigrant membership base. The organization argued for black nationalism and socialist policies, using its newspaper, *The Crusader*, to spread its message. Other African American newspapers, such as the *Chicago Whip* and the UNIA-run *Negro World*, echoed a black nationalist theme.

Some in the emerging African American middle class distanced themselves from Garvey and his push for racial separation. The FBI saw UNIA as a dangerous catalyst for African American uprisings. Marcus Garvey was convicted of mail fraud in 1923. He served time in federal prison and was deported to Jamaica in 1927.

Despite Garvey's failure to keep his movement alive, he gave millions of African Americans a sense of pride in their heritage and inspired hope for the future. These feelings reemerged strongly in the 1950s and played a vital role in the civil rights movement of the 1960s, especially in the beliefs of Malcolm X and the Nation of Islam.

✓ **CHECK FOR UNDERSTANDING**

Contrasting How did African American leaders differ in their approaches to political actions during this decade?

The Harlem Renaissance

GUIDING QUESTION

What does the Harlem Renaissance reveal about African American culture in the 1920s?

During World War I and the 1920s, hundreds of thousands of African Americans joined the Great Migration from the South to industrial cities in the North. Populations swelled in large Northern cities, but city leaders used laws to deny African Americans the ability to settle in any neighborhood they wished. In the predominantly African American neighborhoods created by this discrimination, including New York City's Harlem, new visions of African American culture and politics were created despite the forces working against African Americans.

Explaining the Harlem Renaissance

The word *renaissance* means "a time of great revival." The Harlem Renaissance was a time of great literary, artistic, and intellectual change in the United States. Artistic development, racial pride, and political organization combined in a flowering of literature, music, and art, which helped to create a new black cultural identity. Although Harlem was the focal point of this new movement, its influences came from the Caribbean, Europe, the American South, and other northern American cities. In fact, the same cultural movement that became Harlem Renaissance had already blossomed in other places, such as Boston; Washington, D.C.; Chicago; and Atlanta, though Harlem became its epicenter.

For example, **jazz**—a musical style influenced by Dixieland and ragtime with syncopated rhythms and improvisational elements—first emerged in New Orleans's African American community before flourishing in cities like Memphis, St. Louis, and Chicago. And because Northern cities like Chicago and Cleveland had been popular destinations for African Americans during the Great Migration out of the Deep South, these cities experienced similar cultural resurgences as those of the Harlem Renaissance. As artists traveled to other American cities throughout the North and South—and to other countries—the influence of this early twentieth century artistic and cultural renaissance expanded.

The creative works of this renaissance helped to instill a strong sense of pride, defiance, and confidence in African Americans. It encouraged resistance to racism and challenged stereotypes, and it also reminded African Americans of their roots and the difficulties they had already overcome. It helped lay the foundation for the civil rights movement that would begin after World War II.

jazz American style of music that developed from ragtime and features syncopated rhythms and improvisation

Everett Collection Historical/Alamy Stock Photo

BIOGRAPHY

AARON DOUGLAS (1899–1979)

Aaron Douglas was one of the most successful and influential visual artists of the Harlem Renaissance. Douglas was born in Topeka, Kansas, and attended a segregated primary school before attending an integrated high school. After graduating, Douglas had several jobs before enrolling at the University of Nebraska. In 1922 Douglas graduated with a degree in fine arts and then taught art at a high school in Kansas City. He helped define a new identity for African Americans that was not connected to the nation's slavery and segregationist past.

JOINING THE MOVEMENT Douglas learned about the emerging African American cultural and artistic scene in Harlem by reading magazines like *The Crisis* and *Opportunity*. He quit his teaching job and moved to Harlem in 1925. Douglas was supported by W.E.B. Du Bois and Charles S. Johnson who soon began publishing Douglas's illustrations in their magazines. Douglas also studied African art to help him visualize and convey the African American experience in America. In addition, he explored new forms of European artistic expression to create his own unique style.

WORKS AND INFLUENCE Douglas's first major work was providing illustrations for *The New Negro*, an influential book featuring fiction, nonfiction, poetry, and dramatic pieces about the lives of African Americans that reclaimed their culture separate from enslavement. In the 1930s, Douglas turned his vision to completing several large-scale murals. These included works for Fisk University in Nashville and Bennett College in North Carolina, along with a four-panel mural for the Texas Centennial Exposition in Dallas, Texas. One of Douglas's most famous works—the four-mural piece *Aspects of Negro Life*—was commissioned by the Works Progress Administration during the Great Depression and completed for the 135th Street branch of the New York Public Library, a creative gathering center for Harlem Renaissance artists.

By 1940, Douglas was living in Nashville and teaching at Fisk University. He eventually became chairman of the university's art department and taught emerging artists until retiring in 1966.

Identifying What types of art served as Douglas's main influences?

New Writing and Literature

Claude McKay was the first influential writer of the Harlem Renaissance. In his 1922 poetry collection, *Harlem Shadows*, McKay expressed a proud defiance and bitter contempt of racism, two major characteristics of Harlem Renaissance writing.

Langston Hughes was a prolific and versatile writer. Zora Neale Hurston wrote some of the first stories featuring African American women as central characters. Hurston presented an insightful and often quite humorous perspective of the African American experience. She was also an accomplished traveler, anthropologist, and an instructor at the North Carolina College for Negroes. In 1942 Hurston published her autobiography, *Dust Tracks on a Road*, to great acclaim. Other notable writers of the Harlem Renaissance include the poet Countee Cullen, the influential writer and proclaimed father of the Harlem Renaissance Alain Locke, and novelist Dorothy West.

Harlem also offered a safe space for people to explore their identity. Many notable members of the Harlem Renaissance, such as Alain Locke, Gladys Bentley, and Richard Bruce Nugent, were open about their sexual orientation and identities. In helping to instill pride and confidence, the literature of the Harlem Renaissance also helped create a distinct and separate African American culture apart from the wider culture of the nation. Other movements took note and began to seek space in order to protect themselves and preserve their own identities.

The Importance of Jazz

Jazz reflected the characteristics of the 1920s era in many ways. With its emphasis on improvisation, it reflected the feelings of many people that the 1920s was a time of experimentation and a breaking from old rules and values. It expressed the individualism of the era, and because many of the popular jazz singers were women, it also reflected the new role of women in society. Blues and soul music also enabled African Americans to give voice to their difficult social and economic position in American society.

In 1922 New Orleans native Louis Armstrong moved to Chicago, where he introduced an early form of jazz. Armstrong broke away from the New Orleans tradition of group playing by performing highly imaginative solos on the cornet and trumpet.

Composer, pianist, and band leader Edward "Duke" Ellington blended improvisation and orchestration. Like many other African American entertainers, Ellington's fame grew at the Cotton Club, the well-known nightclub in Harlem, which served only white customers.

Bessie Smith, known as the Empress of the Blues, innovated the musical style called soul. Smith sang of unfulfilled love, poverty, and oppression—the classic themes of the **blues,** a soulful style of music that involved syncopated rhythms, bending tones whether vocal or instrumental to symbolize grief, and a very formal chord progression. The elements in blues, evolved from African American spirituals, have made their way to subsequent musical genres, including country music. Jazz built a sense of community and created a connection between African American culture and the rest of American society. Listening to jazz records on the radio introduced a larger population to the Harlem Renaissance.

American jazz music had a significant impact on the world. Artists like James Reese Europe, who toured France during World War I, helped spread ragtime and jazz music. In part because of America's role in ending World War I, many Europeans, especially in France, became fascinated with American culture. Many American jazz musicians visited Europe after World War I and helped develop a European audience for the music. Josephine Baker, an American-born dancer, stunned audiences in Paris but refused to perform for segregated audiences in America. Paris became a center for jazz in Europe just as it became home to many American expatriate writers in the years after the war.

Theater flourished, and films were produced. Musicals like *Shuffle Along*, written, produced, and performed by African Americans, were performed on Broadway. The show's success helped launch several careers, including that of Paul Robeson, who gained wide acclaim for his performance in Eugene O'Neill's *Emperor Jones,* and Florence Mills, a singer and dancer, who paved the way for African Americans in mainstream theater. Oscar Micheaux produced the first African American feature, *The Homesteader*, in 1919. Between 1919 and 1948, he wrote, produced, directed, and distributed more than 45 films for African American audiences.

✓ **CHECK FOR UNDERSTANDING**

1. **Identifying** What characteristics of jazz made it such a unique musical form?

2. **Making Connections** What did the Harlem Renaissance reveal about African American culture in the 1920s?

LESSON ACTIVITIES

1. **Informative/Explanatory Writing** Write a short essay describing the growth of African American civil rights organizations and cultural forms during the 1920s and 1930s. Describe why these two movements might have flourished at the same time.

2. **Collaborating** With a partner, research the life of an author from the Harlem Renaissance. Then, develop a short screenplay for one of this author's works. Share your screenplay with the class.

---

blues style of music evolving from African American spirituals and noted for its melancholy sound

06

Analyzing Sources: The Harlem Renaissance

? COMPELLING QUESTION

Was the Harlem Renaissance a time of hope for African American artists and musicians?

Plan Your Inquiry

In this lesson, you will investigate how the cultural movement known as the Harlem Renaissance reflected the lives of African Americans during the 1920s.

DEVELOP QUESTIONS

Developing Questions About the Harlem Renaissance Read the Compelling Question for this lesson. Consider what you have learned about the Roaring Twenties and the Jazz Age. Then, think about the experiences and contributions of African American artists, writers, and musicians during this time. Develop a list of Supporting Questions that would help you answer the Compelling Question in this lesson.

APPLY HISTORICAL TOOLS

Analyzing Primary and Secondary Sources You will work with a variety of primary and secondary sources in this lesson. These sources focus on the inspiration and influence of the Harlem Renaissance. As you read, use a graphic organizer like the one below to record information about the sources that will help you examine them and check for historical understanding. Note ways in which each source helps you answer your Supporting Questions.

Supporting Questions	Primary Source	How this source helps me answer the Supporting Question
Question 1:		
Question 2:		
Question 3:		

After you analyze the sources, you will:
- use the evidence from the sources.
- communicate your conclusions.
- take informed action.

Background Information

During World War I, more than 380,000 African American men served in segregated regiments. Back home, millions of African Americans joined the Great Migration to northern and western cities, where they took jobs in the nation's factories, mills, offices, and ports to supply and support the war effort and hoped for greater equality. However, at war's end, the realities of discrimination and segregation set in. Those who had fought did not enjoy the rights for which they had fought. Those who had looked to the North for liberation from oppression found themselves locked out of jobs, unions, and neighborhoods, often experiencing racial harassment and violence.

The Harlem Renaissance developed as a cultural branch of a larger New Negro Movement that sought to celebrate African American heritage and to win greater rights and freedoms for African Americans as U.S. citizens. The Harlem Renaissance came, in part, from the burgeoning African American communities of New York City, but its vision and voice swept the nation. As with progressivism, the Harlem Renaissance was not just one vision with one goal; it included many scholars, artists, writers, musicians, and other producers of creative works.

» The film *Hallelujah* featured a black cast and new cinematic techniques that blended dialogue, music, and sound effects. Harlem, 1929.

©John Springer Collection/Corbis Historical/Getty Images

A

Effects of the Great Migration

Dr. Alain Locke, an African American scholar, editor, philosopher, and educator, became known as the "Father of the Harlem Renaissance" following the publication of *The New Negro: An Interpretation* in 1925. This work collected the stories, essays, poetry, plays, music, and art of Harlem Renaissance figures. This collection and Locke's own work launched the New Negro Movement, a celebration of the African heritage of African American culture and the individual voices of its artists, writers, and musicians.

PRIMARY SOURCE : BOOK

66 . . . [T]he life of the Negro community is bound to enter a new **dynamic** phase . . . The migrant masses, shifting from countryside to city, hurdle several generations of experience at a leap, but more important, the same thing happens spiritually in the life-attitudes and self-expression of the Young Negro, in his poetry, his art, his education and his new outlook, with the additional advantage, of course, of the poise and greater certainty of knowing what it is all about. . . .

A main change has been, of course, that shifting of the Negro population which has made the Negro problem no longer exclusively or even predominantly Southern. Why should our minds remain sectionalized, when the problem itself no longer is? Then the trend of migration has not only been toward the North and the Central Midwest, but city-ward and to the great centers of industry—the problems of adjustment are new, practical, local and not particularly racial. Rather they are an integral part of the large industrial and social problems of our present-day democracy. 99

—Alain Locke, *The New Negro*, 1925

---

dynamic active and changing, energetic

EXAMINE THE SOURCE

1. **Identifying Cause and Effect** What effects of migration does the author identify?

2. **Interpreting** How does the author consider African American life dynamic? What does he consider obsolete, and why?

B

Building Urban Neighborhoods

In 2013 scholar Nicholas L. Gaffney published an article entitled "'He Was a Man Who Walked Tall Among Men': Duke Ellington, African American Audiences, and the Black Musical Entertainment Market, 1927–1943" in *The Journal of African American History*. Gaffney examines the life, work, and historical and cultural context of Ellington, a renowned jazz musician and composer who played in Harlem.

SECONDARY SOURCE : BOOK

66 Harlem was full of new faces during the 1920s and 1930s. . . . Between the turn of the 20th century and the outbreak of the Second World War, thousands upon thousands of African Americans escaped the rural South and headed for urban areas in the northern and western United States. The lure of industrial job opportunities in urban centers gave black southerners a compelling **incentive** to abandon the cotton fields of the South, the financial slavery of sharecropping, and the social, political, and economic oppression of Jim Crow segregation. . . . New York City's black population continued its rapid expansion between 1910 and 1930, growing from approximately 91,000 to over 300,000, mostly concentrated in upper Manhattan. Harlem was likewise a **beacon** for Afro-Caribbean immigrants streaming into the United States during the same period. Between 1900 and 1930 over 40,000 black immigrants, mostly from the British West Indies, poured into Harlem. Typically blending into pre-existing African American neighborhoods, Afro-West Indians represented nearly a quarter of Manhattan's black population. 99

—*The Journal of African American History*, *Vol.* 98, No. 3 (Summer 2013)

---

incentive something to encourage action
beacon a signal fire or light to guide one's way

EXAMINE THE SOURCE

1. **Identifying Cause and Effect** What push and pull factors for the Great Migration does the author identify?

2. **Speculating** What do you think the growing African American communities in New York City were like?

(l)Locke, Alain. ed. The New Negro. Albert & Charles Boni, Inc. 1925. (r)Gaffney, Nicholas L. "He Was a Man Who Walked Tall Among Men": Duke Ellington, African American Audiences, and the Black Musical Entertainment Market, 1927–1943." The Journal of African American History 98. no. 3 (2013): 367-91. Accessed April 7, 2020. doi:10.5323/jafriamerhist.98.3.0367.

PHOTO: Album/Alamy Stock Photo; TEXT: Grainger, Porter and Robbins. Everett. "Tain't Nobody's Biz-ness If I Do, [sheet music] New York: Clarence Williams, 1922.

C

"Tain't Nobody's Business If I Do"

Bessie Smith has been called the Empress of the Blues. She was born in Chattanooga, Tennessee, and lived in poverty for much of her youth. Bessie Smith also worked as a street musician to earn money. Smith's work as a professional singer was helped by touring with another female musician of this time period—Ma Rainey. Smith moved to the Harlem neighborhood in 1923. The lyrics of this song reflect Smith's confident personality. These lyrics can also be interpreted as symbolic of the growing power and independence of women during these early decades of the twentieth century.

PRIMARY SOURCE : LYRICS

" There ain't nothing I can do or nothing I can say
That folks don't criticize me
But I'm going to do just as I want to anyway
And don't care if they all despise me

If I should take a **notion**
To jump into the ocean
Ain't nobody's bizness if I do

If I go to church on Sunday
Then shimmy down on Monday
Ain't nobody's bizness if I do, if I do

If my friend ain't got no money
And I say 'Take all mine, honey'
Tain't nobody's bizness If I do, do, do do

If I give him my last nickel
And it leaves me in a **pickle**
Tain't nobody's bizness if I do, if I do . . . "

—Bessie Smith, 1923

---

notion a quick impulse or action
pickle a difficult situation

» A portrait of Bessie Smith from 1923

EXAMINE THE SOURCE

1. **Analyzing Perspectives** What is the subject of the song?
2. **Interpreting** How does Smith's song lyrics reflect the changing culture of the Jazz Age decade?

Abundant African American Art

In 1925 Langston Hughes was working as a hotel busboy. Though he had already begun publishing poems, he struggled because of the limited opportunities for African Americans and wrote the NAACP for help to pay for college. Soon after, he won a scholarship to attend Lincoln University. While there, he wrote this essay, articulating the spirit of the Harlem Renaissance and defending the need to celebrate African American voices. It appeared in *The Nation* magazine in 1926.

PRIMARY SOURCE : ESSAY

" Certainly there is, for the American Negro artist who can escape the restrictions the more advanced among his own group would put upon him, a great field of unused material ready for his art. Without going outside his race, and even among the better classes with their 'white' culture and conscious American manners, but still Negro enough to be different, there is sufficient matter to furnish a black artist with a lifetime of creative work. And when he chooses to touch on the relations between Negroes and whites in this country, with their innumerable overtones and undertones surely, and especially for literature and the drama, there is an inexhaustible supply of themes at hand. To these the Negro artist can give his racial individuality, his heritage of rhythm and warmth, and his **incongruous** humor that so often, as in the Blues, becomes ironic laughter mixed with tears. . . . And within the next decade I expect to see the work of a growing school of colored artists who paint and model the beauty of dark faces and create with new technique the expressions of their own soul-world. And the Negro dancers who will dance like flame and the singers who will continue to carry our songs to all who listen—they will be with us in even greater numbers tomorrow. . . . We younger Negro artists who create now intend to express our individual dark-skinned selves without fear or shame. If white people are pleased, we are glad. If they are not, it doesn't matter. We know we are beautiful. And ugly, too. . . . We build our temples for tomorrow, strong as we know how, and we stand on top of the mountain, free within ourselves. "

–"The Negro Artist and the Racial Mountain," Langston Hughes, 1926

» Drawing of poet Langston Hughes by Winold Reiss around 1925

EXAMINE THE SOURCE

1. **Identifying Themes** What is the main idea of this excerpt? What underlying theme does Hughes's statement address?

2. **Determining Context** How does Hughes evoke historical context and current events and conditions to make his point?

incongruous inappropriate to the occasion

PHOTO: Science History Images/Alamy Stock Photo; TEXT: Hughes, Langston, "The Negro Artist and the Racial Mountain" from The Collected Works of Langston Hughes, published by University of Missouri Press. Copyright © 2002 by The Estate of Langston Hughes. Reprinted with the permission of Harold Ober Associates Incorporated.

Drawing in Two Colors

Winold Reiss emigrated from Germany to the United States in 1913. In 1924 a magazine hired him to paint the portraits of prominent Harlem Renaissance figures, including Countee Cullen, Langston Hughes, and Zora Neale Hurston. His work led Dr. Alain Locke to commission him to illustrate his upcoming collection *The New Negro: An Interpretation* in 1925. This piece, titled *Drawing in Two Colors* is also known by the title *Interpretation of Harlem Jazz.*

PRIMARY SOURCE : PAINTING

Drawing in Two Colors   Winold Reiss

EXAMINE THE SOURCE

1. **Analyzing Perspective** What details do you notice in the painting? What comparison do you think Reiss was making, and why?

2. **Drawing Conclusions** What do you think the painter intends to show about the culture and experience of African Americans with this artwork? Explain.

"America"

Born in Jamaica, Claude McKay moved to the United States in 1912. By then, he had already published two collections of poetry, written in his native dialect. He attended school in the South and the Midwest before moving to New York, where he published two more collections, including *Harlem Shadows*. This poem, originally published in *The Liberator* in 1921, appears in that book. Written as a Shakespearean sonnet, it serves as a testament to his conflicted feelings. McKay next spent more than a decade in Europe, during which time he wrote three novels. *Home to Harlem*, which explored the life of a soldier returning home from war, became the most widely read novel by a black author at that time. In 1934 he returned to Harlem, and became a U.S. citizen six years later.

PRIMARY SOURCE : POEM

" Although she feeds me bread of bitterness,
And sinks into my throat her tiger's tooth,
Stealing my breath of life, I will confess
I love this cultured hell that tests my youth!
Her vigor flows like tides into my blood,
Giving me strength erect against her hate.
Her bigness sweeps my being like a flood.
Yet as a rebel fronts a king in state,
I stand within her walls with not a shred
Of terror, malice, not a word of jeer.
Darkly I gaze into the days ahead,
And see her might and granite wonders there,
Beneath the touch of Time's unerring hand,
Like priceless treasures sinking in the sand. "

—"America," from *Harlem Shadows: The Poems of Claude McKay,* 1922

EXAMINE THE SOURCE

1. **Analyzing** What does the author personify in this poem? How does he describe "her" in conflicting ways?

2. **Drawing Conclusions** How might this poem reflect the experience or feelings of other African Americans in the 1920s? Explain.

PHOTO: Library of Congress; TEXT: McKay, Claude. "America." Harlem Shadows: The Poems of Claude McKay. New York: Harcourt, Brace and Company, 1922

"Criteria of Negro Art"

Born in 1868 in Massachusetts, W.E.B. Du Bois became one of the leading and most prolific figures of the African American civil rights movement. He helped start the National Association for the Advancement of Colored People (NAACP) in 1909 and served as the editor of its magazine, *The Crisis*, for fourteen years. He is best known for authoring a collection of essays, entitled *The Souls of Black Folk* (1903), in which he sought to rebuff Booker T. Washington's accommodationist approach. Instead, he advocated action to win equal rights and an end to segregation. He gave this speech at an NAACP conference in honor of another African American author-historian, Carter G. Woodson, in 1926. In the speech, he references Roland Hayes, the son of enslaved African Americans who became an internationally acclaimed singer.

PRIMARY SOURCE : SPEECH

66 We have, to be sure, a few recognized and successful Negro artists; but they are not all those fit to survive or even a good minority. They are but the remnants of that ability and genius among us whom the accidents of education and opportunity have raised on the tidal waves of chance. We black folk are not altogether peculiar in this. After all, in the world at large, it is only the accident, the remnant, that gets the chance to make the most of itself; but if this is true of the white world it is infinitely more true of the colored world. It is not simply the great clear tenor of Roland Hayes that opened the ears of America. We have had many voices of all kinds as fine as his and America was and is as deaf as she was for years to him. Then a foreign land heard Hayes and put its imprint on him and immediately America with all its imitative snobbery woke up. We approved Hayes because London, Paris and Berlin approved him and not simply because he was a great singer. 99

—W.E.B. Du Bois, 1926

EXAMINE THE SOURCE

1. **Analyzing** What does the author mean when he describes America as "deaf"?

2. **Making Generalizations** What does this statement suggest about the experiences and potential of African American artists, including writers and musicians?

Your Inquiry Analysis

EVALUATE SOURCES AND USE EVIDENCE

Reflect back to the Compelling Question and the Supporting Questions you developed at the beginning of this lesson.

1. **Gathering Sources** Refer back to the Graphic Organizer you created as you read through the sources. Which sources most helped you answer the Supporting Questions you wrote? Circle or highlight those sources in your graphic organizer. What questions, or parts of your questions, did your sources not answer?

2. **Evaluating Sources** Looking at the sources that help you answer the Supporting Questions, evaluate the credibility of each source. How reliable do you consider the source as an authority on the subject, and why? What additional information would you like to know about or from each source?

3. **Comparing and Contrasting** Compare and contrast two of the sources in this lesson more closely. What does each source reveal about the Harlem Renaissance? How does each reflect the experiences and goals of African Americans in the 1920s?

COMMUNICATE CONCLUSIONS

Presenting Work with your group to identify the main idea expressed in each text or piece of artwork. Then, create a multimedia collage—combining text and visual elements—that reflects these core concepts about the Harlem Renaissance. Write a statement explaining your collage as a response to the Compelling Question. Present your work to the class.

TAKE INFORMED ACTION

Promoting Alternative Voices Identify a community or group of people today that you feel is underrepresented in art, literature, music, film, or another creative field. Research one or more artists from that group or community and analyze the content of their message and their means of expression. Then write an essay that could serve as a letter to a newspaper or arts organization explaining why this community should have a platform for expression. Use examples from the artist or artists you researched.

Du Bois, W.E.B. "Criteria of Negro Art." The Crisis. Vol. 32. October 1926. pp. 290–297. http://www.webdubois.org/dbCriteriaNArt.html

Longworth, Alice Roosevelt. 1933. Crowded Hours: Reminiscences of Alice Roosevelt Longworth. New York: Charles Scribner's Sons.

READING STRATEGY

Analyzing Key Ideas and Details As you read about Americans' reactions to immigrants during the 1920s, complete a graphic organizer similar to the one here by filling in the causes and effects of anti-immigrant prejudices.

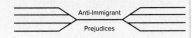

Anti-Immigrant
Prejudices

1920s Politics

GUIDING QUESTION

How was Warren Harding's presidency impeded by scandals?

Following Woodrow Wilson's eight years as president, people were resistant to progressivism after the years of experimentation and increased government intervention in the economy—including more taxes on the wealthy in America. This desire to change the reforms of the previous administrations was just one aspect of an eagerness by some Americans to return to a more traditional America. Perhaps this was a reaction to a developing modern, urban society. The tension of stopping the changes of the recent past was reflected in a variety of social and cultural disagreements during this decade.

The Harding Administration

Warren G. Harding began his career in Ohio state politics. In 1903 he became Ohio's lieutenant governor before being elected a U.S. senator in 1914. After serving one term, Harding ran for and won the presidency in 1920. In his presidential campaign, Harding promised "a return to normalcy" following the war. For Harding and his administration, returning to normalcy meant ending progressive reforms, decreasing economic regulation, and lowering taxes on the wealthy. But this would weaken government protections for children, the poor, and other disadvantaged groups. People applauded the easygoing atmosphere of the Harding administration, replacing the reform and war fervor of President Wilson's last years.

Harding made several notable appointments to the cabinet. These included former Supreme Court Justice Charles Evans Hughes as secretary of state, former Food Administrator Herbert Hoover as secretary of commerce, and business tycoon Andrew Mellon as secretary of the treasury. Many of his other appointments, however, were disastrous. He gave cabinet posts and other high-level jobs to friends and political allies from Ohio. Harding felt comfortable among his old friends, known as the Ohio Gang. Alice Roosevelt Longworth, daughter of President Theodore Roosevelt, described a typical evening in Harding's White House study:

❝ The air [would be] heavy with tobacco smoke, trays with bottles containing every imaginable brand of whiskey . . . cards and poker chips at hand—a general atmosphere of waistcoat unbuttoned, feet on desk, and spittoons alongside. ❞

–from *Crowded Hours*, 1933

Several of these men used their influential posts for their own gain. Colonel Charles R. Forbes, an Ohio acquaintance of Harding's, sold scarce medical supplies from veterans' hospitals and kept the money for himself. He cost the public about $250 million.

The most famous scandal, known as Teapot Dome, began in early 1922. Harding's secretary of the interior, Albert B. Fall, took bribes from private oil companies to drill on public lands at Teapot Dome, Wyoming, and Elk Hills, California. In return, Fall received bribes totaling more than $300,000. After the *Wall Street Journal* broke the story, the Senate launched an investigation that took most of the 1920s to complete. In 1929, Secretary Fall became the first cabinet secretary to go to prison. Attorney General Harry Daugherty was investigated for accepting bribes from a German agent seeking to buy a

The Senate Committee hears testimony during its investigation of the Teapot Dome oil lease scandal, 1924.

German-owned company that had been seized by the U.S. government during World War I. Daugherty refused to open Justice Department files to a congressional committee. He also refused to testify under oath, claiming immunity, or freedom from prosecution, on the grounds that he had confidential dealings with President Harding. Daugherty was later dismissed by President Coolidge.

Teapot Dome and the other scandals of the Harding administration increased Americans' distrust of the federal government and political leaders. This distrust hindered the goals of progressives as many progressive ideas and policies depended on efficient, honest government to be effective. If the government was corrupt, it helped make the case for reducing the role of government in the economy.

In June 1923, while traveling from Alaska to California, Harding became ill with what was probably a heart attack. He died in San Francisco on August 2. Early the next morning, the vice president, Calvin Coolidge, took the oath of office and became president.

"Silent Cal" Takes Over

Though Calvin Coolidge shared many of Harding's views on government, he had a different personality than President Harding. A critic joked that Coolidge could be "silent in five languages." Coolidge worked quickly to distance himself from Harding's scandals. However, he asked the most capable cabinet members—Hughes, Mellon, and Hoover—to remain. Like his Republican predecessor, Coolidge believed that prosperity rested on business leadership and that government should interfere with business and industry

as little as possible, which was a direct pushback to the reforms promoted by others in the Progressive Era.

> 66 After all, the chief business of the American people is business. They are profoundly concerned with producing, buying, selling, investing and prospering in the world. . . . In all experience, the accumulation of wealth means the multiplication of schools, the encouragement of science, the increase of knowledge, the dissemination of intelligence, the broadening of outlook, the expansion of liberties, the widening of culture. 99
>
> –Calvin Coolidge, from a speech to newspaper writers, quoted in the *New York Times*, January 18, 1925

In the year following Harding's death and the **revelations** of the scandals, Coolidge avoided crises and adopted policies intended to keep the nation prosperous. He easily won the Republican nomination for president in 1924. The Republicans promised the American people that the policies that had brought prosperity would continue. Coolidge won the election.

Republican Economic Policies

Andrew Mellon, a successful banker and industrialist, was secretary of the treasury under President Harding and his chief architect of economic policy. Mellon had three major goals when he took office: to balance the budget, to reduce the government's debt, and to cut taxes. Mellon argued that if taxes were lower, businesses and consumers would spend and invest their extra money. The economy would grow, Americans would earn more, and the government then would collect more in taxes. This idea is known today as **supply-side economics.** At Mellon's urging, Congress dramatically reduced tax rates. By 1928 Congress had reduced the income tax rate most Americans paid to 0.5 percent, down from 4 percent. They cut the rate for the wealthiest Americans to 25 percent, down from 73 percent. The federal budget fell from $6.4 billion to less than $3 billion in seven years.

Secretary of Commerce Herbert Hoover also sought to promote economic growth. He tried to balance government regulation with his philosophy of **cooperative individualism.** This idea involved encouraging businesses to form trade associations that would voluntarily share information with the federal government. Hoover believed this system would reduce costs and promote economic efficiency.

revelation an act of revealing to view or making known

supply-side economics an economic theory that lower taxes and decreased regulation will boost the economy as businesses and individuals invest their money, thereby creating higher tax revenue

cooperative individualism the idea that business would form trade associations that would in turn voluntarily share information with the federal government

PHOTO: Bettmann/Getty Images; TEXT: Coolidge, Calvin. 1925. President Calvin Coolidge's Address to the American Society of Newspaper Editors, Washington D.C., January 17, 1925. The New York Times, January 18, 1925.

Before World War I, the United States was a debtor nation. By the end of the war, wartime allies owed the United States more than $10 billion in war debts. By the 1920s, the United States was the dominant economic power in the world. Under Secretary of State Charles Evans Hughes, the nation tried to use its economic power to encourage peace and stability.

Isolationism

Following the turmoil of World War I, many Americans were tired of being entangled in European politics. Some of the nations' leaders did not wish to join the League of Nations and the Senate did not ratify the Treaty of Versailles. But in fact, the United States was too powerful and too interconnected with other countries economically to be truly isolated from the rest of the world. Instead of relying on armed force and the collective security of the League of Nations, the United States tried to promote peace by using economic policies and arms control agreements. This meant that while the United States was still active in the world, it was not limited by the League of Nations.

America's former allies, Britain and France, had difficulty making the payments on their immense war debts. Meanwhile, Germany was trying to make huge cash payments to these nations as punishment for starting the war—payments that were crippling the German economy. To address this problem, in 1924 American diplomat Charles G. Dawes negotiated an agreement with France, Britain, and Germany. American banks would make loans to Germany to help it to make reparations payments. In exchange, Britain and France would accept less in reparations and pay back more of their war debts to the United States.

Despite their debts, the major powers were involved in a costly postwar naval arms race. In 1921, the United States invited representatives from eight major countries—Britain, France, Italy, China, Japan, Belgium, the Netherlands, and Portugal—to Washington, D.C., to discuss disarmament. Secretary of State Charles Evans Hughes proposed a 10-year halt on the construction of new warships. This resulted in three agreements.

In the Five-Power Naval Limitation Treaty, Britain, France, Italy, Japan, and the United States essentially formalized Hughes's proposal. The Four-Power Treaty between the United States, Japan, France, and Great Britain recognized each country's island possessions in the Pacific. Finally, all the participant countries signed the Nine-Powers Treaty, which guaranteed China's independence. As a long-term effort to prevent war, the Washington Conference had some serious shortcomings. It did nothing to limit land forces. Japan was emerging as an economic and military power in the 1920s. It was offended because it wished to be treated equal to Great Britain and the

United States. The conference did, however, give Americans cause to look forward to a period of peace, recovery, and prosperity.

The Washington Conference inspired U.S. Secretary of State Frank Kellogg and French Foreign Minister Aristide Briand to propose a treaty to outlaw war altogether. On August 27, 1928, the United States and 14 other nations signed the Kellogg-Briand Pact. All signing nations agreed to abandon war and to settle all disputes by peaceful means.

From January to April 1930, five nations met in London to extend the Washington Conference. The United States, Britain, France, Italy, and Japan agreed on ratios for war ships, halting the arms race through 1936. In 1934 Japan declined to extend the treaty past 1936. It was pursuing imperial expansion into China. The United States, Britain, and France agreed to sign the treaty again in December 1935, but Italy refused.

✓ CHECK FOR UNDERSTANDING

1. **Identifying Cause and Effect** What were some consequences after Harding appointed members of the Ohio Gang, his friends and political allies from Ohio?

2. **Making Connections** What initiatives did the United States take in the 1920s to help ensure economic stability and peace in Europe?

New Values, New Cultures

GUIDING QUESTION

Why did nativism strengthen during the 1920s, and how did the government deal with the tension?

The 1920s was a time of economic growth, but it was also a time of turmoil. An economic recession immediately after World War I, a rise in suspicions toward immigrants as expressed in the Red Scare, a renewal of **nativism,** and weariness toward progressive reforms and rapid cultural change combined to create an atmosphere of disillusionment and intolerance.

Nativism and Immigration Policies

During World War I, immigration to the United States had dropped sharply. By 1921, however, it had returned to prewar levels. Many Americans chose to scapegoat immigrants for the post–World War I bombings, labor strikes, and economic recession that occurred around 1919 and 1920. Many of these same people believed that immigrants were taking jobs that would otherwise have gone to soldiers returning home from the war.

The Sacco-Vanzetti case reflected the prejudices and fears of the era. On April 15, 1920, two men

---

nativism hostility toward immigrants

robbed and murdered two employees of a shoe factory in Massachusetts. Police subsequently arrested two Italian immigrants, Nicola Sacco and Bartolomeo Vanzetti, for the crime. The case created a furor when newspapers revealed that the two men were **anarchists,** or people who opposed government, private property, and capitalism.

They also reported that Sacco owned a gun similar to the murder weapon and that the bullets used in the murders matched those in Sacco's gun. The evidence was questionable, but the fact that the accused men were anarchists and foreigners led many people to assume they were guilty, including the jury. On July 14, 1921, Sacco and Vanzetti were found guilty and sentenced to death. After six years of appeals, Sacco and Vanzetti were executed on August 23, 1927.

The group that most wanted to restrict immigration was the newly re-formed Ku Klux Klan, but such nativism and white supremacy was not limited to members of the KKK alone. As the Klan targeted Roman Catholics, Jews, immigrants, and other groups deemed "un-American," organizations emerged to fight the KKK. The Anti-Defamation League (ADL), which formed in 1913 to combat attacks on Jewish citizens, viewed the Klan and its nativist goals as a danger to individual liberty. Klan membership began to decline in the late 1920s due to scandals and power struggles among its leaders. In addition, new restrictions on immigration deprived the Klan of one of its major issues.

American immigration policies became more restrictive in response to nativist groups like the KKK. Even some business leaders, who had favored immigration as a source of cheap labor, now saw the new immigrants as radicals. In 1921 President Harding signed the Emergency Quota Act, which restricted annual admission to the United States by ethnic group. In 1924 the National Origins Act made immigration restriction a permanent policy. The law set quotas at 2 percent of each national group represented in the U.S. Census of 1890—long before the heavy wave of Catholic and Jewish immigration from southern and eastern Europe. As a result, new quotas favored immigrants from northwestern Europe.

Employers still needed immigrants as a source of cheap labor for agriculture, mining, and railroad work. Mexican immigrants could fill this need because the National Origins Act exempted natives of the Western Hemisphere from the quotas. Large numbers of Mexican immigrants had moved to the United States due to the Newlands Reclamation Act of 1902, which funded irrigation projects in the Southwest and led to the creation of large farms that needed thousands of workers. By the end of the 1920s, nearly 700,000 Mexicans had immigrated.

Many nonwhite immigrants who had moved to the United States and had lived and worked in the country for years were not safe from nativist attacks or from the nation's courts. Two important Supreme Court cases, *Takao Ozawa* v. *United States* (1922) and *United States* v. *Bhagat Singh Thind* (1923), established the U.S. government's definition of citizenship. These cases deal with **naturalization** and cultural preferences implied by racial definitions. At the time, naturalization only applied to free white people and people of African descent. Ozawa argued that as a Japanese man who had lived in America for 20 years, he should be properly classified as a free white person. The Court denied Ozawa, instead ruling that "free white person" meant Caucasian. Thind argued that his Indian heritage shared ancestry with what would be defined as a free white person, especially since it originated in the Caucasus Mountains from which the term *Caucasian* comes from. He also argued that his Indo-Aryan language belonged to the same linguistic family as English. The Court said that while Thind might share a common cultural understanding, he did not fit the popular understanding of a free white person.

By denying certain groups from becoming citizens based on notions of race, the rulings in *Ozawa* and *Thind* reinforced nativist ideas. The rulings also helped pass exclusionist immigration policies such as the National Origins Act, which denied entry to any person who would be ineligible for citizenship based on race.

Cultural Clashes

Groups that wanted to restrict immigration also wanted to preserve what they considered to be traditional values. This desire to preserve a more conservative culture and reject change reflected similar impulses in politics and increased rejection of progressive actions. They feared that a "new morality" was taking over. This trend glorified youth and personal freedom and brought big changes—particularly to the status of women.

Having won the right to vote in 1920, many women sought to escape the trappings of traditional roles. Women who attended college often found support to pursue careers. Many working-class women took jobs because they needed the wages, but work also allowed them to break away from parental authority and establish financial independence. Women's fashions changed during the 1920s: women "bobbed," or shortened, their hair and wore flesh-colored silk stockings. Some women, known as flappers, smoked cigarettes, drank prohibited liquor, and wore makeup and sleeveless dresses with short skirts.

Sigmund Freud, a neurologist who pioneered psychoanalysis, developed theories on human sexuality

---

anarchist a person who rejects modern government, capitalism, and private wealth

naturalization the process through which a foreigner becomes a citizen of a country

that affected people's ideas about relationships. It became more socially acceptable to talk about sexual desire. Romance, pleasure, and friendship became linked to successful marriages. Dating became more common, and the concept of a companionate marriage, a marriage based on mutual respect and equality between partners, became the norm. Records show that during the 1920s, women living together as domestic partners and a couple became more visible. This arrangement was often called a "Boston marriage," from the title of Henry James's 1886 novel *The Bostonians*.

Many women made major contributions in science, medicine, law, and literature. Florence Sabin's research led to a dramatic drop in death rates from tuberculosis. Public-health nurse Margaret Sanger believed that families could improve their standard of living by limiting the number of children they had. She founded the American Birth Control League in 1921 to promote knowledge about birth control. The use of birth control increased dramatically, particularly in the middle class.

Sanger's birth control movement overlapped with the philosophy of eugenics that tried to improve the genetic composition of societies by using selective breeding techniques. Eugenicists categorized people as either "fit" or "unfit." American eugenicists generally classified middle- and upper-class native white people as "fit" while determining nonwhites and those with physical or mental health issues as "unfit." The acceptance of the unproven theories of eugenics by many mainstream U.S. scientific communities eventually led to the forced sterilization of roughly 60 thousand Americans, the majority of whom were either poor, African American, or confined to mental health institutions.

Cars offered the modern woman of the 1920s mobility and independence.

Explaining How does this photograph illustrate the changing roles of women in the 1920s?

The growth of cities also brought new freedoms to the LGBTQ community. Boarding houses and residential hotels were often maintained with single-gender rules, to provide distant parents peace of mind when allowing young adults the freedom to live outside the traditional family structure in the growing cities. Supporting oneself through independent work and wages also provided urban dwellers the freedom to explore new identities and seek out people with similar interests. New communities, such as Greenwich Village in New York City and the North Beach neighborhood in San Francisco, allowed LGBTQ individuals an opportunity to express their identities.

The theater and Hollywood also offered some opportunity for LGBTQ expression. Performers such as Julian Eltinge and Gladys Bentley became known for their gender-bending performances. Different sexual orientations and gender identities appeared in some of the art of the time. These small communities of social disruption laid the foundation for people such as Christine Jorgensen, who in the 1950s became the first American to have gender reassignment surgery.

Religious Fundamentalism

While many Americans embraced the new morality of the 1920s, others feared that the country was losing its traditional values. They viewed the consumer culture, relaxed ethics, and changing roles of women as evidence of the nation's moral decline. Many, especially evangelical Christians, grew more vocal in their opposition to a changing morality. These evangelicals embraced the Fundamentalist religious views that had existed in the nation since the nineteenth century.

Fundamentalists in the 1920s and today believe in a literal interpretation of the Bible. They defend the Protestant faith against the implication that human beings derive their moral behavior from society and nature, not God. In particular, they reject the principle of **evolution,** which is that human beings developed from lower forms of life over the course of millions of years. Instead, they believe in **creationism**—the belief that God created the world as described in the Bible.

In 1925 Tennessee outlawed any teaching that denied "the story of the Divine Creation of man as taught in the Bible" or taught that "man descended from a lower order of animals." The American Civil Liberties Union (ACLU) advertised for a teacher willing to be arrested for teaching evolution. John T. Scopes, a biology teacher in Dayton, Tennessee, volunteered. At Scopes's trial, William Jennings Bryan, a three-time presidential candidate, was the prosecutor representing the creationists. Clarence Darrow, one of the country's most celebrated trial lawyers, defended Scopes. Scopes was found guilty and fined $100, although the

PHOTO: Library of Congress, Prints and Photographs Division [LC-USZ62-100382]; TEXT: Public Acts of the State of Tennessee. Chapter No. 27, House Bill No. 185. Tennessee General Assembly, March 13, 1925.

evolution the scientific theory that humans and other forms of life have evolved over time

creationism the belief that God created the world and everything in it, usually in the way described in the Bible

The Women's Christian Temperance Union (WCTU) was influential in Prohibition efforts. This 1929 *New York Daily News* photo shows WCTU members with barrels of liquor seized in raids.

conviction was later overturned on a technicality. The trial was broadcast over the radio, and Darrow's blistering cross-examination of Bryan hurt the Fundamentalist cause.

Two popular evangelical preachers, Billy Sunday and Aimee Semple McPherson, preached in very nontraditional ways. Sunday, a former professional baseball player, drew huge crowds with his rapid-fire sermons and on-stage showmanship. McPherson conducted her revivals and faith healings in Los Angeles in a flamboyant theatrical style, using stage sets and costumes that expressed the themes of her highly emotional sermons.

McPherson was one of the most influential preachers in the emerging Pentecostal movement in the early twentieth century. Pentecostals were evangelical Protestants who did not stress traditional customs or doctrines. Women and African Americans became active in the Pentecostal movement as a way to shed the prejudices of traditional churches. Elder Lucy Smith was the first African American woman to lead a huge congregation in Chicago, and her church, Langley Avenue All Nations Pentecostal Church, helped many Chicagoans through the Great Depression. With thriving congregations in urban centers such as Los Angeles, Cleveland, and Memphis, as well as more rural areas like Kansas, Pentecostal preachers used mass media to spread their messages and to offer an alternate expression of the Jazz Age.

The push to control alcohol consumption also mixed into the cultural issues of the 1920s. The movement to ban alcohol sales had begun during the progressive reform years. Many people believed that prohibiting alcohol would help reduce unemployment, domestic violence, and poverty. Religious groups had long been leading voices in the temperance movement since the 1800s.

For many, prohibition was a tool to fight what they perceived as immoral behavior. Others blamed alcohol-related problems on the large wave of immigrants flowing into the United States. In their view, many immigrants held more permissive attitudes toward alcohol consumption and were emerging as leaders in the brewing industries. Prohibition, consequently, became an attempt to control the culture of immigrant communities. The Eighteenth Amendment went into effect January 1920, banning the manufacture and sale of alcohol. The Volstead Act gave the U.S. Treasury Department the power to enforce Prohibition, marking a dramatic increase in federal police powers.

In the 1920s, Treasury Department agents made more than 540,000 arrests, but Americans still ignored the law. People flocked to secret bars called **speakeasies** to purchase alcohol. In New York City alone, an estimated 32,000 such bars sold illegal liquor. Liquor also was readily available in rural areas through bootlegging—the illegal production and distribution of alcohol. Huge profits could be made smuggling liquor from Canada and the Caribbean. Organized crime became big business, and gangsters used their money to corrupt local politicians. Al Capone, one of the most successful and well-known gangsters of the era, had many police officers, judges, and other officials on his payroll.

The battle to repeal Prohibition began almost as soon as the Eighteenth Amendment was ratified, and the amendment was repealed in 1933. Though diseases and some social problems were reduced, Prohibition did not improve society as dramatically as its supporters had hoped. In fact, with the introduction of organized crime to smuggle alcohol in response to Prohibition, it was an experiment that failed.

✓ **CHECK FOR UNDERSTANDING**

1. **Summarizing** Why did nativism strengthen during the 1920s, and how did the government deal with the tensions?

2. **Explaining** How did obtaining the right to vote in the 1920s help many women break free from traditional roles?

LESSON ACTIVITIES

1. **Argumentative Writing** Suppose it is the 1920s. Write a letter to your senator to persuade him to support Prohibition or its repeal.

2. **Evaluating Claims** In small groups, discuss whether you think the 1920s were ultimately a return to normalcy. Provide reasons to support your answer.

---

speakeasies places where alcoholic beverages are sold illegally

New York Daily News Archive/Getty Images

Reviewing Progressivism and the Jazz Age

Summary

Progressive Reforms

Industrial growth, increased immigration, and other societal changes led to new problems in American society. Progressive reformers sought to address social issues such as crime, illiteracy, alcohol abuse, child labor, and health and safety through a variety of methods including the founding of charities. In many cases, privileged women were the champions of these causes and worked to protect families, women, and children from the vulnerabilities caused by poverty. Progressive reformers also sought to bolster democratic values and eliminate corruption through political and government reforms. These reformers tackled government at all levels—from decentralizing control in local governments, to allowing citizens to take active roles in introducing legislature, to countering corruption within Congress.

Women's Suffrage

Women's reform efforts in the late nineteenth and early twentieth centuries resulted in a major achievement of the Progressive Era—a constitutional amendment protecting women's right to vote. Women's rights activists had been lobbying for suffrage since the Seneca Falls Convention of 1848. Many early suffrage activists were also abolitionists who were disappointed that women were not included in the Fifteenth Amendment, which protected voting rights for African American men. During the late nineteenth century, different groups led by women such as Elizabeth Cady Stanton, Susan B. Anthony, Lucy Stone, and Julia Ward Howe tried to garner support for women's suffrage. Eventually most of the activists combined their efforts and formed the National American Woman Suffrage Association (NAWSA). This group lobbied to expand women's voting rights on local and state levels while building support for a constitutional amendment. However, white suffragists often excluded African American suffragists, who went on to form the National Association of Colored Women's Clubs (NACWC).

By the turn of the century, some younger activists such as Alice Paul were growing impatient with the slow pace of change. Organizing as the National Woman's Party (NWP), they engaged in confrontational protests to bring attention to their cause. After some protesters were arrested, they staged prison hunger strikes, gaining media attention. When World War I broke out, many suffrage activists encouraged women's service to their country. Movement leaders used the example of women's patriotism and war work to lobby for a constitutional amendment. In 1919 the Senate approved the amendment, which quickly gained the approval it needed from three-fourths of the states. The Nineteenth Amendment protecting women's right to vote was ratified in 1920, however, African American women would face barriers to voting until the Voting Rights Act of 1965 and beyond.

Presidential Progressive Reform

Laws passed under Progressive presidents from Theodore Roosevelt to Woodrow Wilson expanded government oversight of businesses in order to improve health and safety conditions for workers and to make the free market system fairer for small businesses and consumers. Roosevelt established the Department of Commerce and Labor, which focused on business regulation, labor disputes, and antitrust oversight. Roosevelt also established the U.S. Department of Agriculture to protect consumer rights around food and medicine. Roosevelt is also widely remembered for his environmental conservation efforts which led to the establishment of the U.S. Forest Service and the first national parks.

The Wilson administration brought tax reform and the establishment of an income tax that would tax the wealthy at a higher rate than the poor. The introduction of income tax allowed for reduced tariffs, positioning the United States for stronger trade. Wilson also modernized the nation's banking system and created the Federal Reserve, a centralized entity that set monetary policy. The Federal Reserve's monetary policy had the power to influence the nation's economy greatly through adjusting interest rates. Wilson also continued the work of his predecessors to address antitrust regulation and child labor reforms.

Economic Growth

Although the United States experienced a recession immediately following the end of World War I, the economy recovered. By the early 1920s, the economy entered a booming period marked by several years of growth and job expansion. Many of these jobs came from the manufacturing sector. Business innovators such as Henry Ford used assembly lines in their factories to mass produce more consumer goods at a lower cost. Ford's automobiles and credit policies enabled many American families to purchase automobiles for the first time. The auto industry not only

A Growing Economy

Elements of the New Consumer Economy
Industrialized Mass Production
Rising Standard of Living
New Consumer Products Created

changed the ways in which people lived and worked, it also spurred growth in numerous other industries.

By the 1920s, job growth and expanded credit created a cycle of prosperity that depended increasingly on consumer purchasing. However, this prosperity was not spread equally among all. The growth in consumer spending also benefited from growth in advertising and mass media. Most homes had access to the newly invented radio, which brought popular entertainment and commercials for new products into daily life. Movies also grew in popularity. Increasingly, advertisements and popular entertainment encouraged Americans to purchase goods to copy the styles and tastes of celebrities from radio, films, and sports.

African American Politics and Culture

African Americans began to move from the South to Northern industrial cities. Known as the Great Migration, this demographic shift continued throughout the 1920s. The Great Migration galvanized African American efforts to fight for greater political rights and freedoms. The NAACP furthered the work it had started before the war in exposing injustices and opposing racist laws through the courts. W.E.B. Du Bois continued to be one of the most prominent voices for the NAACP. Increasingly, however, new voices emerged calling for greater African American unity in the face of discrimination. Marcus Garvey was a leading proponent of black nationalism. He argued that African Americans should focus on supporting one another rather than integrating with whites. Garvey's ideas encouraged pride in African American heritage and would influence some later civil rights leaders in the 1960s.

Although African Americans still faced discrimination and segregation, they developed thriving communities and cultural connections. African American writers, musicians, and visual artists reflected the voices and cultures of their community. Collectively, their artistic expression became known as the Harlem Renaissance, named after the African American neighborhood in New York City. Langston Hughes,

Countee Cullen, and Zora Neale Hurston were some of the most famous Harlem Renaissance writers. Visual artists such as Aaron Douglas and Augusta Savage changed perceptions with their art that reflected the African American experience. Even the music that distinguished the Jazz Age emerged from African American communities. Musicians such as Louis Armstrong and Duke Ellington transferred the jazz sound from New Orleans to northern urban clubs and soon to the entire country. The radio and phonograph further popularized African American musical forms, including soul and the blues.

Cultural Clashes

The rapid changes in American culture before and after World War I prompted a cultural backlash. President Warren Harding promised a "return to normalcy" in his 1920 campaign. In politics, that meant a retreat from some of the reform efforts of the Progressive Era period, a shift back toward isolationism, and economic policies that favored American businesses over global trade. During the 1920s, nativism, racism, and fears about radicalism and immigration increased, as reflected in the Sacco-Vanzetti Case. Congress responded by enacting strict quotas on immigration from certain countries.

Along with increased nativism and isolationism, a conservative culture emerged amongst fears of the changing styles and freedoms. With newfound freedoms, some independent women became flappers, shocking society by wearing short skirts and bobbing their hair. Some cultural critics and politicians railed against what they perceived as a loss of values among the younger generation.

Fundamentalists, who adhered to strict behavioral rules and rigid interpretations of the Bible, raised alarms over cultural developments such as the widespread violations of Prohibition laws and the teaching of evolution in schools, challenged in the widely followed Scopes Trial.

Clashing Values

Traditional Values	Modern Values
• Religious fundamentalism	• More freedom for women
• Support of prohibition	• New scientific and cultural ideas

Apply What You Have Learned

A Understanding Multiple Perspectives

The "Roaring Twenties" was a period of widespread economic prosperity and cultural advancement for some parts of United States society in the early twentieth century. However, not everyone experienced the economic benefits of the United States's overall economic growth. Some pockets of the economy struggled.

Also, not all of the people living in the nation viewed the cultural and social developments of the 1920s as positive. These cultural critics questioned whether the cultural developments of this decade were actually positive or might instead reflected a decline in the traditional morals of previous generations.

Trying to evaluate and understand the competing points of view of a complex society is a key skill to learning history.

ACTIVITY **Make a Game** Working in small groups, create an "Agree/Disagree" game about the 1920s. Write a series of opinion statements about the period with which one might agree or disagree. An example might be: "Coolidge's economic policies were good for everyone." After your group has developed at least five opinion statements, exchange your statements with that of another group. Have your group play a game in which one person reads aloud each given statement. Have members of your group vote on whether or not the following people living in the 1920s would agree or disagree with each statement: a southern agricultural worker, a recent immigrant from southeastern Europe, a single woman living in a city, a Fundamentalist minister, and a Wall Street investment banker. Discuss why each person in your group voted the way they did.

B Making Connections to Art

The artists and art forms of the Harlem Renaissance reached a wider and more appreciative audience because of the developing mass media technology of the early twentieth century. Films, recordings, radio broadcasts, and magazines introduced their works across the country and throughout the world.

ACTIVITY **Create a Playlist** Using library and Internet resources, research film or audio recordings of music, songs, dances, or spoken-word performances from the Harlem Renaissance. Using this information, create a playlist of performances that you would use to teach someone else about the time period. When you are finished, work in pairs to exchange playlists with another student in your class. Discuss why you selected the particular performances you chose.

C Analyzing Change

During the 1920s, many women were able to break from traditional roles and take advantage of new opportunities. However, for the women who had worked for years to expand women's rights, the newfound freedoms available to young women in the 1920s stood in stark contrast to the opportunities that had been available when they were young.

ACTIVITY **Write a Monologue** Review the names of women involved in the long fight to secure suffrage for women and choose one of these women. Then, using your textbook, library, and Internet resources, research more information about her life and the changes that occurred during her lifetime. Using this information, write a spoken-word monologue that compares the opportunities that young women in the 1920s had with those your subject might have had in her youth.

D Making Connections to Today

Many of the issues that caused friction and social divisions during the Progressive Era and the Jazz Age are still being debated by Americans today.

For example, politicians still debate whether the United States should limit immigration from certain countries or enact tariffs on imported goods. These were political disagreements during the early decades of the twentieth century, and they remain debatable topics today, even if the people and the details that the debates center around have changed.

ACTIVITY **Compare and Contrast Issues Over Time** Reexamine the information that you have learned in this topic and choose one issue that divided society in the 1920s and still divides Americans today. Using library or Internet resources, research your chosen issue. Using that information, create a Venn diagram to compare and contrast how the issue was debated in the Progressive Era or the Jazz Age and how it is debated today.

A September 5, 2017, rally in Portland, Oregon, protests President Donald Trump's decision to end the Deferred Action for Childhood Arrivals (DACA) program that protects young adult immigrants from deportation.

Diego G Diaz/Shutterstock

Franklin D. Roosevelt (center) takes the presidential oath of office in 1933, in the depth of the Great Depression.

The Great Depression and the New Deal 1929–1941

INTRODUCTION LESSON

01 Introducing the Great Depression and the New Deal 234

LEARN THE EVENTS LESSONS

02 Hoover's Response to the Depression 239

04 Life During the Great Depression 249

05 The First New Deal 253

06 The Second New Deal 259

INQUIRY ACTIVITY LESSONS

03 Turning Point: The Stock Market and the New Deal 245

07 Analyzing Sources: Roosevelt's Political Critics 265

REVIEW AND APPLY LESSON

08 Reviewing the Great Depression and the New Deal 271

National Archive/Hulton Archive/Getty Images

THE HOOVER DAM

As a way to alleviate the economic crisis known as the Great Depression, the federal government planned and supported hundreds of public works projects during the 1930s. Many of these projects lasted only a few years, but what they produced often still exists today. One of the most impressive public works projects created during the Great Depression is the Hoover Dam along the Arizona-Nevada border. Even though it is something as ordinary as a hydroelectric dam, it attracts nearly seven million tourists each year.

Describing the Hoover Dam as a massive feat of engineering is an understatement. At 726 feet tall, the structure is the highest concrete **arch dam** in the United States. The dam's crest is 1,244 feet (379 meters) long, and it contains nearly 4.5 million cubic yards (3.4 million cubic meters) of concrete. Around 20,000 people were hired to build the dam during a time when jobs were scarce.

Lake Mead, the lake created by Hoover Dam, is one of the largest artificial lakes in the world. By 1939, more than 8 trillion gallons (30 trillion liters) of water were stored in the lake. Four intake towers above Hoover dam divert water from Lake Mead into huge steel pipes. The water falls about 500 feet (152 meters) into a giant hydroelectric power plant at the dam's base.

The power plant generates enough electrical energy to provide power to southern California, including Los Angeles, as well as parts of Nevada and Arizona. By 1940, the total annual electric power generation of the dam was about 3 billion kilowatt-hours.

The dam was built on the Colorado River, which is an important source of water for seven states— Arizona, California, Colorado, Nevada, New Mexico, Utah, and Wyoming. These states worked together to enact legislation for the Boulder Canyon Project, which would control, store, and distribute water from the Colorado River. Although Arizona was unhappy with the water distribution, the Boulder Canyon Project Act passed.

In 1931 the Bureau of Reclamation awarded the project to Six Companies, a construction and engineering firm, for $48,890,995. This made it the most expensive water project of its time. Users of the electricity produced paid back the cost to the Federal Treasury by 1987. The dam is so named to honor President Herbert Hoover, who was in office during the beginning of construction. On September 30, 1935, the Hoover Dam was considered officially complete and was dedicated by President Franklin D. Roosevelt.

> **"** . . . to take each problem and integrate it to the whole . . . **"**

The streamlined look of the dam is attributed to Gordon B. Kaufmann, an architect known for his design of the *Los Angeles Times* building, and a mural artist named Allen True. Kaufmann later explained "there was never any desire or attempt to create an architectural effect or style, but rather to take each problem and integrate it to the whole in order to secure a system of plain surfaces relieved by shadows here and there." True helped Kaufmann with the interior designs and colors. True is responsible for the inclusion of geometric designs in the **terrazzo** floors. Inspired by Native American designs, such as the Acoma bowl and the Pima basket, True linked art with engineering.

For more than eighty years, the Hoover Dam has delighted visitors with its power, magnificence, and subtle elegance. It stands as a symbol of the power of government cooperation during a difficult time of economic depression. Projects such as the Hoover Dam provided needed jobs for thousands of unemployed people and created economic improvements that provided a foundation for modern American innovation.

arch dam a dam that is curved upstream in order to transmit the major part of the water load to the abutments, or the part of a structure that directly receives pressure

terrazzo a mosaic flooring that has pieces of marble or granite set in mortar and is then highly polished

Rhinehart, Julian. "The Grand Dam." U.S. Bureau of Reclamation: Hoover Dam. 2015.

bluejayphoto/iStock/Getty Images Plus

The federal government founded Boulder City, Nevada, for the 20,000 workers who built the Hoover Dam.

Analyzing Visuals What does this photo reveal about the dangers of building Hoover Dam?

Understanding the Time and Place: The United States, 1931–1941

The Great Depression was the worst economic crisis that the nation had yet faced. American optimism reached a new height in the 1920s, but it was replaced by fears and worries when the stock market failed in 1929. By 1933, nearly a quarter of the population was unemployed. The crisis lasted until America entered World War II.

Consumerism and Overproduction

Many factors led to the Great Depression. The beginning of the twentieth century was marked by rapid industrialization and increasing consumerism. Factories and farms produced many goods, but not enough families had disposable incomes to purchase these goods. By 1929, about two-thirds of families earned less than $2,500 a year. Farmers in particular suffered economic disadvantages in the 1920s. During World War I, many farmers bought new land or equipment with loans to meet wartime demand. But by the 1920s, prices fell at the same time many farmers were growing and selling more goods to pay their debts, taxes, and living expenses. The extra supply drove prices so low that many farmers went bankrupt and lost their farms.

The growing consumerism of the early twentieth century meant many Americans wanted items that they could not afford. They were still able to purchase high-cost items, such as cars and refrigerators, through **installment plans,** where purchasers paid some money up front and then had a monthly bill due until the entire purchase was paid off. However, relying too much on installment plans increased debt. Eventually, buyers stopped making new purchases to keep their debt under control. As demand for their products decreased, manufacturers cut production and laid off employees. The unemployed and those struggling for more work could no longer afford to keep up with their monthly debt payments.

The interconnection of manufactured products rippled in industries throughout the country. When radio sales slumped, orders for copper wire, wood cabinets, and glass radio tubes slowed. Montana copper miners, Minnesota lumberjacks, and Ohio glassworkers lost jobs. Jobless workers had to cut back on purchases, further reducing sales. This put even more out of work. In 1930 alone, about 26,000 businesses failed.

World Markets and Federal Policies

U.S. banks engaged in the practice of loaning money to **speculators** throughout the 1920s. At the same time, banks cut loans to foreign countries. European nations had depended on U.S. loans to help recover from World War I. Loans also helped secure foreign markets for goods manufactured in the United States. When banks stopped making these foreign loans, foreign buyers purchased fewer American-made products. In 1929 President Hoover wanted to lower tariffs to encourage global trade, but Congress disagreed. Republican legislators believed higher tariffs would protect American manufacturing from foreign competition. The 1930 Hawley-Smoot Tariff raised tariffs to an all-time high. Foreign countries retaliated by raising their tariffs, reducing American exports by more than half by 1932.

Cyclical Effect

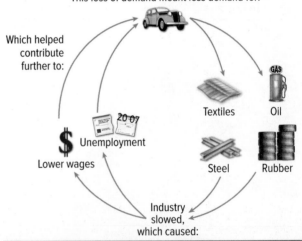

Automobile sales declined. This loss of demand meant less demand for:

Which helped contribute further to:

Textiles

Oil

Unemployment

Lower wages

Steel

Rubber

Industry slowed, which caused:

The U.S. economy grew worse rapidly because of a cycle of interconnected factors. Companies borrowed money to expand and produce more goods than the general public could afford to buy. High tariffs prevented those goods from being sold to foreign countries. Companies production decreases affected a wide variety of industries and employees lost wages and jobs.

Analyzing What effect did the decline in automobile sales have on related industries?

---

installment plans monthly plan made to pay off the cost of an item when buying it on credit

speculators a person who risks money in hopes of a financial profit

Fleeing the Effects of the Dust Bowl

The effects of the Great Depression were made worse by erosion and drought in the Great Plains, a vast grassland that is roughly one-third of the United States. Many of the hardest hit people in the Plains abandoned their homes because of the environmental destruction caused by the dust storms.

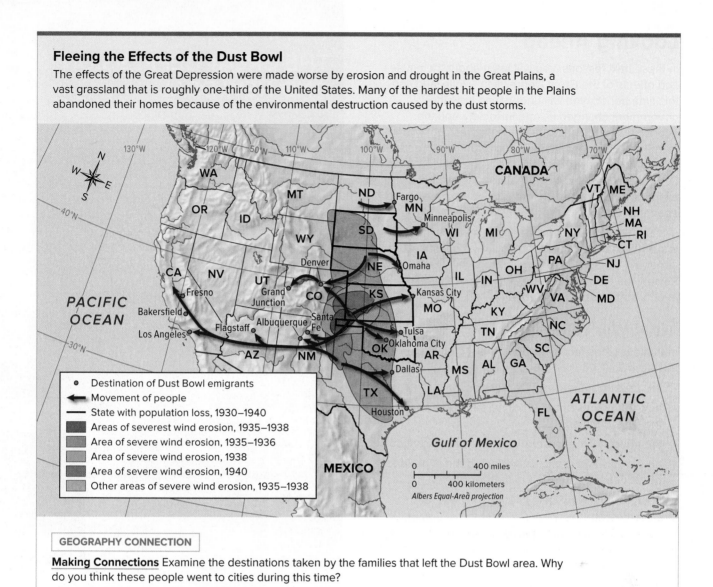

Legend:
- Destination of Dust Bowl emigrants
- ← Movement of people
- — State with population loss, 1930–1940
- Areas of severest wind erosion, 1935–1938
- Area of severe wind erosion, 1935–1936
- Area of severe wind erosion, 1938
- Area of severe wind erosion, 1940
- Other areas of severe wind erosion, 1935–1938

Albers Equal-Area projection

GEOGRAPHY CONNECTION

Making Connections Examine the destinations taken by the families that left the Dust Bowl area. Why do you think these people went to cities during this time?

Federal Reserve Policies

During the 1920s, the Federal Reserve Board kept interest rates low, which prompted more people to borrow money. Low interest rates motivated member banks to make risky loans to people or businesses without concrete security that the loan would be paid back. The low interest rates also encouraged business leaders to borrow money to expand production. Businesses borrowed more money to expand production, which contributed to the massive overproduction that characterized the 1920s.

The Market and the Dust Bowl

The beginning of the Great Depression is often attributed to the stock market crash in 1929, although, as discussed previously, many other factors were involved. By 1929 a growing number of American households owned stocks. By the end of the 1920s, many buyers were speculating that the market would

continue to climb. In September 1929 the market peaked. Then, prices unevenly began to slide downward, causing many to believe it was time to sell. As more people sold, the market plummeted and finally crashed on October 29. Investors and businesses lost billions of dollars. By 1932, about one out of every four banks in the United States had gone out of business.

The Great Depression was worsened by what became known as the Dust Bowl. Farmers in the Great Plains had been stressing the soil for years with their methods of farming, which eventually led to land that was unable to sustain crops. Without enough plants to keep the soil down, erosion increased. In addition, a severe drought affected the area, resulting in dust storms that destroyed more soil and more crops. Many farmers could no longer support themselves, and a mass exodus from the Great Plains took place as some 2.5 million people moved west in search of food and work.

Looking Ahead

In these next lessons, you will learn about the causes and effects of the Great Depression. While studying this time period, you will understand how the government changed its role in society and the economy as a result of the Great Depression. You will learn how President Herbert Hoover initially reacted to the economic crisis. You will also lean about Franklin D. Roosevelt and his New Deal policies. And you will examine how arts and culture continued, despite the economic crisis.

You will examine Compelling Questions in the Inquiry Lessons and develop your own questions about the Great Depression and the New Deal. Review the time line to preview some of the key events that you will learn about.

What Will You Learn

In these lessons focused on the Great Depression and the New Deal, you will learn:

- the causes of the Great Depression.
- how the events of the stock market crash affected the United States.
- the effects of the Dust Bowl and farmer migration.
- how artists and musicians reflected the experience of the Great Depression in their work.
- how the First New Deal changed the role of government.
- the political pressures Roosevelt faced and how he responded to their criticisms.
- how the Second New Deal was different than the First New Deal.

? COMPELLING QUESTIONS

- **Was the stock market crash of 1929 a turning point?**
- **How did people view the New Deal?**

1928 — 1928 Herbert Hoover elected president

1929 U.S. stock market crashes on October 24 and October 29

1930 Hawley-Smoot Tariff enacted

1931 National Credit Corporation established to aid failing banks

1932 Bonus Army marchers arrive in Washington, D.C., to protest

1932 Unemployment peaks at 22.9 percent

1933 — 1933 Franklin D. Roosevelt elected president

1934 Securities and Exchange Commission (SEC) created

1935 Social Security Act passed (image from Social Security poster right)

1936 — 1936 Franklin Roosevelt wins reelection for second term

1937 Sit-down strike by GM workers ends, forcing the automaker to recognize the United Auto Workers union

1938 Fair Labor Standards Act sets minimum wage law and 44-hour work week

1940 — 1940 First Social Security checks mailed

MORE SECURITY FOR THE AMERICAN FAMILY

WHEN AN INSURED WORKER DIES, LEAVING DEPENDENT CHILDREN AND A WIDOW, BOTH MOTHER AND CHILDREN RECEIVE MONTHLY BENEFITS UNTIL THE LATTER REACH 18.

FOR INFORMATION WRITE OR CALL AT THE NEAREST FIELD OFFICE OF THE
SOCIAL SECURITY BOARD

Everett Collection/Shutterstock

Sequencing Time Identify the events that reflect changes enacted by the federal government to improve the lives of American workers and explain how these changes most likely affected workers.

(t) Public Papers of the Presidents of the United States: Herbert Hoover, March 4 to December 31, 1929. Washington, D.C.: United States Government Printing Office, 1974; (b)Hoover, Herbert. Inaugural address, March 4, 1929. Reproduced by The Avalon Project: Yale Law School - Lillian Goldman Law Library.

02

Hoover's Response to the Depression

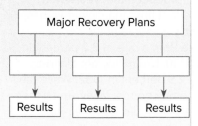

READING STRATEGY

Key Ideas and Details As you read about Herbert Hoover's response to the Depression, create a graphic organizer such as this listing his major initiatives and their results.

Major Recovery Plans

Results   Results   Results

The Long Bull Market Ends

GUIDING QUESTION

What economic choices caused the economy to become unstable in the 1920s?

The economic collapse that began in 1929 seemed unimaginable months before. The consumerism of the 1920s—built on increased productivity, higher wages, and credit—fueled a booming economy. In the 1928 election both presidential candidates painted a rosy picture of the future. Republican presidential nominee Herbert Hoover declared, "We are nearer to the final triumph over poverty than ever before in the history of any land."

The Election of 1928

For the presidential election of 1928 the Democrats chose Alfred E. Smith, governor of New York, as their candidate. Smith was the first Roman Catholic to win a major party's presidential nomination. He faced a tough challenger, as Herbert Hoover was Secretary of Commerce and former head of the Food Administration.

Smith's religious beliefs became a campaign issue, with some Protestants claiming the Catholic Church financed Smith's campaign and would have inappropriate influence on American politics. The attacks embarrassed Hoover, a Quaker, and he tried to quash them, but the charges damaged Smith's candidacy.

The prosperity of the 1920s—for which the Republicans took full credit—was a bigger challenge to Smith's candidacy. Hoover won in a landslide, and on March 4, 1929, an estimated 50,000 onlookers stood in the rain to listen to Hoover's Inaugural Address. "I have no fears for the future of our country," proclaimed Hoover. "It is bright with hope."

The Stock Market Soars

The optimism that swept Hoover into office also drove stock prices to new highs. Sometimes the **stock market** has a long period of rising stock prices, or a bull market. The **bull market** of the 1920s convinced many of the strength of the economy. As a result, a growing number of Americans began purchasing stocks. Before the late 1920s, stock prices generally reflected their true values, but in the late 1920s, many investors failed to consider a company's earnings and profits. Buyers engaged in **speculation,** or betting the market would continue to climb, thus enabling them to sell stock and make money quickly.

Many investors bought stocks on **margin,** making only a small cash down payment (as low as 10 percent of the price). With $1,000, an investor could buy a sum of $10,000 worth of stock. The remaining $9,000 came as an interest-bearing loan from the stockbroker. Quick profits were possible as long as

stock market a system for buying and selling stocks in corporations

bull market a long period of rising stock prices

speculation act of buying stocks at great risk with the anticipation that the prices will rise

margin buying a stock by paying only a fraction of the stock price and borrowing the rest

Shanty towns sprung up across the country as the financial situation worsened and the unemployed and displaced migrated in search of work and shelter. This makeshift community was in Seattle, Washington.

Identifying Main Ideas Why were so many people forced to live in these types of homes?

stock prices kept rising, but problems came when prices began to fall. To protect a loan, a broker could issue a **margin call,** demanding the investor repay the loan at once.

The Great Crash

The bull market lasted only as long as investors continued putting new money into it. In September 1929 the market peaked, and prices then began an uneven downward slide known as a bear market. As investors decided the boom was over, they sold more stock, causing prices to decline even further.

On Monday, October 21, 1929 the comedian Groucho Marx—one of the most successful stars of his time—was awakened by a telephone call from his broker. "You'd better get down here with some cash to cover your margin," the broker said. The stock market had plunged. The dazed comedian had to pay back the money he had borrowed to buy stocks, which were now selling for far less than he had paid for them. Other brokers made similar margin calls, leading customers to put stocks up for sale at a frenzied pace, driving the market into a tailspin. On October 24, a day that came to be called Black Thursday, the market plummeted further. Marx was totally broke, because he had put all his money in stocks.

The following week, on October 29, prices took the steepest dive yet. That day, more than 16 million

shares of stock were sold, and the value of the industrial index (a measure of the value of leading industrial companies) dropped by 10 percent. By mid-November, the market price of stocks had dropped by more than one-third. Some $30 billion was lost, a sum roughly equal to the total wages Americans earned in 1929.

Although the stock market crash was not the main cause of the Great Depression, it undermined the economy's ability to overcome other weaknesses. Fearful of the future, corporations quit investing money in economic growth, and as consumer spending declined, they cut production. By the end of 1930 Gross Domestic Product (GDP)—the value of all the goods and services produced that year—was already down 8.5 percent. Rather than lower wages, many corporations simply let some of their workers go. Unemployment rose from a rate of 3.2 percent in 1929 to 8.7 percent in 1930. Unemployment increased each year, peaking at 22.9 percent in 1932. While the employed had money to buy goods, many saved their money for fear that they too would lose their jobs.

Banks Begin to Close

The stock market crash also revealed problems with the nation's banks. One problem was that by 1929, banks had over-extended themselves by lending billions of dollars to stock speculators. Making matters worse, banks themselves had invested depositors' money in the stock market, hoping for high returns. When stock values collapsed, banks lost money on their investments, and speculators defaulted on their loans. The serious losses led banks to drastically reduce the money they were willing to loan. With less credit available, consumers and businesses were not able to borrow money, sending the economy into a recession.

Some banks could not absorb the losses they suffered and had to close. The government did not insure bank deposits at the time, so if a bank failed, customers, including those who did not invest in the stock market, lost their savings. As a growing number of banks closed in 1929 and 1930, a severe crisis of confidence in the banking system further destabilized the economy.

News of bank failures worried Americans, leading some depositors to make runs on banks, thus causing the banks to fail. A **bank run** takes place when many depositors decide to withdraw their money at the same time, usually out of fear that the bank will collapse. Most banks make a profit by lending money received from depositors and collecting interest on the loans. The bank keeps only a fraction of

---

margin call demand by a broker that investors pay back loans made for stocks purchased on margin

bank run persistent and heavy demands by a bank's depositors, creditors, or customers to withdraw money

PHOTO: Bettmann/Getty Images; TEXT: 1929: The Year of the Great Crash, by William K. Klingman. Copyright © 1989 by Harper and Row, Publishers. With excerpts from Life with Groucho, by Arthur Marx. Copyright © 1954 by Simon and Schuster.

PHOTO: Bettmann/Getty Images; TEXT:(1)Public Papers of the Presidents of the United States: Herbert Hoover: March 4 to December 31, 1929. Washington, D.C.: United States Government Printing Office, 1974; (2)Hoover, Herbert. Address, March 8, 1930. Congressional Record. Proceedings and Debates of the Second Session of the Seventy-First Congress. v. LXXII, part 8. 1930; (3)Hoover, Herbert. "Campaign Speech, October 22, 1928." The Public Papers of the Presidents of the United States: Herbert Hoover. Washington: United States Government Printing Office, 1929.

depositors' money in reserve, and usually that reserve is enough to meet the bank's needs. If too many people withdraw their money, however, the bank will collapse. By 1932, about one in four banks in the United States had gone out of business.

✓ **CHECK FOR UNDERSTANDING**

1. **Describing** What economic choices caused the economy to become unstable in the late 1920s?
2. **Identifying Cause and Effect** How did the stock market crash play into the chain of events that led to the Great Depression?

Herbert Hoover's Political Philosophy

GUIDING QUESTION

How did President Hoover's governing philosophy influence his efforts to combat the Great Depression?

On Friday, October 25, 1929, President Herbert Hoover declared that "the fundamental business of the country . . . is on a sound and prosperous basis." On March 7, 1930, he told the press that "the worst effects of the crash upon employment will have passed during the next sixty days." Critics derided his optimism as conditions worsened. Hoover was not oblivious to the seriousness of the situation; rather, he hoped to downplay the public's fears and to avoid more bank runs and layoffs. He urged consumers and business leaders to make rational decisions. In the end, his efforts failed to inspire the public's confidence, and the economy continued its downward slide.

Hoover believed that American "rugged individualism" would keep the economy moving and that the government should not step in to help individuals. After World War I, many European countries implemented a form of socialism, which Hoover felt contributed to their lack of economic recovery, and Hoover also believed that socialism infringed on individual liberty.

66 You cannot extend the mastery of the government over the daily working life of a people without at the same time making it the master of the people's souls and thoughts. . . . Free speech does not live many hours after free industry and free commerce die. . . . Every step of bureaucratizing of the business of our country poisons the very roots of liberalism— that is, political equality, free speech, free assembly, free press, and equality of

opportunity. It is the road not to more liberty, but to less liberty. 99

—Herbert Hoover, from a speech delivered October 22, 1928

In 1922 Hoover had written a book, *American Individualism,* explaining why the American system of individualism was the best social, political, spiritual, and economic system. His philosophical stance made it difficult for him to propose more government control.

Despite public statements that the economy was not in trouble, Hoover was worried. He organized a series of conferences, bringing together heads of banks, railroads, and other big businesses, as well as labor leaders and government officials, to come up with solutions. Industry leaders pledged to keep factories open and to stop slashing wages, but, by 1931, they had broken those pledges. Hoover encouraged Congress to increase funding for **public works,** or government-financed building projects, but the resulting construction jobs employed a small fraction of the millions of unemployed. The only way the government could create enough new jobs was through massive spending, which Hoover refused to do.

Someone had to pay for public works projects. If the government raised taxes, consumers would have even less money to spend, further hurting business. If the government kept taxes low and ran a budget deficit—spending more than it collected—it would have to borrow money, making less available for consumer and business loans. As the 1930 congressional elections approached, most Americans blamed the party in power for the ailing economy. The Republicans lost 49 seats and their majority in the

President Hoover and members of Congress passed a Farm Relief Bill to help fight the effects of the Depression.

---

public works projects such as highways, parks, and libraries built with public funds for public use

House of Representatives; they held on to the Senate by a single senator.

To get the economy growing, Hoover wanted to increase the money supply to help banks make loans to corporations. The president asked the Federal Reserve Board to put more currency into circulation, but the Board refused. To ease the money shortage, Hoover set up the National Credit Corporation (NCC) in October 1931. The NCC created a pool of money that allowed troubled banks to continue lending money in their communities; however, the program failed to meet the nation's needs.

In 1932 Hoover requested Congress set up the Reconstruction Finance Corporation (RFC) to make loans to businesses. By early 1932, the RFC had lent about $238 million to banks, railroads, and building-and-loan associations. However, the RFC was overly cautious and failed to increase its lending sufficiently. The economy continued its decline.

Hoover strongly opposed the federal government's participation in **relief**—money given directly to impoverished families. He believed that only state and local governments should dole out relief with any other needs being met by private charity. By the spring of 1932, however, state and local governments were running out of money, and private charities lacked the resources to handle the growing crisis.

Support for a federal relief measure increased, and Congress passed the Emergency Relief and Construction Act in July. The new act, which Hoover reluctantly signed, called for $1.5 billion for public works and $300 million in emergency loans to the states for direct relief. For the first time in American history, the federal government was supplying direct relief funds. By this time, however, the new program could not reverse the damage that had been done.

✓ CHECK FOR UNDERSTANDING

Identifying What two major strategies did President Hoover use to promote economic recovery?

Anger Leads to Change

GUIDING QUESTION

How did citizens respond to the government's efforts during the early years of the Depression?

In the months after the Wall Street crash, most Americans were resigned to bad economic news. By 1931, however, many were becoming increasingly discontent with the situation.

Hunger Marches and Protests

In January 1931, about 500 residents of Oklahoma City looted a grocery store, and the following month, hundreds of unemployed citizens smashed the windows of a Minneapolis grocery store and helped themselves to meat, produce, and canned goods.

Crowds began showing up at rallies and "hunger marches" organized by the American Communist Party. On December 5, 1932, in Washington, D.C., a group of about 1,200 hunger marchers chanted, "Feed the hungry, tax the rich." Police herded them into a cul-de-sac and denied them food and water. When some members of Congress insisted on the marchers' right to petition their government, the marchers made their way to Capitol Hill.

The hungry poor were not the only people who began to protest conditions during the Depression. During the agricultural boom that took place during World War I, many farmers had heavily mortgaged their land to pay for seed, equipment, and food for livestock. After the war, prices sank so low that farmers began losing money.

Between 1930 and 1934, creditors **foreclosed** on nearly one million farms, taking ownership of the land and evicting families. Some farmers began destroying their crops, desperately trying to raise prices by reducing the supply. In Nebraska farmers burned corn to heat their homes, and in Georgia dairy farmers blocked highways and stopped milk trucks, dumping the milk into ditches.

World War I veterans protested on the steps of the Capitol Building in Washington, D.C., in 1932 to force Congress to deliver promised bonus checks.

Making Connections Why were these veterans angry with the legislators?

ullstein bild Dtl./ullstein bild/Getty Images

---

relief aid in the form of money or supplies for those in need

foreclose to take possession of a property because of defaults on payments

The Bonus Marchers

After World War I, Congress had enacted a $1,000 bonus for each veteran to be distributed in 1945. In 1929 Texas congressman Wright Patman introduced a bill that would authorize early payment of these bonuses. In May 1932 several hundred Oregon veterans began marching to Washington, D.C., to lobby for passage of the legislation. As they moved eastward, other veterans joined them until they numbered about 1,000. Wearing ragged military uniforms, they trudged along the highways or rode the rails, singing old war songs. The press termed the marchers the "Bonus Army."

Once in Washington, the veterans camped in "Hoovervilles," a derisive term for shantytowns that had cropped up nationwide. The term implied that people largely blamed Hoover's inaction for the extreme poverty faced by many. At the Bonus Army camp more veterans joined the original marchers until the Bonus Army swelled to an estimated 15,000 people. President Hoover acknowledged the veterans' right to petition but refused to meet with them. When the Senate voted down the bonus bill, veterans outside the Capitol began to grumble. In a statement, Hoover said, "Congress made provision for the return home of the so-called bonus marchers who have for many weeks been given every opportunity of free assembly, free speech and free petition to the Congress." After Hoover's speech, many returned home, but some stayed on, living in the camps or squatting in vacant buildings downtown.

In late July Hoover ordered the buildings cleared. The police tried to clear out the remaining Bonus Marchers, but when an officer panicked and fired into a crowd, killing two veterans, authorities asked if Hoover could send in army troops. General Douglas MacArthur ignored Hoover's orders to clear the buildings but to leave the camps alone, instead sending in cavalry, infantry, and tanks to clear the camps. Soon, unarmed veterans were running away, pursued by some 700 soldiers. The soldiers teargassed stragglers and burned the shacks. National press coverage of troops assaulting veterans further harmed Hoover's reputation and hounded him throughout the 1932 campaign.

Although Hoover failed to resolve the economic crisis, he did more than any prior president to expand the federal government's role in the economy. The Reconstruction Finance Corporation was the first federal agency created to stimulate the economy during peacetime. The rout of the Bonus Army marchers and the lingering Depression, however, tarnished Hoover's public image.

The Rise of Roosevelt

Hoover faced Democrat Franklin Delano Roosevelt in the 1932 presidential election. Roosevelt, a distant cousin of Theodore Roosevelt, grew up in Hyde Park, New York. In his youth Franklin learned to hunt, ride horses, and sail; he also developed a lifelong commitment to conservation and a love of rural areas

PHOTO: Bettman/Getty Images in credit with Illustrated London News Ltd/Pantheon/Superstock; TEXT: Hoover, Herbert. 28 July, 1932. "Statement About the Bonus Marchers." Online by Gerhard Peters and John T. Woolley, The American Presidency Project. http://www.presidency.ucsb.edu/ws/?pid=23184.

BIOGRAPHY

ELEANOR ROOSEVELT (1884–1962)

Born Anna Eleanor Roosevelt on October 11, 1884, Eleanor was the daughter of Anna Hall and Elliot Roosevelt, the younger brother of Theodore Roosevelt. Eleanor was orphaned before the age of ten after her mother and father died within two years of each other. She and her surviving brother were raised by her maternal grandmother.

FIRST LADY Eleanor married Franklin Delano Roosevelt in 1905 and became First Lady after he was inaugurated as president in 1933. Eleanor Roosevelt transformed the role of First Lady. She traveled, toured factories and coal mines, and met with workers, then told her husband what people were thinking. She was a strong supporter of civil rights and urged him to stop discrimination in New Deal programs.

HUMAN RIGHTS ADVOCATE After President Roosevelt's death, she was appointed a delegate to the United Nations in 1946. There, she helped draft the Universal Declaration of Human Rights.

Citing Text Evidence How did Eleanor Roosevelt transform the role of First Lady?

in the United States. Roosevelt was educated at Harvard College and then gained more education at Columbia Law School. While he was continuing his studies as a Harvard student, Franklin Roosevelt became friends with former president Theodore Roosevelt's niece, Eleanor Roosevelt. Franklin and Eleanor married in 1905. Franklin Roosevelt's charming personality, his deep rich voice, and his wide smile allowed him to present a public personality that showed strong confidence and plenty of optimism. In short, Franklin Roosevelt's persona was a very good fit for a life in politics.

Roosevelt began his political career in 1910 when he was elected to the New York State Senate, where he earned a reputation as a progressive reformer. Three years later, Roosevelt became assistant secretary of the navy in the Woodrow Wilson administration. In 1920 his reputation—aided in part by his well-known and famous family name—helped him win the vice presidential nomination on the unsuccessful Democratic ticket.

After losing that election, Roosevelt temporarily withdrew from politics. The next year, in 1921, he was diagnosed with the paralyzing disease **polio.** Although there was no cure, Roosevelt began a vigorous exercise program that helped him restore muscle control and maintain strength as long as possible. By using heavy steel braces on his legs, he was able to walk short distances while leaning on a cane and with another's support. He was able to swing his legs forward from his hips. Roosevelt avoided appearing in a wheelchair in public for as long as possible.

While recovering from polio, Roosevelt depended on his wife Eleanor and his aide, Louis Howe, to keep his name prominent in the New York Democratic Party. Eleanor Roosevelt became an effective public speaker, and her efforts kept her husband's political career alive.

By the mid-1920s, Roosevelt was again active in the Democratic Party. In 1928 he ran for governor of New York. Roosevelt campaigned hard to show that his illness had not slowed him down, and he narrowly won the election. In 1930 he was reelected as New York's governor in a landslide victory. As governor, Roosevelt oversaw the creation of the first state relief agency to aid the unemployed.

Franklin Roosevelt's popularity in New York paved the way for his presidential nomination in 1932. Roosevelt's energy, serenity, and optimism gave Americans hope despite the tough economic times. When one aide commented on his attitude, Roosevelt replied, "If you had spent two years in bed trying to wiggle your big toe, after that anything else would seem easy."

In mid-June 1932, when the country was deep in the Depression, Republicans gathered in Chicago and nominated Herbert Hoover to run for a second term as president. Later that month, the Democrats also held their national convention in Chicago. When Roosevelt won the nomination, he broke with tradition by flying to Chicago to accept it in person. His speech set the tone for his campaign:

66 Let it be from now on the task of our Party to break foolish traditions. . . . [I]t is inevitable that the main issue of this campaign should revolve about . . . a depression so deep that it is without precedent. . . . Republican leaders not only have failed in material things, they have failed in national vision, because in disaster they have held out no hope. . . . I pledge you, I pledge myself, to a new deal for the American people. 99

–speech delivered to the Democratic National Convention, July 2, 1932

From that point forward, Roosevelt's policies for ending the Depression became known as the New Deal. Roosevelt's confidence that he could make things better contrasted sharply with Herbert Hoover's apparent failure to do anything effective. On Election Day, Roosevelt won in a landslide, winning the electoral vote in all but six states.

✓ CHECK FOR UNDERSTANDING

1. **Summarizing** How did some citizens respond to the government's efforts during the early years of the Depression?

2. **Analyzing** What characteristics did Roosevelt have that made him popular with Americans?

LESSON ACTIVITIES

1. **Argumentative Writing** Suppose you are a Bonus Army marcher. Write a letter to MacArthur questioning his decision to defy Hoover and clear the Bonus Army camps.

2. **Presenting** Work in small groups to prepare a short theater piece in which workers, farmers, and veterans meet with a member of Congress to express their needs and plead for help. Set your piece within the context of the Great Depression, and make reasoned arguments for the positions of both the unemployed and the member of Congress.

polio abbreviated term for poliomyelitis, an acute infectious disease affecting the skeletal muscles, often resulting in permanent disability and deformity

(b) Roosevelt, Franklin D. In Sunstein, Cass R. The Second Bill of Rights: FDR's Unfinished Revolution and Why We Need It More Than Ever. New York: Basic Books, 2004; (t)Roosevelt, Franklin D. 1932. Address Accepting the Presidential Nomination at the Democratic National Convention in Chicago, July 2, 1932. Hyde Park: Franklin D. Roosevelt Library and Presidential Museum, U.S. National Archives and Records Administration.

03

Turning Point: The Stock Market and the New Deal

? COMPELLING QUESTION

Was the Stock Market Crash of 1929 a turning point?

Plan Your Inquiry

In this lesson, you will investigate the stock market crash and its aftereffects.

DEVELOP QUESTIONS

Developing Questions About the Stock Market Crash Read the Compelling Question for this lesson. Think about the immediate and long-term effects of the stock market crash. Consider, too, the responses made and policies adopted by President Herbert Hoover and President Franklin Delano Roosevelt. Then, develop a list of Supporting Questions to help you answer the Compelling Question in this lesson.

APPLY HISTORICAL TOOLS

Analyzing Primary Sources You will work with a variety of primary sources in this lesson. These sources focus on the effects of the stock market crash as well as the differing responses of two U.S. presidents. As you read, use a graphic organizer like the one below to record information about the sources that will help you examine them and check for historical understanding. Note ways in which each source helps you answer your Supporting Questions.

Supporting Questions	Primary Source	What this source tells me about....	Questions the source leaves unanswered
	A		
	B		
	C		
	D		
	E		

After you analyze the sources, you will:

- use the evidence from the sources
- communicate your conclusions
- take informed action

Background Information

Throughout the 1920s, the stock market climbed steadily in value. Recall that the stock market is where investors buy and sell shares in companies. Only a small percentage of Americans actually owned stock during this time; however, many people saw the growth of the stock market as an indicator of the nation's economic health and success. So when the stock market started to slide, people began to worry—and then panic.

By 1929, risky lending and investing practices had shaken faith in the market. In September professional investors sensed danger and started selling their stocks. When other investors did the same, the price of stocks declined rapidly. The stock market fully "crashed" in October 1929. Stock prices fell so fast that they were worth far less than the money investors had borrowed to purchase stock in the first place. On October 29 almost 16 million shares of stock were sold, and about $14 billion of their value disappeared. As the economy collapsed, people rushed to take out their savings, but the banks closed their doors. Other businesses soon followed, and millions of people lost their jobs. The Great Depression had begun.

» A crowd gathers around the closed American Union Bank in New York City, on April 26, 1932.

National Archives and Records Administration.

Stock Prices, 1920–1932

Throughout the 1920s, stock market prices—and values—rose steadily. Hoping to get rich quick, more Americans started to buy stocks. Many bought stocks on credit, which falsely inflated the value of the stocks. In 1929 investors started to realize that their stocks were not worth as much as they thought. They rushed to sell. As a result, on October 29, the value of the **Dow Jones Industrial Average** dropped by 10 percent.

The graph below is taken from data collected by Standard & Poor's *Security Price Index Record*. You can see the sharp decline that is marked by that dramatic drop in October. By mid-November, the market price of stocks had dropped by more than one-third. Some $30 billion was lost, a sum roughly equal to the total wages that Americans earned in 1929. As the economy weakened, stocks continued to drop into the 1930s.

PRIMARY SOURCE : GRAPH

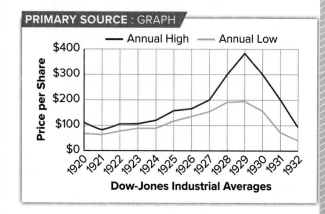

Dow-Jones Industrial Averages

Dow Jones Industrial Average an index, or tool, that measures the performance of the stocks of 30 large companies

EXAMINE THE SOURCE

1. **Interpreting** Look at the labels on the x-axis and y-axis. What do the lines in this line graph represent?

2. **Analyzing** How does the graph change in 1929? What does that indicate?

A Collapsing Financial System

Today, stocks can be traded online. In the 1920s and 1930s, investors had to buy and sell stocks through a **broker,** or agent who manages stock sales. The New York Stock Exchange (NYSE) formed as an agreement among 24 brokers in May 1792. By 1865, it had become the busiest financial exchange center in the United States. That year, it found a permanent home in the building at 11 Wall Street. In the days leading up to the crash, investors rushed to the NYSE wanting to sell their stocks. The days following saw many people milling outside the NYSE, waiting to trade their stocks and recover whatever money they could.

PRIMARY SOURCE : PHOTOGRAPH

broker an agent who negotiates an exchange between a buyer and a seller

EXAMINE THE SOURCE

1. **Describing** What do you see in the photograph? Describe the people, location, and other elements of the image.

2. **Analyzing Perspectives** What do you think the photographer wants to show with this image?

New York Daily News Archive/Getty Images

C

Number of Bank Failures

As confidence in the economy fell, people lined up outside banks with suitcases and paper bags, desperate to withdraw their money. By March 1933, bank runs had caused more than 4,000 banks to collapse, in turn wiping out individual savings accounts. In response, President Roosevelt signed the Banking Act of 1933. This act included the creation of the Federal Deposit Insurance Corporation (FDIC), which **insures** bank deposits. This graph shows the reduction in bank failures that occurred after the new legislation was implemented.

PRIMARY SOURCE : GRAPH

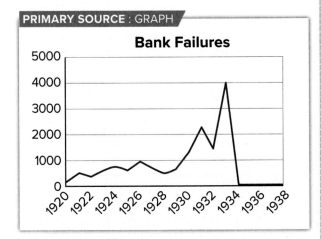

Bank Failures

Source: John R. Walter, *Depression-Era Bank Failures: The Great Contagion or the Great Shakeout?*

insure to cover financial losses

EXAMINE THE SOURCE

1. **Interpreting** How does the graph change in the periods from 1920 to 1929, from 1929 to 1933, and after?

2. **Analyzing** What does this data suggest about the economy and the experiences of Americans during each period?

D

"Put People to Work"

In 1932 Franklin D. Roosevelt campaigned on the promise to extend unemployment and farm relief and to put people back to work. His first Inaugural Address expressed a belief in finding ways to solve the economic problems ahead.

PRIMARY SOURCE : SPEECH

66 So, first of all, let me assert my firm belief that the only thing we have to fear is fear itself—nameless, unreasoning, unjustified terror which paralyzes needed efforts to convert retreat into advance. In every dark hour of our national life a leadership of frankness and vigor has met with that understanding and support of the people themselves which is essential to victory. . . .

In such a spirit on my part and on yours we face our common difficulties. . . . Values have shrunken to fantastic levels; taxes have risen; our ability to pay has fallen; government of all kinds is faced by serious curtailment of income; the means of exchange are frozen in the currents of trade; the withered leaves of industrial enterprise lie on every side; farmers find no markets for their produce; the savings of many years in thousands of families are gone.

More important, a host of unemployed citizens face the grim problem of existence, and an equally great number toil with little return. Only a foolish optimist can deny the dark realities of the moment.

. . . Our greatest primary task is to put people to work. . . . It can be accomplished in part by direct recruiting by the Government itself, treating the task as we would treat the emergency of a war, but at the same time, through the employment, accomplishing greatly needed projects to stimulate and reorganize the use of our natural resources. 99

–Franklin Delano Roosevelt, from his first Inaugural Address, March 4, 1933

EXAMINE THE SOURCE

1. **Explaining** What problems does Roosevelt identify?

2. **Drawing Conclusions** What does he see as the biggest problem? How does he intend to solve it?

Roosevelt, Franklin D. "First Inaugural Address," March 4, 1933.

Social Welfare Expenditures Under Public Programs

When President Roosevelt took office in 1933, he launched the New Deal, a package of programs aimed at relieving hardship and stabilizing the economy. The New Deal launched many social welfare benefits—including social security, unemployment insurance, food stamps, and subsidized housing—that still exist today. These programs are intended to guarantee a minimum level of income to people who might otherwise be unable to support themselves. As a result of the New Deal, government expenses on public services rose dramatically, and the relationship between citizens and the federal government changed fundamentally. Roosevelt initiated a second package of reforms, called the Second New Deal, in 1935.

PRIMARY SOURCE : GRAPH

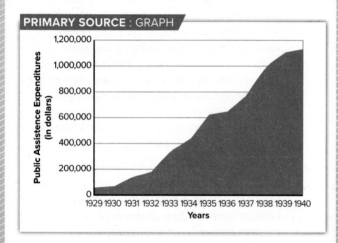

Source: *Historical Statistics of the United States*

EXAMINE THE SOURCE

1. **Making Inferences** What do you suppose the graph looked like before 1929? Explain.

2. **Evaluating** Roosevelt's New Deal programs began in 1933 and 1935. What relationship between those programs and public spending does the graph support?

Your Inquiry Analysis

EVALUATE SOURCES AND USE EVIDENCE

Reflect back to the Compelling Question and the Supporting Questions you developed at the beginning of this lesson.

1. **Gathering Sources** Refer back to the Graphic Organizer you created as you read through the sources. How did each source help you answer the Supporting Questions you wrote? What information do you still need to answer your Supporting Questions and where might you find it?

2. **Evaluating Sources** Looking at the sources that help you answer the Supporting Questions, evaluate the reliability of each source. Consider the source and implications of the quantitative data as well as how that data correlates to events about which you have learned. What factors influenced Roosevelt's perspective on conditions in the country?

3. **Comparing and Contrasting** Compare and contrast two of the sources in this lesson more closely. How does each relate to the stock market crash? What does each show or say about life before and after 1929?

COMMUNICATE CONCLUSIONS

Analyzing Information Work with a partner to analyze the data and information provided by the sources. Share your Supporting Questions and your responses to the graphic organizer. Then, discuss whether you have sufficient evidence to designate 1929 as a turning point in American history. Together, state a clear position in response to the Compelling Question. Identify the two most significant pieces of evidence that you believe supports this position. Change partners and take turns sharing your response and evidence with your new partner.

TAKE INFORMED ACTION

Evaluating Benefits and Drawbacks of Social Welfare Programs Public funding for social welfare programs remains a hotly debated topic today—for continuing or expanding current programs or for creating new ones, such as a universal healthcare system. Ask yourself: What does the federal government owe to its citizens and where do its obligations end? Brainstorm a few ideas. Then, investigate one current or proposed social welfare program. Write a letter to a Congressional representative in which you express your support or opposition to the program and explain your reasoning based on considerations of need and practicality as well as on your ideological views about government.

04
Life During the Great Depression

READING STRATEGY

Key Ideas and Details As you read, use a graphic organizer like the one below to describe the effects of the Depression.

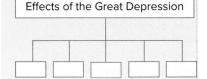

Effects of the Great Depression

Struggling to Get By

GUIDING QUESTION

How did economic changes affect everyday life during the 1930s?

The Depression grew steadily worse during President Hoover's administration. In 1930 1,352 banks suspended operations across the nation, more than twice the number of bank failures in 1929. In 1932 alone some 30,000 companies went out of business, and by 1933, roughly one-fourth of the workforce was unemployed. Of those who were employed, one-third could only find part-time jobs.

The jobless often went hungry. When possible, they stood in breadlines for free food or lined up outside soup kitchens. People who could not pay their rents or mortgages lost their homes. Some, paralyzed by fear and humiliation, did not move and were evicted by court officers called **bailiffs.**

Throughout the country, newly homeless people put up shacks on unused or public lands. They built shantytowns, which they called Hoovervilles after the president they blamed for their plight. In search of work or a better life, many homeless, unemployed Americans began walking, hitchhiking, or, most often, "riding the rails" across the country. These wanderers, called **hoboes,** would sneak into open boxcars on freight trains. Hundreds of thousands of people, mostly boys and young men, wandered from place to place in this way.

Impacts on Immigrants

The Depression also caused many immigrants to return to their native countries. In some cases, this repatriation was voluntary as jobs became scarce. The Filipino Repatriation Act of 1935 offered Filipino residents in the United States free transportation back to the Philippines. The act was not without its problems. It paid for the transportation of single adults, which forced families to split up, and strict immigration quotas meant it was very difficult to reunite families afterwards.

In other cases, repatriation was forced. The federal government launched repatriation drives to send poor immigrants back to their home countries and stepped up efforts to deport immigrants who had violated the law. In the Southwest, federal officials rounded up Mexicans, often without regard to their citizenship status, and forcibly returned them to Mexico. Although estimates vary, historians believe that during the Mexican Repatriation, between 500,000 and 2 million people of Mexican heritage, perhaps more than half American citizens, were forced to move to Mexico. Hispanics were one of the most visible immigrant minorities remaining after the immigration laws of the 1920s had restricted immigration from other nations.

In 2005 the California State legislature issued an apology to all those who had been affected by the Mexican Repatriation, acknowledging the impact these actions had on many people, immigrants and citizens alike:

---

bailiffs minor officers of the courts

hoboes a homeless and usually penniless wanderer

> Beginning in 1929, government authorities . . . in California and throughout the United States undertook an aggressive program to forcibly remove persons of Mexican ancestry from the United States. . . . Throughout California, massive raids were conducted on Mexican-American communities, resulting in the clandestine removal of thousands of people, many of whom were never able to return to the United States, their country of birth. . . . These raids targeted persons of Mexican ancestry, with authorities and others indiscriminately characterizing these persons as 'illegal aliens' even when they were United States citizens or permanent residents. **"**

—"Apology Act for the 1930s Mexican Repatriation Program," 2005

Both Mexican Repatriation and the Filipino Repatriation Act were meant to control illegal immigration. However, it is debatable whether the policies actually had this result.

The Indian Reorganization Act was also passed around this time. Also known as the Wheeler-Howard Act of 1934, the law loosened federal control of Native American affairs by instituting tribal self-government, returning lands to tribal control, and providing funding for economic development and educational opportunities.

The Dust Bowl

Already suffering before the Great Depression, farmers soon faced a new disaster. The Great Plains tended to be arid and experienced high wind speeds. Topsoil was held in place by deep rooted prairie grasses that preserved moisture in times of low rainfall. The Homestead Act encouraged large-scale settlement of the region, and tractors and combines were widely used. As a result, much of the Great Plains were extensively deep-plowed, making the topsoil susceptible to rapid erosion.

Erosion was not a problem at first, as the Great Plains experienced higher than normal rainfall from the late 1800s to the 1920s. But many farmers left their fields uncultivated when crop prices fell in the 1920s. At the same time, temperatures climbed and rainfall declined, so when a severe drought hit in the early 1930s, there was nothing to anchor the soil, and it turned to dust. Human and physical geographic factors had combined to create a disaster.

Winds blew the arid soil aloft, blackening the sky for hundreds of miles. Dust buried crops and livestock. Humans and animals caught outdoors sometimes died of suffocation when the dust filled their lungs. During most of the 1930s, an average of 50 dust storms a year hit the Plains.

Some farmers managed to hold on to their land, but others were not so lucky. If their land was mortgaged,

A dust storm approaching Stratford, Texas, April 18, 1935

Making Generalizations How does this photo illustrate the Depression experience of some Americans?

PHOTO: Photo by George E. Marsh, NOAA, Dept. of Commerce; TEXT: California State Legislature. 2005. Apology Act for the 1930s Mexican Repatriation Program, Title 2, Division 1, Chapter 8.5, Article 8721, effective January 1, 2006.

the loss of crops meant that they could not pay the mortgage payments and had to turn their property over to the banks. Nearly penniless, many families headed west, hoping for a better life in California. With a milder climate and longer growing season, California looked like a haven to the farming families fleeing the Dust Bowl. However, in California their struggles continued. Many migrants—called "Okies" because most were from Oklahoma—were turned away at California's borders. Those who did make it settled in Hoovervilles and competed with each other for too few jobs. While Okies took up some of the jobs recently vacated by repatriated Mexicans and Mexican Americans, the effects of the Depression and the large numbers of migrants drove down wages for farm workers and severely limited the number of jobs available.

Many of Roosevelt's advisers believed that both farmers and businesses were suffering because prices were too low and production too high. To help the nation's farmers, Congress passed the Agricultural Adjustment Act, which was based on a simple idea that prices for farm goods were low because farmers had been growing too much food since they increased production capacities for World War I. Under this act, the government's Agricultural Adjustment Administration (AAA) would pay farmers not to raise certain livestock, grow certain crops, and produce dairy products. Over the next two years, farmers withdrew millions more acres from cultivation and received more than $1 billion in support payments. The program met its goal, although raising food prices in a depression drew harsh criticism.

Not all farmers benefited from the program. Thousands of tenant farmers, many of them African Americans, lost their jobs and homes when landlords took their fields out of production. The Agricultural Adjustment Administration had paid landowners for what they did not produce. Those landowners were then supposed to distribute the funds to tenant farmers affected by the program, but most landlords kept the funds for themselves.

The Southern Tenant Farmers Union formed to help tenant farmers and led protests to force landlords to give tenant farmers their portion of AAA funds. The union had been started by both African American and white farmers and was racially integrated during a time when most unions would not accept African Americans. However, this meant that the union faced more harassment and violence than other similar unions did.

In June 1933 the government turned its attention to manufacturing with the National Industrial Recovery Act (NIRA). This law authorized the National Recovery Administration (NRA) to suspend antitrust laws and allowed business, labor, and government to cooperate with rules, or codes of fair competition, for each industry. Codes set prices, established minimum wages, shortened workers' hours to create more jobs, permitted unionization, and helped businesses develop industry-wide rules of fair competition. The NRA revived a few industries, but the codes were difficult to administer. Employers disliked that the NRA allowed workers to form unions, and they also argued that paying minimum wages forced them to raise prices. After the NRA began, industrial production continued to fall. The Supreme Court declared the NRA unconstitutional in 1935.

 CHECK FOR UNDERSTANDING

Summarizing How did economic changes affect everyday life during the 1930s?

Arts and Entertainment

GUIDING QUESTION

In what ways did culture reflect the Depression experience?

The hard times of the 1930s led many Americans to try to escape their worries temporarily through entertainment. Most people could scrape together the money to go to the movies, or they could sit with their families and listen to one of the many radio programs broadcast across the country.

Movies and radio programs grew increasingly popular. During the 1930s, more than 60 million Americans went to the movies each week. Child stars delighted viewers, and comedies provided a relief from daily worries. The Marx Brothers amused audiences in such films as *Animal Crackers*. Walt Disney produced the first feature-length animated film, *Snow White and the Seven Dwarfs*, in 1937.

Serious films often celebrated ordinary people and the values of small-town America. In *Mr. Smith Goes to Washington*, Jimmy Stewart played a decent but naive senator who refuses to compromise his principles and exposes the corruption of some of his colleagues. Although few movies portrayed the hard times of the era, dramas tended to show heroes, often regular people, standing up to corruption or powerful forces. These films resonated because they relieved the helplessness many felt during the Depression, and portrayed characters like the audience as victims of corruption among the wealthy and powerful.

In 1939 MGM produced *The Wizard of Oz,* and that same year, Vivien Leigh and Clark Gable attracted large audiences in *Gone with the Wind*, a Civil War epic that won nine Academy Awards. The movie promoted an idealized version of American slavery, but also offered Hattie McDaniel the opportunity to become the first African American to win an Academy Award.

While movies captured the imagination, radio offered both information and entertainment. Tens of millions listened to the radio daily. Comedians such as Jack Benny were popular, as were the adventures of

In *Young Corn*, 1931, Grant Wood presents an idealized vision of the American landscape.

Analyzing Perspectives Why do you think Grant Wood chose a vision of the American landscape that was in such sharp contrast to the reality of rural Midwestern life in the 1930s?

superheroes such as the Green Hornet. Daytime dramas continued their story lines from day to day. One such program, *The Guiding Light*, presented the personal struggles of middle-class families. Often sponsored by makers of laundry soaps, these dramas became known as soap operas. Radio also exposed listeners to a variety of musical styles, such as songs from movies and Broadway musicals, swing music, and country.

Literature

Literature flourished during the 1930s. Writers and artists tried to portray life around them, and novelists developed new writing techniques. In *The Sound and the Fury*, William Faulkner showed what characters are thinking and feeling using a stream of consciousness technique, and through this, he exposed hidden attitudes of the residents of a fictional Mississippi county. Another Southern writer named Thomas Wolfe used his own life to examine the theme of artistic creation in his powerful novels, including *Look Homeward, Angel*. In her novel *Their Eyes Were Watching God*, author Zora Neale Hurston referenced many aspects of African American folk culture, using her work as an ethnographer for the Works Progress Administration (WPA) as inspiration for her writing.

Perhaps no writer did more to capture the Depression than reporter and novelist John Steinbeck. Steinbeck focused on the rural poor, particularly agricultural workers and farmers, and created a sense of realism with rich, detailed descriptions. Steinbeck's writings added depth to journalists' reports of poverty

and misfortune and evoked sympathy for his characters. In *The Grapes of Wrath* (1939), Steinbeck describes the experiences of the Joad family who headed to California after losing their farm in the Dust Bowl.

Photography and Painting

Photographers roamed the nation with the new 35-millimeter cameras seeking new subjects. In 1936 *TIME* magazine publisher Henry Luce introduced *LIFE*, a weekly photojournalism magazine that enjoyed instant success. The striking pictures of photojournalists Dorothea Lange and Margaret Bourke-White showed how the Great Depression affected average Americans.

Lange photographed homeless people in San Francisco and poor migrant agricultural workers in California's Central Valley. Her most famous photo, "Migrant Mother" (1936), depicts a sad, weary woman with three of her seven children.

Like Lange, Margaret Bourke-White was a master at using photography to capture the era's ironies and contrasts. In 1937 *LIFE* magazine carried one of her most famous photographs. It showed a line of poor African American flood victims waiting for help in front of a billboard that declared "World's Highest Standard of Living" and showed a white family happily driving a car.

Painters of the 1930s included Thomas Hart Benton and Grant Wood, whose styles were referred to as the regionalist school. Their work emphasized traditional American values, especially those of the rural Midwest and South. Wood's best-known painting is *American Gothic*, which portrays a stern farmer and his daughter in front of their humble farmhouse. The portrait pays tribute to no-nonsense Midwesterners while gently making fun of their severity.

✓ **CHECK FOR UNDERSTANDING**

Making Connections In what ways did culture reflect the Depression experience?

LESSON ACTIVITIES

1. **Informative/Explanatory Writing** Choose a figure from Depression-era movies, radio, or literature. Write a one-page essay describing your choice. Give a brief overview of his or her career and explain how he or she was significant. Research as needed.

2. **Presenting** Work in groups of four to research, write, and present brief monologues describing the effect of the Great Depression. You may each play the role of a business owner, an unemployed worker, an "Okie," an immigrant, a radio or movie star, or any other person of the time. Ask your classmates to take notes for a class discussion. Prepare at least two questions for each character presented.

Print Collector/Hulton Archive/Getty Images

05
The First New Deal

(t)Roosevelt, Franklin D. "First Inaugural Address." March 4, 1933. (b)Franklin D. Roosevelt, Address at Oglethorpe University, May 22, 1932, The Franklin D. Roosevelt Presidential Library and Museum.

READING STRATEGY

Analyzing Key Ideas and Details As you read about Roosevelt's first three months in office, complete a time line like the one below to record the major problems addressed during this time.

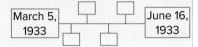

Projecting Confidence

GUIDING QUESTION

How did New Deal legislation try to stabilize the nation's banks?

Franklin Roosevelt won the presidency in November 1932, but the economy grew worse between the election and his inauguration. Unemployment continued to rise and bank runs increased. People feared that Roosevelt would abandon the **gold standard** and reduce the value of the dollar to fight the Depression. Under the gold standard, one ounce of gold equaled a set number of dollars; at this time, an ounce of gold was worth a little over 20 dollars. To reduce the value of the dollar, the United States would have to stop exchanging dollars for gold. By reducing the value of the dollar, however, the government would also leave people with less purchasing power—an unpopular concept among people still reeling from the stock market crash and a loss of funds.

Many Americans and foreign investors with deposits in American banks decided to take their money out and convert it to gold before it lost its value. Across the nation people stood in long lines with paper bags and suitcases, waiting to withdraw their money from banks. By March 1933, more than 4,000 banks had collapsed, wiping out nine million savings accounts. In 38 states, governors declared **bank holidays**—closing the remaining banks before bank runs could put them out of business.

By the day of Roosevelt's inauguration, most of the nation's banks were closed, and one in four workers was unemployed. Roosevelt knew he had to restore the nation's confidence. "First of all," he declared in his Inaugural Address, "let me assert my firm belief that the only thing we have to fear is fear itself. . . . This nation asks for action, and action now!"

Roosevelt and his advisers came into office bursting with ideas about how to end the Depression. The president had an agenda that matched his political ideology but he was not afraid to stretch his goals as well. He argued, "The country needs bold, persistent experimentation. . . . Above all, try something." Roosevelt sent bill after bill to Congress. Between March 9 and June 16, 1933—which came to be called the Hundred Days—Congress passed 76 laws in total, including 15 major acts to resolve the economic crisis. These programs made up what would be called the First New Deal. This idea of informally marking the accomplishments of a new president during the first hundred days in office has since been applied to subsequent administrations.

Although Roosevelt alone made the final decision about what policies and programs to pursue, he depended on his advisers for new ideas. Roosevelt deliberately chose advisers who disagreed with one another because he wanted to hear many different points of view.

One influential group of advisers believed that if government agencies worked with businesses to regulate wages, prices, and production, they could lift the economy out of the Depression. A second group of advisers, who distrusted big business and felt business leaders had caused the Depression, wanted government planners to run key parts of the economy.

---

gold standard a monetary system in which the value of currency is defined in terms of gold

bank holidays closing of banks during the Great Depression to avoid bank runs

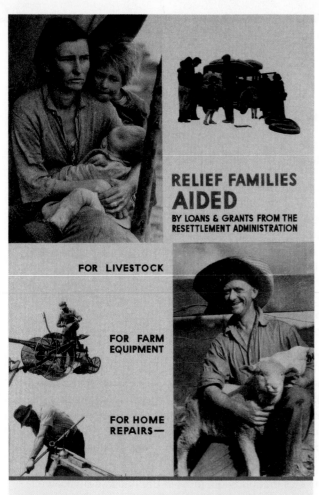

A poster from the United States Resettlement Administration advertises relief services to aid families and farmers, a result of the Federal Emergency Relief Act that passed during Roosevelt's Hundred Days.

Evaluating Why might the photograph "Migrant Mother" by Dorothea Lange be a good choice for this poster?

A third group of advisers supported former president Woodrow Wilson's "New Freedom" philosophy of restraining the overall power of the federal government. They wanted Roosevelt to break up big companies and allow competition to set wages, prices, and production levels. This group of advisers also thought that the government should impose regulations to keep economic competition fair.

Regulating the Banking System

Roosevelt knew that very few of the new programs would work as long as the nation's banks remained closed and that he had to restore people's confidence in the banking system. Within a week of his taking office, the Emergency Banking Relief Act was passed.

The new law required federal examiners to survey the nation's banks and issue Treasury Department licenses to those that were financially sound. On March 12 1933 Roosevelt addressed the nation by radio. Sixty

million people listened to this first of many **"fireside chats."** He said, "I assure you that it is safer to keep your money in a reopened bank than under the mattress." When banks opened on March 13, deposits far outweighed withdrawals, and the banking crisis was over.

As banking system confidence strengthened, Roosevelt began using powers granted in the Emergency Banking Relief Act to take the dollar off the gold standard. In June Congress went further by passing a law that made all contracts payable only in legal tender. No one could demand gold in payment or use gold to pay for things.

Almost immediately, inflation began. This was exactly what the president wanted because his purpose for going off the gold standard was to cause inflation. Roosevelt called it "reflation" because he believed the dollar was overvalued from decades of deflation, and that inflation would help people in debt.

When inflation occurs, money loses value. Debts become easier to pay because the money owed is not worth as much as when the loan was issued. At the same time, inflation causes prices to go up. As Roosevelt had hoped, the increase in prices earned more money for farmers and others who were suffering from low prices for their goods. The United States stayed off the gold standard for about nine months, until the administration thought the dollar's value had fallen far enough. In early 1934 Roosevelt set a new price for the gold standard in which one ounce of gold equaled 35 U.S. dollars.

Many of the president's advisers wanted to go further and pushed for new regulations for banks and the stock market. Roosevelt supported the Securities Act of 1933 and the Banking Act of 1933, commonly known as the Glass-Steagall Act. The Securities Act required companies that sold stocks and bonds to provide complete and truthful information to investors. The Securities and Exchange Commission (SEC) was created to regulate the stock market and stop fraud. The Glass-Steagall Act separated commercial banking from investment banking. Commercial banks that handled everyday transactions could no longer risk depositors' money through stock speculation. The act also created the Federal Deposit Insurance Corporation (FDIC) to provide government insurance for bank deposits. The creation of the FDIC increased public confidence in the banking system.

In creating the FDIC and the SEC, Congress changed the historical role of state and federal governments in financial matters. Until the New Deal, the regulation of banks had been the responsibility of state governments. Today banks can have a federal charter or a state charter and are subject to both federal and state regulations. Similarly, the operation of stock markets had been generally unregulated

fireside chats radio broadcasts made by President Franklin D. Roosevelt to Americans

PHOTO: Everett Collection Inc/Alamy Stock Photo; TEXT: Roosevelt, Franklin D. Fireside Chat 1: On the Banking Crisis. March 12, 1933.

before 1933. Under the laissez-faire ideas of the late 1800s, the idea that the federal government should impose rules on a market where people met to buy and sell stocks was never seriously considered. The great crash of 1929 changed people's thinking.

The FDIC still exists today. It guarantees bank deposits up to $250,000 for all member banks and is funded by insurance premiums paid by the banks, not by taxpayer money. The FDIC supervises the operations of over 4,500 banks nationwide, making sure they are sound and comply with all financial regulations and consumer protection laws. You can tell if a bank is FDIC insured by looking for the "Member FDIC" logo on bank windows, paper documents, and websites.

The SEC also still regulates the operations of the nation's stock markets, inspecting stock brokers, investment advisors, and agencies that rate stocks. It investigates reports of fraud and insider trading, and works to prevent companies from misleading investors with false information. The SEC does not insure investments. Investing in companies always carries risk and investors can lose their money. The SEC's role is not to protect investments, but to prevent fraud and make sure investors are given correct information so they can make good investment decisions.

Debt Relief

Many Americans cut back on their spending because they were terrified of losing their homes and farms. Roosevelt responded by introducing policies to help Americans with their debts. For example, the Home Owners' Loan Corporation (HOLC) bought the mortgages of home owners who were behind in their payments. It then restructured the loans with longer repayment terms and lower interest rates. The Farm Credit Administration (FCA) helped farmers refinance their mortgages, saving millions of farms from foreclosure. Although the FCA may have slowed economic recovery by making less money available to lend to more efficient businesses, it did help many desperate and impoverished people hold onto their land. Both the HOLC and the FCA represented a dramatic expansion of the federal government's role in the economy. Never before had the federal government been involved in helping people with their mortgages.

Not everyone benefited equally from these mortgage relief programs, however. African Americans who were trying to purchase their own homes were often subjected to unequal treatment by banks and community laws. This meant that banks sometimes refused these prospective homeowners the ability to use a mortgage entirely or only approved them for sub-prime loans with harsh terms. Such discrimination made it much more difficult for African Americans to invest in home ownership and created economic inequality that contributed to generational financial instability.

Helping Rural Areas

The New Deal led to several large-scale water management projects. These projects all served different purposes but building dams and other water management systems helped employ large amounts of unemployed workers during the Great Depression, allowed for flood control and better irrigation, and provided hydroelectric power.

The Tennessee Valley Authority (TVA) was a project that built dams to control floods, conserve forestlands, and bring electricity to rural areas. Today, TVA brings power to nearly 8 million people in a seven-state region. However, the TVA was not without its controversies. Thousands of family homes and even some towns were displaced to make room for these dams and reservoirs. Also, while the project tried to conserve the local environment, dams did impact fish migrations.

In the arid West, where water management was critical, California's Central Valley Project (CVP) was built to move water from northern California into the San Joaquin Valley to help with irrigation. This turned the valley into the agricultural region it is now. Like the TVA, the CVP also provided hydroelectric power to the region, but the massive dams interrupted salmon migrations and severely affected fish populations. Even worse, the Shasta Dam's reservoir flooded most of the land belonging to the Winnemem Wintu Native Americans. The Bonneville Dam, located on the Columbia River in Oregon, was built as a Public Works Project that provided employment and hydroelectric power. But that dam's reservoir also flooded over the villages, burial grounds, and fishing locations of the Columbia River Native Americans.

✓ CHECK FOR UNDERSTANDING

1. **Speculating** Why were the first hundred days so important for President Roosevelt?
2. **Summarizing** How did the government restore confidence in the banking system?

Relief Programs

GUIDING QUESTION

How did New Deal programs differ from President Hoover's attempts to fight the Depression?

Many of President Roosevelt's advisers believed adjusting prices and providing debt relief would solve the Depression. Others maintained that the Depression's fundamental cause was low consumption. The supporters of the low consumption theory thought that getting money into the hands of needy individuals would be the fastest way to fix the economy. Because neither Roosevelt nor his advisers wanted to give

The TVA, 1940

The Tennessee Valley Authority (TVA) was created to help control flooding, bring electricity to rural areas, and improve the quality of life in the region.

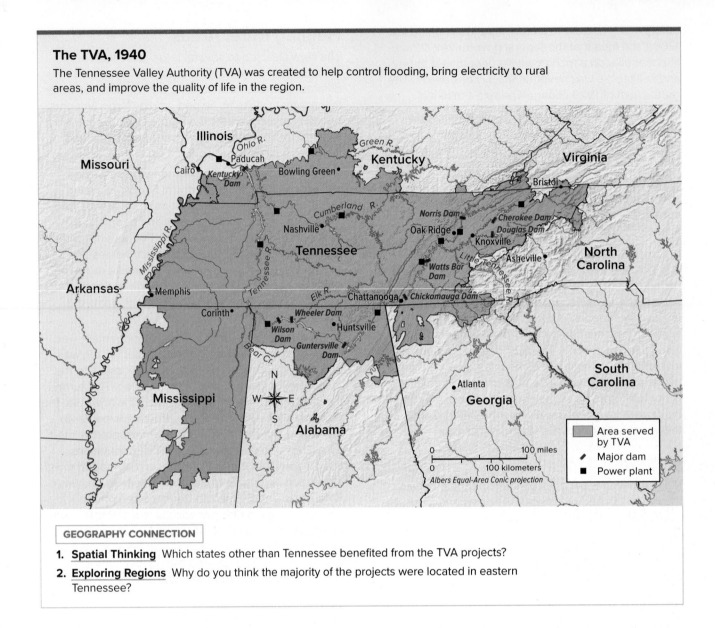

GEOGRAPHY CONNECTION

1. **Spatial Thinking** Which states other than Tennessee benefited from the TVA projects?
2. **Exploring Regions** Why do you think the majority of the projects were located in eastern Tennessee?

money to the unemployed, they supported work programs to hire the unemployed.

The decision to create federal work programs marked yet another change in the historical roles of state and federal government. Before the Depression, government relief programs had been rare and, when set up, had always been funded and managed by state and local governments. The first time relief aid had been sent from the federal government to state governments to help fund programs for jobs was during the Hoover administration. But the New Deal went even further by creating several federally managed job programs that bypassed the state governments entirely.

New Deal Agencies

The most highly praised New Deal work relief program was the Civilian Conservation Corps (CCC). The CCC offered unemployed young men from 18 to 25 years old the opportunity to work under the direction of the forestry service planting trees, fighting forest fires, and building reservoirs.

The young men lived in camps near their work areas and earned $30 a month, $25 of which was sent directly to their families. The average CCC worker returned home after six to twelve months better nourished and with greater self-respect. CCC programs also taught more than 40,000 of their recruits to read and write. By the time the CCC closed down in 1942, it had put 3 million young men to work outdoors—including 80,000 Native Americans, who helped reclaim land they had once possessed. After a second Bonus Army march on Washington in 1933, Roosevelt added some 250,000 veterans to the CCC as well.

A few weeks after authorizing the CCC, Congress established the Federal Emergency Relief Administration (FERA). Roosevelt chose Harry Hopkins, a former social worker, to run FERA. Initially, it did not create projects for the unemployed.

Instead, it gave money to state and local agencies to fund their relief projects. After meeting with Roosevelt to discuss his new job, Hopkins spent $5 million on relief projects. When critics charged that some of the projects did not make sense in the long run, Hopkins replied, "People don't eat in the long run—they eat every day."

In June 1933 Congress authorized another relief agency, the Public Works Administration (PWA). One-third of the nation's unemployed were in the construction industry. The PWA began building highways, dams, schools, and other government facilities. The PWA also insisted that contractors not discriminate against African Americans. In this way, the agency broke down some of the racial barriers in the construction trades, though it did not completely eradicate them.

By the fall of 1933, neither FERA nor the PWA had reduced unemployment significantly, and Hopkins realized that unless the federal government acted quickly, a huge number of unemployed citizens would be in severe distress once winter began. After Hopkins explained the situation, President Roosevelt authorized him to set up the Civil Works Administration (CWA).

Hiring workers directly, the CWA employed 4 million people, including 300,000 women. The agency built or improved 1,000 airports; 500,000 miles of roads; 40,000 school buildings; and 3,500 playgrounds and parks. The program spent nearly $1 billion in just five months. Although the CWA helped many people get through the winter, President Roosevelt was alarmed by how quickly the agency was spending money, and did not want Americans to get used to the federal government providing them with

jobs. Warning that the Civil Works Administration would "become a habit with the country," Roosevelt insisted that it be shut down the following spring. Hopkins summarized what the CWA had accomplished:

66 Long after the workers of CWA are dead and gone and these hard times are forgotten, their effort will be remembered by permanent useful works in every county of every state. 99

–from *Spending to Save: The Complete Story of Relief*, 1936

Effects on Native Americans

Prior to the Roosevelt administration, in the mid-1920s the U.S. government had conducted a survey on the state of Native American tribal lands. The results showed that Native Americans suffered from poverty, poor health outcomes, inadequate education, and a disconnection from mainstream American culture.

Like others throughout the country, Native Americans also experienced severe financial hardships during the Great Depression. The Roosevelt administration aimed to alleviate these struggles through the 1934 Indian Reorganization Act. Major goals of the Indian New Deal, as it later became known, included reducing federal control of tribal communities and promoting Native American self-governance, responsibility, and restoration of tradition cultures. Tribal lands that had been previously allocated to individuals or lost through the Dawes Act were now available for purchase by tribal authorities. Anthropologists and photographers were hired to document Native American cultures and

PHOTO: Herbert Gehr/The LIFE Images Collection/Getty Images; TEXT: (l)Federal Power Commission Oversight: Natural Gas Curtailment Priorities : Hearing Before the Committee on Commerce, United States Senate, Ninety-third Congress, Second Session .... United States: U.S. Government Printing Office, 1974.; (r)Hopkins, Harry L. Spending to Save: The Complete Story of Relief. New York: W. W. Norton & Company, 1936.

These members of the Civilian Conservation Corps are creating road signs for locations and directions leading to Flagstaff, Arizona.

Making Connections In what ways is this photograph a testimony to the success of the CCC?

The Tlinget people restore totem poles in the Tongass National Forest, Alaska. This work is another example of the Civilian Conservation Corps that was created by the First New Deal.

Making Connections How does this image help explain the goals of the First New Deal?

languages, and thousands of unemployed Native Americans found work with the CCC-ID, a branch of the Civilian Conservation Corps specifically created for Native Americans.

Success of the First New Deal

During his first year in office, Roosevelt convinced Congress to pass an astonishing array of legislation. The First New Deal did not restore prosperity, but it reflected Roosevelt's zeal for action and his willingness to experiment. Banks were reopened, many more people retained their homes and farms, and more people were employed. Perhaps the most important result of the First New Deal was a change in the spirit of the American people. Roosevelt's actions had inspired hope and restored Americans' faith in their nation. Writer Ervin E. Lewis captured this sense of hope, as well as the uncertainty surrounding Roosevelt's New Deal programs:

66 The fate of the 'New Deal' is up to us—as well as to our leaders. Right here is the challenge of these exciting times to every live man or woman, boy or girl. History is being made NOW. There is taking place before our very eyes a more comprehensive revolution than any we can read about in a history book. If there ever was a time when the average person could learn from personal experience how the world is run, is now. . . . Let us measure the 'New Deal' by the economic

security it will give us. This is the road we should travel. Will it bring us into the new era of abundance and abundant living for which we are ready? Will it guarantee to all of us alike, in the near future, not a bare subsistence but the nobler and richer life which our vast natural resources and our machine civilization now make possible? 99

—Ervin E. Lewis from *A Primer of the New Deal*, 1933

✓ **CHECK FOR UNDERSTANDING**

1. **Making Connections** What kinds of projects were done under New Deal relief programs? Which projects are still important today?

2. **Identifying** Which New Deal programs were specifically helpful to Native Americans? Explain.

LESSON ACTIVITIES

1. **Argumentative Writing** If you were an adviser to President Roosevelt, what ideas would you suggest to end the Depression? Provide an argument for why your ideas would work.

2. **Using Multimedia** Work with a group to create a slideshow advertising one of the programs created under the First New Deal. Use text and graphics to show what the program does and why people should join or take advantage of it.

PHOTO: National Archives and Records Administration; United States Forest Service; TEXT: Lewis, Ervin Eugene. 1933. A Primer of the New Deal: What It Means to You. Columbus (OH) and New York: American Education Press, Inc.

06

The Second New Deal

Long, Huey. In Kennedy, David M. Freedom From Fear. Oxford History of the United States, v.9. Oxford: Oxford UP, 1999.

READING STRATEGY

Analyzing Key Ideas and Details As you read about President Roosevelt's Second New Deal, complete a graphic organizer similar to this one by filling in his main legislative successes during this period.

Legislation	Provisions

Continuing the Economic Recovery

GUIDING QUESTION
How did the Wagner Act and the Social Security Act affect Americans?

President Roosevelt was tremendously popular during his first two years in office, but opposition to his policies began to grow. New Deal programs had created more than 2 million new jobs. More than 7 million workers remained unemployed, however, and the nation's total income was about half of what it had been in 1929.

Criticism from Right and Left

Roosevelt faced disagreements from both the political right and the left. The right wing believed that the New Deal regulated business too tightly. Opponents thought that it gave the federal government too much power over the states. By late 1934,conservatives increased their opposition as Roosevelt started **deficit spending,** abandoning a balanced budget and borrowing money to pay for his programs and to get the country on the path to economic stability. Many business leaders became alarmed at the growing deficit.

Some on the left, however, believed that the New Deal had not gone far enough. They wanted even more economic intervention to shift wealth from the rich to middle-income and poor Americans. One such critic was Huey Long. As governor of Louisiana, Long had championed the poor. He improved schools, colleges, and hospitals, and built roads and bridges. These **benefits** made him popular, and he built a powerful but corrupt political machine. In 1930 Long was elected to the U.S. Senate. In 1934 he established the Share Our Wealth Society to "pull down these huge piles of gold until there shall be a real job, not a little old sow-belly, black-eyed pea job but a real spending money, beefsteak and gravy, Chevrolet, Ford in the garage, new suit, Thomas Jefferson . . . red, white, and blue job for every man." Long planned to run for president in 1936.

Roosevelt also faced a challenge from Catholic priest and popular radio host Father Charles Coughlin. Once a New Deal supporter, Coughlin called for inflating the currency and nationalizing the banking system. In 1934 Coughlin organized the National Union for Social Justice, which some Democrats feared would become a new political party.

A third challenge came from California physician Francis Townsend. He proposed that the federal government pay citizens over age 60 a pension of $200 a month. Recipients would have to retire and spend the entire check each month. Townsend believed that the plan would increase spending and free up jobs for the unemployed.

The Works Progress Administration

In 1935 Roosevelt launched a series of programs, now known as the Second New Deal, to generate greater economic recovery. Among these new programs was the Works Progress Administration (WPA), the New Deal's largest public works program. Between 1935 and 1941, the WPA employed 8.5 million workers and spent $11 billion to construct about 650,000 miles of roadways, 125,000

deficit spending government practice of spending borrowed money rather than raising taxes to boost the economy

benefit something that promotes well-being or is a useful aid

Louisiana Senator Huey Long criticizes the New Deal and promotes his motto, "Every Man a King," during a nationally broadcasted speech, 1934.

public buildings; 853 airports; more than 124,000 bridges; and more than 8,000 parks.

One WPA program, called Federal Project Number One, financed artists, musicians, those working in theater, and writers. Artists created murals and sculptures for public buildings; musicians set up orchestras and smaller musical groups; playwrights, actors, and directors wrote and staged plays; and writers, including Zora Neale Hurston, recorded the stories of those who had once been enslaved and others whose voices had not often been heard.

The Supreme Court's Role

In May 1935 in *Schechter Poultry Corporation* v. *United States*, the Supreme Court struck down the authority of the National Recovery Administration. The Schechter brothers had been convicted of violating the NRA's poultry code. The Court ruled that the Constitution did not allow Congress to delegate its legislative powers to the executive branch, and therefore the NRA's codes were unconstitutional. Roosevelt worried that the ruling suggested the Supreme Court could strike down the rest of the New Deal. Roosevelt knew he needed a

new series of programs to keep voters' support. He called congressional leaders to a White House conference and angrily demanded that Congress not go home until it passed his new bills. That summer, Congress passed Roosevelt's programs.

Unionizing Workers

When the Supreme Court struck down the NRA, it also invalidated the section of the National Industrial Recovery Act (NIRA) of 1933 that gave workers the right to organize. Democrats knew that the working-class vote was key to winning reelection in 1936. They also believed that unions could help end the Depression because high union wages would give workers more money to spend, thereby boosting the economy. Opponents disagreed, arguing that high wages forced companies to charge higher prices and hire fewer people. Despite these concerns, Congress pushed ahead with new labor legislation.

In July 1935 Congress passed the National Labor Relations Act, also called the Wagner Act. This act guaranteed workers the right to unionize and bargain collectively. It also established the National Labor Relations Board (NLRB), which organized factory elections by secret ballot to determine whether workers wanted a union. The NLRB could also investigate employers' actions and stop unfair practices. The Wagner Act also set up a process called **binding arbitration,** whereby dissatisfied union members took their complaints to a neutral party who would listen to both sides and decide on the issues.

The Wagner Act led to a burst of labor activity. In 1935 John L. Lewis, leader of the United Mine Workers, helped form the Committee for Industrial Organization (CIO). The CIO set out to organize unions that included all workers, skilled and unskilled, in a particular industry. First, it focused on the automobile and steel industries, two of the largest industries in which workers were not yet unionized. Organizers used new tactics to get employers to recognize the unions. For example, during **sit-down strikes,** employees stopped work inside the factory and refused to leave. This technique prevented management from sending in replacement workers. It was a common CIO tactic for several years.

In late December 1936 the United Auto Workers (UAW), a CIO union, began a sit-down strike at General Motors' plant in Flint, Michigan. Family, friends, and others passed food and other provisions to them through windows.

66 Beds were made up on the floor of each car, the seats being removed if necessary. . . . I could not see—and I looked for it carefully—the

binding arbitration process whereby a neutral party hears arguments from two opposing sides and makes a decision that both must accept

sit-down strike method of boycotting work by sitting down at work and refusing to leave the establishment

PHOTO: Bettmann/Getty Images; TEXT: Sitting Down in Flint, Bruce Bliven. The New Republic. Vol. LXXXIX, No. 1156. January 27, 1937.

Members of the Department Store Employees Union (CIO) strike for better wages from Woolworth Company, a chain of general merchandise stores.

Drawing Conclusions What was the atmosphere outside the Woolworth store during the strike?

slightest damage done anywhere to the General Motors Corporation. The nearly completed car bodies, for example, were as clean as they would be in the salesroom, their glass and metal shining. 99

–Bruce Bliven, from "Sitting Down in Flint," *The New Republic*, January 27, 1937

Violence broke out when police launched a tear gas assault on strikers, wounding 13, but the strike held. On February 11, 1937, General Motors recognized the UAW as its employees' sole bargaining agent. The UAW became one of the most powerful unions in the United States.

U.S. Steel, the nation's largest steel producer and a long-standing opponent of unionizing, decided it did not want a repeat of General Motor's experience. In March 1937, the company recognized the CIO's steelworkers union. By 1941, the steelworkers union had won contracts throughout the industry.

Smaller steel producers did not follow suit and suffered bitter strikes. On May 30, 1937, striking Republic Steel workers tried to set a picket line in front of a mill in southeast Chicago. The protest became violent when police used tear gas, bullets, and clubs to repel the protesters. Known as the Memorial Day Massacre, the incident resulted in 10 deaths and some 90 injuries. It remains one of the most violent labor incidents in U.S. history. In the late 1930s, employees in other industries worked hard to gain union recognition from their employers. Union membership tripled from roughly 3 million in 1933 to about 9 million in 1939. In 1938 the CIO changed its name to the Congress of

Industrial Organizations and became a federation of industrial unions.

Creating Social Security

After passing the Wagner Act, Congress began work on one of the United States's most important pieces of legislation. This was the Social Security Act, which provided some financial security for older Americans, unemployed workers, and others. Roosevelt and his advisers viewed the bill primarily as an insurance measure. Workers earned the right to receive benefits because they paid special taxes to the federal government, just as they paid premiums in buying a life insurance policy. The legislation also provided modest welfare payments to others in need, including people with disabilities and poor mothers with dependent children.

Some critics did not like the fact that the money came from payroll taxes imposed on workers and employers, but to Roosevelt these taxes were crucial:

66 We put those payroll contributions there so as to give the contributors a legal, moral, and political right to collect their pensions and their unemployment benefits. With those taxes in there, no . . . politician can ever scrap my social security program. 99

–quoted in "Memorandum on Conference with FDR Concerning Social Security Taxation," 1941

What Roosevelt did not anticipate was that Congress would later borrow from the Social Security fund to pay for other programs without raising payroll taxes. The core of Social Security was the monthly retirement benefit, which people collected when they stopped working at age 65. Unemployment insurance supplied a temporary income to workers who had lost their jobs.

Social Security continues to be a part of American life today. When Americans find themselves unemployed, they can draw on their unemployment insurance from Social Security for many weeks while they look for a new job. In addition, Americans who have contributed to the Social Security system are eligible for a pension benefit when they retire. In 2019 Social Security paid those who had contributed to the program through qualifying work just under $1.4 trillion, more than 30 percent of the government's total budget.

Social Security dramatically changed the role of the federal government. It was the first example of what came to be called "entitlement" programs. An entitlement program is not simply a form of welfare or relief. It is a payment from the government that Americans are entitled to receive in part because they have paid into the system regularly with deductions from their paychecks and in part because the law imposes a requirement on the government to make the payments.

PHOTO: Bettmann/Getty Images; TEXT: Gulick, Luther. 1941. Luther Gulick's Memorandum on Conference with FDR Concerning Social Security Taxation, Summer 1941. Franklin D. Roosevelt Presidential Library, National Archives and Records Administration.

A poster from the Social Security Board, 1935

Identifying Cause and Effect How might Social Security have changed Americans' sense of personal economic security?

Social Security was controversial at the time it was passed, and it remains a source of political debate today. The Social Security Act also included provisions to exclude farm workers and domestic staff, which in effect excluded many African Americans from its benefits. Even though Americans are entitled to their Social Security payments, the federal government has borrowed against the Social Security fund in the past, and it is now forced to borrow more money to pay its Social Security obligations. Social Security established the principle that the federal government should be responsible for those who, through no fault of their own, are unable to work.

✓ CHECK FOR UNDERSTANDING

1. **Summarizing** What were some benefits of the Wagner Act and the Social Security Act for the American public?

2. **Explaining** What unanticipated development occurred that has made it necessary for the federal government to borrow money to pay out its Social Security obligations?

Roosevelt's Second Term

What impact has the New Deal legislation had on federal and state governments?

In 1936 millions of voters owed their jobs, mortgages, and bank accounts to the New Deal. Many African Americans, who had reliably voted Republican since Reconstruction, switched their allegiance to the Democratic Party. They recognized that the New Deal was working for their interests.

A Roosevelt coalition emerged, including not just the white South, but also African Americans, farmers, workers, immigrants, and women, as well as progressives and intellectuals across all groups. In the 1936 presidential election, Republican nominee Alfred Landon could not convince most voters that change was needed. Roosevelt won more than 60 percent of the popular vote.

Second Term Stumbles

Although the New Deal had popular support, the Supreme Court saw things differently. In January 1936 the Supreme Court declared the Agricultural Adjustment Act unconstitutional. Cases pending on Social Security and the Wagner Act meant that the Court might strike down other New Deal programs. Roosevelt was furious. After his reelection, he tried to change the Court's political balance. He sent Congress a bill that would increase the number of justices and allow the president to appoint an additional justice if a sitting justice who had served 10 years did not retire within six months of reaching age 70. The bill, if passed, would have allowed Roosevelt to appoint up to six new justices.

President Roosevelt's request of Congress to allow him to add additional justices sparked controversy throughout the nation. Rallies erupted in opposition and constituents flooded their congressional representatives with letters—both in support and opposition to the plan. Many accused the president of showing authoritarian tendencies and of threatening the independence of the judiciary.

Some even questioned whether he was hampering his own goals and subverting the Constitution by setting dangerous precedents for future presidents:

66 To President Roosevelt, packing the Supreme Court is merely the quickest means of achieving a desirable end. It is but a preliminary step to what the President regards as essential control over farming, working conditions and other major economic problems which he believes to be national in scope. But the step he advised Congress to take is of such a dangerous character that is has almost

PHOTO: Library of Congress Prints and Photographs Division [LC-DIG-ppmsca-07216]; TEXT: Pusey, Merlo J. 1937. The Supreme Court Crisis. New York: The Macmillan Company

completely diverted attention from the social and economic program it is designated to facilitate. **99**

–from Merlo J. Pusey, *The Supreme Court Crisis* (1937)

The **court-packing** plan, as it was called, was a major political misstep. Many Southern Democrats feared new justices would overturn segregation. African American leaders worried future justices might oppose civil rights. The Court appeared to back down, narrowly upholding the constitutionality of both the Wagner Act and the Social Security Act. Soon after, a conservative justice's resignation allowed Roosevelt to appoint a justice who supported the New Deal. Even so, the court-packing plan hurt the president's reputation and caused conservative Democrats to join Republicans to block further New Deal efforts.

In early 1937 the economy seemed to be on the verge of recovery. Industrial output was almost back to pre-Depression levels, and many people believed the worst was over. Concerned about rising debt, Roosevelt ordered the WPA and the PWA to be cut significantly. Unfortunately, he cut spending just as the first Social Security payroll taxes took $2 billion out of the economy. By the end of 1937, about two million people were out of work.

A debate over the value of government spending arose within the administration. The leaders of the WPA and the PWA cited a new economic theory called Keynesianism (KAYN • zee • uh • nih • zuhm), which held that government should spend heavily in a recession to jump-start the economy.

At first, Roosevelt was reluctant to begin deficit spending again. Some critics believed the recession proved the public was becoming too dependent on government spending. But in early 1938, with no recovery in sight, Roosevelt asked Congress for $3.75 billion for the PWA, the WPA, and other programs.

Final Reforms

One of the president's goals for his second term was to provide better housing for the nation's poor. Eleanor Roosevelt, who had toured poverty-stricken Appalachia and the rural South, strongly urged the president to do something.

Roosevelt responded with the passage of the National Housing Act, which established the United States Housing Authority. This organization received $500 million to subsidize loans to builders willing to construct low-cost housing.

In his second Inaugural Address, Roosevelt pointed out that despite progress in climbing out of the Depression, many Americans were still poor:

66 I see one-third of a nation ill-housed, ill-clad, ill-nourished. . . . The test of our progress is not whether we add more to the abundance of those who have much; it is whether we provide enough for those who have too little. **99**

–from *The Public Papers and Addresses of Franklin D. Roosevelt: The Constitution Prevails*, 1937

Roosevelt also sought to help the nation's tenant farmers. About 150,000 white and 195,000 African American tenant farmers were expelled from farms when landlords took their land out of production under the AAA. To stop this trend Congress created the Farm Security Administration to give loans to tenants so they could purchase farms. The last major piece of New Deal reform was the Fair Labor Standards Act, which abolished child labor, limited the workweek to 44 hours for most workers, and set the first federal minimum wage at 25 cents an hour.

Despite these efforts, the recession of 1937 enabled Republicans to win seats in Congress in the midterm elections of 1938. Together with conservative

Do We Want A Ventriloquist Act In The Supreme Court?

President Franklin D. Roosevelt is depicted with new judges in this 1937 cartoon, "Do We Want A Ventriloquist Act in the Supreme Court?"

Interpreting What is this political cartoon saying about Roosevelt's relationship with the United States Supreme Court?

PHOTO: Fotosearch/Archive Photos/Getty Images; TEXT: Roosevelt, Franklin D. Second Inaugural Address, January 20, 1937. Hyde Park: Franklin D. Roosevelt Library, National Archives and Records Administration.

court-packing the act of changing the political balance of power in a nation's judiciary system whereby a national leader, such as the president, appoints judges who will rule in favor of his or her policies

These African American farmers wait in a tobacco warehouse in Durham, North Carolina. The Farm Security Administration hoped to provide money to farmers so that they could continue growing crops.

Making Connections Which programs in the New Deal were created to help farmers, such as the men pictured here?

Southern Democrats, they began blocking further New Deal legislation. By 1939, the New Deal era had come to an end.

Legacy of the New Deal

The Great Depression was a major turning point in American history. This economic crisis led to the New Deal, which fundamentally changed the relationship between the American people and the federal government. The power of the federal government to intervene in the economy significantly increased. At the same time, the historical role of state governments and their relationships to the federal government began to shift as well. Increasingly the federal government took on a regulatory role that had previously been left to state governments. State governments also began to look to the federal government to help them pay for state programs and provide aid in difficult economic times.

The New Deal did not end the Depression, but it did give many Americans a stronger sense of security and stability. The New Deal tried to balance competing economic interests. Supreme Court decisions in 1937 and 1942 further increased federal power over the economy and allowed it to **mediate** between competing groups. In taking on this mediating role, the New Deal established what some have called the **broker state,** in which the government works out conflicts among different interests. Roosevelt's programs had succeeded in creating a **safety net**—safeguards and relief

programs that protected people against economic disaster. Throughout the hard times of the Depression, most Americans maintained a surprising degree of confidence in the American system.

✓ **CHECK FOR UNDERSTANDING**

1. **Identifying** What impact has New Deal legislation had on federal and state governments?

2. **Identifying Cause and Effect** How did Supreme Court decisions help increase the power of the federal government during this period?

LESSON ACTIVITIES

1. **Argumentative Writing** Write a short essay in which you evaluate Roosevelt's solution to the 1937 recession. Do you think he took the best course of action, or do you think he should have taken a different approach? Give details and reasons to support your opinions.

2. **Collaborating** In small groups, discuss the programs and reforms that were created under the New Deal. Which do you consider most important? What do you think about the objections raised by opponents of the New Deal?

mediate to attempt to resolve conflict between hostile people or groups

broker state role of the government to work out conflicts among competing interest groups

safety net something that provides security against misfortune; specifically, government relief programs intended to protect against economic disaster

Universal History Archive/Universal Images Group/Getty Images

07

Analyzing Sources: Roosevelt's Political Critics

? COMPELLING QUESTION

How did people view the New Deal?

Plan Your Inquiry

In this lesson, you will investigate critical perspectives on President Franklin D. Roosevelt and his New Deal policies and programs.

DEVELOP QUESTIONS

Developing Questions About Roosevelt and the New Deal Read the Compelling Question for this lesson. Think about the goals of specific New Deal policies and programs. Consider, too, how the New Deal might have affected different groups within the United States. Then, develop a list of Supporting Questions to help you answer the Compelling Question in this lesson.

APPLY HISTORICAL TOOLS

Analyzing Primary Sources You will work with a variety of primary sources in this lesson. These sources present critical views of President Roosevelt and the New Deal. As you read, use a graphic organizer like the one below to record information about the sources that will help you examine them and check for historical understanding. Note ways in which each source helps you answer your Supporting Questions.

Supporting Questions	Source	Description/ Notes	Which Supporting Question does this source help me answer?
	A		
	B		
	C		
	D		
	E		
	F		
	G		

After you analyze the sources, you will:

- use the evidence from the sources.
- communicate your conclusions.
- take informed action.

Background Information

In 1932 Democrat Franklin D. Roosevelt overwhelmingly defeated incumbent Republican President Herbert Hoover. With more than 22 million popular votes and 472 electoral college votes, Roosevelt took office as the 32nd president in March 1933. In his first 100 days, Roosevelt's administration sent numerous bills to Congress to launch the promised New Deal. These measures included a "bank holiday," subsidies for farmers, and massive government spending to create jobs on public works projects, like dam construction. A large percentage of the American population supported these measures as necessary to stabilize the economy, help workers, and spur recovery. Roosevelt argued that institutions like the National Recovery Administration would bring together workers and big business to resolve their differing interests and find solutions to shared problems. The two waves of New Deal programs created some economic successes but also faced political criticisms. Conservatives and others decried measures like the NRA as too intrusive, complicated and even unconstitutional. Roosevelt went on to win three reelections, but business interests and others continued to challenge policies that they considered dangerous to economic and individual liberty.

» "The Spirit of the New Deal!" by Clifford Kennedy Berryman, 1933, shows a New Deal program as the solution for bringing together the interests of big business and workers.

Science History Images/Alamy Stock Photo

"The Challenge to Liberty"

In 1934 President Roosevelt proposed a new set of measures called the Second New Deal. These new proposals, which included the creation of the Social Security program, sought to respond to a variety of protests and challenges. Many conservatives, including former President Herbert Hoover, forcefully objected. Hoover wrote a lengthy article touting the fundamental principles of individual liberty and its applications to business, industry, and finance.

» Herbert Hoover criticized Roosevelt's New Deal as a dangerous expansion of presidential power.

PRIMARY SOURCE : ARTICLE

66 . . . The first step of economic **regimentation** is a vast centralization of power in the Executive. Without tedious recitation of the acts of Congress delegating powers over the people to the executive or his assistants, and omitting relief and regulatory acts, the which have been assumed include the following: . . .

3. To expend enormous sums from the **appropriations** for public works, relief and agriculture upon projects not announced to the Congress at the time appropriations were made;

4. To create corporations for a wide variety of business activities, heretofore the exclusive field of private enterprise; . . .

9. To establish minimum wages; to fix maximum hours and conditions of labor;

10. To impose **collective bargaining**; . . .

Most of these powers may be delegated by the Executive to any appointee and the appointees are mostly without the usual confirmation by the Senate. The staffs of most of the new organizations are not selected by the merit requirements of the Civil Service. These powers were practically all of them delegated by the Congress to the executive upon the representation that they were 'emergency' authorities, limited to a specific time for the purpose of bringing about national recovery from the depression.

At some time or place all of these authorities already have been used. Powers once delegated are bound to be used, for one step drives to another. Moreover, some group somewhere gains benefits or privilege by the use of every power. Once a power is granted, therefore, groups begin to exert the pressure necessary to force its use. Once used, a **vested** interest is created which thereafter opposes any relaxation and therefore makes for permanence. But beyond this, many steps once taken set economic forces in motion which cannot be retrieved. Already we have witnessed these processes in action. 99

—"The Challenge to Liberty," Herbert Hoover, *The Saturday Evening Post*, September 8, 1934

regimentation strict structuring for the purpose of control
appropriations money set aside or reserved for a specific use
collective bargaining negotiations between employers and unions of workers over wages and other matters
vested guaranteed under the law

EXAMINE THE SOURCE

1. **Summarizing** What parts of the New Deal does Hoover call out as part of an effort to centralize executive power?

2. **Analyzing Perspectives** What does Hoover suggest is a danger of granting presidential emergency powers?

PHOTO: Everett Collection/Newscom. TEXT: Hoover, Herbert. "The Challenge to Liberty." The Saturday Evening Post. V. 207. No. 10. September 8, 1934.

Long, Huey, "Statement of the Share Our Wealth Movement," Congressional Record, 74th Cong., 1st sess., Vol. 79, 8040-43.

Statement of the Share Our Wealth Movement

Criticism of President Roosevelt did not come from just conservatives. Democrat Huey Long served as governor of Louisiana from 1928 to 1932, during which time he implemented even more stringent government controls and interventions in the state economy. In 1932 Long became a U.S. Senator, and proposed "Share the Wealth" policies that many viewed as radically socialist. Long charged that the concentration of wealth in a small percentage of the population made economic recovery impossible. On February 23, 1934 he delivered a national radio address unveiling his proposals, and iterated key points in a speech to Congress in May 1935. By then, more than 7 million Americans had joined thousands of Share Our Wealth clubs across the nation. Long's rising popularity—and a potential run against Roosevelt for president—likely helped push Roosevelt to introduce key parts of the Second New Deal.

PRIMARY SOURCE : BOOK

66 The whole line of any political thought has always been that America must face the time when the whole country would shoulder the obligation which it owes to every child born on earth—that is, fair chance to life, liberty, and happiness. . . .

Here is the whole sum and substance of the share-our-wealth movement:

1. Every family to be furnished by the Government a homestead allowance . . . of not less than one-third the average family wealth of the country. . . . No person to have a fortune of more than 100 to 300 times the average family fortune. . . .

2. . . . No yearly income shall be allowed to any person larger than from 100 to 300 times the size of the average family income, which means that no person would be allowed to earn in any year more than from $600,000 to $1,800,000, all to be subject to present income-tax laws.

3. To limit or regulate the hours of work to such an extent as to prevent overproduction; the most modern and efficient machinery would be encouraged, so that as much would be produced as possible so as to satisfy all demands of the people, but to also allow the maximum time to the workers for recreation, convenience, education, and luxuries of life.

4. An old-age **pension** to the persons over 60.

5. To balance agricultural production with what can be consumed . . . which includes the preserving and storage of surplus commodities to be paid for and held by the Government for the emergencies when such are needed. . . .

6. To pay the veterans of our wars what we owe them and to care for their disabled.

7. Education and training for all children to be equal in opportunity in all schools, colleges, universities, and other institutions for training in the professions and **vocations** of life; to be regulated on the capacity of children to learn, and not on the ability of parents to pay the costs. . . .

8. The raising of revenue and taxes for the support of this program to come from the reduction of swollen fortunes from the top, as well as for the support of public works to give employment whenever there may be any slackening necessary in private enterprise. 99

–Huey Long, *Congressional Record,* 74th Congress, 1st session, vol. 79, May 23, 1935

pension a fixed sum paid regularly to a person following retirement from work
vocation line of work

EXAMINE THE SOURCE

1. **Determining Central Ideas** How does Long propose to pay for the programs that he suggests?

2. **Drawing Conclusions** Whom would these proposals most likely benefit? Who is most likely to object, and why?

The Townsend Plan

During the Great Depression, Dr. Francis Townsend argued that the New Deal did not do enough to help elderly people in poverty. He proposed an old-age pension of $200 a month for persons over the age of 60, paid for by a sales tax. It sparked an outcry among conservative and business interests. This image shows a citizen petition among supporters of Townsend's idea in Otwell, Arkansas.

PRIMARY SOURCE : IMAGE

A PETITION FAVORING LEGISLATION
FOR THE TOWNSEND PLAN OF
Old Age Revolving Pensions
A National Plan For Recovery and Permanent Prosperity

TO THE HONORABLE *Hattie Caraway*

District _____ State of *Arkansas*

The undersigned legal voters of your district request you to introduce in the Congress of the United States at your earliest opportunity the following bills and use your utmost effort to obtain their passage into law:

FIRST: A bill obligating the government of the United States to pay every citizen of said government whose record is free of criminality and who has attained the age of sixty years, a monthly pension of $200 until the end of his life upon the sole condition that he agree, under oath, to spend the entire amount of the pension within the confines of the United States during the current month in which it is received.

SECOND: A bill creating a Nation-wide Federal Retail Sales Tax calculated at a rate sufficiently high to produce the revenue necessary to meet the requirements of Bill No. 1. It is obvious that the passage of these acts and the beginning of their operation will discharge the Nation's obligation to a class of her citizens deserving this reward for past services and at the same time place immediate buying power in the hands of the general public, thus stimulating every avenue of commerce and trade. A quick cure for this depression and a sure prevention of recurring ones.

Name _____ Address _____ City _____ State _____
Name _____ Address _____ City _____ State _____

PLAN DESCRIBED IN BRIEF ON OPPOSITE SIDE.

EXAMINE THE SOURCE

1. **Interpreting** Why do you think this petition uses the language it does, including "Old Age Revolving Pensions" and "National Plan for Recovery and Permanent Prosperity"?

2. **Analyzing Information** Based on the petition's description of how the plan works, would you categorize it as economic recovery or worker relief?

Coughlin's Warnings

Throughout the 1920s, a Roman Catholic priest and radio host named Father Charles Coughlin rapidly gained in popularity. At the onset of the Great Depression, he supported newly-elected President Roosevelt and his New Deal promises. However, he soon came to view them as too limited in scope. Coughlin called for more drastic measures, like inflating the currency and nationalizing banking. In 1934 Coughlin organized the National Union for Social Justice. Many Democrats feared Coughlin meant to start a new political party.

PRIMARY SOURCE : BOOK

> I shall not be one, either today or at any future date, to break down your confidence in the outcome of this new deal. My constant prayer is for its success. Soft words and insincere praise, however, must have no more place at this present hour . . . Two years hence [the Democratic Party] will leave the courtroom of public opinion vindicated and with a new lease on life, or will be condemned to political death if it fails to answer the simple question of why there is want in the midst of plenty.
>
> Truly, democracy itself is on trial. It has been given the final mandate to face the real causes of this depression and to end them. . . .
>
> Today the American people are the judge and jury who will support this Administration and accord it a sportsman's chance to make good. It has already subscribed to the principle that human rights must take precedence over financial rights. It recognizes that these rights far outweigh in the scales of justice either political rights or so-called constitutional rights.

—Reverend Charles E. Coughlin, *A Series of Lectures on Social Justice*, November 11, 1934

EXAMINE THE SOURCE

1. **Determining Central Ideas** What challenges does Coughlin make to the Democratic Party?

2. **Interpreting** What does he imply are the "real causes of this depression"?

PHOTO: National Archives and Records Administration; TEXT: Coughlin, Charles E. "The National Union for Social Justice." A Series of Lectures on Social Justice. New York: Da Capo Press, 1971.

(l)Gannett, Frank. "A Statement By Frank E. Gannett, Publisher Gannett Newspapers." February 23, 1937; (r)La Follette, Robert. "In Support of FDR's Court-Packing Plan." February 13, 1937.

A Statement by Frank E. Gannett

In 1937 President Roosevelt tried to counter the conservative Supreme Court Justices with a "court-packing" plan to add more justices to the Court if justices over the age of 70 did not retire. Frank E. Gannett, a newspaper publisher in Rochester, responded with a lengthy criticism.

PRIMARY SOURCE : EDITORIAL

❝ . . . A year ago I predicted that this is exactly what would happen if Roosevelt was reelected. The Supreme Court having declared invalid many of the administration measures the President now resorts to a plan of creating a Supreme Court that will be entirely sympathetic with his ideas. . . .

The Supreme Court has been the anchor that has held America safe through many storms. Its absolute independence and integrity must never be in doubt.

Our government is composed of three departments, Legislative, Executive, and Judiciary. . . . As a result of the election and the transfer of powers by so-called emergency measures, the Executive now dominates the Legislative Department. The President now proposes also to dominate the Judiciary. Do we want to give to this man or any one man complete control of these three departments of our Government which have from the beginning of the Republic been kept entirely separate and independent?

This proposal should give every American grave concerns for it is a step towards **absolutism** and complete dictatorial power. ❞

–Frank E. Gannett, "Regarding President Franklin D. Roosevelt's Attempt to Pack the Supreme Court," February 23, 1937

absolutism system of government in which one person holds total power

EXAMINE THE SOURCE

1. **Making Connections** What fundamental principles of the U.S. Constitution does Gannett invoke?

2. **Interpreting** How does Gannett view Roosevelt's proposed judicial reforms as a "step towards absolutism"?

La Follette Supports the Court-Packing Plan

During President Roosevelt's first several years in the White House, all nine Supreme Court justices had been appointed by other presidents. Roosevelt and his supporters believed that these justices were not willing to confront the emergency of the Depression. Wisconsin Senator Robert La Follette was one of many officials to speak out to refocus the public debate.

PRIMARY SOURCE : RADIO SPEECH

❝ A beautiful and historic example is what happened to the minimum wage legislation. It has been before the Supreme Court three times. On the basis of the recorded votes of the individual justices, there have been seven who have voted in favor of its constitutionality, and six against it. Yet the legislation was invalidated, simply because a bare majority of the particular set of justices who happen to be on the court at the time was opposed to that kind of legislation. Congress wanted it, the people wanted it. Seven out of thirteen justices wanted it, but the other six did not, so the law went into the ash can. If that is not government by men, I would like to know what it is. Even the Republican Party refused to defend such a flagrant act of judicial usurpation. Ten days after the Supreme Court's decision arbitrarily brushing aside the New York Minimum Wage Act For Women, the Republican Party solemnly pledged itself to support state minimum wage legislation for women, and recorded its belief that such legislation is within the Constitution as it now stands. This is but one more public recognition of the fact that our Constitution is what the justices choose to make it. ❞

–Robert M. La Follette, "In Support of FDR's Court-Packing Plan," February 13, 1937

EXAMINE THE SOURCE

1. **Identifying Main Ideas** What happened when Congress passed legislation regarding a minimum wage?

2. **Interpreting** How does La Follette use this instance as evidence to support Roosevelt's plan?

Interview with Henry Gill

In 1938 a knife maker named Henry Gill sat down to talk with members of the Federal Writers' Project. During one interview, Gill read from and responded to an article in an independent newspaper leaflet being distributed around his town—*The American Guardian*.

PRIMARY SOURCE : TRANSCRIPT

❝ Near's I can make out, it's some new plan for the revision of the capitalist system. They've got it figured out that it's lack of buying power that's responsible for the depression, and they're goin' to give every family 'ead an income of at least twenty eight dollars a week while e's out of work and a minimum of fifty when 'e goes back to work, no matter what 'e does. They're also goin' to repeal taxes. Don't ask me how they're goin' to got the money. When I read that far I got dizzy.

. . . [reading from the newspaper] 'The American Foundation for Abundance— (that's what they call the plan—the AFA) would not break up [monopolies]. It proposes that the public take them over and put them under scientific management for the common good. . . . The only intelligent solution of the monopoly problem in the public ownership and public operation of the monopoly. . . .'

Sounds almost like Communism, don't it. Only it goes a bit farther than Communism. They believe in the New Deal but they don't think it goes far enough. . . . [reading] 'We are supporters of the New Deal as just a tiny step on the road toward a New Day. However, we recognize that if the majority of our people continue to be content with just tiny steps like the New Deal that it will be centuries before the people come into their own.' ❞

—Henry Gill, No. 3, Federal Writers' Project, 1938

EXAMINE THE SOURCE

Analyzing Perspectives What question does Gill pose about the plan laid out in the article? What does that suggest about his own concerns about the New Deal?

Your Inquiry Analysis

EVALUATE SOURCES AND USE EVIDENCE

Reflect back to the Compelling Question and the Supporting Questions you developed at the beginning of this lesson.

1. **Gathering Sources** Refer back to the Graphic Organizer you created as you read through the sources. How did each source help you answer the Supporting Questions you wrote? How did the information they provided reflect different perspectives on the New Deal? What other information do you think you might need to answer the Compelling Question?

2. **Evaluating Sources** Looking at the sources that help you answer the Supporting Questions, evaluate the credibility of each source. Consider the bias and intent of each source as well as the content provided. What evidence does each source offer (or fail to offer) to defend a position? How does each source's goal influence the content?

3. **Comparing and Contrasting** Compare and contrast two sources that express a similar criticism of Roosevelt or the New Deal. How are their arguments and methods alike and different? Which do you think is more effective or persuasive, and why?

COMMUNICATE CONCLUSIONS

Identifying Arguments Work with a partner to analyze the sources and write a response to the Compelling Question. One partner should identify and explain a key criticism of Roosevelt or the New Deal from progressives, and the other partner should focus on a criticism from conservatives. Present your analyses orally to the class.

TAKE INFORMED ACTION

Investigating Social Security The Social Security system was a hallmark program of the New Deal that remains in effect today. However, as in the 1930s, citizens, special interests, and politicians continue to debate the efficacy and sustainability of the program. With a partner, learn more about the present provisions of Social Security benefits, and research two contrasting perspectives on potential reforms of Social Security. Write an editorial or a radio address of your own in which you and your partner explain the present debate surrounding Social Security and defend a clear position on what changes, if any, you think need to be made going forward.

Gill, Henry. Mr.Gill no. 3. Federal Writer's Project, 1938. PDF. https://www.loc.gov/item/wpalh000337/.

08

Reviewing the Great Depression and New Deal

Summary

The presidential election of 1928 pitted Democrat Al Smith against Republican Herbert Hoover. The economy was flourishing, and Hoover easily won in a landslide. Within months after entering office, however, Hoover's administration faced significant challenges as the country slid into one of the greatest economic crises it had ever faced.

The Stock Market's Role

The expansion of credit and consumer purchasing spurred an economic boom and a rise in stock market prices during the 1920s. However, some investors had started using credit to buy stocks in companies with inflated values. When stock market prices plummeted in October 1929, brokers began to call in the loans of clients who had purchased now-worthless stocks on margin. Reaction to the crash in combination with other underlying weaknesses in the economy prompted a rapid economic downturn. Banks that had funded risky loans closed. This caused bank customers to lose the money in their accounts. Consumer spending slowed. Companies scaled back on production or shut down completely, and many people lost their jobs. Without reliable and regular income, many Americans could not pay loans they had taken out to purchase homes, cars, and other goods.

Hoover and the Depression

At first, the federal government did little to try to slow the downturn. President Hoover, like many others, believed that it was just a typical part of the ups and downs of a market economy. He thought that it was better for the federal government to avoid trying to influence the economy. As unemployment rose and more Americans called for action, Hoover backed the creation of the Reconstruction Finance Corporation and the Emergency Relief and Construction Act to help stabilize the economy. However, these efforts had limited effects.

The Bonus Army

As poverty and homelessness intensified, many people participated in "hunger marches" to make their voices heard. In 1932 unemployed World War I veterans and their families launched a protest to demand early payment of bonuses for their service that the federal government was scheduled to pay. Over several months this "Bonus Army" grew, and eventually thousands were camped out in the nation's capital. President Hoover finally authorized the U.S. military to clear out the Bonus Army. The violent confrontation that took place shocked the nation. It further weakened Hoover's chances at re-election and boosted his opponent, Democrat Franklin D. Roosevelt.

Life During the Great Depression

The economic downturn soon affected almost all aspects of daily life, and some groups were hit harder than others. Some immigrants, such as Filipino and Mexican field workers, returned to their home countries as jobs became scarce. The federal government supported repatriation efforts, and it also forcibly removed hundreds of thousands of people of Mexican heritage without regard to their citizenship status.

Many farm families started migrating westward after the Dust Bowl. That disaster, caused by drought and years of strain on the land, had destroyed farm life across the Great Plains. During the Depression, Americans found some relief in popular entertainment such as going to the movies or listening to the radio. Many artists, including writers, dramatists, and musicians, used their skills to document the experiences and struggles of Americans.

Hoover's Response to the Depression

Cautious Beginnings	Reluctant Public Relief	Reconstruction Finance Corporation
National Credit Corporation • Started in October 1931 • Increased money supply for banks to lend to business	**Emergency Relief and Construction Act** • Passed by Congress in July 1932 • $1.5 billion in public works finances provided • $300 million in emergency loans provided to state governments	• Begun in 1932 • Over $230 million loaned to lenders, railroads

The First New Deal

When Franklin Roosevelt won the 1932 election and entered the White House, his administration immediately prepared to tackle the economic issues of the Great Depression. With the help of expert cabinet members and advisers, Roosevelt presented a New Deal to the American public. His administration's plan included a variety of programs and government agencies to bring about relief, recovery, and reform. Beginning with his inaugural address and then through "fireside chats" on the radio, the president helped restore the confidence of the American public.

The Hundred Days

The first 100 days of Roosevelt's administration witnessed a flurry of activity. Within a week of taking office, the Emergency Banking Relief Act passed, which helped end the nation's "bank holiday" and restore confidence in reopened banks. Between March and June, Roosevelt quickly sent several bills to Congress, resulting in fifteen major acts to help resolve the economic crisis. These programs became what would be called the First New Deal.

An "Alphabet Soup"

Under Roosevelt's leadership, the federal government was characterized by an "alphabet soup" of new entities. Among the first of these were the Securities and Exchange Commission (SEC) and the Federal Deposit Insurance Corporation (FDIC) targeted at protecting investors from risky stock and banking practices. The Agricultural Adjustment Administration (AAA) and Tennessee Valley Authority (TVA) helped expand opportunities for farmers and others in rural areas. Relief programs, such as the Civilian Conservation Corps (CCC), Public Works Administration (PWA), and Civil Works Administration (CWA), created thousands of jobs for Americans.

A Lasting Legacy

While the New Deal helped bring some relief to Americans' lives and improvements to the economy, critics from both the right and left attacked Roosevelt's efforts. Some disagreed with the reliance on deficit spending, in which the federal government spent more money than it collected in revenues. Others argued the programs did not go far enough. Some believed the federal government should tax the very wealthy to provide direct monetary payments to families. Others challenged New Deal programs in court. Responding to some of these concerns, Roosevelt launched a new series of efforts known as the Second New Deal. It included the Works Progress Administration (WPA), which created more jobs.

The Supreme Court struck down some provisions of the First New Deal. Congress and the administration responded by including new laws designed to help protect workers' bargaining power. The administration also supported the creation of Social Security to provide for Americans after retirement and during periods of unemployment. After Roosevelt won reelection in 1936, he tried to protect New Deal programs by packing the Supreme Court with several new justices. Although his plan failed, the Court was more favorable towards New Deal legislation during his second term.

As the economy began to improve, Roosevelt's administration pulled back on spending, which led to a new recession in 1937. Clearly, the economy was not yet strong enough to fully recover on its own.

The Great Depression and New Deal left a lasting legacy of how the federal government operated and what citizens expected from it. The federal government continued to play a much larger role in directing and regulating the economy and providing a safety net to better protect citizens from future economic disasters.

WPA photographer Gordon Parks created *American Gothic, Washington, D.C.* This photo provides an alternate view of Grant Wood's famous *American Gothic* painting with a portrait of Ella Watson, a cleaning woman for the offices of the Farm Security Administration.

Library of Congress Prints & Photographs Division, FSA/OWI Collection [LC-DIG-ppmsca-05809]

Apply What You Have Learned

A Understanding Multiple Perspectives

By the time the Great Depression reached its peak in 1932, many Americans blamed slow action by the Hoover administration for worsening the crisis. Hoover, like other presidents before him, believed that too much federal government intervention in the economy was a threat to liberty. Even so, he oversaw the largest increase in federal programs to "prime the pump" of the economy by any president prior to Franklin Roosevelt.

The New Deal administration ushered in a period of unprecedented federal government intervention in the economy. Still, some critics believed the government should have gone further, increasing fears in some that the crisis would lead the United States down a path towards communism or socialism. In 1934 Hoover wrote an essay warning of the long-term effects government intervention in the economy might have on the stability of the political system.

ACTIVITY **Draw a Conclusion** Read the following excerpt from Hoover's 1934 essay.

Based on Hoover's essay, draw a conclusion about whether Hoover would have agreed or disagreed with President Roosevelt's attempts to prime the economic pump with his many different New Deal agencies and programs. Write a paragraph summarizing your conclusion.

" Even if the government conduct of business could give us the maximum of efficiency instead of least efficiency, it would be purchased at the cost of freedom. It would increase rather than decrease abuse and corruption, stifle initiative and invention, undermine the development of leadership, cripple the mental and spiritual energies of our people and the forces which make progress. . . . The nation seeks for solution of its many difficulties. These solutions can come alone through the constructive forces from the system built upon Liberty. They cannot be achieved by the destructive forces of Regimentation. The purification of Liberty from abuses, the restoration of confidence in the rights of men, the release of the dynamic forces of initiative and enterprise are alone the methods by which these solutions can be found and the purpose of American life assured. . . . "

–Herbert Hoover, *The Challenge to Liberty,* 1934.

B Making Connections to Art

One of the unique aspects of New Deal work projects was that many of them capitalized on the work skills and training American workers already had. Some projects included hiring artists from various fields to enhance public works.

The federal government hired hundreds of visual artists to create beautiful murals that decorated public buildings, such as post offices that were being built through federal work programs. These murals were often sweeping in nature, reflecting stories about the history and heritage of local residents. The artists' underlying messages were often uplifting in nature.

ACTIVITY **Describing a Mural** Using the library or Internet resources, research and examine at least five examples of murals created on New Deal public works projects. Consider what story or message the artists were trying to convey. Using what you have learned, design a mural that could be created to adorn a public building in your community. You do not have to draw or visualize your mural design unless you want to. But your work should carefully describe the content of your mural and clearly reflect something specific about the history or heritage of your community.

Hoover, Herbert. The Challenge to Liberty. 1934. In Herbert Hoover Reassessed: Essays Commemorating the Fiftieth Anniversary of our Thirty-First President. Washington: US Government Printing Office, 1981.

C Making Connections to Today

The United States has experienced many stock market crashes since 1929, some of which have involved larger one-day losses of stock values than the days that precipitated the Great Depression. In some cases, these more recent crashes were followed by economic downturns, which many economists still consider natural "corrections" to bull markets.

Even with these continued ebbs and flows of the market-based system, none of the twentieth century economic downturns following a stock market crash were as severe as the Great Depression. Many of the reforms put in place during the New Deal era continued to help protect the economy against the worst effects of a stock market crash. However, in the twenty-first century, several stock market crashes tested the economic foundations of the country.

ACTIVITY **Create a Venn Diagram** Using library or Internet resources, research information about a stock market crash that occurred during the twenty-first century. Examine why that crash occurred, what industries were involved, and the impact the crash had on the economy in the months afterwards. Then create a Venn diagram comparing and contrasting elements of the 1929 crash with the more recent crash you researched. Include elements the crashes share in the middle of the diagram.

» Traders at the New York Stock Exchange react to a tumbling stock market that saw investors fleeing the market to find safer assets, February 27, 2020.

D Geographic Reasoning

The economic crisis of the Great Depression was compounded by the environmental devastation of the Dust Bowl. Unlike a hurricane or tornado, this natural disaster was many years in the making. Decades of poor farming practices that wore out topsoil combined with drought and high winds, creating a perfect storm of conditions that ravaged huge sections of the Great Plains and the South. It led to a huge emigration of people fleeing their worn-out farmlands in search of better opportunities further west.

Even many areas not located directly in the worst of the Dust Bowl experienced severe erosion due to the combination of human activities and severe weather patterns. Federal programs such as the tree-planting programs of the CCC addressed some of the environmental problems that led to the Dust Bowl.

Government researchers examined ways to better understand the causes of and remedies for the Dust Bowl to prevent such a disaster from happening again. They promoted practices that would help the land heal and support healthy farming. Despite these efforts, it took many years for some of the hardest-hit areas of the Dust Bowl to recover.

ACTIVITY **Write an Environmental Study** An environmental study is an assessment of environmental conditions, problems, or solutions. Such studies can help researchers, legislators, or the public better understand issues related to the environment. They rely on expert scientific practices for their analyses. Sometimes such studies summarize research by other scientists. Working in small groups, use library or Internet resources to research information about the causes, effects, and long-term remedies for the environmental issues of the Dust Bowl in the 1930s. Using that information, work as a team to write an environmental study summarizing your findings.

CHINE NOUVELLE/SIPA/Newscom

World War II was fought in Europe and in the Pacific, but it affected nations around the world. This U.S. squadron is shown in a war-ravaged town in Italy in April 1945.

World War II 1933–1945

INTRODUCTION LESSON

01   Introducing World War II   276

LEARN THE EVENTS LESSONS

02   The Origins of World War II   281

03   The Holocaust   287

05   The United States Mobilizes for War   299

06   World War II in Europe   305

07   World War II in the Pacific   311

INQUIRY ACTIVITY LESSONS

04   Understanding Multiple Perspectives
     About American Neutrality   293

08   Turning Point: The D-Day Invasion   319

REVIEW AND APPLY LESSON

09   Reviewing World War II   323

Galerie Bilderwelt/Hulton Archive/Getty Images

THE REMARKABLE VERNON BAKER

Vernon Baker, who would go on to become a hero of World War II, was born on December 17, 1919, in Cheyenne, Wyoming. At the age of four, Baker was orphaned when he lost his parents in a car accident. Baker and his two sisters were raised by their grandparents, who eventually moved to Clarinda, Iowa, where Baker graduated from high school in 1937. The town had very limited jobs for African Americans, and Baker eventually worked at the same railroad where his grandfather was a brakeman. However, Baker's dissatisfaction with employment opportunities led him to an army recruiting office in April 1941, where he was rejected by the recruiting officer because of the color of his skin. Baker recalled that "when I walked out the door I swore I wasn't coming back . . . I was living with my sister and it kind of **rankled** me that I needed to support myself. So, I swallowed my pride and I went back to the recruiting office."

Baker successfully enlisted in the army on July 26, 1941, and was sent to Texas to train. Following basic training, Baker was sent to Officer Candidate School in Georgia, where he faced deep-seated racism. Less than two years later, Baker was commissioned as a second lieutenant and was assigned to the 370th Regiment of the 92nd Infantry Division, a segregated African American division in the armed forces. Baker's division landed in Naples, Italy, in June 1944. In the thick of heavy combat, they made their way north toward central Italy.

On April 5, 1945, First Lieutenant Vernon Baker and his platoon advanced toward Castle Aghinolfi, a German stronghold near Viareggio, Italy. Baker and about 25 others moved ahead of the group, and Baker successfully destroyed an observation post, a dugout, and three machine gun positions. He also managed to cut the Germans' communication network. During the attack, Baker's platoon lost 19 men, so he quickly set up a defensive position while waiting for reinforcements. Baker soon realized, however, that his superiors had no intention of sending help. He then organized a withdrawal, and when his platoon was stopped by an entrenched machine gun nest, Baker crawled ahead of his men and destroyed it. He then attacked a German observation post and killed or wounded the four enemy soldiers occupying it. Baker and one of his men successfully destroyed two more machine gun nests, and then Baker drew enemy fire so that wounded soldiers in his platoon could be evacuated. The next night, Baker volunteered to lead the advance through enemy mine fields and heavy fire until the division reached its objective.

> **"I just feel I was a soldier and I did my job . . ."**

For Baker's heroic actions on April 5 and 6, 1945, the army awarded him a Purple Heart, Bronze Star, and Distinguished Service Cross. However, the military's greatest award—the Medal of Honor—was largely reserved for white soldiers, something not **rectified** until 1997, when President Bill Clinton awarded the Medal of Honor to seven African American veterans from World War II. By then, Baker was the only one of the seven recipients still alive. In a CNN interview after the Medal of Honor ceremony, Baker said, "I still don't feel like a hero. I just feel I was a soldier and I did my job, and I think I was rewarded for it." He was saddened, however, by having to wait more than 50 years for that award: "As I look back on it, it really makes me feel sad that we did our job, we fought, but we weren't appreciated."

Baker remained on active duty until 1968, and then worked for the Red Cross for more than 20 years. He died in 2010 at the age of 90.

rankle to cause anger or irritation

rectify to set right

(1)United States Department of Agriculture. Natural Resources Conservation Service Idaho. "World War II Congressional Medal of Honor Recipient First Lieutenant Vernon J. Baker, US Army."; (2)Baker, Vernon. Quoted in Shaugnessy, Larry. "Vernon Baker, Extraordinary Hero and Victim of Racism, Dies." CNN.com. July 15, 2020.

Jesse Tinsley/The Spokesman-Review/AP Photo

Vernon Baker received the Medal of Honor in 1997. The Medal of Honor is awarded sparingly to those who risk their lives above and beyond the call of duty while in combat against an armed enemy of the United States.

Evaluating From what you have learned about Vernon Baker, how well did the photographer capture him in this portrait?

Understanding the Time and Place: The World, 1933–1945

World War I had been a global conflict that caused massive death and destruction. Including those who were killed, wounded, taken as prisoners, or missing in action, the Allied Power countries suffered combined casualties of just over 22 million members of the military; the Central Power countries had casualties totaling nearly 37.5 million. Civilian casualties are harder to tally because no agencies existed to record the numbers, but experts estimate around 13 million civilians died. Understandably, in the 1930s people were wary of fighting another world war.

World War II in Europe

The effects of World War I and the global Great Depression that followed led to the rise of **dictators** in several countries, including Benito Mussolini in Italy, Joseph Stalin in the Soviet Union, and Adolf Hitler in Germany. In Japan, the military took control of the country during this period. In 1935 Hitler took actions that directly defied the Treaty of Versailles that ended World War I, such as building a new air force and beginning a military draft. European leaders desperately wanted to avoid another global conflict, so they sought to negotiate with Hitler instead of taking military action to stop him. Hitler wanted to unite all German-speaking countries, and was willing to do so by force. He began by occupying Austria and Czechoslovakia. When Hitler invaded Poland on September 1, 1939, Britain and France knew negotiation was no longer an option and declared war on Germany. This marked the beginning of World War II.

The United States, however, did not join the war in 1939. After the hardship of World War I, the United States had been passing legislation to protect its own neutrality throughout the 1930s, making it illegal to sell arms to any countries at war. As tensions and conflict increased throughout Europe, the United States passed more laws to attempt to keep the country isolated from another global conflict.

Despite America's movement towards isolation, President Roosevelt sought to support Britain once World War II had officially begun. The Lend-Lease Act, for example, was passed by Congress in 1941 and allowed America to supply Britain with arms and other supplies. This act also enabled America to aid the Soviet Union when Hitler invaded that country in June 1941. The American people were divided on the issue. Some wanted the United States to join the war to help Britain and its allies in their fight against Germany, while others remained firm in the idea that America should not get involved. The debate about American neutrality ended when Japan attacked Pearl Harbor on December 7, 1941. The following day, Roosevelt asked Congress to declare war on Japan, which it did, and the United States was no longer neutral.

World War II in America

America was ready for war by 1941. Roosevelt had been building up the U.S. military since Hitler's invasion of Poland in 1939, and 60,000 men enlisted in the weeks following the attack on Pearl Harbor. Jim Crow laws still reigned, however, including in the military. Soldiers were segregated, and many African Americans who served never saw combat but were assigned to service or mechanical jobs. There was also hostility against other minority soldiers, including Latinos, Native Americans, Jewish Americans, and Japanese Americans. Members of all of these groups

This World War II poster from 1943 shows the flags of the Allied Forces on the cannon barrels.

Library of Congress Prints & Photographs Division [LC-USZC4-12529]

---

dictator one who rules with absolute power, often in an oppressive way

Global Scale of World War II

Although World War I is often referred to as the "Great War," World War II involved many more countries, and people around the globe—directly or indirectly—were affected by the epic conflict.

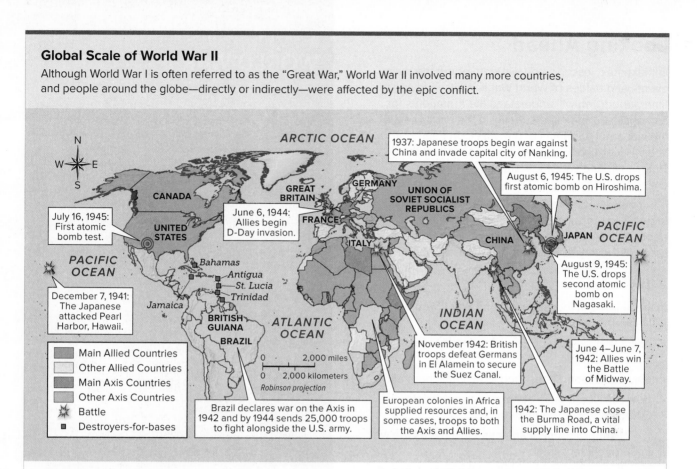

1937: Japanese troops begin war against China and invade capital city of Nanking.

July 16, 1945: First atomic bomb test.

June 6, 1944: Allies begin D-Day invasion.

August 6, 1945: The U.S. drops first atomic bomb on Hiroshima.

December 7, 1941: The Japanese attacked Pearl Harbor, Hawaii.

August 9, 1945: The U.S. drops second atomic bomb on Nagasaki.

November 1942: British troops defeat Germans in El Alamein to secure the Suez Canal.

June 4–June 7, 1942: Allies win the Battle of Midway.

Brazil declares war on the Axis in 1942 and by 1944 sends 25,000 troops to fight alongside the U.S. army.

European colonies in Africa supplied resources and, in some cases, troops to both the Axis and Allies.

1942: The Japanese close the Burma Road, a vital supply line into China.

Legend:
- Main Allied Countries
- Other Allied Countries
- Main Axis Countries
- Other Axis Countries
- Battle
- Destroyers-for-bases

0 — 2,000 miles
0 — 2,000 kilometers
Robinson projection

GEOGRAPHY CONNECTION

Spatial Thinking Which large Allied country was located to the east of Europe?

distinguished themselves in the military during World War II. Many of those who served were members of the **second generation.** The military was fully desegregated in 1948, due in large part to the important contributions and successes of minority fighters.

With so many men off fighting, women filled many positions that had once been available only to men. Women could also enlist in the armed forces, serving in a variety of noncombat roles. Many jobs were clerical, but women also served as pilots, flying planes from factories to the bases where they were needed. Female units existed in the army, coast guard, navy, and marines, and about 68,000 women served as nurses in the army and navy.

The rapid mobilization of the armed forces and the industries that supported them created about 19 million new jobs, effectively ending the Great Depression. Because so many white men were away fighting, employment opportunities opened up for people normally passed over for these jobs, including African Americans, Latinos, and women. Roosevelt made sure positions in the government and defense

industries were filled by issuing an executive order that prohibited job discrimination in these sectors based on "race, creed, color, or national origin."

America's industrial and military might proved assets to the war effort. In the early months of 1945, the end of the war was achievable. American and British troops focused on liberating France from German occupation as the Soviets moved toward Berlin, the German capital. Once France was free, American troops attacked Germany from the west. On April 30, 1945, Hitler committed suicide, and Germany accepted the terms of unconditional surrender on May 7.

World War II in Europe was over, but the war still raged in the Pacific. To expedite its end, President Truman made the difficult decision to use atomic bombs—one on Hiroshima on August 6, 1945, and another on Nagasaki three days later. Tens of thousands died instantly, and tens of thousands more died later from injuries and the effects of radiation. The Japanese government surrendered on August 15, marking the end of one of the world's most destructive, expensive, and deadly wars.

second generation   the children of immigrants, who are often called the "first generation"

Executive Order 8802: Prohibition of Discrimination in the Defense Industry (1941). National Archive and Records Administration.

Looking Ahead

In these next lessons, you will learn about the main events and battles of World War II. While studying this time period, you will understand the arguments for and against American neutrality in the early years of the war and the effects of the attack on Pearl Harbor. You will learn about Hitler's Nazi regime and the Holocaust. And you will examine how the war changed U.S. society.

You will examine Compelling Questions in the Inquiry Lessons and develop your own questions about World War II. Review the time line to preview some of the key events that you will learn about.

What Will You Learn

In these lessons focused on World War II, you will learn:

- how the policy of appeasement failed to preserve peace in Europe.
- why the United States tried to maintain neutrality.
- how Nazi leadership attempted to annihilate Europe's Jewish population.
- the changes in American neutrality laws as the war in Europe intensified.
- how the government mobilized the economy and transformed it for wartime manufacturing.
- how minorities and women contributed to the armed forces and the economy.
- how some Americans were discriminated against and detained during the war.
- the military strategies used in Europe and the Pacific.
- the debate surrounding the atomic bombing of Japan.
- why the Normandy invasion was a turning point in World War II.

? COMPELLING QUESTIONS

- **Should the United States have entered World War II?**
- **What made D-Day a turning point?**

KEY EVENTS OF THE
WORLD WAR II

1933 ○ **1933** Hitler becomes chancellor of Germany

1935 First Neutrality Act bars sale of weapons to warring nations

1935 Mussolini orders Abyssinia invasion

1937 ○ **1937** Neutrality Act limits trade with all warring nations

1939 Germany invades Poland

1939 United States denies S.S. *St. Louis* permission to dock

1940 Roosevelt makes Destroyers-for-Bases deal with Britain

1941 ○ **1941** Congress passes Lend-Lease Act

1941 Japan attacks Pearl Harbor (right); United States enters World War II

1942 Japanese American relocation and internment

1944 D-Day invasion begins

1945 ○ **MAY 8, 1945** V-E (Victory in Europe) Day

AUGUST 1945 United States drops atomic bombs on Japan

AUGUST 15, 1945 V-J (Victory Over Japan) Day

Sequencing Time Identify the events that reflect America's attempts to stay neutral before and during World War II and the event that brought America into the war.

Everett Collection/Shutterstock

READING STRATEGY

<u>Analyzing Key Ideas and Details</u> As you read, use a graphic organizer like the one below to create an outline using the major headings of the lesson.

Origins of World War II

   I. The Rise of Dictators

      A.

      B.

   II.

The Rise of Dictators

GUIDING QUESTION

What economic and political conditions following World War I encouraged dictatorships?

After World War I, the unintended consequences of the Treaty of Versailles, along with the economic depression that followed the war, contributed to the rise of antidemocratic governments in both Europe and Asia. These antidemocratic states would eventually break the peace agreement that ended World War I.

Militarists Control Japan

In Japan difficult economic times helped undermine the political system. Japanese industry imported most of the raw materials needed for production. A conservative faction associated with the Japanese army grew in power throughout the 1920s, calling for acquiring resources from the Asian mainland. When the Great Depression struck, the United States and European nations responded by raising their tariffs, further harming Japan's economy.

Japanese leaders also worried about the Soviets' growing influence in China. In 1931 a group of Japanese colonels in Korea decided to take matters into their own hands and stage an incident that they used to justify an invasion of Manchuria, in northern China. The Japanese tried to stop them. One of the advocates of expansion was Minister of War Hideki Tōjō. The Japanese military gained power throughout the 1930s, and the military proceeded further into China in 1937. In Nanking (now Nanjing), the Japanese destroyed the city and killed as many as 300,000 of its residents. The incident became known as the "Rape of Nanking." In October 1941 Tōjō took over as prime minister.

Mussolini, Stalin, and Hitler Rise to Power

One of Europe's first dictatorships arose when in 1919 Benito Mussolini founded Italy's Fascist movement. **Fascism** is an aggressive nationalistic movement that considers the nation more important than the individual. Fascists believe that orderly society and national greatness come through a dictator who leads a strong government.

Mussolini's fascism was strongly anti-communist. After the Russian Revolution, many Europeans feared that Communists, allied with labor unions, would bring down their governments. Mussolini exploited these fears by portraying fascism as a bulwark against communism, claiming that it protected private property and the middle class and pledging to return Italy to the glories of the Roman Empire.

In 1922 Mussolini threatened to march on Rome, claiming he was defending Italy against a communist revolution. The Italian king refused liberals' request to declare martial law, and the cabinet quit. Conservative advisers then persuaded the king to appoint Mussolini as the premier. Once in office, Mussolini embarked on a program of imposing his control over Italy.

fascism a political system headed by a dictator that calls for extreme nationalism and often racism and no tolerance of opposition

Around the same time, Joseph Stalin rose to power in the Soviet Union. The Soviet Union, or the Union of Soviet Socialist Republics (USSR), was established by the Communist Party in 1922 after the Russian Revolution. The Communists instituted a one-party rule, suppressed individual liberties, and punished opponents. Their leader, Vladimir Lenin, died in 1924. By 1926, Stalin had become the new Soviet dictator. Stalin began a massive effort to industrialize his country using Five-Year Plans. Steel production increased, but industrial wages declined by 43 percent from 1928 to 1940. Family farms were turned into **collectivized** farms. Peasants who resisted faced show trials or death from starvation. Stalin sought to expand Soviet influence and used concentration camps to imprison his opposition. Between 15 and 20 million people died under Stalin's rule, which lasted until his death in 1953.

Just as Mussolini rose to power in Italy and Stalin rose to power in the Soviet Union, Adolf Hitler was attempting to gain power in Germany. Hitler was a fervent nationalist who hated both the victorious Allies and the German government that had accepted their peace terms at the end of World War I. He became the leader of the National Socialist German Workers' Party, or Nazi Party, which called for Germany to expand its territory and to reject the terms of the Treaty of Versailles. The party was also anti-Semitic, meaning that it held very negative views of the Jewish people and used Jews as political scapegoats for Germany's problems. In November 1923, the Nazis tried to seize power by marching on the city hall in Munich, Germany. The plan failed, the Nazi Party was banned for a time, and Hitler was arrested.

While in prison, Hitler wrote *Mein Kampf* ("My Struggle"), in which he claimed that Germans, particularly blond, blue-eyed Germans, belonged to a "master race" called Aryans. He argued that the Slavic peoples of Eastern Europe belonged to an inferior race that Germans should enslave. He also blamed the Jews for many of the world's problems, especially for Germany's defeat in World War I. After his release, Hitler changed tactics. He focused on getting Nazis elected to the Reichstag, the lower house of the German parliament. The Nazis gained support from desperate German voters during Germany's economic depression. By 1932, the Nazis were the largest party in the Reichstag. The following year, the German president appointed Hitler as chancellor.

After taking office, Hitler called for new elections. Through military intimidation of voters, the Nazis dominated the Reichstag after the elections, and Hitler gained dictatorial powers. In 1934 Hitler became president, gaining control of the army.

✓ CHECK FOR UNDERSTANDING

Explaining What economic and political conditions following World War I encouraged dictatorships?

Benito Mussolini gained power in Italy by convincing voters that by giving the government strong power, voters would allow him to fix the nation's social and political problems.

Attempts to Appease Hitler

GUIDING QUESTION

How did European nations try to prevent war?

In 1935 Hitler defied the Treaty of Versailles when he announced that Germany would build a new air force and begin a military draft to greatly expand its army. Rather than enforce the treaty by going to war, however, European leaders tried to negotiate.

Europe's leaders had several reasons for wanting to believe that they could reach a deal with Hitler to avoid war. First, they wanted to avoid a repeat of World War I. Second, they thought some of Hitler's demands were reasonable, including his demand that

collectivized describing an economic system with centralized control of production and distribution

SeM/Universal Images Group/Getty Images

Leaders gathered at the Munich Conference including, from right to left, French Premier Edouard Daladier, Adolf Hitler, Benito Mussolini (center), British Prime Minister Neville Chamberlain, and Hermann Göring, a leader in the Nazi Party.

Explaining What important figure is missing from this gathering at the Munich Conference? Explain.

all German-speaking regions be united. Third, they assumed that the Nazis would want peace once they gained more territory.

The Austrian *Anschluss*

In late 1937, Hitler again called for the unification of all German-speaking people, including those in Austria and Czechoslovakia. He believed that Germany could expand its territory only by force. In February 1938, Hitler threatened to invade German-speaking Austria unless Austrian Nazis were given important government posts. Austria's chancellor gave in to this demand but then tried to put the matter of unification with Germany to a democratic vote. Fearing the outcome, Hitler sent troops into Austria in March and announced the *Anschluss,* or unification, of Austria and Germany.

The Munich Crisis

Hitler next announced German claims to the Sudetenland, an area of Czechoslovakia with a large German-speaking population. The Czechs resisted these demands. France threatened to fight if Germany attacked Czechoslovakia, and the Soviet Union also promised aid. Prime Minister Neville Chamberlain pledged Britain's support to France, its ally.

Representatives of Britain, France, Italy, and Germany met in Munich, Germany, to decide Czechoslovakia's fate. At the Munich Conference, on September 29, 1938, Britain and France agreed to Hitler's demands, a policy that came to be known as **appeasement.** They believed that if they gave Hitler what he wanted, they could avoid war. Czechoslovakia

had to give up the Sudetenland or fight Germany on its own. When Chamberlain returned home, he stated, "My good friends, for the second time in our history, a British Prime Minister has returned from Germany bringing peace with honor. I believe it is 'peace for our time.' Go home and get a nice quiet sleep."

Appeasement failed to preserve the fragile peace. In March 1939, Germany sent troops into Czechoslovakia and divided the country. Slovakia became independent in name but was under German control. Czech lands became a German protectorate. A month after the Munich Conference, Hitler demanded that the city of Danzig be returned to German control. Danzig was more than 90 percent German, and it had been part of Poland since World War I. Hitler also requested a highway and railroad across the Polish Corridor, which had been carved out after World War I to give Poland sea access. Hitler's new demands convinced Britain and France that war was inevitable.

On March 31, 1939, Britain announced that if Poland went to war to defend its territory, Britain and France would come to its aid. This declaration encouraged Poland to refuse Hitler's demands. In May 1939, Hitler ordered the German Army to prepare to invade Poland. He also ordered his foreign minister to begin negotiations with the Soviet Union. If Germany was going to fight Britain and France, Hitler did not want to have to fight the Soviets, too.

✓ CHECK FOR UNDERSTANDING

Summarizing How did European nations try to prevent war?

War Begins in Europe

GUIDING QUESTION

Why did Germany make a pact with the Soviet Union, and why did the pact surprise people?

When Germany proposed a nonaggression treaty to the Soviets, Stalin agreed. He believed the best way to protect the Soviet Union was to turn the capitalist nations against each other and that establishing peace with Germany would turn Hitler's aggression toward Britain and France. The pact, signed on August 23, 1939, shocked the world. Communism and Nazism were supposed to be opposed to each other. Leaders in Britain and France saw the agreement as a sign that Hitler was ready to go to war. They did not know that the treaty called for dividing Poland between Germany and the Soviet Union.

Invading Poland

On September 1, 1939, Germany invaded Poland. Two days later, Britain and France declared war on Germany.

---

appeasement giving in to the unjust demands of a belligerent leader in order to avoid war

PHOTO: Everett Collection Inc/Alamy Stock Photo; TEXT: Neville Chamberlain, "Peace for Our Time," September 30, 1938.

The British Expeditionary Force evacuates from the French seaport of Dunkirk to England aboard a naval vessel, June 1940. Hundreds of civilian boats also aided in the Dunkirk evacuation of British, French, and Belgian troops.

Determining Context Why would this image of soldiers retreating from the enemy be remembered as a successful event?

World War II had begun. The Germans used a new type of warfare called *blitzkrieg*, or "lightning war." Instead of the more defensive trenches that were the hallmark of World War I, the *blitzkrieg* was all about offensive speed. The strategy took advantage of Germany's advancements with internal combustion engines and communication technologies. Tanks, combined with waves of aircraft and paratroopers, were used to break through and encircle enemy positions. By October 5, 1939, the Germans had defeated the Polish military.

While German forces overtook Poland, Western Europe remained quiet. British and French troops in France waited for the inevitable German attack. On May 10, 1940, Hitler launched a new *blitzkrieg* in the west. German troops parachuted into the Netherlands and German tanks moved into Belgium and Luxembourg. British and French forces raced north into Belgium to oppose the Nazi soldiers. German soldiers crossed the Ardennes Mountains of Luxembourg and eastern Belgium. German tanks smashed through the French lines and moved west across northern France, trapping British and French forces in Belgium.

Dunkirk and France's Fall

Meanwhile, German troops were driving Allied forces toward the English Channel. The port of Dunkirk

became the Allies' only way out. As German forces moved in on Dunkirk, Hitler mysteriously ordered them to stop. Historians think that Hitler was nervous about risking his tank forces. Whatever his reasons, this decision provided a three-day delay that allowed Allied forces to evacuate. When the evacuation ended on June 4, an estimated 338,000 British and French troops had been saved during the "Miracle at Dunkirk."

Less than three weeks later, on June 22, 1940, France surrendered and became Nazi-occupied territory. Germany set up a puppet government at the town of Vichy and made France's Marshal Philippe Pétain the leader. Hitler did not, however, give Pétain any actual power. French general Charles de Gaulle led the Free French resistance forces from the French colony of Algiers. De Gaulle worked with Allied leaders and refused to recognize the defeat of France.

✓ **CHECK FOR UNDERSTANDING**

Identifying Why did Hitler and Stalin sign a nonaggression pact?

American Neutrality

GUIDING QUESTION

How did President Roosevelt assist Britain while maintaining U.S. neutrality?

The rise of dictatorships and militarism in Europe discouraged many Americans. The sacrifices they had made during World War I seemed pointless. In addition, during the Depression, most European nations announced they would no longer repay their war debts to the United States. In response, many Americans once again began supporting isolationism and trying to avoid involvement in international conflicts.

Meanwhile, arms manufacturers were accused of tricking the United States into entering World War I. In 1934 Senator Gerald P. Nye investigated these allegations. The Nye Committee report documented the huge profits that arms factories had made during the war and created the impression that these businesses had influenced the decision to go to war, causing more Americans to turn toward isolationism.

Legislating Neutrality

In response to growing Italian and German aggression in Europe, Congress passed the Neutrality Act of 1935. This legislation made it illegal for Americans to sell arms to any country at war.

In October 1935, as part of his dream to build a new Roman empire, Mussolini ordered the Italian military to invade Ethiopia, then known as Abyssinia. The war was short; the Abyssinian forces were no match for the better armed Italian troops, and the

CORBIS/Corbis Historical/Getty Images

emperor, Haile Selassie, was forced into exile. Knowing that the American people and Congress would not support action to stop Italy, Roosevelt supported the passage of a new law, the Neutrality Act of 1936, which extended the ban on arms sales imposed by the Neutrality Act of 1935 and also banned loans to nations at war. The 1936 act was far more likely to hurt Italy than Abyssinia, which would not have been able to borrow much money anyway.

In 1936 the Spanish Civil War erupted. Rebel Nationalists led by General Francisco Franco and supported by Germany and Italy fought against the Republicans, supported by the Soviet Union and thousands of volunteers from Europe and the United States who went to Spain to fight. The Spanish Civil War was widely portrayed as the first clash between the forces of fascism and western democracy. Franco's forces eventually won the civil war, and Franco became the leader of Spain until his death in 1975.

Soon after the Spanish Civil War began, Hitler and Mussolini pledged to cooperate on several international issues, and Japan aligned itself with Germany and Italy. The three nations became known as the Axis Powers. As European tensions worsened, Congress passed the Neutrality Act of 1937, continuing the ban on selling arms to warring nations and also requiring them to buy all nonmilitary supplies from the United States on a "cash-and-carry" basis. Countries had to send their own ships to pick up goods and had to pay in cash; loans were not allowed. Isolationists knew that attacks on American ships had helped bring the country into World War I and wanted to prevent the United States from being pulled into another European war.

Roosevelt's Internationalism

Despite the government's stand on neutrality, President Roosevelt supported **internationalism,** the idea that trade between nations creates prosperity and helps prevent war. He warned that the neutrality acts "might drag us into war instead of keeping us out," but he did not veto the bills. When Japan invaded China in July 1937 without declaring war, Roosevelt claimed the Neutrality Act of 1937 did not apply. He authorized the sale of weapons to China, warning that America should not let an "epidemic of lawlessness" infect the world:

66 There is no escape through mere isolation or neutrality. . . . When an epidemic of physical disease starts to spread, the community . . . joins in a quarantine of the patients in order to protect the health of the community against the spread of the disease. . . . War is a contagion, whether it be declared or undeclared. 99

—from *The Public Papers and Addresses of Franklin D. Roosevelt*

Testing Neutrality

Roosevelt wanted to help Britain and France in their struggle and asked Congress to revise the neutrality laws to allow the sale of weapons to warring nations. Congress passed the Neutrality Act of 1939, permitting the sale of weapons, but only on a "cash-and-carry" basis. In the spring of 1940 the United States faced the first test of its neutrality. Britain asked Roosevelt for old American destroyers to replenish its fleet, and the president used a loophole in the cash-only requirement for purchases. He sent 50 ships to Britain in exchange for America's use of British bases in the Atlantic. Because the deal did not involve an actual sale, the Neutrality Act did not apply.

Widespread acceptance of the Destroyers-for-Bases deal indicated a change in public opinion. By July 1940, most Americans favored offering limited aid to the Allies, but debate continued over the scope of that aid. The Fight for Freedom Committee wanted the repeal of neutrality laws and stronger actions against Germany. On the other side, the America First Committee opposed any intervention to help the Allies. After winning reelection in 1940, Roosevelt expanded the nation's role in the war. Speaking to Congress, he listed the Four Freedoms for which both

Clifford K. Berryman's cartoon, published in *The Evening Star* on September 7, 1939, takes aim at senators William Borah of Idaho, Gerald Nye of North Dakota, and Hiram Johnson of California, who shared a long history of opposing U.S. involvement in international alliances and wars.

Analyzing Points of View What position is Berryman taking on the issue of U.S. isolationism?

PHOTO: National Archives and Records Administration; TEXT:(t) Roosevelt, Franklin D. "Statement on Neutrality Legislation." August 31, 1935; (2) Address at Chicago, Franklin D. Roosevelt, October 5, 1937, The Franklin D. Roosevelt Presidential Library and Museum, National Archives and Records Administration.

internationalism a national policy of actively trading with foreign countries to foster peace and prosperity

the United States and Britain stood: freedom of speech, freedom of worship, freedom from want, and freedom from fear.

The Lend-Lease Act

By December 1940, Great Britain had run out of funds to fight the war, and Roosevelt oversaw efforts to keep Britain supplied with arms and other materials. He proposed the Lend-Lease Act, which Congress passed on March 11, 1941, by a wide margin. The Lend-Lease Act allowed the United States to sell, loan, or transfer military and other assets to any country considered a necessary part of America's defense:

66 SEC. 3. (a) Notwithstanding the provisions of any other law, the President may, from time to time, when he deems it in the interest of national defense, authorize the Secretary Of War, the Secretary of the Navy, or the head of any other department or agency of the Government—

(1) To manufacture in arsenals, factories, and shipyards under their jurisdiction, or otherwise procure, to the extent to which funds are made available therefor, or contracts are authorized from time to time by the Congress, or both, any defense article for the government of any country whose defense the President deems vital to the defense of the United States. 99

—from the Lend-Lease Act, 1941

Lend-Lease aid eventually went to the Soviet Union after Hitler invaded the Soviet Union in June 1941. Roosevelt followed Britain's lead in supporting any state fighting the Nazis. The problem of getting American arms and supplies to Britain remained. German submarines in the Atlantic sank hundreds of thousands of tons of cargo each month. The British Navy lacked the ships to stop them. Because the United States was still officially neutral, Roosevelt could not order the navy to protect British cargo ships. Instead, he developed the idea of a hemispheric defense zone, declaring that the entire western half of the Atlantic was part of the Western Hemisphere and therefore neutral. He then ordered the U.S. Navy to patrol the western Atlantic and reveal the location of German submarines to the British.

The Atlantic Charter

In August 1941, Roosevelt and Churchill met and developed the Atlantic Charter, which committed both nations to a postwar world of democracy, nonaggression, free trade, economic advancement, and freedom of the seas. Churchill later said that Roosevelt "made it clear that he would look for an 'incident' which would justify him in opening hostilities" with Germany.

Despite Roosevelt's support for the British and French, many Americans believed that fighting another war overseas was against the nation's interests.

Predicting Would you expect isolationists' feelings to change if the United States suffered a direct attack?

In early September, a German submarine, or U-boat, fired on an American destroyer that had been radioing the U-boat's position to the British. Roosevelt promptly responded by ordering American ships to follow a "shoot-on-sight" policy toward German submarines. The Germans escalated hostilities the following month, targeting two American destroyers. One of them, the *Reuben James*, sank after being torpedoed, killing over 100 sailors. As the end of 1941 drew near, Germany and the United States continued a tense standoff.

✓ **CHECK FOR UNDERSTANDING**

1. **Explaining** How did Roosevelt assist Britain while maintaining U.S. neutrality?

2. **Summarizing** What was the central idea of the Atlantic Charter?

LESSON ACTIVITIES

1. **Informative/Explanatory Writing** Write a paragraph explaining why the Nazi-Soviet Nonaggression Pact was such a surprise to the world.

2. **Presenting** In small groups, use the Internet and other available resources to research the rise of dictatorships in Italy, the Soviet Union, or Germany in the years leading up to World War II. Make sure you use only accurate, credible sources. Create a short slide show to explain how the dictatorship took hold in your assigned country in the time between the world wars. Share your presentation with the class.

PHOTO: Bettmann/Getty Images; TEXT: (1)U.S. Congress. March 11, 1941. Lend-Lease Act of 1941 (55 Stat. 31). Accessed April 27, 2017 at https://www.ourdocuments.gov/doc.php?doc=71&page=transcript; (2) Dallek, Robert. 1995. Franklin D. Roosevelt and American Foreign Policy, 1932-1945. New York: Oxford University Press..

03

The Holocaust

Key Ideas and Details As you read, use a graphic organizer like the one below to list examples of Nazi persecution of European Jews.

Examples of Persecution	

Nazi Persecution of the Jews

GUIDING QUESTION

What legal and political actions were used to persecute European Jews?

During the Holocaust, the Nazis murdered nearly 6 million Jews, two-thirds of the Jews in Europe. The Nazis also murdered millions of people from other groups they considered inferior. The Hebrew term for the Holocaust is Shoah, meaning "catastrophe," but it is often used specifically to refer to the Nazi campaign to exterminate the Jews during World War II. The Holocaust was a genocide, the systematic murder of members of a group with the intent to destroy its existence.

The Nuremberg Laws

Although the Nazis persecuted anyone who dared oppose them—as well as people with disabilities, Roma (previously known as "gypsies"), homosexuals, and Slavic peoples—they reserved their strongest hatred for the Jews. This loathing went far beyond the European anti-Semitism that was common at the time. In the Middle Ages, Jews had been subjected to discrimination, mob violence, and expulsions. But in nineteenth- and twentieth-century Western and Central Europe, both the frequency and intensity of anti-Jewish government policies diminished.

After the Nazis took power, however, they quickly moved to deprive German Jews of many established rights. In September 1935, the Nuremberg Laws took citizenship away from Jewish Germans and banned marriage between Jews and other Germans. Two months later, another decree barred Jews from holding public office or voting, and another law compelled Jews with German-sounding names to adopt "Jewish" names. Soon the passports of Jews were marked with a red J to identify them as Jewish.

By the summer of 1936, at least half of Germany's Jews were jobless, having lost the right to work as civil servants, journalists, farmers, and actors. In 1938 the Nazis also banned Jews from practicing law and medicine and from operating businesses. With no source of income, life became very difficult. Well integrated into German society before this time, many Jewish families were reluctant to leave and give up the lives they had built there, even as their political and social conditions worsened. Many also thought that conditions would surely improve after a time, but in fact, conditions soon became worse.

Kristallnacht

On November 7, 1938, a young Jewish refugee named Herschel Grynszpan shot and killed a German diplomat in Paris. Grynszpan's parents and more than 14,000 other Polish Jews had been deported from Germany to Poland, and the young man was seeking revenge for this act and for the persecution of the Jews in general.

Using this as a pretext, Hitler ordered his minister of propaganda, Joseph Goebbels, to stage attacks against the Jews that would seem like a spontaneous popular reaction to news of the murder. On the night of November 9, this plan played out in a spree of destruction. In Vienna, a Jewish child named Frederic Morton watched in terror as Nazi storm troopers broke into his family's apartment:

On *Kristallnacht*, Nazi storm troopers destroyed Jewish property, such as this Jewish-owned shop in Berlin, and terrorized Jewish families.

Interpreting How do you think publication of photographs showing the aftermath of *Kristallnacht* would have affected world opinion toward the Nazis?

> 66 They yanked out every drawer in every one of our chests and cupboards, and tossed each in the air. They let the cutlery jangle across the floor, the clothes scatter, and stepped over the mess to fling the next drawer. Their exuberance was amazing. . . . 'We might be back,' the leader said. On the way out he threw our mother-of-pearl ashtray over his shoulder, like confetti. We did not speak or move or breathe until we heard their boots against the pavement. 99

—quoted in *Facing History and Ourselves*

The anti-Jewish violence that erupted throughout Germany and Austria that night came to be called *Kristallnacht*, or "night of broken glass," because afterward broken glass littered the streets. By the following morning, more than ninety Jews were dead, hundreds were badly injured, and thousands more were terrorized. The Nazis had forbidden police to interfere while roving bands of Nazis destroyed 7,500 Jewish businesses and hundreds of synagogues.

The lawlessness of *Kristallnacht* lasted longer than a single night. Following the initial night of violence, the Gestapo, the Nazi government's secret police, arrested about 30,000 Jewish men. The Nazi government also confiscated insurance payments owed to Jewish owners of ruined businesses.

Jews Try to Escape

Kristallnacht and its aftermath marked a significant escalation of Nazi persecution against the Jewish people. Many Jews, including Frederic Morton's family, decided that it was time to leave and fled to the United States. Between 1933, when Hitler took power, and the start of World War II in 1939, some 250,000 Jews escaped Nazi-controlled Germany.

These emigrants included prominent scientists, such as Albert Einstein, and business owners like Otto Frank, who resettled his family in Amsterdam in 1933. Otto's daughter Anne kept a diary of her family's life in hiding after the Nazis overran the Netherlands, and the "secret annex," as she called their hiding place, has become a museum.

By 1938, one U.S. consulate in Germany had a backlog of more than 100,000 visa applications from Jews trying to leave for the United States. Following the Nazi *Anschluss*, some 3,000 Austrian Jews applied for U.S. visas each day. Most never received visas to the United States or to the other countries where they applied. As a result, millions of Jews remained trapped in Nazi-dominated Europe.

Several factors limited Jewish immigration to the United States. Nazi orders prohibited Jews from taking more than about four dollars out of Germany, while U. S. immigration law forbade granting a visa to anyone "likely to become a public charge." Customs officials tended to assume that the description "public charge" applied to Jews because Germany had forced them to leave behind any wealth. High unemployment rates in the 1930s also made

German-Jewish refugees onboard the SS *St. Louis* arrive in Antwerp, Belgium after over a month at sea, first traveling from Hamburg, Germany to Cuba and the United States.

Drawing Conclusions Considering the people onboard the SS *St. Louis,* what conclusions can you draw about the reasons Cuba and the United States gave for turning them away?

PHOTO: (tl)Hulton Archive/Getty Images; (br)Three Lions/Hulton Archive/Getty Images; TEXT: "Kristallnacht," by Frederic Morton, published November 10, 1978. Copyright © 1978 by The New York Times.

immigration unpopular with many Americans, even to accommodate European refugees. Some Americans held anti-Semitic beliefs and did not want to admit Jewish immigrants into the United States. The existing immigration policy allowed only 150,000 immigrants annually, with a fixed quota from each country, and the law permitted no exceptions for refugees or victims of persecution.

At an international conference on refugees in 1938, several European countries, the United States, and Latin America stated their regret that they could not take in more of Germany's Jews without raising immigration quotas. Meanwhile, Nazi propaganda chief Joseph Goebbels announced, "[I]f there is any country that believes it has not enough Jews, I shall gladly turn over to it all our Jews." Hitler also declared himself "ready to put all these criminals at the disposal of these countries . . . even on luxury ships."

As war loomed in 1939, many ships departed from Germany crammed with Jews desperate to escape. Some of their visas, however, had been forged or sold illegally, and Mexico, Paraguay, Argentina, and Costa Rica all denied access to Jews with such documents, as did the United States.

On May 27, 1939, the SS St. Louis entered the harbor in Havana, Cuba, with 937 Jewish refugees on board. Most of these passengers hoped to go to the United States eventually, but they had certificates improperly issued by Cuba's director of immigration giving them permission to land in Cuba. When the ships arrived in Havana, the Cuban government refused to let the refugees come ashore. For several days, the ship's captain steered his ship in circles off the coast of Florida, awaiting official permission to dock at a U.S. port.

Denied permission, the ship turned back toward Europe, reaching Antwerp, Belgium, on June 17, 1939. Belgium, France, the Netherlands, and Great Britain agreed to take some of the refugees. Within two years, the first three of these countries fell under Nazi domination.

✓ **CHECK FOR UNDERSTANDING**

1. **Identifying Cause and Effect** Why did many Jews remain in Nazi Germany and within Axis-controlled areas of Europe?

2. **Explaining** How did the German law forbidding Jews from taking their wealth out of the country have an impact on the ability of Jews to escape Nazi Germany?

The Voyage of the SS St. Louis, May 13–June 17, 1939

German-Jewish refugees boarded the SS St. Louis to escape persecution. Their hopes were dashed when Cuba, then the United States and Canada, refused to honor their visas.

The SS St. Louis departs Hamburg, Germany, on May 13 with about 900 German-Jewish refugees on board. The ship stops in Cherbourg, France, to take on additional refugees, for a total of 937 passengers. One elderly refugee dies en route and is buried at sea.

June 6, 1939: Returns to Europe; June 17, 1939: Arrives in Antwerp

May 13, 1939: Departs Hamburg; Destination Havana

ATLANTIC OCEAN

0   1,000 miles
0   1,000 kilometers
Miller Cylindrical projection

Cuba only honors 28 visas. One passenger tries to commit suicide and is taken to the hospital in Havana. The remaining 908 refugees are turned away. On June 2, the ship sails toward Florida, but is denied permission to dock. On June 6, the ship heads back to Europe, reaching Antwerp, Belgium, on June 17.

GEOGRAPHY CONNECTION

1. **Exploring Place** Why did the SS St. Louis stop in Cherbourg, France?

2. **Patterns and Movement** How long was the return trip to Europe?

(1)Goebbels, Josef. In Kennedy, David M. Freedom From Fear. Oxford History of the United States, v.9, pt. 1. Oxford: Oxford UP, 2004; (2)Landau, Ronnie S. The Nazi Holocaust. New York: I. B. Tauris, 2006.

The Holocaust, 1939–1945

Nazi concentration camps and extermination camps extended across several countries.

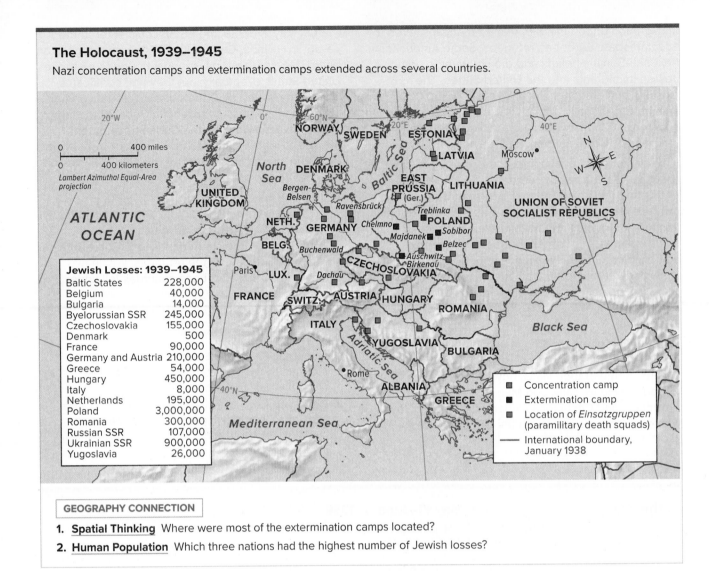

Jewish Losses: 1939–1945

Baltic States	228,000
Belgium	40,000
Bulgaria	14,000
Byelorussian SSR	245,000
Czechoslovakia	155,000
Denmark	500
France	90,000
Germany and Austria	210,000
Greece	54,000
Hungary	450,000
Italy	8,000
Netherlands	195,000
Poland	3,000,000
Romania	300,000
Russian SSR	107,000
Ukrainian SSR	900,000
Yugoslavia	26,000

Legend:
- ■ Concentration camp
- ■ Extermination camp
- ■ Location of *Einsatzgruppen* (paramilitary death squads)
- — International boundary, January 1938

GEOGRAPHY CONNECTION

1. **Spatial Thinking** Where were most of the extermination camps located?

2. **Human Population** Which three nations had the highest number of Jewish losses?

The Final Solution

GUIDING QUESTION

How did the Nazis try to exterminate Europe's Jewish population?

On January 20, 1942, Nazi leaders met at the Wannsee Conference to coordinate the "final solution of the Jewish question." Previous "solutions" had included rounding up Jews, Roma, Slavs, and others from conquered areas, shooting them, and piling them into mass graves. A different inhumane method forced Jews and other "undesirables" into trucks and then piped in exhaust fumes to kill them. These methods, however, had proven too slow and inefficient for the Nazis.

At Wannsee, the Nazis made plans to round up Jews from the vast areas of Nazi-controlled Europe.

Jews were taken to detention centers known as **concentration camps,** where healthy individuals would work as slave laborers until they often died of exhaustion, disease, or malnutrition. Most others, including the elderly, young children, and the infirm (among them laborers who could no longer work) would be sent to **extermination camps,** attached to many of the concentration camps, to be executed in massive gas chambers.

Concentration Camps

The Nazis had established their first concentration camps in 1933 to jail political opponents. After the war began, the Nazis built concentration camps throughout Europe.

As one of the largest concentration camps, Buchenwald had more than 200,000 prisoners

---

concentration camp a place where people are detained or confined

extermination camp a place where people are sent to be executed

PHOTO: Wojtek Laski/Hulton Archive/Getty Images; TEXT: (1)Luther D. Fletcher quoted in World War II: From the Battle Front to the Home Front, by Kay B. Hall. University of Arkansas Press, 1995; (2)Night by Elie Wiesel. Copyright © 1960 by Hill and Wang.

Concentration camp survivors are helped through a gate at Auschwitz during liberation, 1945. Prisoners passed through this gate upon arrival, under a sign reading "Work Sets You Free."

Determining Context
This sign has become one of the most recognizable symbols of the holocaust. Why do you think that is?

working 12-hour shifts as forced laborers in nearby factories. Although Buchenwald had no gas chambers, hundreds of prisoners died there every month from exhaustion and horrible living conditions. As a U.S. Army chaplain wrote in his diary in 1945:

66 One thousand Weimar citizens toured the Buchenwald camp in groups of 100. They saw blackened skeletons and skulls in the ovens of the crematorium. In the yard outside, they saw a heap of white human ashes and bones. . . . Those who were dead were stripped of their clothing and lay naked, many stacked like cordwood waiting to be burned in the crematory. At one time, 5,000 had been stacked on the vacant lot next to the crematory. 99

—Captain Luther D. Fletcher, quoted in *World War II: From the Battle Front to the Home Front*

Extermination Camps

In late 1941, the Nazis built extermination facilities at the Chelmno and Auschwitz camps in Poland. After the Wannsee Conference, extermination facilities were built at four other camps in Poland.

At these camps, including the infamous Treblinka, Jews were the Nazis' main victims. Auschwitz alone housed about 100,000 people in 300 prison barracks. Its gas chambers, built to kill 2,000 people at a time, could gas 12,000 people in a day. Of the estimated 1,600,000 people who died at Auschwitz, about 1,300,000 were Jews, and most others were Poles, Soviet prisoners of war, or Roma.

Upon arrival at Auschwitz, healthy prisoners were selected for slave labor. Elderly or disabled people, the sick, and mothers and children went immediately to the gas chambers, after which their bodies were burned in giant crematoriums.

When Elie Wiesel was fifteen, the Nazis occupied Hungary. Wiesel and his family, who were Jewish, were rounded up and deported to the extermination camp at Auschwitz. Many of Wiesel's family did not survive. He wrote about his experiences during the Holocaust in his book, *Night*. Wiesel vividly described prisoners' desperation and the targeted inhumane treatment of Jews:

66 The snow fell thickly. We were forbidden to sit down or even to move. The snow began to form a thick layer over our blankets. They brought us bread—the usual ration. We threw ourselves upon it. Someone had the idea of appeasing his thirst by eating the snow. Soon the others were imitating him. As we were not allowed to bend down, everyone took out his spoon and ate the accumulated snow off his neighbor's back. A mouthful of bread and a spoonful of snow. The SS who were watching laughed at this spectacle. 99

—Elie Wiesel, *Night*

In only a few years Jewish culture, which had existed in Europe for more than a thousand years, had been virtually obliterated by the Nazis in the lands they conquered. The Holocaust has been intensively studied to attempt to understand why and how such as event could have occurred.

After weeks of fierce resistance, Jews in the Warsaw ghetto in Poland are rounded up for deportation to concentration camps in May 1943.

Evaluating What details in the photograph suggest what might happen when these people reach the concentration camps?

Most historians point to a number of factors that contributed to the Holocaust. First, the German people felt a strong sense of injury after World War I and looked for someone to blame for their suffering. In addition, Germany experienced severe economic problems in the years after World War I—transitioning from a wartime economy, a devastated economic infrastructure, and global economic depression. Also, Adolf Hitler's unprecedented level of control over the German nation combined with the lack of a strong tradition of representative government in Germany made it easier for a singular point of view to become dominant. The German citizens of Hitler's secret police also encouraged people to ignore abuses happening around them. And finally, there was a long history of anti-Jewish prejudice and discrimination in Europe.

 CHECK FOR UNDERSTANDING

Summarizing How did the Nazis try to exterminate Europe's Jewish population?

The Nuremberg Trials

GUIDING QUESTION

What was the purpose of the Nuremberg Trials?

At the war's end in August 1945, the United States, Britain, France, and the Soviet Union created the International Military Tribunal (IMT) to punish German military leaders and others for war crimes. The tribunal held trials in Nuremberg, Germany, where Hitler had staged Nazi Party rallies. Twenty-two German leaders were prosecuted at the Nuremberg Trials. Three were acquitted, and seven were given prison sentences. Twelve were sentenced to death. Trials of lower-ranking leaders continued until April 1949, leading to 24 more executions and 107 prison sentences.

Although some of these trials addressed Holocaust-related crimes, only one made the Holocaust its focus: Case #9 of the Subsequent Nuremberg Proceedings. This trial, conducted by the United States, tried 22 members of the *Einsatzgruppen,* a mobile task force created by the German SS to exterminate Jews, Roma, and other groups deemed undesirable by the Nazis.

In Case #9, the IMT charged the defendants with three counts: crimes against humanity, war crimes, and membership in organizations designated criminal by the International Military Tribunal. All of the defendants pleaded not guilty, claiming they were acting under orders as soldiers. Nevertheless, the IMT convicted 20 of the 22 defendants on all three counts and the remaining two defendants on the third count alone.

Fourteen of these defendants were sentenced to death, although only four were eventually executed. The remaining 10 had their sentences commuted to prison time. The IMT sentenced the rest of the defendants to various lengths of prison time, with one being released for time served. Even though some defendants were sentenced to life terms, all were released from prison by 1958.

 CHECK FOR UNDERSTANDING

Identifying What was the purpose of Case #9 of the Subsequent Nuremberg Proceedings?

LESSON ACTIVITIES

1. **Argumentative Writing** Imagine that you are living in the United States during the 1930s. You believe that more Jewish immigrants should be allowed to come into the country. Write a letter to your representative or senator in Congress to express your point of view using appropriate language.

2. **Presenting** Work with a small group to research transcripts from the Nuremberg Trials. Choose an excerpt from the transcripts and perform a careful analysis of the information. Each group should participate in a class discussion about their analysis.

PHOTO: Keystone/Hulton Archive/Getty Images

04

Understanding Multiple Perspectives About American Neutrality

? COMPELLING QUESTION

How did the United States respond to the events of World War II in Europe?

Plan Your Inquiry

In this lesson, you will investigate the American response to the outbreak of war in Europe and contrast perspectives leading up to the United States entering World War II.

DEVELOP QUESTIONS

Developing Questions About American Neutrality Read the Compelling Question for this lesson. What key events led to World War II? How did those events involve or affect the United States and the American people? Develop a list of Supporting Questions that would help you answer the Compelling Question in this lesson.

APPLY HISTORICAL TOOLS

Analyzing Primary Sources You will work with a variety of primary sources in this lesson. These sources provide perspectives from 1936 through 1941, the years leading up to U.S. entry into the war. As you read, use a graphic organizer like the one below to record information about the sources that will help you examine them and check for historical understanding. Note ways in which each source helps you answer your Supporting Questions.

Source	Author/ Creator	Description/ Notes	Which Supporting Question does this source help me answer?
A			
B			
C			
D			
E			
F			
G			
H			

After you analyze the sources, you will:

- use the evidence from the sources
- communicate your conclusions
- take informed action

Background Information

In the mid-1930s the United States was struggling to recover from the Great Depression. President Franklin D. Roosevelt's New Deal programs and policies had some limited success. As tensions rose in Europe and gave way to conflict, many Americans feared another foreign war. World War I had led to a great loss of life and the seeming post-war prosperity had not proven sustainable.

President Roosevelt won a second term—by a landslide—in 1936. At the time, his focus remained on the hardships caused by farm and business failures and widespread unemployment. He knew that many Americans needed help and expected the federal government's focus to be on domestic concerns. His Inaugural Address promised an ongoing effort to put people back to work and bolster the U.S. economy.

But Roosevelt and many others knew that trouble was brewing in Europe and Asia. Like World War I, the Great Depression had shown the strong ties between the United States and the rest of the world. What happened overseas would inevitably affect the American people. Still, in the 1930s, public opinion was strongly set against devoting resources to what many perceived as the problems of others.

» The city of London experienced substantial bombing damage during World War II.

Popperfoto/Getty Images

Findings of the Nye Committee

Fueling the nation's sentiment to stay out of foreign wars were public accusations that arms manufacturers had tricked the United States into entering World War I. From 1934 into 1936, Senator Gerald P. Nye held dozens of hearings to investigate these allegations. The Nye Committee report documented the huge profits made during the war, but no firm proof was gathered to show conspiracy. Nye was among several members of Congress who pushed for passage of the Neutrality Act of 1935. By the time the Nye report was completed, Adolf Hitler had become Führer, or the sole leader, of Germany and reintroduced military conscription, an act prohibited under the Treaty of Versailles in 1919.

PRIMARY SOURCE : REPORT

66 I. NATURE OF THE MUNITIONS COMPANIES

The committee finds . . . that almost none of the **munitions** companies in this country confine themselves exclusively to the manufacture of military materials. Great numbers of the largest suppliers to the Army and Navy (Westinghouse, General Electric, du Pont, General Motors, Babcock & Wilcox, etc.) are predominantly manufacturers of materials for civilian life. Others, such as the aviation companies and Colt's Patent Firearms Co., supply the greatest portion of their output to the military services. In addition to the manufacturers there are several sales companies which act as agents for various manufacturers. There are also brokers dealing largely in old and second-hand supplies. In case of war, other companies, not at present producing any munitions, would be called upon to furnish them. . . .

IV. THE EFFECT OF ARMAMENTS ON PEACE

The committee finds . . . that some of the munitions companies have occasionally had opportunities to intensify the fears of people for their neighbors and have used them to their own profit.

[T]he very quality which in civilian life tends to lead toward progressive civilization, namely the improvements of machinery, has been used by the munitions makers to scare nations into a continued frantic expenditure for the latest improvements in devices of warfare. The constant message of the traveling salesman of the munitions companies to the rest of the world has been that they now had available for sale something new, more dangerous and more deadly than ever before and that the potential enemy was or would be buying it.

While the evidence before this committee does not show that wars have been started solely because of the activities of munitions makers and their agents, it is also true that wars rarely have one single cause, and the committee finds it to be against the peace of the world for selfishly interested organizations to be left free to **goad** and frighten nations into military activity 99

—The Nye Report, February 24, 1936

munitions arms, weaponry, and ammunition
goad to incite or rouse to action

EXAMINE THE SOURCE

1. **Summarizing** What information does this report provide? Summarize the key points.
2. **Analyzing Points of View** What connection does the report imply between munitions companies and war-making?

United States Senate, Special Committee on Investigation of the Munitions Industry, Munitions Industry, Report No. 944, Part 8, 74th Congress, 2d Session, February 24, 1936.

PHOTO: Sueddeutsche Zeitung Photo/Alamy Stock Photo; TEXT: Sound Recording RLXA30: President Franklin Roosevelt's "Quarantine" Speech; 10/5/1937; Sound Recordings of Franklin D. Roosevelt's Speeches, 1933- 1944; Washington Records, Incorporated; National Archives at College Park, College Park, MD. [Online Version, https://www.docsteach.org/documents/document/fdr-quarantine-speech, May 1, 2020]

B

"The Tug of War"

Spurred by support for isolationism, Congress passed a series of Neutrality Acts from 1935 to 1939 that barred direct aid to nations engaged in war. However, as international tensions grew, so did the tension at home over whether to remain neutral or assist U.S. allies against a growing threat. This cartoon, published in the *Chicago Tribune* in 1939, illustrates that push and pull.

PRIMARY SOURCE : POLITICAL CARTOON

THE TUG OF WAR

EFFORTS TO DRAG AMERICA INTO EUROPEAN QUARRELS

CONGRESS

EXAMINE THE SOURCE

1. **Analyzing Visuals** Who are the opposing teams depicted in the cartoon, and who does FDR side with?

2. **Interpreting** What message is the artist trying to convey?

C

FDR's Quarantine Speech

Roosevelt believed that trade between nations created prosperity and helped prevent war, but he did not veto the Neutrality Acts passed between 1935 and 1937. In March 1936, Nazi forces took control of the demilitarized zone in the Rhineland while Italy led an assault on Ethiopia. A year later, Japan invaded China. President Roosevelt responded with this speech.

PRIMARY SOURCE : SPEECH

66 The political situation in the world, which of late has been growing . . . worse, is such as to cause grave concern . . . to all the peoples and nations who wish to live in peace and amity with their neighbors. . . .

It seems to be unfortunately true that the epidemic of world lawlessness is spreading.

When an epidemic of physical disease starts to spread, the community approves and joins in a **quarantine** . . . to protect . . . against the spread of the disease.

It is my determination to pursue a policy of peace. . . . It ought to be inconceivable that in this modern era, . . . any nation could be so foolish and ruthless as to run the risk of plunging the whole world into war by invading and violating, in contravention of solemn treaties, the territory of other nations that have done them no real harm and are too weak to protect themselves . . . Yet the peace of the world and the welfare and security of every nation, including our own, is today being threatened. . . .

War is a contagion, whether it be declared or undeclared. . . . We are adopting such measures as will minimize our risk of involvement, but we cannot have complete protection in a world of disorder in which confidence and security have broken down. 99

—Franklin D. Roosevelt, October 5, 1937

quarantine a state of isolation to prevent the spread of disease

EXAMINE THE SOURCE

1. **Analyzing** What extended metaphor does Roosevelt use in this passage? How does that metaphor relate to his main idea?

2. **Drawing Conclusions** What does Roosevelt suggest about the nature of war and its potential impact on the United States?

D

Destroyers for Bases Agreement

In 1940, after France and other Western European nations had fallen to Germany, Winston Churchill pressured the United States to provide more aid. Because of the United States's official neutrality, the attempts to help the Allies in the fight against Germany involved creativity. In 1940 the British ambassador agreed to give land in British territory to the United States for military use. In exchange President Roosevelt authorized Secretary of States Cordell Hull to transfer 50 U.S. Navy destroyer ships.

PRIMARY SOURCE : DIPLOMATIC AGREEMENT

66 . . . in view of the desire of the United States to acquire additional air and naval bases in the Caribbean and in British Guiana, and without endeavouring to place a monetary or commercial value upon the many tangible and intangible rights and properties involved, His Majesty's Government will make available to the United States for immediate establishment and use naval and air bases and facilities for entrance thereto and the operation and protection thereof, on the eastern side of the Bahamas, the southern coast of Jamaica, the western coast of St. Lucia, the west coast of Trinidad in the Gulf of Paria, in the island of Antigua and in British Guiana within fifty miles of Georgetown, in exchange for naval and military equipment and material which the United States Government will transfer to His Majesty's Government. 99

—communication between The Marquess of Lothian and Secretary of State Hull, September 2, 1940

EXAMINE THE SOURCE

Explaining Why did Great Britain not try to assign a monetary value to the land it was providing the United States?

E

"The Four Freedoms Speech"

President Roosevelt gave this speech on January 6, 1941, in which he called for a world founded on "four essential human freedoms": freedom of speech and expression, freedom of worship, freedom from want, and freedom from fear. Roosevelt's support for neutrality is echoed in the speech, but he also warns that neutrality does not mean meek acceptance of outside events.

PRIMARY SOURCE : SPEECH

66 Our national policy is this:

First, by an impressive expression of the public will and without regard to partisanship, we are committed to all-inclusive national defense.

Second, . . . we are committed to full support of all those resolute peoples, everywhere, who are resisting aggression and are thereby keeping war away from our Hemisphere. . . .

Third . . . we are committed to the proposition that principles of morality and consideration for our own security will never permit us to **acquiesce** in a peace dictated by aggressors. . . .

Let us say to the democracies: 'We Americans are vitally concerned in your defense of freedom. We are putting forth our energies, our resources, and our organizing powers to give you the strength to regain and maintain a free world. We shall send you, in ever increasing numbers, ships, planes, tanks, guns. This is our purpose . . . [W]e will not be intimidated by the threats of dictators that they will regard as a breach of international law and as an act of war our aid to the democracies which dare to resist their aggression. . . . 99

—Franklin D. Roosevelt, January 6, 1941

acquiesce agree or submit to

EXAMINE THE SOURCE

1. **Summarize** What three points of national policy does Roosevelt identify?
2. **Analyzing Perspectives** What promise does Roosevelt implicitly make to Britain and other democratic nations?

296

The America First Committee

The America First Committee (AFC) formed in September 1940 as pressure increased on the United States to commit more foreign aid to Britain. As Roosevelt expanded the cash-and-carry policy and then the Lend-Lease Act, prominent figures throughout the country helped form and supported the AFC and its isolationist principles.

PRIMARY SOURCE : TEXT FLYER

" 1. The United States must build an **impregnable** defense for America. With such a defense no foreign power, or group of powers, can successfully attack us.

2. With proper safeguards for the distribution of supplies and the maintenance of our neutrality, Americans should . . . give humanitarian aid to the suffering and needy people of England and the occupied countries.

3. The cash and carry provisions of the existing Neutrality Act are essential to American peace and security. Within the limits of that Act Americans may properly aid Great Britain. Aid to her beyond the limitations of the present Neutrality Act would weaken our defense at home, and might . . . involve us in conflict. We oppose any change in the law which would permit American vessels to enter the combat zone or which would permit the American navy to convoy merchant ships through that zone, as any such course would . . . plunge this country into Europe's war.

4. Americans should and do cherish the ideals of democracy and abhor dictatorship, but the welfare of one hundred thirty million Americans and the preservation of democracy on this continent demand that the United States keep out of foreign wars. "

—America First Committee, 1941

impregnable incapable of being conquered

> **EXAMINE THE SOURCE**
>
> 1. **Contrasting** What type of foreign aid does the AFC support and what type does it oppose?
> 2. **Analyzing Perspectives** What reason does the flyer give for limiting U.S. involvement in foreign wars?

Describing the America First Committee

The AFC seized the public's attention not only because of its messaging but also because of its messengers. The popular aviator Charles Lindbergh—who had made the first non-stop solo flight across the Atlantic Ocean—traveled the country in 1940 and 1941, speaking on behalf of the movement. He urged Americans to stay out of a war that he considered a squabble among European nations. The activities of the AFC soon caught the attention of popular society columnist Evelyn Peyton Gordon.

PRIMARY SOURCE : NEWSPAPER

" 'There is nothing so secure as a settled mind.' That's what Genevieve Champ Clark Thomson, sister of Sen. Bennett Champ Clark says, and that's about right. Genevieve was discussing the conditions of the American mind today.

At least that's what her sister-in-law Mrs. Bennett Clark said yesterday when she spoke to more than a hundred people who had met at the home of former Undersecretary of State William R. Castle.

Those people, capitalists, labor union members, Democrats, Republicans, authors and one orchestra leader, were meeting to hear the story of 'America First.' An organization which started some time ago and which seems to be growing by leaps and bounds. . . . [C]hapters of the movement have sprung up in many cities. . . .

'It's not 'anti' anything. It's not 'pro' anything either, except American,' said Mr. Castle as he opened the meeting in the oak-paneled library of his home. 'We'll welcome any American as a member unless he is a Communist or Fascist and then he is not a real American. We're trying to keep out of this war and to build a big defense.' "

—Evelyn Peyton Gordon, *Washington Daily News,* December 12, 1940

> **EXAMINE THE SOURCE**
>
> 1. **Describing** What event motivated Gordon to write this column, and how does she describe the event?
> 2. **Making Inferences** What two key ideas can you infer from Gordon's description of the event and the quote from Mr. Castle?

(l)America First Committee, "The Principles of the America First Committee," 1941; (r)Gordon, Evelyn Peyton, "Washington Society Leaders Organizing America First" Unit," Washington Daily News, December 12, 1940.

Trying to Prepare for War

At its peak, the America First Committee boasted more than 800,000 members spread across various classes and occupations. This included Senator Gerald P. Nye of the Nye Committee. By late 1940, Germany, Italy, and Japan had formed an alliance and the bombing of Britain had begun. War seemed more imminent than ever. This memorandum appears in the files of the Federal Bureau of Investigation (FBI), which was monitoring AFC activities. The reference to "Mrs. Gordon's column" is a reference to the excerpt provided in Source G.

PRIMARY SOURCE : MEMORANDUM

66 At the meeting referred to in Mrs. Gordon's column, Former Undersecretary of State Castle made the statement that if we go to war then everyone in attendance who is a member of America First Committee should forget about the movement, that they are not against giving aid to England but that they were in favor of maintaining a strict cash and carry policy, a strict policy of neutrality, building adequate defense and that they would not tolerate any Communists or Fascists in the group.

Respectfully, L. B. Nichols 99

—December 16, 1940

EXAMINE THE SOURCE

1. **Synthesizing** How does this memo reinforce the ideas highlighted in the AFC flyer and in Evelyn Peyton Gordon's column?

2. **Drawing Conclusions** In what way does the memo deviate from those sources? What does that distinction suggest about the broader historical context?

Your Inquiry Analysis

EVALUATE SOURCES AND USE EVIDENCE

Reflect back to the Compelling Question and the Supporting Questions you developed at the beginning of this lesson.

1. **Gathering Sources** Refer back to the Graphic Organizer you created as you read through the sources. Which sources provided answers to the Supporting Questions you wrote? Circle or highlight those sources in your graphic organizer. If any sources raised additional questions, note those questions in the margin.

2. **Evaluating Sources** Looking at the sources that help you answer the Supporting Questions, evaluate the strength of each source. Put a star next to those that provide the most helpful information. Make notes regarding the bias revealed by each source and consider how the bias affects the content. Do any sources fail to provide what you consider helpful evidence? Why?

3. **Comparing and Contrasting** Compare and contrast two of the sources in this lesson more closely. What position does each source take? What evidence does the source provide to support that position? Record your ideas in a quick Venn diagram.

COMMUNICATE CONCLUSIONS

Identifying Arguments With a partner, discuss each of your Supporting Questions and explain their relationship to the Compelling Question. Together, review the sources and use them to help you write a response to the Compelling Question. Share your response with the class.

TAKE INFORMED ACTION

Presenting on Foreign vs. Domestic Issues Foreign versus domestic obligations remains a key point of debate in the United States today. What obligation does the United States have to help foreign trade partners and allies as well as to assist countries struggling with natural disasters, military conflict, and other crises? Skim a recent edition of a print or online newspaper. Identify a current world event of concern to the United States. Then, use appropriate print and online resources to learn about arguments for and against U.S. aid or intervention. Prepare a multimedia slideshow in which you examine the issue, outline the main perspectives, and state and explain a position on what role you think the nation should take. Be sure to include texts and visuals in your project. Present your slideshow in class or in an online format.

Federal Bureau of Investigation. Nichols, L.B. "Memorandum for Mr. Tolson." December 16, 1940.

05

The United States Mobilizes for War

READING STRATEGY

Key Ideas and Details Use a graphic organizer like the one below to list changes for women and minorities during the war.

	Changes
Women	
African Americans	
Native Americans	
Hispanic Americans	
Japanese Americans	

Japan Attacks Pearl Harbor

GUIDING QUESTION

How did the United States try to slow Japan's advances in the Pacific?

Despite the growing tensions in Europe, it was the Japanese attack on Pearl Harbor that finally brought the United States into World War II. Ironically, Roosevelt's efforts to help Britain fight Germany contributed to Japan's decision to attack the United States.

As German submarines sank British ships in the Atlantic, the British began moving warships from Southeast Asia, leaving India and other colonial possessions vulnerable to Japanese attack. To hinder Japanese aggression, Roosevelt began applying economic pressure. Japan depended on the United States for many key materials, including scrap iron, steel, and especially oil. In July 1940 Congress gave the president the power to restrict the sale of **strategic materials**—items important for fighting a war. Roosevelt then blocked the sale of airplane fuel and scrap iron to Japan. Furious, the Japanese signed an alliance with Germany and Italy, becoming a member of the Axis.

In 1941 Roosevelt began sending lend-lease aid to China, hoping to enable the Chinese to tie down the Japanese and prevent them from attacking elsewhere, but the strategy failed. By July 1941, Japan had sent military forces into southern Indochina, threatening the British Empire. Roosevelt froze all Japanese assets in the United States, reduced oil shipments to Japan, and sent General Douglas MacArthur to the Philippines to improve American defenses.

With its war against China in jeopardy because of a lack of resources, the Japanese military planned to attack the resource-rich British and Dutch colonies in Southeast Asia. They also decided to seize the Philippines and to attack the American fleet at Pearl Harbor. Negotiations with the Americans continued, but neither side would back down. In late November 1941 six Japanese aircraft carriers, two battleships, and several other warships set out for Hawaii.

The Japanese government appeared to be continuing negotiations with the United States in good faith. American intelligence, however, had decoded Japanese messages that made it clear that Japan was preparing to go to war against the United States. On November 27, American commanders at the Pearl Harbor naval base received a war warning from Washington, D.C., but it did not mention Hawaii as a possible target. Because of its great distance from Japan, officials doubted that Japan would attack Hawaii.

The U.S. military's inability to interpret the intelligence correctly left Pearl Harbor an open target. Japan's surprise attack on December 7, 1941, was devastating. Eight battleships, three cruisers, three destroyers, and four other vessels were damaged or sunk. The attack destroyed over 180 aircraft, killed 2,403 Americans, and injured another 1,178. That night, a gray-faced Roosevelt met with his cabinet, telling them the country faced the most serious crisis since the Civil War. The next day, he asked Congress to declare war. The Senate voted 82 to 0 and the House 388 to 1 to declare war on Japan.

Hitler had hoped that Japan would attack the United States so that most U.S. forces would go to the Pacific front. He had previously expected the United States to enter the European war as incidents between German submarines and the United States rose in the Atlantic.

strategic materials items needed during wartime

Hitler underestimated the U.S. strategy, which was to view Germany as the larger threat yet fight the Japanese with the U.S. Navy. By helping Japan, he hoped for Japanese support against the Soviet Union after defeating the Americans. On December 11, Italy and Germany both declared war on the United States.

✓ CHECK FOR UNDERSTANDING

Identifying Cause and Effect What sequence of events led the United States to a declaration of war?

Building the Military

GUIDING QUESTION

What roles did minorities and women play in the armed forces during World War II?

Within days of Germany's attack on Poland in 1939, President Roosevelt expanded the army to 227,000 soldiers. Earlier many Americans had opposed a peacetime draft, but opinions changed after France surrendered to Germany in June 1940. In September of that year Congress approved—by a wide margin—the Selective Training and Service Act, a plan for the first peacetime draft in American history.

The man responsible for taking the flood of recruits and building a large modern army capable of engaging the armed forces of Germany and Japan

was General George C. Marshall, chief of staff of the U.S. Army and Roosevelt's chief military adviser. Marshall would guide the largest expansion of the army in American history from fewer than 190,000 men at the time the war began in Europe in 1939 to over 8 million men by the war's end.

You're in the Army Now

More than 60,000 men enlisted in the month after the attack on Pearl Harbor, initially overwhelming the army's training facilities, equipment, and supplies. New bases, such as the Naval Air Station in Jacksonville, Florida, were built, and existing ones, such as Eglin Air Force Base, were expanded. Many recruits lived in tents rather than barracks, carried sticks representing guns, and practiced maneuvers with trucks labeled "TANK."

New recruits were given physicals and vaccinated against smallpox and typhoid. They were issued boots, uniforms, and equipment and sent to basic training for eight weeks. Trainees drilled and exercised constantly and learned how to work as a team. Recruits came from all over the country, and training together created tight relationships.

A Segregated Military

Although basic training promoted unity, most recruits did not encounter Americans from every part of society since at the start of the war, the U.S. military was segregated. African Americans were organized into their own units, but white officers generally commanded them. Military leaders typically assigned them to construction and supply units.

Not all African Americans wanted to support the war. As one African American college student noted: "The Army jim-crows us. . . . Employers and labor unions shut us out. Lynchings continue. We are **disenfranchised** . . . [and] spat upon. What more could Hitler do to us than that?" Nevertheless, most agreed that they should support their country. One leading African American newspaper, the *Pittsburgh Courier*, launched the "Double V" campaign to urge readers to support the war to win a double victory over Hitler's racism abroad and racism at home.

Under pressure from African American leaders, President Roosevelt prohibited government defense contractors from discriminating on the basis of race, although he did not officially desegregate the armed forces. He promoted Colonel Benjamin O. Davis, Sr., the highest-ranking African American officer, to the rank of brigadier general. Even so, the vast majority of African Americans continued to serve in support roles. Many white military officers and government officials, including Roosevelt's secretary of war, falsely believed that African Americans were incapable of mastering modern military weaponry.

U.S. ARMED FORCES, 1939–1946

Military Personnel (millions) — Year: 1939, 1940, 1941, 1942, 1943, 1944, 1945, 1946

—— Army —— Navy ⋯⋯ Marines

Source: Historical Statistics of the United States.

CIVICS CONNECTION

1. **Analyzing Visuals** In which years were the armed forces at the highest and lowest levels?

2. **Drawing Conclusions** Between which two years was there the greatest increase in the armed services? What happened during this time period that might account for the increase?

disenfranchise to deprive of the right to vote

A People's History of the United States: 1492 - Present by Howard Zinn. Copyright © 1980, 1995, 1998, 1999, 2003 by Howard Zinn. Published 2010 by HarperCollins.

Then in early 1941, the air force created its first African American unit, the 99th Pursuit Squadron. Trained in Tuskegee, Alabama, the pilots became known as the Tuskegee Airmen. Under the command of Lt. Colonel Benjamin O. Davis, Jr., the squadron helped win the Battle of Anzio in Italy. Three other Tuskegee squadrons, known as the 332nd Fighter Group, protected American bombers as they flew to their targets. The African American 761st Tank Battalion was commended for service during the Battle of the Bulge.

Although Japanese Americans were barred from enlisting in the military for a period of time after Pearl Harbor, eventually some Japanese Americans were allowed to serve in the 100th Infantry Battalion and the 442nd Regimental Combat Team. Almost half had been in detention camps in the Southwest. These units became the most decorated in the history of the United States military. Approximately 500,000 Hispanic Americans served in the armed forces despite racial hostility against them. By the end of the war, 17 Hispanic Americans had received the Medal of Honor. About one-third of all able-bodied Native American men aged 18 to 50 served in the military during the war. More than 400 Navajo marines served as "code talkers," relaying critical information and orders over field radios as spoken messages coded in their own language. Of the half million Jewish Americans who served in the military, approximately 52,000 were decorated for bravery.

Although the military did not end all segregation during the war, it did integrate military bases in 1943 and steadily expanded the role of African Americans within the armed forces. These successes paved the way for President Truman's decision to fully integrate the military in 1948.

Women Join the Armed Forces

Women also joined the armed forces in noncombat roles. Many army jobs were administrative and clerical, and filling these jobs with women freed more men for combat. Congress first allowed women in the military in May 1942 by creating the Women's Army Auxiliary Corps (WAAC). It appointed War Department official Oveta Culp Hobby as WAAC's first director. Many women were unhappy that WAAC was not part of the regular army, however. About a year later, the army replaced the WAAC with the Women's Army Corps (WAC), and Hobby became a colonel. The coast guard, navy, and marines followed suit and set up women's units. Another 68,000 women served as nurses in the army and navy. About 300 women serving as Women Airforce Service Pilots (WASPs) made more than 12,000 flights to deliver planes to the war effort.

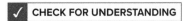

✓ CHECK FOR UNDERSTANDING

1. **Summarizing** What roles did women play in the armed forces during World War II?
2. **Making Connections** What domestic issues led some African Americans to resist supporting the war effort?

American Economy in Wartime

GUIDING QUESTION

How did the U.S. government mobilize the economy for war?

Fighting a global war troubled President Roosevelt but not British prime minister Winston Churchill who knew that victory depended on industry. He compared the American economy to a gigantic boiler: "Once the fire is lighted under it there is no limit to the power it can generate."

Converting the Economy

War production increased rapidly after the attack on Pearl Harbor, helped by existing government plans to build thousands of warplanes and a "Two-Ocean" navy. Roosevelt believed that government and business had to work together to prepare for war. He created the National Defense Advisory Commission and asked business leaders to serve on the committee. Known as "dollar-a-year men," some business leaders left their upper-level corporate jobs to work for the government for a token salary of $1. Many union leaders also contributed by pledging not to strike during the war, and much of the strike activity that did occur was not sanctioned by union leadership. As a result of an increased number of jobs, union membership soared. After the war, pent up worker demands led to massive strikes in 1946. Congress responded by passing the Taft-Hartley Act in 1947, which placed limits on the power of unions and their right to strike.

The president and his advisers believed that giving industry incentives to produce goods quickly was the best way to rapidly mobilize the economy. Normally, the government asked companies to bid on contracts to produce military equipment, which was a slow process. Instead, the government signed **cost-plus** contracts, agreeing to pay a company the cost to make a product plus a guaranteed percentage as profit. Under the cost-plus system, the more—and faster—a company produced, the more money it made. Although not cheap, the system got war materials produced quickly and in quantity. Cost-plus convinced many companies to convert to war production, and Congress authorized the

Grey, Edward. In Winston S. Churchill. The Second World War, vol. 3. London: Cassell, 1948-1954. Lessing J. Rosenwald Collection, Rare Book and Special Collections Division, Library of Congress. (142.1)

cost-plus a government contract to pay a manufacturer the cost to produce an item plus a guaranteed percentage

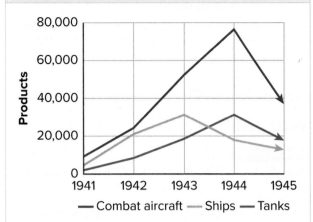

Mobilizing Industry

Products

80,000
60,000
40,000
20,000
0

1941 1942 1943 1944 1945

— Combat aircraft — Ships — Tanks

ECONOMICS CONNECTION

1. **Making Connections** When did tank production begin to drop? Why might this be so?
2. **Inferring** How might the changes in industrial production toward the end of the war have affected employment in the late 1940s?

Reconstruction Finance Corporation (RFC) to make loans to companies wanting to convert.

Getting the Job Done

By the fall of 1941, much had already been done to prepare the economy for war, but it was still only partially mobilized. The attack on Pearl Harbor changed everything, and by the summer of 1942, almost all major industries and some 200,000 companies had converted to war production, making the nation's wartime "miracle" possible.

The automobile industry was uniquely suited to mass-producing military goods, so automobile plants began making trucks, jeeps, and tanks. Mass production was critical because the country that could move troops and supplies most quickly usually won the battle. Automobile factories also produced rifles, helmets, artillery, and dozens of other pieces of military equipment. Henry Ford created an assembly line near Detroit for the enormous B-24 "Liberator" bomber. The factory went on to build more than 8,600 aircraft. Overall, the auto industry made nearly one-third of all wartime military equipment.

Ford's remarkable achievement in aircraft production was more than matched by Henry Kaiser's shipyards. German submarines were sinking American cargo ships at a terrifying rate, so the United States had to find a way to build cargo ships as quickly as possible. Kaiser's method emphasized speed and results. Instead of building an entire ship in one place from the keel up, parts were prefabricated and

brought to the shipyard for assembly. Kaiser's shipyards built many kinds of ships, but they were best known for basic cargo ships called Liberty ships. When the war began, it took 244 days to build the first Liberty ship. After Kaiser shipyards applied their mass-production techniques, average production time dropped to 41 days. Kaiser's shipyards built 30 percent of all American ships constructed during the war. As war production grew, controversies between business leaders, government agencies, and the military increased. President Roosevelt created the War Production Board (WPB) to direct priorities and production goals. Later he set up the Office of War Mobilization to settle disputes.

Mobilizing the economy finally ended the Great Depression, creating almost 19 million new jobs and nearly doubling the average family's income. This improvement in the economy did not come without a price. Families had to move to where the defense factories were located, and housing conditions were terrible. The pressures and prejudices of the era led to strikes, race riots, and rising juvenile delinquency. Goods were rationed and taxes were higher. Workers earned more money but also worked longer hours. When the war began, American defense factories wanted to hire white men; however, with so many white men in the military, employers began to recruit women and minorities instead.

Women in Defense Plants

During the Great Depression, the public opinion was that married women should not work outside the home, especially if they took jobs that could go to men trying to support their families. Most working women were young, single, and employed in traditional female jobs such as domestic work or teaching. The wartime labor shortage, however, forced factories to recruit married women for industrial jobs traditionally reserved for men.

Although the government hired nearly 4 million women, primarily for clerical jobs, women working in factories captured the public imagination. The great symbol of the campaign to hire women was "Rosie the Riveter," a character from a popular song by the Four Vagabonds. The lyrics told of Rosie, who worked in a factory while her boyfriend served in the marines. Eventually 2.5 million women worked in shipyards, aircraft factories, and other manufacturing plants. By the end of the war, the number of working women had increased from 12.9 million to 18.8 million. Though most were laid off or left their jobs voluntarily after the war, their success changed American attitudes about women in the workplace.

✓ CHECK FOR UNDERSTANDING

1. **Summarizing** How did the U.S. government mobilize the economy for war?
2. **Identifying** How did World War II change life for women?

Supporting the War Effort

GUIDING QUESTION

How did the government promote the war effort to citizens at home?

Both wages and prices began to rise quickly during the war because of the high demand for workers and raw materials. Worried about inflation, Roosevelt created the Office of Price Administration and Civilian Supply (OPACS) and the Office of Economic Stabilization (OES) to regulate wages and certain prices. As a result, prices rose only about half as much as they had during World War I. While OPACS and OES controlled inflation, the War Labor Board (WLB) tried to prevent strikes. Most American unions issued a "no strike pledge," instead asking the WLB to mediate wage disputes. By the end of the war, the WLB had helped settle more than 17,000 disputes.

High demand for raw materials and supplies created shortages. OPACS began rationing many products to make sure enough were available for military use. Households picked up a book of rationing coupons every month for different kinds of food. When people bought food, they had to have enough coupon points to cover their purchases. Meat, sugar, fats, oils, processed foods, coffee, shoes, and gasoline were all rationed. Driving distances were restricted, and the speed limit was set at 35 miles per hour to save gas and rubber.

Americans also planted gardens in backyards, schoolyards, city parks, and empty lots to produce more food for the war effort. The government encouraged **victory gardens** by praising them in film reels, pamphlets, and official statements. The government organized scrap drives to collect rubber, tin, aluminum, and steel.

The federal government spent more than $300 billion during World War II—more money than it had spent from Washington's administration to the end of Franklin Roosevelt's second term. Congress raised taxes, although not as high as Roosevelt requested due to public opposition to large tax increases. As a result, the extra taxes collected covered only 45 percent of the war's cost. To make up the difference, the government issued war bonds. Buying bonds is a way to loan money to the government. In exchange for the money, the government promised to repay the bonds' purchase price plus interest at some future date. Individual Americans demonstrated their patriotism and commitment to winning the war by buying nearly $50 billion worth of war bonds. Banks, insurance companies, and other financial institutions bought the rest—more than $100 billion worth of bonds.

In 1942 President Roosevelt created the Office of War Information (OWI) to improve the public understanding of the war and to act as a liaison office with various media. The OWI established detailed guidelines for filmmakers, including a set of questions to be considered before making a movie, such as "Will this picture help win the war?"

✓ CHECK FOR UNDERSTANDING

Determining Central Ideas How did the government encourage and promote the war effort at home?

Racial Upheavals at Home

GUIDING QUESTION

How did the wartime detention of many Americans affect U.S. government and society?

Many African Americans left the South for jobs in war factories in the North and West, but they often faced suspicion and intolerance. Racial violence erupted in Detroit on Sunday, June 20, 1943. Fighting between white and African American teens sparked a citywide riot that left 25 African Americans and 9 whites dead.

In Los Angeles, the fear of juvenile crime and racism against Mexican Americans became linked in the "zoot suit" riots. Popular with Mexican American teenagers, **zoot suits** had very baggy, pleated pants and an overstuffed, knee-length jacket with wide lapels. Most men, to conserve fabric for the war, wore a "victory suit" with no vest, no cuffs, a short jacket, and narrow lapels. In June 1943, after hearing rumors that zoot suiters had attacked several sailors, some 2,500 soldiers and sailors attacked Mexican American neighborhoods in Los Angeles.

Minorities During the War

Frustrated by factories' resistance to hiring African Americans, A. Philip Randolph, the head of the Brotherhood of Sleeping Car Porters—a major union for African American railroad workers—decided to act. He informed President Roosevelt that he was organizing a march on Washington "in the interest of securing jobs . . . in the national defense and . . . integration into the . . . military and naval forces."

Propaganda in Hollywood movies had contributed to this discrimination against minorities and had also minimized the defense industry's system of segregation. The U.S. Navy, for example, initially excluded African American women from joining Women Accepted for Volunteer Military Service (WAVES) and only rescinded the exclusion shortly before the war ended.

---

victory garden a garden planted by civilians during war to raise vegetables for home use, leaving more of other foods for the troops

zoot suit men's clothing of an exaggerated cut consisting of an oversized jacket with wide, padded shoulders, and baggy pants

A. Philip Randolph, as quoted in "Constructing G.I. Joe Louis: Cultural Solutions to the 'Negro Problem' during World War II" by Lauren Rebecca Sklaroff, The Journal of American History, Vol. 89, No. 3 (Dec. 2002).

KOREMATSU V. UNITED STATES, 1944

BACKGROUND TO THE CASE During World War II, President Roosevelt's Executive Order 9066 and other legislation gave the military the power to exclude people of Japanese descent from areas that were deemed important to U.S. national defense and security. In 1942 Toyosaburo Korematsu refused to leave San Leandro, California, which had been designated as a "military area." Korematsu was convicted under the executive order but petitioned the Supreme Court to review the decision.

HOW THE COURT RULED In their decision, the majority of the Supreme Court, with three dissenting, found that, although exclusion orders based on race are constitutionally suspect, the government is justified in time of "emergency and peril" to suspend citizens' civil rights. The case was reviewed in 1983 and the verdict overturned when it was discovered that government prosecutors deliberately withheld evidence and presented false evidence at the trial.

1. **Explaining** Why did the Supreme Court find in favor of the government in this case, even though the justices were suspicious of exclusion based on race?

2. **Identifying** Why was the case eventually overturned?

» This photography shows a group of Japanese-Americans arriving at the Manzanar internment camp in Owens Valley, California, in 1942.

On June 25, 1941, Roosevelt issued Executive Order 8802, which stated, "there shall be no discrimination in the employment of workers in defense industries or government because of race, creed, color, or national origin." To enforce the order, he created the Fair Employment Practices Commission, the first federal civil rights agency since Reconstruction.

The wartime economy also benefited Mexicans. In 1942 the federal government arranged for Mexican farmworkers to help harvest crops in the Southwest as part of the Bracero Program, which continued until 1964. More than 200,000 Mexicans came to work during the war. Many also helped build and maintain railroads. Migrant workers thus became important to the Southwest's economic system.

Restricting Freedoms

Thousands of people of German and Italian descent also had their freedom restricted. All unnaturalized residents of German and Italian descent aged 14 years or over were deemed enemy aliens and subject to regulations including travel restrictions and the seizure of personal property. More than 5,000 were arrested and sent to live in military detention camps. In addition, the Alien Registration Act of 1940 began registering and fingerprinting millions of resident aliens.

Most American propaganda was directed at Hitler himself rather than people of German descent. But when Japan attacked Pearl Harbor, many Americans turned their anger against Japanese immigrants and Japanese Americans, and propaganda against the Japanese featured many racial stereotypes. On February 19, 1942, President Roosevelt signed

Executive Order 9066 allowing the War Department to declare any part of the United States a military zone and to remove people from that zone as necessary. Most of the West Coast was declared a military zone, and people of Japanese ancestry were evacuated to 10 detention camps farther inland. In 1988 after decades of activism by Japanese Americans and the findings of the Commission on Wartime Relocation and Internment of Civilians, President Ronald Reagan apologized to Japanese Americans on behalf of the U.S. government and signed legislation granting $20,000 to each surviving Japanese American who had been held in the camps.

✓ **CHECK FOR UNDERSTANDING**

Describing How did the wartime detention of many Americans affect U.S. government and society?

LESSON ACTIVITIES

1. **Informative/Explanatory Writing** Write a short essay identifying two or three groups in society that benefited from the war effort. Explain the ways in which they benefited.

2. **Analyzing Information** In a small group, discuss the restrictions that certain groups were subjected to during the war. What types of restrictions were imposed? Who was affected? What reasoning did the Supreme Court give in allowing the suspension of the civil rights of some groups? Under what circumstances, if any, do you think the government should be able to suspend civil liberties of all or specific groups of U.S. citizens or noncitizens?

PHOTO: Eliot Elisofon/The LIFE Picture Collection/Getty Images; TEXT: Executive Order 8802: Prohibition of Discrimination in the Defense Industry (1941). National Archive and Records Administration.

READING STRATEGY

Analyzing Key Ideas and Details Use a graphic organizer like the one below to record the major battles discussed and when each was fought.

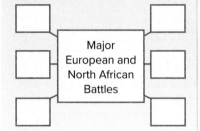

Major European and North African Battles

The War in Europe

GUIDING QUESTION

What were the goals of strategic bombing in Germany and the invasion of Sicily?

Since 1940, U.S. military strategists had discussed with President Roosevelt the pressures of a two-front war. After Germany declared war against the U.S. in 1941, Roosevelt wanted to get U.S. troops into battle in Europe, but Prime Minister Churchill did not believe the United States and Britain were ready to invade Europe. Instead, the prime minister wanted to attack the periphery of the German empire. Roosevelt eventually agreed, and in July 1942, he ordered the invasion of Morocco and Algeria—two French territories indirectly under German control.

Halting Germany's Advances

Roosevelt decided to invade North Africa for two reasons. The invasion would give the army some experience without requiring a lot of troops, and it would help the British troops fight the Germans in Egypt. Most of Britain's Empire, including India, Hong Kong, Singapore, Malaya, and Australia, sent supplies to Britain through Egypt's Suez Canal.

German field marshal Erwin Rommel, whose success earned him the nickname "Desert Fox," commanded the "Afrika Korps." After two battles in the summer and the fall at the Egyptian coastal city of El Alamein, the British secured the Suez Canal and forced Rommel to retreat in November 1942. Despite this defeat, German forces remained a serious threat in North Africa.

Later that month, American troops commanded by General Dwight D. Eisenhower invaded North Africa. When the Americans advanced into the mountains of western Tunisia, they fought the German army for the first time. At the Battle of Kasserine Pass, the Americans were outmaneuvered, suffering roughly 7,000 casualties and losing nearly 200 tanks. Eisenhower fired the general who led the attack and put General George Patton in command. The American and British forces finally pushed the Germans back, and on May 13, 1943, the last German troops in North Africa surrendered.

German submarines began entering American coastal waters. American cargo ships were easy targets, especially at night when the glow from cities in the night sky silhouetted the vessels. To protect the ships, citizens on the East Coast dimmed their lights every evening and put up special "blackout curtains" to prevent the ships from being silhouetted.

By August 1942, German submarines had sunk about 360 American ships and oil tankers along the East Coast. So many tankers were sunk that gasoline and fuel oil had to be rationed within the nation's domestic economy. To keep oil flowing, the federal government built the first long-distance pipeline, running some 1,250 miles (2,010 km) from Texas oil fields to Pennsylvania.

The loss of so many ships convinced the U.S. Navy to use a **convoy system** in which cargo ships traveled in groups escorted by

convoy system a system by which merchant ships travel with naval vessels for protection

GO ONLINE Explore the Student Edition eBook and find interactive maps, time lines, and tools.

305

The War in Europe, 1942–1945

The war against Germany and Italy was fought on three fronts.

GEOGRAPHY CONNECTION

1. **Spatial Thinking** How much west-to-east territory did the Axis control near the end of 1942?

2. **Exploring Regions** What Allied victories are shown in North Africa?

warships, making it more difficult for a submarine to torpedo a cargo ship and escape without being attacked.

The spring of 1942 marked the high point of the German submarine campaign. In May and June alone, German submarines sunk more than 1.2 million tons of shipping. Yet in those same two months, American and British shipyards built more than 1.1 million tons of new shipping. American airplanes and warships also began to use new technology—including radar, sonar, and depth charges—to locate and attack submarines, which turned the Battle of the Atlantic in the Allies favor.

On the Eastern Front, Hitler was convinced that defeating the Soviet Union depended on destroying the Soviet economy, so in May 1942, he ordered his army to capture strategic oil fields, factories, and farmlands in southern Russia and Ukraine. The city of Stalingrad, on the Volga River and a major railroad junction, was key to the attack. If the German army captured Stalingrad, they would cut off the Soviets from the resources they needed to stay in the war.

When German troops entered Stalingrad in mid-September, Stalin ordered his troops to hold the city at all costs. The Germans were forced to fight from house to house, losing thousands of soldiers in the process. Unlike the Soviets, they were not equipped to fight in the bitter cold Russian winter.

On November 23, Soviet reinforcements arrived and surrounded Stalingrad, trapping almost 250,000 German troops. When the battle ended in February 1943, some 91,000 Germans had surrendered. Only 5,000 of them survived the Soviet prison camps, and each side lost nearly half a million soldiers in the conflict.

Although the Battle of Stalingrad put the Germans on the defensive, the Soviet Army and the citizens of Stalingrad paid a heavy price for the victory, and the Soviet Union would continue to suffer staggering losses for the remainder of the war. Although the exact number is debated, historians estimate that between 22 and 28 million Soviet soldiers and civilians died during World War II, or roughly 14 percent of the population. In contrast, roughly 420,000 Americans died in the war, or about 0.32 percent of the American population.

Strategies in Europe

The Allied invasion of North Africa in November 1942 had shown that a large-scale invasion from the sea was possible, and the success of the landings convinced Roosevelt to meet again with Churchill to plan the next stage of the war.

In January 1943 Roosevelt headed to Casablanca, Morocco, to meet the prime minister. At the Casablanca Conference, Roosevelt and Churchill agreed to step up the bombing of Germany, with the goal of this new campaign being "the progressive destruction of the German military, industrial, and economic system, and the undermining of the morale of the German people." The Allies also agreed to attack the Axis on the island of Sicily. Churchill called Italy the "soft underbelly" of Europe, and he was convinced that the Italians would quit the war if the Allies invaded their homeland.

The Allies had been bombing Germany even before the Casablanca Conference. Britain's Royal Air Force had dropped an average of 2,300 tons of explosives on Germany every month for more than three years, and the United States Eighth Army Air Force had dropped an additional 1,500 tons of bombs during the last six months of 1942. These numbers were small, however, compared to the massive new campaign. Between January 1943 and May 1945, the Royal Air Force and the U.S. Eighth Army Air Force dropped about 53,000 tons of explosives on Germany every month.

The bombing campaign did not destroy Germany's economy or undermine German morale, but it did cause a severe oil shortage, wreck the railroad system, and destroy so many aircraft factories that Germany's air force could not replace its losses. By the time the Allies landed in France, they had control of the air, ensuring that their troops would not be bombed.

As the bombing campaign against Germany intensified, plans to invade Sicily also moved ahead. General Eisenhower commanded the invasion, with General Patton and British general Bernard Montgomery heading the ground forces. The invasion began before dawn on July 10, 1943. Despite bad weather, the Allied troops made it ashore with few casualties. Eight days after the troops came ashore, American tanks smashed through enemy lines and captured the western half of the island. Patton's troops then headed east, while the British attacked from the south, and by August 17, the Germans had evacuated the island.

The attack on Sicily created a crisis within the Italian government. The king of Italy, Victor Emmanuel, and a group of Italian generals decided that it was time to depose Mussolini. On July 25, 1943, the king invited the dictator to his palace.

"My dear Duce," the king began, "it's no longer any good. Italy has gone to bits. Army morale is at rock bottom. The soldiers don't want to fight anymore. . . . You can certainly be under no illusion as to Italy's feelings with regard to yourself. At this moment, you are the most hated man in Italy." The king then arrested Mussolini, and the new Italian government began negotiating a surrender to the Allies.

Following Italy's surrender, however, German troops seized control of northern Italy, including Rome, and returned Mussolini to power. The Germans then took up positions near the heavily fortified town of Cassino, where the terrain was steep, barren, and rocky. Rather than attack such difficult terrain, the Allies landed at Anzio, behind German lines. Instead of retreating, however, as the Allies had hoped, the Germans surrounded the Allied troops near Anzio.

It took the Allies five months to break through the German lines at Cassino and Anzio. Finally, in late May 1944, the Germans retreated, and less than two weeks later, the Allies captured Rome. Fighting in Italy continued, however, for another year. The Italian campaign was one of the bloodiest in the war, with more than 300,000 Allied casualties.

Roosevelt wanted to meet with Stalin before the Allies invaded France, and in late 1943, Stalin agreed, proposing that Roosevelt and Churchill meet him in Tehran, Iran. The leaders reached several agreements. Stalin promised to launch a full-scale offensive against the Germans when the Allies invaded France in 1944.

Roosevelt and Stalin then agreed to divide Germany after the war so that it would never again threaten world peace. Stalin promised that once Germany was defeated, the Soviet Union would help the United States against Japan, and he also accepted Roosevelt's proposal of an international peacekeeping organization after the war.

Part of the agreement proclaimed:

> 66 The common understanding which we have here reached guarantees that victory will be ours.
>
> And as to peace—we are sure that our concord will win an enduring Peace. We recognize fully the supreme responsibility resting upon us and all the United Nations to make a peace which will command the goodwill of the overwhelming mass of the peoples of the world and banish the scourge and terror of war for many generations.
>
> With our diplomatic advisers we have surveyed the problems of the future. We shall

(1)The Strategic Air War Against Germany 1939-1945: Report of the British Bombing Survey Unit. London: Frank Cass, 1998; (2)King Victor Emmanuel III of Italy, as quoted in Benito Mussolini Memoirs, 1942-1943, with Documents Relating to the Period. Translated by Frances Lobb. Edited by Raymond Klibansky. Copyright © 1975 by H. Fertig; (3) Bevans, Charles I., ed. 1968. Treaties And Other International Agreements of the United States of America, 1776-1949. Washington, DC: United States Government Printing Office.

seek the cooperation and active participation of all nations, large and small, whose peoples in heart and mind are dedicated, as are our own peoples, to the elimination of tyranny and slavery, oppression and intolerance. We will welcome them, as they may choose to come, into a world family of democratic nations. **"**

—from the Tehran Declaration, December 1, 1943

✓ **CHECK FOR UNDERSTANDING**

Summarizing Why did Churchill and Roosevelt want to attack German-controlled areas in North Africa before areas in Europe?

The D-Day Invasion

GUIDING QUESTION

What if D-Day had failed and Germany had defeated the Allies in Europe?

After the conference in Tehran, Roosevelt headed to Cairo, Egypt, where he and Churchill continued planning an invasion of France that would force

Germany to again fight the war on two fronts. One major decision, however, still had to be made. The president had to choose the commander for Operation Overlord—the code name for the invasion. Roosevelt selected General Eisenhower.

Operation Overlord

Hitler had fortified the French coast along the English Channel, but he did not know when or where the Allies would land. The Germans believed the landing would be in Pas-de-Calais—the area of France closest to Britain. The Allies encouraged this belief by placing dummy equipment along the coast across from Calais. The real target was farther south, a 60-mile stretch of five beaches along the Normandy coast.

The selection of a site for the largest amphibious landing in history was one of the biggest decisions of World War II. Allied planners considered coastlines from Denmark to Portugal in search of a sheltered location with firm flat beaches within range of friendly fighter planes in England. There also had to be enough roads and paths to move jeeps and trucks off the beaches and to accommodate the hundreds of thousands of American, Canadian, and British troops

Throughout D-Day, Coast Guard landing barges brought wave after wave of American soldiers across the English Channel to reinforce the beachheads of Normandy, France.

Predicting What would happen as soon as these soldiers landed in Normandy?

National Archives and Records Administration

set to stream ashore following the invasion. An airfield and a seaport that the Allies could use were also needed, but a reasonable expectation of achieving the element of surprise was most important.

Planners also discussed who should lead France after the invasion. General Eisenhower had informed Brigadier General Charles de Gaulle, the leader of the French Resistance movement against Nazi occupation, that the French Resistance forces would assist in the liberation of Paris, but President Roosevelt was not sure he trusted de Gaulle and refused to recognize him as the official French leader.

By the spring of 1944, more than 1.5 million American soldiers, 12,000 airplanes, and 5 million tons of equipment had been sent to England. Setting the invasion date and giving the command to go were all that remained of the preparations. The invasion had to begin at night to hide the ships crossing the English Channel, and the ships had to arrive at low tide so that they could see beach obstacles. The low tide had to come at dawn so that gunners bombarding the coast could see their targets, and paratroopers, who would be dropped behind enemy lines, needed a moonlit night to see where to land. Most important of all was good weather. A storm would ground the airplanes, and high waves would swamp landing craft.

Given all these requirements, there were only a few days each month to begin the invasion. The first opportunity was from June 5 to 7, 1944. Eisenhower's planning staff referred to the day any operation began by the letter D. The invasion date came to be known as D-Day.

Heavy cloud cover, strong winds, and high waves made June 5 impossible. The weather was forecast to improve slightly a day later. The Channel would still be rough, but the landing ships and aircraft could operate. After looking at forecasts one last time, shortly after midnight on June 6, 1944, General Eisenhower gave the final order: "OK, we'll go."

The Longest Day

Nearly 7,000 ships carrying more than 100,000 soldiers headed for Normandy's coast. At the same time, 23,000 paratroopers were dropped inland, east and west of the beaches. Allied fighter-bombers raced up and down the coast, hitting bridges, bunkers, and radar sites, and at dawn, Allied warships began a tremendous barrage. Thousands of shells rained down on the beaches, code-named "Utah," "Omaha," "Gold," "Sword," and "Juno."

The American landing at Utah Beach went well. The German defenses there were weak, and in less than three hours, the troops had captured the beach and moved inland, suffering fewer than 200 casualties. On the eastern flank, the British and

Canadian landings also went well, and by the end of the day, British and Canadian forces were several miles inland.

Omaha Beach, however, was a different story. Surrounded at both ends by cliffs that rose wall-like from the sea, Omaha Beach was only four miles long. A 150-foot-high bluff overlooked the entire beach, and there were only five ravines that allowed any sort of access from the beach to the top of the bluff. The Germans had made full use of the geographic advantage the high bluff gave them. They dug trenches and built concrete bunkers for machine guns at the top of the cliffs and positioned them to guard the ravines leading from the bluff to the beach. Under intense German fire, the American assault almost disintegrated.

General Omar Bradley, commander of the American forces landing at Omaha and Utah, began making plans to evacuate. Slowly, however, the American troops began to knock out the German defenses. More landing craft arrived, ramming their way through the obstacles to get to the beach. Nearly 2,500 Americans were either killed or wounded on Omaha, but by early afternoon, Bradley received this message: "Troops formerly pinned down on beaches . . . [are] advancing up heights behind beaches."

By the end of the day, nearly 35,000 American troops had landed at Omaha, and another 23,000 had landed at Utah. More than 75,000 British and Canadian troops were on shore as well. The invasion had succeeded.

✓ CHECK FOR UNDERSTANDING

Contrasting How were the landings at Utah Beach and Omaha Beach different from each other?

The Third Reich Collapses

GUIDING QUESTION

Why was the Battle of the Bulge so important to Allied forces?

Although D-Day had been a success, it was only the beginning. Surrounding many fields in Normandy were hedgerows—dirt walls, several feet thick, covered in shrubbery—built to fence in cattle and crops. They also enabled the Germans to fiercely defend their positions. The battle of the hedgerows ended on July 25, 1944, when 2,500 U.S. bombers blew a hole in the German lines, enabling U.S. tanks to race through the gap.

As the Allies broke out of Normandy, the French Resistance—French civilians who had secretly organized to resist the German occupation—staged a

Gerow, Leonard. In Warfare History Network. "'They Laid It All On the Line': Why Omaha Beach at D-Day Was Total Hell." [blog post]. The National Interest. June 6, 2019.

U.S. troops march near Murrigen, Belgium, during the Battle of the Bulge in January 1945.

Drawing Conclusions Based on this photograph, what can you infer about the conditions soldiers faced the Battle of the Bulge?

rebellion in Paris. When the Allies liberated Paris on August 25, the streets were filled with French citizens celebrating their victory.

The Battle of the Bulge

As the Allies advanced toward the German border, Hitler decided to stage one last desperate offensive. His goal was to cut off Allied supplies coming through the port of Antwerp, Belgium.

The attack began just before dawn on December 16, 1944. Six inches (15 cm) of snow covered the ground, and the weather was bitterly cold. Moving rapidly, the Germans caught the American defenders by surprise. As the German troops raced west, their lines bulged outward, and the attack became known as the Battle of the Bulge.

Eisenhower ordered General Patton to the rescue. Three days later, faster than anyone expected in the midst of a snowstorm, Patton's troops slammed into the German lines. As the weather cleared, Allied aircraft began hitting German fuel depots.

On Christmas Eve, out of fuel and weakened by heavy losses, the German troops driving toward Antwerp were forced to halt. Two days later, Patton's troops broke through the German line. Fighting continued for three weeks, but the United States had won the Battle of the Bulge.

On January 8, the Germans began to withdraw, having suffered more than 100,000 casualties. They had very few resources left to prevent the Allies from entering Germany.

The War Ends in Europe

While American and British forces fought to liberate France, the Soviets attacked German troops in Russia. By the end of the Battle of the Bulge, the Soviets had driven Hitler's forces out of Russia and across Poland. By February 1945, the Soviets were only 35 miles (56 km) from Germany's capital, Berlin.

Soviet troops crossed Germany's eastern border, while American forces attacked its western border. By the end of February 1945, American troops had reached the Rhine River, Germany's last major line of defense in the west, and on March 7, American tanks crossed the Rhine. As German defenses crumbled, American troops raced east to within 70 miles (113 km) of Berlin. On April 16, Soviet troops finally smashed through the German defenses and reached the outskirts of Berlin five days later.

Deep in his Berlin bunker, Adolf Hitler knew the end was near. On April 30, 1945, he committed suicide. On May 7, 1945, Germany accepted the terms for an unconditional surrender. The next day May 8, 1945, was proclaimed V-E Day for "Victory in Europe."

✓ **CHECK FOR UNDERSTANDING**

Describing Why was the Battle of the Bulge so important to the Allied forces?

LESSON ACTIVITIES

1. **Narrative Writing** U.S. soldiers invading Normandy on D-Day showed extreme bravery in the face of enormous difficulties. Imagine that you are one of the first soldiers approaching Omaha Beach by water. Use the information in the text and the visuals to help you write a description of the beach and the atmosphere at that moment. Be sure to include sensory words that are tied to the facts and source material that is provided in this lesson.

2. **Collaborating** Work with a partner to find photos, newsreels, and newspaper accounts of one of the battles described in the lesson. Discuss how they support or add to the information in the lesson. Make note of details from the sources you find that help expand your understanding of the battle. Write a summary describing the most useful or interesting sources you found and how they add to your knowledge of the battle. Cite the sources that you consulted.

CORBIS/Corbis Historical/Getty Images

07

World War II in the Pacific

Rose Meier, as quoted in Angels of Mercy: The Army Nurses of World War II by Betsy Kuhn. Copyright © 1999 by Betsy Kuhn. Published by Atheneum Books for Young Readers, an imprint of Simon & Schuster Children's Publishing.

Analyzing Key Ideas and Details Use a graphic organizer such as this one to record the major battles discussed and the victor in each.

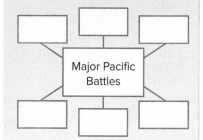

The Fight in the Pacific

GUIDING QUESTION

Why was the Doolittle Raid important for U.S. forces in the Pacific?

Admiral Chester Nimitz, the commander of the United States Navy in the Pacific, began planning operations against the Japanese Navy. Although the Japanese had badly damaged the American fleet at Pearl Harbor, they had missed the American aircraft carriers, which were at sea on a mission. The United States had several carriers in the Pacific, and Nimitz was determined to use them. In the days just after Pearl Harbor, however, Nimitz could do little to stop Japan's advance into Southeast Asia.

The Philippines Fall

A few hours after bombing Pearl Harbor, the Japanese attacked American airfields in the Philippines. Two days later, they landed troops. The American and Filipino forces defending the Philippines were badly outnumbered. Realizing MacArthur's capture so soon after Pearl Harbor would demoralize the American people, President Roosevelt ordered General MacArthur to evacuate to Australia. Instead, MacArthur retreated to the Bataan Peninsula.

By March, the troops had eaten cavalry horses and mules in desperation. The lack of food and supplies, along with diseases such as malaria, scurvy, and dysentery, took its toll. The women of the Army Nurse Corps worked on Bataan in primitive conditions. Patients slept in the open air. One nurse, Rose Meier, reported, "If we needed more room, we got our axes and chopped some bamboo trees down." MacArthur did then leave American troops behind on Bataan—but he vowed to return and rescue them.

On April 9, 1942, the weary defenders of the Bataan Peninsula finally surrendered. Nearly 78,000 prisoners of war were forced to march—sick, exhausted, and starving—65 miles (105 km) to a Japanese prison camp. Almost 10,000 troops died on this march, which would later be called the Bataan Death March. The troops in the Bataan Peninsula surrendered, but a small force held out on the island of Corregidor in Manila Bay until May 1942. The Philippines had finally fallen to the Japanese.

The fall of the Philippines did not end resistance for large numbers of Filipinos, who fled to the islands' jungles and mountains to engage in guerrilla warfare against the occupying Japanese forces. An estimated 300,000 Filipinos, including Filipino guerrilla units, fought the Japanese for three years, until MacArthur's return. About one million Filipinos lost their lives by the end of the war in 1945.

In 1941 a presidential order brought all military forces in the Philippines under American control. President Roosevelt promised Filipino soldiers that they would receive full U.S. military veterans' benefits. However, in 1946 these benefits were denied when Congress passed the Rescission Act, which canceled the benefits for the Filipino veterans and their families. It was not until the early 1990s that some Filipino veterans were granted U.S. citizenship. Starting in 2009, surviving Filipino veterans who were American citizens and Filipino noncitizens received one-time payments for their service in the war.

1st Filipino Regiment (1942–1946)

On December 8, 1941, fewer than ten hours after Japanese aircraft bombed Pearl Harbor, U.S. airbases near Manila, the capital of the Philippines, were also attacked by the Japanese air force. As war broke out, tens of thousands of Filipinos living in the United States either volunteered for service or were recruited into the armed forces. Thousands of Filipinos still living in the Philippines also enlisted to fight with the U.S. forces under American command.

FORMING THE REGIMENT In February 1942 Secretary of War Henry L. Stimson established a unit made up of Americans of Filipino ancestry and Filipinos living in the U.S. who were not yet citizens to serve together in the U.S. Army. This unit became the 1st Filipino Regiment. The regiment's motto was *Laging Una*, which means "Always First" in the Tagalog language, one of the major languages spoken in the Philippines. Almost 9,000 Filipino Americans and Filipinos served in and fought with the U. S. Army 1st and 2nd Filipino Infantry Regiments during World War II. Members of the 1st Regiment also received special training in intelligence, sabotage, and demolition in Australia. These soldiers were sent to the Philippines to coordinate actions with Filipino guerrilla armies fighting the Japanese.

TAKING BACK THE PHILIPPINES Following training in mid-1944, the 1st Regiment arrived in New Guinea, located in the South Pacific, and fought in numerous battles before landing in the Philippines at Tacloban, Leyte, in early February 1945. The regiment fought under General MacArthur and helped liberate the Philippines, eventually earning battle honors for its actions at New Guinea, Leyte, and the Southern Philippines. In addition, the 1st earned the Philippine Presidential Unit Citation. Members of the 1st and 2nd Filipino regiments were awarded more than 50,000 decorations for their actions in the war. In 2016 Congress awarded a collective Congressional Gold Medal to Filipino veterans in recognition of their service.

» The coat of arms of the 1st Filipino Regiment features the colors and stars from the flag of the Philippines, and the weapons on the shield represent two island tribes.

Speculating Why might the 1st Filipino Regiment have played an invaluable role in helping to take back the Philippines?

The Doolittle Raid

Even before the Philippines fell, President Roosevelt was searching for a way to raise the morale of the American people. He wanted to bomb Tokyo, but American planes could reach Tokyo only if an aircraft carrier brought them close enough. However, Japanese ships in the North Pacific prevented carriers from getting near Japan. In early 1942 a military planner suggested replacing the carrier's usual short-range bombers with long-range B-25 bombers that could attack from farther away. The only problem was that, while B-25s could take off from a carrier, the bombers could not land on its short deck. After attacking Japan, they would have to land in China.

President Roosevelt put Lieutenant Colonel James Doolittle in command of the mission to bomb Tokyo. At the end of March, a crane loaded sixteen B-25s onto the aircraft carrier *Hornet*. The next day,

the *Hornet* headed west across the Pacific. On April 18, American bombs fell on Japan for the first time. While Americans rejoiced in this small success, the Japanese were aghast at the raid. Those bombs could have killed Emperor Hirohito, who was revered as a god.

The Doolittle Raid convinced Japanese leaders to change their strategy. Officers in charge of the navy's planning wanted to cut American supply lines to Australia by capturing the south coast of New Guinea. But commander of the fleet, Admiral Yamamoto, wanted to attack Midway Island—the last American base in the North Pacific west of Hawaii. He believed that attacking Midway would lure the American fleet into battle and enable his fleet to destroy it.

After Doolittle's raid, the Japanese war planners dropped their opposition to Yamamoto's idea. The American fleet had to be destroyed to protect Tokyo

National Archives and Records Administration

Albert Smith, a Navajo Code Talker, is interviewed during a reception that preceded the Congressional Gold Medal ceremony honoring code talkers.

Identifying Themes How does Albert Smith and the event honoring code talkers exemplify the experiences of minorities serving in the U.S. military during World War II?

The Navajo Code Talkers

When American marines stormed an enemy beach, they used radios to communicate; however, that meant the Japanese could intercept and translate the messages. Amid battle, there was no time to use a code-machine. Acting upon the suggestion of Philip Johnston, an engineer who had lived on a Navajo reservation as a child, the marines recruited Navajos to serve as "code talkers." Native American Choctaw and Cherokee soldiers provided these same assignments in the fighting on the Western Front in 1918 in World War I.

The Navajo language had no written alphabet and was known only to the Navajo and a few missionaries and anthropologists. The Navajo recruits developed code words, using their own language, that stood for military terms. For example, the Navajo word *jay-sho*, or "buzzard," was code for bomber; *lo-tso*, or "whale," meant battleship; and *ni-ma-si*, or "potatoes," stood for grenades.

Code talkers proved invaluable. They could relay a message in minutes that would have taken a code-machine operator hours to encipher and transmit. During the Battle of Iwo Jima, code talkers transmitted more than 800 messages during the first forty-eight hours as the marines struggled to get ashore under intense bombardment. Sworn to secrecy, their mission was not revealed until 1968. In 2001 Congress awarded code talkers the Congressional Gold Medal for their unique contribution during the war.

✓ **CHECK FOR UNDERSTANDING**

1. **Summarizing** Why was the Doolittle Raid important for U.S. forces in the Pacific?
2. **Describing** What was the outcome of the Battle of the Coral Sea? How did this battle impact the broader war in the Pacific?

Driving Back Japan

GUIDING QUESTION

What was the strategic thinking behind island hopping?

Back at Pearl Harbor, the code-breaking team learned of the plan to attack Midway. With so many ships at sea, Admiral Yamamoto transmitted the plans for the Midway attack by radio, using code the Americans had already cracked.

Admiral Nimitz had been waiting for the chance to ambush the Japanese fleet. He immediately ordered carriers to take up positions near Midway. Unaware that they were heading into an ambush, the Japanese launched their aircraft against Midway on June 4,

---

from bombing. The attack on New Guinea would still go ahead, but only three aircraft carriers were assigned to the mission. All of the other carriers were ordered to assault Midway.

The Battle of the Coral Sea

The Japanese believed that they could safely proceed with two attacks at once because they thought their operations were secret. What the Japanese did not know was that an American team of **code** breakers based in Hawaii had already broken the Japanese navy's secret code for conducting operations.

In March 1942 decoded Japanese messages alerted the United States to the Japanese attack on New Guinea. Admiral Nimitz sent two carriers in response, the *Yorktown* and the *Lexington*, to intercept the Japanese in the Coral Sea. There, in early May, carriers from both sides launched all-out airstrikes against each other. Although the Japanese sank the *Lexington* and badly damaged the *Yorktown*, the American attacks prevented the Japanese from landing on New Guinea's south coast and kept the supply lines to Australia open.

---

code a signal or symbol used to represent something that is to be kept secret

Tom Williams/Roll Call/Getty Images

The Battle of Midway

The Battle of Midway was fought predominantly by aircraft.

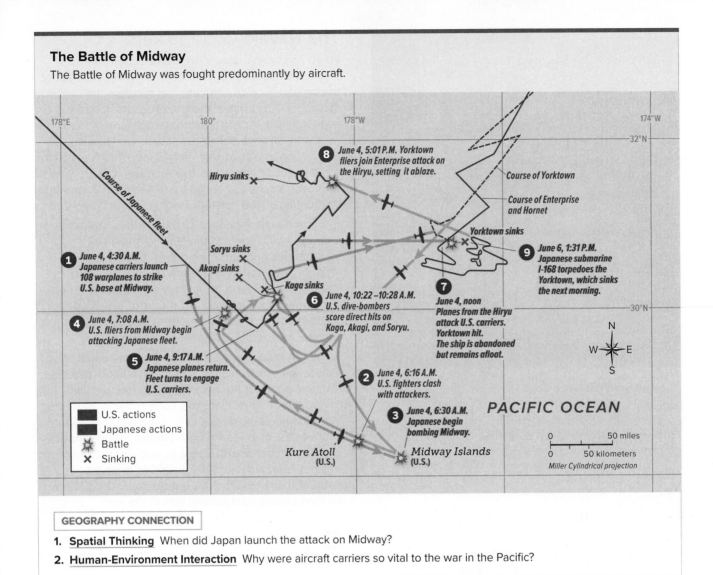

1 June 4, 4:30 A.M. Japanese carriers launch 108 warplanes to strike U.S. base at Midway.

4 June 4, 7:08 A.M. U.S. fliers from Midway begin attacking Japanese fleet.

5 June 4, 9:17 A.M. Japanese planes return. Fleet turns to engage U.S. carriers.

6 June 4, 10:22–10:28 A.M. U.S. dive-bombers score direct hits on Kaga, Akagi, and Soryu.

8 June 4, 5:01 P.M. Yorktown fliers join Enterprise attack on the Hiryu, setting it ablaze.

Hiryu sinks

Soryu sinks

Akagi sinks

Kaga sinks

2 June 4, 6:16 A.M. U.S. fighters clash with attackers.

3 June 4, 6:30 A.M. Japanese begin bombing Midway.

7 June 4, noon Planes from the Hiryu attack U.S. carriers. Yorktown hit. The ship is abandoned but remains afloat.

Yorktown sinks

9 June 6, 1:31 P.M. Japanese submarine I-168 torpedoes the Yorktown, which sinks the next morning.

Course of Japanese fleet

Course of Yorktown

Course of Enterprise and Hornet

Kure Atoll (U.S.)

Midway Islands (U.S.)

PACIFIC OCEAN

- ■ U.S. actions
- ■ Japanese actions
- ✳ Battle
- ✕ Sinking

50 miles

50 kilometers

Miller Cylindrical projection

GEOGRAPHY CONNECTION

1. **Spatial Thinking** When did Japan launch the attack on Midway?
2. **Human-Environment Interaction** Why were aircraft carriers so vital to the war in the Pacific?

1942. The Japanese ran into a blitz of antiaircraft fire, and 38 planes were shot down. As the Japanese prepared a second Midway attack, aircraft from the American carriers *Hornet, Yorktown,* and *Enterprise* launched a counterattack. The American planes caught the Japanese carriers with fuel, bombs, and aircraft exposed on their flight decks. Within minutes, three Japanese carriers were reduced to burning wrecks. A fourth was sunk a few hours later, and Yamamoto ordered his remaining ships to retreat.

The Battle of Midway was a turning point in the war. The Japanese navy lost four large carriers—the heart of its fleet. Just six months after Pearl Harbor, the United States had stopped the Japanese advance. The victory, however, was not without cost. The battle killed 362 Americans and 3,057 Japanese.

Island Hopping in the Pacific

The American plan to defeat Japan called for a two-pronged attack. The Pacific Fleet, commanded by Admiral Nimitz, would advance through the central Pacific by "hopping" from one island to the next, closer

and closer to Japan. Meanwhile, MacArthur's troops would advance through the Solomon Islands, capture the north coast of New Guinea, and then launch an invasion to retake the Philippines.

By the fall of 1943, the navy was ready to launch its island-hopping campaign, but the geography of the central Pacific posed a problem. Many of the islands were coral reef atolls, or places where the reefs create islands. The water over the coral reef was not always deep enough to allow landing craft to get to the shore. If the landing craft ran aground on the reef, the troops would have to wade to the beach, risking exposure and high casualties.

At Tarawa, when the landing craft hit the reef, at least 20 ships ran aground. The marines had to plunge into shoulder-high water and wade several hundred yards to the beach. Raked by Japanese fire, only one marine in three made it ashore. Once the marines reached the beach, the battle was still far from over.

The fighting was brutal. As one soldier, Robert Sherrod, recounted:

> Two more Marines scaled the seawall, [one] carrying a twin-cylindered tank strapped to his shoulders, the other holding the nozzle of the flamethrower. . . . [A] khaki-clad figure ran out . . . The flamethrower . . . caught him in its withering stream of intense fire. As soon as it touched him, the [Japanese soldier] flared up like a piece of celluloid. He was dead instantly . . . charred almost to nothingness.

—Robert Sherrod, from *Tarawa: The Story of a Battle*

Although many troops died wading ashore, one boat was able to cross the reef and deliver troops to the beaches. The vehicle nicknamed the "Alligator," or **amphtrac,** was invented in the 1930s to rescue people in Florida swamps. Never used in combat, the navy decided to buy only 200 of them in 1941. If more had been at Tarawa, American casualties likely would have been much lower. More than 1,000 marines lost

their lives there. Photos of bodies lying crumpled next to burning landing craft shocked Americans at home, and people wondered how many lives would be lost in defeating Japan.

The next assault—Kwajalein Atoll in the Marshall Islands—went more smoothly. This time all the troops went ashore in amphtracs. Although the Japanese resisted fiercely, the marines captured Kwajalein and nearby Eniwetok with far fewer casualties.

After the Marshall Islands, the navy targeted the Mariana Islands. American military planners wanted to use the Marianas as a base for a new heavy bomber, the B-29 Superfortress. The B-29 could fly farther than any other plane in the world. From airfields in the Marianas, B-29s could bomb Japan. Admiral Nimitz decided to invade three of the Mariana Islands: Saipan, Tinian, and Guam. Despite strong Japanese resistance, American troops captured all three by August 1944. A few months later, B-29s began bombing Japan.

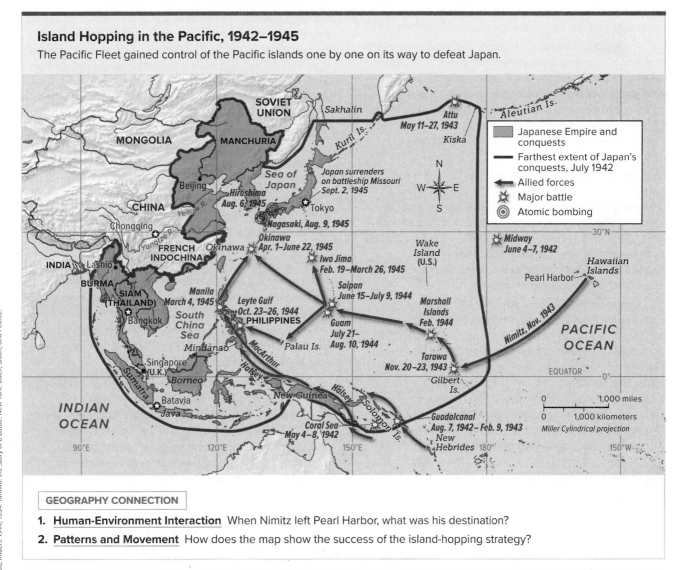

Island Hopping in the Pacific, 1942–1945

The Pacific Fleet gained control of the Pacific islands one by one on its way to defeat Japan.

GEOGRAPHY CONNECTION

1. **Human-Environment Interaction** When Nimitz left Pearl Harbor, what was his destination?
2. **Patterns and Movement** How does the map show the success of the island-hopping strategy?

Sherrod, Robert. 1944, 1954. Tarawa: the Story of a Battle. New York: Duell, Sloan, and Pearce.

amphtrac an amphibious tractor used to move troops from ships to shore

Returning to the Philippines

As the forces under Admiral Nimitz hopped across the central Pacific, MacArthur's troops began their own campaign in the southwest Pacific. By early 1944, MacArthur's troops finally captured enough islands to surround the main Japanese base in the region. The Japanese withdrew their ships and aircraft from the base, although they left 100,000 troops behind to hold the island. Worried that the navy's advance across the central Pacific was leaving him behind, MacArthur ordered his forces to leap nearly 600 miles (966 km) to capture the Japanese base at Hollandia on the north coast of New Guinea. Shortly after securing New Guinea, MacArthur's troops seized the island of Morotai—the last stop before the Philippines.

To take back the Philippines, the United States assembled an enormous invasion force. In October 1944, over 700 ships carrying more than 160,000 troops sailed for Leyte Gulf in the Philippines. On October 20, the troops began to land on Leyte, an island on the eastern side of the Philippines. A few hours after the invasion began, MacArthur waded ashore. He made a radio broadcast: "People of the Philippines, I have returned. . . . [O]ur forces stand again on Philippine soil."

To stop the American invasion, the Japanese sent four aircraft carriers toward the Philippines from the north and secretly dispatched another fleet from the west. Most of the American carriers protecting the invasion left Leyte Gulf and headed north to stop them. The Japanese warships to the west raced through the Philippine Islands into Leyte Gulf and ambushed the remaining American ships.

The Battle of Leyte Gulf was the largest naval battle in history. It was also the first time that the Japanese used **kamikaze** attacks. Kamikaze pilots would deliberately crash their planes into American ships, inflicting severe damage. Luckily for Americans, as the situation was becoming desperate, the Japanese commander, believing more American ships were on the way, ordered a retreat.

Although the Japanese fleet had retreated, the campaign to recapture the Philippines from the Japanese was long and grueling. More than 80,000 Japanese were killed; fewer than 1,000 surrendered. MacArthur's troops did not capture Manila until March 1945. The battle left the city in ruins and more than 100,000 Filipino civilians dead. The remaining Japanese retreated into the rugged terrain north of Manila; they were still fighting in August 1945 when word came that Japan had surrendered.

✓ CHECK FOR UNDERSTANDING

1. **Summarizing** What was the military strategy behind "island-hopping"? Was it successful?

2. **Describing** How did the U.S. Navy successfully drive back Japanese forces in the Pacific?

kamikaze during World War II, a Japanese suicide pilot whose mission was to crash into his target

Ending the War

GUIDING QUESTION

Why did Truman decide to use the atomic bomb?

President Roosevelt died of a stroke on April 12, 1945 while vacationing in Warm Springs, Georgia. His vice president, Harry S. Truman, became president. The next day, Truman told reporters: "Boys, if you ever pray, pray for me now. . . . When they told me yesterday what had happened, I felt like the moon, the stars, and all the planets had fallen on me." Truman began to make decisions about the war. Although Germany surrendered a few weeks later, war with Japan continued, and Truman was forced to make some of the most difficult decisions of the war, and of his life, during his first six months in office.

The Battle of Iwo Jima

On November 24, 1944, bombs fell on Tokyo. Eighty B-29 Superfortress bombers traveled more than 1,500 miles (2,414 km) from new American bases in the Mariana Islands. By the time the B-29s reached Japan, however, they did not have enough fuel left to fix their navigational errors or to adjust for high winds. Many of their bombs missed the targets. The pilots needed an island closer to Japan so the B-29s could refuel. American military planners chose Iwo Jima. It was halfway between the Marianas and Japan, but its geography was formidable. It had a dormant volcano at its southern tip and rugged terrain with rocky cliffs, jagged ravines, and dozens of caves. Volcanic ash covered the ground. Even worse, the Japanese had built a vast network of concrete bunkers connected by miles of tunnels.

On February 19, 1945, some 60,000 marines landed on Iwo Jima. As the troops leapt from the amphtracs, they sank up to their ankles in soft ash and were pounded by Japanese artillery. The marines crawled inland, attacking the Japanese bunkers with flamethrowers and explosives. More than 6,800 marines were killed capturing the island. Admiral Nimitz later wrote that on Iwo Jima, "uncommon valor was a common virtue."

While American engineers prepared airfields on Iwo Jima, General Curtis LeMay, commander of the B-29s based in the Marianas, changed strategy. To help the B-29s hit their targets, he ordered them to drop bombs filled with **napalm**—a type of jellied gasoline. The bombs would not only explode but would also start fires. Even if the B-29s missed their targets, the fires they started would spread to the intended targets.

The use of firebombs was controversial because the fires would also kill many civilians; however, LeMay

napalm a jellied gasoline used for bombs

(1)General Douglas MacArthur, as quoted in United States Army in World War II: The War in the Pacific, Leyte: The Return to the Philippines by M. Hamlin Cannon. Published by Office of the Chief of Military History, Department of the Army, 1954; (2)Truman, Harry S. "Swearing in of Harry Truman," April 12, 1945; (3)Fleet Admiral Chester W. Nimitz, CINCPACFLT Communique No. 300, World War II Command File, Papers of Chester W. Nimitz, Operational Archives Branch, Naval Historical Center, Washington, D.C.

could think of no other way to quickly destroy Japan's war production. Loaded with firebombs, B-29s attacked Tokyo on March 9, 1945. As strong winds fanned the flames, the firestorm grew so intense that it sucked the oxygen out of the air, asphyxiating thousands.

The firebombing of Tokyo killed more than 80,000 people and destroyed more than 250,000 buildings. By the end of June 1945, Japan's six key industrial cities had been firebombed. By the end of the war, the B-29s had firebombed 67 Japanese cities.

Unconditional Surrender

There were few signs in the spring of 1945 that Japan was ready to quit. Many American officials believed Japan must be invaded. To prepare for the invasion, the United States needed a base near Japan to stockpile supplies and build up troops. Military planners chose Okinawa—only 350 miles (563 km) from mainland Japan.

American troops landed on Okinawa on April 1, 1945. Japanese troops took up positions in the island's rugged mountains. To force the Japanese out of their caves and bunkers, the American troops had to fight their way up steep slopes against constant machine gun and artillery fire. More than 12,000 American soldiers, sailors, and marines died during the fighting, but by June 22, 1945, Okinawa had finally been captured.

Shortly after the United States captured Okinawa, Japanese emperor Hirohito urged his government to find a way to end the war. American officials knew that the fate of Hirohito was the most important issue for the Japanese. Demands for unconditional surrender might mean that the emperor would step down. Many Japanese leaders were willing to surrender, but only on the condition that Hirohito stay in power. Most Americans, however, wanted to remove the emperor from power. President Truman was reluctant to go against public opinion. Furthermore, he knew the United States was almost ready to test the new atomic bomb that might drive Japan to surrender.

Using the Atomic Bomb

In 1939 Leo Szilard, a Jewish physicist who had fled Nazi persecution, learned that German scientists had split the uranium atom. Szilard had been the first scientist to suggest that splitting the atom might release enormous energy. Szilard convinced the world's best-known physicist, Albert Einstein, to sign a letter Szilard had drafted and send it to President Roosevelt. The letter warned that by using uranium, "extremely powerful bombs of a new type may . . . be constructed."

Roosevelt responded by setting up a scientific committee to study the issue. In 1941 the committee met with British scientists who were already working on an atomic bomb. The Americans convinced Roosevelt to launch a program to build an atomic bomb.

The secret American program to build an atomic bomb was code-named the Manhattan Project and was headed by General Leslie R. Groves. The first breakthrough came in 1942, when Szilard and Enrico Fermi, another physicist, built the world's first **nuclear** reactor at the University of Chicago. Groves then organized a team of engineers and scientists to build

Marines raise the American flag at the highest point on Iwo Jima, February 23, 1945. This photograph has appeared on magazine covers, postage stamps, films, and sculptures since that time.

Analyzing Visuals Why do you think this photograph immediately became an iconic image?

PHOTO: PF-(aircraft)/Alamy Stock Photo; TEXT: Letter from Albert Einstein to President Franklin D. Roosevelt, August 2, 1939.

nuclear used in or produced by a nuclear reaction

The city of Nagasaki, Japan, was devastated after the atomic bombing of August 9, 1945.

Analyzing Visuals What details in the photograph illustrate the effect of the atomic bomb?

an atomic bomb at a secret laboratory in Los Alamos, New Mexico. Physicist J. Robert Oppenheimer led the team. On July 16, 1945, they detonated the world's first atomic bomb in New Mexico.

Even before the bomb was tested, officials began debating how to use it. Admiral William Leahy, chairman of the Joint Chiefs of Staff, opposed using the bomb because it would kill civilians. He believed an economic blockade and conventional bombing would convince Japan to surrender. Secretary of War Henry Stimson wanted to warn the Japanese about the bomb and tell them their emperor could stay in power if they surrendered. Secretary of State James Byrnes, however, wanted to drop the bomb on Japan without any warning.

President Truman later wrote that he "regarded the bomb as a military weapon and never had any doubt that it should be used." His advisers had warned him to expect massive casualties if the United States invaded Japan. Truman believed it was his duty as president to use every weapon available to save American lives. The Allies threatened Japan with "prompt and utter destruction" if the nation did not surrender, but the Japanese did not reply. Truman then ordered the military to drop the bomb. On August 6, 1945, a B-29 bomber named *Enola Gay* dropped an atomic bomb, code-named "Little Boy," on Hiroshima, an important industrial city.

The bomb destroyed about 63 percent of the city. Between 80,000 and 120,000 people, including children, died instantly, and thousands more died later from burns and radiation sickness. Three days later, on August 9, the Soviet Union declared war on Japan. Later that day, the United States dropped another atomic bomb, code-named "Fat Man," on the city of

Nagasaki, killing between 35,000 and 74,000 people. Faced with such massive destruction and the shock of the Soviets joining the war, Hirohito ordered his government to surrender. On August 15, 1945—V-J Day—Japan surrendered. The long war was finally over.

Putting the Enemy on Trial

In August 1945, the United States, Britain, France, and the Soviet Union created the International Military Tribunal (IMT) to punish German and Japanese leaders for war crimes. The tribunal held trials in Nuremberg, Germany, where Hitler had staged Nazi Party rallies.

In January 1946, the International Military Tribunal for the Far East (IMTFE) was created in Tokyo, authorized by an agreement among the United States, the Soviet Union, and the United Kingdom. Like the trials held in Nuremberg, the purpose of the Tokyo War Crimes trials was to punish Japanese leaders.

The IMTFE prosecuted nine senior Japanese leaders and 18 military leaders. During the trials, which lasted from 1946 to 1948, all defendants were found guilty. Punishments ranged from imprisonment to death. Hirohito was not indicted by the IMTFE, as some feared that any attempt to put the emperor on trial would lead to an uprising. The emperor was allowed to remain on the throne, but in a ceremonial role only.

The IMT trials punished many of the people responsible for World War II and the Holocaust, but they were also part of the American plan for building a better world. As Robert Jackson, chief counsel for the United States at Nuremberg, said in his opening statement to the court: "The wrongs we seek to condemn and punish have been so calculated, so malignant and so devastating, that civilization cannot tolerate their being ignored because it cannot survive their being repeated."

✓ **CHECK FOR UNDERSTANDING**

3. **Describing** What made Iwo Jima a strategically important target for the United States?

4. **Analyzing** What factors complicated the issue of Japan's surrender when the emperor asked to end the war after the fall of Okinawa?

LESSON ACTIVITIES

1. **Informative/Explanatory Writing** Suppose you are a journalist in 1968 reporting on the government's disclosure about the Navajo code talkers. Write a newspaper article informing Americans how the code talkers assisted the marines at the Battle of Iwo Jima.

2. **Interpreting Information** With a partner, prepare an annotated time line of the war in the Pacific. Include important battles, key figures, and images and text that convey significant details about the events you include.

PHOTO: Roger Viollet/Getty Images; TEXT: (l)President Harry S. Truman, as quoted in Voices of the American Past: Documents in U.S. History by Raymond M. Hyser and J. Chris Arndt. Copyright © 2008, 2004 by Thomson Wadsworth, a part of The Thomson Corporation; (2)"Second Day, Wednesday, 11/21/1945, Part 04", in Trial of the Major War Criminals before the International Military Tribunal. Volume II. Proceedings: 11/14/1945-11/30/1945. [Official text in the English language.] Nuremberg: IMT, 1947. pp. 98-102.

08

Turning Point: The D-Day Invasion

 COMPELLING QUESTION

What made D-Day a Turning Point?

Plan Your Inquiry

In this lesson you will investigate the events surrounding the Allied invasion of Western Europe that began on June 6, 1944. You will consider the impact of what became widely known as D-Day to determine how the events on that date marked a turning point in World War II.

DEVELOP QUESTIONS

Developing Questions About D-Day Read the Compelling Question for this lesson. How was the war going before D-Day? What changed after the Allies launched their invasion? Develop a list of Supporting Questions that would help you answer the Compelling Question in this lesson.

APPLY HISTORICAL TOOLS

Analyzing Primary and Secondary Sources You will work with a variety of primary and secondary sources in this lesson. These sources provide insight into the events leading up to D-Day as well as the invasion and its aftermath. As you read, use a graphic organizer like the one below to record information about the sources that will help you examine them and check for historical understanding. Note ways in which each source helps you answer your Supporting Questions.

Supporting Questions	Sources	What this source tells me about D-Day...	Questions the source leaves unanswered
	A		
	B		
	C		
	D		
	E		

After you analyze the sources, you will:
- use the evidence from the sources.
- communicate your conclusions.
- take informed action.

Background Information

From 1939 to 1942, Nazi Germany went on a relentless and seemingly unstoppable march. When the United States entered the war at the end of 1941, Germany and its allies had occupied or annexed most of Western, Central, and Eastern Europe and much of North Africa.

The Allied Powers began planning to trap Nazi forces between American, British, and Canadian forces in the west and Soviet forces in the east. Operation Overlord was born and planned for May 1944. However, technical issues with the landing craft required to launch the largest **amphibious** invasion in history delayed the invasion by a month.

On June 5, more than 150,000 troops crossed the English Channel toward five landing points along the Normandy Coast of France. Stormy weather made the seas rough and slowed the approach. Then, at about 6:30 a.m. on June 6, the first troops touched shore. German mines and artillery fire cost thousands of soldiers their lives, but the forces pressed on. By nightfall, the Allies had taken the beaches and were poised to begin retaking Europe.

amphibious involving land and sea forces

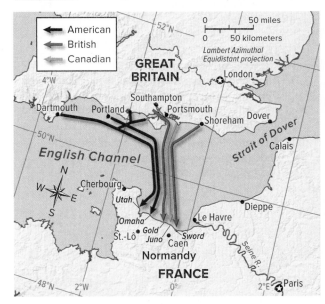

» Allied forces staged a major invasion of the northern French coast as part of Operation Overlord in what became known as the D-Day invasion.

The Scale of the Invasion

More than one D-day took place during World War II. That is because military forces as far back as the first World War began using the label *D-day* to mark the day on which an attack or other military operation would begin. However, the June 6, 1944, D-Day has taken over ownership of the term because of the significance of the invasion and because of its massive scope. More than 6,000 ships and other vessels landed at five beaches in Normandy. More than 11,000 aircraft dropped paratroopers, bombs, and supplies and conducted **reconnaissance.** More would follow. The scale of this operation made this D-Day stand out from all the others.

PRIMARY SOURCE : PHOTOGRAPH

reconnaissance a survey of an area, especially by military forces

EXAMINE THE SOURCE

1. **Analyzing Visuals** What do you see in this picture? Describe the vehicles and the setting. How do you think American citizens would have reacted viewing this photo?

2. **Analyzing Perspectives** Why do you think the photographer took this picture? Explain the photographer's choices.

Eisenhower's Inspiration

Tens of thousands of troops prepared to land in France on D-Day. More than 2 million others waited to follow them. Their commander was General Dwight D. Eisenhower. In February 1944, Eisenhower began drafting the order for the invasion, which he distributed to thousands of the troops on June 5 and later delivered as a speech.

PRIMARY SOURCE : SPEECH

66 Soldiers, Sailors and Airmen of the Allied Expeditionary Force!

You are about to embark upon the Great Crusade, toward which we have striven these many months. The eyes of the world are upon you. The hopes and prayers of liberty-loving people everywhere march with you. In company with our brave Allies and brothers-in-arms on other Fronts, you will bring about the destruction of the German war machine, the elimination of Nazi tyranny over the oppressed peoples of Europe, and security for ourselves in a free world.

Your task will not be an easy one. Your enemy is well trained, well equipped and battle-hardened. He will fight savagely.

But this is the year 1944! Much has happened since the Nazi triumphs of 1940—41. The United Nations have inflicted upon the Germans great defeats . . . Our air offensive has seriously reduced their strength in the air and their capacity to wage war on the ground. Our Home Fronts have given us an overwhelming superiority in weapons . . . and placed at our disposal . . . trained fighting men. The tide has turned! The free men of the world are marching together to Victory!

I have full confidence in your courage, devotion to duty and skill in battle. We will accept nothing less than full Victory! . . . 99

—General Dwight D. Eisenhower, June 6, 1944

EXAMINE THE SOURCE

1. **Describing** What goal does Eisenhower give the troops in this statement?

2. **Interpreting** Eisenhower says, "The tide has turned!" What is the significance of this sentence and of his tone throughout the message?

PHOTO: Library of Congress Prints and Photographs Division [LC-USZ62-111201]; TEXT: Eisenhower, Dwight D. 1944. D-Day Statement to Soldiers, Sailors, and Airmen of the Allied Expeditionary Force, 6/44. Collection DDEEPRE: Dwight D. Eisenhower Library, National Archives and Records Administration.

(l)U.S. House of Representatives. Committee on Veteran's Affairs. Report on Observance of the 50th Anniversary of the D-Day Invasion, 103rd Congress, 2nd sess. Washington: U.S. G.P.O. 1994; (r)Clinton, William J. D-Day National Remembrance Day and Time for the National Observance of the Fiftieth Anniversary of World War II, 1994. In U.S. House of Representatives. Committee on Veteran's Affairs. Report on Observance of the 50th Anniversary of the D-Day Invasion, 103rd Congress, 2nd sess. Washington: U.S. G.P.O. 1994.

C

D-Day Plus 50 Years

In June 1994, people across the world marked the fiftieth anniversary of D-Day. U.S. Representative G.V. Montgomery, Chairman of the Committee on Veterans' Affairs, wrote this foreword to a report on the celebrations and memorials.

SECONDARY SOURCE : COMMITTEE REPORT

❝ On June 6, 1944, a military force of more than 150,000 American, British, and Canadian troops launched along a 60-mile front the most massive assault of its kind ever attempted in the history of the world. Their goal was the liberation of Europe and the preservation and restoration of freedom in the western world. The invasion was massive, brilliant and successful. . . . Few events, if any, have had such a resounding impact on the course of American and European history. The invasion was the beginning of the end of the war against Hitler.

The D-Day assault involved 6,500 naval vessels and 10,000 aircraft. The five separate beaches—code-named by the Allied military Omaha, Utah, Gold, Juno and Sword—where troops landed were fiercely guarded by German defenders. The approaches were filled with underwater obstacles. The beaches were heavily mined and strewn with barbed wire. High ground above the beaches was commanded by German artillery.

The loss in both personnel and materiel was extremely high. Many brave individuals successfully completed an impossible task. Theirs is a story that is a powerful part of both our past and our future. We owe much to our service personnel and allies for their courage and extraordinary efforts in bringing about the defeat of Hitler's armies. ❞

—Committee on Veterans Affairs, October 24, 1994

EXAMINE THE SOURCE

1. **Summarizing** What does the report say about the purpose of D-Day, and how does it describe the events of that day?

2. **Inferring** What can you infer about the impact of D-Day based on this statement and its commemoration? Explain its world-wide impact.

D

D-Day National Remembrance

On June 6, 1994, President Bill Clinton journeyed to Normandy. He met with his counterparts from other nations, toured the historical sites and memorials, and delivered a speech on Omaha Beach. A week before, he had signed this proclamation, declaring June 6, 1944, D-Day National Remembrance Day.

PRIMARY SOURCE : PROCLAMATION

❝ . . . Over 5,000 ships and 10,000 aircraft carried more than 130,000 soldiers, sailors, and airmen from the United States, Great Britain, Canada, Poland, France, Norway, the Netherlands, Czechoslovakia, New Zealand, Australia, Luxembourg, and Belgium to the shores of Normandy. More than 9,000 Americans never returned.

D-Day was considered crucial not only by the Allies, but also by the Axis powers. Field Marshall Erwin Rommel, commander of the enemy forces in the area, dubbed the first 24 hours as 'The Longest Day,' referring to the fact that the Allies were successful in establishing a **beachhead**. . . .

[T]he Allied forces had more than just their will to win urging them on. As defenders of justice, they were driven by the desire to restore the peace and freedom that the Nazi occupation had denied to millions of people. . . .

[M]illions . . . were delivered from oppression and fear. Those who landed on the beaches of Normandy, not only on D-Day but also throughout the rest of the war, were responsible for the liberation of many of the concentration camps as well as cities, towns, and villages throughout Europe that had suffered for so many years. . . . ❞

—President Bill Clinton, June 6, 1994

beachhead an occupied area of shoreline from which to land troops and supplies

EXAMINE THE SOURCE

1. **Explaining** What viewpoint from the Axis Powers does Clinton cite? Why do you think he does so?

2. **Drawing Conclusions** What does the proclamation suggest about the immediate and lasting impact of D-Day?

D-Day at Normandy Revisited

After the Allies secured the Normandy beaches, they fortified their position and began the push inland. At first, they made slow progress, but then the Allies delivered terrible losses to the German forces during the Battle of the Bulge from December 1944 to January 1945. Afterward, Germany proved unable to stop the Allied advance from east and west as they surrounded and captured Berlin.

SECONDARY SOURCE : ARTICLE

" June 1944 was the **climactic** month that set the stage for the final victory in World War II in Europe. Ever since Adolph Hitler invaded Russia in 1941, Joseph Stalin had relentlessly pressed Franklin D. Roosevelt and Winston Churchill for a second front in Europe. Finally, on 6 June 1944 . . . about 5,000 ships, smaller landing craft, and thousands of planes and gliders brought the equivalent of over nine divisions of troops to the sandy soil of Normandy in the largest **armada** in history. . . .

Today, the D-day landings are remembered in heroic, chivalric terms. In spite of recriminations by the Canadians against the *12th SS Panzer Division* following D-day, the Allies conceded that according to the curious morality of the battlefield, the Germans had behaved reasonably during the fighting in Normandy. There were many days and weeks of hard fighting ahead in the hedgerow (*bocage* in French) country of Normandy to secure the hard-won landing beaches. The capture of Cherbourg, the breakout at St. Lo, the battle of the Falaise Gap, the liberation of Paris, and the advance to the Rhine all lay ahead; but, the liberation of Western Europe had begun. "

—Retired Lt. Colonel Thomas D. Morgan, *Army History*, No. 36 (Winter 1996)

climactic referring to the most crucial turning point
armada a fleet of ships

EXAMINE THE SOURCE

1. **Summarizing** Why makes the D-Day landing so historically significant?

2. **Drawing Conclusions** What historical context does he provide for the events of June 6, 1944?

Your Inquiry Analysis

EVALUATE SOURCES AND USE EVIDENCE

Reflect back to the Compelling Question and the Supporting Questions you developed at the beginning of this lesson.

1. **Gathering Sources** Refer back to the Graphic Organizer you created as you read through the sources. Which sources do you consider most helpful for answering your Supporting Questions? Circle or highlight those sources in your graphic organizer. How might you find answers to additional questions the sources raised?

2. **Evaluating Sources** Looking at the sources that helped you answer the Supporting Questions, evaluate the strength of each source. Note the date of each source as well as any credentials that strengthen the reliability of the source. Consider, too, how bias might affect the content. Jot down notes in the margins of your graphic organizer.

3. **Comparing and Contrasting** Compare and contrast two of the sources in this lesson more closely. Summarize the main ideas in each source, and describe the different perspectives offered by each. Then, explain how the two sources reinforce each other or your understanding of the topic.

COMMUNICATE CONCLUSIONS

Analyzing Information Answer each of your Supporting Questions and explain their relationship to the Compelling Question. Make a concept web in which you record details from the sources that support the idea of D-Day as a turning point in World War II. Then, use your web to write a paragraph in which you answer the Compelling Question and cite and explain evidence from the sources to support your response. Share your paragraph with the class.

TAKE INFORMED ACTION

Writing Letters Visit the Department of Veterans Affairs website and scan online or print newspapers to identify an issue of concern to veterans today. Conduct additional research, if needed, to understand that issue. Then, complete one of these activities:

- Write a letter to a veteran in which you express your gratitude for his or her service, share what you have learned about one issue, and inquire what the veteran thinks should be done to address the issue.

- Write a letter to a state or federal official in which you note your interest in the state of veterans' affairs, share what you learned about one issue, and explain what you think should be done regarding this issue.

Morgan, Thomas D. "D-Day at Normandy Revisited." Army History. No. 36, Winter 1996, p.30-35.

09

Reviewing World War II

Summary

The Origin of War

Twenty years after "the war to end all wars," the world found itself engulfed in an even larger and more devastating conflict. Many of the causes of World War II can be traced to events that transpired in the aftermath of World War I. Instability in the years following World War I allowed authoritarian dictatorships to develop in several countries. In Italy fascist leader Benito Mussolini rose to power by playing on fears of a communist revolution and with promises of returning national glory. He and his Blackshirt followers seized and maintained power largely through intimidation and martial law.

As dictator of the Soviet Union, Joseph Stalin tried to expand the nation's industry and organized agriculture through collective farming. He also used fear, mass murder, imprisonment, and even famines to control the Soviet people. In Germany, Adolf Hitler rose to power by appealing to nationalism, racism, anti-Semitism, and anger over the Treaty of Versailles. His Nazi Party and its Stormtroopers targeted groups they deemed "inferior" on their way toward seizing control and establishing a dictatorship.

Authoritarian leadership also developed in Japan. Rather than a dictatorship, a group of military leaders gained increasing influence over the government. Their goal of creating an Asian empire outweighed even the desires of the emperor.

These authoritarian governments expanded their militaries and used them to maintain power and prepare for territorial invasions. Both Italy and Germany expanded their control of lands beyond their borders without threatening one another. Hitler's troops slowly seized more territories as British and French leaders, fearful of another massive war, allowed German expansion through a policy of appeasement. Their inaction only emboldened Hitler. After signing a nonaggression pact with the Soviet Union, Germany invaded Poland in September 1939. The pact finally led Britain and France (the Allied Powers) to declare war against Germany. In turn, Germany allied with Italy and Japan as the Axis Powers. Hitler's troops swept through western Europe. France fell to Germany, but Great Britain held firm.

The United States tried to remain neutral in the conflict. Gradually, Congress passed a series of laws using loopholes such as "cash-and-carry" and Lend-Lease, which allowed the United States to increase its support for the Allies while still officially remaining neutral. President Roosevelt, who won an unprecedented third term in office, began to prepare for the possibility of war.

Time Line of the Events Leading up to World War II

1935	1936	1937	1938	1939	1940
• Hitler violates the Treaty of Versailles by rebuilding Germany's military. • Congress passes the First Neutrality Act. • Mussolini invades Ethiopia.	• Congress renews the Neutrality Act until May of 1937.	• Congress prohibits U.S. merchant ships from transporting arms to warring nations. • The cash-and-carry amendment allows warring nations to buy any materials except arms. • Japanese forces carry out the Rape of Nanking.	• Germany invades Austria. • Britain and France cede the Sudetenland to Germany.	• Congress denies renewal of cash-and-carry. • Germany invades Czechoslovakia. • Germany invades Poland. • Britain and France declare war. • The final U.S. Neutrality Act passes, with the restoration of cash-and-carry, with arms allowed to be sold.	• Denmark, Norway, Belgium, and Holland fall to Germany. • France surrenders to Hitler. • The Battle of Britain rages. • Roosevelt signs the "Destroyers for Bases" agreement.

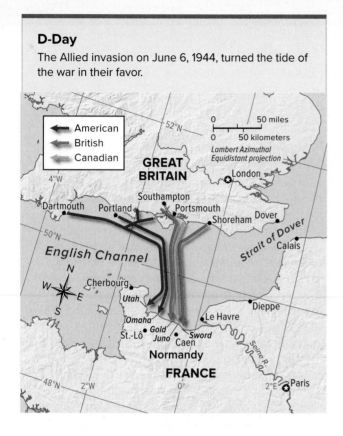

D-Day

The Allied invasion on June 6, 1944, turned the tide of the war in their favor.

The Holocaust

One of the key features of Hitler's philosophy was the scapegoating of various groups, especially Jews, seen as a threat to the ideal "Aryan" race. Once in power, the Nazi government passed laws limiting the rights of Jews and other "undesirables." Jewish individuals and businesses were attacked. One such example was *Kristallnacht.* Jews tried to flee to other nations for safety, but many of them were turned away. Gradually, Nazi forces forced Jews first into ghettos and then into concentration camps, where they were subjected to horrific treatment and acts and were often worked to death. In 1942 Hitler's government launched its Final Solution for the mass extermination of all Jews. In all, about six million Jews perished in what would come to be known as the Holocaust.

The United States and War

Although the United States gradually increased its support for the Allies, most of the American public preferred the country stay out of the conflict. This attitude changed after December 7, 1941, when Japan attacked Pearl Harbor. Because of the attack, Japanese Americans would experience discrimination, including internment in detention camps. The United States quickly mobilized to fight in Europe and the Pacific. The need for such a large fighting force expanded military opportunities for racial minorities, immigrants, and women. On the home front, many women filled important jobs in defense industries.

War in Europe

In Europe, the United States joined the Allies, which now included the Soviet Union, in striking the "soft underbelly" of the Axis. Fighting in North Africa and an Allied invasion into Italy drove back Mussolini's forces. Soviet reserves during the siege of Stalingrad wore down German forces on the Eastern front. Soviet forces began an offensive march toward Germany. The tide turned for the Allies with the D-Day invasion on the beachfronts of Normandy, France, on June 6, 1944. Over the following months, Allied forces would liberate Paris and discover horrifying situations at concentration camps as they drove toward Berlin. In late April 1945, with Allied forces closing in on both sides, Hitler and some of his closest aides committed suicide. New German leaders negotiated a cease-fire to end the war in Europe.

War in the Pacific

Immediately following the attack on Pearl Harbor, Japan swiftly moved to secure key territories throughout Asia, including the Philippines. Japan hoped that by wiping out naval forces and securing Asia quickly, the United States would be willing to negotiate. Americans wanted revenge for the attack, and the Navy recovered much faster than the Japanese had expected.

American forces employed a strategy of island hopping to secure key spots among Japanese-occupied lands. The war in the Pacific turned in the Allies' favor at the Battle of Midway in 1942, but the fighting dragged on. *Kamikaze* pilots destroyed American vessels. Fierce fighting on islands such as Iwo Jima and Okinawa led to huge casualties on both sides. By the summer of 1945, even many Japanese leaders wanted an end to the war, but they resisted the American insistence on unconditional surrender.

After Roosevelt died in 1945, President Harry S. Truman learned of a secret "Manhattan Project" to develop an atomic bomb. Truman weighed the cost of a massive Allied military invasion of mainland Japan against the loss of civilian life that would result from dropping an atomic bomb. He authorized the use of the bomb. In August 1945 the United States dropped a nuclear bomb on the Japanese city of Hiroshima. Despite the devastation, the Japanese government did not surrender. Three days later the United States dropped a second atomic bomb on Nagasaki, after which Japan agreed to unconditional surrender.

The war was over, but the world would never be the same. Nazi leaders who had carried out the Holocaust and Japanese leaders who had tortured prisoners faced trials for crimes against humanity. Unlike the aftermath of World War I, the United States would remain a world leader rather than return to isolationism.

Apply What You Have Learned

A Understanding Multiple Perspectives

The decision to use nuclear weapons against Japan was not an easy one. Even though the use of the bombs led to the Japanese surrender, many people questioned whether Truman made the right decision.

ACTIVITY **Write an Editorial** Read the following quotes from President Harry Truman and from William Leahy, who was chairman of the Joint Chiefs of Staff. Identify the main points each make. Then, write an editorial supporting one of these points of view. The editorial should demonstrate that you understand the other point of view as well.

66 The world will note that the first atomic bomb was dropped on Hiroshima, a military base. . . . If Japan does not surrender, bombs will have to be dropped on her war industries and, unfortunately, thousands of civilian lives will be lost. . . . We have used it against those who attacked us without warning at Pearl Harbor, against those who have starved and beaten and executed American prisoners of war, against those who have abandoned all pretense of obeying international laws of warfare. We have used it in order to shorten the agony of war, in order to save the lives of thousands and thousands of young Americans. 99

—President Truman, August 9, 1945

66 It is my opinion that the use of this barbarous weapon at Hiroshima and Nagasaki was of no material assistance in our war against Japan. The Japanese were already defeated and ready to surrender because of the effective sea blockade and the successful bombing with conventional weapons. . . . The lethal possibilities of atomic warfare in the future are frightening. My own feeling was that in being the first to use it, we had adopted an ethical standard common to the barbarians of the Dark Ages. 99

—William Leahy, from *I Was There*, 1950

B Making Connections to Today

One of the lessons American leaders learned from World War II was that the United States was not sheltered from foreign events. The nation emerged from World War II as one of the world's leading powers. This new power involved increased roles in resolving foreign conflicts both diplomatically and militarily.

Even today, however, debate often rages about when and how the United States should get involved in overseas conflicts that do not directly threaten U.S. citizens. Some leaders believe isolationism is still in the nation's best interests.

ACTIVITY **Analyze a Current Event** Using library or Internet resources, research a current global conflict about which American leaders are debating whether to get involved. Write a summary analyzing facts about the conflict, what the major issues of debate are, and why some Americans do or do not want to get involved. Pair with another student to share your findings and discuss whether and how you think the United States should get involved.

» A U.S. Marine is deployed to strengthen a security post at the Baghdad Embassy Compound in Iraq, January 4, 2020.

PHOTO: Sgt. Kyle Talbot/Associated Press; TEXT: (1)Truman, Harry S. 1945. Radio Report to the American People on the Potsdam Conference, August 9, 1945, in Public Papers of the Presidents of the United States: Harry S. Truman, 1945. Washington: U.S. Government Printing Office; (2)Leahy, William D. 1950. I Was There: The Personal Story of the Chief of Staff to Presidents Roosevelt and Truman Based on His Notes and Diaries Made at the Time, with a Foreword by President Truman. New York: Curtis Publishing Company.

C Building Citizenship

The Nuremberg Trials and the Tokyo War Crimes Trials established that some actions go beyond what can be explained as the horrors of war. Despite cultural differences, the prosecutors argued, most civilized people agree that some actions are unacceptable. These actions came to be known as "crimes against humanity." As Robert H. Jackson, Chief of Counsel for the United States during the Nuremberg Trials explained:

66 The wrongs which we seek to condemn and punish have been so calculated, so malignant, and so devastating, that civilization cannot tolerate their being ignored, because it cannot survive their being repeated.

. . . Civilization can afford no compromise with the social forces which would gain renewed strength if we deal ambiguously or indecisively with the men in whom those forces now precariously survive. 99

ACTIVITY <u>Establish International Principles</u> Working in small groups, discuss some of the ideas established by the post-World War II war crimes trials. Then, as a group, develop a list of five principles for humanity that could apply to almost all people, regardless of where they live. The violation of such principles would amount to a crime against humanity.

D Understanding Data

After the Japanese attack on Pearl Harbor, the United States had to mobilize military forces very quickly. It also had to produce weapons and supplies for these fighting forces. Thousands of civilians, including many women, worked in defense plants as the primarily male fighting force went overseas.

As the war progressed, the military finally reached its quotas for large-scale weapons, but the need for more troops continued because of casualties and the expansion of fighting.

ACTIVITY Explain Visual Information
Analyzing data can reveal more about historical events than numbers alone. The graphs below illustrate American production of large-scale weapons as well as the number of troops in each branch of the service throughout the war. Write a brief explanation of the trends you notice in these graphs. Explain why the production of ships, tanks, and combat aircraft declined earlier than the number of members of the U.S. Army, Navy, or Marines.

The Industry and Troops of World War II

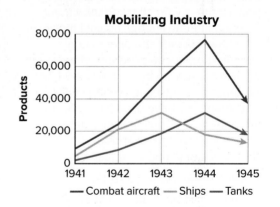

Second Day, Wednesday, 11/21/1945, Part 04", in Trial of the Major War Criminals before the International Military Tribunal. Volume II. Proceedings: 11/14/1945-11/30/1945. [Official text in the English language.] Nuremberg: IMT, 1947, pp. 98-102.

Cold War Foreign Policy 1945–1991

People used their bare hands to pull down barbed wire from the Berlin Wall after the border between East Germany and West Germany opened in November 1989.

INTRODUCTION LESSON

01 Introducing Cold War Foreign Policy   328

LEARN THE EVENTS LESSONS

02 The Early Cold War Years   333

03 Foreign Policy in the 1950s and 1960s   339

05 Foreign Policy in the 1970s and 1980s   351

06 Ending the Cold War   355

INQUIRY ACTIVITY LESSONS

04 Analyzing Sources: The Cold War in Space   345

07 Turning Point: The Soviet Union Collapses   359

REVIEW AND APPLY LESSON

08 Reviewing Cold War Foreign Policy   363

Thomas Imo/Photothek/Getty Images

THE YALTA CONFERENCE

From February 4 to 11, 1945, as World War II neared an end, three leaders of the Allied nations met in Yalta, a city along the Black Sea in Crimea. President Franklin D. Roosevelt, British Prime Minister Winston Churchill, and Premier of the Soviet Union Joseph Stalin discussed the United Nations and world organization, the liberation of Europe, Germany's division, and Germany's reparations. As stated in the text from the conference, the three leaders agreed that the "establishment of order in Europe and the rebuilding of national economic life must be achieved by processes which will enable the liberated peoples to destroy the last vestiges of Nazism and Fascism to create democratic institutions of their own choice."

Germany's unconditional surrender occurred on May 7, 1945, about a month after Roosevelt died and Vice President Harry Truman took office. The war in the Pacific ended in August. Roosevelt and Churchill had trusted Stalin to adhere to the Yalta agreements because they believed Soviet power was necessary to defeat Japan. Stalin agreed to join the war in the Pacific "two or three months after Germany has surrendered and the war in Europe is terminated." But the war ended without Soviet aid when President Truman's choice to deploy atomic bombs on Japan led to its surrender.

The Yalta agreements were made public in 1946 and were met with harsh criticism in the United States. Stalin did not uphold his promise to hold free elections in Czechoslovakia, Poland, Hungary, Romania, or Bulgaria. Instead, communist governments were established and any opposing political parties were suppressed. The Soviet Union's military occupied Eastern Europe, and although there was public and political outrage at Stalin's failure to follow through with the Yalta agreements, the West was not able to enforce those agreements in the aftermath of war.

Historians now believe Roosevelt's failing health played an important role in the mistakes made at Yalta. Roosevelt died on April 12, 1945, from a brain hemorrhage, but he had been suffering from advanced **arteriosclerosis** for more than a year before Yalta. Roosevelt's health had been an issue in his 1944 campaign, but his landslide win indicated that American voters did not view what they knew about his health as a problem. When Roosevelt returned from Yalta, however, he sat while addressing Congress, which was something he had never done before even though he was partially paralyzed as a result of polio. Some critics later pointed to the deal Roosevelt made regarding China as evidence of his failing health.

In return for entering the battle against Japan, Stalin wanted the Japanese Kuril Islands and the territory that had been lost in the Russo-Japanese War in 1904. In addition, he wanted the Soviet Union's interests in Port Dairen in China to be protected, as well as the use of Port Arthur as a naval base. Stalin also secured control over the railroads that led from the Soviet Union to Dairen through "a joint Soviet-Chinese Company." However, this portion of the conference was kept secret, and Roosevelt made no mention of China in his March 1945 report to Congress. Roosevelt's agreement with Stalin on behalf of China—without the permission of Chinese leaders—had long-lasting effects on relations between Russia, China, and the United States.

> 66 ... establishment of order in Europe and the rebuilding of national life must be achieved by processes ... to create democratic institutions of their own choice. 99

(1)U.S. Department of State, Office of the Historian. "Text Proposed by the United States for a Declaration on Liberated Europe, February 9, 1945." Foreign Relations of the United States: Diplomatic Papers, Conferences at Malta and Yalta, 1945; (2) Crimea (Yalta) Conference, 1945: Entry of Soviet Union Into War Against Japan. Agreement signed at Yalta February 11, 1945. 59 Stat. 1823; Executive Agreement Series 498; 1945 For.Rel. (Conferences at Malta and Yalta) 984.

arteriosclerosis a chronic disease that thickens and hardens artery walls, which can restrict the flow of blood to tissues and organs

▶ GO ONLINE Explore the Student Edition eBook and find interactive maps, time lines, and tools.

National Archives and Records Administration (NWDNS-111-SC-260486)

British Prime Minister Winston Churchill, U.S. President Franklin D. Roosevelt, and Soviet Premier Joseph Stalin met at the Yalta Conference in February 1945.

Understanding the Time and Place: The Cold War, 1945–1989

In the first half of the twentieth century, the world experienced two wars and a massive economic depression. Even before World War II ended, global leaders started working together to create ways to ensure these events did not repeat themselves. But cooperation among nations was no easy task, especially as two opposing economic systems—communism and capitalism—took center stage.

Communism Versus Capitalism

World War II did not create the tension between **communism** and **capitalism,** although it did magnify it. The Bolsheviks seized political control of Russia in 1917 during the Russian Revolution and brought down the Romanov dynasty that had ruled for more than 300 years. This contributed to the Red Scare in the United States between 1919 and 1920, when fear of anti-capitalist ideas and mistrust of immigrants ran rampant throughout the country. People particularly feared immigrants from Russia and southern and eastern Europe because some believed that they wanted to overthrow the U.S. government. Raids and arrests of anyone considered an anarchist, a communist, or a socialist occurred in 1920. This culture of fear influenced the trial of Nicola Sacco and Bartolomeo Vanzetti, who were put to death in August 1927. The deeply rooted opposition to communism and socialism that pervaded the United States after World War I also influenced the events that followed World War II.

An "Iron Curtain" Descends

The United States and the Soviet Union were allies during World War II, but this was largely because Hitler violated the nonaggression pact he had signed with the Soviet Union. After the war, the Soviet-U.S. tension solidified. After the Potsdam Conference in 1945, West Berlin was occupied by France, Great Britain, and the United States, while East Berlin was held by the Soviets. West Berlin was rebuilt as a Western power with freedoms and economic growth that Soviets found threatening. Eventually, East Germany's communist government built a wall encircling West Berlin. The Berlin Wall stood as a concrete manifestation of two opposing world views; it did not fall until late 1989 and was not completely removed until 1991.

On March 5, 1946, Winston Churchill was visiting Westminster College in Fulton, Missouri. During the speech that Churchill gave as part of that visit, the former prime minister of Great Britain described the dangers of Communist control occurring in the countries of Eastern Europe. Churchill was concerned about the influence that Communism was exerting across the continent—especially in areas that were being gathered more and more under the umbrella of Soviet influence. Churchill worried even more specifically that the governments in the capital cities of Prague, Budapest, Bucharest, and many others in the region were not simply being influenced by Soviet ideas. He feared that these nations were being directly controlled by the leaders in Moscow. Churchill warned that these areas of Europe falling under Soviet control were disappearing behind an "iron curtain."

The press picked up the term "iron curtain," and for the next 43 years, it described the communist nations

Winston Churchill delivers the 1946 speech in which he coined the term "iron curtain."

Analyzing Visuals What details in the photo suggests that Churchill's speech was considered important?

communism an economic system in which the production of goods is controlled by the state

capitalism an economic system characterized by the private or corporate ownership of goods with the distribution of goods determined by competition in a free market

PA Images/Alamy Stock Photo

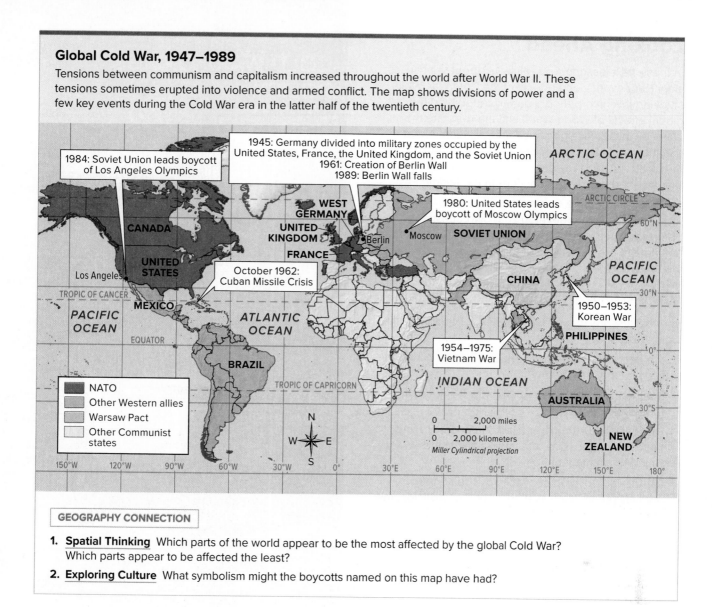

Global Cold War, 1947–1989

Tensions between communism and capitalism increased throughout the world after World War II. These tensions sometimes erupted into violence and armed conflict. The map shows divisions of power and a few key events during the Cold War era in the latter half of the twentieth century.

1984: Soviet Union leads boycott of Los Angeles Olympics

1945: Germany divided into military zones occupied by the United States, France, the United Kingdom, and the Soviet Union
1961: Creation of Berlin Wall
1989: Berlin Wall falls

1980: United States leads boycott of Moscow Olympics

October 1962: Cuban Missile Crisis

1950–1953: Korean War

1954–1975: Vietnam War

NATO
Other Western allies
Warsaw Pact
Other Communist states

0 — 2,000 miles
0 — 2,000 kilometers
Miller Cylindrical projection

GEOGRAPHY CONNECTION

1. **Spatial Thinking** Which parts of the world appear to be the most affected by the global Cold War? Which parts appear to be affected the least?
2. **Exploring Culture** What symbolism might the boycotts named on this map have had?

of Eastern Europe and the Soviet Union. The metaphor effectively emphasized the fierce divisions between communism and capitalism.

U.S. Foreign Policies

The United States followed isolationist policies in the early years of World War II, but these policies changed toward the war's end and after the war. World War II destroyed land, property, industry, lives, and livelihoods throughout Europe and in Japan. Leaders recognized the necessity of global cooperation and worked to create international economic, political, and humanitarian institutions, such as the World Bank, the International Monetary Fund, and the United Nations.

In June 1947 Secretary of State George C. Marshall proposed a program, which became known as the **Marshall Plan,** to aid countries affected by the

war. The United States offered the plan to the Soviet Union and its associated countries, but the Soviets rejected it. The generosity of the Marshall Plan sent billions of dollars in supplies, machinery, and food into Western Europe, aiding in the region's postwar economic recovery. It helped the United States by reducing the appeal of communism in impoverished countries and opened new trade markets. At the same time, it aroused hostilities with the Soviets and their allies.

The Cold War, as these tensions between the United States and the Soviet Union were named, lasted for a half century. The United States pledged to help other nations fight against communist aggression, which led to wars in Korea and Vietnam and shaped American foreign policy throughout those decades.

Marshall Plan a U.S. program of financing to help European nations rebuild after World War II

Looking Ahead

In these next lessons, you will learn about the causes, significant events, and effects of the Cold War. While studying this time period, you will understand the global effects of World War II and the resulting changes in U.S. foreign policy. You will learn about communism in the Soviet Union and its spread throughout Asia, and you will examine how the Cold War affected policies and actions in the Middle East.

You will examine Compelling Questions in the Inquiry Lessons and develop your own questions about foreign policy during the Cold War. Review the time line to preview some of the key events that you will learn about.

What Will You Learn

In these lessons focused on foreign policy during the Cold War, you will learn:

- the decisions made by President Truman during the first years of the Cold War.
- the theory of containment and how it influenced U.S. foreign policy.
- the reasons Eisenhower used brinkmanship and the threat of massive retaliation against the Soviet Union to maintain peace.
- the foreign policy crises faced by the Kennedy administration, such as the Bay of Pigs invasion, the construction of the Berlin Wall, and the Cuban missile crisis.
- how the Nixon Doctrine and détente represented new directions in U.S. foreign policy.
- the political and social reasons for the collapse of the Soviet Union.

? COMPELLING QUESTIONS

- **How was the space race an extension of the Cold War?**
- **Why did the Cold War end?**

KEY EVENTS OF THE

COLD WAR FOREIGN POLICY

1947 ○   **1947** Truman Doctrine declared

1948 Berlin Airlift begins

1949 NATO forms

1954 Eisenhower puts forward domino theory

1957 ○

1960 U.S. spy plane shot down over Soviet Union

APRIL 1961 Soviet astronaut Yuri Gagarin (right) is first person to orbit Earth

APRIL 17, 1961 Bay of Pigs invasion

AUGUST 1961 Construction of the Berlin Wall begins

OCTOBER 1962 Cuban Missile Crisis

1970 ○

FEBRUARY 1972 Richard Nixon visits China

SEPTEMBER 1978 Camp David Accords signed

1989 Fall of Berlin Wall

1990 East and West Germany reunite

1991 ○   **1991** Soviet Union dissolves

Sequencing Time Identify the events that reveal the tension between the United States and the Soviet Union and explain what those events reveal about that tension.

ITAR-TASS News Agency/Alamy Stock Photo

332

READING STRATEGY

Analyzing Key Ideas and Details As you read, use a graphic organizer similar to this one to list early conflicts between the Soviet Union and the United States.

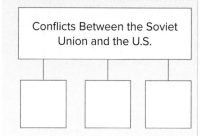

World War II Influences on the Cold War

GUIDING QUESTION

How did the outcome of World War II shape the fault lines of the Cold War?

Well before World War II ended, President Roosevelt began thinking about the world after the war. He was determined to build a new economic and political system that would preserve world peace and promote economic growth.

The Bretton Woods System

President Roosevelt believed that high tariffs were a cause of the Great Depression. He and his advisers thought that the best way to generate postwar economic growth was to increase trade between countries and to create institutions that would stabilize the trade system. In July 1944 Roosevelt helped to organize a conference in Bretton Woods, New Hampshire, for the world's non-Axis nations.

The conference set up two organizations—the World Bank and the International Monetary Fund (IMF). The World Bank's purpose was to help rebuild Europe after the war and help Asian, African, and Latin American nations develop their economies. The IMF was designed to help nations with trade deficits, which occur when a country imports more than it exports, causing more money to flow out of the country than flows in. The conference also set up a new currency system that used the U.S. dollar as the world's reserve currency. All nations set an exchange rate between their currency and the dollar, and the dollar was put on a gold standard, with one ounce of gold equaling 35 U.S. dollars. The United States vowed to keep enough gold in reserve to redeem dollars for gold on demand. One benefit of the Bretton Woods system was that it prevented nations from using inflation to avoid debts as Germany had done with its World War I reparation debts.

Creating the United Nations

Roosevelt believed one cause of World War II had been the U.S. decision to stay out of the League of Nations after World War I. Because of this, Roosevelt wanted to create an international organization that would take an active role in preserving peace. He was assisted by Secretary of State Cordell Hull. Delegates from 39 countries met at the Dumbarton Oaks estate in Washington, D.C., in 1944 to discuss a new organization called the United Nations (UN). Delegates agreed that the UN would have a General Assembly, where every member nation in the world would have one vote, as well as a Security Council with eleven members. The delegates named five countries as permanent members of the Security Council: Great Britain, France, China, the Soviet Union, and the United States, and each would have veto power. By including all of the great powers on the UN Security council, the countries had to consult with each other whenever the United Nations took action. However, any one member of the Security Council had veto power to stop the UN from taking action.

On April 25, 1945, delegates from 50 countries, including educator and activist Mary McLeod Bethune who represented the United States, went to San Francisco to officially organize the United Nations and design its **charter.** The General Assembly was given the power to vote on resolutions and to choose the non-permanent members of the Security Council. The Security

charter a constitution

GO ONLINE Explore the Student Edition eBook and find interactive maps, time lines, and tools.

333

Council—responsible for international peace and security—could ask its members to use military force to uphold a UN resolution.

Declaration of Liberated Europe

In February 1945 Roosevelt, Churchill, and Stalin met at Yalta—a Soviet resort on the Black Sea—to plan the postwar world. Several agreements reached at Yalta later played important roles in causing the Cold War. One key issue was that Poland had two governments claiming the right to govern—a Soviet-backed Communist one and a non-Communist one. President Roosevelt and Prime Minister Churchill argued that the Poles should choose their own government, but Stalin pointed out that every time invaders entered Russia from the west, they came through Poland. Eventually, the three leaders compromised by recognizing the Communist government that included members of the prewar Polish government and that promised to hold free elections as soon as possible.

The three leaders then issued the Declaration of Liberated Europe, which echoed the Atlantic Charter, asserting "the right of all people to choose the form of government under which they will live." The statement promised that the people of Europe would be allowed "to create democratic institutions of their own choice" and to create temporary governments that represented "all democratic elements." The Declaration also pledged "the earliest possible establishment through free elections of governments responsive to the will of the people."

Roosevelt, Churchill, and Stalin agreed to divide Germany into four zones, with Great Britain, the United States, the Soviet Union, and France each controlling a zone. The same countries would also divide the German capital city of Berlin into four zones, even though it was set within the Soviet zone. Stalin demanded that Germany pay heavy reparations for the damages it had caused during the war. The Allies finally agreed that Germany could pay war reparations with trade goods and products, half of which would go to the Soviet Union. The Allies would also remove industrial machinery, railroad cars, and other equipment from Germany as reparations. Later arguments about reparations greatly increased the growing tensions between the United States and the Soviet Union.

Rising Tensions

Problems arose just two weeks after Yalta when the Soviets pressured the Romanian king to appoint a Communist government. The United States accused the Soviets of violating the Declaration of Liberated Europe. The Soviets refused to allow more than three non-Communist Poles to serve in the 18-member Polish

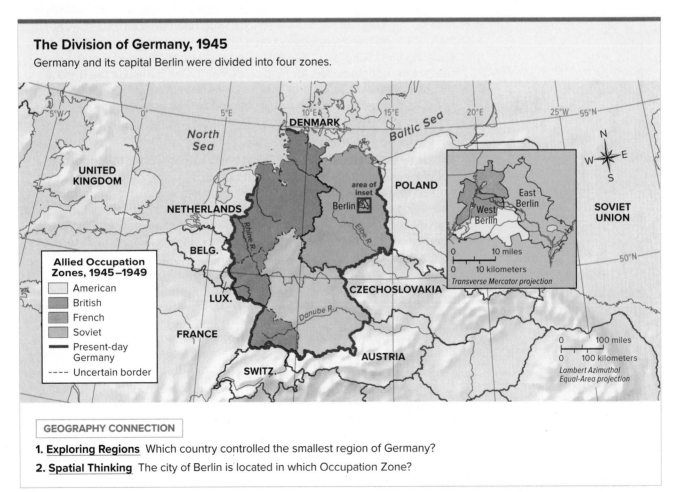

The Division of Germany, 1945
Germany and its capital Berlin were divided into four zones.

Allied Occupation Zones, 1945–1949
- American
- British
- French
- Soviet
- — Present-day Germany
- ---- Uncertain border

A Decade of American Foreign Policy: Basic Documents, 1941-49. 1950. Washington, D.C.: Government Printing Office.

GEOGRAPHY CONNECTION

1. **Exploring Regions** Which country controlled the smallest region of Germany?

2. **Spatial Thinking** The city of Berlin is located in which Occupation Zone?

government and showed no indication of holding free elections as promised. On April 1 Roosevelt informed the Soviets that their actions were unacceptable.

Roosevelt hoped that an Allied victory and the creation of the United Nations would lead to a more peaceful world. Instead, as the war came to an end, the United States and the Soviet Union grew more hostile toward each other, even as they avoided direct military confrontation. Postwar tensions grew into the **Cold War,** an era of confrontation and competition between the nations lasting from about 1946 to 1991.

The Soviets wanted to keep Germany weak and make sure that countries between Germany and the Soviet Union remained under Soviet control to serve as a buffer if Germany started a third war. They were also suspicious of capitalist nations. The Soviets believed that communism was a superior economic system that would one day replace capitalism, and thought capitalist countries would eventually try to destroy it.

While the Soviets focused on security, the American leaders focused on economics. They believed that reduced trade had increased the severity of the Great Depression. They also believed that a lack of trade forced nations into war to get resources. Roosevelt and his advisers regarded economic growth through world trade as the key to peace, and the free enterprise system, with private property rights and limited government intervention in the economy, as the best route to prosperity.

Truman Takes Control at Potsdam

Eleven days after confronting the Soviets about Poland, Roosevelt died and Harry Truman became president. Truman was strongly anti-Communist. In a meeting with the Soviet foreign minister, Truman demanded that Stalin hold free elections in Poland as promised at Yalta. The meeting marked an important shift in Soviet-American relations.

In July 1945 Truman finally met Stalin at Potsdam, near Berlin, to work out a deal on Germany. With the Soviet economy devastated by war, Stalin needed reparations from Germany. But Truman was firmly against heavy reparations, insisting that Germany's industry needed time to recover. Truman suggested the Soviets take reparations from their zone, while the Allies allowed industry to be revived in the other zones, but Stalin opposed this idea since the Soviet zone was mostly agricultural. Truman then offered Stalin a small amount of industrial equipment from the other zones and acceptance of the German-Polish border the Soviets had established. Stalin thought the Americans were limiting reparations to keep the Soviets weak, but he had to accept the terms because the Americans and the British controlled Germany's industrial heartland.

The decisions increased tensions between the United States and the Soviet Union.

Responses to the War

In response to the atrocities of World War II, the UN held a General Assembly in December 1946 that made genocide punishable internationally. The text of the Convention on the Prevention and Punishment of the Crime of Genocide became the first UN human rights treaty. Former First Lady Eleanor Roosevelt, who was well-known in the states and abroad for her activism in U.S. politics, chaired a UN Commission on Human Rights in 1948. As a delegate to the United Nations, she delivered a speech in Paris, France, advocating for a Universal Declaration of Human Rights that same year:

66 I have chosen to discuss this issue in Europe because this has been the scene of the greatest historic battles between freedom and tyranny. I have chosen to discuss it in the early days of the General Assembly because the issue of human liberty is decisive for the settlement of outstanding political differences 99

–Eleanor Roosevelt, from "The Struggle for Human Rights," September 28, 1948

The commission drafted the Universal Declaration of Human Rights, promoting the inherent dignity of every human being, and committing to end discrimination.

World War II also prompted the adoption of four Geneva Conventions in 1949. The first two conventions protected wounded and sick soldiers on land and sea, while the third convention protected prisoners of war. These were revisions of existing conventions. In response to the atrocities of World War II a new fourth convention protected civilians in war.

✓ CHECK FOR UNDERSTANDING

1. **Summarizing** How did the conferences at Bretton Woods, Dumbarton Oaks, and Yalta attempt to shape the postwar world?

2. **Identifying** Why did the Potsdam Conference further increase tensions between the United States and the Soviet Union?

The Global Iron Curtain

GUIDING QUESTION

How did the alliances and pacts during this time indicate increasing Cold War tensions?

Although Truman won the reparations argument, he had less success on other issues at Potsdam. The Soviets refused to pledge stronger commitments to uphold the Declaration of Liberated Europe.

Roosevelt, Eleanor. 1948. "The Struggle for Human Rights," speech delivered September 28, 1948, at the Sorbonne, Paris, in The Department of State Bulletin, Volume 19, Office of Public Communication, Bureau of Public Affairs, 1948. Washington: U.S. Government Printing Office.

Cold War conflict over ideological differences that does not involve warfare or overt military action

The presence of the Soviet army in Eastern Europe ensured that pro-Soviet Communist governments would be established in the nations of Poland, Romania, Bulgaria, Hungary, and Czechoslovakia. The Communist countries of Eastern Europe came to be called **satellite nations** because they were controlled by the Soviets—as satellites are tied by gravity to the planets they orbit. Although not under direct Soviet control, these nations had to remain Communist and friendly to the Soviet Union and follow Soviet-approved policies.

After watching the Communist takeover in Eastern Europe, the former British prime minister Winston Churchill referred to an "iron curtain" falling across Eastern Europe in a March 5, 1946, speech in Fulton, Missouri. The press picked up the term, and for the next 43 years it described the Communist nations of Eastern Europe and the Soviet Union. With the **Iron Curtain** separating Eastern Europe from the West, the World War II era came to an end and the Cold War began.

Containing Communism

Increasingly frustrated by the Soviets' refusal to cooperate, officials at the U.S. State Department asked the American Embassy in Moscow to explain Soviet behavior. On February 22, 1946, diplomat George Kennan responded with what became known as the

Long Telegram—which laid out his views of the Soviets. According to Kennan, the Soviets' view of the world came from a traditional "Russian sense of insecurity" and fear of the West, intensified by the communist ideas of Lenin and Stalin. Because Communists believed they were in a historical struggle against capitalism, Kennan argued, it was impossible to reach any permanent settlement with them.

Kennan proposed what became basic American policy throughout the Cold War: "a long-term, patient but firm and vigilant **containment** of Russian expansive tendencies." In Kennan's opinion, the Soviet system had major economic and political weaknesses. If the United States could keep the Soviets from expanding their power, it would only be a matter of time before their system would fall apart, allowing the United States to defeat communism without going to war. The Long Telegram circulated widely in Truman's administration and became the basis for the U.S. policy of containment—limiting the spread of communism through diplomatic, economic, and military actions.

While Truman's administration discussed Kennan's ideas, a series of crises erupted during the spring and summer of 1946 that seemed to prove Kennan right.

The first crisis began in Iran. During World War II the United States had troops in southern Iran while Soviet

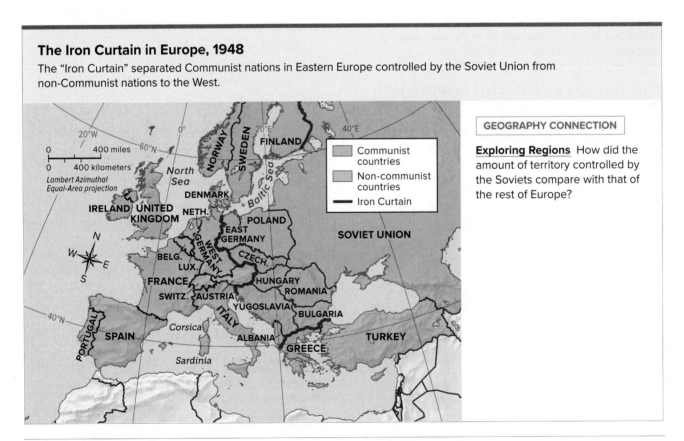

The Iron Curtain in Europe, 1948

The "Iron Curtain" separated Communist nations in Eastern Europe controlled by the Soviet Union from non-Communist nations to the West.

GEOGRAPHY CONNECTION

Exploring Regions How did the amount of territory controlled by the Soviets compare with that of the rest of Europe?

satellite nations nations politically and economically dominated or controlled by another more powerful country

Iron Curtain the political and military barrier that isolated Soviet-controlled countries after World War II

containment the policy or process of preventing the expansion of a hostile power

Kennan, George F. Sources of Soviet Conduct. In Foreign Affairs, Volume 25, Number 4, July 1947. New York: Council on Foreign Relations, 1947.

troops held northern Iran to secure a supply line from the Persian Gulf. After the war, instead of withdrawing as promised, Soviet troops remained in northern Iran, and Stalin began demanding access to Iran's oil supplies. To increase the pressure, Soviet troops helped local Communists in northern Iran establish a separate government. American officials saw these actions as a Soviet push into the Middle East. The secretary of state sent Stalin a strong message demanding that Soviet forces withdraw. At the same time the battleship USS *Missouri* sailed into the eastern Mediterranean. The pressure seemed to work. Soviet forces withdrew, having been promised a joint Soviet-Iranian oil company, although the Iranian parliament later rejected the plan.

The Truman Doctrine

Frustrated in Iran, Stalin turned northwest to Turkey where the straits of the Dardanelles were a vital shipping route from Soviet ports on the Black Sea to the Mediterranean. In August 1946 Stalin demanded joint control of the Dardanelles with Turkey. Presidential adviser Dean Acheson saw this move as part of a Soviet plan to control the Middle East. He advised Truman to make a show of force. The president ordered the new aircraft carrier *Franklin D. Roosevelt* to join the *Missouri* and protect Turkey and the eastern Mediterranean.

Meanwhile, Great Britain tried to help Greece. In August 1946 Greek Communists launched a guerrilla war against the Greek government. British troops helped fight the guerrillas, but in February 1947 Britain informed the United States that it could no longer continue helping Greece due to the weakened British economy. Truman then asked Congress for $400 million to fight Communist aggression in Greece and Turkey. His speech outlined a policy that became known as the Truman Doctrine. The president pledged to fight the spread of communism worldwide:

❝ [I]t must be the policy of the United States to support free peoples who are resisting attempted subjugation by armed minorities or by outside pressures. I believe that we must assist free peoples to work out their own destinies in their own way. ❞

—President Truman, from his address to Congress, March 12, 1947

The Marshall Plan

Postwar Western Europe faced grave problems. The war had ruined economies, left people starving, and caused political chaos in many countries. In June 1947 Secretary of State George C. Marshall proposed the European Recovery Program, commonly called the Marshall Plan, which gave European nations American aid to rebuild. Truman saw both the Marshall Plan and the Truman Doctrine as essential for containment.

Recommendation for Assistance to Greece and Turkey: Address of the President of the United States, Harry Truman, March 12, 1947.

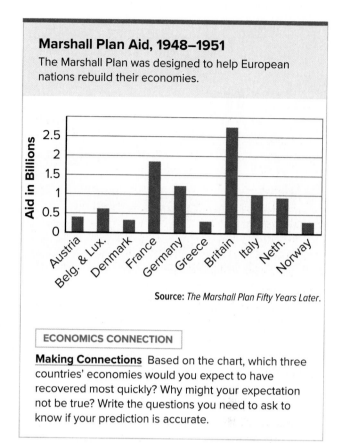

Marshall Plan Aid, 1948–1951

The Marshall Plan was designed to help European nations rebuild their economies.

Source: *The Marshall Plan Fifty Years Later.*

ECONOMICS CONNECTION

Making Connections Based on the chart, which three countries' economies would you expect to have recovered most quickly? Why might your expectation not be true? Write the questions you need to ask to know if your prediction is accurate.

Although the United States offered the Marshall Plan to the Soviet Union and its satellite nations, the Soviets rejected it and developed their own economic program. The result was a further separation of Europe into competing regions. The Marshall Plan pumped billions of dollars in supplies, machinery, and food into Western Europe. With this aid, the region recovered, making it more appealing than the communist region. The actions of the Marshall Plan also opened new markets for trade.

The expansion of trade was also aided by establishment of the General Agreement on Tariffs and Trade (GATT). Meeting in Geneva in 1947, 23 countries signed the trade agreements. GATT reduced tariffs among the signing nations. In his 1949 Inaugural Address Truman proposed the Point Four Program to assist underdeveloped countries outside the war zone. The program aimed to provide these countries with "scientific advances and industrial progress" for improvement and growth. The Department of State administered the program until its merger with other foreign aid programs in 1953.

Truman and his advisers believed Western Europe's prosperity depended on Germany's recovery, but the Soviets still wanted Germany to pay reparations. This dispute brought the nations to the brink of war. By early 1948, American officials had concluded that the Soviets were trying to undermine Germany's economy.

As Berliners watch, an American cargo plane flies into the city bringing much-needed supplies.

Analyzing Visuals Which details in the photograph help you understand why the Marshall Plan was considered necessary to restore the economy of Western Europe?

In response the United States, Great Britain, and France merged their German zones. This merger allowed the Germans to have their own government, the Federal Republic of Germany, known as West Germany. The United States, Britain, and France also agreed to merge their zones in Berlin and make West Berlin part of West Germany. The Soviet zone became the German Democratic Republic, or East Germany. West Germany was mostly independent but not permitted to have a military.

Crises in Berlin

The creation of West Germany convinced the Soviets they would never get the reparations they wanted. In June 1948 Soviet troops blockaded West Berlin, intending to force the United States to abandon West Berlin. Truman sent bombers capable of carrying atomic weapons to bases in Britain. Hoping to avoid war with the Soviets, he ordered the Air Force to fly supplies rather than troops into Berlin. The Berlin Airlift began in June 1948 and continued through the spring of 1949 and carried more than two million tons of supplies to the city. Stalin lifted the blockade on May 12, 1949. The airlift symbolized American determination to contain communism and not give in to Soviet demands.

This was not the only conflict involving Berlin. In June 1961 President John F. Kennedy faced another foreign policy challenge. To stop Germans from leaving East Germany for West Berlin, the Premier of the Soviet Union Nikita Khrushchev demanded that Western powers recognize East Germany and withdraw from Berlin. Kennedy refused, reaffirming the West's

commitment to West Berlin. Khrushchev retaliated by building a wall through Berlin, cutting off the flow between the Soviet sector and the rest of the city. Soviet guards along the wall shot at those attempting to cross from East to West Berlin. The Berlin Wall stood until 1989 as a symbol of Cold War divisions.

The Creation of NATO

The Berlin blockade convinced many Americans that the Soviets were bent on conquest. The public began to support a military alliance with Western Europe. By April 1949, the United States, Canada and much of Western Europe had agreed to form the North Atlantic Treaty Organization (NATO)—a mutual defense alliance. General Dwight D. Eisenhower, who had led the Allied forces in Western Europe during World War II, became the first Supreme Allied Commander Europe of the NATO forces. NATO initially included 12 countries: the United States, Canada, Great Britain, France, Italy, Belgium, Denmark, Portugal, the Netherlands, Norway, Luxembourg, and Iceland. NATO members agreed to come to the aid of any member who was attacked. For the first time, the United States had committed itself to maintaining peace in Europe. Six years later, alarming Soviet leaders, NATO allowed West Germany to rearm and join its organization. The Soviets responded by organizing a military alliance in Eastern Europe known as the Warsaw Pact.

The Soviets formed the Warsaw Pact on May 14, 1955, with eight members: the Soviet Union, Albania, Bulgaria, Czechoslovakia, East Germany, Hungary, Poland, and Romania. Like NATO, Warsaw Pact members pledged to support each other if attacked. While members supposedly had equal decision-making powers, the Soviet Union actually controlled most decisions and used the pact to control unrest among its satellite nations. The development of NATO and the Warsaw Pact made it clear that both sides aimed to extend their spheres of influence.

✓ **CHECK FOR UNDERSTANDING**

1. **Explaining** What was the policy of containment?
2. **Analyzing** How did NATO and the Warsaw Pact signal increasing Cold War tensions?

LESSON ACTIVITIES

1. **Informative/Explanatory Writing** Use primary sources such as news articles, editorials, and radio or newsreel coverage, from the time to write an analysis of the Yalta or Potsdam Conferences. Consider both the purposes of the conferences and the short-term consequences.

2. **Collaborating** With a partner, research and prioritize incidents in the Cold War. After prioritizing, cite your reasoning for which incident was most important and which was least important.

Charles Fenno Jacobs/The LIFE Images Collection/Getty Images

03
Foreign Policy in the 1950s and 1960s

READING STRATEGY

<u>Analyzing Key Ideas and Details</u> As you read, complete a concept web like the one below that lists features of President Eisenhower and President Kennedy's Cold War policies.

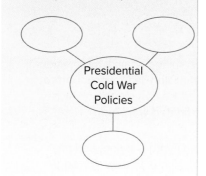

The Korean War

GUIDING QUESTION

Why was the Korean War a major turning point in the Cold War?

The Cold War would eventually spread to Asia. A communist revolution in China and conflicts over reuniting Korea led to American troops being sent back to Asia less than five years after World War II had ended.

The Chinese Revolution

In China Communist forces led by Mao Zedong had been struggling against the Nationalist government led by Chiang Kai-shek since the late 1920s. During World War II, the two sides suspended their conflict to resist Japanese occupation. As World War II ended, civil war broke out again. Although Mao and the Communist forces made gains, neither side could win.

To prevent a communist revolution in Asia, the United States sent the Nationalist government $2 billion in aid beginning in the mid-1940s. The Nationalists, however, squandered this advantage through poor military planning and corruption. By 1949, the Communists had captured the Chinese capital of Beijing, while support for the Nationalists declined. In August 1949, the U.S. State Department discontinued aid to the Chinese Nationalists. The defeated Nationalists then fled to the small island of Formosa (now called Taiwan), and the victorious Communists established the People's Republic of China in October 1949.

China's fall to communism shocked Americans, and to make matters worse, in September 1949, the Soviet Union announced that it had successfully tested its first atomic weapon. Then, early in 1950, the People's Republic of China and the Soviet Union signed a treaty of friendship and alliance. Many Western leaders feared that China and the Soviet Union would support communist revolutions in other nations.

The United States kept formal diplomatic relations with only the Nationalist Chinese in Taiwan and used its veto power in the UN Security Council to keep representatives of the new Communist People's Republic of China out of the UN, allowing the Nationalists to retain their seat.

The Chinese Revolution brought about a significant change in American policy toward Japan. At the end of World War II, General Douglas MacArthur controlled occupied Japan. His mission was to introduce democracy and keep Japan from threatening war again. Once the United States lost China as its chief ally in Asia, it adopted policies to encourage the rapid recovery of Japan's industrial economy. Just as the United States viewed West Germany as the key to defending all of Europe against communism, it saw Japan as the key to defending Asia.

The Korean War

At the end of World War II, both American and Soviet forces had entered Korea to disarm the Japanese troops stationed there. The Allies divided Korea at the 38th parallel of latitude. Soviet troops controlled the north, while American troops controlled the south. As the Cold War began, talks to reunify Korea broke down. Both a Communist government in the north and a U.S.-backed government in the south claimed authority over Korea, and border clashes were common. The Soviets provided military aid to the North Koreans, who quickly

In this November 1950 photograph, soldiers of the US Army's 2nd Infantry Division observe the position of enemy troops during the Korean War.

Analyzing Visuals Based on the photograph, what challenges does the Korean terrain pose for the soldiers fighting there?

built an army. On June 25, 1950 North Korean troops invaded the south, driving back the poorly equipped South Koreans.

President Truman saw the Communist invasion of South Korea as a test of the containment policy and ordered U.S. naval and air power into action. Rather than ask Congress to declare war, he called on the United Nations to act. With the pledge of UN troops, the president ordered General Douglas MacArthur to send U.S. troops from Japan to Korea. The American and South Korean troops were driven back into a small pocket of territory near the port of Pusan. Inside the "Pusan perimeter," troops stubbornly resisted the North Koreans, buying time for MacArthur to organize reinforcements. On September 15, 1950, MacArthur ordered a daring invasion behind enemy lines at the port of Inchon. The Inchon landing took the North Koreans by surprise, and within weeks they were in full retreat. Truman then gave the order to pursue the North Koreans beyond the 38th parallel. MacArthur pushed the North Koreans north to the Yalu River, the border with China.

The Communist People's Republic of China saw the advancing UN troops as a threat and warned them to halt their advance. When warnings were ignored, Chinese forces crossed the Yalu River in November. Hundreds of thousands of Chinese troops flooded across the border, driving the UN forces back across the 38th parallel. MacArthur asked for a blockade of Chinese ports, the use of Chiang Kai-shek's Nationalist forces, and the bombing of Chinese cities with atomic weapons. Truman refused, not wanting to expand the war into China or to use the atomic bomb. MacArthur publicly criticized President Truman and argued that it was a mistake to keep the war limited. He equated a limited war with appeasement and argued that appeasement "begets new and bloodier war."

Determined to maintain control of policy, Truman fired MacArthur for insubordination in April 1951. MacArthur returned home to parades and a hero's welcome. Public opinion shifted against the president. However, Congress and military leaders supported Truman's decision and his Korean strategy, which remained committed to **limited war**. Truman later explained his position:

66 The Kremlin [Soviet Union] is trying, and has been trying for a long time, to drive a wedge between us and the other nations. It wants to see us isolated. It wants to see us distrusted. It wants to see us feared and hated by our allies. Our allies agree with us in the course we are following. They do not believe we should take the initiative to widen the conflict in the Far East. If the United States were to widen the conflict, we might well have to go it alone. 99

–from an address to the Civil Defense Conference, May 7, 1951

By mid-1951, UN forces had pushed the Chinese and North Korean forces back across the 38th parallel. In July 1951 peace negotiations began at Panmunjom. As talks continued, the war became increasingly unpopular in the United States. After Dwight D. Eisenhower was elected to the presidency in 1952, the former general traveled to Korea to talk with commanders and their troops. Eisenhower quietly hinted to the Chinese that the United States might use a nuclear attack in Korea. The threat seemed to work. In July 1953 negotiators signed an armistice. The battle line between the two sides became the border between North Korea and South Korea. A "demilitarized zone" (DMZ) separated them. American troops are still based in Korea, helping to defend South Korea's border. There has never been a peace treaty to end the war. More than 33,600 American soldiers died in action, and over 20,600 died in accidents or from disease.

The Korean War marked a turning point in the Cold War. Until 1950 the United States had preferred to use political pressure and economic aid to contain

limited war a war fought with limited commitment of resources to achieve a limited objective, such as containing communism

PHOTO: National Archives and Records Administration [NWDNS-111-SC-353469]; TEXT: (t) MacArthur, Douglas. Address to Congress. April 19, 1951; (2)Truman, Harry. 1951. Address at a Dinner of the Civil Defense Conference, May 7, 1951. National Archives and Records Administration, Public Papers of the Presidents, Harry S. Truman Library, Independence, Missouri.

communism, and it had focused its efforts on Europe. But after the Korean War began, the United States embarked on a major military buildup and expanded the Cold War into Asia. By 1954, the United States had signed defense agreements with Japan, South Korea, and Taiwan, and in 1954 it formed the Southeast Asia Treaty Organization (SEATO). Aid also began flowing to French forces fighting Communists in Vietnam.

✓ CHECK FOR UNDERSTANDING

Making Connections Why was the Korean War a major turning point in the Cold War?

Mutually Assured Destruction

GUIDING QUESTION

How did Eisenhower use the possible consequences of a nuclear war to keep the Soviets in check?

Eisenhower's presidential victory was driven by the belief that Truman's foreign policy was failing. The Soviet Union had tested an atomic bomb and consolidated its hold on Eastern Europe. China had fallen to communism and Americans were fighting in Korea.

Massive Retaliation

The Cold War shaped Dwight Eisenhower's thinking from the moment he took office. He felt that the key to victory was not just military might but a strong economy. The United States had to show the world that the free enterprise system could produce a better society than communism. At the same time, economic prosperity would prevent Communists from gaining support in the United States and protect society from subversion.

The Korean War convinced Eisenhower that the United States could not contain communism by fighting a series of small wars. Instead, wars had to be prevented. He believed the best way to do that was threatening to use nuclear weapons. This policy came to be called **massive retaliation.** Eisenhower wanted to make sure that the United States could wage nuclear war even if the Soviets destroyed U.S. bases in Europe or Asia. The United States began to build the nuclear triad: a three-part system made up of long-range bombers, land-based missiles, and missile-carrying submarines. This approach enabled Eisenhower to cut military spending by reducing the size of the army. He then increased the U.S. nuclear arsenal from about 1,000 bombs in 1953 to about 18,000 bombs in 1961. This led to a new arms race as the United States and Soviet Union competed to expand the size and power of their nuclear arsenals.

massive retaliation a policy that involves threatening the use of nuclear weapons to avoid a potential war

brinkmanship the willingness to go to the brink of war to force an opponent to back down

Brinkmanship

President Eisenhower's willingness to threaten nuclear war to maintain peace worried many people. Critics called this **brinkmanship**—the willingness to go to the brink of war to force the other side to back down—and critics argued that this strategy was too dangerous.

Although Communists had taken power in mainland China, Chinese Nationalists still controlled Taiwan and several small islands along China's coast. In the fall of 1954 China threatened to seize two of the islands. When China began shelling the islands, Eisenhower, who saw Taiwan as part of the "anti-Communist barrier" in Asia, asked Congress to authorize the use of force to defend Taiwan. He then warned that an attack on Taiwan would be resisted by U.S. naval forces and hinted at the use of nuclear weapons. China backed down.

The following year a crisis erupted in the Middle East. Eisenhower wanted to prevent Arab nations from aligning with the Soviet Union. To build support among Arabs, Secretary of State John Foster Dulles offered to help Egypt finance the construction of a dam on the Nile River, but the deal ran into trouble in Congress because Egypt had bought weapons from Communist Czechoslovakia. A week after Dulles withdrew the offer, Egyptian troops seized control of the Suez Canal from the Anglo-French company that had controlled it. The Egyptians intended to use the canal's profits to pay for the dam.

In October 1956 British and French troops invaded Egypt. The situation grew worse when the Soviet Union threatened rocket attacks on Britain and France and offered to send troops to help Egypt. Eisenhower immediately put U.S. nuclear forces on alert, noting, "if those fellows start something, we may have to hit 'em—and, if necessary, with *everything* in the bucket." Pressured by the United States, the British and French called off the invasion. The Soviet Union had won a major diplomatic victory by supporting Egypt. Soon other Arab nations began accepting Soviet aid.

Covert Operations

President Eisenhower relied on brinkmanship on several occasions, but he knew it could not work in all situations. It could not prevent Communists from staging revolutions within countries. To resist this, Eisenhower used **covert,** or hidden, operations conducted by the Central Intelligence Agency (CIA). Several CIA operations took place in **developing nations**—nations with primarily agricultural economies. Many of these formerly colonial nations blamed European imperialism and American capitalism for their

covert not openly shown or engaged in; secret

developing nation a nation whose economy is mainly agricultural and is creating a basis for industrial development

Eisenhower, Dwight. In United States Submarine Veterans. United States Submarine Veterans, Inc: The First 40 Years. Nashville: Turner Publishing, 2006.

problems and looked to the Soviet Union as a model of industrialization. They often threatened to nationalize, or put under government control, foreign businesses operating in their countries.

If the threat of communism seemed strong, the CIA ran covert operations to overthrow anti-American leaders and replace them with pro-American leaders. For example, Iranian prime minister Mohammed Mosaddegh had nationalized the Anglo-Iranian Oil Company by 1953 and seemed ready to make an oil deal with the Soviet Union. The pro-American shah of Iran tried to force Mosaddegh out of office, but the shah failed and fled into exile. The CIA sent agents to organize street riots and arrange a coup that ousted Mosaddegh and returned the shah to power.

In 1950 Jacobo Arbenz Guzmán was elected president of Guatemala with Communist support. After Arbenz Guzmán assumed office in 1951, his land-reform program took over large estates and plantations, including those of the American-owned United Fruit Company. In May 1954 Communist Czechoslovakia delivered arms to Guatemala. The CIA responded by arming the Guatemalan opposition and training them at secret camps in Nicaragua and Honduras. Shortly after the CIA-trained forces invaded Guatemala, Arbenz Guzmán left office.

Stalin died in 1953, creating a power struggle in the Soviet Union. By 1956, Nikita Khrushchev emerged as the Soviet leader. He delivered a secret speech to Soviet officials that attacked Stalin's policies and insisted that there were many ways to build a communist society. The CIA obtained a copy of the speech and distributed it throughout Eastern Europe and the world. Many Eastern Europeans who had been frustrated with Communist rule led riots in Eastern Europe in June 1956. By late October, a full-scale uprising was happening in Hungary but Soviet tanks rolled into the capital of Hungary to end the rebellion.

The Eisenhower Doctrine

The United States was not the only nation using covert means to support its foreign policy. President Gamal Abdel Nasser of Egypt had emerged from the Suez crisis as a hero to the Arab people, and by 1957 he had begun working with Jordan and Syria to spread pan-Arabism—the idea that all Arab people should be united into one nation. Eisenhower and Dulles worried about Nasser's links to the Soviets and feared he was laying the groundwork to take control of the Middle East. In late 1957 Eisenhower asked Congress to authorize the use of military force whenever the president thought it necessary to assist Middle East nations resisting Communist aggression. The policy, which came to be called the Eisenhower Doctrine, essentially extended the Truman Doctrine and the policy of containment to the Middle East. In July 1958 Eisenhower's concerns appeared to be confirmed when left-wing rebels, believed to be backed by Nasser and the Soviets, seized power in Iraq. The president of Lebanon sought help, and Eisenhower ordered 5,000 marines to Beirut, the Lebanese capital. Once the situation stabilized, the U.S. forces withdrew.

After a Hungarian uprising, Khrushchev sought to reassert Soviet power and the superiority of communism. In 1958 Khrushchev demanded the withdrawal of Allied troops from West Berlin. Dulles rejected Khrushchev's demands. If the Soviets threatened Berlin, Dulles announced, NATO would respond, "if need be by military force." Brinkmanship worked again, and Khrushchev backed down. Eisenhower invited Khrushchev to visit the United States in late 1959, and the visit's success led the two leaders to agree to hold a summit in Paris. Shortly before the 1960 summit convened, the Soviet Union shot down an American U-2 spy plane. At first Eisenhower claimed that the aircraft was a weather plane that had strayed off course. Then Khrushchev produced the pilot, Francis Gary Powers. Eisenhower refused to apologize, saying the flights had protected American security. In response, Khrushchev canceled the summit.

As Eisenhower prepared to leave office in January 1961, he delivered a farewell address in which he pointed out that a new relationship had developed between the military establishment and the defense industry. He warned Americans to be on guard against the influence of a "**military-industrial complex**" in a democracy. Although he had avoided war and

U.S. marines rest after landing in Beirut, Lebanon. Marines arrived in the country in 1958 to help protect the nation against a possible Communist takeover.

Bettmann/Getty Images

---

military-industrial complex an informal relationship that some people believe exists between the military and the defense industry to promote greater military spending and influence government policy

contained communism, he was frustrated, stating, "I confess that I lay down my official responsibilities in this field with a definite sense of disappointment. As one who has witnessed the horror and the lingering sadness of war . . . I wish I could say tonight that a lasting peace is in sight."

✓ **CHECK FOR UNDERSTANDING**

1. **Summarizing** In what ways did Eisenhower use threats to prevent war?
2. **Describing** Why did President Eisenhower want to use covert operations to combat the spread of communism?

Kennedy's Cold War Strategies

GUIDING QUESTION

How did the Cuban missile crisis illustrate the fragility of power balances during the Cold War?

When John F. Kennedy entered the White House in 1961, the Cold War with the Soviet Union dominated all other concerns. He used a range of programs to try to stop the spread of communism.

A More Flexible Response

Kennedy felt that Eisenhower had relied too heavily on nuclear weapons. To allow for a "**flexible response,**" the president pushed for a buildup of troops and conventional weapons. He also expanded the army's Special Operations Forces (known as the Green Berets), an elite unit used in limited conflicts. Despite his commitment to flexible response, Kennedy had warned against a "missile gap" during his campaign. Although no gap existed, the United States began a massive build-up of intercontinental ballistic missiles (ICBMs) armed with nuclear warheads. At the time Kennedy took office, less than 20 ICBMS were deployed by the United States, and only 50 new Minuteman missiles were planned. The Soviet Union had less than 10 ICBMs ready to fire at the United States. Nonetheless, Kennedy decided to build 1,000 Minutemen ICBMS.

Kennedy sought another approach in Latin America, where the wealthy controlled governments and many people lived in extreme poverty. These conditions spurred the growth of left-wing movements aimed at overthrowing governments. During the Cold War, U.S. involvement in Latin America often consisted of helping existing governments stay in power and preventing Communist movements from flourishing. Latin Americans resented this, just as they resented the presence of U.S. corporations, which were seen as imperialistic. To improve relations, Kennedy proposed the Alliance for Progress, a series of cooperative aid projects with Latin American governments designed to create a "free and prosperous Latin America" that would be less likely to support Communist-inspired revolutions. In some countries, the Alliance did promote real reform by funding schools, housing, health care, and fairer land distribution. In others, local rulers used the money to keep themselves in power.

Kennedy launched another program aimed at fighting poverty. The Peace Corps, established in 1961, sends Americans to provide humanitarian services in developing nations. Volunteers spend two years in countries that request assistance. Among other projects, volunteers build roads, teach English, lay out sewage systems, and train medical technicians.

The Cold War in Space

The Cold War also fueled a space race between the United States and the Soviet Union. On October 4, 1957, the Soviets launched *Sputnik I*, the first artificial satellite to orbit Earth. Less than four months later, the United States launched its first satellite, *Explorer I*. Determined not to be beaten by the Soviets, Eisenhower proposed the National Aeronautics and Space Administration, or NASA, in late 1958 to begin developing a civilian space program for the United States. *Sputnik I* marked a turning point in history and the beginning of a new era—the use of satellites in space to assist in communications and to spy on other nations. These developments and technology expanded science education in the United States.

Crises in Cuba

President Kennedy's efforts to combat Communist influence in Cuba, located only 90 miles (145 km) from American shores, led to some of the most intense crises of the Cold War. Fidel Castro had overthrown the corrupt Cuban dictator Fulgencio Batista in 1959. Castro quickly established ties with the Soviet Union, instituted drastic land reforms, and seized foreign-owned businesses, many of which were American. While still in office, President Eisenhower, fearing that the Soviets might use Cuba as a base to spread revolution from, had authorized the CIA to secretly train and arm a group of Cuban exiles, known as *La Brigada*, to invade the island and set off a popular uprising against Castro. When Kennedy became president, he agreed to the operation with some changes. On April 17, 1961, about 1,400 armed Cuban exiles landed at the Bay of Pigs on the south coast of Cuba, but the invasion was a disaster. Contrary to U.S. expectations, Cubans did not revolt. Within two days, Castro's forces had killed or captured almost all the members of *La Brigada*.

Then, during the summer of 1962, American intelligence learned that Soviet technicians and

---

flexible response a military approach that relies more heavily on conventional means than it does on nuclear weapons

President Dwight D. Eisenhower, "Farewell Radio and Television Address to the American People, January 17, 1961".

The Cuban Missile Crisis, October 1962

The Cuban missile crisis brought the United States and the Soviet Union to the brink of war.

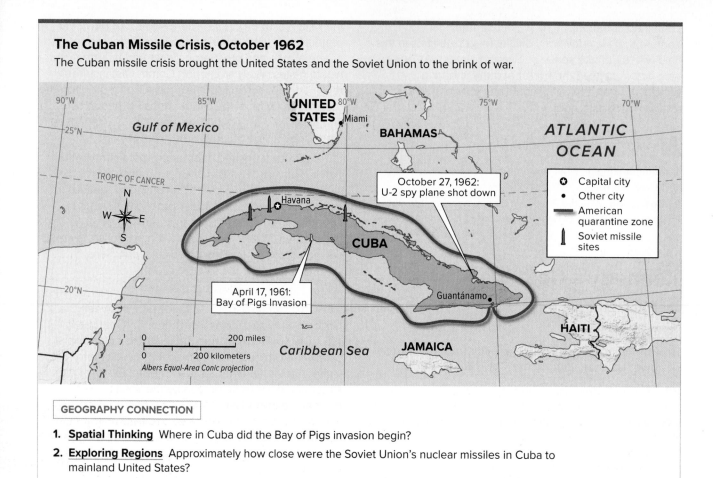

GEOGRAPHY CONNECTION

1. **Spatial Thinking** Where in Cuba did the Bay of Pigs invasion begin?
2. **Exploring Regions** Approximately how close were the Soviet Union's nuclear missiles in Cuba to mainland United States?

equipment had arrived in Cuba and that military construction was in progress. In October Kennedy announced that the Soviet Union had placed long-range nuclear missiles in Cuba and ordered a naval quarantine to stop the delivery of more missiles. He demanded the existing missile sites be dismantled and warned that if attacked, the United States would respond fully against the Soviet Union. Still, work on the missile sites continued. Nuclear warfare seemed more possible than ever. After a flurry of secret negotiations, the Soviet Union offered to remove the missiles if the United States promised not to invade Cuba. The U.S. also agreed to remove its missiles from Turkey near the Soviet border. On October 28, the leaders reached an agreement, and the world could breathe again.

Negotiating Nuclear Weapons

The Cuban missile crisis forced the United States and the Soviet Union to consider the consequences of nuclear war. Understanding that they had come very close to nuclear war, Kennedy and Soviet leader Khrushchev agreed to resume high-level negotiations aimed at banning nuclear testing. Earlier negotiations had stalled because of Soviet concerns over inspections to verify underground testing.

On July 25, 1963, after only 12 days of negotiations, the United States and the Soviet Union

agreed to ban nuclear testing under water, in the atmosphere, and in space, and on August 5, 1963, the two nations, along with the United Kingdom, signed the Limited Nuclear Test Ban Treaty, which the Senate ratified on September 23 and Kennedy signed on October 7. The treaty promoted the idea of eventual nuclear disarmament.

✓ **CHECK FOR UNDERSTANDING**

1. **Explaining** Why did the United States organize *La Brigada*? What were the goals of this group?
2. **Making Connections** How did the Cuban missile crisis exemplify the dangerous conditions that existed between countries during the Cold War?

LESSON ACTIVITIES

1. **Informative/Explanatory Writing** Write a short essay in which you explain Eisenhower's foreign policy goals and practices. Be sure to include details about how these policies influenced historical events.

2. **Collaborating** With a partner, research events in Cuba that contributed to Cold War tensions during the Kennedy administration. Then use your research to construct a time line of the major events.

04

Analyzing Sources: The Cold War in Space

 COMPELLING QUESTION

How was the space race an extension of the Cold War?

Plan Your Inquiry

In this lesson, you will investigate how the space race evolved out of competition between the United States and the Soviet Union during the Cold War.

DEVELOP QUESTIONS

Developing Questions About the Space Race Think about the Cold War and how competition between the United States and the Soviet Union influenced politics, technology, and public attitudes in the United States. Develop a list of Supporting Questions that would help you answer the Compelling Question in this lesson.

APPLY HISTORICAL TOOLS

Analyzing Primary and Secondary Sources You will work with a variety of primary and secondary sources in this lesson. These sources focus on the causes and effects of the space race. As you read, use a graphic organizer like the one below to record information about the sources that will help you examine them and check for historical understanding. Note ways in which each source helps you answer your Supporting Questions.

Supporting Questions	Primary Source	How this source helps me answer the Supporting Question
Question 1:		
Question 2:		
Question 3:		

After you analyze the sources, you will:

- use the evidence from the sources.
- communicate your conclusions.
- take informed action.

Background Information

In October and November 1957 the Soviet Union launched two satellites into orbit. These successes stunned the American public and galvanized U.S. investment in space flight and exploration to catch up with Soviet advancements. The United States made its first launch attempt in December, but the satellite exploded. A second U.S. satellite successfully made orbit on January 31, 1958. President Dwight D. Eisenhower convened an advisory committee and subsequently sent a bill to Congress to establish the National Aeronautics and Space Administration (NASA). Congress passed and Eisenhower signed the Space Act, establishing the goals of the new agency.

Then, not long after President John F. Kennedy took office in 1961, the Soviets sent the first human into space. Kennedy and his advisors took this success as a challenge. The space race was on.

By the 1960s, the United States had established itself as a global superpower with unmatched military, technological, and economic might. U.S. officials had no intention of yielding that spot; they perceived Soviet successes in space as a threat to U.S. influence. At the height of the Cold War, American leaders resolved to stay ahead of the Soviets in every way possible. This included developing and demonstrating superior scientific capability. Americans also worried that space exploration could easily be used to support a military attack during the Cold War.

» NASA assembled its first group of astronauts, shown here, in the late 1950s.

NASA

A

Reaction to the Soviet Satellite

By the 1950s, the Cold War had begun in earnest. The Federal Civil Defense Administration (FCDA) had launched a campaign of "duck and cover" drills, flyers, and animated films, teaching the American public to fear nuclear war. Some people bought or built shelters to protect themselves from air raids and nuclear fallout. So, when the Soviets launched *Sputnik I*, the government interpreted the accomplishment as a new kind of threat, and the news media popularized it.

PRIMARY SOURCE : MEMORANDUM

" One week after the USSR announced that it had launched an earth satellite, a number of broad major effects on world public opinion appeared clear:

1. Soviet claims of scientific and technological superiority over the West and especially the U.S. have won greatly widened acceptance.

2. Public opinion in friendly countries shows decided concern over the possibility that the balance of military power has shifted or may soon shift in favor of the USSR. . . .

3. American **prestige** is viewed as having sustained a severe blow, and the American reaction, so sharply marked by concern, discomfiture and intense interest, has itself increased the impact of the satellite. "

—October 16, 1957, "Reaction to the Soviet Satellite: A Preliminary Evaluation," from the Dwight D. Eisenhower Presidential Library

prestige high standing; position of respect and authority

EXAMINE THE SOURCE

1. **Describing** According to the memo, how did the launch of *Sputnik I* affect American public opinion?

2. **Inferring** What concern on the part of U.S. officials does this memo suggest?

B

Impact of *Sputnik*

The Office of the Secretary of Defense circulated this memo, which describes the results of a public opinion poll conducted by the media. The survey polled 1,000 adults and 117 newspaper editors regarding the launch of *Sputnik I*. The poll and memo addressed concerns that the American public might have lost confidence in U.S. leadership and technological and military capabilities.

PRIMARY SOURCE : MEMORANDUM

" The news of Sputnik's launch was known to 95% of the public, but 40% noted the news and dismissed it without serious thought as to what it might mean to them and their country.

After Sputnik, 80% thought we were 'at least even' with the Soviets or would 'catch up before long'; editors had a more alarmed point of view.

. . . The launching of Sputnik had little if any effect on the prestige of the Eisenhower administration. The September poll indicated that this popularity had already fallen due to rising prices and high taxes, and fell no further as a result of Sputnik.

The blame for our missile lag was attributed to the following, in order:

1. Our schools have placed too little stress on science. (69%)

2. We Americans have been too smug and **complacent** about our national strength. (67%)

3. There's been too much rivalry between the Army, Navy and Air Force. (63%)

4. We have failed to give scientists the salaries and recognition their importance deserves. (61%). "

—O.M. Gale, Special Assistant, April 14, 1958

complacent lacking interest or concern

EXAMINE THE SOURCE

1. **Contrasting** According to the memo, how did the general public and newspaper editors feel differently about the launching of *Sputnik I*?

2. **Analyzing** What concerns among the American people does the poll reveal?

[1]United States Information Agency, "Reaction to the Soviet Satellite: A Preliminary Evaluation," White House Office of Special Assistant for National Security Affairs files, Eisenhower Library, Abilene, Kansas, October 16, 1957; [2]Gale, O. M. "Memorandum for Mr. McElroy," Office of the Secretary of Defense, Washington, D.C. April 14, 1958.

C

Kennedy's Address to Congress

President John F. Kennedy took office in January 1961. By this time, the Soviets had succeeded in launching and returning living plants and animals to and from space and had put a probe on the Moon. The United States, too, had launched satellites and Ham, a chimpanzee, into space. However, Kennedy perceived the nation as lagging behind the Soviet Union. Then, less than three months later, Soviet cosmonaut Yuri Gagarin became the first human to orbit Earth. Kennedy spoke about the accelerating space race in this speech to Congress.

PRIMARY SOURCE : SPEECH

66 . . . [I]f we are to win the battle that is now going on around the world between freedom and **tyranny**, the dramatic achievements in space which occurred in recent weeks should have made clear to us all, as did the Sputnik in 1957, the impact of this adventure on the minds of men everywhere, who are attempting to make a determination of which road they should take. Since early in my term, our efforts in space have been under review. . . .

Recognizing the head start obtained by the Soviets with their large rocket engines, which gives them many months of lead time . . . we nevertheless are required to make new efforts on our own. For while we cannot guarantee that we shall one day be first, we can guarantee that any failure to make this effort will make us last. . . . But this is not merely a race. Space is open to us now; and our eagerness to share its meaning is not governed by the efforts of others. We go into space because whatever mankind must undertake, free men must fully share. 99

—President John F. Kennedy, Address to Joint Session of Congress, May 25, 1961

tyranny a state of oppression; domination

EXAMINE THE SOURCE

1. **Explaining** Why does Kennedy say that the United States must explore space?

2. **Interpreting** What does Kennedy mean when he says that people everywhere must decide "which road they should take"?

D

Address at Rice University

In 1962 Kennedy made this speech to 35,000 people in the stadium at Rice University. By then, American astronaut Alan Shepard had gone into space and Kennedy had issued a challenge to the nation to be the first to send people to the Moon. At the same time, other aspects of the Cold War had heated up, increasing political pressure. Construction on the Berlin Wall had started, the first U.S. troops had gone to Vietnam, and the Soviet Union had begun sending arms to Cuba.

PRIMARY SOURCE : SPEECH

66 We choose to go to the moon. We choose to go to the moon in this decade and do the other things, not because they are easy, but because they are hard, because that goal will serve to organize and measure the best of our energies and skills, because that challenge is one that we are willing to accept, one we are unwilling to postpone, and one which we intend to win, and the others, too. . . .

The growth of our science and education will be enriched by new knowledge of our universe and environment, . . . by new tools and computers for industry, medicine, the home as well as the school. Technical institutions, such as Rice, will reap the harvest of these gains. . . .

Many years ago the great British explorer George Mallory, who was to die on Mount Everest, was asked why did he want to climb it. He said, 'Because it is there.'

Well, space is there, and we're going to climb it, and the moon and the planets are there, and new hopes for knowledge and peace are there. And, therefore, as we set sail we ask God's blessing on the most hazardous and dangerous and greatest adventure on which man has ever embarked. 99

—President John F. Kennedy, Address at Rice University, September 12, 1962

EXAMINE THE SOURCE

1. **Summarizing** Why does Kennedy say that the United States must send people to the Moon?

2. **Interpreting** Why does Kennedy quote George Mallory, and how does this reflect the nature of the Cold War competition?

(1)President John F. Kennedy, Special Message to the Congress on Urgent National Needs, May 25, 1961, Delivered in person before a joint session of Congress, John F. Kennedy Presidential Library & Museum; (2)Kennedy, John F. 1962. Address at Rice University, September 12, 1962. NASA.gov.

Kennedy's Views on Space

James E. Webb served as the administrator of NASA from 1961 to 1968. This transcript records a discussion between Webb, President John F. Kennedy, and Kennedy's science adviser, Jerome Wiesner, during a meeting at the White House. Members of the administration gathered to discuss the time line and the budget for the Apollo lunar program, NASA's effort to put American astronauts on the Moon. Some officials, including Webb, worried that the time line was too ambitious and favored spreading funding across multiple NASA programs. Kennedy insisted that they focus funding on Apollo and push for a 1967 moon landing. Other officials questioned whether they should be investing in the program at all.

PRIMARY SOURCE : TRANSCRIPT

> **JFK:** Jim, I think [the manned moon mission] is a top priority. I think we ought to have that very clear. . . . [S]ome of these other programs can slip six months or nine months and nothing particularly is going to happen that's going to make it. But this is important for political reasons, international political reasons, and this is, whether we like it or not, a race. If we get second to the moon, it's nice, but it's like being second anytime. So that if you're second by six months because you didn't give it the kind of priority, then, of course, that would be very serious. So I think we have to take the view that this is the top priority.
>
> **WEBB:** Number one, there are real unknowns as to whether man can live under the weightless condition and you'd ever make the lunar landing. This is one kind of political vulnerability I'd like to avoid such a flat commitment to.
>
> **JFK:** I agree that we're interested in this, but we can't wait six months on all of it.
>
> **WEBB:** But you have to use that information to do these things.
>
> **WIESNER:** We don't know a damn thing about the surface of the moon, and we're making the wildest guesses about how we're going to land on the moon, and we could get a terrible disaster from putting something down on the surface of the moon that's very different than we think it is, and the scientific programs that find us that information have to have the highest priority. . . .
>
> **JFK:** [W]e ought to get, you know, really clear that the policy ought to be that this is the top priority program of the agency and one of the two—except for defense—the top priority of the United States government. I think that that's the position we ought to take. Now, this may not change anything about that schedule, but at least we ought to be clear, otherwise we shouldn't be spending this kind of money, because I'm not that interested in space. I think it's good. I think we ought to know about it. We're ready to spend reasonable amounts of money, but we're talking about fantastic expenditures which wreck our budget and all these other domestic programs, and the only justification for it, in my opinion is to do it because we hope to beat them and demonstrate that starting behind as we did, by a couple of years, by God, we passed them.

—White House Cabinet Room, November 21, 1962

EXAMINE THE SOURCE

1. **Analyzing Points of View** On what points do Kennedy, Webb, and Wiesner seem to agree and disagree?
2. **Drawing Conclusions** Why does Kennedy want to make the Apollo lunar program one of the nation's two top priorities? What relationship might he see between the two?

Kennedy, John F. Recording of Meeting with James Webb, November 21, 1962. In McNaught, Tom. Listening In: JFK's Secret Tapes. Kennedy Library Forum, October 4, 2012.

PHOTO: NASA; TEXT: National Aeronautics and Space Administration (NASA). July 20, 1969. One Giant Leap for Mankind. [blog post]. July 20, 2019.

Reacting to the Moon Landing

On July 20, 1969, Neil Armstrong and Buzz Aldrin descended in the landing module and became the first humans to walk on the Moon's surface. The moonwalk aired live across the world. As many as 600 million people watched.

EXAMINE THE SOURCE

1. **Describing** What does the image show?
2. **Drawing Conclusions** What does the public interest and reaction to the Moon landing suggest about the significance of the space race? What effect did the space race have on the American public?

PRIMARY SOURCE : PHOTOGRAPH

» Flight controllers celebrate the successful Moon landing.

NASA Apollo 11 Mission Summary

To mark the 50th anniversary of the Apollo 11 mission, NASA published this summary.

SECONDARY SOURCE : PRESS RELEASE

66 At 10:56 p.m. EDT Armstrong is ready to plant the first human foot on another world. With more than half a billion people watching on television, he climbs down the ladder and proclaims: 'That's one small step for a man, one giant leap for mankind.'

Aldrin joins him shortly, and offers a simple but powerful description of the lunar surface: 'magnificent **desolation**.' They explore the surface for two and a half hours, collecting samples and taking photographs.

They leave behind an American flag, a patch honoring the fallen Apollo 1 crew, and a plaque on one of *Eagle's* legs. It reads, 'Here men from the planet Earth first set foot upon the moon. July 1969 A.D. We came in peace for all mankind.'

Armstrong and Aldrin blast off and dock with Collins in *Columbia*. Collins later says that 'for the first time,' he 'really felt that we were going to carry this thing off.'

In an interview years later, Armstrong praises the . . . people behind the project. 'Every guy that's setting up the tests, cranking the torque wrench, and so on, is saying, man or woman, "If anything goes wrong here, it's not going to be my fault."' 99

–from "July 20, 1969: One Giant Leap for Mankind"

---

desolation a state of barrenness or absolute solitude

EXAMINE THE SOURCE

1. **Analyzing** What did the astronauts leave behind on the Moon? Describe the significance of one of the items.
2. **Synthesizing** Why do Armstrong's words and the words on the plaque matter?

Space Program Spinoffs

In his speech at Rice University, President John F. Kennedy references the knowledge and tools to be gained from space exploration. Today, many schools and other institutions invest in STEM (science, technology, engineering and math) programming. That push began with the space race. Since its inception, NASA and its partners have been the driving forces behind scientific education and innovation.

SECONDARY SOURCE : WEB PAGE

66 . . . **Improved Radial Tires** Goodyear Tire and Rubber Company developed a fibrous material . . . for NASA to use in parachute shrouds to soft-land the Viking [landers] on the Martian surface. The fiber's chain-like molecular structure gave it incredible strength in proportion to its weight. Recognizing the increased strength and **durability** of the material, Goodyear expanded the technology and went on to produce a new radial tire with a tread life expected to be 10,000 miles greater than conventional radials. . . .

Firefighter Gear Firefighting equipment widely used throughout the United States is based on a NASA development . . . A project that linked NASA and the National Bureau of Standards resulted in a lightweight breathing system including face mask, frame, harness, and air bottle, using an aluminum composite material developed by NASA for use on rocket casings. . . .

Enriched Baby Food Commercially available infant formulas now contain a nutritional enrichment ingredient that traces its existence to NASA-sponsored research that explored the potential of algae as a recycling agent for long-duration space travel. [They] can be found in over 90 percent of the infant formulas sold in the United States. . . 99

—from *NASA Technologies Benefit Our Lives*

durability ability to last for a long time

EXAMINE THE SOURCE

1. **Describing** What does this passage describe?
2. **Making Connections** How did the space race influence other aspects of life?

Your Inquiry Analysis

EVALUATE SOURCES AND USE EVIDENCE

Reflect back to the Compelling Question and the Supporting Questions you developed at the beginning of this lesson.

1. **Gathering Sources** Refer back to the Graphic Organizer you created as you read through the sources. Which sources most help you answer the Supporting Questions you wrote? Circle or highlight those sources in your graphic organizer. Which sources do you think offer unique insights into the space race? Put a star next to these sources.

2. **Evaluating Sources** Looking at the sources that help you answer the Supporting Questions, evaluate the credibility of each source. Make notes about the potential bias of each author or creator and consider how that bias might affect the content. Write down which sources you consider most objective and/or informative, and why.

3. **Comparing and Contrasting** Compare and contrast two sources that you identified. What central idea does each source convey? How does each influence your understanding of the space race?

COMMUNICATE CONCLUSIONS

Collaborating Answer each of your Supporting Questions. Then, use what you have learned to write a short paragraph in response to the Compelling Question. Share your paragraph with a partner, and together, draw and write a storyboard for a short, animated video explaining causes, events, and effects of the space race. Present your storyboard to the class.

TAKE INFORMED ACTION

Supporting a Position on Space Exploration Consider the motivations that led the United States to prioritize space exploration during the Cold War. Then consider the political and technological consequences of U.S. participation. Should the United States prioritize space exploration today? Use library or online sources to find out what motivations currently inspire people to support or oppose making space exploration a priority for time, effort, and budgeting. Then write an essay arguing for or against expanding today's space program.

NASA Technology Transfer Program. "NASA Technologies Benefit Our Lives."

(1)Nixon, Richard. "U.S. Foreign Policy for the 1970s: A New Strategy for Peace." Report to Congress. February 18, 1970; (2)Nixon, Richard. 1980. The Real War. London: Sidgwick & Jackson.

READING STRATEGY

Analyzing Key Ideas and Details As you read, use a graphic organizer like the one below to take notes on foreign policies during this lesson.

Nixon's foreign policies	
Carter's foreign policies	
Reagan's foreign policies	

Nixon's Foreign Policy

GUIDING QUESTION

How did Nixon's foreign policy help ease the tensions of the Cold War?

When President Richard Nixon was elected in 1968, the United States was deeply involved in the Vietnam War. The Cold War and all of its related conflicts was more than twenty years old. Nixon expressed his hope that a qualified cabinet of advisers could run the country, allowing him to focus on foreign affairs.

The Détente Policy

In a move that would greatly influence his foreign policy, Nixon chose Henry Kissinger, a Harvard professor in the Department of Government, as his national security adviser. Kissinger had served under Presidents Kennedy and Johnson as a foreign policy consultant. Although Secretary of State William Rogers outranked him, Kissinger soon took the lead in shaping Nixon's foreign policy. Nixon and Kissinger spent much of their foreign policy focus on ending the Vietnam War in the 1970s. They worked toward a gradual withdrawal of U.S. troops from the area while training the South Vietnamese to defend themselves.

This policy of Vietnamization, as it was called, was extended globally in what came to be known as the Nixon Doctrine. In July 1969, only six months after taking office, Nixon announced that the United States would honor all the alliances it had signed. The nation would continue to provide military aid and training to allies. Yet, it would no longer "conceive all the plans, design all the programs, execute all the decisions and undertake all the defense of the free nations of the world." America's allies would have to take responsibility for maintaining peace and stability in their own areas of the world.

The Soviet Union was not pleased when Nixon became president. He was known to be strongly anti-Communist. Yet Nixon and Kissinger believed the United States needed to adjust to the growing role of China, Japan, and Western Europe. This emerging "multipolar" world demanded a different approach to American foreign policy.

Both Nixon and Kissinger wanted to continue to contain communism, but they believed that negotiation with Communists was a better way for the United States to achieve its international goals. They developed a new approach called **détente,** or relaxation of tensions, between the United States and its two major Communist rivals, the Soviet Union and China. Nixon said that the nation had to build a better relationship with its main rivals for world peace:

66 We must understand that détente is not a love fest. It is an understanding between nations that have opposite purposes, but which share common interests, including the avoidance of a nuclear war. Such an understanding can work—that is, restrain aggression and deter war—only as long as the potential aggressor is made to recognize that neither aggression nor war will be profitable. 99

—quoted in *The Real War*, 1980

The successes of détente were diminished due to upheavals in smaller nations. In Chile, President Salvador Allende was killed during a coup

détente a policy that attempts to relax or ease tensions between nations

BIOGRAPHY

HENRY KISSINGER (1923–)

Henry Kissinger was born in Fürth, Germany, in 1923 and lived there until 1938, when he and his family fled to escape Nazi anti-Jewish restrictions. After arriving in New York City, Kissinger worked to help support his family, while attending high school and learning English. In 1940 he graduated and then enrolled at the City College of New York to study accounting.

CITIZENSHIP AND WWII Kissinger was naturalized as an American citizen in 1943 and was drafted into the U.S. Army during World War II. He first served as a rifleman and later as a military intelligence officer in both France and his former homeland of Germany. During his service in the war, Kissinger decided to study political history with the hope of teaching at a university.

POLITICAL CAREER Following the war, Kissinger attended Harvard University, earning degrees in 1950 and 1954 before joining the faculty. He first served as a consultant on national security issues for the administrations of Presidents Kennedy and Johnson. President Richard Nixon then appointed Kissinger as the national security adviser in 1969 and secretary of state in 1973. While serving in the Nixon administration, Kissinger helped establish the policy of détente with the Soviet Union and China. He negotiated the cease-fire with North Vietnam and was awarded the Nobel Peace Prize in 1973. In 1977 Kissinger received the Presidential Medal of Freedom.

Explaining How did Henry Kissinger influence foreign policy in the 1970s?

---

supported by the CIA. Similarly, the Angolan Civil War, which began in 1975, featured secret aid from the United States. These were examples of proxy war—Cold War conflicts that did not directly involve the United States and the Soviet Union but advanced political goals of these two superpowers. Much of the Cold War was fought through other nations that were establishing their own national regimes.

The Cold War in China

Détente began with an effort to improve American-Chinese relations. Since 1949, when Communists took power in China, the United States had refused to recognize the Communists as the legitimate rulers. Instead, the U.S. government recognized the exiled regime on the island of Taiwan as the Chinese government. Nixon now set out to reverse this policy, and China concluded it was time to engage with capitalist Western nations.

After secret negotiations between Kissinger and Chinese leaders, Nixon announced that he would visit China in February 1972. During the historic trip, the leaders of both nations agreed to establish "more normal" relations between their countries. Nixon's visit to China was part of his foreign policy known as

triangulation. Nixon exploited the contentious relationship between China and the Soviet Union to strengthen American interests and relationships with each of the Communist superpowers.

Tensions Ease With Soviets

Nixon's strategy toward the Soviet Union worked. Shortly after the public learned of American negotiations with China, the Soviets proposed an American-Soviet **summit,** or high-level diplomatic meeting, to be held in May 1972. On May 22, President Nixon flew to Moscow for a weeklong summit. Nixon was the first American president since World War II to visit the Soviet Union. During the historic summit, the two superpowers signed the first Strategic Arms Limitation Treaty, or SALT I, a plan the two nations had been working on for years. The treaty temporarily froze the number of strategic nuclear weapons. Nixon and Soviet premier Leonid Brezhnev also agreed to increase trade and the exchange of scientific information. Détente had helped ease tensions between the two countries. One Soviet official admitted that by the end of Nixon's presidency, "the United States and the Soviet Union had their best relationship of the whole Cold War period."

---

triangulation a policy in which two countries' hostilities toward one another are exploited to the benefit of a third country

summit a meeting between government leaders

PHOTO: Mondadori Portfolio/Getty Images; TEXT: Yuri Barsukov quoted in Nixon: An Oral History of his Presidency, by Gerald S. Strober and Deborah H. Strober. Copyright © 1996 by Harper Perennial.

Another highlight of détente was a series of meetings that created the Helsinki Accords. In 1975 the United States, Canada, and most of the countries of Eastern and Western Europe committed to three sets of recommendations focusing on security, economic, and human rights issues. In one section, the signing states agreed to "respect human rights and fundamental freedoms, including the freedom of thought, conscience, religion or belief, for all without distinction as to race, sex, language or religion."

✓ **CHECK FOR UNDERSTANDING**

1. **Making Connections** What was the policy of Vietnamization, and how did it relate to the Nixon Doctrine?

2. **Contrasting** What difficulties did Nixon face in conducting diplomacy with China? In what ways was he successful in negotiating with the Soviet Union?

The Cold War in the Middle East

GUIDING QUESTION

How did U.S. aid to foreign countries and groups resisting Communism affect Cold War tensions?

A man of strong religious and humanitarian beliefs, President Jimmy Carter, who entered the White House in 1977, argued that the United States must try to be "right and honest and truthful and decent" in dealing with other nations. Yet it was on the international front that Carter suffered a devastating defeat. In his Inaugural Address, Carter gave his foreign policy a focus by saying:

66 Our commitment to human rights must be absolute . . . the powerful must not persecute the weak, and human dignity must be enhanced. . . . We pledge perseverance and wisdom in our efforts to limit the world's armaments to those necessary for each nation's own domestic safety 99

–from his Inaugural Address, January 20, 1977

Carter and his foreign policy team—including Andrew Young, the first African American ambassador to the United Nations—strove to achieve these goals.

Triumph and Failure in the Middle East

In 1978 Carter helped broker peace between Israel and Egypt through the Camp David Accords. The treaty, signed in 1979, established peace between Israel and Egypt—nations that had been bitter enemies for decades. This was the first time Israel traded land and removed settlements for peace. Although many Arab nations did not support the treaty, it helped to begin the slow Middle East peace process.

Just months after the treaty was signed, Carter faced a crisis in Iran. The United States had long supported Iran's monarch, the shah, because Iran was a major oil supplier and a buffer against Soviet expansion. The shah had grown increasingly unpopular in Iran due to his repressive rule and Westernizing reforms. The Islamic clergy opposed the shah's reforms. In January 1979 protesters forced him to flee. An Islamic republic was then declared. Led by religious leader Ayatollah Khomeini, this new regime distrusted the United States. In November 1979 revolutionaries stormed the American embassy in Tehran, taking 52 Americans hostage. The Carter administration unsuccessfully tried to negotiate the hostages' release. In April 1980 Carter approved a rescue attempt that failed when several helicopters malfunctioned and one crashed in the desert. Eight servicemen died. Hamilton Jordan, President Carter's chief of staff, described the gloomy atmosphere in the White House the day after the crash:

PHOTO: David Hume Kennerly/Archive Photos/Getty Images; TEXT: (1)Commission for Security and Cooperation in Europe. The Final Act of The Conference on Security and Cooperation in Europe, August 1, 1975, 14 I.L.M. 1292. (2)Carter, Jimmy. 1977. Inaugural Address. Washington, D.C., January 20. Jimmy Carter Library, National Archives and Records Administration.

One of Carter's major policy successes was the meetings he coordinated between Egyptian President Anwar Sadat and Israeli Prime Minister Menachem Begin. This 1978 photograph shows the three men together soon after the meetings concluded.

Identifying What Middle East diplomatic events were not as successful for the Carter administration?

> He looked exhausted and careworn, sitting behind the big wooden desk in the Oval Office as he spoke. 'It was my decision to attempt the rescue operation. It was my decision to cancel it when problems developed. . . . The responsibility is fully my own.' The mood at the senior staff meeting was somber and awkward. I sensed that we were all uncomfortable, like when a loved one dies and friends don't know quite what to say. "

The crisis continued. Every night, news programs reminded viewers how many days the hostages had been held. Carter's inability to free them cost him support in the 1980 election. On January 20, 1981, the day Carter left office, Iran released the Americans, ending their 444 days in captivity.

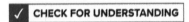 CHECK FOR UNDERSTANDING

Summarizing How would you describe the philosophy of Carter's foreign policy?

The Cold War in the 1980s

GUIDING QUESTION

Why did Reagan expand military spending?

When Ronald Reagan assumed the presidency in January 1981, he adopted a new foreign policy that rejected both containment and détente. He called the Soviet Union "an evil empire" and believed the United States should defeat evil, not contain or negotiate with it. Reagan believed the only way to deal with the Soviet Union was "peace through strength," a phrase he used during his campaign. Reagan launched a $1.5 trillion military buildup, which he believed was needed to keep up with Soviet military development. However, despite Reagan's hardline rhetoric, he was willing to negotiate with Soviet leaders.

The United States tried to stop nations from supporting terrorism. During his first term, Reagan authorized the use of U.S. Marines as part of a multinational force trying to deescalate violence during the civil war in Lebanon. In October 1983 Lebanese terrorists attacked the Marines' barracks in Beirut, Lebanon, using a truck filled with explosives. The attack killed 241 Marines. In February 1984 Reagan pulled the Marines out of the country and withdrew U.S. military support for the peacekeeping force. Then on April 14, 1986, the United States launched an air attack on Libya after it backed a terrorist bombing in Berlin.

Reagan's military buildup created new jobs in defense industries. Supply-side economists thought that despite the spending, lower taxes and cuts in government programs would generate enough revenue to balance the budget. Though tax revenues rose, they were not enough to balance the budget without

requiring drastic cuts in social programs. The annual deficit went from $80 billion to over $200 billion.

The Reagan Doctrine

Reagan believed the United States should support guerrilla groups that were fighting to overthrow Communist or pro-Soviet governments, a policy that became known as the Reagan Doctrine. The most visible example of the policy was in Afghanistan, when Soviet troops invaded in 1979. Reagan sent hundreds of millions of dollars in covert military aid to Afghan guerrillas fighting the Soviets. The war strained the Soviet economy, and in 1988 the Soviets withdrew.

In Grenada, radical Marxists overthrew the left-wing government in 1983. Reagan sent in troops, quickly defeating the Grenadian and Cuban soldiers. A new anti-Communist government was installed.

Reagan was also concerned about Soviet influence in Nicaragua when Sandinista rebels overthrew a pro-American dictator in 1979, set up a socialist government, and accepted Cuban and Soviet aid. The Reagan administration secretly armed anti-Sandinista guerrillas known as the contras. When Congress discovered this, it banned further aid to the contras.

The Iran-Contra Scandal

Despite the congressional ban, Reagan's administration illegally continued to support the Nicaraguan rebels. The administration also secretly sold weapons to Iran, considered an enemy and sponsor of terrorism, in exchange for the release of American hostages in the Middle East. Profits from the weapons sales were then sent to the contras. News of these operations broke in November 1986. U.S. Marine colonel Oliver North and senior National Security Council members and CIA officials admitted to covering up their actions. President Reagan had approved the sale of arms to Iran, but the congressional investigation concluded he had no direct knowledge about the diverted money.

 CHECK FOR UNDERSTANDING

Describing Describe the diplomatic approach known as the Reagan Doctrine.

LESSON ACTIVITIES

1. **Informative/Explanatory Writing** Take on the role of a journalist assigned to cover the 1972 American-Soviet summit in Moscow. Write a newspaper article about the events and outcomes of this meeting.

2. **Presenting** Work in groups of four to research, write, and present brief monologues describing various events and milestones of the Reagan administration. Each should be written and presented from the perspective of someone who was personally affected.

Jordan, Hamilton. 1982. Crisis: The Last Year of the Carter Presidency. New York: G. P. Putnam's Sons.

06

Ending the Cold War

Reagan, Ronald. Remarks at Brandenberg Gate, Berlin, Germany [President's Speaking Copy], 06/12/1987 [National Archives Identifier: 198491];
White House Office of Records Management Subject File folder SP1107 439177 (1), Collection RR-WHORM: White House Office of Records
Management File Systems (White House Central Files), 01/20/1981 - 01/20/1989; Ronald Reagan Library (NLRR); National Archives and Records Administration.

Analyzing Key Ideas and Details As you read, complete a graphic organizer similar to this one by listing key events that led to the end of the Cold War and their effects.

Event	Effects

The Weakening Soviet Union

GUIDING QUESTION

What events do you think played the most critical role toward the end of the Cold War?

As Reagan's second presidential term rolled on, he continued to build up the military, but he also pushed Soviet leaders to address economic and social reforms. Decisions made by new Soviet leadership would lead to significant changes in the lives of Soviet citizens and for people around the world.

Nuclear Disarmament

As part of the military buildup, Reagan decided to place missiles in Western Europe to counter Soviet missiles. When protests erupted worldwide, he offered to cancel the new missiles if the Soviets removed their missiles from Eastern Europe. He also proposed Strategic Arms Reduction Talks (START) to cut the number of missiles on both sides in half. The Soviets refused. Reagan disagreed with the military strategy known as nuclear deterrence, sometimes called "**mutual assured destruction.**" Reagan and his advisers argued that if nuclear war did begin, there would be no way to defend the United States. In March 1983 he proposed the Strategic Defense Initiative (SDI), nicknamed "Star Wars," to develop weapons that could intercept incoming missiles.

In 1985 Mikhail Gorbachev became the leader of the Soviet Union and agreed to resume arms-control talks. Gorbachev believed that the Soviet Union could not afford another arms race with the United States. Reagan and Gorbachev met in a series of summits. At the first summit Gorbachev promised to cut back nuclear forces if Reagan gave up SDI, but Reagan refused. Reagan then challenged Gorbachev to make reforms. In West Berlin, Reagan stood at the Brandenburg Gate of the Berlin Wall—the symbol of divided Europe—and declared: "General Secretary Gorbachev, if you seek peace, if you seek prosperity for the Soviet Union and Eastern Europe . . . tear down this wall!"

Antinuclear activists in the United States and Europe also played a significant role in defusing tensions during the Cold War. Fear of a nuclear war motivated many Americans to demand that their government pursue diplomatic efforts rather than strictly relying on nuclear deterrent policies. Protests by the antinuclear movement in the United States and Europe, such as the large public gathering in 1979 of more than 100,000 activists in Bonn, West Germany, applied pressure on Western and Soviet leaders to seek nuclear disarmament agreements and to limit or completely shut down nuclear power plants in Europe.

In December 1987 Reagan and Gorbachev signed the Intermediate Range Nuclear Forces (INF) Treaty. Gorbachev then pushed ahead with economic and political reforms, which eventually led to the collapse of the Soviet Union. As Reagan's second term was ending, some people were getting very rich, the military was growing, and the Soviet threat seemed to be less of a danger than it had for several years.

mutual assured destruction the strategy assuming that as long as two countries can destroy each other with nuclear weapons, they will be afraid to use them

Gorbachev's Reforms

By the late 1980s, the Soviet economy was suffering from years of inefficient central planning and huge expenditures on the arms race. To save the economy, Gorbachev instituted **perestroika,** or "restructuring," which allowed some private enterprise and profit making. As part of economic reform, Gorbachev cut military spending. Beginning in 1988, and without reciprocal cuts from the United States, Gorbachev began decreasing the size of the military. By 1990, more than half a million soldiers had been cut from the military.

Gorbachev's perestroika policy also tried to decentralize control of the Soviet economy to help the Soviets catch up to the powerful Western and Asian economies. New laws permitted state enterprises some measure of autonomy. Plant and factory managers could determine production levels and decide how to allocate surplus materials. Other perestroika reforms allowed Soviet citizens to engage in some private ownership of businesses in the services, manufacturing, and foreign-trade industries. Soviet manufacturers and local government agencies were given permission to engage in foreign trade and would not have to deal with the inefficient Soviet central government.

Through perestroika, Gorbachev also restructured the Soviet political system. Democratic elections were held for the first time since 1917, and congresses were established in each of the Soviet republics, allowing for more local control.

Gorbachev also established **glasnost**, or "openness," to allow more freedom of religion, speech, and the dissemination of information. Glasnost was established in part to help "sell" the economic and political reforms of perestroika to the public. Initially aimed at bringing Soviet citizens into the political process to a degree, the new freedoms of

BIOGRAPHY

MIKHAIL GORBACHEV (1931–)

Mikhail Gorbachev was born in Stavropol territory in southern Russia. The son of peasants, he drove tractors as a teenager to help support his family. He then studied law at Moscow State University, graduating in 1955.

RISE TO LEADERSHIP As a talented party administrator, Gorbachev quickly rose through the ranks. He became first secretary of the regional party committee as a member of the Young Communist League in 1970, and 10 years later became a member of the Politburo, the supreme law-making body in the Soviet Union. His status grew, and in 1985, upon the death of Soviet leader Konstantin Chernenko, the Politburo chose Gorbachev as general secretary of the Communist Party.

REBUILDING THE SOVIET UNION Domestically, Gorbachev implemented significant reforms to democratize the Soviet political and economic systems through his perestroika and glasnost policies. In foreign affairs, he forged closer relationships with countries in the West and in Asia, including signing significant nuclear arms reduction treaties. Gorbachev's reforms helped lead to the rise of noncommunist countries in Eastern Europe and the formation of new countries from former Soviet republics. Elected as the first president of the Soviet Union in 1990, Gorbachev could not maintain stability or power. On December 25, 1991, he resigned, and the Soviet Union dissolved on December 31. For his efforts in helping to end the Cold War, Gorbachev received the Nobel Prize for Peace in 1990.

> **Explaining** What role did Gorbachev play in the breakup of the Soviet Union?

Francois Lochon/The LIFE Images Collection/Getty Images

perestroika a policy of economic and government restructuring instituted by Mikhail Gorbachev in the Soviet Union in the 1980s

glasnost a Soviet policy permitting open discussion of political and social issues and freer dissemination of news and information

expression also led to another reaction. Disgruntled citizens and the news media criticized the inefficient Soviet regime and the problems it created for society. Citizens' newfound abilities to protest the government, along with failing perestroika reforms, prompted some groups to seek autonomy or independence throughout the Soviet bloc.

✓ CHECK FOR UNDERSTANDING

Identifying Cause and Effect What were the effects of Gorbachev's attempts to revive the Soviet Union's economy through perestroika and glasnost?

After the Soviet Union

GUIDING QUESTION

How did the region of Eastern Europe respond to the collapse of the Soviet Union?

The countries of Eastern Europe had been controlled by the Soviet Union for more than 40 years. Mikhail Gorbachev's restructuring of the Soviet economy and political system in the late 1980s loosened the Soviet grip on the Iron Curtain countries.

The Reunification of Germany

Under the umbrella of glasnost, pro-democracy independence movements spread throughout Eastern Europe. In 1989 revolutions replaced Communist rulers with democratic governments in Bulgaria, Czechoslovakia, Hungary, Poland, and Romania. At midnight on November 9, 1989, guards at the Berlin Wall opened the gates. Soon, bulldozers began leveling the symbol of Communist repression. East Germany and West Germany soon reunited.

Germany officially reunified on October 3, 1990, and in December, the first all German free elections since the 1930s were held. The West German Chancellor Helmut Kohl assumed the head of the unified government, Bundestag, and Berlin was again the capital.

Economic disparities between the former countries hampered a smooth reunification. The former East German economy had collapsed and unemployment skyrocketed. Monetary concerns troubled reunification for many years.

Social issues also festered during the reunification process. The release of secret informant files collected over 40 years by East Germany's powerful security and police agency, the Stasi, revealed that East Germans had been spied on by family, neighbors, friends, and even prominent citizens. The revelations of betrayals by family members, neighbors, and friends traumatized people, damaged relationships, and undermined communities.

The End of the Soviet Union

As Eastern Europe abandoned communism, Gorbachev faced mounting criticism at home. In August 1991, a group of Communist Party officials and army officers tried to stage a coup. They arrested Gorbachev and sent troops into Moscow. However, Boris Yeltsin, the president of Russia (then a country within the Soviet Union) defied the coup leaders. President George H.W. Bush telephoned Yeltsin to express U.S. support. The coup soon collapsed, and Gorbachev regained control.

The end of the Soviet Union had begun. All 15 Soviet republics declared their independence from the Soviet Union. In late December 1991, Gorbachev announced the end of the Soviet Union. Most of the former Soviet republics joined in a federation called the Commonwealth of Independent States (CIS). Although member states remained independent, they eventually formed a common economic zone in 1993.

To help the new CIS states and to protect its interests and security, the Bush administration worked to avert a nuclear crisis and to prevent dangerous groups from acquiring weapons. It also focused on limiting the possibility of ethnic violence and engaged in diplomatic efforts to establish stable new governments. The United States quickly recognized the independence of the new republics of the former Soviet Union and worked to forge diplomatic relations with them.

Support from the United States was not enough, however. Conflicts and power struggles within the republics flared up soon after the Soviet breakup. Civil wars broke out in several republics, killing thousands and displacing even more. In addition, fighting erupted over control of the new governments in Azerbaijan, Georgia, Moldova, and Tajikistan.

As president of the Soviet Republic of Russia, Boris Yeltsin gained fame and western support for his support of a market-based economy within the Soviet Union. After the USSR collapsed, Yeltsin became the first duly elected president of an independent Russia.

Nikolai Ignatiev/Alamy Stock Photo

Carving Up the Soviet Union, 1991

The breakup of the Soviet Union led to the establishment of several new independent countries across eastern Europe and central Asia.

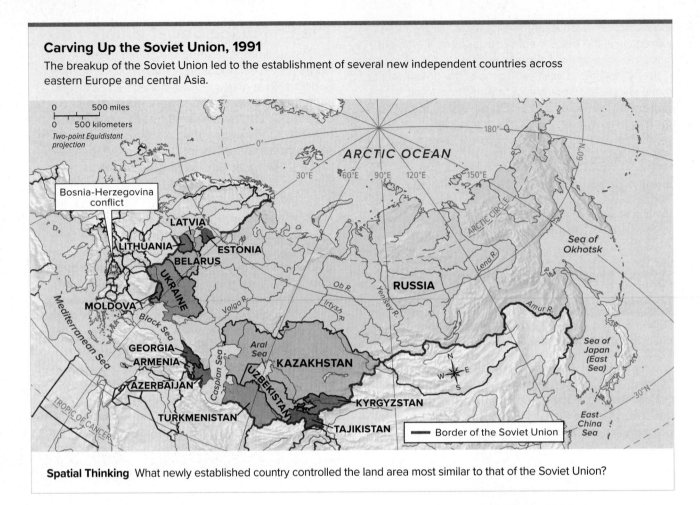

Spatial Thinking What newly established country controlled the land area most similar to that of the Soviet Union?

Bosnia and Kosovo

The United States also was concerned about mounting tensions in southeastern Europe. During the Cold War, Yugoslavia had been a nation of many ethnic groups under a strong Communist government. In 1991 Yugoslavia began to split apart. In the new republic of Bosnia and Herzegovina, a civil war erupted among Orthodox Christian Serbs, Catholic Croatians, and Bosnian Muslims. The Serbs began the brutal expulsion of non-Serbs from a geographic area by what is called **ethnic cleansing.** In some cases, Serbian troops slaughtered Bosnian Muslims instead of moving them.

The United States convinced its NATO allies to take military action. NATO warplanes attacked the Serbs in Bosnia, forcing them to negotiate. President Bill Clinton's administration arranged peace talks in Dayton, Ohio, where the participants signed a peace plan known as the Dayton Accords. In 1996 about 60,000 NATO troops entered Bosnia to enforce the plan.

Another war erupted in 1998, this time in the Serbian province of Kosovo. Kosovo has two major ethnic groups—Serbs and Albanians. Many Albanians wanted Kosovo to separate from Serbia. To keep Kosovo in Serbia, Serbian leader Slobodan Milošević, a staunch nationalist, purged thousands of Albanians

and murdered political opponents. Worried about Serbian violence against Albanian civilians, Clinton asked European leaders to intervene. In March 1999 NATO began bombing Serbia, and Serbia pulled its troops out of Kosovo.

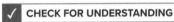

Making Connections Why was the Berlin Wall opened after nearly 30 years?

LESSON ACTIVITIES

1. **Narrative Writing** Suppose that you were a citizen of East Berlin who was present on the night of November 9, 1989, when the Berlin Wall was opened. Write a detailed account in which you describe what happened, how you felt, and how you thought your life would change.

2. **Using Multimedia** In small groups, use the Internet to research one of the new countries that emerged following the breakup of the Soviet Union. Locate information, images, and videos that show life in the country before and several years after the breakup of the Soviet Union. Create a short digital report that presents your findings. After presenting your reports, lead a class discussion in which you discuss the positive and negative impacts.

---

ethnic cleansing the expulsion, imprisonment, or killing of ethnic minorities by a dominant majority group

07

Turning Point: The Soviet Union Collapses

? COMPELLING QUESTION

Why did the Cold War end?

Plan Your Inquiry

In this lesson, you will investigate events leading to the collapse of the Soviet Union and the end of the Cold War.

DEVELOP QUESTIONS

Developing Questions About the Collapse of the Soviet Union Think about the events and conditions that led to the decline in Soviet power and the events that signaled the end of the Cold War. Read the Compelling Question for this lesson. Develop a list of Supporting Questions that would help you answer the Compelling Question in this lesson. Write these in a graphic organizer.

APPLY HISTORICAL TOOLS

Analyzing Primary Sources You will work with a variety of primary sources in this lesson. These sources focus on the collapse of the Soviet Union and the end of the Cold War. As you read, use a graphic organizer like the one below to record information about the sources that will help you examine them and check for historical understanding. Note ways in which each source helps you answer your Supporting Questions. Not all sources will help you answer each of your Supporting Questions.

Supporting Questions	Primary Source	What this source tells me about the end of the Cold War	Questions the source leaves unanswered
	A		
	B		
	C		
	D		
	E		

After you analyze the sources, you will:
- use the evidence from the sources.
- communicate your conclusions.
- take informed action.

Background Information

The Berlin Wall stood as a marker of the divisions between east and west for much of the Cold War, from 1961 to 1989. In October 1989 pro-democracy forces swept the Communist government from power in East Germany. It was part of a wider wave of changes that signaled the decline of Soviet influence. Where once the Soviet Union had dominated the regimes of satellite nations in Eastern Europe, it was now losing its grip. Communist-controlled governments in Hungary, Poland, Romania, and Czechoslovakia each lost power. Why?

For years, change had been brewing in the Soviet Union. In 1985 Mikhail Gorbachev had advanced to General Secretary of the Politburo, the main governing body of the Communist Party. Looking to revive the struggling Soviet economy, Gorbachev undertook daring reforms. Among them were glasnost, or a new "openness" to more freedom of expression and communication, and perestroika, or economic reforms that began to roll back central planning of the economy and introduce multiple candidates and the secret ballot in some elections.

The following sources provide insight into the shifting political climate within the Soviet Union as well as changes to the balance of power in the Cold War.

» In November 1989, Germans tore down the Berlin Wall, uniting the city for the first time in more than four decades.

INTERFOTO/Alamy Stock Photo

A

Mikhail Gorbachev Describes the Need for Change

Until 1989, East Germany was a satellite state under the influence of the Soviet Union. That year, Mikhail Gorbachev met with members of the East German government. He believed that reforms, such as perestroika (restructuring), were needed for Communist countries to survive.

PRIMARY SOURCE : SPEECH

" [O]ur perestroika is also a response to the challenge of the time. In the end we, Communists, think about what we leave behind, what we prepare for the generations to come. . . .

[T]o make a decision to undertake political reforms is also not an easy thing to do. In the future you will have to make courageous decisions. I am speaking about it from our own experience. Remember, Lenin used to say that in turbulent revolutionary years people get more experience in weeks and months than sometimes in decades of normality.

Our perestroika led us to the conclusion that the revolutionary course would not receive the support of the working class if [its] living standards were not improving. But it turned out that the problem of sausage and bread is not the only one. The people demand a new social atmosphere, more oxygen in the society, especially because we are talking about the socialist regime. . . . Figuratively speaking, people want not only bread but the entertainment also. If you take it in a general sense, we are talking about the necessity to build not only the material but also the socio-spiritual atmosphere for the development of the society. I think it is a lesson for us. . . . Life itself will punish us if we are late. "

—Mikhail Gorbachev, Address to the Politburo of the Central Committee of the Socialist United Party of Germany, October 7, 1989

EXAMINE THE SOURCE

1. **Describing** What does Gorbachev say that the working class and other people need and want?

2. **Analyzing Points of View** What overarching idea does Gorbachev try to convey?

B

"Mr. Gorbachev, Tear Down This Wall"

President Ronald Reagan took office in 1980. At first, he sought to ramp up U.S. defense spending and take a harsher stance toward the Soviet Union, even calling it "the evil empire." By 1987, Gorbachev had come to power and begun implementing reforms. Reagan and Gorbachev met to discuss arms reductions in 1986 and signed a treaty to eliminate some of their nation's missiles in 1987. Reagan's administration saw the changes happening in the Soviet Union. So, in 1987, when Reagan visited West Berlin, he delivered these words in front of the Brandenburg Gate, not far from the Berlin Wall, to a crowd of perhaps 20,000 people.

PRIMARY SOURCE : SPEECH

" There is one sign the Soviets can make that would be unmistakable, that would advance dramatically the cause of freedom and peace.

General Secretary Gorbachev, if you seek peace—if you seek prosperity for the Soviet Union and Eastern Europe—if you seek **liberalization**: come here, to this gate.

Mr. Gorbachev, open this gate.

Mr. Gorbachev, tear down this wall.

I understand the fear of war and the pain of division that afflict this continent—and I pledge to you my country's efforts to help overcome these burdens. To be sure, we in the West must resist Soviet expansion. So we must maintain defenses of unassailable strength. Yet we seek peace. So we must strive to reduce arms on both sides. "

—Ronald Reagan, Brandenburg Gate, West Berlin, Germany, June 12, 1987

liberalization the removal or reduction of restrictions placed upon (a particular sphere of) economic activity

EXAMINE THE SOURCE

1. **Explaining** What does Reagan ask Gorbachev to do? In what ways does he suggest doing so is in the Soviet Union's best interest?

2. **Analyzing Points of View** What immediate and broader audience does Reagan address? How do you think this shapes his statement?

(1)Gorbachev, Mikhail. Document 6. Record of Conversation between Mikhail Gorbachev and Members of the Central Committee of the Socialist United Party of Germany, 7 October 1989. In Savranskaya, Svetlana, Blanton, Thomas, Zubok, Vladislav, eds. Masterpieces of History: The Peaceful End of the Cold War in Europe, 1989 Budapest: Central European University Press, 2010; (2)Reagan, Ronald. Remarks at Brandenburg Gate, Berlin, Germany [President's Speaking Copy], 06/12/1987 (National Archives Identifier: 198491); White House Office of Records Management Subject File folder SP107 439177 (1), Collection RR-WHORM: White House Office of Records Management File Systems (White House Central Files), 01/20/1989; Ronald Reagan Library (NLRR); National Archives and Records Administration.

"Developments in the USSR"

Brent Scowcroft, a former general in the U.S. Air Force, served as National Security Advisor to President George H.W. Bush. He wrote this memo to the president following the attempted coup against Mikhail Gorbachev by Communist hard-liners in August 1991.

(1)Scowcroft, Brent. Memorandum for the President: Developments in the USSR. September 5, 1991; (2)Memorandum of Telephone Conversation: Telcon with President Yeltsin of the Republic of Russia. December 8, 1991.

PRIMARY SOURCE : MEMORANDUM

❝ Today's decision by the Congress of People's Deputies to step aside in favor of an **interim** bicameral legislature giving a dominant role to representatives of the republics concludes the first phase of the revolution triggered by last month's failed coup. The major decisions now seem to be made, and the next few months will be devoted to finalizing them in a new union treaty and constitution which formally create a voluntary union of probably ten republics. . . .

In this new world it will be much more important than in the past for us to be aware of political, economic, and social conditions in the republics. In the past a republican leader's position on key issues was determined by Central Committee staff in Moscow. Now it will be determined in the ballot boxes, and in some cases on the streets, of his republic. . . .

This is where active engagement by individual countries and international institutions . . . can make a difference. This revolution is very much a victory for those who seek to integrate into the global system, and a defeat for those who feared western influence. The fluidity of the situation, and the search for a model, gives us now more influence than we have ever had in the Soviet Union. The issue for us is if, and how, we choose to use that influence. ❞

—Brent Scowcroft, Memorandum for the President, September 5, 1991

interim temporary; for a limited time

EXAMINE THE SOURCE

1. **Summarizing** What events does Scowcroft report?
2. **Analyzing Perspectives** What opportunity does Scowcroft see in these events?

Yeltsin's Call to Bush

Yeltsin started out as a supporter of Gorbachev, but he did not think change was happening fast enough. As Russian President, Yeltsin opposed Gorbachev's plan to maintain the Soviet Union. Following the failed coup, Yeltsin moved quickly to take control of the Russian government. On December 8, he signed a declaration with two other leaders announcing the dissolution of the Soviet Union. Then, he called President Bush to share the news.

PRIMARY SOURCE : TRANSCRIPT

❝ . . . We got together today, Mr. President, the leaders of the three states—Byelorussia, Ukraine, and Russia. We gathered and after many lengthy discussions that lasted about two days agreed that the system in place and the Union Treaty everyone is pushing us to sign does not satisfy us. And that is why we got together and literally a few minutes ago signed a joint agreement. . . . [T]he community of independent states of Byelorussia, Ukraine, and Russia, have signed an accord. This accord, consisting of 16 articles, is basically a creation of commonwealth. . . .

The members of this commonwealth have a goal for strengthening international peace and security. They also guarantee all international obligations under agreements and treaties signed by the former Union, including foreign debt. We are also for the unitary control of nuclear weapons and nonproliferation. . . .

Mr. President, I must tell you confidentially, President Gorbachev does not know these results. He knew that we were to meet. . . . We . . . feel there is only one possible way out of this critical situation. We don't want to do anything secretly—we will give a statement immediately to the press. We are hoping for your understanding. ❞

—Boris Yeltsin, in a conversation with President George H.W. Bush, December 8, 1991

EXAMINE THE SOURCE

1. **Summarizing** What does Yeltsin tell Bush that he has done?
2. **Evaluating** What is significant about the final paragraph?

Memorandum of Last Phone Call

At the end of 1991, Gorbachev's efforts at restructuring had outpaced him. While Gorbachev pushed for reforms within the Soviet system, other leaders like Yeltsin worked to break up the Soviet Union and form new governments. The attempted coup and Gorbachev's compromises had weakened his authority. Gorbachev chose not to oppose the republics as they withdrew from the Soviet Union. On December 25, he stepped down as president of the Soviet Union, which ceased to exist. He called Bush to share his decision.

PRIMARY SOURCE : TRANSCRIPT

66 . . . [I]n about two hours I will speak on Moscow TV and will make a short statement about my decision. I have sent a letter to you, George. I hope you will receive it shortly. I said in the letter a most important thing. And I would like to reaffirm to you that I greatly value what we did working together with you, first as Vice President and then as President of the United States. I hope that all leaders of the Commonwealth and, above all, Russia understand what kind of assets we have **accrued** between the leaders of our two countries. . . .

The debate in our union on what kind of state to create took a different track from what I thought right. But let me say that I will use my political authority and role to make sure that this new commonwealth will be effective.

. . . I will be active politically, in political life. My main intention is to help all the processes here begun by Perestroika and New Thinking in world affairs. . . . 99

—Mikhail Gorbachev, in a phone conversation with George H.W. Bush, December 25, 1991

accrue to accumulate or gain

EXAMINE THE SOURCE

1. **Analyzing Perspectives** What hope does Gorbachev express, and what promise does he make?

2. **Making Connections** How does this statement from Gorbachev mark the end of an era?

Your Inquiry Analysis

EVALUATE SOURCES AND USE EVIDENCE

Reflect back to the Compelling Question and the Supporting Questions you developed at the beginning of this lesson.

1. **Gathering Sources** Refer back to the graphic organizer you created as you read through the sources. Which sources most help you answer the Supporting Questions you wrote? Circle or highlight those sources in your graphic organizer. Then explain which two sources you found most helpful and why as well as what questions you still want to answer and how you plan to find those answers.

2. **Evaluating Sources** Looking at the sources that help you answer the Supporting Questions, evaluate the credibility of each source. What opinion does each speaker or author express on his topic? What bias does each source reveal? How does that bias influence the message?

3. **Comparing and Contrasting** Compare and contrast one American source with one Soviet source. What purpose does each source have? What tone does each use? How do the two sources relate to each other and work together to inform your understanding of the collapse of the Soviet Union?

COMMUNICATE CONCLUSIONS

Presenting Share your Supporting Questions in a small group. As a group, write a response to each of the Supporting Questions. Then, use what you have learned to make an illustrated time line of events related to the end of the Cold War and write a response to the Compelling Question. Present your time lines and response to the class.

TAKE INFORMED ACTION

Writing a Speech Think about a current relationship between the United States and another nation that might be considered rocky or uncertain or even thought of as a "cold war"—a situation with mistrust on both sides but not overt military confrontations. Use library or online sources to learn more about the conflict from both sides. Then write a speech spelling out what actions the other nation should take regarding issues such as trade or nuclear development to repair relations and what the United States might be willing to do in return. For inspiration, revisit the speeches, transcripts, and memorandums to consider how issues might be resolved and how ideas could be conveyed for maximum impact.

Memorandum of Telephone Conversation: Telcon with Mikhail Gorbachev, President of the Soviet Union. December 25, 1991.

08

Reviewing Cold War Foreign Policy

Summary

The Early Cold War

The United States and the Soviet Union had been allies during World War II. However, after peace agreements were signed, the two countries immediately positioned themselves to protect their own interests and extend their influence around the world. The political and military conflicts that followed would become known as the Cold War.

Fearing the expansion of communism, in 1947 President Truman focused on a policy of containment, which was the effort to try to keep communism confined and stop its spread to new countries. He issued the Truman Doctrine, promising that the United States would aid countries fighting communist influence. The United States and its allies established the NATO alliance for mutual protection.

Germany had been divided into four zones after World War II, and Great Britain, the United States, France, and the Soviet Union each controlled a zone. Berlin, located within the borders of the Soviet-controlled zone, was also divided up into sections controlled by the four nations. When Cold War tensions escalated and the Soviet Union tried to blockade the portions of West Berlin controlled by the other nations, U.S. forces organized the Berlin Airlift to supply the city.

For his part, Stalin refused to yield control of Eastern Europe. In 1955 the Soviet Union established the Warsaw Pact, a defense treaty that included seven satellite nations in Central and Eastern Europe that the Soviet Union controlled. The Warsaw Pact was in response to the NATO alliance.

Policy in the 1950s and 1960s

The Cold War quickly expanded beyond Europe. Asia became the next focal point in the struggle between communism and democracy. This area came to the forefront of the Cold War after Chinese Communists won a revolution against the Nationalists. American leaders feared China becoming Communist would lead to other Communist governments in Asia.

Korea had been occupied by both American and Soviet forces during World War II in order to disarm the Japanese troops stationed there. During the war, the two counties had divided the nation along the 38th parallel of latitude. Soviet troops controlled the north, while American troops controlled the south. Following World War II, talks about the future of Korea broke down. Both a Communist government in

the north and a U.S.-backed government in the south claimed authority over Korea.

What was meant to be a temporary division of the country became permanent with the Soviets backing North Korea and the U.S. supporting South Korea. When the North Koreans invaded South Korea in 1950, the United States and its UN allies came to South Korea's defense.

The Korean War continued into the presidency of Dwight Eisenhower with fighting that lasted until the summer of 1953. The peace agreement that followed left the two Koreas separated by a demilitarized zone. The border between North Korea and South Korea was roughly aligned with the 38th parallel—the same border that had existed before the bloody Korean War.

In this political cartoon from December 1985 titled "Joy to the World," Caspar Weinberger, Reagan's Secretary of Defense, distributes defense contracts and the wealth they bring throughout the nation and the world. The rocket he rides is labeled "Star Wars Programs."

Library of Congress, Prints & Photographs Division [LC-DIG-ppmsca-21957]. Reprinted with permission, Herb Block Foundation.

President Eisenhower won the presidency in part because the public believed Truman's foreign policy was failing. Eisenhower, who had been a general during World War II, expanded the nuclear arms race. He believed the threat of massive retaliation would keep Communist powers in check. Aides referred to this approach as "brinkmanship" because it relied on the risk of bringing the country to the brink, or edge, of nuclear war. Eisenhower also expanded the use of covert operations in different parts of the world, including using the CIA to suppress revolutions in developing countries. His Eisenhower Doctrine promised U.S. aid to Middle Eastern countries that resisted Communism.

In 1957 the Soviet Union launched the satellite *Sputnik I* into space. United States leaders and the public were concerned that by launching a satellite, the Soviets had an edge in the arms race and a new platform from which to attack. Early in his administration, President Kennedy set the ambitious goal of being the first nation to put a person on the moon.

Like his predecessor, Kennedy used covert operations in various parts of the world to contain Communism. A newly Communist neighbor, Cuba, became an ongoing concern, especially when the Soviet Union began shipping Soviet technicians and military equipment to Cuba. Eisenhower had authorized the CIA to secretly train and arm a group of Cuban exiles, known as *La Brigada*, to invade the island and set off a popular uprising. When Kennedy became president, he agreed to continue the operation. However, the members of *La Brigada* were captured within two days, contrary to U.S. expectations. Kennedy's successful use of brinkmanship in the Cuban missile crisis, however, led Soviet leader Nikita Khrushchev to back down from the edge of nuclear war.

Policy in the 1970s and 1980s

When Republican Richard Nixon was elected president in 1968, he ushered in a new approach to Cold War policy. Nixon's national security adviser, Henry Kissinger, shaped much of the administration's foreign policy strategy.

Responding to growing concerns about the dangers the nuclear arms race posed to the world, Nixon followed a strategy leading to disarmament. In his most daring move, Nixon opened diplomatic ties with China. This effort concerned leaders of the Soviet Union, who were not friendly with neighboring China despite it also being a Communist nation. The Soviets engaged in discussions to limit the expansion of the arms race. This thawing of relations became known as détente.

The U.S. role in the Middle East also increased in the 1970s. The crisis carried over into the presidency of Jimmy Carter, who helped ease some tensions by brokering the Camp David Accords between Egypt and Israel. The Iran hostage crisis weakened Carter's presidency and helped lead to his defeat in 1980.

The Reagan Years

President Reagan reversed course on the Cold War, reigniting the nuclear arms race. He called his approach "Peace through Strength." His Reagan Doctrine supported guerrillas fighting Communist powers. This support included helping people in Afghanistan defeat invading Soviet troops. The Reagan administration's secret support for rebels in Nicaragua led to the Iran-Contra scandal.

By Reagan's second term, the cost of the arms race and the failed Afghanistan campaign had weakened the Soviet Union. After a new Soviet leader, Mikhail Gorbachev, instituted massive reforms in the Soviet Union, Reagan initiated new talks on disarmament.

The End of the Cold War

Gorbachev's reforms, perestroika and glasnost, granted greater freedoms to the Soviet people and established a more diverse economy. During the presidency of George H.W. Bush, the Cold War began to take a different shape as Eastern Bloc nations instituted their own reforms. Emboldened by global trends and the weakening of the Soviet Communist regime, numerous grassroots movements launched rebellions that led to the overthrow of Communist governments.

One by one, Communist governments throughout Eastern Europe fell. In 1989 the world watched in amazement as East and West Germans tore down the Berlin Wall. By 1991, the Soviet Union had collapsed. It reorganized into several independent nations. The dissolution of the Soviet Union marked the end of the Cold War.

End of the Soviet Union
Glasnost allows more freedom of speech in USSR and perestroika increases private enterprise and profit in economy.
Several Eastern European satellite nations revolt against Soviet control.
A coup is attempted against leadership within the Communist Party in Moscow.
Fifteen Soviet republics declare independence.

Apply What You Have Learned

A Making Connections to Science

During the Cold War, the Soviet Union and the United States engaged in a space race. As each nation tried to outdo the other in its bid to push the limits of space exploration, they devoted resources and made significant investments in the sciences. While the space race goal for each country was to be the first to put a human on the moon, the technology developed on the path toward that goal had long-lasting effects on other sciences and on daily life. Many inventions created to solve problems in space exploration influenced technology that would be used by ordinary citizens in their work and homes.

ACTIVITY   **Sketch an Invention** In an accident in 1962, astronaut Gus Grissom lost his headset when he had to escape his space capsule. In response, NASA asked researchers to devise a lightweight device that could remain attached to the astronauts, allowing them to communicate with mission control in case of future emergencies. The result was the first headset used in space, shown in the image. Using your textbook,

library, or Internet resources, create a sketch of an invention for daily use that evolved from, or could have evolved from, space race technology.

» Neil Armstrong puts on his space suit before the launch of Apollo 11, on July 16, 1969.

B Understanding Multiple Perspectives

Nine U.S. presidents served during the Cold War years. Each took a different approach to dealing with the ongoing conflict with the Soviet Union. The goal for each was to expand democracy and limit Soviet influence but also to avoid direct war with the Soviets—and the danger of nuclear annihilation. For some presidents, achieving these goals required tough stands and greater military involvement in third-party nations. Others focused on expanding diplomacy and forging strategic alliances, even with other Communist nations.

ACTIVITY   **Draw Conclusions** Using your textbook and additional research, copy and complete the following chart to summarize the different approaches each U.S. president took during the Cold War. As you complete the chart, include the strengths and weaknesses of each

approach. When you have completed the chart, write a paragraph that draws a conclusion about which set of policies you think was the wisest based on the strengths and weaknesses you identify.

President	Policies	Strengths	Weaknesses
Truman			
Eisenhower			
Kennedy			
Johnson			
Nixon			
Ford			
Carter			
Reagan			
Bush			

NASA/Kennedy Space Center

C Making Connections to Today

After the Soviet Union dissolved at the end of the Cold War, Russia remained the largest and most powerful nation of the former Soviet Union. Despite initial efforts to expand civil liberties and open the economy, during the twenty-first century the Russian government reverted to some aspects of the authoritarian rule that had dominated Soviet life during the Cold War.

For more than two decades following his election as president in 2000, Vladimir Putin dominated Russian culture and politics. Putin gained power by appealing to Russian nationalism and glory. He also tightly controlled the media and suppressed political opposition.

Despite establishing a positive working relationship with some recent American presidents, Putin's government was often accused of engaging in Cold War–style attempts to weaken the United States This behavior included influencing the 2016 U.S. presidential election with social media aimed at swaying American voters.

ACTIVITY **Write a News Story** Using library and Internet resources, research recent news stories about the current relationship between Russia and the United States. Relying on your research and information from this lesson, write a news story describing how the relationship between the leaders of the Soviet Union, Russia, and the United States has evolved since the end of the Cold War.

» U.S. president Donald Trump and Russian president Vladimir Putin gave a joint press conference as part of their meeting in Helsinki, Finland, on July 16, 2018.

D Geographic Reasoning

The Cold War shaped the world in many ways. At times the events of the Cold War created the need to redraw national borders and update maps and geographic data. Some of the initial disputes in the Cold War grew out of the mutual desires of the Soviet Union and the United States to influence global events and build alliances with other nations. Although the Soviet Union and the United States never directly attacked one another throughout the many decades of the Cold War, they often engaged in indirect conflicts in third-party nations, whose future (and borders) were determined by the outcome of these armed conflicts.

ACTIVITY **Compare Maps** The geopolitical shape of the world looked very different at the beginning of the Cold War during the late 1940s and the 1950s. By the end of the era of political tension, in the early 1990s, many nations had appeared and disappeared, and other nations saw different border configurations. Use your textbook, library, and Internet resources to locate at least two world maps—one showing the nations that existed in 1946 and the other showing the world in 1996. Take a careful look at these maps and compare the different countries and border configurations. Identify a list of countries that either changed names, experienced borders adjustments, or ceased to exist during this time period.

Anadolu Agency/Getty Images

Postwar Domestic Issues `1945–1980`

Economic growth in the 1950s led entrepreneurs in homebuilding and real estate to promote the glories of suburban life.

INTRODUCTION LESSON

01 Introducing Postwar Domestic Issues   368

LEARN THE EVENTS LESSONS

02 Cold War Fears at Home   373

03 Truman and Eisenhower   377

04 Postwar American Society   383

INQUIRY ACTIVITY LESSONS

05 Turning Point: The Warren Court   391

06 Analyzing Sources: The Great Society   395

REVIEW AND APPLY LESSON

07 Reviewing Postwar Domestic Issues   401

H. ARMSTRONG ROBERTS/ClassicStock/Alamy Stock Photo

01

DUCK AND COVER!

During the Cold War era, the threat of an **imminent** nuclear attack concerned many Americans daily. The fear was so prevalent that the government developed safety precautions and trainings to help put Americans at ease.

For example, in 1951 the Federal Civil Defense Administration—started by President Truman in 1950 after the outbreak of war with Korea—created a film to teach students how to "duck and cover" in the event of a nuclear attack. According to the film, "We all know the atomic bomb is very dangerous. Since it may be used against us, we must get ready for it, just as we are ready for many other dangers that are around us all the time."

The film compares the duck-and-cover drill to other safety measures children already knew, including fire drills and other common safety measures, such as pedestrian crosswalks. As the narrator of the film explains, the atomic bomb is "such a big explosion" that it can "break windows all over town." But "if you duck and cover," the film assures students, then "you will be much safer."

The duck-and-cover drill is just like the name sounds: A warning siren indicated that enemy planes were coming, and students were told to duck under a desk or table and cover the back of their head with their hands. If they were outside when they heard the signal, then they were told to get to the nearest safe building as fast as they could. The film explains the bomb could be dropped without any warning at all; in that situation, people were told to duck and cover as soon as the bomb's flash was seen.

Although the duck-and-cover training film makes children aware of the great danger of an atomic bomb, it does so without going into the gory details. The film tries to compare the dangers of a nuclear bomb to events more familiar to the students practicing the

drill. It mentions, for example, that "the atomic bomb flash can burn you worse than a terrible sunburn."

This training film was part of the Alert America campaign that created more than 400 million pieces of literature, such as pamphlets, advertisements, and films, that told Americans how to protect themselves in the event of a nuclear attack. One pamphlet outlines "things to do before, during, and after the bomb explodes" and opens with the helpful advice that "When the bomb goes off—don't BE there!" Government officials mailed maps displaying evacuation routes to people. The government also encouraged families to build their own bomb shelters and sent them construction guides as well as a list of materials to store in their shelters.

> **"** We all know the atomic bomb is very dangerous. **"**

The Alert America materials represented an attempt to exert some control over what seemed an impossible situation and to provide Americans with some solace during a tense and turbulent time. However, ducking and covering would only help someone who was far from the blast of an atomic bomb.

The bomb the United States had used on Hiroshima at the end of World War II heavily damaged nearly everything within a three-mile radius, completely destroying everything within a smaller radius, and the Nagasaki bomb caused total destruction over an area of about three square miles. It's estimated that more than 70,000 people died immediately or soon after the Hiroshima bomb, and illnesses due to radiation in both cities greatly increased the initial death toll—as many as 166,000 people in Hiroshima and 80,000 people in Nagasaki died within the first few months after the bombing.

People understandably feared the power of nuclear weapons, and the intensity of the Cold War era reverberated throughout American society, culture, and politics.

(l)United States Office Of Civil Defense, and Archer Productions. Duck and Cover. 1951. Video. https://www.loc.gov/item/mbrs01836081; (r)Office of Civil Defense. "When the Bomb Goes Off — Don't Be There!"

---

imminent ready to take place; happening soon

Bettmann/Getty Images

This 1951 photograph shows school children practicing the duck-and-cover drill.

Understanding the Time and Place:
The United States, 1945–1966

World War II helped end the Great Depression, and an economic boom occurred throughout the country in the decades after the war. Coupled with advancements in science and technology, this newfound wealth altered American society in ways that still resonate today. The prevalence of wealth, however, did not mean it was evenly distributed.

Growth of the Middle Class

World War II was followed by a time of prosperity. The wartime increase in manufacturing and industrialization continued after the war was over, and people found steady work that paid well, allowing many working-class people to move into the middle class. In addition, the **GI Bill** legislation passed in 1944 provided benefits to veterans such as money for college, job training, and low-interest home loans. These benefits created opportunities for veterans of World War II, with benefits later extended to anyone who served in the armed forces. Not every veteran, however, had equal access to these opportunities; African Americans and other non-white veterans were denied full access to the benefits they had earned through their military service.

Advancements in technology made luxury products such as cars, washing machines, refrigerators, and ovens more affordable. People had more free time, often spent traveling by car as roads and highway systems expanded and improved. The idea for an interstate highway system like we have today was first described in a report to Congress in 1939, but the idea did not truly come to fruition until President Eisenhower took office in January 1953. He made revitalizing the nation's highway system a top priority, and the Federal-Aid Highway Act of 1956 represented an important step toward that goal.

Cars allowed people to live farther away from their jobs, resulting in mass-produced suburban neighborhoods that sprang up around cities. These suburbs boasted quiet streets and large, newly built houses with manicured lawns, often bordered by the now-iconic white picket fence. This material wealth and the exploding U.S. birthrate led to the baby boom era from 1946 to 1964. During the height of the baby boom a child was born every seven seconds.

But not all families were living lives of convenience and luxury. Nearly one in five Americans, or roughly 30 million people, lived below the poverty line. Most of these people were African Americans, Latinos, and Native Americans. They tended to live in urban areas or in impoverished rural areas. Many lived in the southern or western United States.

The American Dream of home ownership, a car in the garage, and green space for children to play became attainable for many working-class and middle-class families during the post-World War II economic boom. At the same time, this American Dream was inaccessible to many Americans. African Americans in urban areas, for example, were segregated into overcrowded neighborhoods with dilapidated buildings. Inadequate plumbing and sanitation lead to slum conditions.

<u>Comparing and Contrasting</u> Based on the two photographs, how was a child's life in an urban area similar to or different from a child's life in a suburb?

GI Bill The GI Bill is the popular name for the Servicemen's Readjustment Act that allowed military personnel to get loans, job training, hiring privileges, and tuition incentives from the Veterans Administration

(l)Steven Gottlieb/Corbis Historical/Getty Images; (r)Mildred Mead/Chicago History Museum/Getty Images

The Interstate Highway System

Advances in technology allowed more people to be able to afford cars, and the 1950s marked the dawn of the automobile age. Roads, fast-food restaurants, drive-in theaters, shopping malls, roadside hotels, and tourist attractions popped up throughout America to support the country's love of traveling by car.

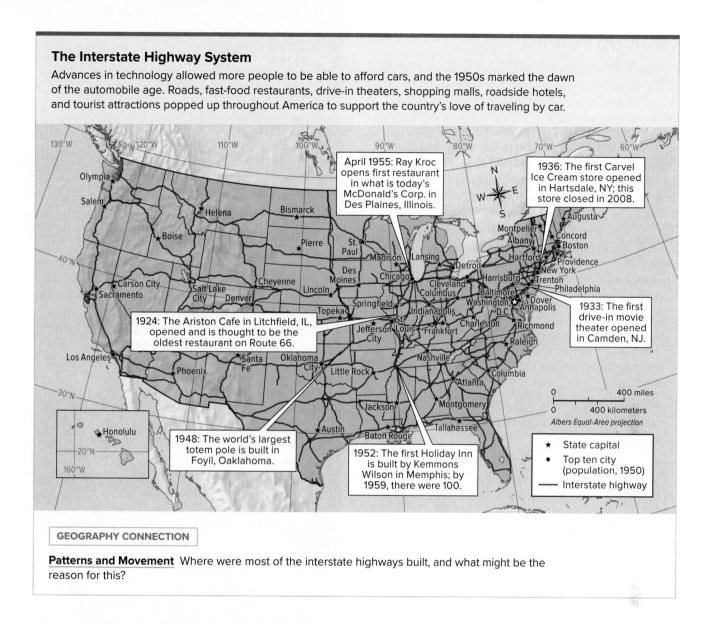

April 1955: Ray Kroc opens first restaurant in what is today's McDonald's Corp. in Des Plaines, Illinois.

1936: The first Carvel Ice Cream store opened in Hartsdale, NY; this store closed in 2008.

1924: The Ariston Cafe in Litchfield, IL, opened and is thought to be the oldest restaurant on Route 66.

1933: The first drive-in movie theater opened in Camden, NJ.

1948: The world's largest totem pole is built in Foyil, Oaklahoma.

1952: The first Holiday Inn is built by Kemmons Wilson in Memphis; by 1959, there were 100.

0 — 400 miles
0 — 400 kilometers
Albers Equal-Area projection

★ State capital
● Top ten city (population, 1950)
— Interstate highway

GEOGRAPHY CONNECTION

Patterns and Movement Where were most of the interstate highways built, and what might be the reason for this?

Science, Technology, and Medicine

Great technological and medical advancements occurred during the Cold War era. In the 1950s cancer treatments using radiation and chemotherapy were discovered, and medical professionals invented a cardiopulmonary resuscitation technique, better known as CPR. Researchers also discovered treatments for polio, a highly contagious viral illness, and tuberculosis, an infectious disease usually affecting the lungs.

Tensions between the Soviet Union and the United States resulted in a "space race," with the ultimate goal of being first to put a man on the moon. Scientists in both nations worked to outwit and outperform the other. On October 14, 1947, U.S. Air Force officer Chuck Yeager became the first man to exceed the speed of sound in flight. However, the Soviet Union won several early victories in the race to the moon. The Russian cosmonaut Yuri Gagarin

became the first human in space on April 12, 1961. Less than a month later, American Alan Shepard accomplished the same feat.

As part of the effort to defeat the Russians in the race to the moon, the National Aeronautics and Space Administration (NASA), an independent U.S. government agency, was created in 1958. In 1969 astronaut Neil Armstrong became the first person to walk on the moon, but he could not have done so without the help of about 100 members of his rocket-development team. One key member was Wernher von Braun, a German engineer who worked for Hitler's army before coming to the United States. In desperation to beat the Soviet Union, the United States was willing to overlook von Braun's Nazi past and bring him to America. Eventually von Braun became the director of NASA's Marshall State Flight Center in Huntsville, Alabama. Von Braun and his team developed the Saturn V rocket that was used to get the historic Apollo 11 mission off the ground.

Looking Ahead

In these next lessons, you will learn about the effects of the Cold War on American life and the changes in American society in the decades after World War II. While studying this time period, you will understand the American policies that were enacted to stop the perceived and feared spread of Communism and the influence of several presidents on American society and politics. You will learn about the space race and how advances in medicine, technology, and science affected the United States. And you will understand the widening gap between the rich and the poor.

You will examine Compelling Questions in the Inquiry Lessons and develop your own questions about postwar domestic issues. Review the time line to preview some of the key events that you will learn about.

What Will You Learn?

In these lessons focused on postwar domestic issues, you will learn:

- about McCarthyism and the second Red Scare.
- about the influence of the Cold War on American life and popular culture.
- about the causes and effects of the growth of suburbs in America.
- how the events of this era are reflected in music, film, art, and literature.
- how advances in medicine, technology, and science affected America.
- how the changing economy touched different groups of people.

? COMPELLING QUESTIONS

- **How did the Warren Court rulings change a person's legal protections?**
- **Why did President Johnson promote the federal Great Society effort?**

1944 ○ — **1944** GI Bill gives financial aid to veterans

1946 ENIAC becomes the first electronic computer

1946–1964 Baby boom swells U.S. population

1953 ○ — **1953** Julius and Ethel Rosenberg are executed

1954 Army–McCarthy hearings

1955 Jonas Salk's polio vaccine becomes widely available (right)

1956 Congress passes Federal-Aid Highway Act

1961 ○ — **1961** Peace Corps is founded

1965 ○ — **1965** Congress establishes Medicare and Medicaid

1965 Department of Housing and Urban Development is created to improve urban life and investigate housing discrimination

ITAR-TASS News Agency/Alamy Stock Photo

Sequencing Time Identify the events that reveal the negative impact of Cold War fears on American policies and explain how the events reveal those fears.

02

Cold War Fears at Home

Analyzing Key Ideas and Details As you read, summarize the lesson content by using the major headings to create an outline similar to this one.

Cold War Fears at Home

I. The Second Red Scare

    A. The Search for Communists

    B.

The Second Red Scare

GUIDING QUESTION

How did the post–World War II Red Scare compare with the one that followed World War I?

The Red Scare began in September 1945 when a clerk named Igor Gouzenko walked out of the Soviet Embassy in Ottawa, Canada, and **defected.** He carried with him documents showing a Soviet effort to infiltrate government agencies in Canada and the United States to obtain information about the atomic bomb. The case stunned Americans, and soon the search for spies in the American government escalated into a general fear of Communist **subversion,** or effort to weaken a society and overthrow its government.

The Search for Communists

In early 1947, President Truman established a **loyalty review program** to screen all federal employees. Between 1947 and 1951, over 6 million federal employees were tried before loyalty boards, which were established in every department and agency of the federal government to consider whether employees had Communist sympathies. A person might become a suspect for reading certain books, belonging to specific groups, traveling overseas, or seeing particular foreign films. The Federal Bureau of Investigation (FBI) scrutinized some 14,000 people. About 2,000 quit their jobs, many under pressure. Federal authorities fired another 212 for "questionable loyalty" without indisputable evidence.

FBI director J. Edgar Hoover urged the House Un-American Activities Committee (HUAC) to hold public hearings to expose Communists, "Communist sympathizers," and "fellow travelers." The FBI sent agents to infiltrate groups suspected of subversion and wiretapped thousands of telephones. Dozens were prosecuted for violating the 1940 Smith Act, which made it illegal to

Ronald Reagan appeared as a "friendly" witness in the HUAC hearings in 1947. Friendly witnesses cooperated with the Committee and supported its investigations.

Determining Context How does the photograph show that the hearings became a media event?

defect to desert a country or cause

subversion a systematic attempt to overthrow a government by using persons working secretly from within

loyalty review program a policy established by President Truman that authorized the screening of all federal employees to determine their loyalty to the U.S. government

AP Photo

"advocate, abet, advise, or teach" the destruction of the government. The Supreme Court upheld the decision to prosecute, saying it did not violate the First Amendment.

One of HUAC's first hearings in 1947 focused on the film industry as a cultural force that Communists might manipulate to spread their ideas and influence. Future American president Ronald Reagan, then head of the Screen Actors Guild, testified that there were Communists in Hollywood. During the hearings ten screenwriters, known as the "Hollywood Ten," used their Fifth Amendment right to protect themselves from self-incrimination and refused to testify. The incident led producers to blacklist, or agree not to hire, anyone who was believed to be a Communist or who refused to cooperate with the committee. Other industries also adopted blacklists, creating an atmosphere of distrust.

In 1948 Whittaker Chambers, a magazine editor and former Communist Party member, told HUAC that several government officials were also former Communists or spies. Chambers's list included Alger Hiss, a diplomat who had served in Roosevelt's administration, attended the Yalta Conference, and helped organize the United Nations. Hiss sued Chambers for libel, but Chambers testified that in 1937 and 1938 Hiss had given him secret State Department documents. Hiss denied being a spy or Communist Party member. He even denied knowing Chambers. The committee was ready to drop the investigation until California representative Richard Nixon pushed for continued hearings. Chambers produced copies of secret documents, along with microfilm that he had hidden in a hollow pumpkin. These "pumpkin papers," Chambers claimed, proved Hiss was lying. A jury convicted Hiss of **perjury,** or lying under oath. The national attention Richard Nixon received helped launch his political career. He went on to become a U.S. senator, vice president, and eventually president.

Another spy case centered on accusations that American Communists had sold atomic bomb secrets to the Soviets in 1949 to help them produce a bomb. In 1950 the FBI arrested Julius and Ethel Rosenberg, a New York couple who were members of the Communist Party. The government charged them with spying for the Soviets. Although the Rosenbergs denied the charges, they were condemned to death for espionage. Many people believed that they were victims caught in the wave of anti-Communist frenzy. Appeals and pleas for clemency failed, however, and the Rosenbergs were executed in June 1953.

In 1946 American and British cryptographers, working for a project code-named "Venona," cracked the Soviet Union's spy code, enabling them to read approximately 3,000 messages between Moscow and the United States collected during the Cold War. These messages confirmed extensive Soviet spying and ongoing efforts to steal nuclear secrets. The U.S. government did not reveal Project Venona's existence until 1995. The Venona documents provided strong evidence that Julius Rosenberg was guilty of spying, but they did not show that Ethel was also a spy.

The Red Scare Spreads

Many state and local governments, universities, businesses, unions, and churches began efforts to identify Communists among their groups. The University of California required its faculty to take loyalty oaths stating that they did not advocate the overthrow of the United States government and were not members of the Communist Party. California state officials fired a total of 157 faculty members for refusing to sign the loyalty oath. Roman Catholic groups became anti-Communist and urged members to identify Communists within the Church. Many union leaders, who were required by the Taft-Hartley Act of 1947 to take oaths saying that they were not Communists, purged their own organizations, eventually expelling 11 unions that refused to remove Communist leaders.

In the South, segregationists targeted civil rights activists. The Communist Party in the United States had often promoted the rights of African Americans, and some activists became party members. The Red Scare thus became another avenue of persecution used against civil rights reformers. Thousands of federal employees of different sexual orientations were fired. Labeled the Lavender Scare, the government justified the purge, without evidence, by claiming that the employees' need for secrecy—due to society's view on diverse sexual orientations at the time—made those employees prone to blackmail by America's enemies.

✓ CHECK FOR UNDERSTANDING

Comparing and Contrasting Compare and contrast the Second Red Scare with the one after World War I.

McCarthyism

GUIDING QUESTION

Why did many Americans believe Senator McCarthy's accusations?

In 1949 the Red Scare intensified as the Soviet Union successfully tested an atomic bomb, and China turned to communism. Many Americans felt that the United States was losing the Cold War. In February 1950, little-known senator Joseph R. McCarthy gave a speech to a Republican women's group in West Virginia. Halfway through his speech, McCarthy made a surprising claim:

66 While I cannot take the time to name all the men in the State Department who have been

perjury lying when one has sworn under oath to tell the truth

374

Speech of Joseph McCarthy, Wheeling, West Virginia, February 9, 1950.

ESTHER BRUNAUER (1901–1959)

Esther Caukin was born and raised in California. She attended Mills College and later Stanford University where she earned a PhD in history. Esther focused on international relations throughout most of her career, beginning her work with the American Association of University Women (AAUW), a group dedicated to the continuing education of women college graduates. She married Stephen Brunauer, an immigrant research chemist from Hungary, in 1931. As a student, Stephen Brunauer had belonged to the Young Workers' League, a Communist group. However, both he and Esther became critical of communism.

STATE DEPARTMENT Esther Brunauer left the AAUW's International Relations program in 1944 to join the U.S. State Department as an international organizational affairs specialist. She helped draft plans for the United Nations and went on to represent the United States in the United Nations Educational, Scientific, and Cultural Organization (UNESCO).

MCCARTHY'S ATTACK On February 11, 1950, Senator Joseph McCarthy accused Esther Brunauer of being one of the Communists in the State Department. Although investigations declared Esther loyal, the State Department considered her a security risk and fired her in 1952, likely because of her husband's alleged Communist ties. The Brunauers moved to Evanston, Illinois, where Esther died of a heart condition in 1959.

> **Explaining** How does Esther Brunauer's story illustrate the damaging effect of McCarthyism?

PHOTO: UN Photo/Rosenberg; TEXT: Speech of Joseph McCarthy, Wheeling, West Virginia, February 9, 1950.

named as members of the Communist Party and members of a spy ring, I have here in my hand a list of 205 . . . that were made known to the Secretary of State as being members of the Communist Party and who nevertheless are still working and shaping the policy of the State Department. 99

—quoted in the *Wheeling Intelligencer*, 1950

The list never appeared. McCarthy proclaimed that Communists posed a danger at home and abroad. He distributed a booklet accusing Democratic Party leaders of corruption and of protecting Communists. McCarthy often targeted Secretary of State Dean Acheson, calling him incompetent and a tool of Stalin. He also accused George C. Marshall, former army chief of staff and secretary of state, of disloyalty. Anxious about Communism, many Americans accepted his claims.

The McCarran Act

In 1950 Congress passed the Internal Security Act, also called the McCarran Act. Similar in intent to the 1940 Smith Act used to prosecute communists and socialists, the new act made it illegal to attempt to establish a totalitarian government in the United States and required all Communist-related organizations to publish their records and register with the United States attorney general. Communists could not have passports and, in cases of a national emergency, could be arrested and detained. President Truman vetoed the bill, but Congress easily overrode his veto in 1950. Later Supreme Court cases limited the act's scope.

McCarthy's Rise and Fall

In 1953 McCarthy became chairman of the Senate Subcommittee on Investigations, which forced government officials to testify about alleged Communist influences. Investigations were based on weak evidence and irrational fears. McCarthy's tactic of damaging reputations with vague, unfounded charges became known as McCarthyism. McCarthy's sensational accusations put him in the headlines, and the press quoted him often and widely. He badgered witnesses and then refused to accept their answers. His tactics left a cloud of suspicion that he and others interpreted as guilt. With the exception of Senator Margaret Chase Smith, who spoke out against McCarthy's tactics without naming him in a 1950 Senate speech, people were afraid to challenge him. But in 1954, McCarthy began looking for Soviet spies in the United States Army. During weeks of televised hearings, Americans watched McCarthy accuse officers of misconduct. His popular support began to wane.

To strike back at the army's lawyer, Joseph Welch, McCarthy brought up the past of a young lawyer in

Welch's firm who had been a member of a Communist-front organization while in law school. Welch exploded at McCarthy for possibly ruining the young man's career: "Until this moment, I think I never really gauged your cruelty or your recklessness. . . . Have you no sense of decency, sir?" Spectators cheered. Welch had said what many Americans had been thinking. Later that year, the Senate passed a vote of **censure,** or formal disapproval, against McCarthy. While he remained a senator, McCarthy had lost all influence.

✓ **CHECK FOR UNDERSTANDING**

Analyzing Why did many Americans believe Senator McCarthy's accusations?

Fears of an Atomic Age

GUIDING QUESTION

How did the anxiety of nuclear war affect American society?

The Red Scare and the spread of nuclear weapons had a profound impact on American life in the 1950s. Fears of Communism and war affected both ordinary Americans and government leaders.

Living With the Bomb

Already upset by the 1949 Soviet test of atomic weapons, Americans were shocked when the Soviets tested the much more powerful hydrogen bomb, or H-bomb, in 1953. The United States had tested its own H-bomb less than a year earlier.

Americans feared a surprise Soviet attack. Schools created bomb shelters and held drills to teach students to "duck-and-cover" in the event of a nuclear attack. Although "duck-and-cover" might have made people feel safer, it would not have protected them from nuclear radiation. Experts have noted that for every person killed outright by a nuclear blast, four more would die later from **fallout,** the radiation left over after a blast. Some families built backyard fallout shelters and stocked them with canned food and water.

In the 1950s, the United States performed nuclear tests at a site in Nevada northwest of Las Vegas. The tests used model towns and mannequins to determine the effects of an atomic blast on the populace and to figure out the best ways to deal with a Soviet attack. The mushroom clouds from the tests were visible from Las Vegas. Unfortunately, winds spread the fallout and affected both civilians and military personnel by increasing cancer rates well into the 1970s.

Like the Soviets, Americans wanted nuclear weapons that could be used on the battlefield, such as the M28/M29 Davy Crockett nuclear weapon system developed in the 1950s. Requiring only three soldiers to operate, this lightweight system could launch a 76-pound nuclear warhead up to 2.5 miles but with limited accuracy and significant danger from fallout. Because of these limitations, the system was phased out by 1971 without being used in combat.

Cold War Pop Culture

As worries about nuclear war and Communist infiltration filled the public imagination, Cold War themes soon appeared in films, plays, television, the titles of dance tunes, and popular fiction. Matt Cvetic, an FBI undercover informant who secretly infiltrated the Communist Party, captivated readers with reports in the *Saturday Evening Post* in 1950. His story was later made into the movie *I Was a Communist for the FBI* (1951). Another film, *Walk East on Beacon* (1952), featured the FBI's activities in a spy case. In 1953 Arthur Miller's thinly veiled criticism of the Communist witch-hunts, *The Crucible,* appeared on Broadway. The play remains popular as a cautionary tale of how hysteria can lead to false accusations. In 1953 a weekly television series, *I Led Three Lives,* about an undercover FBI counterspy who was also a Communist Party official, debuted. Popular tunes such as "Atomic Boogie" and "Atom Bomb Baby" played on the radio. The next year, author Philip Wylie published *Tomorrow!,* a novel describing the horrific effects of nuclear war on an unprepared American city. Wylie wrote his novel to educate the public about the horrors of atomic war.

John Hersey's nonfiction book *Hiroshima* was originally published as the August 31, 1946, edition of the *New Yorker* magazine. The book provides six firsthand accounts of the United States dropping the atomic bomb on Hiroshima, Japan. *Hiroshima* not only made Americans question the use of the bomb but also underscored the personal horrors of a nuclear attack.

✓ **CHECK FOR UNDERSTANDING**

Summarizing How did fears of nuclear war affect American society?

LESSON ACTIVITIES

1. **Argumentative Writing** Consider the historical events surrounding the early Cold War era. Were HUAC and Senator McCarthy justified in investigating people who were suspected of being Communists? Why or why not?

2. **Collaborating** In small groups, work together to write a statement describing how the Cold War affected American society. In particular, discuss the impact of alarmism and government restrictions that were dictated by fearmongering.

censure to express a formal disapproval of an action

fallout radioactive particles dispersed by a nuclear explosion

Joseph Welch, U.S. Senate, Committee on Government Operations, Special Senate Investigation on Charges and Countercharges Involving Secretary of the Army Robert T. Stevens, John G. Adams, H. Struve Hensel and Senator Joe McCarthy, Roy M. Cohn, and Francis P. Carr, 83rd Cong., 2nd Sess., part 59 (Washington: U.S. Government Printing Office, 1954), pp 2428-2429.

03

Truman and Eisenhower

READING STRATEGY

Analyzing Key Ideas and Details As you read, use a graphic organizer like the one below to list characteristics of the postwar economy.

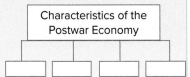

The Truman Administration

GUIDING QUESTION

How did the government try to ease the transition into a peacetime economy?

After World War II, many Americans were apprehensive about a peacetime economy. They worried about unemployment and a recession because military production had stopped just as millions of former soldiers needed work. Despite such worries, the economy continued to grow after the war. Increased consumer spending helped ward off a recession. After years of economic depression and wartime shortages, Americans rushed to buy consumer goods.

The Servicemen's Readjustment Act of 1944, popularly called the GI Bill, also boosted the economy. Many veterans struggled after World War I because no provisions had been made help them return to civilian life. The GI Bill was created to help World War II veterans reintegrate into civilian society. The federal GI Bill provided unemployment benefits and gave veterans the opportunity to further their education, buy houses and farms, and establish businesses. However, programs funded by federal money were directed by local officials who favored white applicants over African Americans, especially in the South. Thousands of African American veterans were denied admission to colleges, loans for housing and business, and enrollment in job-training programs offered by the GI Bill, and thus were denied economic opportunities available to white veterans.

About 7.8 million veterans took advantage of the GI Bill's educational opportunities either by attending trade schools, colleges, and universities or by participating in farming or on-the-job training. The 2.2 million veterans who pursued college degrees caused enrollments to skyrocket, forcing schools to expand to meet the demand. Colleges and universities rushed to hire more faculty, add night and summer courses, and increase class sizes. California set up a three-tier system consisting of junior colleges, state colleges, and the nine-campus University of California system. Similarly, New York created its own higher education system—the State University of New York (SUNY).

Return to a Peacetime Economy

The postwar economy encountered problems in the early years after the war. A greater demand for goods led to higher prices. The resulting inflation soon triggered labor unrest. As the cost of living rose, workers in the automobile, steel, electrical, and mining industries went on strike for better pay.

Truman was afraid that the miners' strikes would drastically reduce the nation's energy supply. He ordered the government to take control of the mines. He also pressured mine owners to grant the union most of its demands. Truman even stopped a strike that shut down the nation's railroads by threatening to draft the striking workers into the army. Labor unrest and high prices prompted many Americans to call for change. The Republicans seized on these feelings during the 1946 congressional elections and won control of both houses of Congress for the first time since 1930.

The new conservative Congress quickly set out to limit the power of organized labor. In 1947 legislators passed the Taft-Hartley Act outlawing the **closed shop,** or the practice of forcing business owners to hire only union

closed shop a system in which union membership is a condition of employment

members. This law also allowed states to pass **right-to-work laws,** which outlawed **union shops** (shops requiring new workers to join the union), and prevented using union money to support political campaigns. Truman vetoed the act, arguing that it was a mistake:

66 [It would] reverse the basic direction of our national labor policy, inject the Government into private economic affairs on an unprecedented scale, and conflict with important principles of our democratic society. Its provisions would cause more strikes, not fewer. 99

–from a message to the U.S. House of Representatives, June 20, 1947

Congress passed the Taft-Hartley Act in 1947 over the president's veto. Supporters claimed that the law held irresponsible unions in check. Labor leaders viewed it as an unfair law, insisting that it erased many of the gains that unions had made since 1933.

Women also faced workplace changes. Those who had filled traditionally male jobs during the war were asked to leave or were fired to make room for returning male veterans. Many of these women needed the income. Some were first-time employees, while others had left lower-paying service jobs. Armed with new skills, they were reluctant to give up their independence and higher income for less lucrative jobs as domestics, secretaries, and waitresses.

Employers, advertisers, the media, and even the government encouraged women–particularly middle-class white women–to stay at home and raise families. Still, as the main purchasers of household consumer goods, women helped fuel the booming economy. By 1952, two million more married women worked outside the home than during the war. Some were middle-class women working to enable their families to enjoy a better economic quality of life. The numbers of single working women also rose rapidly during the 1950s, reaching 40 percent of all women aged 16 and older by the end of the decade.

Truman's Legislative Agenda

The Democratic Party's loss of control in Congress in the 1946 elections did not dampen Truman's plans. After taking office, Truman proposed domestic measures to continue the work of Roosevelt's New Deal. This included expanding Social Security benefits and raising the minimum wage. He also proposed public housing construction; a program to ensure full employment through federal spending and investment; a system of national health insurance; and long-range environmental and public works planning, including the Federal Water Pollution Control Act of 1948.

While Truman focused on other aspects of his agenda, Congress amended Executive Order 8802. President Roosevelt had issued this order to prevent discrimination of federal employees by reason of "race, creed, color, or national origin." In February 1948 Truman asked Congress to pass a broad civil rights bill that would protect African Americans' right to vote, abolish poll taxes, and make lynching a federal crime. He also issued executive orders 9980 and 9981 barring discrimination in federal employment and ending segregation in the armed forces. Most of Truman's legislative efforts failed as a coalition of Republicans and conservative Southern Democrats defeated many of his proposals.

The Election of 1948

As the 1948 presidential election neared, observers gave Truman little chance of winning. Some Southern Democrats, angry at Truman's support of civil rights,

The *Chicago Daily Tribune* incorrectly declared President Truman's defeat in the tight 1948 presidential race.

Interpreting How would you explain Truman's response to the headline in this photo?

PHOTO: Underwood Archives/Alamy Stock Photo; TEXT: Harry S. Truman. 120 - Veto of the Taft-Hartley Labor Bill. June 20, 1947. John T. Woolley and Gerhard Peters, The American Presidency Project [online]. Santa Barbara, CA. Available from World Wide Web: http://www.presidency.ucsb.edu/ws/index.php?pid=12675

right-to-work laws laws that make it illegal to require employees to join a union

union shops businesses that require employees to join a union

formed the States' Rights, or Dixiecrat, Party and nominated South Carolina governor Strom Thurmond for president under the slogan "Segregation Forever!" Liberal Democrats, frustrated by Truman's ineffective domestic policies and critical of his anti-Soviet foreign policy, formed a new Progressive Party, choosing Henry A. Wallace as their presidential candidate. Besides these two new challengers, Truman faced his Republican opponent, New York governor Thomas Dewey, who seemed unbeatable.

Truman remained confident of re-election, however. He traveled more than 20,000 miles by train and made more than 200 speeches. He attacked the majority Republican Congress as "do-nothing, good-for-nothing" for refusing to enact his legislative agenda. However, his attacks were not entirely accurate. The "Do-Nothing Congress" had passed his aid program to Greece and Turkey and the Marshall Plan. Congress had created the Department of Defense, the National Security Council, and the CIA. It had permanently established the Joint Chiefs of Staff and set up the air force as an independent branch of the military. It also had passed the Twenty-second Amendment, which limited a president to two terms in office. But because Congress's actions were in areas that did not affect most Americans directly, Truman's charges began to stick. Supported by laborers, African Americans, and farmers, Truman won a narrow but stunning victory over Dewey. In addition, the Democratic Party regained control of both houses of Congress.

The Fair Deal

Truman repeated his previous domestic agenda in his 1949 State of the Union address.

66 As we look around the country, many of our shortcomings stand out. . . . Our minimum wages are far too low. . . . Our farmers still face an uncertain future. And too many of them lack the benefits of our modern civilization. Some of our natural resources are still being wasted. We are acutely short of electric power. . . . Five million families are still living in slums and firetraps. . . . Proper medical care is so expensive that it is out of the reach of the great majority of our citizens. Our schools . . . are utterly inadequate. Our democratic ideals are often thwarted by prejudice and intolerance. . . . [E]very individual has a right to expect from our Government a fair deal. 99

–from President Truman's State of the Union address, January 5, 1949

Whether intentional or not, the president had coined a name—the Fair Deal—to set his program apart from the New Deal.

The 81st Congress did not completely support Truman's Fair Deal. Legislators did raise the legal

minimum wage to 75¢ an hour. They increased Social Security benefits by over 75 percent and extended them to 10 million additional people. Congress also passed the National Housing Act of 1949 which provided for the construction of low-income housing and for long-term rent subsidies. Congress refused, however, to pass national health insurance or to provide aid for farmers or schools.

Led by conservative Republicans and Dixiecrats, legislators also opposed Truman's civil rights legislation. When Truman first became president, Southern Democrats believed they now had someone in the White House who was sympathetic to segregation. Truman had grown up in segregated Missouri, and both sets of his grandparents had been slaveholders. Although not without prejudice, Truman also believed in fairness and in his duty as president. He was moved by stories of African American soldiers being beaten upon their return from the war. Urged on by African American voters and civil rights leaders, Truman decided to take a stand.

On December 5, 1946, Truman signed an executive order creating the President's Committee on Civil Rights to investigate mob violence and propose civil rights legislation. The committee's 1947 report outlined discrimination in housing, public accommodations, education, and voting rights. That same year Truman became the first president to address the NAACP. In his speech he declared that all Americans should have equal opportunities. Although his proposals to abolish poll taxes, protect African Americans' right to vote, and make lynching a federal crime were stalled by Congress, Truman nonetheless laid the foundation for future legislation through his executive orders barring discrimination in federal employment and ending segregation in the armed forces.

✓ CHECK FOR UNDERSTANDING

1. **Summarizing** How did the GI Bill affect the postwar economy?

2. **Making Connections** How did President Truman seek to continue the New Deal goals?

The Eisenhower White House

GUIDING QUESTION

How did Eisenhower's presidency signal a more conservative direction for government?

In 1950 the United States went to war in Korea. The war consumed the nation's attention and resources, ending Truman's Fair Deal. By 1952, with the war at a bloody stalemate and his approval rating dropping quickly, Truman decided not to run for reelection. With

Truman, Harry S. 1949. Annual Message to the Congress on the State of the Union, January 5, 1949. National Archives and Records Administration. Harry S. Truman Library, Independence, Missouri.

no Democratic incumbent to face, Republicans pinned their hopes on a popular World War II hero: Dwight Eisenhower, former commander of the Allied Forces in Europe. The Democrats nominated Illinois governor Adlai Stevenson.

The Republicans adopted the slogan "It's time for a change!" The warm and friendly Eisenhower, known as "Ike," promised to end the war in Korea. "I like Ike" became the Republican rallying cry. Eisenhower won the election in a landslide. The Republicans also gained an eight-seat majority in the House, and a one vote majority in the Senate.

Eisenhower's "Dynamic Conservatism"

President Eisenhower had two favorite phrases. "Middle of the road" described his political beliefs, and **"dynamic conservatism"** meant balancing economic conservatism with activism that would benefit the country. Under the guidance of a cabinet filled with business leaders, Eisenhower ended government price and rent controls. Many conservatives viewed these as unnecessary federal regulations of the economy. Eisenhower's administration believed business growth was vital to the nation. His secretary of defense, the former president of General Motors, declared that "what is good for our country is good for General Motors, and vice versa."

Eisenhower believed that the federal government risked the future of American democracy when it spent more than it took in. Thus, he balanced the federal budget three times during his presidency by cutting federal spending.

To cut federal spending, Eisenhower vetoed a school construction bill and agreed to slash aid to public housing. He also targeted aid to businesses, or what he called "creeping socialism." Shortly after taking office, he abolished the Reconstruction Finance Corporation (RFC), which loaned money to banks, railroads, and other large institutions in financial trouble. Another agency, the Tennessee Valley Authority (TVA), also came under Eisenhower's scrutiny. During his presidency, federal spending for the TVA fell from $185 million to $12 million. Eisenhower also endorsed some modest tax cuts.

The president even supported cutting military spending, believing that it took money away from more worthy causes. As the stockpiles of atomic weapons increased, Eisenhower pushed for the peaceful use of atomic energy. He expressed this view in his "Atoms for Peace" speech to the United Nations:

66 The United States knows that if the fearful trend of atomic military build-up can be reversed, this greatest of destructive forces can be

developed into a great boon, for the benefit of all mankind. The United States knows that peaceful power from atomic energy is no dream of the future. That capability, already proved, is here—now—today. **99**

–from President Eisenhower's speech before the United Nations, December 8, 1953

In some areas of domestic policy Eisenhower took an activist role. He especially pushed for two large government projects. As more Americans owned cars, the need for better roads increased. In 1956 Congress passed the Federal Highway Act, the largest public works program in American history. The act provided for a $25 billion, 10-year project to create an Interstate Highway System (IHS) of more than 40,000 miles (64,400 km) of roads. Congress also authorized the construction of the St. Lawrence Seaway. This project included building a series of locks along the St. Lawrence River that would allow ships to travel from the Great Lakes to the Atlantic Ocean. The three previous administrations had failed to accomplish this feat because of differences with Canada over the waterway.

In 1955 Congress passed the Air Pollution Control Act to help investigate and control air pollution, though the primary responsibility of enforcement would fall to the states. States were also investing in projects during this era. The GI Bill had driven growth in higher education. In 1960 California passed its Master Plan for Higher Education, which was intended to help make higher education available to all Californians despite their economic means. High-performing high school graduates were guaranteed tuition-free enrollment at a University of California campus. The state's community colleges were also made more available to other high school graduates, and upon graduation, they could transfer to the university system to complete their bachelor's degree requirements.

Extending Social Security

Despite cutting federal spending and attempting to limit the government's role in the economy, President Eisenhower agreed to extend the Social Security system to an additional 10 million people. He also supported extending unemployment payments to 4 million more citizens. Eisenhower even agreed to raise the minimum wage and to continue to provide some government aid to farmers.

By the time Eisenhower ran for a second term in 1956, the nation had successfully shifted back to a peacetime economy. The battles between liberals and conservatives over whether to continue New Deal policies would continue. In the meantime, most

"dynamic conservatism" an approach that involves balancing economic conservatism with more radical changes in other areas

(1)U.S. Senate Armed Services Committee. Nominations : hearings, 83d Congress, 1st session, on nominee designates. Washington, D.C., 1953. (Y 4.AR 5/3:N 72/2/); (2)Eisenhower, Dwight D. "Text of the Address Delivered by the President of the United States Before the General Assembly of the United Nations in New York City Tuesday Afternoon, December 8, 1953."

Americans focused their energy on enjoying what had become a decade of tremendous prosperity.

✓ CHECK FOR UNDERSTANDING

Determining Central Ideas How did Eisenhower's presidency signal a more conservative direction for the government?

America's Postwar Abundance

GUIDING QUESTION

How did the lives of Americans change after World War II?

After World War II, the postwar economy grew and allowed Americans to spend much more than they could spend after World War I. Between 1940 and 1955, the average income of U.S. families roughly tripled. People in all income brackets experienced a rapid rise in income. New business techniques and technology enabled the production of abundant goods and services, dramatically raising the U.S. standard of living. With more disposable income than ever, Americans began spending on new consumer goods. Advertising helped fuel the spending spree and became the country's fastest-growing industry. Manufacturers employed new, carefully planned marketing techniques to prompt consumer demand for their products.

Suburban Growth

Advertisers targeted wealthy consumers, many of whom lived in new mass-produced suburbs that developed around cities in the 1950s. Levittown, New York, was one of the earliest of the mass-produced suburbs with hundreds of simple, similar-looking homes built 10 miles east of New York City. Between 1947 and 1951, families rushed to buy the homes that some considered to be comparatively inexpensive. Similar suburbs were duplicated throughout the nation. The suburban population doubled, while the population of cities rose only 10 percent.

The GI Bill and the government's decision to give income tax deductions for mortgage and property tax payments made home ownership more attractive than ever. In addition to the economic incentives for moving to the suburbs, many white Americans sought to flee more racially diverse neighborhoods in cities for predominantly white suburbs, often citing reasons such as crime and city congestion to justify the moves. Others were drawn by the better living conditions and financial aid, like the GI Bill, that both made the suburbs more affordable for white homeowners and unobtainable for African Americans.

While suburban living appealed to many, African Americans encountered discrimination when they tried to buy houses in the suburbs. Many of these communities were funded through guaranteed bank loans from the FHA on the condition that no homes be sold to African Americans and that every deed have a clause prohibiting resale to African Americans—a practice referred to as redlining. At the same time urban neighborhoods that were mostly home to African Americans were demolished to make way for newly constructed interstates, forcing them into increasingly smaller and more crowded communities.

The Baby Boom

The U.S. birth rate exploded after World War II. From 1946 to 1964, more than 65 million children were born in the United States. At the height of this **baby boom,** a child was born every seven seconds. Many factors contributed to the baby boom. First, young couples who had put off getting married during World War II and the Korean War could finally begin their families. Also, the government encouraged the growth of families by offering generous GI benefits for home purchases. Finally, popular culture celebrated pregnancy, parenthood, and large families.

Inner City Decline

Poverty was most apparent in the nation's urban centers. As middle-class families moved to the

Levitt & Sons built so many houses that they reportedly finished a home every 16 minutes at their peak, creating Levittowns in New York, New Jersey, and Pennsylvania.

Evaluating In what ways is the image of a Levittown an accurate depiction of 1950s America, and in what ways is it not?

baby boom a marked rise in birthrate over a certain period of time, especially during the years following World War II

Hulton Archive/Archive Photos/Getty Images

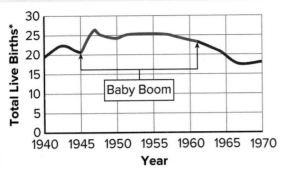

The Birthrate, 1940–1970

per 1,000 Population for 15–44 years old
Source: *Historical Statistics of the United States*

ECONOMICS CONNECTION

Speculating In which years did the greatest increase in the number of live births occur? Why might this be? What economic consequences does a society with a "baby boom" have to face when that generation reaches retirement age?

---

suburbs, those who could not afford to move or were unable to because of redlining remained in cities. Without the middle-class tax base, many city centers deteriorated and could no longer provide adequate public transportation, housing, and other services. The government often made matters worse. **Urban renewal** programs tried to eliminate poverty by tearing down slums and building new high-rises for poor residents. Yet these crowded projects did not address the issue of poverty and often created an atmosphere of violence. The government also unwittingly created a condition supporting poverty by evicting residents of public housing as soon as they began earning a higher income.

Although more than 3 million African Americans had migrated from the South to Northern cities, long-standing patterns of racial discrimination kept many of them poor. In 1958 African Americans' salaries, on average, were only 51 percent of what whites earned.

The Changing Workplace

The postwar booming economy was mainly fueled by consumer demand for manufactured goods and the increase in workers entering the middle class as a

result of labor unions. Ongoing mechanization of farms and factories meant more Americans began working in offices in what came to be called **white-collar jobs** because the mainly male employees typically wore a white dress shirt and a tie to work instead of the blue denim work shirts of factory workers and laborers. In 1956 white-collar workers outnumbered **blue-collar workers** for the first time.

The shift to white-collar jobs was partly the result of new technology and management innovations. In the 1950s, the first business computers came on the market. Payroll, billing, inventory, record-keeping, and calculations could all be done by computers. This allowed companies to consolidate clerical tasks across departments and focus on management tasks.

Many white-collar employees worked for large corporations, including **multinational corporations** that expanded overseas to be near raw materials and benefit from a cheap labor pool. The **franchise** was another corporate innovation. In a franchise, a person owns and runs one or more stores of a larger chain. Believing that consumers valued dependability and familiarity, the owners of chain operations required their franchisees to conform to a uniform look and style. Many other corporate leaders also expected conformity rather than freethinking. In his 1950 book, *The Lonely Crowd,* sociologist David Riesman argued that conformity was changing the way people valued themselves.

✓ CHECK FOR UNDERSTANDING

1. **Explaining** How did the lives of Americans change after World War II?

2. **Summarizing** How did corporations change the lives of Americans?

LESSON ACTIVITIES

1. **Argumentative Writing** Suppose that you are a member of Congress who heard Truman deliver his speech on the Fair Deal. Write a speech convincing your colleagues in Congress to pass or defeat Truman's Fair Deal measures.

2. **Collaborating** In small groups, discuss the political agendas of President Truman and President Eisenhower. How did their agendas differ? How were they similar? Based on what you know of today's society, which president had the most enduring legacy?

---

urban renewal government programs that attempt to eliminate poverty and revitalize urban areas

white-collar jobs professional office jobs

blue-collar workers workers who perform manual labor, particularly in industry

multinational corporations large corporations that operate both domestically and overseas

franchise a business given the authorization to market a company's goods or services in an area

READING STRATEGY

Analyzing Key Ideas and Details As you read, use a time line like the one below to record major events of science, technology, and popular culture during the late 1940s and 1950s.

New Science, Media, and Culture

GUIDING QUESTION

How did technological advances change society?

As the United States experienced social changes during the postwar era, it witnessed important scientific advances in electronics, aviation, and medicine. The computer age also dawned in the postwar era. In 1946 scientists developed one of the earliest computers, ENIAC (Electronic Numerical Integrator and Computer), to make military calculations. Later the UNIVAC (Universal Automatic Computer) model started the computer revolution. In 1947 three U.S. physicists developed the transistor, a tiny electric generator that made it possible to create small portable radios. Aviation progressed rapidly; aircraft designers utilized plastics and light metals, swept-back wings, and new jet engine technology to build planes that could fly farther on the same amount of fuel, making airline travel more affordable.

Medical Breakthroughs

Prior to the 1950s, there were few effective treatments for cancer and heart attacks. In the 1950s, the improved techniques of radiation treatments and chemotherapy, or the use of chemical substances to treat cancer, helped treat cancer patients and extend their years of survival. CPR, cardiopulmonary resuscitation, developed in 1950, helped many survive heart attacks. Doctors also began using artificial valves and implanted the first pacemakers in 1952.

Tuberculosis had frightened Americans for decades. Tuberculosis patients were kept isolated to prevent the spread of the highly contagious lung disease. During the 1950s, a blood test and new antibiotics helped end fears by providing a way to identify carriers of the disease and cure them of it before it spread to others. By 1956, tuberculosis was no longer among the top ten fatal diseases.

Polio is a highly infectious disease caused by a gastrointestinal virus. Polio epidemics would typically occur during the summer months, spreading quickly and disproportionately affecting children. Though many would recover from the disease, others might suffer temporary or permanent paralysis or even death. Parents frantically tried to protect their children, sometimes sending them to the country to avoid excessive contact with others. Public swimming pools and beaches were closed, and parks and playgrounds were deserted. A record 58,000 new cases were reported in 1952. Research scientist Jonas Salk developed an injectable polio vaccine that became available to the public in 1955. Researcher Albert Sabin then developed an oral polio vaccine that was safer and more convenient, making polio nearly disappear.

New Mass Media

Regular television broadcasts had begun in the early 1940s, but there were few stations and television sets were expensive. By 1957, nearly 40 million sets had been sold, and more than 80 percent of families owned at least one TV.

Between 1951 and 1957, Lucille Ball and her husband, Desi Arnaz, starred in one of television's most popular shows ever, a comedy called *I Love Lucy*. One episode attracted an audience of 44 million viewers—more than the audience for the presidential inauguration the following day. Many early comedy shows, such as those starring Bob Hope and Jack Benny, were adapted from radio

Little Richard's unique vocalizations, showmanship, and frenetic piano playing made him an instant hit in the mid-1950s.

audiences in with technology like CinemaScope, and the studios quickly won over large European audiences. Hollywood began playing an important role in spreading American culture globally.

Rock 'n' Roll

In 1951 at a record store in downtown Cleveland, Ohio, radio disc jockey Alan Freed asked his station manager to play more African American rhythm-and-blues music. Freed argued that teenagers were purchasing these records in local music stores and that his station could benefit from the growing mainstream popularity. A new generation of white and African American musicians created an original style of music termed **rock 'n' roll**, combining influences from blues, soul, and country music. With an accentuated beat that made it ideal for dancing and lyrics about themes that appealed to young people, rock 'n' roll became wildly popular. Teens bought recordings from artists such as Buddy Holly and Chuck Berry. In 1956 teenagers found their first rock 'n' roll hero in Elvis Presley.

Presley owed his popularity as much to his moves as to his music, dancing and swinging his hips during his performances in ways that shocked older people. Many adults condemned rock 'n' roll as loud, mindless, and dangerous. The rock 'n' roll hits that teens bought in record numbers united them in a world their parents did not share. Chuck Berry, Little Richard, and Ray Charles all recorded hit songs.

The same era also saw the rise of several female African American groups, including the Shirelles and the Ronettes. The music of these early rock 'n' roll artists profoundly influenced popular music around the world. The Beatles recorded their own versions of several African American-written rock 'n' roll songs during their rise to global fame. But unlike white entertainers, African American entertainers did not quickly find a wide audience in the U.S. With a few exceptions, television tended to shut them out.

The Beat Movement

A group of writers and artists who called themselves *beats*, or *beatniks*, highlighted a values gap in 1950s America. Beat poets, writers, and artists criticized American culture for its sterility, conformity, sexual repression, and emptiness. In 1956 29-year-old poet Allen Ginsberg published a long poem titled "Howl" blasting American life.

The culture of the beat movement, which had started in the bohemian culture of San Francisco, allowed artists such as Ginsberg to be open with their sexual identities. Beat author Jack Kerouac's book *On the Road* (1957), about his freewheeling adventures with a car thief and con artist, shocked some readers.

programs. Variety shows like Ed Sullivan's *Toast of the Town* provided a mix of comedy, music, dance, and acrobatics. Quiz shows and westerns grew quickly in popularity. Viewers also enjoyed police shows, and television news and sports broadcasts became popular.

Prior to television, radio programs provided comedy, drama, and soap operas, but television made these programs obsolete. Radio stations responded by broadcasting music, news, weather, sports, and talk shows. Radio had one audience that television could not reach—people traveling in their cars. People commuting from the suburbs, running errands, or traveling on long road trips relied on radio for news and entertainment. As a result, the number of radio stations more than doubled between 1948 and 1957.

Hollywood Adapts

As television's popularity grew, movies lost viewers. Attendance plunged from 82 million in 1946 to 36 million by 1950. By 1960, one-fifth of the nation's movie theaters had closed. Hollywood used contests, door prizes, and advertising to attract audiences, but failed. Hollywood tried 3-D movies, but viewers tired of the silly plots and the special necessary glasses. CinemaScope—a process that showed movies on large, panoramic screens—finally gave Hollywood something television could not match. Full-color spectacles like *Around the World in 80 Days* were expensive, but drew huge audiences and profits.

As television spread in Europe, it cost European movie studios their audiences, just as it had American movie studios. But because television had spread across the United States sooner than Europe, the Hollywood studios had already adapted by drawing

rock 'n' roll popular music characterized by a persistent, heavily accented beat and simple melodies

Michael Ochs Archives/Getty Images

Although the beat movement was small, it laid the foundations for the widespread cultural rebellion of 1960s youth.

✓ **CHECK FOR UNDERSTANDING**

1. **Explaining** How did technological advances change society?

2. **Identifying** How did television help spread American culture?

Kennedy's New Frontier

GUIDING QUESTION

What were some domestic policies initiated when Kennedy took office?

On September 26, 1960, an estimated 75 million people sat indoors watching the first televised presidential debate, marking a new era of politics.

During the 1960 presidential race, both parties made substantial use of television. The Democrats spent more than $6 million on television and radio spots, while the Republicans spent more than $7.5 million. Television news commentator Eric Sevareid complained that the candidates had become "packaged products." He declared that the "Processed Politician has finally arrived."

The candidates differed in many ways. John F. Kennedy, the Democratic nominee and a senator, appeared outgoing and relaxed. Richard M. Nixon, the Republican nominee and current vice president, struck many as formal and stiff. Although the candidates presented different styles, they differed little on key issues. Both promised to boost the economy, and both portrayed themselves as "Cold Warriors," determined to stop the forces of Communism. Kennedy expressed concern about a suspected **"missile gap,"** claiming the United States lagged behind the Soviets in weaponry, although he knew that was untrue. Nixon warned that the Democrats' fiscal policies would boost inflation and only he had the foreign policy experience needed for the nation.

The series of four televised debates influenced the election's close outcome. Kennedy won the popular vote by 118,574 out of more than 68 million votes cast and the Electoral College by 303 votes to 219. Despite his narrow victory, Kennedy captured the imagination of the American public with his youth and optimism.

Kennedy Takes Office

Kennedy's agenda was called the New Frontier. He hoped to increase aid to education, provide health insurance to the elderly, and create a Department of Urban Affairs. This was no easy task. Although the Democrats had majorities in both houses of Congress, Kennedy was unable to push through many of his programs. His candidacy, which led to only a narrow victory, had not helped elect many Democrats, and those who won felt that they owed him nothing. In addition, conservative Southern Democrats—a large part of the Democrats—saw Kennedy's program as too expensive and, together with Republicans, defeated many of his proposals.

Kennedy achieved some victories, particularly in improving the economy. Although the economy had soared through much of the 1950s, it had slowed by

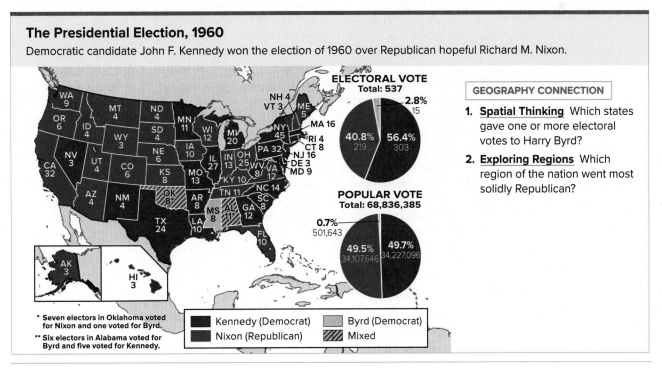

The Presidential Election, 1960

Democratic candidate John F. Kennedy won the election of 1960 over Republican hopeful Richard M. Nixon.

ELECTORAL VOTE
Total: 537
2.8% 15
40.8% 219
56.4% 303

POPULAR VOTE
Total: 68,836,385
0.7% 501,643
49.5% 34,107,646
49.7% 34,227,096

GEOGRAPHY CONNECTION

1. **Spatial Thinking** Which states gave one or more electoral votes to Harry Byrd?

2. **Exploring Regions** Which region of the nation went most solidly Republican?

* Seven electors in Oklahoma voted for Nixon and one voted for Byrd.

** Six electors in Alabama voted for Byrd and five voted for Kennedy.

Kennedy (Democrat) Byrd (Democrat)
Nixon (Republican) Mixed

Sevareid, Eric, in Patterson, James T. Grand Expectations. Oxford: Oxford UP, 1996.

missile gap a discrepancy between the number of missiles the Soviet Union and the United States had

The Presidential Commission on the Status of Women proposed the Equal Pay Act, which Kennedy signed in 1963 at this ceremony.

the end of the decade. To increase economic growth, Kennedy advocated deficit spending and investing more funds in defense and space exploration, which did create jobs and stimulate economic growth.

Kennedy asked businesses to hold down prices and labor leaders to hold down pay increases. The labor unions in the steel industry agreed to reduce their demands for higher wages, but several steel companies raised prices sharply. Kennedy responded by threatening to have the Department of Defense buy cheaper foreign steel. He asked the Justice Department to investigate whether the steel industry was fixing prices. The steel companies backed down and cut their prices, but the victory caused strained relations with the business community.

Kennedy also pushed for tax cuts. When opponents argued that a tax cut would help only the wealthy, Kennedy asserted that lower taxes meant businesses would have more money to expand, which would create new jobs and benefit everyone. Congress refused to pass the tax cut because of fears that it would cause inflation, and also blocked his plans for health insurance for senior citizens and federal aid to education. However, Congress did agree to raise the minimum wage, the proposal for the Area Redevelopment Act, and the Housing Act.

The Kennedy administration initiated crime control programs in urban areas as another method to fight poverty. The President's Committee on Juvenile Delinquency and Youth Crime was established in 1961 to provide low-income citizens in urban areas with basic education, job training, counseling, and other social welfare programs.

Expanding Other Rights

In 1961 Kennedy created the Presidential Commission on the Status of Women, which called for federal action against gender discrimination and affirmed women's

right to equally paid employment. Kennedy never appointed a woman to his cabinet, but a number of women worked in prominent positions in the administration, including Esther Peterson, assistant secretary of labor and director of the Women's Bureau of the Department of Labor.

In 1961 Kennedy convened the President's Panel on Mental Retardation. Though the term *mental retardation* was considered acceptable at the time, terms such as *intellectual disability* are now preferred. Kennedy created the panel in response to his own sister's disability, which resulted from a lobotomy she received to cure her mood swings. The panel's first report called for funding of research into developmental disabilities, and educational and vocational programs for people with developmental disabilities. It also called for a greater reliance on residential, rather than institutional, treatment centers.

Responding to the report, Congress enacted the Mental Retardation Facilities and Community Mental Health Centers Construction Act of 1963. This legislation provided grants to build research centers and helped states construct mental health centers. It also provided funds to train personnel to work with people with developmental disabilities. In 1962 Eunice Kennedy Shriver, the president's sister, began a day camp at her home for children with developmental disabilities. Camp Shriver offered people with disabilities a chance to be physically competitive. The effort later grew into the Special Olympics. The first Special Olympics Games were held in Chicago in 1968.

Warren Court Reforms

In 1953 Earl Warren, the former governor of California, became chief justice of the United States. Under Chief Justice Warren's leadership, the Supreme Court issued several rulings that dramatically reshaped American politics and society for decades to come.

Some of the Court's more notable decisions concerned **reapportionment.** By 1960, more Americans resided in urban than in rural areas, but many states' electoral districts did not reflect this shift. Thus, rural voters often had far more political influence than urban ones. In *Baker* v. *Carr* (1962) the Supreme Court ruled that federal courts had jurisdiction to hear lawsuits seeking to force states to redraw electoral districts. In *Reynolds* v. *Sims* (1964) the Court ruled that states must reapportion electoral districts along the principle of "one person, one vote," so that all citizens' votes would have equal weight. The decision shifted political power from rural areas to urban areas, boosting the political power of urban residents—which included many African Americans and Latinos.

The Supreme Court began to use the Fourteenth Amendment to extend the Bill of Rights to the states rather than only to the federal government. The

reapportionment the establishment of electoral districts based on their populations

UPI/Newscom.

Fourteenth Amendment states "no state shall . . . deprive any person of life, liberty, or property without **due process** of law," meaning that the law may not treat individuals unfairly, arbitrarily, or unreasonably. In 1961 the Supreme Court ruled in *Mapp* v. *Ohio* that state courts could not consider evidence obtained in violation of the Constitution. In *Gideon* v. *Wainwright* (1963), the Court ruled that a defendant in a state court had the right to a lawyer, regardless of his or her ability to pay. In *Escobedo* v. *Illinois* (1964), the Court ruled that suspects must be allowed access to a lawyer and be informed of their right to remain silent before being questioned. *Miranda* v. *Arizona* (1966) required authorities to inform suspects of their right to remain silent, that anything they say can and will be used against them in court, and that they have a right to a lawyer. These warnings are known as Miranda rights.

The Warren Court reaffirmed the separation of church and state in two cases. The Court applied the First Amendment in *Engel* v. *Vitale* (1962), ruling that states could not compose official prayers and require those prayers to be recited in public schools. In *Abington School District* v. *Schempp* (1963), the Court ruled against state-mandated Bible readings in public schools. The Court ruled in *Griswold* v. *Connecticut* (1965) that prohibiting the sale and use of birth control devices violated citizens' constitutional right to privacy.

Kennedy's Assassination

John F. Kennedy's presidency ended shockingly. On November 22, 1963, during a presidential visit in Dallas, Texas, the president was shot. He was sped to a nearby hospital but was pronounced dead at 1 p.m.

Lee Harvey Oswald, the man accused of killing Kennedy, appeared to be an embittered Marxist who had spent time in the Soviet Union. In a bizarre twist, Oswald was shot to death while in police custody two days after Kennedy's assassination. The extraordinary situation led some to speculate that Oswald's killer, a nightclub owner named Jack Ruby, killed Oswald to protect others involved in the crime. In 1964 a national commission headed by Chief Justice Warren concluded that Oswald was the lone assassin. The Warren Commission report, however, left some questions unanswered, in part because many of the investigative documents were sealed and not disclosed to the public. The last of these sealed government papers was not made public until October 2017. Kennedy had been president for little more than 1,000 days, yet he had made a profound impression on most Americans. Kennedy's successor, Vice President Lyndon Baines Johnson, set out to promote many of the programs that Kennedy left unfinished.

Just hours after President Kennedy had been pronounced dead, Lyndon B. Johnson took the oath of office in the cabin of *Air Force One*. Days later, Johnson appeared before Congress and urged the nation to build on Kennedy's legacy. Although the nation was booming, not all Americans shared in its prosperity. In his 1962 book, *The Other America*, Michael Harrington claimed that almost 50 million poor Americans lived largely hidden in slums, Appalachia, the Deep South, and Native American reservations.

Johnson decided to launch an antipoverty crusade. He was born and raised in the impoverished "hill country" of central Texas, near the banks of the Pedernales River. Johnson remained a Texan at heart, and his style posed a striking contrast with Kennedy's. He was a man of impressive stature who spoke directly, convincingly, and even roughly at times. He earned a reputation as a man who got things done. He did favors, twisted arms, bargained, flattered, and threatened in order to find consensus, or general agreement. His ability to build coalitions had made him one of the most effective and powerful leaders in Senate history.

Why was Johnson concerned about the poor? He had known hard times growing up and had seen extreme poverty firsthand in a brief career as a teacher in a low-income area. He also believed that a wealthy, powerful government should try to improve the lives of its citizens. Finally, there was his legacy. He wanted history to portray him as a great president who vastly improved his fellow Americans' lives.

☑ CHECK FOR UNDERSTANDING

1. **Summarizing** What were some domestic policies Kennedy initiated when he took office?
2. **Evaluating** How significant are some of the Warren Court rulings for today's society?

Poverty Amid Prosperity

GUIDING QUESTION

Which groups of the population did not experience the rising abundance of this postwar period?

The 1950s saw a large expansion of the middle class. At least one in five Americans, or about 30 million people, however, lived below the **poverty line.** Many mistakenly thought that the country's prosperity would provide for everyone. But poverty remained a significant problem in urban cities, rural areas, on Native American reservations, and across the United States.

Hispanic and Native American Poverty

Much of the nation's Hispanic population struggled with poverty. Nearly 5 million Mexicans had come to the United States through the Bracero Program to work on

US Const. Amend XIV, § 1., https://www.archives.gov/founding-docs/amendments-11-27.

due process the following of procedures established by law

poverty line a minimum level of income needed to support a family

farms and ranches in the Southwest. Braceros worked long hours in difficult conditions, including poor access to food, substandard housing, prejudice and discrimination, physical mistreatment, exposure to pesticides, and unsatisfactory earnings. Some 350,000 settled permanently in the United States; others returned home. In 1953 nearly a million former Braceros were forcibly rounded up and deported by the U.S. government through a program officially named "Operation Wetback" (*wetback* is a pejorative and offensive term for Mexicans living in the United States), sometimes legally and other times without authorization.

By the 1950s, Native Americans were the poorest ethnic group in the nation. The U.S. government launched a program to bring Native Americans into mainstream society. Under the Termination Policy of 1953, the federal government withdrew all official recognition of the Native American groups as legal entities and made them subject to the same laws as citizens. Another program encouraged Native Americans to relocate from their reservations to cities.

For many Native Americans, relocation was a disaster. For example in the mid-1950s, the Welfare Council of Minneapolis said of Native American living conditions: "One Indian family of five or six, living in two rooms, will take in relatives and friends who come from the reservations seeking jobs until perhaps fifteen people will be crowded into the space." During the 1950s, Native Americans in Minneapolis could expect to live only 37 years compared to 68 years for other Minneapolis residents.

Appalachia and the War on Poverty

Far from urban areas, the poverty-stricken mountainous region of Appalachia, stretching from New York to Georgia, was often overlooked. Coal mining, long the backbone of the Appalachian economy, mechanized in the 1950s, causing soaring unemployment. Some 1.5 million people left Appalachia to seek better lives in cities. Appalachia had fewer doctors than the rest of the country, and rates of nutritional deficiency and infant mortality were high. Because of the area's poverty, education also suffered.

President Johnson, who shared President Kennedy's desire to address the economic and social inequalities in the United States, wanted to expand his predecessor's goals. Before his death, Kennedy had plans for an anti-poverty program and a civil rights bill. Continuing these efforts seemed logical to Johnson, who knew that any program linked to the slain president would be popular. By the summer of 1964, Johnson had convinced Congress to pass the Economic Opportunity Act, which attacked inadequate public services, illiteracy, and unemployment. The act established 10 new programs within a new agency, the Office of Economic Opportunity (OEO). Many of the programs were directed at young, inner-city Americans.

This 1964 photograph shows the living conditions of a family in Appalachia. The region was hit by devastating poverty after the decline of coal mining in the area.

The Neighborhood Youth Corps provided work-study programs to help the underprivileged earn a high school diploma or college degree. The Job Corps helped unemployed people ages 16–21 acquire job skills. The VISTA (Volunteers in Service to America) acted like a domestic Peace Corps, putting young people with skills and community-minded ideals to work in poor neighborhoods and rural areas to help people overcome poverty. Additional programs included Upward Bound, which offered tutoring to high school students, and a work experience program, which provided daycare and other kinds of support for those in poor households so they could work.

The Great Society

Johnson began working with Congress to create the "Great Society" he had promised during his campaign. His goals reflected the times. The civil rights movement had brought racial inequalities to the forefront, and the strong economy encouraged people to believe that poverty could be reduced. Johnson noted the Great Society's goals, aiming not to confine government efforts but to form a society "where the city of man serves not only the needs of the body and the demands of commerce but the desire for beauty and the hunger for community," during a speech in May 1964.

Johnson's vision encompassed more than 60 programs initiated between 1965 and 1968, including Medicare and Medicaid. Medicare had strong support because it was offered to all senior citizens, about half of whom lacked health insurance. Medicare's twin program, Medicaid, financed health care for welfare recipients living below the poverty line. Great Society programs also strongly supported education. The Elementary and Secondary Education Act of 1965 granted millions of dollars to public and private schools.

PHOTO: Time Life Pictures/Getty Images; TEXT: (l)"Indian Affairs - Report - The Minnesota Indian in Minneapolis 1956", Box 121, Folder 1, United Way of Minneapolis Records, Social Welfare History Archives, University of Minnesota; (r)President Lyndon B. Johnson's Remarks at the University of Michigan, May 22, 1964. , Public Papers of the Presidents of the United States: Lyndon B. Johnson, 1963-64. Volume I, entry 357, pp. 704-707. Washington, D. C.: Government Printing Office, 1965.

Education efforts were extended to disadvantaged preschoolers through Project Head Start.

Johnson also urged Congress to act on several pieces of legislation addressing urban issues. One created a new cabinet agency, the Department of Housing and Urban Development (HUD), in 1965. Its first secretary, Robert Weaver, was the first African American to serve in the cabinet. HUD aimed at improving urban centers and investigated reports of housing discrimination. A program known as "Model Cities" authorized federal subsidies to improve cities' transportation, health care, housing, and policing.

This era saw the creation of several environmental regulations. The 1963 Clean Air Act was passed in 1963 to control and improve air quality. In 1965 Congress passed both the Solid Waste Disposal Act to improve waste disposal and protect human and environmental health and the Water Quality Act to protect and maintain waterways. In 1967 an Air Quality Act expanded the 1955 version, giving the government more authority to study pollution.

The Immigration and Naturalization Act of 1965 ended the quota system from the 1920s that preferred Northern European immigrants and replaced it with a system that reunited families and attracted skilled immigrants from Europe, Asia, and Africa.

✓ CHECK FOR UNDERSTANDING

1. **Explaining** What was the intention behind the termination policy?
2. **Identifying** What types of improvements to cities were developed under the Johnson Administration?

Economic Crisis of the 1970s

GUIDING QUESTION

What economic conditions or problems led to a stagnant economy during the 1970s?

After World War II, American prosperity relied on easy access to global raw materials and a strong manufacturing base at home. In the 1970s, however, prosperity gave way to a decade of hard times.

The Economy Slows

Economic troubles began in the mid-1960s. President Johnson increased deficit spending to fund the Vietnam War and the Great Society without raising taxes. By the 1970s, this caused rapid inflation.

Rising oil prices dealt another blow. By 1970 the United States had become dependent on imported oil. In 1973 the Arab members of the Organization of the Petroleum Exporting Countries (OPEC) used oil as a political weapon when war erupted between Israel and its Arab neighbors. Arab members announced an embargo, or trade ban, on petroleum to countries that supported Israel, and they raised the price of crude oil by up to 130 percent. After the embargo ended, oil prices continued rising. Americans had less money for other goods, which contributed to a recession.

Stagnation

Declining manufacturing was another economic problem. In 1971 the nation imported more than it exported for the first time since 1889. Factories closed, and millions of workers lost their jobs. In the early 1970s President Nixon thus faced a new economic problem called "**stagflation,**" or inflation, high unemployment, and a stagnant economy. Because some economists believed inflation could only occur when demand for goods was high, they were not sure what policy the government should follow to fight inflation and the recession. The government tried to cut spending and raise taxes and interest rates. When these methods failed, Nixon ended the gold standard.

As part of the Bretton Woods system, the U.S. dollar was made convertible to gold at the rate of 35 dollars for one ounce of gold. Other world currencies were then pegged to the U.S. dollar at agreed upon exchange rates. The United States maintained gold reserves equal to the amount of currency in circulation. At any time, people who wanted to convert their dollars into gold could do so. The problem with the system was that it limited monetary policy. If the country wanted to circulate more money, it had to make sure there was an equivalent amount of gold in reserve. When inflation began in the late 1960s, which caused the U.S. dollar to be worth less, many believed foreign nations were gouging Americans, or charging them high, unfair prices. OPEC seemed to be an example of this. If the value of the U.S. dollar increased, however, the cost of imported goods would fall.

No major trading partner of the United States wanted to change its exchange rate. Americans were buying lots of imported goods, and foreign countries were earning a lot of U.S. dollars that they could convert to gold. In response, Nixon announced that dollars could no longer be redeemed for gold. The president also imposed a 90-day freeze on wages and prices to prevent the end of the gold standard from increasing inflation. Nixon's actions became known as the New Economic Policy, or the Nixon Shock. The plan was supposed to be temporary, to force other countries to renegotiate their exchange rates. By early 1973, the system had collapsed, and the gold standard came to an end. The country moved to a true fiat currency in which money has value because the government says it does, and people accept it for payment.

---

stagflation high inflation and unemployment combined with stagnant consumer demand

Inflation and Unemployment Rates

President Ford failed to solve the nation's lingering economic problems.

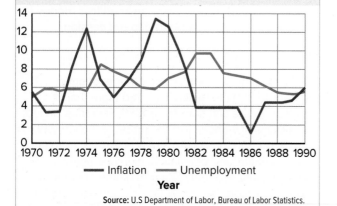

Source: U.S Department of Labor, Bureau of Labor Statistics.

ECONOMICS CONNECTION

1. **Interpreting** What was the trend for both unemployment and inflation in the late 1970s?
2. **Speculating** What effect do you think inflation and unemployment had on Ford's 1976 presidential bid?

Because it was no longer tied to gold, the dollar began to "float" or rise and fall in value compared to other nations' currencies. The end of the gold standard gave the Federal Reserve the ability to use monetary policy without many limitations. It could now freely pump money into the economy to help overcome recessions or slow the expansion of the money supply to control inflation. But critics have argued that it makes the international economy less stable, encourages deficit spending, and has led to sudden swings in the world's stock markets.

Ford's and Carter's Economic Crisis

When Nixon resigned in 1974, inflation was still high, and the unemployment rate was over 5 percent. It would now be up to the new president, Gerald Ford, to confront stagflation. By 1975, unemployment had risen to nearly 9 percent. Ford launched a plan called WIN—"Whip Inflation Now"—but it had little impact on the economic situation. He tried other measures to reduce inflation, but these plans also failed.

The 1976 presidential race pitted Ford against former Georgia governor Jimmy Carter, who had no experience in Washington. Carter ran as an outsider promising to restore honesty to the federal government and create or reform several domestic programs. Carter's moral and upstanding image attracted voters, and he narrowly defeated Ford.

Carter tried to end the recession by increasing government spending and cutting taxes. Then he tried to ease inflation by reducing the money supply and raising interest rates. These measures did not work. Carter believed the nation's most serious economic problem was its dependence on foreign oil, so he asked Americans to fight against rising energy consumption. He also proposed a national energy program to conserve oil and to promote the use of coal and renewable energy sources. Carter even convinced Congress to create a Department of Energy. Some argued that Carter should deregulate the domestic oil industry to decrease dependence on imported oil. Carter supported **deregulation** but called for a tax to prevent overcharging consumers.

In the summer of 1979, instability in the Middle East produced a second major fuel shortage. Carter warned about a "crisis of confidence":

> 66 The erosion of our confidence in the future is threatening to destroy the social and the political fabric of America. The confidence that we have always had as a people is not simply some romantic dream or a proverb in a dusty book that we read just on the Fourth of July. It is the idea which founded our nation and has guided our development as a people. 99

–from the "Crisis of Confidence" speech, July 15, 1979

The address became known as the "malaise" speech. Americans felt that Carter was blaming them for his failures. Carter's economic difficulties lay partly in his inexperience and inability to work with Congress. He had difficulty working with legislative leaders, and many of his energy proposals failed. By 1979, polls showed that Carter's popularity had dropped.

✓ **CHECK FOR UNDERSTANDING**

1. **Summarizing** How did President Carter try to change the domestic oil industry?
2. **Identifying Cause and Effect** How did the economic crisis have both a positive and a negative effect on Jimmy Carter's political fortunes?

LESSON ACTIVITIES

1. **Informative/Explanatory Writing** Write a short essay in which you analyze efforts to extend New Deal goals through the Great Society and evaluate the successes and failures of those efforts.

2. **Presenting** Work in a group to create a multimedia presentation describing the causes of economic problems in the 1970s, including both long-term and short-term causes in your presentation. Illustrate your points using images, music, movie clips, or animations.

---

deregulation the act or process of removing restrictions or regulations

Carter, James. "Crisis of Confidence Speech." July 15, 1979. Public Papers of the Presidents of the United States: Jimmy Carter, 1979. Bk. II. Washington: United States Government Printing Office, 1980.

05

Turning Point: The Warren Court

? COMPELLING QUESTION

How did Warren Court rulings change a person's legal protections?

Plan Your Inquiry

In this lesson, you will investigate the effects of landmark rulings made by the U.S. Supreme Court under the leadership of Chief Justice Earl Warren, from 1953 to 1969.

DEVELOP QUESTIONS

Developing Questions About the Warren Court Read the Compelling Question for this lesson. Think about the cases the Warren Court decided and the precedents they set. Develop a list of Supporting Questions that would help you answer the Compelling Question in this lesson.

APPLY HISTORICAL TOOLS

Analyzing Primary and Secondary Sources You will work with a variety of primary and secondary sources in this lesson. These sources focus on the decisions and legacy of the Warren Court. As you read, use a graphic organizer like the one below to record information about the sources that will help you examine them and check for historical understanding. Note ways in which each source helps you answer your Supporting Questions.

Source	Author/ Creator	Description/ Notes	Which Supporting Question does this source help me answer?

After you analyze the sources, you will:
- use the evidence from the sources.
- communicate your conclusions.
- take informed action.

Background Information

In March 1954 the U.S. Senate confirmed President Dwight D. Eisenhower's appointment of Earl Warren as Chief Justice of the U.S. Supreme Court. Warren held the position until his retirement in June 1969. During that time, the Court, made up of nine justices, decided some of the most politically charged and precedent-setting cases in the nation's history. In at least one case, *Brown* v. *Board of Education of Topeka, Kansas*, the Court overturned precedent.

The Court not only decided key questions on segregation, racial equality, and civil rights laws but also issued rulings on other cases involving personal liberties. Among these were apportionment of representation; criminal justice protections, including due process; personal privacy; and the freedom of religion and separation of church and state. These cases dealt with fundamental freedoms and represented a major shift from earlier courts.

Conservative critics accused Warren and the other liberal justices of "judicial activism," or using their positions to redefine constitutional law according to their political leanings. Supporters countered that the Court was finally taking steps to uphold constitutional rights and protections against decades of ill-conceived and unjustly applied state and federal laws. In this inquiry, you will study primary and secondary sources about some of the Warren Court's landmark cases and decide for yourself what impact they had.

» Beginning in the mid-1950s, the U.S. Supreme Court under the leadership of Chief Justice Earl Warren made a series of critical decisions that reshaped American life.

Bettmann/Getty Images

Engel v. Vitale

In 1959 parents in New York challenged a state law requiring the recitation of a specific prayer at the start of each school day. Steven Engel led the suit against the local school board's president, William Vitale. The First Amendment protects both the freedom of religious worship as well as the separation of church and state, known as the Establishment Clause. The Court ruled 6-1 in favor of the parents.

PRIMARY SOURCE : COURT RULING

66 We think that by using its public school system to encourage recitation of the Regents' prayer, the State of New York has adopted a practice wholly inconsistent with the Establishment Clause. . . . The nature of such a prayer has always been religious, none of the respondents has denied this . . .

The petitioners contend among other things that the state laws requiring or permitting use of the Regents' prayer must be struck down as a violation of the Establishment Clause because that prayer was composed by governmental officials as a part of a governmental program to further religious beliefs. For this reason, petitioners argue, the State's use of the Regents' prayer in its public school system breaches the constitutional wall of separation between Church and State. We agree with that contention since we think that the constitutional prohibition against laws respecting an establishment of religion must at least mean that in this country it is no part of the business of government to compose official prayers for any group of the American people to recite as a part of a religious program carried on by government. . . . 99

—Justice Hugo Black, Opinion of the Court, June 25, 1962

EXAMINE THE SOURCE

1. **Explaining** Why does the Court rule that the Regents' prayer is unconstitutional?

2. **Drawing Conclusions** What type of prayer in schools might still be allowed given this ruling?

Miranda v. Arizona

In 1963 Ernesto Miranda was arrested and interrogated at length during which he was not advised of his constitutional rights and protections. He confessed to the crimes, was charged and later convicted based on that confession. The Court ruled 5-4 in a decision that established the reading of one's Miranda Rights.

PRIMARY SOURCE : COURT RULING

66 The cases before us raise questions which go to the roots of our concepts of . . . criminal **jurisprudence:** the restraints society must observe consistent with the . . . Constitution in prosecuting individuals for crime. More specifically, we deal with the admissibility of statements obtained from an individual who is subjected to custodial police interrogation and the necessity for procedures which assure that the individual is accorded his privilege under the Fifth Amendment . . . not to be compelled to incriminate himself.

We dealt with certain phases of this problem recently in *Escobedo* v. *Illinois*[.] There . . . law enforcement officials took the defendant into custody and interrogated him in a police station for the purpose of obtaining a confession. The police did not effectively advise him of his right to remain silent or of his right to consult with his attorney. Rather, they confronted him with an alleged accomplice who accused him of having perpetrated a murder. When the defendant denied the accusation . . . they handcuffed him and took him to an interrogation room. There . . . he was questioned for four hours until he confessed. During this interrogation, the police denied his request to speak to his attorney, and they prevented his retained attorney, who had come to the police station, from consulting with him. 99

—Chief Justice Earl Warren, Opinion of the Court, October 1965

jurisprudence a body of law and legal precedents

EXAMINE THE SOURCE

1. **Identifying** What rights does the ruling indicate that the police and the courts violated?

2. **Analyzing** How was this ruling intended to affect police and suspect interactions?

(1)Engel v. Vitale, 370 US 421 (1962); (2)Miranda v. Arizona, 384 U.S. 436 (1966).

C

"Some Are More Equal Than Others"

Herbert Block drew this cartoon on the issue of apportionment in 1961. Apportionment determines the geographic area and number of citizens represented by each state representative. At the time, urban areas had swelled in population. Soon after, the Warren Court decided two landmark cases on reapportionment of state electoral districts. In 1962 *Baker* v. *Carr* established that the Court could hear cases on state apportionment. In 1964 *Reynolds* v. *Sims* determined that the inequitable apportionment in Alabama violated the equal protections clause of the Fourteenth Amendment. This cartoon alludes to the novella *Animal Farm*, written by George Orwell. Published in 1945, the novella tells the story of a rebellion among farm animals seeking freedom and equality. However, the revolt backfires, and one powerful pig institutes a dictatorship.

PRIMARY SOURCE : POLITICAL CARTOON

PHOTO: Library of Congress, Prints & Photographs Division, [LC-DIG-ppmsc-03534]; Used by permission of Herb Block Foundation; TEXT: Stone, Geoffrey, and Strauss, David A. "The Legacy of the Warren Court." American Heritage. v. 64 no. 1, Winter 2020.

EXAMINE THE SOURCE

1. **Interpreting** What do the text and visual elements together say about voting?

2. **Analyzing Perspectives** How does the artist's opinion support the Court's rulings in *Baker* v. *Carr* and *Reynolds* v. *Sims*?

D

The Legacy of the Warren Court

In 1803 Chief Justice Marshall established judicial review, which affirms the Court's right to check legislative power by judging the constitutionality of laws. This article discusses the Warren Court's relationship with judicial review.

SECONDARY SOURCE : ARTICLE

66 . . . [T]he Warren Court had a vision of the role that the highest court should play in American government. But the justices of the Warren Court did not simply impose that vision on society. To the contrary, even their most controversial decisions had deep roots in American law and traditions.

Critics often portray . . . the Warren Court as judicial imperialists who took over policymaking from elected representatives. . . . The Warren Court was, in fact, . . . reluctant to strike down Acts of Congress.

Many of the Warren Court's greatest decisions did reject laws enacted by the states. But those decisions, too, reflected a deep commitment to democracy. The Warren Court acted on the premise that the role of the Supreme Court is to intervene when . . . democracy was not truly democratic: when some groups were marginalized or excluded and denied their fair share of democratic political power. . . .

The Warren Court protected political dissidents, stating unequivocally that free and open debate is a central commitment of any democratic government. In its 'one person, one vote' decisions, the Warren Court put an end to manipulative and unjustified disparities in people's ability to elect their representatives. [It] acted on behalf . . . of minority religious groups whose interests were disregarded by the majority, and of criminal defendants who were often also members of discriminated-against minority groups and who lacked any effective voice in politics. . . . 99

–Geoffrey R. Stone and David A. Strauss,
   in *American Heritage*, Winter 2020

EXAMINE THE SOURCE

Summarizing How do the authors say that the Warren Court sought to uphold the fundamental principles of democracy?

Oral History Project Interview

From 1967 to 1974, historian Joe B. Frantz served as director of the Lyndon B. Johnson Oral History Project for the University of Texas at Austin. He conducted hundreds of interviews, including this one with Chief Justice Earl Warren.

PRIMARY SOURCE : INTERVIEW

66 **Frantz:** . . . You must have felt at times terribly isolated and exposed in some of those decisions.

Warren: We did indeed. And a lot of people are of the opinion that the Supreme Court just reached out and grabbed onto those issues and decided them in opposition to Congress and so forth. But, really, all the court was doing was filling a vacuum because Congress had not acted.

Now I don't lay all that blame on Congress, because Congress had passed the Civil Rights Act and the Supreme Court had watered it down in the 19th Century, you know. And as a result there was just a great gap there from that time on until the time Lyndon Johnson came on. Up to that time we just had to deal with the bare bones of the Constitution on the question of equal protection of the laws, what the limits of that were, and due process of law; those were the two things we had to be guided by as they appeared in the 14th Amendment. But when the Voting Rights Act came along and the Public Facilities Act came along, . . . it greatly helped the Court. I was delighted to see that legislation, because then we could deal with acts of Congress, don't you see; and if we decided something that the Congress didn't like particularly, they could change their act. But when we're dealing with just the Constitution itself the relationship between the different agencies of government is thrown out of kilter. . . . 99

—Joe B. Frantz and Earl Warren, recorded September 21, 1971

EXAMINE THE SOURCE

1. **Determining Context** What "vacuum" does Warren suggest that the Supreme Court was filling?

2. **Making Inferences** What does Warren suggest changed with the election of Lyndon Johnson?

Your Inquiry Analysis

EVALUATE SOURCES AND USE EVIDENCE

Refer back to the Compelling Question and the Supporting Questions you developed at the beginning of this lesson.

1. **Gathering Sources** Refer back to the Graphic Organizer you created as you read through the sources. Which sources provide concrete facts to answer the Supporting Questions you wrote? Circle or highlight those sources in your graphic organizer. Which provide key insights and opinions that help you answer your Supporting Questions? Put a star next to these sources. Write a sentence explaining which two sources you consider the most helpful, and why. If you need more information to answer the questions, where might you look for that information?

2. **Evaluating Sources** Looking at the sources that help you answer the Supporting Questions, evaluate the credibility of each source. Write down the main idea or opinion of each source. Then list facts provided by the source to support those opinions. What prior knowledge, gained from your study of previous lessons, also supports each source's position?

3. **Comparing and Contrasting** Compare and contrast two sources. What does each suggest about the impact of the Warren Court? How do the two sources support, complement, or counter each other's perspectives?

COMMUNICATE CONCLUSIONS

Using Multimedia With a partner, answer your Supporting Questions. Then, use what you have learned to write a paragraph in response to the Compelling Question. Identify pieces of key evidence from the sources that support your response. Develop that evidence into a multimedia presentation containing four to five slides. Incorporate excerpts from the sources as well as appropriate images or video clips.

TAKE INFORMED ACTION

Applying Precedent Think about a civil rights issue in the news today, such as: laws that make it difficult for certain groups to vote, gerrymandering, access to education, discrimination against a minority group, and others. Use online or library resources to learn more about specific decisions made by the Warren Court. Then consider how one or more of those decisions could be used as a precedent to argue a position about the current issue.

Transcript, Earl Warren Oral History Interview I, 9/21/71, by Joe B. Frantz, Internet Copy, LBJ Library.

06

Analyzing Sources: The Great Society

 COMPELLING QUESTION

Why did President Johnson promote the federal Great Society effort?

Plan Your Inquiry

In this lesson, you will investigate the principles, policies, and impact of President Lyndon B. Johnson's Great Society.

DEVELOP QUESTIONS

Developing Questions About the Great Society Read the Compelling Question for this lesson. Think about the promises Lyndon Johnson made as part of the Great Society and how he tried to fulfill those promises. Develop a list of Supporting Questions that would help you answer the Compelling Question in this lesson.

APPLY HISTORICAL TOOLS

Analyzing Primary Sources You will work with a variety of primary sources in this lesson. These sources focus on the legislation that Johnson promoted as part of the Great Society campaign. As you read, use a graphic organizer like the one below to record information about the sources that will help you examine them and check for historical understanding. Note ways in which each source helps you answer your Supporting Questions.

Supporting Questions	Primary Source	What this source tells me about . . .	Questions the source leaves unanswered
	A		
	B		
	C		
	D		
	E		
	F		
	G		
	H		

After you analyze the sources, you will:
- use the evidence from the sources.
- communicate your conclusions.
- take informed action.

Background Information

President Lyndon B. Johnson took office following the assassination of President John F. Kennedy in 1963. He inherited a thriving economy fraught with disparity, a conflict in Vietnam, and a nation struggling with the civil rights movement as it intensified. Kennedy had been an immensely popular president, so Johnson set out first to fulfill his predecessor's promises to expand civil rights and end poverty.

Johnson championed economic, social, and environmental policies that reshaped the government's relationship with its citizens. Many programs launched as part of Johnson's Great Society remain today, including Medicare, Medicaid, and Project Head Start. The Child Nutrition Act expanded school lunch programs and added school breakfasts. The Clean Air Act and the Water Quality Act provided a framework to establish standards for safe air and water. The Housing and Urban Development Act expanded public housing and federal subsidies to improve urban infrastructure. The Immigration Act ended the use of quotas that favored immigrants from Northern Europe.

Supporters hailed Johnson's efforts, but critics charged Johnson's policies overextended the federal government's budget and role. Others argued his policies did not go far enough to correct the nation's deep social and economic ills.

» First Lady "Lady Bird" Johnson appeared at a ceremony for National Head Start Day on June 30, 1965. Head Start is a school readiness program that seeks to meet the needs of preschool children from low-income families.

LBJ Library photo by Unknown

Toward the Great Society

During his 1964 campaign, Johnson promised to pursue policies that would create a "great society."

PRIMARY SOURCE : SPEECH

" World affairs will continue to call upon our energy and our courage. But today we can turn increased attention to the character of American life.

We are in the midst of the greatest upward surge of economic well-being in the history of any nation. . . . We worked for two centuries to climb this peak of prosperity. But we are only at the beginning of the road to the Great Society. Ahead now is a summit where freedom from the wants of the body can help fulfill the needs of the spirit.

We built this Nation to serve its people. We want to grow and build and create, but we want progress to be the servant and not the master of man.

We do not intend to live in the midst of abundance, isolated from neighbors and nature, confined by blighted cities and bleak suburbs, stunted by a poverty of learning and an emptiness of leisure.

The Great Society asks not how much, but how good; not only how to create wealth but how to use it . . .

It proposes as the first test for a nation: the quality of its people.

This kind of society will not flower spontaneously from swelling riches and surging power. It will not be the gift of government or the creation of presidents. It will require of every American, for many generations, both faith in the destination and the fortitude to make the journey.

And like freedom itself, it will always be challenge and not fulfillment. And tonight we accept that challenge. "

—President Lyndon B. Johnson,
    State of the Union Address, January 4, 1965

EXAMINE THE SOURCE

1. **Summarizing** What Great Society does Johnson envision? Describe what he wants to accomplish.

2. **Interpreting** What does Johnson suggest Americans must do to achieve the Great Society?

Project Head Start

One of the goals of Project Head Start was to provide pre-school education opportunities to low-income families. The Head Start organizers believed that giving more educational opportunities to young children also improved their social and emotional development. All of these improved services would give children the skills and abilities they needed to avoid poverty as they grew into adulthood.

PRIMARY SOURCE : PHOTOGRAPH

» First Lady Lady Bird Johnson visits a Project Head Start pre-school classroom.

EXAMINE THE SOURCE

1. **Analyzing Images** What is happening in the photograph? What do you notice about the people shown?

2. **Analyzing Images** How does this image reflect Johnson's stated goal to build a Great Society?

PHOTO: LBJ Library photo by Robert Knudsen/White House Photo Office; TEXT: Johnson, Lyndon Baines. Annual Message to the Congress on the State of the Union, January 4, 1965. Public Papers of the Presidents of the United States: Lyndon B. Johnson, 1965. Volume I, entry 2, pp. 1-9. Washington, D.C.: Government Printing Office, 1966.

C

"New Approaches to Old Problems"

As part of his "war on poverty," Johnson sought to provide more funding for struggling schools and increase equal access to education. This federal report highlights the variety of programs pursued under the Elementary and Secondary Education Act of 1965. Title I, the first provision of the law, allocates funds to districts with a large number of students whose families earn low incomes. This excerpt includes a term that is no longer considered acceptable to describe cognitive disabilities but was commonly used at the time this report was produced.

PHOTO: LBJ Library photo by Cecil Stoughton/White House Office Photo TEXT: US Department of Health, Education, and Welfare. A Chance for a Change: New School Programs for the Disadvantaged. Washington: Government Printing Office, 1966.

PRIMARY SOURCE : REPORT

66 These are a few of the innovative uses of Title I funds through which school officials across the nation are attempting to solve their diverse education problems.

Pairing college students on a one-to-one basis with first graders in Tucson, Arizona. . . .

Training mentally retarded teenagers in a Bloomington, Indiana, work-study project so they may continue in a meaningful school curriculum and, at the same time, qualify for promised jobs in the community. . . .

Providing a special course of study for the 100 to 200 children of migrant Mexican-American families that arrive each spring in Wasco, California. . . .

Offering a new physical education program to Greencastle, Indiana, educationally deprived children, including the provision of necessary gym clothing and shoes to youngsters who cannot afford them. . . .

Hiring a child development specialist to work closely with the parents of 70 youngsters scheduled to attend Woodward-Granger, Iowa, kindergarten classes next fall. . . .

Purchasing a four-wheel-drive bus in Pecos, New Mexico, so that school-age residents of an almost inaccessible and poverty-stricken mountain village may be transported down narrow winding roads each day to attend classes. . . .

Using Neighborhood Youth Corps high-schoolers in an East Chicago, Indiana, Title I project to serve as 'liaison agents' between the home and the school. . . . 99

—United States Office of Education, 1966

EXAMINE THE SOURCE

1. **Identifying** What are some services and opportunities provided by Title I of the law?
2. **Identifying Cause and Effect** What effect are these policies intended to have?

D

Anti-Poverty Tour

Johnson's Great Society led to the creation of many new programs and agencies to address social welfare. This resulted in a massive expansion of government services, spending, and employment. Johnson traveled to see some of the people whom he hoped would benefit from his programs and their living conditions. This 1964 photograph shows him meeting with a man in Appalachia.

PRIMARY SOURCE : PHOTOGRAPH

EXAMINE THE SOURCE

1. **Analyzing Visuals** How might the people, including those watching from a distance, have interpreted Johnson's visit?
2. **Speculating** Why might Johnson have wished to travel personally to Appalachia?

SNCC Criticism

The Student Nonviolent Coordinating Committee (SNCC) was instrumental during the civil rights movement. Jack Minnis ran the group's research arm and compiled reports challenging the motivations of Johnson's programs.

PRIMARY SOURCE : REPORT

" . . . Lyndon announced that $101 million of war-on-poverty money has been allocated. A total of $22,670, .02% of the allocations, actually went to poor people in the form of . . . loans. The balance, 99.98%, went to the poverty warriors themselves. A typical *grant* (no loans to the warriors—only the poor must repay) was . . . to the Systems Development Corporation. . . . This corporate poverty warrior got $85,000 to 'operate a computer based information processing and retrieval system.'

In his . . . message on January 4, Lyndon declared that the fate of the nation depends upon the availability of adequate medical treatment for all Americans. In his Inaugural Address on January 20, Lyndon said, 'In a land of healing miracles, neighbors must not suffer and die untended. . . . [E]very sick body made whole—like a candle added to an altar—brightens the hope of all the faithful.' Meanwhile, Lyndon had lighted his own little candle . . . by closing 14 . . . hospitals . . . to cut $25 million from his budget.

. . . [T]he Federal Trade Commission announced the filing of a complaint against Merck & Co. The charge is that Merck has lied to the public about the healing qualities of its 'Sucrets' cough drops. . . . [T]he Senate confirmed Lyndon's appointment of Merck president John T. Connor as Secretary of Commerce. Connor, having been policy-maker for Merck when it lied about its cough drops, will now be policy-maker for the business department. . . . They are all honorable men. "

—SNCC Report, January 22, 1965

EXAMINE THE SOURCE

1. **Analyzing Points of View** What tone does the author take in this report? Explain.

2. **Distinguishing Fact from Opinion** What implied opinion does the author convey?

F

Remarks Upon Signing the Economic Opportunity Act

Johnson made these remarks when he signed the Economic Opportunity Act, a key part of his "war on poverty." The 1964 law created programs and agencies to relieve what were deemed underlying causes of unemployment and poverty. Among these were the Office of Economic Opportunity, the Job Corps, Head Start, VISTA, and the Neighborhood Youth Corps.

PRIMARY SOURCE : SPEECH

" This is not in any sense a cynical proposal to exploit the poor with a promise of a handout or a **dole.**

We know—we learned long ago—that answer is no answer.

The measure before me this morning for signature offers the answer that its title implies—the answer for opportunity. . . .

For the million young men and women who are out of school and . . . out of work, this program will permit us to take them off the streets, put them into work training programs, to prepare them for productive lives, not wasted lives. . . .

We will work with them through our communities . . . to develop comprehensive community action programs—with **remedial** education, with job training, with retraining, with health and employment counseling, with neighborhood improvement. We will strike at poverty's roots.

This is by no means a program confined just to our cities. Rural America is afflicted deeply by rural poverty, and this program will help poor farmers get back on their feet. . . . "

—President Lyndon Johnson, August 20, 1964

dole money given by the government to people in need

remedial corrective; meant as a remedy

EXAMINE THE SOURCE

1. **Identifying** What purpose does Johnson suggest that the law serves? What does he believe it will do?

2. **Analyzing Perspectives** What main point does Johnson try to make by invoking words like "dole"?

(1)Minnis, Jack. "Life with Lyndon in the Great Society." Student Nonviolent Coordinating Committee mimeo report. January 1965. Cleveland L. Sellers, Jr. Papers, 1934-2003. Avery Research Center at the College of Charleston; (2)Johnson, Lyndon B. "Remarks Upon Signing the Economic Opportunity Act." August 20, 1964. Public Papers of the Presidents of the United States: Lyndon B. Johnson, 1963-64. Washington: Government Printing Office, 1965.

Report on the Effectiveness of Government Health Programs

As a part of the Great Society's War on Poverty, the Office of Economic Opportunity and the Department of Health, Education, and Welfare used federal tax money to fund health programs, including services for migrants and youth. Supporters believed that if people did not suffer from chronic illness, they would be able to improve their earning potential and overcome poverty. They also believed that having smaller families would help reduce poverty. This belief led to the availability of family planning programs—but also to the sterilization, often without their consent, of Native American women as well as African American, Latina, and poor white women. The battle for reproductive rights for African American, Latina, and Native American women continues to this day. This report, published in 1969, points out the lack of previous data on the health care effort and indicates the complexities of these types of reform efforts. The General Accounting Office is charged with reviewing and evaluating federal government expenditures.

Resource Management Corporation. Evaluations of the War on Poverty: Health Programs. RMC Report UR-047. Prepared for General Accounting Office Under Contract No. GA-654. March 1969.

PRIMARY SOURCE : REPORT

66 This paper examines the problems associated with evaluating the effectiveness of public-health programs in the **amelioration** of poverty. While it is generally accepted that poor health and poverty reinforce each other, it has not been possible to establish definitive relationships between providing health services and diminishing poverty. It is not clear that raising the health status of the poor to the mean level maintained by the rest of the population would significantly reduce the incidence of poverty in the U.S. The exception to this generalization would, of course, be that fraction of the poor whose **indigency** can be related to a specific disability that does not permit them to work or is absorbing a large part of their income. Stated differently, the disabilities associated with poor health may impair the effectiveness of other poverty-alleviation programs.

Fortunately, good health, or at least good health care, for every citizen in the country is a worthwhile goal in itself. It is thus possible, as a minimum, to judge public-health programs on the basis of their contribution to improving the health status of the poor relative to the rest of the population without regard to the impact of such an improvement upon personal income.

Furthermore, it is not at all certain which programs, characteristics, or mixes of programs would be most effective in reducing poverty. In part, this is because the specific nature and unique characteristics of the health problems of the poor are not fully understood. The report of the National Advisory Commission on Health Manpower could identify 'no clear-cut solution for care of the disadvantaged. . . . Successful programs,' they said, 'will have to be unique, intensive, and designed with recognition of the special problems of this particular segment of the population.' It is not surprising, therefore, that there are many public-health programs and that other types of anti-poverty programs—whose primary function, for example, may be manpower development or education—frequently have a health component. This multiplicity of approaches increases the difficulty of evaluation and makes the assessment of the effectiveness of public-health programs as anti-poverty efforts a formidable and unique problem. 99

—U.S. General Accounting Office, 1969

amelioration the process of making something better or more tolerable

indigency a state of extreme poverty and hardship

EXAMINE THE SOURCE

1. **Explaining** What does the author mean by saying that "poor health and poverty reinforce each other"?

2. **Drawing Conclusions** What does this report suggest about efforts to evaluate Great Society programs?

H

Continuing the Change

In 1968 Johnson entered the final year of his first full term as the death toll in Vietnam and criticism of the country's foreign policy mounted. That spring Johnson announced that he would not seek re-election. In January 1969, he gave this State of the Union shortly before his successor took office.

PRIMARY SOURCE : SPEECH

66 . . . The effort to meet the problems must go on, year after year, if the momentum that we have all mounted together in these past years is not to be lost.

Although the struggle for progressive change is continuous, there are times when a watershed is reached—when there is—if not really a break with the past—at least the fulfillment of many of its oldest hopes. . . . I think the past 5 years have been such a time.

. . . I wish it were possible to say that everything that this Congress and the administration achieved during this period had already completed that cycle. But a great deal of what we have committed needs additional funding to become a tangible realization.

Yet the very existence of these commitments . . . are achievements in themselves, and failure to carry through on our commitments would be a tragedy for this Nation. . . .

I hope it may be said, a hundred years from now, that by working together we helped to make our country . . . more just for all of its people, as well as to insure . . . the blessings of liberty for all of our posterity.

That is what I hope. But I believe that at least it will be said that we tried. 99

—President Lyndon Johnson, State of the Union Address, January 14, 1969

EXAMINE THE SOURCE

1. **Determining Context** How would you characterize this address and the way Johnson talks about his administration's programs?

2. **Analyzing Perspectives** To what immediate and broader audiences does Johnson address his comments, and what main message does he try to communicate to them?

Your Inquiry Analysis

EVALUATE SOURCES AND USE EVIDENCE

Reflect back to the Compelling Question and the Supporting Questions you developed at the beginning of this lesson.

1. **Gathering Sources** Refer back to the Graphic Organizer you created as you read through the sources. Circle the sources that you consider most helpful in answering the Supporting Questions that you wrote. Then identify which of your lingering questions you would most like to have answered. Brainstorm how you might find answers to those questions.

2. **Evaluating Sources** Looking at the sources that help you answer the Supporting Questions, evaluate the credibility of each source. Write a statement summarizing the main position and any apparent bias for each source. Then categorize the sources as for, against, or neutral on Johnson's Great Society programs. How does each source's stance on the Great Society shape its content?

3. **Comparing and Contrasting** Compare and contrast two sources. Explain similarities and differences in tone, audience, message, purpose, and key points or conclusions.

COMMUNICATE CONCLUSIONS

Identifying Arguments Write an answer to each of your Supporting Questions. Then use those responses to write a short response (3–5 sentences) in response to the Compelling Question. Finally, identify and explain one argument in support of Johnson's Great Society programs and one argument against the programs. List evidence from the source documents to support each argument. Take turns sharing your argument outlines in a small group. Discuss which argument you support and why.

TAKE INFORMED ACTION

Tracing Programs Several laws and programs begun as part of the War on Poverty and the Great Society still exist, often in modified form, today. Select one of the laws or programs you read about that most interests you. Use appropriate print and online resources to trace its development from the Johnson administration through today. List key developments and changes on a time line. Then use what you have learned to take a position on whether you support, oppose, or would like to see additional changes made to the present policy or law. Cite evidence from your research to support your reasoning and present your time line and findings as a written or oral report.

Johnson, Lyndon B. "Annual Message to the Congress on the State of the Union, January 14, 1969." Public Papers of the Presidents of the United States: Lyndon B. Johnson, 1968-69. Volume II, entry 676, pp. 1263-1270. Washington, D. C.: Government Printing Office. 1970.

07

Reviewing Postwar Domestic Issues

Summary

The Domestic Cold War

The generation that came of age during the Great Depression and World War II experienced many hardships. By the end of the war, Americans were ready for security and stability. Thanks to a flourishing postwar economy, many built better lives for themselves and their families with new homes and educational opportunities. American society and politics were not without challenges, however.

The GI Bill gave some returning World War II veterans financial assistance for education, job training, and low-interest home loans. However, African Americans and other nonwhite veterans were denied full access to the benefits they had earned through their military service. African Americans would also be denied access to the suburbs that grew during this era through a practice called redlining.

McCarthy and the New Red Scare

As the Cold War between the United States and the Soviet Union escalated, fears increased about communist spies trying to undermine America. The United States experienced another Red Scare, and this one was more intense and longer than the one that followed World War I.

President Truman established a loyalty review program in 1947 to screen all federal employees. Officials such as those on the House Un-American Activities Committee (HUAC) and Senator Joseph McCarthy tried to prove that spies lurked in the federal government and Hollywood. Many people were wrongly accused and lost their jobs and reputations because of the hysteria. The Red Scare was also used to target civil rights activists and LGBTQ individuals.

Aspects of the 1950s Second Red Scare

- Investigations of the House Un-American Activities Committee (HUAC)
- Alger Hiss espionage trial
- Controversy over Julius and Ethel Rosenberg's accusations of espionage
- Project Venona report

The Atomic Age and Pop Culture

As the United States and Soviet Union built up their nuclear arsenals, concerns about the dangers of atomic energy increased. Government officials tried to reassure the public that they could survive a nuclear war.

Students practiced "duck-and-cover" safety drills in school, although the drill would have done little to actually protect them from the dangers of a nuclear attack. Some families built and stocked backyard bomb shelters. In the 1950s, nuclear testing at a site in Nevada spread fallout to nearby population centers that increased cancer rates in the area well into the 1970s.

Popular culture was filled with monster movies and science fiction stories about the dangerous outcomes of atomic experiments gone awry, an extension of the anxiety many felt about the Cold War. There were also many stories about communist spies, including *I Led Three Lives*, a show about an undercover FBI counterspy who was also a Communist Party official.

Truman's Challenges

Democratic President Harry Truman continued to expand upon Roosevelt's New Deal reforms. However, some believed that the time had come to scale back government spending.

After Republicans took control of both houses of Congress in 1946, they tried to institute more conservative approaches to the federal budget. Some Southern Democrats broke away from the national party over Truman's support for civil rights. Despite strong opposition, Truman unexpectedly won the presidential election of 1948, largely due to a coalition of Northern laborers, farmers, and African Americans. Truman expanded the power of workers and civil rights for nonwhites, including desegregating the U.S. military.

For many Americans, but not all, the GI Bill, suburban growth, and the baby boom marked a new era of affluence and improved standards of living. The needs of the postwar economy created multiple new middle-class jobs for workers throughout innovative industries. However, as more people moved to suburbs, some urban neighborhoods experienced decline and neglect.

Ike's America

President Eisenhower's election in 1952 marked the first time in 20 years that a Republican president held the White House. The slogan "I Like Ike" summed up most Americans' feelings about the popular war hero. By the time Eisenhower took office, the American economy was booming. His "dynamic conservatism" sought to keep prosperity flowing while balancing a fiscally conservative budget. He also pushed forward innovative ideas such as the creation of the Interstate Highway System (IHS).

The 1950s witnessed numerous scientific breakthroughs, including the development of a vaccine to prevent polio. American jobs were shifting from the blue-collar jobs that had marked previous eras, to white-collar jobs that often involved office jobs and new technologies like computers.

Television reshaped entertainment and popular culture, and filmmakers began to experiment with CinemaScope and 3-D technology to enhance the theatrical movie experience. New musical styles such as rock 'n' roll—combining influences from blues, soul, and country music—thrilled teenagers and horrified parents. Beat writers such as Jack Kerouac challenged the older generations' seeming conformity, laying the foundations for the widespread cultural rebellion of 1960s youth.

Kennedy's New Frontier

The presidential election of the youthful and charismatic John F. Kennedy in 1960 represented the optimism of the postwar era. Kennedy proposed a bold set of goals, promising a New Frontier for Americans. His administration supported efforts to expand rights for women and to help people with disabilities. During his administration, the U.S. Supreme Court under Chief Justice Earl Warren made several rulings that significantly expanded civil liberties.

Despite Kennedy's successes, some of his reform goals stalled in a resistant Congress. In November 1963 Kennedy was still struggling with Congress and preparing for his re-election campaign when he was assassinated in Dallas. Shortly after the assassination, Jack Ruby shot and killed the suspected gunman, Lee Harvey Oswald, on live television. This string of events shocked the nation.

Johnson's Great Society

President Lyndon B. Johnson quickly leveraged his years of experience in the legislature and mourning over Kennedy's death to push several stalled items through Congress. After winning election in 1964, Johnson proposed a series of reforms to create a Great Society in America. The reforms included a War on Poverty to eliminate economic suffering in the

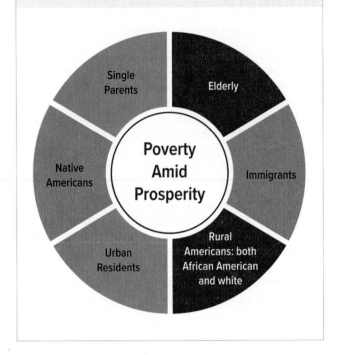

The Other America
Despite the overall economic prosperity of the postwar era, many Americans still struggled. Many of the Great Society programs attempted to address such inequities.

affluent nation. Johnson's Great Society efforts marked the busiest era of domestic reform since the New Deal.

A Crisis of Confidence

By the 1970s, the economy was starting to slow down. An oil embargo led to an energy crisis that further dragged down the economy. Soon the unusual phenomenon of stagflation set in. The economic and energy crises weighed heavily on the presidencies of Republicans Richard Nixon and Gerald Ford. Nixon tried to address the economic issues by taking the U.S. dollar off the gold standard in an attempt to strengthen the economy and renegotiate foreign exchange rates. Ford tried to address the continuing economic crisis through a plan called WIN—"Whip Inflation Now"—but it had little impact on the economic situation.

The economic problems continued after Democratic outsider Jimmy Carter won the presidency in 1976. Carter attempted to fix the economic crisis through increased government spending, reduced taxes, and a decrease in American reliance on foreign oil, but the economic crisis persisted. By 1979, as Carter's popularity was plunging, he declared that the country was suffering from a "crisis of confidence."

Apply What You Have Learned

A Analyzing Primary Sources

Advertising played a prominent role in The postwar era and was a lucrative industry. Many ads featured an ideal lifestyle based on filling one's home with the "right" consumer products. Such advertisements also often promoted rigid gender and family roles and "keeping up with the Jones's," or competition between neighbors to have a home as nice or better than the one next door.

ACTIVITY **Interpreting an Advertisement**
Examine the advertisement from the postwar era shown here. Consider the direct and indirect messages it is promoting. Then, write a paragraph explaining what you think the ad does and does not reflect about lifestyles and values during the postwar period.

Happy traveling! with modern highways and HOWARD JOHNSON'S
"LANDMARK FOR HUNGRY AMERICANS"

B Understanding Multiple Perspectives

Senator McCarthy claimed in a speech on February 9, 1950, that more than two hundred State Department employees were Communists. Two days later, he sent a telegram to President Truman claiming that he had a list of fifty-seven supposed Communists working in the department and demanding the president take action:

66 I would suggest . . . that you simply pick up your phone and ask Mr. Acheson how many of those whom your board had labeled as dangerous he failed to discharge. . . . [Y]ou signed an order forbidding the State Department's giving any information in regard to the disloyalty or the communistic connections of anyone in that Department, despite . . . [this] blackout, we have been able to compile a list of 57 Communists in the State Department. . . . 99

On March 31, 1950, Truman drafted a reply:

66 [T]his is the first time in my experience, and I was ten years in the Senate, that I ever heard of a Senator trying to discredit his own Government before the world.

You know that isn't done by honest public officials. Your telegram is not only not true and an insolent approach to a situation . . . but it shows conclusively that you are not even fit to have a hand in the operation of the Government. . . .

I am very sure that the people of Wisconsin are extremely sorry that they are represented by a person who has as little sense of responsibility as you have. 99

McCarthy continued to insist that Communists had infiltrated the U.S. government. Despite these many statements, he never proved his claims nor produced the list of names he said he had.

ACTIVITY **Connecting Historical Events** Review the excerpts and identify the main points of each writer. As you learned in previous lessons, the first Red Scare occurred following World War I. Using materials from those lessons and other resources, find examples of an exchange from the first Red Scare that are similar to the McCarthy-Truman exchange. Write a summary comparing the various points of view expressed during both Red Scares.

PHOTO: Blank Archives/Hulton Archive/Getty Images; TEXT: (l)McCarthy, Joseph R. 1950. Telegram from Senator Joseph R. McCarthy to President Harry S. Truman, with Truman's Reply, February 11, 1950. National Archives, Collection HST-PSF: President's Secretary's Files (Truman Administration), 1945-1960; (2) Truman, Harry S. 1950. Telegram from Senator Joseph R. McCarthy to President Harry S. Truman, with Truman's Reply, February 11, 1950. National Archives, Collection HST-PSF: President's Secretary's Files (Truman Administration), 1945-1960.

C Making Connections to Today

The postwar baby boom dramatically shaped American society. Between 1946 and 1964, the birthrate increased significantly. As they matured into teenagers and young adults in the 1960s and 1970s, the baby boom generation had an enormous impact on American culture.

Raised during one of the longest periods of economic growth in American history, many baby boomers were more highly educated and found it easier than previous generations to obtain good-paying jobs. In addition, because of their overall affluence and good health, the members of this generation generally have a longer life-expectancy than previous generations.

Retiring baby boomers can collect full Social Security after the age of 66. In recent years, many economists have warned that the coming wave of retirees could put severe strains on the Social Security and Medicare systems. Some economists and politicians have argued that without reforms, these systems might "run out of money" before later generations retire.

ACTIVITY **Interpreting Statistical Data** Examine the chart below. Identify the years when most baby boomers can start collecting full Social Security benefits. Include that information in a paragraph describing what the chart reveals about the continued impact the baby boomers might have on American society.

Number of People Age 65 and Older (millions)

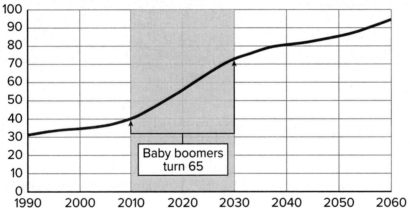

Baby boomers turn 65

Sources: U.S. Census Bureau, *National Intercensal Estimates*, *2016 Population Estimates*, June 2017; and 2017 *National Population Projections*, September 2018.

D Connecting to Music

The postwar period witnessed a quick expansion of artistic creativity. During this time of peace and rebuilding after World War II, some in the younger generation could spend their time indulging in creative expression in the arts--especially in the popular rock 'n' roll music of the 1950s. The language and styles of rock 'n' roll songs baffled many parents, who reacted negatively to made up words and sounds. Take for example this portion of lyrics from Little Richard's song "Tutti Frutti":

66 Tutti frutti, oh rutti
Awop-bop-a-loo-mop alop-bam-boom 99

ACTIVITY **Interpreting Music** Using library and Internet resources, research the lyrics of a rock 'n' roll song written between 1946 and 1959. Write a paragraph explaining the meaning of the song in your own words. Then explain how you think different audiences might have reacted to the piece when it was first released.

Music by Little Richard, Lyrics co-written by Little Richard and Dorothy LaBostrie. "Tutti Frutti." Sony ATV Music Publishing, 1955

Library of Congress Prints & Photographs Division [LC-DIG-ppmsca-37229]

The Civil Rights Movement 1954–1978

Protesters march in support of civil rights at the March on Washington in 1963.

INTRODUCTION LESSON

01 Introducing the Civil Rights Movement   406

LEARN THE EVENTS LESSONS

03 The Civil Rights Movement Begins   417

04 Challenging Segregation   423

06 The Civil Rights Movement Continues   435

INQUIRY ACTIVITY LESSONS

02 Understanding Multiple Perspectives About Discrimination and Segregation   411

05 Analyzing Sources: Civil Rights Movement Activists   429

REVIEW AND APPLY LESSON

07 Reviewing the Civil Rights Movement   441

ROSA PARKS TAKES A STAND

On December 1, 1955, Rosa Parks left her job as a tailor's assistant in Montgomery, Alabama, and boarded a city bus to go home.

Buses were segregated in most Southern cities. If no whites were on the bus, African Americans could sit in the middle and front, but they were forced to move to the back if there were no seats available for white people at the front of the bus. In Montgomery, however, African Americans were barred from sitting at the front of the bus even when it was empty and could be forced to give up their seat in the segregated section if the bus was full.

The bus grew crowded. When the bus driver noticed a white man standing at the front of the bus, he told Parks and three other African Americans in her row to get up and let the white man sit down. Nobody moved. The driver cautioned them, "Y'all better make it light on yourselves and let me have those seats." The other three African Americans moved, but Parks did not. She was tired of giving in to the system of segregation that treated her and other African Americans as second-class citizens over 70 years after the end of the Civil War.

She had many years of experience as an activist resisting segregation, including learning resistance techniques from the Highlander Folk School in Tennessee. Her action was one of many instances of citizens fighting back against inequality and discrimination during the civil rights movement.

The bus driver called the city police, who arrested Parks and took her to jail. News of her arrest soon reached E.D. Nixon, a former president of the local chapter of the National Association for the Advancement of Colored People (NAACP).

Nixon had long wanted to challenge bus segregation laws in court, and he told Rosa Parks, "With your permission we can break down segregation on the bus with your case."

Parks told Nixon: "If you think it will mean something to Montgomery and do some good, I'll be happy to go along with it."

The details of this incident might seem surprising to some people today. A bus driver demands that a woman give up her seat on a bus to a man who boarded the bus after her. When she refuses, not only is she publicly shamed by the bus driver, but she is also arrested and jailed. Yet for African Americans living in the South during the early 1950s, an event like this was not uncommon.

> **"With your permission we can break down segregation on the bus with your case."**

During the 1950s, numerous African American activists like Rosa Parks, alongside the NAACP, fought these unjust laws. This specific bus incident, however, would capture national attention and lead to a turning point in modern American history.

After Parks's arrest, African American citizens of Montgomery, Alabama, worked together to challenge their community's bus segregation laws by staging a boycott. This boycott, which lasted for over a year, was led by local minister and leader of the then newly formed Montgomery Improvement Association, Dr. Martin Luther King, Jr.

Rosa Parks's act of civil disobedience was one of many choices made by African Americans across the United States to fight for their equality. Alongside the Montgomery bus boycott, these important actions were among the early efforts to seek equal treatment under the law for African Americans. Historians now call this period of activism and change the civil rights movement.

(1)Blake, J.P. Quoted in Branch, Taylor. 1988. Parting the Waters: America in the King Years, 1954-63. New York: Simon & Schuster, Inc.; (2)Nixon, E.D. Quoted in Anderson, Jennifer Joline. 2011. The Civil Rights Movement. Edina: ABDO Publishing. 2011; (3)Parks, Rosa. Quoted in. Branch, Taylor. 1988. Parting the Waters: America in the King Years, 1954-63. New York: Simon & Schuster, Inc.

This photograph by a United Press International photojournalist shows Rosa Parks sitting on a Montgomery bus after the courts declared the city's segregated seating system illegal. The people of Montgomery fought for more than a year to end this discrimination in public transportation.

Bettmann/Getty Images

Understanding the Time and Place:
The United States, 1865–1954

The civil rights reform movement of the 1950s and 1960s was a response to a long history of racial inequality in the United States. During the Reconstruction period after the Civil War (from about 1865 to 1877) Constitutional amendments gave African Americans the rights of citizenship. However, in the years following 1877, state governments denied African Americans their rights and legalized segregation and discrimination across the United States. The civil rights movement formed to protest this inequality and aimed to overturn this systemic discrimination.

Reconstruction, 1865–1877

After the Civil War, the Constitution was revised to protect the rights of African Americans through three important amendments. The Thirteenth Amendment legally ended slavery throughout the United States. The Fourteenth Amendment granted citizenship to African Americans and provided legal protections. The Fifteenth Amendment gave African American men the right to vote.

African Americans who had served in the Union Army gave public speeches to the formerly enslaved and helped bring new people into politics. Many recently freed African Americans ran for public office, won elections, and served as legislators and administrators in almost all levels of government.

African Americans created strong social and religious community networks and emphasized education, especially after it had been denied to so many enslaved people shortly before Reconstruction. Several African American academies formed during this time grew into a network of African American colleges and universities referred to today as Historically Black Colleges and Universities (HBCUs). This includes Hampton Institute in Virginia and Morehouse College in Georgia. Just over ten years after the Civil War's end, almost 40 percent of African American children were enrolled in schools.

Southern white Democrats who opposed these changes during the Reconstruction period fought against African Americans and their political allies in the Republican Party. White militia groups who wished to **redeem** the South from "Black Republican" rule used intimidation and physical violence against African Americans. By 1877, this brief period of African American political reform ended.

Legalizing Segregation, 1880s–1890s

After the Compromise of 1877 ended Reconstruction, **Jim Crow laws**—which existed throughout the South but also took hold in much of the North—made it legal to discriminate against African Americans. Literacy tests, poll taxes, and **grandfather clauses** were created to target the African American population and weaken their constitutional right to vote under the Fifteenth Amendment. African Americans challenged the variety of restrictions of their freedoms, but several important Supreme Court rulings denied their legal claims and weakened the protections first granted by the Fourteenth Amendment. The 1896 *Plessy* v. *Ferguson* Supreme Court ruling allowed systemic segregation by saying the Fourteenth Amendment's equal protection clause allowed two sets of "separate but equal" public facilities. In the following decades, divided facilities for public transportation, restrooms, water fountains, schools, and other places were created throughout the United States.

During these years, African Americans spoke out against segregation and other forms of discrimination. Ida B. Wells headed a strong political effort to end

Library of Congress Prints & Photographs Division [LC-DIG-ppmsc-00199].

African Americans stand near a restricted "Colored Waiting Room" at a North Carolina bus station. Segregation required separate facilities for whites and African Americans in almost every aspect of public life.

---

redeem to win back; to restore

Jim Crow laws statutes enacted to enforce segregation

grandfather clause an exemption in a law

Segregation in the United States, Mid-Twentieth Century

Segregation was strongest in the Southern states, but it was also present in other parts of the United States before the civil rights movement.

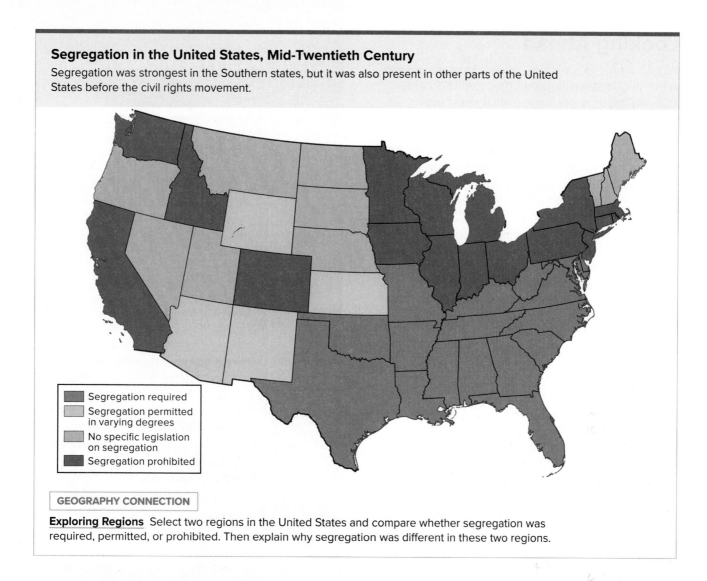

Legend:
- Segregation required
- Segregation permitted in varying degrees
- No specific legislation on segregation
- Segregation prohibited

GEOGRAPHY CONNECTION

Exploring Regions Select two regions in the United States and compare whether segregation was required, permitted, or prohibited. Then explain why segregation was different in these two regions.

African American lynchings. She published books and spoke in public to denounce mob violence. Wells demanded all African Americans get the right to a fair trial and the use of legally approved forms of punishment. Booker T. Washington founded the Tuskegee Institute in 1881, while W.E.B. Du Bois and a host of other reformers created the Niagara Movement in 1905 to fight racial discrimination, lynching, and race-based voting restrictions. In 1909 many of these same leaders established the National Association for the Advancement of Colored People (NAACP).

Segregation in the United States, Early 1950s

As shown in the map, much of the United States, not only the South, required segregation by law during the early 1950s. Few states had laws prohibiting segregation; most of these states were in the Northeast and Midwest. Even in those Northern states that prohibited segregation, however, **de facto segregation** remained the reality for many communities. African Americans and white Americans lived in separate communities because of housing discrimination against African Americans. Employment discrimination for African Americans was common in both the South and the North. It was in the context of segregation and discrimination that the civil rights movement gained momentum.

In 1954 the NAACP gained a major legal victory against segregation. The U.S. Supreme Court ruled in *Brown* v. *Board of Education of Topeka* that segregation in public schools was unconstitutional and violated the equal protection clause of the Fourteenth Amendment, reversing the decision in *Plessy* v. *Ferguson*. Even though the Court's decision applied only to public schools, it implied that segregation was illegal in other public facilities.

de facto segregation segregation by custom and tradition

Looking Ahead

You will learn the history of the civil rights movement in the United States between 1954 and 1978. While studying this time period, you will learn about segregation and other forms of discrimination that African Americans endured, and the strategies civil rights movement activists employed. You will see how the leaders of the modern civil rights movement were motivated by past struggles against inequality. And you will understand the changes that came about because of these protests.

You will examine Compelling Questions and develop your own questions about the civil rights movement in the inquiry lessons. Review the time line to preview some of the key events, people, and organizations that you will learn about.

What Will You Learn

In these lessons focused on the civil rights movement, you will learn:

- the historical causes of the civil rights movement.
- the key events in the history of the civil rights movement.
- the actions taken by significant individuals and important organizations within the civil rights movement.
- the effects of the civil rights movement.
- the legacy of the civil rights movement in the United States.

? COMPELLING QUESTIONS

- **How did discrimination affect the daily life of African Americans before the civil rights movement?**
- **How did activists move the civil rights movement forward?**

CIVIL RIGHTS MOVEMENT

1941 — **JANUARY 25, 1941** A. Philip Randolph proposes a March on Washington to highlight segregation and Jim Crow discrimination

1954 — **MAY 17, 1954** Supreme Court rules against public school segregation in *Brown* v. *Board of Education of Topeka*

DECEMBER 1955 Montgomery, Alabama, bus boycott begins

SEPTEMBER 1957 Federal troops ensure integration of African American students at Central High School in Little Rock, Arkansas

SEPTEMBER 1957 Civil Rights Act passed to ensure that all Americans could exercise their right to vote

1960 — **FEBRUARY 1960** Greensboro sit-ins begin

AUGUST 1963 March on Washington for Jobs and Freedom (right)

JULY 1964 Civil Rights Act passed that ends segregation in public places and banned employment discrimination

1965 — **AUGUST 1965** Voting Rights Act passed to remove legal barriers of voter discrimination at the local and state levels

APRIL 4, 1968 Dr. Martin Luther King, Jr., assassinated in Memphis

APRIL 11, 1968 Civil Rights Act passed prohibiting housing discrimination

Civil Rights March on Washington, D.C. [A wide-angle view of marchers along the mall, showing the Reflecting Pool and the Washington Monument.] August 28, 1963. National Archives and Records Administration National Archives and Records Administration

Sequencing Time List the events about education and explain how each event contributed to school desegregation.

02

Understanding Multiple Perspectives About Discrimination and Segregation

 COMPELLING QUESTION

How did discrimination affect the daily life of African Americans before the civil rights movement?

Plan Your Inquiry

In this lesson, you will investigate how discrimination affected African Americans before the civil rights movement.

DEVELOP QUESTIONS

Developing Questions About Discrimination Think about how segregation and the discrimination experienced by African Americans throughout the United States motivated the civil rights movement. Then read the Compelling Question for this lesson. Develop a list of three Supporting Questions that would help you answer the Compelling Question for the lesson. Write these in a graphic organizer like the one below.

APPLY HISTORICAL TOOLS

Analyzing Primary and Secondary Sources You will work with a variety of primary and secondary sources in this lesson. These sources focus on African American experiences of discrimination in different locations throughout the United States. Use a graphic organizer like the one below to record and organize information about each source. Note ways in which each source helps you answer the Supporting Questions you created. Not all sources will help you answer each of your supporting questions. Only include relevant sources in your graphic organizer.

Supporting Questions	Primary Source	How this source helps me answer the Supporting Question
	A	
	B	
	C	
	D	
	E	
	F	
	G	
	H	

After you analyze the sources, you will:
- use the evidence from the sources.
- communicate your conclusions.
- take informed action.

Background Information

Despite the promise of Reconstruction, African Americans throughout the country still experienced discrimination, segregation, and violence. Their writings and remembrances told of the pain and mistreatment they faced in their everyday lives: the jobs they were denied, the public spaces they could not use, and their experiences in segregated schools. These experiences motivated them to demand the civil rights they were being denied, starting a movement to bring about lasting change. The following writings, interviews, and images reflect those experiences. Please note that these sources reflect the language and terminology of the time period and may contain terms that are offensive.

Source H — Dickinson, ND
Sources E,G — New York City, NY
Source F — Prince Edward County, VA
Source A — Oklahoma City, OK
Source C — Fort Huachuca, AZ
Source B — Portsmouth, VA
Source D — Norwood, AL

» This map shows the geographic distribution of the different sources you will analyze.

🖱 **GO ONLINE** Explore the Student Edition eBook and find interactive maps, time lines, and tools.

411

Segregation at the Water Cooler

Under Jim Crow laws in the American South, separate public facilities for whites and African Americans—including waiting rooms, restrooms, and water coolers—were required. This photo was taken at a streetcar terminal in Oklahoma City, Oklahoma, in 1939.

PRIMARY SOURCE : PHOTOGRAPH

» This photograph by Russell Lee shows a young man drinking from a water fountain meant for African Americans only. These separate facilities were usually of lower quality than those reserved for whites.

EXAMINE THE SOURCE

1. **Analyzing Visuals** What is occurring in this photograph? How does it reflect the racial policies and attitudes of the period?

2. **Comparing and Contrasting** Compare the signs and the messages in this photo with the treatment of African Americans during slavery. How had things changed, what were the changes, and what were the similarities between outright slavery and Jim Crow laws?

Segregation in the Workplace During World War II

The massive national effort required to fight World War II brought economic and social changes and new opportunities for African Americans. In this excerpt from an interview, Lucy Overton of Portsmouth, Virginia, describes the issues facing African Americans as they went to work in war-related industries.

PRIMARY SOURCE : INTERVIEW

❝ I was one of the persons who worked, was employed in the Naval Shipyard during World War II. . . . [T]he need for workers was great, because the men were bein' called off to the Army, and therefore, they placed the ladies into jobs that men usually did. My job was in the Shipfitters Shop. . . . [T]here was some problems in the shipyard, some racial problems. First . . . of all . . . the Navy Yard needed welders, and . . . burners, the personnel said they didn't have . . . toilet facilities, so they couldn't hire black men. Well, at that time, Franklin Delano Roosevelt was president. . . . [H]e got the news somehow and came down. . . . He went directly to the Navy Yard, and had conferences with . . . the Admirals and those persons in charge, and in a couple of days, they had facilities for blacks. Ah, separate . . . facilities. To begin with they didn't have any at all for blacks, therefore they couldn't hire blacks as welders, . . . burners and chippers . . . . They had separate water fountains, they had separate . . . , toilet facilities for the ladies. They had on the door, 'White Ladies,' 'Colored Women.' And we didn't like that at all, but we, we couldn't do anything about that, then. ❞

—from Lucy Overton interview, in *Lower Tidewater in Black and White*, 1982

EXAMINE THE SOURCE

Analyzing Why did the Navy Yard begin to hire African Americans? Why was Overton dissatisfied with the situation when African Americans were hired?

PHOTO: Library of Congress Prints & Photographs Division [LC-DIG-fsa-8a26761]; TEXT: Lucy Overton, Transcript, interviewed on October 27, 1981, Lower Tidewater in Black and White (Portsmouth, VA: Portsmouth Public Library, 1981), 1-12.

PHOTO: Internet Archive; TEXT: Trimmingham, Rupert. "What is the Negro soldier fighting for?. Letter to the editor of Yank. Brinkley, Douglas, ed. World War II: The Allied Counteroffensive, 1942-1945. New York: Henry Holt, 2003.

An African American Soldier Faces Segregation

Yank magazine was a weekly publication distributed to members of the American armed forces during World War II. The magazine was designed as a morale booster and featured cartoons and pin-up girls along with news stories. It also included a section with letters from soldiers. In this 1944 letter, an African American corporal described an especially upsetting experience with segregation while traveling with other African American soldiers. Remember that even as African American soldiers were fighting for world democracy, U.S. federal law kept them segregated within the armed forces.

PRIMARY SOURCE : LETTER

66 Dear YANK:

Here is a question that each Negro soldier is asking. What is the Negro soldier fighting for? On whose team are we playing? Myself and eight other soldiers were on our way from Camp Claiborne, La., to the hospital here at Fort Huachuca. We had to layover until the next day for our train. On the next day we could not purchase a cup of coffee at any of the lunchrooms around there. As you know, Old Man Jim Crow rules. The only place where we could be served was at the lunchroom at the railroad station but, of course, we had to go into the kitchen. But that's not all; 11:30 a.m. about two dozen German prisoners of war, with two American guards, came to the station. They entered the lunchroom, sat at the tables, had their meals served, talked, smoked, in fact had quite a swell time. I stood on the outside looking on, and I could not help but ask myself these questions: Are those men sworn enemies of this country? Are they not taught to hate and destroy . . . all democratic governments? Are we not American soldiers, sworn to fight for and die if need be for this our country? Then why are they treated better than we are? Why are we pushed around like cattle? If we are fighting for the same thing, if we are to die for our country, then why does the Government allow such things to go on? Some of the boys are saying that you will not print this letter. I'm saying that you will. . . .

Cpl. Rupert Trimmingham,
Fort Huachuca, Ariz. 99

—*Yank: The Army Weekly,* April 28, 1944

» An example of a *Yank* magazine cover.

EXAMINE THE SOURCE

1. **Analyzing** Describe the situation experienced by Corporal Trimmingham. Why did he find that experience especially upsetting?

2. **Inferring** How did Corporal Trimmingham challenge the editors of *Yank*? What effect may the letter have had on fellow soldiers and Army policy?

Remembering Segregated Schools

Charles Gratton lived in Norwood, Alabama, during the Depression and World War II. His childhood memories of living in the segregated South highlighted the struggles he faced with unequal school opportunities.

PRIMARY SOURCE : TRANSCRIPT

66 They also had a park. It was about a block from where I was born and raised and where I lived, and it was known as the white person's park. They had a tennis court there and nice park trees, and blacks weren't allowed in that park. I mean we just couldn't go there. You know, it's just one of those things.

Some days I would be sick, and I could hear the schoolchildren playing during their lunch hour down at Norwood Elementary School, which was all white, and that's what really stuck in my mind. I'd say, 'It's a shame that I have to walk so far to school every day.' When I'd hear those schoolchildren playing, I'd say, 'Here I am a block and a half from the elementary school, and I've got to walk six or seven miles to school every day.'

Even now, I can almost hear those kids, those white kids down at this elementary school playing, and the noise and laughing and playing, and I'm at home sick basically from the exposure of walking those six and seven miles to school every day. Whether it was raining or not, I had to go. So those are some of the memories that I have of my childhood growing up over at Norwood. 99

—Charles Gratton, in *Remembering Jim Crow: African Americans Tell About Life in the Segregated South*

EXAMINE THE SOURCE

Interpreting Text Does Charles Gratton have the same feelings toward the segregated park as he does toward the unequal school access? Why or why not?

Running Out of Patience

On May 12, 1958, President Eisenhower addressed a meeting of African American leaders sponsored by the National Newspaper Publishers Association. Jackie Robinson, the first African American baseball player in the twentieth century to play in the major leagues, was in the audience. The next day, he sent the president a letter expressing his frustration with Eisenhower's advice to "have patience and forbearance" as the nation tackled the difficult problem of racial discrimination.

PRIMARY SOURCE : LETTER

66 I was sitting in the audience at the Summit Meeting of Negro Leaders yesterday when you said we must have patience. On hearing you say this, I felt like standing up and saying, 'Oh no! Not again.'

I respectfully remind you sir, that we have been the most patient of all people. When you said we must have self-respect, I wondered how we could have self-respect and remain patient considering the treatment accorded us through the years.

17 million Negroes cannot do as you suggest and wait for the hearts of men to change. We want to enjoy now the rights that we feel we are entitled to as Americans. This we cannot do unless we pursue aggressively goals which all other Americans achieved over 150 years ago. . . . 99

—Jackie Robinson, letter to President Eisenhower, May 13, 1958

EXAMINE THE SOURCE

1. **Interpreting Text** To what is Robinson referring when he mentions pursuing goals other Americans achieved over 150 years ago?
2. **Inferring** What point do you think Robinson hopes to convey by making this connection to the goals that others achieved in the past?

(l)Gratton, Charles. In: William H. Chafe, Raymond Gavins, and Robert Korstad, eds., Remembering Jim Crow: African-Americans Tell about Life in the Segregated South. New York: The New Press, 2001; (r)Robinson, Jackie. Letter to President Dwight Eisenhower May 13, 1958.

Comparing White and African American Schools in Virginia

While *Plessy* v. *Ferguson* allowed for "separate but equal" facilities for whites and African Americans, the racially based inequality of schools in the South was plainly obvious, even to children. John Stokes described his memories of school in Virginia in the 1940s for an oral history project. John Stokes led a student strike against poor schools. This led to a court case that became part of the *Brown* v. *Board of Education* decision against segregated "separate but equal" schools.

PRIMARY SOURCE : INTERVIEW

66 There were two buses for whites only that passed by our house every morning and picked up Jack Jeffreys, Bill Schueler, these were the white boys that I played with, these were the kids that's [sic] I played with, and yet my twin sister and I could not ride those buses.

. . . [T]hose buses were going to the wrong schools. They were going to all white schools. But we wondered why the blacks did not have buses. . . .

Now, there were around 10 or 12 [schools for African American children] scattered throughout Prince Edward County at that time of wood construction, outdoor toilets, none of them had indoor plumbing, of course, and yet, in each of the districts for the white kids there was a school there, but it was of brick construction. And those students would have, of course, the privilege of having a bus that would take them to and from those schools. They built the schools for the blacks, we found out later, very closely knitted to the churches so that the kids would not have to walk too far, but some of them still had to walk pretty long distances to get to those schools.

But the most amazing thing was the fact that in our minds we just wondered how come the white kids had these beautiful brick buildings, with heat, number one, and no one had to go out there and gather wood every morning to start the fire; number two, they had running water, and when December came, they didn't have to go outdoors to the toilet. 99

—from John A. Stokes interview, for *Voices of Freedom*, Virginia Commonwealth University

---

EXAMINE THE SOURCE

1. **Contrasting** What differences does Stokes recall between the white and the African American educational experiences during his childhood?

2. **Making Connections** Explain how the differences between the schools might affect learning outcomes.

The NAACP Calls Attention to Lynchings

Extralegal lynchings of African Americans occurred in the United States for decades. Between 1877 and 1950, more than 4,000 lynchings are documented, and the vast majority of those lynched were African American. In the 1920s and 1930s, the National Association for the Advancement of Colored People (NAACP) flew the flag (shown in the image) on days when it learned that an African American in the United States had been lynched. The flag was raised at the NAACP's office in New York City. This photo was taken in 1936. The United States still does not have an anti-lynching law passed by Congress.

PRIMARY SOURCE : PHOTOGRAPH

» This flag was in use from 1920 to 1938.

EXAMINE THE SOURCE

Evaluating Information What purpose did the NAACP have for flying this flag?

PHOTO: Library of Congress Prints and Photographs Division; Visual Materials from the National Association for the Advancement of Colored People Records [LC-DIG-ppmsca-09705]; TEXT: Carrington, Ronald E. interviewer. "Interview with John A. Stokes (Transcript)." March 21, 2003

Excerpt From a Travel Guidebook for African Americans

Because of Jim Crow laws, travel for African Americans in many parts of the country was difficult or even dangerous. The *Negro Motorist Green Book* listed, by state and city, places to stay and restaurants that were either owned by or welcomed African Americans. In the following excerpt from the 1948 edition, a contributor describes travel to a town in North Dakota.

PRIMARY SOURCE : GUIDEBOOK

❝ From DICKINSON, NORTH DAKOTA:

. . . Several places of business, while they are glad to provide for Negro customers, do not care to advertise for Negro trade.

The attitude of a majority of those I contacted was that, while they themselves had no color prejudice, some of their regular customers did have. This was the impression I gained from hotel operators, barbers, and others contacted. They were all eager to provide whatever services were required by Negroes visiting Dickinson. . . .

Upon occasion, Negroes have been accommodated in Dickinson hotels. However, a Negro tourist would have an easier time getting accommodations at Dickinson's motels and in several **tourist camps.** North Dakotans, generally, are friendly, and I am sure that a Negro tourist would be pleased with his reception in Dickinson. ❞

—*The Negro Motorist Green Book,* 1948

---

tourist camps lodging for travelers often consisting of small individual cabins

EXAMINE THE SOURCE

1. **Analyzing Text** What is the writer attempting to accomplish with this contribution to the *Green Book*? According to the writer, does Dickinson seem like a welcoming destination for African Americans?

2. **Inferring** In what circumstances might the *Green Book* not be helpful or be misleading?

Your Inquiry Analysis

EVALUATE SOURCES AND USE EVIDENCE

Reflect back to the Compelling Question and the Supporting Question you developed at the beginning of this lesson.

1. **Gathering Sources** Which sources helped you answer the Compelling Question and your Supporting Questions most directly? Which sources, if any, challenged the answers you thought you were going to arrive at when you first created your supporting questions? Were there details you still need more information on, and where might you look to find that information?

2. **Evaluating Sources** Looking at the sources that helped you answer your Supporting Questions, evaluate the credibility of each source. What details made that source a particularly useful one to answer your question? Are there further details you may need in order to better evaluate the authority of these sources?

3. **Comparing and Contrasting** Compare and contrast two of the sources in this lesson more closely. What area of life does each source examine? What tone is expressed by each writer, speaker, or photographer? Is the person angry, sad, or merely conveying information? Explain.

COMMUNICATE CONCLUSIONS

Presenting Work with a partner to compare the Supporting Questions each of you wrote at the beginning of the lesson. Choose three of these Supporting Questions to answer using the sources. Then, prepare a short multimedia presentation on how the sources helped you answer the Supporting Questions you chose. Consider including quotes from the sources in your presentation. Give your presentation in front of your classmates.

TAKE INFORMED ACTION

Writing a Letter Think about an issue or cause that you care deeply about. How could showing the impacts of that cause, such as the sources in this lesson have done, help motivate improvements in that cause? Consider if you have seen any similar examples in recent media. Write a letter to your local elected officials that explains the impacts of the injustice you identified and suggests solutions for the problem.

The Negro Motorist Green Book: 1948. New York: Victor H. Green & Co., 1948. New York Public Library Digital Collections. Accessed June 10, 2020. http://digitalcollections.nypl.org/items/70651400-8931-0132-f4b5-58d385a7bbd0

03

The Civil Rights Movement Begins

READING STRATEGY

Analyzing Key Ideas and Details As you read, complete a graphic organizer similar to the one here by listing the techniques used to challenge segregation.

The Origins of the Civil Rights Movement

GUIDING QUESTION

What role did the NAACP play in the civil rights movement?

The National Association for the Advancement of Colored People (NAACP) was established in 1909 to fight for the rights of African Americans. The NAACP convinced the military to allow African American pilots to fly in World War II. This allowed the Tuskegee Airmen, a unit filled with black pilots, to be established. The accomplishments of these and other black soldiers during the war encouraged the civil rights movement.

The NAACP gave African Americans the institutional support to fight racial discrimination and injustice. One founder in this movement was A. Philip Randolph—a union leader since the 1920s as well as a civil rights activist—who compelled President Franklin Roosevelt to issue an executive order ending discrimination in wartime industries during World War II. The NAACP emboldened people to commit acts of defiance against segregated bus laws—including Rosa Parks's famous refusal to give up her seat to a white person on a Montgomery, Alabama bus in December 1955.

These victories were in contrast to the entrenchment of segregation. Back in 1896, the Supreme Court had declared segregation to be constitutional in *Plessy* v. *Ferguson*, which established the **"separate but equal"** doctrine. Laws that segregated African Americans were permitted as long as "equal" facilities were provided for all races. The facilities provided for African Americans, however, were usually of poorer quality than those provided for whites. Offering separate facilities is an example of **de jure segregation,** or segregation based on laws. After Reconstruction, local and state laws in the South allowed for the segregation of many facets of life, including transportation, education, neighborhoods, restaurants, theaters, libraries, pools, restrooms, drinking fountains, and even cemeteries. Areas without such laws often had de facto segregation—segregation by custom and tradition.

Pushing for Desegregation

The civil rights movement had been building for a long time. Since its founding, the NAACP had supported court cases aimed at overturning segregation with some success. For example, the Supreme Court ruled in *Norris* v. *Alabama* (1935) that the exclusion of African Americans from juries violated their rights to equal protection under the law.

African Americans also gained political power as northern politicians increasingly sought their votes. In response to the New Deal, many African Americans began supporting the Democratic Party in the 1930s, giving the party new strength in the North. The northern wing of the party was now able to counter Southern Democrats, who often supported segregation.

During World War II, African American leaders began to use their political power to help end discrimination in wartime factories. They also increased opportunities for African Americans in the military. After the war, many African

"separate but equal" a doctrine established by the 1896 Supreme Court case *Plessy* v. *Ferguson* that permitted laws segregating African Americans as long as equal facilities were provided

de jure segregation segregation by law

BROWN V. BOARD OF EDUCATION, 1954

BACKGROUND TO THE CASE One of the most important Supreme Court cases in American history began in 1952, when the Supreme Court agreed to hear the NAACP's case *Brown* v. *Board of Education of Topeka,* and three other cases. These cases all dealt with the question of whether the principle "separate but equal," established in *Plessy* v. *Ferguson,* was constitutional with regard to public schools.

HOW THE COURT RULED In a unanimous decision in 1954, the Court ruled in favor of Linda Brown and the other plaintiffs. In doing so, it overruled *Plessy* v. *Ferguson.* It rejected the idea that equivalent but separate schools for African American and white students was constitutional. The Court held that racial segregation in public schools violated the Fourteenth Amendment's equal protection clause. Chief Justice Earl Warren summed up the Court's decision, declaring: "[I]n the field of public education, the doctrine of 'separate but equal' has no place. Separate educational facilities are inherently unequal." The Court's rejection of the separate but equal doctrine was a major victory for the civil rights movement. It led to the overturning of laws requiring segregation in other public places.

» The children involved in the *Brown* case, photographed in 1953. From l to r, Vicki and Donald Henderson, Brown, James Emanuel, Nancy Todd, and Katherine Carper.

1. **Making Connections** Why did the Supreme Court find in favor of Linda Brown?
2. **Summarizing** Why was the ruling in *Brown* v. *Board of Education* so important?

American soldiers returned home optimistic that their country would appreciate their loyalty and sacrifice. In the 1950s, when change did not come, their determination to change prejudices led to protests—and to the emergence of the civil rights movement.

In 1942 James Farmer and George Houser founded the Congress of Racial Equality (CORE) in Chicago. CORE began using sit-ins, a form of protest first popularized by union workers in the 1930s, to desegregate restaurants that refused to serve African Americans. Using the sit-in strategy, members of CORE went to segregated restaurants. If they were denied service, they sat down and refused to leave. The sit-ins were intended to shame restaurant managers into integrating their restaurants. CORE successfully integrated many restaurants, theaters, and other public facilities in Northern cities, including Chicago, Detroit, Denver, and Syracuse.

Brown v. Board of Education

The NAACP continued to use the courts to challenge segregation. From 1939 to 1961, the NAACP's chief counsel and director of its Legal Defense and Educational Fund was African American attorney Thurgood Marshall. After the war, Marshall focused his efforts on ending segregation in public schools.

In 1954 the Supreme Court decided to combine several cases and issue a general ruling on segregation in schools. One of the cases involved a young African American girl named Linda Brown, who was denied admission to her neighborhood school in

Topeka, Kansas, because of her race. She was told to attend an all-black school across town. With the help of the NAACP, her parents sued the Topeka school board. On May 17, 1954, the Supreme Court ruled unanimously in *Brown* v. *Board of Education of Topeka,* that segregation in public schools was unconstitutional. This ruling extended the 1950 decision in *Sweatt* v. *Painter* that declared segregation in university graduate schools unconstitutional if the facilities were not truly equal.

One of the cases combined with *Brown* was *Davis* v. *County School Board of Prince Edward County.* Oliver W. Hill, the lead NAACP lawyer in Virginia, helped shepherd the case through federal court and write the brief for the Supreme Court case. *Davis* was one of many lawsuits Hill brought in Virginia in his efforts to dismantle segregation.

Southern Resistance

The *Brown* decision marked a dramatic reversal of the precedent established in the *Plessy* v. *Ferguson* case in 1896. *Brown* v. *Board of Education* applied only to public schools, but the ruling threatened the entire system of segregation. Thus, it angered many white Southerners, causing them to become even more determined to defend segregation, regardless of what the Supreme Court ruled.

Although some school districts in the Upper South integrated their schools, anger and opposition was a far more common reaction to integration. Senator Harry F. Byrd of Virginia called on Southerners to adopt

PHOTO: Carl Iwasaki/The LIFE Images Collection via Getty Images/Getty Images; TEXT: Brown v. Board of Education of Topeka, 347 U.S. 483 (1954), Supreme Court of the United States.

"massive resistance" against the ruling. South Carolina's Strom Thurmond, who was elected to the Senate in 1954, joined Senator Byrd in helping draft the "Southern Manifesto" in 1956. It denounced the Supreme Court's ruling as "clear abuse of judicial power" and pledged to use "all lawful means to bring about a reversal of this decision." In Georgia former restauranteur Lester Maddox, who sold his restaurant rather than serve African Americans, won the governorship on a segregationist ticket in 1966 and fought against integrating the state's public schools. Across the South, hundreds of thousands of white Americans joined citizens' councils to pressure their local governments and school boards into defying the Supreme Court.

Conversely, *Brown* helped convince many African Americans that the time had come to challenge segregation. Medgar Evers was among those to take up the fight. Evers was born in Mississippi and fought in World War II in both Germany and France. He married while still in college, and he and his wife, Myrlie, eventually had three children.

Evers was denied admission to the University of Mississippi law school in 1954. He sued for admission and, although he lost, it was the beginning of his involvement with the NAACP. Evers worked tirelessly for African American equality while he and his family faced constant threats and violence. In May 1963, his home was firebombed. The following month, on June 11, he was murdered outside his home by a man named Byron De La Beckwith, a founder and longtime member of Mississippi's White Citizens Council.

✓ **CHECK FOR UNDERSTANDING**

1. **Examining** What two types of segregation were practiced in the South?

2. **Describing** What techniques did the civil rights movement use to challenge segregation?

Beginning the Movement

GUIDING QUESTION

How was the civil rights movement a combination of local protest and government reform?

In the midst of the uproar over the *Brown* v. *Board of Education* case, Rosa Parks challenged segregation of public transportation. Jo Ann Robinson, head of a local group called the Women's Political Council, called on African Americans to boycott Montgomery's buses on the day Rosa Parks appeared in court.

The Montgomery Bus Boycott

Several African American leaders formed the Montgomery Improvement Association to run the boycott and to negotiate with city leaders. They elected a 26-year-old pastor named Martin Luther King, Jr., to

African Americans walk to work during the third month of the Montgomery bus boycott.

Analyzing Visuals How does this photograph demonstrate the boycott's effectiveness?

lead them. Dr. King encouraged the people to continue to protest but cautioned that it had to be peaceful:

66 Now let us say that we are not advocating violence. . . . The only weapon that we have in our hands this evening is the weapon of protest. . . . If we were incarcerated behind the iron curtains of a communistic nation—we couldn't do this. If we were trapped in the dungeon of a totalitarian regime—we couldn't do this. But the great glory of American democracy is the right to protest for right. 99

—quoted in *Parting the Waters: America in the King Years*, 1989

King's theology education and the influence of other reformers, such as Quaker pacifist Bayard Rustin, produced an emphasis on nonviolent resistance as the best way to end segregation. He urged African Americans to tell racists, "[W]e will soon wear you down by our capacity to suffer. And in winning our freedom we will so appeal to your heart and conscience that we will win you in the process." In November 1956, over a year into the boycott, the Supreme Court declared Alabama's laws requiring segregation on buses unconstitutional. After the Court's ruling, the Montgomery boycott was ended. Many other cities in the South, however, successfully resisted integrating their public transportation systems for years.

The Women's Political Council, led by Jo Ann Robinson, contributed greatly to the Montgomery bus boycott's success. The group printed and distributed leaflets advertising the boycott, organized carpools, and coordinated with civil rights groups.

Eisenhower and the Crisis in Little Rock

President Eisenhower was not sympathetic to the civil rights movement. He feared that a court ruling overturning segregation would anger white voters and

PHOTO: ©Don Cravens/The LIFE Images Collection/Getty Images; TEXT: (1)The Southern Manifesto. From Congressional Record, 84th Congress Second Session. Vol. 102, part 4 (March 12, 1956), Washington, D.C.: Government Printing Office, 1956: 4459-4460; (2)Martin Luther King, Jr., "Address to the Montgomery Improvement Association," December 5, 1955, reprinted in The Papers of Martin Luther King, Jr., vol. 3, ed. Clayborne Carson (Berkeley: University of California Press, 1994), 72; (3)Martin Luther King, Jr., The Papers of Martin Luther King, Jr.: Volume IV: Symbol of the Movement, January 1957-December 1958. (Berkeley, University of California Press, 2000) Pg 341.

EMMETT TILL (1941–1955)

Emmett Till was born in Chicago on July 25, 1941, to working-class parents. In August of 1955 Till, then 14, traveled from his home in the South Side of Chicago to Money, Mississippi, to visit family. While there, he and his cousins visited a country store, where he allegedly flirted with Carolyn Bryant, the store owner's white wife.

TILL'S MURDER When Roy Bryant, Carolyn Bryant's husband, learned of the incident, he and his half brother, J.W. Milam, went to the home of Moses Wright, Till's great-uncle, and kidnapped the boy at gunpoint. They beat him, shot him, then weighed his body down before throwing it into the Tallahatchie River. Moses Wright reported Till's disappearance to the police, and Roy Bryant and Milan were arrested the following day—August 29. Mamie Till Bradley, Emmett's mother, kept her son's casket open at his funeral so everyone could see the brutality he had suffered.

THE TRIAL Roy Bryant and Milam stood trial on September 19, 1955. Moses Wright identified the two men as the kidnappers. After hearing evidence over four days, the all-white, all-male jury took only about an hour to find Bryant and Milam not guilty. The two later sold their story to *Look* magazine, admitting to the murder and even bragging that they had delivered Southern justice to protect white womanhood. Late in her life, Carolyn Bryant admitted she had lied in court about Till's actions. The anger African Americans felt over Till's murder was another critical motivational point for many who joined the years-long protest and action of the civil rights movement.

Analyzing How does Emmett Till's death and trial show the injustice of the Jim Crow South?

---

cost him reelection. The military, however, was one area he was comfortable pushing through desegregation. In 1948 President Truman had issued Executive Order 9981, which called for the full integration of all branches of the military, but the military had been slow to comply. In response, Eisenhower ordered navy shipyards and veterans' hospitals to desegregate.

At the same time, Eisenhower disagreed with using protests and court rulings. He believed segregation and racism would end gradually as values changed. With the nation in the midst of the Cold War, he worried that challenging white Southerners might divide the nation. Publicly, he refused to endorse the *Brown* v. *Board of Education* decision, remarking, "I don't believe you can change the hearts of men with laws or decisions." However, Eisenhower knew he had to uphold the authority of the federal government, and became the first president since Reconstruction to send troops into the South to protect the rights of African Americans.

In September 1957 the school board in Little Rock, Arkansas, was under a federal court order requiring that nine African American students be admitted to Central High. The governor of Arkansas Orval Faubus, determined to win reelection, began to campaign as a defender of white supremacy. Faubus ordered troops from the Arkansas National Guard to prevent the nine students from entering the school. As the National Guard troops surrounded the school, an angry white mob gathered to intimidate students.

Faubus had used the armed forces of a state to oppose the federal government—the first such challenge to the Constitution since the Civil War. Eisenhower knew that he could not allow Faubus to defy the federal government. After a conference between Eisenhower and Faubus proved fruitless, the district court ordered the governor to remove the troops. Instead of ending the crisis, however, Faubus simply left the school to the mob of segregationists. After the African American students entered the building, angry whites beat at least two African American reporters and broke many windows.

The violence convinced Eisenhower that federal authority had to be upheld. He immediately ordered the U.S. Army to send troops to Little Rock and federalized the Arkansas National Guard. By nightfall more than 1,000 soldiers of the 101st Airborne Division had arrived. By 5:00 A.M., the troops had encircled the school, bayonets ready. A few hours later the nine African American students arrived in an army station wagon and walked into the high school. Federal authority had been upheld, but in September 1958, one year after Central High was integrated, Faubus closed Little Rock's high schools for the entire year rather than allow African American students to attend school.

The same year that the Little Rock crisis began, Congress passed the Civil Rights Act of 1957—the first civil rights law since Reconstruction—to protect the right of African Americans to vote. Eisenhower believed

PHOTO: Bettmann/Getty Images; TEXT: Eisenhower, Dwight D. The President's News Conference of June 26, 1957. Public Papers of the Presidents of the United States: Dwight D. Eisenhower, 1957, entry 119, pp 505. Washington, D.C.: Government Printing Office, 1958.

firmly in the right to vote and in his responsibility to protect voting rights. He also knew that if he sent a civil rights bill to Congress, conservative Southern Democrats would try to block the legislation. In 1956 he sent the bill to Congress, hoping not only to split the Democratic Party but also to convince more African Americans to vote Republican.

Several Southern senators tried to stop the Civil Rights Act of 1957, but Senate majority leader Lyndon Johnson put together a compromise that enabled the act to pass. Although its final form was much weaker than originally intended, the act still brought the power of the federal government into the civil rights debate. It created a Civil Rights Division within the Department of Justice and gave it the authority to seek court injunctions against anyone interfering with the right to vote. It also created the United States Commission on Civil Rights to investigate any denial of voting rights. After the bill passed, the Southern Christian Leadership Conference (SCLC)—a group that had been founded to help organize the Montgomery bus boycotts—announced a campaign to register two million new African American voters.

 CHECK FOR UNDERSTANDING

Explaining How did President Eisenhower respond to the crisis in Little Rock, Arkansas?

Challenging Segregation Across the South

GUIDING QUESTION

What were the goals of the Student Nonviolent Coordinating Committee?

In the fall of 1959 four young African Americans—Joseph McNeil, Ezell Blair, Jr., David Richmond, and Franklin McCain—enrolled at North Carolina Agricultural and Technical College, an African American college in Greensboro. The four freshmen often talked about the civil rights movement. In January 1960 McNeil suggested a sit-in. "All of us were afraid," Richmond later recalled, "but we went and did it."

On February 1, 1960, the four friends entered the nearby Woolworth's department store. They purchased school supplies and then sat at the whites-only lunch counter and ordered coffee. When they were refused service, Blair asked, "I beg your pardon, but you just served us at [the checkout] counter. Why can't we be served at the counter here?" The students stayed at the counter until it closed. They then stated that they would sit there daily until they got the same service as white customers. They left the store excited. McNeil recalled, "I just felt I had powers within me, a superhuman strength that would come forward."

McCain noted, "I probably felt better that day than I've ever felt in my life."

The Sit-In Movement

News of the daring sit-in spread quickly. The following day, twenty-nine African American students arrived at Woolworth's determined to sit at the counter until served. By the end of the week more than 300 students were taking part. The sit-in proved to be a dramatic protest technique for civil rights that caught the public's attention. Within two months, sit-ins had spread to fifty-four cities in nine states. They were staged at segregated stores, restaurants, hotels, and movie theaters. By 1961, sit-ins had been held in more than one hundred cities. The sit-in movement brought large numbers of college students into the civil rights struggle. Many were discouraged by the slow pace of desegregation. Sit-ins offered them a way to dictate the pace of change.

At first, the leaders of the NAACP and the SCLC were nervous about the sit-in campaign. Those conducting sit-ins were heckled, punched, kicked, beaten with clubs, and burned with cigarettes, hot coffee, and acid. Most practiced nonviolence in response. Many, including Rosa Parks, participated in nonviolence training at the Highlander Folk School in Tennessee. This school, founded by Myles Horton, played an important role in teaching skills and providing inspiration to many civil rights activists.

Urged on by former NAACP official and SCLC executive director Ella Baker, students established the Student Nonviolent Coordinating Committee (SNCC) in 1960. Baker organized a conference at Shaw University in Raleigh, North Carolina, to encourage formation of the group and plan future efforts. She believed that young activists would bring new energy into the movement. African American college students from all across the South made up the majority of SNCC's members. Many whites also joined. SNCC became an important civil rights group.

Volunteer Robert Moses urged SNCC to start helping rural Southern African Americans who often faced violence if they tried to register to vote. Many SNCC volunteers, including Moses, bravely headed south as part of a voter education project. During a period of registration efforts in 1964 known as Freedom Summer, the Ku Klux Klan brutally murdered three SNCC workers with the complicity of local officials.

SNCC organizer Fannie Lou Hamer was evicted from her farm after registering to vote. Police arrested her in Mississippi as she was returning from a voter registration workshop in 1963, and the police beat her while she was in jail. She still went on to help organize the Mississippi Freedom Democratic Party and challenged the legality of the state's segregated Democratic Party at the 1964 national convention.

(1)David Richmond; (2)Ezell Blair, Jr.; (3)Joseph McNeil; (4)Franklin McCain. All quoted in Civilites and Civil Rights: Greensboro, North Carolina, and the Black Struggle for Freedom by William Henry Chafe. Copyright © 1980, 1981 by Oxford University Press.

Freedom Riders traveling from Washington, D.C., to New Orleans whose bus was set on fire by a white mob as they arrived in Anniston, Alabama, in May 1961.

Analyzing Perspectives Why might it be important for journalists to be traveling with the Freedom Riders?

The Freedom Riders

Despite rulings outlawing segregation in interstate bus service, bus travel remained unintegrated in much of the South, including Alabama. Alabama's governor, John Patterson, was known to be in favor of segregation. As attorney general of the state, he had banned NAACP activity in Alabama, and he had fought the bus boycotts.

In early May 1961, teams of African American and white volunteers who became known as Freedom Riders boarded several southbound interstate buses. These buses were met by angry white mobs in Anniston, Birmingham, and Montgomery, Alabama. The mobs slit bus tires and threw rocks at the windows. In Anniston, someone threw a firebomb into one bus. Fortunately, no one was killed.

In Birmingham riders emerged from a bus to face a gang of young men armed with baseball bats, chains, and lead pipes. The gang beat the riders viciously. Birmingham public safety commissioner Theophilus Eugene "Bull" Connor claimed that there had been no police at the bus station because it was Mother's Day, and he had given many officers the day off. FBI evidence later showed that Connor told the local Klan to beat the riders until "it looked like a bulldog got a hold of them." The violence made national news, shocking many Americans and drawing the federal government's attention to the plight of African Americans in the South.

Kennedy's Civil Rights Response

While campaigning for the presidency in 1960, John F. Kennedy made promises to support civil rights. Civil rights leaders, such as NAACP executive director Roy Wilkins, urged Kennedy to support civil rights legislation after taking office, but Kennedy tried to avoid strong actions supporting racial equality. He wanted to keep the support of Southern senators to get other programs through Congress. Kennedy's response disappointed civil rights leaders.

Kennedy supported civil rights in other ways. He appointed Thurgood Marshall to a federal judgeship on the Second Circuit Appeals Court in New York. Kennedy also created the Committee on Equal Employment Opportunity (CEEO) and allowed the Justice Department, run by his brother Robert, to actively support the civil rights movement. The department tried to help African Americans register to vote by filing lawsuits across the South.

After the Freedom Riders were attacked in Montgomery, both Kennedys publicly urged the civil rights protesters to have a "cooling off" period. CORE leader James Farmer rejected the idea and announced that the riders would head into Mississippi. To stop the violence, President Kennedy made a deal with Mississippi senator James Eastland. As a result, no violence occurred when buses arrived in Jackson, but Kennedy did not protest the riders' arrests.

When Thurgood Marshall learned that the cost of bailing the Freedom Riders out of jail used up most of CORE's funds, he offered Farmer the use of the NAACP Legal Defense Fund's bail-bond account to keep the rides going. When President Kennedy found that the Freedom Riders were still active, he ordered the Interstate Commerce Commission (ICC) to tighten its regulations against segregated bus terminals, and Attorney General Robert Kennedy ordered the Justice Department to take legal action against Southern cities that maintained segregated bus terminals. By late 1962, the committed work of activists began eliminating segregated interstate bus travel.

✓ **CHECK FOR UNDERSTANDING**

1. **Making Connections** What were the goals of the Student Nonviolent Coordinating Committee?
2. **Summarizing** How did the Kennedy administration's Justice Department help the civil rights movement?

LESSON ACTIVITIES

1. **Informative Writing** Assume the role of a journalist at a college newspaper in 1960. Write an article for the newspaper describing the sit-in movement, including its participants, goals, and achievements.

2. **Presenting** Work in groups of four to research, write, and present brief monologues describing various events and milestones of the civil rights movement. Each monologue should be written and presented from the perspective of an actual participant. Ask your classmates to take notes for an after-presentation class discussion. Prepare at least two discussion questions for each event presented.

PHOTO: Bettmann/Getty Images; TEXT: Freedom Bound: A History of America's Civil Rights Movement by Robert Weisbrot. Copyright © 1990 by Robert Weisbrot. Published by W.W. Norton & Company, Inc. All rights reserved.

04

Challenging Segregation

Bettmann/Getty Images

The Civil Rights Act of 1964

GUIDING QUESTION

What were the causes and effects of the Civil Rights Act of 1964?

During the civil rights movement, the U.S. Congress passed two pieces of civil rights legislation before passing the historic Civil Rights Act of 1964. President Eisenhower signed the first act on September 9, 1957. It tried to protect voting rights and created the Civil Rights Division within the Justice Department. The U.S. Commission on Civil Rights was also created to investigate accusations of voter infringement. On May 6, 1960, Eisenhower signed a new law that extended the life of the Civil Rights Commission and strengthened other elements in the 1957 law.

But neither of these laws gave the federal government enough authority to enforce the spirit of the law. Civil rights activists continued planning protests that increased the pressure on Washington, D.C. Martin Luther King, Jr., Ralph Abernathy, Fred Shuttlesworth, and other activists made Birmingham, Alabama, the focus of a massive effort to expose and end the city's network of separate and unequal laws that discriminated against its African American citizens.

The Birmingham Campaign

The protests in Birmingham began in March 1963, but the momentum was slow, and the nation did not immediately pay attention. Birmingham police first arrested Dr. King and other activists in mid-April for marching without a permit. While King sat in jail, eight of the city's religious leaders wrote to the

READING STRATEGY

<u>Key Ideas and Details</u> As you read, use a graphic organizer like the one below to take notes.

EVENT	EFFECT
The Birmingham Campaign →	
The Civil Rights Act of 1964 →	
Selma March →	
Voting Rights Act of 1965 →	

The water pressure of the fire hoses used against protesters could be intense enough to lift people into the air, roll bodies down the street, and rip the shirts off the protesters.

Analyzing Visuals Why is this photograph unsettling?

Birmingham Times, describing the protests as untimely and unwise. This letter is sometimes called "A Call for Unity." The protests in Birmingham seemed like they might fall apart before they truly started.

While Dr. King was in solitary confinement, he responded to the criticism by writing in the margins of newspapers and scraps of paper and paper towels. King's lawyer smuggled this series of notes out of the jail and published them as the "Letter from Birmingham Jail." King wanted to motivate his fellow activists to continue resisting Birmingham's segregated society and to persuade government leaders in Washington, D.C., to support new civil rights legislation.

Birmingham activists increased the pressure on the Kennedy Administration by putting African American children at the front of the protests. In May 1963 children began marching daily through the streets of Birmingham singing "We Shall Overcome." They were arrested for lacking city-granted parade permits and were quickly taken off the streets and into waiting police vans. But the continuing waves of children overwhelmed the city's police. The number of children marching grew larger each day, and the city ran out of police vans. School buses were called into service to transport each day's new crowd to the jail, but the jail cells quickly overflowed. The Birmingham police then used fire department water hoses and police dogs to hold back the youth. King sent a telegram asking President Kennedy: "Will you permit this . . . violence in Birmingham to threaten our lives and deny our rights?"

Birmingham's brutal reputation was firmly established after World War II, as African American families began moving into formerly all-white neighborhoods. Segregationists responded by bombing their homes, businesses, and churches. Newly desegregated neighborhoods were targeted so often that one became known as "Dynamite Hill," and Birmingham was nicknamed "Bombingham." The violence culminated in 1963 when Addie Mae Collins, Cynthia Wesley, Carole Robertson, and Carol Denise McNair were killed and more than 20 other churchgoers were injured in the bombing of the 16th Street Baptist Church. It took more than three decades to bring all the perpetrators to justice.

Kennedy Takes Action

Events in Alabama grew more tense. At his inauguration as Alabama's governor, George Wallace stated, "I draw the line in the dust and toss the gauntlet before the feet of tyranny. And I say, Segregation now! Segregation tomorrow! Segregation forever!"

On June 11, 1963, Wallace stood in front of the University of Alabama's admissions office, blocking two African Americans from enrolling in the school. Federal officials ordered Wallace to move away from the door. When Wallace refused, President Kennedy sent troops from the Alabama National Guard to help the officials. Wallace stepped down to avoid an outbreak of violence.

That same night, President Kennedy announced on national television his support for a new civil rights bill that was moving through the House of Representatives and the Senate.

❝ It ought to be possible, in short, for every American to enjoy the privileges of being American without regard to his race or his color. In short, every American ought to have the right to be treated as he would wish to be treated, as one would wish his children to be treated. But this is not the case. . . .

This is not a sectional issue. Difficulties over segregation and discrimination exist in every city, in every State of the Union . . .

I am, therefore, asking the Congress to enact legislation giving all Americans the right to be served in facilities which are open to the public—hotels, restaurants, theaters, retail stores, and similar establishments. ❞

—President John F. Kennedy's speech on civil rights, June 11, 1963

Kennedy's action encouraged the activists who had worked so hard in Birmingham. They knew, however, that moving an effective civil rights bill through Congress would be a slow and difficult political process.

Hours after Kennedy's address, a white segregationist murdered civil rights activist Medgar Evers in Mississippi. Evers had been the National Association for the Advancement of Colored People's (NAACP) first field secretary in Mississippi. He had helped organize voter registration efforts and

Martin Luther King, Jr., acknowledges the crowd at the March on Washington.

PHOTO: Francis Miller/The LIFE Picture Collection/Getty Images; TEXT: (1)King, Jr., Martin Luther, In Risen, Clay, The Bill of the Century: The Epic Battle for the Civil Rights Act. London: Bloomsbury, 2014; (2)Wallace, George C. "Inaugural Address." 1963 Governor Inaugural. Montgomery, Alabama, 14 Jan. 1963. Alabama Governor, Inaugural addresses and programs, SP194, Alabama Department of Archives and History; (3)John F. Kennedy, Report to the American People on Civil Rights, 11 June 1963. John F. Kennedy Presidential Library & Museum.

PHOTO: Library of Congress Prints and Photographs Division [LC-DIG-ds-04118]; TEXT: Martin Luther King, Jr., "I Have a Dream," August 28, 1963. Reprinted by arrangement with The Heirs to the Estate of Martin Luther King Jr., c/o Writers House as agent for the proprietor New York, NY. , Copyright 1963 Dr. Martin Luther King Jr; copyright renewed 1991 Coretta Scott King.

BIOGRAPHY

JAMES FARMER (1920–1999)

James L. Farmer, Jr., grew up in Marshall, Texas. Pearl Houston, his mother, graduated from Florida's Bethune-Cookman Institute and worked as a teacher. His father, James Farmer, Sr., was a Methodist preacher with a doctorate degree in theology and taught at the historic black educational institute Wiley College. James Farmer graduated from Wiley College in 1938 when he was just 18. He earned a second degree in Divinity from Howard University in 1941. Farmer was very aware of the segregationist policies surrounding him as he grew up, and he formed an early commitment to end such discrimination. While studying at Howard, Farmer also grew interested in nonviolent methods of protest to create social change. He was a conscientious objector during World War II.

ACTIVISM IN ACTION During World War II, Farmer helped found the Congress of Racial Equality (CORE) in Chicago, Illinois. A key principle of CORE, according to Farmer, was that it was led by regular citizens instead of experts, and it took direct action against segregation through nonviolence. One of CORE's largest direct-action efforts was the Freedom Rides in 1961 to force integration on interstate bus travel. Farmer himself was one of the riders jailed in Jackson, Mississippi, in 1961.

BIG SIX As a leader of CORE, Farmer was considered one of the "Big Six" who helped organize the March on Washington. The other five activists were Martin Luther King, Jr., of the Southern Christian Leadership Conference (SCLC), John Lewis of the Student Nonviolent Coordinating Committee (SNCC), Roy Wilkins of the NAACP, Whitney Young of the National Urban League, and A. Philip Randolph.

Understanding Significance What leadership role did Farmer play in the civil rights movement?

boycotts. Evers was seen by many to be a **martyr** of the civil rights movement.

The March on Washington

Civil rights leaders searched for a way to speed the legislative process while also growing national support. When A. Philip Randolph suggested a march on Washington D.C. Bayard Rustin was named Deputy Director of the event and began the process of planning and organizing the march.

On August 28, 1963, more than 200,000 demonstrators of all races converged on the nation's capital. The audience heard speeches and sang hymns and songs as they gathered peacefully near the Lincoln Memorial. The most memorable moment was Dr. King's "I Have a Dream" speech describing his vision of freedom and equality for all Americans.

    I have a dream that one day this nation will rise up and live out the true meaning of its creed: 'We hold these truths to be self-evident, that all men are created equal.'

I have a dream that one day on the red hills of Georgia, the sons of former slaves and the sons of former slave owners will be able to sit down together at the table of brotherhood. . . .

I have a dream that my four little children will one day live in a nation where they will not be judged by the color of their skin but by the content of their character.

—Martin Luther King, Jr., from the "Address in Washington," August 28, 1963

That speech and the dignity of the March on Washington built momentum for the civil rights bill that was already being debated In Congress. The bill's opponents continued to slow down the bill, dragging out their committee investigations and using procedural rules to delay votes.

Legislative Delays

President Kennedy was not able to push the civil rights legislation to a final vote before his shocking

martyr a person who sacrifices greatly or perhaps gives their life for the sake of important principles

assassination in November 1963. Vice President Lyndon Johnson—a former member of the Senate Democrats—became president. Johnson had helped pass the Civil Rights Acts of 1957 and 1960 but only by weakening their provisions through compromises with other Southern senators.

On November 27, 1963, the newly sworn-in President Johnson spoke to a joint session of Congress. Johnson pledged to continue Kennedy's work and made the passage of a new civil rights bill a key piece of honoring Kennedy's legacy.

The bill, however, was stuck in the House of Representatives Rules Committee—where all House versions of bills must begin. The chairman of the Rules Committee, Howard W. Smith of Virginia, was a determined segregationist and had effectively blocked civil rights bills since 1955. This delaying tactic was a key component of the Southern Democrats' anti-civil rights strategy. They believed that if they could hold up legislation long enough, frustrated civil rights activists might initiate more violent militant actions, causing a backlash against desegregation and diminishing the public passion for Kennedy's memory.

While Southern senators worked openly to oppose the civil rights bill, many of them realized that they were fighting a losing battle against changes that would soon transform the nation.

66 I believe the Negro has been imposed upon. He has been subjected to indignities. But we shouldn't upset the whole scheme of constitutional government and expect people to swallow laws governing their most intimate social relations. The tempo of change is the crux of the whole matter. Any realist knows that the 'separate but equal' doctrine is finished. 99

—Senator Richard Russell, *Congressional Record*, August 1963

The civil rights bill passed the House of Representatives in February 1964. It then moved to the Senate, where the bill's opponents used another tactic to delay passage.

Democrats used the **filibuster,** a tactic in which senators speak continuously to prevent a vote. On March 30, the full Senate began its debate on the legislation. To carry out the filibuster, the bill's opponents divided themselves into three teams. One team controlled the debate on the Senate floor, then passed off speaking time to another team. Each day a new team took over from the senators who spoke on the previous day, while another group rested.

Southern Senators including (l to r) Sam Ervin, James Eastland, Allen Ellender, Harry Byrd, and Olin Johnston meet before a Senate session to plan their strategy to filibuster the Civil Rights bill in March 1964.

Analyzing Visuals Based on the Senators' expressions, what attitude toward the filibuster did they hold?

Democrats held onto the debate for the next sixty days. The key members of this so-called Southern Resistance group included Sam Ervin of North Carolina, John Stennis and James Eastland from Mississippi, Richard Russell from Georgia, Spessard Holland from Florida, Allen Ellender and Russell Long from Louisiana, A. Willis Robertson from Virginia, and Strom Thurmond from South Carolina.

While the filibuster was going on, Senator Hubert Humphrey of Minnesota, the Democratic Whip, was working against his more conservative-leaning Southern party members to get the sixty-seven votes needed to achieve **cloture**—the procedure needed to end a filibuster debate and force a vote. Illinois Senator Everett Dirksen also tried to increase the chances of compromise by introducing a revised version of the Senate bill that weakened the scope of the federal government's regulations on private businesses and civil rights.

On June 10, the Senate voted 71 to 29 to stop the filibuster delay and call a final approval vote. The Senate then easily passed Dirksen's revised bill.

filibuster an attempt to kill or delay a bill by having a group of senators take turns speaking continuously so that a vote cannot take place

cloture a motion that ends debate and calls for an immediate vote

PHOTO: Bettmann/Getty Images; TEXT: Russell, Richard. August 14, 1963. In Congressional Record. 88th Congress, First Session. Vol. 109, pt. 11.

On July 2, 1964, Johnson signed the final version of the Civil Rights Act of 1964 into law.

The Law Changes the Nation

The Civil Rights Act of 1964 was the most comprehensive civil rights law ever enacted by Congress. The law made segregation illegal in most places and banned racial discrimination in places that served the general public, specifically any type of hotel, restaurant, theater, or entertainment venue. Yet, it was unclear whether the federal government had jurisdiction to regulate these businesses—so the passage of the Civil Rights Act of 1964 immediately raised constitutional issues.

The owner of the Heart of Atlanta Motel refused to allow African Americans to stay at his hotel and filed suit in federal court. In *Heart of Atlanta Motel* v. *United States* (1964), the Supreme Court ruled that the interstate commerce clause (Article I, Section 8, of the Constitution) did give Congress the power to ban discrimination in facilities serving the public. The Civil Rights Act also gave the U.S. attorney general more power to enforce school desegregation, and it required private employers to end workplace discrimination. It also established the Equal Employment Opportunity Commission (EEOC) as a permanent federal agency.

The Civil Rights Act went further than simply banning discrimination based on race. It also banned discrimination based on religion, gender, and national origin. For religious minorities, immigrants, and women, the act represented a dramatic step forward in expanding their political rights and economic opportunities.

✓ **CHECK FOR UNDERSTANDING**

1. **Analyzing Effects** What happened as a result of the Birmingham campaign? Was the campaign successful?
2. **Summarizing** How did the Civil Rights Act of 1964 give the federal government new authority to fight discrimination?

The Voting Rights Struggle

GUIDING QUESTION

Why was the passage of the Voting Rights Act of 1965 a turning point in the civil rights movement?

In December 1964, Dr. King received the Nobel Peace Prize in Oslo, Norway, for his work in the civil rights movement. Yet, despite the passage of the Civil Rights Act of 1964, African Americans still faced voting barriers.

The Twenty-fourth Amendment, ratified in 1964, helped by eliminating poll taxes in federal (but not state) elections. As the SCLC and the SNCC stepped up their voter registration efforts in the South, their members were often attacked and beaten, and several were murdered. A few weeks later, King announced, "We are not asking, we are demanding the ballot." Convinced that a new law was needed to protect African American voting rights, Dr. King decided to hold another dramatic protest.

The Selma March

To keep pressure on the president and the Congress to pass voting legislation, Dr. King joined with SNCC activists and organized a march for freedom from Selma, Alabama, to the state capitol in Montgomery about 50 miles (80 km) away. Selma was the focal point for this voting rights campaign because although African Americans made up most of Selma's population, they only made up one or two percent of registered voters.

The march began on Sunday, March 7, 1965. The SCLC's Hosea Williams and SNCC's John Lewis led some 600 protesters toward Montgomery. As the protesters approached the Edmund Pettus Bridge, which led out of Selma, Sheriff Jim Clark and a deputized group of armed white citizens ordered them to disperse. Lewis and the marchers refused to stop the protest, and Clark's posse responded violently.

Many protesters were beaten in full view of television cameras. This brutal attack, known later as "Bloody Sunday," left 17 marchers hospitalized and another 70 injured. The nation was shocked by the media's footage of law enforcement officers beating peaceful demonstrators. Watching the events from the White House, President Johnson grew furious. Eight days later, he appeared before a nationally televised joint session of Congress to propose a new voting rights law. When King would march across the Edmund Pettus Bridge with a second group of protesters, they would be protected by federal troops to prevent the same violence.

The Voting Rights Act of 1965

On August 3, 1965, the House of Representatives passed the voting rights bill by a wide margin. The following day, the Senate also passed the bill. The Voting Rights Act of 1965 authorized the U.S. attorney general to send federal examiners to register qualified voters, bypassing local officials who often refused to register African Americans. The law also suspended discriminatory devices, such as literacy tests, in counties where less than half of all adults were registered to vote.

The Voting Rights Act of 1965, like the Civil Rights Act of 1964, immediately raised constitutional questions. Article 1, Section 2, of the Constitution says that each state must use the same rules for choosing members of Congress as for choosing state legislators. When the Voting Rights

Martin Luther King, Jr., "Selma March," January 2, 1965.

Percentage Change of Southern African Americans Registered to Vote

The Voting Rights Act of 1965 was a turning point of the civil rights movement that resulted in immediate changes to voter registration in the Southern states.

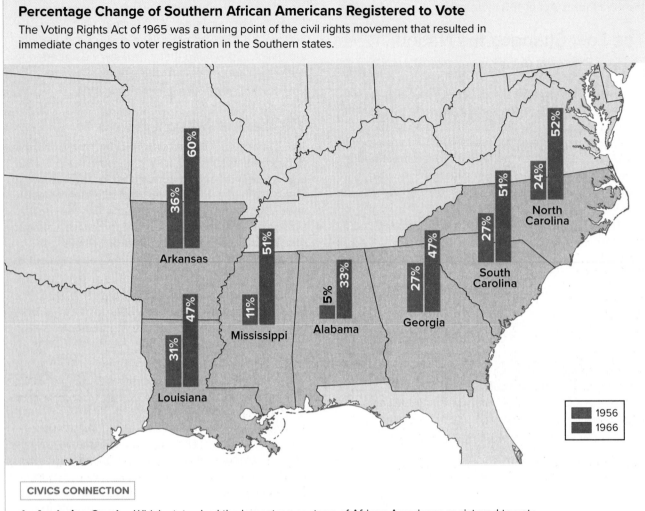

Arkansas — 36%, 60%
Louisiana — 31%, 47%
Mississippi — 11%, 51%
Alabama — 5%, 33%
Georgia — 27%, 47%
South Carolina — 27%, 51%
North Carolina — 24%, 52%

1956
1966

CIVICS CONNECTION

1. **Analyzing Graphs** Which states had the largest percentage of African Americans registered to vote in 1956 and 1966? Which had the lowest? What can you infer about the states that show the least changes?

2. **Drawing Conclusions** How might the Voting Rights Act of 1965 have changed political campaigns in these states?

Act of 1965 banned literacy tests, Congress created a new voting rule for the states. This made it legally unclear if the newly-created federal ban on literacy tests violated the other voting rules already established by the states. If it did, then the Voting Rights Act of 1965 would conflict with the Constitution.

The Supreme Court resolved this in 1966 when it ruled in the *Katzenbach* v. *Morgan* case. With a 7-2 majority, Justice William Brennan explained that the Fourteenth Amendment did allow Congress to ban literacy tests and impose similar voting rules on state governments.

By the end of 1965, almost 250,000 African Americans had registered as new voters. Between 1960 and 2018, the number of African American members of Congress rose from 4 to 52.

CHECK FOR UNDERSTANDING

Explaining What was the Selma March and why was it significant?

LESSON ACTIVITIES

1. **Writing an Informative/Explanatory Essay** Why was the civil rights movement successful at achieving legislation to extend and protect civil rights for African Americans?

2. **Collaborating** Imagine you and a partner are newspaper reporters in 1966 and have been assigned to write an article about the effects of the Voting Rights Act of 1965 in your community. Work together to create a profile of someone you would have wanted to interview and create a list of interview questions.

05

Analyzing Sources: Civil Rights Movement Activists

 COMPELLING QUESTION

How did activists move the civil rights movement forward?

Plan Your Inquiry

In this lesson, you will investigate the role and contributions of key civil rights activists.

DEVELOP QUESTIONS

Developing Questions About Civil Rights Activists Read the Compelling Question for this lesson. Think about the key events that made up the civil rights movement and how different individuals and groups contributed to these events. Develop a list of Supporting Questions that would help you answer the Compelling Question in this lesson.

APPLY HISTORICAL TOOLS

Analyzing Primary Sources You will work with a variety of primary sources in this lesson. These sources focus on contributions of several key civil rights activists in the 1960s. As you read, use a graphic organizer like the one below to record information about the sources that will help you examine them and check for historical understanding. Note ways in which each source helps you answer your Supporting Questions.

Source	Author/ Creator	Description/ Notes	Which Supporting Question does this source help me answer?
A			
B			
C			
D			
E			
F			
G			

After you analyze the sources, you will:

- use the evidence from the sources
- communicate your conclusions
- take informed action

Background Information

Beginning in 1909, the National Association for the Advancement of Colored People (NAACP) mounted legal challenges against segregation laws. W.E.B. Du Bois and Ida B. Wells-Barnett were among its founders. They also served as editors and writers for *The Crisis*, which argued the NAACP's civil rights platform. In 1942 James Farmer launched the Congress of Racial Equality (CORE), which began holding sit-ins to call attention to discrimination and protest segregation. Their actions helped inspire the Student Nonviolent Coordinating Committee (SNCC), founded by Diane Nash, John Lewis and others, which led the lunch counter sit-ins and the Freedom Rides in the 1960s.

You have read about the actions led by Medgar Evers, Rosa Parks, Ella Baker, and Dr. Martin Luther King, Jr., founder of the Southern Christian Leadership Conference (SCLC). In this Inquiry, you'll learn about the actions and goals of civil rights activists in their own words.

» Organizing picket lines, such as this one in front of a school board office, was a strategic activity in the civil rights movement.

RBM Vintage Images/Alamy Stock Photo

Interview with C.T. Vivian

Inspired by the nonviolent acts of civil disobedience practiced by India's Mohandas Gandhi, activist Reverend James M. Lawson supported a nonviolent approach in the struggle for civil rights in the South. He developed workshops in Nashville, Tennessee, on effective nonviolent protest and trained many leaders of the Southern Christian Leadership Conference (SCLC) and the Student Nonviolent Coordinating Committee (SNCC), including Diane Nash, John Lewis, and Reverend C.T. Vivian. In this interview excerpt, conducted in Atlanta, Georgia, in 2011, Vivian recalls Lawson's workshops and how his message was received at the time.

PRIMARY SOURCE : INTERVIEW

❝ **Interviewer:** [A] number of the people that I've talked to who were in [James] Lawson's workshops said that there were psychological aspects to [nonviolent protests] as well, besides the religious, the patriotic, that what you were doing was that they'd come into the workshops thinking that nonviolence meant a kind of curling into the fetal position and that sort of thing to protect yourself and Lawson would tell them no, you need to make eye contact and keep eye contact with people. They have a harder time being violent with you when you're looking at them and making human contact with them. . . .

Reverend Vivian: Well, see, the thing, there was a lot of conversation about it. It was easy to understand it, but you see here again are these various parts of the movement . . . SNCC was the one that wanted to curl up and get beaten and put over your head and all that sort of thing. . . . That was not true with SCLC at any point. ❞

—Interview with Reverend C.T. Vivian, Civil Rights History Project, 2011

EXAMINE THE SOURCE

1. **Explaining** What self-defense technique does Lawson advise against? Why?
2. **Interpreting** Based on what Vivian says about SNCC and SCLC, what do you think is a difference he sees between the two groups?

Letter to the DNC

In 1964 civil rights groups organized the Mississippi Freedom Democratic Party and sent their own elected delegates to the Democratic National Committee (DNC) convention.

PRIMARY SOURCE : LETTER

❝ Dear Convention Delegate:

Three mother's sons who sought to secure political democracy for the people of Mississippi probably lie buried beneath the murky swamps near Philadelphia, a small town in that state.

If they have paid with their lives for believing in the right . . . to have a voice in the election . . . all Democrats who can register and vote with freedom are now challenged as never before. The long and systematic denial of the Negro's right to vote in Mississippi, and the flagrant disloyalty of the 'regular' Mississippi Democratic Party to the principles of the National Democratic Party demand that new channels be created through which all the people of Mississippi can be represented in the 1964 Democratic National Convention. To do less at this historic moment would be a disgrace.

The Freedom Democratic Party parallels the structure and the proceedings of the existing Democratic Party, with the notable exceptions that it is open to all citizens. . . .

We urge that your entire delegation use the full weight of its . . . voting strength to see that the challenge raised by the Mississippi Freedom Democratic Party receives a full and open hearing before the Credentials Committee of the Convention, and if the . . . Committee fails to seat the Freedom Democratic Party, that your delegation call for . . . a roll-call vote to permit the Mississippi issue to be discussed on the floor of the convention. . . . ❞

—Ella J. Baker, July 20, 1964

EXAMINE THE SOURCE

1. **Drawing Conclusions** What does Baker ask the DNC to do, and to what end?
2. **Identifying Cause and Effect** What conditions led Baker and other activists to take this action?

(l)Branch, Taylor, interviewer. Reverend C.T. Vivian oral history interview. Atlanta, GA, March 29, 2011. Civil Rights History Project, Smithsonian Institute's National Museum of African American History & Culture and the Library of Congress, 2011; (r)Baker, Ella J. "Mississippi Freedom Democratic Party Letter to Democratic National Convention Delegates." July 20, 1964

The Courage of the Freedom Riders

In 1946 the U.S. Supreme Court ruled segregation of interstate transportation unconstitutional in *Morgan* v. *Virginia.* Then in *Boynton* v. *Virginia* (1960), the Court ruled that segregation in facilities that served interstate travelers was also unconstitutional. CORE and then SNCC decided to enforce these rulings within the South with the Freedom Rides. The first Freedom Riders—seven of whom were African American and six white—departed Washington, D.C., for New Orleans on May 4, 1961. The riders first met with resistance in Virginia and encountered violence in South Carolina. In Alabama an angry mob beat the riders and firebombed one of the buses. The bus journey ended, and the group flew on to New Orleans. John Seigenthaler was an assistant to Attorney General Robert F. Kennedy (RFK), and Diane Nash was a key leader of SNCC involved in orchestrating the Freedom Rides. PBS produced the documentary *Freedom Riders,* excerpted below, in 2011.

PRIMARY SOURCE : FILM TRANSCRIPT

❝ John Seigenthaler, Assistant to RFK: I went to a motel to spend the night. And you know, I thought, 'What a great hero I am, you know? How easy this was, you know? I just took care of everything the President and the Attorney General wanted done. Mission Accomplished.'

My phone in the hotel room rings and it's the Attorney General. He has received word from the FBI in Nashville that another wave of Freedom Riders is coming down to Birmingham from Nashville to continue the Freedom Rides. And he opened the conversation, 'Who the hell is Diane Nash?'. . .

Diane Nash, Student, Fisk University: It was clear to me that if we allowed the Freedom Ride to stop at that point, just after so much violence had been inflicted, the message would have been sent that all you have to do to stop a nonviolent campaign is inflict massive violence. It was critical that the Freedom Ride not stop, and that it be continued immediately. . . .

Seigenthaler: So I called her. I said, 'I understand that there are more Freedom Riders coming down from Nashville. You must stop them if you can.' Her response was, 'They're not gonna turn back. They're on their way to Birmingham and they'll be there, shortly.'

You know that spiritual—'Like a tree standing by the water, I will not be moved'? She would not be moved. And, and I felt my voice go up another decibel and another and soon I was shouting, 'Young woman, do you understand what you're doing? You're gonna get somebody . . . [D]o you understand you're gonna get somebody killed?'

And, there's a pause, and she said, 'Sir, you should know, we all signed our last wills and testaments last night before they left. We know someone will be killed. But we cannot let violence overcome non-violence.'

That's virtually a direct quote of the words that came out of that child's mouth. Here I am, an official of the United States government, representing the President and the Attorney General, talking to a student at Fisk University. And she in a very quiet but strong way gave me a lecture. **❞**

—Diane Nash and John Seigenthaler,
   in *Freedom Riders*

EXAMINE THE SOURCE

1. **Determining Central Ideas** Why does Nash say that she insisted on the Freedom Rides going forward?

2. **Analyzing Perspectives** How did Seigenthaler react to Nash's comments, and how might his exchange with her have influenced events?

» The Birmingham Freedom Riders wait to board a bus.

PHOTO: Donald Uhrbrock/The LIFE Images Collection/Getty Images; TEXT: "Freedom Riders." [video] American Experience. WGBH Educational Foundation, 2011.

Black Panther Party Leaflet

The Black Panther Party for Self Defense was founded in 1966 in Oakland, California, by Huey P. Newton and Bobby Seale. The Black Panthers believed that nonviolent methods and tactics were not always enough to liberate African Americans, give them control over their lives, or to protect them from police brutality. The following excerpt comes from a leaflet handed out at a Black Panther Party meeting in Greensboro, North Carolina, in the spring of 1969.

PRIMARY SOURCE : LEAFLET

❝ You must discipline yourselves to concentrate because revolution is not a party or a joke. There will be no revolution without a revolutionary party. The Black Panther Party is truly a revolutionary party. We must work very hard. Please feel free to ask about anything you don't understand and don't be afraid to challenge your instructor at any point.

You must memorize and understand the TEN POINT PROGRAM.
You must memorize and understand the POLITICAL DEFINITIONS.
You must memorize and understand the 3 RULES OF DISCIPLINE & 8 POINTS OF ATTENTION.
You must obtain or liberate a copy of CHAIRMEN MAO TSE-TUNG QUOTATION (REDBOOK).
You must obtain or liberate a BERET.

During the six week training period you will be put through test and given special assignments to test your fiber. You will be expected to do some community work and help get together a community organizational chart. We must always have the respect of the community. A Panther must always carry him self like a gentleman. We are the peoples heroes and the peoples liberation force. The first army that black people have ever had. ❞

—Federal Bureau of Investigation, File 105-165706-8

EXAMINE THE SOURCE

Summarizing Why does this leaflet emphasize that the Black Panthers must "always have the respect of the community"?

Learning More About Living Conditions

Gloria Hayes Richardson worked with the Cambridge Nonviolent Action Committee in Cambridge, Maryland in the early 1960s. One of her leadership tasks was to create and help distribute a survey of the living conditions of African Americans in Cambridge. The survey was handed out to school children who then took them home for completion by parents. Student volunteers from Swarthmore College evaluated the data and used it to persuade government leaders.

PRIMARY SOURCE : TRANSCRIPT

❝ **Joseph Mosnier:** Yeah, so you surveyed, you sampled—I think, uh, the same children who were—high school students and others—who were active in the community in the Movement . . . [t]ook the survey cards to high schools across the Second Ward.

Gloria Hayes Richardson: Took the survey, and it really was more the grammar school kids, because in the summer the high school kids were out working, picking up jobs.

JM: Yeah. And your card, you had—so, on the whole series of questions on the card: your priorities in the Movement, aspects about your—the condition of the house you live in, are you employed, all those things. . . . So, you really did a, in a sense, a basic solid systematic survey of conditions in—

GR: . . . And then after they . . . wrote it up and did the correlations . . . I think that's what changed Robert Kennedy's mind, was it was perfectly clear that it was just abysmally poor people, that most of the component to them being poor over generations was racism. ❞

—interview by the Southern Oral History Program, for the Smithsonian Institute's National Museum of African American History & Culture, July 19, 2011

EXAMINE THE SOURCE

Interpreting How does this interview help you understand the types of tactics that were used by participants in the civil rights movement?

(l) "Never, Never Surrender Brothers: Power To You." Black Panther Party - North Carolina. FBIHQ File 105-165706-8 (r)Mosnier, Joseph. Interview with Gloria Hayes Richardson. July 19, 2011. Civil Rights History Project. National Museum of African American History & Culture, 2011.

Conflict Between SNCC and the NAACP

Ella Baker, a prominent member of the NAACP and SCLC, organized the 1960 students' conference that created SNCC. She sent Bob Moses to recruit young activists to participate in what they hoped would become a student-led counterpart to the NAACP. One of these recruits, Fannie Lou Hamer, grew up in a sharecropper's family in Mississippi. Angry at the treatment of African American voters, she joined SNCC. She was fired when her employer learned that she had attempted to register to vote despite failing a required literacy test. In 1963 Hamer participated in a sit-in at a segregated bus station restaurant. Then, in 1966 she helped start the Mississippi Freedom Democratic Party (MFDP).

PRIMARY SOURCE : NEWSPAPER

66 **Hamer:** . . . I haven't seen Bob [Moses, of the NAACP] in quite a while. I miss that man. . . . I've seen so many . . . things in this country. What we thought were different things. . . . Bob became sick of it all, I guess. . . .

Interviewer: What did he do? That's one of the things we've been interested in . . . interviewing people . . . different style that SNCC brought in Mississippi when they first came in and so different from NAACP.

Hamer: It worked with the people. NAACP didn't work with the people. You know, I used to write membership for the [NAACP] and they don't care. They care about folk. You see I'm not particular about working with nobody that don't say yes sir to everything to Mr. Charlie, and that's all [NAACP] does. . . . Now the legal affairs. I don't fight the legal affairs because they have some good attorneys. . . . The [NAACP] is different from everything, 'cause the people in the [NAACP], most of 'em is white man. . . . But [SNCC treated me] for the first time I ever been treated like a human being, whether the kids was white or black. I was respected with the kids and they never told nobody what to say. . . . Everything you heard, us screaming and saying . . . nobody tell us to say that. This is what's been there all the time and we had a chance to get it off our chests and nobody else had ever give us that chance. . . .

Interviewer: When did you first meet up with SNCC kids? When did they first come in?

Hamer: In '62 and before '62 . . . I'd never heard of a mass meeting in my life. . . . [NAACP] was all over the state then. They didn't tell nobody but the people here in town that had their own homes. **99**

—Fannie Lou Hamer, interviewed by Anne and Howard Romaine, 1966

» Fannie Lou Hamer speaks out for the members of the Mississippi Freedom Democratic Party delegation to the 1964 Democratic National Convention in Atlantic City, New Jersey.

EXAMINE THE SOURCE

1. **Comparing and Contrasting** How does Hamer say that SNCC differed from the NAACP?

2. **Speculating** What gap might SNCC have filled that the NAACP did not?

PHOTO: Bettmann/Getty Images; TEXT: Romaine, Anne. Interview with Mrs. Fannie Lou Hamer. Anne Romaine Interviews, 1966-1967; Archives Main Stacks, SC 1069, Folder 1; WIHVR2050-A. Wisconsin Historical Society. 1966.

Julian Bond's Campaign

In 1964 a Supreme Court ruling barred states from gerrymandering districts to weaken the votes of African American citizens. Georgia redrew its districts to create three new majority-African American districts. Julian Bond of SNCC ran for a seat in the Georgia House of Representatives, and in early 1965, he and six other African American leaders were elected. *The Student Voice,* a newspaper produced by SNCC, reported on his campaign.

PRIMARY SOURCE : NEWSPAPER

66 The successful campaign of a young SNCC worker for the Georgia House of Representatives has begun a new phase of political organizing for SNCC. . . .

'The campaign was a new one for Atlanta for several reasons,' Bond said. 'For one, we tried to run on issues and not labels, on people's concerns and not their prejudices. Atlanta has never had a house-to-house, block meeting campaign like this one, where people knew the candidate and got a chance to question him.'

'The next step,' a campaign worker said, 'is to put people inside Julian's District in touch with each other, so they can use each other to get things for themselves.' . . .

'But more important,' Bond says, 'they've begun to talk about including in the strike others across the city who live in the same kind of houses. They want to organize everyone who wants a better house through their actions.'

The campaign was unique because Bond and his campaign workers asked residents of the District—voters and non-voters alike—what it was that they expected from a State Representative and what they were prepared to do themselves. . . .

'The state of Georgia says anyone who is 21-years old and who has $500 is 'qualified' . . .' Bond said, 'and I agree with them completely. The real qualification is interest and a willingness to work.' 99

—*The Student Voice,* July 5, 1965

EXAMINE THE SOURCE

1. **Inferring** What roles did Bond play in civil rights?
2. **Drawing Conclusions** How did Bond and his campaign influence the political climate in Georgia?

Your Inquiry Analysis

EVALUATE SOURCES AND USE EVIDENCE

Reflect back to the Compelling Question and the Supporting Questions you developed at the beginning of this lesson.

1. **Gathering Sources** Refer back to the graphic organizer you created as you read through the sources. Which sources most helped you answer the Supporting Questions you wrote? Circle or highlight those sources in your graphic organizer. Then, write a sentence or two in which you explain how helpful your Supporting Questions were in guiding your inquiry. Note any additional questions that you might have as well as any questions that were left unanswered.

2. **Evaluating Sources** Review the sources that you found the most helpful, and evaluate their credibility. What biases does each source reveal, and how do those biases shape the content of each source? What additional research might you do to confirm the details provided by each source? What insights do these personal perspectives offer?

3. **Comparing and Contrasting** Select two of the activists from the sources. Compare and contrast the roles that they played, the goals that they had, and the ideas that they espoused, as related in the sources.

COMMUNICATE CONCLUSIONS

Using Multimedia Write an answer to each of your Supporting Questions. Then share your responses with a partner. Together, write a paragraph in response to the Compelling Question in which you cite evidence from the sources. Locate images and quotes from each of the sources, and assemble these in a slideshow along with your response to the Compelling Question. Present your slideshow to the class.

TAKE INFORMED ACTION

Teaching the Value of Nonviolent Action
Protests remain an important part of civil action and discourse today. Research the history of nonviolence as a tool of political and social protest, including its use during the civil rights movement and in response to current events. Then, write a guide for your own nonviolent protest workshop in which you explain the value and intent of nonviolent protest as well as at least three strategies for sustaining a nonviolent position in the face of critical or violent opposition. Your instruction should include what NOT to do during nonviolent protest and why and should discuss the legal implications of some forms of protest. Present your plan as a tutorial guide, website, or workshop session.

"Bond Attempts to Hear Voice of People." The Student Voice. v.6, no. 4. July 5, 1965.

06

The Civil Rights Movement Continues

National Advisory Commission on Civil Disorders, Report of the National Advisory Commission on Civil Disorders. Washington, DC: U.S. Government Printing Office, 1968.

READING STRATEGY

Analyzing Key Ideas and Details As you read, use a graphic organizer like the one below to list major violent events in the civil rights movement and their results.

Event	Result

Urban Problems Outside the South

GUIDING QUESTION

How did the methods and the goals of the civil rights movement change in the 1960s and what were the results?

Despite the passage of civil rights laws in the 1950s and 1960s, **racism** still existed across the United States and was not confined to the South. Such racism created a series of disadvantages that placed African Americans in poverty. In 1960, only 15 percent of African Americans held professional or managerial white collar jobs, as compared to 44 percent of whites. African Americans held low-paying jobs and the average income of African American families was 55 percent of the income of a white family. These income disadvantages and existing legal restrictions prevented African Americans from freely moving out of the depressed urban centers to the growing suburbs.

Several northern cities also saw civil rights protests erupt. In 1963 Ruth Batson and members of the NAACP led protests against school segregation in Boston, culminating in multiple school boycotts by thousands of African American high school students. In 1964 nearly half a million students in New York City boycotted school to protest segregation policies.

The Watts Riot and the Kerner Commission

Just five days after President Johnson signed the Voting Rights Act, a riot erupted in Watts, a predominantly African American neighborhood in Los Angeles. Allegations of police brutality along with existing housing segregation, job discrimination, and social and economic inequality sparked an uprising. This revolt lasted six days and more than 14,000 National Guard members and 1,500 law officers were sent to restore order. Uprisings broke out in dozens of American cities between 1965 and 1968. In Detroit alone during 1967, burning, looting, and conflicts with police and the National Guard resulted in 43 deaths and more than 1,000 wounded. Property loss was estimated at almost $200 million.

That same year President Johnson appointed the National Advisory Commission on Civil Disorders, headed by Governor Otto Kerner of Illinois, to study the causes of the urban riots. The Kerner Commission, as it became known, blamed racism for most urban problems. The commission reported that "[o]ur nation is moving toward two societies, one black, one white—separate and unequal." The commission recommended the creation of inner-city jobs and the construction of new public housing, but due to the spending for the Vietnam War, Johnson never endorsed these recommendations.

The Poor People's Campaign

In the mid-1960s, Dr. Martin Luther King, Jr., decided to focus on the economic problems that African Americans faced. King was inspired by the work of Albert Raby, an organizer for the Coordinating Council of Community Organizations (CCCO) in Chicago. The CCCO contained various groups that worked to reform Chicago's public school policies. Raby led a school boycott in 1963. Two years later, King joined Raby for a series of rallies in Chicago, and King later relocated to the city in 1966. To call attention to deplorable housing conditions, Dr. King and his wife Coretta moved into a slum apartment in an

---

racism prejudice or discrimination against someone of a particular racial or ethnic group

Heart of Atlanta Motel, Inc. v. United States, 1964

BACKGROUND OF THE CASE Title II of the Civil Rights Act of 1964 made it illegal for establishments engaged in interstate commerce to discriminate based on race. All businesses or establishments that provided goods, facilities, or services to the public were bound by Title II. Prior to the passage of the Civil Rights Act of 1964, the owner of the Heart of Atlanta Motel refused to rent rooms to African American customers. Intending to continue this practice in violation of the law, the motel's owner sued the government in federal court, challenging the Civil Rights Act and arguing that Congress had exceeded its power to regulate interstate commerce. The motel owner also argued that his Fifth Amendment rights were violated because he was not allowed to run the business as he saw fit, such as by choosing his own customers. After a federal district court ruled against the owner, the case was taken up by the U.S. Supreme Court.

» Morton Rolleston, owner, stands outside the Heart of Atlanta Motel.

HOW THE COURT RULED The Court explained that the motel was engaged in interstate commerce because, due to its location near two interstate highways, most of its patrons were from out of state. In addition, the motel advertised on a national scale. The Court's opinions noted that, because racial discrimination impeded interstate commerce, Congress was authorized to prohibit it. In its decision, the Court affirmed the right of the federal government to regulate local private businesses, not just state or government entities. This decision would set a precedent later used to revoke Jim Crow laws.

1. **Citing Text Evidence** What text evidence supports the idea that the Heart of Atlanta Motel engaged in interstate commerce?

2. **Explaining** What was especially significant about the Supreme Court's ruling?

African American neighborhood. He and the SCLC hoped to improve the economic status of African Americans in poor neighborhoods.

The Chicago Movement made some headway in the face of adversity, although it never fully achieved its goals. When Dr. King led a march for open housing through the all-white neighborhood of Marquette Park, he was met by angry whites more hostile than those in Birmingham and Selma.

Mayor Richard J. Daley met with King to discuss a new program to clean up the slums, and realtors and bankers also agreed to promote open housing. In theory, mortgages and rental property would be available to everyone. In practice, little changed. Dr. King had been drawn to Chicago partly in response to Al Raby's work with the Coordinating Council of Community Organizations (CCCO). The CCCO partnered with the SCLC and conducted sit-ins, boycotts, and marches.

✓ **CHECK FOR UNDERSTANDING**

Identifying Cause and Effect Why did riots break out in dozens of U.S. cities in the late 1960s?

Black Power and the Black Panthers

GUIDING QUESTION

What attracted some African Americans to the Black Power movement?

Dr. King's lack of progress in Chicago convinced some activists that nonviolent protests could not solve economic problems. Even before this, some members of SCLC had promoted more drastic measures to enact change. After 1965, many African Americans began to turn away from King. Some called for more aggressive forms of protest, and organizations such as CORE and SNCC believed that African Americans alone should lead their struggle. Many young African Americans called for black power, a term with many meanings. A few, including Robert F. Williams and H. Rap Brown, interpreted black power to include the idea that physical self-defense was an appropriate response when threatened.

In 1964 Stokely Carmichael, a young African American activist and Freedom Rider, traveled to Alabama, where he organized an independent

Bettmann/Getty Images

Members of the Black Panther Party assemble in front of the courthouse in Oakland, California, in 1968 to support leader Huey P. Newton, who was charged with killing a police officer. After several trials, the charges were dropped.

Making Connections How does this image of the Black Panther Party reflect the values and purpose of the party?

PHOTO: CSU Archives/Everett Collection Historical/Alamy Stock Photo; TEXT: What We Want, by Stokely Carmichael. Copyright © 1966 by Santa Clara County Friends of SNCC.

political party called the Lowndes County Freedom Organization (LCFO). White supremacists in the mostly African American county had a history of terrorizing African Americans who attempted to vote, and the LCFO sought to empower African Americans to claim that constitutional right. The organization's symbol was a black panther. In 1966 Carmichael first spoke of a new Black Power movement, which both promoted African American pride and advocated the necessity of self-defense in violent situations.

In 1966 most supporters of the black power movement believed African Americans should control the social, political, and economic direction of their civil rights struggle:

66 This is the significance of black power as a slogan. For once, black people are going to use the words they want to use—not just the words whites want to hear. . . . The need for psychological equality is the reason why SNCC today believes that blacks must organize in the black community. Only black people can . . . create in the community an aroused and continuing black consciousness. 99

—from "What We Want," the *New York Review of Books*, September 1966

Black power emphasized racial distinctiveness instead of adapting to the dominant culture. African Americans showed pride in their racial heritage through "Afro" hairstyles and African-style clothing. Many also took African names. Dr. King and some other civil rights leaders criticized black power as a philosophy of hopelessness and despair.

By the early 1960s, a young man named Malcolm X had become a symbol of the black power movement. Born Malcolm Little in Omaha, Nebraska, he experienced a difficult childhood and adolescence. In 1946 he was imprisoned for burglary. While in prison, Malcolm educated himself and played an active role in the prison debate society.

Eventually he joined the Nation of Islam, commonly known as the Black Muslims. Despite its name, the Nation of Islam is very different from mainstream Islam. It preached black nationalism. After joining the Nation of Islam, Malcolm Little became Malcolm X. The X symbolized the unknown family name of his enslaved African ancestors. He declared that his true name had been stolen from him by enslavement, and he would no longer use his former name. Malcolm X's criticisms of white society and the mainstream civil rights movement gained national attention for the Nation of Islam.

By 1964, however, Malcolm X had broken with the group. Discouraged by scandals involving the Nation of Islam's leader, he went to the Muslim holy city of Makkah (Mecca) in Saudi Arabia. After seeing Muslims from many races worshiping together, he no longer promoted separatism. After Malcolm X left the Nation of Islam, he continued to criticize it. Organization members shot and killed him in February 1965.

Malcolm X's speeches and ideas influenced a new generation of militant African American leaders who supported black power, black nationalism, and economic self-sufficiency. In 1966 in Oakland, California, Huey P. Newton and Bobby Seale organized the Black Panther Party for Self Defense. Black Panther leaders called for an end to racial oppression and for control of major institutions in the African American community, such as schools, law enforcement, housing, and hospitals.

Like Malcolm X, the Black Panthers believed that nonviolent methods and tactics were not always enough to liberate African Americans or give them control over their lives. California law permitted citizens to openly carry firearms. Black Panther members sent armed patrols into neighborhoods to protect citizens from police misconduct and brutality. In 1967 Seale led a small group of armed Black Panthers into the California state capitol to protest legislation prohibiting the Panthers' armed patrols.

Originally founded to fight police brutality, the Black Panther Party later established and promoted social reform, creating dozens of community assistance programs in cities with Black Panther chapters. These programs featured health care services, legal aid, clothing, and education for children. One of the party's most successful offerings was the Free Breakfast for Children Program for school-aged children. This idea spread across the country and helped lead to an increase in federal food programs.

Many of these events were organized by women, who made up about half of the party's membership. Some, like Kathleen Neal Cleaver, Ericka Huggins, Lynn French, and Elaine Brown, held leadership roles within the party, while radical scholar and activist Angela Davis taught political education classes to party members.

✓ CHECK FOR UNDERSTANDING

Summarizing Why did many young African Americans join the black power movement?

Dr. King is Assassinated

GUIDING QUESTION

How did Dr. King's assassination affect the civil rights movement?

In March 1968, Dr. King went to Memphis, Tennessee, to support a strike of African American sanitation workers. At the time, the SCLC planned a national Poor People's Campaign to promote economic advancement for impoverished Americans. The campaign planned to lobby the federal government to commit billions of dollars to end poverty and unemployment in the United States. People of all races and nationalities converged on Washington, D.C., to camp out until both Congress and President Johnson passed the legislation to fund the proposal.

On April 4, 1968, as he stood on his hotel balcony in Memphis, Dr. King was assassinated by a gunshot. In a speech the previous night, King had told a gathering at a local church, "I've been to the mountaintop. . . . I've looked over. And I've seen the promised land. I may not get there with you, but I want you to know tonight that we as a people will get to the promised land." Dr. King's death touched off both national mourning and violence in more than 100 cities, including Washington, D.C., where President Johnson sent almost 14,000 federal troops to suppress the protests.

Dr. King's death ignited the violence, but frustration over the continuing issues of segregation, police brutality, school and housing inequalities, and unemployment fueled the anger. People were reacting to the long-standing systemic disparities that Dr. King and the civil rights movements had spent over a decade trying to end. Around 27,000 people were arrested during the violence and 3,500 were injured. About 125 fires blazed throughout Chicago, while city leaders in Baltimore called in 5,000 federal soldiers to prevent arson in their neighborhoods. Not all cities experienced such violence. Los Angeles and New York City brought together city and social leaders to reach out to citizens to diffuse the anger.

The Reverend Ralph Abernathy served as a trusted assistant to Dr. King for many years, and led the Poor People's Campaign in King's absence.

However, the demonstration was a very public failure. It did not achieve any of the major objectives that either King or the SCLC had hoped it would.

In the wake of Dr. King's death, Congress passed the Civil Rights Act of 1968. This law, sometimes known as the Fair Housing Act of 1968, outlawed discrimination on the basis of race, color, religion, or national origin when selling, renting, or financing housing. In many communities across the nation, African Americans were prevented from purchasing homes in defined neighborhoods. Banks would not approve loans because of racist attitudes or assumptions made by the loan officers. The Civil Rights Act of 1968 tried to end these practices, but additional legislation was later passed to strengthen the attempt.

The law also benefited immigrants and religious minorities. Historically, in many places in the United States, Jewish Americans had encountered rules preventing them from buying or renting property in certain neighborhoods. The Civil Rights Act of 1968 expanded their economic opportunities as well.

The assassination of Dr. King was a turning point in the civil rights movement. After his death, the movement began to fragment. With formal laws in place banning segregation and discrimination and guaranteeing voting rights, the movement lost some of its unity of purpose. The shift to economic rights was already underway at the time of his death, and it was clear that the struggle to end poverty and provide more economic opportunity would have to involve different approaches than those used before.

✓ CHECK FOR UNDERSTANDING

Identifying Cause and Effect What was the nation's reaction to Dr. King's assassination?

A funeral procession of over 100,000 mourners accompany the casket of Dr. Martin Luther King, Jr., for a public memorial service.

PHOTO: Bettmann/Getty Images; TEXT: Dr. Martin Luther King, Jr., I've Been to the Mountaintop delivered April 3, 1968, Mason Temple.

Seeking Greater Opportunities

GUIDING QUESTION

How did African American civil rights reformers change their focus?

Although various forms of racial discrimination had become illegal, many African Americans saw little improvement in their daily lives. Access to good jobs and equal schooling remained prevalent issues. Civil rights leaders began to focus on these problems.

Equal Access to Education

In the 1970s, African Americans and their allies began to push harder for improvements in public education and access to good schools. In the 1954 case *Brown* v. *Board of Education,* the Supreme Court had ordered an end to segregated public schools. In the 1960s, however, many schools remained segregated as communities moved slowly to comply with the Court. Since children usually attended a school in their neighborhood, segregation in public schools reflected the racial segregation of neighborhoods.

In many cases where such segregation existed, the white schools were superior, as Ruth Batson of the NAACP noted about Boston schools in 1965:

❝ When we would go to white schools, we'd see . . . a small number of children in each class. The teachers were permanent. We'd see wonderful materials. When we'd go to our schools, we would see overcrowded classrooms, children sitting out in the corridors, and so forth. And so then we decided that where there were a large number of white students, that's where the care went. That's where the books went. That's where the money went. ❞

—quoted in *Voices of Freedom*, 1990

Courts began ordering local governments to bus children to schools outside their neighborhoods to achieve greater racial balance. The practice led to protests and even riots in several white communities. The Supreme Court, however, upheld the constitutionality of **busing** in the 1971 case *Swann* v. *Charlotte-Mecklenburg Board of Education*.

In response, many white parents took their children out of public schools or moved to suburban districts with no busing. For example, thousands of white students left Boston's public school system to attend parochial and private schools. By late 1976, minorities made up the majority of Boston's public school students. This "white flight" also occurred in other cities. The city of Detroit, Michigan, tried to address the issue of continuing school inequality by busing students between districts in 1974. However, the Supreme Court ruled in *Milliken* v. *Bradley* that busing across district lines was unconstitutional unless it was proven that those school district boundaries had been purposely drawn to create segregation.

Affirmative Action and the *Bakke* Case

In addition to supporting busing, civil rights leaders began advocating **affirmative action** as a new way to solve discrimination. Political leaders such as President Kennedy and President Johnson supported the strategy as an effective solution to address racial inequality.

Affirmative action was enforced through executive orders and federal policies. It called for companies, schools, and institutions doing business with the federal government to recruit African Americans candidates for new hiring positions and for educational enrollment. Supporters hoped that this intentional targeting of African American candidates would improve their social and economic status. Officials later expanded affirmative action to include other minority groups and women.

Through affirmative action, the city of Atlanta, Georgia, witnessed a significant increase in minority job opportunities. In 1974 Maynard Jackson took office as Atlanta's first African American mayor. When Jackson was elected, African Americans made up a large part of Atlanta's population, but only a few city contracts went to African American companies. Through Jackson's efforts, small companies and minority-owned firms took on a higher percentage of all city contracts. This helped these African American business owners experience financial success.

Some critics argued that an unintended consequence of affirmative action programs was reverse discrimination against white males. They claimed that affirmative action led to the use of quotas on the basis of race or gender. They argued that white men were denied opportunities because slots were set aside for minorities or women.

In 1978 the Supreme Court addressed affirmative action in *Regents of the University of California* v. *Bakke*. Officials at the University of California at Davis medical school had twice denied the application of Allan Bakke. When Bakke learned that slots had been set aside for minorities, he sued the school. Bakke pointed out that the school had admitted minority applicants with lower exam scores than his. He claimed that the school had discriminated against him because he was Caucasian.

---

busing the practice of transporting children to schools outside of their neighborhoods to achieve a more equal racial balance

affirmative action an approach used to improve employment or educational opportunities for minorities and women

Ruth Batson quoted in Voices of Freedom: An Oral History of the Civil Rights Movement from the 1950s through the 1980s, by Henry Hampton and Steve Fayer with Sarah Flynn. Copyright © 1990 by Bantam Books.

Protesters demonstrated as the Supreme Court deliberated the *Regents of the University of California v. Bakke* case.

Summarizing What is the meaning of the sign that the protester is carrying?

In a 5-to-4 ruling, the Supreme Court declared that the university had violated Bakke's civil rights. It said that schools should encourage racial diversity and could consider race as an admissions criteria, but that they could not set aside "fixed quotas," for minorities.

Affirmative action policies have regularly been challenged and debated in the decades since *Bakke*. In the 2003 case *Grutter* v. *Bollinger,* the Court ruled that affirmative action is allowed when race is used as one factor in admissions decisions to promote student diversity. But that same year, in *Gratz* v. *Bollinger*, the Court prohibited a points- or quota-based system of affirmative action, upholding *Bakke*. In the 2016 case *Fisher* v. *University of Texas at Austin*, the Court, referring back to the language of the *Grutter* decision, determined that affirmative action policies are constitutional and allowed when they are "narrowly tailored" to serve the state's compelling interest in "the educational benefits that flow from student body diversity."

New Political Leaders

New political leaders emerged in the African American community in the 1970s to continue fighting for economic, social, and political equality for African Americans. For the first time since Reconstruction, African Americans became more influential in national politics. Jesse Jackson, a former aide to Martin Luther King, Jr., was among this new generation of activists. In 1971 Jackson founded Operation PUSH (People United to Save Humanity). Operation PUSH was dedicated to developing African American businesses, educational opportunities, and social and political development. Jackson sought the Democratic presidential nomination and lost in 1984 and 1988. Yet he won over millions of voters.

In 1971 African American members of Congress organized the Congressional Black Caucus (CBC) to more clearly represent their concerns. One of the CBC's founding members was Shirley Chisholm of New York, the first African American woman to serve in Congress. In 1972 Chisholm entered the race for the Democratic nomination for president, becoming the first woman and the first African American to run for a major party's nomination. Chisholm received the votes of 152 delegates at the Democratic National Convention but did not win the nomination.

In 1977 another former assistant to Dr. King, U.S. Representative Andrew Young, became the first African American to serve as U.S. ambassador to the United Nations. He later served as the mayor of Atlanta. By the mid-1980s, African American mayors had been elected in Atlanta, Detroit, Chicago, Los Angeles, New Orleans, Philadelphia, and Washington, D.C.

In 1990 Virginia voters elected L. Douglas Wilder, who became the first African American governor of a state. That same year, David Dinkins took office as the first African American mayor of New York City.

✓ **CHECK FOR UNDERSTANDING**

1. **Identifying** How was busing used to desegregate public schools?
2. **Explaining** What was the goal of affirmative action?

LESSON ACTIVITIES

1. **Informative/Explanatory Writing** Write a paragraph in which you summarize the issues involved in the Supreme Court cases of *Swann* v. *Charlotte-Mecklenburg Board of Education* and *Regents of the University of California* v. *Bakke*.

2. **Presenting** Work in small groups to prepare a short theater piece in which newscasters relate three to five highlights of civil rights history set between the years 1954 and 1968. Ask your classmates to take notes for an after-presentation class discussion.

PHOTO: Bettmann/Getty Images; TEXT: Grutter v. Bollinger, 539 U.S. 306 (2003).

07

Reviewing the Civil Rights Movement

Summary

Origin of the Movement

During Reconstruction, Congress took some steps to protect African Americans' civil rights. But in 1896 the *Plessy* v. *Ferguson* decision allowed those rights to be severely curtailed by state statutes known as Jim Crow laws. These laws legalized segregation, restricting African American mobility, labor, and voting rights. Even where it was not enforced by law, de facto segregation limited African Americans' lives.

In response to institutional racism and segregation, the National Association for the Advancement of Colored People (NAACP) and other organizations began to chip away at Jim Crow laws by challenging them in court. The NAACP scored a major victory in 1954 when the U.S. Supreme Court struck down segregation in public education in *Brown* v. *Board of Education*. The decision caused some Southern governors to increase their resistance to integration.

The Montgomery Bus Boycott

One year after *Brown* v. *Board,* Rosa Parks's refusal to yield her seat on a city bus to a white man led to the Montgomery Bus Boycott. A young minister named Dr. Martin Luther King, Jr., emerged as a leading voice of the civil rights movement during the boycott. After more than a year, the boycott and legal challenges achieved the desegregation of the city transportation system. That success inspired more resistance throughout the South and led to the formation of the Southern Christian Leadership Conference (SCLC).

Also in 1955, two white men murdered 14-year-old Emmett Till. Till's death highlighted the dangers of racist violence protected by the Southern judicial system.

The Little Rock Nine

President Eisenhower had been reluctant to get involved in civil rights issues. After the governor of Arkansas used the National Guard to try to prevent nine African American students from integrating Little Rock's Central High School, Eisenhower intervened, ordering federal forces to protect the students and enforce integration at Central High School in 1957.

Sit-Ins and Freedom Rides

Civil rights activism continued into the 1960s, spearheaded by young college students. One group in Greensboro, North Carolina, used sit-ins to challenge segregation in public restaurants. Soon activists throughout the South staged sit-ins to protest segregation, many of them part of groups like the Congress of Racial Equality (CORE) and the Student Nonviolent Coordinating Committee (SNCC), led by young leaders such as John Lewis and Diane Nash.

In 1961 a group of African American and white students challenged de facto segregation on interstate buses and terminals. The Freedom Riders were attacked by violent mobs and arrested in several cities. More Freedom Riders expanded the effort. President Kennedy finally sent in federal marshals to protect the riders, but tensions continued until the Interstate

---

Challenging Segregation

The activism of individuals and organizations led to nation-wide legal changes. Pictured below (l to r) James Farmer, Roy Wilkins, Dr. Martin Luther King, Jr., and Ella Baker.

CORE

1943: Founded by members such as James L. Farmer on a principle of nonviolence

1961: Organized the Freedom Rides to force integration in interstate bus travel

NAACP

1909: Founded to protest lynchings and advocate for justice

1954: Argued against school segregation in *Brown* v. *Board of Education*

1955–1956: Supported the Montgomery bus boycotts

SCLC

1957: Created from the Montgomery bus boycott efforts

1963: Helped organize the March on Washington

1964: Organized voter registration drives in the South

1965: Helped organize the Selma March

SNCC

1960: Established by African American and white college students

1963–1964: Organized voter registration drives in the South

1965: Helped organize the March for Freedom

(1) Library of Congress Prints and Photographs Division [LC-DIG-ds-04118]; (2)Library of Congress Prints and Photographs Division Washington [LC-DIG-ppmsc-01273]; (3)Library of Congress Prints and Photographs Division [LC-DIG-ppmsca-49864]; (4)Everett Collection/Newscom

 **GO ONLINE** Explore the Student Edition eBook and find interactive maps, time lines, and tools.

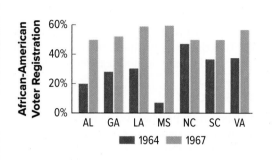

African American Voter Registration in Selected Southern States, 1964 and 1967

The Voting Rights Act of 1965 had an almost immediate impact on African American voter registration.

Commerce Commission issued prohibitions on segregation in the interstate bus system.

The Battle Continues

Although President Eisenhower had signed civil rights bills in 1957 and 1960, they did not go far enough in protecting African American rights. Some civil rights leaders called on President Kennedy to support stronger civil rights protections, and others continued to challenge segregation directly.

The movement focused a series of protests on key Southern cities, including Birmingham, Alabama. Dr. King and others were arrested during the protests. Soon more protesters joined in, many of them children. At the direction of Bull Connor, city law enforcement forcefully attacked the peaceful protesters with hoses and dogs, and the news images shocked the public across the country.

On June 11, 1963, President Kennedy sent federal troops to Alabama to enforce integration on public college campuses. He also announced support for a strong new civil rights bill. In the early hours of June 12, a white segregationalist murdered civil rights activist Medgar Evers in Mississippi. Activists organized a March on Washington. In August Dr. King delivered his "I Have a Dream" speech to over 250,000 demonstrators at the Lincoln Memorial in Washington, D.C.

Segregationists continued to stall the civil rights legislation in Congress. After Kennedy's assassination, President Lyndon Johnson pressed Congress to send him a bill, which resulted in the Civil Rights Act of 1964. The act represented the most extensive civil rights legislation ever passed by Congress, but it still did not explicitly protect voting rights. The movement next focused on securing federal voting rights protection. Those who tried to help African Americans register to vote faced resistance and, in some cases, murder. Activists marched from Selma to Montgomery in Alabama to bring national attention to the cause. On "Bloody Sunday" authorities violently attacked the

protesters. A few months later, Johnson signed the Voting Rights Act of 1965 into law.

The Movement Changes

The movement faced competing priorities from groups who disagreed on the most important focus. Some wanted to address long-term effects of segregation, such as inadequate housing and low incomes. Frustration with systemic racism and police brutality sparked numerous uprisings in cities throughout the country. Al Raby's Chicago Freedom Movement drew Dr. King to put more emphasis on economic inequality through the Poor People's Campaign.

Some younger activists, inspired by figures such as Stokely Carmichael and Malcolm X, lent their voice and efforts to the Black Power movement. There were always activists who disagreed with an emphasis on nonviolent resistance. The Black Panther Party called for self-empowerment among African American communities. After Dr. King's assassination in 1968, some lost hope that further change could be achieved. Despite many successes, the movement experienced some setbacks in the 1970s, including the *Bakke* case, which limited the use of affirmative action in education.

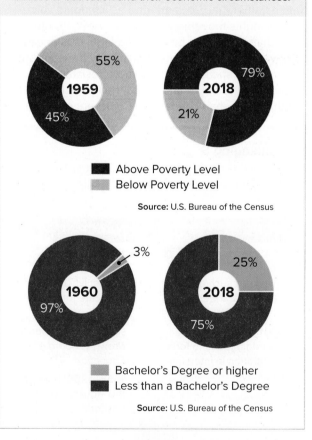

African American Poverty Rates and Education Status

The civil rights movement affected African Americans' access to education and their economic circumstances.

Source: U.S. Bureau of the Census

Source: U.S. Bureau of the Census

Apply What You Have Learned

Understanding Chronology

The civil rights movement spanned more than a decade of time and involved a great many people and events. Organizing these events in a simple, logical fashion can help you better understand the most important moments of this historical era. Listing the events in chronological order will also allow you to visualize change over time and understand cause-and-effect relationships.

ACTIVITY **Create a Group Time Line** Work in small groups of four people each. Each person should list what they think are the ten most important events of the civil rights movement that they learned during their studies of this topic. After each person has finished their list, compare lists with one another and discuss why each person chose their events. Be sure to add the month, days, and year for the events listed. Combine the group's events into a single list, eliminating any duplicates. Then work as a group to chronologically sequence the final events in a time line. Create either a time line poster or a digital time line with the events. Then compare and contrast the time line you created with the one found in Lesson 1 of this topic.

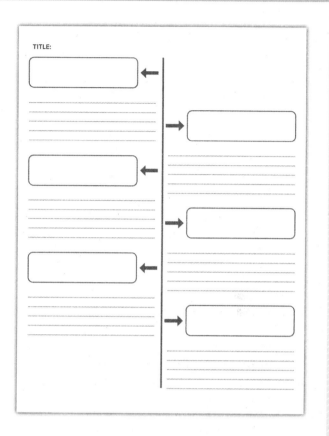

TITLE:

Understanding Multiple Perspectives

Segregation affected all African Americans, but how people experienced it often depended on other aspects of their identities. For example, think about how segregation might have affected African American men, women, and children differently because of their age or gender.

ACTIVITY **Write an Informative/Explanatory Essay** Select two famous African Americans of different genders and research their experiences and responses to segregation. Compare and contrast their experiences and report on your findings. Prepare an essay that explains your findings. Your essay should include an introduction, a thesis statement, a presentation of your evidence, and a conclusion. Cite the sources that you used to support your thesis, evidence, and conclusion.

Connecting to Music

Several popular songs became closely associated with the civil rights movement. Participants in the movement sang at their meetings, as they marched, and even as they were taken to jail. Other forms of music including folk and soul also became part of the soundtrack of the times with lyrics that called for equality and freedom.

ACTIVITY **Evaluate Evidence** Choose a song from the 1950s or 1960s that is associated with the civil rights movement. Analyze the song's lyrics and how they relate to the movement's purpose and goals. Evaluate the song's effectiveness as a motivating force to bring about change.

D Making Connections to Today

The 50th anniversary of "Bloody Sunday" in Selma, Alabama, was remembered on March 7, 2015. President Barack Obama delivered a speech explaining the significance of Selma to the civil rights movement:

> " . . . [T]here are places and moments in America where this nation's destiny has been decided. . . .
>
> Selma is such a place. In one afternoon 50 years ago, so much of our turbulent history—the stain of slavery and anguish of civil war; the yoke of segregation and tyranny of Jim Crow; the death of four little girls in Birmingham; and the dream of a Baptist preacher—met on this bridge. . . .
>
> The Americans who crossed this bridge, they were not physically imposing. But they gave courage to millions. . . .
>
> Because of what they did, the doors of opportunity swung open not just for black folks, but for every American. Women marched through those doors. Latinos marched through those doors. Asian Americans, gay Americans, and Americans with disabilities—they all came through those doors. "
>
> —President Obama, "Bloody Sunday" 50th Anniversary Speech

As President Obama notes in his speech, the civil rights movement, directly and indirectly, inspired other activist movements in the United States. Movements for Latino and Native American civil rights as well as the modern feminist and the LGBTQ movements learned from its original example.

ACTIVITY **Podcast Presentation** Select one of the other movements President Obama referenced in his speech and create a podcast that compares and contrasts it to the civil rights movement of the 1950s and 1960s. In what ways has the civil rights movement inspired this other movement? How were the movements similar? In what ways did they differ?

As you seek to answer these questions, focus on the following topics and explain the similarities and differences between the movements:

- The goals of each movement
- The methods used by each movement to achieve these goals
- The judicial or legislative successes of each movement

Use your student text, library, and online sources to research the movement. Then, for your podcast, describe events that help the listeners to visualize the significant moments captured in videos or photographs. Create and submit a bibliography citing the sources you used for your podcast. Publish and share your podcast with family, friends, or a larger audience.

» The right photo shows people reenacting the 1965 march across the Edmund Pettus Bridge. The left photo, taken March 7, 2015, shows President Barack Obama (center left, in white shirt), civil rights leaders from several generations, and former President and First Lady, George W. Bush and Laura Bush. They are commemorating the 50th anniversary of "Bloody Sunday" in Selma, Alabama.

PHOTO: (l)National Archives and Records Administration; (r)National Park Service; TEXT: Obama, Barack. "Remarks by the President at the 50th Anniversary of the Selma to Montgomery Marches." Selma, Alabama. March 7, 2015.

The Vietnam War 1954–1975

United States Marines patrol in Vietnam in 1965.

INTRODUCTION LESSON

01 Introducing the Vietnam War   446

LEARN THE EVENTS LESSONS

02 American Involvement in Vietnam Begins   451

03 The Antiwar Movement   457

05 The Vietnam War Ends   467

INQUIRY ACTIVITY LESSONS

04 Turning Point: The Pivotal Year of 1968   463

REVIEW AND APPLY LESSON

06 Reviewing the Vietnam War   473

SAUER Jean-Claude/Paris Match/Getty Images

 GO ONLINE   Explore the Student Edition eBook to find interactive maps, time lines, and tools.

THE HORRORS OF VIETNAM

War is always brutal, and the Vietnam War was no exception. It was one of the longest and most controversial wars in American history. Nearly 3.5 million people were deployed to Southeast Asia, more than 50,000 American soldiers died in battle, and just over 153,000 more were wounded. At least a quarter of these American soldiers were drafted into service. At home, antiwar protests often erupted into violence.

Many people believed the war was doomed to fail from the start. For example, Daniel Ellsberg, who served in the Pentagon under Secretary of Defense Robert McNamara, wrote in his book *Secrets: A Memoir of Vietnam and the Pentagon Papers* that, "In the fall of 1961 it didn't take very long to discover in Vietnam that we weren't likely to be successful there. It took me less than a week, on my first visit. . . . You didn't have to speak Vietnamese, or know Asian history or philosophy or culture, to learn that nothing we were trying to do was working or was likely to get better."

Nevertheless, the U.S. sent an increasing number of military advisers to Vietnam in the early 1960s and began bombing North Vietnam in 1965. That same year, troops were sent to the South. The war did not end until April 30, 1975, when North Vietnamese troops successfully entered Saigon, the capital city of South Vietnam, which was renamed Ho Chi Minh City in 1976.

Soldiers on the ground experienced horrendous conditions in an unfamiliar and unforgiving terrain. Karl Marlantes, for example, explains the difficulty of the situation in his book *What It Was Like To Go To War*:

❝ . . . nothing we were trying to do was working . . . ❞

"I was the commander of a Marine rifle platoon. A rifle platoon at full strength consisted of forty-three Marines, but that winter we struggled against **malaria, jungle rot, dysentery,** and the North Vietnamese Army to keep our strength above thirty. . . . We patrolled hard and ceaselessly in terrain so steep and difficult we often had to use rope to get up and down the cliffs. On the radio we pretended to be a company so the enemy wouldn't know how vulnerable we were to attack. At night no one slept longer than an hour at a time."

The United States used a military draft during the Vietnam War—although some voluntarily enlisted. Soldiers in Vietnam sometimes found the separation between military forces they were fighting and civilians unclear.

For example, in *Bloods: Black Veterans of the Vietnam War: An Oral History*, Reginald "Malik" Edwards recalls, "All of a sudden, this Vietnamese came runnin' after me, telling me not to shoot: 'Don't shoot. Don't shoot.' See, we didn't go in the village and look. We would just shoot first. . . . So he ran out in front of me. I mean he's runnin' into my line of fire. I almost killed him. But I'm thinking, what is wrong? So then we went into the hut, and it was all these women and children huddled together. I was gettin' ready to wipe them off the planet. In this one hut. I tell you, man, my knees got weak. I dropped down, and that's when I cried. First time I cried in the 'Nam. I realized what I would have done. I almost killed all them people. That was the first time I had actually had the experience of weak knees."

malaria a disease caused by a parasite that is transmitted through mosquito bites

jungle rot a skin infection that is often contracted in tropical environments

dysentery a disease characterized by severe diarrhea

(1)Ellsberg, Daniel. Secrets: A Memoir of Vietnam and the Pentagon Papers. New York: Viking Press, 2002; (2)Marlantes, Karl. What It Is Like to Go to War. New York: Atlantic Monthly Press, 2011; (3)Edwards, Reginald. In Terry, Wallace, ed. Bloods: Black Veterans of the Vietnam War: An Oral History. New York: Random House, 2013.

National Archives and Records Administration.

In November 1967 these U.S. Army troops embarked on a search-and-destroy mission near Cat Lai in the Republic of Vietnam. To get there, they had to wade through a deep irrigation canal.

Understanding the Time and Place: Southeast Asia, 1950s through 1970s

Cold War tensions went far beyond the borders of America and the Soviet Union. Conflicts between communism and capitalism erupted around the globe, and one of the United States's primary goals during the decades following World War II was to contain the spread of communism.

Vietnam and the Cold War

Vietnam is a country along the eastern portion of mainland Southeast Asia that shares borders with China, Laos, and Cambodia. In the latter half of the nineteenth century, Vietnam, along with Cambodia and Laos, was ruled as a colony of France known as **Indochina.** During World War II, after France's fall to Nazi Germany, Indochina became ruled by the Japanese military and was an important base of operations for Japan. Independence movements within Vietnam, however, had been taking place for years and finally achieved success when Japan surrendered in August 1945. Vietminh, a broad national alliance led by the Communist Party that had been formed in 1941, rose to power and became the Democratic Republic of Vietnam.

But the Vietminh did not have power over all of Vietnam. The French seized power in the central and southern regions, where they had once ruled as a colonial power, and Vietnam was split in two: a Communist north controlled by the Vietminh, led by Ho Chi Minh, and a non-Communist south controlled by the French.

The French attempted peaceful solutions with the Vietminh, but these were largely unsuccessful. Fighting began in 1946 with the United States providing financial support to France. Peace was finally reached in 1954, when France left Indochina and the split became official as North Vietnam and South Vietnam.

The two countries began to restore the war-torn land with China and the Soviet Union supporting the North and the United States and its allies supporting the South. But the peace between North Vietnam and South Vietnam did not last. Communist forces in the North, which became known as the Vietcong, sought to reunify the country, and the government of the South struggled against the threat. The United States increased its military advisers in the region as the years progressed, eventually sending thousands of troops in 1965.

Although American troops were intended to serve as support for South Vietnam's military, U.S. forces and firepower dominated the conflict from 1965 until the war's end. North Vietnam proved to be a fierce opponent, however, and the struggle lasted much longer than many believed it would. As the years went on, dissatisfaction with the war among American civilians continued to rise. The U.S. government under President Johnson refused to relent, fearing the appearance of weakness at home and in the global community amid the fierce Cold War tensions.

The Anti-War Movement

By 1967, many Americans, particularly college students and academics, disagreed with the Vietnam War. They believed that the war was unjust and caused far too many civilian casualties in North and South Vietnam.

Campus protests were common, and these grew larger as the war continued. Images of the war were shown on the nightly news, which brought the conflict right into people's living rooms and caused many to question the government's claim that the U.S. was

The Vietnam Veterans Memorial on the National Mall in Washington, D.C., is a long wall of black granite etched with the names of more than 58,000 Americans who gave their lives in the Vietnam War. The memorial was designed by Maya Lin.

Speculating Family, friends, and others often bring personal items to place at the wall in memory of those lost. How might a memorial like this bring comfort or closure to mourners?

Indochina a colony consisting of Vietnam, Cambodia, and Laos ruled by France in the second half of the nineteenth century

Denise Kappa/Shutterstock.

Why did Vietnam matter to the United States?

Southeast Asia was an important part of America's trade network, and the U.S. government did not want communism to spread there.

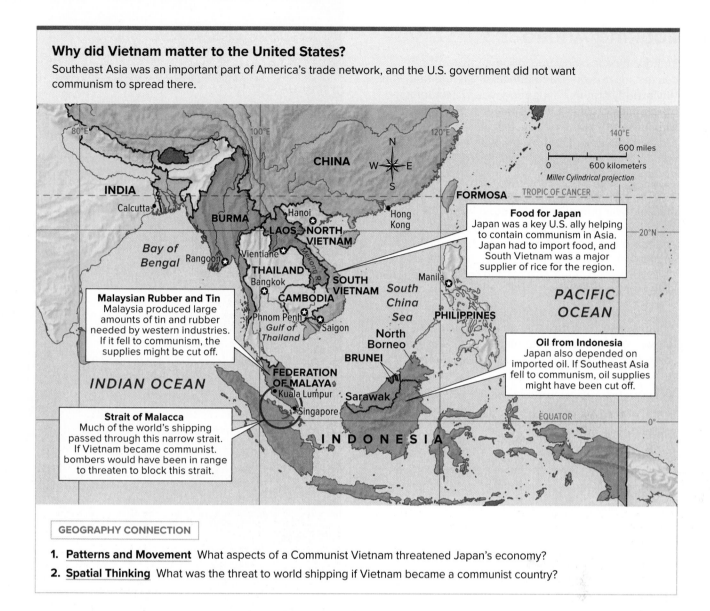

Food for Japan
Japan was a key U.S. ally helping to contain communism in Asia. Japan had to import food, and South Vietnam was a major supplier of rice for the region.

Malaysian Rubber and Tin
Malaysia produced large amounts of tin and rubber needed by western industries. If it fell to communism, the supplies might be cut off.

Oil from Indonesia
Japan also depended on imported oil. If Southeast Asia fell to communism, oil supplies might have been cut off.

Strait of Malacca
Much of the world's shipping passed through this narrow strait. If Vietnam became communist, bombers would have been in range to threaten to block this strait.

GEOGRAPHY CONNECTION

1. **Patterns and Movement** What aspects of a Communist Vietnam threatened Japan's economy?
2. **Spatial Thinking** What was the threat to world shipping if Vietnam became a communist country?

winning the war. By the summer of 1967, less than 50 percent of Americans polled agreed with the government's handling of the war.

One major cause of discontent was the draft. Most of those who fought in the Vietnam War were drafted, and many saw the draft process as unfairly biased because it was more likely to send minorities and the poor to fight and die for reasons that were unclear, implausible, or immoral.

The draft had been used since the Civil War to replenish military personnel when too few volunteered. The draft system for Vietnam changed in December 1969, when a lottery system was instituted to make the draft more fair. Local draft boards assigned each eligible man a random number between 1 and 366. After turning 18, men had thirty days to register for the draft, and then they waited to see whether their number was chosen.

There were, however, ways to get out of the draft that added to the draft's bias against minorities and the poor. Being enrolled in college or obtaining an exemption due to work responsibilities excluded some Americans from the draft. In addition, those who had documented medical conditions were exempted from the draft.

By the 1970s, the U.S. moved toward lessening its military presence in Vietnam. The decision had been driven in large part by the antiwar protests at home. After a complex series of events, negotiations, and secret and public meetings, the war was ended and the country was officially united as the Socialist Republic of Vietnam on July 2, 1976.

The United States failed to achieve its goal of halting the spread of communism in Southeast Asia, and the brutality of the conflict altered U.S. culture, politics, and military-civilian relations.

Looking Ahead

In these next lessons, you will learn about the causes, main events, and effects of the Vietnam War. While studying this time period, you will understand the policies of different presidents in relation to Vietnam and Southeast Asia. You will learn about the anti-war movement and its effect on American culture. And you will understand the great human toll the Vietnam War took.

The Vietnam War reflected the political tensions of the Cold War period and it occurred within the protest period of 1960s United States domestic politics. The lessons in this topic will examine both the global implications of the Vietnam War and the ways that the Vietnam War changed political and social movements within the United States.

You will examine the Compelling Question in the Inquiry Lesson and develop your own questions about the Vietnam War. Review the time line to preview some of the key events that you will learn about.

What Will You Learn?

In these lessons focused on the Vietnam War, you will learn:

- how the United States became involved in Vietnam.
- how American involvement in Vietnam changed during the Kennedy and Johnson administrations.
- the problems that the Vietnam War caused at home.
- why 1968 was such an important year during this era.
- the steps President Nixon took to end the conflict in Vietnam.
- the impact the Vietnam War had on American culture and politics.

? COMPELLING QUESTION

- What made 1968 a turning point?

KEY EVENTS OF THE
VIETNAM WAR

1954
1954 France leaves Indochina

1955 U.S. military aid and advisers sent to South Vietnam

1964 Congress passes Gulf of Tonkin Resolution

1965
1965 Military leaders oust civilian government in South Vietnam

1965 U.S. combat troops land in Vietnam

JANUARY 1968 Tet Offensive begins

AUGUST 1968 Anti-war protest at the Democratic National Convention in Chicago (right)

1970
APRIL 1970 Nixon orders invasion of Cambodia

MAY 1970 National Guard troops kill four students at Kent State University

JANUARY 1973 Paris Peace Accords signed to establish peace in Vietnam

MARCH 1973 Last U.S. troops leave Vietnam

1975
1975 Saigon falls to North Vietnamese invasion

Sequencing Time Identify the events that reveal the tension between the U.S. government's actions in Vietnam and the reaction of Americans to the Vietnam War.

Everett Collection/SuperStock.

450

02

American Involvement in Vietnam Begins

AFP/Getty Images.

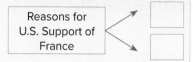

READING STRATEGY

Analyzing Key Ideas and Details Complete a graphic organizer similar to the one here by providing the reasons the United States aided France in Vietnam.

Reasons for U.S. Support of France

Vietnam's Struggles Begin

GUIDING QUESTION

Why did the United States provide military aid to the French in Indochina?

In 1940 Japan invaded Vietnam and became one of a series of foreign nations to rule the Asian country. Prior to the Japanese, the Chinese had controlled the region for hundreds of years. Then, beginning in 1887 and lasting until World War II, the French colonized Vietnam, Laos, and Cambodia—a region then known as French Indochina.

The Growth of Vietnamese Nationalism

By the early 1900s, nationalism became a powerful force in Vietnam. Several political parties pushed for independence or for reform of French colonial rule. Among the nationalist leaders was Nguyen That Thanh—better known by his assumed name, Ho Chi Minh. After years working in Communist politics in Europe, China, and the Soviet Union, he returned to Southeast Asia where he helped found the Indochinese Communist Party in 1930 and worked for independence.

Ho Chi Minh's activities forced him to flee Indochina, but after several years in exile in the Soviet Union and China, he returned to Vietnam in 1941. By then, Japan had seized control of the country. Ho Chi Minh organized a nationalist group called the Vietminh, which united Communists and non-Communists in the effort to expel the Japanese. Soon afterward, the United States began sending aid to the Vietminh to help put pressure on Japan during World War II.

Ho Chi Minh (center, on the shoulders of the crowd) was affectionately referred to as "Uncle Ho" by his followers. In this photo, he was cheered by members of the Vietminh during a unification congress in Vietnam in 1951.

Analyzing Visuals How does this photograph illustrate the feelings the members of this crowd had for Ho Chi Minh? How do you think he feels about them?

◥ **GO ONLINE** Explore the Student Edition eBook and find interactive maps, time lines, and tools.

451

America Aids the French

When Japan surrendered to the Allies in 1945, it gave up control of Indochina. Ho Chi Minh quickly declared Vietnam's independence. France, however, had no intention of losing its former colony, which provided it with a wealth of natural resources and inexpensive labor. French troops returned to Vietnam in 1946 and drove the Vietminh into hiding.

The Vietminh fought back against the French-dominated regime. Their familiarity with the terrain and conditions slowly helped them gain control of large areas of the country. As the fighting escalated, France appealed to the United States for help. The request put American officials in a difficult position because the United States opposed colonialism. It had pressured the Dutch to give up their empire in Indonesia and supported the British decision to give India independence in 1947. American officials, however, feared that Vietnam would fall to communism.

China's shift to communism and the outbreak of the Korean War helped convince President Truman to aid France. President Eisenhower continued Truman's policy and defended his decision with what became known as the **domino theory**—the idea that if Vietnam fell to communism, the rest of Southeast Asia would follow, like a line of dominoes falling over.

Defeat at Dien Bien Phu

Despite aid from the United States, the French continued to struggle against the Vietminh, who used hit-and-run and ambush tactics. These are the tactics of **guerrillas,** irregular troops who blend into the civilian population and are difficult for regular armies to fight. Rising casualties and a lack of victories made the war unpopular with the French public.

The turning point came in the mountain town of Dien Bien Phu, which the French seized in order to cut the Vietminh's supply lines and force them into open battle. The French forces fell to the Vietminh on May 7, 1954, after a huge Vietminh force surrounded and began bombarding the town. The defeat convinced the French to make peace and withdraw from Indochina.

Geneva Accords

Negotiations to end the conflict were held in Geneva, Switzerland. The resulting Geneva Accords provided for a temporary division of Vietnam along the 17th parallel. Ho Chi Minh and the Vietminh controlled North Vietnam, and a pro-Western regime led by the fiercely anti-Communist Ngo Dinh Diem (ehn•GOH DIHN deh•EHM) held the South. French troops soon left, and the United States became the principal protector of the new government in South Vietnam.

The accords called for elections to be held in 1956 to reunite the country under a single government. Diem refused to permit the elections, however, fearing Ho Chi Minh would win. Eisenhower approved of Diem's actions and increased American aid to South Vietnam.

✓ **CHECK FOR UNDERSTANDING**

1. **Citing Text Evidence** Why did the United States provide military aid to the French in Indochina?
2. **Identifying Cause and Effect** Why was the United States put in a difficult position when the French asked for aid?

American Involvement Deepens

GUIDING QUESTION

How did American involvement in Vietnam change during the Kennedy and Johnson administrations?

After Ngo Dinh Diem refused to hold national elections, Ho Chi Minh and the Communists began an armed struggle to reunify the nation. They organized a new guerrilla army of South Vietnamese Communists, which became known as the Vietcong.

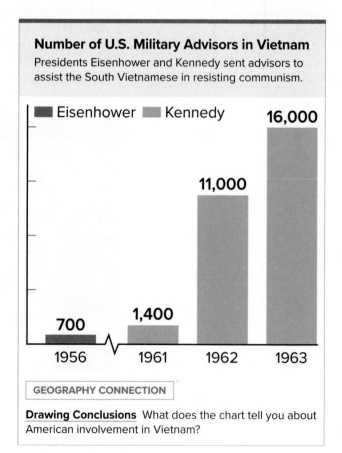

Number of U.S. Military Advisors in Vietnam
Presidents Eisenhower and Kennedy sent advisors to assist the South Vietnamese in resisting communism.

| Eisenhower | Kennedy |

1956	1961	1962	1963
700	1,400	11,000	16,000

GEOGRAPHY CONNECTION

Drawing Conclusions What does the chart tell you about American involvement in Vietnam?

---

domino theory the belief that if one nation in Asia fell to the Communists, neighboring countries would follow

guerrilla member of an armed band that carries out surprise attacks and sabotage rather than open warfare

SPUTNIK/Alamy Stock Photo.

BIOGRAPHY

HO CHI MINH (1890–1969)

Ho Chi Minh was born on May 19, 1890, in the province of Nghe An in central Vietnam to Hoang Thi Loan, the daughter of a village scholar, and Nguyen Sinh Sac, a scholar and civil servant. In line with custom, Ho's name was changed at age 10 from Nguyen Sinh Cung to Nguyen That Thanh, meaning "Nguyen who is destined to succeed."

EARLY YEARS Ho was born shortly after Vietnam fell under French colonial rule. His father, who had strong nationalist views, was fired from his civil service job for anti-French activities. Yet Sinh Sac sent his son to the National School in Hue, which the French had built to train people for colonial government service. His father reasoned that Ho needed to understand the French in order to defeat them. Ho was eventually expelled for participating in revolutionary activities. After leaving the school, Ho taught briefly and entered a vocational school before traveling the world as a crew member on a French ship. He stayed for a time in New York and London before settling in Paris, taking a variety of jobs to survive.

NATIONALIST EFFORTS While in Paris, Ho organized Vietnamese immigrants and sent a petition to the Versailles Peace Conference in 1919, demanding that the Vietnamese be given equal rights under French colonial rule. The petition was ignored. Ho also turned to communism, joining the French Communist Party in 1920, after being inspired by Lenin's writings on colonial powers. His work with the Communist Party led to his participation in founding the Indochinese Communist Party in 1930. When Ho returned to Vietnam in 1941, he took the name Ho Chi Minh, which means "Bringer of Light." Ho died on September 2, 1969, in Hanoi. The North Vietnamese mourned the president they called Uncle Ho.

Making Connections What does the name "Uncle Ho" suggest about Ho Chi Minh's approach to leadership?

Eisenhower sent hundreds of military advisers to train South Vietnam's army, but the Vietcong continued to grow more powerful because many Vietnamese opposed Diem's government. By 1961, the Vietcong had established control over much of the countryside.

When President Kennedy took office in 1961, he continued to support South Vietnam, believing the country was vital in the battle against communism. From 1961 to late 1963, the number of U.S. military personnel in South Vietnam jumped from about 1,400 to around 16,000, yet they failed to shore up the Diem regime, which struggled due to unpopular programs. One such program was the creation of strategic hamlets. The government moved villagers into these fortified villages despite the peasants' resentment at being uprooted.

The Overthrow of Diem

American officials blamed Diem, who made himself even more unpopular by discriminating against and repressing Buddhism, one of the country's most widely practiced religions. In the spring of 1963 he banned the traditional religious flags for the Buddha's birthday. When Buddhists protested in the streets, Diem's police killed nine people. In response, a Buddhist monk poured gasoline over his robes and set himself on fire, the first of several to do so. Images of their self-destruction horrified Americans as they watched the footage on nightly television news reports.

In August 1963 U.S. ambassador Henry Cabot Lodge learned that several Vietnamese generals were plotting to overthrow the unpopular Diem. Lodge expressed American sympathy for their desire to overthrow Diem, but President Kennedy supported the generals' plot privately. The generals launched a military coup, seizing power on November 1, 1963, and executed Diem soon after. Despite his unpopularity, Diem had been a respected nationalist. The chaos created by his death weakened South Vietnam's government.

Johnson Takes Over

Just three weeks after Diem's death, Kennedy was assassinated in Dallas, Texas. The presidency—and the growing problem of Vietnam—now belonged to President Lyndon B. Johnson. Although he approached Vietnam cautiously at first, Johnson wanted to keep the country from falling to the Communists. Additionally, some had blamed Democrats when China became a Communist country in 1949, which led Johnson to fear that the Democrats' loss of Vietnam might "shatter my Presidency, kill my administration, and damage our democracy."

On August 2, 1964, Johnson announced that North Vietnamese torpedo boats had fired on two U.S. destroyers in the Gulf of Tonkin, and two days later he reported another attack. Publicly, Johnson insisted that these were unprovoked and ordered American aircraft to attack North Vietnamese ships and naval facilities. However, historians generally conclude that Johnson knew that these attacks on U.S. ships were not unprovoked. Johnson then asked Congress for the authority to defend American forces and allies in Southeast Asia. Congress readily agreed, and on August 7, 1964, it passed the Gulf of Tonkin Resolution authorizing the president to "take all necessary measures to repel any armed attack against the forces of the United States and to prevent further aggression." Soon after, the Vietcong began to attack bases where American advisers were stationed in South Vietnam. After one particularly damaging attack, Johnson sent American aircraft to bomb North Vietnam.

Although the American public and Johnson's advisers generally supported these actions, some officials disagreed. Undersecretary of State George Ball, who initially supported involvement in Vietnam, warned that if the United States got too involved, it would be difficult to get out. "Once on the tiger's back, we cannot be sure of picking the place to dismount."

Other advisers, such as National Security Advisor McGeorge Bundy, believed that success in Vietnam was important to protect American interests and maintain stability in Southeast Asia. In a memo to the president, he argued:

> 66 The stakes in Vietnam are extremely high. The American investment is very large, and American responsibility is a fact of life which is palpable in the atmosphere of Asia, and even elsewhere. The international prestige of the U.S. and a substantial part of our influence are directly at risk in Vietnam. 99

—quoted in *The Best and the Brightest*, 1972

In March 1965 Johnson again expanded American involvement by ordering a sustained bombing campaign against North Vietnam. That same month he sent the first U.S. combat troops into Vietnam.

✓ CHECK FOR UNDERSTANDING

Analyzing How did American involvement in Vietnam change during the Kennedy and Johnson administrations?

A Bloody Stalemate

GUIDING QUESTION

What military tactics were used by the Vietcong, and how did American troops respond?

By the end of 1965, more than 180,000 U.S. combat troops were fighting in Vietnam, and that number doubled in 1966. The U.S. military entered Vietnam with great confidence. "America seemed omnipotent then," wrote one of the first marines to arrive, Philip Caputo, in his prologue to *A Rumor of War*. "[W]e saw ourselves as the champions of 'a cause that was destined to triumph.'"

Lacking the firepower of the Americans, the Vietcong used ambushes, booby traps, and other guerrilla tactics. Ronald J. Glasser, an American army doctor, described the devastating effects of one trap:

> 66 Three quarters of the way through the tangle, a trooper brushed against a two-inch vine, and a grenade slung at chest high went off, shattering the right side of his head and body. . . . Nearby troopers took hold of the unconscious soldier and, half carrying, half dragging him, pulled him the rest of the way through the tangle. 99

—in *365 Days*, 1971

U.S. troops used flamethrowers such as this one to spray napalm throughout the countryside. The tank in this photo is targeting bunkers along Route 13 in Vietnam in 1967.

Identifying Cause and Effect How might the use of chemical weapons such as napalm have encouraged the South Vietnamese populace to support the Vietcong?

PHOTO: Co Rentmeester/The LIFE Picture Collection/Getty Images; TEXT: (1)Johnson, Lyndon. in Zelizer, Julian E. Arsenal of Democracy: The Politics of National Security - From World War II to the War on Terrorism. New York: Basic Books, 2010; (2)Tonkin Gulf Resolution; Public Law 88-408, 88th Congress, August 7, 1964; General Records of the United States Government; Record Group 11; National Archives; (3)"How Valid Are the Assumptions Underlying our Vietnam Policies?" by Under Secretary of State George Ball, October 5, 1964; Vietnam Memos; Records of Under Secretary of State George W. Ball, compiled 1961 - 1966; General Records of the Department of State; Record Group 59; National Archives; (4)Memorandum From the President's Special Assistant for National Security Affairs McGeorge Bundy to President Johnson, February 7, 1965. Foreign Relations of the United States, 1964-1968, Volume II: Vietnam, January-June 1965, Document 84. Office of the Historian, Bureau of Public Affairs, United States Department of State; (5)Caputo, Philip. A Rumor of War. New York: Henry Holt and Company, 1977; (6)Glasser, Ronald J. 365 Days. New York: Bantam Books, 1971.

The Vietcong also frustrated American troops by blending in with the general population and then quickly vanishing. "It was a sheer physical impossibility to keep the enemy from slipping away whenever he wished," explained one American general.

"Search and Destroy"

To counter these tactics, American troops tried to find enemy troops, bomb their positions, destroy their supply lines, and force them out into the open for combat. American planes dropped **napalm,** a jellied gasoline that explodes on contact. They also used **Agent Orange,** a chemical that strips leaves from trees and shrubs, turning farmland and forest into wasteland. Agent Orange was intended to devastate the jungles to remove food sources and places to hide from the Vietcong, but the chemical agent also had negative health impacts for Vietnamese civilians and for American troops.

American military leaders underestimated the Vietcong's strength and misjudged the enemy's stamina and the support they had among the South Vietnamese. American generals believed that bombing and killing large numbers of Vietcong would destroy their morale and lead them to surrender. The guerrillas, however, had no intention of surrendering, and they willingly accepted huge losses to achieve their goals.

The Huey helicopter played a major role for the American forces. Weighing in at nearly four tons and capable of flying 130 miles per hour, the Huey was first used in Vietnam in 1963. When used as a transport, it could carry nine fully armed soldiers to and from battle or evacuate six stretchers of wounded soldiers. When used as a gunship, it could carry a formidable combination of rockets, grenades, automatic weapons, and ammunition. Over 7000 of these helicopters were active during the war. Over 3000 were destroyed by enemy fire, mechanical failure, or accidents. In some battles, over a hundred helicopters might be in the air, laying down fire or transporting soldiers or the wounded.

The Hueys were essential in the dense jungle and mountain terrain of Vietnam. When delivering troops and equipment to the battlefield, the helicopters often flew in tight formation, which was increasingly dangerous as they neared their landing zones. Medical evacuation could be especially treacherous since the medical helicopters were unarmed. Even with the danger, most wounded soldiers were evacuated within an hour.

If the wounded received attention within that span of time, known as the "golden hour," the rate of survival greatly improved. The use of long-range radios made it possible to quickly dispatch helicopters to the wounded and to alert the crew to the types of wounds. Crew members were trained in pre-hospital medical care, much like Emergency Medical Technicians (EMTs) today. For example, the crews treated the wounded for shock and started life-saving blood transfusions using the universal donor blood type, O negative.

Ho Chi Minh Trail

North Vietnamese support was a major factor in the Vietcong's war effort. Although the Vietcong included many South Vietnamese, North Vietnam provided arms, advisers, and leadership. As Vietcong casualties mounted, North Vietnam began sending North Vietnamese Army units to fight. North Vietnam sent arms and supplies south by way of a network of jungle paths known as the Ho Chi Minh Trail. The trail wound through Cambodia and Laos, bypassing the border between North Vietnam and South Vietnam.

The North Vietnamese used trucks, bicycles, and even people to carry loads on their backs to transport arms and supplies south along the trail. Underground barracks, workshops, fuel drops, and storage facilities were positioned along the trail. Although the Ho Chi Minh Trail included roads, most paths were concealed by jungle, making it difficult for Americans forces to destroy the trail, even from the air. When parts were destroyed, new paths and roads quickly took their place. Northwest of Saigon, the Vietcong built the underground Cu Chi tunnels to transport supplies and messages and to house troops and mount attacks.

Huey helicopters airlift soldiers from a rubber plantation to transport them to a new staging area for a search-and-destroy mission near Cu Chi, South Vietnam, in 1966.

Explaining Based on the photograph, why were helicopters particularly efficient in moving troops from one area of operations to another?

napalm a jellied gasoline used for bombs

Agent Orange a chemical defoliant used to clear Vietnamese jungles during the Vietnam War

PHOTO: Pictures from History/CPA Media Pte Ltd/Alamy Stock Photo; TEXT: Rogers, Bernard William. Cedar Falls -- Junction City: A Turning Point. Washington, D.C.: United States Dept. of the Army, 1974.

The Ho Chi Minh Trail

The North Vietnamese used the Ho Chi Minh Trail to supply the Vietcong fighting in South Vietnam.

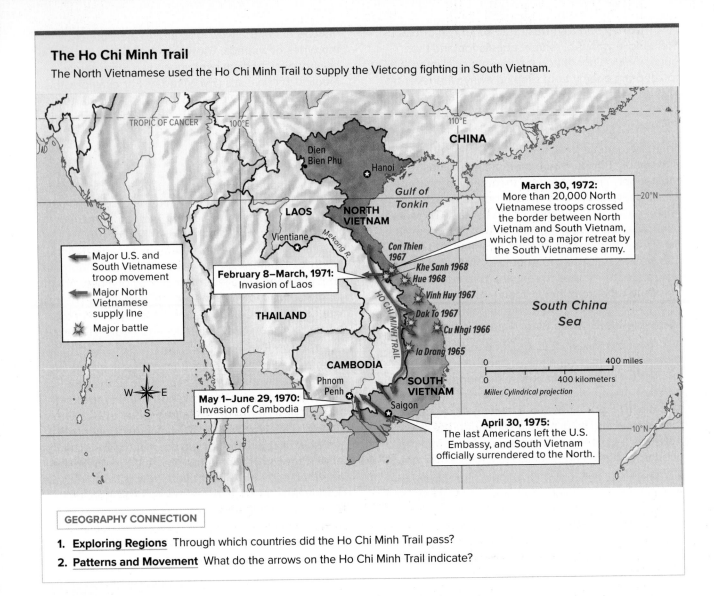

GEOGRAPHY CONNECTION

1. **Exploring Regions** Through which countries did the Ho Chi Minh Trail pass?
2. **Patterns and Movement** What do the arrows on the Ho Chi Minh Trail indicate?

North Vietnam itself received weapons and other support from the Soviet Union and China. The Soviet-supplied AK-47s worked much more efficiently than the M16s Americans used, which tended to become jammed and fail to extract. Johnson feared that directly attacking North Vietnam would bring China into the war, as had happened in the Korean War.

Instead of conquering territory, American troops had to fight a war of attrition—defeating enemy forces by wearing them down. This strategy led troops to conduct grisly body counts after battles to determine how many enemy soldiers had been killed. The American military began measuring "progress" in the war by comparing the number of enemy dead to the number of American soldiers lost.

Bombing from American planes killed many thousands of Vietnamese, and American soldiers were also dying in increasing numbers. As the notion of a quick and decisive victory grew increasingly remote, many citizens back home began to question the nation's involvement in the war.

✓ **CHECK FOR UNDERSTANDING**

Identifying Cause and Effect What military tactics were used by the Vietcong, and how did American troops respond?

LESSON ACTIVITIES

1. **Argumentative Writing** Take on the role of a member of Congress in 1964. Write a statement supporting or opposing the Gulf of Tonkin Resolution. Use details from the lesson and further research, either in a library or on the Internet, to support your position.

2. **Using Multimedia** With a partner, develop a digital slide presentation that illustrates main points along the Ho Chi Minh Trail. Make sure you include a map with the points you have chosen to illustrate. When possible, consider why the trail took the path it did, and note whether the trail changed based on American military actions.

03

The Antiwar Movement

PHOTO: Tim Page/CORBIS/Corbis Historical/Getty Images; TEXT: Westmoreland, William C. "National Press Club Address." Address, November 21, 1967. In Willbanks, James H., ed. Vietnam War: The Essential Reference Guide. Santa Barbara: ABC-CLIO, 2013.

READING STRATEGY

Analyzing Key Ideas and Details As you read, use a graphic organizer like the one below to take notes.

Reasons for Opposition to Vietnam War

A Growing Credibility Gap

GUIDING QUESTION

How did the difference between government reports on the Vietnam War and the media coverage of the war affect public opinion?

When the first U.S. combat troops arrived in Vietnam in the spring of 1965, about 66 percent of Americans approved of U.S. policy in Vietnam. Congress had previously granted Johnson a great deal of power with the Gulf of Tonkin Resolution. Now Congress began to seek greater involvement in the war, suspicious of disparities between the Johnson administration's depiction of events in Vietnam and that of journalists and troops. Beginning in February 1966, the Senate Foreign Relations Committee held televised "educational" hearings on Vietnam, primarily designed to obstruct the administration from sending additional troops to the country. The committee called in policy makers and critics to discuss the administration's military strategy. The televised hearings successfully swayed public opinion about the war's direction.

As the war dragged on, public support continued to wane. Media accounts seemed to contradict government reports. For example, in late 1967 the American commander in South Vietnam, General William Westmoreland, reported that the "enemy's hopes are bankrupt" and "the end begins to come into view." Yet millions saw images of American casualties on television in their living rooms each day as Vietnam became the first "television war." For many people a **credibility gap** had developed between what the government was claiming and what the nightly news was showing.

Westmoreland, who had assumed command in 1964, pushed the Johnson administration to send more troops to Vietnam and refocused the country's mission. The United States would move away from its advisory role to take on

General William Westmoreland consults with the troops at a military base in Vietnam in 1968.

Inferring Based on the photograph, what may you infer about Westmoreland's leadership style? Explain why.

credibility gap a perceived difference between what is said and what is true

more combat operations. By 1967, half a million U.S. soldiers were in Vietnam.

Despite suffering heavy casualties the Vietcong and North Vietnamese forces were able to continually replace their losses and remain a constant threat. High-ranking members of the Johnson administration began questioning the war and privately doubting prospects for victory.

Johnson launched a public relations campaign in response to shore up public support for the war and recalled Westmoreland back to the United States to provide assistance in this effort. Under Westmoreland's leadership, the Military Assistance Command, Vietnam (MACV) used its influence and war data to present an image to the media of weakening Communist forces and a victorious United States. Although influential U.S. journalists published the MACV's claims, they, along with some U.S. commanders on the ground in Vietnam, did not agree with this assessment. Instead, they believed the MACV was misleading the public.

By the mid-1960s, the national television networks had expanded their evening news programs from 15 minutes to 30 minutes to provide greater coverage of the front lines in Vietnam. In addition, more than 600 journalists were reporting on the war from Vietnam by 1968. What Americans saw on television and read in their newspapers contradicted what Westmoreland and the MACV were saying.

To highlight these contradictions, a group of faculty members and students at the University of Michigan joined together in March 1965 in a **teach-in.** They discussed issues surrounding the war and reaffirmed their reasons for opposing it. In May 1965 122 colleges broadcast a "National Teach-In" to more than 100,000 antiwar demonstrators via campus radio stations.

People opposed the war for different reasons. Some saw the conflict as a civil war in which the United States should not interfere. Others saw South Vietnam as a corrupt dictatorship and believed defending it was immoral.

✓ CHECK FOR UNDERSTANDING

Analyzing How did print and broadcast journalism affect Americans' perceptions of the war in Vietnam?

Anger at the Draft

GUIDING QUESTION

Why did Americans disagree about the Vietnam War?

As the war continued, thousands of demonstrators held public protests against the war. Students for a Democratic Society (SDS) organized a march on Washington, D.C., that drew more than 20,000 people in April 1965. A rally at the Lincoln Memorial drew tens of thousands of protesters as well. One of the largest demonstrations was in Washington, D.C., when almost 100,000 people gathered. More than half of them stormed toward the Pentagon, and 500 demonstrators were arrested. Many conscientious objectors declared that not only would they refuse the draft, but they would help others avoid it.

❝ Today I am making public my total disaffiliation with the so-called Selective Service System. I wish to make it perfectly clear that I do not recognize the Selective Service System as having any moral or legal control over my person.

I will not now or ever allow myself to be conscripted, indoctrinated, or trained to kill my brothers and sisters.

I will not now or ever allow myself to be directed, influenced or deferred by a system designed to brutalize the spirit of men by forcing them into servitude in agencies designed for mass murder.

I will not now or ever carry on my person or maintain in my possession any card or document that states I am registered with, or deferred by, any agency of conscription.

Further: I counsel all of you to do as I am doing. Repudiate and refuse to cooperate with the so-called Selective Service System. And I will aid anyone who does so.

I willfully will cause or attempt to cause, any man now imprisoned in the military forces of the United States, to refuse all duty, and to be disloyal to the system that is being disloyal to his spirit, and I will distribute literature to that effect.

I urge all military personnel to desert the agencies that are brutalizing you. I will aid, harbor, conceal and protect all deserters who come to me. . . . ❞

—Jerry D. Coffin, from FBI Records: The Vault "Clergy and Laity Concerned about Vietnam"

Many protesters focused on what they saw as an unfair draft system. Until 1969, college students could often defer military service until after graduation. Young people from working-class families unable to afford college were more likely to be drafted. Draftees were most likely to be assigned to combat units, and they commonly made up more than half of the casualties. At least a quarter of the American soldiers who fought in Vietnam entered the military through the draft

The draft intended to arrive at decisions fairly. Nevertheless, a disproportionate number of

Coffin, Jerry D. "Public Statement of Selective Service Dis-Affiliation." Philadelphia. October 16, 1967. Clergy and Laity Concerned about Vietnam.

teach-in an informal extended discussion about a social or political issue

Dan Rather, then a news reporter for CBS, accompanied U.S. troops into battle in Vietnam in 1966 and reported on the action while he and his crew were under fire.

Analyzing Perspectives How do you think watching a reporter file a news story from the middle of a battle might affect the viewers on the home front? Why?

working-class and minority youths went to war. Between 1961 and 1966, African Americans constituted about 10 percent of military personnel, but because they were more likely to be assigned to combat units, they accounted for almost 20 percent of combat-related deaths. The high number of African American and poor Americans dying in Vietnam angered people such as Martin Luther King, Jr. Dr. King had refrained from specifically speaking out against the war in earlier years. This was because King feared that doing so would draw media and political attention away from his main focus on the civil rights movement. Still, the skewed death rate angered African American leaders because statistically African Americans only accounted for about 10 percent of the population in 1967.

One organization that spoke out against the social tensions of the Vietnam era was Students for a Democratic Society (SDS). The SDS defined its views in a 1962 declaration known as the Port Huron Statement. Written largely by Tom Hayden, editor at the University of Michigan's student newspaper, the declaration called for an end to apathy and urged citizens to stop accepting the current situation.

66 . . . [H]uman degradation, symbolized by the Southern struggle against racial bigotry . . . the Cold War symbolized by the presence of the Bomb, brought awareness that we ourselves, and our friends, and millions of abstract 'others' . . . might die at any time. . . . Our work is guided by the sense that we may be the last generation in the experiment with living. 99

—from the *Port Huron Statement*, 1962

SDS chapters focused on protesting the Vietnam War and other issues including poverty, campus regulations, nuclear power, and racism.

ANALYZING SUPREME COURT CASES
TINKER V. *DES MOINES,* 1969

BACKGROUND TO THE CASE In December 1965, 13-year-old Mary Beth Tinker, her 15-year-old brother John, and their friend Christopher Eckhardt wanted to express their opposition to the Vietnam War by wearing black armbands to their public schools in Des Moines, Iowa. When school administrators heard about the plan, however, they quickly passed a new policy banning black armbands and vowed to suspend any students who refused to take them off while at school. Students also would be forbidden from returning to school until they agreed not to wear the armbands. Aware of the new policy, the Tinkers and Eckhardt nonetheless arrived at school wearing their armbands and refused to remove them. The three students were subsequently expelled for violating the policy.

HOW THE COURT RULED The students, led by their parents, challenged their expulsion as a violation of their First Amendment right to free speech. A U.S. District Court upheld the suspensions, stating that the district's actions were reasonable so as to limit disruptions in schools. The Tinkers appealed to the U.S. Court of Appeals, but a tie vote allowed the lower court's decision to stand. The Tinkers then appealed to the U.S. Supreme Court, which in 1969 ruled 7 to 2 in favor of the students, holding that wearing black armbands was a form of "symbolic expression" covered by the First Amendment. As long as their symbolic protest was not disruptive, they had a right to express their opinions.

» Mary Beth and John Tinker display the armbands they wore to protest the conflict in Vietnam.

1. **Citing Text Evidence** What rationale did the schools use to ban students from wearing black armbands?

2. **Making Connections** How does the Tinker decision affect your right to wear a T-shirt at school supporting a cause you believe in?

PHOTO: (tl)CBS Photo Archive/CBS/Getty Images; (br)Bettmann/Getty Images; TEXT: Port Huron Statement of the Students for a Democratic Society, 1962. In Fernlund, Kevin J. Documents for America's History. 7th ed. v2: Since 1865. Boston: Bedford/St. Martin's, 2011.

As the war escalated, an increased draft call put many college students at risk of being drafted. An estimated 500,000 draftees refused to go. Some burned their draft cards, did not show up for induction, or fled the country. From 1965 to 1968, officials prosecuted over 3,000 Americans who refused to serve. In 1969 a lottery system was instituted in which dates of birth were randomly assigned lottery numbers, so only those with low numbers were subject to the draft. Many draftees argued that if they were old enough to fight, they were old enough to vote. In 1971 the Twenty-sixth Amendment to the Constitution was ratified, giving all citizens age 18 and older the right to vote in all state and federal elections.

As war opposition grew, President Johnson remained determined to continue fighting and saw the effort as resistance to communism. He assailed his critics in Congress as "selfish men who want to advance their own interests" and dismissed the college protesters. Johnson was not alone in his views.

The nation was divided into two camps of opinions on the war. "Doves" wanted to leave Vietnam. "Hawks" wanted the nation to stay and fight. Like Johnson, hawks saw communism as a real threat. They challenged the patriotism of the doves and supported the post–World War II "containment theory," which predicted that if Vietnam fell to Communists, other countries in Southeast Asia could fall as well. Some hawks supported the bombing of North Vietnamese cities or the invasion of the Communist country. Johnson tried to straddle a middle position between the hawks and doves. As the two groups debated, the war took a dramatic turn for the worse.

✓ CHECK FOR UNDERSTANDING

Contrasting How did hawks and doves differ?

The Tet Offensive

GUIDING QUESTION

What impact did the Tet Offensive have on the direction of the Vietnam War?

On January 30, 1968, during Tet, the Vietnamese New Year, the Vietcong and North Vietnamese launched a massive surprise attack. In what was called the Tet Offensive, guerrilla fighters attacked most American airbases in South Vietnam and most of the South's major cities. Vietcong even blasted their way into the American embassy in Saigon.

After a month of fighting, U.S. and South Vietnamese soldiers repelled the enemy troops, inflicting heavy losses on them. The American people were shocked that an enemy supposedly on the verge of defeat could launch such a large-scale attack. The media openly criticized the war. "The American people

should be getting ready to accept, if they haven't already, the prospect that the whole Vietnam effort may be doomed," declared the *Wall Street Journal*.

Dr. Benjamin Spock, a pediatrician, who was trusted among Americans due to his popular parenting book, *Baby and Child Care*, was one of the first public figures to march in an anti-war demonstration with Dr. Martin Luther King, Jr. In 1968 Dr. Spock was convicted for counseling draft evasion—a conviction later overturned on appeal. Dr. Spock said about his stance:

66 I am opposed to this war, not only because I think it is morally and legally wrong, but because I think it is destroying the good name and the leadership of the United States. Furthermore, I believe that the war is militarily unwinnable. If we should succeed in bombing Vietnam to rubble, we will only find ourselves up against the Chinese. I believe that thousands of American young men are being asked to die to save Lyndon Johnson's face. He must know by now that this war is unwinnable but he does not know how to give up. Therefore, I believe that young men are not only justified but to be thanked if they point this out by refusing to take part in such an outrageous war any longer. 99

—Dr. Benjamin Spock, October 2, 1967, press conference, New York City

✓ CHECK FOR UNDERSTANDING

Describing Why was the Tet Offensive such a significant event during the Vietnam War?

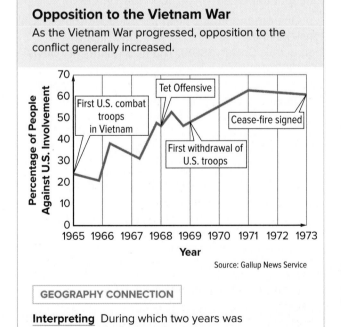

Opposition to the Vietnam War

As the Vietnam War progressed, opposition to the conflict generally increased.

Source: Gallup News Service

GEOGRAPHY CONNECTION

Interpreting During which two years was opposition to the war lowest? What event occurred around that time?

(1)United States Congress, Congressional Record: Proceedings and Debates of the United States Congress, Volume 114, Part 1, Page 611, U.S. Government Printing Office, 1968. (2)"The Logic of the Battlefield." The Wall Street Journal, February 23, 1968; (3)Spock, Benjamin, 1968. Speech at an anti-Vietnam draft rally, May 22, 1968. U.S. Department of Justice, File Unit: Coffin, Spock, et al Transcript Vol III 5/22/1968, 1928 - 1976; Series: Precedent Case Files, 1928 - 1976; Record Group 118: Records of U.S. Attorneys, 1821 - 1994.

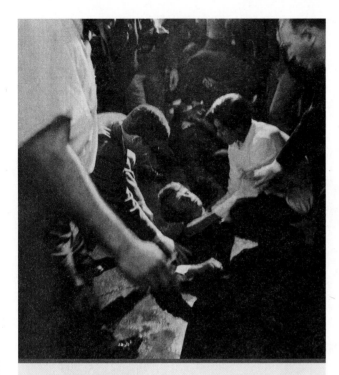

After Robert Kennedy was shot, the people around him, including busboy Juan Romero, tried to assist him until medical help could arrive.

Analyzing Visuals What do the various activities going on in the photograph tell you about the atmosphere at the scene as it unfolded?

PHOTO: Bill Eppridge/The LIFE Picture Collection/Getty Images; TEXT: "The President's Address to the Nation Announcing Steps To Limit the War in Vietnam and Reporting His Decision Not To Seek Reelection, March 31, 1968." Public Papers of the Presidents of the United States: Lyndon B. Johnson, 1968-69. Volume I, entry 170, pp. 469-476. Washington, D. C.: Government Printing Office, 1970.

Johnson Leaves the Race

GUIDING QUESTION

What events can you identify that affected the 1968 presidential election?

Both President Johnson and the Vietnam War had become increasingly unpopular. With the presidential election of 1968 on the horizon, some Democratic politicians made surprising moves. In November 1967, Eugene McCarthy, a little-known liberal senator from Minnesota, declared that he would challenge Johnson for the Democratic presidential nomination.

At first McCarthy's candidacy was mostly dismissed, but he attracted support from those who opposed the war. In March 1968, McCarthy made a strong showing in the New Hampshire primary, winning more than 40 percent of the vote. Realizing that Johnson was vulnerable, Senator Robert Kennedy, who also opposed the war, quickly entered the race for the Democratic nomination.

With the country and his own party deeply divided, Johnson announced on television on March 31, 1968, "I have concluded that I should not permit the presidency to become involved in the partisan divisions that are developing in this political year. Accordingly, I shall not seek, and I will not accept, the nomination of my party for another term as your President."

A Season of Violence

More shocking events followed Johnson's announcement. On April 4, Dr. Martin Luther King, Jr., was assassinated in Memphis, Tennessee, by James Earl Ray, an escaped convict and an admirer of Adolf Hitler. Then on June 5, Robert Kennedy was shot and killed by Sirhan Sirhan, a Palestinian nationalist. Sirhan became a fierce critic of Kennedy following Kennedy's support of Israel after the 1967 Six-Day War, during which Israel took control of Sirhan's birthplace, the Old City of Jerusalem. Kennedy had won five out of six Democratic primaries until his assassination and was the presumptive nominee. But with Kennedy gone, the Democratic primary race was thrown into turmoil.

The violence that plagued the country in 1968 culminated with a well-publicized clash between antiwar protesters and police at the Democratic National Convention in Chicago. Thousands of young activists surrounded the convention center to protest the war. Despite these protests, the delegates selected Vice President Hubert Humphrey as the Democratic nominee. Meanwhile, in a park not far from the convention, protesters and police began fighting. Demonstrators taunted police with the chant, "The whole world is watching!" as the officers tried to force them to disperse.

Nixon Wins the Presidency

At a much more sedate convention, Republicans selected former vice president and 1960 presidential hopeful Richard Nixon as their candidate. A third candidate, Governor George Wallace of Alabama, decided to run in 1968 as an independent.

An outspoken segregationist, Wallace sought to attract Americans who supported his segregationist and anti-civil rights views. In an attempt to gain national notoriety, Wallace tried to take advantage of the resentment white Americans felt at the fight for civil rights and the antiwar protests.

Public opinion polls gave Nixon a wide lead over Humphrey and Wallace. Nixon's campaign promise to unify the nation and "restore law and order" appealed to Americans who feared their country was spinning out of control. He claimed to represent a silent majority of Americans who had been overshadowed in recent years by social and political turmoil.

This promise to restore "law and order" specifically appealed to those with racist leanings who believed that doing so would return the nation to the racial hierarchy of previous eras. Nixon also promised that he had a secret plan to bring "peace with honor" in Vietnam.

The Vietnam War and a return to social order were key issues during the campaign. Humphrey argued in support of "order for justice," in contrast to the "law and order" slogan used by Nixon and Wallace.

The Election of 1968

The Election of 1968 revealed regional differences in the attitude of American voters toward the Vietnam War.

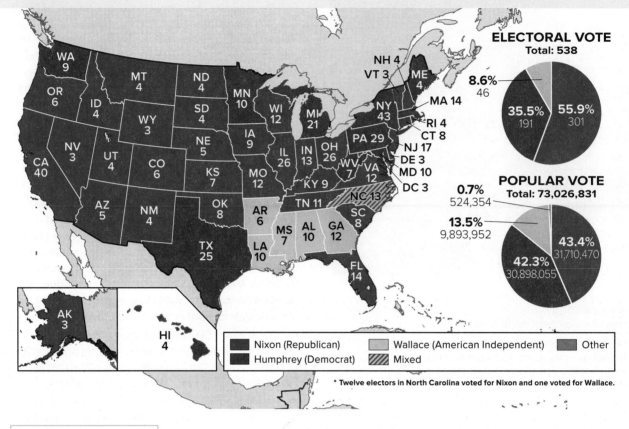

ELECTORAL VOTE
Total: 538

- 8.6% — 46
- 35.5% — 191
- 55.9% — 301

POPULAR VOTE
Total: 73,026,831

- 0.7% — 524,354
- 13.5% — 9,893,952
- 43.4% — 31,710,470
- 42.3% — 30,898,055

Legend:
- Nixon (Republican)
- Humphrey (Democrat)
- Wallace (American Independent)
- Mixed
- Other

*Twelve electors in North Carolina voted for Nixon and one voted for Wallace.

GEOGRAPHY CONNECTION

1. **Exploring Regions** In what region of the country did George Wallace receive all of his votes?

2. **Human Population** Given the results, what might you infer about people's attitudes in the Northeast toward the Vietnam War? Explain.

Nixon, sensing that more southern white Democrats might abandon their party, courted these voters. He assured them his administration would not intrude in local matters, such as school busing to desegregate local schools. Nixon's "southern strategy" would prove successful and would lead to a shift in party alignment that broke the Democratic hold on the South.

Humphrey's campaign faced significant challenges, but by October 1968, his increasingly anti-war stance and strong campaigning helped turn his numbers around. A week before the election, President Johnson announced that the bombing of North Vietnam had halted and that a cease-fire would follow. These boosts came too late for Humphrey. Nixon defeated him by more than 100 electoral votes, although he only won the popular vote by a slim margin of 43 percent to 42 percent.

✓ **CHECK FOR UNDERSTANDING**

Explaining Why did many Americans find Nixon's campaign appealing?

LESSON ACTIVITIES

1. **Argumentative Writing** Suppose that you were living in 1968. Write an article for a student newspaper in which you present an argument for or against U.S. involvement in the Vietnam War.

2. **Presenting** In small groups, use the Internet to research more about protests around the country in response to the Vietnam War. Choose one protest and prepare a short slideshow about the protest. Include information about where it happened, who organized it, and what effect it may have had. Share your presentation with the class.

04

Turning Point: The Pivotal Year of 1968

 COMPELLING QUESTION

What made 1968 a turning point?

Plan Your Inquiry

In this lesson, you will investigate events happening in Vietnam in 1968 and the official and the public response in the United States.

DEVELOP QUESTIONS

Developing Questions About 1968 Read the Compelling Question for this lesson. Think about key events that occurred in Vietnam that year and how U.S. officials responded. Develop a list of Supporting Questions that will help you answer the Compelling Question in this lesson.

APPLY HISTORICAL TOOLS

Analyzing Primary and Secondary Sources You will work with a variety of primary and secondary sources in this lesson. These sources focus on the conditions and events in Vietnam in 1968 as well as the policy responses in the United States. As you read, use a graphic organizer like the one below to record information about the sources that will help you examine them and check for historical understanding. Note ways in which each source helps you answer your Supporting Questions.

Supporting Questions	Source	How this source helps me answer the Supporting Question
Question 1:		
Question 2:		
Question 3:		

After you analyze the sources, you will:

- use the evidence from the sources.
- communicate your conclusions.
- take informed action.

Background Information

During World War II, Japan invaded French-controlled Vietnam. Ho Chi Minh, founder of the Vietnamese Communist Party, organized the Vietminh to fight the Japanese. After World War II, France sought to re-exert colonial rule, but the Vietminh refused to yield.

Officially, the United States opposed imperialism; however, U.S. officials worried about the spread of communism in the region. The United States had important economic interests in Southeast Asia as well. The United States sent aid and advisors to assist France. Then France lost.

For a while, the country was divided as North Vietnam, led by Minh's Communist Party, and South Vietnam, led by Ngo Dinh Diem, a pro-Western, anti-Communist leader who refused to hold national elections. The North responded by supporting the Vietcong opposition in the South. When conflict erupted, the United States increased military aid to the South.

In 1964 Lyndon B. Johnson inherited the escalating situation in Vietnam. By then, military leaders had overthrown Diem and taken control of the South. A year later, the United States began bombing North Vietnam, and the first U.S. combat troops arrived. Officials soon realized that they had underestimated the strength of North Vietnam and their support in the South as they became mired in a devastating guerrilla war.

» Chicago police officers and antiwar protesters clashed violently in Grant Park during the August 1968 Democratic National Convention.

National Archives and Records Administration.

Walter Cronkite's Tet Broadcast

On January 30, 1968, the North Vietnamese and Vietcong launched the devastating attacks known as the Tet Offensive. Long-time CBS news anchor Walter Cronkite gave his assessment of the war effort on national television. The excerpt below describes the impact of that report.

SECONDARY SOURCE : ARTICLE

❝ Wearing a dark suit with matching tie, Cronkite took to the airwaves on February 27, 1968, at 10 p.m. In the half-hour 'Report from Vietnam,' he calmly and objectively presented the facts, providing a penetrating illustrated briefing that covered everything from U.S. air raids to villages in ruin. Millions of Americans tuned in.

After the last commercial break, Cronkite turned to look straight into the camera . . . indicating his desire to speak 'personally' to the viewers in a speculative and subjective fashion. In his closing words . . . he told the American people what he now firmly believed: from a U.S. military perspective, the Southeast Asian war was 'unwinnable.'

Cronkite's editorial wasn't radical: in many ways, calling the war a 'stalemate' was a middling position in 1968. But in the highly polarized national dialogue on Vietnam, it placed Cronkite squarely as a dove. He had lent his august name to the antiwar movement and thereby put it into mainstream America.

» Walter Cronkite, host of CBS Evening News

His words resonated deeply with millions of viewers. His opinion was widely quoted in the press . . . Even the conservative *Wall Street Journal's* editorial page said, 'The whole Vietnam effort may be doomed.' ❞

—Douglas Brinkley, "The Sage of Black Rock," *American Heritage*, Spring 2012

EXAMINE THE SOURCE

Summarizing How did Cronkite's report shift public opinion on Vietnam in 1968?

A Tense Meeting

President Johnson supported military engagement in Vietnam as part of the containment policy. By the end of 1967, tens of thousands of Americans had died in the fight, and President Johnson was asking Congress for more money to fight the war. Then came the Tet Offensive.

EXAMINE THE SOURCE

1. **Analyzing Visuals** How do Johnson and McNamara appear to be responding to news of events in Vietnam?

2. **Speculating** How might the American public have responded to Cronkite's broadcast and images like this one?

PRIMARY SOURCE : PHOTOGRAPH

» On February 7, following the Tet Offensive, President Johnson and Secretary of Defense Robert McNamara attend a National Security Council meeting.

PHOTO: (tr)CBS Photo Archive/CBS/Getty Images; (b)LBJ Library photo by Yoichi Okamoto; TEXT: Brinkley, Douglas. "The Sage of Black Rock." American Heritage. v. 62:1, Spring 2012.

President Johnson's Televised Address

President Lyndon Johnson swept the electoral and popular votes in the 1964 election. During his campaign, Johnson affirmed that he did not want to involve American troops in a war in Southeast Asia—but that soon changed. As more troops went to Vietnam, public support for the war and for the president declined. The Tet Offensive only deepened the doubts of the American people, encouraging Senator Eugene McCarthy to run against Johnson for the Democratic nomination in 1968. In the New Hampshire primary, McCarthy did surprisingly well, pulling more than 40 percent of the vote, largely as a result of mounting opposition to the war. Johnson delivered this speech just two weeks later.

PRIMARY SOURCE : SPEECH

❝ Good evening, my fellow Americans:

Tonight I want to speak to you of peace in Vietnam and Southeast Asia.

No other question so preoccupies our people. No other dream so absorbs the 250 million human beings who live in that part of the world. No other goal motivates American policy in Southeast Asia.

For years, representatives of our Government and others have traveled the world—seeking to find a basis for peace talks.

Since last September, they have carried the offer . . . [that] the United States would stop its bombardment of North Vietnam when that would lead promptly to productive discussions—and that we would assume that North Vietnam would not take military advantage of our restraint.

Hanoi denounced this offer, both privately and publicly. Even while the search for peace was going on, North Vietnam rushed their preparations for a savage assault on the people, the government, and the allies of South Vietnam.

Their attack—during the Tet holidays—failed to achieve its principal objectives. . . .

They are, it appears, trying to make 1968 the year of decision in South Vietnam—the year that brings, if not final victory or defeat, at least a turning point in the struggle. . . .

So, tonight . . . I am taking the first step to deescalate the conflict. We are reducing—substantially reducing—the present level of hostilities.

And we are doing so **unilaterally,** and at once. . . .

With America's sons in the fields far away, with America's future under challenge right

» From the Oval Office, President Johnson delivered a speech in which he announced an end to bombing in Vietnam and his decision not run for reelection in 1968.

here at home, with our hopes and the world's hopes for peace in the balance every day, I do not believe that I should devote an hour or a day of my time to any personal partisan causes or to any duties other than the awesome duties of this office—the Presidency of your country.

Accordingly, I shall not seek, and I will not accept, the nomination of my party for another term as your President.

But let men everywhere know, however, that a strong, a confident, and a vigilant America stands ready tonight to seek an honorable peace—and stands ready tonight to defend an honored cause—whatever the price, whatever the burden, whatever the sacrifice that duty may require. . . . ❞

—President Lyndon Johnson, March 31, 1968

unilaterally something done by one person, country, or other party without regard to what others do

EXAMINE THE SOURCE

1. **Determining Central Ideas** Why does Johnson say that he will not seek reelection?

2. **Analyzing** Why do you think Johnson begins by saying he wants to talk about peace in Vietnam?

PHOTO: LBJ Library photo by Yoichi Okamoto; TEXT: "The President's Address to the Nation Announcing Steps To Limit the War in Vietnam and Reporting His Decision Not To Seek Reelection, March 31, 1968." Public Papers of the Presidents of the United States: Lyndon B. Johnson, 1968-69. Volume I, entry 170, pp. 469-476. Washington, D.C.: Government Printing Office, 1970.

Letter to End the War in Vietnam

The National Mobilization Committee to End the War in Vietnam first met in 1966 to organize rallies opposing the war. Committee chairs Dave Dellinger, Donald Kalish, and Sidney Peck wrote this letter in August 1968 as delegates prepared for the Democratic National Convention in Chicago.

PRIMARY SOURCE : LETTER

66 We are sure that you realize that this is a testing time in Chicago. . . . Mayor Daley and the Democratic Party have turned Chicago into an armed camp of national guardsmen, . . . barbed wire, tanks, mace and every conceivable weapon of intimidation and repression. . . . [W]e are appealing to people to make it clear that we will not lose our democratic rights by default. We plan to assert our right to march to the Convention and to hold public hearings there. At these public hearings, we will hear victims of war and racism—returned veterans from Vietnam (both black and white), welfare mothers, . . . etc. It is our hope that the pressure of tens of thousands . . . ready to march and the pressure from people all over the country will cause the city Administration and the Democratic Party to draw back from the brink and avoid this disgrace. . . .

But we need other persons too—persons who come not to confront the repressive machinery but to assemble peacefully in a park, to hold a meeting for which we have a permit and where, whatever happens elsewhere, there should be no likelihood of trouble of any kind.

A mass People's Assembly will convene on Wednesday August 28, at 1:00 P.M. near the bandshell at Grant Park. . . . Thousands of people . . . coming in for the day, can make a tremendous witness for peace and racial equality. . . . 99

—National Mobilization Committee to End the War in Vietnam, August 1968

EXAMINE THE SOURCE

1. **Summarizing** What plan does the Committee outline, and for what purpose?
2. **Analyzing** What does this source suggest about the public's response to events in Vietnam as well as domestic challenges in 1968?

Your Inquiry Analysis

EVALUATE SOURCES AND USE EVIDENCE

Refer back to the Compelling Question and the Supporting Questions you developed at the beginning of this lesson.

1. **Gathering Sources** Refer back to the Graphic Organizer you created as you read through the sources. Which sources helped you answer the Supporting Questions you wrote? Circle or highlight those sources in your graphic organizer. What additional questions did these sources raise? Write down at least two questions.

2. **Evaluating Sources** Looking at the sources that help you answer the Supporting Questions, evaluate the credibility of each source. Rank each source in terms of level of bias and quality of information. Write two to three sentences explaining which sources you found most helpful and why.

3. **Comparing and Contrasting** Compare and contrast two of the sources in this lesson more closely. What position does each take? What purpose does each serve? What tone is expressed by the writer, speaker, or photographer? What does each suggest about the significance of the events in 1968?

COMMUNICATE CONCLUSIONS

Identifying Arguments Answer each of your Supporting Questions. Share your responses with a partner. Then, identify a significant argument made or suggested by two of the sources. Write a paragraph in which you explain how those arguments help you understand 1968 as a turning point. Display or present your responses in class.

TAKE INFORMED ACTION

Evaluating Multiple Media Perspectives The media reports on and influences events and conditions. It both responds to and encourages thoughts, feelings, beliefs, opinions, and actions among readers or viewers. Identify one current issue of importance to you. Then locate three media sources from print and digital publications as well as radio, television, and Internet broadcasts. Review at least one report or story related to your subject from each source. Then, make a chart comparing and contrasting 1) what information each source shares, 2) what bias each shows, 3) what tone each takes, and 4) how each influences your thoughts or opinions. Write a short essay explaining how you think the media are both responding to and influencing public perceptions of the event. Share your work with the class or on a class board or website.

Letter from National Mobilization Committee to End the War in Vietnam; 8/1/1968; Records of District Courts of the United States, Record Group 21. [Online Version, https://www.docsteach.org/documents/document/letter-from-national-mobilization-committee, June 22, 2020].

05

The Vietnam War Ends

(1–2)Nixon, Richard M. "A Progress Report on Our Plan for Peace in Viet-Nam." The Department of State Bulletin. v. LXII, no. 1593. January 5, 1970.; (3)Nixon, Richard. "Remarks of the President on Vietnam." November, 1969. U.S. Senate. Briefing on Vietnam. Hearings Before the Committee on Foreign Relations. Ninety-First Congress, First Session. November 18-19, 1969.; (4)"Address to the Nation on the War in Vietnam." November 3, 1969. https://www.nixonlibrary.gov/forkids/speechesforkids/silentmajority/silentmajority_transcript.pdf.

READING STRATEGY

Analyzing Key Ideas and Details As you read, use a graphic organizer like the one below to list the steps that President Nixon took to end American involvement in Vietnam.

Steps Nixon Took

Nixon Moves to End the War

GUIDING QUESTION

What policies did Nixon employ to end the war?

During his 1968 election campaign, Nixon stated that he had a secret plan to quickly end the Vietnam War. This claim, however, was not borne out by events. As a step toward ending the war, Nixon appointed Henry Kissinger as special assistant for national security affairs. Kissinger embarked upon a policy called linkage, or improving relations with the Soviet Union and China to persuade them to reduce their aid to North Vietnam. In August 1969 Kissinger entered into secret negotiations with North Vietnam's representative, Le Duc Tho.

Meanwhile, Nixon began **Vietnamization.** This process involved the gradual withdrawal of U.S. troops while the South Vietnamese assumed more of the fighting. He announced the withdrawal of 25,000 soldiers on June 8, 1969. At the same time, Nixon increased air strikes against North Vietnam and began secretly bombing Vietcong sanctuaries in neighboring neutral Cambodia to disrupt North Vietnamese supply lines along the Ho Chi Minh Trail.

As opposition to the war steadily increased, Nixon rejected calls for a complete and immediate withdrawal of all U.S. forces from Vietnam. He believed this would be a humiliation for the United States, and he remained committed to finding an "end to the war and to achieve a just peace."

The Nixon administration's plan for Vietnamization involved three key considerations: "progress in the Paris negotiations, progress in the training of South Vietnamese forces, and the level of enemy activity." As peace talks stalled, the Nixon administration turned to training the South Vietnamese forces. Nixon shifted the focus of U.S. troops from proactive combat missions to enabling the South Vietnamese to assume the full responsibility for the security of South Vietnam. He also outlined the gradual withdrawal of American troops.

In a speech to Americans, Nixon described the process as one that "will be made from strength and not from weakness. As South Vietnamese forces become stronger, the rate of American withdrawal can become greater." Vietnamization also involved programs designed to strengthen the South Vietnamese government. This included helping the government implement effective election processes and strengthening social and economic development. Nixon summarized Vietnamization by saying:

> 66 The defense of freedom is everybody's business—not just America's business. And it is particularly the responsibility of the people whose freedom is threatened. In the previous administration, we Americanized the war in Vietnam. In this administration, we are Vietnamizing the search for peace. 99

— "Address to the Nation on the War in Vietnam," November 3, 1969

Turmoil at Home Continues

In late 1969 Americans learned that in the spring of 1968, an American platoon under the command of Lieutenant William Calley had massacred unarmed

Vietnamization the process of making South Vietnam assume more of the war effort by slowly withdrawing American troops from Vietnam

Shortly after noon on May 4, 1970, the Ohio National Guard first fired tear gas canisters into a crowd of Kent State University protesters to disperse them. The soldiers then marched forward with fixed bayonets to force the demonstrators to retreat.

Analyzing Visuals What can be learned about this event from the photograph?

South Vietnamese civilians in the hamlet of My Lai. Most of the victims were old men, women, and children. Calley eventually went to prison for his role in the killings.

Jan Barry, a founder of the Vietnam Veterans Against the War, viewed My Lai as a symbol of the dilemma his generation faced in the conflict:

66 To kill on military orders and be a criminal, or to refuse to kill and be a criminal is the moral agony of America's Vietnam war generation. It is what has forced upward of sixty thousand young Americans, draft resisters and deserters, to Canada, and created one hundred thousand military deserters a year. . . . 99

—Jan Barry, "Why Veterans March Against the War," April 23, 1971, *New York Times*

In April 1970 Nixon announced that American troops had invaded Cambodia to destroy Vietcong bases there. Many believed this invasion expanded the war, which led to more protests. On May 4, 1970, Ohio National Guard soldiers armed with tear gas and rifles fired on demonstrators at Kent State University, killing four students.

The Kent State shootings were preceded by protests, which began days earlier. After receiving calls from the city's mayor, the governor of Ohio sent in the National Guard. About 1,200 troops dispersed demonstrators on the nights of May 2 and 3, sometimes by using tear gas and bayonets.

By noon on May 4, nearly 3,000 demonstrators had gathered near the Kent State Commons. After demonstrators refused to disperse, guardsmen advanced on the protesters, who scattered in all directions. A group of guardsmen, feeling threatened, then fired more than 60 shots at the protesters, killing four and wounding nine others. Lorrie J. Accettola was a 23-year-old senior at Kent State and was on campus that day:

66 When they (Guardsmen) came to the crest of the hill, approximately 30 feet from where the Iron sculpture stands, they started shooting for what I thought was no apparent reason. I was just down the hill in the parking lot at this time. I remember the sounds of the bullets flying through the air. They sizzled and hissed as they flew by my head. I immediately fell to the ground. After the shooting stopped I got up and ran. The thought actually crossed my mind that it might be very possible that they would shoot everyone. I ran for my life. 99

—Lorrie Accettola, Kent State University Special Collections and Archives, submitted November 13, 1999

Of the four dead students, only one was within 60 feet of the Guardsmen. The shootings sparked student demonstrations across the country.

Ten days after the Kent State killings, police shot and killed two African American students at the predominantly black Jackson State College in Mississippi. African American students protesting the war and the shootings at Kent State were met with confrontations from white townspeople and law enforcement. Responding to reports of rocks being thrown at passing cars driven by white citizens, police arrived at a women's dormitory on the Jackson State campus.

As a fire blazed near the scene, students and nonstudents began throwing rocks and bricks at the police officers. Officers then fired 150 rounds into the building in 30 seconds, killing a Jackson State student, a local high school senior, and wounding 12 others. In their defense, the officers claimed that a sniper within the dorm had opened fire on them. An official government report completed after the shootings, however, could provide no evidence for that claim.

PHOTO: Everett Collection/SuperStock; TEXT: (1)"Why Veterans March Against the War," by Jan Barry in The New York Times, April 23, 1971; (2)Lorrie J. Accettola, Personal Narrative. November 13, 1999.

NEW YORK TIMES V. UNITED STATES, 1971

BACKGROUND TO THE CASE In the late 1960s, Daniel Ellsberg was working as a military analyst when he helped create a high-level government report titled *History of U.S. Decision-Making in Vietnam, 1945–68*. The report contained classified information revealing that the country's involvement in the Vietnam War was greater than the government had publicly acknowledged. The report, along with Ellsberg's previous experience working with American troops in Vietnam, convinced him that the war was not only unwinnable but misguided and wrong.

In early 1971, Ellsberg leaked related classified documents, known as the Pentagon Papers, to the *New York Times* and the *Washington Post*. When the newspapers attempted to publish these documents, the Nixon administration argued that publication would threaten national security and obtained a restraining order to stop further publication. After a Court of Appeals upheld the restraining order, the *New York Times* appealed to the Supreme Court, which agreed to hear the case the next day. The case centered on the First Amendment guarantee of a free press.

HOW THE COURT RULED In a 6-to-3 per curiam opinion—meaning that the decision was issued by the whole Court and not specific justices—the Court found that the Nixon administration had failed to prove that publication of the Pentagon Papers would imperil the nation in any way. The *New York Times* could publish the Pentagon Papers. The case is generally considered a confirmation of the rights of an uncensored free press in the United States.

1. **Speculating** Why do you think Daniel Ellsberg leaked the Pentagon Papers to the press?
2. **Explaining** Do you think the government can ever justify media censorship, even based on national security concerns?

An angry Congress began to work to end the president's control of the war. In December 1970, it repealed the Gulf of Tonkin Resolution, which had given the president nearly complete power in directing the conflict.

The following year a former employee of the Department of Defense, Daniel Ellsberg, leaked what became known as the Pentagon Papers to the *New York Times*. The documents contained details about decisions to expand the war and confirmed what many Americans had long believed: the government had not been honest with them.

Prisoners of War

Between 1964 and 1973, more than 700 U.S. military personnel were held as prisoners of war (POWs). More than 80 percent were aircrew or aviators with the Air Force or Navy who had been shot down while flying missions. The POWs were held in 13 camps in North Vietnam, most near Hanoi, the capital city.

Many prisoners spent years living in squalid cells, often in solitary confinement for long periods of time. POWs were often tortured, psychologically abused, and used as propaganda for the North Vietnamese

government, even though this treatment was against international law. Among the American POWs was future Republican senator and 2008 presidential candidate John McCain, who spent more than five years in captivity, including time at the Hoa Loa prison, nicknamed the "Hanoi Hilton" by American POWs.

At the Paris Peace Talks, one of the American conditions for ending the war was the release of all POWs within 60 days of signing the agreement. The parties reached their agreement in January 1973, and the first American POWs were sent home beginning on February 12. The last known POW was released by April. That same year, the U.S. government reported that approximately 2,500 American military and civilian personnel were considered "missing in action" (MIA). As of 2020, almost 1,587 Americans still remain "unaccounted-for."

The United States's Involvement Ends

Americans were increasingly ready for the war to end as the presidential election of 1972 approached. Nixon faced Democratic challenger George McGovern, an outspoken critic of the war. Less than a month before the election, however, Kissinger emerged from his

Everett Collection Historical/Alamy Stock Photo.

The U.S. Military Presence in Vietnam

The United States' involvement in Vietnam spanned three presidential administrations. President Nixon began a gradual troop withdrawal in an effort to end the war.

US Military Personnel in South Vietnam on December 31, 1961–1972

Kennedy   Johnson   Nixon   — Number of troops

GEOGRAPHY CONNECTION

Drawing Conclusions What does the chart tell you about American involvement in Vietnam?

secret talks with Le Duc Tho to announce that "peace is at hand." Nixon soundly defeated McGovern.

Soon, Kissinger's peace negotiations broke down over disagreements about the presence of North Vietnamese troops in the South. In December 1972, to force North Vietnam to resume negotiations, the Nixon administration began the most destructive air raids of the war. American B-52s dropped thousands of tons of bombs on North Vietnamese targets for 11 straight days in what became known as the "Christmas bombings." Then negotiations resumed.

On January 27, 1973, the warring sides signed an agreement "ending the war and restoring the peace in Vietnam." The United States promised to withdraw its troops, and both sides agreed to exchange prisoners of war. After almost eight years of war, the nation ended its direct involvement in Vietnam.

The Domino Effect

Peace did not last. Cambodia fell under the control of the Communist group, the Khmer Rouge in January 1975. The North Vietnamese army invaded South Vietnam in March 1975. Nixon had resigned in August 1974 following Watergate, a scandal that broke as the war was winding down. When the new president, Gerald Ford, asked for funds to aid the South Vietnamese, Congress refused.

By the end of April 1975, North Vietnamese troops were outside Saigon. On April 29, U.S. personnel scrambled to evacuate by helicopter the remaining Americans in the city and bring them to U.S. ships waiting along the coast. During Operation Frequent Wind, 81 U.S. helicopters airlifted more than 1,000 Americans and more than 5,000 Vietnamese within 19 hours. The last U.S. Marines left the American embassy before dawn on April 30. Later that day, the North Vietnamese captured Saigon,

South Vietnam's capital. They renamed it Ho Chi Minh City.

Laos, another country in the region, was also affected by the Vietnam War. Though Laos was run by a neutral coalition government during most of the war, the effects of bombings on the parts of the Ho Chi Minh Trail in Laos destabilized that neutrality. Communists took over Laos after the fall of Saigon. In the end, the domino effect took place despite the American government's efforts to prevent it.

✓ **CHECK FOR UNDERSTANDING**

1. **Making Connections** How did the repeal of the Gulf of Tonkin Resolution affect presidential control of the war effort?

2. **Speculating** Why did Congress refuse to give Gerald Ford the funds he requested to aid the South Vietnamese?

The Legacy of the Vietnam War

GUIDING QUESTION

How would you describe the political and cultural aftermath of the Vietnam War?

"The lessons of the past in Vietnam," President Ford declared in 1975, "have already been learned—learned by Presidents, learned by Congress, learned by the American people—and we should have our focus on the future." Vietnam had a profound effect on America.

The War's Human Toll

America paid a heavy price for its involvement in Vietnam, far more than the estimated $173 billion in

TEXT: (1)Agreement on Ending the War and Restoring Peace in Viet-Nam. [Treaty.] January 27, 1973; (2)Ford, Gerald R. 6 May 1975. "The President's News Conference." The American Presidency Project.

direct costs. Approximately 58,000 young Americans died, and some 300,000 were injured. An estimated 1 million North Vietnamese and South Vietnamese soldiers died, as did millions more civilians. Back home, some soldiers had trouble readjusting. Army Specialist Doug Johnson recalled:

> 66 It took a while for me to recognize that I did suffer some psychological problems in trying to deal with my experience in Vietnam. . . One evening . . . I went to see a movie on post. I don't recall . . . what it was about, but I remember there was a sad part, and that I started crying uncontrollably. It hadn't dawned on me before this episode that I had . . . succeeded in burying my emotions. 99

—quoted in *Touched by the Dragon*, 1998

Because many people considered the war a defeat and wanted to put it behind them, the veterans' sacrifices often went unrecognized. They received relatively few welcome-home parades and celebrations.

The war remained unresolved for the American families whose relatives and friends were classified as prisoners of war (POWs) or missing in action (MIA). Despite many official investigations, these families were not convinced that the government had told the truth about POW/MIA policies.

Vietnam remained on the nation's mind nearly a decade later. In 1982 the nation dedicated the Vietnam Veterans Memorial in Washington, D.C., a large black granite wall inscribed with the names of those killed and missing in action in the war. American architect Maya Lin designed the memorial.

The Vietnam War continues to influence American popular culture. The tumultuous era still fascinates artists, writers, musicians, and filmmakers. Hundreds of films and literary and musical works have explored people and events in the war and, in a larger sense, how the war changed the country and what that means for Americans looking to the future.

The War's Impact on the Nation

The war also left a mark on national politics. In 1973 Congress passed the War Powers Act as a way to reestablish some limits on executive power. The act required the president to inform Congress of any commitment of troops abroad within 48 hours, and to withdraw them in 60 to 90 days, unless Congress explicitly approved the troop commitment. No president has recognized this limitation, however, and

PHOTO: B Christopher/Alamy Stock Photo; TEXT: Johnson, Doug. In Gryzb, Frank L. 1998. Touched by the Dragon: Experiences of Vietnam Veterans from Newport County, Rhode Island. West Lafayette: Purdue University Press.

Visiting the Vietnam Veterans Memorial is a solemn and emotional experience for all who come, and especially for the veterans and families who touch the names of those they lost.

Identifying Themes Over time, the emotional response to Maya Lin's wall has transcended the Vietnam War, with visitors coming from all over the world and of all ages. Why do you think that is?

Refugees Arriving in the United States of America by Year, 1975-1989

The end of the Vietnam War and the Refugee Act of 1980 impacted the number of refugees arriving in the United States.

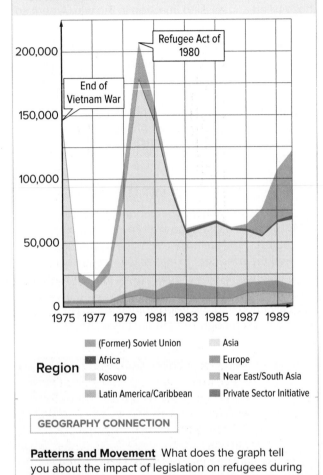

Region
- (Former) Soviet Union
- Africa
- Kosovo
- Latin America/Caribbean
- Asia
- Europe
- Near East/South Asia
- Private Sector Initiative

GEOGRAPHY CONNECTION

Patterns and Movement What does the graph tell you about the impact of legislation on refugees during the 1980s?

Refugees from South Vietnam who were evacuated in Operation Frequent Wind were allowed to bring only one bag of possessions aboard the helicopters.

Making Connections What challenges do you think these refugees will face in the United States?

United States. Most had either been in the South Vietnamese military or government, or they had family members who had worked with American personnel during the war. The opposition government saw them as the enemy. The social and political disruption caused by the war in both Vietnam and other countries in the region led to a second, larger wave of immigrants or refugees arriving in the late 1970s, many of whom fled by sea. Since 1975 more than 1.2 million refugees from Southeast Asia immigrated to the United States. The majority were from Vietnam, but large numbers of Laotians and Cambodians also made the journey.

CHECK FOR UNDERSTANDING

Identifying Cause and Effect Why do you think the war shook the nation's confidence?

LESSON ACTIVITIES

1. **Narrative Writing** Suppose that you are a college student in 1970. Write a journal entry expressing your thoughts and feelings about the events at Kent State University and Jackson State College.

2. **Using Multimedia** With a partner, use the Internet to research the Vietnam Veterans Memorial, the Three Soldiers statue, or the Women's Vietnam Memorial in Washington, D.C. Use presentation software to prepare a short presentation to explain its design, how many people visit it each year, and other facts about the memorial.

the courts have tended to avoid the issue. Almost every president since the act's passage has disregarded or found ways to get around provisions in the act, leading some critics to suggest either repealing or amending the War Powers Act. Nonetheless, every president since the law's passage has asked Congress to authorize the use of military force before committing ground troops to combat. In general, the war shook the nation's confidence and made some begin to question American foreign policies.

On the domestic front, the Vietnam War increased Americans' cynicism about their government. Together with Watergate, Vietnam made many Americans feel that the nation's leaders had misled them.

The war also had a significant impact on immigration, specifically that of refugees, to the United States. Following the fall of Saigon, the United States helped evacuate nearly 125,000 Vietnamese to the

Pictures from History/CPA Media Pte Ltd/Alamy Stock Photo.

06

Reviewing the Vietnam War

Summary

Vietnam was subject to occupation by other nations throughout its history. For centuries, China dominated the country. In the twentieth century, the country was the battleground for several different conflicts.

Vietnam and France

In 1887 France colonized Vietnam, Laos, and Cambodia. During World War II, the Japanese occupied this resource-rich land but faced fierce resistance from the Vietminh, Vietnamese nationalists led by Communist Ho Chi Minh. After the war, the Vietminh declared independence, but France sought to reclaim its colony. Fearing that a Communist Vietnam would mark another fallen domino in the Cold War, the United States backed France in its long, bloody fight to retake Vietnam.

The Vietminh wore down French forces through guerrilla tactics. After being defeated at Dien Bien Phu in 1954, France called for a truce and gave up its claim to Indochina. Still fearing a Communist takeover, the United States played a leading role in the Geneva Accords, which would temporarily divide the country into North Vietnam, led by Ho Chi Minh's Communist government, and South Vietnam, a republic led by anti-Communist Ngo Dinh Diem.

Increasing U.S. Involvement

An 1956 election was planned for the Vietnamese to choose a unified government, but Diem feared the popular Ho Chi Minh would win. With backing from the U.S. government, Diem refused to participate in the election. Ho Chi Minh responded by organizing a rebel army known as the Vietcong to oppose the South Vietnamese government and unify the country. Because the corrupt Diem was unpopular, many South Vietnamese citizens secretly supported the Vietcong.

President Eisenhower gradually committed more U.S. military personnel to train South Vietnamese soldiers. President Kennedy continued this trend after becoming president. Kennedy, like other U.S. officials, believed South Vietnam was a crucial piece in the Cold War. Over time, however, Diem became even more unpopular among his people by launching a violent campaign against those of the Buddhist faith, who were the majority. When President Kennedy learned of a plot to overthrow Diem, he ordered American forces not to intervene. In November 1963, a military coup overthrew and executed Diem.

Three weeks after Diem's death, Kennedy was assassinated. President Johnson, relying on Kennedy's foreign policy advisers, continued the same Cold War policies. Following the Gulf of Tonkin incident in 1964, Congress gave Johnson the ability to increase both funding and direct military support for the South Vietnamese government. U.S. forces expanded search-and-destroy missions to find Vietcong and their supporters. Meanwhile, the North

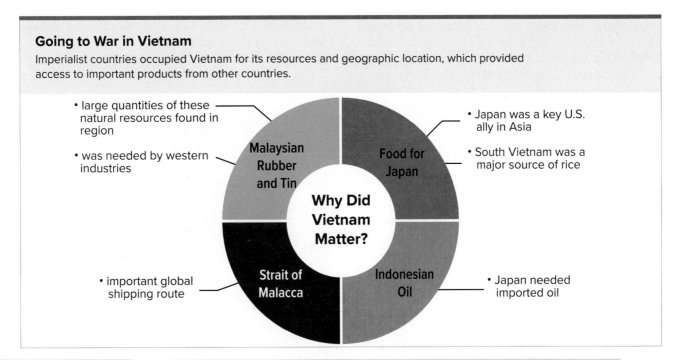

Going to War in Vietnam

Imperialist countries occupied Vietnam for its resources and geographic location, which provided access to important products from other countries.

- large quantities of these natural resources found in region
- was needed by western industries

Malaysian Rubber and Tin

- Japan was a key U.S. ally in Asia
- South Vietnam was a major source of rice

Food for Japan

Why Did Vietnam Matter?

- important global shipping route

Strait of Malacca

Indonesian Oil

- Japan needed imported oil

Vietnamese sent supplies to rebels in the South through the Ho Chi Minh Trail.

Opposition to the War

For many years, most Americans supported U.S. policy in Vietnam. As the war dragged on, public support waned. As the first televised war, images of the conflict were broadcast into people's homes every night. Positive reports about the war's progress—especially those coming from the American commander in South Vietnam, General William Westmoreland—seemed to conflict with the bloody reality the public saw on television. This credibility gap eroded public trust.

An Organized Movement

The anti-war movement first emerged on college campuses. Inspired by the civil rights movement, groups of young activists organized protests to make their voices heard. One of the most outspoken of these groups was the Students for a Democratic Society (SDS). A group of SDS members issued the Port Huron Statement, linking the ideals of the civil rights movement to the human rights violations the students believed were being carried out in the Vietnam conflict. Anti-war groups soon focused on the draft. Some young men refused to fight for what they believed was an unjust war. Opposition to the draft fueled support for ratification of the Twenty-sixth Amendment, which lowered the voting age to 18 throughout the country. Increasingly the country was divided into pro-war hawks and anti-war doves.

The Turning Point

By 1968, the United States had its highest number of soldiers embedded in Vietnam. Officials assured the public that victory was near. Then the Vietcong and North Vietnamese launched a surprise attack during the Vietnamese Tet holiday. Although American and South Vietnamese forces eventually repelled the attack, the attack shocked the nation and further eroded trust in official reports about the war's progress. Antiwar protesters focused their anger at President Johnson. Realizing his support was waning, in late March 1968, Johnson announced he would not run for another term.

Shortly after Johnson's announcement, on April 4, Martin Luther King, Jr., was assassinated. On June 5, Robert F. Kennedy was assassinated. That summer, antiwar protesters clashed with police in violent confrontations outside the Democratic National Convention in Chicago. It seemed there was no escape from violence. Within this context, Republican Richard Nixon won the presidency by promising to restore "law and order" to the country and establish peace with honor in Vietnam.

The War's Legacy

National Security Advisor Henry Kissinger led Nixon's so-called secret plan for winning the war. Under a plan of Vietnamization, U.S. troops slowly began to withdraw while gradually turning over more of the fighting to the South Vietnamese. Meanwhile U.S. bombings of the Ho Chi Minh Trail expanded the war into neighboring Cambodia.

Media reports of atrocities carried out by U.S. soldiers in the My Lai massacre horrified the public. Further shock and outrage occurred after the deaths of students during anti-war protests at Kent State and Jackson State universities. Congress soon repealed the Gulf of Tonkin Resolution, checking the president's power to expand the war. The Pentagon Papers revealed the extent to which the government had been lying about the war. Nixon won reelection in 1972, promising that peace negotiations were making progress. In 1973 the United States reached an agreement to withdraw its troops from Vietnam.

Two years later, Cambodia fell to a Communist regime, and North Vietnam invaded South Vietnam. With the capture of Saigon, soon renamed Ho Chi Minh City, the country reunified as an independent nation. Communists soon took over Laos, which had become destabilized because of the conflict in the region.

The Vietnam War left deep scars and costs billions of dollars and countless lives. In the United States, disagreements over the war had divided families. Many U.S. soldiers who served in Vietnam were ignored or mistreated upon their return. Families of missing POWs were left with unanswered questions. Mistrust of the government remained high for many years. Congress tried to prevent future presidents from waging undeclared war.

The war caused a massive refugee crisis as thousands from Vietnam, Laos, and Cambodia fled after their countries became communist. Those refugees, many of whom moved to the United States, paid a high price for the international conflict that had taken place in their homelands.

As Saigon was about to fall to the North Vietnamese, a massive airlift was orchestrated by the United States to evacuate 1,373 Americans and 5,595 South Vietnamese in less than 24 hours on April 29, 1975.

HUGH VAN ES/UPI Photo Service/Newscom.

Apply What You Have Learned

 ## Analyzing Graphs

Initially, most Americans supported U.S. policy in Vietnam. As U.S. military involvement expanded and the conflict dragged on, more Americans began to question U.S. policies in the region.

ACTIVITY **Interpret Historical Data** Many researchers point to the Tet Offensive as a turning point in support for the war in Vietnam. Although U.S. and South Vietnamese forces successfully repelled the offensive, the attack shocked many. Government

reports had indicated that Americans and their allies had virtually annihilated the opposition. The surprise attack on the Tet holiday undermined faith in the government's portrayal of how the war was progressing.

Analyze the graph below, which reflects public opinions about U.S. involvement in Vietnam. Based on this information, write a summary statement explaining whether the Tet Offensive was the key turning point in opposition to the war.

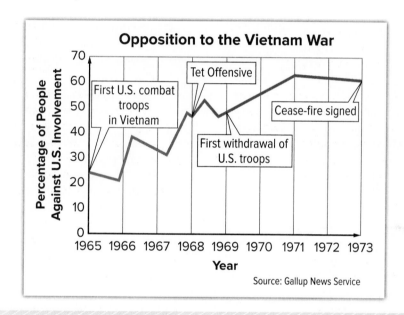

Opposition to the Vietnam War

Source: Gallup News Service

 ## Understanding Multiple Perspectives

One of the most controversial aspects of Cold War policy toward Vietnam was the extent to which Western powers made decisions for the Vietnamese people and ignored the voices of those they claimed to want to liberate. Many nationalists saw the conflict as a civil war that should have been left to the Vietnamese to resolve among themselves.

ACTIVITY **Compare and Contrast Points of View** Working in a small group, use library and Internet resources to find different perspectives on the Vietnam War. Before you research, decide which perspective each group member will try to track down. For example, one

member might try to find an antiwar protestor's perspective on the war, another group member could track down the perspective of a Vietnamese person who lived through the war, and a third group member may find a primary source from a soldier that fought in the war.

Once you have gathered your sources, write a summary of each source and then compare and contrast their points of views. Note differences in their backgrounds and experiences that might have influenced their different attitudes about American involvement in the conflict. Present your findings to the class.

C Making Connections to Today

The conflict in Vietnam had long-lasting effects on all the nations of Southeast Asia. Following the fall of Saigon, thousands of refugees fled to the United States from Vietnam, Cambodia, and Laos, where they settled in communities throughout the country. Many of these refugees and their descendants have made significant contributions to American life.

Dat Nguyen was one such success story. His family fled South Vietnam after the fall of Saigon. Dat was born in an Arkansas refugee camp shortly after their arrival. The family eventually settled along the Texas gulf coast, where Dat fell in love with football. He became a star linebacker for Texas A&M and the first Vietnamese American to play for the NFL. Dat's efforts opened the door for more Asian American football players. He retired from the game after seven seasons with the Dallas Cowboys. Dat was elected to the College Football Hall of Fame in 2017. He still lives in Texas, where he is a successful businessman, sports commentator, and supporter of numerous civic organizations.

ACTIVITY **Write a Biographical Summary** Using library or Internet resources, research information about an Asian American individual or family who came to live in the United States as a result of resettlement after the fall of Saigon. Write a brief summary about their lives, including how they or their family came to America and how their refugee experience shaped their lives.

» Dat Nguyen warms up before the start of the Dallas Cowboys and Seattle Seahawks football game, December 6, 2004.

D Geographic Reasoning

The U.S. military's use of chemicals like Agent Orange significantly damaged the environment and the health of both the Vietnamese and the American forces. Some of the areas affected by these chemicals have still never fully recovered.

ACTIVITY **Draw an Environmental Map** Using library and Internet resources, research information about the areas in Vietnam where U.S. forces sprayed defoliants to clear the jungle growth and expose supply lines. Use this research to create an environmental map of Vietnam that highlights the areas affected by such chemicals. Include sources for your map.

Jesse Beals/Icon SMI 560/Newscom

Disability rights activists, such as these protestors at a 1977 rally, sought improved accommodations for physical challenges and legal protection from employment discrimination, among other goals.

More Civil Rights Voices 1968-PRESENT

INTRODUCTION LESSON

01   Introducing More Civil Rights Voices   478

LEARN THE EVENTS LESSONS

02   The Modern Feminist Movement   483

03   Organizing for Latino Rights   489

04   The Civil Rights Movement Expands   495

INQUIRY ACTIVITY LESSONS

05   Turning Point: The Americans with Disabilities Act   501

06   Analyzing Sources: Building New Freedom Movements   505

REVIEW AND APPLY LESSON

07   Reviewing More Civil Rights Voices   511

Wally McNamee/Corbis Historical/Getty Images

FIGHTING FOR THE ERA

Could a constitutional amendment first proposed in the 1920s finally be ratified almost 100 years later? That may be the case for the Equal Rights Amendment (ERA), first introduced to Congress in 1923. The amendment states that, "Equality of rights under the law shall not be denied or abridged by the United States or by any state on account of sex." Today we are more likely to substitute the word *gender* for *sex*, because *sex* generally refers to the biological aspects, such as reproductive organs, while *gender* is a societal construct that affects how a person identifies. Still, the idea behind the amendment is the same as it was in 1923: all people should be treated equally under the law.

While this idea of equality may seem an accepted tenet of American society, generations of women have fought for and against the ERA. The amendment was first proposed by feminists Alice Paul and Crystal Eastman in 1923.

Renewed enthusiasm for the ERA came in the 1960s and 1970s when more women were elected to political office and the social movements encouraged people to fight for change. The ERA was approved by the U.S. Senate in March 1972, then sent to the states for ratification. When 30 states ratified the ERA within a year, it seemed like passage of the amendment would be easy. But the battle for the remaining 8 states was fiercely fought.

Advocates of the ERA believed federal and state laws made women too dependent on men. They felt decisions regarding divorce and child support should be based on individual cases and not determined by sex alone. The National Organization for Women (NOW) fought hard for the passage of the ERA. Founded in 1966, NOW was headed by President Betty Friedan, who had gained attention with her best-selling 1963 book *The Feminine Mystique*. In the book, Friedan explored her own life experiences as a mother and housewife as well the overt and subtle forms of discrimination that women in America experienced. Friedan's popularity made her an obvious leader in the women's rights movement.

Other key figures in the feminist movement included lawyer and former Congresswoman Bella Abzug, co-founder of the feminist *Ms.* magazine Gloria Steinem, and Republican political activist Jill Ruckelshaus. Shirley Chisholm, the first African American woman elected to Congress, was also instrumental. Chisholm even took the fight to her run for president in 1972, making her the first black candidate to run for nomination in a major political party and the first woman to run for president as a Democrat. These women, along with countless others, fought for the ERA at conventions and marches and lobbied representatives to support the ERA.

> **" Equality of rights under the law shall not be denied . . . on account of sex. "**

However, the ERA had strong opponents. Chief among them was Phyllis Schlafly, a conservative activist who organized like-minded American women around her STOP ERA campaign. Schlafly and her followers argued that if the ERA passed, women would be subject to being drafted into the military. They also believed the ERA would cause women to lose economic support from their husbands, particularly in divorce cases. Schlafly and her STOP ERA followers fought a hard anti-ERA campaign to persuade states not to ratify the amendment. As a result, 15 states had not ratified by the 1982 deadline, making the total number of ratifying states three short of the 38 needed to ratify.

Since 1982, various states have passed ratification bills. In January 2020, the state of Virginia became the thirty-eighth state to ratify. Shortly thereafter, the U.S. House of Representatives voted to remove the ratification deadline. Passage of the ERA might be possible.

Alice Paul. Equal Rights Amendment, sec. 1, 1943.

In the 1970s women gathered in mass demonstrations such as this 1976 protest in Pittsburgh, Pennsylvania, to support the passage of the Equal Rights Amendment. By 2020, the amendment still had not been officially ratified.

Barbara Freeman/Hulton Archive/Getty Images

Understanding the Time and Place: United States, 1968–1990

While African American men had been granted the right to vote with the passage of the Fifteenth Amendment in 1870, voter suppression techniques denied many voting rights. The passage of the 1964 Civil Rights Act and the 1965 Voting Rights Act almost one hundred years after the passage of the Fifteenth Amendment protected more African Americans' right to vote. These successes inspired other marginalized groups, each of whom had their own unique agenda and effort, to fight for the expansion of civil rights in America.

The Modern Feminist Movement

With the widespread enthusiasm for social change, the women's movement took on a new energy. People were fighting for women's rights long before the 1960s, but great strides were made toward equality of the sexes during the decades after World War II.

During the war, many women worked and held traditionally masculine jobs while men served overseas. Many of these women lost their jobs when men returned from war—they were expected to become mothers and housewives, not factory workers. The ideal of a hardworking husband being supported by a hardworking housewife remained prevalent for middle-class and wealthy families during the 1950s, even if it was often not the case for many. This iconic image also presupposed that a family could subsist on a single income. For many Americans, this was not possible, and many women went to work during the 1950s to make ends meet or to find professional fulfillment.

By 1960, about one-third of married women were part of the paid workforce. Work was often separated by gender, however, and many opportunities were closed to women because of preconceived notions about masculine and feminine strengths. For example, men were believed to be rational and intelligent, while women were viewed as emotional and less capable, thus diminishing women's opportunities in careers. Job opportunities for women unable to afford an education were even more limited, and most women were paid less than men working the same jobs. This economic disparity inspired many men and women to support legislation that sought to make the genders more equal under the law, such as the 1963 Equal Pay Act, the inclusion of gender in the 1964 Civil Rights Act, and the Equal Rights Amendment in 1972.

Immigration

Documented and undocumented immigrants also faced changes after World War II. The Immigration Act of 1965 ended the quota system, which limited the number of people from a particular country allowed to immigrate to the United States. Instead, preference was given to skilled people and people who already had family living in the United States. The act, passed as an attempt to make the United States appear more welcoming than its communist adversaries, opened the door to more refugees from Cuba and Vietnam. Unfortunately, the act also closed the door on immigration for many Mexican Americans.

Immigrants who were allowed entry into the country could apply for residency after legally living in the country for five years. Refugees fleeing war-torn countries affected by World War II as well as those fleeing communist countries were often granted **amnesty.** Along with legal immigrants, many illegal immigrants sought refuge and a better life for their families in the United States. Much debate and legislation resulted from differing perspectives about how to deal with illegal immigration, an issue that would continue well into the twenty-first century.

National Woman's Party members gather from around the United States to honor Alva Belmont, president of the National Woman's Party, in front of her home in New York City on May 21, 1922.

Analyzing Perspectives How do you think the perspectives of these women differ from those of the demonstrators shown previously who gathered in Pittsburgh in 1976? How do you think their perspectives are the same?

---

amnesty an act of an authority by which a pardon is granted to a large number of people

Library of Congress Manuscript Division, Records of the National Woman's Party [mnwp000413]

Estimated Unauthorized Resident Population, 2000

In 2000 there were an estimated 8.4 million unauthorized residents in the United States.

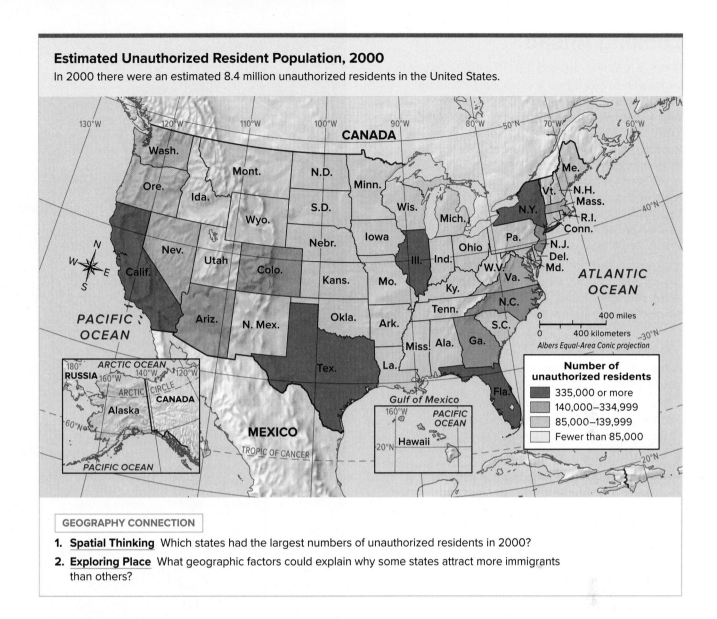

Number of unauthorized residents
- 335,000 or more
- 140,000–334,999
- 85,000–139,999
- Fewer than 85,000

Albers Equal-Area Conic projection

GEOGRAPHY CONNECTION

1. **Spatial Thinking** Which states had the largest numbers of unauthorized residents in 2000?

2. **Exploring Place** What geographic factors could explain why some states attract more immigrants than others?

Expanding Civil Rights

Just as the women's movement had successes before the middle of the twentieth century, so too did the fight for increased rights related to sexual orientation and gender identity. The Society for Human Rights, founded in 1924; the Mattachine Society, founded in 1950; and the Daughters of Bilitis, formed in 1955, are organizations dedicated to protecting the rights and improving the lives of people in the LGBTQ (lesbian, gay, bisexual, transgender, and queer) community.

A pivotal moment in the history of LGBTQ rights was the Stonewall riots of 1969. Stonewall Inn was a New York City bar raided by police on June 28, 1969. Police were used to people retreating during these raids, but this time was different—the LGBTQ bar-goers in attendance that night fought back against the police for the next five days. This is now seen as a turning point in the fight for equality and increased social and political visibility for the LGBTQ community.

Native Americans and Americans with disabilities are two additional groups of people who protested for rights and recognition during this time period. Native Americans had been struggling to protect their rights from the U.S. government since before the country's beginning, and this struggle continued in the 1960s and 1970s through protests, treaties, and new legislation. The 1968 Indian Civil Rights Act, for example, recognized tribal courts while granting those living on reservations the protections of the U.S. Bill of Rights. Native Americans continued to win additional rights through legislation such as the Indian Self-Determination and Educational Assistance Act of 1975, during the 1970s.

The struggle for disability rights also experienced some successes in the 1970s, but it was the 1990 Americans with Disabilities Act (ADA) that banned discrimination against persons with disabilities in employment, transportation, public education, and telecommunication. However, disability rights advocates still struggle to get the ADA enforced.

Looking Ahead

In these next lessons, you will learn the history of this expansion of civil rights. You will learn about the movements in the second half of the twentieth century that worked to expand civil rights for more Americans. While studying this time period, you will understand how the feminist movement, the LGBTQ rights movement, and the disability rights movement all advocated for more legal protection. You will also learn about expanding civil rights for immigrants, Latinos, Asian Americans, and Native Americans. And you will understand the important legal victories that these movements accomplished.

You will examine Compelling Questions in the Inquiry Lessons and develop your own questions about more civil rights voices. Review the time line to preview some of the key events that you will learn about.

What Will You Learn?

In these lessons focused on more civil rights voices, you will learn:

- how different civil rights movements were connected and influenced by one another.
- the American policies that affected the treatment and rights of minority groups.
- about U.S. immigration legislation and how it affected immigrants coming to America.
- the main events of the civil rights movements taking place during this time period.
- how civil rights movements changed American politics, society, and culture.

? COMPELLING QUESTIONS

- **How did the Americans with Disabilities Act help address accessibility issues?**
- **How did Latinos, Asians, women, and other disadvantaged groups build upon the African American civil rights movement?**

MORE CIVIL RIGHTS VOICES

1966 O — **1966** National Organization for Women founded

1968 Congress passes Indian Civil Rights Act

1969 *La Raza Unida* founded

1970 United Farm Workers wins contract with grape growers

1971 Equal Rights Amendment reintroduced

1972 O — **1972** Title IX introduced within Education Amendment of 1972

1973 American Indian Movement (AIM) protests for 30 days at Wounded Knee, South Dakota (right)

1973 *Roe* v. *Wade* Supreme Court decision

1980 O — **1982** Equal Rights Amendment fails to meet Constitutional requirements

1988 President Reagan signs legislation granting federal payments to surviving Japanese Americans interned during World War II

1990 O — **1990** Congress passes Americans with Disabilities Act (ADA)

Kevin McKiernan/ZUMA Press/Newscom

Sequencing Time Identify the events that reveal fundamental changes to U.S. law and explain the group of people most affected by each event.

02

The Modern Feminist Movement

Universal Art Archive/Alamy Stock Photo

READING STRATEGY

Analyzing Key Ideas and Details As you read about the feminist movement, complete a graphic organizer similar to this one by listing the main arguments for and against the Equal Rights Amendment (ERA).

Arguments For and Against the ERA	
For ERA	Against ERA

A Renewed Women's Movement

GUIDING QUESTION

What events revitalized the women's movement?

African Americans and college students were not the only groups seeking to change American society in the 1960s. By the middle of the decade, the feminist movement was making itself a strong presence in national conversations. **Feminism** is the belief that men and women should be equal politically, economically, and socially.

Although the post–World War II emphasis on establishing families discouraged some women from seeking employment, the number of women who held jobs outside the home actually increased during the 1950s. Many women went to work outside the home to make ends meet, to have a career, or to help their families maintain comfortable lifestyles. By 1960, about one-third of all married women were part of the paid workforce. Yet many people continued to believe that women could better serve society by remaining in the home to influence the children of the next generation.

Origins of the Movement

By the early 1960s, many women were increasingly resentful of a world where newspaper ads separated jobs by **gender,** banks denied women credit, and female employees often were paid less for the same work. Nearly half of American women worked by the mid-1960s, but three-fourths of these women worked in lower-paying clerical, sales, or factory jobs or as janitors and hospital attendants.

One development that invigorated the women's movement was the President's Commission on the Status of Women established by President Kennedy in 1961. The Commission's report highlighted the problems women faced in the workplace and helped create a network of feminist activists who

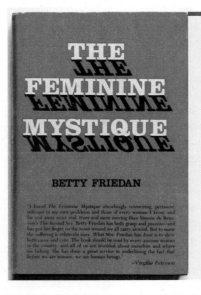

The first edition of *The Feminine Mystique*, published in 1963, featured a review of the book on the dust cover.

Inferring Why do you think the publishers decided to print a review on the front of *The Feminine Mystique*?

feminism the belief that men and women should be equal politically, economically, and socially

gender term applied to the characteristics of a male or female

lobbied for legislation. In 1963 they won passage of the Equal Pay Act, which in most cases outlawed paying men more than women for the same job. But even so, pay inequality between men and women remained an ongoing problem.

Many women who had stayed home to tend to their families were also discontented. Betty Friedan tried to describe the reasons for this discontent in her 1963 book *The Feminine Mystique*. Friedan interviewed women who graduated with her from Smith College in 1942. The book reported that while most of these women had much social and economic success, they felt unfulfilled.

Friedan herself was financially secure and had many reasons to be happy with her life, but she realized that something was fundamentally wrong about her situation:

66 I was an educated young woman. . . . I got married . . . and had three children, and was fired because I was pregnant with my second child. And so then, I was a suburban housewife . . . I was living the life that most women of my generation were living in those years after World War II, when . . . the fulfillment of women, was solely in terms of the wife, mother, housewife, server of the physical needs of husband, children, home—and not as a partner defining herself by her own actions in society. And that's who I was. I was simply living a life that was the dream life, supposedly, of American women at that time. And I called that image the 'feminine mystique.' 99

—Betty Friedan, interview with Voice of America, 1984

As the book became a best seller, women began reaching out to one another. They poured out their anger and sadness in what came to be known as consciousness-raising sessions. While they talked about their unhappiness, they were also building the base for a nationwide mass movement.

At the same time, ideas about sexuality and relationships were also changing. The Kinsey Reports, two university studies from the 1950s on the sexual behavior of men and women based on thousands of interviews, helped bring the topic of sexuality and desire into public dialogue. The reports included discussion of the spectrum of human sexuality. Because birth control was becoming more readily available, women had greater control over their sexuality and family planning. The ability to plan if and when to have children gave women the option to focus on advancing their education and careers before becoming parents if they chose. As a result, more women were able to advance up the career ladder.

Congress gave the women's movement another boost by including gender in the Civil Rights Act of 1964. Title VII of the act outlawed job discrimination not only on the basis of race, color, religion, and national origin but also on the basis of gender. This provided a strong legal basis for the changes the women's movement later demanded.

But simply having the law on the books was not enough. Even the agency charged with administering the Civil Rights Act—the Equal Employment Opportunity Commission (EEOC)—ruled in 1965 that gender-segregated help-wanted ads were legal.

The Time is NOW

By June 1966, Betty Friedan had returned to an idea that she and other women had been considering—the need for an organization to promote feminist goals. Friedan and others then set out to form the National Organization for Women (NOW). A group of about 30 women and men held the founding conference of NOW in October 1966.

66 [T]he time has come to confront, with concrete action, the conditions that now prevent women from enjoying the equality of opportunity and freedom of choice which is their right, as individual Americans, and as human beings. 99

—from NOW Statement of Purpose, 1966

The new organization responded to their members' growing frustration by demanding greater educational and career opportunities for women. NOW leaders denounced the exclusion of women from certain professions and from most levels of politics. NOW was also against the practice of paying women less than men for equal work—which had been prohibited by the Equal Pay Act but was still commonplace.

When NOW set out to pass an Equal Rights Amendment to the Constitution, its membership rose to over 200,000. By July 1972, the movement had its own magazine, entitled *Ms.* The cofounder and editor of *Ms.* was Gloria Steinem, an author who became one of the movement's leading figures.

Gloria Steinem (left) examines a copy of *Ms.* with staff members Freada Klein and Karen Savigne in 1977.

PHOTO: Bettmann/Getty Images; TEXT: (l)Friedan, Betty. 1985. Voice of America Interviews with Eight American Women of Achievement, by Chantal Mompoullan, VOA Africa Field Service. Washington: Voice of America, United States Information Agency; (r)The National Organization for Women 1966 Statement of Purpose.

PHOTO: DONNA DIETRICH/KRT/Newscom; TEXT: Gloria Steinem, Testimony before Senate hearings on Equal Rights Amendment, May 6, 1970. The "Equal Rights" Amendment, Hearings before the Subcommittee on Constitutional Amendments of the Committee on the Judiciary United States Senate Ninety-First Congress, Second Session, on S. J. Res. 61 5-7 May 1970 (Washington, D. C.: U. S. Government Printing Office, 1970), 335-7.

GLORIA JEAN WATKINS (1952–2021)

Feminist, author, and educator Gloria Jean Watkins was born in Hopkinsville, Kentucky, on September 25, 1952. She wrote under the name bell hooks, which she wrote in lowercase letters in order to place the emphasis on her message rather than on herself. She took the name from Bell Blair Hooks, her great-grandmother, to honor her female heritage.

ACADEMIC WORK Hooks began writing her first book, *Ain't I a Woman: Black Women and Feminism*, when she was 19. The book was published in 1981 when she was 29. During the intervening years, she received undergraduate and graduate degrees in English literature from Stanford University, the University of Wisconsin, and the University of California, Santa Cruz. She taught English, African American and ethnic studies, and women's studies at a variety of universities before beginning to serve as professor in residence at Berea College in Berea, Kentucky, in 2004.

WRITING In the 1980s, she started the Sisters of Yam, a support group for African American women. Over the years, she published many books on feminism, race, and class, including *Feminist Theory from Margin to Center* (1984) and *Where We Stand: Class Matters* (2000). Her books focus on how the combination of gender, race, and economics affect systems of privilege and oppression.

Understanding Supporting Details How did Gloria Jean Watkins advance the cause of feminism?

African American feminists played an important role in pushing the movement in new directions. Like Sojourner Truth in the 1800s, many modern African American feminists saw the struggle for racial, gender, and class equality as linked. This was the view taken by legal scholar and activist Pauli Murray, a cofounder of NOW. Murray had been open about her same-sex relationships until the era of McCarthyism. At that point, concerned that her past affiliation with communism and her work as a human rights lawyer would make her a target of the Red Scare, Murray chose to stop discussing her sexual preference for fear it would draw even more attention to her. She never talked about her sexual orientation again. Murray focused her activism on fighting discrimination based on race, gender, and sexual orientation. Critical of the male-centered leadership in the civil rights movement, she coined the term "Jane Crow" to describe the double discrimination faced by African American women. Murray eventually became disillusioned with NOW as the organization moved away from advocating for racial and economic justice. Today, African American feminists still advocate for racial and economic justice and gender equality.

✓ **CHECK FOR UNDERSTANDING**

Identifying Cause and Effect What events revitalized the women's movement?

Successes and Failures

GUIDING QUESTION

What political and economic gains did women make during this time?

During the late 1960s and early 1970s, the women's movement fought to amend the Constitution and enforce Title VII of the Civil Rights Act. It also worked to repeal laws against abortion and pass legislation against gender discrimination in employment, housing, and education. As a leading voice in the movement, Steinem explained the need for such legislation.

❝ The truth is that all our problems stem from the same sex based myths. We may appear before you as white radicals or the middle-aged middle class or black soul sisters, but we are all sisters in fighting against these outdated myths. Like racial myths, they have been reflected in our laws. ❞

—Gloria Steinem, from testimony before a Senate subcommittee in support of the ERA, May 1970

The Equal Rights Amendment

Members of the women's movement pushed for passage of the Equal Rights Amendment (ERA). Shirley

Chisholm, the first African American woman elected to Congress and a fierce advocate for the rights of women and minorities, spoke in defense of the amendment:

> 66 Discrimination against women . . . is so widespread that is seems to many persons normal, natural, and right. . . . It is time we act to assure full equality of opportunity . . . to women. The argument that this amendment will not solve the problem of sex discrimination is not relevant. Of course laws will not eliminate prejudice from the hearts of human beings. But that is no reason to allow prejudice to continue to be enshrined in our laws. 99

—Representative Shirley Chisholm, August 10, 1970

The women's movement seemed to be off to a strong start when Congress passed the Equal Rights Amendment in March 1972. The amendment had to be ratified by 38 states within seven years to become part of the Constitution. Many states did so—35 by 1979, when Congress extended the ratification

deadline until 1982. But then significant opposition to the amendment began to build.

Opponents argued that the amendment would take away some women's rights. These included the right to alimony in divorce cases and the right to have single-sex colleges. They feared it would eliminate women's exemption from the draft and do away with laws that provided special protection for women in the workforce.

One outspoken opponent was Phyllis Schlafly. Schlafly was an attorney who unsuccessfully ran for Congress in 1952. She became a conservative political activist and formed the organization STOP ERA, which campaigned to defeat the Equal Rights Amendment.

> 66 This amendment will absolutely and positively make women subject to the draft. Why any woman would support such a ridiculous and un-American proposal as this is beyond comprehension. . . . Another bad effect of the Equal Rights Amendment is that it will abolish a woman's right to child support and alimony. . . . Under present American laws, the man is

ERA Ratification, 1972–1982
The ERA sought to ensure women equal rights under the law.

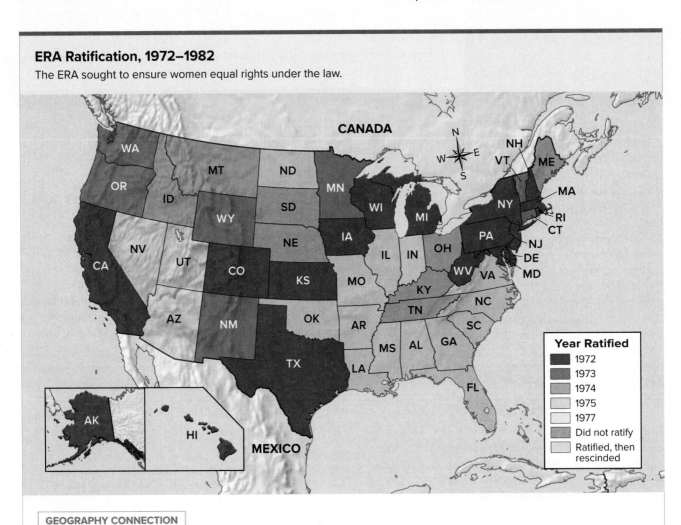

Year Ratified
- 1972
- 1973
- 1974
- 1975
- 1977
- Did not ratify
- Ratified, then rescinded

GEOGRAPHY CONNECTION

1. **Spatial Thinking** Which states rescinded their ratification of the ERA?

2. **Exploring Places** How many states did not ratify the amendment?

(1)"For the Equal Rights Amendment," Shirley Chisholm to the U.S. House of Representatives, August 10, 1970, Congressional Record, 91st congress, 2nd session. Copyright © U.S. Government Printing Office; (2)Phyllis Schlafly, "What's Wrong with Equal Rights 'for Women?' Phyllis Schlafly Report 5, no. 7, February 1972.

always required to support his wife and each child he has caused to be brought into the world. Why should women abandon these good laws . . . ?"

—Phyllis Schlafly, February 1972

By the end of 1979, five states had voted to rescind their approval. Many people had become worried that the amendment would give federal courts too much power to interfere with state laws. Unable to achieve ratification by three-fourths of the states by the deadline set by Congress, the ERA finally failed in 1982.

Equality in Education

One major achievement of the movement came in education. Kathy Striebel's experience illustrated the discrimination female students often faced in the early 1970s. Striebel, a junior high school student in St. Paul, Minnesota, wanted to compete for her school's swim team in 1971, but the school did not allow girls to join. Kathy's mother, Charlotte Striebel, was a member of the local NOW chapter. Through it, she learned that St. Paul had recently banned gender discrimination in education. She filed a grievance with the city's human rights department, and officials required the school to allow Kathy to swim. Shortly after joining the team, Kathy beat out one of the boys and earned a spot at a meet. As she stood on the block waiting to swim, the opposing coach declared that she was ineligible because the meet was outside St. Paul and thus beyond the jurisdiction of its laws.

Leaders of the women's movement lobbied to ban gender discrimination in education. In 1972 Congress responded by passing a law known collectively as the Educational Amendments. One section, Title IX, prohibited federally funded schools from discriminating against women in nearly all aspects of school operations, from admissions to athletics.

Title IX increased opportunities for women. Within just a few years, the number of women attending college surged, and the majority of people attending college were women by 1978. By 2014, women made up approximately 58 percent of all college students. Title IX also created new opportunities for women in college athletics. It required that women and men have equal opportunities to participate in sports and receive sports-related scholarships. Women's participation in sports grew dramatically as a result. The demand generated by the growing number of women's sports teams as well as increased funding and prestige drew many new coaches, including men, to the women's sports.

Right to Privacy and *Roe v. Wade*

The feminist movement also worked to secure the right to make private decisions, including reproductive decisions. A constitutional right to marital privacy was introduced in 1965 when the Supreme Court outlawed state bans on contraceptives for married couples in *Griswold v. Connecticut.*

The right to privacy was expanded beyond married couples when activists began challenging laws against abortion. Until 1973, the right to regulate abortion was reserved to the states. The original plan of the Constitution gave states most of the authority to enact laws impinging on personal or property rights in the interest of safety, health, welfare, and morality. Early in the country's history, some abortions were permitted in the early stages of pregnancy. By the nineteenth century, however, states had passed laws prohibiting abortion except to save the life of the mother. Some states began adopting more liberal abortion laws in the late 1960s. For example, several states allowed abortion if carrying a pregnancy to term might endanger the woman's mental health or if she was a victim of rape or incest.

The 1973 Supreme Court decision in *Roe* v. *Wade* was a major legal development. The decision stated that state governments could not regulate abortion during the first three months of pregnancy, a time that was ruled to be within a woman's constitutional right to privacy. During the second three months of pregnancy, states could regulate abortions on the basis of the health of the mother. In the final three months, states could regulate or outlaw abortions except in the cases of a medical emergency. Those in favor of abortion rights cheered *Roe* v. *Wade* as a victory, but the issue was far from settled politically. The Supreme Court ruling galvanized the right-to-life movement, whose members consider abortion morally wrong and work toward its total ban.

Title IX helped promote women's basketball games, such as this one played in the 1970s between Queens College and Immaculata College at Madison Square Garden in New York City.

Analyzing Visuals Based on the photo, do you think women's basketball was popular at the time? What leads you to that opinion?

Bettmann/Getty Images.

Women in the Workplace

The number of women in the workforce climbed steadily from the 1950s through the 1990s before beginning to decline.

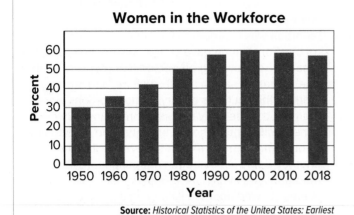

Women in the Workforce

Source: *Historical Statistics of the United States: Earliest Times to the Present, Volume 2*; Bureau of Labor Statistics

ECONOMICS CONNECTION

1. **Calculating** By how much did the percentage of working women increase between 1950 and 2000?

2. **Determining Context** What general trend do you see in women's participation in the workforce?

After the *Roe* v. *Wade* ruling, the two sides began an impassioned legal and political battle that continues today. In the 1992 case *Planned Parenthood* v. *Casey*, the Supreme Court modified *Roe* v. *Wade*. The Court decided that states could place some restrictions on abortions. For example, doctors could be required to explain the risks and have patients give "informed consent." Underage girls might now be required to inform their parents before getting an abortion, although the Court did strike down laws requiring women to notify their husbands before having an abortion. It also abandoned the rule that states could ban abortion only in the final trimester. Technology had enabled a fetus to be viable outside the womb much earlier in a pregnancy. States could now restrict abortion based on the viability of the fetus.

The Impact of the Feminist Movement

The women's movement profoundly changed society. Since the 1970s, many women have pursued college degrees and careers outside of the home. Since the women's movement began, two-career families are much more common, although a need for greater family income may be a factor in that increase. Mothers working outside the home are more accepted, and many employers now offer options to help women make work life more compatible with family life, including flexible hours, on-site childcare, and job sharing.

Even with those changes, a significant income gap between men and women still exists. About one-third of the wage gap is due to the uneven distribution of men and women among various occupations. For example, more men than women tend to work in higher-paying construction and engineering trades. Likewise, more women than men tend to work in lower-paying household service and office occupations.

Women have made the most dramatic gains in professional jobs since the 1970s. By 2010, women made up more than 50 percent of the nation's graduates receiving medical or law degrees.

Today, the women's movement remains strong and strives for more inclusivity with its focus on intersectional feminism. Intersectional feminism is the belief that discrimination is based on multiple factors, including gender, race, sexual orientation, class, and religion.

✓ CHECK FOR UNDERSTANDING

1. **Citing Text Evidence** What political and economic gains did women make during this time?

2. **Summarizing** What arguments did opponents of the ERA advance?

LESSON ACTIVITIES

1. **Argumentative Writing** Take a position either for or against the ratification of the Equal Rights Amendment. Then write a newspaper editorial convincing readers to support your position.

2. **Collaborating** With a small group, discuss how feminism impacted the United States in the 1960s and 1970s. Do you think the women's movement achieved its goals? Do any of the issues that the women's movement worked on in the 1960s and 1970s still exist today? What do you think are the mainstream beliefs and expectations about the roles of women and men in the United States today?

03

Organizing for Latino Rights

Galarza, Ernesto. 1971. Barrio Boy. Notre Dame, IN: University of Notre Dame Press.

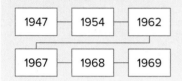

READING STRATEGY

Analyzing Key Ideas and Details Complete a time line like the one below by recording major events in the struggle of Latinos for equal civil and political rights.

1947	1954	1962

1967	1968	1969

Migrating North

GUIDING QUESTION

How did Mexican migration affect American society in the twentieth century?

Americans of Mexican heritage have lived in what is now the United States since before the founding of the republic. In the twentieth century, Mexican immigration to the United States rose greatly, partly due to the turmoil of the Mexican Revolution that began in 1910. During the 1920s, half a million Mexicans immigrated to the United States through official channels and an unknown number entered the country by other means.

While some people of Mexican heritage moved to northern states, most remained concentrated in the areas that were once the northern provinces of Mexico. In 1930 90 percent of ethnic Mexicans in the United States lived in areas of the West and Southwest. As a result of heavy Mexican immigration, the ethnic Mexican population in Texas grew from 71,062 in 1900 to 683,681 in 1930. Likewise, Southern California also had a large Spanish-speaking population.

Mexicans Face Discrimination

Across the urbanized Southwest, most Mexican Americans lived in barrios—neighborhoods comprised of primarily Mexican immigrant and Mexican American populations. Barrios were the product of the region's history and discrimination against Mexican immigrants.

Los Angeles was founded as a Spanish town in 1781. A century later when English-speaking settlers arrived, they built around the older Spanish-speaking district. From 1900 to 1930, Mexican immigration increased the ethnic Mexican population of the city from as many as 5,000 to around 150,000. By then, the Spanish-speaking population was segregated in the eastern part of the city, where the housing was in poor condition and the infant mortality rate was high.

66 For the Mexicans the barrio was a colony of refugees. We came to know families from Chihuahua, Sonora, Jalisco, and Durango. . . .

As poor refugees, their first concern was to find a place to sleep, then to eat and find work. In the barrio they were most likely to find all three, for not knowing English, they needed something that was even more urgent than a room, a meal, or a job, and that was information in a language they could understand. 99

—Ernesto Galarza, from *Barrio Boy*, 1971

In California and across the Southwest, employment discrimination meant that most ethnic Mexicans could find work only in low-paying jobs, such as by working as agricultural laborers. During the Great Depression, many Mexican Americans faced increased hostility and discrimination as unemployment rates soared. About one-third of the nation's Mexican population returned to Mexico. Some left voluntarily, believing it would be easier to get by in Mexico. Others left as part of the **repatriation**—a series of deportations was carried out at the federal, state, and local levels. This included not only immigrants but often their American-born children as well.

During World War II, labor shortages in the Southwest led to the creation of the Bracero Program, which let Mexican workers enter short-term labor

repatriation being restored or returned to the country of origin, allegiance, or citizenship

Growth of Latino Population in the United States

The Latino population of the United States increased in the last hundred years.

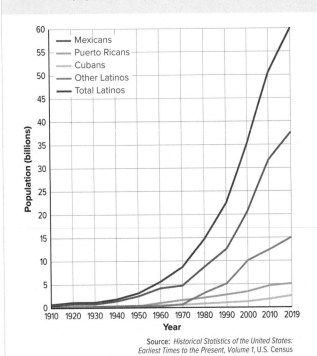

Legend:
- Mexicans
- Puerto Ricans
- Cubans
- Other Latinos
- Total Latinos

Y-axis: Population (billions) — 0 to 60
X-axis: Year — 1910, 1920, 1930, 1940, 1950, 1960, 1970, 1980, 1990, 2000, 2010, 2019

Source: *Historical Statistics of the United States: Earliest Times to the Present, Volume 1*, U.S. Census

CIVICS CONNECTION

1. **Interpreting** How has the overall Latino population changed since 1950?
2. **Inferring** Based on the chart, what can you infer about the U.S. Latino population in the future?

contracts, mostly as low-wage farmworkers. Meanwhile, illegal immigration increased. In 1954 President Eisenhower's administration launched a program to deport undocumented Latino immigrants. Police swept through immigrant neighborhoods seeking illegal immigrants. As a result, more than 3.7 million Mexicans were deported over the next three years.

The raids were criticized in the United States and in Mexico for intimidating people for simply "looking Mexican." In addition, the program often failed to distinguish between individuals legally in the country—including U.S. citizens—and those who had entered illegally.

Other Latinos Arrive

The terms *Latino* (male), *Latina* (female), and *Latinx* (gender neutral) refer to anyone born in or with ancestors from Latin America, which includes Mexico, Central America, and South America. The term Hispanic generally applies to Spanish-speaking people who are often Latin American but might also be from other Spanish-speaking regions. The terms Chicano and Chicana more specifically refer to those of Mexican origin or descent.

Although Mexicans remained the largest group of Spanish-speaking newcomers to the United States in the 1950s, large numbers of Puerto Ricans arrived as well. Puerto Rico is an American territory and its residents are U.S. citizens. After World War II, economic troubles prompted more than a million

Puerto Ricans to move to the U.S. mainland. The majority settled in New York City, where they faced racial discrimination and high poverty levels.

The nation became home to more than 350,000 Cuban immigrants in the decade after the Cuban Revolution of 1959. Many were professionals and business owners who settled in the Miami, Florida, area, where they were typically welcomed as refugees fleeing Communist oppression. By 1970, more than 9 million Latinos lived in the United States.

✓ CHECK FOR UNDERSTANDING

Identifying Cause and Effect Why did many Mexicans migrate to the United States from the early to the mid-1900s, and how did this affect U.S. society?

Changes in Immigration Law

GUIDING QUESTION

How have important immigration laws affected legal and undocumented immigration to the United States?

After the introduction of the national origins quota system in the 1920s, immigration to the United States changed dramatically. For the next few decades, the total number of immigrants arriving annually remained markedly lower. The quota system, which favored immigrants from northern and western Europe, remained largely unchanged until the mid-1960s.

The Immigration Act of 1965 abolished the national origins quota system. It gave preference to skilled persons and persons with close relatives who are U.S. citizens—policies that remain in place today. The preference given to the children, spouses, and parents of U.S. citizens meant that **migration chains** were established. As newcomers became citizens, they could send for relatives in their home country. However, the legislation also introduced the first limits on immigration from the Western Hemisphere. These new legal limits resulted in a rise of undocumented Mexicans because it became harder to earn legal citizenship.

Few people expected that the new law would cause much change in the pattern or volume of immigration to the United States. Supporters of the law presented it as an extension of America's growing commitment to equal rights for all people, regardless of race or ethnicity. U.S. Representative Phillip Burton of California explained:

> 66 Just as we sought to eliminate discrimination in our land through the Civil Rights Act, today we seek by phasing out the national origins quotas to eliminate discrimination in immigration to this Nation composed of the descendants of immigrants. 99

—from a speech before Congress, August 25, 1965

Supporters of the new law also assumed that the new equal quotas for non-European nations would generally go unfilled, but immigration from non-European countries soared. Some newcomers arrived in the United States as **refugees.** Beginning in 1948, refugees from countries ravaged by World War II were admitted, although they were counted as part of their nation's quota. The Cold War brought more refugees. According to the McCarran-Walter Act of 1952, anyone who was fleeing a Communist regime could be admitted as a refugee. The Refugee Act of 1980 further broadened U.S. policy by defining a refugee as anyone leaving his or her country due to a "well-founded fear of persecution on account of race, religion, nationality, membership in a particular group, or political opinion."

The growing problem of illegal immigration led to changes in immigration law. During the Reagan administration, Congress passed the Immigration Reform and Control Act of 1986, establishing penalties for employers who knowingly hired unauthorized immigrants and strengthening border controls to prevent illegal entry. It also set up a process to grant **amnesty,** or a pardon, to any undocumented immigrant who could prove that he or she had entered the country before January 1, 1982, and had since lived in the United States. There was a short decline in illegal immigration between 1986 and 1990 but it did

not stop. By 1990, an estimated 3.5 million unauthorized immigrants resided in the United States.

During the George H.W. Bush administration, Congress passed the Immigration Act of 1990, which instituted major reforms. The act raised the limit on the number who could legally immigrate each year. It also established a diversity lottery system to provide slots for immigrants from underrepresented countries, and it set up a skilled worker program that enabled employers to hire skilled foreign workers using temporary visas.

By the mid-1990s, Congress was debating new ways to combat illegal immigration during the Clinton administration. It passed the Illegal Immigration Reform and Immigrant Responsibility Act of 1996, which made several changes to immigration law. First, it required families sponsoring an immigrant to have an income above the poverty level. Second, it allocated more resources to stop illegal immigration, authorizing an additional 5,000 U.S. Border Patrol agents and calling for the construction of a 14-mile fence along the border near San Diego. Third, the law toughened penalties for smuggling people or providing fraudulent documents. Finally, the law made it easier for authorities to deport undocumented immigrants.

More recently, the divide over immigration has widened between the Democratic Party and the Republican Party. During the 1990s, Democrats and Republicans more or less held similar views, with some members of each party viewing immigrants as a

Between April and October 1980, Fidel Castro—the dictator of Cuba—allowed more than 125,000 Cuban refugees to leave their island nation for the United States. Because they left from the port of Mariel on small vessels provided by private citizens, the event is called the Mariel boat lift.

Analyzing Visuals Based on this photograph, what were some immediate challenges would refugees have faced upon arriving in the United States?

PHOTO: TIM CHAPMAN (KRT)/Newscom; TEXT: (1)Representative Phillip Burton (D-CA), Congressional Record, Aug. 25, 1965, p. 21783; (2)An Act to Amend the Immigration and Nationality Act to Revise the Procedures for the Admission of Refugees, to Amend the Migration and Refugee Assistance Act of 1962 to Establish a More Uniform Basis for the Provision of Assistance to Refugees and for Other Purposes. Public Law 96-212, U.S. Statutes at Large 94 (1980).

migration chains the practice of immigrants who have acquired U.S. citizenship sending for relatives in their home country to join them

refugees people who leave their home countries to escape persecution, war, or natural disasters

amnesty a pardon granted to political prisoners

positive force in the country and other members seeing immigrants as a burden. However, Democrats are now viewed as stronger defenders of immigrants' rights.

✓ CHECK FOR UNDERSTANDING

Making Connections How have important immigration laws affected legal and illegal immigration to the United States?

Latinos Organize

GUIDING QUESTION

How did the Latino approach to gaining civil rights compare to the African American approach?

Regardless of their citizenship status, people of Mexican heritage were often treated as outsiders by the English-speaking majority. Latinos formed organizations to work for equal rights and fair treatment.

In 1929 a number of Mexican American organizations came together to create the League of United Latin American Citizens (LULAC). The organization's purpose was to fight discrimination against persons of Latin American ancestry. At first LULAC limited membership to those of Latin American heritage who were U.S. citizens. The group encouraged assimilation into American society and adopted English as its official language to avoid the appearance of being un-American. It wanted its members to take an active role in society by securing the right to vote, serving on juries, and running for office. In the 1960s it dropped its emphasis on assimilation and adopted more assertive tactics, such as protests.

Prior to the 1960s, Latino organizations generally used institutional channels like the courts and the ballot box to fight for change. Several lawsuits filed in the 1920s and 1930s pushed for educational reforms, and LULAC had several notable legal successes in the 1940s and 1950s. In *Mendez* v. *Westminster* (1947), a group of Mexican parents won a lawsuit challenging school segregation in California. Two years later, LULAC filed a similar lawsuit that aimed to end the practice of segregating Spanish-speaking children into "Mexican schools" in the state of Texas. During the 1950s the organization was a vocal critic of the abuses of deportation authorities. In 1954 the Supreme Court's ruling in *Hernández* v. *Texas* extended more rights to Latino citizens. The case ended the exclusion of Mexican Americans from juries in Texas.

66 The petitioner established that 14% of the population of Jackson Country were persons with Mexican or Latin American surnames, and that 11% of the males over 21 bore such names. The County Tax Assessor testified that 6 or 7 percent of the freeholders on the tax rolls of the County were persons of Mexican descent. The State of Texas stipulated that 'for the last twenty-five years there is no record of any person with a Mexican or Latin American name having served on a jury commission, grand jury or petit jury in Jackson County.' . . . [It] taxes our credulity to say that mere chance resulted in there being no member of this class among the over six thousand jurors called in the past 25 years. 99

—from the Supreme Court decision in *Hernández* v. *Texas*

Another Latino organization, the American GI Forum, was founded by Dr. Héctor P. García. The purpose of the GI Forum was to protect the rights of Mexican American veterans. After World War II Latino veterans were excluded from veterans' organizations, and they were also denied medical services by the Veterans Administration.

The GI Forum's first effort to combat racial injustice involved a Mexican American soldier killed during World War II. A funeral home refused to hold his funeral because he was Mexican American. The GI Forum drew national attention to the incident, and the soldier's remains were buried in Arlington National Cemetery.

Under Dr. García's leadership, the organization began to challenge discrimination against all Latinos. It helped pay the poll taxes of poor Hispanics so that they could vote, fought against segregated schools, helped fund the attorneys arguing *Hernández* v. *Texas*, and worked to register Latino voters. In 1968 García was appointed to the U.S. Commission on Civil Rights. Today the GI Forum has nearly 160,000 members across the United States.

Protests and Progress

Latino Americans continued to face prejudice and were denied access to adequate education, employment, and housing. Encouraged by the African American civil rights movement, Latinos launched a series of campaigns beginning in the 1960s. These campaigns, which included direct action and radical rhetoric, differed from tactics used in earlier efforts.

In the early 1960s César Chávez and Dolores Huerta organized the National Farm Workers Association (NFWA). Another group, the Agricultural Workers Organizing Committee (AWOC), was organized by Larry Itliong and mostly comprised Filipino and Filipino American farmworkers. In 1965 the AWOC began a strike against table grape growers demanding union recognition, increased wages, and better benefits. When employers resisted, NFWA joined the strike. The two groups merged to form the United Farm Workers of America in 1966. Between 14 and 17 million stopped buying grapes, and industry profits tumbled.

To bring attention to the movement and promote a philosophy of nonviolence, Chávez held a hunger strike in 1968. A UFW spokesman described the impact the hunger strike had on Chávez and the farmworkers:

Hernandez v. The State of Texas, 346 U.S. 811 (1954).

PHOTO: Bob Fitch photography archive, © Stanford University Libraries; TEXT: Larned, Marianne. 1998. By Giving our Lives, We Find Life, Told by Marc Grossman, in Stone Soup for the World: Life Changing Stories of Everyday Heroes. Newburyport, MA: Conari Press.

BIOGRAPHY

CÉSAR CHÁVEZ (1927–1993) & DOLORES HUERTA (1930–)

An Arizona native, labor leader César Chávez grew up a Mexican American migrant farm laborer. He was a community organizer during the 1950s before cofounding the National Farm Workers Association, a forerunner of the United Farm Workers, with Dolores Huerta. He led peaceful strikes and boycotts that were usually successful. His contributions earned Chávez a Presidential Medal of Freedom the year following his death.

CSO In 1955 Dolores Huerta also helped found the Stockton chapter of the Community Service Organization (CSO). Huerta led voter registration drives and worked for improved public services for farmworkers and other community residents. It was through the CSO that Huerta met César Chávez, who was then an executive director of the group.

NFWA In 1962 Huerta and Chávez formed the National Farm Workers Association (NFWA). When the NFWA became the United Farm Workers (UFW), Huerta played a central role in the development of the organization, lobbying in Sacramento and Washington, D.C., against the farm owners' use of toxic pesticides that harmed workers; organizing strikes of field workers; and campaigning for candidates favorable to the farmworkers' causes.

Summarizing How did Chávez and Huerta help advance the rights of farmworkers?

> ❝ After twenty-five days, César was carried to a nearby park where the fast ended during a mass with thousands of farmworkers. He had lost thirty-five pounds, and there was no more talk about violence among the farmworkers. ❞
>
> —Marc Grossman, "By Giving our Lives, We Find Life," from *Stone Soup for the World: Life-Changing Stories of Everyday Heroes*

Young Latinos also became involved. In 1967 college students in San Antonio, Texas, led by José Angel Gutiérrez, founded the Mexican American Youth Organization (MAYO). One walkout protest organized by MAYO led to the creation of bilingual education at a local Texas high school.

In 1969, Gutiérrez founded *La Raza Unida*, or "the United People" to mobilize Mexican American voters. By the early 1970s, it had elected Latinos to local offices in several cities and small towns with large Latino populations. A larger civil rights movement that fought against discrimination and celebrated Latino pride emerged among Mexican Americans.

In the late 1960s, Latino leaders promoted **bilingualism,** and in 1968 Congress passed the Bilingual Education Act, dictating that school districts set up classes for immigrants in their own languages while they were learning English. The act was controversial, and an English-only movement began in the 1980s. By the 2000s, more than half of the state legislatures had passed laws or amendments making English the official language of their states.

The Chicano Mural Movement

Efforts to defend civil rights and promote economic opportunity within the Hispanic American community encouraged a renewed sense of ethnic and cultural identity. In the 1960s, the Chicano Mural Movement began depicting Mexican American culture. Drawing upon the art of Mexican master artists, such as Diego Rivera, David Siqueiros, and later Frida Kahlo, it reflected the tone and issues of the 1960s and 1970s. The Chicano Mural Movement—while portraying economic and social issues of the day—helped remind Hispanics of their identity, cultural heritage, and contributions to the United States and encouraged them to continue to advocate for their rights.

✓ **CHECK FOR UNDERSTANDING**

Making Connections How was the Latino approach to gaining civil rights similar to and different from the African American civil rights movement?

bilingualism the use of two languages

Chicano Murals
The Chicano Legacy 40 Años mural is found at the U.C. Santa Barbara. The mural is constructed with many tiny pieces of colored glass. It depicts symbols of the strong Chicano heritage of the California area.

Immigration Near the Turn of the Century

GUIDING QUESTION

How did the federal government address immigration reform at the turn of the century?

Certain states experienced a larger influx of immigrants than others. In 1990 California, Texas, New York, New Jersey, and Florida had the largest populations of foreign-born residents. High numbers of immigrants increased the ethnic diversity of these states as their Latino and Asian populations grew. Among the immigrants who arrived during the 1990s, just over 10 percent came from Europe. More than half of new immigrants came from Latin America, while about another 25 percent came from Asia. By 2001, the top five countries of origin for legal immigrants to the United States were Mexico, India, China, the Philippines, and Vietnam.

Refugees added to the growing immigrant population. In the 25 years following the Cuban Revolution of 1959, more than 800,000 Cubans arrived in the United States. So many settled in the Miami, Florida, area that the only city that is home to more Cubans is Havana, Cuba. The Vietnam War also created refugees, and some 600,000 immigrants from Vietnam, Laos, and Cambodia arrived in the decade after 1974. Other immigrants arrived without official permission, and the largest number came from Mexico, El Salvador, and Guatemala.

The amnesty program established in 1986 had been designed to solve the problem of illegal immigration, yet over the next 20 years, the number of unauthorized immigrants more than tripled.

Americans were divided over whether unauthorized immigrants should be able to obtain driver licenses, send their children to public schools, or receive government services. Some believed that unauthorized immigrants should be deported, while others favored allowing them to apply for temporary work visas so the government could keep track of them. Some supported permitting them to earn permanent residence if they learned English, paid back taxes, and had no criminal record.

In 2006 President George W. Bush made immigration reform a top priority. A bipartisan majority of the Senate favored legislation that blended tougher enforcement of immigration laws with some form of earned citizenship. The Senate bill included a provision that allowed undocumented immigrants who grew up in the United States and graduated from high school to apply for citizenship. Conservative Republicans who held the majority in the House objected that this would reward illegal behavior. Republicans rejected any form of amnesty and called for the United States to build a wall along its Mexican border. Advocates of immigration reform promoted alternatives such as expanding quotas through a guest-worker program and establishing a legalization process for those already in the country.

✓ **CHECK FOR UNDERSTANDING**

Describing How has the federal government addressed immigration reform in the twenty-first century?

LESSON ACTIVITIES

1. **Creating a Timeline** Create a timeline of key achievements for Latinos in the United States in the twentieth century. Each entry should provide a brief summary of the event's significance.

2. **Using Multimedia** With a partner, use the Internet to research recent immigration statistics in the United States. Use presentation software to prepare a short presentation to explain how immigration laws have changed over the years.

Norm Olson/Alamy Stock Photo

04

The Civil Rights Movement Expands

READING STRATEGY

Analyzing Key Ideas and Details Complete a time line like the one below by recording people and groups in the civil rights movements and their actions.

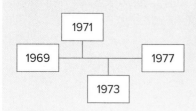

New Civil Rights Movements

GUIDING QUESTION

How did other groups of people adopt approaches similar to the African American civil rights movement?

The African American civil rights movement helped inspired other underrepresented groups to further champion for their own civil rights with new strategies, though many groups had already been advocating for their rights in the years before the civil rights movement. These groups often intentionally learned from and applied the tactics developed and used by the civil rights movement.

In the 1960s Native Americans and Asian Americans faced many challenges. Native American unemployment was ten times the national rate with an annual family income $1,000 less than that of African Americans. Native Americans often faced crushing poverty, especially on reservations. Cultural misunderstandings of Asian Americans had existed for decades but were heightened by the Vietnam War. Bigotry against Asian Americans was common during this time, and immigration quotas for Asians remained very limited.

Native American Protests

In 1961 more than 400 members of 67 Native American groups gathered in Chicago to discuss their concerns and to develop strategies to address inequalities. They developed a Declaration of Indian Purpose, which requested more economic opportunities for Native Americans and called on the federal government to honor existing treaties and respect **self-determination.** In 1968 the Indian Civil Rights Act passed and guaranteed reservation residents the Bill of Rights protection while also recognizing tribal courts and laws.

Native Americans who viewed the government's efforts as inadequate formed more militant groups. After a fire destroyed San Francisco's American Indian Center in 1969, an activist group known as Indians of All Tribes occupied the shuttered federal penitentiary on Alcatraz Island in November of that year. In a public manifesto, they outlined their plans to create an Indian school, a cultural center, and a museum on the island. The Indians of All Tribes claimed that the abandoned Alcatraz Island was theirs "by right of discovery," a phrase intentionally meant to echo the language European explorers had used to justify taking Native American land.

On November 20, 1969, Native American activists and supporters arrived at Alcatraz Island, reaching 600 occupiers at one point. The occupation was originally organized by Richard Oakes, Native American students, and Native American groups from around San Francisco, but as the protest gained media attention, more and more joined the occupation on the island in the middle of the San Francisco harbor.

Internal leadership issues eventually weakened the occupation, and the federal government forced the final protesters off the island in June 1971. The occupation, however, helped persuade the federal government to return millions of acres of tribal lands and introduce dozens of legislative proposals supporting Native American sovereignty over their lands.

self-determination the right of a native peoples to make decisions about their society free of outside government influence

Native American protesters arrived on Alcatraz in December 1969 to join the occupation of federal land.

Analyzing Visuals What do the items the protesters carry tell you about their plans for the occupation? Why?

PHOTO: RWK/AP Images; TEXT (1)U.S. Congress. House of Representatives. Committee on Interior and Insular Affairs. Subcommittee on Mines and Mining. Regulation of Strip Mining: Hearing. 92nd Congress, 1st Session. 1971; (2)Nixon, Richard. Special Message on Indian Affairs. July 8, 1970. Public Papers of the Presidents of the United States: Richard Nixon, 1970.

Occupiers used spray paint to alter signs, including one alteration that reads "Indians Welcome" above the sign declaring Alcatraz a United States penitentiary. The changes are still there.

Native activists also organized the American Indian Movement (AIM), which mounted a protest at Wounded Knee, South Dakota, the site of a famous attack upon Sioux by federal troops in 1890. AIM seized control of the town for 70 days in 1973 and demanded a series of reforms in reservation administration. It also demanded that the government honor its past treaty obligations. Before the siege ended, two Native Americans were killed and both the federal troops and the protesters suffered injuries.

Other Native American groups in the southwest, such as the Hopi and the Navajo, objected to federal leases that the government issued to mining companies that then stripped the land of mineral resources, displaced families, and threatened sacred Native American spaces. The organization wrote letters of protest to the government:

66 Today the sacred lands where the Hopi live are being desecrated by men who seek coal and water from our soil that they may create more power for the white man's cities. This must not be allowed to continue for if it does, Mother Nature will react in such a way that almost all men will suffer the end of life as they now know it. . . . The Great Spirit, said not to take from the Earth. . . . Your government has almost destroyed our basic religion which is actually a way of life for all our people in this land of the Great Spirit. 99

—quoted in testimony before Congress in hearings on the regulation of strip mining, 1972

Native American Gains

One of the first victories for Native American rights was the suspension of the U.S. government's termination policy. This policy tried to break up Native American nations by forcing them to assimilate into the broader culture of the United States. In 1970 President Richard Nixon announced that "the Indian future is determined by Indian acts and Indian decisions" and called for "self-determination without termination." Nixon's statement set a different course for relations between the federal government and Native Americans.

By the mid-1970s, the Native American movement had begun to achieve more of its goals. In 1975, Congress passed the Indian Self-Determination and Educational Assistance Act. This act encouraged tribal participation in and management of federal programs, such as social services, law enforcement, and health services. It also increased funds for Native American education.

Native Americans also won several court cases involving land and water rights. The Pueblo of Taos, New Mexico, regained control of property rights to

LOVING v. *VIRGINIA*, 1967

BACKGROUND TO THE CASE Throughout U.S. history, laws banning interracial marriage were commonplace. The plaintiffs in the *Loving* v. *Virginia* case were Richard and Mildred Loving, a white man and a woman of African American and Native American ancestry. In 1958 while both were living in Virginia, the couple traveled to Washington, D.C., to get married. After returning to Virginia, they were arrested and charged with breaking Virginia's interracial marriage law.

After pleading guilty the following year, the Lovings were sentenced to one year in prison. If they left the state and did not return as a married couple for 25 years, however, their sentence would be suspended. As a result, the Lovings moved to Washington, D.C., where they lived for the next several years.

The couple began the legal process to appeal their convictions in 1963, but both a Virginia state court and the Virginia Supreme Court of Appeals rejected their case. The U.S. Supreme took the case and heard oral arguments in April 1967.

HOW THE COURT RULED In a 9–0 decision, the Court ruled that state laws forbidding interracial marriages were unconstitutional under the Fourteenth Amendment. Writing for the Court, Chief Justice Earl Warren stated that these kinds of laws violated the equal protection clause and denied "citizens of liberty without due process of law." Warren also explained, "Under our Constitution, the freedom to marry, or not marry, a person of another race resides with the individual, and cannot be infringed by the state." *Loving* v. *Virginia* is often viewed as a key event in the march toward removing Jim Crow race laws. The case has also been used to argue for the rights of same-sex couples.

1. **Determining Central Ideas** Why did the Supreme Court strike down Virginia's law against interracial marriage?
2. **Making Connections** How might proponents of same-sex marriage use the *Loving* v. *Virginia* decision to defend their position?

PHOTO: Francis Miller/The LIFE Picture Collection/Getty Images; TEXT: Loving v. Virginia, 388 U.S. 1 (1967).

Blue Lake, a location sacred to their religion. Instead of seizing Native lands, the government paid the Passamaquoddy and the Penobscot peoples $81.5 million in 1980 to give up their claim to land in Maine. Other court decisions gave tribal governments the power to tax businesses on reservations.

Since Native Americans began to organize, many reservations have improved their economic conditions. Businesses such as electric plants, resorts and casinos, cattle ranches, and oil and gas wells have been developed on Native American nations.

In addition to economic gains, Native Americans expanded their political rights as a religious minority. In 1978 Congress passed the American Indian Religious Freedom Restoration Act. This law protects the rights of Native Americans

as well as Native Hawaiians and the native peoples of Alaska to practice their traditional religions. It also protects their right to be given access to sacred sites for purposes of religious ceremonies.

However, in a series of cases in the 1980s, the Supreme Court ruled that laws that burdened a person's religion did not violate the First Amendment if those laws affected all religious practices and did not single out a specific faith to discriminate against. For example, when Native Americans tried to stop the Forest Service from building a road through sacred land claiming it violated their First Amendment rights, the Court held that the road was not specifically targeting their faith practices.

In response to the Court's ruling, a coalition of civil rights and religious organizations pressured Congress to pass a new Religious Freedom Restoration Act in

Richard Aoki is seen here being arrested in Berkeley, California in February 1969. During World War II, his Japanese American family was put in Utah internment camps from 1942 to 1945. Aoki also served in the U.S. military for eight years. In the late 1960s, he helped organize political protests for Asian American educational improvements in California.

Analyzing Information Why did these activists believe that organizing under the term "Asian American" would benefit their efforts for equality?

1993. This act stated that laws could not impose burdens on a person's religion, regardless of whether the laws were general in nature and not aimed at a person's religious beliefs. The law strengthened the rights of Native Americans and other religious groups.

Increased Asian American Voices

When Congress passed the Immigration and Nationality Act of 1965, the act removed the quotas that had limited the number of Asian immigrants in the 1880s and 1920s. This allowed Asian American citizens to apply for their family members to move to the United States. According to Census Bureau data, more than 300,000 immigrants in the United States during the 1960s had been born in the Philippines, China, Japan, or Korea.

In addition to a population increase, Chinese Americans, Filipino Americans, Japanese Americans, and others found common cause with other 1960s movements. African Americans, Asian Americans, and other college students used protest action to secure rights and expand their social influence.

College student activists recognized the importance of ensuring everyone had access to

higher education and of giving African Americans, Asian Americans, and other similar groups a more formal place in academia. The San Francisco State College strike, which started in November 1968 and lasted until March 1969, was the longest student strike in U.S. history. Its goal was to open admissions and create a Black Studies and an Ethnic Studies department at San Francisco State College. A similar strike occurred at the University of California, Berkeley, in 1969.

The growing awareness of race-based discrimination in the 1960s led politically active youths at the University of California, Berkeley, to coin the term "Asian American" as a mechanism for uniting students across various Asian identities to make them a more potent group to advocate for change. They eventually founded the Asian American Political Alliance (AAPA) to demand collective rights. AAPA was involved in the student strikes at colleges in the San Francisco area. It also helped coordinate anti–Vietnam War protests.

The Philippine American Collegiate Endeavor (PACE) was established in 1967 at San Francisco State College. PACE wanted to help address issues that affected the Filipino American community. It worked with other groups to create the Third World Liberation Front (TWLF). This combined group helped lead the protests that eventually resulted in the establishment of the first ethnic studies departments on college campuses.

The increase in Asian American rights and social influence was not driven by a single leader—it was an effort undertaken by many different activists who represented a variety of goals reflecting the needs of separate cultures. Yet the methods used were like those of African Americans, women, Native Americans, and other minority groups demanding that their points of view be heard as part of the American experience.

The LGBTQ Rights Movement

The effort to end violence and discrimination based on sexual orientation and gender identity had started long before the 1960s. However, during this period, in part because of the civil rights movement, the movement for equality for people of differing sexual orientations and gender identities gained momentum, media attention, and influence.

The Mattachine Society was one of the first gay rights organizations. It was established in Los Angeles in 1950. In its mission statement, the society called for a grassroots movement of gay people to challenge antigay discrimination. The group actively advocated for the formation of a gay community.

Founded in 1955, the Daughters of Bilitis emerged as the first national political and social organization for lesbians. Until the organization

Media Group/Oakland Tribune/Getty Images

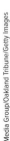

Beginning in early April 1977, demonstrators staged a successful sit-in at San Francisco's Health, Education, and Welfare Office to protest the lack of civil rights for the disabled. This protest lasted over 20 days.

Drawing Conclusions Based on what you can see in the photo, what led to the success of the protest?

disbanded in the early 1970s, the Daughters of Bilitis provided social support and a community for lesbians who felt isolated.

Throughout the 1970s and 1980s, more gay rights groups formed to advocate for change. In recognition of the complexity of sexual orientation and identity, the term LGBTQ—which stands for lesbian, gay, bisexual, transgender, and queer—eventually evolved to describe the many different groups affected by discrimination based on sexual orientation and gender identity.

The 1969 Stonewall riots were a pivotal event that helped bring the issue of LGBTQ equality into a broader, more mainstream context. The Stonewall Inn in the Greenwich Village neighborhood of New York City was a frequent target for police raids. During one raid in June 1969, some patrons and neighborhood residents refused police orders to disperse. Confrontations turned violent when crowds began protesting police brutality by throwing objects at the officers.

Clashes between police and activists outside the club continued for five more days. Stonewall marked a major change and acted as a catalyst for many to join in the LGBTQ movement. Activists began to demand equal rights more vocally and publicly, and more groups, such as the Gay Liberation Front (GLF), formed after the Stonewall incident. It helped ignite a stronger antidiscrimination movement among LGBTQ people. In 2016 President Barack Obama designated the Stonewall Inn as a national monument to recognize that event's role in the equality movement. In 1977 Harvey Milk, a gay rights activist and prominent member of San Francisco's gay community, was elected to a seat on the city's Board of Supervisors. He became one of the first openly gay elected official in the country, and while he was in office, he sponsored legislation to ban discrimination in public

accommodations, housing, and employment based on sexual orientation.

The next year, Milk and Mayor George Moscone were gunned down by a former city supervisor in San Francisco's City Hall. Milk's presence in politics and the LGBTQ movement helped highlight the role of gay men in society.

✓ **CHECK FOR UNDERSTANDING**

1. **Summarizing** What civil rights gains have Native Americans and Asian Americans achieved since the 1960s?
2. **Explaining** Why are the Stonewall riots considered a turning point in the history of the LGBTQ movement?

The Disability Rights Movement

GUIDING QUESTION

How did federal legislation protect the civil rights of people with disabilities?

While the movement for disability rights has roots in movements that date back to the 1800s, the more modern disability rights movement rose to prominence through such efforts as the independent living movement that began at the University of California at Berkeley in the early 1970s. The independent living movement, primarily led by those with disabilities, advocated for people of all levels of abilities to have the right to choose to live freely in society without architectural or societal barriers.

By the late 1980s, more than 300 independent living centers had sprung up across the country. These centers provided many services to people with disabilities, including peer counseling, help with

Jim Palmer/AP Images

wheelchair repair and ramp construction, and housing and employment assistance. These developments reflected a new attitude that encouraged people who had disabilities to live independently.

Within the deaf community, activists advocated for deaf and hard of hearing students to be given access to sign language as a primary language. These advocates argued that there were communities of deaf individuals in places like Martha's Vineyard as far back as American colonial history. These colonists began developing the foundations of what would become American Sign Language (ASL). However, around the 1880s, a movement called oralism, spearheaded by individuals such as Alexander Graham Bell, insisted that deaf students should be taught how to reproduce spoken language. This policy led to many deaf students growing up without many language skills at all.

Beginning in the late 1950s, activists like William Stokoe, a professor at Gallaudet University, fought against oralism and argued that it was vital for deaf people to have the full access to language that ASL provides them. Gallaudet University is a university aimed at the education of the deaf and hard of hearing. It became an epicenter in the deaf rights movement when student activists used protest and civil disobedience to advocate for a deaf individual to lead the university. On March 6, 1988, students began a campaign that led to the hiring of the first deaf person to lead an American university, I. (Irving) King Jordan.

People with disabilities also looked to the federal government to protect their civil rights. They sought access to public facilities and demanded equality in employment. One victory was the 1968 Architectural Barriers Act, which required that new buildings constructed with federal funds be accessible to persons with disabilities. The Rehabilitation Act of 1973 was even more significant. Section 504 states that no person with a disability can be discriminated against in any way by an entity that receives federal funding.

As of 1977, the Department of Health, Education, and Welfare (HEW) had no procedures to enforce the Rehabilitation Act. Frustrated, the American Coalition of Citizens with Disabilities organized protests. On April 5, 1977, some 2,000 persons with disabilities in 10 cities began sit-ins at regional HEW offices to support passage of Section 504. Protesters in San Francisco kept up their sit-in for over three weeks, with many foregoing vital medical care. Finally, on April 28, HEW's director signed the regulations banning discrimination.

Changes also occurred in special education. In 1966 Congress created the Bureau for the Education of the Handicapped. The bureau provided grants to develop programs for educating children with disabilities. In 1975 the Education for All Handicapped Children Act required that all students with disabilities receive a free, appropriate education. As a result, many schools began bringing students with disabilities into regular classrooms.

Disability activists began pushing for the Americans with Disabilities Act (ADA) in 1988. Advocates, including House Representative Tony Coelho from California and disability rights activist Judith Heumann, testified before a joint House and Senate hearing about the barriers they had experienced based on perceptions of their disabilities rather than their actual abilities. Two years later in 1990, Congress enacted the Americans with Disabilities Act (ADA). This far-reaching legislation banned discrimination against persons with disabilities in employment, transportation, public education, and telecommunications.

Disability advocacy is ongoing. Groups advocate to ensure that deaf students have access to the sign language skills they need. Activists still fight for recognition and accommodation for mobility aids and service animals. Today, technologies such as closed-captioned television broadcasts, devices for telephones, and screen readers help people with disabilities access information in new ways. There are sign language translation services for video calls and sign language news channels. Online streaming services include both closed-captioning and audio description tracks to better serve all users.

✓ CHECK FOR UNDERSTANDING

Explaining How did federal legislation protect the civil rights of people with disabilities?

LESSON ACTIVITIES

1. **Informative/Explanatory Writing** Take on the role of a journalist covering the 1969 Stonewall riots. Use the Internet to find resources that describe the events in more detail. Then write a newspaper article about the uprising.

2. **Collaborating** In a group of four, discuss the similarities and differences between the tactics used and the results achieved by activists advocating for the civil rights of African Americans, Native Americans, Asian Americans, and people with disabilities during this period. Following the discussion, individually write paragraphs summarizing the tactics used and the results achieved for each of the four cases. Once you have written your paragraphs, take turns to read them to one another and provide constructive feedback to each other.

05

Turning Point: The Americans with Disabilities Act

 COMPELLING QUESTION

How did the Americans with Disabilities Act help address accessibility issues?

Plan Your Inquiry

In this lesson, you will investigate the provisions of and responses to the Americans with Disabilities Act (ADA).

DEVELOP QUESTIONS

Developing Questions About the ADA Read the Compelling Question for this lesson. Consider what motivated passage of the ADA and what the law entails. Develop a list of Supporting Questions that would help you answer the Compelling Question in this lesson. Write these in a graphic organizer.

APPLY HISTORICAL TOOLS

Analyzing Primary Sources You will work with a variety of primary sources in this lesson. These sources focus on the provisions of the ADA as well as its effects on citizens and businesses. As you read, use a graphic organizer like the one below to record information about the sources that will help you examine them and check for historical understanding. Note ways in which each source helps you answer your Supporting Questions.

Supporting Questions	Primary Source	What this source tells me about the ADA	Questions the source leaves unanswered
	A		
	B		
	C		
	D		

After you analyze the sources, you will:
- use the evidence from the sources.
- communicate your conclusions.
- take informed action.

Background Information

Following strategies used by African American protest groups, disability activists joined together to form activist organizations to mobilize support and resources. They staged marches, rallies, and sit-ins. They filed court cases and contacted lawmakers.

The federal government had provided some assistance to people living with disabilities under the Social Security Act of 1935 and the Medicaid Act of 1965. But these laws did not guarantee their rights as citizens of the United States. In New York, activists founded Disabled in Action to challenge barriers, both physical and social, that prevented disabled people from full and equal participation in society. These and other groups aligned their efforts in 1975 under the umbrella organization the American Coalition of Citizens with Disabilities (ACCD). The ACCD helped win passage of a new law—the Rehabilitation Act—versions of which were twice vetoed by President Richard Nixon before he signed it in 1973. Two years later the Education for All Handicapped Children Act followed.

Neither of these laws provided the kind of sweeping "equal protections" that disability rights activists sought, but the Americans with Disabilities Act, passed in 1990, was an important step in that direction.

» The Americans with Disabilities Act (ADA) requires that all places of public accommodation built after January 1992 be fully accessible.

Andersen Ross/Blend Images/Getty Images

Hearings on the ADA

On September 27, 1988, disability advocates went before Congress to advocate for the passage of the Americans with Disabilities Act (ADA) of 1988. Judith Heumann had been denied many opportunities because of her disability.

PRIMARY SOURCE : SPEECH

66 My disability has made me a target for arbitrary and capricious prejudices from any person with whom I come into contact. . . . [E]xperience has taught us that we must be constantly aware of people's attempts to discriminate against us. . . .

Neither I, nor any one of the 42 million other people with disabilities, can wait for the 200 million nondisabled Americans to become educated to the fact that disability does not negate our entitlement to the same constitutional right as they have. Just as other civil rights legislation has made previously sanctioned discrimination illegal, so too will the passage of the Americans with Disabilities Act of 1988. . . .

We . . . are here today to insure for the class of disabled Americans the ordinary daily life that nondisabled Americans too often take for granted. The right to ride a bus or a train, the right to any job for which we are qualified, the right to enter any theater, restaurant or public accommodation, the right to purchase a home or rent an apartment, the right to appropriate communication. . . .

You have all heard our testimony today, but you have also been aware of these stories for many years. As elected representatives, you must act without delay to end these reprehensible acts of discrimination. To do any less is immoral. 99

—Judith Heumann, from a statement before Congress on September 27, 1988

EXAMINE THE SOURCE

1. **Explaining** Why does Heumann say that disability activists "must be constantly aware of people's attempts to discriminate against us"?

2. **Analyzing Points of View** What connections does Heumann make between the disability rights movement and the civil rights movement?

Disability Rights Protests

The Ford administration had done little to uphold the provisions of the Rehabilitation Act of 1973. No people with disabilities served on President Carter's task force to address the issue. Many worried that officials planned to change (and weaken) proposed regulations to uphold Section 504. On April 5, 1977, the American Coalition of Citizens with Disabilities (ACCD) launched a sit-in at the Health, Education, and Welfare (HEW) building in San Francisco. Hundreds of activists and their supporters participated. On April 28, HEW Secretary Joseph Califano signed the 504 regulations. This photograph is from April 7, 1977, during those protests.

PRIMARY SOURCE : PHOTOGRAPH

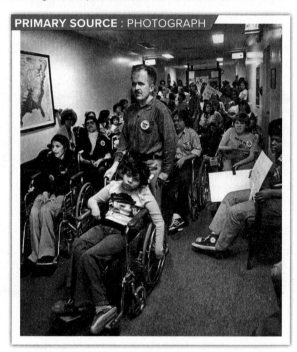

» Protesters line the hallway outside the U.S. Department of Health, Education, and Welfare to demand better support for people with disabilities.

EXAMINE THE SOURCE

1. **Analyzing Visuals** What key message and purpose does the photograph convey?

2. **Drawing Conclusions** What does this photograph suggest about the disability rights movement?

PHOTO: John Prieto/The Denver Post/Getty Images; TEXT: Heumann, Judith. Quoted in "Americans with Disabilities Act of 1988." Joint Hearing Before the Subcommittee on the Handicapped of the Committee on Labor and Human Resources, United States Senate, and the Subcommittee on Select Education of the Committee on Education and Labor, House of Representatives, One Hundredth Congress, Second Session on S. 2345 September 27, 1988.

Remarks by President George H.W. Bush

On July 26, 1990, President George H.W. Bush made these remarks during a ceremony at the White House in which he signed the Americans with Disabilities Act (ADA). The law, based on the Civil Rights Act of 1964 and the Rehabilitation Act of 1973, defines disability, in part, as "a physical or mental impairment that substantially limits one or more major life activities." Its provisions prohibit discrimination against persons with disabilities in most areas of life—not just by federally funded agencies and programs.

PRIMARY SOURCE : SPEECH

66 With today's signing of the landmark Americans for Disabilities Act, every man, woman and child with a disability can now pass through once-closed doors into a bright new era of equality, independence and freedom.

As I look around at all these joyous faces, I remember clearly how many years of dedicated commitment have gone into making this historic new civil rights Act a reality. It's been the work of a true **coalition.** A strong and inspiring coalition of people who have shared both a dream and a passionate determination to make that dream come true. It's been a coalition in the finest spirit. . . . Of public officials and private citizens. Of people with disabilities and without.

This historic Act is the world's first comprehensive declaration of equality for people with disabilities. . . . Its passage has made the United States the international leader on this human rights issue. Already, leaders of several other countries . . . have announced that they hope to enact now similar legislation. . . .

[F]or too many Americans, the blessings of liberty have been limited or even denied. The Civil Rights Act of '64 took a bold step towards righting that wrong. But the stark fact remained that people with disabilities were still victims of segregation and discrimination, and this was intolerable.

. . . Legally, [this Act] will provide our disabled community with a powerful expansion of protections and then basic civil rights. . . . [T]he ADA ensures that employers covered by the Act cannot discriminate against qualified individuals with disabilities. Second, the ADA ensures access to public accommodations such as restaurants, hotels, shopping centers and offices. And third, the ADA ensures expanded access to transportation services. . . . 99

—President George H.W. Bush, July 26, 1990

coalition a temporary alliance of individuals and groups for a common purpose

EXAMINE THE SOURCE

1. **Identifying Problems and Solutions** What problem(s) does President Bush say the ADA addresses? How does he suggest it provides solutions?

2. **Interpreting** What does Bush mean when he says, "every man, woman and child with a disability can now pass through once-closed doors into a bright new era of equality, independence and freedom"? Why do you think he chose the "door" metaphor?

» President George H.W. Bush signed the Americans with Disabilities Act into law on July 26, 1990.

PHOTO: MediaPunch Inc/Alamy Stock Photo; TEXT: Bush, George H. W. "Remarks on Signing the Americans with Disabilities Act of 1990." Weekly Compilation of Presidential Documents. Vol. 26, No. 30, July 30, 1990.

ADA Fact Sheet

The Office of the Press Secretary for President George H.W. Bush issued this press release on July 26, 1990.

PRIMARY SOURCE : DOCUMENT

❝ The President today signed the Americans with Disabilities Act of 1990, the broadest expansion of the nation's civil rights laws since the Civil Rights Act of 1964.

The legislation extends the framework of Federal civil rights laws that currently apply to women and minorities to the 43 million Americans who have some form of disability. This allows an unprecedented opportunity to bring Americans with disabilities into the mainstream of American life.

. . . The ADA prohibits discrimination against qualified persons with disabilities because of their disability. The prohibition applies to job application procedures, the hiring, advancement, or discharge of employees, employee compensation, job training, and other terms, conditions, and privileges of employment. Employees must reasonably accommodate the disabilities of qualified applicants or employees, unless an undue hardship would result.

. . . Public accommodations are prohibited from discrimination on the basis of disability in the full and equal enjoyment of goods, services, facilities, privileges, advantages, or accommodations. The prohibition extends to denying participation, offering disabled persons unequal or separate benefits, and requires accommodation of disabled persons in an integrated setting, unless an undue burden results.

In addition, public accommodations are required to remove architectural and communication barriers where removal is readily achievable. New construction and alterations must be accessible. . . .❞

—from "ADA Fact Sheet," July 26, 1990

EXAMINE THE SOURCE

1. **Explaining** What goal(s) does the source identify?
2. **Analyzing** What exceptions or conditions does the source specify for the law? What effect do these exceptions have?

Your Inquiry Analysis

EVALUATE SOURCES AND USE EVIDENCE

Refer back to the Compelling Question and the Supporting Questions you developed at the beginning of this lesson.

1. **Gathering Sources** Refer back to the Graphic Organizer you created as you read through the sources. Which sources help you answer the Supporting Questions you wrote? Circle or highlight those sources in your graphic organizer. What questions do you still have? Explain how you might find answers to these questions.

2. **Evaluating Sources** Looking at the sources that help you answer the Supporting Questions, evaluate the credibility of each source. How does the creator of each source relate to the subject? What opinion or bias does the source reveal? Explain which two sources you find most helpful and reliable in answering your Supporting Questions.

3. **Comparing and Contrasting** Compare and contrast the two sources that you described above. How do the two sources support or reinforce each other, if at all? What does each source tell you that the other does not? Explain why it's important to investigate multiple sources about this topic.

COMMUNICATE CONCLUSIONS

Collaborating Write one of your Supporting Questions at the top of a sheet of paper. In a small group, each group member passes the question to the next student, who writes a short response. Continue rotating papers until all group members have answered each chosen question. When your paper is returned to you, look over the responses. Then, take turns sharing your response to your Supporting Question and explaining how it helps you answer the Compelling Question. Finally, as a group, write a response to the Compelling Question. If time permits, select one group member to present your response to the class.

TAKE INFORMED ACTION

Investigating the ADA at Work Investigate your community for evidence of the ADA at work. Find three examples of accommodations that provide equal access. If possible, interview an individual with a disability or a member of a local disability rights group to learn how the ADA has impacted that person's life and what changes, if any, would be helpful for disabled people in your community, the state, or the nation. Use what you have learned to a) write a news feature article or b) prepare a slideshow presentation about the impact of the ADA.

White House Office of the Press Secretary. "FACT SHEET: The Americans with Disabilities Act of 1990." July 26, 1990.

06

Analyzing Sources: Building New Freedom Movements

 COMPELLING QUESTION

How did Latinos, Asians, women, and other disadvantaged groups build upon the African American civil rights movement?

Plan Your Inquiry

In this lesson, you will investigate the efforts of women, Native Americans, Asians, Latinos, and other marginalized groups to attain greater civil rights protections.

DEVELOP QUESTIONS

Developing Questions About New Freedom Movements
Read the Compelling Question for this lesson. Think about the goals of the new freedom movements and the methods they used to achieve those goals. Develop a list of Supporting Questions that will help you answer the Compelling Question in this lesson. Write these in a graphic organizer like the one below.

APPLY HISTORICAL TOOLS

Analyzing Primary and Secondary Sources You will work with a variety of primary and secondary sources in this lesson. These sources focus on the efforts of marginalized groups other than African Americans to achieve expanded civil rights protections. As you read, use a graphic organizer like the one below to record information about the sources that will help you examine them and check for historical understanding. Note ways in which each source helps you answer your Supporting Questions.

Source	Author/ Creator	Description	Which Supporting Question does this source help me answer?
A			
B			
C			
D			
E			
F			
G			

After you analyze the sources, you will:
- use the evidence from the sources.
- communicate your conclusions.
- take informed action.

Background Information

The African American civil rights movement did not begin on a certain day, with a certain person or group, at a certain event. For hundreds of years, free and enslaved African Americans struggled for freedom, human and civil rights, and fair and equitable opportunities and protections under the nation's laws.

The activism of the 1960s and 1970s signified a sea change in the African American civil rights movement because of the sheer scope—the vast number of people, including many non–African American supporters; the level of organization across various established groups, from students to labor unions to religious communities; their sharpened focus on strategies, methods, and goals, particularly through their commitment to nonviolent rallies, marches, sit-ins, strikes, and boycotts; their media exposure, which reached people across the nation; and their notable achievements, such as the Civil Rights Act of 1964, the Voting Rights Act of 1965, and the Fair Housing Act of 1968.

The efforts and successes of the African American civil rights movement spurred increased activity among other marginalized and persecuted groups, including women, Asian Americans, Latino Americans, Native Americans, and LGBTQ individuals. Their movements did not begin with a single person or event, either, but drew on the energy and momentum of the time.

» Demonstrators march in support of women's rights and the Black Panther Party in New Haven, Connecticut, in November 1969.

David Fenton/Archive Photos/Getty Images

"Asian Pacific Americans and the New Minority Politics"

In the 1960s many Asian Americans aligned with and supported the African American, Latino, and Native American civil rights movements. In the process, they formed their own organizations and movement. Among these was the Asian American Political Alliance (AAPA), founded in 1968. Students like Emma Gee and Yuji Ichioka sought to unify the many people who descended from various diverse groups of the largest continent and to magnify their voices.

SECONDARY SOURCE : ARTICLE

❝ The Asian American movement of the late 1960s—which coined the term 'Asian-American,' in 1969—recognized that all Asian ancestry groups shared a history of racial discrimination. As with other groups of color, [Asian Pacific Americans] APAs are liable to experience 'racial lumping'; which emphasizes a general **panethnic** identity, regardless of how specific individuals identify themselves. Just as some West Indian immigrants have found that outsiders usually view them as 'black,' APAs usually find that most Americans fail to note ethnic distinctions. . . . Panethnic marginalization has provided a powerful incentive for cooperation between APA subgroups, who have worked together on issues such as anti-Asian violence, college admissions controversies, and the '**glass ceiling**' for APAs. ❞

> —Andrew L. Aoki and Don T. Nakanishi, "Asian Pacific Americans and the New Minority Politics," in *PS: Political Science and Politics*, September 2001

panethnic a wide range of ethnic groups lumped together based on related origins

glass ceiling an invisible barrier that prevents certain groups of people from advancing to higher professional levels

EXAMINE THE SOURCE

1. **Explaining** What shared circumstances motivated different groups to organize the Asian American movement?

2. **Determining Context** What do the authors mean by "panethnic marginalization"?

Examining African American Feminism

The African American feminist movement grew out of the African American civil rights and the feminist movements. Many African American women activists were dissatisfied with these movements, which they felt overlooked the intersection of distinct forms of oppression that shaped their lives, including gender, sexuality, race, and class. Gloria Jean Watkins took the name of her grandmother—bell hooks—to challenge perceptions of African American women and to explore and challenge multiple forms of discrimination. The title of this book alludes to a speech by Sojourner Truth.

PRIMARY SOURCE : BOOK

❝ Although the women's movement motivated hundreds of women to write on the woman question, it failed to generate in depth critical analyses of the black female experience. Most feminists assumed that problems black women faced were caused by racism—not sexism. The assumption that we can divorce the issue of race from sex, or sex from race, has so clouded the vision of American thinkers and writers on the 'woman' question that most discussions of sexism, sexist oppression, or woman's place in society are distorted, biased, and inaccurate. We cannot form an accurate picture of woman's status by simply calling attention to the role assigned females under **patriarchy.** More specifically, we cannot form an accurate picture of the status of black women by simply focusing on racial **hierarchies.** ❞

> —bell hooks, *Ain't I a Woman: Black Women and Feminism*, 1981

patriarchy control by men of a disproportionately large share of political, economic, and social power

hierarchies a set of ranked groups based on perceived superiority

EXAMINE THE SOURCE

1. **Analyzing Perspectives** What criticism does hooks make about the broader feminist movement?

2. **Drawing Conclusions** How does hooks build on and respond to the broader African American civil rights and feminist movements?

[1]Aoki, Andrew L., and Don T. Nakanishi. "Asian Pacific Americans and the New Minority Politics." PS: Political Science and Politics 34, no. 3 (2001): 605-10. Accessed July 7, 2020. www.jstor.org/stable/1353547.
[2]hooks, bell. Ain't I a Woman: Black Women and Feminism. 2nd ed. New York: Routledge. 2015.

Robert Kennedy's Support of Farmworkers

From the 1500s to 1848, Mexico (and before Mexico, Spain) claimed most of the American Southwest, from Texas to California. In the early 1900s many Latino Americans still called this region home, and in the 1940s many more came as migrant workers under the Bracero Program. Others soon followed, fleeing hardship and persecution in their countries of origin. During the 1900s many Asian immigrants—particularly from the former U.S. colony of the Philippines—crossed the Pacific for the same reason. But few protections existed for these workers and their families until Dolores Huerta (WEHR•tuh) and César Chávez (Ce•sahr CHAH•vehz) organized the National Farm Workers Association (NFWA) and Larry Itliong (IHT•lee•ahng) founded the Agricultural Workers Organizing Committee (AWOC). Senator Robert Kennedy delivered this speech at an event honoring Chávez.

PRIMARY SOURCE : SPEECH

66 We have come here out of respect for one of the heroic figures of our time—Cesar Chavez. But I also come here to congratulate all of you, you who are locked with Cesar in the struggle for justice for the farmworker, and the struggle for justice for the Spanish-speaking American. I was here two years ago, almost to the day. Two years ago your union had not yet won a major victory. Now, elections have been held on ranch after ranch and the workers have spoken. They have spoken, and they have said, 'We want a union.'

You are the first—not the first farm workers to organize—but the first to fight and triumph, over all the odds, without proper protection from Federal law. . . .

Others, inspired by your example, have come to offer help—and they have helped. But the victories are yours and yours alone. You have won them with your courage and perseverance. You stood for the right—you would not be moved. . . .

The world must know, from this time forward, that the **migrant** farm worker, the Mexican-American, is coming into his own rights. You are winning a special kind of citizenship; no one is doing it for you . . . and therefore no one can ever take it away. . . .

But the struggle is far from over. And now, as you are at midpoint in your most difficult organizing effort, there are suddenly those who question the principle that underlies everything you have done so far—the principle of non-violence. There are those who think violence is some shortcut to victory.

Let me say that violence is no answer. And those who organized the steel plants and the auto plants and the coal mines a generation ago learned from bitter experience that that

was so. For where there is violence and death and confusion and injury, the only ones who benefit are those who oppose your right to organize. . . .

But if you come here today from such great distances and at such great sacrifice to demonstrate your commitment to nonviolence, we in Government must match your commitment. That is our responsibility.

We must have a Federal law which gives farm workers the right to engage in **collective bargaining**—and have it this year.

We must have more adequate regulation of **green-card** workers, to prevent their use as strikebreakers—and we must have that this year.

We must have equal protection of the laws. Those are the words of the Fourteenth Amendment to the Constitution of the United States. The California Labor Code, the Federal Immigration Laws, the Federal Labor Department Regulations—these are laws which are supposed to protect you. They must be enforced. From now on. . . . 99

—Robert Kennedy, March 10, 1968

migrant a person who moves around to find work

collective bargaining negotiation between an employer and a labor union on work issues such as wages

green card relating to an identity card affirming the residency status of an immigrant to the United States

EXAMINE THE SOURCE

1. **Explaining** What does Kennedy say that Chávez and the migrant farmworkers movement have achieved? What methods did they use?

2. **Analyzing Perspectives** What does Kennedy feel the next steps should be, and who would be responsible for them?

Kennedy, Robert F. "Statement of Senator Robert F. Kennedy." Delano, CA. March 10, 1968.

Kennedy and Chávez

Born to a prominent and wealthy New England family, Robert Kennedy attended prestigious universities, joined the U.S. Navy, served as the U.S. Attorney General, and then became a U.S. Senator. César Chávez grew up in a migrant farmworkers' family in Arizona. He also served in the U.S. Navy. In the 1950s, Chávez became a community organizer before turning his attention to organizing farmworkers. In 1966 Kennedy—a member of the Senate Subcommittee on Migratory Labor—met Chávez and witnessed the hardships experienced by the farmworkers.

PRIMARY SOURCE : PHOTOGRAPH

» Robert Kennedy (seated, left) and César Chávez (seated, center) attend a United Farm Workers rally in 1968. Chávez has just ended a long hunger strike.

EXAMINE THE SOURCE

1. **Analyzing Visuals** What do you notice about the individuals in this photo, their expressions, and their arrangement?

2. **Evaluating** What does this image suggest about the methods and success of the migrant farmworkers' movement?

International Women's Year

In 1966 women organized the National Organization for Women (NOW) to campaign for passage of the Equal Rights Amendment (ERA). Both houses of Congress passed the amendment in 1972, but it failed to achieve the required number of state ratifications to become law. In 1975, shortly after Gerald Ford became president following Richard Nixon's resignation, he issued this executive order.

PRIMARY SOURCE : EXECUTIVE ORDER

66 There is increasing recognition of, and interest in, the contributions of women to the national life of this country in all its important aspects—cultural, political, economic, and social. Significant progress continues in advancing the rights and responsibilities of women, in opening new opportunities, and in overcoming political, legal, social, and economic **handicaps** to which women have long been subject. Americans must now deal with those inequities that still linger as barriers to the full participation in our Nation's life. We must also support and strengthen the laws that prohibit discrimination based on sex.

The United Nations General Assembly, by proclaiming 1975 as International Women's Year, has offered us an exceptional opportunity to focus attention . . . on the rights and responsibilities of women. Presidential Proclamation No. 4262 of January 30, 1974, called upon the Congress and the people of the United States, . . . officials of the Federal Government and of State and local governments, . . . to provide for the national observance of International Women's Year. . . . 99

—The White House, "Establishing a National Commission on the Observance of International Women's Year," January 9, 1975

handicap a disadvantage that makes achievement difficult

EXAMINE THE SOURCE

1. **Summarizing** How does the order describe the experience of women in the United States?

2. **Synthesizing** What does Ford's response to the UN proclamation suggest about the feminist movement?

PHOTO: Photo by Michael Rougier/©Time & Life Pictures/Getty Images; TEXT: Ford, Gerald. "President Establishes Commission on International Women's Year." The Department of State Bulletin. Vol. 72, No. 1863. March 10, 1975.

The Alcatraz Protest

In 1961 members of diverse Native American groups began working together to achieve recognition not only of their rights but also of existing treaties. In 1968 President Lyndon B. Johnson signed the Indian Bill of Rights, but many Native Americans felt that it did not go far enough. From November 20, 1969, to June 11, 1971, a group of Native Americans called Indians of All Tribes occupied Alcatraz Island, known as "the Rock."

SECONDARY SOURCE : BOOK

66 In the early morning hours of November 20, 1969, eighty-nine American Indians landed on Alcatraz Island in San Francisco Bay. Identifying themselves as 'Indians of All Tribes,' these young urban college students claimed the island by 'right of discovery,' demanded clear title to Alcatraz Island, and called for the establishment of an American Indian university, an American Indian cultural center, and an American Indian museum. Their nineteen-month occupation, a culmination of two previous attempts at seizing the island, ushered in a new era of American Indian activism that continued well into the mid-1970s and kept national attention focused on Indian rights and grievances. For the Indians, Alcatraz Island would serve as a symbol of everything they had been promised but never received from the government, their lost land, and government waste. This symbolism proved strong because Native Americans remembered the importance of this island to their people. 99

—from *The Occupation of Alcatraz Island: Indian Self-Determination and the Rise of Indian Activism*, by Troy R. Johnson

EXAMINE THE SOURCE

1. **Identifying Main Idea and Details** What was the main purpose of the Alcatraz protest?
2. **Comparing and Contrasting** How was this protest similar to and different from other civil rights-era protests?

» Alcatraz protesters unload supplies from a boat in December 1969.

PHOTO: Ralph Crane/The LIFE Picture Collection/Getty Images; TEXT: Johnson; Troy R. The Occupation of Alcatraz Island: Indian Self-determination and the Rise of Indian Activism. Champaign: University of Illinois Press, 1996.

Testimony of Gwenn Craig, 1980

In the 1970s, new groups formed to protect the rights of LGBTQ individuals, partially in response to police raids on LGBTQ people and the riots at Stonewall Inn in 1969. Gwenn Craig, an African American lesbian activist, appeared before a Congressional committee to testify about discrimination based on sexual orientation.

PRIMARY SOURCE : CONGRESSIONAL TESTIMONY

" . . . [A]s one who has experienced **bigotry** in varied forms, . . . with many other experiences to relate **gleaned** from the case files of lawyers, social [researchers], and political activists. . . . unrestricted hatred that gay people face is evidenced in big cities . . . where gangs . . . roam our neighborhoods to harass and beat identifiable gays, while police protection is often nonexistent.

. . . [W]hat is most frightening is that we have little or no **recourse** if we are arbitrarily forced from our jobs, our livelihoods. . . .

Does discrimination exist? . . . Ask Robert Murdoch, a corporate lawyer for 7 years with the Atlantic Richfield Oil Company . . . employed until ARCO found he was gay and then he was simply fired. "

—Gwenn Craig, testimony before the Subcommittee on Employment Opportunities of the Committee on Education and Labor, House of Representatives, October 10, 1980

bigotry stubborn devotion to one's opinions, especially one's prejudices, or preconceived judgments about others

glean to gather information bit by bit

recourse way to seek help

EXAMINE THE SOURCE

1. **Explaining** What point does Craig try to make in her testimony?
2. **Determining Context** To what immediate audience does Craig speak? To what broader audience does she express her argument?

Your Inquiry Analysis

EVALUATE SOURCES AND USE EVIDENCE

Reflect back to the Compelling Question and the Supporting Questions you developed at the beginning of this lesson.

1. **Gathering Sources** Refer back to the graphic organizer you created as you read through the sources. Which sources help you answer the Supporting Questions you wrote? Circle or highlight those sources in your graphic organizer. Write a sentence describing the most important information that you learned from each source.

2. **Evaluating Sources** Looking at the sources that help you answer the Supporting Questions, evaluate the credibility of each source. Summarize the perspective, role, and bias of each source's subject or creator.

3. **Comparing and Contrasting** Compare and contrast two of the sources that helped you answer your Supporting Questions in detail. Sketch a Venn diagram in which you record similarities and differences between the authors/creators, subjects, and goals and methods of the movements described.

COMMUNICATE CONCLUSIONS

Using Multimedia With a partner, take turns sharing and answering your Supporting Questions. Then, together, write a paragraph in response to the Compelling Question. Use the paragraph to develop a multimedia presentation in which you combine visual, text, and audio resources to share your response. If time permits, present your slideshow to the class.

TAKE INFORMED ACTION

Understanding Precedent Select one of the liberation movements discussed in the inquiry. Use appropriate reference materials to learn more about two laws or court cases related to that movement, one before 1980 and one that is more recent (preferably within the past 20 years). Then, write a short report in which you explain a) the context for each law or case; b) the provisions or key points of each; and c) any consistencies or changes between the two and the likely reasons for them. Finally, explain whether you agree or disagree with the most recent law or ruling, and why or why not; however, be sure to explain how the nation's laws and principles support your position. Take turns presenting your reports and opinions in groups or to the full class.

Craig, Gwenn. Statement of Gwenn Craig, Vice President, Harvey Milk Gay Democratic Club, in Hearing Before the Subcommittee on Employment Opportunities of the Committee on Education and Labor, House of Representatives, 96th Congress, 2nd Session, H.R. 2074. Washington: U.S. Government Printing Office.

07

Reviewing More Civil Rights Voices

Summary

Expanding the Movement

The African American civil rights movement inspired numerous other movements for civil rights based on ethnicity, gender, sexual orientation, and disability. Nonviolent protests remained the most common tactic among all these various groups.

Modern Feminism

African American women in the civil rights movement drew attention to the gender discrimination they experienced, even as the movement advocated for full equality of all citizens. In the mid-1960s, women began to organize to end discrimination based on gender. This new wave of feminists represented a diverse cross-section of the population, and African American feminists played an important role in pointing out the connections between racial, gender, and sexual equality.

The National Organization for Women (NOW)

The publication of Betty Friedan's 1963 book *The Feminine Mystique* was one of the founding works of the modern wave of feminism. Friedan wrote about the frustration many white, well-educated women like herself experienced when they confronted limited career opportunities in a society that assumed their primary roles did not go beyond housewife and mother. The movement was acknowledged when gender was included in the Civil Rights Act of 1964. Friedan and other feminists, including younger activists like Gloria Steinem, created the National Organization for Women (NOW). This group lobbied to strengthen laws to end inequality based on gender, especially in the workplace, schools, and the political realm.

The Equal Rights Amendment

One of NOW's goals became completing the work of early-twentieth-century feminists by getting the Equal Rights Amendment ratified. Ratification required 38 states. However, organized opposition arose against the ERA, led by anti-feminists including Phyllis Schlafly, who argued that the amendment would wipe out gender-based laws that protected women, such as authorizing special accommodations for pregnant workers. The opposition led Congress to set a ratification deadline of 1982. Without reaching 38 states by that year, the amendment appeared dead.

Social and Political Changes

The feminist movement both reflected and brought about many changes in society. Legal challenges highlighting unequal opportunities for female students led to language prohibiting gender discrimination in public schools and universities in Title IX of the Education Amendments Act of 1972.

The Feminist Movement

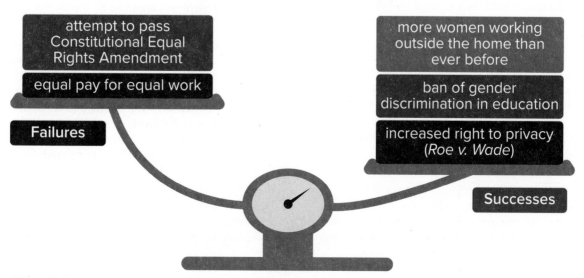

attempt to pass Constitutional Equal Rights Amendment

equal pay for equal work

Failures

more women working outside the home than ever before

ban of gender discrimination in education

increased right to privacy (*Roe v. Wade*)

Successes

The U.S. Supreme Court upheld protection of women's right to abortion, citing patient privacy in the 1973 decision in *Roe* v. *Wade*. The anti-feminist movement strengthened in response to outrage over *Roe* v. *Wade*, and it also fueled an organized right-to-life movement set on overturning the Court's decision.

The feminist movement brought attention to gender discrimination and helped increase women's participation in the workforce and in politics. Although women still lag behind men in wages and other opportunities, women today have significantly more career and life choices than they did in 1960.

Rights of Ethnic Groups

Mexican Americans had maintained a significant presence throughout the Southwest for generations. However, they continued to experience segregation and discrimination. By the 1960s, political and economic upheaval in various Central and South American countries led to increased immigration. The growing Latinx populations were lending strength to their cause for equal rights. However, the changing populations also led to a backlash from nativists who feared the transformation.

The League of United Latin American Citizens (LULAC), which worked to end discrimination for Latinos, and the American GI Forum, which focused on discrimination against Latino veterans, helped challenge discrimination. Activists César Chávez and Dolores Huerta began organizing farmworkers, many of whom were Latino, who were often exploited and underpaid by major food producers, in the Southwest. Their boycott against California grape producers brought national attention to the cause and launched the United Farm Workers Union.

By the late 1960s, younger activists, such as the Mexican American Youth Organization, organized walkouts and other protests against discrimination in daily life. Groups such as *La Raza Unida* encouraged Latino political participation. Younger activists brought attention to issues such as the need for bilingual education, and they encouraged ethnic pride through efforts such as the Chicano mural project.

Immigration from Mexico, Central and South America, and Asia increased over the next several decades. The Immigration and Nationality Act of 1965 ended the quota system established in the 1920s. The act also limited immigration from the Western Hemisphere, which resulted in a rise of undocumented immigration from Mexico and Central and South America.

For some people, the rising numbers of immigrants caused anxiety, so they focused on undocumented immigration. Despite numerous efforts at immigration reform—including attempts to expand opportunities for refugees and to provide a path to citizenship for undocumented immigrants who have lived in the United States since childhood—this issue remains a hotly debated topic among U.S. leaders.

Civil Rights for All

Other minority groups applied the tactics of the African American civil rights organizers. Native American leaders organized and lobbied to pass the Indian Civil Rights Act of 1968. Over the years, Native American groups sought more self-determination with court challenges. The American Indian Movement (AIM) took a more confrontational approach. In 1973 a violent stand-off at Wounded Knee took place between AIM members and government officials.

Immigration from Asian countries increased after the Immigration and Nationality Act of 1965 removed numerical quotas that limited the number of Asian immigrants in the early twentieth century. As the cultural presence of Asians and the Asian American children of previous immigrants came of age in the 1960s, they began advocating for equality and an end to discrimination. College-aged Asian American students in California found common cause with the African American protests of the 1960s. These students recognized the importance of a strong education. They organized a five month strike in 1968 and 1969 at San Francisco State College. The goal of the students was to expand admissions criteria to a wider minority population. They also wanted to create a Black Studies and Ethnic Studies department at the college. Their success inspired a similar strike at the University of California, Berkeley, also in 1969.

Across the country, Americans who identified as part of the LGBTQ community were forced to hide their identities for fear of being prosecuted under discriminatory laws. After a violent confrontation in 1969 between police and members of the LGBTQ community at New York's Stonewall Inn, lawyers and activists joined together to fight discrimination based on sexual orientation. Openly gay politicians such as Harvey Milk inspired others to be themselves and be involved.

Another civil rights movement launched during this period advocated for disability rights. Without laws to address discrimination and inaccessibility, many people with disabilities, such as those with seeing and hearing impairments or the inability to walk, faced limited options in the workforce and society. Efforts to improve equity of access and opportunity for those with disabilities led to important legislation, such as the Rehabilitation Act of 1973, the 1975 Education for All Handicapped Children Act, and the Americans with Disabilities Act of 1990. These laws have helped improve equity in educational settings and the workplace for millions of people with disabilities.

Apply What You Have Learned

 ## A Building Citizenship

The Voting Rights Act of 1975 required areas with a certain percentage of voting-age citizens to provide election materials in the primary language of that group. The inclusion of this provision has been a huge help to citizens whose first language is not English. Decisions about when and in which languages to provide the materials are based upon demographic information gathered by the U.S. Census Bureau, and that information is updated every five years. In addition to examining how many citizens might not speak English as their first language, the law also requires examining education levels within the community. The assumption among lawmakers is that, especially for immigrant citizens with less than a fifth-grade level of education, election materials would be easier to understand if presented in their primary languages. After the passage of the Voting Rights Act of 1975, Congress repeatedly extended this provision.

ACTIVITY **Write an Informative Essay** Examine the map below, which shows the current locations that are required to provide election materials in languages other than English. Choose a county or city in one of these areas. Using library and Internet resources, research the history of this location. Then write an informative essay explaining how and why this area is required to comply with the language provisions of Voting Rights Act of 1975. Conclude your essay by noting what effects this legislation might have on citizens in the community.

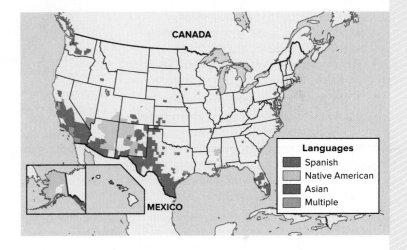

B Understanding Multiple Perspectives

The feminist movement launched in the 1960s sought to expand opportunities for all women. Differences of age, class, race, ethnicity, sexual orientation, and disability shaped the points of view of many feminists.

ACTIVITY **Complete a Table** This table lists the women featured in this topic who had different backgrounds and focuses for their activism. Use your textbook and other resources to complete each category of the table.

Person	Background	Main Focus of Activism/Accomplishment
Betty Friedan	White, WWII generation, Jewish, college-educated, upper-middle class	*The Feminine Mystique,* cofounded NOW, supported the ERA, advocated for advances for women in the workplace and in politics
Gloria Steinem		
Shirley Chisholm		
bell hooks		
Phyllis Schlafly		
Dolores Huerta		

C Making Connections to Today

The disability rights movement increased awareness of and pride among people with disabilities. It also led to laws that help protect the rights of people with disabilities in the workplace. Yet even with these various protections, many people with disabilities still face many barriers. For example, despite laws requiring access for people with disabilities in new buildings, many older buildings are still not fully accessible. Loopholes, slow construction timelines, costs, and other issues might lead decision makers to delay upgrading older buildings to meet accessibility standards. The inability of those without disabilities to appreciate how such decisions affect those with disabilities is a type of discrimination called "ableism."

» Ali Stroker, Tony Award–winning actress, performs a song from the musical *Oklahoma!*

In 2019 actor Ali Stroker made history by becoming the first person who requires a wheelchair to win a Tony Award for a performance on Broadway. Her role in the classic musical *Oklahoma!* changed the way many people viewed the possibilities for performers with physical disabilities. In her acceptance speech, she dedicated the award to "every kid who is watching tonight who has a disability, who has a limitation or a challenge, who has been waiting to see themselves represented in this arena."

Despite joy over her win, the event highlighted lack of access in the theater where the awards show was held. There was no wheelchair ramp leading from where nominees usually sat, the audience area, and the stage. Stroker had to wait backstage while the nominations were called. Stroker used the controversy to highlight accessibility issues that still exist in many theaters, especially for performers.

ACTIVITY  Using library and Internet resources, identify a building in your community that was constructed before 1990. Research information about the building. Visit it, if possible. Using the results from your research, write an assessment about how accessible you think the building is for people with disabilities. Include in your assessment any improvements that you think could be made to the building to improve accessibility for all.

D Making Connections to the Arts

Inspired by the African American civil rights movement, Hispanic Americans, women, Asian Americans, Americans with disabilities, and the LGBTQ community all expressed pride in their identity or heritage during the 1960s and 1970s. The protest movements of this time reflects the symbols, colors, and designs that helped celebrate each group's identity and culture.

ACTIVITY **Create Protest Art** Using your textbook, library, and Internet resources, create protest art that reflects various ways people in the 1970s celebrated pride in their gender, race, ethnicity, ability, or sexual orientation. Include details such as graphically designed elements, vibrant colors, and relevant cultural symbols.

PHOTO: Sara Krulwich/The New York Times/Redux; TEXT: Stroker, Ali. In "Representation Matters." [blog post] Spina Bifida Association. July 29, 2019.

Political Divisions

1970–2000

President Ronald Reagan met formally with the Soviet leader Mikhail Gorbachev as part of diplomatic meetings such as the Washington Summit, depicted in this 1987 photograph. As the Cold War drew to a close, political and cultural shifts began both in the United States and abroad that reshaped the nation's relations with the world.

INTRODUCTION LESSON

01 Introducing Political Divisions   516

LEARN THE EVENTS LESSONS

02 The 1970s and Watergate   521

04 The Reagan Revolution   531

05 The New World Order   537

07 The Clinton Administration   547

INQUIRY ACTIVITY LESSONS

03 Analyzing Sources: The Senate Watergate
    Committee Hearings   525

06 Turning Point: The Computer Changes
    Society   543

REVIEW AND APPLY LESSON

08 Reviewing Political Divisions   553

National Archives and Records Administration

THE FIRST FEMALE JUSTICE

The Supreme Court is the highest judicial institution in the United States. Since 1789, there have been seventeen Chief Justices and 102 Associate Justices on the Court. The first woman to serve on the Supreme Court, Sandra Day O'Connor, was appointed by President Ronald Reagan and took the judicial oath on September 25, 1981.

Sandra Day was born in El Paso, Texas, on March 26, 1930. Although her family owned a large ranch near Duncan, Arizona, she was sent to live with her grandmother in El Paso because educational opportunities for young women were better there. She excelled in school, graduating from high school two years early and entering Stanford University at sixteen. She graduated from Stanford with a bachelor's degree in economics and entered Stanford Law School in 1950. She completed law school in only two years rather than in the three years it typically takes.

Despite being third in her graduating class, Day struggled to find a job; no law firms would hire her because she was a woman. Eventually she was hired to serve as deputy district attorney in San Mateo County, California.

In 1954 Day and her husband, a Stanford law classmate named John Jay O'Connor III, moved to Germany. For three years, Day O'Connor worked as a civil attorney for the army. After returning to the United States and settling in Arizona, she began a private law practice with another lawyer. Eight years later, she became Assistant Attorney General of Arizona. Over the next two decades, she was elected to serve in the Arizona State Senate and the Superior Court of Maricopa County. She was also appointed to the Arizona Supreme Court of Appeals. Then, her career reached a **pinnacle** when President Reagan nominated her for the Supreme Court in 1981.

During his presidential campaign, Ronald Reagan promised to appoint a woman to the Supreme Court, and Sandra Day O'Connor helped him fulfill his promise. He wanted to appoint a conservative female judge, and options were few. O'Connor had attended Stanford Law with Justice William Rehnquist, and he enthusiastically supported her nomination. O'Connor had no experience with constitutional law, however. In preparation for the confirmation hearings, she studied relentlessly, which paid off. The confirmation hearings were publicized, and the American public fell in love with a smart woman who competently answered questions and carefully avoided controversial subjects. The Senate voted unanimously to approve her.

> **❝** It's good to be first, but you don't want to be the last. **❞**

Although appointed to be the voice of conservative America, O'Connor became known throughout her time in the Court as a critical swing vote. This means that she frequently served as a tiebreaker between liberal and conservative justices. She consistently made rulings that were aimed at promoting gender equality. Her first ruling on the Court, for example, supported a man who claimed discrimination when denied access to a traditionally all-female nursing school. Justice O'Connor supported his admission because to do otherwise perpetuated the stereotype that nursing was a female-only profession.

O'Connor retired from the Supreme Court in 2006 to care for her husband, who had been diagnosed with Alzheimer's. She often remarked that, "It's good to be first, but you don't want to be the last." O'Connor's concern never came to pass, and she successfully paved the way for more women to serve on the nation's highest court.

pinnacle highest point of achievement or development

O'Connor, Sandra Day. In Thomas, Evan. First: Sandra Day O'Connor. New York: Random House, 2019.

David Hume Kennerly/Getty Images

Sandra Day O'Connor, shown speaking at her 1981 confirmation hearing in the U.S. Senate, made history as the first woman to sit on the U.S. Supreme Court.

Understanding Information How did Justice O'Connor's confirmation affect Supreme Court rulings?

Understanding the Time and Place: United States, 1970–2000

The social and political movements of the 1960s and 1970s expanded civil rights, but these tumultuous decades also increased people's fears and insecurities. As a result, conservatism resurged in the 1970s and 1980s, causing the divisions in American society to deepen.

Nixon's Rise and Fall

Not all Americans supported the antiwar and social justice protests of the 1960s and 1970s. Much of the population saw these movements as shifting the country away from traditional values. Richard Nixon capitalized on these sentiments when he ran as the Republican presidential candidate in 1968. One of Nixon's strategies was to win support from Southern states. He chose Spiro Agnew, Maryland's governor, as his vice president and promised to put Southerners and conservatives in positions of power. Nixon claimed Virginia, Tennessee, Kentucky, and the Carolinas in the election, and he strengthened his appeal to Southern voters after becoming president. He overturned civil rights legislation, worked toward slowing desegregation, targeted antiwar protests and protesters, and imposed conditions for states and local agencies to receive federal funds. Yet he also favored some causes championed by liberals, such as a guaranteed income and regulations to protect the environment.

Although Nixon was elected to serve a second term as president, he resigned in 1974 because of his role in the Watergate scandal and the looming threat of impeachment. Nixon had gained power by supporting conservative views and appealing primarily to voters who rejected the period's progressive movements; however, his disgrace meant the Republicans had to find a new leader.

America's Changing Population

The success Nixon achieved by appealing to conservative values represented a fundamental shift in American politics, one that could be partly attributed to changes in the population. The Northeast had long been the focus of those with political hopes because so many people lived there. However, this started to change after World War II, when population dramatically increased in the Southern and Southwestern states.

During World War II, many people moved south and west to what became known as the **Sunbelt** to find jobs in wartime factories. Many military bases also attracted people to these areas. After the war, this trend continued as Midwestern industries in places like Pennsylvania, Michigan, and Ohio failed. The entertainment industry boomed in California, as did the tourist industry in places with alluring beaches and temperate year-round climates. As the problems associated with industry, such as pollution and overcrowding, affected people in the Northeast, state and local governments sought the aid of the federal government. People in these regions often supported the expansion of federal policies and programs.

The South and West, however, had long been opposed to strong federal regulation. In addition, the **arid** Southwestern climate meant states often fought for water rights, and farmers and ranchers throughout the region resented any government involvement that would mean a reduction in production or profit. The seven states along the Colorado River—Wyoming, Colorado, Utah, New Mexico, Nevada, Arizona, and California—regularly battled one another to increase their legal allotment of water. However, western states also depended on federal aid to build the highways, dams, and other public works projects that made their expansion possible.

During the 1970s, cities such as Dallas, shown here, experienced growth as the U.S. population shifted toward the Sunbelt.

Speculating Why do you think people moved in such great numbers to the Sunbelt region of the United States?

R. KRUBNER/ClassicStock/Alamy Stock Photo.

Sunbelt region of the Southern and Southwestern United States characterized by a mild winter climate

arid dry, with very little or no rainfall

The Rise of the Sunbelt, 1950–1980

New job opportunities in new industries contributed to population growth in the Sunbelt.

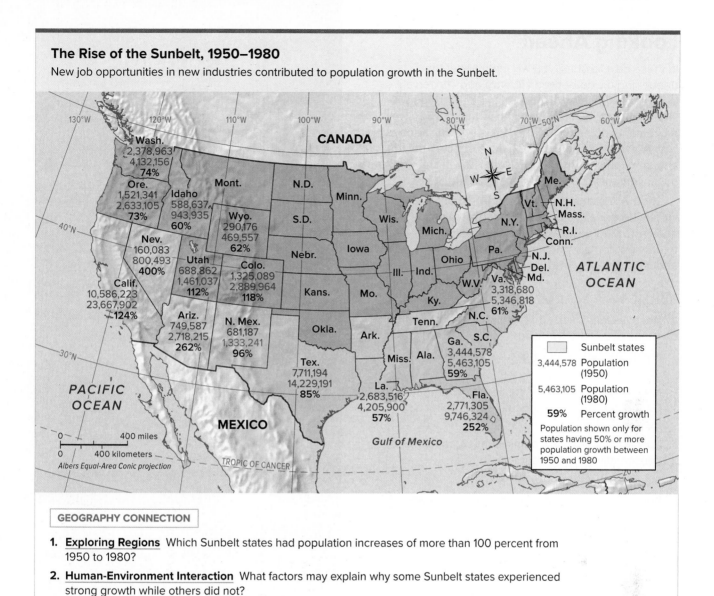

CANADA

Wash.
2,378,963
4,132,156
74%

Ore.
1,521,341
2,633,105
73%

Idaho
588,637
943,935
60%

Nev.
160,083
800,493
400%

Calif.
10,586,223
23,667,902
124%

Utah
688,862
1,461,037
112%

Wyo.
290,176
469,557
62%

Colo.
1,325,089
2,889,964
118%

Ariz.
749,587
2,718,215
262%

N. Mex.
681,187
1,333,241
96%

Tex.
7,711,194
14,229,191
85%

La.
2,683,516
4,205,900
57%

Va.
3,318,680
5,346,818
61%

Ga.
3,444,578
5,463,105
59%

Fla.
2,771,305
9,746,324
252%

PACIFIC OCEAN

MEXICO

Gulf of Mexico

ATLANTIC OCEAN

0 — 400 miles
0 — 400 kilometers
Albers Equal-Area Conic projection

TROPIC OF CANCER

	Sunbelt states
3,444,578	Population (1950)
5,463,105	Population (1980)
59%	Percent growth

Population shown only for states having 50% or more population growth between 1950 and 1980

GEOGRAPHY CONNECTION

1. **Exploring Regions** Which Sunbelt states had population increases of more than 100 percent from 1950 to 1980?

2. **Human-Environment Interaction** What factors may explain why some Sunbelt states experienced strong growth while others did not?

As more people moved to states with more available land, the number of new suburban areas being built increased, continuing the trend of suburbanization that had begun during World War II. Many people sought to escape what they saw as the chaotic urban landscape. New technologies allowed more people to find good jobs, leading to an expanding middle class that became very concerned with the amount of federal and state taxes they had to pay. Thus, cutting taxes became a primary concern for many voters. Other issues central to Southern and Southwestern conservative voters were immigration, gun control, and the *Roe* v. *Wade* decision.

Reagan's Rise

America's changing demographics—and much of the political, social, and economic turmoil of the decades following World War II—set the stage for Ronald Reagan to become the hero the Republican Party

had been waiting for. Reagan was a Hollywood actor during the 1930s and 1940s, and his experiences with communism during the Second Red Scare pushed him toward conservative values.

He had traveled the country in the 1950s at the expense of General Electric, which hired him to promote capitalism. During his travels, he often heard people complain about too much government oversight. Thus, when he ran for governor of California in 1966 and 1970, he won by appealing to conservative voters, a strategy that helped him become president in 1980. Reagan sought to alleviate people's fears by cutting taxes and expanding the military to make the country safer. He attracted a rising conservative political movement by promising a return to traditional values. Reagan also appealed to people's sense of self-reliance by claiming that big government was the problem, not the solution. The American dream, after all, was that anyone could achieve success on their own by working hard.

Looking Ahead

In these next lessons, you will learn about the deepening divide between liberals and conservatives in America. While studying this time period, you will learn how conservatives reacted to the progressive movements of the 1960s and 1970s. You will also learn how America's changing population affected politics and government. And you will learn how technological advancements changed life in the United States.

You will examine Compelling Questions in the Inquiry Lessons and develop your own questions about growing political divisions. Review the time line to preview some of the key events that you will learn about.

What Will You Learn

In these lessons focused on the growing political divisions of the late twentieth century, you will learn:

- about the events and individuals of the Watergate scandal.
- how media coverage of the Senate Watergate Committee Hearings affected public opinion of President Nixon.
- how Ronald Reagan's administration popularized conservative Republican political goals.
- the important events of the 1980s.
- how new global political challenges arose after the fall of the Soviet Union.
- about the domestic challenges of George H.W. Bush's presidential administration.
- about the rising importance of a globalized economy.
- about the rising influence of congressional Republicans and the meaning of the Contract with America.
- the important foreign policy events of the Clinton presidency.
- why Bill Clinton was impeached.

? COMPELLING QUESTIONS

- **How did the Watergate hearings shape the public's view of the federal government?**
- **To what extent has the invention of the computer transformed society?**

1980 ○ **NOVEMBER 1980** Ronald Reagan wins presidential election

AUGUST 1981 IBM begins selling new personal computer to retail customers

1981 First reported cases of AIDS

1984 ○ **JANUARY 1984** Apple Macintosh introduces the mouse and graphic-user interface

1991 ○ **JANUARY 1991** Operation Desert Storm begins

JULY 1991 President George H.W. Bush nominates Clarence Thomas (right) to Supreme Court vacancy

APRIL 1993 Mosaic, the first popular Web browser, released

DECEMBER 1998 House of Representatives impeaches Bill Clinton

2000 ○ **NOVEMBER 2000** Contested presidential election between Al Gore and George W. Bush

Sequencing Time Identify the events that reveal technological transformations and explain how these events most likely affected people at the time.

Hulton Archive/Getty Images.

02

The 1970s and Watergate

Kleindienst, Richard. In Congressional Record: Proceedings and Debates of the 91st Congress, First Session. August 12, 1969. Washington: U.S. Government Printing Office, 1969.

READING STRATEGY

Analyzing Key Ideas and Details Use the headings in this lesson to create an outline similar to this one by recording information about the Watergate scandal.

The 1970s and Watergate

I. Nixon Appeals to Middle America

   A.

   B.

II.

   A.

   B.

Nixon Appeals to Middle America

GUIDING QUESTION

What were Nixon's keys to victory in the 1968 presidential election?

Americans who longed for an end to the turmoil of 1968 turned to Republican presidential candidate Richard Nixon. He aimed his campaign messages at this group, whom he referred to as "Middle America" and the "silent majority." Nixon promised "peace with honor" in Vietnam and "law and order" at home. He also promised a more streamlined government and a return to traditional values.

Nixon faced Johnson's vice president Hubert Humphrey and third-party candidate, George Wallace, an experienced Southern politician and supporter of segregation. Wallace captured 13.5 percent of the popular vote. Yet Nixon managed to win with 43.4 percent of the popular vote to Humphrey's 42.7, and 301 electoral votes to Humphrey's 191.

The Southern Strategy

Nixon partially owed his victory to a surprisingly strong showing in the South. The South had long been a Democratic stronghold, but Nixon worked hard to build Southern support. This effort became known as the "Southern strategy." He had met with powerful South Carolina senator Strom Thurmond and won his support by promising to support political actions that resisted the reforms of the civil rights movement. Nixon agreed to appoint only conservatives to the federal courts and to name a Southerner to the Supreme Court. He also promised to oppose court-ordered busing and to choose a vice-presidential candidate that the South could support. Nixon chose Spiro Agnew, governor of Maryland.

Election Day results indicated large numbers of white Southerners left the Democratic Party. Humphrey's only Southern victory was in Johnson's home state of Texas. Wallace claimed most of the states in the Deep South, but Nixon captured Virginia, Tennessee, Kentucky, and North Carolina. Thurmond's support delivered his state of South Carolina to the Republicans as well.

A Law-and-Order President

Nixon had promised to uphold law and order, and his administration went after antiwar protesters. In Nixon's view, there was little difference between peaceful marches and destructive riots. Attorney General John Mitchell warned that he stood ready to prosecute anyone who crossed state lines to start riots. His deputy, Richard Kleindienst, declared, "We're going to enforce the law against draft evaders, against radical students, against deserters, against civil disorders, against organized crime, and against street crime."

Nixon attacked the recent Supreme Court rulings that expanded the rights of accused criminals and openly criticized the Court and its chief justice, Earl Warren. The president promised to fill vacancies on the Court with judges who would support the rights of law enforcement over the rights of the accused.

Earl Warren retired soon after Nixon took office. The president replaced him with a respected conservative judge, Warren Burger. Nixon would place three other conservative justices on the Court, including one from the South. The Burger Court did not reverse Warren Court rulings on suspects' rights, but it refused to expand those rights. For example, *Stone* v. *Powell* (1976) limited defendants' rights to appeal state convictions to the federal judiciary. The Burger Court also reaffirmed capital punishment.

Nixon's New Federalism

Nixon had also promised to reduce the size of the Great Society government. He planned to end several federal programs and give more control to state and local governments. Nixon called this the "New Federalism." He argued that such an approach would make government more effective. "I reject the patronizing idea that government in Washington, D.C., is inevitably more wise, more honest and more efficient than government at the local or State level," Nixon declared. "The idea that a bureaucratic elite in Washington knows what's best for people . . . is really a contention that people cannot govern themselves."

Under President Nixon's New Federalism plan, Congress passed a series of **revenue-sharing** bills granting federal funds to state and local agencies. As states came to depend on federal funds, the federal government could impose conditions on states. Unless states met those conditions, funds would be cut. When Congress appropriated money for programs he opposed, Nixon **impounded,** or refused to release, the funds. By 1973, it was estimated that he had impounded as much as $18 billion. The Supreme Court eventually declared impoundment acts unconstitutional.

One federal program Nixon wanted to reform was the nation's **welfare** system—Aid to Families with Dependent Children (AFDC). In 1969 Nixon proposed replacing the AFDC with the Family Assistance Plan. The plan called for providing needy families a yearly grant of $1,600, which could be supplemented by outside earnings. Many liberals applauded the plan as a significant step toward expanding federal responsibility for the poor. The program won approval in the House in 1970, but welfare recipients complained that the federal grant was too low. Conservatives disapproved of guaranteed income. Such opposition led to the program's defeat in the Senate.

Nixon convinced Congress to enact a series of progressive environmental objectives. In 1970 he signed the National Environmental Policy Act, which created the Environmental Protection Agency (EPA). The EPA set and enforced pollution standards, promoted research, and directed antipollution activities with state and local governments. In 1970 Nixon signed a new Clean Air Act into law, which established emissions standards for factories and cars, and aimed to improve national air quality within five years.

Congress passed two more pieces of significant environmental legislation. The Clean Water Act of 1972 restricted the discharge of pollutants into the nation's lakes and rivers. The Endangered Species Act of 1973 established measures for saving threatened animal and plant species. These laws succeeded in reducing smog, as well as curbing pollution in many lakes, streams, and rivers. This environmental legislation balanced out Nixon's concessions to conservative voters, making him an overall moderate Republican.

The Endangered Species Act did, however, pose a constitutional question. Because it imposed restrictions on the use of land where endangered species existed, did the act interfere with the Fifth Amendment property rights of individuals, businesses, or communities? The Constitution specifies that private property cannot be taken for public use without just compensation. Many cases have gone to court, but no general rule has emerged. In some cases courts have required the government to compensate property owners for the losses they have suffered when the Endangered Species Act is applied to their properties.

✓ **CHECK FOR UNDERSTANDING**

1. **Identifying Cause and Effect** What movement did Nixon oppose? Why was his opposition to this movement popular with Nixon voters?

2. **Summarizing** How did Nixon try to establish a new relationship between federal and state governments?

Men working in South Carolina as part of Job Corps, established by Lyndon B. Johnson in 1964. The program offered job training for at-risk and low-income Americans.

Making Connections Why do you think Job Corps was an important program?

---

revenue-sharing federal tax money that is distributed among the states

impound to take possession of

welfare aid in the form of money or necessities for those in need, especially disadvantaged social groups

PHOTO: National Archives and Records Administration; TEXT: President Richard Nixon, Annual Message to the Congress on the State of the Union, January 22, 1971, Nixon Presidential Library & Museum, National Archives and Records Administration.

The Roots of Watergate

GUIDING QUESTION

Why did Nixon's advisers order a break-in at the Democratic Party's headquarters?

The Watergate scandal began on the early in the morning of June 17, 1972, when five men were caught after they broke into the Democratic National Committee (DNC) headquarters in Washington's Watergate apartment and office complex. Later that day, a young *Washington Post* reporter named Bob Woodward was assigned to cover the seemingly insignificant but bizarre incident. Woodward went to the hearing to see if the story of the break-in was worth reporting.

As Woodward listened to the bail proceedings for the five defendants, the judge asked each of the accused to state his occupation. One of the men, James McCord, responded that he was retired from government service. "Where in government?" asked the judge. "CIA," McCord whispered.

When Woodward heard this, he sprang to attention. Why was a former CIA agent involved in what seemed to be a simple burglary? Over the next two years, Woodward and his journalist colleague Carl Bernstein—with the support of *Washington Post* publisher Katharine Graham—investigated the scandal that eventually forced Nixon to resign.

Mounting a Reelection Fight

The Watergate scandal revealed the Nixon administration's efforts to cover up its involvement in the break-in at the DNC headquarters and other illegal actions. Many scholars believe the roots of the scandal lay in President Nixon's character. Nixon had fought hard to become president. Along the way, he had grown defensive of his political position in Washington D.C. Nixon grew secretive of his decisions, and records of conversations show that he was resentful of his critics and the press. He became so consumed with his opponents that he made an "enemies list."

As the 1972 presidential election approached, Nixon's reelection prospects seemed promising but not certain. He had just finished triumphant trips to China and the Soviet Union, but the Vietnam War still raged, and staffers remembered the close 1968 election. Determined to win, Nixon campaign leadership authorized spying on the opposition and spreading rumors about political opponents. Nixon's advisers ordered five men to break into the Democratic Party's headquarters at the Watergate complex and place wiretaps on the office phones to collect sensitive campaign information. While the burglars worked, a security guard spotted a piece of tape holding a door lock and quickly called police, who arrested the men.

The Cover-Up Begins

After the break-in, the media discovered that McCord was not only an ex-CIA officer, he was also a member of the Committee for the Re-election of the President (CRP). Reports surfaced that the burglars had been paid from a secret CRP fund controlled by the White House. Nixon may not have ordered the break-in, but he did approve the cover-up. White House officials destroyed incriminating documents and gave investigators false testimony.

With Nixon's consent, administration officials asked the CIA to stop the FBI from investigating the source of money paid to the burglars. The CIA told the FBI that the investigation threatened national security. FBI deputy director W. Mark Felt then secretly leaked information about Watergate to the *Washington Post*. Nixon's press secretary dismissed the incident as trivial, and Nixon denied White House involvement. Most believed Nixon. Few paid attention to Watergate during the 1972 presidential campaign and Nixon won reelection by one of the largest margins in history.

Making Connections What effect did the CIA have on the FBI's investigation of the burglars in the Watergate break-in?

The Cover-Up Unravels

GUIDING QUESTION

How did the Watergate cover-up confuse the line between acceptable and unacceptable use of executive power?

In early 1973, the Watergate burglars went on trial. Under prodding from Judge John J. Sirica, McCord agreed to cooperate with the grand jury investigation and to testify before the newly created Senate Select Committee on Presidential Campaign Activities.

The Case of the Tapes

McCord's testimony opened a floodgate of confessions. Presidential counsel John Dean confessed that former attorney general John Mitchell had ordered the Watergate break-in and that Nixon had taken part in the cover-up. The Nixon administration strongly denied the charges, and Dean had no evidence. The Senate committee spent weeks trying to determine the truth. The answer came in July when White House aide Alexander Butterfield testified that Nixon had ordered a taping system installed in the White House to record all conversations to help him write his memoirs.

Nixon refused to hand over the tapes, pleading **executive privilege,** the principle that White House conversations should remain confidential to protect

---

executive privilege a legal exemption from disclosing communications that might endanger national security

All the President's Men, by Carl Bernstein & Bob Woodward. Copyright © 1974, 4987, 1994 by Touchstone.

Fred Clow of Boston listens to President Nixon's address to the nation on April 30, 1973.

Drawing Conclusions Why do you think Clow is watching the TV and reading the paper so intently?

national security. **Special Prosecutor** Archibald Cox took Nixon to court in October 1973 to press him to give up the tapes. Nixon ordered Attorney General Elliot Richardson to fire Cox, but Richardson refused and resigned. Nixon then ordered Richardson's deputy to fire Cox, but he, too, resigned. Nixon's solicitor general, Robert Bork, finally fired Cox, but the incident—known as the Saturday Night Massacre—damaged Nixon's reputation. Vice President Spiro Agnew resigned after it was found he had taken bribes while in office. Nixon appointed and Congress confirmed Gerald Ford, Republican leader of the House of Representatives, as vice president.

Nixon appointed a new special prosecutor, Leon Jaworski, who proved determined to obtain the tapes. In July, the Supreme Court ruled that Nixon had to surrender the tapes:

66 We conclude that when the ground for asserting privilege as to subpoenaed materials sought for use in a criminal trial is based only on the generalized interest in confidentiality, it cannot prevail over the fundamental demands of due process of law in the fair administration of criminal justice. 99

—Chief Justice Warren Burger, *United States* v. *Nixon*, 1974

The House Judiciary Committee voted to impeach Nixon, or officially charge him with misconduct. Charges included obstructing justice, misusing federal agencies to violate the rights of citizens, and defying the authority of Congress. Then new evidence emerged that Nixon had ordered the CIA to stop the FBI probe into the Watergate burglary. Impeachment and conviction were inevitable. On August 9, 1974, Nixon resigned. Republican National Committee chairman George H.W. Bush was present that day:

66 President Nixon looked just awful. He used glasses—the first time I ever saw them. Close to breaking down. . . . Everyone in the room in tears. . . . The Nixon speech was masterful. In spite of his inability to totally resist a dig at the press, that argument about hating—only if you hate do you join the haters. 99

—George H.W. Bush diary entry, August 9, 1974

Vice President Gerald Ford took office as president. Urging Americans to put the scandal behind them, he said, "Our long national nightmare is over." On September 8, 1974, Ford announced a full pardon for Nixon, drawing criticism and diminishing his popularity.

✓ CHECK FOR UNDERSTANDING

1. **Analyzing** Why did Nixon decide he had to resign?
2. **Speculating** Why might Ford's decision to pardon Nixon be viewed as a mistake?

LESSON ACTIVITIES

1. **Argumentative Writing** Find two or more reactions to President Ford's pardon of Nixon and identify the author and when the reaction was written. Evaluate the validity, reliability, and bias of each source, and write a paragraph comparing the sources.

2. **Collaborating** In a small group, discuss the principle of executive privilege. Use the Internet to find information about how other presidents have claimed executive privilege. Consider different perspectives that support the principle and those that dismiss or limit it. Continue your group discussion to reach a conclusion on the necessity of executive privilege. Give your conclusion as a short presentation to your classmates.

Special Prosecutor a lawyer from outside the government appointed to investigate a government official for misconduct while in office

PHOTO: Bettmann/Getty Images; TEXT: (1)United States v. Nixon, 418 U.S. 683 (1974); (2)Bush, George H.W. 1974. Diary entry, August 9, 1974, National Archives and Records Administration, George Bush Presidential Library and Museum, College Station, Texas; (3)President Gerald Ford, Remarks on taking the oath as president, August 9, 1974, Gerald R. Ford Library, National Archives and Records Administration.

03

Analyzing Sources: The Senate Watergate Committee Hearings

? COMPELLING QUESTION

How did the Watergate hearings shape the public's view of the federal government?

Plan Your Inquiry

In this lesson, you will investigate primary sources focused on the U.S. Senate's Watergate committee hearings.

DEVELOP QUESTIONS

Developing Questions About the Watergate Hearings
Read the Compelling Question for this lesson. Think about how the Watergate hearings informed the public and affected their views on the government. Develop a list of Supporting Questions that would help you answer the Compelling Question in this lesson.

APPLY HISTORICAL TOOLS

Analyzing Primary and Secondary Sources You will work with a variety of primary and secondary sources in this lesson. These sources focus on the role of the media in disseminating information about the Watergate hearings. As you read, use a graphic organizer like the one below to record information about the sources that will help you examine them and check for historical understanding. Note ways in which each source helps you answer your Supporting Questions.

Supporting Questions	Source	How this source helps me answer the Supporting Question
Question 1:		
Question 2:		
Question 3:		

After you analyze the sources, you will:
- use the evidence from the sources.
- communicate your conclusions.
- take informed action.

Background Information

On August 9, 1974, President Richard M. Nixon became the first president in U.S. history to resign from office. Vice President Gerald Ford took the oath of office shortly after, and a month later, Ford pardoned Nixon for any crimes committed in office.

Nixon's resignation followed a series of escalating events that began with an early-morning break-in at the headquarters of the Democratic National Committee at the Watergate hotel and office complex on June 17, 1972. With an administration that was increasingly criticized for its handling of the war in Vietnam, the burglary took place just five months before the presidential election in which Nixon would face Democrat George McGovern. Five men were arrested for the crime, and two reporters took a special interest when one suspect revealed himself to be a former member of the Central Intelligence Agency (CIA).

The news media—in print, on the radio, and most dramatically, on television—proved crucial not only in launching a more comprehensive investigation of the curious break-in but also in bringing the investigation and its revelations live to the American public.

» In May 1973 interest in the Watergate hearings was so great that customers gathered around televisions in stores that were tuned to the broadcast.

Bettmann/Getty Images

A

Origins of the Watergate Scandal

Congressional committees exercise the powers of oversight and investigation over the executive branch. This overview of the 16-month-long Watergate affair appears on the Senate website "A History of Notable Senate Investigations."

SECONDARY SOURCE : ARTICLE

" Early on the morning of June 17, 1972, five men broke in the Democratic National Committee headquarters at the Watergate hotel and office complex in Washington, D.C. A security guard discovered the team and alerted the metro police, who arrested the burglars, who carried more than $3,500 in cash and high-end **surveillance** and electronic equipment.

While the burglars awaited their **arraignment** in federal district court, the FBI launched an investigation of the incident. The dogged reporting of two *Washington Post* journalists, Bob Woodward and Carl Bernstein, raised questions and suggested connections between Nixon's reelection campaign and the men awaiting trial in federal district court. The White House denied any connection to the break-in, and President Richard Nixon won reelection in a landslide in November 1972.

On January 10, 1973, the trial of the Watergate burglars and two accomplices began. . . . Chief Federal District Judge John Sirica expressed skepticism that all the facts in the case had been revealed. Five men pleaded guilty and two were convicted by a jury. . . . "

—"The Watergate Committee," U.S. Senate: Select Committee on Presidential Campaign Activities

---

surveillance keeping a close watch over a person or place, often in secret
arraignment the process of appearing in court to answer charges of criminal activity

---

EXAMINE THE SOURCE

1. **Explaining** What key events triggered the Watergate scandal?

2. **Inferring** How did the media contribute to the escalation and exposure of the investigation?

B

Public Television's Role

The 1967 Public Broadcasting Act created the nonprofit Corporation for Public Broadcasting (CPB). In 1969 CPB then launched the Public Broadcasting Service (PBS) mainly as a network for educational programs.

SECONDARY SOURCE : ARTICLE

" What remains clear is that [the National Public Affairs Center for Television's] coverage of the hearings was an . . . success for public broadcasting. Letters, phone calls, . . . and newspaper clippings from around the country flooded national and local offices praising the coverage. . . .

In an April 19 press release [NPACT President Jim Karayn] . . . stated his vision of the . . . value of public affairs programming:

'This is precisely the kind of event which public television should put before the American viewer. By providing complete coverage of these hearings, millions will be able to see that the hearings have a significance far beyond alleged wrongdoings by a political party. They should provide insight into the basic workings of American government by dealing with such issues as congressional procedure, the investigative process, and executive privilege.' . . .

Throughout April and May, public television laid plans for the upcoming hearings. The networks, on the other hand, did not even decide to air the hearings until the week before. During this time, the member stations voted on whether they would prefer live or delayed coverage. The result of the poll set the start time at 8 p.m. Eastern time. On May 10, PBS was persuaded to offer a 'live feed' during the day to the 46-station Eastern Educational Network at additional cost. . . . "

—"Gavel-to-Gavel: The Watergate Scandal and Public Television," American Archive of Public Broadcasting website

EXAMINE THE SOURCE

Contrasting How did PBS's coverage differ from that of commercial networks? Why did PBS make this choice?

(1)Senate Select Committee on Presidential Campaign Activities (The Watergate Committee), U.S. Senate Historical Office, Washington, D.C.; (2)Reichenbach, Amanda, curator. "Gavel-to-Gavel": The Watergate Scandal and Public Television: Watergate and Public Broadcasting, American Archive of Public Broadcasting.

PHOTO: Arnie Sachs/CNP/Polaris/Newscom; TEXT: (1)Inouye, Daniel K. "Opening Statement of Senator Inouye of Hawaii," Presidential Campaign Activities of 1972, Hearings Before the Select Committee on Presidential Campaign Activities of the United States Senate, 93rd Congress, First Session. Book 1. Washington: U.S. Government Printing Office, 1973. (2)Nixon, Richard. Letter to Committee. July 23, 1973. Document courtesy of the Center for Legislative Archives, National Archives, Select Committee on Presidential Campaign Activities, Minutes, Feb 21- Nov 13, 1973, Box A 13.

C

Opening Statement

Hawaii Democrat Daniel Inouye joined the U.S. Army in 1943. He went on to represent the territory-turned-state first in the U.S. House of Representatives and then in the U.S. Senate. He became a leading member of the Watergate committee.

PRIMARY SOURCE : SPEECH

66 At stake is the very integrity of the election process. Unless we can safeguard that process from broad manipulation, deception, and other illegal or unethical activities, one of the most precious rights—the right to vote—will be left without meaning. . . .

As I see it, our mission is two-fold: First, to thoroughly investigate all allegations of the improper activities during the 1972 presidential election so that the full truth will be known; and secondly, to take steps to prevent future recurrences of such activities.

Our effort should not be directed toward punishing the guilty—judicial processes with that aim are under way in at least four cities—but to initiate a national public debate on our elections and how they work or fail to work.

Like most Americans, I have been truly shocked by the revelations and allegations of this scandal. . . .

These hearings should enlighten and inform and provide the groundwork

for a reaffirmation of faith in our American system. 99

—Senator Daniel Inouye, Opening Statement, May 17, 1973

EXAMINE THE SOURCE

1. **Analyzing Perspectives** What focus does Inouye want the hearing to take, and why?
2. **Drawing Conclusions** What impact might televising this speech have had on many Americans? Explain.

» Senator Daniel K. Inouye listens to testimony during the Senate Watergate hearings.

D

Nixon's Refusal to Comply

In July 1973, President Nixon sent a letter to Sam J. Ervin, Jr., the chairman of the Select Committee on Presidential Campaign Activities. Nixon stated his decision to not release audio recordings on the grounds of executive privilege.

PRIMARY SOURCE : LETTER

66 I have considered your request that I permit the Committee to have access to tapes of my private conversations with a number of my closest aides. . . . I shall not do so. . . .

If release of the tapes would settle the central questions at issue in the Watergate inquiries, then their disclosure might serve a substantial public interest that would have to be weighed very heavily against the negatives of disclosure.

The fact is that the tapes would not settle the central issues before your Committee. Before their existence became publicly known, I personally listened to a number of them. The tapes are entirely consistent with what I know to be the truth and what I have stated to be the truth. . . . [T]he tapes could be accurately understood or interpreted only by reference to an enormous number of other documents and tapes, so that to open them at all would begin an endless process of disclosure and explanation of private Presidential records totally unrelated to Watergate, and highly confidential in nature. They are the clearest possible example of why Presidential documents must be kept confidential. . . . 99

EXAMINE THE SOURCE

Explaining How does Nixon justify not releasing the tapes to the Watergate Senate Hearing Committee?

E

Subpoenaing President Nixon

In 1973 lawyer Rufus Edmisten served on the staff of North Carolina Senator Samuel Ervin, Jr. When the Senate selected Ervin to chair the Watergate committee, Edmisten became Deputy Chief Counsel. Rose Mary Woods worked as President Nixon's assistant for more than 20 years. The tapes to which Edmisten refers are recordings of conversations between Nixon and his Chief of Staff H.R. "Bob" Haldeman in the Oval Office.

PRIMARY SOURCE : INTERVIEW

" I knew enough to have a number, we regularly call the White House when you need to provide this witness or that witness. We have this little anteroom beside the committee room. The committee is in there talking and jabbering around and I dialed the number and finally they get me to who I suppose is Rose Mary Woods. I suppose because I always thought that she was the one with whom I talked because she was his personal secretary. I said, 'Ms. Woods, this is Rufus Edmisten. I'm the deputy chief counsel for the Senate Watergate committee.' . . . 'Senator Ervin and Senator Baker would like to speak with the President.' She says, 'Hold on, I'll be back.' . . .

Senator Ervin gets on the phone. It's one-sided conversation. . . . He was saying 'But Mr. President, we have a right to the tapes. You don't have anything to fear if there is nothing on them that's **incriminating.** We need to verify the truth of the matter. . . .' Nixon obviously says, 'No.' Then that's when [the Senate Watergate committee voted]. They voted there in the room and then they voted unanimously in public at one point to do it. But they voted in the room that day, as I recall, to **subpoena** the president. "

—Rufus Edmisten, interviewed by Kate Scott, Senate historian, September 8, 2011

incriminating suggesting of guilt or wrongdoing

subpoena a writ commanding someone to appear in court, usually to testify

EXAMINE THE SOURCE

1. **Summarizing** Which events does Edmisten describe?
2. **Analyzing** In what way does this excerpt exemplify the checks and balances of the U.S. government?

F

Justice Department Memo

In 1973 Leon Jaworski became the special prosecutor in the Watergate investigations. Carl Feldbaum worked as an assistant special prosecutor in the Justice Department.

PRIMARY SOURCE : MEMORANDUM

" There is a presumption . . . that Richard M. Nixon, like every citizen, is subject to the rule of law. Accordingly, one begins with the premise that if there is sufficient evidence, Mr. Nixon should be indicted and prosecuted. The question then becomes whether the presumption for proceeding is outweighed by the factors mandating against indictment and prosecution.

The factors which mandate against indictment and prosecution are:

1. His resignation has been sufficient punishment. . . .

5. There would be . . . difficulty in achieving a fair trial because of massive . . . publicity.

The factors which mandate in favor of indictment and prosecution are:

. . . 2. The country will be further divided . . . unless there is a final disposition of charges of criminality outstanding against him so as to forestall the belief that he was driven from his office by erosion of his political base. . . .

3. Article I, Section 3, clause 7 of the Constitution provides that a person removed from office by impeachment and conviction 'shall nevertheless be liable and subject to Indictment, Trial, Judgment, and Punishment, according to Law.' . . .

5. The modern nature of the Presidency necessitates massive public exposure of the President's actions. . . . A bar to prosecution on the grounds of such publicity effectively would immunize all future Presidents for their actions, however criminal. . . . "

—Feldbaum to Jaworski, August 9, 1974

EXAMINE THE SOURCE

1. **Interpreting** What arguments does the memo make for and against prosecuting Nixon?
2. **Analyzing Perspectives** How do you think publicity about Watergate might have affected a trial? Does that outweigh the right for the public to be informed?

(1)Edmisten, Rufus. Interview by Kate Scott. September 8, 2011; (2) Feldbaum, Carl B. "Memorandum to the Special Prosecutor." Watergate Special Prosecution Force, Department of Justice, August 9, 1974.

PHOTO: Block, Herbert. Artist. Late Returns, 1973. [5/18] Publication Date] Photograph. https://www.loc.gov/item/2012638696/. TEXT: Reichenbach, Amanda, curator. "Gavel-To-Gavel": The Watergate Scandal and Public Television: Watergate and Public Broadcasting. American Archive of Public Broadcasting.

G

Effects on the Public

The Senate hearings on the break-in and presidential cover-up lasted 16 months, from May 17, 1973, to November 15, 1974. Following are excerpts from a statement by PBS broadcast reporter Jim Lehrer at the close of the first day of hearings in May and two viewers' letters read aloud during the June 5 broadcast.

PRIMARY SOURCE: BROADCAST

❝ **Jim Lehrer:** 'We are running it all each day because we think these hearings are important and because we think it is important that you get a chance to see the whole thing and make your own judgments. Some nights, we may be in competition with a late, late movie. We are doing this as an experiment, temporarily abandoning our ability to edit, to give you the whole story, however many hours it may take.'

James Wilmeth, Ft. Worth, Texas: 'I am sick of press and TV reporters' opinions on Watergate. You are the one station that gives it to us as it is and allows us to form our own opinions.'

June Wilson, Atlanta, Georgia: 'Since the Watergate gavel-to-gavel rebroadcast began, I have not sewed on a button, taken up a hem, or put the yogurt on to make, since I work during the day I would be hard pressed to keep up with the testimony and the nuances which undeniably show themselves in such a hearing. Thus I arrive red-eyed and sleepy to work now and don't care.' ❞

—quoted in "Gavel-to-Gavel: The Watergate Scandal and Public Television," American Archive of Public Broadcasting Web site

nuance subtlety; fine distinction

EXAMINE THE SOURCE

1. **Analyzing Perspectives** What are the pros and cons of PBS's decision to air "gavel-to-gavel" coverage?

2. **Synthesizing** What do all three sources suggest about the nature of the PBS coverage as distinguished from other media networks? How might you describe PBS's role in the national conversation?

H

"Late Returns"

In November 1972 President Richard Nixon won reelection by more than 18 million votes. He famously declared this win by signing V-for-victory with both hands. Two months later, five defendants in the Watergate trial pled guilty, and soon after, two more were convicted. Then the Senate Select Committee on Presidential Campaign Activities formed, and several administration officials resigned or were dismissed. In May the televised Senate hearings began.

PRIMARY SOURCE : POLITICAL CARTOON

Late Returns

©1973 HERBLOCK

» Cartoonist Herbert Block, known as Herblock, published this cartoon in the *Washington Post* on May 19, 1973.

EXAMINE THE SOURCE

1. **Analyzing Visuals** What shift in American public opinion does this visual suggest? How do you know?

2. **Making Connections** How does this image relate to other sources in the inquiry?

Final Report of the Senate Select Committee

The Senate committee investigating Watergate released its report in the summer of 1974. The report detailed all the evidence and information gathered during the committee's investigation into the break-in of the Watergate Hotel during the 1972 election. It concluded that some members of Nixon's campaign staff committed crimes to gather evidence against Nixon's Democratic opposition.

PRIMARY SOURCE : REPORT

66 It thus must be stressed that the committee's hearings were not conducted, and this report not prepared, to determine the legal guilt or innocence of any person or whether the President should be impeached. . . . Its conclusions, therefore, must not be interpreted as a final legal judgment. . . .

The Watergate affair reflects an alarming indifference displayed by some in the high public office . . . to concepts of morality and public responsibility and trust. Indeed, the conduct of many Watergate participants seems grounded on the belief that the ends justified the means, that the laws could be flaunted to maintain the present administration in office. . . .

Its major legislative recommendations relate to the creation of new institutions necessary to safeguard the electoral process, to provide the requisite checks against the abuse of executive power and to ensure the prompt and just enforcement of laws that already exist. Surely one of the most penetrating lessons of Watergate is that campaign practices must be effectively supervised and enforcement of the criminal laws vigorously pursued against all offenders— even those of high estate—if our free institutions are to survive. 99

—Senate Select Committee on Presidential Campaign Activities, June 1974

EXAMINE THE SOURCE

1. **Summarizing** What did the Senate Select Committee conclude?

2. **Drawing Conclusions** What does the committee suggest broadly to prevent future abuse of executive power?

Your Inquiry Analysis

EVALUATE SOURCES AND USE EVIDENCE

Refer back to the Compelling Question and the Supporting Questions you developed at the beginning of this lesson.

1. **Gathering Sources** Refer back to the graphic organizer you created as you read through the sources. Consider how the sources you recorded for each of your Supporting Questions most help you answer those questions. Circle or highlight key details from your notes in the graphic organizer, such as the names of media outlets.

2. **Evaluating Sources** Looking at the sources that help you answer the Supporting Questions, evaluate the credibility of each source. In the margins of the graphic organizer, note key opinions and elements of bias.

3. **Comparing and Contrasting** Compare and contrast two of the sources in this lesson more closely. How informative, credible, and influential might the American public in the early 1970s have found these two sources? Explain similarities and differences in the content, authorship, and platform.

COMMUNICATE CONCLUSIONS

Evaluating Claims Write a short response to each of your Supporting Questions. Then, with a partner, explain how your responses to the Supporting Questions help you answer the Compelling Question. Take turns pointing out strengths and weaknesses (at least one each) in one another's gathered evidence. Together, write a paragraph in response to the Compelling Question in which you answer not only the question but also assess whether you have sufficient information to fully address the issue. Present your response to the class or in larger groups.

TAKE INFORMED ACTION

Understand the Process Local, state, and federal government bodies provide processes for investigating and removing elected officials. Individually or in groups, investigate and report on one of these processes. Research the legal framework at your assigned level of government for investigating charges of corruption and abuse of power. What types of misconduct might lead to removal from office? What steps can officials and voters take to hold public officials accountable? How might citizens evaluate the veracity of news reports on the matter? Prepare a digital "citizens' guide" to public accountability. As a class, discuss similarities and differences at the local, state, and federal levels.

United States Senate. Select Committee on Presidential Campaign Activities. Final Report. Washington: U.S. Government Printing Office, 1974.

04

The Reagan Revolution

"Looting and Liberal Racism," by Midge Decter, published September 1977, copyright © Commentary.

READING STRATEGY

Analyzing Key Ideas and Details As you read about the resurgence of conservatism, complete a graphic organizer like the one below. Use the major headings of this section to outline information about the rise of the new conservatism in the United States.

The Reagan Revolution

I. Conservatism Revives

   A.

   B.

II.

   A.

Conservatism Revives

GUIDING QUESTION

How do liberals and conservatives view the role of government?

Conservative writer Midge Decter was appalled at the looting and arson that rocked New York City during a blackout on the night of July 13, 1977. City officials and the media blamed the events on the anger and despair of youth in neglected areas. Decter disagreed:

> ❝ [T]hose young men went on their spree of looting because they had been given permission to do so. They had been given permission to do so by all the papers and magazines, movies and documentaries—all the outlets for the purveying of enlightened liberal attitude and progressive liberal policy—which had for years and years been proclaiming that race and poverty were sufficient excuses for lawlessness. ❞

—from "Looting and Liberal Racism," *Commentary*, September 1977

Decter's article blaming liberalism for the New York riots illustrates one side of a debate in American politics that continues today. On one side are people who call themselves **liberals**; on the other side are those who identify as **conservatives.** In the 1960s, liberal ideas dominated U.S. politics. Conservative ideas gained support in the 1970s. In 1980 conservative Ronald Reagan was elected president.

Liberalism

Modern liberals generally believe that government should regulate the economy to protect people from the power of corporations and wealthy elites. Unlike radicals, who promote state ownership, liberals favor capitalism as the government philosophy of economic affairs. They seek to expand access to American prosperity and democracy equitably through civil rights measures. Liberals also believe that the federal government should help disadvantaged Americans through social programs and by putting more of society's tax burden on wealthier people. They believe that those with greater assets should take on more of the costs of government.

Although liberals favor government intervention in the economy, they do not support the government regulating social behavior. They are opposed to the government supporting or endorsing religious beliefs, no matter how indirectly. They believe that a society with ethnic and cultural diversity tends to be more creative and energetic.

Conservatism

Conservatives distrust government regulation of the economy and wish to limit social welfare programs. They also believe that government regulation makes the economy less efficient and that free enterprise is the best economic system. They argue that increased economic regulation could lead to regulation in every aspect of people's behavior. Conservatives are in favor of strengthened national security as well as expanded spending of tax dollars on defense. They also favor laws and policies that enforce traditional structures of marriage and

---

liberal a person who supports socially progressive policies and government-funded social programs

conservative a person who promotes free enterprise, private ownership, and limited government involvement

---

Barry Goldwater, Republican candidate for president, campaigns on the steps of the Idaho State Capitol in Boise in September 1964.

Analyzing Visuals What can you observe about the spectators at Goldwater's campaign stop? How might you interpret this information?

family. Conservatives generally oppose high taxes and government programs, such as Project Head Start and the Child Nutrition Act that were part of President Johnson's Great Society.

Conservatives generally believe that social problems result from issues of morality and character. They often argue that such issues are best addressed through commitment to a religious faith and through the private efforts of churches, individuals, and communities to help those in need. Despite this general belief, conservatives often support the use of police powers to regulate social behavior.

The Role of the Cold War

The Cold War had helped rekindle support for conservative ideas. First, the struggle against communism revived the debate about the role of the government in the economy. Some Americans believed that liberal economic ideas were leading the United States to communism. They also thought the United States had failed to stop the spread of Soviet power because liberals did not fully support a strong anticommunist foreign policy, even though liberal presidents like Truman, Kennedy, and Johnson had promoted strong foreign policies against communism. Some Americans viewed the Cold War in religious terms and saw communism as a contest between good and evil. Liberalism gradually lost the support of these Americans as they turned to conservatism.

Conservatives Organize

In 1955 a young conservative, William F. Buckley, founded a magazine called *National Review*, which promoted conservative ideas. In 1960 some 90 young conservative leaders met at Buckley's family estate and founded Young Americans for Freedom (YAF). This independent conservative group supported conservative candidates. By 1964, the new conservative movement had achieved enough influence within the Republican Party to enable the conservative Barry Goldwater to win the nomination for president. President Lyndon Johnson defeated him by a landslide.

Sunbelt Conservatism

In the 1950s and early 1960s the South and the West were more conservative than other regions. Southern conservatives, however, generally voted for Democrats, while conservatives in the West voted for Republicans. Thus, the party that won the populous Northeast would win the presidential election. Since the Northeast supported liberal ideas, both parties leaned liberal.

This pattern changed during World War II, when large numbers of Americans moved south and west for jobs in war factories. Sunbelt states experienced dramatic population growth. The movement was fueled by states with warmer climates, such as California and Florida, where tourism increased job opportunities. As the Sunbelt's economy expanded, some of its residents began thinking differently about the government than Northeasterners did.

The declining economy of Midwestern industrial centers such as Pennsylvania, Michigan, and Ohio led to the region's nickname as the Rust Belt. Northeasterners looked to the government to help them solve unemployment, congestion, and pollution. In contrast, many Americans in the Sunbelt opposed high taxes and federal regulations that might interfere with their region's growth, even as government spending had provided the highway infrastructure that made Sunbelt growth possible.

Many white Southerners grew angry with Democrats for supporting civil rights and equal status for African Americans—something they saw as a governmental imposition. During the 1964 election, Southerners began consistently voting for Republicans in large numbers for the first time since Reconstruction because they opposed new federal laws that eliminated segregation policies.

The Religious Right

Some were drawn to conservatism because they feared that society had lost touch with traditional values. Americans of conservative religious faiths were dismayed by Supreme Court decisions protecting a woman's choice for abortion, limiting prayer in public schools, and expanding protections for people accused of crimes.

The push for the Equal Rights Amendment (ERA) also upset some religious conservatives because it challenged traditional family roles. In 1972 Phyllis Schlafly founded the Eagle Forum, a political interest

Bettmann/Getty Images

group, to educate voters and lobby the government on behalf of conservative social issues, particularly involving the family and women's role in society.

Protestant evangelicals represented the largest group of religious conservatives. After World War II, Protestants in the United States experienced a religious revival. Ministers such as Billy Graham and Oral Roberts built national followings, and some owned newspapers, magazines, radio stations, and television networks. Through television, evangelical ministers reached a nationwide audience. These **televangelists** included Marion "Pat" Robertson and Jerry Falwell, founders of the Moral Majority—a network of ministers that registered 2 million new voters in the 1980 election.

Gun Control and the NRA

For many Christians, their single defining issue was the *Roe* v. *Wade* decision upholding the right to abortion. For conservatives, particularly in the South and West, the passage of the Gun Control Act of 1968 became the focus of their concern about growing federal power. Rising crime rates in the 1960s convinced Congress to impose additional regulations and controls on gun sales and ownership. For many gun owners, the law seemed to be a step toward taking away their Second Amendment rights. In response, the National Rifle Association (NRA) began to focus on politics.

The NRA was originally formed in 1871 to help improve people's skills in the use of firearms. It did not engage in extensive lobbying until the 1970s, when conservatives within the organization began an intensive effort to lobby Congress whenever legislation involving gun control was proposed. The NRA's large membership and organizational skills have continued to play an important role in the electoral success of conservative political leaders since then.

The Rise of Think Tanks

Many conservative leaders in the 1970s worried that there was no mechanism for taking broad conservative ideas and turning them into specific policy solutions that the government could implement. Conservatives had been disappointed with Richard Nixon, who had used conservative rhetoric in his speeches, but often supported liberal approaches in governing. Nixon had backed the Family Assistance Plan, the New Economic Policy, and the creation of the EPA, in part because those were the only solutions to specific problems being proposed.

In 1973 several leading conservatives established the Heritage Foundation, the first in a series of think tanks that conservatives created in the 1970s and 1980s. The purpose of the Heritage Foundation, and think tanks in general, is to provide political leaders with research papers, policy ideas, and recommendations

for how to change the law in support of the think tank's values and beliefs. In 1981 the Heritage Foundation published a report with 2,000 specific suggestions on how to reduce the size of the federal government and move government in a conservative direction. President Ronald Reagan's administration realized many of these proposals, and many people at the Heritage Foundation joined the Reagan administration.

With the support of wealthy donors, think tanks have proliferated in the years since. There are dozens of conservative and liberal think tanks today.

The United States had seen political scandal, economic worries, growing federal power, and social turmoil. International events such as the exit from Vietnam made the nation look weak. Those who rejected the turmoil caused by the equality reforms of the 1960s argued that the country had lost its way. All these different political, economic, and social concerns came together as a new conservative coalition in American politics.

✓ CHECK FOR UNDERSTANDING

1. **Speculating** What might a conservative find objectionable about liberal ideas? What might a liberal find objectionable about conservative ideas?
2. **Determining Central Ideas** Why are some regions of the country more conservative or liberal than other areas?

Reagan's Domestic Policies

GUIDING QUESTION

How did Reagan's early personal experiences influence his political beliefs?

As a younger man Ronald Reagan did not hold to the conservative beliefs he would later have. When he was a college student in Eureka, Illinois, he pushed for a student strike. But, over time, his political beliefs also shifted and Reagan began supporting a public philosophy of self-reliance and independence.

After graduating from Eureka College in 1932, Reagan worked as a radio broadcaster and, later, a Hollywood actor. In 1947 Reagan became president of the Screen Actors Guild. As president of the Screen Actors Guild, he testified before the House Un-American Activities Committee. Dealing with Communists in the union motivated Reagan's shift toward conservative ideas.

In the 1950s Reagan traveled the nation to promote the General Electric Company, which sponsored a television program that he hosted. During these travels, Reagan said he met many people who complained about big government. By the time he ran for governor of California in 1966, Reagan was a committed conservative. He made radical student

---

televangelist an evangelical preacher who conducts televised religious sermons

protests a target of his campaign. Reagan won that election and was reelected in 1970. Ten years later, he won the Republican presidential nomination.

Reagan's campaign appealed to frustrated Americans by promising to cut taxes and to make America safer. He appealed to the growing Religious Right and social conservatives by calling for a constitutional amendment banning abortion. Reagan won the election easily. For the first time since 1954, Republicans also gained control of the Senate.

Reaganomics

Reagan believed that the key to restoring the economy was for Americans to believe in themselves again. "In this present crisis," he claimed, "government is not the solution to our problem; government is the problem."

Reagan first turned to the lingering problem of stagflation. Some conservative economists supported the philosophy of **supply-side economics.** They believed that tax cuts could provide extra money to expand businesses and create new jobs. They also believed lower taxes would reward business innovation and strengthen the economy by pushing more money back into the marketplace. The result would be a larger supply of goods for consumers, who would have more to spend. Critics coined this Reaganomics or "trickle-down economics." They believed this policy would help corporations and wealthy Americans, but little wealth would "trickle down" to the middle-class or poor.

Reagan asked Congress to pass a massive 30 percent tax cut. Lower taxes and higher military spending, another of Reagan's priorities, would increase the budget deficit—the amount by which expenditures exceed income. To control the deficit, Reagan proposed cuts to social programs.

After vigorous debate, Congress passed a 25 percent tax cut and some cuts to social programs that benefited low-income Americans, including school lunch programs, food stamp programs, and Aid to Families with Dependent Children. The fight convinced Reagan that Congress would never cut spending enough to balance the budget. He decided building up the military and cutting taxes were more important than a balanced budget. The national debt tripled during his presidency.

Reagan believed that excessive government regulation was another reason for the economy's problems. His first act as president was to sign an executive order to end price controls on oil and gasoline. Deregulation in broadcasting, banking, and automotive industries soon followed. Increased oil drilling, mining, and logging on public land angered

environmentalists, as did EPA decisions easing regulations on pollution-control equipment and reducing safety checks on chemicals and pesticides.

Unemployment climbed to almost 11 percent as the result of a recession in 1982, but by 1984, the nation entered the biggest economic expansion in its history. Incomes climbed and unemployment fell, but the wealthiest Americans experienced the greatest gains. The economic recovery boosted Reagan's popularity, and he won the 1984 election in a landslide against Democrats Walter Mondale and Representative Geraldine Ferraro, the first woman nominated as vice president by a major party.

Shifting the Judicial Balance

Reagan tried to bring a strict constructionist outlook to the judiciary and sought judges who followed the original intent of the Constitution. He nominated Sandra Day O'Connor, who became the first female justice in 1981. In 1986 Reagan chose conservative associate justice William Rehnquist to succeed retiring chief justice Warren Burger, and named conservative judge Antonin Scalia to fill Rehnquist's vacancy. In 1987, after his nomination of the conservative Robert Bork failed, Reagan nominated moderate Anthony Kennedy as a new associate justice.

✓ **CHECK FOR UNDERSTANDING**

Summarizing What did Reagan think was the least important aspect of his fiscal policy: balancing the budget, cutting taxes, or building up the military?

A Booming Economy

GUIDING QUESTION

How did discount retailing and new forms of media contribute to the economic boom of the 1980s?

The strong economic growth of the 1980s mostly benefited middle- and upper-class Americans. From 1967 to 1986, the amount of money earned by the top 5 percent of Americans fluctuated between 14.4 and 16.5 percent of the nation's aggregate family income. In the late 1980s, their share of the nation's income began to rise. By the mid-1990s, the top 5 percent of Americans earned over 20 percent of the nation's income.

A Revolution in Retail and Media

In addition to the booming real estate and stock markets, the economy witnessed a revolution in retail sales with the growth of **discount retailing.** Discount retailers sold large quantities at low prices, turning over their entire inventory in a short time. This ability to sell cheaper goods also depended on selling foreign

supply-side economics an economic theory that lower taxes and decreased regulation will boost the economy as businesses and individuals invest their money, thereby creating higher tax revenue

discount retailing selling large quantities of goods at very low prices to turn over inventory in a short period of time

Ronald Reagan, Inaugural Address, January 20, 1981, The Ronald Reagan Presidential Library, National Archives and Records Administration.

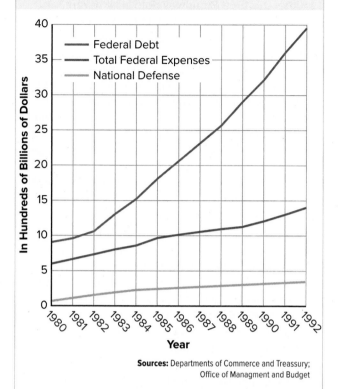

The Budget Deficit

As a result of Reagan's economic policies, the national debt increased rapidly.

In Hundreds of Billions of Dollars (y-axis)

Legend:
- Federal Debt
- Total Federal Expenses
- National Defense

Year (x-axis): 1980, 1981, 1982, 1983, 1984, 1985, 1986, 1987, 1988, 1989, 1990, 1991, 1992

Sources: Departments of Commerce and Treassury; Office of Managment and Budget

GEOGRAPHY CONNECTION

Explaining Why do you think the federal debt rose faster than total expenses?

imports from companies that paid very low labor costs. Discount retailers made more money than traditional retailers who sold fewer products at higher prices.

The most successful discount retailer was Sam Walton, the founder of Walmart. Annual sales at Walmart increased from about $2 billion in 1980 to over $20 billion by 1988. By 1985, he had become the richest person in the United States. Walton was one of the first retailers to track inventory and sales with a computer database. He also used distribution centers to resupply stores. New "superstores" created millions of jobs in the 1980s and helped fuel economic growth.

Until the late 1970s, television viewers were limited to three national networks, local stations, and the public television network. In 1970 Ted Turner bought a failing television station in Atlanta, Georgia. He pioneered a new type of broadcasting by creating WTBS in 1975. WTBS was the first television station that sold low-cost sports and entertainment programs via satellite to cable companies across the nation. In 1980 entrepreneur Robert Johnson created Black Entertainment Television (BET). In 1981 Music Television (MTV) began broadcasting music videos. Music videos boosted the careers of artists such as Madonna and Michael Jackson.

Oprah Winfrey, a former news reporter for an African American radio station, became an influential media personality in the late 1980s. Her show was syndicated on more than one hundred channels nationwide. She expanded her reach with Oprah's Book Club and launched Oxygen Media in 1998, *O: The Oprah Magazine* in 2000, and the Oprah Winfrey Network (OWN) in 2011. Rap music was the new sound of the 1980s. Originating in local clubs in New York City's South Bronx, rap emphasized heavy bass and rhythmic sounds and lyrics that frequently focused on the African American experience in the inner city. Its popularity made rap a multimillion-dollar industry.

New Technologies

Until the 1980s, most people listened to music on home stereo systems or relied on the car radio when they were driving. The new Sony Walkman made music portable. In the 1990s, portable compact disc (CD) players replaced the Walkman, and in the early 2000s, digital audio players, such as the iPod and MP3 players, advanced the technology even further.

Videocassette recorders (VCRs) allowed people to tape television shows or watch taped films whenever they wished. By the early 2000s, digital video disc (DVD) recorders began replacing VCRs. Initially the entertainment industry worried that VCRs would lead to copyright violations, but when the Supreme Court ruled in *Sony Corp. of America* v. *Universal City Studios* that people could record shows and movies for home use, Hollywood quickly adapted. Studios realized that the VCR created a demand for home editions of movies. VCRs helped spread American culture around the globe. By the 1980s, Hollywood movies were often making more money overseas than they were in the U.S.

Video games grew out of military computer technology. The first video arcade game, released in 1972, was *Pong*. Home video games developed quickly. In the early 1980s, sales reached about $3 billion with the popularity of games such as *Pac-Man* and *Space Invaders*. By the mid-1980s, home video games competed with arcade games in graphics and speed.

The Global Positioning System (GPS) also emerged in the 1980s. The GPS is composed of a series of satellites in low-earth orbit that allow users to precisely determine their location and navigate accurately. The first GPS satellite went into orbit in 1989, and the system was completed in 1994. Technology companies quickly and widely adopted it for air and sea navigation. They found ways to build inexpensive GPS units that drivers could use in their cars. Modern cell phones began incorporating GPS signals.

✓ **CHECK FOR UNDERSTANDING**

Summarizing How did discount retailing and new forms of media contribute to the economic boom of the 1980s?

New Social Activism

Why did new activist groups form in the 1980s?

Drug abuse in the 1980s made many urban neighborhoods dangerous. The rising use of crack cocaine, a highly addictive and inexpensive street drug, particularly ravaged African American communities. Drug use and trafficking contributed to rising crime and incarceration rates as drug users often committed crimes to get money for drugs.

President Reagan launched a "War on Drugs" that relied on tough policing and increased prison sentences. Young African American men were disproportionately arrested and imprisoned in growing numbers. By the late 1980s, the criminal justice system had placed some 25 percent of African American men between the ages of 20 and 29 under some form of formal supervision, such as imprisonment, probation, or parole. The prison population, especially those incarcerated for drug offenses, increased dramatically.

To reduce teen drug use, some schools began searching student bags and lockers for drugs. In 1984 one teen who had been arrested for selling drugs challenged the school's right to search her purse without a warrant. In 1985 the Supreme Court case *New Jersey* v. *T.L.O.* upheld the school's right to search without a warrant if it had probable cause. Similarly, the 1995 case *Vernonia School District* v. *Acton* held that random drug tests do not violate students' Fourth Amendment rights.

Alcohol abuse was also a serious concern. In 1980 Mothers Against Drunk Driving (MADD) was founded to try to stop underage drinking and drunk driving, and "[t]o increase public awareness of the problem of drinking and drugged driving." In 1984 Congress cut highway funds to any state that did not raise the legal drinking age to 21.

Activist Groups

In 1981 researchers identified a deadly disease that they named "acquired immunodeficiency syndrome," or AIDS. AIDS weakens the immune system. In the United States, AIDS was first noticed among gay men. Soon, though, it was noted throughout the general population. Many people were infected by their sexual partners. Between 1981 and 1988, the Centers for Disease Control and Prevention identified more than 100,000 cases in the country. In part because of the disease's early association with gay men, the government was slow to respond.

The number of AIDS-related deaths, combined with the lack of government assistance, led to increased activism in the gay and lesbian community. This increase in activism resulted in the creation of organizations such as AIDS Coalition To Unleash Power (ACT UP). The fight against AIDS increased the visibility of the country's gay and lesbian community, but LGBTQ activists had been active well before the 1960s.

After the 1969 Stonewall riots in New York, organizations such as the Gay Liberation Front began efforts to increase tolerance of differing sexual orientations and diverse gender identities. Some of the frustrations in the LGBTQ community stemmed from Reagan's conservative political opposition to the rights the community wanted, including the right to marry. Many conservatives did not wish to grant the right of marriage to same-sex couples. But the AIDS crisis motivated LGBTQ activists to request marriage protections as their partners died of the disease. Conservatives responded by defining marriage legally as a union between a man and a woman. This fight would continue for the next several decades.

The anti-abortion, or pro-life, movement, also grew in the 1980s. A surge in evangelical Christians joining these groups led to a sustained effort to outlaw or limit abortion through legislation. Some anti-abortion groups employed radical methods, such as blockading reproductive health clinics, threatening staff, and even committing acts of violence.

Senior citizens became politically active in the 1980s. Improvements in medicine had resulted in more Americans surviving to an older age. The birthrate had also declined, so younger people represented a comparatively smaller proportion of the population. The fact that more Americans were receiving Social Security payments created budget pressures for the government. Older Americans became very vocal in the political arena, opposing cuts in Social Security or Medicare. Because they tend to vote in large numbers, senior citizens are an influential interest group. Their lobbying organization is AARP, formerly the American Association of Retired Persons.

✓ CHECK FOR UNDERSTANDING

Comparing and Contrasting How have the social issues that affected the United States during the 1980s changed?

LESSON ACTIVITIES

1. **Informative/Explanatory Writing** Select one technological innovation from the 1980s, state whether it is part of everyday life today, and if so, explain whether it has or has not changed. Use descriptive language to convey your information.

2. **Collaborating** As a group, research the role of religion as a political factor in recent presidential elections. When researching, consider if there is regional data that indicates the importance of religion. How has religion played a role in the major party presidential nominees in the most recent four elections? Discuss your research as a class.

MADD's Articles of Incorporation, 1980.

05

The New World Order

Uprisings Following the Soviet Union's Fall

GUIDING QUESTION

How did the end of the Cold War lead to more global U.S. military conflicts?

<table>
<tr><td colspan="2">READING STRATEGY</td></tr>
<tr><td colspan="2"><u>Analyzing Key Ideas and Details</u> As you read, use a graphic organizer like the one below to take notes on U.S. foreign policy in each of the places listed.</td></tr>
</table>

Place	Foreign Policy
Soviet Union	
China	
Panama	
Middle East	

When Ronald Reagan left office, his domestic policies remained popular. In 1988 Republicans nominated Vice President George H.W. Bush, who promised to do just that. Bush easily won the general election against Democrat Michael Dukakis. Though voters had focused on domestic issues during the campaign, President Bush had to focus on foreign policy soon after taking office.

After the Cold War, President Bush noted that a "new world order" was emerging that introduced new military challenges around the globe. For example, U.S. troops led Operation Restore Hope, providing humanitarian assistance and famine relief to refugees in Somalia. Western aid had supported Somalia during the 1980s due to its strategic location near Middle Eastern oil fields, but with the end of the Cold War, its importance—and U.S. aid—waned.

In South Africa, a system of apartheid, or racial segregation, had kept black and white citizens separated since the early 1900s. This system grew and intensified in the late 1940s, when the white Nationalist Party began blocking political protests by nonwhites. In the 1960s, black leaders of the African National Congress (ANC), such as Nelson Mandela, were facing lifetime imprisonment for their political activism.

The U.S. government had long endured the apartheid system because it saw an ally in the anti-communist South African government. In 1986, however, Congress overrode President Reagan's veto and passed legislation that imposed economic sanctions on South Africa. Spurred by protests, U.S. companies began to divest from the country. After suffering from pressure by the United States and other countries, South Africa finally brought the system of apartheid to an end in the early 1990s.

Panama

In 1978 the United States agreed to transfer control of the Panama Canal to Panama by the year 2000. Given the canal's importance, U.S. officials wanted to make sure Panama's government was both stable and pro-United States. But by 1989, Panama's dictator, General Manuel Noriega, was aiding drug traffickers and harassing American military personnel defending the canal. In December 1989, U.S. troops invaded Panama and seized Noriega, who was sent to the United States to stand trial on drug charges. The troops then helped the Panamanians hold elections and organize a new government.

The Persian Gulf War

President Bush faced perhaps his most serious crisis in the Middle East when Iraqi dictator Saddam Hussein invaded oil-rich Kuwait in August 1990. U.S. officials feared that the invasion might be only the first step in Iraq's ultimate goal of capturing Saudi Arabia and its vast oil reserves. Bush persuaded other United Nations member countries from Europe, the Middle East, and Canada to join a coalition to stop Iraq. The United Nations set a deadline for Iraqi withdrawal from Kuwait, after which the coalition would use force to remove them, and Congress also voted to authorize force if Iraq did not withdraw.

The Persian Gulf War, 1991

After its invasion of Kuwait, Iraq was defeated by a U.S.-led coalition of troops.

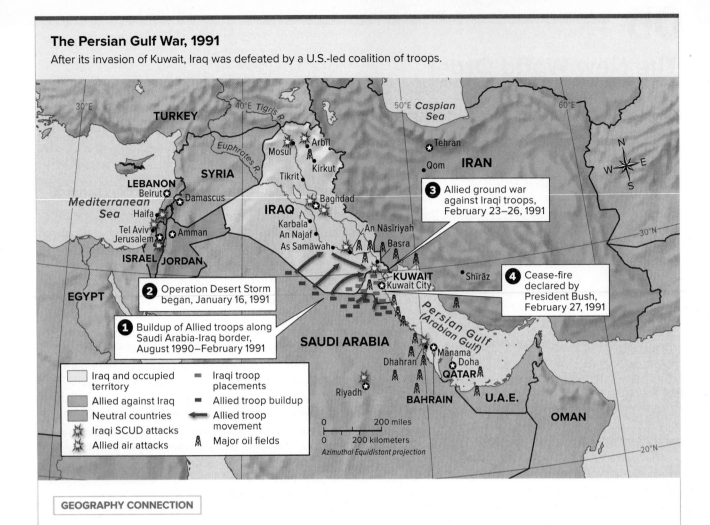

Colin Powell, Oral History interview, "The Gulf War". Courtesy of WGBH Boston. Copyright © WGBH Educational Foundation.

GEOGRAPHY CONNECTION

1. **Exploring Regions** What is the most likely reason that Allied troops staged their invasion of Iraq from Saudi Arabia?

2. **Human-Environment Interaction** Which Middle East nations remained neutral during the war, and which nations did Iraq attack with SCUD missiles?

By October 31, 1990, General Colin Powell, chairman of the Joint Chiefs of Staff, Secretary of Defense Dick Cheney, and other high-ranking officials met with President Bush. It was clear that Iraq would not comply with the UN deadline. Powell presented the plan for attacking Iraq. "Mr. President," Powell began, "[w]e've gotta take the initiative out of the enemy's hands if we're going to go to war." Cheney later recalled that Bush "never hesitated." He looked up from the plans and simply said, "Do it."

On January 16, 1991, coalition forces launched Operation Desert Storm. Cruise missiles and laser-guided bombs fell on Iraq, destroying its air defenses, bridges, artillery, and other military targets. After about six weeks, the coalition launched a massive ground attack. Thousands of Iraqi soldiers died, but fewer than 300 coalition troops were killed. Just 100 hours after the ground war began, Bush declared Kuwait to be liberated. Iraq accepted the cease-fire terms, and American troops returned home to cheering crowds.

The quick U.S. withdrawal left Hussein in power but kept Kuwait's oil fields out of Iraqi control.

✓ **CHECK FOR UNDERSTANDING**

Identifying Cause and Effect How did the end of the Cold War lead to more global U.S. military conflicts?

Domestic Challenges

GUIDING QUESTION

Why did President George H.W. Bush lose his bid for reelection in 1992?

President Bush spent much of his time dealing with foreign policy, but he could not ignore domestic issues due to a growing deficit and a slowing economy inherited from his predecessor. With the Persian Gulf crisis, the economy plunged into a recession and unemployment rose.

The recession that began in 1990 was partly due to the end of the Cold War. As the Soviet threat faded, the nation cut back on military spending, and soldiers and defense industry workers were laid off. Other companies also began **downsizing**—laying off workers to become more efficient.

The nation's high level of debt made the recession worse. The huge deficit forced the government to borrow money to pay for its programs, keeping money from being available to businesses. The government also had to pay interest on its debt, using money that might otherwise have helped fund programs or boost the economy. The collapse of many savings and loan institutions added to the deficit. After Congress allowed them to deregulate, many had made risky or even dishonest investments. When these investments failed, depositors collected from federal programs that insured deposits. The cost to the public may have reached $500 billion.

As president, Bush tried to improve the economy by calling for a cut in the **capital gains tax**—the tax paid by businesses and investors when they sell stocks or real estate for a profit. Bush believed that the tax cut would encourage businesses to expand, but Democrats in Congress defeated it, calling the idea a tax break for the rich. Aware that the growing federal deficit was hurting the economy, Bush broke his "no new taxes" pledge, and after meeting with congressional leaders, he agreed to a tax increase in exchange for cuts in spending. This decision turned many voters against Bush, damaging his chances for reelection in 1992.

Racial Tensions

Racial tensions added to the nation's domestic upheaval as riots broke out in Los Angeles in the spring of 1992. The riots followed the acquittal of four Los Angeles police officers charged in the beating of African American motorist Rodney King. On March 3, 1991, the four officers had dragged King from his car after a high-speed chase and repeatedly kicked him and beat him with their batons for a reported 15 minutes. King suffered broken teeth and bones and a skull fracture that led to permanent brain damage. A witness captured the beating on video, and the officers were charged with assault with a deadly weapon and use of excessive force.

The officers went on trial in 1992. Unconvinced that the video illustrated and conveyed the entire event, the predominately white, twelve-member jury acquitted the officers. The verdict was announced around 3 p.m. on April 29, and protests and rioting broke out soon after. That night and for several days afterward, rioters looted, set fire to buildings, and destroyed stores and other property.

In response to the riots, Tom Bradley, the mayor of Los Angeles, issued a state of emergency, and Governor Pete Wilson called in National Guard troops. As the rioting increased, shutting down much of the city, Rodney King called for calm. President Bush sent several thousand federal military troops and law enforcement officers to help combat the rioting. By May 4, the rioting had stopped, leaving more than 50 dead and around $1 billion in property damage. Two of the officers were later convicted in civil court of infringing on King's civil rights.

The Clarence Thomas Hearings

The nation was also riveted by the 1991 Senate confirmation hearing of Clarence Thomas, an African American judge whom President Bush nominated to fill Thurgood Marshall's seat on the U.S. Supreme Court. During Thomas's controversial confirmation, his former aide, Anita Hill, testified that he had sexually harassed her when she worked for him at the Department of Education and the Equal Employment Opportunity Commission.

The televised hearings shocked many Americans, not only because of Hill's frank explanation of events, but also because of the response of the all-male, all-white Senate committee. The committee members were unsympathetic toward Hill, and some were even antagonistic. Thomas vehemently denied the allegations, and some witnesses attacked Hill's mental stability and character. In the end, the Senate narrowly confirmed Thomas. Nevertheless, Hill's allegations emphasized the ongoing problem of sexual harassment in the workplace and helped spur women to run for state and national offices to have a stronger

On April 29 angry residents of Los Angeles protested the acquittal of four police officers charged with the beating of Rodney King.

Analyzing Visuals What does the photograph show about the relationship between the police and people of Los Angeles after the Rodney King verdict?

---

downsizing reducing the size of a company by laying off its employees

capital gains tax a federal tax that businesses and investors pay when they sell stocks or real estate

Gene Blevins/ZUMA Press/Newscom.

voice in creating laws to protect those who experience sexual harassment.

The 1992 Election

Although the recession had hurt his popularity, Bush won the Republican nomination. He promised to address voters' economic concerns and blamed congressional Democrats for the government's gridlock. The Democrats nominated Arkansas governor William Jefferson Clinton, despite stories questioning his character and evasion of military service. Calling himself a "New Democrat," Clinton promised to reduce government spending, to cut middle-class taxes, and reform the nation's health care and welfare programs. His campaign blamed Bush for the recession. An independent candidate, billionaire Texas businessman H. Ross Perot, was also a strong challenger. He stressed the need to end deficit spending. His no-nonsense style appealed widely, and a **grassroots movement**— groups of people organizing at the local level—put Perot on the ballot in all 50 states.

Clinton won the election with 43 percent of the popular vote and 370 electoral votes. Bush won 37 percent of the popular vote, and Perot 19 percent.

The Democrats also retained control of Congress. At 46 years old, Clinton was the first baby boomer to occupy the White House. It was his task to revive the economy and guide the United States in a rapidly changing world.

✓ CHECK FOR UNDERSTANDING

1. **Summarizing** Why did President George H.W. Bush lose his bid for reelection in 1992?
2. **Making Connections** Who did Bush blame for his inability to initiate his economic reforms?

The New Global Economy

GUIDING QUESTION

How did NAFTA and other regional trading blocs affect the global economy?

During the 1990s, economies of individual nations became more interdependent as new technology helped link the world monetarily and culturally. Many world leaders were convinced that free trade and the global exchange of goods contributed to prosperity and economic growth. The concept of the world becoming increasingly interconnected is called globalism, and the process is globalization.

Selling American-made goods abroad has long been important to U.S. prosperity. American businesses make money selling goods abroad, and consumers benefit by having the option to buy cheaper imported goods. Opponents, however, argue that global trade comes at the expense of American worker's jobs. The debate is still an ongoing part of American politics.

Regional Blocs

Regional trade pacts, such as the North American Free Trade Agreement (NAFTA), increase international trade. Approved by Congress in 1993, NAFTA linked Canada, the United States, and Mexico in a free-trade zone that increased trade between the three countries. Because there were no tariffs to impede free trade, factories in Mexico would import raw materials from the United States, use the materials to produce finished products, and then export the finished products—often back to the country in which the materials originated. These factories, known as *maquiladoras*, were often located in zones called export processing zones that were set up to encourage exports and encourage foreign companies to invest and build factories.

Many Americans feared that NAFTA would cause industrial jobs to move to Mexico, where labor costs were lower. Jobs were lost as low-skill manufacturing was **outsourced,** but the U.S. unemployment rate actually fell and wages rose. Many U.S. businesses upgraded their technology, and workers shifted to more skilled jobs or to the service industry. However, because the regional agreement undercut the price of Mexican-grown agricultural products, many Mexican farmers were pushed off their land and crossed the border into the United States for work.

In 1993 the European Union (EU) was created to promote economic and political cooperation among European nations. It encouraged free trade, established a common bank, and created a common currency called the **euro,** adopted by some nations. The Asia-Pacific Economic Cooperation (APEC) formed in 1989 to promote economic cooperation and lower trade barriers, but major political differences kept its members from acting together.

The World Trade Organization

In 1994, 121 nations signed an agreement to form the World Trade Organization (WTO) to represent them in negotiations on international trade agreements and trade disputes. U.S. supporters of the WTO cited benefits for American consumers, including cheaper

---

grassroots movement a group of citizens organizing at the local or community level

outsourced having moved labor to another country to lower its costs

euro the currency shared by members of the European Union

Clinton, William. 2000. "Address at Vietnam National University." Hanoi, November 17. The William J. Clinton Presidential Library, National Archives and Records Administration.

World Trading Blocs

Global trading blocs have formed to increase international trade.

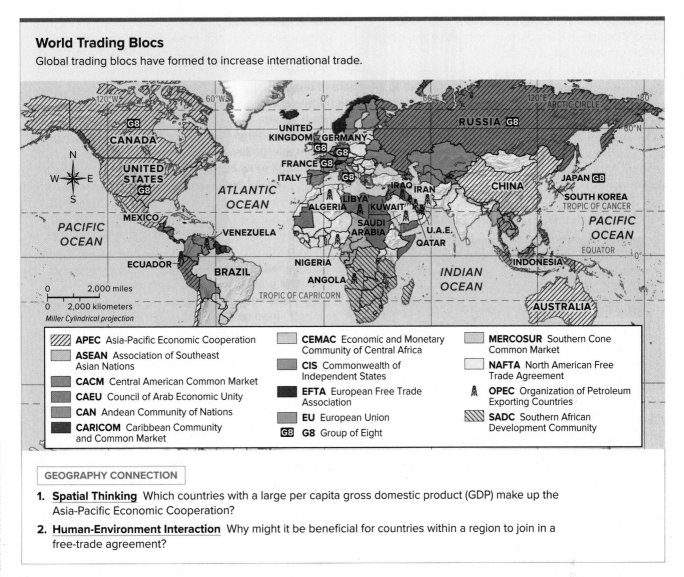

APEC Asia-Pacific Economic Cooperation

ASEAN Association of Southeast Asian Nations

CACM Central American Common Market

CAEU Council of Arab Economic Unity

CAN Andean Community of Nations

CARICOM Caribbean Community and Common Market

CEMAC Economic and Monetary Community of Central Africa

CIS Commonwealth of Independent States

EFTA European Free Trade Association

EU European Union

G8 Group of Eight

MERCOSUR Southern Cone Common Market

NAFTA North American Free Trade Agreement

OPEC Organization of Petroleum Exporting Countries

SADC Southern African Development Community

GEOGRAPHY CONNECTION

1. **Spatial Thinking** Which countries with a large per capita gross domestic product (GDP) make up the Asia-Pacific Economic Cooperation?

2. **Human-Environment Interaction** Why might it be beneficial for countries within a region to join in a free-trade agreement?

imports, new markets, and copyright protection. Opponents argued that the United States would have to accept the WTO's rulings in trade disputes even if the rulings hurt the U.S. economy.

Trade with China

China presented a huge potential market for U.S. goods, but made a worrisome trading partner due to its poor human rights record. President Clinton nevertheless urged Congress to grant China permanent normal trade relation status, and despite objections, Congress passed the bill in late 2000. Clinton spoke in favor of globalization:

66 Even as people take pride in their national independence, we know we are becoming more and more interdependent. The movement of people, money, and ideas across borders, frankly, breeds suspicion among many good people in every country. They are worried about globalization because of its unsettling and unpredictable consequences.

Yet, globalization is not something we can hold off or turn off. It is the economic equivalent of a force of nature, like wind or water. We can harness wind to fill a sail. We can use water to generate energy. We can work hard to protect people and property from storms and floods. But there is no point in denying the existence of wind or water, or trying to make them go away. The same is true for globalization. We can work to maximize its benefits and minimize its risks, but we cannot ignore it and it is not going away. 99

—President Bill Clinton, from an address at Vietnam National University, November 17, 2000

Tiananmen Square

Despite the collapse of communism elsewhere, China's Communist leaders remained determined to stay in power. China's government had relaxed controls on the economy but continued to repress political speech. In April and May 1989 Chinese students and workers held pro-democracy demonstrations at Tiananmen Square in Beijing, China's capital. In early June, government tanks and soldiers crushed the protests.

Troops killed several hundred demonstrators. Hundreds more pro-democracy activists were arrested and later sentenced to death. Shocked, the United States and several European countries halted arms sales and curtailed diplomatic contacts with China, and the World Bank suspended loans. President Bush resisted harsher sanctions, preferring to rely on trade and diplomacy.

The Computer Changes Society

Globalization was not the only change that altered the world. Technological innovation in the form of computers, telecommunications, and the Internet also revolutionized how people lived and worked.

The first electronic digital computer began operation in 1946 and was the size of a small house. In 1959 Robert Noyce designed the first integrated circuit—a whole electronic circuit on a single silicon chip. In 1968 Noyce's company, Intel, put several integrated circuits on a single chip, making circuits much smaller and easier to manufacture. By the late 1960s, manufacturers were making microprocessors, or single chips with many integrated circuits containing both memory and computing functions. These microprocessors made computers smaller and faster.

Using microprocessor technology, Steve Jobs and Stephen Wozniak set out to build a small computer suitable for personal use. They founded Apple Computer in 1976, and the following year they launched the Apple II—the first practical and affordable home computer. In 1981 International Business Machines (IBM) introduced the "Personal Computer," or PC. In 1984 Apple put out the Macintosh, which used on-screen icons that users could manipulate with a mouse.

As Jobs and Wozniak were creating Apple, Bill Gates cofounded Microsoft with Paul Allen. In 1980 IBM hired Microsoft to make an operating system for its new PC. The system was called MS-DOS, and Microsoft came out with the "Windows" operating system in 1985. Computers became essential tools for almost all businesses. By the late 1990s, many workers were able to telecommute, or work from home via computer.

Telecommunications also underwent a revolution. In 1996 Congress passed a law breaking up the telephone monopoly and allowing phone companies to compete with one another and to send television signals. It also allowed cable companies to offer telephone service. Soon wireless digital technology made it possible to produce small, inexpensive satellite dishes for home use.

Cell phones, invented in the 1940s, became popular as technology made phones smaller and service cheaper. As technology advanced, companies developed connectible digital music players, cameras, radios, televisions, and music and video recorders.

The Rise of the Internet

The Internet began as a system of networked computers of a U.S. Department of Defense agency that linked to a system of networked supercomputers of the National Science Foundation. Similar networks grew across the world, and this communications system became known as the Internet. As personal computer ownership rose, individuals—rather than just government agencies—began connecting to the Internet, and by 2007 more than 1 billion people around the world were regularly using the Internet.

In 1990 researchers in Switzerland developed a new way to present information on Internet-linked computers. Known as the World Wide Web, this system used hypertext, or "links," and was accessed by Web browser software. Users could post information on Web pages and use links to move between sites.

Enthusiasm for the World Wide Web spawned a "dot-com" economy, and the stock of Internet-related companies helped fuel the prosperity of the 1990s. It fell dramatically in 2000 when many unprofitable online companies failed, but a few "dot-com" companies were very successful. This new economy also required American workers to acquire new skills. This retraining increased productivity as well as the nation's gross domestic product (GDP). Driven by the information technology industry, the GDP rose more than 20 percent during the mid- to late 1990s.

☑ **CHECK FOR UNDERSTANDING**

1. **Identifying** How did NAFTA and other regional trading blocs affect the global economy?

2. **Explaining** How did the computer revolution change the workplace?

LESSON ACTIVITIES

1. **Narrative Writing** Imagine what your life would be like without technological developments such as the Internet and the cell phone. Write a short narrative in which you describe how your typical day would be different without these types of technology.

2. **Presenting** Work in groups of four to research, write, and present brief monologues describing the life experiences of various people during the 1990s. You may each play the role of a Bush supporter, a Perot supporter, a Clinton supporter, a Soviet citizen, a Tiananmen Square protester, a Panamanian citizen, an Iraqi citizen, a U.S. citizen, or any other person of the time. Ask your classmates to take notes for an after-presentation class discussion. Prepare at least two discussion questions for each character that is presented.

Turning Point: The Computer Changes Society

 COMPELLING QUESTION

To what extent has the invention of the computer transformed society?

Plan Your Inquiry

In this lesson, you will investigate the impact of computer technology on the United States.

DEVELOP QUESTIONS

Developing Questions About the Impact of Computers Read the Compelling Question for this lesson. Consider how computer technology developed in the late 1900s and early 2000s and how computers changed life in the United States. Develop a list of Supporting Questions that would help you answer the Compelling Question in this lesson.

APPLY HISTORICAL TOOLS

Analyzing Primary and Secondary Sources You will work with a variety of primary and secondary sources in this lesson. These sources focus on the development of computer technology and its impact on the American economy and society. As you read, use a graphic organizer like the one below to record information about the sources that will help you examine them and check for historical understanding. Note ways in which each source helps you answer your Supporting Questions.

Source	Author/ Creator	Description/ Notes	Which Supporting Question does this source help me answer?
A			
B			
C			
D			

After you analyze the sources, you will:

- use the evidence from the sources.
- communicate your conclusions.
- take informed action.

Background Information

Today, computer technology is a pervasive and integral part of our daily lives. As of 2016, the U.S. Census Bureau reported that about 89 percent of American households had at least one personal computer or laptop, and the Pew Research Center estimates that about 81 percent of Americans own smartphones. We use computer-based, or digital, technology like the Internet to learn, communicate, buy and sell goods, get directions, get X-rays, watch movies, and more.

Technology has come a long way since 1946 when the first digital computer—known as ENIAC (Electronic Numerical Integrator and Computer)—powered up. ENIAC was huge; made of 40 tall panels, it took up an entire 50-by-30-foot (15-by-9-meter) basement. Rapid innovations produced smaller and faster computers, largely through the development of components like microprocessors, which combined multiple functions in a single chip. In the 1970s companies such as IBM, Commodore, and Apple rolled out the first personal computers. Then came giant leaps in software: Microsoft's MS-DOS in 1981, Apple's first graphic user interface (GUI) in 1983, and Microsoft Windows software in 1985.

Meanwhile, other scientists had been developing a new way to network computers. Although the first connection was in 1969, the Internet remained a well-kept secret for years. Then, in the 1990s, the World Wide Web launched the digital age of e-mail, e-commerce, social media, emojis, and near-instantaneous global connectivity.

» Personal computers such as the Apple II revolutionized commerce, communication, and other facets of American society.

MIKE BLAKE/REUTERS/Newscom

Government Support for Computing Research

The U.S. government funded computer research during World War II, largely to improve weapons and communications. After the war, the government expanded research and development to include applications across a wide range of civil, economic, and scientific areas.

SECONDARY SOURCE : BOOK

66 Between 1993 and 1994, 1,619 patents were issued in the United States containing references to papers published in computing-related journals. . . . Despite the fact that 75 percent of these patents were issued to U.S. companies, the majority of the papers cited by these patents were written by university or government researchers. . . . Moreover, of the papers for which funding information is available, 51 percent acknowledged funding from the federal government, whereas 37 percent acknowledged industry funding. NSF [National Science Foundation] support was acknowledged in 22 percent of the papers, DARPA [Defense Advanced Research Projects Agency] support in 6 percent. These data . . . suggest that federally sponsored research . . . continue to contribute to innovation in computing. . . .

[T]he federal government has played an important role in helping to create the research infrastructure needed to support the nation's computing industry. The federal government became the primary source of funding for university research in computer science and electrical engineering. . . . It also became the primary supporter of graduate students studying . . . in these fields. 99

—National Research Council, *Funding a Revolution: Government Support for Computing Research,* 1999

EXAMINE THE SOURCE

1. **Describing** Describe the roles of government and business in the development of the computing industry during the early 1990s.
2. **Drawing Conclusions** What does this source suggest about the importance of computer technology?

Creating the Internet

In 1916 the National Academy of Sciences launched the National Research Council to coordinate efforts among government, industry, and academic institutions.

SECONDARY SOURCE : BOOK

66 Digital transmission became possible throughout the telephone network with the deployment of optical fiber. . . . In April 1995, all commercialization restrictions on the Internet were lifted. Although still primarily used by academics and businesses, the Internet was growing, with the number of hosts reaching 250,000. Then the invention of the Web catapulted the Internet to mass popularity almost overnight.

The idea for the Web was simple: provide a common format for documents stored on server computers, and give each document a unique name that can be used by a browser program to locate and retrieve the document. Because the unique names (called universal resource locators, or URLs) are long, including the DNS [Domain Name System] name of the host on which they are stored, URLs would be represented as shorter hypertext links in other documents. When the user of a browser clicks a mouse on a link, the browser retrieves and displays the document named by the URL."

—National Research Council, *Funding a Revolution: Government Support for Computing Research,* 1999

EXAMINE THE SOURCE

1. **Explaining** How did the World Wide Web change the Internet?
2. **Making Connections** What effect did the World Wide Web have on Internet usage?

» Network servers are a key technology supporting digital communication.

PHOTO: dotsinock/Shutterstock; TEXT: (both)Committee on Innovations in Computing and Communications: Lessons from History, Computer Science and Telecommunications Board, Commission on Physical Sciences, Mathematics, and Applications, National Research Council, Funding a Revolution. Government Support for Computing Research. Washington, DC: National Academy Press, 1999.

How Computers Affected the Workforce

Eric Jaffe is an author and journalist based in New York City and the editorial director of Sidewalk Labs, an urban design and technology company. He has worked and written for numerous publications, including *Psychology Today, Los Angeles Times, Boston Globe, Smithsonian Magazine, The Atlantic,* and *Slate*. In this article, Jaffe explores the effects of computer technology on urban life—particularly in relation to jobs, career opportunities, and workplaces.

SECONDARY SOURCE : ARTICLE

" The rise of computer technology led to all sorts of winners and losers in the modern labor force. Some jobs (bank tellers, telephone operators, typists and the like) became easier to replace with machines; others (programmers, engineers, data analysts, etc.) became more valuable with their arrival. But it wasn't just the fortunes of people that changed with these times—those of entire cities shifted, too, according to a new study of urban labor in the personal computer era.

The key to success, it seems, came down to whether or not residents of a given metro area possessed 'abstract' skills capable of **complementing** computer technology, such as problem-solving, analytical reasoning, and complex communication. Metros with an abstract knowledge-base prospered, report University of Oxford researchers Thor Berger and Carl Benedikt Frey in *Regional Science and Urban Economics*. Those with more 'routine' workforces didn't.

'Although the computer revolution arrived everywhere, it had very different effects based on what types of work cities specialized in,' says Berger via email. 'In cities with an abundance of abstract skills, the computer led to the creation of a wide variety of new work, whereas in cities specializing in routine manufacturing work it led to the displacement of middle-skill workers.'

. . . Berger and Frey reached their conclusion after analyzing U.S. census labor and residential data from 1970 to 2000, alongside trends in new types of jobs and specific job tasks. They characterized these tasks as manual, routine, or abstract labor, then calculated the share of workers in a given city employed in jobs requiring these various skills. All told they included 321 U.S. cities in their study sample.

Crunching those numbers led, first, to a broad insight on changes in the U.S. labor force

» Office workers in the 1990s.

during this time. The researchers found a 'previously undocumented shift' in the skills required for new jobs after 1980, concurrent with enormous improvements in the personal computer. During those decades, computer-related jobs became more popular, computer-related industries experienced the most job growth, and jobs that did grow fast were associated with abstract skills. . . .

'There is a sharp shift in new job creation around 1980—a shift that is intimately associated with the **advent** of the computer,' says Berger. "

—Eric Jaffe, "How the Computer Revolution Changed U.S. Cities," *Bloomberg*, December 28, 2015

complement to enhance or make better by adding a different quality or element
advent coming into being; birth

EXAMINE THE SOURCE

1. **Identifying** What main idea does Jaffe want to express about the unequal impact of technology on different groups? Cite two details that support this idea.

2. **Analyzing** For what purpose does Jaffe use evidence from Berger and Frey's report? How does this information aid your understanding?

PHOTO: Horizon International Images Limited/Alamy Stock Photo; TEXT: Jaffe, Eric. "The Computer Revolution and the Fates of U.S. Cities." Bloomberg CityLab. December 28, 2015.

D

Mobile Phones and Teens

Graduate student Shanthi Ravichandran submitted a thesis based on data gathered through questionnaires and interviews with 115 parents and caregivers of teenagers (aged 13 to 19).

PRIMARY SOURCE : RESEARCH PAPER

66 Parents/caregivers [PACG] of this study express both positive and negative impact towards teenagers' mobile phone usage.

On a positive note, PACG perceive that mobile phones are very useful devices for communication and co-ordination of activities. They also find that they are compulsory as they are used as safety devices especially in emergencies. Voice and text features are considered as the basic required facilities in teenagers' mobile phones by PACG.

On the negative side, PACG express that teenagers are addicted and obsessed with texting, while some of the PACG feel that it distracts the teenagers from their study time and other important activities. Some PACG hold the service providers responsible for this because of texting plans. Bullying and abusive messages have been perceived as the major problem mediated by mobile phones. PACG express that teenagers with their mobile phones are out of control for them. . . .

The overall findings from this study reveal that parents/caregivers' perceptions of teenagers' mobile phone usage are not satisfactory. Although they express a mixed opinion, they lean towards negative impacts. A very high number of interview participants expressed the view that negative impacts outweighing positive purposes with teenagers' mobile phone usage. . . . 99

—S.V. Ravichandran, "Mobile phones and teenagers: Impact, consequences and concerns—parents/caregivers perspectives," Unitec Institute of Technology, 2009

EXAMINE THE SOURCE

1. **Explaining** What benefits and drawbacks to cell phone use among teens does the study identify?

2. **Evaluating** What might be some limitations of this source?

Your Inquiry Analysis

EVALUATE SOURCES AND USE EVIDENCE

Refer back to the Compelling Question and the Supporting Questions you developed at the beginning of this lesson.

1. **Gathering Sources** Refer back to the Graphic Organizer you created as you read through the sources. Consider how the sources you recorded for each of your Supporting Questions most help you answer those questions. Rank each source from most helpful (1) to least (4) for each Supporting Question. What other information or viewpoints would you like to investigate?

2. **Evaluating Sources** Looking at the sources that help you answer the Supporting Questions, summarize the technological changes that each describes. Then, explain how those innovations relate to economic, social, and political changes. What other types of sources might be helpful in answering your Supporting Questions or other lingering questions?

3. **Comparing and Contrasting** Compare and contrast the technologies discussed in three sources. List potential benefits and drawbacks for each. Circle similarities and box differences. Explain how these sources, together, help you answer the Compelling Question.

COMMUNICATE CONCLUSIONS

Collaborating With a partner, review your answers to your Supporting Questions and work together to answer the Compelling Question. Discuss how computers signify a turning point in recent history. Then identify five ways in which computers have transformed daily life, economics, social interactions, politics, the environment, or some other significant aspects of life in the past few decades. Prepare a poster presentation (e.g., collage, concept web, infographic, illustrated time line) in which you share your conclusion and evidence with the class.

TAKE INFORMED ACTION

Civic Uses of Technology With a small group, brainstorm a list of ways that citizens, officials, businesses, and organizations use computer technology to improve society, pursue reforms, or benefit specific groups of people. Together, research three examples and prepare short descriptions of each. Use what you have learned to brainstorm a volunteer civic technology project in which you can use digital technology to pursue what you consider to be a positive change in the community, state, or nation. Prepare a detailed proposal with visual aids to present to the class. If permitted, develop your project and evaluate and report on its effects.

Ravichandran, S. V. (2009). Mobile phones and teenagers: Impact, consequences and concerns - parents/caregivers perspectives. Unpublished thesis submitted in partial fulfillment of the degree of Master of Computing, Unitec Institute of Technology, New Zealand.

07

The Clinton Administration

READING STRATEGY

Analyzing Key Ideas and Details As you read about President Clinton's administration, use the section headings to create an outline similar to the one here

The Clinton Administration

I. Clinton's Domestic Agenda

  A.

  B.

II.

Clinton's Domestic Agenda

GUIDING QUESTION

During his first presidential term, what domestic policy areas did President Clinton focus on?

Just 46 years old when he became president, Bill Clinton was the first baby boomer to reach the Oval Office. He set out an ambitious domestic agenda focusing on the economy, the family, education, crime, and health care.

Raising Taxes and Stumbling on Health Care

Clinton first focused on the economy. He saw the massive federal deficit as the main source of the economy's weakness because it forced the government to borrow heavily, which helped to drive up interest rates. Clinton believed that lowering interest rates would enable businesses and consumers to borrow more money for business investment and increase consumer purchasing that would then promote growth.

About half of all government spending went to entitlement programs—such as Social Security and veterans' benefits—that could not easily be cut because so many people relied on them and, in the case of Social Security, had contributed to the system for years. Facing these constraints, Clinton's 1993 plan for reducing the deficit proposed raising taxes on middle and upper incomes and placing new taxes on gasoline, heating oil, and natural gas. Congressional Republicans refused to support the unpopular tax increases. Clinton pressured Democrats, however, and after many amendments, a modified version of the plan narrowly passed.

During his campaign, Clinton had promised to reform the health care system in recognition of the fact that some 40 million Americans, or roughly 15 percent of the nation, did not have health insurance. The president created a task force and appointed his wife, Hillary Rodham Clinton, to head it—an unprecedented role for a First Lady. The task force developed a plan that put much of the burden of paying for benefits on employers. Small business owners feared they could not afford paying benefits, and the insurance industry and doctors' organizations mounted a nationwide advertising campaign to build public opposition to the plan. Republican opposition and a divided Democratic Party led to the plan being dropped without a vote.

Families, Education, and Gun Control

During his campaign, Clinton had stressed the need to help American families. His first success was the Family Medical Leave Act. This law gave workers up to 12 weeks per year of unpaid leave for the birth or adoption of a child or for the illness of a family member. He also persuaded Congress to create AmeriCorps, a national service program in which student volunteers work in rural and urban areas to improve low-income housing, teach children to read, and clean up the environment. AmeriCorps incorporated the VISTA program that John F. Kennedy envisioned. Students earn a salary and are awarded a scholarship to continue their education. In September 1994, some 20,000 AmeriCorps volunteers began serving in more than 1,000 communities.

Clinton strongly endorsed new gun control laws. Despite opposition from many Republicans and the National Rifle Association (NRA), Congress passed a gun control law known as the Brady Bill. This law established a five-day waiting period and required a criminal background check before purchasing a handgun from a licensed dealer. In 1994 Clinton introduced a far-reaching crime bill to fund new prisons and add 100,000 more police officers. It also banned nineteen kinds of assault weapons and funded crime prevention programs.

After several clashes between federal agents and right-wing militant groups in the 1990s as well as a domestic terrorist attack in Oklahoma City, Oklahoma, in 1994, American officials began investigating the tactics and composition of right-wing militant groups.

 CHECK FOR UNDERSTANDING

Summarizing Which domestic policy areas did Clinton focus on during his first presidential term?

Members of the AARP advocate for issues important to older Americans at rallies such as this one in Michigan.

Drawing Conclusions What reforms are these activists seeking? Why might this issue be of particular importance to AARP members?

The Rise of Advocacy Groups

GUIDING QUESTION

How did advocacy groups affect the political decisions of the 1990s?

Debates erupted over Clinton's agenda. During this period, political and social advocacy groups grew in power and influence. In one sense, advocacy groups have always been part of American history. Whenever citizens join together in a formal organization to push for new laws or changes to society, they form an advocacy group. In the 1800s, abolitionists formed political advocacy groups as did supporters of woman suffrage.

These new advocacy groups grew in response to the changing political landscape. Increasingly, the nation found itself divided, with liberals and progressives aligned with the Democratic Party and conservatives and libertarians aligned with the Republican Party. Both sides began to form organizations to advocate for their issues.

Advocacy groups use a variety of methods to bring about change. They lobby politicians, donate a great deal of money to political campaigns, try to educate voters and change their opinions, and their leaders appear on news shows and engage in public debates. Advocacy groups also file lawsuits and write briefs to influence court decisions, and, of course, they stage protests, organize marches, and conduct public events to raise awareness of their causes and issues.

Political Advocacy

Political issues involving taxation, economic policy, social reform, and government programs have always been contentious and have led to a host of advocacy

groups across the political spectrum. Prominent conservative groups include the policy and research group known as Heritage Foundation and the advocacy group Americans for Tax Reform (ATR), led by Grover Norquist. The ATR opposes tax increases and advocates reducing the amount of money collected by the government.

The United States Chamber of Commerce serves as a powerful advocacy group on economic issues. Representing many of the nation's businesses, the Chamber is one of the nation's largest lobbying groups. Another very powerful and effective political advocacy group is the National Rifle Association (NRA). Hollywood actor Charlton Heston—elected president of the NRA in 1998—raised the profile of the organization. After Heston's death, Wayne LaPierre became the NRA's primary spokesman for defending the right of gun ownership.

The American Association of Retired Persons (AARP) has fought to prevent cuts in Social Security and Medicare spending and has lobbied for health care reforms. With approximately forty million members, AARP is among the most powerful advocacy groups in the United States.

Liberal and progressive advocacy groups, including People for the American Way, were founded in response to the rise of the religious right. Other major progressive organizations include MoveOn.org, originally founded to fight the effort to impeach President Bill Clinton, and the Center for American Progress, a liberal alternative to the Heritage Foundation. Liberal advocacy groups are also prominent in pushing for environmental laws. The most prominent environmental advocacy groups include Greenpeace, the Sierra Club, and the Natural Resources Defense Council.

Jim West/Alamy

PHOTO: Richard Ellis/Alamy Stock Photo; TEXT: Clinton, William J. "Remarks on Signing the National and Community Service Trust Act of 1993." Public Papers of the Presidents of the United States: William J. Clinton. Washington: United States Government Printing Office, 1994.

During the late twentieth century, the Human Rights Campaign sought to resist laws that permitted discrimination of gay, lesbian, and bisexual Americans and encourage the election of officials who supported LGBTQ rights. By the end of the 1990s, the organization's membership numbered more than 300,000.

Analyzing Visuals How do the activists shown here at a 1996 rally in Washington, D.C., seek to share their message?

Social Advocacy

Social issues, including reproductive rights, have generated their own group of social advocacy organizations. On the liberal side is NARAL Pro-Choice America which defends a woman's right to choose abortion. Planned Parenthood provides reproductive health care services and safe abortions. On the opposite side of the issue is the National Right to Life Committee (NRLC), which seeks to eliminate abortions through education and legislation. Other social issues and concerns have led to a range of both liberal and conservative advocacy organizations. The Human Rights

Campaign is the largest social and political advocacy group working to expand rights for lesbian, gay, bisexual, transgender, and queer individuals.

Another important aspect to the rise of political and social advocacy organizations has been the growing support of wealthy Americans for these groups. Because campaign finance laws limit the amount of money people can give directly to candidates, many wealthy Americans donate heavily to advocacy groups in order to promote political and social issues that matter to them.

By the 1990s, there were thousands of political and social advocacy groups in the United States promoting many issues, and their numbers have continued to grow. When studying the history of the United States from Bill Clinton's presidency to the present, an important part of the analysis should always be to look at the advocacy groups on both sides of the issue and determine how they have influenced the democratic process.

In 1993 President Clinton spoke of the importance of social advocacy through community service:

66 I saw the wreckage, the insanity, the lost human potential that you can find now not only in our biggest cities but in every community. And yet, I saw even in the most difficult circumstances the light in the eyes of so many young people, the courage, the hunger for life, the desire to do something to reach beyond themselves and to reach out to others and to make things better.

I listened and learned from so many people. I saw the examples of the service programs that you have represented here on this stage. I watched people's dreams come to life. I watched the old and the young relate in ways they hadn't. I watched mean streets turn into safer and better and more humane places. I saw all these things happening, and I realized that there was no way any Government program could solve these problems, even if we had the money to spend on them, which we don't, but that the American people, if organized and directed and challenged and asked, would find a way. 99

—President Bill Clinton from "Remarks on Signing the National and Community Service Trust Act of 1993," September 21, 1993

✓ CHECK FOR UNDERSTANDING

Making Connections What was the connection between the turmoil of the 1960s and 1970s and the rise of new advocacy groups of the 1990s?

President Bill Clinton (center) hosted a pivotal meeting between Israeli Prime Minister Yitzhak Rabin (left) and Palestine Liberation Organization leader Yasir Arafat (right) at the White House in 1993.

Clinton's Foreign Policy

GUIDING QUESTION

How did the Clinton administration provide foreign aid to areas of conflict around the world?

Although Clinton's domestic policies would become bogged down in struggles with Congress, he was able to engage in a series of major foreign policy initiatives. Several times he used force to try to resolve regional conflicts.

Haitian Intervention

In 1991 military leaders in Haiti overthrew the country's democratically elected president Jean-Bertrand Aristide. Seeking to restore democracy, the Clinton administration convinced the United Nations to impose a trade embargo on Haiti. The embargo caused a severe economic crisis in Haiti, and many Haitians fled to the United States. Clinton then ordered an invasion of Haiti, but former president Carter convinced Haiti's rulers to step aside, and American troops landed to serve as peacekeepers.

Peacemaking in the Middle East

Although the United States had defeated Iraq in the 1991 Persian Gulf War, Iraqi president Saddam Hussein continued to display his power. In 1996 Iraqi forces attacked the Kurds, an ethnic group that set up a de facto state in northern Iraq following the 1991 Gulf War. To stop the attacks, the United States fired cruise missiles at Iraqi military targets.

Relations between Israel and the Palestinians had been volatile for many years despite attempts at accords and compromise. In 1993 Israeli Prime Minister Yitzhak Rabin and Palestine Liberation Organization (PLO) leader Yasir Arafat reached an agreement. This was the first direct agreement

between Israel and the PLO, the first time the PLO recognized Israel's right to exist, and the first time Israel recognized the PLO as the representative of the Palestinians. President Clinton then invited Arafat and Rabin to the White House, where they signed the Declaration of Principles—a plan for creating a Palestinian government. Extremist opposition to the peace plan surfaced on both sides. Radical Palestinian terrorists exploded bombs in Israel, killing hundreds of civilians, and in 1995 a right-wing Israeli assassinated Prime Minister Rabin.

In 1994 Jordan and Israel signed a peace treaty with help from the United States. In 1998 Israeli and Palestinian leaders met with Clinton at the Wye River Plantation in Maryland. The agreement they reached, however, did not address the contested status of Jerusalem or the ultimate parameters of a projected Israeli withdrawal from the West Bank and Gaza.

In July 2000, President Clinton invited Arafat and Israeli Prime Minister Ehud Barak to Camp David to discuss unresolved issues. Barak agreed to the creation of a Palestinian state in all of Gaza and over 90 percent of the West Bank, but Arafat rejected the deal. In late September 2000, a Palestinian uprising began. The region remained as far from peace as ever.

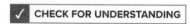

✓ CHECK FOR UNDERSTANDING

Explaining What were the effects of the Declaration of Principles?

Republicans and Clinton Battle

GUIDING QUESTION

How did the Republican Party respond to its victory in the 1994 midterm election?

President Clinton's popularity had fallen by late 1994. He had raised taxes and failed to fix health care, and while the economy was improving, many companies were still downsizing. Also, several women accused Clinton of past sexual harassment, causing public confidence in the president to weaken. As a result, the Republican won more seats in the midterm election.

The Contract with America

In the 1994 midterm elections, congressional Republicans led by Representative Newt Gingrich of Georgia proposed a campaign platform called the "Contract with America." Signed on September 27, 1994, on the Capitol steps in Washington, D.C., the Contract with America outlined legislation to be enacted by the House of Representatives within the first 100 days of the 104th Congress. The platform included proposals on tax cuts, welfare reform,

mark reinstein/Alamy Stock Photo

permanent line-item vetoes, measures to reduce crime, and middle-class tax relief. It also included constitutional amendments that required term limits and a balanced budget.

The Contract with America was delivered by Newt Gingrich:

66 As Republican Members of the House of Representatives and as citizens seeking to join that body we propose not just to change its policies, but even more important, to restore the bonds of trust between the people and their elected representatives. That is why, in this era of official evasion and posturing, we offer instead a detailed agenda for national renewal, a written commitment with no fine print. 99

—Republican Members of the House of Representatives

In the 1994 elections Republicans won a majority in both houses of Congress for the first time in 40 years. Led by Newt Gingrich, who became Speaker of the House, Republicans representatives quickly passed almost the entire program, with the exception of the amendment for term limits, but the Senate defeated several proposals, and the president vetoed others.

The Contract with America and the results of the 1994 midterm elections had a lasting impact on American politics. In the short term Republicans won back both Houses of Congress for the first time since 1954. But, more importantly, the Contract with America helped unify the Republican Party around a conservative agenda that gave candidates a clear national message. This united message, and Gingrich's unwillingness to compromise, helped build the extreme partisan divide between Republicans and Democrats that is still evident today.

The Budget Battle

In 1995 congressional Republicans and President Clinton clashed over the new federal budget. Clinton vetoed several Republican budget proposals, saying they cut into social programs too much. Gingrich believed if Republicans stood firm, Clinton would approve the budget rather than let the government shut down for lack of funds. Clinton, however, called Gingrich's bluff and allowed the federal government to shut down.

The public blamed Gingrich and the Republicans for the federal job layoffs that resulted. Public anger at the shutdown helped Clinton regain much of his previously lost support, and Republicans tried harder to work with the president to pass legislation. Clinton and Congress soon agreed to balance the budget. The next year, Congress passed the Health Insurance Portability

PHOTO: Erik Freeland/Corbis Historical/Getty Images; TEXT: Contract with America, quoted in Congressional Record: Proceedings and Debates of the 104th Congress, First Session. Vol. 141. No. 58. March 29, 1995, p. H3921.

Republican Congressman Newt Gingrich announced a conservative legislative platform called the Contract with America in 1994.

Speculating Based on this photograph, how did Gingrich hope to appeal to Americans through the Contract with America?

and Accountability Act (HIPAA) to improve health coverage for people who changed jobs and to reduce discrimination against those with pre-existing illnesses.

Reforming Welfare

Congress also passed the Welfare Reform Act, which limited people to no more than two consecutive years on welfare and required them to work to receive benefits. The law also increased child-care spending and gave tax breaks to companies hiring new employees who had been on welfare. The act built on welfare policies initiated by the Reagan administration that were designed to cut welfare spending. It focused on the concept of personal responsibility, including punishments for recipients who did not meet the act's requirements. It also shifted the task of distributing welfare benefits from the federal government to the states. States were given block grants, which, along with their own matching funds, they distributed to recipients.

Tragedy in Oklahoma City

President Clinton's first term in office suffered the deadliest terrorist attack perpetrated on U.S. soil to that date. On April 19, 1995, a homemade bomb concealed inside a rental truck ripped apart the Alfred P. Murrah Federal Building in Oklahoma City, Oklahoma, killing 168 people, including 19 young children, and injuring more than 500. The bomb was the work of Timothy McVeigh and Terry Nichols, two men sympathetic toward the Patriot movement, an extreme far-right collective of anti-government groups and militias. Both men had military and survivalist backgrounds. Found guilty of the bombings, McVeigh was sentenced to death and Nichols was sentenced to life in prison.

Like others in the early Patriot movement, McVeigh and Nichols claimed to have been radicalized by two deadly confrontations involving federal agents. The first was the 1992 Ruby Ridge, Idaho, shoot-out between federal agents and survivalist Randy Weaver. The second was the 1993 siege of the Branch Davidian compound near Waco, Texas, in which 75 members of the religious sect died. McVeigh and Nichols timed the Oklahoma bombing to coincide with the second anniversary of the Waco siege.

✓ CHECK FOR UNDERSTANDING

1. **Identifying Cause and Effect** How did the Republican Party respond to its 1994 midterm election victory?
2. **Understanding Supporting Details** Why did Clinton veto several Republican budget proposals?

Second Term Problems

GUIDING QUESTION

Why was President Clinton's domestic agenda less aggressive during his second term?

During President Clinton's second term, the economy expanded. The gross domestic product continued to grow, unemployment rates decreased, average hourly wages and median household incomes increased, and poverty rates dropped. In 1997 the president submitted a balanced budget to Congress, and in 1998 the government began to run an economic surplus. That means that the government collected more money than it spent. Despite these economic and financial achievements, much of the attention of Bill Clinton's second term was devoted to congressional struggles against a personal scandal.

Putting Children First

During President Clinton's second term, one area of domestic policy he focused on was helping the nation's children. He asked the Congress to authorize a $500 per child tax credit, and he signed into law the Adoption and Safe Families Act. Clinton also asked Congress to ban cigarette advertising aimed at children. In August 1997, President Clinton signed the Children's Health Insurance Program to provide health insurance for children whose parents could not afford it on their own.

The president also focused on students. At a commencement address at Carleton College in Northfield, Minnesota, he told graduating students:

❝ I came from a family where nobody had ever gone to college before. . . . When I became President, I was determined to do what I could to give every student that chance. I am well

aware, if it hadn't been for that chance . . . I wouldn't be standing here today. ❞

—President Bill Clinton, commencement address at Carleton College, Northfield, Minnesota, June 10, 2000

Clinton asked for a tax credit, a large increase in student grants, and expansion of Head Start for disadvantaged preschoolers.

Clinton Is Impeached

Clinton's popularity soon faltered. Banking regulators investigated charges that he had arranged illegal loans while he was governor for Whitewater Development, an Arkansas real estate company. Attorney General Janet Reno called for an independent counsel to investigate, and a three-judge panel appointed former federal judge Kenneth Starr to this role. In early 1998, new allegations emerged about Clinton's relationship with a White House intern. Some evidence suggested that he had committed **perjury,** or had lied under oath, about the relationship.

In September 1998, Starr argued that Clinton had obstructed justice, abused his power as president, and committed perjury. Clinton's supporters argued that Starr was playing politics, while opponents claimed Clinton should face charges if he had committed a crime. Ultimately, Starr found no evidence to formally charge Clinton in the Whitewater accusations.

On December 19, 1998, the House of Representatives passed two articles of impeachment: one for perjury and one for obstruction of justice. The vote split along party lines, and the case moved to the Senate. On February 12, 1999, the senators voted 55 to 45 that Clinton was not guilty of perjury, and 50-50 on obstruction of justice. Both votes fell short of the two-thirds needed to remove Clinton from office; however, his reputation and his political career suffered.

✓ CHECK FOR UNDERSTANDING

Contrasting Why was President Clinton's domestic agenda less aggressive during his second term?

LESSON ACTIVITIES

1. **Argumentative Writing** Suppose that you are a member of Congress. Write a speech in which you attempt to persuade other lawmakers to vote for or against the Contract with America.

2. **Presenting** In small groups, use the Internet to research and learn more about Clinton's domestic and foreign policy. Decide whether you think President Clinton was more successful in domestic or in foreign policy. Provide details to support your answer and present your findings to the class.

perjury lying when one has sworn under oath to tell the truth

Clinton, William. 2000. Commencement Address, 126th Carleton College Commencement Exercises. Northfield, MN, June 10. Public Papers of the President of the United States. Washington, DC: GPO.

08

Reviewing Political Divisions

Summary

Nixon and Public Confidence

Richard Nixon's election in 1968 promised to usher in "law and order" following a chaotic election year. His "Southern strategy" involved appealing to white Southerners who were upset with the Democratic Party's support for civil rights legislation. Despite Nixon's New Federalism campaign, which aimed to reduce the size of the federal bureaucracy, his administration expanded a number of domestic agencies, including regulatory authority to curb pollution and protect endangered species.

Although polls predicted Nixon would easily win reelection in 1972, the president wanted to ensure victory. Some of his advisers engaged in unethical tricks and tactics to try to undermine the opposition. They directed five men to break into the Democratic Party headquarters to steal information and plant wiretapping devices. After the burglars were caught, reporters realized they had ties to the White House.

Nixon won reelection in a landslide, but scrutiny into what would become known as the Watergate scandal continued. Some participants in the burglary revealed they had been paid by White House officials to hide what they knew. Although Nixon denied involvement, suspicion grew. In 1973 a special Senate committee launched public hearings during which the committee learned that Nixon secretly recorded conversations in his office. When officials requested that Nixon turn over the tapes, he refused.

The Supreme Court finally ordered Nixon to provide the secret tapes, which revealed incriminating evidence. As Congress prepared to impeach the president, Nixon resigned, and Gerald Ford became president. Although Ford tried to restore public trust, his pardoning of Nixon coupled with an economic downturn weakened his image. In 1976 voters elected a Washington outsider, Georgia Governor Jimmy Carter, as president. While Carter was a deeply religious and highly ethical man, his inability to improve the economy and his handling of the Iranian hostage crisis upset many Americans.

Ronald Reagan's Revolution

By 1980, public confidence in the federal government was low. Republican Ronald Reagan, a former actor and governor of California, won election by promising to restore America's image. Reagan was a charismatic and motivating speaker. He supported a domestic agenda of cutting taxes and decreasing regulatory agencies and social services. Reagan's theory of supply-side economics, or Reaganomics, rested on the belief that by cutting corporate taxes and regulations, businesses would create jobs and boost the economy.

While cutting some spending, Reagan increased military budgets as part of his Cold War "peace through strength" strategy. Reagan also supported rebels fighting socialist governments. This type of support led to the Iran-Contra scandal in which White House aides illegally sold arms to Iran to funnel money to the Contra rebels of Nicaragua.

Socially conservative ideas and values flourished during the 1980s, and the country experienced a mid-decade economic boom fueled by consumer spending. New technologies and celebrity entrepreneurs such as Oprah Winfrey emerged. An effort to fight the AIDS virus galvanized calls for research into the deadly disease.

THE WATERGATE SCANDAL

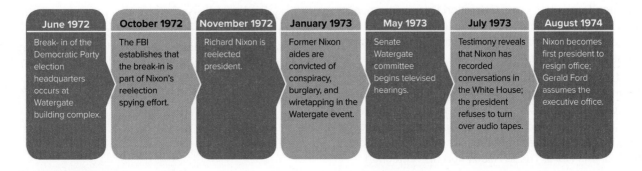

June 1972	October 1972	November 1972	January 1973	May 1973	July 1973	August 1974
Break-in of the Democratic Party election headquarters occurs at Watergate building complex.	The FBI establishes that the break-in is part of Nixon's reelection spying effort.	Richard Nixon is reelected president.	Former Nixon aides are convicted of conspiracy, burglary, and wiretapping in the Watergate event.	Senate Watergate committee begins televised hearings.	Testimony reveals that Nixon has recorded conversations in the White House; the president refuses to turn over audio tapes.	Nixon becomes first president to resign office; Gerald Ford assumes the executive office.

President George H. W. Bush met with top military and government advisors during the United States invasion of Iraq during 1991's Operation Desert Storm.

Bush's New World Order

Ronald Reagan's vice president, George H.W. Bush, won the presidency in 1988. Bush, who had extensive foreign affairs experience, declared a "New World Order" following the end of the Cold War and the division of the Soviet Union in many separate nations. Because of the end of the decades long Cold War, and without the Soviet Union's military rivalry, the United States stood in the 1990s as the world's strongest "superpower."

This change in the United State's global position meant increased involvement in military and humanitarian efforts around the world. U.S. military forces helped combat famine in Somalia and invaded Panama in 1989 to take down its dictatorial leader Manuel Noriega, facilitating a peaceful transfer of the Panama Canal to local control. A crackdown on anti-communist protests in China, however, showed the limits of some Western efforts to expand democracy.

President Bush's most significant foreign operation during his time in the White House was launched after Iraqi dictator Saddam Hussein invaded the nation of Kuwait to gain control of its oil supplies. Neighboring Saudi Arabia asked for assistance in repelling the attack. The United States led a United Nations coalition of countries who sent troops into the region. When Hussein refused to retreat from Kuwait, coalition forces launched Operation Desert Storm, an attack that quickly drove back the Iraqi forces and liberated Kuwait. Within six weeks Iraq agreed to the terms of a cease-fire.

Despite President Bush's successes in foreign affairs, his presidency faced domestic challenges and an economic recession that began in 1990. Despite having promised "no new taxes," Bush supported a tax hike, angering some supporters who felt he had gone back on his word. These issues hurt his reelection campaign. In the election of 1992, Bush faced an independent candidate, Texas billionaire H. Ross Perot, and former Arkansas governor Bill Clinton. Governor Clinton ran as a centrist "New Democrat" who tried to appeal to moderate voters who did not always vote for Republicans or for Democrats. Clinton won the election and became the first baby boomer to be elected president.

Clinton's Highs and Lows

Bill Clinton came into office with ambitious reform goals. He tackled the sluggish economy by raising taxes and cutting spending in key areas. He also proposed an initiative to reform the health care system. Led by First Lady Hillary Rodham Clinton, the plan faced strong opposition and ultimately failed to gain congressional support. Clinton garnered support for other reforms, and the economy started to improve by the end of his first term.

The 1990s witnessed the rise of many advocacy groups—outside of traditional political parties—that focused on passing legislation for specific causes. These groups often supported political candidates who backed their issues. Advocacy groups played a significant role in the success of Republican candidates who managed to gain control of both houses of Congress in 1994. Promising to fulfill a "Contract with America," congressional Republicans led by Newt Gingrich challenged many of Clinton's reform efforts, leading to standoffs over the federal budget. Despite such political conflicts, Clinton won a second term in 1996, riding a wave of support in a booming economy that led to a federal surplus.

During his second term, Clinton's political opponents accused him of involvement in potentially illegal real estate investments when he had been a governor. During this investigation, the special prosecutor uncovered evidence that Clinton had engaged in an affair with a White House intern and tried to cover it up, including lying under oath about it. Although the special prosecutor found no evidence to charge Clinton with any crimes, House Republicans issued articles of impeachment against him for perjury and obstruction of justice related to the affair. The Senate failed to get close to the two-thirds vote needed to convict Clinton, but his legacy suffered due to the scandal.

Overall, the 1990s witnessed a thriving economy, limited military entanglements overseas, and technological advances in an American society that was becoming more racially and ethnically diverse.

Corbis Historical/Getty Images

Apply What You Have Learned

 ## A Understanding Multiple Perspectives

As the investigation into Watergate unfolded, Nixon refused to comply with a subpoena for tapes of recorded conversations. Nixon cited executive privilege, claiming a president could refuse to produce materials to protect national security. In an interview after his resignation, he even declared, "[W]hen the president does it, that means that it is *not* illegal." The Supreme Court disagreed. In a unanimous 8-0 decision (Justice Rehnquist did not take part) in *United States* v. *Nixon* (1974), the Court found that executive privilege did not protect Nixon's recordings.

The ruling stated that while the president has a right to protect military secrets and other sensitive material, the needs of a criminal trial must take precedence.

ACTIVITY **Draw Political Cartoons** Review the views of Nixon and the Supreme Court regarding the limits of executive privilege. Working in pairs, draw two political cartoons—one representing Nixon's views on executive privilege and one representing the Supreme Court's view. When you are finished, compare your cartoons with the rest of the class and discuss.

 ## B Connecting to Science

The AIDS epidemic caused widespread anxiety because of how quickly the disease emerged, its high fatality rate, and the mystery surrounding how it spread. Because doctors first documented it among gay men, fears about the disease increased discrimination. Biases against the LGBTQ community slowed public investment in identifying the causes of and potential treatments for AIDS. Researchers believe this delay contributed to a higher death toll because from the outset the disease was not treated as a medical science issue but as a values issue.

Ryan White, a thirteen-year-old who contracted AIDS from a blood transfusion in 1984, served as a turning point for public opinion. White waged a legal fight to keep attending public school. His mother, Jeanne White-Ginder, recalled the discrimination he faced:

66 Through court hearings, we thought it would take one court hearing, and we'd have all these medical experts in so to speak, and then everybody would be educated, but it didn't happen that way. It was really bad. People were really cruel, people said that . . . he had to have done something bad or wrong, or he wouldn't have had it. . . . 99

Although initially given a prognosis of six months, Ryan lived until 1990, dying just a month before his high school graduation. White's courage inspired four-time Olympic gold medalist diver Greg Louganis to disclose his own status. In 1994 Louganis came out as a member of the LGBTQ community, revealing he had AIDS and had been diagnosed with HIV prior to the 1988 Olympics. Thanks to progress made in treating the disease, Louganis has survived and remains an LGBTQ activist.

ACTIVITY **Create a Graph** Using library and Internet resources, research information about the number of people globally who died of AIDS each year between 1980 and 2000. Identify the year scientists identified HIV as the virus that causes AIDS.

» Image of Ryan White meeting Greg Louganis in the 1980s

PHOTO: Taro Yamasaki/The LIFE Images Collection/Getty Images; TEXT: (1)Nixon, Richard. Transcript of David Frost's Interview with Richard Nixon. Teaching American History. 1977; (2)Ginder, Jeanne White. Interview in Who Was Ryan White? Ryan White & Global HIV/AIDS Programs, Health Resources & Services Administration. https://hab.hrsa.gov/about-ryan-white-hivaids-program/who-was-ryan-white.

C Geographic Reasoning

One of the most dramatic shifts in global politics in the 1990s was the end of the Cold War. The Cold War had heated up during the first Reagan administration, and it culminated with the dissolution of the Soviet Union in 1991. The end of the Cold War led to a realignment of alliances and shifting of global power. Eventually most members of what had been the Soviet-allied Warsaw Pact joined the North Atlantic Treaty Organization (NATO) as U.S. allies.

ACTIVITY **Label a Map** Using library and Internet resources, research information about the Warsaw Pact and NATO. During your research, locate and label a global map of current NATO members. On your map, indicate which NATO members had once been part of the Soviet Union or the Warsaw Pact.

D Making Connections to Today

Technology changed tremendously between 1980 and 2000. Most of the technology that we use almost every day originated during this time. Although government agencies had worked with computer technology for years, the first personal computers (PCs) came to market in 1981. The World Wide Web was introduced in 1990. While much smaller than the often room-sized mainframe computers that preceded them, the first personal computers look quite large and boxy compared to the small, sleek personal devices of the twenty-first century. Most people who grew up prior to 1980 could not have imagined life in which virtually any person could find information on Internet systems connected throughout the world, all while using a computer that fits into the palm of one's hand.

ACTIVITY **Conduct an Interview** Find a family member, friend, or teacher who graduated from high school before 1980. Prepare a list of questions to for interviewing the person about what life was like growing up prior to the availability of personal computers, cell phones, or Internet technology. Conduct the interview. As you speak with the person, take notes comparing his or her life then and now. After completing the interview, write a summary paragraph that compares and contrasts the way your interview subject grew up to your life today. Be prepared to present your findings to the class.

» The desktop computer that was a special purchase in the 1980s is less powerful than the common smart phone that is purchased by many today.

(l)John Robertson/Alamy Stock Photo; (r)Manuel Breva Colmeiro/Getty Images

The New Millennium 2000–PRESENT

This "Tribute in Light" took place on the 5-year anniversary of the September 11, 2001, attacks. The two beams of light serve as a reminder of the World Trade Center towers that fell.

INTRODUCTION LESSON

01   Introducing The New Millennium   558

LEARN THE EVENTS LESSONS

02   The Election of 2000   563

03   The War on Terrorism   567

04   Bush's Domestic Challenges   573

05   The Modern Environmental Debate   577

06   Obama's Presidency   581

08   Trump Takes Office   595

09   Resistance and Protest During the Trump Years   603

10   The 2020s Begin   609

INQUIRY ACTIVITY LESSONS

07   Understanding Multiple Perspectives on Immigration   589

11   Analyzing Sources: The 2020 Campaign   617

REVIEW AND APPLY LESSON

12   Reviewing The New Millennium   623

US Navy Photo/Alamy Stock Photo

THE GREAT RECESSION

Guelaguetza, which means "to give or share," is the name of a restaurant in Los Angeles, California, which became famous for its authentic Oaxacan cuisine. Oaxaca is a city in southern Mexico, but Oaxacan people and culture, including food ingredients and preparation, are connected to the region's indigenous peoples from thousands of years ago, long before Spanish colonization.

Guelaguetza first opened its doors for business in 1994. After a slow start, the restaurant's reputation began to spread quickly, and over the years, the family-owned business expanded to include several new locations.

Then the Great **Recession** hit in 2008, and soon only the original restaurant remained open. Battered by the economic crash, Guelaguetza's founders decided to retire and return to Oaxaca. But their three children refused to give up, and they were able to buy the restaurant from their parents in 2012. Their hard work and focus on traditional flavors earned the restaurant the James Beard Award, one of the highest honors in the culinary world.

Not all tales of impacts of the Great Recession ended as happily as this one. Although the Great Recession technically occurred from December 2007 to June 2009, its effects on many lasted far longer. About one in five people lost their jobs. Many of those who lost their jobs were not able to find comparable employment for years after and had to work for far less money. Young people just about to enter the job market had their plans disrupted.

Over the next decade, many of those who graduated college during the Great Recession have

delayed buying houses or having children because of the recession's long lasting effects on their income.

At a town hall meeting in Henderson, Nevada, on February 20, 2010, President Barack Obama observed that "the way I measure our economy's strength—the way you measure it—is by whether jobs and wages and incomes are growing. But the other way we measure is by whether families have a roof over their heads and whether folks are living out that American Dream of owning a home. That dream has been jeopardized in this recession for a lot of people, especially right here in Nevada."

The road to recovery following the recession proved to be a long one. Homeownership in 2004 was 69 percent; in 2015, it was 63.4 percent; and it rose to 67.9 percent in 2020.

> ❝ That dream has been jeopardized in this recession for a lot of people . . . ❞

In 2008 the *New York Times* interviewed people to see how the recession had affected them and then followed up to see how these same people fared ten years later. One man remembered being hungry and nearly homeless. He survived by sleeping on friends' couches. Luckily, he was able to start a new life as a real estate agent and used his experiences to prioritize saving money in preparation for the next crash.

A woman from Kentucky was not so lucky. She lost her job in a factory in 2008 and never found a full-time replacement job. She worked on and off for the next eight years, eventually driving 50 miles each way for a job that paid far less than what she had earned in the factory. She once believed she would be retired by the age of 60, but the recession made that dream impossible.

Obama, Barack. "Remarks by the President at Town Hall Meeting in Henderson, Nevada." February 20, 2010.

recession period of reduced economic activity

National Archives and Records Administration

President Barack Obama makes a telephone call from the Oval Office during his first 100 days in office. In dealing with the economic crisis, the Obama Administration worked to create the Consumer Financial Protection Bureau to advocate for average Americans.

Understanding the Time and Place: United States, 2000–Present

The transition into the twenty-first century brought many changes to the United States. But many conflicts and concerns from the twentieth century remained. Deeply divisive issues—such as racial justice, gender equality, immigration, tax reform, and foreign policies—remained a central part of the nation's political and social landscape.

The George W. Bush Administration

On January 20, 2001, George W. Bush followed the path of his father, George H.W. Bush, and became the forty-third president of the United States. His road to the White House was not without controversy. In the 2000 election, Bush won the electoral college, but former Vice President Al Gore, Jr., the Democratic candidate for president, won the popular vote by over 500,000 votes.

The result of the election hinged on Florida's electoral votes, where the vote count was extremely close and there had been reported issues with confusing ballots. A number of recounts and lawsuits connected with Florida's voting procedures eventually led to the Supreme Court's intervention. The Supreme Court ruled that further recounts must stop, which ended the contest. George W. Bush won Florida's electoral votes, which gave him the election.

Bush faced a number of challenges during his two terms in office. The most devastating challenge occurred on September 11, 2001, when terrorist attacks killed nearly 3,000 people.

Following the events of September 11, President Bush and the U.S. Congress made significant changes to the structure of the federal government. A new cabinet-level agency, the Department of Homeland Security was created. The federal government's investigation and surveillance powers were expanded. These initiatives aimed to more effectively fight terrorism. But they had lasting, wide-reaching effects, and many critics questioned their necessity.

During this time, the Bush administration and Congress authorized the invasion of Iraq and Afghanistan as part of what became known as the War on Terror. Osama bin Laden, the leader of the terrorist group al-Qaeda, had planned the 2001 terrorist attacks. U.S. intelligence agents believed he was hiding in Afghanistan, which was then ruled by the Taliban. These wars in Iraq and Afghanistan made an **indelible** mark on the Middle East, with effects that would be felt long after Bush's time in office. The war in Afghanistan, for example, replaced the Vietnam War as the longest-running foreign conflict in which the United States fought.

Hurricane Katrina inflicted another domestic disaster during Bush's presidency. One of the most powerful Atlantic storms on record, Hurricane Katrina destroyed large areas of Mississippi and Louisiana along the Gulf of Mexico. Although the storm did not directly hit New Orleans, Louisiana, its rainfall and storm surge overwhelmed the city's **levee** system and flooded about 80 percent of the city. The storm and its aftermath claimed the lives of more than 1,800 Americans. The Federal Emergency Management Agency (FEMA) struggled to respond to the scale of this disaster, and the people of New Orleans in particular suffered from the slow response for aid and rescue.

The Barack Obama Administration

The election of Barack Obama to the White House marked one of the most historic events in United States history. As Obama started his administration, Americans were facing problems, including escalating tensions in the Middle East and an economic disaster comparable to the Great Depression.

In October 2008, before Obama became president, President Bush and Congress authorized $700 billion to help America's financial institutions. During Obama's first year in office, the economic situation worsened. President Obama signed the American Recovery and Reinvestment Act in February 2009, which provided tax cuts to working families and small businesses.

President Obama focused on fixing the American health care system and specifically wanted to address the large percentage of the country that had no health insurance to deal with medical issues. Obama's plan depended on increasing taxes on the wealthy in order to pay for the expansion of health care. Republicans argued that these health care reforms spent too much federal money and expanded the power of the federal government too much. In the 2010 midterm elections, the Republican Party won a majority in the House of Representatives and gained six seats in the Senate. The division between the Republicans in Congress and the Democratic president would greatly affect the rest of Obama's time as president.

---

indelible lasting; unforgettable

levee an embankment used to prevent flooding

COVID-19 in the United States, 2020

Coronaviruses are a type of virus that includes the common cold. In late 2019, however, a new coronavirus appeared in China. This virus, named COVID-19, was declared a global pandemic by the World Health Organization in March 2020. COVID-19 spread throughout the United States and affected people in every state.

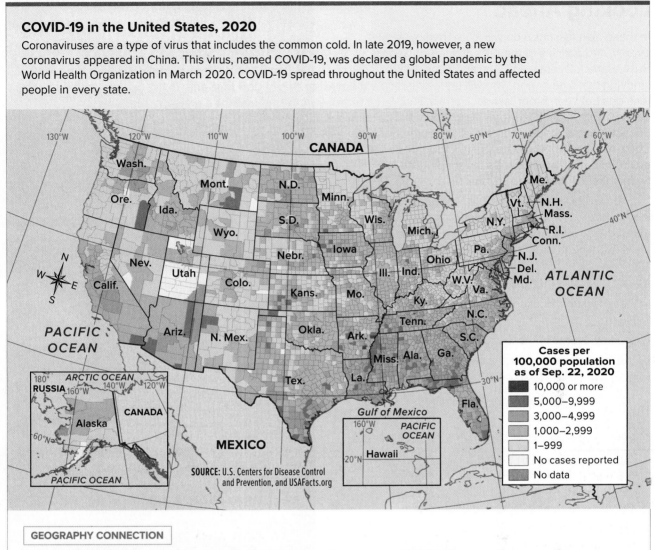

Cases per 100,000 population as of Sep. 22, 2020
- 10,000 or more
- 5,000–9,999
- 3,000–4,999
- 1,000–2,999
- 1–999
- No cases reported
- No data

SOURCE: U.S. Centers for Disease Control and Prevention, and USAFacts.org

GEOGRAPHY CONNECTION

1. **Spatial Thinking** Which state had the largest land area with no cases of COVID-19 reported?
2. **Exploring Regions** Which region of the United States had the greatest concentration of cases on September 22, 2020?

The Donald Trump Administration

Like George W. Bush, Donald Trump won the presidential election without winning the popular vote. Trump's opponent, Democrat Hillary Clinton, won the popular vote by a substantial margin—Clinton won almost 2.9 million more votes than Trump. But Trump won the electoral college, winning 304 electoral votes to Clinton's 227 electoral votes.

Donald Trump touted his lack of government experience as an asset. Many people responded to Trump's aggressive personality and his critical view of Washington D.C. Trump supporters believed he would bring a fresh point of view to government leadership and improve economic conditions for small businesses. Trump cultivated the dissatisfaction of those Americans who felt ignored by the policies of previous administrations and who thought Hillary Clinton would continue the same policy goals of Obama's time in the White House.

The effects of the Great Recession could still be felt throughout the nation in 2016. Many Americans had not recovered—and they worried they never would, unless something drastically changed. They hoped that a vote for Trump would bring about improvements in their lives.

Looking Ahead

In these next lessons, you will learn the key details, events, and policies of the presidencies of George W. Bush, Barack Obama, and Donald Trump. While studying this time period, you will understand how the tensions between progressives, liberals, and conservatives continued to deepen. You will also learn how the United States changed after September 11, 2001. And you will understand the important social, environmental, and global issues shaping life in twenty-first century United States.

You will examine Compelling Questions in the Inquiry Lessons and develop your own questions about the new millennium. Review the time line to preview some of this time period's key events.

What Will You Learn

In these lessons focused on the new millennium, you will learn:

- the key events of the 2000 presidential election.
- the legal reasoning for the case of *Bush* v. *Gore.*
- the historical events of September 11, 2001.
- how the United States government addressed the threat of terrorism.
- how the War on Terror affected civil liberties in the United States.
- the economic and social effects of the Great Recession of 2008.
- the key events and impacts of the modern environmental movement.
- how the slow recovery from the Great Recession created political and public protests surrounding wealth inequality.
- how different presidents have enforced security on the United States's southern border.
- about President Donald Trump's domestic priorities and how the coronavirus pandemic affected those priorities.
- how Donald Trump was impeached twice by the House.
- the key moments of the 2020 presidential election.

❓ COMPELLING QUESTIONS

- **How have debates over immigration shaped policy in recent decades?**
- **What issues and concerns influenced the 2020 presidential election?**

NEW MILLENNIUM

2000 ○
NOVEMBER 2000 Close vote in Florida causes a contested presidential election

SEPTEMBER 11, 2001 Terrorists attack the World Trade Center and the Pentagon

2003 ○
MARCH 2003 United States invades Iraq

AUGUST 2005 Hurricane Katrina devastates Louisiana and Mississippi and floods New Orleans (right)

OCTOBER 2008 Emergency Economic Stabilization Act passed

NOVEMBER 2008 Barack Obama elected

2010 ○
JUNE 2015 *Obergefell* v. *Hodges* allows same-sex marriages

NOVEMBER 2016 Donald Trump elected president

DECEMBER 18, 2019 Trump impeached

DECEMBER 2019 COVID-19 pandemic begins to affect nations

2020 ○
FEBRUARY 5, 2020 Trump is acquitted by Senate

NOVEMBER 2020 Joe Biden wins presidential election

JANUARY 6, 2021 Angry crowd of Trump supporters break into U.S. Capitol in attempt to halt election certification

Sequencing Time Identify the events that have had the most direct impact on your life and explain how they have affected you.

Library of Congress Prints & Photographs Division, photograph by Carol M. Highsmith [LC-DIG-highsm-04024]

02

The Election of 2000

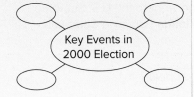

READING STRATEGY

Analyzing Key Ideas and Details Use a graphic organizer like the one below to identify the key events of the 2000 presidential election.

Key Events in 2000 Election

A Close Vote

GUIDING QUESTION

Why was the presidential election of 2000 controversial?

In the election of 2000, the division between liberals and conservatives expanded even further. The election itself was one of the closest in American history and was decided by a Supreme Court ruling.

The Candidates Campaign

In 2000 Democrats nominated Vice President Al Gore for president. Gore had competition in the Democratic primary from just one other candidate: the former senator from New Jersey Bill Bradley. Gore easily won the nomination and chose as his running mate Senator Joseph Lieberman, the first Jewish American on a major party ticket. The Republican candidate was Texas governor George W. Bush, son of former president George H.W. Bush. Bush had beaten out a considerably more crowded field in the Republican primary—one that included Senator John McCain from Arizona and Senator Orrin Hatch from Utah, among others. For his vice-presidential candidate, Bush chose Dick Cheney, who had served as George H.W. Bush's secretary of defense.

The campaign between Bush and Gore revolved around the question of what to do with surplus tax revenues. Both agreed that Social Security needed reform, but they disagreed on the details. Both promised to cut taxes, to improve public education, and to support plans to help senior citizens pay for prescription drugs. In the public's mind, however, Gore would forever be associated with President Clinton, whose impeachment tarnished his otherwise high ratings as president. This was an association Gore found difficult to overcome during the election.

Consumer advocate Ralph Nader also entered the race as a third-party candidate running on the Green Party ticket. Third parties often draw "protest votes" from voters who are frustrated by the actions and disagreements of the major parties.

The Green Party had origins in the antinuclear, pro-peace movement. In 1996 Ralph Nader ran for president alongside vice presidential candidate Winona LaDuke, a Native American activist and environmentalist. The party received only about 685,000 popular votes that year, but the campaign helped raise awareness of its platform of political reform, social justice, ecology, and peace.

In 2000 Nader again ran for president on the Green Party ticket. Nader saw little difference between Democratic and Republican candidates, claiming that both parties accepted money from corporations and political action committees (PACs). Nader believed that the contributions from corporations and PACs corrupted the political system and resulted in politicians ignoring the needs of the people in favor of campaign contributions.

Democrats viewed Nader's presence as a third-party candidate as harmful to Gore. Nader received nearly 2,883,000 votes—a total far higher than he had gotten in the 1996 election. In the highly contested Florida election, Nader received 97,488 votes, or 1.63 percent of the vote, more than the difference between Bush and Gore.

Unclear Election Day

No candidate won a majority in the 2000 election, but Gore received the most popular votes, winning 48.4 percent of the popular vote compared to 47.9 percent for Bush. To win the presidency, however, candidates must win a majority of votes in the Electoral College.

The election came down to the results in Florida. Both Bush and Gore needed its 25 electoral votes to exceed the 270 Electoral College votes required for the election. The ballot count margins in Florida were so close that state law required a recount of the ballots using vote-counting machines. Yet there were thousands of ballots the machines could not read accurately. Gore then asked for a manual recount of ballots in several strongly Democratic counties. After the machine recount showed Bush still ahead, a legal battle began over how to conduct recounts by hand.

Most Florida ballots required voters to cast a vote by punching a small piece of cardboard out of the ballot beside the candidate's name. This small piece is called a **chad.** Vote counters were forced to interpret the intent of a voter if the chad on the ballet was still partially attached. On some, the chad had not been punched out at all, and the voter had left only a dimple on the ballot's surface. Vote counters had to determine what the voter intended—and different Florida counties used different standards.

Under state law, Florida officials had to certify the results by a certain date. When it became clear that not all of the manual recounts could be finished in time, Gore went to court to challenge the deadline. The Florida Supreme Court agreed to set a new deadline. The Bush campaign then made its own legal challenge against the Florida Supreme Court's new deadline. This challenge went to the U.S. Supreme Court to decide if the Florida Supreme Court had acted constitutionally.

✓ **CHECK FOR UNDERSTANDING**

Summarizing What were the platforms of the Republican, Democratic, and Green Party candidates?

Election workers in Florida conducted a hand recount during the election of 2000. In at least one county, election workers were about 30 minutes from finishing the recount when the U.S. Supreme Court ordered it to be halted.

Speculating Based on this photograph, what were some challenges election workers faced in conducting a hand recount?

Sylvia Buchholz/REUTERS/Alamy Stock Photo

chad a piece of cardboard removed when punching a type of physical election ballot

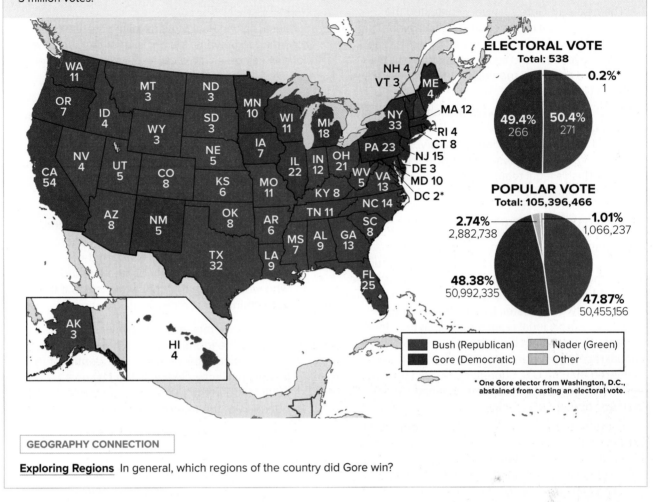

Presidential Election, 2000

The election of 2000 was a very close race that saw Green Party candidate Ralph Nader earn almost 3 million votes.

ELECTORAL VOTE
Total: 538

0.2%* 1
49.4% 266
50.4% 271

POPULAR VOTE
Total: 105,396,466

2.74% 2,882,738
1.01% 1,066,237
48.38% 50,992,335
47.87% 50,455,156

Bush (Republican)
Gore (Democratic)
Nader (Green)
Other

* One Gore elector from Washington, D.C., abstained from casting an electoral vote.

 **GEOGRAPHY CONNECTION**

Exploring Regions In general, which regions of the country did Gore win?

Bush v. Gore

GUIDING QUESTION

What was the legal reason for the Supreme Court's intervention in the 2000 election?

The results of the presidential election of 2000 were so close that the U.S. Supreme Court intervened. Its landmark ruling was both unprecedented and controversial.

An Attempted Recount

In the early hours of November 8, 2000, the night after the election, the major news networks reported that Bush had won Florida and the presidential election. Gore called Bush to concede the election. Less than an hour later, however, Gore received information that indicated Bush's lead in Florida had dropped to only a few thousand votes. Gore retracted his concession, and the major networks also retracted their reports that Bush was the president-elect.

On November 10, the completed machine recount revealed Bush as the winner in Florida by only 327 votes. Two days later, officials in Palm Beach County and Volusia County began conducting a recount by hand. Bush's legal team went to federal court in an attempt to block manual recounts, and both parties filed numerous lawsuits over the next few days, seeking either to block the recounts or allow them to proceed.

On November 15, the Florida Secretary of State Katherine Harris announced she would not accept any further recounts and asked the state supreme court to halt manual recounts. But the state Supreme Court ruled that manual counts must continue and that counties had five days to complete them.

On November 23, officials in Miami-Dade stopped the manual recount, claiming that it would not be completed by the state Supreme Court's deadline. Democrats believed this decision by the county election board was due to a Republican demonstration meant to intimidate the board into quitting, though Republicans denied this accusation. Finally, on November 26, Secretary of State Harris certified Florida's results, which gave Bush a lead by 537 votes. New recount results from Palm Beach and Miami-Dade Counties were not included in the total, allowing earlier results to stand.

The next day, Gore's lawyers contested the election results at a circuit court in Tallahassee. This court eventually ruled against Gore, saying that he failed to prove that hand recounts could affect the results. Gore appealed the decision to the Florida Supreme Court.

On December 8, the Florida Supreme Court voted 4 to 3 to order manual recounts in all counties with a significant number of presidential undervotes, or ballots not counted because of an unclear marking by the voter. Bush's legal team appealed this decision to the U.S. Supreme Court.

The Supreme Court Intervenes

On December 9, 2000—a month after Election Day—the U.S. Supreme Court voted 5 to 4 to issue a stay on the manual recounts that the Florida Supreme Court had ordered. The Supreme Court held a hearing on the case two days later. During this hearing, George W. Bush's legal team argued that the Florida Supreme Court did not have the authority to order a manual recount of undervotes. Gore's legal team countered that the U.S. Supreme Court did not have reason for intervening in a matter that had already been decided at the state level.

In the end the U.S. Supreme Court overturned the ruling of the Florida Supreme Court and ruled in favor of George W. Bush. This meant that the official Florida ballot count remained with Bush's 537 ballot lead, awarding him Florida's 25 electoral votes. It was the first time since 1888 that a president had won the electoral vote but not the popular vote.

The Florida Supreme Court had ordered any recounts to use a general standard set forth in Florida law to discern the "clear intent of the voter." In a 7 to 2 ruling, the U.S. Supreme Court declared that because different vote counters used different standards, the recount did not treat all voters equally. This, the majority of justices argued, violated the equal protection clause of the U.S. Constitution.

In addition, both federal law and the Constitution require the electoral votes for president to be cast on a certain day. If Florida missed that deadline, its electoral votes would not count. The Court ruled 5 to 4 that there was not enough time left to conduct a manual recount that would pass constitutional standards.

According to the Court's minority, who rejected *Bush* v. *Gore*'s final ruling, the flaws in Florida's recount process did not mean the process should be prevented from proceeding. Dissenting justices believed that the protection of each vote guaranteed by the Constitution should not be subject to a time line.

Justice Ruth Bader Ginsburg was one of the dissenting justices. Her disagreement with the Court's ruling was so adamant that she signed her written dissent with "I dissent," rather than the traditional "I respectfully dissent."

Justice John Paul Stevens joined Justice Ginsburg. According to Stevens, the decision of the Supreme Court in this case would cause the country's citizens to lose confidence in the nation's justice system:

66 In the interest of finality, however, the majority effectively orders the disenfranchisement of an unknown number of voters whose ballots reveal their intent—and are therefore legal votes under state law—but were for some reason rejected by ballot-counting machines. . . .

What must underlie petitioners' entire federal assault on the Florida election procedures is an unstated lack of confidence in the impartiality and capacity of the state judges who would make the critical decisions if the vote count were to proceed. . . .

Although we may never know with complete certainty the identity of the winner of this year's Presidential election, the identity of the loser is perfectly clear. It is the Nation's confidence in the judge as an impartial guardian of the rule of law. 99

—Justice John Paul Stevens, *Bush* v. *Gore*, December 12, 2000

Al Gore finally conceded the election to George W. Bush on December 13, 2000. In a televised address, Gore stated his acceptance—but disagreement—with the results.

✓ CHECK FOR UNDERSTANDING

Explaining What were the views of the Supreme Court justices in the decision *Bush* v. *Gore*?

LESSON ACTIVITIES

1. **Informative/Explanatory Writing** Write a short essay summarizing why the presidential election of 2000 was controversial. Be sure to include the views of both presidential candidates' campaigns in your essay.

2. **Presenting** Working in groups, debate the *Bush* v. *Gore* Supreme Court case. One group will take the position of the Supreme Court's majority, and the other group will take the position of the Supreme Court's minority. Conduct online research to locate statements written by the justices involved in the case and use these statements in your debate. Then present the debate to your class.

(1 & 2)Bush v. Gore 531 U.S. 98 (2000).

03

The War on Terrorism

READING STRATEGY

Analyzing Key Ideas and Details Use a graphic organizer like the one below to show the causes of terrorist acts and groups.

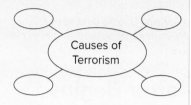

Causes of Terrorism

September 11, 2001

GUIDING QUESTION

What contributed to the rise in terrorist groups, and why did these groups resort to violent attacks?

On September 11, 2001, two passenger jets slammed into the twin towers of the World Trade Center in New York City. Soon afterward, a third plane crashed into the Pentagon in Washington, D.C. Within about two hours, the World Trade Center towers collapsed in a billow of dust and debris, killing nearly 3,000 people. The airplanes did not crash accidentally; terrorist hijackers deliberately flew them into the buildings. Hijackers had also seized a fourth airplane. Passengers on that flight learned of the earlier attacks while in flight. The passengers decided to fight back against their hijackers, and the plane crashed in a field in Pennsylvania.

The attacks shocked everyone. Americans rallied together and donated food, money, supplies, and their own time toward the recovery effort. On September 14, President Bush declared a national emergency. Congress authorized the use of force to fight whomever had planned the attacks. Intelligence agencies soon identified Osama bin Laden and the al-Qaeda (al KY•duh) terrorist organization as the plotters behind the attacks.

Terrorism and the United States

The September 11 attacks were acts of **terrorism,** which is the use of violence by nongovernmental groups and some individuals to achieve a political goal. Since World War II, many terrorist attacks on Americans outside the United States had been carried out by groups in the Middle East.

More than 400 police and firefighters lost their lives in the aftermath of the World Trade Center attacks.

Speculating Why was it so dangerous for rescue workers at the World Trade Center in the aftermath of the terrorist attacks there?

terrorism the use of violence by nongovernmental groups and some individuals to achieve a political goal

Library of Congress Prints & Photographs Division [LC-DIG-ppmsca-02155]

In the 1920s, American and European oil companies invested in Middle Eastern oil. The ruling families in some kingdoms grew rich, but most other people stayed poor. Many Muslims feared that Western influences would weaken their traditional values. In Middle Eastern countries, new political movements arose, calling for a strict interpretation of the Quran—the Muslim holy book—and a return to traditional religious laws. Some militant supporters used terrorism to achieve their goals.

The United States's support of Israel had also angered many in the Middle East. In 1947, as a response to global outrage over the Holocaust, the United Nations proposed to divide the British Mandate of Palestine into an Arab state and a Jewish state. The Jews accepted the UN plan and established Israel in 1948. Arab states responded by attacking Israel. The territory that the UN had proposed as an Arab state came under the control of Israel, Jordan, and Egypt. In the 1950s, Palestinians began staging guerrilla raids and terrorist attacks against Israel. The United States gave aid to Israel, which made the U.S. a target of Muslim hostility. In the 1970s, several Middle Eastern nations fought Israel and the United States by providing terrorists with money, weapons, and training. This is called **state-sponsored terrorism.** The governments of Libya, Syria, Iraq, and Iran have all sponsored terrorists in the past.

The Rise of Al-Qaeda

In 1979 the Soviet Union invaded Afghanistan. In response, Muslims from across the world headed to Afghanistan to help fight the Soviets. In the context of the Cold War, the United States supported the Soviets' enemies, in this case, fundamentalist Muslim rebels in Afghanistan, and provided them with funds and training. One of them was a 22-year-old named Osama bin Laden who came from one of Saudi Arabia's wealthiest families. He used his wealth to support the Afghan resistance. In 1988 he founded an organization called al-Qaeda, or "the Base." Al-Qaeda recruited Muslims and channeled money and arms to the Afghan resistance.

Bin Laden's experience in Afghanistan convinced him that superpowers could be beaten. He also believed that Western ideas had contaminated Muslim society, and he was outraged by Saudi Arabia's decision to allow American troops to establish military bases on Saudi soil after Iraq invaded Kuwait.

At first bin Laden ran al-Qaeda from camps in Sudan, but he moved back to Afghanistan in 1996 after the Taliban, a militant Muslim fundamentalist group, took power there. Bin Laden dedicated himself to driving Westerners out of the Middle East. In 1998 he called on Muslims to kill Americans. Soon afterward his followers set off bombs at the American embassies in Kenya and Tanzania.

President Bill Clinton ordered cruise missile attacks upon terrorist camps in Afghanistan and

Sudan, but bin Laden was not deterred. In 1999 al-Qaeda terrorists were arrested while trying to smuggle explosives into the United States in an attempt to bomb Seattle, Washington. In October 2000, al-Qaeda terrorists crashed a boat loaded with explosives into the warship USS *Cole* while it was docked in Yemen. Then, on September 11, 2001, al-Qaeda struck again, hijacking four American passenger planes and executing the most devastating terrorist attack in U.S. history.

✓ CHECK FOR UNDERSTANDING

1. **Explaining** How did the Soviet invasion of Afghanistan lead to the rise of al-Qaeda?
2. **Making Connections** Why was Osama bin Laden focused on defeating Western superpowers, and how did he try to achieve this goal?

The War on Terror Begins

GUIDING QUESTION

What major actions marked the beginning of the United States's war on terrorism?

On September 20, 2001, President Bush demanded that the Taliban regime in Afghanistan turn over bin Laden and his supporters and shut down all terrorist camps. The United States began building international support against terrorism and deploying troops to the Middle East. President Bush argued that this was a war that had to be fought:

❝ Great harm has been done to us. We have suffered great loss. And in our grief and anger we have found our mission and our moment. . . . Our Nation—this generation—will lift a dark threat of violence from our people and our future. ❞

—President George W. Bush, Address to Joint Session of Congress, September 20, 2001

Homeland Security

One effective way to fight terrorist groups is to cut off their funding. On September 24, 2001, President Bush issued an executive order freezing the financial assets of individuals and groups suspected of terrorism. He asked other nations to help, and soon some 80 nations had issued orders to freeze the assets of the organizations and individuals on the American list.

President Bush proposed the formation of the new Office of Homeland Security. Bush also asked Congress to pass legislation to help law enforcement agencies locate terrorist suspects. Congress's new legislation had to balance Fourth Amendment protections against unreasonable search and seizure with increased security. In October 2001, Bush signed the anti-terrorist bill called the USA PATRIOT Act, which was an acronym

Bush, George. 2001. Address Before a Joint Session of the Congress on the United States Response to the Terrorist Attacks of September 11, 2001. In Public Papers of the Presidents of the United States: George W. Bush, 2001, Book II, July 1 to December 31, 2001. Washington, DC: Government Printing Office.

---

state-sponsored terrorism the act of one nation fighting another by providing terrorists with money, weapons, and training

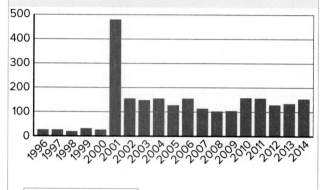

Hate Crimes against Muslims, 1996–2014

The United States experienced a sharp increase in hate crimes against Muslim Americans following the terrorist attacks of September 2001.

CIVICS CONNECTION

1. **Calculating** How did the number of hate crimes change between 2000 and 2001?
2. **Making Generalizations** What trend in attitudes toward Muslim Americans does this graph show?

for "Uniting and Strengthening America by Providing Appropriate Tools Required to Intercept and Obstruct Terrorism." The act made it easier for government agencies to wiretap suspects, track Internet communications, and seize voice mail. Authorities could conduct secret searches and obtain a nationwide search warrant. Civil libertarians worried that the powers granted in the USA PATRIOT Act threatened people's rights, especially privacy rights.

On October 5, 2001, a new threat arose when a newspaper editor in Florida died from an anthrax infection. **Anthrax,** a type of bacteria, has been used to create biological weapons. Antibiotics can cure anthrax, but if left untreated, anthrax can quickly become lethal. Anthrax was also found in offices in New York and Washington, D.C. It became clear that these anthrax attacks had been delivered via the postal service. As a result of these attacks, 5 people died and 17 became ill.

On October 7, 2001, the United States began bombing al-Qaeda camps and Taliban military forces in Afghanistan. Addressing the nation, President Bush explained that Islam and the Afghan people were not the enemy and that the United States would send aid to refugees. He also declared that this war on terrorism would continue until victory was achieved.

An Economic Crisis

Even before the September 11 terrorist attacks, the American economy showed signs of weakening. The attacks triggered an economic crisis. Stock markets plunged and the Dow Jones Industrial Average

suffered its biggest one-week loss in history up to that point. Unemployment, which had already begun to rise, became even worse.

Three months earlier, the president had convinced Congress to pass a major tax cut in order to help the economy. The Bush tax cuts reduced tax rates for all Americans and cut the capital gains tax. The economy remained weak throughout 2002, in part because of the uncertainty that the war caused. Bush pushed Congress to pass a second tax cut in 2003 that accelerated the cuts passed in the first bill. By mid-2003, the economy was recovering and unemployment numbers were no longer rising. Critics argued that cutting taxes while funding the war on terrorism helped turn the budget surpluses of the late 1990s into a deficit by the end of 2002. Supporters argued that the tax cuts prevented the recession from becoming much worse and causing even greater deficits.

✓ **CHECK FOR UNDERSTANDING**

Summarizing What major actions marked the beginning of the U.S. war on terrorism?

Afghanistan and the Taliban

GUIDING QUESTION

Why did the United States want to overthrow the Taliban regime?

Less than a month after the September 11 attacks, the United States launched a war in Afghanistan with the goal of bringing down the Taliban leadership sheltering Osama bin Laden and other al-Qaeda terrorists. Americans wanted to capture bin Laden and put him on trial in the United States.

While American warplanes bombed the Taliban's forces, the U.S. sent military aid to the Northern Alliance, a coalition of Afghan groups that had been fighting the Taliban for several years. U.S. Special Forces also entered Afghanistan to advise the Northern Alliance and identify targets for American aircraft. The American bombing campaign quickly shattered the Taliban's defenses. The Northern Alliance then launched a massive attack. In December 2001, the Taliban government collapsed and surviving Taliban members fled to the mountains of Afghanistan.

Tracking Down Al-Qaeda

American intelligence agencies believed that, early in the U.S. invasion of Afghanistan, Osama bin Laden crossed into Pakistan to hide in the mountainous region of Waziristan, where the local people were friendly to al-Qaeda and the Taliban. Between 2002 and 2006, bin Laden released several audio tapes and one videotape

---

anthrax common name for an infectious bacteria that can be fatal if not treated and has been used as a biological weapon

urging his followers to continue the fight. Pakistan did not officially allow American troops into its territory to find bin Laden, although U.S. Special Forces operated in the area. Pakistan itself launched several military operations in Waziristan in search of al-Qaeda and Taliban forces.

In 2003 Pakistan and the United States captured Khalid Sheikh Mohammed—one of the highest-ranking members of al-Qaeda and the man suspected of planning the September 11 attacks. Despite the arrest of many other al-Qaeda operatives in Pakistan, bin Laden remained at large.

In the summer of 2010, during President Barack Obama's first term, intelligence and military reports indicated that bin Laden was hiding north of Pakistan's capital city of Islamabad. In May 2011, bin Laden's exact location was verified. President Obama ordered U.S. troops to attack, and bin Laden was killed after a brief firefight. Obama announced to the nation that DNA tests confirmed that it was bin Laden who had been killed during the attack. Former President George W. Bush responded to bin Laden's death by reminding the nation that "the fight against terror goes on, but . . . [n]o matter how long it takes, justice will be done."

During the almost decade-long search for bin Laden, the U.S. and its allies captured or killed hundreds of al-Qaeda members. The U.S. government estimated that it prevented other major al-Qaeda attacks between 2002 and 2006, including at least three on the United States and two on Great Britain. But the American people were also growing more skeptical about seemingly endless military deployments.

Rebuilding Afghanistan

After the Taliban fled, the United States and its allies helped local Afghan leaders create a new government. Meanwhile, thousands of American and allied troops arrived to act as peacekeepers. In 2003 NATO took command of peacekeeping in Afghanistan. Since 2002, Afghanistan has slowly recovered from decades of war. Its economy grew rapidly, although the people remain very poor. The United States and its allies have donated $24 billion to rebuild the country. In December 2004, Afghanistan held its first nationwide democratic election, and Hamid Karzai was elected president. One year later, the Afghan people elected a National Assembly. Afghanistan, however, continued to suffer from violence. Taliban insurgents staged guerrilla attacks and suicide bombings. The Afghan government had little control over the mountainous regions of southern Afghanistan.

✓ CHECK FOR UNDERSTANDING

Identifying Cause and Effect Why did the U.S. go to war in Afghanistan, and what were some effects of this war?

Confronting Iraq

GUIDING QUESTION

What factors led to the U.S. invasion of Iraq?

After the September 11 terrorist attacks, President Bush and his advisers grew deeply concerned that terrorists might acquire **weapons of mass destruction (WMD)**—including nuclear, chemical, and biological weapons—that could kill large numbers of people all at once. During the Cold War, the United States relied upon deterrence to prevent the use of such weapons. The rise of state-sponsored terrorism created a new problem. If a nation secretly gave weapons to terrorists who then used them against the United States, the U.S. military might not know whom to attack in response. Between 1991 and 1998, Iraq appeared to be hiding weapons of mass destruction from UN inspectors. In 1998 the Iraqi government expelled the inspectors. Still, American intelligence agencies suspected that Iraq was hiding weapons of mass destruction.

In 2002 Bush warned that an "axis of evil," consisting of Iraq, Iran, and North Korea, posed a grave threat. Each nation had been known to sponsor terrorism and was suspected of developing weapons of mass destruction. The president and his advisers believed Iraq to be the most immediate danger because it had used chemical weapons against the Kurds, an ethnic group in northern Iraq. After the 1991 Gulf War, UN inspectors found evidence that Iraq had developed biological weapons and had been working on a nuclear bomb.

On September 12, 2002, President Bush asked the UN for a new resolution against Iraq. Iraq's dictator, Saddam Hussein, would have to give up Iraq's weapons of mass destruction, readmit UN weapons inspectors, stop supporting terrorism, and stop oppressing his people. Bush made it clear that the U.S. would act with or without UN support. Bush asked Congress to authorize the use of force against Iraq, which it did. Later, the United Nations approved a new resolution against Iraq that threatened "serious consequences" if Iraq did not comply.

In November 2002, Iraq agreed to readmit UN weapons inspectors. It then admitted it had weapons of mass destruction before the Gulf War but denied it currently had them. Secretary of State Colin Powell said that Iraq's declaration contained lies and was in "material breach" of the UN resolution. As the United States and a coalition of some 30 nations prepared for war with Iraq, others in the UN Security Council argued that inspectors should be given more time to find evidence of Iraq's WMD. By March 2003, inspectors had found nothing, and the United States began pressing the UN to authorize the use of force.

(1)Statement by President George W. Bush on bin Laden's Death, May 1, 2011.

weapons of mass destruction (WMD) weapons that could kill a large number of people at once

U.S. soldiers, like this one shown in the Kirkuk region, patrolled Iraqi communities during the war.

Analyzing Visuals What does this photograph suggest about relations between U.S. forces and Iraqi civilians during the conflict?

France and Russia, two UN Security Council members with veto power, refused to back such a resolution. Around the world, anti-war protesters staged rallies and marches. Several nations that had supported the United States in this war on terror and had sent troops to Afghanistan—including France, Germany, and Canada—refused to join the coalition against Iraq. Saudi Arabia and Turkey—both American allies—refused to allow the United States to attack Iraq from their territories. The only nation bordering Iraq that granted permission to use its territory was Kuwait.

On March 20, 2003, more than 150,000 U.S. troops, some 45,000 British troops, and a few hundred special forces from Australia and Poland took part in the invasion of Iraq. Much of the Iraqi army dissolved as soldiers refused to risk their lives for Saddam Hussein. A few fierce battles took place, but the Iraqis could not stop the coalition advance. Hussein was captured in late 2003, found guilty of ordering mass executions, and executed in 2006.

Insurgent Attacks

The majority of Iraq's population is Shia Muslim, but there is also a large Sunni Muslim minority. The Sunni were themselves divided between Sunni Arabs, who ruled the country under Saddam Hussein's leadership, and Sunni Kurds. The collapse of Hussein's dictatorship renewed old hostilities among these groups, known as **sects,** due to their differences in religious beliefs. Coalition troops were forced to protect them from attacks from each other's militias. Soon after the coalition took control of the country, small groups of Iraqi insurgents began staging bombings, sniper attacks, and sporadic battles against coalition forces.

Having aimed to overthrow a tyrant and eliminate the use of WMD (which were never discovered), the United States found itself trying to suppress an insurgency, prevent a civil war, and establish a new Iraqi government. The United States and its allies spent more than $30 billion to improve infrastructure, but insurgent attacks slowed these efforts.

If the U.S. troops left Iraq too soon, the country might fall into civil war and provide a safe haven for terrorist groups. Yet, the longer the United States stayed, the more its presence stirred up resentment and support for terrorist groups. The best solution seemed to be to get a functioning, democratic Iraqi government in place as quickly as possible and then train its forces to take over the country's security. In January 2005, the Iraqi people went to the polls in huge numbers for the first free elections in their country's history. After much debate, voters overwhelmingly approved a new constitution in October 2005.

Problems in Iraq

American policymakers were encouraged when large numbers of Iraqis turned out to vote in democratic elections, but hope for peace in Iraq soon faded. The Bush administration had expected the war to end quickly, but between 2003 and 2006, insurgents killed more than 3,000 U.S. soldiers. As the fighting dragged on, support for the war declined. The failure to find any WMD added to growing controversy as to whether the war had been a mistake. The elections were followed by a rise in sectarian violence as Sunni and Shia militias turned against each other. Ongoing suicide bombings, kidnappings, and attacks on U.S. soldiers turned a majority of Americans against the war.

National Archives and Records Administration

sect a subgroup within a religious community whose beliefs differ from the larger group

Defense Secretary Donald Rumsfeld had been an architect of the Iraqi war. In 2006 he resigned, and President Bush appointed Robert Gates to replace him. Bush then announced a plan to send a "surge" of some 20,000 more troops to Iraq to restore order in Baghdad, where the violence was concentrated. These new troops began holding areas of Baghdad that had been plagued by crime and insurgent attacks. U.S. forces also reached out to Sunni groups in western Iraq that had been opposed to the American presence.

In the western province of Anbar, a militant group known as al-Qaeda in Iraq (AQI) tried to impose a militant version of Islam through murder and intimidation. The Sunni groups worked with U.S. forces to fight AQI, which helped change the course of the war. By the fall of 2008, violence in Iraq had been dramatically reduced. Coalition forces had handed over control of 12 of Iraq's 18 provinces to the Iraqi government, and coalition casualties were lower than at any time since the war began in 2003. In August 2010, Operation Iraqi Freedom officially ended as the number of U.S. troops remaining in Iraq was reduced to about 50,000. Their job was primarily to train Iraqi troops.

✓ CHECK FOR UNDERSTANDING

1. **Explaining** What factors led to the U.S. invasion of Iraq?
2. **Summarizing** How did the invasion of Iraq lead to a more complicated situation than anticipated?

The Continuing War on Terror

GUIDING QUESTION

What factors led to the formation of ISIS?

The wars in Iraq and Afghanistan heightened tensions between the United States and some Muslims, and violent extremists sought to exploit the situation. In 2009 President Obama spoke at Egypt's Cairo University. There he called for a "new beginning" based on mutual respect between the United States and the Muslim world. He pledged to pursue a peaceful settlement of the long dispute between Israelis and Palestinians and to promote democracy and human rights in the face of ruthless governments.

In 2011 popular unrest in the Middle East led to a series of revolutions against oppressive governments. The movement known as the "Arab Spring" overthrew dictators in Tunisia, Libya, and Egypt. Since American troops were engaged in combat in Afghanistan, Obama was reluctant to provide American military support to the rebels in these nations. Instead, he relied on other NATO nations to provide the air support. Overthrowing dictators caused widespread political instability that posed serious problems for U.S. policy in the Middle East. Some of the governments that fell had been security partners with the U.S. There was a risk that

religious extremists might gain power, which would complicate relations with the U.S., make U.S. negotiations with Israel more difficult, and jeopardize the supply of oil and other commerce from the Middle East. Another unsettling danger was the possibility that Iran had the capability to develop nuclear weapons.

Fighting the Islamic State

After President Obama completed the withdrawal of U.S. troops from Iraq in 2011, another problem in the Middle East drew the U.S. back once again. A splinter group of al-Qaeda known as the Islamic State in Iraq and Syria (ISIS), or the Islamic State, assembled an army and set out to create a new Muslim state. ISIS ignored international borders, and it rapidly seized control of large areas of northern Iraq and eastern Syria. ISIS targeted Christians, non-Sunni Muslims, and religious minorities. Its forces destroyed churches and Shia Muslim shrines and committed public executions. Large numbers of refugees fled from ISIS-controlled areas.

Abu Bakr al-Baghdadi emerged as the leader of the Islamic State in 2010. He had earlier been part of AQI, which fought the Iraqi government and attacked Iraq's Shia Muslims. In 2014 ISIS militants kidnapped more than 100 Kurdish schoolboys in Syria and forced them to study radical Islamic teachings. ISIS repeated this pattern of forced religious conversion as it moved through Syria and northern Iraq. The United Nations estimated that because of ISIS, more than 1 million Iraqi citizens had fled from their homes. The Pentagon agreed to increase U.S. advisory troops in Iraq to 800. These military advisers aided the Iraqi forces fighting against ISIS and guarded the U.S. Embassy and airport in Baghdad.

President Obama authorized targeted airstrikes within Iraq to push back ISIS forces and to provide protection for religious minorities targeted by ISIS. When ISIS released public videos of the execution of captured American and British journalists, President Obama pledged to increase the number of U.S. troops in Iraq to more than 1,000 and to continue air and drone strikes against ISIS-controlled areas.

✓ CHECK FOR UNDERSTANDING

Identifying What is the "Arab Spring"?

LESSON ACTIVITIES

1. **Informative/Explanatory Writing** Write an explanation of the effects of Operation Iraqi Freedom on the people of Iraq. Address the positive and negative outcomes in your response.

2. **Collaborating** In small groups, discuss the events of September 11 and the consequences of those events. Based on what you know of today's society, which consequences of September 11 have had the most lasting impact?

04

Bush's Domestic Challenges

READING STRATEGY

Analyzing Key Ideas and Details Use a graphic organizer similar to the one shown here to create an outline of the major headings of the lesson.

Domestic Challenges

I. Security vs. Liberty

   A.

   B.

II.

Security Versus Liberty

GUIDING QUESTION

How did the September 11 terrorist attacks and the wars in Afghanistan and Iraq increase tension between the need for national security and protecting civil liberties?

In early 2004, President Bush's approval ratings began to fall. The ongoing war in Iraq and the failure of inspectors to find any weapons of mass destruction (WMD) there weakened his support as did the scandal at the Iraqi prison of Abu Ghraib, where prisoners were abused by American soldiers.

These events gave Democrats the opportunity to mount a serious challenge in the 2004 election. The Democrats nominated Massachusetts senator John Kerry for president and North Carolina senator John Edwards for vice president. Despite the problems in Iraq, Bush won both the popular and the electoral votes.

War on Terror Concerns

The war on terror heightened the tension between national security and civil liberties. Americans questioned whether terrorist attacks justified limits on civil liberties and whether captured terrorists had any rights at all.

In 2004 President Bush decided to hold captured members of al-Qaeda at the American military base in Guantanamo Bay, Cuba, where they could be interrogated. This decision proved extremely controversial. Critics argued that the prisoners should be formally charged and have the right to a lawyer and a proper trial. The Bush administration called the prisoners enemy combatants, not suspects charged with a crime, and insisted they did not have the right to appeal their detentions to an American court. The administration also declared that the procedures regarding the treatment of prisoners, as specified in the Geneva Conventions, did not apply to terrorists since they were not part of any nation's armed forces.

The Supreme Court disagreed. In *Rasul* v. *Bush* (2004), the Court ruled that foreign prisoners who claimed that they were unlawfully imprisoned had the right to have their cases heard in court. In response, the Bush administration created military tribunals to hear detainee cases. The Supreme Court struck this plan down in 2006 in *Hamdan* v. *Rumsfeld*. Bush then asked Congress to establish new tribunals that met the Court's objections. Congress passed the Military Commissions Act, which stated that noncitizens captured as enemy combatants had no right to file writs of habeas corpus. In *Boumediene* v. *Bush* (2008), the Supreme Court ruled that detainees had a right to habeas corpus and declared that section of the Military Commissions Act unconstitutional.

Domestic Surveillance

As part of the war on terror, the National Security Agency (NSA) began wiretapping domestic telephone calls made to overseas locations when they believed one party in the call was a member of al-Qaeda or affiliated with al-Qaeda. When the news media revealed the monitoring program in 2005, the wiretapping sparked a controversy. Civil rights groups argued that the program violated the Fourth Amendment. In 2006 a federal judge declared the wiretapping to be unconstitutional, but the following year an appeals court overturned the judge's decision. When Congress began drafting legislation to address the issue, the Bush administration suspended the program and announced that future wiretaps would require a warrant from the Foreign Intelligence Surveillance Court.

✓ CHECK FOR UNDERSTANDING

Making Connections How did the September 11 terrorist attacks and the wars in Afghanistan and Iraq increase tension between needing national security and protecting civil liberties?

A Stormy Second Term

GUIDING QUESTION

What were the successes and failures of President George W. Bush's second term?

President Bush's reelection convinced him that he had a mandate to continue his policies:

> 66 "[W]hen you win, there is a feeling that the people have spoken and embraced your point of view. And that's what I intend to tell the Congress . . . I earned capital in the campaign, political capital. And now I intend to spend it. 99
>
> —President Bush, November 4, 2004

A major priority of Bush's second term was Social Security reform. He proposed that workers be allowed to put 4 percent of their income in private accounts rather than in Social Security. He believed that private accounts would grow rapidly and help cover the expected shortfall in Social Security accounts, but Democrats argued that privatizing any part of Social Security was dangerous. With the public unenthusiastic about the changes to the program, the plan never came to a vote in Congress. Although this plan failed, Bush convinced Congress to enact a new prescription drug program for seniors. Under the new program provided by Medicare, people age 65 and older could sign up for insurance to help cover the cost of prescription drugs.

Hurricane Katrina

On August 29, 2005, Hurricane Katrina spread devastation from Florida to Louisiana. The storm surges destroyed buildings, roads, and electrical lines, left thousands of people homeless, and cost at least 1,200 lives. Rising flood water breached levees protecting New Orleans and flooded the low-lying city. These levees, built by the Army Corps of Engineers, were not properly maintained to handle the volume of flood water. Thousands sought shelter in the convention center and at the Superdome sports arena. Some 30,000 people had evacuated to the Superdome, while another 25,000 sought refuge at the convention center. Some displaced residents were sent to a Red Cross shelter in the Astrodome arena in Houston, Texas.

Tens of thousands of stranded residents required rescue by the U.S. Coast Guard, the Louisiana National

Families found temporary shelter in places such as Houston's Astrodome when the destruction of Hurricane Katrina forced them from their homes.

Analyzing Visuals What were conditions like in temporary hurricane shelters?

PHOTO: National Archives and Records Administration; TEXT: President George W. Bush, The Next 4 Years-Press Conference, November 4, 2004.

KELO V. CITY OF NEW LONDON, 2005

BACKGROUND TO THE CASE The Fifth Amendment states that the government cannot take property for public use without giving property owners just compensation. In 2000 the city of New London, Connecticut, seized property from several homeowners and gave the land to a corporation in order to have it redeveloped as part of a plan to rejuvenate the city's economy. The homeowners challenged the taking of their land, arguing that it was not being seized for public use as specified in the Constitution.

HOW THE COURT RULED In 2005 the Supreme Court, in a 5-4 decision, interpreted the term "public use" in a broad way. The Court interpreted the phrase "public use" to mean the government can take property if it serves a public purpose, even if it is not truly for public use. In other words, if government wants to promote development in a community so as to create new jobs, or increase tax revenue, it can take property from one private owner and give it to another.

The case outraged people across the political spectrum. Many conservatives saw it as example of the Court violating rights by going beyond what they believed was the actual meaning of the Constitution. Many liberals were outraged that government could take land from individual homeowners and give it to large corporations. After the decision, more than 40 states passed laws restricting the ability of state and local jurisdictions to take land away from homeowners for "economic development" by businesses.

1. **Describing** Why were people outraged by the Court's ruling?
2. **Identifying Cause and Effect** What was the significance of the Court's ruling?

Guard, and private citizens. Some of the rescued were left with no food, water, or medical attention. Some of those affected waited for days with little food, clean water, or information from authorities. The difficult conditions survivors faced were broadcast on television news. The unsanitary conditions, floodwaters, and high daily temperatures quickly created a public health emergency.

Reporters asked why the government was slow to respond. The mayor of New Orleans was faulted for not issuing a mandatory evacuation order until the storm was less than a day away and for not providing public transportation out of the city for more than 100,000 residents who did not have access to cars. The Federal Emergency Management Agency (FEMA), led by Michael Brown, took days to set up operations in New Orleans. With polls showing a sharp drop in confidence in his administration, President Bush traveled to New Orleans to pledge federal funds for rebuilding the city. Congress approved $200 billion for the massive task, but Michael Brown resigned as the head of FEMA.

New Supreme Court Judges

In 2005 President Bush filled two vacancies on the Supreme Court. In the spring of 2005, Justice Sandra

Day O'Connor announced her retirement. Although appointed by President Reagan, Justice O'Connor had been a pivotal **swing vote** on the Court, sometimes siding with conservatives, sometimes with liberals. As her replacement, Bush nominated federal judge John G. Roberts, Jr. Before the Senate could act, however, Chief Justice William Rehnquist died. Bush then named Roberts to replace him. Again attempting to fill Justice O'Connor's vacancy, President Bush nominated, and the Senate confirmed, federal judge Samuel Alito, Jr.

Chief Justice Roberts generally avoided judicial activism, instead focusing on interpreting the existing laws. He also has upheld past Supreme Court decisions. These approaches have sometimes led him to side with the more liberal judges on the Court. Justice Alito reliably sided with his fellow conservative justices in his legal interpretations.

The 2006 Midterm Elections

The first two years of President Bush's second term had not gone well. At the same time, Americans had also grown frustrated with Congress. Congress seemed unable to control spending, partly because Republicans and Democrats had been adding an

Mark Wilson/Getty Images

swing vote a vote that may sometimes lean conservative and other times liberal

Foreclosure rates increased around the United States as subprime loans and adjustable rate mortgages offered by banks left many homeowners vulnerable to losing their homes.

increasing number of special funding requests to spending bills.

Voters expressed their unhappiness with the president and the Republican Congress in 2006. The Democrats won a majority in both the House and the Senate for the first time since 1992. House Democrats then elected California representative Nancy Pelosi to be the first female Speaker of the House of Representatives. She summed up Democrats' interpretation of their victory:

66 The election of 2006 was a call to change, not merely to change the control of Congress, but for a new direction for our country. . . . Our Founders envisioned a new America driven by optimism, opportunity, and courage. . . . Now it is our responsibility to carry forth that vision of a new America into the 21st century. 99

—from a speech to the House of Representatives, January 4, 2007

Despite promises to end the wars in the Middle East and change how Congress operated, Speaker Pelosi and other Democrats were not able to get enough votes to cut funding, set a deadline for pulling troops out of Iraq, or reduce spending.

Economic Recession

By 2008, the American economy was in crisis. In the early 2000s, reductions in the prime rate—the rate banks charge low-risk borrowers—had helped fuel a boom in home sales. As housing prices rose, banks were eager for more borrowers. In response they began issuing subprime loans, which were loans offered at higher interest rates to people who did not have the credit to get a traditional loan. Many financial institutions bought up these loans, hoping to turn a quick profit by bundling them and selling them as

mortgage-backed investments. These investments—in hindsight—were much riskier than their ratings suggested. The flow of money allowed the banks to issue even more subprime loans.

Lenders also came up with new types of loans with low up-front terms but with ballooning payments after several years. Such loans were fine if housing values continued to rise and interest rates remained low. Borrowers could refinance their homes before their payments ballooned. However, when the economy began to turn, many people with these and other risky loans began defaulting on their mortgage payments. At the same time, housing prices began to fall. People could no longer borrow against their home values because many homeowners owed more on the house than what the property was worth. This caused housing foreclosures to increase rapidly.

Banks across the country that had relied on mortgage-backed investments did not know what their investments were worth. This uncertainty caused banks to doubt the financial health of other banks, leading to credit freezes between banks. As a result, beginning in 2007, a number of well-known investment banks and mortgage lenders faced bankruptcy and some eventually collapsed. Without adequate "real" funds to lend, banks reduced the amounts they lent, and many businesses feared they could not borrow enough money to keep operating. Companies began laying off workers in response to the financial crisis. In December 2007, the unemployment rate was 5 percent. By January 2009, the unemployment rate had climbed to 7.2 percent, and by October it had peaked at 10 percent. As home prices and the stock market fell, many saw their net worth and retirement funds decline, and the poverty rate increased. The country was in a recession that would rival the Great Depression.

✓ CHECK FOR UNDERSTANDING

1. **Summarizing** What were the successes and failures of President Bush's second term?

2. **Explaining** How did Bush's Supreme Court appointments reflect his political principles?

LESSON ACTIVITIES

1. **Narrative Writing** Write a journal entry describing President Bush's second term that will be read by students 50 years in the future. Be clear and concise with your descriptions of these events.

2. **Presenting** Work with a small group to conduct research about Hurricane Katrina and the response that followed. Trace developments in New Orleans in the years since the disaster, including what happened to residents who were displaced and whether homes were rebuilt. With your group, create a short presentation that summarizes your findings.

PHOTO: MARK AVERY/REUTERS/Newscom; TEXT: "Pelosi Calls for a New America, Built on the Values that Made Our Country Great," Nancy Pelosi, January 4, 2007, 110th Congress.

05

The Modern Environmental Debate

Silent Spring by Rachel Carson. Copyright © 1962, 1990, 2002 by Mariner Books.

READING STRATEGY

Analyzing Key Ideas and Details As you read, complete a graphic organizer like the one below by including actions taken to combat the nation's environmental problems in the 1960s and 1970s.

Actions Taken

The Origins of Environmentalism

GUIDING QUESTION

What concerns inspired the environmental movement?

In 1966 Carol Yannacone of Patchogue, a small community on Long Island, New York, learned that officials were using the powerful pesticide DDT as part of a mosquito control operation at a local lake. Yannacone and her husband Victor, an attorney, were concerned that the pesticide might be poisonous. They decided to contact local scientists who confirmed their suspicions.

The Yannacones then successfully sued to halt the use of the pesticide. In so doing, they had discovered a new strategy for addressing environmental concerns. Shortly after the Yannacones' court victory, the scientists involved in the case established the Environmental Defense Fund. They used its contributions for a series of legal actions across the country to halt DDT spraying. Along with those of other environmental organizations, their efforts led to a nationwide ban on DDT in 1972.

The effort to ban DDT was only one part of a new environmental movement that took shape in the 1960s and 1970s. Rachel Carson, a soft-spoken marine biologist, helped start the movement. Carson had planned to be a writer until a college biology course strengthened her sense of wonder about the natural world. She earned a master's degree in zoology from Johns Hopkins University, taught zoology, became an aquatic biologist, and eventually chief editor of publications at what would become the U.S. Fish and Wildlife Service. She continued to write about science and nature, and by 1952, she had won a National Book Award for her book, *The Sea Around Us*. Carson's writings inspired many people to become active in protecting the environment.

Carson's 1962 book *Silent Spring* assailed the increasing use of pesticides, particularly DDT. She argued that while pesticides curbed insect populations, they also killed birds, fish, and other creatures that might ingest them. Carson warned Americans of a "silent spring" in which there would be no birds left to usher spring in with their songs. "No . . . enemy action had silenced the rebirth of new life in this stricken world. The people had done it themselves. . . . A grim specter has crept upon us almost unnoticed, and this imagined tragedy may easily become a stark reality we all shall know," she warned.

Silent Spring became a best seller and one of the most controversial and influential books of the 1960s. The chemical industry was outraged and began an intense campaign to discredit Carson and her arguments. Many Americans believed Carson's warnings, however, largely because of what they were seeing around them and reading in news reports. It was becoming apparent to many that people needed to learn more about the environment.

Rivers across the nation were no longer safe for fishing or swimming. In the Northwest, timber companies were cutting down acres of forest. In 1969 a major oil spill off Santa Barbara, California, ruined miles of beach and killed many birds and aquatic animals. Land development in Florida's Everglades destroyed large portions of the environment. Pollution and garbage killed many fish in Lake Erie. Major cities were suffering from increasingly severe smog. **Smog,** or fog made heavier and darker by smoke and chemical fumes, was the one environmental problem that many Americans could see and experience every day. In a few locations, such as the Los Angeles region,

smog fog combined with smoke or other pollutants

This photo from 1970 shows children and adult leaders in the Dallas, Texas, area who joined together to improve their community environment. The Clean Dallas Project focused on picking up litter and garbage.

Making Connections What other examples can you list from this lesson that show an increased awareness of improving the environment during this time?

smog was the result of a very large population with inhabitants using millions of motor vehicles in a small area that is surrounded by mountains and a warm desert. The geography of the region trapped the automobile exhaust over the city. Elsewhere smog was simply the result of a growing population and its distribution into dense urban areas. By 1970, approximately 75 percent of Americans lived in cities. As they watched the air quality grow steadily worse, many citizens became convinced it was time to do something about protecting the environment.

A Grassroots Effort Begins

Many observers point to April 1970 as the beginning of the environmentalist movement. That month the nation first observed Earth Day, a day devoted to environmental concerns. The response was overwhelming: on college campuses, in secondary schools, and in communities, Americans actively showed their environmental awareness. After Earth Day, many citizens formed local environmental groups, which joined existing organizations such as the Audubon Society, the Sierra Club, and the Wilderness Society in efforts to protect the environment and promote the conservation of natural resources. In 1970 activists started the Natural Resources Defense Council to coordinate a nationwide network of scientists, lawyers, and activists.

Many communities and businesses responded to these organizations. They tried to make communities and buildings more environmentally friendly and worked to restore damaged natural spaces.

The Movement Grows

In 1970 President Nixon signed the National Environmental Policy Act, which created the Environmental Protection Agency (EPA). The EPA set and enforced pollution standards, promoted research, and directed antipollution activities with state and local governments. In 1970 President Nixon signed a new Clean Air Act into law. This act established emissions standards for factories and automobiles. It aimed to improve national air quality within five years and set guidelines and timetables for states and cities to meet.

In the following years, Congress passed two more pieces of environmental legislation. The Clean Water Act of 1972 restricted the discharge of pollutants into the nation's lakes and rivers. The Endangered Species Act of 1973 established measures for saving threatened animal and plant species. These laws succeeded in reducing smog, and the pollution of many lakes, streams, and rivers declined.

The Endangered Species Act did pose a constitutional question. Because it imposed restrictions on the use of land where endangered species existed, did the act interfere with the Fifth Amendment property rights of individuals, businesses, or communities? The Constitution specifies that private property cannot be taken for public use without just compensation. In subsequent years, many cases have gone to court, but no general rule has emerged. The courts examine each case on its own merits. In some cases, courts have required the government to compensate property owners for the losses they have suffered when the Endangered Species Act is applied to their property.

Love Canal

Despite increasing federal legislation, Americans also worked for change at the community level throughout the 1970s. One of the most powerful displays of community activism occurred in a housing development near Niagara Falls, New York, known as Love Canal.

Ralph Morse/The LIFE Picture Collection/Getty Images.

During the 1970s, residents of Love Canal began to notice an increasingly high number of health problems in their community, including nerve damage, blood diseases, cancer, miscarriages, and birth defects. The residents soon learned that their community sat atop a decades-old toxic waste dump. Over time its hazardous contents had spread through the ground. Led by a local woman, Lois Gibbs, the residents joined together and demanded that the government take steps to address these health threats. Gibbs later wrote about the importance of organizing to protect the environment:

66 It will take a massive effort to move society from corporate domination, in which industry's rights to pollute and damage human health and the environment supersede the public's right to live, work, and play in a safe environment. This is a political fight, since the science is already there showing that people's health is being placed at risk. To win the political fight, we need to continue to build the movement, to network with one another, and to plan, strategize, and keep moving forward. 99

—from *Love Canal: The Story Continues . . .* , 1998

Residents struggled against uncooperative officials and worked to increase awareness of their plight. The state finally relocated more than 200 families in 1978, and President Carter declared Love Canal a limited disaster area. In 1980 Carter called for emergency aid and moved approximately 500 families who remained to new locations. In 1983 Love Canal residents sued the company that had created the dump site and settled the case for around $20 million. The site was cleaned up by sealing the waste within an underground bunker and demolishing homes located above the site.

Concerns About Nuclear Energy

During the 1970s, a number of citizens became concerned about the use of nuclear reactors to generate electricity, especially as the number of nuclear power plants increased. Supporters of nuclear energy hailed it as a cleaner and less expensive alternative to **fossil fuels,** such as coal, oil, and natural gas, which are in limited supply. Opponents warned of the risks nuclear energy posed, particularly the devastating consequences of radiation released into the air.

The nuclear debate gained national attention in 1979. In the early hours of March 28, one of the reactors at the Three Mile Island nuclear facility outside Harrisburg, Pennsylvania, overheated. The problem occurred after its cooling system failed. That night, as plant officials scrambled to fix the problem, low levels of radiation began to escape from the reactor.

State officials evacuated many nearby residents, while others fled on their own. Citizens and community groups expressed outrage at protest rallies. Officials closed down the reactor and sealed the leak, but the Nuclear Regulatory Commission, the federal agency that regulates the nuclear power industry, eventually declared the plant safe. President Carter arranged a visit to the site to allay the public's concerns.

The accident at Three Mile Island had a powerful impact politically. It left much of the public with grave doubts about the safety of nuclear energy.

✓ **CHECK FOR UNDERSTANDING**

1. **Identifying Cause and Effect** What events or people inspired the environmental movement?
2. **Explaining** How did the new laws passed during this period protect the environment?

Global Environment

GUIDING QUESTION

How have nations around the world tried to address global environmental issues?

Environmental concerns are not limited to a single country. Environmental activism has become a global affair as nations grapple with the effects of fossil fuels, ozone depletion, and climate change.

The Focus on Oil

Many of the largest multinational corporations that shaped the world's economy predate the digital revolution. Of the 25 largest companies in the world in 2013, 11 were oil companies, and 4 were car companies, underscoring that energy and transportation continues to drive economic growth.

The primary sources of the world's energy remain fossil fuels: oil, coal, and natural gas. In the 1990s, hydraulic fracturing, also known as fracking, was developed to extract gas from shale. The technology triggered what has been called the "shale boom"—the rapid growth of the gas and oil industry where large shale formations exist. Fracking technology has helped reduce American dependence on foreign energy and played an important role in the economy's recovery from the 2008 recession. After critics raised concerns about its impact, debates erupted in several states as to whether to allow fracking operations to proceed.

Global Politics of Environmentalism

The rise of a global economy also increased awareness of environmental issues. Environmentalists began thinking of the environment as a global system. In the 1980s, scientists discovered that

Gibbs, Lois Marie. 1998. Love Canal: The Story Continues . . . Gabriola Island, BC: New Society Publishers.

fossil fuel a fuel formed in the Earth from decayed plant or animal remains

GRETA THUNBERG (2003–)

#FRIDAYSFORFUTURE Environmental activist Greta Thunberg was born January 3, 2003, in Stockholm, Sweden, to an opera singer mother and actor father. Thunberg, who has Asperger syndrome, developed a deep interest in climate change around the age of 8. She first put her concerns into action by becoming a vegan and sacrificing air travel as a result of the harmful gases produced by livestock and airplanes. In 2018, at the age of 15, Thunberg took a more public step by skipping school to protest climate change. She sat outside Sweden's parliament building holding a sign that read *Skolstrejk för Klimatet*— School Strike for Climate. She was soon joined by other students, first in Sweden and then around the world, urged on by the hashtag #FridaysForFuture.

A CALL TO ACTION Beginning in 2019, Thunberg took a year off school to spread her message about climate change. During that time she led protests and addressed such groups as the European Parliament, the United Nations, and the World Economic Forum in Davos, Switzerland. Her message was blunt: the older generation is robbing the younger generation of a future through their inaction on climate change. Thunberg's efforts have earned her the respect of environmentalists and the honor of being *Time* magazine's 2019 Person of the Year. In 2020 she was awarded the Gulbenkian Prize for Humanity for her work in mobilizing the younger generation in the fight against climate change. Rather than keep the $1.5 million prize, Thunberg donated it to environmental groups working to combat climate change and other ecological problems.

Identifying Why is Greta Thunberg frustrated by older generations?

chlorofluorocarbons (CFCs) were affecting the layer of ozone in Earth's atmosphere. Ozone blocks many of the sun's ultraviolet rays. At that time, CFCs were widely used in air conditioners and refrigerators. In that same decade, scientists documented a large hole in the ozone layer over Antarctica. In 1987 the United States and many other nations agreed to phase out CFCs and other chemicals that might be weakening the ozone layer.

During this time, scientists warned that climate change could lead to more droughts and extreme weather. Most experts concluded that carbon dioxide emissions from factories and power plants contributed to global warming. The issue became controversial for some because they worried about the potential economic impacts of restrictions on emissions, although experts warned that the detrimental economic impacts of global warming would also be severe. Concern about global warming led the European Union and many other nations to sign the Kyoto Protocol in 1997, promising to reduce emissions. U.S. representatives signed the agreement, but the Senate did not ratify it. President Bush withdrew the United States from the agreement in 2001, citing flaws in the treaty.

In 2015 countries met in Paris to create a stronger agreement known as the Paris Climate Agreement. Countries pledged to lower carbon emissions with the intent of limiting global warming to fewer than 2°C. President Obama ratified the agreement by executive action, bypassing Senate approval. In 2017 President Trump announced that the United States would withdraw from the agreement. When he took office in 2021, President Biden signed an executive order for the U.S. to rejoin the Paris Agreement.

✓ **CHECK FOR UNDERSTANDING**

Summarizing How has the United States responded to global environmental issues?

LESSON ACTIVITIES

1. **Informative/Explanatory Writing** Write a short essay describing how community activism brought the environmental disaster at either Love Canal or Three Mile Island to the nation's attention.

2. **Collaborating** Work as a group to create a public advertising campaign promoting a new environmental law. Be sure to describe the issue being addressed and the benefits of the law.

Abaca Press/Roses Nicolas/Abaca/Sipa USA/Newscom

Sylvia Buchholz/REUTERS/Alamy Stock Photo

READING STRATEGY

Analyzing Key Ideas and Details As you read, use the major headings of the lesson to create an outline like the one below, listing key events in the Obama candidacy and presidency.

The Obama Presidency

I. The Election of 2008

   A.

   B.

II.

   A.

   B.

The Election of 2008

GUIDING QUESTION

What issues and events attracted support for Barack Obama's presidential election?

In 2007 millions of Americans found themselves unable to make payments on their home mortgages. Financial institutions failed, which came as a shock since many of these banks were considered "too big to fail." As the 2008 election approached, the economy replaced the war in Iraq as the most important issue for voters.

Senator John McCain of Arizona, a widely admired hero of the Vietnam War, won the Republican nomination for president. Surprisingly, he chose Sarah Palin, governor of Alaska and a lesser-known politician, as his running mate.

Illinois senator Barack Obama bested New York senator Hillary Clinton to win the Democratic nomination. Obama's delivery of the keynote address at the 2004 Democratic National Convention impressed Democrats and made him a national political figure. Senator Joe Biden was Obama's running mate, and his 35 years in the Senate helped balance criticism of Obama's inexperience.

In October 2008, President Bush and Congress passed a $700 billion bailout for the nation's financial institutions. Many Americans opposed it because it seemed to reward those who had been responsible for the crisis. With the approval ratings of the president and Congress at all-time lows, McCain and Obama both promised change. McCain ran a more traditional campaign, but Obama's campaign was one of the first to take full advantage of the Internet and social media to build a strong grassroots network of young supporters. Obama won 53 percent of the popular vote and 365 electoral votes. It was the biggest

President-elect Barack Obama addresses his supporters on November 4, 2008. More than 125,000 people gathered at Grant Park in Chicago to celebrate Obama's victory on election night.

victory for a Democratic candidate since 1964. Obama, the first African American to win the presidency, exulted:

> **❝** This is our moment . . . to put our people back to work and open doors of opportunity for our kids; to restore prosperity and promote the cause of peace; to reclaim the American Dream and reaffirm that fundamental truth—that out of many, we are one; that . . . where we are met with . . . those who tell us that we can't, we will respond with that timeless creed that sums up the spirit of a people: Yes We Can. **❞**

—from the Address at Grant Park, November 4, 2008

✓ **CHECK FOR UNDERSTANDING**

Identifying What issues and events attracted support for Barack Obama's presidential campaign?

Financial Meltdown

GUIDING QUESTION

How did the economic recession and housing crisis affect Obama's domestic goals?

Despite the wars and recessions that destabilized the world after 2001, the world's economy increasingly became interconnected. Yet these interconnections posed a danger. The world learned in 2008 that economic problems in one part of the globe could have a sweeping impact in other parts of the world.

This interconnectivity was driven by the on-going revolution in digital technology. The use of cell phones, the Internet, and computers converged in a way that allowed people to connect, interact, research, create, and work from anywhere, at any time. This new level of interactivity, sometimes called hyperconnectivity, transformed society and the economy.

Several new corporations found ways to profit from the new interconnectivity. Steve Jobs led Apple, Inc., to enormous success through the introduction of new digital devices, including the iPhone and the iPad. Another key entrepreneur in the early twenty-first century was Jeff Bezos, who founded Amazon.com in 1995 as an online bookstore. Amazon revolutionized online retailing and rapidly became one of the top 500 companies in the world. Google, founded in 1998 by Sergey Brin and Larry Page, began as a search engine for the Internet that focused on organizing the world's information and making it accessible and useful.

Obama's Economic Response

When Americans voted President Obama into office, many expected an immediate improvement in the shaky economy. Obama's domestic agenda proposed to create jobs, help families, assist homeowners, and ease the financial crisis. Yet as the economy worsened, Obama's specific plans drew criticism. Some thought he was not doing enough, while others argued that he was misusing government authority by doing too much. Despite the Bush administration's 2008 bailout of financial institutions and insurance companies, the American economy continued to weaken. More Americans lost their homes, and banks closed. Many large companies reported record losses and laid off workers, contributing to a spike in unemployment. As the crisis spread worldwide, global trade declined, and the world economy shrank.

In response, Obama signed the American Recovery and Reinvestment Act in February 2009. The act provided tax cuts to working families and small businesses. It allocated federal funds for growth and investment as well as for education, health, and other entitlement programs. The act also set up a system to monitor how the recovery money was spent. In July 2010, Obama pushed additional legislation through the Democrat-controlled Congress that provided protection for consumers and created more government oversight of financial institutions and large companies.

Early signs indicated that Obama's measures were working. The nation's gross domestic product (GDP) climbed. Some of the businesses that had accepted stimulus funds, including the automobile industry, reported improvements. But the unemployment rate continued to rise as did the federal deficit. By 2010, however, GDP began to rise and unemployment started to decline, signaling the end of the Great Recession. These trends would continue for the remainder of Obama's presidency. Still, conservative critics were uncomfortable with what they viewed as a rapidly growing role of the federal government in the economy.

Other Economic Concerns

The national debt grew alarmingly. In 2001 when President George W. Bush took office, the national debt totaled close to 6 trillion dollars. By the time Obama became president in 2009, the debt was 10 trillion dollars. By January 2015, the debt had grown to 18 trillion dollars. The causes included President Obama's stimulus plan, President Bush's tax cuts, the two wars in Iraq and Afghanistan, an expansion of Medicare to cover prescription drugs, the housing crisis, and the recession. Unemployment was a significant factor because those who lost their jobs, or who took lower-paying employment, paid less in taxes. Federal deficits required more borrowing, which meant that the government had to pay more interest on its debts.

The issues of deficit spending, the national debt, and taxes drove the political parties further apart. The president appointed a commission to reach a compromise, but its proposed solutions of cutting spending and raising taxes won little support in Congress. Rather than directly confronting economic problems, Congress delayed addressing these problems, shelving them for future consideration.

Obama, Barack. 2008. Victory Speech. Chicago, November 4. Accessed May 23, 2017. http://www.cnn.com/videos/politics/2017/01/10/barack-obama-2008-acceptance-speech-chicago-sot.cnn

Home Foreclosures

Before the housing crisis, home foreclosures averaged between 4%–6%. This chart shows the increase in delinquent mortgages, or mortgages where the owners missed one or more payments, and foreclosures.

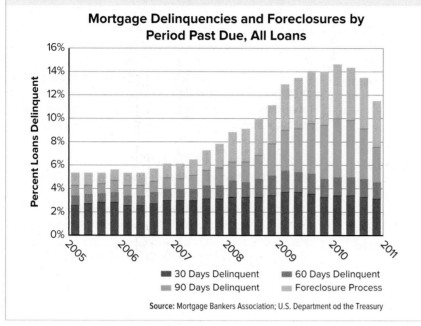

Mortgage Delinquencies and Foreclosures by Period Past Due, All Loans

Legend:
- ■ 30 Days Delinquent
- ■ 60 Days Delinquent
- ■ 90 Days Delinquent
- ■ Foreclosure Process

Source: Mortgage Bankers Association; U.S. Department od the Treasury

ECONOMICS CONNECTION

1. **Interpreting** What was the percentage increase in delinquent mortgages and foreclosures between 2007 and 2009?

2. **Making Connections** Why was there a steady rise in foreclosures beginning in 2007?

The Income Gap

The recession widened the gap between the income levels in the United States. Although the economy began improving, slow wage growth and lingering unemployment hit those in middle and lower incomes the hardest. Wealthier individuals recovered from the recession faster and their share of the nation's total income increased. Middle-income families' share of income fell from 62 percent in 1970 to 45 percent in 2010. The share of income from the wealthiest rose from 29 percent in 1970 to 46 percent in 2010.

Middle-income Americans cut back on their spending, which further restrained recovery. The decline in manufacturing jobs hit this group hardest. The family home was usually their biggest investment. When housing values fell sharply, some people found themselves paying home mortgages that were higher than what their homes were worth. Rising costs of health care and college tuition also put additional stress on those in the middle incomes.

Occupy Wall Street

The widening gap between income groups sparked a movement called "Occupy Wall Street." Protesters claimed that they represented "the 99 percent" of the population against the wealthiest 1 percent. They began by occupying a park in New York City's financial district. Occupy Wall Street drew attention to economic inequality, tax breaks for the wealthy, and corporate greed. Most of the protesters were young and identified themselves as political independents.

President Obama acknowledged that the movement expressed people's frustrations with the financial crisis. After police moved demonstrators out of the parks they had occupied, the movement dwindled. Although the Occupy Wall Street movement expressed popular anger, it suffered from a lack of leadership and specific solutions to the nation's economic problems.

✓ CHECK FOR UNDERSTANDING

1. **Summarizing** Explain the goals of the American Recovery and Reinvestment Act.

2. **Making Connections** How did the Great Recession lead to the Occupy Wall Street movement?

Partisan Conflicts

GUIDING QUESTION

What issues defined the conflict between Obama and the Republicans in Congress?

Despite the financial crisis and a growing political divide, Obama made several significant proposals during the first years of his presidency.

Health Care Reform

One priority was to reform and expand the health care system. Obama's health care reform plan, the Affordable Care Act (ACA), aimed to lower health care costs, introduce better procedures for delivering care, and provide health insurance for all Americans. In a speech delivered to Congress in 2009, he said,

"We are the only advanced democracy on Earth—the only wealthy nation—that allows such hardships for millions of its people. There are now more than thirty million American citizens who cannot get coverage."

Obama wanted to pay for the plan through higher taxes on the wealthy and by reducing wasteful spending. Yet conservatives opposed this as another expensive government intrusion. Months of heated debate took place in Congress. No Republican voted for the final bill that passed in March 2010, and many vowed to overturn it. Though Obama had promised to reform the system of **earmarks,** the bill contained many in order to pass.

The ACA extended health care coverage to 32 million more Americans who could not previously afford it. It prevented insurers from denying insurance to people with preexisting medical conditions. It allowed young adults to remain on their family's health insurance until they were 26 years old. It also gave tax credits to small businesses that provided health care to their employees. The Obama administration predicted that the plan would lower costs, strengthen the Medicare program, and expand the Medicaid program.

Supreme Court Issues

Obama filled two vacancies on the Supreme Court in his first term in office. In 2009 Justice Sonia Sotomayor became the first Hispanic Supreme Court justice and the third woman to serve on the Court. A year later Obama nominated Elena Kagan. Kagan previously served the Obama administration as U.S. solicitor general, the first woman to hold the position. Obama's appointments marked a shift to a more diverse Court.

In 2002 the McCain-Feingold Act put new limits on campaign contributions. A conservative nonprofit group called Citizens United challenged some of these campaign restrictions and the case eventually appealed to the Supreme Court. In 2010 the Court ruled that the government may regulate a business corporation's political speech but cannot suppress it totally. Justice Anthony Kennedy's majority opinion in *Citizens United* v. *Federal Election Commission* said that First Amendment protections of speech should not be based on the identity of speakers and that a corporation should not be limited in its campaign spending. Those who opposed the ruling feared that the financial power of corporations could unfairly tilt the power of elections toward the concerns of the wealthy and diminish the ability of individuals to speak out during campaigns.

Tea Party Challenges

As the 2010 midterm elections approached, Obama's approval rating was at a low point. Conservatives felt that the stimulus and health care bills had been too expensive and had not strengthened the economy. A grassroots populist movement called the "Tea Party" sprang up to protest the Obama administration. The movement took its name from a reference to the Boston Tea Party protests against British taxation. Most in the movement opposed what they called "big government"—including taxes, the health care program, and the economic stimulus plans of Bush and Obama. Yet they disagreed on many other issues.

Republicans won sweeping victories in the 2010 elections, gaining control of the House by winning 63 new seats. They also added 6 seats in the Senate, although Democrats retained the majority. Polls showed that the weakened economy, especially the unemployment rate, remained the leading issue for the voters. But President Obama defeated his Republican opponent Mitt Romney. Obama owed his reelection to support from women, minorities, and young voters.

Tea Party supporters protested taxation and other policies of the Barack Obama Administration at an April 15, 2009, protest in Staten Island, New York. A series of Tea Party protests across the United States on this day that drew more than 250,000 people.

Making Connections Based on this photograph, how did Tea Party supporters connect their ideals to those of Americans in the past?

PHOTO: EMMANUEL DUNAND/AFP/Getty Images; TEXT: President Barack Obama, "Address to a Joint Session of Congress on Health Care." Congressional Record. September 9, 2009.

earmark specific spending measures for particular projects that members of Congress include in bills

These elections left Congress politically divided. Major issues of deficits, taxes, immigration, and the environment remained unresolved. Citizens challenged both parties to break the legislative gridlock. Obama argued for raising the federal minimum wage and reforming immigration laws, but the division in Congress prevented any significant legislative action. Republicans continued to criticize the Affordable Care Act, dubbing it "Obamacare," attacked the president's foreign policy, and launched investigations into a series of controversies in Obama's administration.

All of these factors combined in the midterm election of 2014 to give the Republicans their largest majority in the House of Representatives since the 1920s. The Republicans also took control of the Senate for the first time since 2007. With Congress back under their control beginning in January 2015, Republicans hoped to start advancing their legislative agenda.

✓ CHECK FOR UNDERSTANDING

1. **Summarizing** What were the benefits of the Affordable Care Act according to the Obama administration?

2. **Identifying** What issues were raised by the Tea Party movement?

Foreign Policy

GUIDING QUESTION

How did President Obama change American diplomatic history?

President Obama inherited two ongoing wars in Iraq and Afghanistan that required much of his attention. But he also made notable changes in other areas of global diplomacy.

Iraq and Afghanistan

When campaigning for the 2009 election, Obama said he would withdraw American military forces from Iraq as soon as possible. He followed through on this promise the month after his inauguration by announcing a plan to reduce troop numbers to 50,000 by the summer of 2010. He wanted all troops withdrawn from Iraq by 2011. This effort proceeded well—in part because President George W. Bush's 2007 surge of troops had stabilized Iraq to allow for Obama's plan to succeed. By 2012 less than 200 Americans troops remained in the country.

President Obama also faced the military situation in Afghanistan, but the circumstances in that country were not as stable as in Iraq. The United States did not want the Taliban to gain new strength after its initial defeat in the early months of the start of the War on Terror in 2003 and 2004. Obama increased U.S. troop

numbers in Afghanistan by 21,000 in the first year of his presidency and he placed General David Petraeus in charge of the campaign. General Petraeus had guided the successful surge of troops in Iraq under President Bush. The U.S. military presence in Afghanistan rose to nearly 100,000 soldiers in the first two years of the Obama administration.

After this rapid increase of soldiers in Afghanistan helped stabilize the situation, Obama did reduce the number of soldiers throughout his terms. He accomplished this effort by placing more reliance upon the use of drone technology. A relatively new technology, the drones were piloted remotely by soldiers far from the combat zone. Shifting emphasis to this type of new technology allowed the military to use a smaller number of soldiers in the field. These soldiers targeted locations using lasers to mark an area or a specific building. A soldier in a distant location then piloted a drone via camera viewscreens to the laser-guided target to strike the area with drone mounted missiles. President Obama supported these tactics because it used fewer American soldiers and helped remove them from the immediate dangers of a battlefield gun fight.

The president authorized over 500 such drone attacks during his time in the White House. Most of these attacks were carried out to locate and kill members of al-Qaeda or other leaders of terrorist groups in the War on Terror. Drone strikes especially benefitted counterterrorism actions because their remote nature allowed for a small group of soldiers to operate more covertly than large numbers of forces. This was helpful when locating terrorist leaders who would quickly hide if they heard a large force of soldiers on the move. But because terrorists often hid within civilian areas, drone strikes sometimes resulted in civilian casualties and unwanted deaths. For those Americans who wished to end the many years of the War on Terror, Afghan civilian casualties became a source of criticism for the reliance on drones.

Though President Obama began a withdrawal of troops throughout the rest of his administration, the situation in Afghanistan was not resolved during his time in office. Even though a highlight of the president's leadership was the capture and killing of al Qaeda leader Osama bin Laden, the U.S. war in Afghanistan was the longest running conflict of the nation's military history.

Syria's Civil War

In March 2011, after the Syrian government violently suppressed peaceful pro-reform, pro-democratic protests in Damascus and Aleppo, an armed uprising began against President Bashar al-Assad. After months of fighting, President Obama froze Syrian government assets and called for al-Assad's resignation. But attempts to create a Syrian National

In 2016 President Barack Obama and Cuban President Raúl Castro acknowledge the honor guard at the Palace of the Revolution in Havana, Cuba. Obama became the first president to visit Cuba since the 1959 Communist Revolution.

Making Connections
What was the United States's position toward Cuba before Obama's administration?

Coalition, which would bring together all opposing factions, failed. A civil war began in 2012. Within a year, the number of Syrian refugees who were fleeing the war-torn area topped two million.

In 2014, fighting between the various rebel groups began to spread, while UN peace talks repeatedly broke down. One of the rebel groups—a breakaway al-Qaeda group called Islamic State of Iraq and the Levant (ISIL, or ISIS)—seized large portions of northern and western Iraq while committing atrocities against the populations there. In September of 2014, the U.S. and five Arab countries launched airstrikes against Islamic State targets in Syria.

In 2015, Russia entered the conflict by launching airstrikes in Syria. U.S. leaders were suspicious of Russia's involvement, believing that they had aimed their attacks more at anti-Assad rebels. In September 2016, the U.S. stopped cooperating with Russia's continued bombing of the city of Aleppo. The crisis in Syria resulted in millions of refugees displaced from their homes and seeking safety in other countries.

Other Diplomatic Efforts

Obama also focused on seeking improvements in the areas of economics and trade, diplomacy, and global stability. One example was the United States's decision to participate in negotiations for the Trans-Pacific Partnership (TPP), a multi-national agreement between the United States, Canada, and nine other nations in Asia and across the Pacific Ocean region. The TPP's goal was to establish a mutually beneficial trade agreement that aided economic development and economic growth for all of the participants.

Obama believed that joining the TPP would increase American exports into this Asia-Pacific region. Because this region also included China and Japan, the economic output in this partnership

represented about two-fifths of the world's total GDP. President Obama reasoned that the TPP agreement would help guarantee high-quality jobs for Americans that manufactured goods for export to the other TPP member nations.

Obama also focused on the global issue of nuclear security by promoting a nuclear weapons agreement with Iran in 2013. The deal that was signed by the U.S., Iran, Germany, France, and the United Kingdom limited Iranian development of weapons-grade plutonium and uranium enrichment. Iran also agreed to allow more frequent and numerous inspections of industries and supply chains that could be used in nuclear weapons manufacturing.

Iran agreed to this deal to reduce economic sanctions that the United States and the United Nations had placed upon it. The United States had placed such limitations on Iran for a variety of reasons in the past including the 1979 hostage crisis during the Carter administration, terrorist actions in the 1980s, and to weaken Iran's ability to create a nuclear weapons program in the 1990s. These sanctions weakened Iran's economy. But critics of the Obama administration's cooperation in this nuclear deal warned that lifting the sanctions could allow the Iranian government to use its growing economy to resume nuclear weapons development in secret by evading inspectors.

President Obama achieved a historic diplomatic milestone in March 2016 by restoring diplomatic relations with Cuba—for the first time since 1959, when the Cuban Revolution established a communist government under the leadership of Fidel Castro. For many decades afterwards, the United States had banned U.S. citizens' and residents' right to travel to Cuba and banned all banking transactions and trade between the nations. The United States had closed its

White House Photo/Alamy Stock Photo.

embassy in Cuba in 1961. Obama reopened the embassy in 2015. President Obama and his family visited in March 2016, making him the first president to visit Cuba since Calvin Coolidge in 1928.

The United States also sought diplomatic advancements with China during the Obama administration. In 2014 China and the United States reached an agreement to fight climate change by reducing carbon emissions. The United States agreed to shrink its carbon emissions into the atmosphere by 28 percent by the year 2025. China agreed for its part to achieve a peak of carbon dioxide emissions around 2030 and to increase its percentage of non-fossil fuels in its primary energy output to about 20 percent by the same year of 2030. President Obama and President Xi Jinping hoped that by setting these emission targets they—as two of the largest industrial nations on the planet—would inspire other nations to also set their own ambitious carbon emission reduction goals.

✓ CHECK FOR UNDERSTANDING

1. **Summarizing** What were the major foreign policy efforts of Barack Obama's administration?
2. **Making Connections** What strategies did Obama use to begin withdrawing military forces from Afghanistan?

Social and Racial Unrest

GUIDING QUESTION

Were there any common threads that connected the various protest groups?

The challenges within the United States during the Obama presidency were not just economic and political. The nation also faced significant social and cultural conflicts that further divided Americans.

New Civil Rights Issues

Civil rights issues expanded during the first decades of the twenty-first century. The 1998 murders of Matthew Shepard, a gay man, and James Byrd, Jr., an African American prompted the Hate Crimes Prevention Act of 2009, which President Obama signed. The nature of these murders had attracted national attention. The law expanded the definition of **hate crimes**, provided funds to state and local authorities to encourage investigation of hate crimes, and gave federal authorities greater power to examine possible hate crimes when local authorities chose not to follow up.

The gay and lesbian civil rights movement also promoted the right to same-sex marriage. In 2003

Massachusetts became the first state to legalize same-sex marriage. Laws regulating marriage have historically been a responsibility of state governments. As a result, the campaign for same-sex marriage took place largely at the state level.

The problem facing gay and lesbian couples was that while their marriage might be legal in one state, if they moved to another state with different laws, their marriage might not be recognized. In 1996 Congress, with the support of President Clinton, had passed the Defense of Marriage Act (DOMA), defining marriage for federal purposes as a union between one man and one women and specifying that states could refuse to recognize same-sex marriages allowed in other states.

In 2012, in *Windsor* v. *United States*, the Supreme Court struck down part of DOMA, saying that the federal government could not limit marriage to one man and one woman. The Court ruled that limiting marriage deprived people of their Fifth Amendment rights under the due process clause because it meant treating people from different states in different ways. The Court's decision, however, did not overturn state laws regarding marriage. Thirty states had previously amended their constitutions to define marriage as between one man and one woman. By 2015, same-sex marriage had become legal in 37 states and the District of Columbia.

In June 2015, the Supreme Court ruled in *Obergefell* v. *Hodges* that the Fourteenth Amendment's equal protection clause meant that if a same sex couple were married in a state where it was legal, that marriage must be officially recognized in all states. This made same-sex marriage legal in all 50 states. The *Obergefell* ruling also overruled the 1996 DOMA law. While many publicly celebrated the ruling, critics complained that the Supreme Court justices had stretched the constitutional rights of gays and lesbians too far. Among those critics was dissenting Chief Justice John Roberts, who wrote "[the Court] is not a legislature. Whether same-sex marriage is a good idea should be of no concern to us."

The Black Lives Matter Movement

In 2012 an African American teen named Trayvon Martin was shot and killed in Florida on his way home from a nighttime trip to the convenience store. George Zimmerman, a neighborhood watch volunteer had followed Martin and called 911 to report suspicious activity, before shooting him. The outrage surrounding Martin's death created a social media hashtag that grew into the Black Lives Matter movement. Three African American women—Alicia Garza, Patrisse Cullors, and Opal Tometi—began the movement. Then Michael Brown was shot and killed by police officer Darren Wilson in the summer of 2014. Protest began in

hate crime a crime that includes acts of physical harm or threats motivated by hostility toward a person's race, color, national origin, religion, gender, sexual orientation, gender identity, or disability

Obergefell v. Hodges, 576 U.S. 644 (2015).

Ferguson, Missouri and then spread to other cities across the country. These protests exposed the unequal treatment of African Americans suspects by local police departments and revealed a great deal of anger. When Officer Wilson was not indicted for the death of Brown, protests in Ferguson turned violent. Curfews attempted to maintain peace and President Obama made a public statement that urged calm. Black Lives Matter supporters were angry that African Americans too often faced a danger of being killed when stopped by the police for even minor infractions. The arrest-related death of Freddie Gray in Baltimore in April 2015 further motivated protesters. More protests followed Gray's funeral.

In June, more violence shocked the nation in Charleston, South Carolina. A white supremacist killed nine African Americans at a church prayer meeting. The resulting protests motivated South Carolina to take down the Confederate battle flag, which had flown on the State House building grounds since the 1960s. President Obama stated that this action and an increased use of body cameras by police, was "a signal of good will and healing, and a meaningful step towards a better future."

The Black Lives Matter movement, begun by Garza, Cullors, and Tometi, started as a social media hashtag. But it has expanded its goals and its reach beyond one incident or one city. It now draws attention to the incidents of police violence and exposes the economic and social inequality of African Americans in society.

Gun Violence and Public Safety

Gun violence repeatedly stunned the nation. In December 2012, a twenty-year-old gunman killed twenty elementary school children and six staff members at the Sandy Hook Elementary School in Newtown, Connecticut. The following month, the Obama administration called on Congress to strengthen gun control legislations, including better background checks during gun purchases to identify those with criminal records, a history of violent mental problems, or known terrorist ties.

Former Arizona Representative Gabrielle Giffords, who was shot and seriously wounded at a public event in 2011, urged the Obama administration to ban the commercial sale of assault weapons that use high-capacity bullet magazines. The supporters of such restrictions claimed that reducing the number of bullets a shooter could carry would reduce the possibility of mass violence. Gun rights advocates contended that people intent on enacting public shootings were not law-abiding citizens in the first place and would not be deterred by tougher laws.

President Obama asked Republican and Democratic members of the House and the Senate to pass stronger gun control legislation. Yet some members of Congress strongly supported the right to own guns and the protections of the Second Amendment. Other members may have feared voters penalizing them in the next election by not voting them back in office, so proposed gun control measures failed in Congress.

Gun control supporters had limited options to advance their agendas, primarily because of Supreme Court rulings involving the Bill of Rights. In 2008, in the case of *District of Columbia* v. *Heller*, the Supreme Court ruled for the first time that the Second Amendment to the Constitution gives individuals the right to own firearms. The Second Amendment states: "A well regulated militia, being necessary to the security of a free state, the right of the people to keep and bear arms, shall not be infringed." For decades, supporters of gun control had cited the reference to a well-regulated militia as evidence that the right extended only to militias organized by state and federal governments. In *Heller*, the Supreme Court argued for the first time that an individual has the right to bear arms.

In 2010, in *McDonald* v. *Chicago*, the Court ruled that the Second Amendment also applies to the states, and that state laws must recognize the right of individuals to bear arms. For many conservatives and organizations such as the National Rifle Association (NRA), the decisions represented major victories in their decades-long effort to assert individual rights under the Second Amendment.

✓ **CHECK FOR UNDERSTANDING**

1. **Identifying** What values or themes did protest groups share during this era?
2. **Making Connections** How did the murder of African American churchgoers in Charleston lead to change in South Carolina? Explain the significance of this change.

LESSON ACTIVITIES

1. **Narrative Writing** Write a journal entry describing the events of the Obama presidency, to be read by students fifty years in the future. Be clear and concise with your description of these events.

2. **Presenting** With a partner, choose one of the movements or events discussed in the lesson. Conduct research to learn more details. Prepare a short presentation for your class, explaining details of the movement or event and why you consider it important or interesting. Remember to consult several reliable sources and to prepare your presentation so that your audience can follow and understand your ideas.

(l)Obama, Barack. Tweet, July 10, 2015; (r)The Second Amendment to the Constitution.

07

Understanding Multiple Perspectives on Immigration

? COMPELLING QUESTION

How have debates over immigration shaped policy in recent decades?

Plan Your Inquiry

In this lesson, you will investigate issues surrounding and debates about immigration today.

DEVELOP QUESTIONS

Developing Questions About Immigration Think about the reasons that people immigrate to the United States today as well as recent changes to immigration policy. Then read the Compelling Question for this lesson. Develop a list of three supporting questions to help you answer the Compelling Question for the lesson. Write these in a graphic organizer like the one below.

APPLY HISTORICAL TOOLS

Analyzing Primary Sources You will work with a variety of primary sources in this lesson. These sources provide insight into immigration policies, immigration statistics, and myths about immigration. Use a graphic organizer like the one below to record and organize information about each source. Note ways in which each source helps you answer the supporting questions you created. Not all sources will help you answer each of your supporting questions. Only include relevant sources in your graphic organizer.

Supporting Questions	Source	How this source helps me answer the Supporting Question
Question 1		
Question 2		
Question 3		

After you analyze the sources, you will:

- use the evidence from the sources.
- communicate your conclusions.
- take informed action.

Background Information

During the 1800s and 1900s, the United States encouraged immigration to provide labor for work in factories, on building railroads, work in agriculture, and more. However, each new wave of immigrants also spurred debate about whether limits on immigrants were necessary and how to address the problems of illegal immigration.

By the 1980s, millions of immigrants had entered the United States without following prescribed procedures. A 1986 law, signed by President Ronald Reagan, granted amnesty to many in the country who were undocumented, but his actions did not resolve ongoing debates over how many people could come, from where, and under what circumstances. As the number of immigrants rose, so too did contentious discourse over immigration policy. In the 2010s, it became one of the most fiercely debated issues. Americans argued over whether immigration helped or hurt the economy. Some contended that immigrants posed a national security threat in the wake of the September 11 terrorist attacks, contributed to crime, or drained public services. Others countered that immigrants were often fleeing danger and hardship and just wanted to keep their families safe. Among the most heated topics were demands to better secure the nation's southern border and to give those brought to the country as children a path to citizenship.

» New American citizens take part in a naturalization ceremony at Harriet Tubman National Park on August 8, 2019.

Mary O'Neill/NPS

The Bush Administration Busts Immigration Myths

President George W. Bush took office in 2000. The U.S. Census Bureau reported more than 31 million foreign-born individuals living in the nation at that time. About 40 percent had become naturalized citizens. Others came on student and work visas, or legal passes; had green cards, or permanent residency documents; had applied for asylum; or had entered or stayed without legal permission. Bush's administration struggled to define policies that would secure borders, provide a path to citizenship, support economic needs met by immigrants, and honor the nation's strong tradition of immigration. This infographic was created by the Bush administration.

PRIMARY SOURCE : INFOGRAPHIC

Busting Immigration Myths

Immigrants played a leading role in building what has become the most prosperous nation in the history of the world. However, legal immigrants are many times misrepresented or their role in the U.S. economy is misunderstood.

MYTH: Immigrants are taking over
FACT: Immigrants actually only account for 13.5% of the total U.S. population, which is in line with historical norms

MYTH: Immigrants are all Mexican
FACT: 30% of immigrants come from Asia, and currently more are coming from China than Mexico

MYTH: Immigrants don't work
FACT: 72.5% of immigrants believe hard work is how you succeed in America and are responsible for half of the total U.S. labor force growth over the last decade

MYTH: Immigrants don't help the economy
FACT: Immigrant-owned businesses with employees have an average of 11 employees

MYTH: Immigrants take American jobs
FACT: 7.6% of immigrants were self-employed compared to 5.6% of native-born Americans and they founded more than 40% of Fortune 500 companies

MYTH: Immigrants are too young or old to work
FACT: More than 70% of immigrants are between the ages of 25 and 64 compared to less than 50% of native-born Americans. By 2035, the working age of immigrants will increase by 18 million.

MYTH: Immigrants take advantage of welfare
FACT: 62.2% of immigrants aged 16 and older were employed compared to 58.1% of native-born Americans

MYTH: Immigrants aren't educated
FACT: Recent immigrants are more likely to have college degrees than native-born Americans and are more likely to have advanced degrees

All data has been sourced from the Bush Institute's immigration handbook *America's Advantage: A Handbook on Immigration and Economic Growth.*

GEORGE W. BUSH INSTITUTE

—George W. Bush Institute

ART: George W. Bush Presidential Center; TEXT: George W. Bush Institute. Busting Immigration Myths. [Infographic]. From Denhart, Matthew. *America's Advantage: A Handbook on Immigration and Economic Growth.* 3rd ed. Dallas, TX. 2017.

EXAMINE THE SOURCE

1. **Summarizing** What overall message does the infographic convey?
2. **Analyzing** How might this information reflect, respond to, or influence public debate and policy on immigration?

(1)U.S. Citizenship and Immigration Services, "Consideration of Deferred Action for Childhood Arrivals (DACA)," 2018; (2) Obama, Barack "Strengthening Enforcement," Taking Action on Immigration.

B

DACA Guidelines

In 2001 Republican Orrin Hatch and Democrat Dick Durban cosponsored the DREAM Act to give minors brought to the country illegally a path to citizenship. Intended beneficiaries became known as DREAMers, but the bill stalled in the U.S. Senate. In 2012 President Obama issued a memorandum establishing the Deferred Action for Childhood Arrivals (DACA) program. *Deferred action* refers to a special protected status granted to immigrants in the country illegally to delay deportation.

PRIMARY SOURCE : GOVERNMENT DOCUMENT

66 You may request DACA if you:

1. Were under the age of 31 as of June 15, 2012;

2. Came to the United States before reaching your 16th birthday;

3. Have continuously resided in the United States since June 15, 2007, up to the present time;

4. Were physically present in the United States on June 15, 2012, and at the time of making your request for consideration of deferred action with USCIS;

5. Had no lawful status on June 15, 2012;

6. Are currently in school, have graduated or obtained a certificate of completion from high school, have obtained a general education development (GED) certificate, or are an honorably **discharged** veteran of the Coast Guard or Armed Forces of the United States; and

7. Have not been convicted of a felony, significant misdemeanor, or three or more other misdemeanors, and do not otherwise pose a threat to national security or public safety. 99

—U.S. Citizenship and Immigration Services, 2012

discharged released from service in the military

EXAMINE THE SOURCE

1. **Analyzing** Whom does this program try to protect?

2. **Inferring** Why does the program include conditions such as those described in items 6 and 7?

C

Deporting Felons, Not Families

In late 2014 President Barack Obama announced executive actions to address a growing immigration crisis. Deemed unconstitutional by critics, the measures sought to slow and prevent illegal immigration, delay deportation for several million unauthorized immigrants, and refocus efforts to apprehend and remove those here illegally.

PRIMARY SOURCE : GOVERNMENT WEBSITE

66 **Focusing on the removal of national security, border security, and public safety threats.** . . . Secretary Johnson is issuing a new DHS-wide memorandum that makes clear that the government's enforcement activity should be focused on national security threats, serious criminals, and recent border crossers. DHS will direct all of its enforcement resources at pursuing these highest priorities for removal. . . .

Accountability—Criminal Background Checks and Taxes: The President is also acting to hold accountable those **undocumented** immigrants who have lived in the U.S. for more than five years and are parents of U.S. citizens or Lawful Permanent Residents. By registering and passing criminal and national security background checks, millions of undocumented immigrants will start paying their fair share of taxes and temporarily stay in the U.S. without fear of deportation for three years at a time. DHS is also expanding the existing Deferred Action for Childhood Arrivals (DACA) policy so that individuals who were brought to this country as children ('DREAMers') can apply if they entered before January 1, 2010, regardless of how old they are today. Going forward, DACA relief will also be granted for three years. 99

—Obama White House, "Taking Action on Immigration," November 20, 2014

undocumented lacking appropriate documents to prove legal immigration or residence

EXAMINE THE SOURCE

1. **Explaining** The source describes measures requiring the Department of Homeland Security (DHS) to focus on which immigrants for deportation?

2. **Drawing Conclusions** What effect might provisions for taxation and accountability have on public opinion?

Benefits of Immigration Outweigh the Costs

After leaving office, former President George W. Bush established a policy, education, and research institute devoted to significant contemporary issues, such as immigration. Immigration continued to grow throughout the Obama administration. During the 2016 presidential campaign, immigration became a fiercely contested issue. The outgoing Obama administration and the Democratic nominee, Hillary Clinton, defended DACA and argued for reform that provided for a path to citizenship. On the opposing side, Republican nominee Donald Trump forcefully promised to overturn DACA and impose severe restrictions on immigration. In this excerpt from an essay from the George W. Bush Institute, the author weighs the costs and benefits of immigration.

PRIMARY SOURCE : ESSAY

" . . . Immigration fuels the economy. When immigrants enter the labor force, they increase the productive capacity of the economy and raise **GDP.** Their incomes rise, but so do those of natives. It's a phenomenon dubbed the 'immigration surplus,' and while a small share of additional GDP **accrues** to natives—typically 0.2 to 0.4 percent—it still amounts to $36 to $72 billion per year.

In addition to the immigration surplus, immigrants grease the wheels of the labor market by flowing into industries and areas where there is a relative need for workers—where bottlenecks or shortages might otherwise damp growth.

Immigrants are more likely to move than natives, and by relieving these bottlenecks to expansion, immigrants increase the speed limit of the economy. Growth accelerates as slack falls, a desirable scenario that follows from the improved **allocation** of resources in the economy. . . .

If immigration makes the economy larger, more efficient and productive, what's the problem? Why do we, as a nation, strictly limit immigration?

. . . Immigration changes factor prices—it lowers the wages of competing workers, while raising the return to capital and the wages of complementary workers. In other words, the immigration surplus does not accrue equally to everyone. It goes primarily to the owners of capital, which includes business and land-owners and investors.

Complementary workers also benefit. The demand for these workers rises with more immigration. They may be construction supervisors, translators, pharmaceutical reps, or immigration lawyers. And consumers benefit from the lower prices of the goods and services that immigrants produce. But competing workers' wages fall, at least in the initial transition period as the economy adjusts to the new labor inflow. . . .

Immigration is thus a positive but also disruptive change. There are lots of historical examples of positive yet disruptive change. The Industrial Revolution displaced millions of farm workers and resulted in the great urban migrations and the birth of mega-cities to which we now ascribe all kinds of positive attributes, including creativity and innovation and higher wages.

No great change is without some short-term cost. What is costly in the long term is preventing market forces from funneling resources to their best use. The adjustment of wages and prices to the changing demand and supply in the economy are the levers of capitalism that direct resources to their best allocation.

Immigration has net benefits. The fact that it has some costs is not a reason to bar it, but rather to manage it. "

—Pia Orrenius, George W. Bush Institute, Spring 2016

GDP gross domestic product; the monetary value of goods and services produced in a country

accrue to come about or accumulate

allocation the process of setting something aside for a specific purpose

EXAMINE THE SOURCE

1. **Explaining** What effect does the essay say that immigration has on the economy?

2. **Analyzing** What immigration policies might this information be used to support?

Orrenius, Pia. "Benefits of Immigration Outweigh the Costs." The Catalyst. Issue 2, Spring 2016.

Remarks on Building the Border Wall

The border between the United States and Mexico extends more than 1,900 miles from southern Texas to the Pacific Ocean. Much of the border runs along the Rio Grande, which serves as a natural boundary. Other parts of the border pass through treacherous landscapes, like the Sonoran Desert. Before 2016, about 700 miles of wall, fencing, and outposts served as barriers against illegal crossing. President Donald J. Trump promised to build a steel and concrete wall across the entire border. By mid-2020, just more than 200 miles of new wall had been built.

PRIMARY SOURCE : TRANSCRIPT

66 . . . [W]e **concur** that border security is national security. It's just commonsense. We have to know who and what is coming through our borders and to our borders, and we have to be able to defend that.

With every new mile of new wall system, the operational capacity of [U.S. Customs and Border Protection] CBP, specifically Border Patrol, is increased. Our ability to enforce the rule of law has increased. Our ability to maintain integrity in the immigration system has increased. Our ability to improve border security has increased. And our ability to shape and drive the behavior of the **cartels** has also increased. Our ability to **impede,** deny, and stop the vast threats that we have increased because of [President Trump's] leadership and providing us the tools, like the wall system.

And I think this is also important, and we— we've talked about this before: It's not just a wall. I keep saying 'wall system' on purpose, because what you have delivered is something that has not been delivered before. It's not just a bunch of steel in the ground. It's that plus access roads, technology, other attributes that really makes it an effective wall system and gives us a capability that we have not had before.

And that's why I stay true to the fact when I'm asked—the 220 miles of wall system we have in right now are 220 new miles of wall system that give us an enhanced capability that we never had.

Stopping drugs at the border, that's what we should do. That helps reduce the tens of thousands of American citizens that have died every year at the hands of the cartels smuggling drugs across this border.

Stopping human smuggling at the border prevents and reduces the ability of women

» Construction crews build a border wall near Yuma, Arizona, on August 20, 2019.

and children to be lost, abandoned, and further exploited by the cartels.

Stopping criminals and gangs at the border reduces violent crime in every city in this country. . . .

And that's why we say all the time that every town, city, and state is a border town, border city, border state. Everything that touches our border touches every city, town, and state in this country, and that's why we have said and will continue to say borders matter; the wall matters. . . . 99

—Commissioner of U.S. Customs and Border Protection Mark Morgan, Yuma, Arizona, June 23, 2020

concur to agree

cartel syndicate that controls a business, such as the drug trade in a region

impede to hinder; slow

EXAMINE THE SOURCE

1. **Identifying** What problem(s) is the southern border wall intended to address?

2. **Distinguishing Fact From Opinion** What opinions does Morgan express? What facts does he provide to support those opinions?

PHOTO: Glenn Fawcett/APFootage/Alamy Stock Photo; TEXT: Morgan, Mark: "Remarks by President Trump in Roundtable on Border Security," Yuma, AZ, June 23, 2020.

Letter from the Attorney General

In 2017 President Donald J. Trump took office. His campaign had focused on building a wall along the southern border, deporting people in the country illegally, and reducing immigration.

PRIMARY SOURCE : LETTER

❝ I write to advise that the Department of Homeland Security (DHS) should rescind the June 15, 2012, DHS Memorandum entitled 'Exercising Prosecutorial Discretion with Respect to Individuals Who Came to the United States as Children,' as well as any related memoranda or guidance. This policy, known as 'Deferred Action for Childhood Arrivals' (DACA), allows certain individuals who are without lawful status in the United States to request and receive a renewable, two-year presumptive reprieve from removal, and other benefits such as work authorization and participation in the Social Security program.

DACA was effectuated by the previous administration through executive action, without proper statutory authority and with no established end-date, after Congress' repeated rejection of proposed legislation that would have accomplished a similar result. Such an open-ended circumvention of immigration laws was an unconstitutional exercise of authority by the Executive Branch. . . .

As Attorney General . . . I have a duty to defend the Constitution and to faithfully execute the laws passed by Congress. Proper enforcement of our immigration laws is, as President Trump consistently said, critical to the national interest and to the restoration of the rule of law in our country. The Department of Justice stands ready to assist and to continue to support DHS in these very important efforts. ❞

—Attorney General Jeff Sessions to DHS Acting Secretary Duke, September 4, 2017

EXAMINE THE SOURCE

1. **Analyzing Perspectives** What argument does this letter make? What is its intent?
2. **Citing Evidence** What reasoning and evidence does Sessions provide to support his position?

Your Inquiry Analysis

EVALUATE SOURCES AND USE EVIDENCE

Reflect back to the Compelling Question and the Supporting Question you developed at the beginning of this lesson.

1. **Gathering Sources** Which sources helped you answer the Compelling Question and your Supporting Questions most directly? Which sources, if any, raised additional concerns or questions? Where might you look to find additional information? Which sources complement or contradict each other? Group them by policy position or type of information.

2. **Evaluating Sources** Looking at the sources that helped you answer your supporting questions, evaluate the credibility of each source. What biases did each reveal, and how did this shape the content? Consider the authors and purposes of each. What evidence does each source provide to support its opinions?

3. **Comparing and Contrasting** Compare and contrast two of the sources in this lesson more closely. Consider the purpose, tone, author/creator, and nature of each source. How do the two sources relate to each other and work together to help you understand issues surrounding modern immigration?

COMMUNICATE CONCLUSIONS

Collaborating Find another student who has the same or a similar Supporting Question as one of yours. Exchange your responses. Then, together, write a response to the Compelling Question in which you cite evidence or examples from at least three of the sources. In your response, describe the relationship between issues surrounding immigration and public policy. Share your response as a brief oral report, an infographic, or a blog.

TAKE INFORMED ACTION

Understanding Immigration Investigate the role of immigrants and the effects of immigration in your state. Conduct additional research to learn about recent (past 10 years) immigration to the state, including data about employment, taxation, voting, small business ownership, and welfare. Then research at least two key policies or policy proposals related to immigrants in your state (or federal policies that affect your state). Read, watch, or listen to two contrasting perspectives. Use what you have learned to a) plan a public service campaign about immigration and policy in your state today or b) write a letter to relevant public official in which you express your position on one or more of the policies or propose a policy solution. For either task, be sure to cite appropriate evidence from your research.

Office of the Attorney General. "Letter from Attorney General Sessions to Acting Secretary Duke on the Rescission of DACA." September 4, 2017.

08

Trump Takes Office

READING STRATEGY

Analyzing Key Ideas and Details As you read, use a graphic organizer like the one below to take notes.

Trump Takes Office

I. The Election of 2016

   A.

   B.

II.

   A.

   B.

The Election of 2016

GUIDING QUESTION

How was Donald Trump different from previous candidates?

In 2016, Hillary Clinton made history by winning the Democratic Party nomination. This was the first time a major party had nominated a woman to run for president. Clinton had served as Secretary of State under Obama and been a senator from New York. She was married to President Bill Clinton and had been First Lady of the United States from 1993 to 2001. The Republican Party also made history by nominating Donald Trump. Trump was the first person nominated by a major party who had neither held elective office nor served as a commander in the military. Trump was a billionaire businessman and a well-known celebrity, having appeared regularly on radio and television since the 1980s.

Although Hillary Clinton won her party's nomination, she faced a major challenge from Vermont senator Bernie Sanders, a long-time advocate for socialist and progressive ideas. His campaign focused on income inequality, workers' rights, and social justice, and he supported government-run health care and government-paid college tuition. Sanders defeated Clinton in 23 states and won 43 percent of Democratic votes nationwide. His success, especially among younger voters, suggested the party's voters might have started to shift from supporting traditional liberal policies to supporting more progressive policies.

Trump's nomination came as a surprise. He defeated 16 candidates, many of whom were well-known Republican senators and governors. His criticism of free trade and his focus on immigration, the decline of American industry, and the need to end foreign wars appealed to more Republican voters than expected and suggested the Republican coalition of voters might also be changing. His campaign brought many new voters to the party. Turnout for the Republican primaries was the highest in 50 years.

Trump's Style: Salesman, Liar, or Populist?

Trump adopted a controversial campaign style. He was blunt, rude, sarcastic, and prone to exaggeration. He spoke in generalized terms such as *huge* and *very big*, perhaps reflecting a lifetime in business focused on "making the sale" rather than sticking to the facts. Trump did not ignore criticism or accept it with grace. He gave insulting nicknames to opponents, attacked their personalities as much as their ideas, and disparaged their accomplishments. During debates, he interrupted, talked over opponents, and argued with the moderators. He was an active user of Twitter, where he had tens of millions of followers. He filled his Twitter feed with jokes, insults, and criticisms of opponents, government policies, and the news media.

Trump's style polarized the nation. It angered those Americans who saw him as a liar, a con artist, and a bully. But to many others, his style seemed honest and direct compared to typical politicians. He did not mince words or hide his true feelings. He was enthusiastic and full of energy. Trump claimed that because he was so rich, political donors and lobbyists could not influence him the way they influenced other politicians. He referred to Washington as "the swamp" and pledged, if elected, to drain it.

On October 9, 2016, Hillary Clinton and Donald Trump held a presidential debate at Washington University in St. Louis. This was the second of three debates in advance of the 2016 election.

Drawing Conclusions What was the relationship between the two candidates based on this photograph?

Some commentators described Trump's style as **populism**. Populism is an approach to campaigning where candidates portray themselves as defenders of the people against a powerful elite at the top of society. Populists argue the government is controlled by this elite and their campaigns focus on putting government back into the hands of the people.

The first populist candidate in American history was President Andrew Jackson. He took power at a time when the right to vote was expanding from property owners to all white men, many of whom resented men of property. The next populist era began in the late nineteenth century when the nation was industrializing and many Americans distrusted the power of bankers and big business. During this era, Democrat presidential candidate William Jennings Bryan and President Teddy Roosevelt each used a populist style in their presidential campaigns. Both Jackson and Roosevelt, like Trump, had intensely loyal voters and were also strongly disliked by people at the top of American society.

Trump Takes Office

Most polls predicted that Hillary Clinton would win the election. Trump's lack of experience was expected to hurt his chances, and the economy was doing well after recovering from the Great Recession of 2007 to 2009. As the election approached, President Obama's popularity was above 50 percent, suggesting that voters would be comfortable choosing another Democrat who promised to continue and expand Obama's policies.

Contrary to the polls, Donald Trump won the election. Clinton won 48 percent of the popular vote to Trump's 46 percent, but Trump won the Electoral College. Trump won the Southern and Plains states that Republicans had won for several decades. But he also won Ohio and Florida, states that had swung back and forth in recent elections. Trump became the first Republican since 1988 to win Pennsylvania, Michigan, and Wisconsin. Voter data analysis showed two major changes compared to 2012 when Obama defeated Romney. In the states Trump won that had previously voted for Obama, white working-class turnout increased while African American turnout decreased.

At his inauguration Trump issued a promise that became the theme of his administration:

> We assembled here today are issuing a new decree to be heard in every city, in every foreign capital, and in every hall of power, from this day forward: a new vision will govern our land, from this day forward, it's going to be only America first. America first. Every decision on trade, on taxes, on immigration, on foreign affairs will be made to benefit American workers and American families. We must protect our borders from the ravages of other countries making our products, stealing our companies and destroying our jobs. Protection will lead to great prosperity and strength.

—Donald Trump, Inaugural Address, January 20, 2017

Some people expected Trump to change his style once elected, but he did not. He continued to use Twitter to attack and insult opponents. He routinely criticized the media, accusing them of "fake news." He also rapidly fired members of his administration if they seemed to be ineffective or disloyal. By the end of his

populism a political philosophy where politicians defend the people against a society's powerful elite

PHOTO: Chip Somodevilla/Getty Images; TEXT: Trump, Donald. 2017. Remarks of President Donald J. Trump - As Prepared for Delivery. Inaugural Address. January 20, 2017. Reprinted by The White House: Office of the Press Secretary.

term, Trump had fired and replaced more members of his cabinet and White House advisors than any previous president in the same amount of time.

✓ CHECK FOR UNDERSTANDING

1. **Identifying** What was the outcome of the 2016 presidential election?
2. **Describing** Describe populism, and explain why Trump's style might be called populist.

Trump and "America First"

GUIDING QUESTION

How did concerns about globalism affect Trump's policies?

The year before he ran for president, Trump published a book, *Crippled America: How to Make America Great Again*.

The phrase "Make America Great Again," or "MAGA," became the slogan for his campaign. Trump argued that the United States had lost its way by supporting **globalism**. After World War II, many American leaders, both Democrats and Republicans, embraced the idea of increasing trade between nations and building an interconnected global economy. They believed this would stop nations from fighting over resources and prevent another world war by improving everyone's standard of living and creating interdependence among the world's people. This idea was called internationalism in the early twentieth century. More recently it has been called globalism. In many ways, Trump's approach resembled U.S. policies before World War II. In the early twentieth century, opponents of internationalism were referred to as nationalists, or protectionists, both terms Trump frequently used. Protectionists believe government should regulate trade and impose **tariffs** to protect U.S. companies from competition and discourage them from moving their factories and jobs overseas where wages are lower. During the primaries, both Trump and Bernie Sanders raised concerns about trade and the need to protect U.S. workers. Trump's victory, and Sanders's primary wins in several states that had suffered from jobs moving out of the country, suggested many voters agreed.

When describing his approach, Trump used the phrase "America First" to explain his decisions. "America First" was first used by President Woodrow Wilson to explain why the U.S. should stay neutral in World War I, and then by President Warren G. Harding to explain why the U.S. did not join the League of Nations in the 1920s. It was also used by a lobby group, the America First Committee, that tried to prevent the U.S. from entering World War II. The phrase is also associated with isolationism, the idea that America should not join alliances or go to war unless the nation's safety is directly threatened. For Trump, the phrase meant finding a way to disentangle the nation from what he called the "forever wars" in the Middle East, to bring troops home from overseas, and to reduce the amount of money the U.S. spent defending allies in Europe and East Asia.

Tariffs, Trade, and Taxes

Trump strongly criticized several previous presidents, saying they had signed "unfair" trade deals that let other nations take advantage of the United States. He also strongly criticized the Chinese government, saying it had manipulated the value of China's currency so that trade deals worked to China's advantage. He also accused China of stealing American intellectual property, especially computer technology.

Upon taking office, Trump withdrew from negotiations on the Trans-Pacific Partnership (TPP), a trade deal with eleven other countries. He also warned Canada and Mexico that the U.S. would withdraw from NAFTA (North American Free Trade Agreement) unless the treaty was renegotiated. He then imposed tariffs on steel and aluminum from Canada and Mexico. Negotiations to amend NAFTA began soon after, and in late 2018, the three countries signed a new trade deal called the United States-Mexico-Canada Agreement (USMCA). Congress ratified the agreement with bipartisan support in early 2020.

To pressure China into a new deal, President Trump imposed tariffs on steel, aluminum and a few other products made in China, and then steadily expanded the list of goods when China did not respond. The tariffs led to a trade war, a conflict in which countries try to hurt each other by restricting trade in goods that the other country wants to buy or sell. China imposed tariffs on American cars, airplanes and soybeans—the top farm product the United States sells to China. The trade war eventually led to new negotiations. In early 2020 the two nations signed the U.S.-China Phase One trade deal that set new rules for currency exchange rates, intellectual property, and the transfer of technology and set targets for the quantities of goods China would import from the United States.

In addition to negotiating new trade deals, the president pushed for new tax cuts. Trump had long argued that one reason U.S. companies moved factories and jobs to other countries was because American corporations paid some of the highest taxes

---

globalism increased trade between nations and an interconnected global economy

tariff a tax added to imported or exported goods

President Trump and Kim Jong-Un meet at the Demilitarized Zone between North and South Korea in 2019.

Identifying the Main Idea Why did Trump want to conduct face-to-face negotiations with North Korea?

in the world. In late 2017, the Republican-controlled Congress passed Trump's plan, the Tax Cuts and Jobs Act, the largest overhaul of the tax code since Ronald Reagan's tax reforms in 1986. By cutting tax rates and changing deductions, the act significantly reduced the amount of federal income tax most Americans paid. The act also cut corporate tax rates from among the highest in the world to among the lowest when compared to other industrial nations.

Ending "Forever Wars"

When President Trump entered the White House, his primary foreign policy goal was to end the ongoing wars in the Middle East. The first step that he took was to defeat the terrorist group ISIS. ISIS had seized control of a large part of Syria and Iraq in early 2014, and carried out terrorist attacks around the world. After meeting with military leaders, President Trump increased the troops in Syria and allowed local commanders to make more decisions on the use of force. This led to a dramatic increase in airstrikes and made it easier for American troops to support local forces fighting ISIS. By early 2018, an estimated 98 percent the territory controlled by ISIS had been taken back by coalition forces.

With the defeat of ISIS, Trump began pushing to bring the troops home, but Congress and military leaders resisted. They thought pulling out troops would give Russia, Iran, and Turkey too much power in the region and hurt American allies, including the Kurds and the Syrian forces fighting to make Syria more democratic. Trump's Secretary of Defense James Matthis resigned rather than implement Trump's decision. The debate led to a reduction of American troops in Syria but not a full withdrawal.

Trump also pushed to end the war in Afghanistan. The war had been underway for nearly 16 years when Trump took office. The Taliban, the radical Islamic group that controlled Afghanistan in 2001 and supported Osama bin Laden and al-Qaeda, had been driven from power. But they had kept fighting, and neither side seemed able to win. Trump did not think the war was worth fighting anymore. Others disagreed, believing the Taliban would continue to support terrorism and might destroy Afghanistan's fragile democracy.

After Trump ordered 3,000 more troops to Afghanistan and the U.S. increased airstrikes, the Taliban agreed to negotiate. In February 2020 they agreed if the U.S. withdrew its troops, the Taliban

Handout/Dong-A Ilbo/Getty Images.

would not allow its members, or members of al-Qaeda or ISIS, to use its territory to prepare attacks against the U.S. or its allies. Soon afterward, U.S. troops began coming home. When Trump left office, only 2,500 troops remained in Afghanistan, the lowest number since the war began. The war between the Taliban and the Afghan government continued, however, and the U.S. continued airstrikes to support Afghan forces fighting the Taliban.

Maximum Pressure on Iran

The Trump administration believed Iran was responsible for much of the ongoing violence in the Middle East that kept American troops in the region. In 2015, the U.S., Britain, France, Germany, Russia, and China had signed a deal with Iran. Iran agreed to stop trying to build a nuclear weapon in exchange for an end to economic sanctions. Trump believed the deal was a mistake. Iran remained hostile to the United States, hostile to Israel, and continued to support terrorist groups. In spring 2018, he withdrew the U.S. from the deal, imposed sanctions, and shifted to a policy of "maximum pressure" on Iran.

Almost immediately, tensions began to rise. Terrorist groups supported by Iran attacked oil tankers in the Persian Gulf. In response, the U.S. sent warships into the region. Iran then shot down a U.S. military drone, and militia groups supported by Iran attacked U.S. bases in Iraq. In January 2020, Trump authorized an airstrike that killed Qasem Soleimani, an Iranian general who coordinated Iran's support for militia groups and terrorists in the Middle East. Soleimani was a hero in Iran with close ties to Iranian leaders. In response to his death, Iran fired missiles at two Iraqi airbases where Americans were stationed, injuring many American soldiers. With the two countries on the edge of war, Trump rejected further military escalation. He imposed more sanctions but also proposed new negotiations. Although Iran rejected the offer, both countries backed away from war.

The Abraham Accords

During his campaign, Trump had stressed his support for Israel and in late 2017, he kept a campaign promise by officially recognizing Jerusalem as Israel's capital and directing the American embassy to be moved to Jerusalem. Bill Clinton, George W. Bush, and Barack Obama all made the same promise when campaigning but did not follow through after being elected. In response, the Palestinian government cut off diplomatic relations with the United States. Congress then responded by cutting off all aid to the Palestinians.

Opponents of Trump's decision believed it would hurt U.S. relations with the Arab states. By 2018, Iran had begun supporting terrorist groups hostile to Saudi Arabia and its Arab allies. After several Iranian-backed terrorist attacks on their territory and shipping, Saudi Arabia and its allies decided to improve relations with Israel and cooperate more closely with the U.S. to counter Iran. In 2020, the Trump administration brokered a series of agreements known as the Abraham Accords between Israel and several Arab states. The United Arab Emirates, Bahrain, Morocco, and Sudan all signed the accords, established normal relations with Israel, and committed to cooperation, tolerance, and dialogue to end conflict in the Middle East.

Negotiating with North Korea

American troops had been stationed on the border of North Korea for nearly 70 years when Trump took office, and in recent years, relations had been growing worse. North Korea began building nuclear weapons during the Bush administration and testing long range missiles during the Obama administration. The U.S. had responded by imposing sanctions and working to keep North Korea isolated.

Trump continued the policy in public, but behind the scenes, his administration reached out to see if a deal was possible. To the surprise of many, North Korea's leader Kim Jong-Un agreed to discussions. Trump became the first president to meet with a North Korean leader. He met Kim Jong-Un three times: in Singapore in 2018, in Vietnam in early 2019, and then at the border of North and South Korea in June 2019, where Trump became the first president to set foot in North Korea. The two sides were not able to agree on a deal, but the meetings reduced tensions. North Korea did not conduct any new tests of nuclear weapons or long-range missiles for the rest of Trump's term.

✓ CHECK FOR UNDERSTANDING

1. **Summarizing** How does globalism differ from Trump's America First policies?
2. **Explaining** Why did Trump think his trade and tax policies would help the U.S.?

Immigration and the Border

GUIDING QUESTION

What were the main goals of Trump's immigration policies?

From the beginning of his campaign, Trump criticized U.S. immigration policies. His views were one of the reasons critics accused him of being racist. He asserted that by failing to control its borders, the U.S. made it easy for terrorists, violent criminals, and illegal drugs to enter the country. 2016 polls showed that while a majority of Americans believed immigrants were good for the country, the number of people who thought illegal immigration was a serious issue had risen during Obama's second term. Those concerns shaped the immigration policies Trump tried to implement after taking office.

The Travel Ban

The events of 9/11, the wars in Iraq and Syria, and the gruesome attacks by ISIS in 2015 and 2016 convinced many people, including Trump, that immigrants from regions associated with terrorism should be kept out of the United States. One week after taking office, Trump signed an order banning travel from seven Muslim-majority nations that supported terrorist groups or were experiencing ongoing civil war and terrorist activity.

The ban was immediately challenged in court. Opponents argued it violated immigration law and was unconstitutional because the immigrants were being discriminated against based on their religion. In *Trump v. Hawaii*, the Supreme Court ruled 5–4 that the president could issue the ban for reasons of national security. Justice Sonia Sotomayor criticized the decision, comparing it to the *Korematsu* decision in World War II that let President Roosevelt move Japanese Americans to internment camps. Chief Justice Roberts disagreed with Sotomayor's

comparison, but he did issue a statement saying for the first time that the Supreme Court considered the *Korematsu* case to have been wrongly decided. He also said that Roosevelt's actions to forcibly remove people on the basis of race had been "morally repugnant" and outside the scope of presidential authority.

Crisis at the Southern Border

Although the number of people crossing the border without authorization declined dramatically during the Bush and Obama administrations, events at the southern border during Obama's second term helped revive the issue for the 2016 election. Central America has four of the five poorest countries in the Western Hemisphere. The region has experienced many civil wars and military coups, along with rising crime, gang violence, drug trafficking, human trafficking, and government corruption. Desperate to improve their lives and help their children escape the violence and poverty, many Central Americans, especially those in Guatemala, Honduras, and El Salvador, looked for ways to migrate to the United States. Some turned to human smugglers, nicknamed coyotes, who exploited people's desperation and promised to get them into the United States if they paid enough.

In 2017 some Americans publicly gathered to change the nations' immigration policy.

Summarizing Why did family separations become a point of protest during Trump's administration?

Jim West/Alamy Stock Photo.

Beginning in 2012, the number of Central Americans crossing the border illegally began to rapidly increase. Many of these immigrants were young women and children, and children traveling without their parents. More than 130,000 unaccompanied children crossed the border between 2012 and 2014. This rising number of incoming people overwhelmed American customs officials who worked and processed people trying to cross the southern border. The children were moved to overcrowded detention facilities then transported to families that agreed to sponsor them until their cases could be heard.

It was in this context that in June 2015, with stories of immigrants crossing the border still fresh in people's minds, presidential candidate Donald Trump promised to build a wall along the border with Mexico to reduce illegal immigration. The border between the two nations is slightly less than 2,000 miles long. By the time that Donald Trump assumed the presidency, some form of barrier wall or fence covered about 650 miles of the border. The approximately 1,350 miles were monitored by electronic sensors and surveillance devices. This equipment alerted border patrol officers whenever someone tried to cross into the United States without permission.

Once he was in the White House, President Trump ordered work on the wall to begin with the funds for barriers that Congress had already approved. When Congress later agreed to only a small amount of money for the wall, Trump declared an emergency at the border and diverted military funds to build the wall. Opposition to the wall was intense. Civil rights groups, environmentalists, and nineteen state governments went to court to slow its construction. By the end of Trump's term, only 450 miles of new or replacement wall had been built.

"Zero Tolerance"

To deter illegal crossings, Trump announced a "zero tolerance" policy of prosecuting anyone caught. Despite the policy, Central Americans began organizing new caravans of thousands of people in the fall of 2018. The number of people arrested for entering the U.S. without authorization rose to more than 850,000 in 2019, the highest in over ten years. Under zero tolerance, adults were separated from their children and held for trial. The children were sent to overcrowded facilities or placed with sponsors. Parents were sometimes deported without their children. In other cases, the location of children was lost, and they could not be reunited with their parents. As criticism of the separations intensified, Trump ordered them to stop. His administration went to court to ask permission to detain the children with their parents because a previous court ruling did not allow it. Instead the court declared adults with minor children had to be released within three weeks of arrest.

Administration officials had data suggesting that if unauthorized people were released, many would not show up for their court cases and they believed the court decision would encourage more people to come. In response, they developed the Migrant Protection Protocols (MPP), sometimes called the "Remain in Mexico" policy. Trump issued an order requiring all immigrants at the southern border to stay in Mexico until their cases were heard. This prevented families from being released into the U.S. before their hearing. Anyone caught crossing the border without authorization was simply sent back to Mexico.

At first, Mexico rejected the plan, not wanting tens of thousands of refugees remaining on its territory. Trump argued the crisis was partly Mexico's fault as it had not controlled its own southern border. He threatened to impose tariffs on Mexican imports if they did not agree. After tense negotiations, Mexican officials allowed the refugees to remain in Mexico. They also agreed to deploy the Mexican National Guard to Mexico's southern border to stop caravans from coming north. Although the number of immigrants crossing the border dropped rapidly, opponents questioned if the policy was humane. Refugees had no easy access to food, shelter, or medical care, and many had small children. Tent camps were set up, but conditions were difficult and work hard to find. Refugees faced prejudice and were targets for criminals.

The DACA Children

Many immigrants who entered the U.S. illegally over the years brought children with them. In 2012, President Obama issued an executive order creating the Deferred Action for Childhood Arrivals (DACA) program. The order allowed undocumented immigrants who had arrived as children to remain for two years, subject to renewal, and directed immigration officials to give work permits to people who qualified. DACA was controversial. Critics argued that the program violated immigration law and that presidents cannot change federal law by executive order. Supporters pointed out that it was not the children's fault they were in the country without authorization, and that growing up without documentation limited their opportunities for education and jobs.

Trump opposed DACA during his campaign but said he wanted a deal that would let the children stay as part of a new immigration bill. But in June 2017, four states threatened to sue the federal government unless DACA was rescinded. After the attorney general said DACA would not hold up in court, Trump issued an order ending the program in six months. The six-month delay was to give Congress time to pass a new law to solve the problem. Trump's order did not get Congress to act. Instead it led to lawsuits, and in 2020, the Supreme Court reversed Trump's order. The Court did not address DACA's constitutionality. It ruled Trump had not followed a law that requires a good explanation for rescinding a program when people have come to rely on it.

✓ CHECK FOR UNDERSTANDING

1. **Identifying** What was the DACA program and why was it introduced?
2. **Explaining** Why did a crisis develop at the southern border during both the Obama and Trump administrations?

The Supreme Court

GUIDING QUESTION

Why were Trump's appointments of Supreme Court justices so controversial?

Supreme Court Justice Antonin Scalia died in February 2016 while Barack Obama was still in the White House. Justice Scalia had been a conservative justice and his death gave the Democrats a chance to shift the Supreme Court in a more liberal direction. President Obama nominated moderate Judge Merrick Garland to replace him, but the Republican-controlled Senate refused to act on the nomination.

Republican Majority Leader Mitch McConnell said he would follow the "Biden Rule." This referred to a speech Senator Joe Biden had given in 1992. Biden had suggested that if a Supreme Court vacancy occurred in an election year when the president was from one party and the Senate was controlled by a different party, the Senate should not vote on the nominee until the election showed the direction voters wanted for the country.

Biden's argument was theoretical. No rule was put in place, and the Constitution allows the Senate to act on nominations regardless of upcoming elections. But with the balance on the Court at stake, Republicans held firm and refused to act until after the election. Soon after taking office, Trump nominated a conservative judge, Neil Gorsuch, to replace Scalia. Gorsuch was quickly confirmed by the Senate.

The following year, Supreme Court Justice Anthony Kennedy retired and Trump nominated Judge Brett Kavanaugh. During the Senate hearings, Democrats released a letter from Dr. Christine Blasey Ford, in which she accused Kavanaugh of sexual assault when they were in their teens. Kavanaugh strongly denied the charges. Following an FBI investigation, congressional testimony from Dr. Ford and Judge Kavanaugh, and a close vote of 50–48, Judge Kavanaugh joined the Court in October 2018.

Less than two years later, just six weeks before the 2020 election, Justice Ruth Bader Ginsburg died. President Trump nominated Judge Amy Coney Barrett, and Senate Republicans moved rapidly to confirm her before the election, and Barrett was approved 52–48. Democrats criticized Republicans, noting their refusal to vote on Merrick Garland during an election year. McConnell said the situation was different. In 2016, the Senate and presidency were controlled by different parties. In 2020, the Senate and presidency were controlled by the same party so the "Biden rule" did not apply.

Ruth Bader Ginsburg had been a strong liberal member of the Supreme Court. By replacing her with Barrett, a staunch conservative jurist, President Trump had decisively shifted the balance on the Court. Ruth Bader Ginsburg was a hero to Democrats and a role model for many liberal women. Her replacement by a conservative justice under controversial conditions angered Democrats enough that some suggested the Supreme Court should be reformed.

Possible reforms suggested included increasing the size of the Court, setting term limits for justices, changing the Court's processes, giving Congress power to override the Court, or even changing the Court's constitutional role. Joe Biden, running for president at the time, promised, if elected, to create a commission to study possible reforms to the Supreme Court.

✓ CHECK FOR UNDERSTANDING

1. **Identifying** How did the Republicans justify treating the nominations of Merrick Garland and Amy Coney Barrett differently?
2. **Explaining** Why was the replacement of Ruth Bader Ginsburg with Amy Coney Barrett significant?

LESSON ACTIVITIES

1. **Argumentative Writing** Write a letter to the president or a member of Congress explaining whether you agree or disagree with President Trump's policies at the southern border. Provide details and reasons to support your argument.

2. **Presenting** Work with a partner to prepare a presentation describing how President Trump implemented his idea of "America First" and whether you agree with the approach. Use either his trade policies or his actions in the Middle East as evidence for your presentation. Conduct online research to look for additional facts and details that will help you explain your views of the president's policy.

09

Resistance and Protest During the Trump Years

READING STRATEGY

Analyzing Key Ideas and Details As you read, use a graphic organizer like the one below to take notes.

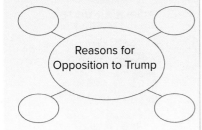

Reasons for Opposition to Trump

Resistance to Trump

GUIDING QUESTION

What ways did Democrats and others try to resist Donald Trump's presidency?

Many Americans, both Democrats and Republicans, feared that Donald Trump was an authoritarian, determined to get what he wanted without concern for the law or the Constitution. They saw him as a threat to the nation and set out to stop him. Some even worried that he was controlled by the Russian government. Others thought he was incompetent, uninformed, and therefore dangerous. Some of those opposed to him began calling themselves "the resistance," a reference to the French resistance in World War II that kept fighting the Nazis after France surrendered. They were determined to do what they could to block Trump's agenda because they believed it was bad for the country.

The FBI Investigates

Suspicion about Trump began before the election. Trump had negotiated business deals with Russian companies in the past, and rumors began to circulate that the Russian government was helping his campaign. In 2016 a law firm working for the Democratic Party hired a company named Fusion GPS to look for damaging information on Donald Trump to sway voters against his candidacy. To investigate the Russia rumors, Fusion GPS hired retired British intelligence officer Christopher Steele, who had contacts in Russia.

Steele sent reports to the FBI suggesting a close relationship between Trump and Russia. At about the same time, it was discovered that Russia had hacked the email of the Democratic National Committee and the Clinton campaign. This led U.S. intelligence to conclude Russia was trying to influence the election. In July 2016, the FBI began an investigation to see if the Trump campaign had connections to the Russian government.

Concerns About the Election

Trump's victory in 2016 was so unexpected that it made many people question the results. The news stories about Russia stealing emails led to suggestions that Russia might have used computer hacking to alter the election results. Given that Clinton had won the popular vote and Trump had won Wisconsin, Michigan, and Pennsylvania by such small margins, many people began to doubt the outcome.

A few weeks after the election, the Clinton campaign supported a request from a bipartisan group of electors for the Electoral College to be briefed on Russian efforts to influence the election. At the same time, editorials and advertisements appeared trying to convince the electors who were supposed to vote for Trump to vote for someone else. The electors received tens of thousands of emails and many reported being threatened and harassed. Ultimately, ten electors tried, and seven succeeded, in casting a vote for a different candidate than who their state had selected. This was the highest number of "faithless" electors in American history. The final Electoral vote was 304 votes for Trump, 227 for Clinton, and 7 for other individuals.

GO ONLINE Explore the Student Edition eBook and find interactive maps, time lines, and tools.

603

Presidential Election of 2016

Donald Trump lost the popular vote but won the Electoral College vote.

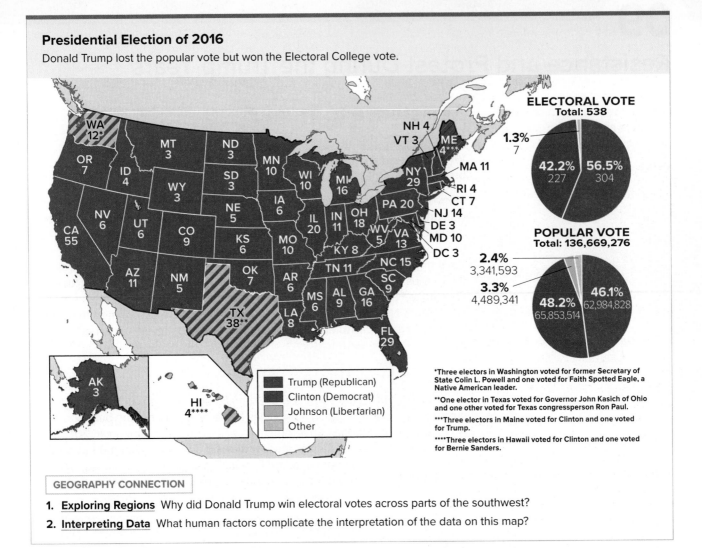

ELECTORAL VOTE
Total: 538

1.3%
7

42.2%
227

56.5%
304

POPULAR VOTE
Total: 136,669,276

2.4%
3,341,593

3.3%
4,489,341

48.2%
65,853,514

46.1%
62,984,828

Trump (Republican)
Clinton (Democrat)
Johnson (Libertarian)
Other

*Three electors in Washington voted for former Secretary of State Colin L. Powell and one voted for Faith Spotted Eagle, a Native American leader.

**One elector in Texas voted for Governor John Kasich of Ohio and one other voted for Texas congressperson Ron Paul.

***Three electors in Maine voted for Clinton and one voted for Trump.

****Three electors in Hawaii voted for Clinton and one voted for Bernie Sanders.

GEOGRAPHY CONNECTION

1. **Exploring Regions** Why did Donald Trump win electoral votes across parts of the southwest?

2. **Interpreting Data** What human factors complicate the interpretation of the data on this map?

When Congress met to count the Electoral votes, 11 Democrats rose to object, expressing concerns about Russian interference as well as possible voter suppression in several states. Their objections were overruled. Millions of Americans however, including a majority of Democrats, did not believe Trump had won fairly, and within weeks of Trump taking office, Democrats in Congress began talking about impeaching him. Even Hillary Clinton, although she conceded the election, stated four years later she still had doubts: "We still don't know what really happened," Clinton said. "But you don't win by three million votes and have all this other shenanigans and stuff going on and not come away with an idea like, 'Whoa, something's not right here.'"

The Mueller Investigation

The FBI continued investigating the Trump campaign after Trump took office. Trump called it a "witch-hunt" and a "hoax." He clashed repeatedly with FBI Director James Comey over the investigation, and in May 2017, Trump fired Comey. Democrats then called for a Special Counsel to continue the investigation and a

week later former FBI Director Robert Mueller was appointed to investigate Russian election interference.

Mueller's investigation took almost two years. His report concluded that Russia had tried to influence the election by hacking the Democratic Party and Clinton campaign and releasing the emails they stole and by posting fake information on Facebook and Twitter to sway voters.

Mueller found no evidence that Russia had hacked voting machines or altered actual votes. Nor did he find evidence of a conspiracy between the Trump campaign and the Russian government to influence the election. Mueller indicted 34 people, including 26 Russians and 7 Americans. Among the Americans charged were Trump's lawyer and 4 members of Trump's campaign team. None of the Americans were charged with crimes related to Russian interference in the election, and Trump eventually pardoned the 4 men who had worked on his campaign.

Trump and many of his supporters believed the investigation had been politically motivated. In 2019 the Justice Department's inspector general issued a

Clinton, Hillary. In Dovere, Edward-Isaac. "Hillary Clinton Says She Was Right All Along." The Atlantic. October 9, 2020.

report critical of the FBI's conduct. Several FBI agents, including the FBI's second-in-command, were fired. The inspector general found the FBI had acted properly in opening an investigation but found instances where the FBI made false statements and falsified evidence to get the court to approve wiretaps and other actions that required court permission.

The inspector general also found some agents were biased against Trump, but did not find evidence they let their personal feelings affect their decisions. Attorney General William Barr appointed District Attorney John Durham to review the FBI's actions. The review became a criminal investigation, and in 2020 one FBI agent pled guilty to altering evidence. The Durham investigation continued into 2021.

Trump is Impeached

The Mueller investigation did not resolve concerns of Trump's critics. In the summer of 2019, a whistleblower in the intelligence community filed a complaint about a call between Trump and the president of Ukraine. The whistleblower claimed that Trump wanted Ukraine to help him win re-election by investigating rumors regarding then-Vice President Joe Biden and Biden's son's connections to a Ukrainian company. The whistleblower also alleged that Trump had threatened to withhold military aid if Ukraine refused.

After the story broke, Democrats in the House of Representatives began an investigation. In response, Trump released a transcript of the call. Although Trump did ask the Ukrainians to investigate the allegations against Biden, he did not reference the election or make a threat to withhold aid, although he had blocked aid to the Ukraine several days before the call.

The Democrats were not convinced. They suspected an informal understanding had been reached. Several diplomats and State Department officials testified they too thought a deal had been made. The House Judiciary Committee then drafted two articles of impeachment. They charged Trump with abuse of power, and obstruction of Congress because he had asserted executive privilege and refused to turn over documents they had subpoenaed.

On December 18, 2019, the House voted in favor of the articles with nearly all Democrats voting in favor and nearly all Republicans opposed. Donald Trump became the third U.S. president to be impeached, Andrew Johnson was impeached in 1868. Bill Clinton was impeached in 1998. Neither of them were convicted by the Senate.

Democrats knew Trump's conviction was also unlikely because a two-thirds vote was needed, Republicans controlled the Senate, and several Republican senators had stated that what mattered was Trump's motive and they did not believe the evidence showed he had a corrupt reason for his actions. On February 5, 2020, by a vote of 52–48, the Senate found Trump not guilty of abuse of power. By a vote of 53–47 they found him not guilty of obstruction of Congress.

✓ CHECK FOR UNDERSTANDING

1. **Summarizing** What steps did opponents of President Trump take to stop him from taking office?
2. **Explaining** Why did the House of Representatives impeach Trump?

Social Protest During the Trump Years

GUIDING QUESTION

How do the protests of the Trump years reflect social justice concerns?

As Democrats and officials inside the government who opposed Trump looked for ways to stall his agenda and weaken his presidency, many other Americans launched protests against the values they believed he represented. Many of them regarded the president as a male chauvinist and a racist. Trump's success worried many liberal and progressive Americans because it suggested there was more acceptance of sexism and racism than they had thought. This led his opponents to protest and take other actions to push back against society's apparent shift toward values they rejected.

The Women's March and #MeToo

Hillary Clinton's campaign put women's issues back in the spotlight in American politics. Many women were deeply disappointed when she lost, partly because her chances looked so good, and partly because of accusations made against Trump during the campaign. Between June and November of 2016, over 20 women accused Donald Trump of lewd and inappropriate behavior toward them. In addition, a recording of Trump from 2005 was released in which he spoke about acting inappropriately toward women. Trump apologized, saying his remarks did not reflect his actual behavior. He denied the accusations the women had made, calling many of them liars seeking publicity or money.

When Trump won the election after these events, opponents set up a Facebook group to organize a Women's March on Washington to protest his inauguration. The march took place on January 21, 2017, the day after Trump was inaugurated. Similar marches were held in cities across the nation and in some 80 other countries. Over 450,000 people marched in Washington, and an estimated three to five million marched in other cities around the U.S. and the world. The Women's March of 2017 was the largest one-day protest in American history.

In the summer of 2020 following George Floyd's death, protests occurred across the U.S. and the world to demand improved and more equal treatment in the criminal justice system for people of color.

Understanding Main Ideas How did the George Floyd marches relate to the wider social justice movement?

The accusations against Trump during the campaign, as well as the women's march, drew attention to how some people with power use their position to sexually harass or abuse others. Later in 2017, a movement known as #MeToo gained national attention as many prominent women began to report their stories of harassment and abuse by major figures in the news, sports, entertainment, and financial industries.

As the movement gained momentum, it encouraged more and more women to come forward. More than 200 prominent men who were accused resigned from their positions. A few were arrested and charged with crimes including rape, sexual abuse, and battery. Several members of Congress faced accusations of sexual harassment, and two of them resigned from Congress as a result. In Congress, several female senators spoke about their own personal experiences with harassment. Because of their public statements, the rules in Congress were changed to make reporting incidents of harassment easier. Many states passed new laws in response to the #MeToo movement. These laws required companies to have mandatory sexual harassment training, banned nondisclosure agreements, gave victims more time to bring their cases, and made it easier for victims to sue perpetrators.

The Social Justice Movement

Social justice is the idea that all people in society should be treated fairly and that society should not have rules that give advantages to some people at the expense of others. Those concerned with social justice look at how wealth and power is distributed in society and analyze who has privilege. They used the word privilege to mean "the advantages some people have over others."

In recent decades, social justice advocates have focused on the privilege of identity. A person has many identities: their name, their family, their nationality, their job, their religion, and so on. A person's identity also includes their race, their gender, and their sexual orientation. Supporters of social justice assert a white identity brings certain privileges and being male and heterosexual brings other privileges. They believe the system has advantages for white men that makes it harder for people of other identities to get their fair share of wealth and power in society. This is the basic idea of systemic racism.

The idea of systemic racism is not new, but it became a controversial term during President Trump's term. **Systemic racism** means that a system—the way people work together to do things—has a built-in bias for or against people depending on their race. A historical example is segregation in the American

systemic racism the way people work together to do things has a built-in bias for or against people depending on their race

Erik Pendzich/Alamy Stock Photo.

South. It did not matter if a person did not agree with segregation; they had to obey their state's law and could not, for example, serve African Americans at lunch counters reserved for whites. The system created a racial hierarchy that gave certain groups advantages over others. Requiring that someone be able to read to vote is another example. If most of those who cannot read are of a different race, the voting system systematically discriminates against them. Many types of systemic racism were ended by the Civil Rights Acts of 1957, 1964, and 1968 as well as the Voting Rights Act of 1965. The introduction of affirmative action in the 1970s tried to address other types of systemic racism that limited African American access to education and jobs.

But by the 2010s, some 50 years after the achievements of the civil rights movement and despite the election of the nation's first African American president, it remained true that African Americans still had not achieved full equality with white people. Although there were many examples of African Americans who had achieved great wealth, power, and success in their careers, the African American community as a whole still did not have an equal share of the nation's wealth or the same rate of higher education, and the community had higher rates of arrest and imprisonment and more medical problems. This suggested to activists that there were other types of systemic racism, perhaps harder to see, embedded in society that gave white people privileges and made it harder for minorities to get to the same level.

Woke Politics

The focus on identity-based politics and systemic racism came to be called "woke" politics. The phrase traces back to African American culture of the 1920s. It referred to the need to stay aware of the racism in society while also embracing African American culture. In 2014 after Michael Brown was killed by police, the #StayWoke movement began online. The term began to refer to the idea that most people are unaware of the systemic racism in society and that activists need to "wake people up" if change is going to happen.

The need to get people's attention led activists to focus on language and symbols, such as flags, statues, slogans, mascots, anthems, music, pop culture advertising, and various other forms of symbolic speech. Activists tried to point out bias, racism, or stereotypes in the symbols, often seeking to have them removed or altered. They also criticized people for their public statements, both past and present, and sometimes filed complaints seeking to have people suspended from social media, expelled from school, or fired from their jobs for expressing ideas the activists felt were contrary to social justice goals.

One prominent symbolic protest that garnered nationwide attention was the decision of many professional athletes from 2016 onward to rest on one knee instead of standing for the national anthem. Taking a knee was intended as a reminder of the nation's history of racism and as a protest of police behavior toward African Americans. As with many of the symbolic actions of woke politics, taking a knee divided Americans. While some applauded the actions, others, including President Trump, saw it as disrespectful to the nation and objected to bringing the divisiveness of politics into sports.

For many, the most prominent symbols that spoke to the nation's history of racism were statues and flags related to the Confederate States of America. The concern with Confederate symbols had been building for a long time, but it erupted in 2014 when white supremacist Dylann Roof killed nine African Americans in a church in Charleston, South Carolina. The attack renewed discussion about racism and Confederate symbols, and over the next few years, protests across the U.S. began demanding the removal of Confederate symbols, including flags as well as statues of Confederate war heroes.

Six months after Trump's inauguration, white supremacist, neo-Nazi, and Ku Klux Klan groups organized a rally in Charlottesville, Virginia, to protest the city's decision to remove a statue of Confederate General Robert E. Lee. As news of the rally spread, counter-protestors traveled to Charlottesville to march in opposition. Violence erupted as the two sides fought each other and one white supremacist, James Alex Fields, Jr., rammed his car into Counter-protestors killing Heather Heyer and wounding 19 others.

Both Democrats and Republicans condemned the violence. But President Trump inflamed the situation when he said, "we condemn in the strongest possible terms this egregious display of hatred, bigotry and violence on many sides, on many sides." This implied that he thought people who opposed racism were no different than those who supported racism. Critics demanded Trump condemn the white supremacists. Trump did so, but his determination not to anger voters who opposed taking down the statue got in the way. He claimed there "were very fine people, on both sides . . . and I'm not talking about the neo-Nazis and the white nationalists—because they should be condemned totally. But you had many people in that group other than neo-Nazis and white nationalists." Former vice president Joe Biden later said this response was what convinced him to run against Trump in 2020.

Racial Protests Sweep the Nation

On May 25, 2020, George Floyd, an African American man, was killed by Derek Chauvin, a white Minneapolis police officer. A video taken during the arrest showed Chauvin restraining Floyd by pressing his knee on

Trump, Donald. "Statement by President Trump." August 14, 2017. Daily Comp. Pres. Docs., 2017.

Floyd's neck. The video captured Floyd telling police, "I can't breathe." Chauvin was arrested and convicted of murder. Three other officers present during the arrest, Tou Thao, J. Alexander Kueng, and Thomas Lane were also charged with aiding and abetting murder.

Floyd's death was the latest in a series of incidents that had focused attention on how police use force in situations involving African Americans. From 2015 to 2020, police in the U.S. killed 5,530 people. About half of those killed were white, and 26 percent were African American. But African Americans are only 12 percent of the population, and they were more than twice as likely to be killed by police. Therefore, protestors began to argue that some sort of systemic racism was producing these different results.

Although African Americans have struggled for decades with how police treat them, the issue began to gain national attention in 2014 with the death of Eric Garner in New York, who died after police used a chokehold on him. Later in 2014 the shooting death of Michael Brown in Ferguson, Missouri brought the Black Lives Matter movement to national prominence. Then came the shootings of Laquan McDonald in Chicago and Tamir Rice in Cleveland. Then in 2015, Walter Scott in Charleston, South Carolina, Samuel DuBose in Cincinnati, Sandra Bland in Texas, and Freddie Gray in Baltimore were killed by police. Then in 2016, Alton Sterling in Baton Rouge and Philando Castile in Minneapolis were killed. In 2018 Stephon Clark in Sacramento was killed, followed in 2020 by Breonna Taylor in Louisville.

In these incidents, police actions toward African Americans provoked outrage, and in almost every case, their behavior was captured on video. Social media spread the videos, and local protests against the police erupted. For many, the video of Floyd's death was the last straw. Within days of Floyd's death, large demonstrations began in Minneapolis and quickly spread nationwide. Some were organized by Black Lives Matter; others began spontaneously.

Over 8,700 protests, the vast majority peaceful, took place in 2020 in all 50 states as well as large demonstrations in Britain, France, Italy, Portugal, Brazil, Canada, and Australia. Some protestors also tried to vandalize or pull down statues that they believed symbolized racist values. This included Confederate statues, statues of Christopher Columbus, and some statues of the nation's founders and early leaders who had been slaveholders, including Presidents Washington, Jefferson, and Jackson. The movement also spread to other countries with large black communities that struggle with the legacy of slavery, poverty, racism, and exclusion.

Rioting Divides the Nation

In addition to the peaceful demonstrations, riots erupted in many cities. Of the 8,700 protests staged in

2020, more than 570 experienced riots as well. Police used tear gas, pepper spray, and rubber bullets to try to control the rioters. Many mayors and governors enacted curfews to decrease the violence, and National Guard troops were sent to many cities. Tens of thousands of people were arrested; more than 2,000 people were injured, and at least 25 were killed. Over $1 billion in property was damaged.

Counter-protesters called for Americans to "Back the Blue" and support police and waved the "Blue Lives Matter" flag that had been created in 2014 after the shooting of two New York police officers. Trump expressed support for the police as well. As a presidential candidate, he had criticized Black Lives Matter, and he continued to do so during the protests, blaming the movement for the rioting and violence. With the 2020 election approaching, Trump stressed his commitment to "law and order," a phrase Richard Nixon used during his campaign to appeal to voters concerned about the violence of the late 1960s.

Police Reforms

In the wake of George Floyd's death, Black Lives Matter and other activists began a call to "defund the police." What this phrase meant varied. Some protestors believed police departments should be abolished. Others suggested police budgets be cut to pressure police departments into making reforms. Still others wanted some of the police budget to be used for social workers and crisis intervention specialists who could train police and even accompany them on calls to prevent violence. Many cities cut police funding and transferred money to other programs intended to reduce violence. Others changed police procedures for restraining suspects, required body cameras to be worn at all times, and implemented training programs to change police behavior.

✓ **CHECK FOR UNDERSTANDING**

1. **Identifying** What is systemic racism?
2. **Summarizing** Explain why social justice activists focus their protests on symbols. What are they trying to accomplish?

LESSON ACTIVITIES

1. **Narrative Writing** Write a brief history describing why many African Americans have become concerned with police behavior toward their communities and outlining some of the solutions that have been proposed.

2. **Presenting** The slogan of the Women's March was "women's rights are human rights." Work with a small group to prepare a poster board showcasing the struggles and achievements of the women's movement in the United States. Go online to find additional information and images to support your presentation.

READING STRATEGY

Analyzing Key Ideas and Details As you read, use a graphic organizer like the one below to take notes.

Effects of the Pandemic

A Global Pandemic

GUIDING QUESTION

What was COVID-19, and why did it worry world health officials?

On December 31, 2019, Chinese health officials reported a contagious disease of unknown origin in Wuhan in central China. A week later, they identified a coronavirus as the cause of the disease. The virus was named Severe Acute Respiratory Syndrome Coronavirus 2. The illness it caused was named Coronavirus Disease 2019. People began calling it "Corona" or "COVID-19."

Coronaviruses were discovered in 1965. Until 2002 there were only three known types that could infect people and would cause cold symptoms. In 2002 a new coronavirus appeared in China, called Severe Acute Respiratory Syndrome, or SARS. SARS was very dangerous and spread to 28 countries but only infected about 8,000 people before being contained. Although the number of people infected was low, nearly 10 percent died. In 2012 another coronavirus appeared, this time in Saudi Arabia. Scientists called it Middle East Respiratory Syndrome, or MERS. Although MERS was less contagious, it was even more deadly. Of the 2,500 people who caught MERS, nearly 35 percent died.

Scientists began to worry that if a coronavirus similar to but more contagious than SARS or MERS emerged, it could lead to a very dangerous **pandemic.** A pandemic occurs when a disease spreads across multiple countries and affects a vast number of people. Pandemics are dangerous not just because many people get sick but because they can overwhelm the medical system's ability to help them. Pandemics can even overwhelm a society, making it unable to function because so many people are sick, or afraid of getting sick, that they stop doing their jobs.

COVID-19 was very contagious. It spread through the tiny droplets of water people exhale when they breathe, cough, sneeze, or talk. Most people who caught COVID-19 experienced mild flu-like symptoms, including cough, fever, fatigue, and difficulty breathing. For a small number of people, the disease could be fatal. It was especially dangerous to older people over 65 and those who had other medical conditions. Although they had limited data, researchers estimated COVID-19's mortality rate, or how likely it was to cause death, was about one percent. This was much lower than SARS or MERS, but still 10 to 20 times more deadly than the flu. If everyone in the world had caught COVID-19, there could have been 70 million deaths, which is why health officials worldwide began urgently sounding the alarm.

In the weeks following its discovery, the number of COVID-19 cases in China began to climb rapidly. Just one month after the first reported cases, COVID-19 had spread to 19 countries, including the United States. The World Health Organization (WHO) declared the outbreak a public health emergency of international concern. Three days later, the Trump administration declared a public health emergency. Several nations, including the U.S., Australia, New Zealand, and Germany, restricted travel to and from China. On March 11, 2020, just ten weeks after it was identified, the WHO declared COVID-19 to be a global pandemic. At that time there were 125,000 cases worldwide and more than 4,600 dead, far surpassing the impact of either SARS or MERS. Most of the world's nations began to impose travel restrictions with other countries.

---

pandemic when a disease spreads across multiple countries and affects a vast number of people

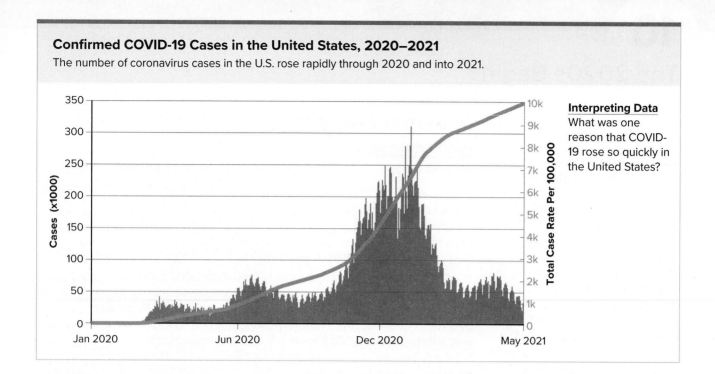

Confirmed COVID-19 Cases in the United States, 2020–2021

The number of coronavirus cases in the U.S. rose rapidly through 2020 and into 2021.

Interpreting Data
What was one reason that COVID-19 rose so quickly in the United States?

The U.S. restricted travel to the European Union the same day the pandemic was declared and to Britain and Ireland three days later. The European Union closed itself to travelers on March 17, 2020.

The travel restrictions came too late. Almost certainly, travelers with COVID-19 had been arriving at international airports before the ban. Later WHO investigations concluded the virus had begun to spread in China as early as October 2019 but was not discovered until late December 2019. European researchers found evidence of COVID-19 in France and Italy a month before the first cases were identified. These findings help explain why measures that had contained SARS and MERS were not as effective against COVID-19. COVID-19 was more contagious and symptoms did not display quickly so some people spread it unawares before response measures were in place.

 **CHECK FOR UNDERSTANDING**

1. **Identifying** What are pandemics? Why are they a serious concern to health officials?

2. **Summarizing** Why did COVID-19 spread so quickly around the world? What steps did the world's nations take to try to slow the spread?

Responding to the Pandemic

GUIDING QUESTION

How did the United States respond to the pandemic?

On January 21, 2020, the state of Washington announced the first case of COVID-19 in the United States. Eight days later, President Trump established the White House Coronavirus Task Force. The president asked Vice President Mike Pence to chair the task force and appointed Dr. Deborah Birx to coordinate the nation's response. Birx had been Obama's coordinator for the nation's response to the AIDS virus. Trump also appointed Dr. Anthony Fauci, Director of the National Institute of Allergy and Infectious Diseases to the task force. Fauci had been part of the U.S. effort to contain SARS and MERS. His expertise helped the task force explain the disease both to officials in the administration and to the American public and media.

On February 28, 2020, the day of the first official American death from the virus, there were only 17 cases in the U.S. By March 11, 2020, the day the WHO declared a pandemic, there were more than 1,000 cases. Two days later, President Trump declared a national emergency. This allowed billions of dollars of emergency aid to be released to fight the virus. Both the Centers for Disease Control and Prevention (CDC) and the White House Task Force began issuing guidelines on how to deal with the disease.

The first concern was to prevent the healthcare system from being overwhelmed. To do that, the nation had to reduce the rate of infection. On March 16, the Task Force recommended Americans not gather in groups greater than ten people and introduced the idea of social distancing. People were asked to stay at home as much as possible and, when out in public, to stay six feet apart from each other.

Throughout March 2020, the United States began to shut down. Schools closed, and companies sent their workers home. Sporting events, concerts, conferences, and weddings were cancelled.

Restaurants, bars, and gyms closed, and curfews were imposed. Airlines and hotels closed. Retailers began limiting how many customers could be inside stores. Millions of people were laid off. For the first time since World War II, Americans experienced widespread shortages of basic supplies as people prepared for the crisis and emptied store shelves of food, toilet paper, and other necessities.

A Politicized Pandemic

From the beginning, the U.S. response to the pandemic was highly politicized. Trump did not trust the media, the Democrats, or the government bureaucracy. The Democrats, having just attempted to impeach Trump, did not trust his judgment, or look to him for leadership during the crisis. Complicating the policymaking was that the risk from COVID-19 was very low for many people but extremely high for others. This posed a basic civics problem that divided Americans: how to balance the public good against individual rights and how to protect the vulnerable without intruding too much on people's freedom.

Trump regularly stressed the cure could not be worse than the disease, and he pushed to reopen the economy every time the situation seemed to be improving. The president even admitted that he diminished the possible severity of the pandemic to protect the economy. For those who resented the restrictions and thought the risks overstated, Trump's impatience seemed appropriate. For others who were worried about the safety of friends and families, he appeared heartless and reckless. Despite the political bickering, the need for action was clear. Although the nation's leaders did not find a way to put their differences aside and present a unified message, they were able to act quickly. It took only a few weeks to implement several important programs to address the pandemic.

Mobilizing the Economy

One week after President Trump declared a national emergency, more than 3 million Americans applied for unemployment aid. To prevent an economic collapse, Congress passed two pieces of legislation. The first was the Families First Coronavirus Relief Act, which provided $104 billion in sick leave and unemployment benefits. The second was the Coronavirus Aid, Relief, and Economic Security Act, or CARES Act, passed on March 27, 2020.

The CARES Act provided $2.2 trillion in government spending. It was the largest spending bill in U.S. history, more than twice the size of any previous bill. It included cash payments to all Americans, increased unemployment benefits, aid to state and local governments, loans for corporations that had lost business, and a program for small businesses to have loans forgiven if they kept people employed.

To fight the pandemic, the Trump administration sought to mobilize U.S. industry. Health care workers needed more masks, gloves, gowns, face shields, and cleaning supplies. They also needed more x-ray machines, CT scanners, ventilators, oxygen masks, and other supplies to help seriously ill patients. A week after the pandemic was declared, Trump invoked the Defense Production Act (DPA). The DPA was first passed in 1950 to help the nation fight the Korean War. It gives the president the authority to order companies to make goods and services needed for national security. Trump used the DPA to order General Motors to make ventilators and General Electric and six other companies to increase production of other medical equipment. To prevent food shortages, he also ordered meat and egg processing plants to stay open and gave them priority in obtaining protective equipment, cleaning supplies, and test kits for their employees.

On May 15, 2020, President Trump announced Operation Warp Speed, a program to accelerate development of vaccines. Normally, vaccines take years to develop, test, and manufacture enough doses for patients. Under Operation Warp Speed, 6 pharmaceutical companies, including Moderna and Johnson & Johnson, received a share of $10 billion to accelerate research and testing and to help scale up their manufacturing. Another company, Pfizer, received $400 million from the German government to develop its "Project Lightspeed" vaccine as well as $2 billion from Operation Warp Speed to manufacture 100 million doses for Americans. In December 2020, just seven months after the effort began, the FDA authorized the Pfizer and Moderna vaccines for emergency use in the U.S. Two months later, they authorized the Johnson & Johnson vaccine for emergency use as well.

Life During the Pandemic

In the early days of the pandemic, life was frantic and uncertain. People stayed home rather then visit elderly relatives or friends to protect each other. They learned how to work remotely while looking after their children, whose schools and day care facilities were closed. They washed their hands frequently, wiped surfaces with sanitizer, and adapted to wearing masks in public. Of all the rules state governments imposed, masks generated the most controversy. Covering their faces with a mask seemed intrusive to some people and they resented being forced to do it. Others were angered by their fellow citizens' reluctance to take a small precaution that made everyone safer. The issue polarized Americans but eventually 39 states issued mandates requiring masks in public and, even in states without mandates, most stores and indoor facilities required masks to enter.

The response to the pandemic also had deep social costs. The imposed isolation increased loneliness, depression, alcoholism, and domestic

As the coronavirus pandemic progressed, state and local officials urged or, in some places, required residents to wear face coverings in public places to reduce the spread of the virus.

Making Connections Why was it important for people to cover their mouth and nose when indoors in public places during the pandemic?

violence. Parents worried that their children were losing ground in their education, and in their social development. The elderly and the terminally ill often died alone as friends or relatives were not allowed to be with them nor could grieving relatives gather at funerals to mourn their loss.

There was also much heroism during the pandemic. Critical parts of the economy had to keep operating to prevent a full-scale economic depression. People who were employed in those critical industries were designated essential workers. These workers were exempt from the stay-at-home rules that affected other members of the nation's labor force.

To do their jobs—especially in the early months of the pandemic when facts about the disease were still being determined—essential workers took the risk of being exposed to the virus. They kept the water and power plants running. They worked in the stores, warehouses, and food processing plants. They loaded the ships, trains, and trucks. They were the first responders racing to help other people in trouble. And they were the medical workers working long, exhausting shifts in hospitals filled to capacity, trying to save as many lives as possible. Together, they prevented the pandemic from overwhelming all of American society.

✓ CHECK FOR UNDERSTANDING

1. **Identifying** What was Operation Warp Speed, and what did it accomplish?

2. **Summarizing** Outline how the United States responded to the COVID-19 pandemic.

The Election of 2020

GUIDING QUESTION

How did Republicans and Democrats respond to the election challenges and its results?

To run against Trump, the Democratic Party nominated Joe Biden, former senator from Delaware and Barack Obama's vice president. At 77 years old, Biden was the oldest person ever nominated for president. He was well known to Americans and had more than four decades of experience in government. Biden, a bit like Trump, was blunt, plain-spoken, and combative at times. He had been born in Pennsylvania and was liked by the working-class voters in the Midwest who supported Trump over Clinton. He had strong support among Democratic leaders in the African American community, and Democrats knew that increasing African American turnout was important if they wanted to win. Biden made history by choosing Senator Kamala Harris to be his running mate. Harris was the first woman of African American and South Asian ancestry to run for vice president.

Trump and Biden took different approaches when campaigning. Biden spoke to Americans who were very worried about the pandemic or suffering economic losses because of it. He stressed the need to come together and heal the divisiveness of the Trump years. He also promised to address the issues raised by the summer's protests against racial injustice. Trump spoke to Americans who resented the loss of freedom from the pandemic and who doubted that extreme measures were necessary. He reminded people the economy had done well in his first three years and promised he would bring that growth back after the pandemic. He also criticized Black Lives Matter and the rioting that had taken place and stressed he supported law and order.

When the votes were counted, Biden won the popular vote with just over 51 percent to Trump's 47 percent. Biden won the states Clinton had won in 2016, but he also won the three states in the upper Midwest that had been key to Trump's 2016 victory: Wisconsin, Michigan, and Pennsylvania. Trump had to win one of those states while winning all the states he had won in 2016 to win reelection in 2020. But Biden also narrowly won Arizona, and to the surprise of many people, the state of Georgia, which had not voted for a Democrat since 1992. These victories gave Biden an Electoral College victory of 306 to Trump's 232. Voter analysis showed that African American turnout had rebounded after declining in 2016, which played an important role in Biden's victories in Georgia, Michigan, and Pennsylvania.

Despite Trump's loss, Republicans gained seats in the House of Representatives, although Democrats kept a slight majority. The Democrats won both Senate seats from Georgia. Raphael Warnock became the first

FamVeld/Shutterstock.

African American senator from Georgia, and Jon Ossoff became the first Jewish senator from Georgia. Their victories resulted in a 50–50 tie in the Senate. This meant the Democrats had gained control because tie votes would be broken by the new vice president, Kamala Harris.

Election Challenges

Election officials faced a challenging situation in 2020 because of the pandemic. Concerns arose that voters would not go to polling stations out of fear of catching the disease. State after state began to modify their election rules to address this problem. They extended early voting, allowed no-excuse absentee voting, allowed people to vote by mail, sent mail-in ballots directly to registered voters whether or not they had requested them, and set up drop-off locations where people could deposit their ballots. Democrats suspected their voters were more likely to be nervous about going to the polls, and they worked hard to get their voters to mail in or drop off their ballots.

As mail-in balloting began, stories appeared in the media describing mail-in ballots being lost or found dumped, people receiving ballots for someone else, ballots being filled out for people who had passed away, people accepting payments in exchange for their ballots, and people being charged with election fraud. The stories were **anecdotes**, personal stories, and they did not prove there were widespread problems. But the sensationalized stories were circulated widely on social media. Trump and his supporters expressed concerns about the election's security and encouraged their voters to vote in person instead of using mail-in ballots to make sure their vote was counted.

The new ways of voting, along with the effort both parties made to get their voters to participate led to the highest percentage of eligible voters turning out since 1900. Over 158 million Americans voted in 2020, more than 66 percent of eligible voters. Half of all votes were sent by mail. Roughly 25 percent were cast during early voting, and 25 percent were cast on Election Day. Because Republicans turned out in larger numbers on election day, Trump built up an early lead in many key states. As the mail-in votes were counted over the next few days, Biden came from behind to win.

This pattern made many Republicans suspicious, and Trump began questioning the outcome almost immediately. At the same time, unsubstantiated reports continued to circulate on social media and were amplified by Trump and his legal team. There were stories that voting machines had been hacked and poll watchers had not been allowed to monitor the count. Other stories suggested signatures on mail-in ballots were not being checked and ballots were accepted that should have been rejected. Within

weeks, a majority of Republicans no longer believed the election outcome was legitimate.

There are always irregularities in an election, and in 2020, people in several states were charged with fraud related to mail-in ballots. But no evidence emerged of a conspiracy that could have altered enough ballots to affect the election even in the close states. No evidence was found of voting machines being rigged either. Ballots were recounted by hand in close states, and they showed voting machines had worked correctly. Some districts made mistakes reporting results, but those were not enough to change the election.

Challenges to the election were widespread. Over 50 cases were filed in Wisconsin, Michigan, Pennsylvania, Arizona, Nevada, and Georgia, all states where the election had been close. Trump and his legal team filed lawsuits as did Republican officials and numerous private individuals and groups. Most lawsuits challenged the changes states had made in response to the pandemic. They claimed the election rules had been changed unfairly, and sometimes unconstitutionally, and that therefore the election results were not legitimate. Trump also lobbied state lawmakers and state officials, trying to get them to refuse to certify their elections or to appoint different electors.

When the lawsuits and lobbying failed, Trump tried to convince Congress to reject some of the Electoral votes when it met to count them. If a member of the Senate and the House of Representatives jointly object to a state's electoral votes, the House and Senate vote on whether to accept the Electoral votes. If both chambers reject a state's Electoral votes, they don't count. If they reject so many votes that no candidate has a majority of the Electoral College, then the House votes by delegation (one vote per state) to pick the president. Because the majority of state delegations were controlled by Republicans, Trump thought he could win.

The Attack on the Capitol

On January 6, 2021, Congress met to count the Electoral votes and certify the winner of the presidential election. As members of Congress gathered for the count, tens of thousands of Trump's supporters gathered for his rally in front of the White House. At the rally President Trump repeated his claims that he had won the election and that there had been enough fraudulent votes to swing the election to Biden. The examples Trump cited were unsubstantiated, and many of these claims had already been proven to be false. Yet Trump seemed to believe the claims he was making were true and that people saying otherwise were lying because they opposed his presidency.

---

anecdotes personal, individual stories that do not provide sufficient proof of larger issues

Kamala Harris and Joe Biden made history in the White House. She was the first female vice president and he was the oldest president to be elected.

Trump urged supporters to march to the Capitol and "peacefully and patriotically make your voices heard." He described watching the results on election night and thinking "something is wrong here, something is really wrong" and that "if you don't fight like hell, you're not going to have a country anymore." He told them to "cheer on our brave senators and congressmen and women," and "to demand that Congress do the right thing and only count the electors who have been lawfully slated."

Even before he finished his speech, crowds of protestors began gathering outside the U.S. Capitol. As the crowd grew, protestors surged past security barriers, overwhelmed police, broke windows and doors, and entered the Capitol building. Warned that a mob had broken into the building, members of Congress took shelter. The rioters roamed through the Capitol, vandalized offices, and entered the Senate chamber. As they broke into a hallway outside the barricaded House chamber, a Capitol officer fired and killed one of the protestors. Over the next few hours, police and National Guard forces regained control and expelled the rioters. Congress immediately reconvened. At 3:40 a.m., January 7, 2021, Congress completed the count, having debated and overruled all objections. Vice President Pence declared that Joe Biden and Kamala Harris would be the next president and vice president of the United States.

Trump is Impeached Again

The attack on the Capitol stunned the nation. Over the years, protestors had broken into federal buildings. There had also been other attacks at the Capitol by terrorists and by people suffering mental illness. But there had never been an attack by a large mob

determined to overturn an election. The protestors used pipes, shields, flag poles, pepper spray, and stun guns to fight with the police, who in turn fought back with truncheons, tear gas, and flash-bang grenades. More than 130 officers were injured, 15 hospitalized, and 5 people, including 1 officer, died. More than 400 people who participated in the attack were identified and arrested over the next few months.

For those who had opposed Donald Trump, the attack confirmed fears that he was an authoritarian. Twitter and Facebook suspended the president's social media accounts saying his words risked inciting further violence and undermining the transition of power to Joe Biden. One week later, the House of Representatives voted 232–197 to impeach Trump. They charged him with "incitement of insurrection." Ten Republicans joined all the Democrats to vote for the impeachment. The Senate was not in session at the time, and Senate Majority Leader Mitch McConnell said he would not call the Senate into an emergency session because he did not believe there was time for a fair trial before Trump left office. Instead, the trial would be held after Biden was inaugurated.

The second impeachment trial began February 9, 2021. The House managers argued that the rally led to the attack on the Capitol after Trump inflamed the crowd with claims the election had been stolen and talked about the need to fight. Trump's defense team pointed to his call for the protestors to peacefully make their voices heard. After listening to the evidence, the Senate acquitted Trump. Although a majority of senators, including all the Democrats and seven Republicans voted to convict, the vote of 57 to 43 was 10 votes short of the two-thirds majority needed for conviction.

PHOTO: JIM WATSON/AFP/Getty Images; TEXT: Trump, Donald. In Naylor, Brian. "Read Trump's Jan. 6 Speech, A Key Part Of Impeachment Trial." NPR.org. Feb. 10, 2021.

Most Republicans, including Mitch McConnell, refused to convict Trump because they did not believe the Constitution allowed someone to be impeached after leaving office. But McConnell stated strongly he believed Trump was responsible: "Former President Trump's actions preceding the riot were a disgraceful dereliction of duty. . . . The leader of the free world cannot spend weeks thundering that shadowy forces are stealing our country and then feign surprise when people believe him and do reckless things."

✓ **CHECK FOR UNDERSTANDING**

1. **Summarizing** Make a list of the reasons that help explain why the number of voters increased so dramatically in 2020.

2. **Explaining** Why did so many Republicans come to believe the election results wrong? What evidence suggests they were mistaken?

President Biden's First 100 Days in Office

GUIDING QUESTION

What were President Biden's priorities once he entered the White House?

With the COVID-19 pandemic still widespread in the United States, and the Capitol ringed with National Guard troops and barbed wire to deter another attack by rioters, President Biden's inauguration was very different from recent presidential inaugurations. The ceremony was small, and the invited guests were spread apart and wearing masks. Biden's goal in his inaugural address was to begin healing the polarization the nation had experienced in recent years:

> Today, on this January day, my whole soul is in this: Bringing America together. Uniting our people. And uniting our nation. I ask every American to join me in this cause. Uniting to fight the common foes we face: Anger, resentment, hatred. Extremism, lawlessness, violence. Disease, joblessness, hopelessness. With unity we can do great things. Important things. We can right wrongs. We can put people to work in good jobs. We can teach our children in safe schools. We can overcome this deadly virus. We can reward work, rebuild the middle class, and make health care secure for all. We can deliver racial justice. We can make America, once again, the leading force for good in the world.

—President Joe Biden, Inaugural Address, January 20, 2021

Joe Biden believed Trump's policies had departed from the nation's core values and that he had to set a new tone for the nation. He deliberately nominated cabinet officers who reflected the diversity of identity in American society. He appointed 6 African Americans, 5 Hispanics, a Native American, an Asian American, and a gay American, making it the most diverse cabinet ever assembled. Of the 24 cabinet-level positions, 11 were women, the largest number of women to serve in the cabinet. His appointments also included the first female secretary of the Treasury, the first Native American secretary of the Interior, and the first African American secretary of Defense. He also ordered the government to develop plans to advance **equity** for all Americans. His order defined equity to mean "the consistent and systematic fair, just, and impartial treatment of all individuals, including individuals who belong to underserved communities." He then established a Gender Policy Council and directed his administration to combat racism against Asian Americans and Pacific Islanders and discrimination based on sexual orientation and gender identity.

Reversing Course on Immigration

One of the first things President Biden did after taking office was issue a series of orders reversing the immigration policies President Trump had implemented. He lifted the travel ban, stopped work on the border wall, ended the "zero tolerance" policy and the "Remain in Mexico" policy, and reaffirmed support for the DACA program. He also set up a task force to reunite families that had been separated at the border.

In the fall of 2020, even before Biden took office, the number of immigrants crossing the southern border illegally had started rising. Within weeks, his administration saw a surge of illegal crossings, many by unaccompanied children, similar to what President Obama and President Trump had faced. By April 2021, the total number of immigrants entering illegally had reached levels not seen since 2001. With detention facilities growing overcrowded, Biden promised his administration he would focus on getting the children processed and moved to sponsors and develop a plan to address the problems in Central America that were causing so many people to come north.

Change and Continuity in Foreign Policy

After taking office, Biden almost immediately sought to reverse Trump's policy of "maximum pressure" on Iran. He offered to lift Trump's sanctions if Iran agreed to return to the nuclear deal and stop trying to develop nuclear weapons. Iran was wary of new negotiations, however, and Biden left the sanctions in place while the two sides talked.

(t)McConnell, Mitch. In Congressional Record. 117th Congress (2021–2022) - 1st Session, Vol. 167, No. 28, February 13, 2021; (b)Biden, Joseph R., Jr., "Inaugural Address by President Joseph R. Biden, Jr." January 20, 2021; (i) Biden, Jr., Joseph R. "Executive Order on Establishment of the White House Gender Policy Council." March 8, 2021.

equity the consistent and systematic fair, treatment of all individuals

Biden did decide to continue Trump's policy of withdrawing from Afghanistan. He noted the U.S. had achieved its original goals of eliminating Osama bin Laden and reducing the power of al-Qaeda. He then set September 11, 2021, as the final date for all troops to return home. Biden also affirmed Trump's decision to move the U.S. Embassy to Jerusalem and said that he supported the Abraham Accords. His administration did announce, however, that it would seek to reopen relations with the Palestinian government and restore aid programs that had been cancelled during the Trump administration.

The American Rescue Plan

Upon taking office, Biden appointed a new COVID-19 response coordinator. He directed the government to improve data collection related to COVID-19 and established a new COVID-19 Pandemic Testing Board to expand testing. He also issued an order requiring all federal workers and people on federal property, as well as all people at airports or traveling on aircraft, trains, ships, or intercity buses, to wear masks. He did not have the authority to order all Americans to wear masks, so he challenged Americans to "mask up" for the first 100 days of his administration, arguing that if everyone wore masks for 100 days, it would have a huge impact on the spread of the pandemic.

As the world entered the second year of the pandemic, many Americans continued to face difficult economic times. Unemployment had spiked to 15 percent in April 2020, then fallen steadily for the rest of the year as the economy adapted to the pandemic. But when Biden took office, unemployment was still at 6.2 percent, nearly twice as high as the previous year. To address these concerns, Congress passed the American Rescue Plan Act, a $1.9 trillion economic aid package. It was the second-largest spending bill in U.S. history, only slightly smaller than the CARES Act passed in the spring of 2020. The CARES Act had increased unemployment benefits. The American Rescue Plan extended those increased benefits into the fall of 2021. It provided cash payments and tax credits to individuals, grants to small businesses to help them stay open, funds to help people cover rent and mortgages, and funds for state, local, and tribal governments to cover budget shortages. It also provided funds to help schools improve ventilation, provide protective equipment, reduce class sizes, improve social distancing, and address any loss of learning students had experienced during the pandemic.

Vaccinations

Biden set a target of 100 million vaccinations by the end of his first 100 days in office. Vaccination rates had begun to rise in December 2020, and they continued to rise rapidly in early 2021. States distributed vaccines in many ways. People got shots at local pharmacies, at doctor's offices, at hospitals, at drive through locations, and at arenas, stadiums, malls, and other centralized locations. Mobile vaccine units were created to take vaccines into neighborhoods and rural areas. National Guard units, firefighters, paramedics, and medical workers were all mobilized to give shots. By the end of Biden's 100 days in office, more than 225 million vaccines had been administered. Approximately 140 million Americans had received at least one dose of a vaccine. More than a third of adults were fully vaccinated, and nearly 70 percent of the people most at risk, those over age 65, had been fully vaccinated.

As vaccinations rose in early 2021, COVID-19 cases rapidly declined. Many Americans began to hope the pandemic was nearing an end, at least in the U.S. Schools began to reopen for in-person instruction, and businesses began planning for workers to return to their offices. Biden's bold request in his inaugural address appeared to be coming true:

66 Now we must step up. All of us. It is a time for boldness, for there is so much to do. And, this is certain: We will be judged, you and I, for how we resolve the cascading crises of our era. Will we rise to the occasion? Will we master this rare and difficult hour? Will we meet our obligations and pass along a new and better world for our children? I believe we must and I believe we will. And when we do, we will write the next chapter in the American story. 99

–President Joe Biden, Inaugural Address, January 20, 2021

✓ CHECK FOR UNDERSTANDING

1. **Identifying** What actions did Biden take to show his values were different than Trump's?
2. **Describing** Describe the actions Biden and Congress took in 2021 to address the COVID-19 pandemic.

LESSON ACTIVITIES

1. **Narrative Writing** Write a brief history of the election of 2020 explaining key events and the results.
2. **Presenting** Work with a small group to prepare a slide show documenting America's response to the COVID-19 pandemics. Go online to find additional information and images to support your presentation. If possible, interview people who played a role in fighting the pandemic in your community and include quotes about their experiences.

Biden, Joseph R., Jr., "Inaugural Address by President Joseph R. Biden, Jr." January 20, 2021.

11

Analyzing Sources: The 2020 Campaign

? COMPELLING QUESTION

What issues and concerns influenced the 2020 presidential election?

Plan Your Inquiry

In this lesson, you will investigate key issues during the presidential election campaign of 2020.

DEVELOP QUESTIONS

Developing Questions About Election 2020 Think about the important political issues and the significant national events that played an important role in the presidential election of 2020. Then read the Compelling Question for this lesson. Develop a list of three supporting questions that would help you answer the Compelling Question for the lesson. Write these in a graphic organizer like the one below.

APPLY HISTORICAL TOOLS

Analyzing Primary Sources You will work with a variety of primary sources in this lesson. These sources focus on events and issues central to the presidential election of 2020. Use a graphic organizer like the one below to record and organize information about each source. Note ways in which each source helps you answer the supporting questions you created. Not all sources will help you answer each of your supporting questions. Only include relevant sources in your graphic organizer.

Source	Author/ Creator	Description	Which Supporting Question does this source help me answer?
A			
B			
C			
D			
E			
F			
G			

After you analyze the sources, you will:

- use the evidence from the sources.
- communicate your conclusions.
- take informed action.

Background Information

In 2016 real-estate mogul Donald J. Trump won the presidential election by promising to "Make America Great Again." Four years later, President Trump faced a tough reelection battle against the Democratic Party nominee—former Vice President Joseph R. Biden, Jr. Biden served for eight years alongside President Barack Obama. Biden also served for decades in the United States Senate.

Some themes from the 2016 presidential election carried over to the 2020 campaign, such as the strength of the nation's economy and debates over the United States's role in the world. But the particularly unusual circumstances and events of 2020 created new arenas for disagreement. This included how best to respond to the COVID-19 pandemic and how to reckon with the consequences—economic hardship, widespread unemployment, school shutdowns, voting safety, and how to maintain safety for Americans across the nation.

At the same time, the nation's long struggle with systemic racism and calls for sweeping civil rights reforms erupted in response to the police killing of George Floyd in May 2020. These issues fueled a deeply divided election campaign and shaped the very processes by which citizens might engage in the voting process.

» Campaign buttons from the 2020 presidential election

chrisdorney/Shutterstock

Important Issues in the 2020 Election

The Pew Research Center is a nonpartisan group that researches and reports about national issues. During the 2020 election, some of the organization's research indicated that while American voters shared many concerns, their party identification and who they supported in the presidential campaign shaped how they ranked these issues' importance.

PRIMARY SOURCE : ARTICLE

66 With the country in the midst of a recession, nearly eight-in-ten registered voters (79%) say the economy will be very important to them in making their decision about who to vote for in the 2020 presidential election—the top issue of 12 included in the survey.

The economy is consistently a top voting issue. In a survey asking a similar, though not identical, list of issues in June 2016, the economy also was the top voting issue.

In the current survey, 68% of voters say health care is very important to their vote, while 64% cite Supreme Court appointments.

As the country continues to grapple with the coronavirus outbreak, 62% of voters say the outbreak will be a very important factor in their decision about who to support in the fall. . . .

There are stark differences in how . . . voters who support Donald Trump and Joe Biden view the importance of these issues. In fact,

of 12 issues included, the only ones that comparable shares of Biden . . . and Trump supporters view as very important are foreign policy and Supreme Court appointments.

For Trump supporters, the economy (88%) and violent crime (74%) are the most salient issues. Roughly six-in-ten Trump supporters cite immigration (61%), gun policy (60%) and foreign policy (57%) as very important to their vote.

By contrast, the largest shares of Biden supporters view health care (84%) and the coronavirus outbreak (82%) as very important. A sizable majority also rates racial and ethnic inequality as important to their vote (76%). 99

–Pew Research Center, August 13, 2020

EXAMINE THE SOURCE

Identifying the Main Idea What segment of the article indicates where Trump supporters and Biden supporters differ in their election priorities?

U.S. Early Voting Options

Early in the nation's history, voting took place over several days to give citizens time to reach the polls. In 1845, Congress set the first Tuesday following the first Monday in November as Election Day. Up until the 1980s, only military personnel and other citizens with a qualifying reason could vote ahead of election day. In 2020 most states provided for some form of early voting, absentee voting, or mail-in voting that did not require citizens to appear in person at the polls on Election Day.

EXAMINE THE SOURCE

1. **Analyzing Visuals** How do procedures in states such as Ohio differ from those in states such as Florida?

2. **Drawing Conclusions** How might this data reinforce arguments for early and absentee voting? What about arguments against early and absentee voting?

PRIMARY SOURCE : INFOGRAPHIC

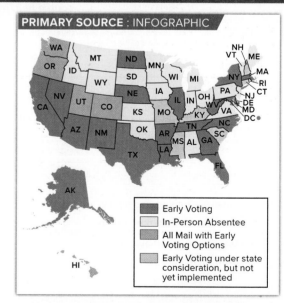

Early Voting
In-Person Absentee
All Mail with Early Voting Options
Early Voting under state consideration, but not yet implemented

» The information shown in the infographic comes from the National Conference of State Legislatures.

Pew Research Center, August, 2020. "Election 2020: Voters Are Highly Engaged, but Nearly Half Expect To Have Difficulties Voting".

(1)Underwood, Lauren. "Let's Make Our Grandchildren Proud." Congressional Record. Vol. 166, No. 117, H2646. June 25, 2020. (2)"President Trump: 'We Have Rejected Globalism and Embraced Patriotism.'" August 7, 2020.

C

Fighting Systemic Racism

George Floyd's death while being arrested by police in May 2020 sparked many protest rallies and marches across the United States. Some protesters demanded significant changes to police funding and police regulations in cities and towns to address concerns of systemic racism and reduce the growing number of African Americans being killed during police actions.

PRIMARY SOURCE : SPEECH

66 . . . Our Nation is facing a critical moment of reckoning. We consider hundreds of important bills in this Chamber every year, but it is not every day that tens of thousands of Americans take to the streets in the middle of a deadly pandemic to demand our attention, . . .

We are here today because Black lives matter. We are here because Rayshard Brooks and Tony McDade and Breonna Taylor and Stephon Clark and Deborah Danner and Philando Castile and Natasha McKenna and Tamir Rice and Laquan McDonald and Eric Garner and Aiyana Stanley-Jones and so many others are not here—because their lives matter.

. . . [T]he fractures in our country demand more from us than police reform. It is not police reform alone that has brought people out into the streets in the middle of a pandemic that disproportionately kills people of color. What is called for in this moment is the courageous and comprehensive reckoning with racism in America past, present, and future. It is Congress' job to deliver policy that answers the call for this transformation.

. . . At this pivotal moment in our Nation's effort to confront its own history, I urge my colleagues to make choices that rise to the gravity of the situation and our responsibility to the American people. It is long past time to bend this arc toward justice in policing and beyond. 99

—Representative Lauren Underwood,
Congressional Record, June 25, 2020

EXAMINE THE SOURCE

Summarizing What is Representative Underwood's goal in making this speech?

D

Staying Focused on America

As COVID-19 spread, Trump's administration faced mounting criticism for shortages of personal protective equipment (PPE) and testing supplies. In August 2020, Trump issued several executive orders to address shortages.

PRIMARY SOURCE : WHITE HOUSE NEWSLETTER

66 Today's executive order directs the Department of Health and Human Services to use the Defense Production Act to buy essential medicines and other equipment from within the United States. Drug prices will be kept low for customers, and American companies will be able to compete more fairly on the world stage as a result. . . .

'It's a great day for America,' [White House Director of Trade & Manufacturing Policy Peter] Navarro said. 'The President has promised that he would bring home the supply chains in production for our essential medicines, and today we're taking a very big step towards fulfillment of that promise.'

President Trump has long made returning blue-collar jobs to America a top priority. Now, the Coronavirus pandemic has made even clearer the risks of becoming overly reliant on foreign nations for our essential supplies. . . .

Here are a few things the new order will accomplish:

- Establish 'Buy American' rules for Federal Government agencies . . .
- Help spark the manufacturing technologies needed to keep drug prices low and move more medicine production onshore. 99

—The White House, "President Trump: 'We Have Rejected Globalism and Embraced Patriotism,'" August 7, 2020

EXAMINE THE SOURCE

1. **Summarizing** What provisions does the executive order include?
2. **Drawing Conclusions** What issues does this executive order suggest might be important during the 2020 presidential election?

Criticizing Amy Coney Barrett's Nomination

In this speech, Senate Minority Leader Chuck Schumer states his belief that because of Judge Amy Coney Barrett's past criticism of the Affordable Care Act, the new conservative balance in the Supreme Court would threaten individuals' health care.

PRIMARY SOURCE : SPEECH

66 Senate Republicans are now rushing through a Supreme Court nominee nearly days before a national election. A Republican majority that once argued the American people should be given a voice in the selection of their next Supreme Court Justice is planning to confirm a nominee in . . . an election that is already underway. You could not design a scenario that would more fully expose the Republicans' double standard . . .

. . . [T]he Republican leader actually mocked the idea that far-right Supreme Court majority might strike down the ACA and that Judge Barrett's judicial philosophy might play a part in that. 'What a joke,' Senator McConnell said, that Justice Barrett might pose any risk to Americans' healthcare.

I guess Judge Barrett must have been joking when she publicly criticized Justice Roberts for upholding the Affordable Care Act. . . .

President Trump said he will pick Supreme Court nominees who will 'terminate the Affordable Care Act.' His administration is in court right now, suing to eliminate it. Senate Republicans tried to repeal the law and replace it with nothing. The Republicans' lawsuit against the Affordable Care Act will be heard by the Supreme Court during the week after the election. There is a reason the Republicans are scrambling to fill this seat so quickly . . . 99

—Senator Charles Schumer, *Congressional Record*, September 29, 2020

EXAMINE THE SOURCE

Interpreting What two main concerns is Senator Schumer pointing out with his speech?

Criticizing Biden's Energy Plan

Senator John Cornyn from Texas spoke against Democratic nominee Joe Biden's national energy proposals. Biden wished to reduce national reliance on fossil fuels such as oil and put more emphasis on renewable energy sources.

PRIMARY SOURCE : SPEECH

66 . . . [I]n Thursday's Presidential Debate, former Vice President Joe Biden said he wants to transition the United States from the oil industry. . . . What Joe Biden is sending is a not too subtly coded message that he wants to end our energy industry as we know it. This is an industry that, according to one study, directly or indirectly supports one out of every six jobs in my State and is a pillar of our State's economy.

Through tax revenue, high-paying jobs, and downstream economic gains, communities across Texas reap substantial benefits from our thriving oil and gas industry every day, and those benefits reach beyond our borders or the borders of any other energy-producing State.

That is because of the hard-working men and women on rigs, in fields, and in refineries. Because of their work, the American people have access to reliable and affordable energy. . . .

In Texas, we literally believe in an 'all of the above' energy policy. We produce more electricity from wind energy, from wind turbines, than any other State in the Nation. But we know the reality of the kind of transition that Vice President Biden has talked about would mean. We got a taste of how disastrous it would be earlier this year. 99

—Senator John Cornyn, *Congressional Record*, October 24, 2020

EXAMINE THE SOURCE

Drawing Conclusions Why is Senator Cornyn critical of former Vice President Biden's national energy plan?

(1)Schumer, Charles. "Supreme Court Nominations." Congressional Record. Vol. 166, No. 169. September 29, 2020. S5901; (2)Cornyn, John. "Presidential Debate." Congressional Record. Vol. 166, No. 183. October 24, 2020. S6428.

2020 Presidential Election Results

The 2020 presidential election results showed a pattern that matched many recent elections, although there were some dramatic flips. The coastal parts of the West and the Northeast voted for the Democratic candidate. The South and the West continued to be strong areas for Republicans. Several states that had trended Republican in past elections, such as Arizona, Georgia, and Nevada, voted Democratic in this election.

PRIMARY SOURCE : MAP

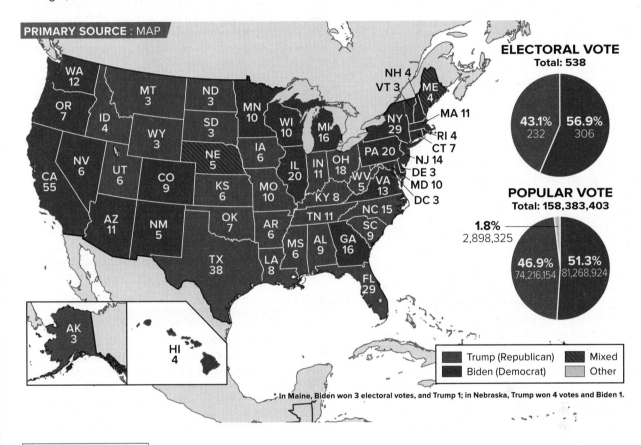

ELECTORAL VOTE
Total: 538

43.1%
232

56.9%
306

POPULAR VOTE
Total: 158,383,403

1.8%
2,898,325

46.9%
74,216,154

51.3%
81,268,924

Trump (Republican)   Mixed
Biden (Democrat)   Other

* In Maine, Biden won 3 electoral votes, and Trump 1; in Nebraska, Trump won 4 votes and Biden 1.

EXAMINE THE SOURCE

1. **Interpreting Visuals** What does it mean when a state is shown as Mixed?

2. **Determining Context** Based on what you have learned about recent presidential elections, what is unusual about the results shown on this map?

H

Joe Biden's Acceptance Speech

On November 7, 2020, after being declared the winner of the presidential election, President-elect Joe Biden gave a victory speech in Wilmington, Delaware.

PRIMARY SOURCE : SPEECH

> 66 Folks, the people of this nation have spoken. They have delivered us a clear victory. A convincing victory. A victory for we, the people. We won with the most votes ever cast on a presidential ticket in the history of the nation. . . . Tonight we are seeing all over this nation, all cities and all parts of the country. Indeed across the world, an outpouring of joy, of hope, renewed faith in tomorrow to bring a better day. And I'm humbled by the trust and confidence you have placed in me. I pledge to be a president who seeks not to divide, but unify. Who doesn't see red states and blue states, only sees the United States.
>
> . . . I sought this office to restore the soul of America. To rebuild the backbone of this nation, the middle class, and to make America respected around the world again. And to unite us here at home. It is the honor of my lifetime that so many millions of Americans have voted for that vision. And now the work of making that vision is real. It is the task of our time.
>
> . . . I will have the honor of serving with the fantastic vice president . . . Kamala Harris, who makes history as the first woman, the first Black woman, the first woman from South Asian descent, the first daughter of immigrants ever elected to this country's [vice presidency]. Don't tell me it's not possible in the United States. It's long overdue. . . . 99

—President-elect Joe Biden, November 7, 2020

EXAMINE THE SOURCE

Summarizing What is the main point of this excerpt from President-elect Biden's acceptance speech?

Your Inquiry Analysis

EVALUATE SOURCES AND USE EVIDENCE

Reflect back to the Compelling Question and the Supporting Question you developed at the beginning of this lesson.

1. **Gathering Sources** Which sources helped you answer your Supporting Questions most directly? Which sources, if any, supported or challenged your preconceptions? Explain what additional information you would like to know to answer the questions and where you might find that information.

2. **Evaluating Sources** Looking at the sources that helped you answer your supporting questions, evaluate the credibility of each source. What opinions did each source state? What evidence did each source provide to support those opinions? How did bias shape the content of each source? Explain which two to three sources you consider most credible and why.

3. **Comparing and Contrasting** Compare and contrast the sources you evaluated as most credible. Note similarities and differences in content, tone, author/creator, and purpose. Explain how these sources work together to help you answer the Compelling Question.

COMMUNICATE CONCLUSIONS

Presenting Make a concept web with the Compelling Question at the center. Record at least one detail from each source that helps you answer the Compelling Question on the web. Write two to three sentences in response to the question, and present your web and response to the class.

TAKE INFORMED ACTION

Choosing a Candidate or Party and a Platform Identify two economic, social, environmental, or other issues that are important to you. Learn what positions the candidates in an upcoming election hold on these issues or how the major parties differ on these issues. Create a display or presentation showing how their policies and/or ideas compare and contrast. Then, write an op-ed column or record a podcast in which you use what you learned to explain why you support one candidate/party or another based on their position on the two issues you researched as well as what you have learned in the inquiry. Be sure to cite evidence from your research as well as from the sources you examined. If your teacher permits, you may collaborate with a partner or small group on your research and presentation.

Biden, Joseph. Joe Biden and Kamala Harris Victory Speeches. November 7, 2020.

12

Reviewing the New Millennium

Summary

A Contested Election

The 2000s began with a heated presidential contest between Republican Party candidate, George W. Bush, governor of Texas and son of President George H.W. Bush, Democrat Party candidate Al Gore, vice president under Bill Clinton, and Green Party candidate Ralph Nader. On Election Day, although Gore won more popular votes overall, the election was so close in some key states that the winner of the Electoral College was uncertain. After a drawn-out recount in the state of Florida and involvement by the Supreme Court, George W. Bush was declared the forty-third president of the United States.

The War on Terror

Bush had many plans for the country, but his entire presidency and the nation's history changed on September 11, 2001, when terrorist hijackers coordinated multiple attack in New York City, Washington, D.C., and Pennsylvania, causing the deaths of more than 3,000 people. It was the worst attack on American soil by a foreign enemy since the Japanese attack on Pearl Harbor in 1941.

The terrorists responsible for these attacks were part of an organization called al-Qaeda, led by Osama bin Laden. The organization was responsible for numerous attacks throughout the world. To fight such an enemy, the U.S. government declared a war on terror, created the Department of Homeland Security, and passed the USA PATRIOT Act, which gave wide-ranging powers to law enforcement officials to prevent future attacks.

Officials believed that the Taliban-controlled government of Afghanistan was hiding bin Laden. When the Taliban refused to hand him over, the United States invaded the country. While the U.S. military quickly defeated the Taliban, the new allied government in Afghanistan faced continued opposition from rebel forces. U.S. troops remained in Afghanistan to help maintain stability. Osama bin Laden eluded capture until 2011. During the presidency of Barack Obama, U.S. troops found and killed bin Laden in Pakistan.

Some U.S. officials worried that terrorists might gain control of weapons of mass destruction (WMD), such as nuclear or chemical weapons. Concerned that Iraqi dictator Saddam Hussein was harboring an arsenal of WMD in violation of UN sanctions, President Bush convinced the United States to launch an invasion of Iraq. The attack led to the overthrow of Hussein, but no WMD were ever recovered. Political instability and unrest followed for many years. U.S. troops continued their presence to maintain order and limit the rise of new terrorist factions.

Domestic Concerns

Bush faced many challenges at home as well. Government activities on behalf of the war on terror raised concerns about citizen privacy and civil liberties. Devastation wrought by Hurricane Katrina and the slow federal response also caused concern among citizens. Bush won a second term in 2004, but the costs of the overseas wars and an extreme economic downturn affected his remaining years in the White House.

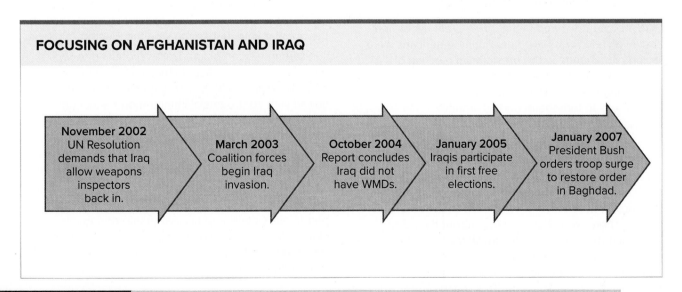

FOCUSING ON AFGHANISTAN AND IRAQ

November 2002 UN Resolution demands that Iraq allow weapons inspectors back in.

March 2003 Coalition forces begin Iraq invasion.

October 2004 Report concludes Iraq did not have WMDs.

January 2005 Iraqis participate in first free elections.

January 2007 President Bush orders troop surge to restore order in Baghdad.

President Barack Obama and his family, shown in the White House Green Room, lived at the nation's top address from 2009 until 2017.

Environmental Concerns

The 2000s witnessed an acceleration of worries about the environment. The roots of the environmental movement began in the 1960s with increased activism, resulting in important environmental regulations in the 1970s.

By the beginning of the new millennium, evidence of the negative impact of climate change led countries to band together to find international solutions. Agreements such as the Kyoto Protocol and Paris Climate Agreement asked countries to commit to actions that would limit environmental hazards. Some business leaders worried such agreements would limit economic activities. Political pressure led the United States to withhold support from some of these international agreements. Meanwhile, young activists such as Greta Thunberg used social media to bring attention to environmental issues and urge political leaders to protect the environment for future generations.

Obama's Historic Presidency

With the country mired in the 2008 Great Recession and involved in wars overseas, many Americans were looking for change in the presidential election of 2008. They elected the country's first African American president, Barack Obama, whose first priority was to turn the economy around.

The trend towards globalization connected the American economy with that of the world. Obama signed legislation to boost recovery and reinvestment. He also wanted to improve consumer protection and regulation of banking practices. The economy began to improve, but recovery was slower than some had hoped. There were also warnings about the rising national debt, taxes, and the growing income gap, which seemed to be narrowing the possibility of financial success for more and more families.

Meanwhile, some activists argued the main problem was the economic system itself, which primarily benefited the wealthiest one percent of society. Noting the negative economic impact of the rising cost of health care, Obama prioritized health care reform legislation that was passed by a Democratic majority Congress. This was the Affordable Care Act.

President Obama's second term was affected by strong Republican opposition in Congress.

Trump's White House

Political polarization had increased tremendously by the 2016 presidential election. Democrat Hillary Clinton made history as the first female candidate nominated for the presidency from a major party. Clinton brought a wealth of experience. Businessman and television celebrity Donald Trump ran as the Republican candidate, promising to "Make America Great Again." Trump's campaign leveraged the power of social media to attract frustrated voters who felt the government was not helping them succeed. It was later revealed that Russian operatives tried to influence voters via social media. On Election Night, Clinton won the popular vote, but Trump won the Electoral College.

During his campaign, Trump promised to repeal the Affordable Care Act, restrict immigration, and build a border wall with Mexico. His administration forged ahead with controversial immigration restrictions. In the second half of his only term in the White House, President Trump was impeached twice by a Democratically controlled House of Representatives but was not convicted by the Republican-held Senate.

As President Trump concluded his term, the world was challenged by the deadly COVID-19 coronavirus pandemic. Criticism of his leadership during this crisis, along with his immigration policies and other factors, resulted in his losing the 2020 presidential election to Democrat Joe Biden.

National Archives and Records Administration

Apply What You Have Learned

 A Understanding Multiple Perspectives

Passed in the aftermath of the September 11 attacks, the Patriot Act granted increased authority to law enforcement officials to spy on individuals without a warrant. Senator Chuck Schumer of New York defended the proposed law:

66 The balance between the need to update our laws given the new challenges and the need to maintain our basic freedoms which distinguish us from our enemies is real. There have been some on the right who have said just pass anything. We just have to go after the terrorists and forget about our freedoms and our civil liberties. There are some on the left who say only look at the civil liberties aspect. . . . [N]either prevailed in this fine piece of work that we have before us. Balance and reason have prevailed. 99

Senator Russ Feingold was the only Senator to vote against the original USA PATRIOT ACT. He has argued:

66 We must redouble our vigilance to ensure our security and to prevent further acts of terror. But we must also redouble our vigilance to preserve our values and the basic rights that make us who we are. The Founders who wrote our Constitution and Bill of Rights exercised that vigilance even though they had recently fought and won the Revolutionary War. They did not live in comfortable and easy times of hypothetical enemies. They wrote a Constitution of limited powers and an explicit Bill of Rights to protect liberty in times of war, as well as in times of peace. 99

ACTIVITY **Write an Editorial** Review the arguments for and against the Patriot Act. Write an editorial in which you take a position on whether the law is needed today or not. Use evidence to support your views.

 B Connecting to Economics

One reason why President Obama and other politicians focused on providing affordable health care for Americans was because the high cost of health care was becoming an economic burden to many families. For those without health insurance, a catastrophic illness or injury could bankrupt a family. For that reason, some politicians called for wider reforms, including "Medicare for All."

ACTIVITY **Compare Data** Using Internet and library resources, research information about the average per capita health care costs for citizens in the United States compared to other Western nations, including the United Kingdom, France, Germany, Canada, the Netherlands, and Switzerland. Write a summary of your findings, including any information about possible reasons for the differences in these health care costs. Write a paragraph explaining what the data reveals about health care in the United States compared to other nations.

1)Schumer, Charles. "H. 3162. 107th Cong., 1st sess." Congressional Record. Vol. 151, pt. 12:20713. October 25, 2001. https://www.gpo.gov/fdsys/pkg/CRECB-2001-pt15/pdf/CRECB-2001-pt15-Pg20669-9.pdf.
(2) Feingold, Russell. "H. 3162. 107th Cong., 1st sess." Congressional Record. Vol. 151, pt. 12:20700. October 25, 2001. https://www.gpo.gov/fdsys/pkg/CRECB-2001-pt15/pdf/CRECB-2001-pt15-Pg20669-9.pdf

C Making Connections to Today

The presidential election of 2016 marked a significant increase in the use of social media and online sources to shape public opinion. After the election, investigations revealed that many stories shared on social media were false.

Such examples of misleading news stories were often created by computer systems or "bots" originating in foreign countries, such as Russia. Researchers have grown increasingly concerned about the ability to sway public opinion with false online reports and stories. Some have called upon social media companies such as Facebook and Twitter to do a better job of monitoring content shared on their platforms.

ACTIVITY **Evaluate Web Sources** Review with your instructor best practices for identifying reliable news sources. Then, working in small groups, research examples of Internet stories and evaluate whether you think the stories are reliable or not. Identify at least one story that your group agrees is probably true based on the reliability of the source and one that is probably fake. Present your findings to the class.

» It is important to evaluate the validity of information, especially from online sources.

D Connecting to Science

The period between 2000 and 2020 witnessed rising concerns over the destruction of the environment and the spread of pandemic diseases. Some of these issues were problems that scientists had been warning about for years. Critics charged that some politicians were ignoring or undermining scientific research that did not align with their political agendas. Many worried that such actions weakened public confidence in scientific expertise at times when it was needed the most.

ACTIVITY **Write a Scientific Summary** Identify one of the topics that concerned environmental activists during the period from 2000 to 2020. Using library or Internet resources, research scientific consensus about the causes and possible solutions for the problem. Write a summary of your findings. Conclude with your recommendations for one way current or future generations could work to fix the problem.

Rawpixel.com/Shutterstock.

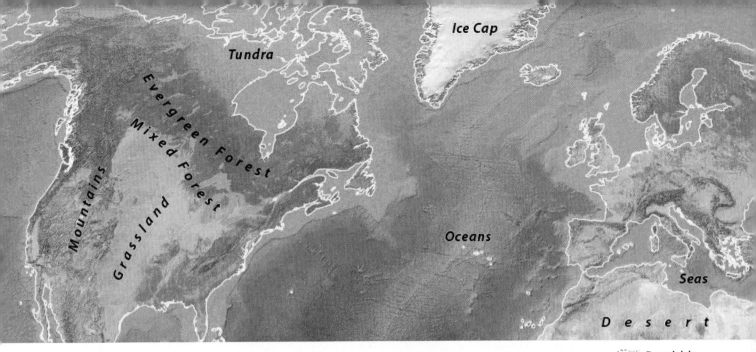

Tundra

Ice Cap

Evergreen Forest

Mixed Forest

Mountains

Grassland

Oceans

Seas

Desert

Atlas and Symbol Key

- ······ Claimed boundary
- —— International boundary (political map)
- —— International boundary (physical map)

- ✪ National capital
- ◦ State/Provincial capital
- • Towns

- ▼ Depression
- ▲ Elevation

 Dry salt lake
Lake
Rivers
~~~~ Canal

Reference Atlas

United States: Political	628
United States: Physical	630
Middle America: Physical/Political	632
Canada: Physical/Political	634
Middle East: Physical/Political	636
World: Political	638
Geographic Dictionary	640

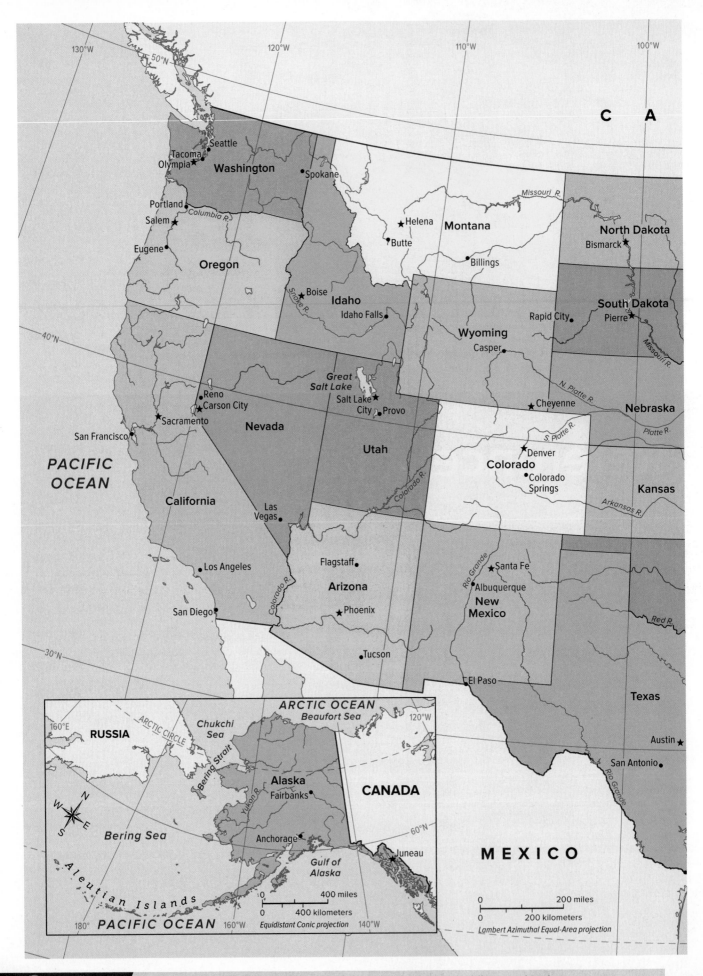

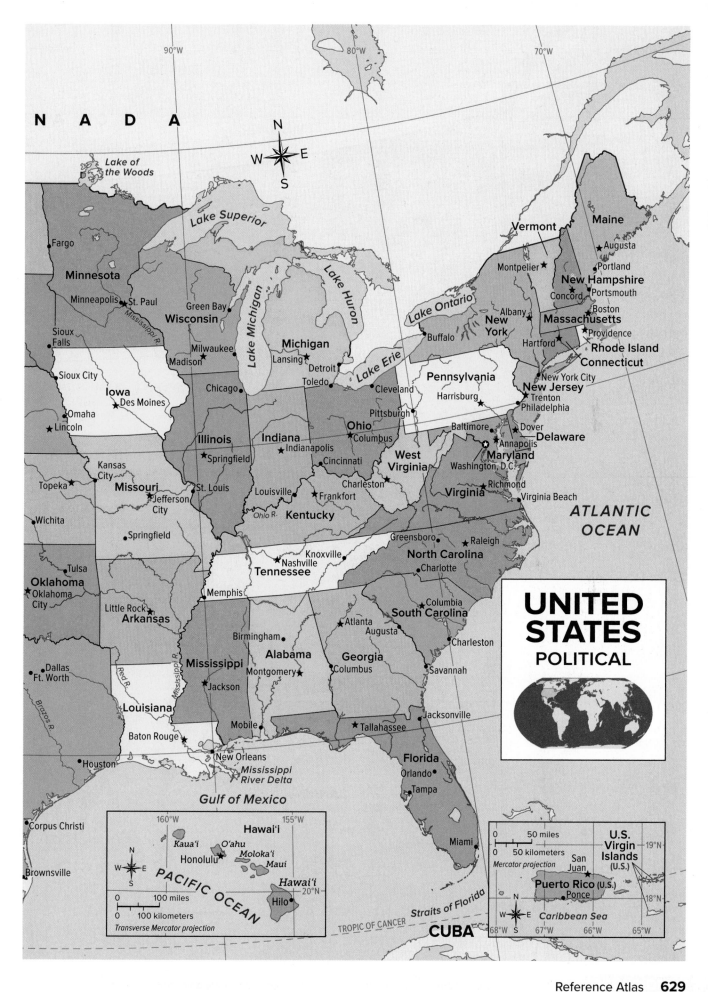

N A D A

Lake of
the Woods

N
W E
S

Lake Superior

Minnesota
• Fargo

Minneapolis • ★ St. Paul

Sioux
Falls

Green Bay •
Wisconsin
Milwaukee •
Madison ★

Lake Michigan

Michigan
Lansing ★

Detroit •
Toledo •

Lake Huron

Lake Ontario

Lake Erie

Cleveland •

Vermont

Montpelier ★

Concord ★

Albany ★

New York

Buffalo •

Hartford ★

Maine
★ Augusta

• Portland

New Hampshire
Portsmouth

Boston ★

Massachusetts
★ Providence

Rhode Island
Connecticut

• New York City

Sioux City •

Iowa
Des Moines ★

• Omaha

• Lincoln

Kansas
City •

Missouri
Jefferson ★
City

Topeka ★

Wichita •

• Springfield

Illinois
Springfield ★

Chicago •

Indiana
• Indianapolis ★

Cincinnati •

St. Louis ★

Louisville •
Frankfort ★

Ohio R.

Kentucky

Ohio
Columbus ★

Pennsylvania

Harrisburg ★

Pittsburgh •

**West
Virginia**

Charleston ★

Baltimore •

Annapolis
Washington, D.C. ★

New Jersey
Trenton ★
Philadelphia •

Dover •
Delaware

Maryland

Virginia
Richmond •

• Virginia Beach

**ATLANTIC
OCEAN**

Knoxville •

Nashville ★

Tennessee

Greensboro •
★ Raleigh

North Carolina
• Charlotte

• Tulsa

Oklahoma
Oklahoma
City ★

Little Rock ★

Arkansas

Memphis •

Birmingham ★

Mississippi
Montgomery ★
★ Jackson

Alabama

Columbia ★

South Carolina

★ Atlanta
Augusta •

Charleston •

Georgia
Columbus •

Savannah •

**UNITED
STATES**
POLITICAL

• Dallas
Ft. Worth •

Louisiana

Baton Rouge ★

Red R.

Brazos R.

Mississippi R.

Mobile •

New Orleans •
*Mississippi
River Delta*

Jacksonville •

Tallahassee ★

Florida
Orlando •

• Houston

Gulf of Mexico

Tampa •

• Corpus Christi

160°W

Hawai'i

155°W

Kaua'i

O'ahu

N
W E
S

Honolulu •

Moloka'i
Maui

Miami •

0   50 miles

0   50 kilometers

Mercator projection

**U.S.
Virgin
Islands**
(U.S.)

19°N

San
Juan ★

Puerto Rico (U.S.)
• Ponce

18°N

PACIFIC OCEAN

0   100 miles

0   100 kilometers

Transverse Mercator projection

Hawai'i

Hilo •

20°N

N
W E
S

Caribbean Sea

68°W   67°W   66°W   65°W

Brownsville •

Straits of Florida

TROPIC OF CANCER

CUBA

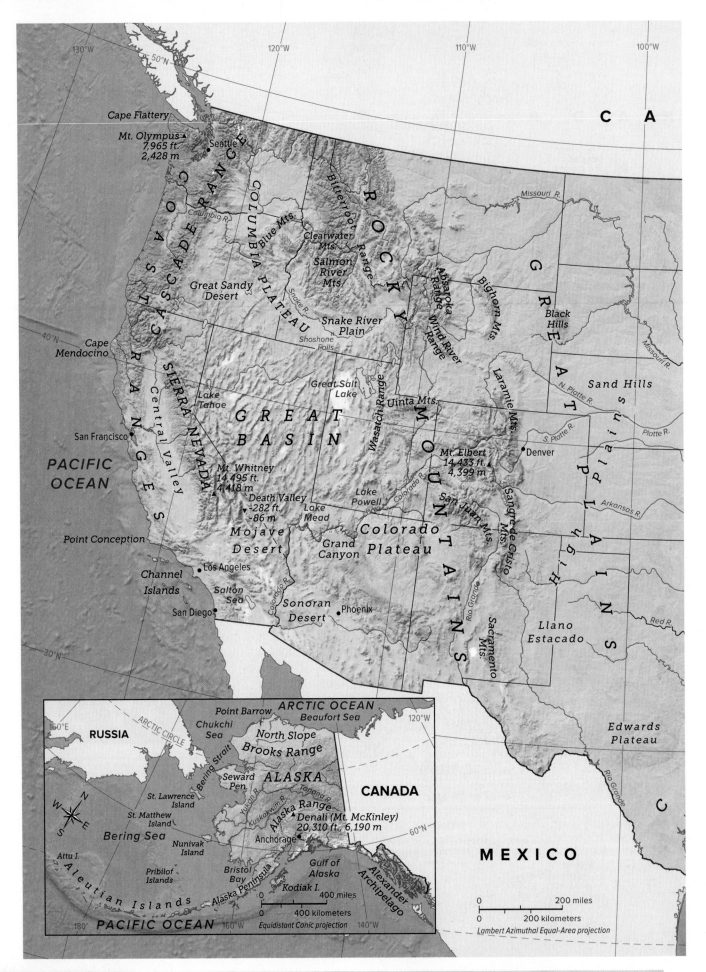

130°W   50°N   120°W   110°W   100°W

C A

Cape Flattery

Mt. Olympus ▲
7,965 ft.
2,428 m   • Seattle

C O A S T   R A N G E S

Columbia R.

COLUMBIA PLATEAU

Blue Mts.

Clearwater
Mts.

Salmon
River
Mts.

Great Sandy
Desert

Snake R.

Snake River
Plain

Shoshone
Falls

R O C K Y

Bitterroot Range

Absaroka
Range

Wind River
Range

Bighorn Mts.

Missouri R.

G R E A T

Missouri R.

40°N

Cape
Mendocino

S I E R R A   N E V A D A

Central Valley

Lake
Tahoe

GREAT SALT
LAKE

GREAT
BASIN

Great Salt
Lake

Wasatch Range

Uinta Mts.

M O U N T A I N S

Laramie Mts.

N. Platte R.

Sand Hills

Black
Hills

S. Platte R.

Platte R.

San Francisco

Mt. Whitney
14,495 ft.
4,418 m ▲

Death Valley
-282 ft.
-86 m ▼

Lake
Powell

Colorado R.

Mt. Elbert
14,433 ft.
4,399 m ▲

• Denver

H i g h

P l a i n s

Arkansas R.

PACIFIC
OCEAN

Point Conception

Mojave
Desert

Lake
Mead

Grand
Canyon

Colorado
Plateau

San Juan Mts.

Sangre de Cristo Mts.

Channel
Islands

Colorado R.

• Los Angeles

Salton
Sea

Sonoran
Desert

• Phoenix

Rio Grande

Sacramento
Mts.

Llano
Estacado

Red R.

San Diego •

MEXICO

Edwards
Plateau

Rio Grande

C

ARCTIC OCEAN

Point Barrow   Beaufort Sea

160°E

RUSSIA

ARCTIC CIRCLE

Chukchi
Sea

North Slope

Brooks Range

120°W

Bering Strait

Seward
Pen.

ALASKA

CANADA

St. Lawrence
Island

Kuskokwim R.

Yukon R.

Tanana R.

Alaska Range

Denali (Mt. McKinley)
20,310 ft., 6,190 m ▲

St. Matthew
Island

Bering Sea

Nunivak
Island

Anchorage •

60°N

Attu I.

Pribilof
Islands

Bristol
Bay

Alaska Peninsula

Kodiak I.

Gulf of
Alaska

Alexander Archipelago

0   400 miles

0   400 kilometers

A l e u t i a n   I s l a n d s

PACIFIC OCEAN

180°   160°W   140°W

Equidistant Conic projection

0   200 miles

0   200 kilometers

Lambert Azimuthal Equal-Area projection

◥ GO ONLINE   Explore the Student Edition eBook and find interactive maps, time lines, and tools.

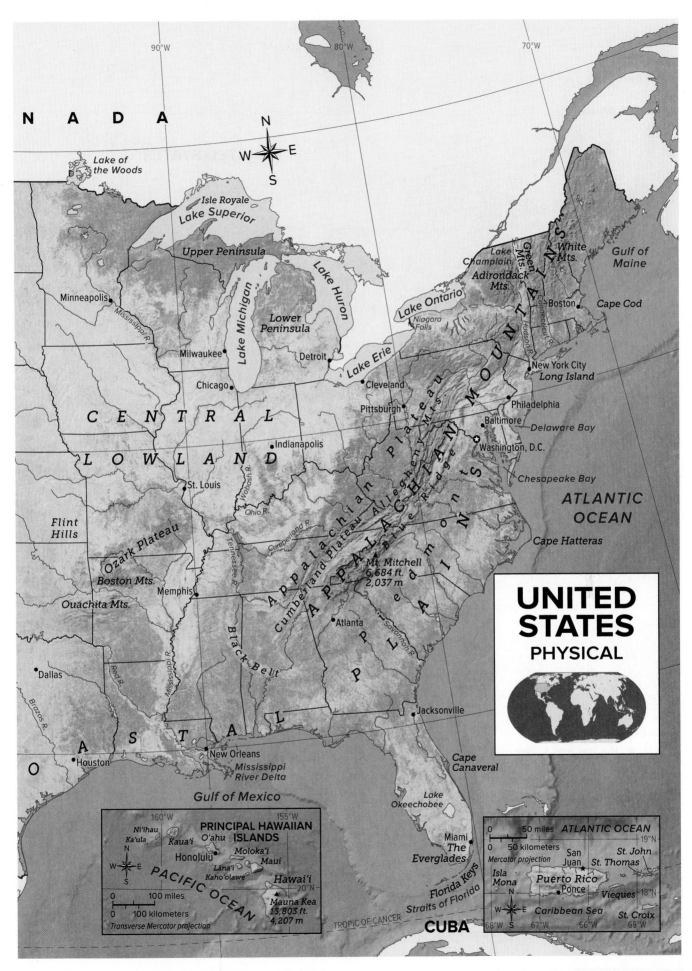

CANADA

Lake of the Woods

Isle Royale

Lake Superior

Upper Peninsula

Lake Michigan

Lake Huron

Lower Peninsula

Minneapolis

Mississippi R.

Milwaukee

Chicago

Detroit

Lake Erie

Cleveland

Lake Ontario

Niagara Falls

Pittsburgh

Lake Champlain

Adirondack Mts.

Green Mts.

White Mts.

Gulf of Maine

Boston

Cape Cod

Connecticut R.

Hudson R.

New York City

Long Island

Philadelphia

Baltimore

Delaware Bay

Washington, D.C.

Chesapeake Bay

ATLANTIC OCEAN

Cape Hatteras

CENTRAL LOWLAND

Indianapolis

Wabash R.

St. Louis

Ohio R.

Flint Hills

Ozark Plateau

Cumberland R.

Tennessee R.

Boston Mts.

Memphis

Ouachita Mts.

Appalachian Plateau

Allegheny Mts.

Cumberland Plateau

Blue Ridge

APPALACHIAN MOUNTAINS

Piedmont

Mt. Mitchell
6,684 ft.
2,037 m

Atlanta

Savannah R.

Black Belt

Mississippi R.

Dallas

Red R.

Brazos R.

COASTAL PLAIN

Houston

New Orleans

Mississippi River Delta

Gulf of Mexico

Jacksonville

Cape Canaveral

Lake Okeechobee

Miami

The Everglades

Florida Keys

Straits of Florida

CUBA

TROPIC OF CANCER

UNITED STATES
PHYSICAL

PRINCIPAL HAWAIIAN ISLANDS

160°W   155°W

Ni'ihau
Ka'ula
Kaua'i
O'ahu
Honolulu
Moloka'i
Lāna'i
Kaho'olawe
Maui

PACIFIC OCEAN

Hawai'i

20°N

Mauna Kea
13,803 ft.
4,207 m

0   100 miles
0   100 kilometers
Transverse Mercator projection

0   50 miles   ATLANTIC OCEAN
0   50 kilometers
Mercator projection

19°N

San Juan

St. John
St. Thomas

Isla Mona

Puerto Rico
Ponce

Vieques

18°N

Caribbean Sea

St. Croix

68°W   67°W   66°W   65°W

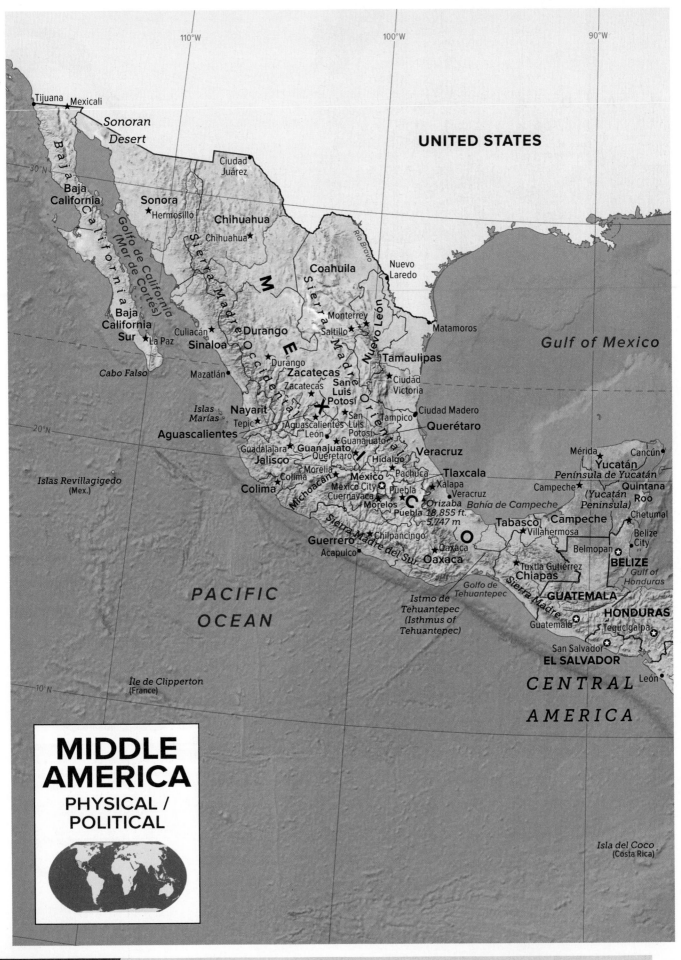

Tijuana Mexicali

Sonoran Desert

UNITED STATES

30°N

Baja California

Baja California

Sonora

Ciudad Juárez

★ Hermosillo

Chihuahua

Chihuahua ★

Golfo de California (Mar de Cortés)

California

Sierra Madre Occidental

Coahuila

Rio Bravo

Nuevo Laredo

Monterrey

Baja California Sur

Culiacán

Durango

Saltillo ★

Nuevo León

★ La Paz

Sinaloa

Cabo Falso

Mazatlán •

Durango

Zacatecas

San Luis Potosí

Matamoros

Gulf of Mexico

Tamaulipas

Ciudad Victoria

Sierra Madre Oriental

Islas Marías

Nayarit

Zacatecas ★

★

Tepic

Aguascalientes

San Luis Potosí

Tampico

Ciudad Madero

20°N

Islas Revillagigedo (Mex.)

Aguascalientes

Guadalajara ★

León ★

Jalisco

Guanajuato

Querétaro

Querétaro ★

Guanajuato

Hidalgo

Mérida ★

Yucatán

Cancún ★

Península de Yucatán

Veracruz

Colima

Colima

Morelia ★

Michoacán

México

Pachuca

Tlaxcala

Campeche

Quintana Roo

Chetumal

Mexico City ✪

Puebla

Veracruz

(Yucatán Peninsula)

Cuernavaca ★

Morelos

Puebla

Orizaba 18,855 ft. 5,747 m

Tabasco

Campeche

Belize City

Villahermosa

Bahía de Campeche

Guerrero

Chilpancingo

Sierra Madre del Sur

Oaxaca ★

Oaxaca

Belmopan ✪

BELIZE

Acapulco •

Istmo de Tehuantepec (Isthmus of Tehuantepec)

Golfo de Tehuantepec

Tuxtla Gutiérrez •

Chiapas

Sierra Madre

Gulf of Honduras

GUATEMALA

HONDURAS

PACIFIC OCEAN

Guatemala ✪

Tegucigalpa ✪

San Salvador ✪

EL SALVADOR

León •

10°N

Île de Clipperton (France)

CENTRAL

AMERICA

MIDDLE AMERICA
PHYSICAL / POLITICAL

Isla del Coco (Costa Rica)

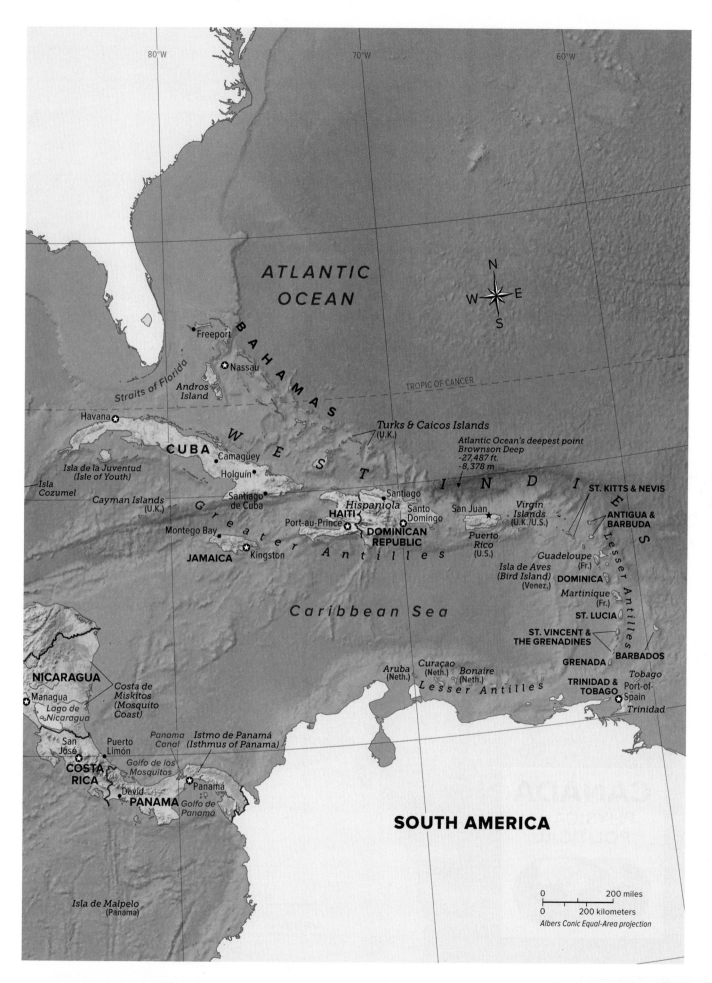

ATLANTIC
OCEAN

N
W E
S

BAHAMAS

Freeport•

☆Nassau

Straits of Florida

*Andros
Island*

TROPIC OF CANCER

Havana☆

CUBA

•Camagüey

*Isla de la Juventud
(Isle of Youth)*

Holguín•

*Isla
Cozumel*

*Cayman Islands
(U.K.)*

Santiago•
de Cuba

Montego Bay•

JAMAICA

Kingston•☆

*Greater
Antilles*

Turks & Caicos Islands
(U.K.)

Atlantic Ocean's deepest point
Brownson Deep
-27,487 ft.
-8,378 m

Santiago•

Hispaniola

HAITI
Port-au-Prince•☆

Santo
Domingo•

**DOMINICAN
REPUBLIC**

San Juan
★

*Puerto
Rico
(U.S.)*

*Virgin
Islands
(U.K./U.S.)*

ST. KITTS & NEVIS

**ANTIGUA &
BARBUDA**

*Guadeloupe
(Fr.)*

DOMINICA

*Isla de Aves
(Bird Island)
(Venez.)*

*Martinique
(Fr.)*

ST. LUCIA

**ST. VINCENT &
THE GRENADINES**

BARBADOS

GRENADA

Lesser Antilles

Caribbean Sea

NICARAGUA

Managua•

*Lago de
Nicaragua*

*Costa de
Miskitos
(Mosquito
Coast)*

San
José•☆

Puerto
Limón•

**COSTA
RICA**

*Panama
Canal*

*Istmo de Panamá
(Isthmus of Panama)*

*Golfo de los
Mosquitos*

David•

☆Panamá

PANAMA

*Golfo de
Panamá*

*Aruba
(Neth.)*

*Curaçao
(Neth.)*

*Bonaire
(Neth.)*

Lesser Antilles

**TRINIDAD &
TOBAGO**

Tobago

Port-of-
Spain☆

Trinidad

SOUTH AMERICA

*Isla de Malpelo
(Panama)*

0   200 miles
0   200 kilometers
Albers Conic Equal-Area projection

80°W   70°W   60°W

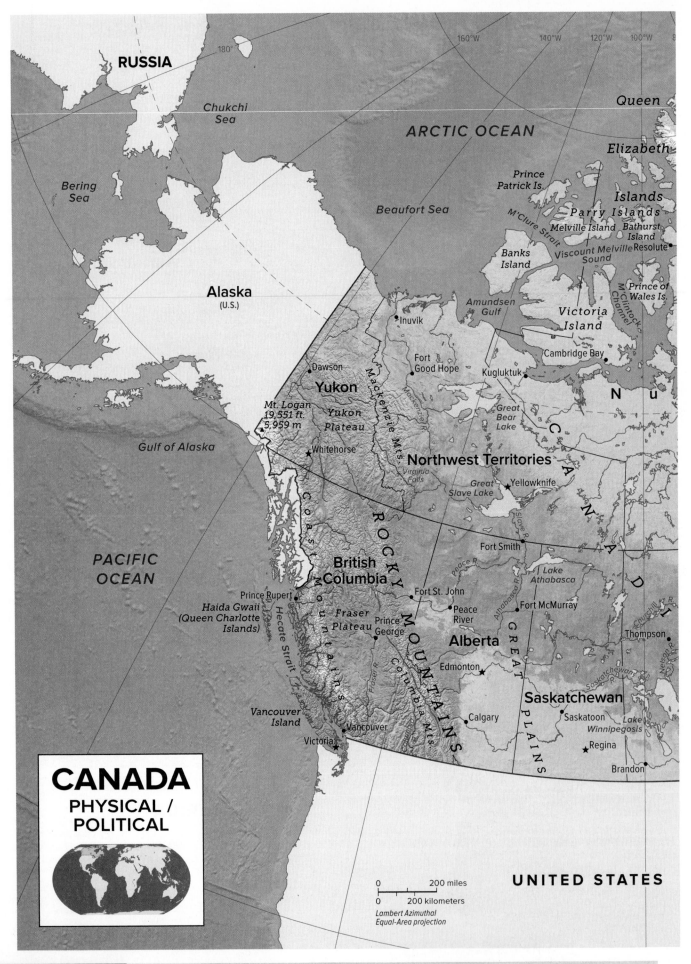

RUSSIA

Chukchi
Sea

ARCTIC OCEAN

Queen

Bering
Sea

Beaufort Sea

Prince
Patrick Is.

Elizabeth

Islands

Parry Islands

M'Clure Strait

Melville Island   *Bathurst*
Island

Viscount Melville   Resolute
Sound

Banks
Island

Alaska
(U.S.)

Amundsen
Gulf

Prince of
Wales Is.

Inuvik

Victoria
Island

Cambridge Bay

Fort
Good Hope

Kugluktuk

N

u

Dawson

Yukon

Yukon
Plateau

Great
Bear
Lake

Mt. Logan
19,551 ft.
5,959 m

Whitehorse

Virginia
Falls

Northwest Territories

Great
Slave Lake

Yellowknife

C

A

N

A

Fort Smith

PACIFIC
OCEAN

Coast

Peace R.

Lake
Athabasca

Fort McMurray

Slave R.

D

I

Athabasca R.

Churchill R.

Prince Rupert

British
Columbia

Fort St. John

Haida Gwaii
(Queen Charlotte
Islands)

Hecate Strait

Fraser
Plateau

Prince
George

Peace
River

R

O

C

K

Y

Thompson

Mountains

M

O

U

N

T

A

I

N

S

Fraser R.

Columbia Mts.

Alberta

G

R

E

A

T

Edmonton

Nelson R.

Saskatchewan R.

Saskatchewan

Vancouver
Island

Vancouver

Calgary

P

L

A

I

N

S

Saskatoon

Lake
Winnipegosis

Victoria

Regina

Brandon

CANADA
PHYSICAL /
POLITICAL

0   200 miles
0   200 kilometers
Lambert Azimuthal
Equal-Area projection

UNITED STATES

180°   160°W   140°W   120°W   100°W

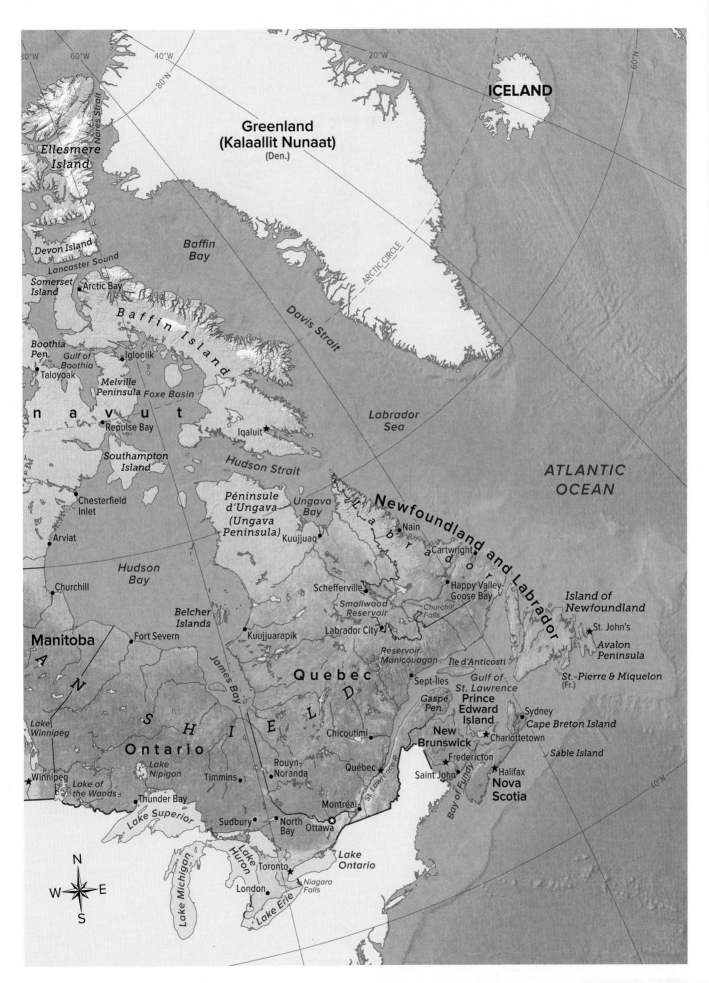

ICELAND

**Greenland
(Kalaallit Nunaat)**
(Den.)

*Ellesmere
Island*

Devon Island

Lancaster Sound

*Somerset
Island*

*Baffin
Bay*

• Arctic Bay

*Boothia
Pen.*

*Gulf of
Boothia*

• Igloolik

• Taloyoak

*Melville
Peninsula* *Foxe Basin*

n a v u t

Davis Strait

ARCTIC CIRCLE

• Repulse Bay

Iqaluit ★

*Southampton
Island*

*Labrador
Sea*

Hudson Strait

Baffin Island

*Péninsule
d'Ungava
(Ungava
Peninsula)*

*Ungava
Bay*

Newfoundland and Labrador

*ATLANTIC
OCEAN*

• Chesterfield
Inlet

Nain •

L

a

b

r

a

d

o

r

• Cartwright

• Arviat

• Kuujjuaq

• Schefferville

*Hudson
Bay*

• Churchill

*Belcher
Islands*

Manitoba

• Fort Severn

James Bay

A

N

*Lake
Winnipeg*

S

H

• Kuujjuarapik

*Smallwood
Reservoir*

Labrador City •

Q u e b e c

Happy Valley-
Goose Bay •

*Churchill
Falls*

*Island of
Newfoundland*

St. John's ★

*Avalon
Peninsula*

St.-Pierre & Miquelon
(Fr.)

*Réservoir
Manicouagan*

Île d'Anticosti

I

E

L

D

Sept-Îles •

*Gulf of
St. Lawrence*

*Gaspé
Pen.*

**Prince
Edward
Island**

• Chicoutimi

Sydney •

Cape Breton Island

O n t a r i o

*Lake
Nipigon*

• Rouyn-
Noranda

Québec ★

**New
Brunswick**

Charlottetown ★

Sable Island

• Timmins

Fredericton ★

★ Winnipeg

*Lake of
the Woods*

• Thunder Bay

Sudbury •

• North
Bay

Lake Superior

*Lake
Huron*

Lake Michigan

Toronto ★

London •

Lake Erie

St. Lawrence R.

Saint John •

Bay of Fundy

Halifax ★

**Nova
Scotia**

Montréal •

Ottawa ✪

*Lake
Ontario*

*Niagara
Falls*

N
W ✦ E
S

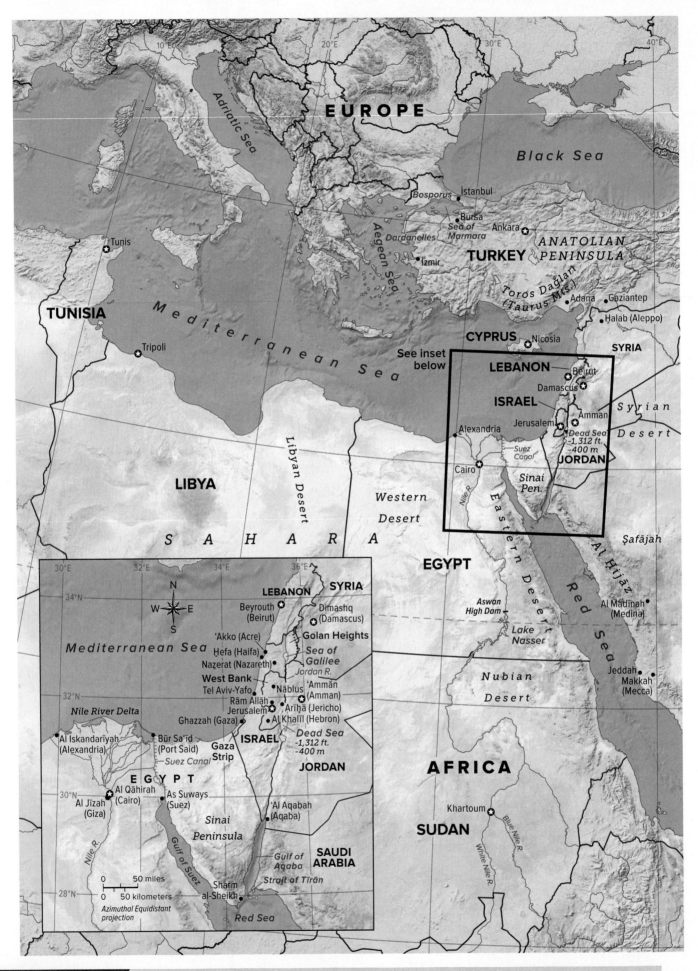

EUROPE

Black Sea

Adriatic Sea

İstanbul
Bosporus
Bursa
Sea of
Marmara
Dardanelles
Ankara
ANATOLIAN
PENINSULA
TURKEY
Tunis
İzmir

Aegean Sea

Toros Dağlari
(Taurus Mts.)
Adana
Gaziantep
Ḩalab (Aleppo)

TUNISIA

M e d i t e r r a n e a n   S e a

CYPRUS
Nicosia

SYRIA

See inset
below

LEBANON
Beirut

Tripoli

Damascus

ISRAEL

Syrian

Alexandria
Jerusalem
Amman
Dead Sea
-1,312 ft.
-400 m

Desert

Suez
Canal

JORDAN

LIBYA

Western
Desert

Cairo

Sinai
Pen.

Libyan Desert

EGYPT

Ṣafājah

SAHARA

Aswan
High Dam
Nile R.
Eastern Desert
Red Sea
Al Ḩijāz
Al Madīnah
(Medina)

Lake
Nasser

Nubian
Desert

Jeddah
Makkah
(Mecca)

AFRICA

Khartoum

SUDAN

Blue Nile R.
White Nile R.

Inset map

N
W E
S

30°E
32°E
34°E
36°E

34°N

SYRIA

LEBANON

Beyrouth
(Beirut)

Dimashq
(Damascus)

Mediterranean Sea

'Akko (Acre)
Golan Heights

Ḩefa (Haifa)
Sea of
Galilee

Naẕerat (Nazareth)
Jordan R.

West Bank
'Ammān
(Amman)

Tel Aviv-Yafo
Nāblus

32°N

Rām Allāh
Jericho)
Arīḩā (Jericho)

Nile River Delta

Jerusalem

Ghazzah (Gaza)
Al Khalīl (Hebron)

Al Iskandarīyah
(Alexandria)

Bûr Saʿīd
(Port Said)

ISRAEL

Dead Sea
-1,312 ft.
-400 m

Suez Canal

Gaza
Strip

JORDAN

E G Y P T

Al Qāhirah
(Cairo)

As Suways
(Suez)

Al Jīzah
(Giza)

30°N

'Al Aqabah
(Aqaba)

Sinai
Peninsula

SAUDI
ARABIA

Gulf of
Aqaba

Gulf of Suez

Strait of Tīrān

0   50 miles
0   50 kilometers

Sharm
al-Sheikh

28°N

Azimuthal Equidistant
projection

Red Sea

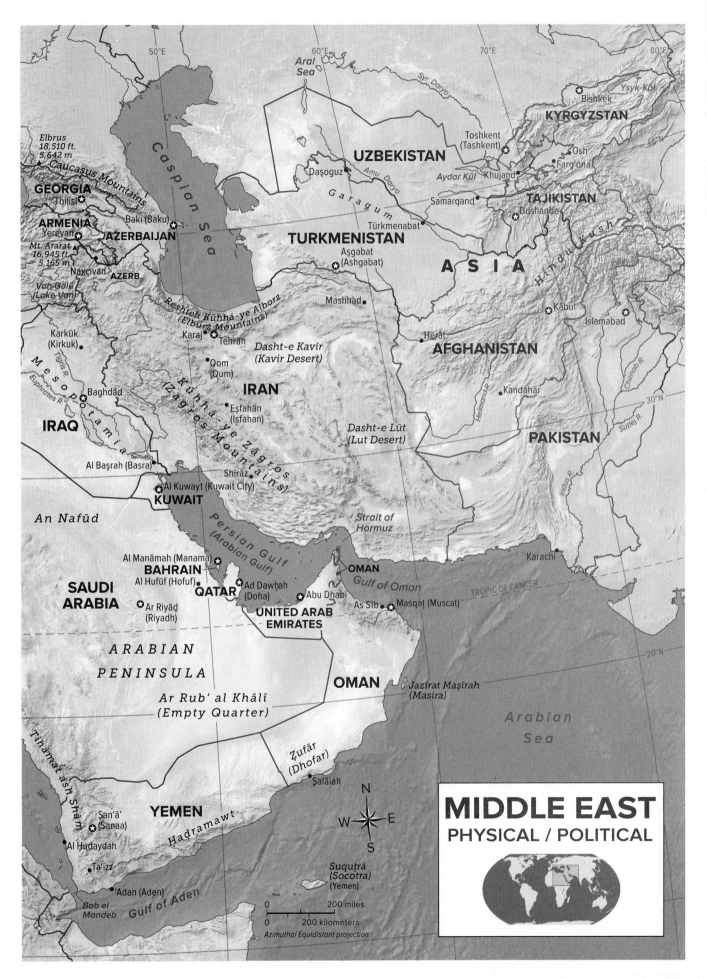

Elbrus
18,510 ft.
5,642 m

Caucasus Mountains

Caspian Sea

GEORGIA
Tbilisi

ARMENIA
Yerevan

Baki (Baku)

AZERBAIJAN

Mt. Ararat
16,945 ft.
5,165 m

Naxçıvan   **AZERB.**

Van Gölü
(Lake Van)

Aral Sea

Syr Darya

Ysyk-Köl

Bishkek

KYRGYZSTAN

Toshkent
(Tashkent)

UZBEKISTAN

Daşoguz

Amu Darya

Garagum

Türkmenabat

TURKMENISTAN

Aşgabat
(Ashgabat)

Aydar Kül

Khujand

Osh

Farg'ona

Samarqand

TAJIKISTAN

Dushanbe

A S I A

Hindu Kush

Mashhad

Reshteh Kühhä-ye Alborz
(Elburz Mountains)

Karaj   Tehrān

Herāt

Kābul

Islamabad

AFGHANISTAN

*Dasht-e Kavīr
(Kavir Desert)*

Karkūk
(Kirkuk)

Tigris R.

Euphrates R.

Mesopotamia

Qom
(Qum)

IRAN

Eşfahān
(Isfahan)

Baghdād

IRAQ

Kühhā-ye Zagros
(Zagros Mountains)

*Dasht-e Lūt
(Lut Desert)*

Kandahār

Helmand R.

Chenab R.

Sutlej R.

PAKISTAN

Indus R.

Al Başrah (Basra)

Shīrāz

Al Kuwayt (Kuwait City)

KUWAIT

An Nafūd

*Persian Gulf
(Arabian Gulf)*

*Strait of
Hormuz*

Karachi

Al Manāmah (Manama)

BAHRAIN

Al Hufūf (Hofuf)

QATAR

Ad Dawḩah
(Doha)

Abu Dhabi

OMAN

Gulf of Oman

TROPIC OF CANCER

**SAUDI
ARABIA**

Ar Riyāḑ
(Riyadh)

**UNITED ARAB
EMIRATES**

As Sīb   Masqaṭ (Muscat)

*ARABIAN

PENINSULA*

*Ar Rub' al Khālī
(Empty Quarter)*

OMAN

Jazīrat Maşīrah
(Masira)

*Arabian
Sea*

Tihāmat ash Sham

*Ẓufār
(Dhofar)*

Şalālah

Şan'ā'
(Sanaa)

YEMEN

Al Ḩudaydah

Hadramawt

Ta'izz

Suquṭrá
(Socotra)
(Yemen)

'Adan (Aden)

*Bab el
Mandeb*

Gulf of Aden

N
W   E
S

0   200 miles

0   200 kilometers

Azimuthal Equidistant projection

MIDDLE EAST
PHYSICAL / POLITICAL

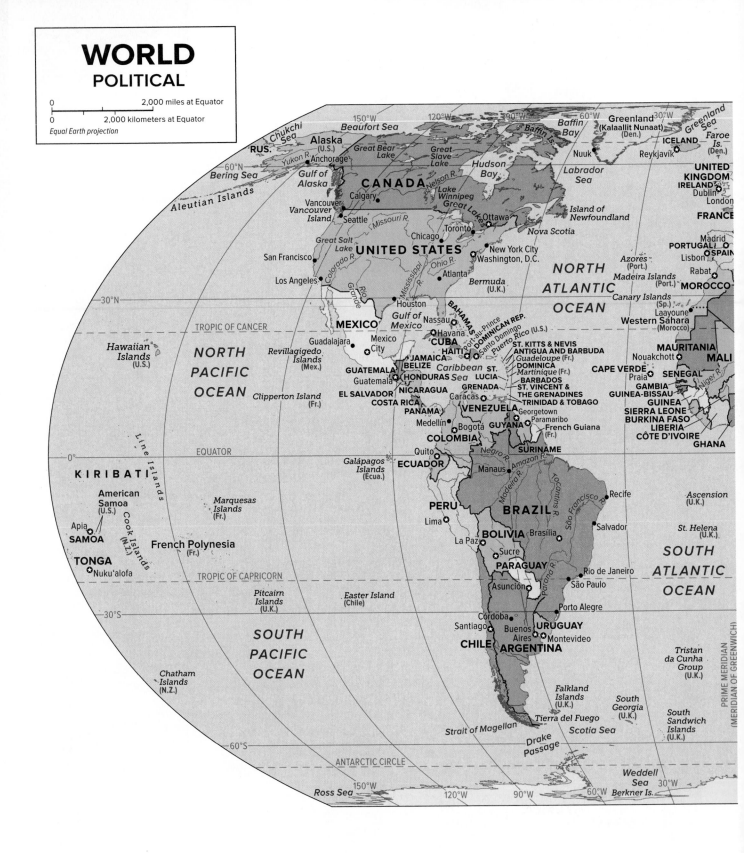

WORLD
POLITICAL

0 _____ 2,000 miles at Equator
0 _____ 2,000 kilometers at Equator
Equal Earth projection

Chukchi Sea
150°W
Beaufort Sea
120°W
90°W
Baffin Bay
60°W
Greenland (Kalaallit Nunaat) (Den.)
30°W
Greenland Sea
Baffin Is.
RUS.
Alaska (U.S.)
Great Bear Lake
Great Slave Lake
Hudson Bay
ICELAND
Faroe Is. (Den.)
Bering Sea
60°N
Yukon R.
Anchorage
Nuuk
Reykjavík
Gulf of Alaska
CANADA
Nelson R.
Labrador Sea
UNITED KINGDOM
Calgary
Lake Winnipeg
Great Lakes
Island of Newfoundland
IRELAND
Vancouver
Vancouver Island
Seattle
Missouri R.
Ottawa
Toronto
Nova Scotia
Dublin
London
FRANCE
Chicago
Great Salt Lake
UNITED STATES
New York City
Washington, D.C.
Azores (Port.)
Madrid
PORTUGAL
Lisbon
SPAIN
San Francisco
Colorado R.
Ohio R.
Atlanta
Bermuda (U.K.)
NORTH ATLANTIC OCEAN
Madeira Islands (Port.)
Rabat
Los Angeles
Rio Grande
Mississippi R.
MOROCCO
30°N
Houston
Canary Islands (Sp.)
TROPIC OF CANCER
MEXICO
Gulf of Mexico
Nassau
BAHAMAS
Western Sahara (Morocco)
Laayoune
Hawaiian Islands (U.S.)
NORTH PACIFIC OCEAN
Guadalajara
Mexico City
Havana
CUBA
Port-au-Prince
DOMINICAN REP.
Santo Domingo
Puerto Rico (U.S.)
ST. KITTS & NEVIS
ANTIGUA AND BARBUDA
MAURITANIA
Nouakchott
MALI
Revillagigedo Islands (Mex.)
HAITI
Guadeloupe (Fr.)
CAPE VERDE
SENEGAL
GUATEMALA
JAMAICA
BELIZE
Caribbean Sea
ST. LUCIA
DOMINICA
Martinique (Fr.)
Praia
GAMBIA
Clipperton Island (Fr.)
Guatemala
HONDURAS
BARBADOS
GUINEA-BISSAU
EL SALVADOR
NICARAGUA
GRENADA
ST. VINCENT &
THE GRENADINES
GUINEA
SIERRA LEONE
COSTA RICA
Caracas
TRINIDAD & TOBAGO
BURKINA FASO
PANAMA
VENEZUELA
Georgetown
LIBERIA
CÔTE D'IVOIRE
Medellín
Bogotá
GUYANA
Paramaribo
French Guiana (Fr.)
GHANA
COLOMBIA
SURINAME
Quito
Negro R.
Amazon R.
0°
EQUATOR
Galápagos Islands (Ecua.)
ECUADOR
Manaus
Madeira R.
Tocantins R.
Recife
Ascension (U.K.)
KIRIBATI
Line Islands
PERU
BRAZIL
São Francisco R.
American Samoa (U.S.)
Marquesas Islands (Fr.)
Lima
BOLIVIA
Brasilia
Salvador
St. Helena (U.K.)
Apia
SAMOA
Cook Islands (N.Z.)
French Polynesia (Fr.)
La Paz
Sucre
TONGA
Nuku'alofa
PARAGUAY
Rio de Janeiro
SOUTH ATLANTIC OCEAN
TROPIC OF CAPRICORN
Paraná R.
São Paulo
Asunción
Pitcairn Islands (U.K.)
Easter Island (Chile)
Porto Alegre
Córdoba
30°S
Santiago
Buenos Aires
URUGUAY
Montevideo
Tristan da Cunha Group (U.K.)
SOUTH PACIFIC OCEAN
CHILE
ARGENTINA
Chatham Islands (N.Z.)
Falkland Islands (U.K.)
South Georgia (U.K.)
South Sandwich Islands (U.K.)
Tierra del Fuego
Strait of Magellan
Scotia Sea
60°S
Drake Passage
PRIME MERIDIAN (MERIDIAN OF GREENWICH)
ANTARCTIC CIRCLE
150°W
Ross Sea
120°W
90°W
60°W
Weddell Sea
Berkner Is.
30°W

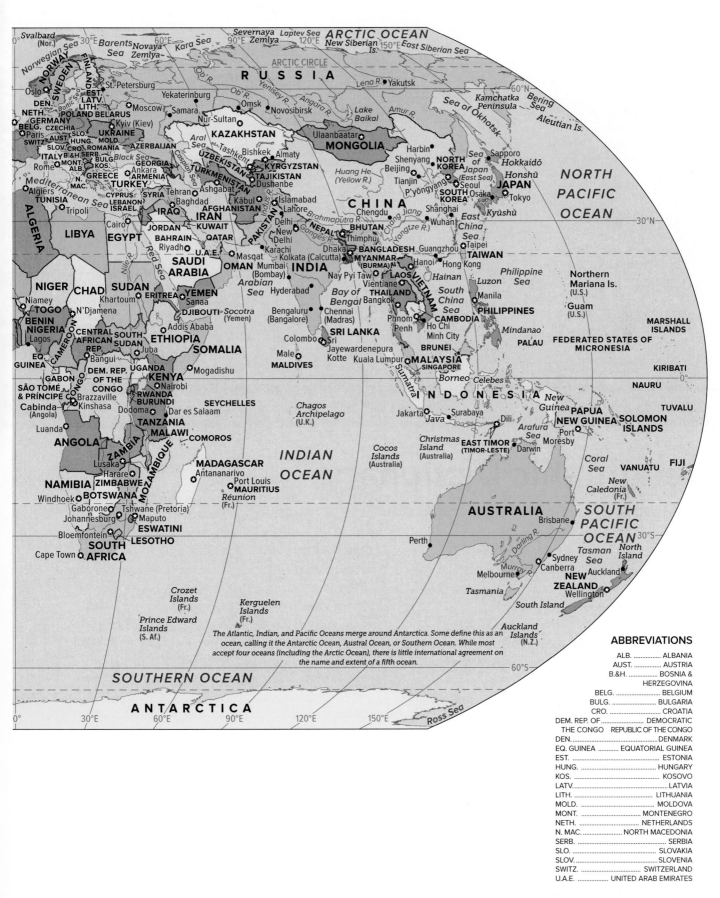

ARCTIC OCEAN

Svalbard (Nor.) *Barents* *Novaya* Kara Sea *Severnaya* Laptev Sea *New Siberian* East Siberian Sea
Norwegian Sea Sea *Zemlya* ARCTIC CIRCLE

NORWAY SWEDEN FINLAND
Oslo DEN. EST. ☆ St. Petersburg R U S S I A Lena R. ● Yakutsk
NETH. LATV. ☆ Moscow Yekaterinburg Kamchatka 60°N Bering
GERMANY POLAND BELARUS Samara Omsk Novosibirsk Peninsula Sea
BELG. CZECHIA LITH. Nur-Sultan Sea of Okhotsk Aleutian Is.
Paris SWITZ. AUST. HUNG. SLO. UKRAINE MOLD. KAZAKHSTAN Ulaanbaatar Harbin Sapporo Hokkaidō
ITALY B.&H. SERB. ROMANIA Aral Tashkent Bishkek Almaty MONGOLIA Shenyang NORTH Sea Honshū NORTH
Rome MONT. ALB. BULG. Black Sea AZERBAIJAN Sea UZBEKISTAN KYRGYZSTAN Beijing KOREA of Osaka PACIFIC
N. MAC. GEORGIA ARMENIA TURKMENISTAN TAJIKISTAN Huang He Tianjin P'yŏngyang Japan Tokyo OCEAN
GREECE Ankara Ashgabat Dushanbe (Yellow R.) CHINA SOUTH (East Sea) Kyūshū
TURKEY CYPRUS SYRIA Tehran Kābul Islamabad Chengdu KOREA Seoul JAPAN 30°N
TUNISIA LEBANON ISRAEL Baghdad AFGHANISTAN Lahore Shanghai East
Mediterranean Sea IRAQ IRAN Delhi New NEPAL BHUTAN Wuhan China
Algiers Cairo JORDAN KUWAIT Delhi Ganges R. Brahmaputra R. Thimphu Yangtze R. Sea Taipei
ALGERIA LIBYA EGYPT BAHRAIN QATAR PAKISTAN Kolkata (Calcutta) BANGLADESH MYANMAR Guangzhou TAIWAN
SAUDI U.A.E. Riyadh Masqat Karachi Dhaka (BURMA) Hanoi Hong Kong
NIGER CHAD ARABIA OMAN Mumbai INDIA Nay Pyi Taw LAOS Hainan South Northern
SUDAN YEMEN Arabian (Bombay) Hyderabad Vientiane VIETNAM China Philippine Mariana Is.
TOGO Khartoum ERITREA Sanaa Sea Bengaluru Chennai THAILAND Sea Luzon Sea (U.S.)
BENIN Niamey N'Djamena DJIBOUTI Socotra (Bangalore) (Madras) Bangkok CAMBODIA Manila Guam (U.S.)
NIGERIA CENTRAL Addis Ababa (Yemen) Colombo SRI LANKA Phnom Ho Chi PHILIPPINES MARSHALL ISLANDS
Lagos AFRICAN SOUTH ETHIOPIA Sri Penh Minh City Mindanao FEDERATED STATES OF
EQ. GUINEA CAMEROON REP. SUDAN Juba SOMALIA Male Jayewardenepura BRUNEI PALAU MICRONESIA
GABON DEM. REP. UGANDA KENYA Bangui Kotte MALDIVES Kuala Lumpur MALAYSIA KIRIBATI
SÃO TOMÉ OF THE Nairobi Borneo SINGAPORE NAURU
& PRÍNCIPE CONGO RWANDA Mogadishu SEYCHELLES Celebes 0°
Cabinda Brazzaville BURUNDI Chagos I N D O N E S I A New TUVALU
(Angola) Kinshasa Dodoma TANZANIA Dar es Salaam Archipelago Jakarta Surabaya Guinea PAPUA SOLOMON
Luanda MALAWI (U.K.) Java Dili NEW GUINEA ISLANDS
ANGOLA ZAMBIA COMOROS INDIAN Christmas Arafura Port
Lusaka MOZAMBIQUE MADAGASCAR OCEAN Island EAST TIMOR Sea Moresby FIJI
NAMIBIA Harare Antananarivo Cocos (TIMOR-LESTE) Darwin Coral VANUATU
ZIMBABWE Port Louis Islands New Sea
Windhoek BOTSWANA MAURITIUS (Australia) Caledonia
Gaborone Tshwane (Pretoria) Réunion (Fr.) AUSTRALIA (Fr.) SOUTH
Johannesburg Maputo (Fr.) Brisbane PACIFIC
Bloemfontein ESWATINI Perth OCEAN 30°S
Cape Town SOUTH LESOTHO Darling R. Sydney Tasman North
AFRICA Crozet Kerguelen Canberra Sea Island
Islands Islands Murray R. Melbourne NEW Auckland
(Fr.) (Fr.) Tasmania ZEALAND
Prince Edward Auckland Wellington
Islands (S. Af.) Islands South Island
(N.Z.)

The Atlantic, Indian, and Pacific Oceans merge around Antarctica. Some define this as an ocean, calling it the Antarctic Ocean, Austral Ocean, or Southern Ocean. While most accept four oceans (including the Arctic Ocean), there is little international agreement on the name and extent of a fifth ocean.

SOUTHERN OCEAN
60°S
A N T A R C T I C A
0° 30°E 60°E 90°E 120°E 150°E Ross Sea

ABBREVIATIONS

ALB.	ALBANIA
AUST.	AUSTRIA
B.&H.	BOSNIA & HERZEGOVINA
BELG.	BELGIUM
BULG.	BULGARIA
CRO.	CROATIA
DEM. REP. OF THE CONGO	DEMOCRATIC REPUBLIC OF THE CONGO
DEN.	DENMARK
EQ. GUINEA	EQUATORIAL GUINEA
EST.	ESTONIA
HUNG.	HUNGARY
KOS.	KOSOVO
LATV.	LATVIA
LITH.	LITHUANIA
MOLD.	MOLDOVA
MONT.	MONTENEGRO
NETH.	NETHERLANDS
N. MAC.	NORTH MACEDONIA
SERB.	SERBIA
SLO.	SLOVAKIA
SLOV.	SLOVENIA
SWITZ.	SWITZERLAND
U.A.E.	UNITED ARAB EMIRATES

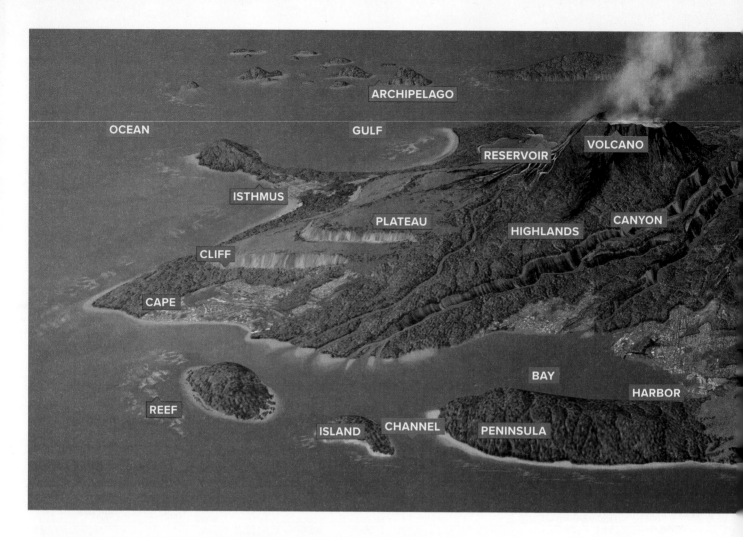

Geographic Dictionary

archipelago a group of islands

basin area of land drained by a given river and its branches; area of land surrounded by lands of higher elevations

bay part of a large body of water that extends into a shoreline, generally smaller than a gulf

canyon deep and narrow valley with steep walls

cape point of land that extends into a river, lake, or ocean

channel wide strait or waterway between two landmasses that lie close to each other; deep part of a river or other waterway

cliff steep, high wall of rock, earth, or ice

continent one of the seven large landmasses on the Earth

delta flat, low-lying land built up from soil carried downstream by a river and deposited at its mouth

divide stretch of high land that separates river systems

downstream direction in which a river or stream flows from its source to its mouth

escarpment steep cliff or slope between a higher and lower land surface

glacier large, thick body of slowly moving ice

gulf part of a large body of water that extends into a shoreline, generally larger and more deeply indented than a bay

harbor a sheltered place along a shoreline where ships can anchor safely

highland elevated land area such as a hill, mountain, or plateau

hill elevated land with sloping sides and rounded (1,000 feet or more) from surrounding land; generally larger and more rugged than a hill summit; generally smaller than a mountain

island land area, smaller than a continent, completely surrounded by water

isthmus narrow stretch of land connecting two larger land areas

lake a sizable inland body of water

lowland land, usually level, at a low elevation

mesa broad, flat-topped landform with steep sides; smaller than a plateau

mountain land with steep sides that rises sharply

GO ONLINE Explore the Student Edition eBook and find interactive maps, time lines, and tools.

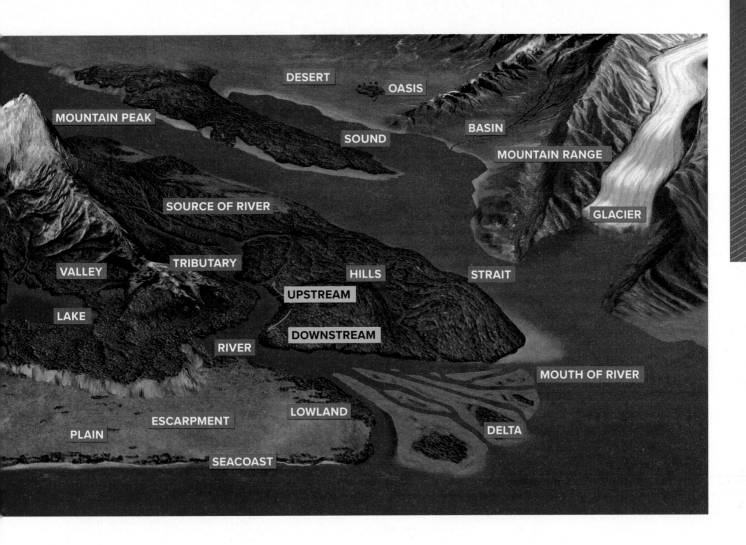

mountain peak pointed top of a mountain

mountain range a series of connected mountains

mouth (of a river) place where a stream or river flows into a larger body of water

oasis small area in a desert where water and vegetation are found

ocean one of the five major bodies of salt water that surround continents

ocean current stream of either cold or warm water that moves in a definite direction through an ocean

peninsula body of land jutting into a lake or ocean, surrounded on three sides by water

physical feature characteristic of a place occurring naturally, such as a landform, body of water, climate pattern, or resource

plain area of level land, usually at low elevation and often covered with grasses

plateau area of flat or rolling land at a high elevation, about 300 to 3,000 feet (90 to 900 m) high

reef a chain of rocks, coral or sand at or near the surface of the water

reservoir a large natural or artificial lake used as a source of water supply

river large natural stream of water that runs through the land

sea large body of water completely or partly surrounded by land

seacoast land lying next to a sea or an ocean

sound broad inland body of water, often between a coastline and one or more islands off the coast

source (of a river) place where a river or stream begins, often in highlands

strait narrow stretch of water joining two larger bodies of water

tributary small river or stream that flows into a large river or stream; a branch of the river

upstream direction opposite the flow of a river; toward the source of a river or stream

valley area of low land usually between hills or mountains

volcano mountain or hill created as liquid rock and ash erupt from inside the Earth

Glossary/Glosario

All vocabulary words are **boldfaced** and **highlighted in yellow** in your textbook.

A		ESPAÑOL
absolute location a global address determined by the intersection of longitude and latitude lines	(p. HT25)	**posición absoluta** *sistema de coordenadas determinado por la intersección de las líneas de longitud y latitud*
affirmative action an approach used to improve employment or educational opportunities for minorities and women	(p. 439)	**acción afirmativa** *medida que se utiliza para incrementar las oportunidades laborales o educativas para minorías y mujeres*
Agent Orange a chemical defoliant used to clear Vietnamese jungles during the Vietnam War	(p. 455)	**Agente Naranja** *defoliante químico usado para limpiar las selvas vietnamitas durante la guerra de Vietnam*
agricultural revolution period when early peoples learned how to plant and raise crops	(p. 4)	**revolución agrícola** *periodo en que los primeros pueblos aprendieron a plantar y cultivar*
allotment a plot of land assigned to an individual or a family for a specified use	(p. 102)	**parcela** *porción de terreno asignada a un individuo o familia para el cultivo*
ambiguous not clear; interpretations may vary	(p. HT14)	**ambiguo** *que no es claro; de diversa interpretación*
Americanization the process of acquiring or causing a person to acquire American traits and characteristics	(p. 91)	**americanización** *proceso de adquirir o lograr que una persona adquiera los rasgos y las características americanas*
amphtrac an amphibious tractor used to move troops from ships to shore	(p. 315)	**amtrac** *vehículo anfibio utilizado para trasladar tropas de los barcos hasta la orilla*
anarchist a person who rejects modern government, capitalism, and private wealth	(p. 226)	**anarquista** *persona que rechaza el gobierno moderno, el capitalismo y la riqueza privada*
anecdotes personal, individual stories that do not provide sufficient proof of larger issues	(p. 613)	**anécdotas** *historias individuales, personales, que no brindan pruebas suficientes respecto de temas más amplios*
annex to incorporate a country or territory into the domain of another country or state	(p. 154)	**anexar** *incorporar un país o territorio al dominio de otro país o estado*
annuity money paid by contract at regular intervals	(p. 99)	**anualidad** *dinero que se paga por contrato a intervalos regulares*
anthrax common name for an infectious bacteria that can be fatal if not treated and has been used as a biological weapon.	(p. 569)	**ántrax** *nombre común de una bacteria infecciosa que resulta fatal si no se trata y que ha sido utilizada como arma biológica*
anthropology the scientific study of human beings through analysis of past cultures, physical characteristics, social relationships, and environmental pressures	(p. HT20)	**antropología** *estudio científico de los seres humanos por medio del análisis de culturas antiguas, características físicas, relaciones sociales y presiones medioambientales*
appeasement giving in to the unjust demands of a belligerent leader in order to avoid war	(p. 285)	**apaciguamiento** *ceder a exigencias injustas de un líder beligerante para evitar la guerra*
archaeology the study of past human life by scientifically studying material remains	(p. HT19)	**arqueología** *estudio de la vida humana del pasado estudiando científicamente restos materiales*
arid dry, with very little or no rainfall	(p. 518)	**árido** *seco, de muy poca o nula pluviosidad*
armistice a temporary agreement to end fighting	(p. 175)	**armisticio** *acuerdo temporal para poner fin a una lucha*

arteriosclerosis a chronic disease that thickens and hardens artery walls, which can restrict the flow of blood to tissues and organs (p. 328)

arterioesclerosis *enfermedad crónica que engrosa y endurece las paredes de las arterias, restringiendo el flujo sanguíneo de tejidos y órganos*

artifact an object made by humans, often from the past (p. HT19)

objeto arqueológico *cualquier objeto hecho por los seres humanos, generalmente del pasado*

assembly line a production system featuring machines and workers in a progressive arrangement of assembly (p. 208)

línea de ensamble *sistema de producción que articula máquinas y trabajadores en un orden progresivo de ensamblaje*

assimilate to absorb a group into the culture of another population (p. 91)

asimilar *incorporar a un grupo en la cultura de otra población*

autonomy the right of self-government (p. 159)

autonomía *derecho al autogobierno*

B | ESPAÑOL

baby boom a marked rise in birthrate over a certain period of time, especially during the years following World War II (p. 381)

boom de natalidad *marcado aumento en la tasa de nacimientos, como el que ocurrió en Estados Unidos después de la Segunda Guerra Mundial*

bailiffs minor officers of the courts (p. 249)

alguacil *oficial inferior de las cortes*

bank holidays closing of banks during the Great Depression to avoid bank runs (p. 253)

cierre bancario *cierre de bancos durante la Gran Depresión para evitar el pánico bancario*

bank run persistent and heavy demands by a bank's depositors, creditors, or customers to withdraw money (p. 240)

pánico bancario *demandas persistentes y considerables por parte de los depositantes, acreedores o clientes de un banco para retirar dinero*

barrio Spanish-speaking neighborhoods in a town (p. 96)

barrios *vecindarios de habla hispana en un pueblo o una ciudad*

benefit something that promotes well-being or is a useful aid (p. 259)

prestación *algo que promueve el bienestar o es una ayuda útil*

bias a personal and sometimes unreasoned judgment about people and events (p. HT11)

prejuicio *juicio subjetivo y a veces irracional acerca de personas y acontecimientos*

bilingualism the use of two languages (p. 493)

bilingüismo *utilización de dos lenguas*

bill a proposed law (p. 27)

proyecto de ley *ley propuesta*

binding arbitration process whereby a neutral party hears arguments from two opposing sides and makes a decision that both must accept (p. 260)

arbitraje obligatorio *proceso mediante el cual una parte neutral oye los argumentos de dos partes opuestas y toma una decisión que ambas partes deben aceptar*

biodiversity the variations of life-forms within an ecosystem (p. HT30)

biodiversidad *variaciones de los seres vivos en un ecosistema*

black codes laws passed in the South just after the Civil War aimed at controlling freedmen and enabling plantation owners to exploit African American workers (p. 77)

códigos negros *leyes aprobadas en el Sur inmediatamente después de la Guerra Civil, que buscaban controlar a los hombres liberados y permitir a los dueños de las plantaciones explotar a los trabajadores afroamericanos*

blue-collar workers workers who perform manual labor, particularly in industry (p. 382)

trabajadores de cuello azul *trabajadores que hacen labores manuales, particularmente en la industria*

English		Español
blues style of music evolving from African American spirituals and noted for its melancholy sound	(p. 216)	**blues** estilo de música que evoluciona a partir de la música espiritual afroamericana, caracterizado por su sonido melancólico
bohemian unconventional; not bound by rules of society	(p. 210)	**bohemio** poco convencional; no atado a las normas de la sociedad
bonanza farm a large, highly profitable wheat farm	(p. 98)	**granja en bonanza** granja de trigo extensa y de alta rentabilidad
brinkmanship the willingness to go to the brink of war to force an opponent to back down	(p. 341)	**política arriesgada** disposición de ir hasta el borde de una guerra para obligar al oponente a retractarse
broker state role of the government to work out conflicts among competing interest groups	(p. 264)	**estado intermediario** papel del gobierno para resolver conflictos entre grupos con conflictos de intereses
bull market a long period of rising stock prices	(p. 239)	**mercado alcista** periodo prolongado de alzas en el valor de las acciones
busing the practice of transporting children to schools outside of their neighborhoods to achieve more equal racial balance	(p. 439)	**busing** práctica de transportar niños y niñas a escuelas fuera de sus vecindarios para lograr un mayor equilibrio racial

C / ESPAÑOL

English		Español
cabinet a group of advisors to the president	(p. 28)	**gabinete** grupo de consejeros del presidente
capital gains tax a federal tax that businesses and investors pay when they sell stocks or real estate	(p. 539)	**impuesto a las ganancias de capital** impuesto federal que pagan los comerciantes e inversionistas cuando venden acciones o bienes raíces
capitalism an economic system characterized by the private or corporate ownership of goods with the distribution of goods determined by competition in a free market	(p. 330)	**capitalismo** sistema económico caracterizado por la propiedad privada o corporativa de bienes que determina la competencia en el mercado libre
carpetbagger name given to any Northerner who moved to the South after the Civil War and supported the Republicans	(p. 78)	**explotador político (carpetbagger)** nombre dado a muchos norteños que se trasladaron al Sur después de la Guerra Civil y apoyaron a los Republicanos
cartographer a mapmaker	(p. HT22)	**cartógrafo** delineante de mapas
categories groups of information	(p. HT15)	**categorías** grupos de información
cause what makes an event happen	(p. HT13)	**causa** lo que hace que algo ocurra
censure to express a formal disapproval of an action	(p. 376)	**censura** expresar formalmente la desaprobación de una acción
chad a piece of cardboard removed when punching a type of physical election ballot	(p. 564)	**pestaña** pedazo de cartón que se desprende al perforarse la papeleta física de votación electoral
chart a way to show facts and numbers in an organized way arranged in rows and columns	(p. HT32)	**tabla** medio de mostrar datos y números organizadamente en filas y columnas
charter a constitution	(p. 334)	**carta constitucional** una constitución
chronology order of dates in which events happened	(p. HT8)	**cronología** orden temporal en el que ocurren los acontecimientos

closed shop an agreement in which a company agrees to hire only union members (p. 119)

taller cerrado *acuerdo en el cual una compañía sólo contrata miembros del sindicato*

cloture a motion that ends debate and calls for an immediate vote (p. 426)

clausura *moción que pone fin a un debate y requiere una votación inmediata*

code a signal or symbol used to represent something that is to be kept secret (p. 313)

código *señal o símbolo usado para representar algo que se debe guardar en secreto*

Cold War a conflict over ideological differences that does not involve warfare or overt military action (p. 335)

Guerra Fría *conflicto por diferencias ideológicas que no conlleva guerras ni acciones militares*

collectivized describing an economic system with centralized control of production and distribution (p. 282)

colectivizado *describe al sistema económico en el que se ejerce un control centralizado de la producción y la distribución*

committee of correspondence committee organized in each colony to communicate with and unify the colonies (p. 9)

comité de correspondencia *comité organizado en cada colonia para comunicarse con las colonias y unificarlas*

communism an economic system in which the production of goods is controlled by the state (p. 330)

comunismo *sistema económico en el cual el Estado controla la producción de bienes*

concentration camp a camp where persons are detained or confined (p. 290)

campo de concentración *campo donde se detienen y confinan personas*

conclusion an understanding based on details or facts (p. HT16)

conclusión *comprensión basada en detalles u hechos*

concurrent powers powers shared by the state and federal governments (p. 26)

poderes concurrentes *poderes que tienen ambos el gobierno nacional y los estandos*

confederacy an alliance for mutual support or common actions (p. 2)

confederación *alianza para darse apoyo mutuo o actuar conjuntamente*

conic projection a map projection based on placing a cone over part of the globe; it accurately shows east-to-west distances near the Equator (p. HT23)

proyección cónica *proyección cartográfica que se obtiene colocando un cono sobre parte del globo; muestra con precisión las distancias de este a oeste cerca del ecuador*

conservative a person who promotes free enterprise, private ownership, and limited government involvement (p. 531)

conservador *persona que promueve la libre empresa, la propiedad privada y la participación limitada del Gobierno*

consumer a person who buys what is produced by an economy (p. 111)

consumidor *persona que compra lo que produce una economía*

containment the policy or process of preventing the expansion of a hostile power (p. 337)

contención *política o proceso para evitar la expansión de una potencia hostil*

continuity continuous or unbroken patterns of occurrence in history (p. HT14)

continuidad *pautas de ocurrencia histórica continuos o ininterrumpidos*

contraband goods whose importation, exportation, or possession is illegal (p. 169)

contrabando *bienes cuya importación, exportación o posesión es ilegal*

convoy system a system by which merchant ships travel with naval vessels for protection (p. 305)

sistema de convoy *sistema en el cual las embarcaciones comerciales viajan con naves de la armada para garantizar su protección*

cooperative a store where farmers buy products from each other; an enterprise owned and operated by those who use its services (p. 138)

cooperativa *tienda donde los agricultores compran productos entre sí; empresa de propiedad de aquellos que usan sus servicios, quienes también la operan*

cooperative individualism the idea that business would form trade associations that would in turn voluntarily share information with the federal government (p. 224)

individualismo cooperativo *idea según la cual las empresas formarían asociaciones comerciales que a cambio compartirían voluntariamente información con el Gobierno federal*

copyright laws laws that prevent the unauthorized use of a writer's work	(p. HT12)	**leyes de derecho de autor** *leyes que evitan el uso no autorizado de la obra de un escritor*	
corporation an organization that is authorized by law to carry on an activity but treated as though it were a single person	(p. 111)	**sociedad anónima** *organización autorizada por la ley para desarrollar una actividad, pero que recibe el tratamiento de un individuo particular*	
cost of living the cost of purchasing goods and services essential for survival	(p. 177)	**costo de la vida** *costo de comprar bienes y servicios esenciales para la supervivencia*	
cost-plus a government contract to pay a manufacturer the cost to produce an item plus a guaranteed percentage	(p. 301)	**contrato de margen fijo** *contrato del gobierno para pagar a un fabricante el costo de producir un artículo más un porcentaje garantizado*	
court-packing national leader, such as the president, appoints judges who will rule in favor of his or her policies	(p. 263)	**reorganización de la corte** *acción de cambiar el equilibrio político del poder en el sistema judicial de una nación mediante la cual un líder nacional, como el presidente de Estados Unidos, nombra a los jueces que fallarán a favor de sus políticas*	
covert not openly shown or engaged in; secret	(p. 341)	**encubierto** *que no se muestra o compromete abiertamente; secreto*	
COVID-19 the name of the illness caused by the SARS-CoV-2 virus	(p. 597)	**COVID-19** *nombre de la enfermedad causada por el virus SARS-CoV-2*	
creationism the belief that God created the world and everything in it, usually in the way described in Genesis	(p. 227)	**creacionismo** *creencia de que Dios creó el mundo y todo lo que hay en él, por lo general de la manera en que se describe en el Génesis*	
credential a degree or association with an institution, agency, or business in a specialized field of study that qualifies someone as an expert	(p. HT11)	**credencial** *grado o asociación con una institución, agencia o empresa en un campo de estudio especializado que califica de experto a alguien*	
credibility gap a perceived difference between what is said and what is true	(p. 457)	**brecha de credibilidad** *diferencia perceptible entre lo que se dice y lo que es verdadero*	
customs duty a tax on imports and exports	(p. 7)	**arancel aduanero** *impuesto a las importaciones y exportaciones*	
cylindrical projection a map projection based on the projection of the globe onto a cylinder shape	(p. HT23)	**proyección cilíndrica** *proyección cartográfica en la que se utiliza la figura de cilindro para proyectar la esfera terrestre*	

D		**ESPAÑOL**	
de facto segregation segregation by custom and tradition	(p. 409)	**segregación *de facto*** *segregación por costumbre y tradición*	
de jure segregation segregation by law	(p. 417)	**segregación *de iure*** *segregación por ley*	
defect to desert a country or cause	(p. 373)	**desertar** *abandonar un país o una causa*	
deficit spending government practice of spending borrowed money rather than raising taxes to boost the economy	(p. 259)	**gasto deficitario** *práctica gubernamental de gastar dinero prestado en lugar de aumentar los impuestos, por lo general en un esfuerzo por estimular la economía*	
deflation a decline in the volume of available money or credit that results in lower prices, and therefore increases the buying power of money	(p. 118)	**deflación** *caída en el volumen de dinero disponible o crédito, que da lugar a precios más bajos y, en consecuencia, aumenta el poder adquisitivo del dinero*	
deport to expel an individual from the country	(p. 178)	**deportar** *expulsar a un individuo de un país*	

deregulation the act or process of removing restrictions or regulations (p. 390)

desregulación *acto o proceso de eliminar restricciones o regulaciones*

détente a policy that attempts to relax or ease tensions between nations (p. 351)

distensión *política orientada a suavizar o aliviar las tensiones entre las naciones*

developing nation a nation whose economy is mainly agricultural and is creating a basis for industrial development (p. 341)

país en desarrollo *país cuya economía es principalmente agrícola y está creando la base para el desarrollo industrial*

diagram special drawing that shows steps in a process, points out the parts of an object, or explains how something works (p. HT32)

diagrama *esquema especial que muestra los pasos de un proceso, señala las partes de un objeto o explica cómo funciona algo*

dictator one who rules with absolute power, often in an oppressive way (p. 278)

dictador *persona que gobierna con poder absoluto, generalmente de manera opresiva*

direct primary a primary, or election, where candidates are nominated for office by a direct vote (p. 194)

primaria directa *elección primaria en la que los candidatos son nominados al cargo por voto directo*

discount retailing selling large quantities of goods at very low prices to turn over inventory in a short period of time (p. 535)

ofertar *vender grandes cantidades de bienes a muy bajo precio para agotar el inventario en poco tiempo*

disenfranchise to deprive of the right to vote (p. 300)

privación del voto *negar el derecho al voto*

dollar diplomacy a policy of using financial power to reap international influence (p. 165)

diplomacia del dólar *política que se valía del poder financiero para obtener influencia internacional*

domino theory the belief that if one nation in Asia fell to the Communists, neighboring countries would follow (p. 452)

teoría dominó *creencia de que si una nación asiática caía ante los comunistas, los países vecinos también lo harían*

downsizing reducing the size of a company by laying off its employees (p. 539)

recortar *reducir el tamaño de una empresa despidiendo empleados*

draft to select a person at random for mandatory military service (p. 174)

reclutar *seleccionar aleatoriamente una persona para el servicio militar obligatorio*

dry farming a way of farming dry land in which seeds are planted deep in the ground where there is some moisture (p. 98)

agricultura de secano *forma de cultivar terreno seco en la cual las semillas se plantan a grandes profundidades en el terreno donde hay un poco de humedad*

due process the following of procedures established by law (p. 30)

debido proceso *seguimiento de los procedimientos establecidos por la ley*

duty a tax on imports (p. 20)

arancel *impuesto a las importaciones*

dynamic conservatism policy of balancing economic conservatism with some activism (p. 380)

conservadurismo dinámico *política que consiste en equilibrar el conservadurismo económico con algún activismo*

dysentery a disease characterized by severe diarrhea (p. 446)

disentería *enfermedad caracterizada por una diarrea aguda*

E

ESPAÑOL

earmark specific spending measures for particular projects that members of Congress include in bills (p. 584)

asignación *disposiciones específicas de gasto para proyectos concretos que los miembros del Congreso incluyen en los proyectos de ley*

English		Español
Eastern Hemisphere the half of the globe east of the Prime Meridian for 180°	(p. HT26)	**hemisferio oriental** *mitad del globo terrestre de 180° ubicada al este del primer meridiano*
economies of scale the reduction in the cost of a good brought about by increased production at a given facility	(p. 112)	**economías de escala** *reducción en el costo de un bien ocasionada por un aumento en la producción en un sector determinado*
ecosystem a community of plants and animals that depend upon one another and their surroundings for survival	(p. HT30)	**ecosistema** *comunidad de plantas y animales que dependen entre sí y de su entorno para sobrevivir*
effect the result of a cause	(p. HT13)	**efecto** *el resultado de una causa*
emancipation the act or process of freeing enslaved persons	(p. 12)	**emancipación** *acción o proceso de liberar a los esclavos*
empresario a person who arranged for the settlement of Texas land grants in the early 1800s	(p. 62)	**empresario** *persona que hacía arreglos para el asentamiento de tierras en Texas en el siglo XIX*
enclave an area within a country or city that is comprised of people who share a nationality or culture	(p. 122)	**enclave** *zona de un país o de una ciudad en la que viven personas que tienen la misma nacionalidad o cultura*
entrepreneur one who organizes, manages, and assumes the risks of a business or enterprise	(p. 115)	**emprendedor** *quien organiza, administra o asume los riesgos de un negocio o una empresa*
enumerated powers powers listed in the Constitution as belonging to the federal government	(p. 26)	**poderes enumerados** *poderes que se enumeran en la Constitución como pertenecientes al gobierno federal*
equity the consistent and systematic fair treatment of all individuals	(p. 615)	**equidad** *tratamiento igual y sistemáticamente justo de todos los individuos*
era time period	(p. HT7)	**era** *lapso de tiempo*
eroded to wear away at something until it disappears	(p. 169)	**erosionar** *desgastar algo hasta que desaparece*
espionage spying, especially to gain government secrets	(p. 175)	**espionaje** *espiar, especialmente para conocer secretos del gobierno*
ethnic relating to large groups of people classed according to a common national or cultural background	(p. 122)	**étnico** *relativo a grandes grupos humanos que se categorizan de acuerdo con un origen nacional o cultural común*
ethnic cleansing the expulsion, imprisonment, or killing of ethnic minorities by a dominant majority group	(p. 358)	**limpieza étnica** *expulsión, encarcelamiento o asesinato de minorías étnicas por parte de una mayoría dominante*
euro the currency shared by members of the European Union	(p. 540)	**euro** *moneda utilizada por los miembros de la Unión Europea*
evolution the scientific theory that humans and other forms of life have evolved over time	(p. 227)	**evolución** *teoría científica según la cual los seres humanos y otras formas de vida han evolucionado con el tiempo*
executive privilege a legal exemption from disclosing communications that might endanger national security	(p. 524)	**privilegio ejecutivo** *excepción legal que impide revelar información que puede poner en riesgo la seguridad nacional*
extermination camp a place where people are sent to be executed	(p. 290)	**campo de exterminio** *lugar al que son enviadas las personas para ser ejecutadas*

F		ESPAÑOL
fallout radioactive particles dispersed by a nuclear explosion	(p. 376)	**lluvia radiactiva** *partículas radiactivas dispersas debido a una explosión nuclear*
fascism a political system headed by a dictator that calls for extreme nationalism and often racism and no tolerance of opposition	(p. 281)	**fascismo** *sistema político encabezado por un dictador que llama al nacionalismo extremo y a menudo al racismo y a la falta de tolerancia hacia la oposición*

648

federalism political system in which power is divided between the national and state governments (p. 25)

federalismo *sistema político en el cual el poder se divide entre los gobiernos nacional y estatal*

feminism the belief that men and women should be equal politically, economically, and socially (p. 483)

feminismo *creencia según la cual hombres y mujeres deben ser iguales en lo político, lo económico y lo social*

filibuster an attempt to kill or delay a bill by having a group of senators take turns speaking continuously so that a vote cannot take place (p. 426)

obstruccionista *intento de impedir la aprobación de un proyecto de ley haciendo que un grupo de senadores se turnen para hablar continuamente para que la votación no pueda tener lugar*

fireside chats radio broadcasts made by President Franklin D. Roosevelt to Americans (p. 254)

charlas íntimas *transmisiones de radio que hacía el presidente Roosevelt para explicar a los estadounidenses sus iniciativas*

flexible response a military approach that relies more heavily on conventional means than it does on nuclear weapons (p. 343)

respuesta flexible *estrategia militar que depende más de métodos convencionales que de armas nucleares*

folklore traditional customs, tales, sayings, dances, or art forms preserved among people, often of a particular time and place (p. 192)

folclor *costumbres, relatos, dichos, bailes u formas artísticas tradicionales preservadas por un pueblo, generalmente de un tiempo y lugar específicos*

foreclose to take possession of a property from a mortgagor because of defaults on payments (p. 242)

ejecutar *tomar posesión de una propiedad de un deudor hipotecario debido al incumplimiento en los pagos*

fossil remains, impression, or trace of past plant or animal life from a previous geological period that has been preserved in Earth's crust (p. HT20)

fósil *restos, impresiones o rastros de plantas o animales extintos, de un periodo geológico anterior, que se preservan en la corteza terrestre*

fossil fuel a fuel formed in the Earth from decayed plant or animal remains (p. 579)

combustible fósil *combustible formado en la Tierra a partir de la descomposición de restos vegetales o animales*

frame of reference experiences and historical and cultural factors that influence a person or a group at a specific time (p. HT11)

marco de referencia *experiencias y factores históricos y culturales que influyen a una persona o un grupo en un tiempo específico*

franchise a business given the authorization to market a company's goods or services in an area (p. 382)

franquicia *negocio que obtiene la autorización para comercializar los bienes o servicios de una compañía en un área*

G | ESPAÑOL

gender term applied to the characteristics of a male or female (p. 483)

género *término aplicado a las características masculinas o femeninas*

geographic information systems a software program that arranges a variety of data in a database and uses those data layers to produce maps (p. HT31)

sistemas de información geográfica *programa de softwareque organiza información diversa en bases de datos y utiliza las capas de datos para producir mapas*

GI Bill the popular name for the Servicemen's Readjustment Act that allowed military personnel to get loans, job training, hiring privileges, and tuition incentives from the Veterans Administration. (p. 370)

Ley del Soldado *nombre más común dado a la Ley de Reajuste del Personal de las Fuerzas Armadas, que permitió al personal militar obtener préstamos, formación profesional, privilegios de contratación e incentivos educativos del Departamentos de Asuntos de los Veteranos*

glasnost a Soviet policy permitting open discussion of political and social issues and freer dissemination of news and information (p. 356)

glasnost *política soviética que permitió la discusión abierta de temas políticos y sociales y la libre difusión de noticias e información*

globalism increased trade between nations and an interconnected global economy (p. 597)

globalismo *aumento en el comercio entre países y la interconexión de la economía global*

globe a scale model of Earth (p. HT22)

globo *modelo a escala de la Tierra*

gold standard a monetary system in which the value of currency is defined in terms of gold (p. 253)

patrón oro *sistema monetario en el cual el valor del dinero se define en términos de oro*

graduated income tax a tax based on the net income of an individual or business, and which taxes different income levels at different rates (p. 139)

impuesto graduado sobre la renta *impuesto que se basa en los ingresos netos de un individuo o empresa, el cual grava con diferentes tasas niveles diferentes de ingreso*

grandfather clause an exemption in a law (p. 408)

cláusula del abuelo *excepción en una ley*

graph a means of summarizing and presenting information visually (p. HT32)

gráfica *medio para resumir y presentar información visualmente*

grassroots movement a group of citizens organizing at the local or community level (p. 540)

movimiento de base *grupos de ciudadanos organizados en el nivel local o comunitario*

great circle route a straight line of true direction on a globe (p. HT22)

arco del círculo máximo *línea recta de dirección real en un globo terrestre*

grid system a pattern of intersecting lines on a map or globe that determines exact location on Earth's surface (p. HT25)

sistema de cuadrícula *patrón de líneas de intersección en un mapa o globo terráqueo que determina la ubicación exacta en la superficie terrestre*

gross national product the total value of goods and services produced by a country during a year (p. 109)

producto nacional bruto *valor total de los bienes y servicios que produce un país durante un año*

guerrilla armed fighters who carry out surprise attacks (p. 166)

guerrilla *combatientes armados que atacan sorpresivamente*

H	ESPAÑOL

Harlem Renaissance a cultural movement of African American artists and writers from about 1918 to 1937 with the Harlem district in New York City as the symbolic capital (p. 192)

Renacimiento Harlem *movimiento cultural de artistas y escritores afroamericanos que duró de 1918 a 1937, aproximadamente, y tuvo por capital simbólica el distrito de Harlem de la Ciudad de Nueva York*

hate crime a crime that includes acts of physical harm or threats motivated by hostility toward a person's race, color, national origin, religion, gender, sexual orientation, gender identity, or disability (p. 587)

crimen de odio *crimen que comprende actos de lesión física o amenazas motivadas por hostilidad hacia la raza, el color, la nacionalidad, la religión, el género, la orientación sexual, la identidad de género o la discapacidad de una persona*

hemisphere one of the halves the geographers divide the Earth into (p. HT25)

hemisferio *una de las mitades en las que los geógrafos dividen la Tierra*

hobo a homeless and usually penniless wanderer (p. 249)

vagabundo *persona errante sin hogar y por lo general sin dinero*

holding company a company whose primary business is owning a controlling share of stock in other companies (p. 112)

sociedad de cartera *compañía cuya actividad principal es poseer una participación accionaria mayoritaria en otras compañías*

homestead a piece of U.S. public land acquired by living on it and cultivating it (p. 97)

posesión de tierras *una porción de terreno público estadounidense adquirió mediante la presentación y que viven en y cultivaría*

hydraulic mining method of mining by which water is sprayed at a very high pressure against a hill or mountain, washing away large quantities of dirt, gravel, and rock and exposing the minerals beneath the surface (p. 94)

minería hidráulica *método de minería mediante el cual se riega con agua a elevadísima presión una colina o montaña; este lavado elimina grandes cantidades de suciedad, grava y roca, y expone los minerales que están bajo la superficie*

I		**ESPAÑOL**
immigrant a person who arrives in a foreign country with the intention of permanently living there	(p. 121)	**inmigrante** *persona que llega a un país extranjero con la intención de vivir permanentemente en él*
imminent ready to take place; happening soon	(p. 359)	**inminente** *a punto de comenzar; que sucede pronto*
impeach to bring formal charges against a federal official	(p. 27)	**acusar** *presentar cargos formales contra un funcionario federal*
imperialism the policy of a powerful nation exercising political and economic control over a weaker one	(p. 157)	**imperialismo** *política de una nación poderosa que ejerce control político y económico sobre una más débil*
impound to take possession of	(p. 522)	**incautar** *tomar posesión*
income tax a tax levied by the government directly on income	(p. 207)	**impuesto sobre la renta** *impuesto tasado por el Gobierno directamente sobre la renta*
indelible lasting; unforgettable	(p. 560)	**indeleble** *perdurable; inolvidable*
individualism the belief that no matter what a person's background is, he or she can still become successful through effort	(p. 133)	**individualismo** *creencia según la cual sin importar cuál sea el entorno de una persona, ésta puede llegar a tener éxito si se esfuerza*
Indochina a colony consisting of Vietnam, Cambodia, and Laos, ruled by France in the second half of the nineteenth century	(p. 448)	**Indochina** *colonia conformada por Vietnam, Camboya y Laos, gobernada por Francia durante la segunda mitad del siglo XIX*
industrial union an organization of common laborers and craft workers in a particular industry	(p. 118)	**sindicato industrial** *organización de obreros comunes y trabajadores calificados de una industria particular*
inference to identify a message not directly stated in a communication by inferring meaning, often based on context	(p. HT16)	**inferencia** *identificar un mensaje que no ha sido expresado directamente en una comunicación deduciendo su mensaje, generalmente a partir del contexto*
inflation the loss of value of money	(p. 8)	**inflación** *pérdida del valor del dinero*
initiative the right of citizens to present legislation for approval by the legislature	(p. 198)	**iniciativa** *derecho de los ciudadanos a proponer leyes para aprobación del legislativo*
injunction a court order whereby one is required to do or to refrain from doing a specific act	(p. 119)	**orden judicial** *orden judicial por la cual se le exige o prohíbe a alguien que realice una acción determinada*
installment plans monthly plan made to pay off the cost of an item when buying it on credit	(p. 236)	**cuota** *plan de pagos mensuales para cubrir el costo de un artículo que se compra a crédito*
internationalism a national policy of actively trading with foreign countries to foster peace and prosperity	(p. 285)	**internacionalismo** *política nacional de comercio activo con países extranjeros para fomentar la paz y la prosperidad*
investor one who puts money into a company in order to gain a future financial reward	(p. 112)	**inversionista** *quien invierte dinero en una compañía con el fin de obtener una retribución económica en el futuro*
Iron Curtain the political and military barrier that isolated Soviet-controlled countries of Eastern Europe after World War II	(p. 336)	**Cortina de Hierro** *barrera política y militar que aisló a los países controlados por la Unión Soviética de Europa del Este durante la Segunda Guerra Mundial*

J		**ESPAÑOL**
jazz American style of music that developed from ragtime and features syncopated rhythms and improvisation	(p. 215)	**jazz** *estilo de música estadounidense que se desarrolló a partir del ragtime y el blues y que usa ritmos y melodías sincopados*

Jim Crow laws statutes enacted to enforce segregation (p. 140)

leyes Jim Crow *conjunto de leyes promulgadas para hacer cumplir políticas de segregación*

jingoism extreme nationalism marked by aggressive foreign policy (p. 160)

jingoísmo *nacionalismo extremo marcado por una política exterior radical*

judicial review the process by which the Supreme Court has the final authority to interpret the Constitution (p. 30)

revisión judicial *facultad de la Corte Suprema para determinar si las leyes expedidas por el Congreso son constitucionales*

jungle rot a skin infection that is often contracted in tropical environments (p. 446)

úlcera tropical *infección cutánea que se suele contraer en ambientes tropicales*

K

ESPAÑOL

kamikaze during World War II, a Japanese suicide pilot whose mission was to crash into his target (p. 316)

kamikaze *durante la Segunda Guerra Mundial, piloto suicida japonés cuya misión era estrellarse contra su objetivo*

L

ESPAÑOL

laissez-faire economic philosophy that government should interfere as little as possible in a nation's economy (p. 90)

laissez-faire *filosofía económica según la cual el Gobierno debe intervenir lo menos posible en la economía de un país*

land grant a grant of land by the federal government especially for roads, railroads, or agricultural purposes (p. 114)

concesión de tierras *terrenos que el gobierno federal cede, especialmente para carreteras, vías férreas o escuelas agrarias*

latitude lines that circle the Earth parallel to the Equator (p. HT25)

latitud *líneas que circunvalan la Tierra de forma paralela al ecuador*

legislation the exercise of the power and function of making rules or laws (p. 194)

legislación *ejercicio del poder y de la facultad de hacer normas o leyes*

levee an embankment used to prevent flooding (p. 560)

dique *escollera utilizada para evitar las inundaciones*

liberal a person who supports socially progressive policies and government-funded social programs (p. 531)

liberal *persona que apoya políticas sociales progresistas y programas sociales financiados por el Gobierno*

limited war a war fought with limited commitment of resources to achieve a limited objective, such as containing communism (p. 340)

guerra limitada *guerra que en la que se participa comprometiendo pocos recursos para alcanzar un objetivo limitado, como contener el comunismo*

lobby to conduct activities with the purpose of influencing public officials, particularly members of a legislative body (p. 200)

cabildear *llevar a cabo acciones con el propósito de influenciar a funcionarios públicos, en especial, miembros de un cuerpo legislativo*

lockout a company strategy to fight union demands by refusing to allow employees to enter its facilities to work (p. 118)

cierre patronal *estrategia de una compañía que consiste en resistir a las exigencias de los sindicatos negando la entrada de los trabajadores a sus instalaciones*

longitude lines that circle the Earth from Pole to Pole (p. HT25)

longitud *líneas que circunvalan la Tierra de polo a polo*

loyalty review program a policy established by President Truman that authorized the screening of all federal employees to determine their loyalty to the U.S. government (p. 373)

programa de verificación de la lealtad *política establecida por el presidente Truman que autorizaba investigar a todos los empleados federales para determinar si eran leales al gobierno de Estados Unidos*

M	ESPAÑOL
malaria a disease caused by a parasite that is transmitted through mosquito bites (p. 448)	**malaria** *enfermedad causada por un parásito que se transmite por picadas de mosquito*
map a symbolic representation of all or part of the planet (p. HT22)	**mapa** *representación simbólica de todo el planeta o parte de él*
map projection placing the round Earth onto a flat surface, which will alter how the shape and size of land forms and other geographic features appear (p. HT23)	**proyección cartográfica** *representación de la esfera terrestre, sobre una superficie plana, que modifica la forma en la que aparecen el contorno y el tamaño del relieve y de otros accidentes geográficos*
margin call demand by a broker that investors pay back loans made for stocks purchased on margin (p. 240)	**margen de garantía** *exigencia de un corredor de bolsa para que los inversionistas paguen los préstamos hechos para la compra de acciones al margen*
margin buying a stock by paying only a fraction of the stock price and borrowing the rest (p. 239)	**margen** *comprar acciones pagando sólo una fracción de su precio y pidiendo en préstamo el saldo*
Marshall Plan a U.S. program of financing to help European nations rebuild after World War II (p. 331)	**Plan Marshall** *programa financiero estadounidense para ayudar a los países europeos en su reconstrucción después de la Segunda Guerra Mundial*
martyr a person who sacrifices greatly or perhaps gives their life for the sake of important principles (p. 424)	**mártir** *persona que se sacrifica mucho o que quizás ofrende su vida en aras de principios importantes*
mass media communication media, such as television and radio, intended to reach a wide audience (p. 212)	**medios masivos de comunicación** *medios de comunicación (como la televisión y la radio) que buscan llegar a una amplia audiencia*
mass production the production of large quantities of goods by way of an automated process (p. 208)	**producción masiva** *producción de grandes cantidades de bienes usando maquinaria y a menudo una cadena de montaje*
massive retaliation a policy that involves threatening the use of nuclear weapons to avoid a potential war (p. 341)	**retaliación masiva** *política que comprende la amenaza de utilizar armas nucleares para evitar una guerra potencial*
mediate to attempt to resolve conflict between hostile people or groups (p. 264)	**mediar** *intento de resolver conflictos entre grupos o personas hostiles*
migration chains the practice of immigrants who have acquired U.S. citizenship sending for relatives in their home country to join them (p. 491)	**cadenas migratorias** *la práctica de los inmigrantes que han adquirido la ciudadanía estadounidense de traer a sus parientes desde su país natal para reunirse con ellos*
militarism a policy of aggressive military preparedness (p. 167)	**militarismo** *política de preparación militar radical*
military-industrial complex an informal relationship that some people believe exists between the military and the defense industry to promote greater military spending and influence government policy (p. 342)	**complejo militar e industrial** *relación informal que algunas personas creen que existe entre el ejército y la industria de defensa para incentivar el gasto militar e influir en las políticas del gobierno*
minutemen companies of civilian soldiers who boasted they were ready to fight at a minute's notice (p. 9)	**minutemen** *compañías de soldados civiles que se jactaban de estar listos para combatir en cuestión de minutos*
missile gap a discrepancy between the number of missiles controlled by the Soviet Union and the United States (p. 385)	**brecha de los misiles** *discrepancia en el número de misiles en poder de la Unión Soviética y Estados Unidos*
Model T car produced from 1908 until 1927 by the Ford Motor Company (p. 209)	**Modelo T** *automóvil construido por la Compañía Automotriz Ford desde 1908 hasta 1927*

monopoly total control of a type of industry by one person or one company	(p. 112)	**monopolio** *control total de un tipo de industria por parte de una persona o compañía*	
multinational corporations large corporations that operate both domestically and overseas	(p. 382)	**empresas multinacionales** *grandes corporaciones que actúan localmente y en ultramar*	
mutual assured destruction the strategy assuming that as long as two countries can destroy each other with nuclear weapons, they will be afraid to use them	(p. 355)	**destrucción mutua asegurada** *estrategia que asume que siempre y cuando dos países puedan destruirse entre sí con armas nucleares, ambos estarán temerosos de usarlas*	

N	ESPAÑOL

napalm a jellied gasoline used for bombs	(p. 317)	**napalm** *gasolina gelatinosa usada para fabricar bombas*	
national self-determination the free choice by the people of a nation of their own future political status	(p. 176)	**autodeterminación de los pueblos** *libre elección por parte de los habitantes de una nación de su situación política futura*	
nativism hostility toward immigrants	(p. 123)	**nativismo** *hostilidad hacia los inmigrantes*	
naturalization the process through which a foreigner becomes a citizen of a country	(p. 226)	**nacionalización** *proceso por el cual se hace uno ciudadano de otro país*	
nonimportation agreement a pledge by merchants not to buy imported goods from a particular source	(p. 8)	**acuerdo contra la importación** *compromiso de los comerciantes de no comprar bienes importados de una fuente en particular*	
Northern Hemisphere the half of the globe north of the Equator	(p. HT26)	**hemisferio norte** *mitad del globo terrestre ubicada al norte del ecuador*	
novel coronavirus a newly identified coronavirus, which is a type of virus that can cause disease in humans	(p. 597)	**nuevo coronavirus** *coronavirus recientemente identificado, que es un tipo de virus que puede causar enfermedad en los seres humanos*	
nuclear used in or produced by a nuclear reaction	(p. 317)	**nuclear** *utilizado en reacciones nucleares o producido por ella*	

O	ESPAÑOL

Open Door policy a policy that allowed all countries to trade freely with China	(p. 162)	**política de puertas abiertas** *política que autorizaba a todos los países a comerciar libremente con China*	
open range vast areas of grassland owned by the federal government	(p. 90)	**terreno abierto** *vastas áreas de praderas de propiedad del gobierno federal*	
opportunity cost the value of the next-best option when considering several alternatives	(p. HT18)	**coste de oportunidad** *valor de la siguiente mejor opción cuando se consideran varias alternativas*	
outsourced having moved labor to another country to lower its costs	(p. 540)	**subcontratado** *haber trasladado trabajo a otro país para disminuir su costo*	
overlander someone who travels over the land to the West	(p. 61)	**viajero terrestre** *persona que viaja por tierra hacia el Oeste*	

P	ESPAÑOL

paleontology a science that relies on the excavation and study of plant and animal remains from previous geological periods	(p. HT19)	**paleontología** *ciencia basada en la excavación y el estudio de restos de plantas y animales de periodos geológicos anteriores*	

pandemic a disease that spreads worldwide; when a disease spreads across multiple countries and affects a vast number of people (p. 175, 609)

pandemia *enfermedad que se propaga mundialmente; enfermedad que se propaga por muchos países y afecta a un vasto número de personas*

party boss the person in control of a political machine (p. 133)

jefe político *persona que controla la maquinaria política*

peacenik an unofficial term for a member of a pacifist movement (p. 458)

pacifista *término no oficial para designar a un miembro de un movimiento en favor de la paz*

perestroika a policy of economic and government restructuring instituted by Mikhail Gorbachev in the Soviet Union in the 1980s (p. 356)

perestroika *política de reestructuración económica y gubernamental instituida por Mijaíl Gorbachov en la Unión Soviética de 1980 a 1990*

perjury lying when one has sworn under oath to tell the truth (p. 374)

perjurio *mentir cuando se ha jurado decir la verdad*

philanthropy providing money to support humanitarian or social goals (p. 134)

filantropía *aportar dinero para apoyar causas humanitarias o sociales*

physical map a map that shows the location and shape of the Earth's physical features (p. HT29)

mapa físico *mapa en el que se muestra la ubicación y forma de los elementos físicos de la Tierra*

pillage to loot or plunder (p. 76)

saquear *apoderarse de todo lo que se encuentra o robar*

pinnacle highest achievement or development (p. 516)

pináculo *máximo logro o desarrollo*

plagiarism to present the ideas or words of another person as your own without offering credit to the source (p. HT12)

plagio *presentar ideas o palabras de otra persona, como si fueran tuyas, sin citar el crédito de la fuente*

planar projection a map projection that presents the Earth centered, resulting in the most accurate projection of the Poles; also called azimuthal projection (p. HT23)

proyección planar *proyección cartográfica que presenta la Tierra en el centro, lo que da lugar a la proyección más precisa de los polos; también se denomina proyección acimutal*

point of view a general attitude about people and life (p. HT11)

punto de vista *actitud general hacia la gente y la vida*

polio abbreviated term for poliomyelitis, an acute infectious disease affecting the skeletal muscles, often resulting in permanent disability and deformity (p. 244)

polio *abreviatura de poliomielitis, una enfermedad infecciosa aguda que afecta los músculos esqueléticos y a menudo produce discapacidad y deformidad permanentes*

political machine an organization linked to a political party that often controlled local government (p. 133)

maquinaria política *organización vinculada a un partido político que a menudo es controlada por el gobierno local*

political map a map that shows the boundaries and location of political units such as counties, states, and cities (p. HT29)

mapa político *mapa que muestra los límites y la ubicación de unidades políticas como condados, estados y ciudades*

poll tax a tax of a fixed amount per person that had to be paid before the person could vote (p. 140)

impuesto de capitación *impuesto de una cantidad fija por persona que debía pagarse para poder votar*

popular sovereignty authority of the people; the idea that people living in a territory had the right to decide by voting whether to allow slavery or not (p. 25)

soberanía popular *autoridad del pueblo; a idea de que las personas que vivían en un territorio tenían derecho a votar para decidir si se debía permitir la esclavitud ahí*

popular vote the number of actual individual votes for a candidate in an election (p. 594)

voto popular *número real de votos individuales por candidato en una elección*

populism a political philosophy where politicians defend the people against a society's powerful elite (p. 596)

populismo *filosofía política en la que políticos defienden al pueblo de la poderosa élite de una sociedad*

poverty line a federal government-determined minimum level of income needed to support a family (p. 387)

línea de la pobreza *nivel mínimo de ingresos, establecido por el Gobierno federal, que se necesita para mantener una familia*

primary sources first-hand pieces of evidence such as written records from people who saw or experienced the events described	(p. HT10)	**fuentes primarias** *evidencias de primera mano, como informes escritos de las personas que vieron o vivieron los acontecimientos descritos*
Prime Meridian the line of longitude set at 0°	(p. HT25)	**primer meridiano** *línea de longitud establecida a 0°*
propaganda the spreading of ideas about an institution or individual for the purpose of influencing opinion	(p. 169)	**propaganda** *difusión de ideas sobre una institución o un individuo con el propósito de influenciar a la opinión*
protectorate a nation that is under the control and protection of another nation	(p. 157)	**protectorado** *nación que se encuentra bajo el control o la protección de otra nación*
public works projects such as highways, parks, and libraries built with public funds for public use	(p. 241)	**obras públicas** *proyectos como carreteras, parques y bibliotecas construidos con fondos públicos para uso público*
pueblo Spanish for "village"; term used by early Spanish explorers to denote large housing structures built by the Anasazi	(p. 4)	**pueblo** *villa; término usado por los exploradores españoles para denotar grandes estructuras de vivienda construidas por los anasazi*

R		**ESPAÑOL**
racism prejudice or discrimination against someone of a particular racial or ethnic group	(p. 435)	**racismo** *prejuicio o discriminación hacia alguien de un grupo racial o étnico específico*
rankle to cause anger or irritation	(p. 276)	**doler** *causar ira o irritación*
reapportionment the establishment of electoral districts based on changing state populations	(p. 386)	**redistribución** *demarcación de distritos electorales con base en los cambios de población en los estados*
recall the removal of an elected official from a government office through petitioning and voting	(p. 198)	**destitución** *remoción de un funcionario electo de su cargo gubernamental mediante solicitud o voto*
recession an economic slowdown; period of reduced economic activity	(p. 21)	**recesión** *desaceleración económica; periodo de escasa actividad económica*
rectify to set right	(p. 276)	**rectificar** *corregir*
redeem to win back; to restore	(p. 408)	**redimir** *recuperar; restituir*
refugees people who leave their home countries to escape persecution, war, or natural disasters	(p. 491)	**refugiados** *personas que dejan su patria huyendo de la persecución, la guerra o los desastres naturales*
relative location the location of one place in relation to another	(p. HT28)	**posición relativa** *ubicación de un lugar en relación con otro*
relief aid in the form of money or supplies for those in need	(p. 242)	**auxilio** *ayuda en forma de dinero o provisiones para los necesitados*
reparation payment by the losing country in a war to the winner for the damages caused by the war	(p. 176)	**indemnización** *pago que el país perdedor en una guerra hace al ganador para compensar los daños ocasionados por la guerra*
repatriation being restored or returned to the country of origin, allegiance, or citizenship	(p. 489)	**repatriación** *acción por la cual se devuelve o regresa a una persona al país de origen, lealtad o ciudadanía*
reserved powers powers retained by the states	(p. 26)	**poderes reservados** *poderes que pertenecen estrictamente a los estados*
revelation an act of revealing to view or making known	(p. 224)	**revelación** *acción de revelar para ver o dar a conocer*

English		Español	
revenue-sharing federal tax money that is distributed among the states	(p. 522)	**participación en los ingresos** *dinero proveniente de los impuestos federales que se distribuye entre los estados*	
right-to-work laws laws that make it illegal to require employees to join a union	(p. 378)	**leyes de derecho al trabajo** *leyes que hacen ilegal exigir que los empleados se unan a un sindicato*	
rock 'n' roll popular music characterized by a persistent, heavily accented beat and simple melodies	(p. 384)	**rocanrol** *música popular que se caracteriza por un ritmo repetitivo, pesado y acentuado y melodías sencillas*	
Rough Rider a volunteer cavalry unit during the Spanish-American War	(p. 152)	***Rough Rider*** *unidad de caballería voluntaria en la guerra hispano-estadounidense*	

S

ESPAÑOL

English		Español	
safety net something that provides security against misfortune; specifically, government relief programs intended to protect against economic disaster	(p. 264)	**red de protección** *algo que brinda seguridad contra las calamidades; en particular, programas de ayuda del gobierno que buscan proteger contra un desastre económico*	
satellite nations nations politically and economically dominated or controlled by another more powerful country	(p. 336)	**naciones satélite** *naciones que están bajo el dominio o control político y económico de un país más poderoso*	
scalawag name given to any Southerner who supported the Republicans and Reconstruction of the South	(p. 78)	***scalawag*** *nombre dado a los sureños que apoyaban la Reconstrucción Republicana del Sur*	
scale a consistent, proportional relationship between the measurements shown on a map and the measurements of Earth's surface	(p. HT28)	**escala** *relación congruente y proporcional entre las medidas que aparecen en un mapa y las medidas de la ubicación de la Tierra*	
scarcity a situation where there is not enough of a resource to provide what people need or want	(p. HT18)	**escasez** *situación en la que se carece de la suficiente cantidad de algo como para proporcionarle a la gente lo que necesita o desea*	
second generation the children of immigrants	(p. 279)	**segunda generación** *los hijos de los inmigrantes*	
secondary sources written documents or media about an event the authors did not experience first-hand	(p. HT10)	**fuentes secundarias** *documentos escritos o medios de comunicación relativos a un acontecimiento que no vivieron los autores*	
sect a group that follows a distinct doctrine or leader	(p. 571)	**secta** *subgrupo en una comunidad religiosa, cuyas creencias difieren del grupo mayor*	
segregation the separation or isolation of a race, class, or group	(p. 139)	**segregación** *separación o aislamiento de una raza, clase o grupo*	
self-determination the right of native peoples to make decisions about their society free of outside government influence	(p. 495)	**autodeterminación** *el derecho de pueblos indígenas a tomar decisiones relativas a su sociedad sin injerencia de gobiernos externos*	
separate but equal a doctrine established by the 1896 Supreme Court case *Plessy* v. *Ferguson* that permitted laws segregating African Americans as long as equal facilities were provided	(p. 417)	**separados pero iguales** *doctrina establecida por la Corte Suprema en el caso* Plessy *contra* Ferguson *de 1896, que permitía las leyes que segregaban a la población afroamericana siempre que se brindaran instalaciones iguales*	
settlement house an institution located in a poor neighborhood that provided numerous community services such as medical care, childcare, libraries, and English classes	(p. 135)	**centro comunitario** *institución localizada en un vecindario pobre que presta numerosos servicios a la comunidad, tales como atención médica, cuidado de niños, bibliotecas y clases en inglés*	

siege a military blockade of a city or fortified place to force it to surrender (p. 75)

sitio *bloqueo militar de una ciudad o lugar fortificado para obligarlo a rendirse*

sit-down strike method of boycotting work by sitting down at work and refusing to leave the establishment (p. 260)

huelga de brazos caídos *método de boicotear el trabajo sentándose en el puesto de trabajo y negándose a abandonar el establecimiento*

skyscraper a very tall building (p. 131)

rascacielos *edificio muy alto*

smog fog combined with smoke or other pollutants (p. 578)

esmog *niebla mezclada con humo y otros contaminantes*

Social Darwinism a philosophy based on Charles Darwin's theories of evolution and natural selection, asserting that humans have developed through competition and natural selection with only the strongest surviving (p. 134)

Darwinismo Social *filosofía basada en las teorías de Charles Darwin sobre la evolución y la selección natural, la cual afirma que los seres humanos se han desarrollado por la competencia y la selección natural y sólo los más fuertes han sobrevivido*

sodbuster a name given to Great Plains farmers (p. 98)

rompeterreno *nombre dado a los granjeros de las Grandes Llanuras*

Southern Hemisphere the half of the globe south of the Equator (p. HT26)

hemisferio sur *mitad del globo terrestre ubicada al sur del ecuador*

sovereign possessing supreme authority (p. 19)

soberano *que detenta la autoridad suprema*

speakeasy place where alcoholic beverages are sold illegally (p. 228)

clandestino *lugar en el que se venden bebidas alcohólicas ilegalmente*

special prosecutor a lawyer from outside the government appointed to investigate a government official for misconduct while in office (p. 524)

fiscal especial *abogado externo al Gobierno designado para investigar a un funcionario gubernamental por mala conducta durante su periodo*

speculation act of buying stocks at great risk with the anticipation that the prices will rise (p. 239)

especulación *compra de acciones con gran riesgo con la expectativa de que los precios subirán*

speculator a person who risks money in hopes of a financial profit (p. 236)

especulador *persona que arriesga dinero con la esperanza de obtener un beneficio económico*

sphere of influence area of a country where a foreign nation enjoys special rights and powers (p. 162)

esfera de influencia *sección de un país donde una nación extranjera goza de derechos y facultades especiales*

stagflation high inflation and unemployment combined with stagnant consumer demand (p. 389)

estanflación *inflación elevada y desempleo conjuntamente con estancamiento de la demanda*

state-sponsored terrorism the act of one nation fighting another by providing terrorists with money, weapons, and training (p. 568)

terrorismo financiado por el Estado *acción de un país que combate con otro que consiste en proveer a terroristas de dinero, armas y entrenamiento*

stock market a system for buying and selling stocks in corporations (p. 239)

mercado de valores *sistema de compra y venta de acciones en las sociedades anónimas*

stockade a line of posts set firmly to form a defense (p. 5)

empalizada *hilera de postes sujetos firmemente a manera de defensa*

strategic materials items needed during wartime (p. 299)

materiales estratégicos *materiales necesarios para participar en una guerra*

subversion a systematic attempt to overthrow a government by using persons working secretly from within (p. 373)

subversión *intento sistemático de derrocar un gobierno valiéndose de personas que trabajan en secreto dentro de ese gobierno*

summary a shortened version of a passage that presents its key ideas or findings (p. HT15)

resumen *versión abreviada de un pasaje que presenta sus ideas o conclusiones principales*

summit a meeting between government leaders (p. 352)

cumbre *reunión entre los jefes de gobierno*

Sunbelt region of the Southern and Southwestern United States characterized by a mild winter climate (p. 518)

Sunbelt *región del Sur y el Sudoeste de Estados Unidos caracterizada por un clima invernal moderado*

supply-side economics an economic theory that lower taxes and decreased regulation will boost the economy as businesses and individuals invest their money, thereby creating higher tax revenue (p. 224)

economía de la oferta *los impuestos y la desregulación impulsarán la economía mientras empresas e individuos invierten su dinero, favoreciendo así una mayor recaudación de impuestos*

swing vote a vote that may sometimes lean conservative and other times liberal (p. 575)

voto flotante *voto que unas veces puede ser conservador y otras veces liberal*

systemic racism the way people work together to do things has a built-in bias for or against people depending on their race (p. 606)

racismo sistémico *sesgo racial sistemático, a favor o en contra de las personas, que se manifiesta en la actuación de la gente*

T

ESPAÑOL

tariff a tax added to imported or exported goods (p. 597)

arancel *impuesto que se aplica a los bienes de importación o exportación*

teach-in an informal extended discussion about a social or political issue (p. 458)

teach-in *discusión informal prolongada acerca de un tema social o político*

televangelist an evangelical preacher who conducts televised religious sermons (p. 533)

televangelista *predicador evangélico que transmite sermones religiosos por televisión*

tenement multifamily apartments, usually dark, crowded, and barely meeting minimum living standards (p. 132)

casa de vecindad *apartamentos multifamiliares, por lo general oscuros, hacinados y que apenas cumplen los estándares mínimos de vivienda*

terrazzo a mosaic flooring that has pieces of marble or granite set in mortar and is then highly polished (p. 234)

terrazo *piso de mosaico, finamente pulido, hecho de fragmentos de mármol o granito aglomerados en cemento*

terrorism the use of violence by nongovernmental groups and some individuals to achieve a political goal (p. 567)

terrorismo *utilización de la violencia por grupos no gubernamentales para alcanzar un objetivo político*

thematic maps maps focused on a specific kind of information or a single idea (p. HT29)

mapas temáticos *mapas enfocados en un tipo específico de información o en una sola idea*

time line diagram that shows the order of events within a period of time (p. HT8)

línea cronológica *esquema que muestra el orden de los acontecimientos en un lapso de tiempo o periodo*

triangulation a policy in which two countries' hostilities toward one another are exploited to the benefit of a third country (p. 352)

triangulación *política en la que las hostilidades entre dos países se explotan para beneficiar a un tercer país*

trust a combination of firms or corporations formed by a legal agreement, especially to reduce competition (p. 114)

trust *asociación de firmas o sociedades anónimas formadas por un acuerdo legal, especialmente para reducir la competencia*

U · ESPAÑOL

unfair trade practices trading practices that derive a gain at the expense of competition (p. 208)

prácticas comerciales desleales *prácticas comerciales que generan ganancias a expensas del bienestar de la competencia*

union shops businesses that require employees to join a union (p. 378)

empresa de afiliación sindical obligatoria *empresa que exige que los empleados se unan a un sindicato*

urban renewal government programs that attempt to eliminate poverty and revitalize urban areas (p. 382)

renovación urbana *programas gubernamentales que buscan eliminar la pobreza y revitalizar las áreas urbanas*

V · ESPAÑOL

victory garden a garden planted by civilians during war to raise vegetables for home use, leaving more of other foods for the troops (p. 173)

huerta de la victoria *huerta plantada por los civiles durante la guerra con el fin de cultivar vegetales para uso doméstico, y dejar más de otros alimentos para las tropas*

Vietnamization the process of making South Vietnam assume more of the war effort by slowly withdrawing American troops from Vietnam (p. 467)

vietnamización *proceso por el cual se hizo que Vietnam del Sur asumiera mayor parte del esfuerzo bélico retirando lentamente las tropas estadounidenses de Vietnam*

W · ESPAÑOL

weapons of mass destruction (WMD) weapons that could kill a large number of people at once (p. 570)

armas de destrucción masiva *armas que pueden aniquilar de inmediato a un gran número de personas*

welfare aid in the form of money or necessities for those in need, especially disadvantaged social groups (p. 522)

asistencia social *ayuda en dinero o en especies para los necesitados, en especial para grupos en desventaja social*

Western Hemisphere the half of the globe west of the Prime Meridian for 180° (p. HT26)

hemisferio occidental *mitad del globo terrestre de 180° ubicada al oeste del primer meridiano*

whistleblower a person who reports inside knowledge of illegal or questionable activities in a government or organization (p. 596)

denunciante *persona que informa confidencialmente de actividades ilegales o cuestionables en un Gobierno o una organización*

white-collar jobs professional office jobs (p. 382)

trabajos de cuello blanco *trabajos profesionales de oficina*

Y · ESPAÑOL

yellow journalism sensational, exaggerated journalism (p. 159)

amarillismo *periodismo sensacionalista, exagerado*

Z · ESPAÑOL

zoot suit men's clothing of an exaggerated cut consisting of an oversized jacket with wide, padded shoulders, and baggy pants (p. 303)

zoot suit *traje para hombre de corte extravagante que consiste en una chaqueta de talla grande, hombreras anchas y acolchadas y pantalón bombacho*

660

Index

Italicized page numbers refer to illustrations. The following abbreviations are used in the index: m = map; c = chart; ptg = photograph, painting, or picture; g = graph; crt = cartoon; q = quote

A

Abernathy, Ralph, 423, 438
Abington School District v. *Schempp*, 387
abortion rights, *c482*, 487–88, 532, 549
absolute location, HT21, HT25, HT28
abstract art, 211
Abu Ghraib prison, 573
Abyssinia, 284–85
Abzug, Bella, 478
Acheson, Dean, 375
acquired immunodeficiency syndrome (AIDS), 536
Adams, John: Committee of Five, 10, 13, *ptg13*; at Constitutional Convention, 21; Treaty of Paris, 11
Adams, Samuel, resisting Townshend and Stamp Acts, 8
Adams, Samuel Hopkins, 201–02
Adamson Act, 208
Addams, Jane, *p136*; anti-annexation, 161; Hull House, 130, 135–36, *c196*; League to Limit Armament, 169; Woman's Peace Party, 169; women's suffrage, 140; Women's Trade Union League (WTUL), 120
Address at Rice University (John F. Kennedy), *q347*
"Address of the Niagara Movement to the Country" (W.E.B. Du Bois), *q142*
Address to Joint Session of Congress (John F. Kennedy), *q347*
Address to the Politburo of the Central Committee of the Socialist United Party of Germany (Mikhail Gorbachev), *q360*
Adoption and Safe Families Act, 552
advertising: after World War II, 381; development of, 112, 209–10; mass, 210
advocacy groups: political advocacy, 548; rise of, 548
affirmative action, 439–40, 607
Affordable Care Act (ACA), 583–84
Afghanistan: military aid, 354; rebuilding of, 570; Soviets attacking, 354; Soviet Union

attacked, 568; Taliban, 568, 585; War on Terror, 560, 569–70, 585
AFL union, *c92*
Africa, apartheid, 537
African American arts, literature and music: Black Entertainment Television (BET), 535; blues, 216; Cotton Club, 216; *Emperor Jones* (Eugene O'Neill), 216; folklore, 192; Harlem Renaissance, 192, *p193*, 215–22; *Homesteader, The* (Oscar Micheaux), 216; jazz, 215, 216; *Oprah Magazine*, 535; Oprah's Book Club, 535; Oprah Winfrey Network (OWN), 535; rock'n'roll, 384, *p384*; Ronettes, 384; Shirelles, 384; *Shuffle Along*, 216; *The Souls of Black Folk* (W.E.B. Du Bois), 222; *Their Eyes Were Watching God* (Zora Neale Hurston), 252
African American people: Abernathy, Ralph, 423, 438; Armstrong, Louis, 216; Baker, Ella, 429, *q430*, 433; Baker, Josephine, 216; Baker, Vernon, 276, *p277*; Bentley, Gladys, 216; Brown, Elaine, 438; Brown, Michael, 587, 588, 607–08; Chisholm, Shirley, 440, 478, *q486*; Cleaver, Kathleen Neal, 438; Craig, Gwenn, *q510*; Cullen, Countee, 216; Davis, Benjamin O., 300–301; Dinkins, David, 440; Douglas, Aaron, 215, *p215*; Du Bois, W.E.B., 141, *q142*, *q145*, 215, 222, *q222*, 429; Ellington, Edward "Duke," 216; Europe, James Reese, 216; Evers, Medgar, 419, 424–25, 429; Farmer, James, 418, 429; Fields, Mary, 98; Floyd, George, 608, 609–10, 617; Foster, Andrew "Rube," 212; French, Lynn, 438; Garvey, Marcus, 214; Hamer, Fannie Lou, 433, *p433*; hooks, bell, 485, *p485*, 506; Houser, George, 418; Huggins, Ericka, 438; Hughes, Langston, 216, 220, *ptg220*; Hurston, Zora Neale, 192, *p193*, 216, 252, 260; Jackson, Jesse, 440; Jackson, Michael, 535; Johnson, Robert, 535; King, Coretta, 435; King, Martin

Luther, Jr., 406, *c410*, 419, 423–25, 427, 429, 435–36, 438, *p438*; Lewis, John L., 427, 429; Locke, Alain, 216; Loving, Mildred, 497, *p497*; Malcolm X, 214, 437; Martin, Trayvon, 587–88; McKay, Claude, *q221*; Micheaux, Oscar, 216; Mills, Florence, 216; Nash, Diane, 429, *p431*, *q431*; Newton, Huey P., 432; Nugent, Richard Bruce, 216; Obama, Barack, 498, 558, *p559*, 560, *c562*, 570, 572, 580, 581–88; O'Neill, Eugene, 216; Parks, Rosa, 406, *c410*, 417, 419, 429; Pollard, Fritz, 212; Raby, Albert, 435–36; Randolph, A. Philip, 303, 417; Robeson, Paul, 216; Seale, Bobby, 432; Shuttlesworth, Fred, 423; Smith, Bessie, 216, *p219*, *q219*; Smith, Lucy, 228; Tanner, Henry Ossawa, 211; Thomas, Clarence, 539–40; Till, Emmett, 420, *p420*; Truth, Sojourner, 485, 506; Turnbo, Annie, 116; Vivian, C.T., *q430*; Walker, Charles J., 116; Walker, Madam C. J., *p116*; Watkins, Gloria Jean, 485, *p485*, 506; Weaver, Robert, 389; Wells, Ida B., 429; West, Dorothy, 216; Wilder, L. Douglas, 440; Williams, Hosea, 427; Winfrey, Oprah, 535; Woods, Granville T., 114; Woodson, Carter G., 222; Young, Andrew, 353
African Americans: during 1920s, 213–22; after Revolutionary War, 12; "Double V" campaign, 300; economic status in 1920s, 210; education in late 1800s, 136; education status, *g442*; Freedmen's Bureau, 78; Great Migration, 174, 195, *m214*; Irving Berlin influenced by, 212; living conditions in Cambridge, MA, 432; Medal of Honor, 276, *p277*; middle class in late 1800s, 141; Nation of Islam, 214; Poro Company, 116; post-World War I, 177; as Spanish vaqueros, 96; suing Massachusetts for freedom, 12; *Sweatt* v. *Painter*, 418; urban life, post-World War II, 381–82; "War on Drugs," 536; Wilson, Darren, 587–88; working class during late 1800s,

132–33. *See also* **enslaved people, African**.
African Americans, civil rights and equality: affirmative action, 439–40; African Blood Brotherhood (ABB), 214; anti-lynching crusade, 140–41; Birmingham Campaign, 423–25, *p423*; Black Lives Matter Movement, 587–88, 610, 621; Black Nationalism, 214, 437–38; Black Panther Party for Self Defense, 432, 437–38, *p437*; Black Power movement, 436–38; Black Wall Street, 213; Brotherhood of Sleeping Car Porters, 303; *Brown* v. *Board of Education of Topeka, Kansas*, 391, 418, 439; Charleston, SC, attack, 588; Chicago Movement, 435–36; children marching in Birmingham, 424; Civil Rights Act of 1957, *c410*, 420–21, 423; Civil Rights Act of 1964, *cHT4*, 200, *c410*, 423–27; Civil Rights Act of 1968, 438; Civil Rights Division, 421; civil rights movements, 142; Colored Farmers' Alliance, 139; Congress for Racial Equality (CORE), 418; Congressional Black Caucus (CBC), 440; *Davis* v. *County School Board of Prince Edward County*, 418; Eatonville, Florida, 192; education of former enslaved people, 78; Equal Employment Opportunity Commission (EEOC), 427; Fair Employment Practices Commission, 303; Fair Housing Act of 1968, 438; feminist movement, 485, 506; Fifteenth Amendment, 50, 78, 140, 199, 408; Fourteenth Amendment, 77–78, 408; Freedom Riders, 422, *p422*, 431, *p431*; Greensboro sit-ins, *c410*; "I Have a Dream" (Martin Luther King, Jr.), *q425*; Jackson State College, antiwar protests, 468; "Jane Crow," 485; Knights of Labor, 119; Legal Defense and Educational Fund, 418; March on Washington in 1941, *c410*; March on Washington in 1963, *p405*, *c410*, 425; National Association for the Advancement of Colored

People (NAACP), 136, 140, 177, 213–14, 222, 406, 409, 415, 417, 418, 419, 422, 424–25, 429, 436, *c441*; National Association of Colored Women, 145; National Negro Committee, *q146*; in national politics, 440; Negro National League, 212; New Negro Movement, 218; Niagara Movement, 142, *p142*; in political office, 440; Poor People's Campaign, 438; progressivism impacting, 194; "Progress of Colored Women, The" (Mary Church Terrell), 145; Public Works Administration (PWA), 257; registering voters campaign, 427; Roosevelt's Executive Order 8802, 303, 417; Selma March, 427; Southern Christian Leadership Conference (SCLC), 421, 427, 430, 435–36, 438; of Southern Christian Leadership Conference (SCLC), *c441*; Southern Tenant Farmers Union, 251; Student Nonviolent Coordinating Committee (SNCC), 398, 421, 427, 429, 430, 433, *p433*, *c441*; suffrage, 77, ptg77, 78; Truman's civil rights proposals, 379; United States Commission on Civil Rights, 421; Voting Rights Act of 1965, 200, *c410*, 427–28, *m428*; women fighting for, 199

African Americans, enslavement of: Emancipation Proclamation, *cHT4*, *c6*, 74–75; in Jamestown, *cHT4*; Three-Fifths Compromise, 23

African Americans, segregation and discrimination of: battling, 213–14; black codes, 77; "Bloody Sunday," 427; bus segregation, 406, *c410*, 417, 419, *p419*, 422, 431, *p431*; during Great Depression, 255; housing discrimination, *c372*, 409, *c410*; inner city decline, 381–82; Jim Crow laws, 140, 143–46, 200, 408, 412, *p412*; Little Rock school desegregation violence, 420–21; *Loving* v. *Virginia*, 497; Montgomery Bus Boycott, 406, *c410*; post-World War II, 370; poverty rates, *g442*; Pullman Railroad Strike, *c92*; during Reconstruction, 408; redlining, 382; Red Scare impacting, 374; reproductive rights of, 399; segregation legalized, 139–40, 143–46; segregation of education, 391, 409, 418, 439; "separate but

equal" doctrine, 140, 144, 408, 415, 417; Separate Car Act, 143; in suburban neighborhoods, 381; tenant farmers, 251; travel guidebook during Jim Crow laws, 416; unions discriminating against, 119; voting barriers, 200; Watts Riot, 435; women excluded from WAVES, 303

African American schools, Provident Hospital and Training School for Nurses, 141

African Americans in military and wars: 761st Tank Battalion, 301; buffalo soldiers, 160; military segregation, 278; Tuskegee Airmen, 301, 417; in Union army, *p74*; in Vietnam War, 459; Virginia Loyalist militia, 10; during World War I, 174; during World War II, 300–301, 303–04, 413, 417; World War II veterans, 370, 377

African Blood Brotherhood (ABB), 214

African Methodist Episcopal Church, 70

African National Congress (ANC), 537

Afrika Korps, 305

Agent Orange, 455

Age of Innocence, The (Edith Wharton), 211

Agnew, Spiro, 518, 521, 524

Agricultural Adjustment Act, 251

Agricultural Adjustment Administration (AAA), 251, 262

agricultural revolution, 4

Agricultural Workers Organizing Committee (AWOC), 492–93, 507

agriculture: A&M colleges, 90, *m91*; Agricultural Adjustment Act, 251; Agricultural Adjustment Administration (AAA), 251, 262; bonanza farms, 98; cattle ranching, 95–96; dry farming, 98; Dust Bowl, 237, *m237*, 250–51, *p250*; Farm Security Administration, 263, *p264*; Food Administration, 173; Hawaii sugar plantations, 158; mechanical reapers, 98; sodbusters, 98; steam tractors, 98, *p99*; threshing machines, 98; westward expansion, 90

Aguinaldo, Emilio, 160

AIDS. *See* **acquired immunodeficiency syndrome (AIDS)**.

AIDS Coalition to Unleash Power (ACT UP), 536

Aid to Families with Dependent Children (AFDC), 522

ailerons, 209

Ain't I a Woman: Black Women and Feminism (bell hooks), 485, 506

Air Commerce Act of 1926, 209

aircraft/airplanes: B-24 "Liberator" bombers, 302, 312; B-29 Superfortress, 315, 316, 317, 318; Huey helicopter, 455, *p455*; invention of, 209; in Vietnam War, 469; in World War I, 172

Air Force: as independent branch, 379; Vietnam War, heavy losses in, 469

airmail service, 209

Air Pollution Control Act, 380

Air Quality Act, 389

Alabama, secedes from U.S., *m66*, 66

Alamo, *c6*

al-Baghdadi, Abu Bakr, 572

Albania, 338, 358

Albany Conference, 7

Albany Plan of Union, 7

Alcatraz Island, 495–96, *p496*, 509, *p509*

alcohol abuse, 536

Aldrin, Buzz, 349

Alert America campaign, 368

Alfred P. Murrah Federal Building, 551–52

Alger, Horatio, 133–34

Algeria, 305

Algiers, 284

Algonquian people, 5

Alien Land Act of 1913, 124

Alien Registration Act of 1940, 304

Alito, Samuel, Jr., 575

Allende, Salvador, 351–52

Alliance for Progress, 343

Allies: American ties to, 169; attacking Sicily and Italy, 307; Battle of the Bulge, 310; bombing Germany, 307; Casablanca Conference, 307; D-Day invasion, 308–09, *p308*; Italy and Sicily invasion, 307; Italy joins, 168; Italy surrendering to, 307; Normandy, 308–09; Operation Overlord, 308–09; Paris liberated, 310; strategies in Europe, 307–08; Tehran Declaration, *q307*–*q08*; Triple Entente becomes, 168; V-E (Victory in Europe) Day, 310; Yalta Conference, 328, *p329*, 334. *See also* **World War I**; **World War II**.

al-Qaeda, 569; bin Laden, Osama, 568; Guantánamo Bay, Cuba, 573; rise of, 568; September 11, 2001, *cHT4*, 567; War on Terror, 560; wiretapping domestic calls to, 573–74

al-Qaeda in Iraq (AQI), 571–72

alternating current (AC), 110

Alvin C. York Foundation, 171

A&M colleges, 90, *m91*

Amazon.com, 582

America First Committee, 285, *q297*, *q298*, 597

"America" from *Harlem Shadows: The Poems of Claude McKay*, *q221*

American Association of Retired Persons (AARP), 536, 548, *p548*, *p554*

American Association of University Women (AAUW), 375

American Birth Control League, 227

American Civil Liberties Union (ACLU), 227–28

American Coalition of Citizens with Disabilities (ACCD), 500, 502

American colonies: American Customs Board, *c8*; Battle of Bunker Hill, 10, *ptg10*; Battle of Saratoga, 10; Boston Massacre, 9; Boston Tea Party, 9; Coercive Acts, 9; Continental Congress, 9; Currency Act of 1764, 7–8; Declaration of Independence, *c6*, 13–18, *p13*; French and Indian War, 7; *Gaspee* affair, 9; government of, 8; Lexington and Concord battle, 9; Olive Branch Petition, 9; smuggling goods, 7; Sons of Liberty, 8; Stamp Act, 8; Stamp Act Congress, 8; Townshend Acts of 1767, 8, *c8*, 9; Treaty of Paris, 11. *See also* **Continental Congress**; **New England colonies**; **Revolutionary War**.

American Communist Party, 242

American Customs Board, *c8*

American diplomacy: in Asia, 162; "big stick" diplomacy, 163–65; Boxer Rebellion, 162; Central America, 160–61; dollar diplomacy, *m164*; Roosevelt, Theodore, 163–65; Roosevelt Corollary, *m164*; Taft, William Howard, 163. *See also* **U.S. foreign policy**.

American Dream, post-World War II, 370, *p370*

American Expeditionary Force (AEF), 175

American Federation of Labor (AFL), 119, 208

American flag, symbolism of, 32

American GI Forum, 492

American Gothic (Thomas Hart Benton), 252

American Gothic, Washington, D.C. (Gordon Parks), *p272*

American Heritage (Geoffrey E. Stone and David A. Strauss), *q393*

American imperialism: economic reasons for, 154, 157; rise of, 154, *m155*. *See also* imperialism.

American Indian Center, 495

American Indian Movement (AIM), *c482*, 496

American Indian Religious Freedom Restoration Act, 497–98

American Individualism (Herbert Hoover), 241

Americanization: education of immigrants, 136; of Native Americans, 91, 102, 103–08, *p103*

American Jewish Joint Distribution Committee, 175

American Party (Know-Nothings), 65

American Railway Union (ARU), 119, *m120*

American Recovery and Reinvestment Act, 560, 582

American Revolution. *See* Revolutionary War.

Americans for Tax Reform (ATR), 548

American Sign Language (ASL), 500

American slavery, foundations of. *See* enslaved people, African; slavery.

American Socialist Party. *See* Socialist Party.

American-Soviet summit, 352–53

American Spirit, The, *q172*

Americans with Disabilities Act (ADA), 481, *c482*, 500, 501–04, *p503*

American Telephone and Telegraph Company (AT&T), 110

American Temperance Society, 70

American Tract Magazine, The, *ptg68*

American Tract Society, *ptg68*, *q72*

American victory parade, *p179*

American Woman Suffrage Association (AWSA), 199

AmeriCorps, 547

Ames, Oakes, 114

amnesty, for refugees, *g472*, 491, 494

Amos 'n' Andy, 212

amphibious invasion, 319, *m319*

amphtrac, 315

anarchists: in late 1800s, 118; Sacco-Vanzetti case, 226

Anasazi people, 4

Anderson, Mary, 201

Angel Island, 123

Anglo-Iranian Oil, 342

Anglo-Saxonism, 154, 157–58

Animal Crackers, 251

Animal Farm (George Orwell), 393

annexation: debate over, 161, *crt161*; for economic reasons, 154, 157; Guam, 154, *c156*; Hawaii, 154, 158, 159; Philippines, 154, *c156*, 161, *crt161*; Puerto Rico, 154, *c156*; Texas, 63

Anthony, Scott, 100

Anthony, Susan B., 140, 199

anthrax attacks, 569

anthropology, HT19

anti-abortion movements, 536

Anti-Defamation League (ADL), 226

anti-lynching bill, 140

anti-lynching crusade, 140–41, 213–14

antipoverty campaign, 387–89, 397

anti-Semitism: in America, 288–89; of Nazis, 282, 287–92

anti-unionism, 118–19

antiwar movement, Vietnam War: after Cambodia invasion, 468; causes of, 448–49, *c450*; credibility gap, 457–58; of draft, 449, 458–60; Kent State University, 468, *p468*; King, Martin Luther, Jr., 460; "National Teach-In," 458; Nixon's resistance to, 521; protesters, *p463*; Spock, Benjamin, *q460*; Students for a Democratic Society (SDS), 458, 459–60; tear gas used against, 468, *p468*; violence of, 446

apartheid, 537

Apollo program, 348–49

"Apology Act for the 1930s Mexican Repatriation Program", *q250*

Appalachian Mountains: colonial settlers west of, 7; poverty of, 387, 388, *p388*; Proclamation of 1763, 7

Apple, Inc., 582

Apple Macintosh, *c520*, 542

Applied Christianity (Washington Gladden), 135

Appomattox Court House, 76

Arabs: Arab Spring, 572; Arab state of Jordan, 568; Organization of the Petroleum Exporting Countries (OPEC), 389; pan-Arabism, 342; Soviet Union and, 341; Sunni, 571

Arab Spring, 572

Arafat, Yasir, 550, *p550*

Arapaho people, 61, 100

arbitration, coal strike of 1902, 117, 201

archaeology, HT19, *pHT19*

arch dam, 234

Architectural Barriers Act, 500

architecture: dumbbell tenement, 132; skyscrapers, 131; streetcar suburbs, 132; tenements, 132, *p132*; upper-class impacting, 131; urbanization impacting, 131

Area Redevelopment Act, 386

Aristide, Jean-Bertrand, 550

Arizona: 2020 elections, 614, 615, *m623*; Boulder Canyon Project Act, 234; mining leading to statehood of, 93, *m94*; water rights, 518

Arkansas, Little Rock school desegregation violence, 420–21

Armed Forces. *See* military.

Armistice, World War I ended, *c156*, 175

armored tanks, 172

arms control agreements, 225

arms race: atomic bombs, 341; before World War I, 167

Armstrong, Edwin, 209

Armstrong, Louis, 216

Armstrong, Neil, 349, 371

army. *See* military.

Army History (Thomas D. Morgan), *q322*

Army Nurse Corps, 174, 279, 301

Arnaz, Desi, 383

Arnold, Benedict, 10

Around the World in 80 Days, 384

arteriosclerosis, 328

Arthur, Chester A., 137

Articles of Confederation: end of, 22; Land Ordinances of 1785, 19; Northwest Ordinance of 1787, 19, *m20*; revision of, 21; trade between states during, 20–21; trade treaties, 19–20; weakness of, 20–21

artifacts, historians using, HT6, HT19, *pHT19*

arts and artisans: during 1920s, 210–11; abstract art, 211; *Banjo Lesson, The* (Henry Ossawa Tanner), 211; Benton, Thomas Hart, 252; Chicano Mural Movement, 493, *p512*; cubism art, 211; Federal Project Number One, 260; during Great Depression, 251–52; Harlem Renaissance, 192, *p193*, 195, 215–22, 252; Hoover Dam, 234; Hopper, Edward, 211; Kahlo, Frida, 493; Marin, John, 211; Modern American Art, 211; O'Keeffe, Georgia, 211; *Persistence of Memory, The* (Salvador Dali), 211; realism art, 211; Rivera, Diego, 493; *Scream, The* (Edvard Munch), 211; Sheeler, Charles, 211; Siqueiros, David, 493; surrealistic art works, 211; Tanner, Henry Ossawa, 211; True, Allen, 234; wealthy patrons funding, 134; Wood, Grant, 252, *ptg252*

Asia: American diplomacy, 162; Asian American Political Alliance (AAPA), 498; Asia-Pacific Economic Cooperation (APEC), 540, *m541*; Southeast Asia Treaty Organization (SEATO), 341. *See also specific countries.*

Asian American Political Alliance (AAPA), 498

Asian Americans: Asian American Political Alliance (AAPA), 498, 506; population increase of, 498; Third World Liberation Front (TWLF), 498

Asian immigrants, *m121*, 123, *p123*, 127

"Asian Pacific Americans and the New Minority Politics," in *PS: Political Science and Politics* (Andrew L. Aoki and Don T. Nakanishi), *q506*

Asia-Pacific Economic Cooperation (APEC), 540, *m541*

Aspects of Negro Life (Aaron Douglas), 215

assassinations: Evers, Medgar, 424–25; Ferdinand, Archduke Franz, *c156*, *p168*; Garfield, James, 137, 194; Kennedy, John F., 387, 425–26; Kennedy, Robert, 461, *p461*; King, Martin Luther, Jr., *c410*, 438, *p438*, 461; Lincoln, Abraham, 76; McKinley, William, 163; Milk, Harvey, 499; Moscone, George, 499; Rabin, Yitzhak, 550

assembly line, 194, 208–09

assimilation, of Native Americans, 102

Astrodome, 574

Atlanta Compromise, 141–42

Atlantic Charter, 286

Atlantic Ocean, Panama Canal, 153–54

"Atom Bomb Baby", 376

Atomic Age, 376

atomic bombs: consequences of nuclear war, 344; development of, 317–18; Hiroshima, *cHT4*, 279, 318, 368; hydrogen bomb (H-bomb), 376; land-based missiles, 341; Limited Nuclear Test Ban Treaty, 344; long-range bombers for, 341; missile-carrying submarines, 341; mutually assured destruction, 341, 355; Nagasaki, *cHT4*, 279, 318, *p318*, 368; Soviet Union developed, 339

"Atomic Boogie", 376

atomic energy, 380

"Atoms for Peace" (Dwight D. Eisenhower), *q380*

ATR. See **Americans for Tax Reform (ATR)**.

attack on the Capitol (January 6, 2021), 613–615

Attorney General Jeff Sessions to DHS Acting Secretary Duke, *q591*

Audubon Society, 578

Auschwitz, 291, *p291*

Australia, 312

Austria: *Anschluss*, 283; Hitler occupying, 278, 283

Austria-Hungary: Archduke Franz Ferdinand, *p168*; Balkans, 167; Bosnia annexed by, 167; Russia, 167; Serbia, war with, *c156*, 168; surrendering in World War I, 175; Triple Alliance, 167

authorship, HT12

auto commuter, 209

automatic dishwasher, 110

automobile industry: B-24 "Liberator" bombers, 302; Committee for Industrial Organization (CIO), 260; development of, 208–09; sit-down strike, 260–61; during World War II, 302

aviation industry, 209

Axis Powers: Germany, 285; Italy, 285; Japan, 285, 299. *See also* **Germany, World War II**; **Italy**; **Japan**.

Ayatollah Khomeini, 353

Aztec people, sun stone, *pHT7*

Aztec people and civilization: Cortés conquering, 5; founding of, 4

B

B-24 "Liberator" bombers, 302, 312

B-29 Superfortress, 315, 316, 317, 318

baby boom, post-World War II, 370, *c372*, 381, *g382*, 540

bailiffs, 249

Bair, Barbara, *pHT6*

Baker, Ella, 429, *q430*, 433

Baker, Josephine, 216

Baker, Vernon, 277, *p277*

Baker v. Carr, 386, 393

Bakke, Allan, 439–40, *p440*

Balkans: nationalism, 167; Ottoman Empire and Austria-Hungary ruling, 167; Russia and Austria-Hungary wanting, 167

Ball, George, 454

Ball, Lucille, 383

Ballinger, Richard A., 202

Banjo Lesson, The (Henry Ossawa Tanner), 211

banking: bank holidays, 253; Banking Act of 1933, 254; commercial banks, 254–55; Emergency Banking Relief Act, 254; failing during Great Depression, 240, 245, *p245*, 247, *g247*, 253; Federal Deposit Insurance Corporation (FDIC), 247, 254–55; Glass-Steagall Act, 254; investment banks, 254–55; Securities Act of 1933, 254; Securities and Exchange Commission (SEC), 254–55. *See also* **National Bank**.

Banking Act of 1933, 247, 254

Bank of the United States. *See* **National Bank**.

bank run, 240, 245, *p245*, 247, *g247*, 253

Barak, Ehud, 550

barbed wire, 95

Barr, William, 607

Barrett, Amy Coney, 602, 618, 622

Barrio Boy (Ernesto Galarza), *q489*

barrios, 96, 489

Barryman, Clifford K., *crt285*

barter, HT18–HT19

baseball: in 1920s, 212; Foster, Andrew "Rube," 212; Negro National League, 212; Ruth, Babe, 212

Bataan Peninsula, 311

Batista, Fulgencio, 343

Batson, Ruth, 436, 439

Battle of Antietam, 74

Battle of Anzio, 301

Battle of Argonne Forest, 171

Battle of Bull Run, First, 74

Battle of Bunker Hill, *ptg10*

Battle of Gettysburg, 75

Battle of Iwo Jima, 313, 316–17, *p317*

Battle of Kasserine Pass, 305

Battle of Leyte Gulf, 316

Battle of Little Bighorn, *c92*, 100

Battle of Midway, 313–14, *m314*

Battle of New Orleans, 74

Battle of Saratoga, 10

Battle of Stalingrad, 306

Battle of the Atlantic, 306

Battle of the Bulge, 301, 310

Battle of the Coral Sea, 313

Battle of Yorktown, 11

Bay of Pigs, *c332*, 343

Bear Flag Republic, 63

bear market, 240

Beatles, the, 384

beat movement, 384

beatniks, 384

Beecher, Catharine, *p70*

Beecher, Charles, *p70*

Beecher, Edward, *p70*

Beecher, Henry Ward, *p70*, 134

Beecher, Lyman, *p70*

Begin, Menachem, *p353*

Beirut, Lebanon, *p342*, 354

Belgium: Battle of the Bulge, 310, *p310*; Dunkirk evacuations, 284, *p284*; Germany attacking, 284; imperialism of, 154, *m155*; NATO, 338; SS *St. Louis*, 289, *m289*; World War I, 168

Bell, Alexander Graham, 110, 500

Bell, John, 65–66

Bellamy, Edward, 135

Bell Telephone Company, 110

Belmont, Alva, *p480*

benevolent societies, 68

Benny, Jack, 251–52, 383–84

Bentley, Gladys, 216, 227

Benton, Thomas Hart, 252

Berlin, Irving, 212

Berlin Airlift, *c332*, 338

Berlin Wall: Berlin Airlift, *c332*; building of, 330, *c332*, 338; tearing down, *p327*, 330, *c332*, 359, *p359*, 360

Bernstein, Carl, 523

Berry, Chuck, 384

Bessemer, Henry, 111

Best and the Brightest, The (McGeorge Bundy), 454

Bethune, Mary McLeod, 333

Bezos, Jeff, 582

bias, HT11

Biden, Joseph R., Jr.: 602, *p616*; 2020 campaign, 607, 614, 626; 2020 election, *c562*, 614–18, *m619*; acceptance speech, 622; "Biden rule", 602; first 100 days in office, 617–18; Covid response, 616; immigration policy, 615; inaugural address,

q618; national energy proposal, 620; Ukraine and, 607; vice-president, 581

big business. *See* **business and corporations**.

"big stick" diplomacy, 163–65

Bilingual Education Act, 493

bilingualism, 493

Bill of Rights, 46–48, *p55*; Americans' rights in, 30; English (Magna Carta), *q60*; ratification of, *c6*; Thomas Jefferson suggesting, *q57*

binding arbitration, 260

bin Laden, Osama, *cHT4*, 560, 567, 568, 569–570; embassy bombings in Kenya and Tanzania, 568; USS *Cole*, 568

biodiversity, HT30

Birmingham Campaign, 423–25, *p423*

birth control: in 1920s, 227; in the 1950s, 484; *Griswold* v. *Connecticut*, 387

Bitter Cry of the Children, The (John Spargo), 197

black codes, 77

blackface, in silent films, 212

Black Hills gold, 93, *m94*

Black Kettle, 100

Black Lives Matter Movement, 587–588, 610, 612

Black Muslims, 437

Black Nationalism, 214, 437–38

Black Panther Party for Self Defense, 432, 437–38, *p437*

Black Power movement, 436–38

Black Thursday, 240, 246

Blaine, James G., 137

Blair, Ezell, Jr., 421

Bland, Thomas, 102

"Bleeding Kansas", 65

blitzkrieg, 284

Block, Herbert, *crt529*

Bloods: Black Veterans of the Vietnam War: An Oral History (Reginald "Malik" Edwards), *q446*

"Bloody Sunday", 427

blue-collar jobs, 382

blues, 216

Board of Indian Commissioners (Merrill Gates), *q104*

bohemian lifestyle, in the 1920s, 210

Bolshevik Party, 175, 330

bombing campaign, 307

bomb shelters, 368, 376

bonanza farms, 98

Bond, Julian, 434

bonds, war bonds, 303

Bonus Army, *c238*, *p242*, 243, 256

bonus marches, *p242*

"boom-and-bust", 90

boomtowns, 93, *m94*

Booth, John Wilkes, 76

Borah, William, *crt285*

border wall: demand for, 494; Illegal Immigration Reform and Immigrant Responsibility Act of 1996, 491, 593

Bork, Robert, 524, 534

Bosnia: assassination of Archduke Franz Ferdinand, 168; Austria-Hungary annexed, 167; civil war in, 358; Dayton Accords, 358; ethnic cleansing, 358; NATO in, 358; Princip, Gavrilo, 168

Bostonians, The (Henry James), 227

Boston marriage, 227

Boston Massacre, *c6*, 9

Boston Tea Party, 9

Boulder Canyon Project Act, 234

Boumediene v. *Bush*, 573

Bourke-White, Margaret, 252

Bow, Clara, 212

Boxer Rebellion, 155, 162

boxing, in 1920s, 212

Boynton v. *Virginia*, 431

Bracero program, 304, 387, 489–90

Braddock, Edward, 7

Bradley, Omar, 309

Bradley, Tom, 539

Brady Bill, 547–48

Branch Davidian, 552

breaker boys, 197

Breckinridge, John C., 65–66

Breedlove, Sarah, 116

Breed's Hill, 10

Brennan, William, *m428*

Bretton Woods System, 333, 389

Brezhnev, Leonid, 352

Briand, Aristide, 225

Brin, Sergey, 582

brinkmanship, 321, 341

Britain: Battle of Bunker Hill, 10, *ptg10*; Battle of Saratoga, 10; Boston Massacre, 9; Boston Tea Party, 9; Coercive Acts, 9; Currency Act of 1764, 7–8; French and Indian War, 7; *Gaspee* affair, 9; Greece communists and, 337; imperialism of, 154, *m155*; Lexington and Concord battle, 9; NATO, 338; navy of, 154; Olive Branch Petition, 9; Oregon territory, 61–62; Proclamation of 1763, *c6*, 7; Stamp Act, 8; surrender at Yorktown, 11; Townshend Acts of 1767, 8, *c8*,

9; Treaty of Paris, 7, 11. *See also* England.

Britain, post-World War II: invading Egypt, 341; in UN Security Council, 333

Britain, World War I: China leaseholds of, 162; entering World War I, 168; militarism, 167; navy of, 167; Triple Entente, 167; World War I propaganda, 169

Britain, World War II: attacking in Algiers and Morocco, 305; attacking Sicily and Italy, 307; bombing Germany, 307; British Expeditionary Force, *p284*; Casablanca Conference, 307; D-Day invasion, 308–09, *p308*; declaring war with Germany, 278, 283–84; Destroyers-for-Bases, *c280*; French ally, 283; Italy and Sicily invasion, 307; Lend-Lease Act, 278, *c280*, 286; London bombings, *p293*; "Miracle of Dunkirk," 284, *p284*; Munich Conference, 283, *p283*; Normandy, 308–09; Operation Overlord, 308–09; SS *St. Louis*, 289, *m289*; Tehran Declaration, *q307–q08*; V-E (Victory in Europe) Day, 310

British East India Company, 9

British Mandate of Palestine, 568

Broadway, 216

brokers, 246

Brotherhood of Sleeping Car Porters, 303

Brown, Elaine, 438

Brown, Henry Billings, *q144*

Brown, H. Rap, 436

Brown, John, 65

Brown, Linda, 418

Brown, Michael, head of FEMA, 575

Brown, Michael, 587–588, 607–608

Brown v. *Board of Education of Topeka, Kansas*, 391, 409, *c410*, 418, 439

Brunauer, Esther, 375, *p375*

Bryan, William Jennings, 139, 161, 169, 227–28, 596

Bryant, Carolyn, 420

Bryant, Roy, 420

Buchanan, James, election of 1856, 65

Buchenwald, 290–91

Buckley, William F., 532

Buddhism, in Vietnam, 453

budget deficit. *See* federal budget.

buffalo, 61

buffalo soldiers, 160

Bulgaria: democratic government replacing communism, 357; Soviet Union controlling, 328,

336; Soviet Union satellite nation, 336; Warsaw Pact, 338

bull market, of 1920s, 239–40, 246

Bureau for the Education of the Handicapped, 500

Bureau of Indian Affairs, 102

Bureau of Mines, 202

Bureau of Reclamation, 234

Bureau of Refugees, Freedmen, and Abandoned Lands. *See* Freedmen's Bureau.

Burger, Warren, 521

Burgoyne, John, 10

Burton, Philip, *q491*

Bush, George H.W.: Americans with Disabilities Act (ADA), *p503*, *q503*; economic recession, 538; election of 1988, 537; election of 1992, 540; Gorbachev, Mikhail, *q362*; Immigration Act of 1990, 491; new world order, 537; Nixon's resignation, *q524*; Operation Desert Storm, 538; Operation Restore Hope, 537; Persian Gulf War, 537–38, *m538*; Somalia, 537; supporting Yeltsin, 357, 361; tax cuts, 539; Thomas, Clarence nomination, *c520*

Bush, George W.: 2000 elections, 560, *c562*, 563–66, *m565*; Address to Joint Session of Congress, *q568*; administration of, 560, *c562*; *Boumediene* v. *Bush*, 573; *Bush* v. *Gore*, 565–66; campaign of, 563–64; contested presidential election, *c520*, 564–66; Department of Homeland Security, 560, *c562*; Gates, Robert, 571–72; Great Recession, 576; *Hamdan* v. *Rumsfeld*, 573; Hurricane Katrina, 560, *c562*, 574–75, *p574*; immigration myths, *p590*; immigration reform, 494; invasion of Iraq, 560, *c562*, 570–71, *p571*; Military Commissions Act, 573; national debt, 582; national security versus civil liberties, 573; Office of Homeland Security, 568; *Rasul* v. *Bush*, 573; Rumsfeld, Donald, 571–72; second term of, 574–76; September 11, 2001, *cHT4*, 560, *c562*, 567, 568; Social Security reform, 574; tax cuts, 569; USA PATRIOT Act, 568–69; War on Terror, 568–72, 573

Bush v. *Gore*, 565–66, *q566*

business and corporations: chain stores, 112; Clayton Antitrust Act, 208; creation of, 111–12; department stores, 112; economies of scale, 111; federal

government laws, 115–16, 201; Federal Trade Commission (FTC), 208; franchise, 382; government interference in, 115–18; holding companies, 112; horizontal integration, 112, *c150*; interstate commerce, 201; Interstate Commerce Commission (ICC), 115–16, 201; laissez-faire, 90, 201; mail-order catalogs, 112; monopoly, 112; multinational corporations, 382; Progressive Era reforms, 201–02; railroads, corruption of, 114; regulating, 117–18; Sherman Antitrust Act, 115; trust, 112; vertical integration, 111–12, *c150*

Butterfield, Alexander, 523

Byrd, Harry F., 418–19, 426, *p426*

Byrd, James, Jr., 587

Byrnes, James, 318

C

cabinet. *See* President of the United States.

cable cars, 131

cable television, 535

Cahokia, *cHT4*, 4

calendars, historians using, HT7

Calhoun, John C., Compromise of 1850, 64

Califano, Joseph, 502

California: Bear Flag Republic, 63; Boulder Canyon Project Act, 234; Central Valley Project (CVP), 255; Compromise of 1850, 64; Dust Bowl migration, 251; "Forty-Niners," 62, 63; gold discovered, 62, 63; Gold Rush, 90, 96; Hispanics in, 96; hydraulic mining, 94; land claim commission, 96; Master Plan for Higher Education, 380; Mexican land grants, 96; Polk's intentions for, 63; Reagan, Ronald, governor, 533–34; slavery-free state, 62, 63; statehood of, 90, 96; three-tier college system, 377; water rights, 518

California Land Act of 1851, 96

Calley, William, 467–68

"Call for Unity, A," *Birmingham Times* (Martin Luther King Jr.), 424

Cambodia: Khmer Rouge, communist group, 470; Nixon orders invasion of, *c450*, 467, 468

Cambridge Nonviolent Action Committee, 432

camera, handheld, 111

Camp David Accords, *c332*, 353, *p353*

Canada: NATO, 338; North American Free Trade Agreement (NAFTA), 540

Canassatego (Onondaga Nation), *q2*

cancer treatments, 371, 383

Cantigny, 175

capital gains taxes, 539

capitalism, communism versus, 330–31

carbon-14, HT20

cardiopulmonary resuscitation technique (CPR), 371, 383

Carlisle School, 104, 108

Carmack, George Washington, 88

Carmichael, Stokely, 436–37

Carnegie, Andrew, 111–12, 134, *q134*, 161

Carnegie Steel, 111–12

Carolina colonies. *See* **South Carolina**.

carpetbaggers, 78

Carranza, Venustiano, 166

cars: gasoline-powered carriage, 111; importance in 1950s, 370, *m371*; women of 1920s, *p227*

Carson, Rachel, 577

Carter, Jimmy: election of 1976, 390; inaugural address, 353; *Love Canal: The Story Continues* (Lois Gibbs), *q578*; Rehabilitation Act of 1973, 502

Casablanca Conference, 307

Cashman, Nellie, 88

Cass, Lewis, 63

Castro, Fidel, 343–44, *m344*, 586

Castro, Raúl, *p590*

categorizing, HT15

Cather, Willa, 211

Catholic Church: Coughlin, Charles, 259, *q268*; expelling Communist Party members, 374; immigrants increasing, 122; Ku Klux Klan (KKK), 195, 213; Smith, Alfred E., 239

Cat Lai, *p447*

Catt, Carrie Chapman: League to Limit Armament, 169; National American Woman Suffrage Association (NAWSA), 200; Woman's Peace Party, 169

cattle ranches: cattle drives, 95–96; open ranges, 90; westward expansion, 90

Cayuga people, 2

CBC. *See* **Congressional Black Caucus (CBC)**.

CCCO. *See* **Coordinating Council of Community Organizations (CCCO)**.

cell phones, 546

Center for American Progress, 548

Central America, 155

Central Intelligence Agency (CIA), 341–42, 379, 523

Central Pacific, 113

Central Pacific Railroad, 123

Central Powers. *See* **Austria-Hungary**; **Bulgaria**; **Germany, World War I**; **Ottoman Empire**; **Triple Alliance**.

Central Valley Project (CVP), 255

Century of Dishonor, A **(Helen Hunt Jackson)**, 102

Chaco Canyon, 4

chad, 563

chain stores, 112

"The Challenge to Liberty," *The Saturday Evening Post* **(Herbert Hoover)**, *q266*

Chamberlain, Neville, 283

Chambers, Whittaker, 374

Chaplin, Charlie, 212

Charleston, SC, white supremacist attack in, 588, 609

Charles Towne, 10, 507

Charlie, Dawson, 88

charts, using, HT32

Château-Thierry, 175

Chávez, César: Kennedy, Robert and, 508, *p508*; National Farm Workers Association (NFWA), 492–93, 507

checks and balances, *c26*, 27

Chelmno, 291

chemotherapy, 371, 383

Cheney, Dick, 538, 563

Cherokee people: code talkers, 313; Mississippi cultural group, 4–5

Cheyenne people, 61, 100, 104

Chicago: Armstrong, Louis, 216; Hull House, 135–36, *c196*; jazz in, 215; Jewish immigrants, 130; King, Martin Luther, Jr., 435–36; race riots of 1919, 177; urbanization and migration, 131; Wells, Ida B., 140, 141; Women's Club of Chicago, 131

Chicago Daily Tribune, 378

Chicago Movement, 435–36

Chicago Whip, 214

Chicana/Chicano, 490

Chicano Mural Movement, 493, *p512*

Chichimec people, 4

child labor, *p198*, *p203*; breaker boys, 197; compulsory education laws, 198; Fair Labor Standards Act, 263; Keating-Owen Child Labor Act, 208; progressive ideals and, 197–98; United States Children's Bureau, 198; in urbanization, 132, *p132*

Children's Bureau, 198, 201

Children's Health Insurance Program, 552

child tax credit, 552

Chilkoot Trail, 88

China: 587; Boxer Rebellion, 155, 162; Chiang Kai-shek, 339; Chinese Revolution, 339; COVID-19 pandemic, *m561*, 609–10; foreign leaseholds, 162; Japan attacking, 285; Japan invading Manchuria, 281; Lend-Lease aid, 299; Mao Zedong, 339; Nationalist government, 339; Open Door Policy, 155, 162; "Rape of Nanking," 281; Society of Righteous and Harmonious Fists, 162; supporting North Vietnam, 456; Taiwan and, 341; Tiananmen Square, 541–42; trade with, 541–42; Trans-Pacific Partnership (TPP), 586, 597; in UN Security Council, 333; war over Korea with Japan, 154, 162; Yalta Conference, 328. *See also* **People's Republic of China**.

Chinese Exclusion Act of 1882, 123, *q127*

Chinese immigrants, 113

Chinese Revolution, 339

Chippewa people, 97

Chisholm, Shirley, 440, 478, *q486*

Chivington, John, 100

chlorofluorocarbons (CFCs), 580

Choctaw people, 313

Christian evolutionists, 134

Christianity: Anglo-Saxonism, 157–58; *Applied Christianity* (Washington Gladden), 135; of conservatives, 532–33; evolution and, 134; Falwell, Jerry, 533; Graham, Billy, 533; Moral Majority, 533; Roberts, Oral, 533; Robertson, Marion "Pat," 533; Salvation Army, 135; settlement house movement, 135–36; Social Gospel movement, 135–36; televangelists, 533; Young Men's Christian Association (YMCA), 135. *See also* **Catholic Church**.

Chrysler, 209

Churchill, Winston: American industry, 301; Atlantic Charter, 286; Casablanca Conference, 307; communist takeover of Eastern Europe, 336; D-Day invasion, 308–09; "Give Us the Tools," *q296*; invading Morocco and Algeria, 305; Iron Curtain, 330, *p330*; Operation Overlord, 308–09; Tehran Declaration,

q307–*q08*; Yalta Conference, 328, *p329*, 334

CinemaScope, 384

citizenship, rights, roles, and responsibilities of, HT19

Citizenship Act, 102

citizens' rights and responsibilities, 30–32

Citizens United v. *Federal Election Commission*, 584

civics, HT18–HT19

civil disobedience. *See* **civil rights movement, African American**; **civil rights movement, Native American**.

Civilian Conservation Corps (CCC), 256–57, *p257*, *p258*

civil rights: Civil Rights Act of 1875, 140, 408; Civil Rights Act of 1957, *c410*, 420–21, 423; Civil Rights Act of 1964, 200, *c410*, 423–27; Civil Rights Division, 421, 423; Executive Order 8802, 378; Executive Order 9980, 378; Executive Order 9981, 378; Great Society, 388–89, 395–400; Kennedy's support of, 422, *q424*; President's Committee on Civil Rights, 379; United States Commission on Civil Rights, 421; Voting Rights Act of 1965, *c410*

civil rights activists: Abernathy, Ralph, 423, 438; Baker, Ella, 429, *q430*, 433; Brown, Elaine, 438; Brown, H. Rap, 436; Carmichael, Stokely, 436–37; Cleaver, Kathleen Neal, 438; Du Bois, W.E.B., 429; Evers, Medgar, 429; Farmer, James, 429; French, Lynn, 438; Hamer, Fannie Lou, 433, *p433*; Huggins, Ericka, 438; Jackson, Jesse, 440; King, Martin Luther, Jr., 429, 435–36, 438, *p438*; Lewis, John L., 429; Malcolm X, 437; Moses, Bob, 433; Nash, Diane, 429, *p431*, *q431*; Newton, Huey P., 432; Oakes, Richard, 495–96, *p496*; Parks, Rosa, 406, *p407*, *c410*, 417, 419, 429; Raby, Albert, 435–36; Seale, Bobby, 432; Seigenthaler, John, *p431*, *q431*; Vivian, C.T., *q430*; Wells, Ida B., 429; William, Robert F., 436

Civil Rights Act of 1875, 140, 408

Civil Rights Act of 1957, *c410*, 420–21, 423, 607

Civil Rights Act of 1964, *cHT4*, 200, *c410*, 423–27, 484, 607

Civil Rights Act of 1968, 438, 607

Civil Rights Division (Department of Justice), 421

civil rights movement, African American: Birmingham Campaign, 423–25, *p423*; Black Panther Party for Self Defense, 432, 437–38, *p437*; Black Power movement, 436–38; "Bloody Sunday," 427; Boston school segregation, 436; Chicago Movement, 435–36; children marching for, 424; Civil Rights Act of 1968, 438; Congressional Black Caucus (CBC), 440; Fair Housing Act of 1968, 438; Freedom Riders, 422, *p422*, 431, *p431*; Greensboro sit-ins, *c410*; Highlander Folk School, 406, 421; "I Have a Dream" (Dr. Martin Luther King, Jr.), *q425*; inspiring others, 495; Lowndes County Freedom Organization (LCFO), 437; March on Washington in 1941, *c410*; March on Washington in 1963, *p405*, *c410*, 425; Medgar Evers's murder, 424–25; Montgomery Bus Boycott, 406, *c410*; National Association for the Advancement of Colored People (NAACP), 136, 140, 177, 213–14, 222, 406, 409, 415, 417, 418, 419, 422, 424–25, 429, 436, *c441*; Niagara Movement, 142, *p142*; Nixon resisting, 521; Operation PUSH (People United to Save Humanity), 440; Poor People's Campaign, 438; Red Scare impacting, 374; registering voters campaign, 427; Selma March, 427; Southern Christian Leadership Conference (SCLC), 421, 427, 430, 435–36, 438, *c441*; Student Nonviolent Coordinating Committee (SNCC), 398, 421, 427, 429, 430, 433, *p433*, *c441*; Voting Rights Act of 1965, 427–28, *m428*; Women's Political Council, 419

civil rights movement, Asian Americans, 498, 506

civil rights movement, LGBTQ, 481, 498–99

civil rights movement, Native American: Alcatraz Island, 495–96, *p496*, 509, *p509*; American Indian Center, 495; American Indian Movement (AIM), 496; American Indian Religious Freedom Restoration Act, 497–98; Bill of Rights protection, 495; Declaration of Indian Purpose, 495; gains of, 496–98; Indian Civil Rights Act, 481, *c482*, 495; Indian Self-Determination and Educational Assistance Act of 1975, 496; Indians of All Tribes, 495–96, *p496*, 509, *p509*; Termination Policy of 1953, 496; Wounded Knee protest, 496

civil service reforms, 137

Civil War: assassination of Lincoln, 76; attrition impacting, 74; attrition in, 74; Battle of Antietam, 74; Battle of Bull Run, First, 74; Battle of Gettysburg, 75; Battle of New Orleans, 74; casualties of, *c76*; cone-shaped bullets, 74; elections of 1864, 76; Emancipation Proclamation, *cHT4*, *c6*, 74–75; end of, 76; Fort Sumter attacked, *cHT4*, 74; General Grant battling General Lee, 76; Grant, Ulysses S., 75; McClellan, George B., 74; Sherman's March to the Sea, 76; siege of Petersburg, 76; siege of Vicksburg, 75; Union army vs. Confederacy army, *c73*; war in the east, 74; women's suffrage after, 199. *See also* **sectional tensions, causes of**.

Civil Works Administration (CWA), 257

Clark, Jim, 427

class structures: middle class, 131; upper-class people, 131; urbanization impacting, 131–32; working class, 131

Clay, Henry: Compromise of 1850, 64; Fugitive Slave Act, 64

Clayton Antitrust Act, *c196*, 208

Clean Air Act, 389, 522, 578

Clean Water Act of 1972, 522, 578

Cleaver, Kathleen Neal, 438

Clemenceau, Georges, 176

Cleveland, Grover, 137, 139, 158, 159

Cleveland riots, 178

Clinton, Henry, 10

Clinton, Hillary Rodham: 547, 605; 2016 elections, 561, *c562*, 581, 595–96; presidential debate, *p596*

Clinton, William "Bill", 596; administration of, 547–52; Adoption and Safe Families Act, 552; advocacy groups, 548–49; Brady Bill, 547–48; Children's Health Insurance Program, 552; China trade, 541–42, *q541*; Dayton Accords, 358; D-Day National Remembrance, *q321*; Defense of Marriage Act (DOMA), 587; election of 1992, 540; embassy bombings in Kenya and Tanzania, 568; Family Medical Leave Act, 547; foreign policy, *q549*; Health Insurance Portability and Accountability Act (HIPAA) 551; Illegal Immigration Reform and Immigrant Responsibility Act of 1996, 491; impeachment of, *c520*, 552; Israeli/Palestinian relationship, 550, *p550*; Oklahoma City bombing, 551–52; perjury, 552; Republicans battling, 550–52; sexual harassment, 550; view on advocacy groups, *q549*; Welfare Reform Act, 551; Whitewater Development, 552

closed-caption television, 500

closed shops, 119, 377–78

cloture, 426

Coal Creek mine, 119

Coal Creek War, 119

cocaine, 536

Cochrane, Josephine, 110

code-breaking in World War II, 313

code talkers, 313

Coelho, Tony, 500

Coercive Acts, 9

Cold War, *m331*; Alliance for Progress, 343; American-Soviet summit, 352–53; Berlin Airlift, 338; Berlin Wall, 338, 360; Central Intelligence Agency (CIA), 341–42; communism versus capitalism, 330–31; conservatism grows during, 532; containing communism, 336–37; covert operations, 341–42; Cuban Missile Crisis, 343–44, *m344*; Détente Policy, 351–52; Eisenhower Doctrine, 342–43; "flexible response," 343; foreign policy during, 328, 331; Gorbachev's reforms, 356–57, 360, 362; Greece, 337; Intermediate Range Nuclear Forces (INF) Treaty, *cHT4*, 355; Iran, 353; Iran and Soviet Union, 336–37; Kennedy's strategies for, 343–44; Korean War and, 339–41; Latin American nations during, 343; Lebanon, 342; Limited Nuclear Test Ban Treaty, 344; Marshall Plan, 331, 337–38, *g337*; massive retaliation, 341; Middle East and, 341, 353–54; missiles, build-up of, 343; mutually assured destruction, 341, 355; Nasser, Gamal Abdel, 342; Nixon Doctrine, 351; North Atlantic Treaty Organization (NATO), 338; nuclear disarmament, 355; pan-Arabism, 342; People's Republic of China, 352; Reagan Doctrine, 354; Reagan's policies, 354; rising tensions, 334–35; Southeast Asia Treaty Organization (SEATO), 341; Soviet Union tensions ease, 352–53; "space race," 371; Strategic Arms Limitation Treaty (SALT I), 352; Strategic Arms Reduction Talks (START), 355; Strategic Defense Initiative (SDI), 355; summit talks, 355, *p515*; Taiwan, 341; Turkey, 337; Vietnamization, 351; Vietnam War and, 448; Warsaw Pact, 338; Yalta Conference role in, 328, 334

Cold War, domestic impact of: African Americans impacted by, 374; bomb shelters, 376; communist subversion fears, 373; duck-and-cover drills, 368, *p369*, 376; fallout shelters, 376; House Un-American Activities Committee (HUAC) hearings, 373–74; Lavender Scare, 374; loyalty review program, 373–74; McCarthyism, 374–76; pop culture of, 376; Red Scare, 373–76

collective bargaining, 119

collectivized farms, 282

college football, 212

Colombia, Panama Canal, 163

Colorado: Boulder Canyon Project Act, 234; mining leading to statehood of, 93, *m94*; Sand Creek Massacre, 100; statehood of, 90; water rights, 518; women's suffrage, 199

Colored Farmers' Alliance, 139

Columbia Broadcasting System (CBS), 209

Columbus, Christopher, *cHT4*

Columbus, New Mexico, 166, *p166*

commercial banks, 254–55

Commissioner of Indian Affairs, 102

Commissioner of U.S. Customs and Border Protection Mark Morgan, Yuma, Arizona, 593

Commissioners of Customs Act, *c8*

Commission of Wartime Relocation and Internment of Civilians, 304

Commission on the Status of Women, 483–84

Committee for Industrial Organization (CIO), 260, 260–61

Committee for the Re-election of the President (CRP), 523

committee of correspondence, 9

Committee of Five, 10, 13, *ptg13*

Committee on Equal Employment Opportunity (CEEO), 422

Committee on Juvenile Delinquency and Youth Crime, 386

Committee on Public Information (CPI), 174–75, 180

Committee on Veterans Affairs, *q321*

Common Sense **(Thomas Paine),** 10

Commonwealth of Independent States (CIS), 357, *m358*

communications: American Telephone and Telegraph Company (AT&T), 110; Bell Telephone Company, 110; telegraph, 110; telephone, 110; trans-Atlantic telegraph cable, 110

communism: Cambodia turning to, 470; capitalism versus, 330–31; Chinese Revolution, 339; containing, 336–37; domino theory, *c332*; Europeans fear of, 281; Laos turning to, 470; Red Scare, *c156*, 178, 183, 185, 186; of Russia, 175; Vietminh, 448, 451–52. *See also* **Cold War.**

Communist Party in America: African Americans in, 374; House Un-American Activities Committee (HUAC) hearings, 373–74; Internal Security Act, 375

Compagnie Universelle du Canal Interocéanique, 153

comparing and contrasting, HT15

Compromise of 1850, 64

Compromise of 1877, *c6*, 78, 79–82, *m80*

compulsory education laws, 198

computers: Apple Macintosh, 542; electronic digital computer, 542; ENIAC, first electronic computer, *c372*; government research, 544; Intel, 542; International Business Machines (IBM), *c520*, 542; Internet, 542, 544; Microsoft, 542; Personal Computers (PC), 542; Windows, 542; workforce impacting, 545

Comstock, Henry, 93, *m94*

Comstock Lode, 90, 93, *m94*

concentration camps: Auschwitz, *p291*; Buchenwald, 290–91; Nazis, 290–91, *m290*

conclusions, HT16

Concord: battles at, 9; minutemen, 9

concurrent powers, 26

cone-shaped bullets, 74

Confederacy: defined, 2; surrender at Appomattox Court House, 76

Confederate army: attrition impacting, 74; Battle of Antietam, 74; Battle of Bull Run, First, 74; Battle of Gettysburg, 75; Battle of New Orleans, 74; casualties of, *c76*; siege

of Vicksburg, 75; Union army compared to, *c73*; war in the east, 74

Confederate States of America. *See* **Confederacy.**

Congress: bills becoming law, 27, *c28*; organization of, *c26*, 27

Congressional Black Caucus (CBC), 440

Congressional Record **(Charles Schumer),** 618

Congressional Record **(John Cornyn),** *q618*

Congressional Record **(Lauren Underwood),** 619

Congressional Record **(Richard Russell),** *q171, q426*

Congressional Record, **74th Congress, 1st session (Huey Long),** *q267*

Congress of Industrial Organizations, 261

Congress of Racial Equality (CORE), 418, 422, 429, *c441*

conic projection, HT23, *mHT23*

Connecticut Compromise (Great Compromise), 22–23

Connecticut Woman Suffrage Association, 70

Connor, Theophilus Eugene "Bull", 422

conservatives/conservatism: 2000 elections, 563–66; Cold War increasing, 532; Gun Control Act of 1968, 533; Heritage Foundation, 533; Nixon, Richard disappointing, 533; organizing, 532; religious rights, 532–33; *Roe* v. *Wade,* 533; of Sunbelt, 532; views of, 531; Young Americans for Freedom (YAF), 532

Constitutional Amendments, 46–54; Eighteenth Amendment, 51; Eighth Amendment, 47; Eleventh Amendment, 48; Fifteenth Amendment, 50, 140, 408; Fifth Amendment, 30–31, 47; First Amendment, 31, 46; Fourteenth Amendment, 49–50, 77–78; Fourth Amendment, 30, 47; Nineteenth Amendment, *cHT4*, 51; Ninth Amendment, 31, 47; Second Amendment, 46; Senate's edits to, 58; Seventeenth Amendment, 50; Sixteenth Amendment, 50; Sixth Amendment, 47; Tenth Amendment, 48; Third Amendment, 46; Thirteenth Amendment, *c6*, 49, 76, 77; Twelfth Amendment, 48; Twentieth Amendment, 51–52; Twenty-Fifth Amendment,

53–54; Twenty-First Amendment, 52; Twenty-Fourth Amendment, 53; Twenty-Second Amendment, 52–53; Twenty-Seventh Amendment, 54; Twenty-Sixth Amendment, 54; Twenty-Third Amendment, 53. *See also* **Bill of Rights.**

Constitutional Convention, *ptg35*; Connecticut Compromise (Great Compromise), 22–23; New Jersey Plan, 22; problems facing, 21–22; Three-Fifths Compromise, 23; Virginia Plan, 22–23

Constitutional Union Party, 65–66

Constitution Handbook: American flag, 32; checks and balances, *c26*, 27; citizens' responsibilities, 31–32; E. Pluribus Unum, 33; executive branch, *c26*, 28–29; federalism, 25–26; "In God We Trust," 34; Great Seal of the United States, 33; individual rights, 27; judicial branch, *c26*, 29–30; legislative branch, *c26*, 27; limited government, 25; a living document, 34; popular sovereignty, 25; republicanism, 25; rights of Americans, 30–31; separation of powers, 26–27, *c26*; Star-Spangled Banner, 33–34

Constitution of the United States, 35–46; amendment process for, 23; Bill of Rights, *c6*; checks and balances, *c26*, 27; citizens' responsibilities, 31–32; drafting of, *cHT4*, *c6*; executive branch, *c26*, 28–29; federalism, 25–26; Fugitive Slave Clause, 23; individual rights, 27; judicial branch, *c26*, 29–30; legislative branch, *c26*, 27; limited government, 25; popular sovereignty, 25; republicanism, 25; rights of Americans, 30–31; separation of powers, 26–27, *c26*; "We the People," 59

Consumer Financial Protection Bureau, *p559*

consumerism, 236

containment, 336, 337, 340, 342, 354, 363, 460

Continental Army, establishment of, 9

Continental Congress: establishing American government, 10, 19; Land Ordinances of 1785, 19; Northwest Ordinance of 1787, 19, *m20*; Second Continental Congress, 10

Continental Navy, 10

"Contract with America", 550–51

Convention on the Prevention and Punishment of the Crime of Genocide, 335

convict lease laws, 119

convoy system, 305

Cook County Insane Asylum, 131

Coolidge, Calvin, *q224*; police force strike, 177; presidency of, 224

cooperative individualism, 224

cooperatives, 138

Coordinating Council of Community Organizations (CCCO), 435–36

copper: Arizona, 93, *m94*; Montana, 93, *m94*

copyright laws, HT12

coral reef atolls, 315

CORE. *See* **Congress of Racial Equality (CORE).**

Cornwallis, General, 10, 11

Cornyn, John, 618

Corporation for Public Broadcasting (CPB), 526

corporations. *See* **business and corporations.**

Cortés, Hernán, 5

cost of living, post-World War I, 177

cost-plus system, 301

Cotton Club, 216

Coughlin, Charles, 259, *q268*

Council Fire and Arbitrator, The, *q105*

council-manager system, 198

court packing, 262–63, *crt263*, 269, *q269*

Covenant of the League of Nations, The, *q181*

covert operations, 341–42

COVID-19 pandemic, 609–12; 2020 elections impacted by, 617; spread of, *m561, c562*; Biden's response, 615–16; relief, 611; vaccines, 611, 616; Trump's response, 610–11, 617, 619, *q619*

Cox, Archibald, 524

Cox, James M.: election of 1920, 178; Progressive Era reforms, 178

Craig, Gwenn, 510

Crane, Stephen, 135

Crazy Horse, 100

creationism, 227–28

credentials, HT11

credit, installment plans, 210, 236

Crédit Mobilier, 114

Creel, George, 174, 180

crime, in late 1800s urban areas, 133

Crisis, The, 215, 429

"Crisis of Confidence" (Jimmy Carter), *q390*

Crocker, Charley, 113

Cronkite, Walter, *p464*

Crowded Hours (Alice Roosevelt Longworth), *q223*

Crucible, The (Arthur Miller), 376

Crusader, The, 214

Crusoe, Robinson, *crt104*

Cuba: Bay of Pigs, 343; Castro, Fidel, 343; Cuban Missile Crisis, *c332*, 343–44, *m344*; economic link to U.S., 158; Havana riots, 159; independence of, 154; *La Brigada*, 343; Mariel boat lift, *p491*; Martí, José, 158, 159; Platt Amendment, 154, 161; refugees from, 490, *p491*, 494; restored relations with, 586, *p586*; slavery in, 158; Spanish-American War, 158–60; SS *St. Louis*, *p288*, 289, *m289*; sugar plantations of, 158; Treaty of Paris, *c156*, 160–61; USS *Maine*, *c156*, 159; war of independence, 159–60

Cuban Missile Crisis, *c332*, 343–44, *m344*

cubism art, 211

Cu Chi tunnels, 455–56, *m456*

Cullen, Countee, 216

Cullors, Patrisse, 587, 588

cultural clashes of 1920s, 226–27

cultural superiority, 157–58

culture (1920s), 210–12

Currency Act of 1764, 7–8

Curtiss, Glenn, 209

Cushing, William, *q12*

Custer, George A., 100

customs duties, 7

customs duty, 7

Cvetic, Matt, 376

cyclical effect on economy, *p236*

cylindrical projection, HT23, *mHT23*

Czechoslovakia: after World War I, 175; democratic government replacing communism, 357; Hitler occupying, 278, 283; Soviet Union controlling, 328, 336; Soviet Union satellite nation, 336; Warsaw Pact, 338

D

Dakotas: Dakota people, 99; Lakota reservation, 100; Native American uprisings in, 99–100; statehood of, 90

Daley, Richard J., 436

Darrow, Clarence, 227–28

Darwin, Charles, 134

Daugherty, Harry, 223–24

Daughters of Bilitis, 498

Davis, Benjamin O., 300–301

Davis, Jefferson: Fort Sumter, 74; war views of, 74

Davis v. County School Board of Prince Edward County, 418

Dawes, Charles G., 225

Dawes Act, *c92*, 102, *q107*

Dawson City: Cashman, Nellie, 88; Klondike Gold Rush, 88

daylight saving time, 173

Dayton Accords, 358

D-Day invasion, *c280*, 308–09, *p308*, 319–22, *m319*, *p320*, *m324*

DDT pesticide, 577

Dead Horse Trail, 88

Deaf community, 500

Dean, John, 523

Debs, Eugene V., 116, 178

Declaration of Independence: document of, 13–18, *p13*; signers of, *cHT4*; writing of, *c6*, 10, 13

Declaration of Independence (John Trumbull), *ptg15*

Declaration of Indian Purpose, 495

Declaration of Liberated Europe, 334

Declaration of Natural Rights, 14

Declaration of Principles, 550

Declaration of Rights and Grievances, 9

Declaration of Sentiments, 199

de facto segregation, 409

Deferred Action for Childhood Arrivals (DACA) program, 591, *q591*, 592, *q594*, 601

deficit spending, 259

deflation, 118, 138

Defoe, Daniel, *crt104*

Deganawida (The Peacemaker), 2

de Gaulle, Charles, 284, 309

de jure segregation, 417

De La Beckwith, Byron, 419

demand, supply and, HT18

demilitarized zone (DMZ), in Korea, 340

democratic government: of Iroquois people, 2; United States established as, 24

Democrats (Democratic-Republicans): 1860 presidential election, 65–66; 2006 midterm elections, 576; 2016 elections, 595–96, 602; 2020 elections, 613, *m621*; African American joining, 262; Cleveland, Grover, 137; Gore, Al, 563–66; in South during Reconstruction, 78; Tammany Hall, 133

Dempsey, Jack, 212

Denmark, 338

Department of Commerce and Labor, 117–18, 201

Department of Defense, 379

Department of Energy, 390

Department of Homeland Security, 560, *c562*

Department of Housing and Urban Development (HUD), *c372*, 389

Department of State, 28

department stores, 112

depth charges, 306

deregulation, 390

desegregation: affirmative action, 439–40; *Brown v. Board of Education of Topeka, Kansas*, 391, 409, *c410*, 418, 439; busing, 439; *Davis v. County School Board of Prince Edward County*, 418; Little Rock school desegregation violence, 420–21; of military, 279, 378, 419–20; resistance against, 418–19; *Sweatt v. Painter*, 418. See also civil rights movement, African American; segregation.

Desert Fox (Erwin Rommel), 305

Destroyers-for-Bases, *c280*, 285

détente, 351–52

Détente Policy, 351–52

developing nations, 341–42

Dewey, George, 160

Dewey, Thomas, *p378*, 379

diagrams, using, HT32

Díaz, Porfirio, 165

Dien Bien Phu, 452

digital audio players, 535

digital technology, hyperconnectivity of, 582

digital video disc (DVD), 535

Dinkins, David, 440

direct election of Senators, 50, *c196*, 198

direct primary nomination, 194, 198

Dirksen, Everett, 426

disability rights activists, 386, *p477*; Americans with Disabilities Act (ADA), 481, *c482*

disabled, rights of. See people with disabilities.

discount retailing, 534–35

discrimination: affirmative action, 439–40; after Revolutionary War, 12; Executive Order 8802, 378; Executive Order 9980, 378; Executive Order 9981, 378; GI Bill administration, 377; against Hispanics, 388; housing discrimination, *c372*, 409, *c410*, 435, 438; against Jews, 287; job, 435; Latinos, 489–94; Mexican Americans, 489–94; in military, 279, 300–301, 413,

419–20; National Advisory Commission on Civil Disorders, 435; of Nazis, 282, 287; against people with disabilities, *p477*, 481; in post-World War II, 370; President's Committee on Civil Rights, 379; redlining, 381, 382; Red Scare impacting, 374; of suburban neighborhoods, 381; during World War II, 279, 300–301, 413. See also civil rights movement, African American; civil rights movement, Asian Americans; civil rights movement, LGBTQ; civil rights movement, Native American; feminist movement, modern; racism/racial tensions; women's rights; women's suffrage.

disease: AIDS, *c520*; Panama Canal construction, 153, 164; during Vietnam War, 446

disenfranchised, 300

Disney, Walt, 251

District of Columbia v. Heller, 588

Dix, Dorothea, 68

Dixiecrat Party, 379

DNA, HT20

The Doctrines and Discipline of the African Methodist Episcopal Church, *q70*

Dodge, Josephine, 200

Dole, Sanford, 158, 159

"dollar-a-year men", 301

dollar diplomacy, *m164*, 165

Dominican Republic, 155, 165

Dominis, John Owen, 159

domino theory, *c332*, 452, 470

Doolittle, James, 312

Doolittle Raid, 312–13

dot-com economy, 542

"Double V" campaign, 300

Douglas, Aaron, 215, *p215*

Douglas, Stephen A.: 1860 presidential election, 65–66; Missouri Compromise, 64

Dow Jones Industrial Average, 246, *g246*

downsizing, 539

draft: during Vietnam War, 446, 449, *m449*, 458–60; during World War II, 300

Drake, Edwin, 109

Drawing in Two Colors (Winold Reiss), *ptg221*

Dred Scott v. Sandford, *c6*, 64, *ptg64*, 65

Dreiser, Theodore, 135

drug abuse, in urban areas, 536

dry farming, 98

Du Bois, W.E.B., 141, *q142*, *q145*, 215, *q222*, 429

duck-and-cover drills, 368, *p369*, 376

due process, 30–31, 386

Dukakis, Michael, 537

dumbbell tenement, 132

Dunmore, governor of Virginia, 10

Durban, Dick, 591

Duryea, Charles, 111

Dust Bowl: causes of, 99, 250; impact of, 237, *m237*, 250–51, *p250*

Dust Tracks on a Road (Zora Neale Hurston), 216

Dutch. *See* Netherlands, the.

Dyea, 88

dynamic conservatism, 380

Dynamic Sociology (Lester Frank Ward), 135

Dynamite Hill, 424

E

Eagle Forum, 532–33

early voting, 613, *m618*

earmarks, 584

Earth Day, 578

East Berlin: Berlin Airlift, *c332*, 338; Berlin Wall, *p327*, 330, *c332*, 338, 359, *p359*; reunification of, 357; Soviet Union controlling, 330, 334, *m334*

Eastern European, racism against, 123, 128–30

Eastern Hemisphere, HT26

Eastern time zone, 114

East Germany: Berlin Airlift, *c332*; Berlin Wall, *p327*, 330, *c332*, 338, 359, *p359*; German Democratic Republic, 338; reunification of, *p327*, *c332*, 357, 359, *p359*; Soviet Union controlling, 330, 334, *m334*; united with West Germany, *c332*; Warsaw Pact, 338

Eastland, James O., 422, 426, *p426*

Eastman, Crystal, 478

Eastman, George, 110–11

Eatonville, Florida, 192

Eckhardt, Christopher, 459

economic crisis: in 1970s, 389–90; dot-com, 542; Great Depression, 239–41, 254, 259; Great Recession, 558, 560, 576, 582, 587; income gap, 583; "Occupy Wall Street" protesters, 583; Panic of 1873, 119; post-World War I, 177; September 11 triggering, 569

economic innovations: assembly line, 208–09; automobile industry, 208–09; aviation industry, 209; mass production, 208–09

Economic Opportunity Act, 388, 398

economic policy, in late 1800s, 137–38

economic reform: Federal Reserve Act of 1913, 207–08; progressive ideals, 197; Roosevelt, Theodore, 201–02; Taft, William Howard, 202

economics: history and, HT18; opportunity costs, HT18; resources and scarcity, HT18; supply and demand, HT18; trade and barter, HT18–HT25

economies of scale, 111

economy: during 1910s and 1920s, 194–95; in the 1950s, *p367*; annexation improving, 154, 157; during Articles of Confederation government, 21; during Civil War, 73–74; Clinton focusing on, 547; conservatives' view of, 531–32; cooperative individualism, 224; cost-plus system, 301; Cuba and U.S. linked, 158; cyclical effect, *p236*; deflation, 118, 138; downsizing, 539; dynamic conservatism, 380; economic policy, 137–38; Federal Reserve Act of 1913, 207–08; during George H.W. Bush administration, 538; global, 540–42; inflation, 138; interconnection of, 582; Kennedy's policies for, 386; Keynesianism, 263; laissez-faire, 90, 111, 112, 115, 255; leading to World War I, 281; liberals' view of, 531; Marshall Plan, 337, *g337*; Point Four Program, 337; post-World War II, 377–78; during Reagan administration, 534–35; Reaganomics, 534; Republican economic policies, 224–25; Spanish-American War impacting, 161–62; stagflation, 389–90; supply-side economics, 224, 534; trickle-down economics, 534; westward expansion post-Civil War, 90; during World War I, 173–74; during World War II, 301

ecosystems and biodiversity, HT30

Edison, Thomas Alva, 109–10

Edison General Electric Company (GE), 110

Edmisten, Rufus, *q528*

Edmund Pettus Bridge, 427

Edo Bay, 158

education: affirmative action, 439; of African Americans in late 1800s, 136, 141, 408; Americanization of Native Americans through, 102, *q104*, 108; Bilingual Education Act, 493; *Brown* v. *Board of Education of Topeka, Kansas*, 391, 409, *c410*, 418, 439; busing, 439; compulsory education laws, 198; *Davis* v. *County School Board of Prince Edward County*, 418; desegregation of, 409, *c410*; Educational Amendment, Title IX, 487, *p487*; Education Amendment of 1972, *c482*; Elementary and Secondary Education Act of 1965, 388–89, 397; equality in, 439, 487; of former enslaved people, 78; GI Bill impacting, 377; Massachusetts reform, 71; Master Plan for Higher Education, 380; Project Head Start, 389, 396, 552; public school, 136; segregation of, 391, 409, *c410*, 414, 415, 418, 439; segregation of Mexican American children, 492; settlement house movement, 136; Social Gospel movement, 135–36; *Sweatt* v. *Painter*, 418; three-tier college system, 377; Title IX, *c482*; vocational education, 136

Educational Amendment, Title IX, 487

Education Amendment of 1972, *c482*

Edwards, John, 573

Eells, Myron, *q105*

Eglin Air Force Base, 300

Egypt: Arab Spring, 572; Britain invading, 341; Camp David Accords, 353, *p353*; France invading, 341; seizing Suez Canal, 341

Eighteenth Amendment, 51, 195, *c196*, 228

Eighth Amendment, 47

Einsatzgruppen, *p292*

Einstein, Albert, 288, 317–18

Eisenhower, Dwight D.: administration of, 379–81; advisors to Vietnam, 453; Air Pollution Control Act, 380; "Atoms for Peace," *q380*; balancing federal budget, 380; Battle of the Bulge, 310; brinkmanship, 341; *Brown* v. *Board of Education of Topeka, Kansas*, 420; Civil Rights Act of 1957, *c410*, 420–21, 423; Civil Rights Division, 423; covert operations, 341–42; D-Day invasion, 308–09, *q320*; deporting illegal immigrants, 490; desegregation of military, 419–20; domino theory, *c332*; dynamic conservatism, 380; election of 1952, 340, 379–80; Federal-Aid Highway Act, 370, *m371*, *c372*, 380; Federal Highway Act, 380; Interstate Highway System, 370, *m371*, *c372*, 380; Italy and Sicily invasion, 307; Korean War, 340; massive retaliation policy, 341; "military-industrial complex," 342; National Aeronautics and Space Administration (NASA), 345; Operation Overlord commander, 308–09; Reconstruction Finance Corporation (RFC), 380; Robinson, Jackie, *q414*; Social Security, expanding, 380–81; Space Act, 345; Supreme Allied Commander NATO Forces, 338; Tennessee Valley Authority (TVA), 380; Warren Court, 391; World War II general, 305

Eisenhower Doctrine, 342–43

elections: 1844, 63; 1856, 65; 1860, 65–66; 1864, 76; 1876, 78, 79–82, *m80*; 1892, 139; 1896, 139; 1912, 207; 1916, 168; 1920, 178; 1928, 209–10, *c238*, 239; 1932, *p233*, *c238*, 243; 1936, *c238*, 262, 293; 1940, 285; 1944, 328; 1948, 378–79; 1952, 340, 379–80; 1960, 343, 385, *m385*; 1964, 532; 1968, 351, 461, *m462*, 467, 518, 521; 1972, 469–70, 478, 523, 529; 1976, 390; 1980, 354, 519, *c520*; 1984, 440, 534; 1988, 440, 537; 1992, 540; 2000, *c520*, 560, *c562*, 563–66, *m565*; 2004, 573; 2006, 575–76; 2008, 581–82, *p581*; 2016, 561, *c562*, 595–97; 2020, *c562*, 602, 612–15, *m619*; Bush and Gore contested, *c520*; Compromise of 1877, 78, 79–82, *m80*

Electoral College: 2000 elections, 563; establishment of, 24

Electoral Commission, *m80*, 81

electoral districts, reapportionment, 386

electric generator, 110

electric power: invention of, 109–10; trolley cars, 131

electronic digital computer, 542

Electronic Numerical Integrator and Computer, 543

Elementary and Secondary Education Act of 1965, 388–89, 397

elevated railroad, 131

Eleventh Amendment, 48

Eliot, T. S., 211
Ellender, Allen J., 426, *p426*
Ellington, Edward "Duke", 216
Ellis Island, 121–22, 129, *p129*
Ellsberg, Daniel, 469, *p469*
Eltinge, Julian, 227
emancipation, Gradual Abolition of Slavery, 12
Emancipation Proclamation, *cHT4*, *c6*, 74–75
Emergency Banking Relief Act, 254
Emergency Economic Stabilization Act, *c562*
Emergency Medical Technicians (EMTs), 455
Emergency Quota Act, 226
Emergency Relief and Construction Act, 242
Emmanuel, Victor, king of Italy, 307
Emperor Jones (Eugene O'Neill), 216
empresarios, 62
Empress of the Blues, 216, 219
Endangered Species Act of 1973, 522, 578
Engel, Steven, 392
Engel v. *Vitale*, 387, 392
England. *See* Britain.
ENIAC, first electronic computer, *c372*
Enlightenment, the, Declaration of Independence influenced by, 10, 13
Enola Gay, 318
enslaved people, African, *cHT4*; African American Loyalist militia, 10; after Revolutionary War, 12; in Cuba, 158; Emancipation Proclamation, *cHT4*, *c6*, 74–75; Fugitive Slave Clause, 23; Gradual Abolition of Slavery, 12; impact of Revolutionary War, 12; in Jamestown, *cHT4*; Scott, Dred, 64, *ptg64*, 65; suing Massachusetts for freedom, 12; Three-Fifths Compromise, 23; Underground Railroad, 64; in westward expansion, 61
entente cordiale, 167
Enterprise, 314
entertainment industry: *Animal Crackers*, 251; development of, 194–95, *m195*; first feature length animated film, 251; Gable, Clark, 251; *Gone with the Wind*, 251; during Great Depression, 251–52; Leigh, Vivien, 251; Marx Brothers, 251; McDaniel, Hattie, 251; motion pictures, *c196*; *Mr. Smith Goes to Washington*, 251; Office of War Information (OWI), 303; *Snow White and the Seven*

Dwarfs, 251; Stewart, Jimmy, 251; *Wizard of Oz, The*, 251
"entitlement" programs: government spending, 547; Social Security Act, 261–62
entrepreneurs, 115
enumerated powers, 26
environmental conservation, 202
Environmental Defense Fund, 577
environmental impact: Dust Bowl, 237; of Great Plains farming, 98; of mining, 94–95
environmentalism: global politics of, 579–80; origins of, 577–79
environmental protection, 579–80; Audubon Society, 578; Carson, Rachel, 577; chlorofluorocarbons (CFCs) bans, 580; Clean Air Act, 389, 522, 578; Clean Water Act of 1972, 522, 578; DDT pesticide ban, 577; Earth Day, 578; Endangered Species Act of 1973, 578; Environmental Defense Fund, 577; Environmental Protection Agency (EPA), 522, 533, 578; global system, 580; Kyoto Protocol, 580; National Environmental Policy Act, 578; Natural Resources Defense Council, 578; Paris Agreement, 580; *Sea Around Us, The* (Rachel Carson), 577; Sierra Club, 578; *Silent Spring* (Rachel Carson), 577; Thunberg, Greta, 580, *p580*; Wilderness Society, 578; Yannacone, Carol and Victor, 577
Environmental Protection Agency (EPA), 522, 533, 578
environment and society, *cHT22*
E. Pluribus Unum, 33
Equal Employment Opportunity Commission (EEOC), 427, 484
Equal Pay Act, 386, 478, 480, 484
Equal Rights Amendment (ERA): opposition to, 478, *q486–q87*, 532–33; origins of, 478, *p480*; ratification failure of, 485–87, *m486*; reintroduction of, *p479*, *c482*, 484
Equator, HT26
eras, HT7
Erie Canal, *ptg1*
Ervin, Samuel, Jr., 426, *p426*, 528
Escobedo v. *Illinois*, 387
espionage: of American Communists, 373–74; House Un-American Activities Committee (HUAC) hearings, 373–74; during World War I, 175, *crt184*

Espionage Act, *c156*, 175, *crt184*, *q184*
"Establishing a National Commission on the Observance of International Women's Year", *q508*
ethnic cleansing, in Bosnia and Kosovo, 358
ethnic communities, 122
eugenics, 227
euro, 540
Europe: after World War II, 334; exploring America, 5, *m5*. *See also* World War I; World War II; *specific countries*.
Europe, James Reese, 212, 216
European immigrants, 121–22, *m121*
European imperialism: Belgium, 154, *m155*; France, 154, *m155*; Germany, 154, *m155*; Great Britain, 154, *m155*; Italy, 154, *m155*; Portugal, 154, *m155*; Spain, 154, *m155*. *See also* imperialism.
European Recovery Program, 337
European Union (EU), 540, *m541*
Evers, Medgar, 419, 424–25, 429
evidence, examining and analyzing, HT10
evolution: discovery of, 134; fundamentalists, 227–28; Scopes trial over, *c196*
exchanges (farms), 138–39
executive branch: Department of State, 28; establishment of, 22, 23–24, *c26*; Executive Office of the President (EOP), 28; president's cabinet, 28; President's role, 28–29
Executive Office of the President (EOP), 28
Executive Order 8802, 378, 417
Executive Order 9066, 304, *p304*
Executive Order 9980, 378
Executive Order 9981, 378, 420
executive privilege, 523
Explorer I, 343
extermination camps, Nazi, 290, *m290*, 291–92

F

Facing History and Ourselves (Frederic Morton), *q288*
factories. *See* manufacturing.
Factory Investigating Commission, 197
Fairbanks, Douglas, 212
Fair Deal, 379
Fair Employment Practices Commission, 303

Fair Housing Act of 1968, 438
Fair Labor Standards Act, *c238*, 263, *q263*
Fall, Albert B., 223
fallout shelters, 376
Falwell, Jerry, 533
Family Assistance Plan, 522, 533
Family Medical Leave Act, 547
family planning programs, 399
Farewell to Arms, A (Ernest Hemingway), 212
Farm Credit Administration (FCA), 255
Farmer, James, 418, 422, 429
Farmers' Alliance, 138–39
farming: in 1920s, 236; in 1930s, 242; Agricultural Adjustment Act, 251; Agricultural Adjustment Administration (AAA), 251, 262; bonanza farms, 98; collectivized farms, 282; Colored Farmers' Alliance, 139; cooperatives, 138; deflation impacting, 138; dry farming, 98; Dust Bowl, 237, *m237*, 250–51, *p250*; economic status in 1920s, 210; exchanges, 138–39; Farm Credit Administration (FCA), 255; Farmers' Alliance, 138–39; Farm Relief Bill, *p241*; Farm Security Administration, 263, *p264*; Federal Farm Loan Act, 208; Fordney-McCumber Act impacting, 210; Grange (Patrons of Husbandry), 138; on Great Plains, 95–96, 98–99; by Mississippian cultures, 4–5; sodbusters, 98. *See also* agriculture.
Farm Relief Bill, *p241*
Farm Security Administration, 263, *p264*
Farragut, David G., Battle of New Orleans, 74
fascism, 281–82
Faubus, Orval, 420–21
Faulkner, William, 252
FBI Records: The Vault, "Clergy and Laity Concerned about Vietnam" (Jerry D. Coffin), *q458*
Federal-Aid Highway Act, 370, *m371*, *c372*, 380
federal budget: balanced, 552; battle over, 551; deficit, *g535*, 539
Federal Bureau of Investigation (FBI), 178; loyalty review program, 373–74; Watergate scandal, 523
Federal Civil Defense Administration, 368, *p369*, 376

Federal Deposit Insurance Corporation (FDIC), 247, 254

Federal Emergency Management Agency (FEMA), 560, 574–75

Federal Emergency Relief Administration (FERA), 256

Federal Farm Loan Act, 208

Federal Highway Act, 380

federalism, 25–26

Federal Republic of Germany, 338

Federal Reserve Act of 1913, 207–08

Federal Reserve Board, 237, 242

federal reserve system, 207–08

Federal Trade Commission (FTC), 208

Feldbaum, Carl, *q528*

Felt, W. Mark, 523

FEMA. *See* **Federal Emergency Management Agency (FEMA)**.

Feminine Mystique, The **(Betty Friedan)**, 478, *p483*, 484

feminist movement, modern: abortion rights, *c482*, 487–88; African American, 506; after World War II, 480; Belmont, Alva, *p480*; career opportunities, 480; Chisholm, Shirley, 440, 478, *q486*; Civil Rights Act of 1964, 484; Commission on the Status of Women, 483–84; Eastman, Crystal, 478; Educational Amendment, Title IX, 487, *p487*; education equality, 487; Equal Employment Opportunity Commission (EEOC), 484; Equal Pay Act, 386, 480, 484; Equal Rights Amendment (ERA), 478, *p479*, *p480*, *c482*, 484, 485–87, *m486*; Friedan, Betty, 478, *p483*, 484, *q484*; hooks, bell, 485, p485, 506; impact of, 488; "Jane Crow," 485; marital privacy rights, 487; #MeToo, 605–06; National Organization for Women (NOW), 478; origins of, 483–85; Paul, Alice, 478; reproductive rights, 487–88; right to privacy, 487–88; *Roe* v. *Wade*, *c482*; Striebel, Charlotte, 487; successes and failures of, 485–88; Watkins, Gloria Jean, 485, *p485*, 506

Ferdinand, Franz, *c156*, 168, *p168*

Ferguson, MO, 587–88, 608

Fermi, Enrico, 317–18

Ferraro, Geraldine, 534

Fetterman, William, 100

Fetterman's Massacre, 100

"Fiddler" (Herb Block), *crt443*

Fields, Cyrus, 110

Fields, Mary, 98

Fifteenth Amendment: African American suffrage, 77, 78, 408; poll tax and literacy tests, 140, 408; voting rights, 50, 199

Fifth Amendment: due process, 30–31; property rights, 575; rights of the accused, 47

Fight for Freedom Committee, 285

filibuster, of Civil Rights Bill, 426, *p426*

Filipino Americans, 492–93

Filipinos: Filipino Regiment I, 312; Filipino Repatriation Act, 249; guerrilla warfare, 160; Philippine American Collegiate Endeavor (PACE), 498; Third World Liberation Front (TWLF), 498; during World War II, 311–12

Fillmore, Millard, 64, 158

Final Solution, 290–92. *See also* **Holocaust, the.**

firefighters (September 11), *cHT4*, 567

"fireside chats", 254

First Amendment, basic freedoms, 31, 46

First Continental Congress, 9

First Neutrality Act, *c280*

First New Deal, 253–58

Fisher v. *University of Texas at Austin*, 440

Fiske, John, 157

Fitzgerald, F. Scott, 212

Five Nations (Iroquois Confederacy), 2–3, *ptg3*

Five-Power Naval Limitation Treaty, 225

Five Themes of Geography, HT21

Five-Year Plans, of Soviet Union, 282

flappers, 212, 226

Florida: 2000 elections, 563–66, *p563*; cattle branding, 96; Everglades land development, 577; secedes from U.S., *m66*, 66; Treaty of Paris, 11

Floyd, George, 606, 607–08, 617, 619

folklore, 192

Food Administration, 173

food stamps, New Deal implementing, 248

football: in 1920s, 212; Pollard, Fritz, 212; Thorpe, Jim, 212

Foraker Act, 161

Forbes, Charles R., 223

Ford, Gerald: economic crisis, 390; International Women's Year, *q508*; Presidency of, 524, 525; Rehabilitation Act of 1973, 502; South Vietnam aid, 470; vice president, 524

Ford, Henry, 174, 194, 208–09, 302

Fordney-McCumber Act, 210

Foreign Intelligence Surveillance Court, 574

foreign loans, 1920s, 236

foreign policy. *See* **U.S. foreign policy.**

Foreign Relations committee, 177

Fort Sumter, *cHT4*, 74

"Forty-Niners", 62, 63, 96

Forum, The **(A. Mitchell Palmer)**, *q186*

fossil fuels, 579. *See also* **oil industry.**

fossils, HT19

Foster, Andrew "Rube", 212

Four Freedoms, 285–86, 296

Four-Power Treaty, 225

Fourteen Points, 176, 181

Fourteenth Amendment: African American citizenship, 77–78; penalty for insurrection, 49; public debt, 49–50; representation in Congress, 49; rights of citizenship, 49, 199; Supreme Court overturning, 140, 408

Fourth Amendment, 30, 47

Four Vagabonds, 302

fracking, 579

frame of reference, HT11

France: Austria-Hungary/Serbia war, 168; Cantigny, 175; Château-Thierry, 175; China leaseholds of, 162; Franco-Russian Alliance, 167; Free French resistance forces, 284; French and Indian War, 7; imperialism of, 154, *m155*; invading Egypt, 341; Iroquois Confederacy and, 2; leaves Indochina, 448, *c450*, 463; leaves Indochina and Vietnam, 452; NATO, 338; Pétain, Marshal Philippe, 284; Prussia and, 167; SS *St. Louis*, 289, *m289*; Treaty of Paris, 7; Triple Entente, 167; in UN Security Council, 333; Vietminh, 452; Vietnam under, 448, 451

France, World War II: D-Day invasion, 308–09; declaring war with Germany, 278, 283–84; de Gaulle, Charles, 284; fall of, 284; "Miracle of Dunkirk," 284, *p284*; Munich Conference, 283, *p283*; Normandy, 308–09; Operation Overlord, 308–09; Paris liberated, 310

franchise, 382

Franco, Francisco, 285

Franco-Russian Alliance, 167

Frank, Otto, 288

Franklin, Benjamin: Albany Plan of Union, 7; Committee of Five, 10, 13, *ptg13*; at Constitutional Convention, 21–22; Treaty of Paris, 11

Frantz, Joe B., *q394*

Free Breakfast for Children Program, 437

Freed, Alan, 384

Freedmen's Bureau: development of, 78; education of former enslaved people, 78; rations provided by, 78

freedom of the seas, 176

Freedom Riders, 422, *p422*, 431, *p431*

Freedom Summer, 421

free enterprise system: communism versus, 341; industrialization due to, 115

Free-Soil Party, 65

free speech, controlling during World War I, 174–75, 180

free trade areas, 115

French, Lynn, 438

French and Indian War: Albany Conference, 7; British triumph, 7; causes of, 7; Treaty of Paris, 7

French Resistance, 309–10

Freud, Sigmund, 226–27

Frick, Henry Clay, 119

Friedan, Betty, 478, *p483*, 484, *q484*

Friends of the Indians, 102

Fuel Administration, 173

Fugitive Slave Act, 64

Fugitive Slave Clause, 23

fugitive slave laws: Fugitive Slave Act, 64; Fugitive Slave Clause, 23

fundamentalists, 227–28

G

Gable, Clark, 251

Gaffney, Nicholas L., 218

Gagarin, Yuri, *c332*, 371

Gage, Thomas, 9

Gannett, Frank E., *q269*

García, Héctor P., 492

Garfield, James, 137, 194, 202

Garland, Merrick, 602

Garvey, Marcus, 214

Garza, Alicia, 587, 588

gasoline-powered carriage, 111

Gaspee **affair**, 9

Gates, Bill, 542

Gates, Horatio, 10

"Gavel-to-Gavel: The Watergate Scandal and Public Television," American Archive of Public Broadcasting website, *q526*, 529

Gay Liberation Front (GLF), 498

gay rights. See **civil rights movement, LGBTQ.**

Gaza, 550

gender identity rights: civil rights movement, 498–99; Stonewall riots, 481, 498, 510

General Agreement on Tariffs and Trade (GATT), 337

General Assembly (United Nations), 333

General Electric Company, 519, 533

General Intelligence Division, 178

generalizations, HT16

General Motors: mass production, 209; sit-down strike, c238, 260–61

Geneva Accords, 452

Geneva Conventions, 335

genocide: concentration camps, 290–91, m290; extermination camps, 290, m290, 291–92; Final Solution, 290–92; Holocaust, the, 287–92, m290; internationally punishable, 335

Geographer's Handbook, HT21–HT32

geographic information systems (GIS), HT31, cHT31

geography: absolute location, HT21; Eastern Hemisphere, HT26; Equator, HT25–HT26; Five Themes of, HT21; hemispheres, mHT22, HT26; latitude, HT25; longitude, HT25; Northern Hemisphere, HT26; Prime Meridian, HT25; relative location, HT21; Six Essential Elements of, HT21–HT22; Southern Hemisphere, HT26; study of Earth's features, HT17; uses of, cHT21; Western Hemisphere, HT26

George, Henry, 134

George, David Lloyd, 176

George III, king of England, 7, 9

George W. Bush Institute (Pia Orrenius), q592

Georgia: 2020 elections, 612, 613, m621; secedes from U.S., m66, 66

German Americans, racism against, 177

German Democratic Republic, 338

German immigrants, 122, 304

Germany, East. See **East Germany.**

Germany, reunified, 357

Germany, West. See **West Germany.**

Germany, World War I: Austria-Hungary/Serbia war, 168; China leaseholds of, 162; division after World War I, 176; imperialism of, 154, m155; Lusitania sinking,

c156, 170; militarism, 167; navy of, 167; Samoan Islands, 158; Sussex sinking, 170; Treaty of Versailles, 176; Triple Alliance, 167; U-boat submarines, 170; World War I reparations, 176; zeppelin fleet, 172; Zimmermann, Arthur, 170

Germany, World War II, m306; Allies bombing, 307; attacking Soviet Union, 306; Austrian Anschluss, 283; Axis Powers, 285; as Axis Powers, 285; Battle of Stalingrad, 306; Belgium attacked by, 284; blitzkrieg, 284; bombing campaign, 307; concentration camps, 290–91, m290; declares war on U.S., 300; division of, 334, m334; Einsatzgruppen, 292; extermination camps, 290, m290, 291–92; Final Solution, 290–92; France and England declaring war on, 278, 283–84; France surrendering to, 284; Goebbels, Joseph, 287; Hitler, Adolf, 278, c280, 282; Hitler's suicide, 310; Holocaust, the, 287–92, m290; invading Poland, 278, c280, 283–84; Jews escaping, 288–89, p288, m289; Kristallnacht, 287–88, p288; Luxembourg attacked by, 284; Munich Conference, 283, p283; Nazi Party gaining power, 282; Netherlands attacked by, 284; nonaggression treaty with Soviet Union, 283, 330; Nuremberg Trials, 292; occupying Austria and Czechoslovakia, 278, 283–84; seizing Northern Italy, 307; submarines, 286, 305–06; surrender of, 310; Third Reich, 309–10; Wannsee Conference, 290

Gestapo during Kristallnacht, 288

Gettysburg, battle of, 75

Gettysburg address, q75

Ghost Dance, 101

ghost towns, 90

Gibbs, Lois, 578

GI Bill: creation of, 370, c372, 377; discrimination, 370, 377

Gideon v. Wainwright, 386–87

Giffords, Gabrielle, 588

Gilded Age, 133

Gilded Age, The: A Tale of Today (Mark Twain and Charles Warner), 133

Gill, Henry, q270

Gingrich, Newt, 550–51, q551

Ginsberg, Allen, 384

Ginsburg, Ruth Bader, 566, 602

"By Giving our Lives, We Find Life," from Stone Soup for the World: Life-Changing Stories of Everyday Heroes (Grossman, Marc), q493

Gladden, Washington, 135

glasnost, 356–57

Glass-Steagall Act, 254

global environment, 579–80

global grid, HT25

Global Iron Curtain. See **Iron Curtain.**

globalism/globalization: computer changing, 542; regional blocs, 540; rejecting globalism, 597; World Trade Organization (WTO), 540–41

globally competent citizen, HT19

Global Positioning System (GPS), 535

global warming, 580

globes, using, mHT22, mHT22–HT29

"In God We Trust", 34

Goebbels, Joseph, 287, 289

gold: Black Hills, 93, m94; in California, 62, 63; California Gold Rush, 90, 96; gold standard, 139, 253, 254, 333, 389–90; Klondike Gold Rush, 88, p89; Pikes Peak, 93, m94

Gold Standard Act, 139

Goldwater, Barry, 532

Gompers, Samuel, 119, 161, 208

Gone with the Wind, 251

Goode's Interrupted Equal-Area projection, HT24, mHT24

Google, 582

Gorbachev, Mikhail: Berlin Wall, 360; Bush, George H.W., q362; glasnost, 356–57; Intermediate Range Nuclear Forces (INF) Treaty, cHT4, 355; life of, 356; perestroika, 356; reforms of, 356–57, 360, 362; resignation of, 356; summit talks, 355, p515

Gore, Al: 2000 elections, 560, c562, 563–66, m565; Bush v. Gore, 565–66; campaign of, 563–64

Gore, Al, contested presidential election, c520

Gorgas, William Crawford, 164

Gorsuch, Neil, 602

Gospel of Wealth, 134

Gospel of Wealth and Other Timely Essays (Andrew Carnegie), 134

Gould, Jay, 114

Gouzenko, Igor, 373

government: big business and corporations, 115–18; Bureau of

Mines, 202; council-manager system, 198; economic policy, 137–38; Great Depression impacting, 264; initiative, 194, 198; Meat Inspection Act of 1906, 202, 205; New Deal expenditures, g248; Progressive Era reforms, 178, 194, 198, 203; Pure Food and Drug Act, 202, 205; recall by voters, 194, 198; referendum, 194, 198

governments, functions and forms of, HT18–HT19

graduated income tax, 139, 207

graft, 133

Graham, Billy, 533

Graham, Katharine, 523

Grand Canyon, pHT5

Grange (Patrons of Husbandry), 138

Grant, Ulysses S.: battling Robert E. Lee, 76; controlling Cumberland and Tennessee Rivers, 74; election of 1868, 78; Lee's surrender to, 76; Native American citizenship, 102, crt104; securing Mississippi River, 75

Grapes of Wrath, The (John Steinbeck), 252

graphs, using, HT32

grassroots movement, Perot, H. Ross, 540

grassroots populist movement, 584–85

Gratz v. Bollinger, 440

Gray, Freddie, 588

"Great American Desert", 97

Great Britain. See **Britain; Britain, World War I; Britain, World War II.**

great circle route, HT23, mHT23

Great Compromise (Connecticut Compromise), 22–23

Great Council of the Six Nations, 2

Great Depression: arts and entertainment, 251–52; bank run, 240, 245, p245; causes of, 236–37; consumerism, 236; economy, 239–41, 259; entertainment industry during, 251–52; federal work programs during Great Depression, 256–57, p257; Filipino Repatriation Act, 249; Gross Domestic Product (GDP), 240; hoboes, 249; Hoover, Herbert, 234, 241–43, 249; Hoover Dam, 234, p235; Hoovervilles, 243, 249; hunger marches, 242; legacy of, 264; life during, 249–52; literature, 252;

Mexican Repatriation, 249–50, 489; movies during, 251–52; National Credit Corporation (NCC), 242; Obama, Barack, 560; overproduction, 236; public works projects, 234, 241; radio during, 251–52; Reconstruction Finance Corporation (RFC), 242; stock market crash, 237, 240; tenant farmers, 251; unemployment, *c238*, 240; World War II ending, 302

Great Gatsby, The (F. Scott Fitzgerald), 212

Great Law of Peace (Gayaneshagowa), 2

Great Migration: (1917-1930), *m214*; of African American workers, 174; Harlem Renaissance, 195; impact of, 218; Jazz Age, 195; start of, *c196*

Great Northern Railroad, 114

Great Plains: bonanza farms, 98; cattle ranches, 95–96; droughts of, 98–99; Dust Bowl, 99, 237, *m237*, 250–51, *p250*; environmental impact of farming, 98; farming, 95–96, 98–99; "Great American Desert," 97; Homestead Acts, *c92*, 97; railroads impacting, 97; tenant farmers, 99

Great Plains native people, Cherokee people, 4–5

Great Railroad Strike, 119, *m120*

Great Recession: 596; American Recovery and Reinvestment Act, 560, 582; home foreclosures, *g583*; impact of, 558; income gap, 583; mortgage-backed investments, 576; national debt, 582; Obama, Barack, 558; "Occupy Wall Street" protesters, 583; subprime loans, 576

Great Seal of the United States, 33

Great Society, 388–89, 395–400

Greece, 337

greenbacks, 138

"Green Berets". See Special Operations Forces.

Green Hornet, 252

Green Party, 563, *m565*

Greenpeace, 548

Greensboro sit-ins, *c410*

Greenwich Village, Manhattan: arts and writers in, 210; LGBTQ community, 227; Stonewall riots, 481, 498, 510

Greenwood District, Tulsa, 213

Grenville, George, 7

Griswold v. *Connecticut*, 387, 487

Groves, Leslie R., 317–18

Grutter v. *Bollinger*, 440

Grynszpan, Herschel, 287

Guadalcanal, 316

Guam: annexation of, 154, *c156*; Spanish-American War, 160; Treaty of Paris, 160–61; World War II, 315

Guantánamo Bay, Cuba, 573

Guatemala, covert operations in, 342

Guelaguetza, 558

guerrilla warfare, in Vietnam War, 452

Guiding Light, The, 252

Gulbenkian Prize for Humanity, 580

Gulf of Tonkin Resolution, *c450*, 454, 457, 469

Gulf War, 570

gun control: Brady Bill, 547–48; Obama administration, 588; voters' concerns about, 519

Gun Control Act of 1968, 533

gun violence, Sandy Hook Elementary School, 588

Gutiérrez, José Angel, 493

Guzmán, Jacobo Arbenz, 342

gypsies, Nazis' treatment of, 287

H

Haitian Intervention, 550

Haitian Revolution, 66, 155

"Halfbreeds", 137

Haldeman, H.R. Bob, 528

Hallelujah, *p217*

Hamdan v. *Rumsfeld*, 573

Hamer, Fannie Lou, *p433*, *q433*

Hamer, Lou, 421

Hamilton, Alexander, at Constitutional Convention, 22

Hancock, John, *p17*

Harding, Warren G.: administration of, 223–24; election of 1920, 178; Emergency Quota Act, 226; radio announcing presidency of, 209

Harlan, Marshall, *q144*

Harlem: African American culture and politics in, 215; African Blood Brotherhood (ABB), 214; Universal Negro Improvement Association (UNIA), 214

Harlem Renaissance: African American artists and writers during, 192, 216, 252; explanations of, 215; Great Migration impacting, 195

Harlem Shadows (Claude McKay), *c196*, 216

Harpers Ferry, 65

Harriet Tubman National Historical Park, *p589*

Harris, Kamala, 612, 614, *p614*

Harris, Katherine, 565–66

Hatch, Orrin, 563, 591

hate crimes, 587

Hate Crimes Prevention Act of 2009, 587

Havana, Cuba, *c156*

Havana riots, 159

Hawaii: annexation of, 154, 158, 159; Dole as governor of, 158; Dominis, John Owen, 159; Hawaiian Republic, 158; Kalākaua, David, 158, 159; Kamehameha III, 159; Kamehameha IV, 159; Leleiohoku, William Pitt, 159; Liliuokalani, 158, 159, *p159*; overthrow of Queen Liliuokalani, *c156*, 158, 159; Pearl Harbor, 158, 278, *c280*, 299–300; sugar plantations of, 158; U.S. annexation of, 158

Hawley-Smoot Tariff, 236, *c238*

Hay, John, 162

Hayes, Rutherford B.: election of 1876, 78, 79–82, *m80*; ending patronage, 137; Great Railroad Strike, 119

Haymarket Riot, *c92*, 119, *m120*

Head Start, 389, 396, 552

health care reform, 583–84

health care system, Obama focusing on, 560

Health Insurance Portability and Accountability Act (HIPAA), 551

health programs, of Great Society, 399

Heart of Atlanta Motel, Inc. v. *United States*, 427, 436

Heatless Mondays, 173

"'He Was a Man Who Walked Tall Among Men': Duke Ellington, African American Audiences, and the Black Musical Entertainment Market, 1927–1943", 218

Helsinki Accords, 353

Hemingway, Ernest, 211, *p211*, 212

hemispheres, *mHT22*, HT26

hemispheric defense zone, 286

Henry, Patrick, 8

Henry Street Settlement, 136

Hepburn Act, 118

Heritage Foundation, 533, 548

Hernández v. *Texas*, 492

Herrera, José Joaquín ("El Capitán"), 95

Herzegovina, 358

Heston, Charlton, 548

Heumann, Judith, 500, *q502*

Hiawatha, Onondaga Chief, *ptg3*

Highlander Folk School, 406, 421

Hill, Anita, 539

Hill, A. P., 75

Hill, James J., 114

Hill, Oliver W., 418

Hine, Lewis, 203, *p203*

HIPAA. See Health Insurance Portability and Accountability Act (HIPAA).

Hirohito, 281

Hirohito, emperor of Japan, 312, 317

Hiroshima, *cHT4*, 279, 318, 368

Hiroshima (John Hersey), 376

Hispanics: in barrios, 96; Bracero program, 304, 387, 489–90; in California, 96; during California Gold Rush, 96; Herrera, José Joaquín ("El Capitán"), 95; *Las Gorras Blancas*, 95; Mexican land grants, 96; in New Mexico territory, 96; "Operation Wetback," 388; poverty of, 387–88; Sotomayor, Sonia, 584; Spanish-speaking people, 490; in Texas territory, 96; in World War II, 301. *See also* Latinos; Mexican Americans.

Hiss, Alger, 374

historians: analyze information, HT16; analyzing sources, HT10; Bair, Barbara, *pHT6*; categorizing, HT15; cause and effects, HT14–HT15; changing interpretations, HT9; comparing and contrasting, HT15; compelling questions, HT9; considering bias, HT11; continuity and change, HT14; dating events, HT7; different interpretations, HT12; drawing conclusions, HT16; error and chance in history, HT14; evaluating relevance, HT9; examining evidence, HT6–HT7; finding main ideas, HT15; frame of reference, HT11; historical inquiry, HT9; identify point of view, HT11; interpreting history, HT13; logical connections, HT14; making generalizations, HT16; making inferences, HT16; measuring and organizing time, HT7–HT8; multiple perspectives, HT11; predicting, HT16; primary and secondary sources, HT10; science and, HT19; sequencing events, HT15; time and place, HT8, HT13–HT14; using charts, graphs, and diagrams, HT32; using past to understand future, HT5–HT7; using time lines, HT8

historical inquiry, HT9

history: civics and, HT18–HT19; continuity and change in, HT14; economics and, HT18; error and chance in, HT14; importance of studying, HT5–HT7; interpreting, HT13; researching and writing about, HT11–HT12; social studies and, HT17

History of U.S. Decision-Making in Vietnam, 1945–68 (Daniel Ellsberg), 469

Hitler, Adolf: arrest of, 282; becomes chancellor, c280, 282; defying Treaty of Versailles, 278, 282–83; invading Poland, 278, c280, 283–84; negotiations with, 278, 282–83; occupying Austria and Czechoslovakia, 278, 283; rise of, 278, c280, 282; suicide of, 310; underestimating U.S. strategy, 300

hoboes, 249

Ho Chi Minh, 448, 451, p451, p453

Ho Chi Minh City, 446, 470

Ho Chi Minh Trail, 455–56, m456, 467

Hohokam people, 4

holding companies, 112

Holland, Spessard, 426

Hollandia, New Guinea, 316

Holly, Buddy, 384

Hollywood: adapts to television, 384; golden age of, 212; "Hollywood Ten," 374; House Un-American Activities Committee (HUAC) hearings, 374; LGBTQ community in 1920s, 227; Reagan, actor in, 519

Holmes, Oliver Wendell, 117

Holocaust, the: Auschwitz, 291, p291; Buchenwald, 290–91; Chelmno, m290, 291; concentration camps, 290–91, m290; *Einsatzgruppen*, 292; extermination camps, 290, m290, 291–92; factors contributing to, 292; Final Solution, 290–92; gas chambers, 290; Jews escaping Nazi Germany, 288–89, p289; *Kristallnacht*, 287–88; Nuremberg Laws, 287; Nuremberg Trials, 292; Treblinka, m290, 291; Wannsee Conference, 290; Warsaw ghetto, p292

home foreclosures, g583

Home Owners' Loan Corporation (HOLC), 255

Homestead Acts, c92, 97, 250

Homesteader, The (Oscar Micheaux), 216

Homestead steel mill strike, 119, m120

Homestead Strike, c92

Hooker, Isabella Beecher, p70

Hooker Chemical Company, The, p578

hooks, bell, 485, p485, 506

Hoover, Herbert: economic policies of, 224–25; election of 1928, c238, 239; election of 1932, 243; Emergency Relief and Construction Act, 242; Farm Relief Bill, p241; Great Depression, 234, 241–43, 249; Hoover Dam, 234, p235; Hoovervilles, 243, 249; inaugural address, 239; political philosophy of, 241–42; public works projects, 234, 241; relief, 242; secretary of commerce, 223; view on socialism, q241

Hoover, J. Edgar, 373–74

Hoover Dam, 234, p235

Hoovervilles, 243, 249

Hope, Bob, 383–84

Hopi people, 496

Hopkins, Harry, 256

Hopkins, Mark, 113

Hopper, Edward, 211

horizontal integration, 112, c150

Hornet, 312, 314

horsecars, 131

Horton, Myles, 421

House Judiciary Committee, 524

House of Burgesses, 8, 9

House of Representatives, establishment of, 23, ptg24, c26, 27, c28

Houser, George, 418

House Un-American Activities Committee (HUAC), 373–74, p373

Housing Act, 386

housing discrimination, c372, 409, c410, 435, 438

housing market during Great Recession, 576

Howe, Julia Ward, 199

Howe, Louis, 244

Howe, William, 10

"Howl" (Allen Ginsberg), 384

"How the Computer Revolution Changed U.S. Cities," *Bloomberg* (Eric Jaffe), q545

How the Other Half Lives (Jacob Riis), 132, 194

"*How Woodrow Wilson's Propaganda Machine Changed American Journalism*" (Christopher B. Daly), q180

Huerta, Dolores, 492–93, p493, 507

Huerta, Victoriano, 155, 165–66

Huey helicopter, 455, p455

Huggins, Ericka, 438

Hughes, Charles Evans, 168–69, q169, 223–24, 225

Hughes, Langston, 192, 216, 220, ptg220

Hull, Cordell, 333

Hull House, q130, 135–36, c196

human/environment interaction, HT21

Human Rights Campaign, 549, p549

human sexuality in 1920s, 226–27

human systems, cHT22

Humphrey, Hubert, 426, 461, m462, 521

Hundred Days, 253

Hungary: after World War I, 175; democratic government replacing communism, 357; Soviet Union controlling, 328, 336; Soviet Union satellite nation, 336; uprising against Soviet Union, 342; Warsaw Pact, 338

hunger marches, 242

hunger strikes: farmworkers' rights, 492, p508; women's rights and suffrage, 200, 229

Huntington, Collis P., 113

Hunton, Eppa, q81

Hurricane Katrina, 560, c562, 574–75, p574; levee system, 560, c562, 574–75

Hurston, Zora Neale, 192, p193, 216, 252, 260

Hussein, Saddam, 537–38, 570

hydraulic mining, 94

hydroelectric dam, Hoover Dam, 234, p235

hyperconnectivity, 582

I

IBM. *See* International Business Machines (IBM).

I Came a Stranger: The Story of a Hull-House Girl (Hilda Satt Polacheck), q130

Iceland, 338

ice-making machine, 110

Idaho, women's suffrage, 199

"I Have a Dream" (Martin Luther King, Jr.), q425

I Led Three Lives, 376

illegal immigrants: differing perspectives about, 480; Eisenhower deporting, 490;

increasing number of, 491; population in 2000, m481

Illegal Immigration Reform and Immigrant Responsibility Act of 1996, 491

I Love Lucy, 383

immigrants/immigration: Alien Registration Act of 1940, 304; antisemitism, 123, 128–30; Asian, m121, 123, p123, 127; border wall, 591, 593; Bracero program, 304, 387, 489–90; changes in laws of, 490–92; Chinese Exclusion Act of 1882, 123, 127; from Cuba, 490, p491, 494; culture of, 121–22; economic status in 1920s, 210; Ellis Island, 121–22, 129, p129; Emergency Quota Act, 226; European, 121–22, m121, g126; factors limiting Jews, 288–89; family separation, p600, 600–01; Filipino Repatriation Act, 249; during Great Depression, 249–50; Hull House, q130, 135–36, c196; illegal, 480, m481, 490, 491, g494; Illegal Immigration Reform and Immigrant Responsibility Act of 1996, 491; Immigration Act of 1882, 123; Immigration Act of 1965, 480, 491; Immigration Act of 1990, 491; Immigration Reform and Control Act of 1986, 491; Jewish immigrants, 122, 128–30, 132; late 1800s, c122, m124, m148; McCarran-Walter Act, 375, g472, 491; Mexican Repatriation, 249–50, 489; migration chains, 491; myths of, p590; National Origins Act, 226; nativism impacting, 123, 225–26; naturalization, 226; 1975-1989, g472; progressivism impacting, 194, p194; quota system, 226, 480, 490–91; racial and ethnic strife over, 125; racial tensions over, 195, 213; Reagan, Ronald, 589; Refugee Act of 1980, g472, 491; refugees, amnesty for, 480, 491; restriction during World War II, 304; from South Vietnam, 472, p472; Trump restricting, 601; urbanization impacted by, p132, 133; voters' concerns about, 519

Immigration Act of 1882, 123

Immigration Act of 1965, 480, 491

Immigration Act of 1990, 491

Immigration and Naturalization Act of 1965, 389

Immigration Reform and Control Act of 1986, 491

imperialism, *m155*; Anglo-Saxonism, 157–58; cultural superiority, 157–58; economic reasons for, 154, 157. *See also* **American imperialism**; **European imperialism**; *specific nations.*

inaugural address: Carter, Jimmy, 353; Hoover, Herbert, 239; Roosevelt, Franklin D., *q247*, 253, *q263*, 293; Truman, Harry S., 337

income gap, 583

income taxes: graduated or progressive, 207; Sixteenth Amendment establishing, 50, *c196*, 207

Indemnity Act, *c8*

Indian boarding schools, 102, 103, 104, 108

Indian Civil Rights Act, 481, *c482*, 495

Indian New Deal, 257–58

Indian Peace Commission, 100

Indian Reorganization Act, 102, 250, 257–58

Indian Rights Association, 102

Indian Self-Determination and Educational Assistance Act of 1975, 481, 496

Indians of All Tribes, 495–96, *p496*, 509, *p509*

Indian Wars, causes of, 97

indigenous people. *See* **Native Americans**.

individualism, during Gilded Age, 133–34

individual rights, 27

Indochina: France leaving, 448, *c450*, 452, 463; Ho Chi Minh's communist politics in, 451

industrialism, 134

Industrial Revolution, second, *m195*; early 1900s, 195; electric power, 109–10; natural resources, 109; workforce, 109; working conditions, 118–20

industrial unions, 118–19. *See also* **unions**.

Industrial Workers of the World (IWW), *c92*, 119–20

industry: consolidating, 111; improved technologies expanding, 90; Office of War Mobilization, 302; "Rosie the Riveter," 302; U.S. advantages in, 109–11; War Production Board (WPB), 302; women during World War II, 302; during World War I, 173–74; during World War II, 301–02, *g302*

inferences, HT16

inflation, 8; cause of, 138; crisis of 1970s, 389; during Great Depression, 254; post-World War II, 377

***Influence of Sea Power Upon History, The* (Alfred T. Mahan)**, 154, 158

influenza pandemic of 1918-1919 (Spanish Flu), *c156*, 175–76, *p176*

information, analyzing: categorizing, HT15; comparing and contrasting, HT15; drawing conclusions, HT16; finding main ideas, HT15; making generalizations, HT15; making inferences, HT16; predicting, HT16; sequencing events, HT15

initiative, 194, 198

innovations in the 1920s, 209

Inouye, Daniel, *q526*

installment plans, 210, 236

insurrection. *See* **Harpers Ferry**.

Intel, 542

interchangeable parts, 111

intercontinental ballistic missiles (ICBMs), 343

Intermediate Range Nuclear Forces (INF) Treaty, *cHT4*, 355

Internal Security Act, 375

International Business Machines (IBM), *c520*, 542

International Harvester, 208

International Ladies' Garment Workers Union (ILGWU), 120

International Military Tribunal (IMT), 292, 318

International Military Tribunal for the Far East (IMTFE), 318

International Monetary Fund (IMF), 333

International Women's Year, 508

Internet, *pHT12*, *c520*, 542, 544

***Interpretation of Harlem Jazz* (Winold Reiss)**, *ptg221*

interpret history, HT12; different interpretations, HT14; time and place, HT13

interracial marriage laws, 497

interstate commerce, 116–17, *crt117*, 201

Interstate Commerce Commission (ICC), 115, 137–38, 201, 422

Interstate Highway System, 370, *m371*, *c372*, 380

inventions. *See* **technology**.

investment banks, 112, 254–55

investors in big businesses, 112

iPads, 582

iPhone, 582

Iran: Ayatollah Khomeini, 353; Cold War crisis in, 336–37, 353; covert operations in, 342; Iran-Contra Scandal, 354; nuclear deal, 586, 599; Tehran hostages, 353–54, 586

Iran-Contra Scandal, 354

Iraq: Abu Ghraib prison, 573; airstrikes in, 572; al-Qaeda (AQI), 571–72; continued violence in, 571; Hussein, Saddam, 537–38, 570; Islamic State in Iraq and Syria (ISIS), 572; left-wing rebels seizing, 342; Obama withdrawing from, 572; Operation Desert Storm, 538, *m538*; Persian Gulf War, 538, *m538*; War on Terror, 560, *c562*, 570–71, *p571*

Irish immigrants, 122

Iron Curtain, *p330*, 335–36

Iron Curtain, descends, 330

Iroquois Confederacy: Canassatego (Onondaga Nation), *q2*; Cayuga people, 2; Deganawida (The Peacemaker), 2; democratic government of, 2; Five Nations (Iroquois Confederacy), 2–3, *ptg3*; French and, 2; in French and Indian War, 7; Great Law of Peace (Gayaneshagowa), 2; Hiawatha, Onondaga Chief, *ptg3*; impact of Revolutionary War, 12; Iroquois Confederacy, *ptg3*; Jigonsaseh, 2; Mohawk people, 2; Oneida people, 2; Onondaga people, 2, *ptg3*; "Peacemaker" story (Iroquois), 2; during Revolutionary War, 10; Seneca people, 2; Six Nations (Iroquois Confederacy), 2–3; Tuscarora people, 2

Iroquois people, 5

"the Irreconcilables", 177

irrigation, of Anasazi people, 4

Islamic State in Iraq and Syria (ISIS), 572

isolationism: following World War I, 225; during World War II, 278, 284–86, *crt285*, 293–98

Israel: Barak, Ehud, 550; Camp David Accords, 353, *p353*; Declaration of Principles, 550; Gaza and West Bank, 550; Jerusalem, 550; Jordan peace treaty, 550; Rabin, Yitzhak, 550, *p550*; relations with Palestinians, 550; Six-Day War, 461; U.S. support for, 568; war of, 389

Italian immigrants, 122

Italy, *m306*; African American regiments attacking, 276; Allies attacking, 307; as Axis Powers, 285; declare war on U.S., 300; Ethiopia invaded by, 284–85; Germany seizing, 307; imperialism of, 154, *m155*; joins Allies, 168; Munich Conference, 283, *p283*; Mussolini, Benito, 278, *c280*, 281–82, *p282*; Mussolini deposed, 307; NATO, 338; surrendering to the Allies, 307; Triple Alliance, 167; war-ravaged towns, *p275*

Itliong, Larry, 492–93, 507

I Was a Communist for the FBI, 376

IWW. *See* **Industrial Workers of the World (IWW)**.

J

Jackson, Jesse, 440

Jackson, Maynard, 439

Jackson, Michael, 535

Jackson, Robert, 318

Jackson State College, antiwar protests, 468

Jaffe, Eric, 545

Jamestown, founding of, *cHT4*

"Jane Crow", 485

Japan: atomic bombs dropped on, *cHT4*, 279, *c280*, 318, 368; attacking Japan, 312–13; as Axis Powers, 285; Battle of Iwo Jima, 316–17, *p317*; Battle of Leyte Gulf, 316; Battle of Midway, 313–14, *m314*; Battle of the Coral Sea, 313; China attacked by, 285; economic and military power of, 225; Hideki Tōjō, 281; Hirohito, emperor of Japan, 281, 312, 317; invading Philippines, 311–12; island hopping in the Pacific, 314, *m315*; joining Axis Powers, 299; kamikaze, 316; MacArthur, Douglas controlling, 339; military control of, 278, 281; Okinawa, 317; Open Door Policy, 155, 162; Pearl Harbor attacked by, *cHT4*, 278, *c280*, 299–300; "Rape of Nanking," 281; Roosevelt declaring war on, 278, *c280*, 299–300; surrender of, *cHT4*, 279, 318; Tokyo bombed, 312, 317; Treaty of Kanagawa, 158; Vietnam under, 448, 451; V-J (Victory Over Japan) Day, *c280*, 318; war over Korea with China, 154, 162; Yamamoto attacking Midway, 312, 313

Japanese Americans: Executive Order 9066, 304, *p304*; internment of, *c280*, 304, *p304*, *c482*; in military in World War II, 279, 301; serving in World War II, 279

Jaworski, Leon, 524, 528

Jay, John, Treaty of Paris, 11

jazz: Armstrong, Louis, 216; development of, 215; Ellington, Edward "Duke," 216; Europe, James Reese, 216; importance of, 216

Jazz Age, Great Migration impacting, 195

Jazz Singer, The (motion picture), *c196*, 212

Jefferson, Thomas: Committee of Five, 10, 13, *ptg13*; House of Burgesses, 8; response to *Gaspee* affair, 9; suggesting Bill of Rights, *q57*

Jerusalem, 550

Jews: Anti-Defamation League (ADL), 226; anti-Semitism of Nazis, 282, 287–92; in Chicago, 130; Civil Rights Act of 1968, 438; concentration camps, 290–91, *m290*; discrimination, 287; *Einsatzgruppen*, 292; Ellis Island arrival, 129; escaping Nazi Germany, 288–89, *p288*, *m289*; extermination camps, 290, *m290*, 291–92; Fair Housing Act of 1968, 438; Final Solution, 290–92; Grynszpan, Herschel, 287; Holocaust, the, 287–92, *m290*; immigration of 1890-1910, 122; Jewish state of Israel, 568; Jewish Welfare Board, 175; *Kristallnacht*, 287–88, *p288*; Ku Klux Klan (KKK) attacking, 195, 213; in New York City, 128, 132; Nuremberg Laws, 287; Shoah, 287–92, *m290*; Warsaw ghetto, *p292*

Jigonsaseh, 2

Jim Crow laws: passing of, 140, 143–46; segregation, 408, 412, *p412*; violent tensions over, 195; voting barriers, 200

Jingoism, 160

Job Corps, *p522*

Jobs, Steve, 542, 582

John Brown's rebellion, 65

Johnson, Andrew: black codes, 77; impeachment of, 78; Reconstruction, 77

Johnson, Charles S., 192, 215

Johnson, Hiram, *crt285*

Johnson, "Lady Bird", *p395*, *p396*

Johnson, Lyndon Baines: affirmative action, 439; antipoverty campaign, 387–89, 397; anti-poverty tour, 397, *p397*; "Bloody Sunday," 427; Civil Rights Act of 1957, 421; Civil Rights Act of 1964, 426; crisis of 1970s, 389–90; Economic Opportunity Act, 388, *q398*; election of 1964, 532; election of 1968, 461; Great

Society, 388–89, 395–400; Indians of All Tribes, 509; Job Corps, *p522*; National Advisory Commission on Civil Disorders, 435; presidency of, 387; Vietnam War, 448, 454, 457, 460, 463, 464–65, *q465*

Johnson, Robert, 535

Johnson's plan, 77

Johnston, Olin D., 426, *p426*

Johnston, Philip, 313

Jones, Bobby, 212

Jones, Mary Harris, 120

Jordan, 550

Jordan, Hamilton, 353

Jordan, I. King, 500

Jorgensen, Christine, 227

Joseph, chief of Nez Perce, 100–101

Journal of African American History, The, *q218*

"Joy to the World", *crt363*

Judah, Theodore, 113

judicial branch: district and appellate courts, 29; establishment of, 22, 23–24, *c26*; judicial review, 30; structure of, 29–30, *c30*; Supreme Court, 29, *c30*

judicial review, 30

Jungle, The (Upton Sinclair), 202

K

Kagan, Elena, 584

Kahlo, Frida, 493

Kaiser, Henry, 302

Kalākaua, David, 158, 159

Kamakaeha, Lydia. *See* **Liliuokalani, queen of Hawaii**.

kamikaze, 316

Kansas: "Bleeding Kansas," 65; cattle drives to, 95; establishment of, 64–65; John Brown's rebellion, 65; Kansas-Nebraska Act, 64; Lawrence, ptg65; two territorial governments of, 65

Kansas-Nebraska Act, 64

Karzai, Hamid, 570

Katzenbach v. Morgan, 428

Kaufmann, Gordon B., 234

Kavanaugh, Brett, 602

Keating-Owen Child Labor Act, 208

Kelley, Florence, 198, *q206*

Kelley, Oliver H., 138

Kelley Act, 209

Kellogg, Frank, 225

Kellogg-Briand Pact, 225

Kelo v. City of New London, 575

Kennan, George, 336

Kennedy, Anthony, 534, 584, 602

Kennedy, John F.: affirmative action, 439; Alliance for Progress, 343; Area Redevelopment Act, 386; assassination of, 387, 425–26; civil rights support, 422, *q424*; Cold War strategies, 343–44; Commission on the Status of Women, 483–84; Committee on Juvenile Delinquency and Youth Crime, 386; disabled, rights of, 386; election of 1960, 343, 385, *m385*; Equal Pay Act, 386, 484; expanding Special Operations Forces, 343; "flexible response," 343; foreign policy crisis, 338; Housing Act, 386; Immigration Reform and Control Act of 1986, 491; minimum wage, 386; missile gap, 385; missiles, build-up of, 343; New Frontier, 385–86; Peace Corps, 343, *c372*; Presidential Commission on the Status of Women, 386, 484; space exploration, 347, 348; support of South Vietnam, 453; VISTA program, 547; Warren Court reforms, 386–87; women's rights, 386

Kennedy, Robert: assassination of, 461, *p461*; Chávez, César and, 508, *p508*; civil rights support, 422; supporting farmworkers, *q507*

Kent State University, antiwar protests, *c450*, 468, *p468*

Kent State University Special Collections and Archives (Lorrie Accettola), *q468*

Kerner Commission, 435

Kerouac, Jack, 384

Kerry, John, 573

Key, Francis Scott, 33

Keynesianism, 263

Khrushchev, Nikita: Berlin Wall, 338; demanded West Berlin, 342; as Soviet Union leader, 342

King, Coretta, 435

King, Martin Luther, Jr.: arrest and imprisonment of, 423–24; assassination of, *c410*, 438, *p438*, 461; Birmingham Campaign, 423–25; "Call for Unity, A," *Birmingham Times*, 424; Chicago Movement, 435–36; civil rights activist, 429; "I Have a Dream," *q425*; "Letter from Birmingham Jail," 424; March on Washington in 1963, 425; Montgomery Bus Boycott, 406, *c410*, 419; Nobel Peace

Prize, 427; nonviolent passive resistance, 419; Selma March, 427; view of Vietnam War, 459

King, Rodney, 539, *p539*

King's Illustrated Portfolio of Our Country, *g126*

Kiowa people, 104

Kissinger, Henry: Détente Policy, 351–52; Le Duc Tho negotiations, 469–70; life of, 352; linkage, 467; Nixon Doctrine, 351; Vietnamization, 351

Klein, Freada, *p484*

Klondike Gold Rush, 88, *p89*

Knights of Labor, 119, 120

Know-Nothings (American Party), 65

Kohl, Helmut, 357

Korea, 155, 162

Korean War, *p340*; Cold War and, 339–41; demilitarized zone (DMZ), 340; Eisenhower, Dwight D., 379–80; limited war, 340; North Korea, 339–41; People's Republic of China, 340; South Korea, 339–41

Korematsu, Toyosaburo, 304

Korematsu v. United States, 304, 600

Kosovo, ethnic cleansing, 358

Kristallnacht, 287–88, *p288*

Ku Klux Klan (KKK): Charlottesville, Virginia, protest, 607; murdering SNCC workers, 421; new Klan in 1915, 195, *c196*, 213; restricting immigration, 226

Kurds, Sunni, 571

Kuwait, 537, 538, 571, 598

Kwajalein Atoll in the Marshall Islands, 315

Kyoto Protocol, 580

L

labor-saving devices, in the 1920s, 209

La Brigada, 343

LaDuke, Winona, 563

Lafayette, Marquis de, 10, 11

La Follette, Robert M., 198, *q269*

laissez-faire, 90, 111, 112, 115

Lake Mead, 234

Lakota people: Americanization of, *p103*; Battle of Little Bighorn, 100; Dakota Territory, 99–100; Great Plains people, 61; Sitting Bull, *c92*, *p92*; Wounded Knee, 101

land-based missiles, atomic bombs, 341

land claim commission, 96
Land-Grant College Act (Morrill Act), 90, *m91*, *c92*
Landon, Alfred, 262
Land Ordinances of 1785, 19
Lange, Dorothea, 252
Langley Avenue All Nations Pentecostal Church, 228
Laos, 470
LaPierre, Wayne, 548
La Raza Unida, *c482*, 493
Las Gorras Blancas, 95
Latimer, Lewis, 110
Latin American nations: Alliance for Progress, 343; during Cold War, 343; Roosevelt Corollary, 155, *m164*; U.S. intervention in, 163–64
Latinos: Bilingual Education Act, 493; Chávez, César, 492–93, *p493*, 507; Chicano Mural Movement, 493, *p512*; Cuban refugee, 490, *p491*; discrimination, 489–94; Gutiérrez, José Angel, 493; Huerta, Dolores, 492–93, *p493*, 507; immigration limits for, 491; *La Raza Unida*, *c482*, 493; from Latin America, 490; League of United Latin American Citizens (LULAC), 492; Mexican American Youth Organization (MAYO), 493; population of, *g490*; post–World War II discrimination, 370; protests and progress for, 492–93; reproductive rights of, 399. *See also* Hispanics; Mexican Americans.
latitude, HT25
Lavender Scare, 374
Lawrence, Kansas, ptg65
Lawson, James M., 430
lead, in Leadville, 93, *m94*
League of Nations: idea of, 176, 181; opposition to, 177, 182
League of United Latin American Citizens (LULAC), 492
League to Limit Armament, 169
Leahy, William, 318
leaseholds, 162
Lebanon, 342, 354
Lecompton constitution, 65–66
Le Duc Tho, 467, 469–70
Lee, Robert E.: Battle of Antietam, 74; Battle of Gettysburg, 75; Grant battling, 76; surrender at Appomattox Court House, 76
Lee, Russell, *p412*
Legal Defense and Educational Fund, 418
legislative branch: bills becoming law, 27, *c28*; establishment of,

23; organization of, *c26*, 27; two-house legislature, 22, 23
Lehrer, Jim, 529
Leigh, Vivien, 251
Leleiohoku, William Pitt, 159
LeMay, Curtis, 317
Lend-Lease Act, 278, *c280*, *q286*, 299
Lenin, Vladimir: death of, 282; seizing power, 175
lesbian, gay, bisexual, transgender, and queer (LGBTQ) community: in 1920s, 227; AIDS Coalition to Unleash Power (ACT UP), 536; civil rights movement, 498–99; Craig, Gwenn, *q510*; Gay Liberation Front (GLF), 498; gender identity rights, 481; homosexuals, Nazis' treatment of, 287; Human Rights Campaign, 549, *p549*; Lavender Scare, 374; marriage rights for, 536; Milk, Harvey, 499; sexual orientation rights, 481; Society for Human Rights, 481; Stonewall riots, 481, 498, 510
Lesseps, Ferdinand de, 153
levee system, 560, *c562*, 574–75
Levittowns, 381, *p381*
Lewis, John L., 260, 427, 429
Lewis, Sinclair, 211
Lexington, 313
Lexington and Concord, battle of, 9
LGBTQ community, same-sex marriages, 587
Libby, Willard Frank, HT20
liberals/liberalism: 2000 elections, 563–66; NARAL Pro-Choice America, 549; views of, 531
Liberty Bonds, 173, *g174*
Liberty ships, 302
Libya, Arab Spring, 572
Lieberman, Joseph, 563
Life magazine, 252
light bulb, 109
Liliuokalani, queen of Hawaii, *c156*, 158, 159, *p159*
limited government, 25
Limited Nuclear Test Ban Treaty, 344
limited war, 340
Lin, Maya, *p448*
Lincoln, Abraham: 1860 presidential election, 66; assassination of, 76; election of 1864, 76; Emancipation Proclamation, *cHT4*, *c6*, 74–75; Gettysburg address, *q75*; Reconstruction plans, 76–77
Lincoln, Benjamin, 21
Lindbergh, Charles, 209
literacy tests, 140, 408

literature: folklore, 192; during Great Depression, 252; Harlem Renaissance, 192; vernacular writing, 192
Little, Malcolm, 437
Little Richard, 384, *p384*
Little Rock, AR, school desegregation violence, *c410*, 419, 420–21
living document (Constitution), 34
Livingston, Robert R., 13, *ptg13*
location, geographical, HT21
Lochner v. New York, 197
Locke, Alain, 216, 218
Locke, John, 14, 221
lockouts, 118
Lodge, Henry Cabot, 177, 453
Logan, Rayford, 140
London, Jack, 135
Lonely Crowd, The (David Riesman), 382
Long, Huey, 259, *p260*, *q267*
Long, Russell, 426
Long, Stephen, 97
Long Day's Journey Into Night (Eugene O'Neill), 211
Longest Day, 309
longitude, HT25
"Long Live the Constitution of the United States," American Socialist Party, *q184*
long-range bombers, for atomic bombs, 341
long-range radios, 455
Long Telegram, 336
Look Homeward, Angel (Thomas Wolfe), 252
Looking Backward (Edward Bellamy), 135
"Looting and Liberal Racism," Commentary (Midge Decter), *q531*
Los Angeles, Spanish roots of, 489
lottery system of draft, 449, 460
Louisiana: Hurricane Katrina, 560, *c562*, 574–75, *p574*; levee system, 560, *c562*, 574–75; secedes from U.S., *m66*, 66; Separate Car Act, 143; voting literacy tests, 140, 408
Love Canal, New York, 578–79, *p578*
Love Canal: The Story Continues (Lois Gibbs), *q578*
Loving, Richard and Mildred, 497, *p497*
Loving v. Virginia, 497
low consumption theory, 255
Lowe, Thaddeus, 110
Lowell, Amy, 211
Lower Tidewater in Black and White (Lucy Overton), *q412*
low interest rates, 237

Lowndes County Freedom Organization (LCFO), 437
loyalty review program, 373–74
Luce, Henry, 252
Lusitania, *c156*, 170
Luxembourg: Germany attacking, 284; NATO, 338

M

M28/M29 Davy Crockett nuclear weapon system, 376
MacArthur, Douglas: Bonus Army, 243; controlling occupied Japan, 339; Korean War, 340; in Philippines, 299, 316; retreating to Bataan Peninsula, 311
machine gun, 172
Maddox, Lester, 419
Madero, Francisco, 165
Madison, James: at Constitutional Convention, 21–22; Jefferson's letter to, *q57*
Madonna, 535
Maggie, A Girl of the Streets (Stephen Crane), 135
Magna Carta, *q60*
Mahan, Alfred T., 154, 158
mail bombs, Red Scare, 178, 185, 186
mail-order catalogs, 112
main ideas, HT15
Main Street (Sinclair Lewis), 211
"Make America Great Again", 597, 617
Malcolm X, 214, 437
Manchuria, 162, 281
Mandela, Nelson, 537
Mangold, Luana, 108
Manhattan Project, 317–18
Manifest Destiny, 157
Manila Bay, 160
Mann-Elkins Act, *c196*
manufacturing: dangers of, 90; impact of, 90; improving quality of life, 111; interchangeable parts, 111; steel mills, 111–12
"The Man Who Is Leading the Fight for Pure Food," Washington Times, *q205*
Mao Zedong, 339
map projections, HT23–HT24
Mapp v. Ohio, 386
maps: absolute location, HT28; cartographer, *HT22*; converting globes to, *mHT22*; projections, HT23, HT24; reading, HT27–HT29; relative location, HT28; scale, HT28; types, *HT22*, HT29
maquiladoras, 540

March on Washington in 1941, *c410*

March on Washington in 1963, *p405*, *c410*, 425

Mariana Islands, 315

Mariel boat lift, *p491*

Marin, John, 211

Marines: Continental Congress establishing, 10; in Vietnam War, *p445*; World War II, growth of, 300–301, *g300*

marital privacy rights, 487

Marshall, George C., 300, 331, 337–38, *g337*, 375

Marshall, Thurgood: federal judgeship of, 422; Legal Defense and Educational Fund, 418

Marshall Islands, 315

Marshall Plan, 331, 337–38, *g337*, 379

Marshall State Flight Center, 371

Martí, José, 158, 159

Martin, Trayvon, 587

Marx, Groucho, 240

Marx, Karl, 118

Marx Brothers, 251

Maryland Toleration Act, 56

Mason, Skookum Jim, 88

Massachusetts: battles at Boston, 10; enslaved people suing for freedom, 12; Massachusetts Provincial Congress, 9; same-sex marriages, 587; Shays's Rebellion, 21

mass advertising, 210

massive retaliation, 341

mass media, 212, 383–84

mass-produced suburbs, 381

mass production, 208–09, 302

mass transit, 131

Master Plan for Higher Education, 380

Mattachine Society, 498

Maya Lin, 471

Mayan people and civilization, 4

McCain, Franklin, 421

McCain, John, 469, 563, 581

McCain-Feingold Act, 584

McCarran-Walter Act, 375, *g472*, 491

McCarthy, Eugene, 461

McCarthy, Joseph R., 374–76, *q374–q75*

McCarthy hearings, *c372*

McCarthyism, 374–76, 485

McClellan, George B., 74

McCord, James, 523

McCormick, Ruth Hanna, 201

McDaniel, Hattie, 251

McDonald v. Chicago, 588

McGovern, George, 469–70

McKay, Claude, 216, 221

McKinley, William: assassination of, 163; Hawaii annexation, 158; McKinley Tariff, 138; Open Door Policy, 162; presidency of, 139; USS *Maine*, 159

McKinley Tariff, 138

McNeil, Joseph, 421

McPherson, Aimee Semple, 228

McVeigh, Timothy, 551–52

Meade, George, 75

Means, Russell, 496

Meat Inspection Act of 1906, *p201*, 202, 205

meatpacking industry, *p201*, 202

mechanical reapers, 98

Medal of Honor: Baker, Vernon, 276, *p277*; York, Alvin Cullum, 171, *p171*

media, during Vietnam War, 457–58

Medicaid, establishment of, *c372*, 388

medical care: cancer treatments, radiation and chemotherapy, 371, 383; cardiopulmonary resuscitation technique (CPR), 371, 383; Great Society's health programs, 399; medical breakthroughs, 383; Medicare and Medicaid, *c372*, 388; oral polio vaccine, 383; polio vaccine, *c372*, *p372*, 383; post-World War II advances in, 371, 383

Medicare, establishment of, *c372*, 388

Mein Kampf (Adolf Hitler), 282

Mellon, Andrew, 223, 224

Memorandum for the President (Brent Scowcroft), *q361*

"Memorandum on Conference with FDR Concerning Social Security Taxation" (Franklin D. Roosevelt), *q261*

Memorial Day Massacre, 261

Memorial to the Legislature of Massachusetts (Dorothea Dix), *q68*

Memphis, jazz in, 215

Memphis Free Speech and Headlight (Ida B. Wells), 141

Mendez v. Westminster, 492

Mental Retardation Facilities and Community Mental Health Centers Construction Act of 1963, 386

Mercator projection, HT24, *mHT24*

Mesoamerican civilizations: Aztec people, 4; Chichimec people, 4; Mayan people, 4; Olmec people, 4; Toltec people, 4

MeToo, 605–06

Mexica, 4

Mexican Americans: in barrios, 489; Bilingual Education Act, 493; Bracero program, 304, 387, 489–90; Chávez, César, 492–93, *p493*, 507; Chicano Mural Movement, 493, *p512*; discrimination, 489–94; Gutiérrez, José Angel, 493; Huerta, Dolores, 492–93, *p493*, 507; Immigration Act of 1965, 480; immigration in 1920s, 226; immigration limits for, 491; *La Raza Unida*, *c482*, 493; Mexican American Youth Organization (MAYO), 493; Mexican Repatriation, 249–50, 489; migration during World War I, 174; migration during World War II, 304; population of, *g490*; protests and progress for, 492–93; "zoot suit" riots, 303

Mexican-American War, 63

Mexican American Youth Organization (MAYO), 493

Mexico: Carranza, Venustiano, 166; Díaz, Porfirio, 165; Huerta, Victoriano, 155, 165–66; Madero, Francisco, 165; North American Free Trade Agreement (NAFTA), 540; Treaty of Guadalupe Hidalgo, 63; Veracruz, 166; war with, 63; Wilson's intervention in, 155, 165–66

Mexico City, Mexican War, 63

Micheaux, Oscar, 216

microprocessors, 542

Microsoft, 542

middle class: in the 1950s, 370; African American in late 1800s, 141; expansion of, 519; leaving urban life, 381; during Reagan administration, 534–35; streetcar suburbs, 132; suburban neighborhoods, 381; urbanization, 131–32

Middle East: Camp David Accords, 353, *p353*; Cold War and, 353–54; Gulf War, 550; pan-Arabism, 342; peacemaking in, 550; terrorist attacks from groups in, 567–68; War on Terror, 560

Midway Island, 312

"Migrant Mother", 252

migration: Dust Bowl, 237, *m237*, 251; Great Migration, 174, 195, *c196*, *m214*, 218; urbanization, 131–33; during World War II, 518

migration chains, 491

Milam, J. W., 420

militarism: of Britain, 167; of Germany, 167; before World War I, 167

military: advisors in Vietnam, 452–53, *g452*; African American pilots in, 417; Air Force, 379; desegregation of, 279, 378, 419–20; Huey helicopter, 455, *p455*; Japanese Americans, 279, 301; segregation of, 300–301, 413; selective service (draft), 174; technology from, 535; during Vietnam War, 446, *p447*, 449; women in, 174, 279, 301; World War I expansion of, 174; World War II, growth of, 300–301, *g300*

Military Assistance Command, Vietnam (MACV), 458

Military Commissions Act, 573

military detention camps, during World War II, 304, *p304*

"military-industrial complex", 342

militia, during Revolutionary War, 9

Milk, Harvey, 499

Millay, Edna St. Vincent, 211

Milliken v. Bradley, 439

Mills, Florence, 216

Milošević, Slobodan, 358

minimum wage: Kennedy's New Frontier, 386; National Recovery Administration (NRA), 251; Truman's Fair Deal, 379

mining: Black Hills gold, 93, *m94*; in California, 90, 96; Coal Creek War, 119; coal strike of 1902, 117, 201; copper and silver in Arizona, 93, *m94*; copper in Montana, 93, *m94*; environmental impacts of, 94–95; gold at Pikes Peak, 93, *m94*; hydraulic mining, 94; impact of, 90; lead and silver in Colorado, 93, *m94*; leading to statehood, 93–94, *m94*; quartz mining, 94–95; Truman controlling, 377; westward expansion, 93, *m94*

Minnis, Jack, 398

minutemen, 9

Minutemen missiles, 343

"Miracle of Dunkirk", 284, *p284*

Miranda rights, 387, 392

Miranda v. Arizona, 387, 392

missile-carrying submarines, for atomic bombs, 341

missile gap, 385

missiles, build-up of, 343

missing in action (MIA), Vietnam War, 469, 471

Mississippi: Hurricane Katrina, 560, *c562*, 574–75; secedes from U.S., *m66*, 66

Mississippian cultures: Cahokia, 4; Cherokee people, 4–5;

farming by, 4–5; women, role in society, 4

Mississippi Freedom Democratic Party, 421, 430, 433, *p433*

Mississippi River: French and Indian War, 7; Mississippian cultures, 4–5

Missouri, cattle drives to, 95

Missouri Compromise, 64

Mitchell, John, 523

mobile phones, 546

"Mobile phones and teenagers: Impact, consequences and concerns-parents/ caregivers perspectives" (S.V. Ravichandran), *q546*

Model T car, 194, 208–09

Modern American Art, 211

Mohammed, Khalid Sheikh, 570

Mohawk people, 2

Mondale, Walter, 534

money: during Articles of Confederation government, 21; Bretton Woods System, 333, 389; debating supply of, 138; euro, 540; Federal Reserve Act of 1913, 208; gold standard, 139, 253, 254, 333, 389; Gold Standard Act, 139; greenbacks, 138; New Economic Policy (Nixon Shock), 389–90; silver standard, 138, 139; world currency system, 333

monopoly: oil industry, 112; steel industry, 111–12

Monroe Doctrine, 155, 158, 164–65, *m164*

Montana: Fields, Mary, 98; mining leading to statehood of, 93, *m94*; statehood of, 90

Montgomery, AL, bus segregation, 406, *c410*, 417, 419, *p419*

Montgomery, Bernard, 307

Montgomery Bus Boycott, 406, *c410*, 419, *p419*

Montgomery Ward, 112

moon landing, 349, *p349*, 371

Moral Majority, 533

Morgan, J. P., *c92*, 112, 116

Morgan v. *Virginia*, 431

Morocco, 305

Morotai, 316

Morrill, Justin, 90

Morrill Act (Land-Grant College Act), 90, *m91*, *c92*

Morrill Tariff, 115

Morris, Dinah, *ptg12*

Morris, Robert, 21

mortgage-backed investments, 576

Mosaddegh, Mohammed, 342

Mosaic web browser, *c520*

Moscone, George, 499

Moses, Bob, 433

Moses, Robert, 421

Mothers Against Drunk Driving (MADD), 536

motion pictures, *c196*

Mountain time zone, 114

movement of people, HT21

MoveOn.org, 548

movies: CinemaScope, 384; full-color, 384; during Great Depression, 251–52; popular culture, 212; silent films, 212

Mr. Smith Goes to Washington, 251

Ms. Magazine, 478, *p483*, 484, *p484*

Muckrakers, 203

Mueller, Robert, 604–05

Mueller Report, 604–05

Mule Bone **(Zora Neale Hurston and Langston Hughes)**, 192

Mules and Men **(Zora Neale Hurston)**, 192

Muller v. *Oregon*, 197

multinational corporations, 382

multiple perspectives, HT11

mutually assured destruction, 341, 355

Munich Conference, 283, *p283*

Murray, Pauli, 485

music videos, 535

Muslims: Ayatollah Khomeini, 353; hate crimes against, *g569*; in Iran, 353; in Middle East, 567–68; Nation of Islam, 214, 437; Quran, 568; sects of, 571; Shia, 571, 572; Sunni Muslims, 571, 572; Taliban, 568

Mussolini, Benito: Italy deposing, 307; rise of, 278, *c280*, 281–82, *p282*

My Lai massacre, 468

N

Nader, Ralph, 563, *m565*

NAFTA. *See* **North American Free Trade Agreement (NAFTA)**.

Nagasaki, *cHT4*, 279, 318, *p318*, 368

napalm, 317, *p454*, 455

NARAL Pro-Choice America, 549

NASA. *See* **National Aeronautics and Space Administration (NASA)**.

NASA Technologies Benefit Our Lives, 350

Nash, Diane, 429, *q431*

Nasser, Gamal Abdel, 342

Nast, Thomas, 133

National Advisory Commission on Civil Disorders, 435

National Aeronautics and Space Administration (NASA), 345, 371

National American Woman Suffrage Association (NAWSA), 145, 199, 200

National Association for the Advancement of Colored People (NAACP): anti-lynching crusade, 213–14, 415; battling segregation and discrimination, 213–14; Boston school segregation, 436; bus segregation, 406; Du Bois, W.E.B., 222; establishment of, 136, 140, 409, *c441*; Evers, Medgar, 419; legal challenges against segregation, 429; Legal Defense Fund, 422; Medgar Evers's murder, 424–25; Nixon, E. D., 406; Parks, Rosa, 406; post-World War I, 177; role in civil rights movement, 417; segregation of education, 418

National Association of Colored Women's Clubs (NACWC), 199

National Association of Colored Women (NACW), 145

National Bank: Federal Reserve Act of 1913, 207–08; federal reserve system, 207–08

National Broadcasting Company (NBC), 209

National Credit Corporation (NCC), *c238*, 242

national debt, 582

National Defense Advisory Commission, 301

national energy program, 390

National Environmental Policy Act, 522, 578

National Farm Workers Association (NFWA), 492–93, 507

national forests, 202

National Housing Act, 263, 379

National Indian Defense Association, 102, 105

National Industrial Recovery Act (NIRA), 251, 260

nationalism, in Balkans, 167

Nationalist government of China, 339

Nationalist Party of South Africa, 537

National Labor Relations Act, 260

National Labor Relations Board (NLRB), 260

National Mobilization Committee to End the War in Vietnam, *q466*

National Negro Committee, *q146*

National Organization for Women (NOW), 478, *c482*, 484, 508

National Origins Act, 226

National Park Service, *c196*

National Recovery Administration (NRA), 251, 260

National Republican, *q81*

National Research Council, *Funding a Revolution: Government Support for Computing Research*, *q544*

National Review, 532

National Rifle Association (NRA), 533, 547–48, 588

National Right to Life Committee (NRLC), 549

National Science Foundation, 542

National Security Agency (NSA), 573–74

National Security Council, 379

national self-determination, Fourteen Points, 176, 181

National Socialist German Workers' Party (Nazi Party). *See* **Nazis**.

"National Teach-In", 458

National Union for Social Justice, 259

National War Labor Board (NWLB), 173

National Woman's Party (NWP), 200

National Woman Suffrage Association (NWSA), 199

Nation of Islam, 214, 437

Native Alaskan, 497

Native Americans: Alcatraz Island, 495–96, *p496*, 509, *p509*; American Indian Center, 495; American Indian Movement (AIM), *c482*, 496; American Indian Religious Freedom Restoration Act, 497–98; Americanization of, 91, 102, 103–08, *p103*; annuities for, 99; Battle of Little Bighorn, *c92*, 100; Bill of Rights protection, 495; Black Kettle, 100; buffalo, 61; Bureau of Indian Affairs, 102; Central Valley Project (CVP), 255; Citizenship Act, 102; Civilian Conservation Corps (CCC), 256; code talkers, 313, *p313*; Crazy Horse, 100; cultural regions of, 4–5; Dakota uprising, 99; Dawes Act, *c92*, 102, *q107*; Declaration of Indian Purpose, 495; economic status in 1920s, 210; Friends of the Indians, 102; Great Plains uprisings, 99–101; Homestead Acts impacting, 97; hunters and gatherers, 4; impact of Revolutionary War, 12; improving life of, 496–97;

Indian Civil Rights Act, 481, *c482*, 495; Indian Peace Commission, 100; Indian Reorganization Act, 102, 250; Indian Rights Association, 102; Indian Self-Determination and Educational Assistance Act of 1975, 481, 496; Indians of All Tribes, 495–96, *p496*, 509, *p509*; Indian Wars of late 1800s, 97; Joseph, chief of Nez Perce, 100–101; Mississippian cultures, 4–5; National Indian Defense Association, 102; Navajo Code Talkers, *p313*; New Deal impacting, 257–58; Northeastern peoples, 5; Oakes, Richard, 495–96, *p496*; Oregon territory, 61–62; post-World War II discrimination, 370; poverty of, 387–88; protesting for rights and recognition, 481; Red Cloud's War, 100; reproductive rights of, 399; during Revolutionary War, 10; Sand Creek Massacre, *c92*, 100; self-determination, 495; Sitting Bull, *c92*, *p92*, 100; as Spanish vaqueros, 96; Termination Policy of 1953, 388, 496; Thorpe, Jim, 212; Treaty of Fort Wise, 100; wagon trains encountering, 61; westward expansion impacting, 91, 99–101; Wheeler-Howard Act of 1934, 250; in World War II, 301; Wounded Knee, 101; Wounded Knee protest, 496. *See also specific* **peoples**.

Native Hawaiians, 497

nativism: immigration policies and, 123–24, 125, 133; in late 1800s, 225–26; post-World War I, 177

NATO. *See* **North Atlantic Treaty Organization (NATO)**.

naturalism, 135

naturalization, 226, *p589*

natural resources, industrial advantage of, 109

Natural Resources Defense Council, 548, 578

"A Nauseating Job, but It Must Be Done", *crt205*

Navajo Code Talkers, *p313*

Navajo people, 4, 496

Naval Air Station, 300

naval arms race, 225

navy: expansion of, 154, 158, 169; of Germany, 167; of Great Britain, 154, 167; Nimitz, Chester, 311; Pacific naval bases, 162; in Pearl Harbor, 158; Samoan Islands base, 158; Spanish-American War impacted by, 154; World War II, growth of, 300–301, *g300*. *See also* **military**.

Nazis: anti-Semitism of, 282; concentration camps, 290–91, *m290*; extermination camps, 290, *m290*, 291–92; Final Solution, 290–92; gaining power in Germany, 282; Goebbels, Joseph, 287; Holocaust, the, 287–92, *m290*; *Kristallnacht*, 287–88, *p288*; National Socialist German Workers' Party, 282; treatment of Slavic people, homosexuals, Roma gypsies, people with disabilities, 287; Wannsee Conference, 290. *See also* **Germany, World War II**.

Nebraska, Kansas-Nebraska Act, 64

"The Negro Artist and the Racial Mountain" (Langston Hughes), *q220*

Negro Motorist Green Book, The, *q416*

Negro National League, 212

Negro World, 214

Neighborhood Youth Corps, 388, 398

Netherlands, the: Germany attacking, 284; NATO, 338; SS *St. Louis*, 289, *m289*

Neutrality Act of 1935, *c280*, 284–85, 294, *crt295*

Neutrality Act of 1936, 284–85, *crt295*

Neutrality Act of 1937, 285, *crt295*

Neutrality Act of 1939, 285, *crt295*

neutrality debate, 168–69

Nevada: 2020 elections, 613, *m621*; Boulder Canyon Project Act, 234; Comstock Lode, 90, 93, *m94*; statehood of, 90; water rights, 518

New Deal: Agricultural Adjustment Administration (AAA), 251, 262; banking and investment programs, 254–55; credit loan programs, 255; Fair Labor Standards Act, 263, *q263*; Farm Security Administration, 263, *p264*; Federal Project Number One, 260; federal work programs, 256–57; first, 253–58; food stamps, 248; Indian New Deal, 257–58; Indian Reorganization Act, 257–58; legacy of, 264; low consumption theory, 255; National Housing Act, 263; National Labor Relations Act, 260; relief programs, 255–58; Roosevelt's policies of, 244; second, 248, 259–64, 266; social security, 248, *cHT4*; Social Security Act, 261–62; social welfare benefits, 248; subsidized housing, 248; unemployment insurance, 248; United States Housing Authority, 263; Wagner Act, 260; water management projects, 255; Works Progress Administration (WPA), 259–60, 263

New Economic Policy, 533

New Economic Policy (Nixon Shock), 389–90

New England colonies: Maryland Toleration Act, 56. *See also specific* **colony**.

New Federalism, 522

New Frontier, Kennedy's policies, 385–86

New Guinea, 312–13, 314

New Imperialism, 157. *See also* **imperialism**.

New Jersey Plan, 22

New Jersey* v. *T.L.O., 536

Newlands Reclamation Act, 202

New Mexico: Boulder Canyon Project Act, 234; Mexican guerrillas attacking, 166, *p166*; mining leading to statehood of, 93, *m94*; water rights, 518

New Negro, The, 215

***New Negro: An Interpretation, The* (Alain Locke)**, *q218*, *ptg221*

New Negro Movement, 217, 218

New Orleans, Louisiana: Armstrong, Louis, 216; jazz in, 215

"New Policy Train", *crt82*

newspapers, during 1920s, 212

Newton, Huey P., 432, 437

new world order, emerging of, 537

New York (state), State University of New York, 377

New York City: Italian, Russian, and Jewish immigrants in, 122, 128–29; "Little Italy," 122; "Lower East Side," 122; party bosses and graft, 133; Plunkitt, George, 133; political machines, 133; Statue of Liberty, *c92*; Tammany Hall, 133; tenements of, 132, *p132*; Tweed, William "Boss," 133; urbanization and migration, 131

***New York Journal*, yellow journalism**, 159

New York Stock Exchange (NYSE), 246

New York Times* v. *United States, 469

***New York World*, yellow journalism**, 159

Nez Perce people, 100–101

Ngo Dinh Diem, 452–53, 463

Nguyen That Thanh. *See* **Ho Chi Minh**.

Niagara Movement, 142, *p142*

Nicaragua: dollar diplomacy, 165; Sandinista rebels, 354

Nicholas II, czar of Russia, 175

Nichols, Terry, 551–52

***Night* (Elie Wiesel)**, *q291*

Nimitz, Chester, 311, 313–14, *m314*, 316–17

Nine-Power Treaty, 225

Nineteenth Amendment, *cHT4*, 51, 195, *c196*, 200–201

Ninth Amendment, 31, 47

Nixon, E. D., 406

Nixon, Richard: Alger Hiss spy case, 374; American-Soviet summit, 352–53; antiwar protests, 521; Cambodia invasion, *c450*, 467, 468; civil rights movement, 521; Clean Air Act, 389, 522, 578; Clean Water Act of 1972, 522, 578; conservatives disappointment in, 533; Détente Policy, 351–52; election of 1960, 385, *m385*; election of 1968, 351, 461–62, *m462*, 467, 518, 521; election of 1972, 469–70, 523, 529; Endangered Species Act of 1973, 522; ending termination policy, 496; Environmental Protection Agency (EPA), 522, 578; Family Assistance Plan, 522; Ford pardoning, 524, 525; impounding funds, 522; Middle America appeal, 521; National Environmental Policy Act, 522, 578; New Economic Policy (Nixon Shock), 389–90; New Federalism, 522; Nixon Doctrine, 351; policies to end Vietnam War, 467; resignation of, 390, 470, 518, 524, 525; resisting Watergate investigation, 523–24, 527, 528; revenue-sharing bills, 522; Saturday Night Massacre, 524; Southern strategy of, 521; stagflation, 389–90; Strategic Arms Limitation Treaty (SALT I), 352; triangulation, 352; Vietnamization, 351, 467, *q467*; visiting China, *c332*, 352; Watergate scandal, 470, 518, 523–24, 525–30, *p525*, *crt529*, *c553*; welfare system, 522

Nixon Doctrine, 351

Nobel Peace Prize: Addams, Jane, 136; Gorbachev, Mikhail, 356; King, Martin Luther, Jr., 427

nonimportation agreement, 8
nonviolent passive resistance, 419
Noriega, Manuel, 537
Normandy, 308–09
Norquist, Grover, 548
Norris v. *Alabama*, 417
North, Oliver, 354
North Africa, halting Germany's advances in, 305
North American Free Trade Agreement (NAFTA), 540, *m541*, 597
North Atlantic Treaty Organization (NATO), *c332*, 338, 358, 570
North Beach, San Francisco, LGBTQ community, 227
North Dakota: mining leading to statehood of, 93, *m94*; statehood of, 90
Northern Alliance, 569
Northern Hemisphere, HT26
Northern Securities, 116–17
Northern Securities v. *United States*, 116, 201
Northern states (The North): Civil War casualties of, *c76*; economy during Civil War, 73–74; established as free states, 19; Fugitive Slave Clause, 23; Three-Fifths Compromise, 23. *See also* Union army.
Northern Whigs, 65
North Korea: communist government of, 339; demilitarized zone (DMZ), 340; Korean War, 339–41
North Vietnam: 599; bombing of, 446, 454, 470; China supporting, 456; Cold War and, 448; Hoa Loa prison "Hanoi Hilton," 469; Ho Chi Minh, 452, 463; Ho Chi Minh City, 446, 470; Ho Chi Minh Trail, 455–56, *m456*, 467; invaded South Vietnam, 470; Le Duc Tho, 467, 469–70; Soviet Union supporting, 456; Tet Offensive, 460, 464; treatment of prisoners of war by, 469; Vietminh, 452, 463
Northwest Ordinance of 1787, 19, *m20*
Northwest Territory: creation of, 19, *m20*; slavery banned in, 19
Norway, NATO, 338
Nova Scotia, vice-admiralty courts, 7
Noyce, Robert, 542
NRLC. *See* National Right to Life Committee (NRLC).
nuclear energy, 579
nuclear power. *See* atomic energy.
nuclear reactor, 317–18

Nuclear Regulatory Commission, 579
nuclear weapons and warfare: consequences of nuclear war, 344; development of, 317–18; duck-and-cover drills, 368, *p369*, 376; fears of, 376; Hiroshima, 279, 318; hydrogen bomb (H-bomb), 376; land-based missiles, 341; Limited Nuclear Test Ban Treaty, 344; long-range bombers for, 341; M28/M29 Davy Crockett system, 376; missile-carrying submarines, 341; mutually assured destruction, 341, 355; Nagasaki, 279, 318, *p318*; Soviet Union developed, 339
Nugent, Richard Bruce, 216
Nuremberg Laws, 287
Nuremberg Trials, 292
nurses: Army Nurse Corps, 174, 279, 301; Provident Hospital and Training School for Nurses, 141; World War I, 174; World War II, 279, 301
N. W. Ayer and Son, 112
Nye, Gerald P., 284, *crt285*, 294
Nye Committee, 284, 294
Nye Report, The, *q294*

O

Oakes, Richard, 495–96, *p496*, 509, *p509*
Oaxacan people, 558
Obama, Barack: *p586*; 2008 elections, 581–82, *p581*; administration of, 560, *c562*; Affordable Care Act (ACA), 583–84; airstrikes in Iraq, 572; American Recovery and Reinvestment Act, 560, 582; bin Laden, Osama, 570; Cairo University speech, 572; Deferred Action for Childhood Arrivals (DACA) program, 591, 601, 615; earmarks, 583–84; economic response, 582–83; first 100 days, *p559*; foreign policy, 585–87; Great Recession, 558, 560; Hate Crimes Prevention Act of 2009, 585; health care reform, 583–84; health care system, 560; immigration, 594; national debt, 582; "Occupy Wall Street" protesters, 583; Paris Agreement, 580; withdrawal from Iraq, 572
Obama White House, "Taking Action on Immigration", *q594*
Obergefell v. *Hodges*, *c562*, 587

Occupation of Alcatraz Island: Indian Self-determination and the Rise of Indian Activism, The (Troy R. Johnson), *q509*
"Occupy Wall Street" protesters, 583
O'Connor, John Jay, 516
O'Connor, Sandra Day, 516, *p517*, 534
Office of Economic Opportunity (OEO), 388, 398
Office of Economic Stabilization (OES), 303
Office of Homeland Security, 568
Office of Price Administration and Civilian Supply (OPACS), 303
Office of War Information (OWI), 303
Office of War Mobilization, 302
Officer Candidate School, 276
The Official Report of the Proceedings of the Sixteenth Republican National Convention (Charles Evan Hughes), *q169*
Ohio Gang, 223
oil fields, development of, 109
oil industry, 112, 579
oil pipelines, during World War II, 305
oil prices: crisis of 1970s, 389; Organization of the Petroleum Exporting Countries (OPEC), 389
O'Keeffe, Georgia, 211
"Okies", 251
Okinawa, 317
Oklahoma City bombing, 551–52
Oklahoma Land Rush, *cHT4*, *c92*, 99
Old Man and the Sea, The (Ernest Hemingway), 211
Olive Branch Petition, 9
Olmec people and civilization, 4
Omaha beach, 309
One Giant Leap for Mankind, *q349*
"One Glass More", *q72*
Oneida people, 2
O'Neill, Eugene, 211, 216
Onondaga people, 2, *ptg3*
Open Door Policy, 155, 162
open ranges, 90, 95–96
Operation Desert Storm, *c520*, 538
Operation Frequent Wind, 470, *p472*, *p474*
Operation Iraqi Freedom, 571–72
Operation Overlord, 308–09
Operation PUSH (People United to Save Humanity), 440
Operation Restore Hope, 537
"Operation Wetback", 388

Oppenheimer, J. Robert, 318
Opportunity (Charles S. Johnson), 192, 215
opportunity costs, HT18
Oprah Magazine, The, 535
Oprah's Book Club, 535
Oprah Winfrey Network (OWN), 535
oralism, 500
Oregon territory: missionaries, 62; Oregon Treaty, 62; westward expansion, 61–62; Willamette Valley, 62
Oregon Treaty, 62
O'Reilly, Leonora, 120
Organization of the Petroleum Exporting Countries (OPEC), 389
organized crime, during prohibition, 228
On the Origin of Species by Means of Natural Selection (Charles Darwin), 134
O'Sullivan, Mary Kenney, 120
Oswald, Lee Harvey, 387
Other America, The (Michael Harrington), 387
Ottawa people, 7
Ottoman Empire: Balkans, 167; surrendering in World War I, 175
outsourcing, 540
overlanders, *m62*
overproduction, Great Depression impacted by, 236
Owen, Ruth Bryan, 201

P

Pacific Railway Act, 113
Pacific time zone, 114
Pac-Man, 535
PACs. *See* Political Action Committees (PACs).
Page, Larry, 582
Paine, Thomas, 10
paleontology, HT19
Palestine Liberation Organization (PLO), 550, *p550*
Palestinians, Israel's relationship with, 550
Palin, Sarah, 581
Palm Beach County, 2000 elections, 565
Palmer, A. Mitchell, 178, 185, 186, *q186*
Palmer, Potter, 131
Palmer Raids, *c156*, 178, 185, 186
Panama: Noriega, Manuel, 537; U.S. aided independence of, 153, 163

Panama Canal: construction of, 153–54, 163–64; Roosevelt inspecting, *p153*; Roosevelt's policy on, 163–64; Senate approves lease of, *c156*

Panama Canal Zone, 153

pan-Arabism, 342

pandemic: of 1918-1919 (Spanish Flu), *c156*, 175–76, *p176*; COVID-19 pandemic, *m561*

Panic of 1873, 119

Panic of 1893, 139

Paris, 310

Paris Agreement, 580

Paris Peace Accords, *c450*, 469

Paris Peace Conference, 179

Parker, Ely S., 102, *q106*

Parker, John J., 213–14

Parks, Gordon, 272

Parks, Rosa, 406, *p407*, *c410*, 417, 419, 429

Parting the Waters: America in the King Years, *q419*

party bosses, 133, 198

Pas-de-Calais, 308

"Passing of the East Side, The," *Menorah Journal*, *q132*

Patman, Wright, 243

Patriot movement, 551–52

patronage, 137

Patterson, John, 422

Patton, George: Battle of the Bulge, 310; Italy and Sicily invasion, 307; World War II general, 305

Paul, Alice, 200, 478

Pawnee people, 104

Payne-Aldrich Tariff, 202

Peace Corps, 343, *c372*

"Peacemaker" story (Iroquois), 2

Pearl Harbor: Japan attacking, 278, *c280*, 299–300; navy base in, 158

Pelosi, Nancy, *q576*

Pendleton Act, 137, 194

Pennsylvania: 2016 elections, 597; 2020 elections, 603, 612, 613; Gradual Abolition of Slavery, 12

Pentagon Papers, 469

Pentecostal movement in 1920s, 228

People for the American Way, 548

People's Party, 139

People's Republic of China: Chinese Revolution, 339; Détente Policy, 352; Korean War, 340; Mao Zedong, 339; Nixon visiting, *c332*, 352

people with disabilities: American Coalition of Citizens with Disabilities (ACCD), 500, 502; Americans with Disabilities Act (ADA), 481, *c482*, 500, 501–04,

p503; Architectural Barriers Act, 500; Bureau for the Education of the Handicapped, 500; Coelho, Tony, 500; fighting for rights of, 481; Heumann, Judith, 500, *q502*; independent living centers, 499–500; Nazis' treatment of, 287; Rehabilitation Act of 1973, 500, 502; rights movement, 499–500

perestroika, 356

perjury, 552

Perot, H. Ross, 540

Perry, Matthew C., 158

Pershing, John L., 166, 175

Persian Gulf War, 537–38, *m538*

Persistence of Memory, The **(Salvador Dalí)**, 211

personal computers (PC), *c520*, 542

Pétain, Marshal Philippe, 284

Peterson, Esther, 386

petroleum. *See* oil fields, development of.

Pew Research Center, 618

Philadelphia: First Continental Congress, 9; Revolutionary battles in, 10

philanthropy, 134

Philippine American Collegiate Endeavor (PACE), 498

Philippines: Aguinaldo, Emilio, 160; annexation of, 154, *c156*, 161, *crt161*; fall to the Japanese, 311–12; Filipino guerrillas, 160; MacArthur recaptures, 316; Spanish-American War, 160; Treaty of Paris, 160–61

phonograph, 109

photographers (Great Depression): Bourke-White, Margaret, 252; Lange, Dorothea, 252; Luce, Henry, 252

physical maps, HT29

physical systems, *cHT21*

Pickett, George E., 75

Pickett's Charge, 75

Pickford, Mary, 212

Pierce, Franklin, 64

pillaging, 76

Pinchot, Gifford, 202

Pinkerton Detectives, 119

Pittsburgh Courier, 300

place, geographical, HT21

places and regions, *cHT21*

plagiarism, HT12

Planned Parenthood, 549

Planned Parenthood **v.** *Casey*, 488

Platt Amendment, 154, 161

Plessy, Homer Adolph, 140, 143, *ptg143*, 408

Plessy v. *Ferguson*, 140, 143–46, 408, 415, 417

Plunkitt, George, 133

Point Four Program, 337

point of view, HT11

poison chlorine gas (weaponized), 172

Poland: after World War I, 175; after World War II, 334; democratic government replacing communism, 357; Hitler invading, 278, *c280*, 283–84; Soviet Union controlling, 328, 336; Soviet Union satellite nation, 336; Warsaw ghetto, *p292*; Warsaw Pact, 338

police, September 11, 2001, *cHT4*, 567

police force strike, 177

polio: Roosevelt, Franklin D., 244; treatments for, 371, 383; vaccine, *c372*, *p372*, 383

Polish immigrants, 122

Political Action Committees (PACs), 563

political advocacy: American Association of Retired Persons (AARP), 548, *p548*; Americans for Tax Reform (ATR), 548; Center for American Progress, 548; Greenpeace, 548; Heritage Foundation, 548; MoveOn.org, 548; Natural Resources Defense Council, 548; National Rifle Association (NRA), 548; People for the American Way, 548; Sierra Club, 548

political machines, in late 1800s urban areas, 133

political maps, HT29

political reforms, 198, 203, 223–24

Polk, James K., 61, 63

Pollard, Fritz, 212

poll tax, 140, 408, 427

Polocheck, Hilda Satt, *q130*

pollution: DDT pesticide, 577; smog, 577

Pong, 535

Pontiac, 7

Poor People's Campaign, 438

popular sovereignty, 25, 63

population: of Asian Americans, 498; changes in, 518, *m519*; illegal immigrants, *m481*; Latinos, *g490*; in Sunbelt, 518, *p518*, *m519*

population growth: after Civil War, 109; baby boom, post-World War II, 370, *c372*, 381, *g382*; due to immigration, 121–22

populism: 596; farmers' political power, 138; People's Party, 139

populist movement, 596

Populist Party, 139

Poro Company, 116

portable compact disc (CD), 535

Port Huron Statement, *q459*

Portugal: imperialism of, 154, *m155*; NATO, 338

postwar American society: Atomic Age, 376; beat movement, 384; beatniks, 384; birthrate, *g382*; Cold War pop culture, 376; Hollywood adapting, 384; Johnson's administration, 387–90; Kennedy's administration, 385–87; mass media, 383–84; medical breakthroughs, 383; poverty, 387–88; rock'n'roll, 384; televisions, 383

postwar domestic issues: baby boom, 370, *c372*, 381, *g382*; changing workplace, 382; Cold War fears, 368, *p369*; discrimination, 370, 374, 378, 379; duck-and-cover drills, 368, *p369*, 376; inflation and labor unrest, 377–78; Lavender Scare, 374; peacetime economy, 377–78; poverty, 370; Red Scare, 373–76; suburban growth, 381; Truman's Fair Deal, 379; women in the workplace, 378

Potsdam Conference, 330, 335

Pound, Ezra, 211

poverty: in the 1950s, 370, 387; of African Americans, 387, 438, *g442*; of Appalachian Mountains, 387, 388, *p388*; of Deep South, 387; of Hispanics, 387–88; of Native Americans, 387–88; post-World War II, 387

Powderly, Terence, 119

Powell, Colin, 538, 570–71

Powers, Francis Gary, 342

Powhatan Confederacy, 5

Pratt, Richard Henry, 102, 104, 108

predicting, HT16

Presidential Commission on the Status of Women, 386, 484

presidential elections, radio campaigning for, 209–10

presidential term limit, 379

President of the United States: cabinet of, 28; qualities of, 29; role of, 28–29

President's Committee on Civil Rights, 379

President's Panel on Mental Retardation, 386

Presley, Elvis, 384

Preston, Thomas, 9

price discrimination, 208

price fixing, 111

primary sources: analyzing visuals, HT10; types of, HT6–HT7, HT10, *cHT10*

Prime Meridian, HT26

Primer of the New Deal, A (Ervin E. Lewis), *q258*

Princip, Gavrilo, 168

Principles of Scientific Management, The (Frederick W. Taylor), 198

prisoners of war (POWs): McCain, John, 469; North Vietnam treatment of, 469; in Vietnam War, 469, 471

Problem of Indian Administration, The, *q107*

Proclamation of 1763, *c6*, 7

Progress and Poverty (Henry George), 134

Progressive Era reforms: African American, 194; collection of different ideas, 197; Cox, James M., 178; economic reform, 197, 201–02; Eighteenth Amendment, 228; goals of, 194, 198, 203; government, 194; immigrants, 194, *p194*; income taxes, 207; Pendleton Act, 194; political and government reforms, 198, 203; Roosevelt, Franklin D., 178; Triangle Shirtwaist Company fire, 197; Wilson, Woodrow, 207–08; women's rights and suffrage, 198–201. *See also* **economic reform**; **social-welfare**.

Progressive Party, 379

progressive tax, 207

progressivism, women in, *p191*

"Progress of Colored Women, The" (Mary Church Terrell), *q145*

Prohibition, 195, *c196*, 228

Project Head Start, 389, 396

Project Venona, 374

pro-life movements, 536

Promontory Point, Utah, *c92*, 113

propaganda, World War I, 169, 180

protectorates, 157

Protestant Church, majority religion of, 122

Provident Hospital and Training School for Nurses, 141

Prussia, France and, 167

Public Broadcasting Act, 526

Public Broadcasting Service (PBS), 526

Public Papers and Addresses of Franklin D. Roosevelt, The, *q285*

Public Works Administration (PWA), 257, 263

public works projects, 234, 241

Pueblo Bonito, 4

pueblos, 4

Puerto Rican Americans, 490

Puerto Rico: annexation of, 154, *c156*; Foraker Act, 161; Spanish-American War, 160; Treaty of Paris, 160–61; U.S. citizenship, 161

Pullen, Harriet, 88

Pullman Railroad Strike, *c92*, 119

pumpkin papers, 374

Pure Food and Drug Act, *c196*, 202, 205

"Puttin' on the Ritz" (Berlin, Irving), 212

Q

Quantrill, William Clarke, ptg65

quartz mining, 94–95

Quebec Act, 9

quota system, immigration, 190, 480, 490–91

Quran, 568

R

Rabin, Yitzhak, 550, *p550*

Raby, Albert, 435–36

racism/racial tensions: 16th Street Baptist Church, 424; during 1920s, 213; Asian immigrants, 123, 127; in Birmingham, AL, 424; Bombingham, 424; against Catholics, 65; early 1900s, 195, 213; Ferguson, MO, 588, 608; Floyd, George, 606, 607–08, 617, 619; German Americans, 177; Greenwood District, Tulsa, 213; against immigrants, 65; Jim Crow laws, 140, 143–46, 408; Know-Nothings (American Party), 65; Ku Klux Klan (KKK), 213; laws not changing, 435; in military during World War II, 300–301; over Rodney King's beating, 539, *p539*; poll tax and literacy tests, 140, 408; post-World War I, 177; race riots of 1919, *c156*; racial stereotypes in 1920s, 212; segregation, 139–40, 143–46, 408; "separate but equal" doctrine, 140, 144, 415, 417; Separate Car Act, 143; in South Africa, 537; systemic racism, 606–08, 617, 619; Tulsa, OK, 213; Watts Riot, 435

radar, 306

radiation, 371, 383

Radical Republicans: impacting the South, 78; Reconstruction plans, 77

radio: adaptation of, 384; beginning of, 209; during Great Depression, 251–52; Green Hornet, 252; *Guiding Light, The*, 252; Jack Benny, 251–52; popular culture, 212; presidential election campaign on, 209–10; sports on, 212

radiocarbon dating, HT20

railroads: Asian immigrants, 113, 123; cattle ranching impacted by, 95; corruption, 114; Crédit Mobilier, 114; government controlled prices, 115–16, 137; Great Northern Railroad, 114; Great Railroad Strike, 119, *m120*; growth of, 113–14; Hepburn Act, 118; Interstate Commerce Commission (ICC), 115–16, 137–38; land grants to, *m113*, 114; mining impacting, 93, *m94*; Pacific Railway Act, 113; Pullman Railroad Strike, 119; robber barons, 114; Separate Car Act, 143; Synchronous Multiplex Railway Telegraph, 114; through Great Plains, 97; time zones for, 114; track gauge, 114; transcontinental railroad, 112–14; Union Pacific, 113; *Wabash, St. Louis & Pacific Railway Company* v. *Illinois*, 115–16, 137; westward expansion, 90, *m91*

Raleigh Hotel, *p183*

ranchos, 96

Randolph, A. Philip, 303, *c410*, 417, 425

"Rape of Nanking", 281

rap music, 535

Rasul v. *Bush*, 573

Rather, Dan, *p459*

rationing coupons, 303

Rauschenbusch, Walter, 135

Ray, James Earl, 461

"Reaction to the Soviet Satellite: A Preliminary Evaluation", *q346*

Reagan, Ronald: Berlin Wall, 360, *q360*; California governor, 533–34; cutting taxes, 534; domestic policies of, 533–34; early life of, 533; election of 1980, 354, 519, *c520*; election of 1984, 534; General Electric Company, 519, 533; Heritage Foundation, 533; Hollywood actor, 519; House Un-American Activities Committee (HUAC) hearings, *p373*, 374; Intermediate Range Nuclear Forces (INF) Treaty, 355, *cHT4*; Iran-Contra Scandal, 354; Japanese Americans,

internment of, 304, 600; Reaganomics, 534; Sandra Day O'Connor appointed by, 516, 534; Screen Actors Guild, 533; Strategic Arms Reduction Talks (START), 355; Strategic Defense Initiative (SDI), 355; summit talks, 355, *p515*; tax reforms, 598; trickle-down economics, 534; "War on Drugs," 536

Reagan Doctrine, 354

Reaganomics, 534

realism art, 211

Real War, The, *q351*

recall by voters, 194, 198

recession: during Articles of Confederation government, 21; Bush, George H.W. administration, 538, 539

Reconstruction: African American rights during, 408; carpetbaggers, 78; Compromise of 1877 ending, *c6*; end of, *crt82*; Lincoln's plan, 76–77; Radical Republicans' plan, 77; scalawags, 78. *See also* **Radical Republicans**.

Reconstruction Finance Corporation (RFC), 242, 243, 380

recruitment posters, World War I, *ptg151*

Red Cloud's War, 99–100

redlining, 381, 382

Red Scare: African Americans impacted by, 374; causes of, 183, 186, 330; Gouzenko, Igor, 373; "Hollywood Ten," 374; House Un-American Activities Committee (HUAC) hearings, 373–74; Internal Security Act, 375; Lavender Scare, 374; loyalty review program, 373–74; mail bombs, 178; McCarran-Walter Act, 375, *g472*; McCarthyism, 374–76; Murray, Pauli, 485; Palmer raids, *c156*, 185; Rosenberg, Julius and Ethel, execution of, 374; spread of, 374

referendum, 194, 198

reform movements: American Tract Society, *ptg68*; in late 1800s, 134–36; Progressive Era reforms, 178, 194

refrigerated railroad car, 110

Refugee Act of 1980, *g472*, 491

refugees. *See* **immigrants/ immigration**.

refugees, amnesty for, 480, 491

"Regarding President Franklin D. Roosevelt's Attempt to Pack the Supreme Court" (Frank E. Gannett), *q269*

Regents of the University of California v. *Bakke*, 439–40, *p440*
region, HT21
regional blocs: Asia-Pacific Economic Cooperation (APEC), 540, *m541*; European Union (EU), 540, *m541*; North American Free Trade Agreement (NAFTA), 540, *m541*
Rehabilitation Act of 1973, 500, 502
Rehnquist, William, *q524*, 534, 575
Reiss, Winold, 221
relative location, HT21, HT28
relief, Hoover's view of, 242
religions: of conservatives, 532–33; in ethnic communities, 122; First Amendment insuring freedom of, 31, 46; freedom of, 56; Maryland Toleration Act, 56; religious fundamentalism in 1920s, 227–28; sects of, 571; Tocqueville's view on, *ptg69*; in Vietnam, 453. *See also* Christianity; *specific religions*.
"Remarks on Signing the National and Community Service Trust Act of 1993" (Bill Clinton), *q549*
Remembering Jim Crow: African Americans Tell About Their Life in the Segregated South (Charles Gratton), *q414*
Reno, Janet, 552
reparations, from Germany for World War I, 176
Reply to the "Remarks" of Thirty-one Boston Schoolmasters on the Seventh Annual Report of the Secretary of the Massachusetts Board of Education (Horace Mann), 71
reproductive rights, 487–88
republicanism, 25
Republican Party: 1860 presidential election, 65–66; 2006 midterm elections, 576; 2010 House majority, 560; 2016 elections, 595–96; beginning of, 65; Bush, George W., 563–66; Clinton's battle with, 550–52; "Contract with America," 550–51; economic policies of, 224–25; "Halfbreeds," 137; reformers, 137; ruling South during Reconstruction, 78; "Stalwarts," 137. *See also* Radical Republicans.
Republic of Cuba. *See* Cuba.
Republic of Texas, 63
Republic Steel workers, 261
Rescission Act, 311

researching history, HT11–HT12
reserved powers, 26
"Resolution of Ratification as Voted on by the Senate", *q182*
resources and scarcity, HT18
Reuben James, 286
Revenue Act, *c8*
Revenue Act of 1913, 207
revenue-sharing bills, 522
Revolutionary War, *c6*; Battle of Bunker Hill, 10, *ptg10*; Battle of Saratoga, 10; Battle of Yorktown, 11; Boston Massacre, 9; Boston Tea Party, 9; Breed's Hill, 10; Coercive Acts, 9; Continental Congress, 9; Declaration of Independence, *c6*, 13–18, *p13*; establishment of Continental Army, 9; *Gaspee* affair, 9; George Washington during, 9; impact of, 12; impact on Native Americans, 12; Lexington and Concord battle, 9; Olive Branch Petition, 9; Treaty of Paris, 11; Valley Forge, 10; women in, 12
Reynolds v. *Sims*, 386, 393
Rhode Island, *Gaspee* affair, 9
Richardson, Elliot, 524
Richardson, Gloria Hayes, 432
Richmond, David, 421
rights of Americans, 30–31
right-to-life movement, 487–88
right to privacy, 487–88
right-to-work laws, 378
Riis, Jacob, *p87*, 132, 194, *p194*
riots: after Martin Luther King, Jr. assassination, 438; Chicago race riots, 177; Cleveland, 178; Greenwood District, Tulsa, 213; Havana riots, 159; Haymarket Riot, *c92*, 119, *m120*; post-World War I, 177; race riots of 1919, *c156*; Rodney King's beating, 539, *p539*; Stonewall riots, 481, 498, 510; urban riots, 435; Watts Riot, 435; "zoot suit" riots, 303
Rivera, Diego, 493
On the Road (Jack Kerouac), 384
robber barons, 114
Roberts, John G., Jr., 575, 587, 600, 620
Roberts, Oral, 533
Robertson, A. Willis, 426
Robertson, Marion "Pat", 533
Robeson, Paul, 216
Robinson, Jackie, *q414*
Robinson, Jo Ann, 419
Robinson Projection, HT24, *mHT24*
Rockefeller, John D., 112, 134
rock'n'roll: development of, 384; Presley, Elvis, 384

Roe v. *Wade*, *c482*, 487–88, 533
Rogers, William, 351
Rolleston, Morton, *p436*
Roma (gypsies), Nazis' treatment of, 287
Roman Catholic Church. *See* Catholic Church.
Romania: democratic government replacing communism, 357; Soviet Union controlling, 328, 334, 336; Warsaw Pact, 338
Rommel, Erwin (Desert Fox), 305
Romney, Mitt, 583, 596
Ronettes, 384
Roosevelt, Edith, *p154*
Roosevelt, Eleanor, *p243*; as First Lady, 243; housing for poor, 263; Roosevelt, Franklin D. dependence on, 244; UN Commission on Human Rights, 335; Universal Declaration of Human Rights, 243, 335
Roosevelt, Franklin D.: 596; Atlantic Charter, 286; atomic bombs, 317–18; Bretton Woods System, 333; Casablanca Conference, 307; Churchill, Winston and, 286, *q296*; court packing, 262–63, *crt263*, 269; D-Day invasion, 308–09; death of, 316; declared war on Japan, 278, *c280*, 299–300; Democratic National Convention speech, *q244*; Destroyers-for-Bases, *c280*, 285; discrimination in wartime industries, 417; Doolittle Raid, 312–13; education of, 243–44; election of 1932, *p233*, *p238*, 243–44, 253; election of 1936, *c238*, 262, 293; election of 1940, 285; election of 1944, 328; Executive Order 8802, 303, 417; Executive Order 9066 (Japanese internment), 304, *p304*; "fireside chats," 254; First New Deal, 253–58; Four Freedoms, 285–86, *q296*; global war troubling, 301; health impacting Yalta Conference, 328; hemispheric defense zone, 286; Hoover Dam, 234; Hundred Days, 253; inaugural address, *q247*, 253, *q263*, 293; internationalism, 285; invading Morocco and Algeria, 305; Lend-Lease Act, 278, *c280*, 286; National Housing Act, 263; New Deal policies, 244; New York governor, 244; Operation Overlord, 308–09; polio, 244; political career, 244; political critics, 265–70; Progressive Era reforms, 178; "Put People to

Work," 247; quarantine speech, *q295*; raising opposition to, 259; Second New Deal, 248, 259–64; second term of, 262–64; "shoot-on-sight" policy, 286; supporting Britain, 278, *c280*, 285–86; Tehran Declaration, *q307–q08*; United Nations, 333; United States Housing Authority, 263; Yalta Conference, 328, *p329*, 334
Roosevelt, Theodore: "big stick" diplomacy, 163–65; coal strike of 1902, 117, 201; Department of Commerce and Labor, 117–18, 201; economic reform, 201–02; elections of 1912, 207; environmental reforms, 202; Hepburn Act, 118; laws governing big business, 115, 116, *crt117*; "Man with a Muck Rake, The," *crt205*; McKinley's assassination, 163; Meat Inspection Act of 1906, *p201*, 202, 205; Newlands Reclamation Act, 202; official international travel, *p154*; Open Door Policy, 162; Panama Canal construction, *p153*; Panama Canal policy, 163–64; Pure Food and Drug Act, 202, 205; Roosevelt Corollary, 155, 164–65, *m164*, *q165*; Rough Riders, 153, 160; Tenement House Commission, 132; trusts and, 115–18; U.S. Forest Service, 202
Roosevelt coalition, 262
Rosenberg, Julius and Ethel, *c372*, 374
Rough Riders, 153, 160
Ruby, Jack, 387
Ruby Ridge shootout, 552
Ruckelshaus, Jill, 478
Rules Committee, 426
Rumor of War, A (Philip Caputo), *q454*
Rumsfeld, Donald, 571–72
Russell, Richard, 426
Russia: 2016 elections, 603–05; Austria-Hungary, 167; Austria-Hungary/Serbia war, 168; Balkans, 167; Franco-Russian Alliance, 167; leaving World War I, 175; Nicholas II, czar of Russia, 175; Open Door Policy, 162; Russian Revolution, 175, 282, 330; Soviet Union dissolved, *m358*; Triple Entente, 167; Yeltsin, Boris, 357, *p357*. *See also* Soviet Union.
Russian immigrants, 122
Rust Belt, 532
Ruth, Babe, 212

S

Sabin, Albert, 383
Sabin, Florence, 227
Sacco, Nicola, 225–26, 330
Sacco-Vanzetti case, 225–26, 330
Sadat, Anwar, *p353*
"The Sage of Black Rock,"
American Heritage (Douglas
Brinkley), *q464*
Saigon, fall of, 446, *c450*, 470
Saipan, 315
Salk, Jonas, *c372, p372*, 383
Salvation Army, 135
same-sex marriages:
Massachusetts legalizing, 587;
Obergefell v. *Hodges*, *c562*,
587
Samoan Islands, 154, 158
Sandburg, Carl, 211
Sand Creek Massacre, *c92*, 100
Sanders, Bernie, 595, 597
Sandinista rebels, 354
San Francisco: Asian immigrants,
123, *p123*; "Migrant Mother,"
252
Sanger, Margaret, 227
San Jacinto, 63
satellites: development of, 343;
satellite dishes, 542; Soviet
Union launching, 345, 346
Saturday Evening Post, 376
Saturday Night Massacre, 524
Saturn V rocket, 371
Saudi Arabia: Operation Desert
Storm, 538; Persian Gulf War,
537–38, *m538*
Savigne, Karen, *p484*
scalawags, 78
Scalia, Antonin, 534, 602
Schechter Poultry Corporation v.
United States, 260
Schenck v. *United States*, 175
Schlafly, Phyllis, 478, *q486–q87*,
532–33
Scholes, 110
Scholes, Christopher, 110
School of Social Work, 136
Schumer, Charles, 618
science, history and, HT19
scientific advances, post-World War
II, 371, 383
SCLC. *See* Southern Christian
Leadership Conference
(SCLC).
Scopes, John T., *c196*, 227–28
Scopes trial, *c196*, 227–28
Scott, Dred, 64, *ptg64*, 65
Scott, Harriet Robinson, *ptg64*
Scott, Winfield, 63
Scowcroft, Brent, 361

Scream, The (Edvard Munch), 211
Screen Actors Guild, 374, 533
SDS. *See* Students for Democratic
Society (SDS).
Sea Around Us, The (Rachel
Carson), 577
Seale, Bobby, 432, 437
search-and-destroy mission,
Vietnam War, *p447*, 455
Sears, Roebuck and Co., 112
secession of states: as to 1860
election, 66; Alabama, *m66*,
66; Florida, *m66*, 66; Georgia,
m66, 66; Louisiana, *m66*, 66;
Mississippi, *m66*, 66; South
Carolina, *m66*, 66; Texas, *m66*,
66
Second Amendment, 46
secondary sources, HT10
Second Continental Congress,
9, 10
Second Great Awakening, 67
Second New Deal, 248, 259–64,
266
*Secrets: A Memoir of Vietnam and
the Pentagon Papers* (Daniel
Ellsberg), *q446*
sectional tensions, causes of:
1860 presidential election,
65–66; "Bleeding Kansas,"
65; Compromise of 1850, 64;
Dred Scott v. *Sandford*, 64, 65;
Fugitive Slave Act, 64; Harpers
Ferry, 65; Kansas-Nebraska
Act, 64, 65; *Uncle Tom's Cabin*
(Harriet Beecher Stowe), 64, 70.
See also Civil War.
sects, 571
Securities Act of 1933, 254
Securities and Exchange
Commission (SEC), *c238*,
254–55
Security Council (United Nations),
333
Sedition Act, 175, *crt184*
segregation: in 1950s, 409, *m409*;
apartheid, 537; of buses, 406,
c410, 417, 419, *p419*, 422, 431,
p431; Civil Rights Act of 1964
banning, 427, 436; Congress for
Racial Equality (CORE), 418; de
facto segregation, 409; de jure
segregation, 417; Dixiecrat Party
promoting, 379; of education,
391, 409, *c410*, 414, 415, 418,
439; Farmer, James, 418;
Houser, George, 418; Jim Crow
laws, 412, *p412*; legalization of,
140, 408; March on Washington
in 1941, *p405, c410*; Mexican
American children, 492;
of military, 300–301, 378,
413; *Norris* v. *Alabama*,
417; Robinson, Jackie,

q414; Southern Manifesto,
419; Student Nonviolent
Coordinating Committee
fighting, 421; Supreme Court
upholding, 140, 143–46, 408,
415, 417; at water coolers, 412,
p412. *See also* desegregation.
Seigenthaler, John, *p431, q431*
Selassie, Haile, 285
selective service: Selective Service
Act, *c156*; Selective Training
and Service Act, 300; during
World War I, 174
self-determination, 495
Selma March, 427
Senate: acquitting Trump, *c562*;
bills becoming law, 27, *c28*;
direct election of senators, 50,
c196, 198; establishment of, 23;
organization of, *c26*, 27
Senate Foreign Relations
Committee, 457–58
Senate Select Committee on
Presidential Campaign
Activities, 523–24, *q526*,
q530
Seneca Falls Convention, 199
Seneca people, 2, 102
senior citizens' activism, 536
"separate but equal" doctrine,
140, 144, 408, 415, 417
Separate Car Act, 143
separation of powers, 26–27, *c26*
September 11, 2001, *cHT4*; Bush,
George W. response to, 560,
c562; Pennsylvania plane
crash, *cHT4*, 567; Pentagon,
cHT4, 567, 568; "Tribute in
Light," *p557*; World Trade
Center, *cHT4, p557*, 567, 568
sequencing events, HT15
Serbia: assassination of Archduke
Franz Ferdinand, 168; Austria-
Hungary, war with, 168; Austria-
Hungary declared war on,
c156; ethnic cleansing, 358;
independence of, 167
*Series of Lectures on Social
Justice, A* (Charles Coughlin),
q268
Servicemen's Readjustment Act of
1944. *See* GI Bill.
settlement house movement,
135–36
Sevareid, Eric, 385
761st Tank Battalion, 301
Seventeenth Amendment, 50,
c196, 198
sewing machines, power-driven,
111
sexual harassment: Clinton
accused of, 550, 552; Thomas,
Clarence, 539

sexual orientation rights:
movement, 498–99; Murray,
Pauli, 485; Stonewall riots, 481,
498, 510
"shale boom", 579
Shame of the Cities, The (Lincoln
Steffens), *q203*
Share Our Wealth Society, 259,
267
Shays, Daniel, 21
Shays's Rebellion, 21
Sheeler, Charles, 211
Shepard, Alan, 347, 371
Shepard, Matthew, 587
Sheppard-Towner Maternity and
Infancy Act, 201
Sherman, Roger, 22
Sherman, William Tecumseh, 75
Sherman Antitrust Act, 115, 116,
crt117
Shia Muslims, 571, 572
Shirelles, 384
Shoah. *See* Holocaust, the.
"shoot-on-sight" policy, 286
Shriver, Eunice Kennedy, 386
Shuffle Along, 216
Shuttlesworth, Fred, 423
Sicily, World War II, 307
siege: siege at Alcatraz, 496; siege
of Branch Davidian compound,
552; siege of Petersburg, 76;
siege of Stalingrad, 324; siege
of Vicksburg, 75
Sierra Club, 548, 578
silent films, 212
Silent Spring (Rachel Carson), 577
silver: Comstock Lode, 90, 93, *m94*;
Leadville, 93, *m94*; Tombstone,
93, *m94*
silver standard, 138, 139
Simmons, William J., 213
Sioux people, 97
Siqueiros, David, 493
Sirhan Sirhan, 461
Sirica, John J., 523
Sister Carrie (Theodore Dreiser),
135
sit-down strike, *c238*, 260–61
sit-in movement: Congress
for Racial Equality (CORE)
organizing, 418, 429;
Greensboro sit-ins, *c410*;
people with disabilities,
502, *p502*; rights for people
with disabilities, *p499*, 500;
Woolworth's sit-ins, 421
Sitting Bull, *c92, p92*, 100, 101
"Sitting Down in Flint," *The New
Republic* (Bruce Bliven),
q260–q61
Six-Day War, 461

Six Essential Elements of Geography, HT21–HT22, *cHT22*

Six Nations (Iroquois Confederacy), 2–3

Sixteenth Amendment, 50, *c196*, 207

Sixth Amendment, 47

Skagway, 88

skyscrapers, 131

slavery: abolition of, *c6*; annexation of Texas, 63; Compromise of 1850, 64; Emancipation Proclamation, *cHT4*, *c6*, 74–75; ending, 76; Fugitive Slave Act, 64; Fugitive Slave Clause, 23; in Jamestown, *cHT4*; John Brown's rebellion, 65; secession of states, 66; Thirteenth Amendment, 49, 75, 77; Underground Railroad, 64; westward expansion of, 61. See also **American slavery, foundations of**.

Slavic people, Nazis' treatment of, 287

Slovakia, 283

From Slovenia to America **(Marie Prisland)**, *q129*

Smith, Albert, *p313*

Smith, Alfred E., 239

Smith, Bessie, 216, *p219*, *q219*

Smith, Howard W., 426

Smith, Lucy, 228

Smith, Margaret Chase, 375

Smith Act, 374

smog, 577

SNCC. See **Student Nonviolent Coordinating Committee (SNCC)**.

Snow White and the Seven Dwarfs, 251

soap operas: *Guiding Light, The*, 252; origin of, 252; on television, 384

social advocacy: Human Rights Campaign, 549; NARAL Pro-Choice America, 549; National Right to Life Committee (NRLC), 549; Planned Parenthood, 549

Social Darwinism, 134–36

Social Gospel movement, 135–36

socialism: Herbert Hoover's view of, *q241*; Industrial Workers of the World (IWW), 119–20; during late 1800s, 116; *Looking Backward* (Edward Bellamy), 135; Red Scare, *c156*, 178, 183

Socialist Party: Debs, Eugene V., 178; *"Long Live the Constitution of the United States,"* American Socialist Party, *q184*

Socialist Republic of Vietnam, 449

social justice movement, 606–08

social justice school, 421

social media: 2020 election, 613, 614; Black Lives Matter movement, 587–88, 607, 608; Obama campaigning on, 581

Social Security: Eisenhower expanding, 380–81; New Deal implementing, *cHT4*, 248; reform, 563, 574; Truman expanding, 378, 379

Social Security Act, *c238*, 261–62, *p262*

social structure, Social Darwinism, 134–36

social studies, HT17, *cHT17*

social-welfare: child labor, 132, *p132*, 197, 197–98, 198, *p198*, *p203*, 208, 263; New Deal implementing, 248; progressive ideals and, 197; women's role in reforms, 195, 197

Society for Human Rights, LGBTQ community, 481

Society of Righteous and Harmonious Fists, 162

society reform, 67

sodbusters, 98

Solid Waste Disposal Act, 389

Solomon Islands, 314, 316

Somalia, Operation Restore Hope, 537

Some Are More Equal than Others, *crt393*

Some Ethical Gains Through Legislation **(Florence Kelley)**, *q206*

sonar, 306

Song of the Lark, The **(Willa Cather)**, 211

Sons of Liberty, 8

Sony Corp. of America v. Universal City Studios, 535

Sony Walkman, 535

Souls of Black Folk, The **(W.E.B. Du Bois)**, 142, *q145*, 222

Sound and the Fury, The **(William Faulkner)**, 252

South Africa: African National Congress (ANC), 537; apartheid, 537; Mandela, Nelson, 537; Nationalist Party, 537

South America, 155

South Carolina: Charles Towne (during Revolutionary War), 10; Fort Sumter, 74; secedes from U.S., *m66*, 66

South Dakota: mining leading to statehood of, 93, *m94*; statehood of, 90

Southeast Asia Treaty Organization (SEATO), 341

Southern Christian Leadership Conference (SCLC): Chicago Movement, 435–36; establishment of, *c441*; nonviolent passive resistance, 430; Poor People's Campaign, 438; registering voters campaign, 421, 427

Southern Democrats: 1860 presidential election, 65–66; anti-civil rights strategy of, 426; Civil Rights Act of 1957, 421; filibuster of Civil Rights Bill, 426, *p426*

Southern Hemisphere, HT26

Southern Manifesto, 419

Southern Oral History Program, for the Smithsonian Institute's National Museum of African American History & Culture, *q432*

Southern Resistance group, 426

Southern states (The South): amnesty after Civil War, 76–77; Civil War casualties of, *c76*; economy during Civil War, 73; established as slave states, 19; Fugitive Slave Clause, 23; Republicans ruling during Reconstruction, 78; Three-Fifths Compromise, 23. See also **Confederacy**; **Confederate army**.

Southern Tenant Farmers Union, 251

Southern Whigs, 65

South Korea: demilitarized zone (DMZ), 340; Korean War, 339–41; U.S.-backed government of, 339

South Side, Chicago, arts and writers in, 210

South Vietnam: Cold War and, 448; Congress refused aid, 470; immigrants from, 472, *p472*; military leaders take over, *c450*, 463; Ngo Dinh Diem, 452–53, 463; training troops of, 467; U.S. military aid and advisers in, *c450*, 452–53, *g452*, 463

South Vietnamese Communists. See **Vietcong**.

Southwestern native people, 4

Soviet Union: Afghanistan, 354; American-Soviet summit, 352–53; Arabs and, 341; arms race, 341; atomic bombs, developed, 339; Battle of Stalingrad, 306; Berlin Wall, *p327*, 330, *c332*, 338, 359, *p359*, 360; Bulgaria, Czechoslovakia, Poland, Hungary, Romania, 328, 336; carving up, *m358*; Cold War tensions ease, 352–53; collectivized farms, 282; Commonwealth of Independent States (CIS), 357; Communist Party coup, 357, 361; Cuban Missile Crisis, 343–44, *m344*; dissolution of, *c332*; economy of, 356; end of, 357–58; Five-Year Plans, 282; Gagarin, Yuri, *c332*, 371; German Democratic Republic, 338; Germany attacking, 306; glasnost, 356–57; Gorbachev's reforms, 356–57, 360, 362; Hungary's uprising against, 342; hydrogen bomb (H-bomb), 376; Intermediate Range Nuclear Forces (INF) Treaty, *cHT4*, 355; in Iran, 336–37; Iron Curtain, 330, *p330*, 335–36; Khrushchev, Nikita, 342; Lend-Lease Act, 278, *c280*, 286; Lenin, Vladimir, 175, 282; Limited Nuclear Test Ban Treaty, 344; nonaggression treaty with Germany, 283, 330; nuclear disarmament, 355; orbiting Earth first, *c332*; perestroika, 356; Potsdam Conference, 330, 335; Reagan's view of, 354; rising tensions with, 334–35; Romania, 334; shooting U-2 spy plane, 342; solider and civilian deaths in World War II, 306; space exploration, 343, 346, 371; Stalin, Joseph, 278, 282; Stalin's death, 342; Strategic Arms Limitation Treaty (SALT I), 352; Strategic Arms Reduction Talks (START), 355; summit talks, 355; supporting North Vietnam, 456; Tehran Declaration, *q307–q08*; in UN Security Council, 333; V-E (Victory in Europe) Day, 310; Warsaw Pact, 338; weakening of, 355–58; Yuri Gagarin, first man in space, *c332*, 371

Space Act, 345

space exploration: Apollo program, 348–49; Armstrong, Neil, 349, 371; Cold War fueling, 343, 346; *Explorer I*, 343; Gagarin, Yuri, *c332*, 371; Kennedy, John F., 347, 348; moon landing, 349, *p349*, 371; Saturn V rocket, 371; Shepard, Alan, 347, 371; Soviet Union orbiting Earth, *c332*; Soviet Union satellites, 345, 346; Space Act, 345; "space race," 371; *Sputnik*, 343, 346; STEM (science, technology, engineering, and math) programs, 350; von Braun, Wernher, 371. See also **National Aeronautics and Space Administration (NASA)**.

Space Invaders, 535

space race, 371
Spain, imperialism of, 154, *m155*
Spanish-American War: Aguinaldo, Emilio, 160; Cuba, 158–60; economic effects of, 161–62; Filipino guerrillas, 160; Guam, 160; navy impacting, 154; Philippines, 160; Puerto Rico, 160; Treaty of Paris, 160–61
Spanish Civil War, 285
Spanish Flu pandemic, *c156*, 175–76, *p176*
Spanish vaqueros, 96
speakeasies, 228
Special Olympics, 386
Special Operations Forces, 343
special prosecutor, 524
speculators, 236, 239–40, 246
Spencer, Herbert, 134
Spending to Save: The Complete Story of Relief, *q257*
sphere of influence, 162
"Spirit of the New Deal, The" (Clifford Kennedy Berryman), *crt265*
Spock, Benjamin, *q460*
sports: in 1920s, 212; baseball in, 212; boxing in, 212; college football, 212; Dempsey, Jack, 212; golf, 212; Negro National League, 212; Ruth, Babe, 212; tennis, 212; women's opportunities in, 487, *p487*
Sprague, Frank J., 131
Sputnik, 343, 346
spy plane, 342
SS *St. Louis*, *p288*, 289, *m289*
stagflation, 389–90
Stalin, Joseph: blockading East Berlin, 338; death of, 342; nonaggression treaty with Germany, 283; Potsdam Conference, 330, 335; rise of, 278, 282; Tehran Declaration, *q307–q08*; Yalta Conference, 328, *p329*, 334
Stalingrad, Germany attacking, 306
"Stalwarts", 137
Stamp Act, *c6*
Stamp Act Congress, 8
Standard & Poor's *Security Price Index Record*, 246, *crt246*
standard of living: in early 1900s, 208; post-Civil War improvements of, 110–11
Standard Oil trust, *c92*, 117
Stanford, Leland, 113
Stanton, Elizabeth Cady, 199
Starr, Ellen, 135–36
Starr, Kenneth, 552
"The Star-Spangled Banner" (Francis Scott Key), 33–34

Stasi, 357
state government: Great Depression impacting, 264; women in office, 201; women's rights and suffrage, 199
State of the Union address (Harry S. Truman), *q379*
State of the Union address (Lyndon B. Johnson), *q396*, *q400*
state-sponsored terrorism, 568, 570
states' rights, 66
States' Rights (Dixiecrat) Party, 379
State University of New York, 377
Statue of Liberty, *c92*
stay-at-home orders, 612
steam tractors, 98, *p99*
steel industry: Carnegie Steel, 111–12; Committee for Industrial Organization (CIO), 260; Memorial Day Massacre, 261; strikes, 261; U.S. Steel, *c92*, 112, 117, 177, *crt185*
Steffens, Lincoln, 203
Stein, Gertrude, 212
Steinbeck, John, 252
Steinem, Gloria, 478, *p484*, *q485*
STEM (science, technology, engineering, and math) programs, 350
Stennis, John, 426
Stevenson, Adlai, 380
Stevenson, Edward, *q127*
Stewart, Jimmy, 251
Stimson, Henry L., 312, 318
St. Lawrence Seaway, 380
St. Louis, jazz in, 215
stock market: bear market, 240; Black Thursday, 240, 246; bull market of 1920s, 239–40, 246; crash of 1929, 237, *c238*, 240, 246; margin call, 240; Securities and Exchange Commission (SEC), 254–55; speculators, 239–40, 246; stocks on margin, 239
Stokoe, William, 500
Stone, Lucy, 199
Stone v. *Powell*, 521
Stonewall riots, 481, 498, 510
STOP ERA organization, 478, 486–87
Stowe, Harriet Beecher, 64, *p70*
St. Peter's Catholic Mission School, 98
Strategic Arms Limitation Treaty (SALT I), 352
Strategic Arms Reduction Talks (START), 355
Strategic Defense Initiative (SDI), 355

strategic materials, 299
Strauss, Samuel, *q210*
streetcar suburbs, 132
Striebel, Charlotte, 487
Striebel, Kathy, 487
strikes: Boston police force strike, 177; in early labor unions, 118; General Motors sit-down, *c238*; Great Railroad Strike, 119, *m120*; Homestead steel mill strike, 119, *m120*; Memorial Day Massacre, 261; post-World War II, 377–78; Pullman Railroad Strike, 119, *m120*; sit-down strike, 260–61; steel industry, 261; steelworkers, 177, *crt185*; textile mills, 120; United Mine Workers (UMW), 117, 201
Strong, Josiah, 157
"Struggle for Human Rights, The" (Eleanor Roosevelt), *q335*
Student Nonviolent Coordinating Committee (SNCC): Baker, Ella, 433; establishment of, 421, 429, *c441*; Freedom Summer, 421; Hamer, Fannie Lou, 433, *p433*; Minnis, Jack, 398; nonviolent passive resistance, 430; Selma March, 427; sit-in movement, 421; voter registration efforts, 427
Students for Democratic Society (SDS), 458, 459–60, *q459*
Student Voice, The, *q434*
submarines: missile-carrying submarines, 341; U-boats, 170, 286, 305–06; World War II, 286, 305–06; during World War II, 305–06
subprime loans, 576
subsidized housing, New Deal implementing, 248
suburban neighborhoods: in the 1950s, *p367*, 370; discrimination in, 381; growth of, 381; mass-produced, 381
subway systems, 131
Sudetenland, 283
Suez Canal: Egypt seizing, 341; World War II, 305
suffrage: of African American men, 77, *ptg77*; Fifteenth Amendment, 199; poll tax and literacy tests, 140, 408; Voting Rights Act of 1965, 427–28. *See also* **Fifteenth Amendment**; **women's suffrage**.
Sullivan, Ed, 384
Sumner, William Graham, 134
Sun Also Rises, The **(Ernest Hemingway)**, 211
Sunbelt: conservatism of, 532; population growth in, 518, *p518*, *m519*, 532

Sunday, Billy, 228
Sunni Arabs, 571
Sunni Kurds, 571
Sunni Muslims, 571, 572
sun stone, *pHT6*
Superdome, 574
supply and demand, HT18
supply-side economics, 224, 534
"In Support of FDR's Court-Packing Plan" (Robert M. La Follette), *q269*
Supreme Court: Alito, Samuel, Jr., 575; Barrett, Amy Coney, 602, 620; Burger, Warren, 521; establishment of, 24; Ginsburg, Ruth Bader, 602; Gorsuch, Neil, 602; judicial review by, 30; Kavanaugh, Brett, 602; Kennedy, Anthony, 534, 584, 602; Rehnquist, William, *q524*, 534, 575; Roberts, John G., Jr., 575; role of, 29–30, *c30*; Roosevelt court packing, 262–63, *crt263*, 269; Sandra Day O'Connor, first female justice, 516, *p517*, 534, 575; Scalia, Antonin, 534, 602; Sotomayor, Sonia, 584, 602; swing vote, 575; Warren, Earl, 386–87, 391, *p391*, *q394*, 418, 521
Supreme Court Crisis, The **(Merlo J. Pusey)**, *q262–q63*
Supreme Court ruling: *Abington School District* v. *Schempp*, 387; *Baker* v. *Carr*, 386, 393; *Boumediene* v. *Bush*, 573; *Boynton* v. *Virginia*, 431; *Brown* v. *Board of Education of Topeka, Kansas*, 391, 409, *c410*, 418, 439; *Bush* v. *Gore*, 565–66; *Citizens United* v. *Federal Election Commission*, 584; *Davis* v. *County School Board of Prince Edward County*, 418; *District of Columbia* v. *Heller*, 588; *Dred Scott* v. *Sandford*, *c6*, 64, 65; *Engel* v. *Vitale*, 387, 392; *Escobedo* v. *Illinois*, 387; *Fisher* v. *University of Texas at Austin*, 440; *Gideon* v. *Wainwright*, 386–87; *Gratz* v. *Bollinger*, 440; *Griswold* v. *Connecticut*, 387, 487; *Grutter* v. *Bollinger*, 440; *Hamdan* v. *Rumsfeld*, 573; *Heart of Atlanta Motel, Inc.* v. *United States*, 427, 436; *Hernández* v. *Texas*, 492; *Katzenbach* v. *Morgan*, 428; *Kelo* v. *City of New London*, 575; *Koremastu* v. *United States*, 304, 600; *Lochner* v. *New York*, 197; *Loving* v. *Virginia*, 497; *Mapp* v. *Ohio*, 386; *McDonald* v. *Chicago*, 588; *Mendez* v. *Westminster*,

492; *Milliken* v. *Bradley*, 439; *Miranda* v. *Arizona*, 387, 392; *Morgan* v *Virginia*, 431; *Muller* v. *Oregon*, 197; *New Jersey* v. *T.L.O.*, 536; *New York Times* v. *United States*, 469; *Norris* v. *Alabama*, 417; *Northern Securities* v. *United States*, 116, 201; *Obergefell* v. *Hodges*, c562, 587; *Planned Parenthood* v. *Casey*, 488; *Plessy* v. *Ferguson*, 140, 143–46, 408, 415, 417; *Rasul* v. *Bush*, 573; *Regents of the University of California* v. *Bakke*, 439–40, p440; *Reynolds* v. *Sims*, 386, 393; *Roe* v. *Wade*, c482, 487–88, 533; *Schechter Poultry Corporation* v. *United States*, 260; *Schenck* v. *United States*, 175; *Sony Corp. of America* v. *Universal City Studios*, 535; *Stone* v. *Powell*, 521; *Swann* v. *Charlotte-Mecklenburg Board of Education*, 439; *Sweatt* v. *Painter*, 418; *Takao Ozawa* v. *United States*, 226; *Tinker* v. *Des Moines*, 459; *Trump* v. *Hawaii*, 600; *United States* v. *Bhagat Singh Thind*, 226; *United States* v. *E.C. Knight*, 116–17; *Vermonia School District* v. *Acton*, 536; *Wabash, St. Louis & Pacific Railway Company* v. *Illinois*, 115–16, 137; *Windsor* v. *United States*, 587

surrealistic art works, 211
Suspending Act, c8
Sussex, 170
Swann v. *Charlotte-Mecklenburg Board of Education*, 439
Sweatt v. *Painter*, 418
Swedish immigrants, 122
Swift, Gustavus, 110
swing vote, 575
Symbols and mottos: American flag, 32; E. Pluribus Unum, 33; "In God We Trust," 34; Great Seal of the United States, 33; Star-Spangled Banner, 33–34
Synchronous Multiplex Railway Telegraph, 114
Syria, 585, 598; civil war, 585; Islamic State in Iraq and Syria (ISIS), 572; Russian air strikes, 586; U.S. air strikes 598–99
systemic racism, 606–08, 617, 619
Szilard, Leo, 317–18

T

Taft, William Howard: diplomacy, 163; economic reform, 202; elections of 1912, 207; laws
governing big business, 115; reforms of, 202; treatment of Filipinos, 161; United States Children's Bureau, 198
Taft-Hartley Act of 1947, 301, 374, 377–78
"Tain't Nobody's Business If I Do" (Bessie Smith), q219
Taiping Rebellion, 123
Taiwan, 339, 341
Takao Ozawa v. *United States*, 226
Taliban: Afghanistan, 568, 599; War on Terror, 560, 569–70
Tammany Hall, 133
Tanner, Henry Ossawa, 211
Tarawa: The Story of a Battle **(Robert Sherrod)**, q315
taxes, Bush tax cuts, 569
taxes/tariffs: Bretton Woods System, 333; capital gains tax cuts, 539; child tax credit, 552; citizens' responsibilities, 31; Clinton, William "Bill" raising, 547; General Agreement on Tariffs and Trade (GATT), 337; Hawley-Smoot Tariff, 236, c238; imperialism and, 157; income taxes, 207; Kennedy's, 386; McKinley Tariff, 138; national government right to, 24; Payne-Aldrich Tariff, 202; Reagan cutting, 534; Revenue Act of 1913, 207; Social Security Act, 261–62, p262; Taft's reforms of, 202; Underwood-Simmons Act, 207; during World War I, 173; during World War II, 303
Taylor, Breonna, 608
Taylor, Zachary, 62, 63, 64
teach-ins, 458
Tea Party, 584–85, p584
Teapot Dome scandal, 223–24
technology: advances of the 1950s, 370; automatic dishwasher, 110; cable television, 535; camera, handheld, 111; Cold War advances in, 371; computer mouse, c520; computers, 542, 543–46; depth charges, 306; digital audio players, 535; digital technology, 582; digital video disc (DVD), 535; during early 1900s, 194; electric generator, 109; electric power, 109–10; electronic digital computer, 542; Electronic Numerical Integrator and Computer (ENIAC), c372, 543; gasoline-powered carriage, 111; during Gilded Age, 133; Global Positioning System (GPS),
535; graphic-user interface, c520; Huey helicopter, 455, p455; hyperconnectivity of, 582; ice-making machine, 110; interchangeable parts, 111; Internet, 542, 544; light bulb, 109; long-range radios, 455; mechanical reapers, 98; microprocessors, 542; personal computers, c520; phonograph, 109; portable compact disc (CD), 535; radar, 306; refrigerated railroad car, 110; satellites, 343; sewing machines, power-driven, 111; shift to white-collar jobs, 382; sonar, 306; Sony Walkman, 535; steam tractors, 98, p99; Synchronous Multiplex Railway Telegraph, 114; telecommunications, 542; telephone, 110; televisions, 383; threshing machines, 98; trans-Atlantic telegraph cable, 110; typewriter, 110; video cassette recorders (VCRs), 535; video games, 535; wireless digital technology, 542; World Wide Web, 542
Tehran Declaration, q307–q08
Tehran hostages, 353–54
telecommunications, 542
telegraph, 110
telephone, 110
televangelists, 533
television: Black Entertainment Television (BET), 535; cable television, 535; first presidential debates on, 385; Hollywood adapted to, 384; mass media, 383; Oprah Winfrey Network (OWN), 535; radio shows adapted to, 384; satellite dishes, 542; Turner, Ted, 535; Vietnam War and, 457–58
Tell My Horse **(Zora Neale Hurston)**, 192
tenant farmers: Farm Security Administration, 263, p264; in Great Depression, 251; in the Great Plains, 99; Southern Tenant Farmers Union, 251
Tenement House Act of 1901, 132
Tenement House Commission, 132
Tenement House Department, 132
tenements, 132
Tennessee Valley Authority (TVA), 255, m255, 380
tennis: Tilden, Bill, 212; Wills, Helen, 212
Tenochtitlán, Cortés conquering, 5
Tenth Amendment, 48
Tenure of Office Act, 78
Ten Years of Missionary Work Among the Indians at
Skokomish, Washington Territory **(Myron Eells)**, q105
Termination Policy of 1953, 388, 496
Terrell, Mary Church, 140, q145, 200
terrorism/terrorist attacks: anthrax attacks, 569; embassy bombings in Kenya and Tanzania, 568; from groups in the Middle East, 567–68; Oklahoma City bombing, 551–52; September 11, 2001, cHT4, 567, 568; state-sponsored terrorism, 568; USS *Cole*, 568
Tet Offensive, c450, 460, 464
Texas: annexation of, 63; secedes from U.S., m66, 66
Texas, Republic of, 63
Texas longhorn cattle, 95
Texas territory: Alamo, c6; American settling in, 62; *empresarios*, 62; Hispanics, 96; independence of, c6
Texas War of Independence: Alamo, 63; San Jacinto, 63
textile mills, 120
Their Eyes Were Watching God **(Zora Neale Hurston)**, 192, 252
thematic maps, HT29
thermoluminescence, HT20
"Things Are in the Saddle," *Atlantic Monthly* **(Samuel Strauss)**, q210
think tanks: development of, 533; Heritage Foundation, 533
Third Amendment, 46
Third Reich. *See* **Germany, World War II**.
Third World Liberation Front (TWLF), 498
Thirteenth Amendment, c6, 49, 76, 77
38th parallel in Korea, 339, 340
Thomas, Clarence: confirmation hearing of, 539–40; sexual harassment charge against, 539; Supreme Court Justice, c520, p520
Thorpe, Jim, 212
Three-Fifths Compromise, 23
Three Mile Island, 579
"3,000 Arrested in Nation-Wide Round-Up of 'Reds,'" *New York Tribune*, q185
three-tier college system, 377
threshing machines, 98
Thunberg, Greta, 580, p580
Thurmond, Strom, 379, 419, 426, 521
Tiananmen Square, 541–42

Tilden, Bill, 212
Tilden, Samuel, 78, 79–82, *m80*
Till, Emmett, 420, *p420*
time lines, historians using, *cHT8*
Time magazine's 2019 Person of the Year, 580
time zones, 114
Tinian, 315
Tinker, John, 459, *p459*
Tinker, Mary Beth, 459, *p459*
Tinker v. *Des Moines*, 459
Tin Pan Alley, 212
Title IX, 487, *p487*
Tlingit people, *p258*
Toast of the Town (Ed Sullivan), 384
Tocqueville, Alexis de, *ptg69*
Tōjō, Hideki, 281
Tokyo War Crimes, 318
Toltec people and civilization, 4
Tombstone, silver in, 93, *m94*
Tometi, Opal, 587, 588
Tomorrow! (Philip Wylie), 376
Touched by the Dragon (Doug Johnson), *q471*
Townsend, Francis, 259, 268
Townshend, Charles, 8
Townshend Acts of 1767, 8, *c8*, 9
Toynbee Hall, 136
Tracy, Benjamin, 34
trade: after World War II, 335; during Articles of Confederation government, 19–20; to China, 162; General Agreement on Tariffs and Trade (GATT), 337; imperialism and, 154, 157; of Iroquois Confederacy, 2; national government regulating interstate commerce, 24; slave trade, *cHT4*; between states before Constitution, 20–21; Townshend Acts impacting, 8, *c8*, 9
trans-Atlantic telegraph cable, 110
transcontinental railroad, *c92*, 112–14
Trans-Pacific Partnership (TPP), 586
transportation: Federal-Aid Highway Act, 370, *m371*, *c372*, 380; gasoline-powered carriage, 111; Interstate Highway System, 370, *m371*, *c372*, 380; mass transit and urbanization, 131; railroads, 90, *m91*, 93, *m94*, 95, 97, 112–14; refrigerated railroad car, 110; St. Lawrence Seaway, 380; transcontinental railroad, 65, *c92*, 112–14
travel bans, 600, 615
Treaty of Brest-Litovsk, 175
Treaty of Fort Wise, 100

Treaty of Guadalupe Hidalgo, 63, 96
Treaty of Kanagawa, 158
Treaty of Paris: American Revolution, *c6*, 7, 11, 20; Cuba, *c156*, 160–61; Guam, 160–61; Philippines, 160–61; Puerto Rico, 160–61; Spanish-American War, 160–61
Treaty of Versailles, 176, 177, 278, 281, 282–83
Treblinka, 291
trench warfare, *m170*, 171–72
Triangle Shirtwaist Company fire, 197
"Tribute in Light", *p557*
trickle-down economics, 534
Triple Alliance: Austria-Hungary, 167; becoming Central Powers, 168; Germany, 167; Italy, 167
Triple Entente, 167, 168
trolley cars, 131
True, Allen, 234
Truman, Harry S.: administration of, 377–79; atomic bombs, 318, 328; containing communism, 336–37; election of 1948, 378–79; Executive Order 9981, 420; Fair Deal, 379; Federal Civil Defense Administration, 368; GI Bill, 377; inaugural address, 337; Internal Security Act, 375; Korean War, 340, *q340*; legislative agenda of, 378; loyalty review program, 373–74; miners' strikes, 377; National House Act, 379; Point Four Program, 337; Potsdam Conference, 330, 335; President's Committee on Civil Rights, 379; Roosevelt's death, 316; Social Security, expanding, 378, 379; Taft-Hartley Act of 1947, 378; Truman Doctrine, *q337*; during World War II, 328
Truman Doctrine, *c332*, *q337*
Trump, Donald: *p598*; 2016 elections, 561, *c562*, 595–96, 603-05, *m604*; 2020 campaign, 599; 2020 election, *c562*, 612–15, *m619*; 2020 election challenges, 613; acquitted, *c562*; administration of, 561, *c562*; "America First," 597; Barrett, Amy Coney, 602, 620; border wall, 591, 593, 601; immigration policy, 599–601; COVID-19 pandemic, 610–12; Deferred Action for Childhood Arrivals (DACA) program, 592, 601; immigration policy, 599–601; impeachment of, *c562*, 604, 605, 611, 614; inaugural address, *q595*; "Make America Great Again,"

597, 617; Paris Agreement, 580; presidential debate, *p596*; tax cut, 598
Trump v. *Hawaii*, 600
trusts: development of, 112; Northern Securities, 116; regulations on, 117–18; Roosevelt, Theodore targeting, 116, *crt117*
Truth, Sojourner, 485, 506
tuberculosis, treatments for, 371, 383
Tula, 4
Tunisia, 305; Arab Spring, 572
Turkey, Soviet Union and, *q337*
Turnbo, Annie, 116
Turner, Frederick Jackson, 99
Turner, Ted, 535
Tuscarora people, 2
Tuskegee Airmen, 301, 417
Tuskegee Institute, 136
Twain, Mark, 133, 161
Tweed, William "Boss", 133
Twelfth Amendment, election of President and Vice President, 48
Twentieth Amendment: "Lame-Duck," 51; succession of president and vice president, 51–52
Twenty-Fifth Amendment, 53–54
Twenty-First Amendment, 52
Twenty-Fourth Amendment, 53, 427
Twenty-Second Amendment, 52–53, 379
Twenty-Seventh Amendment, 54
Twenty-Sixth Amendment, 54, 460
Twenty-Third Amendment, 53
two-house legislature, 22, 23
typewriter, 110

U

U-2 spy plane, 342
U-boat submarines, 170, 286, 305–06
Uncle Tom's Cabin (Harriet Beecher Stowe), 64, 70
Underground Railroad, 64
Underwood-Simmons Act, 207
unemployment insurance, 248, 261
unfair trade practices, 208
Union army: African Americans in, *p74*; attrition impacting, 74; Battle of Antietam, 74; Battle of Bull Run, First, 74; Battle of Gettysburg, 75; Battle of New Orleans, 74; casualties of, *c76*; Confederate army compared to, *c73*; Cumberland River

controlling, 74; McClellan, George B., 74; Meade, George, 75; Sherman, William Tecumseh, 75; Sherman's March to the Sea, 76; siege of Petersburg, 76; siege of Vicksburg, 75; victory of, 76; war in the east, 74
Union of Russian Workers, 178
Union of Soviet Socialist Republics (USSR). *See* **Soviet Union**.
Union Pacific, 113
unions: American Federation of Labor (AFL), 119; American Railway Union (ARU), 119; binding arbitration, 260; Brotherhood of Sleeping Car Porters, 303; closed shops, 119; coal strike of 1902, 117, 201; collective bargaining, 119; early opposition to, 118–19; exempt from Clayton Antitrust Act, 208; expelling Communist Party members, 374; industrial unions, 118–19; Industrial Workers of the World (IWW), 119–20; International Ladies' Garment Workers Union (ILGWU), 120; Knights of Labor, 120; National Labor Relations Act, 260; right-to-work laws, 378; sit-down strike, 260–61; Southern Tenant Farmers Union, 251; Taft-Hartley Act of 1947, 301, 377–78; Union of Russian Workers, 178; United Auto Workers, *c238*; United Auto Workers (UAW), 260–61; United Mine Workers (UMW), 117, 201, 260; Wagner Act, 260; Women's Trade-Union League (WTUL), 120; during World War I, 173; during World War II, 301, 303
United Auto Workers (UAW), *c238*, 260–61
United Farm Workers, *c482*
United Kingdom. *See* **Britain; England**.
United Mine Workers (UMW), 117, 201, 260
United Nations (UN): Convention on the Prevention and Punishment of the Crime of Genocide, 335; creation of, 333–34; first African American ambassador to, 353; General Assembly, 333; invasion of Iraq, 570–71; Korean War, 340; Roosevelt supporting, 333–34; Saudi Arabia, 537; Security Council, 333; trade embargo on Haiti, 550; UN Commission on Human Rights, 335; Universal Declaration of Human Rights, 335

United States, government of: American flag, 32; Articles of Confederation, *c6*, 19–21; birth of, 10, 13; checks and balances, *c26*, 27; citizens' responsibilities, 31–32; computer research, 544; concurrent powers, 26; conservatives' view of, 531–32; Constitutional changes to, 23; Declaration of Independence, 10, 13–18, *p13*; as democratic republic, 13, 24; enumerated powers of, 26; E. Pluribus Unum, 33; establishing branches of, 22, 23–24; executive branch, *c26*, 28–29; federalism, 25–26; "In God We Trust," 34; Great Seal of the United States, 33; individual rights, 27; judicial branch, *c26*, 29–30; legislative branch, *c26*, 27; liberals' view of, 531; limited government, 25; living document (Constitution), 34; popular sovereignty, 25; republicanism, 25; reserved powers, 26; rights of Americans, 30–31; separation of powers, 26–27, *c26*; Star-Spangled Banner, 33–34; two-house legislature, 22; in UN Security Council, 333. *See also* **Constitution of the United States; executive branch; judicial branch; legislative branch.**

United States Commission on Civil Rights, 421, 423

United States Constitution. *See* **Constitution of the United States.**

United States Housing Authority, 263

United States* v. *Bhagat Singh Thind, 226

United States* v. *E.C. Knight, 116–17

Universal Declaration of Human Rights, 243, 335

Universal Negro Improvement Association (UNIA), 214

***Up from Slavery* (Booker T. Washington)**, *q142*

upper-class people: architecture, 131; clothing and lifestyle of, 131; Gospel of Wealth, 134; during Reagan administration, 534–35; women, role in society, 131; women's clubs, 131

Upward Bound, 388

urbanization: class structures impacted by, 131–32; crime impacted by, 133; immigration

and, *p132*, 133; mass transit, 131; migration to cities, 131–33; party bosses, 133; poverty in, 370; problems with, *p132*, 133; rise of political machines, 133; skyscrapers, 131; working class, 135–36

urban life: for African Americans post-World War II, 381–82; drug abuse, 536; in late 1800s, 131–33, *p132*

urban renewal programs, 382

urban riots, Watts Riots triggering, 435

USA PATRIOT Act, 568–69

U.S. Border Patrol, 491

U.S. Citizenship and Immigration Services, *q591*

U.S. Department of Defense, 542

U.S. Department of Agriculture (USDA), 202

U.S. foreign policy: in 1950 and 60s, 339–44; in 1970s and 80s, 351–54; after World War II, 331; Boxer Rebellion, 155; Central America, 155; of Clinton, 550; containing communism, 336–37; Cuban Missile Crisis, *c332*, 343–44, *m344*; Détente Policy, 351–52; Dominican Republic, 155, 165; Haitian Intervention, 550; Haitian Revolution, 155; imperialism, 154, *m155*, 157–62; Intermediate Range Nuclear Forces (INF) Treaty, 355, *cHT4*; Jimmy Carter's, 353; Latin American nations, 155, 163–64; Marshall Plan, 331, 337–38, *g337*; Nixon Doctrine, 351; nuclear disarmament, 355; Panama independence, 153; Point Four Program, 337; Reagan Doctrine, 354; during Roosevelt, Theodore administration, 201; South America, 155; Strategic Arms Reduction Talks (START), 355; in Turkey and Greece, 337; Vietnamization, 351; of Woodrow Wilson, 165–66, 167. *See also* **American diplomacy; Cold War.**

U.S. Forest Service, 202

USS *Cole*, 568

USS *Maine*, *c156*, 159

U.S. spy plane, *c332*

U.S. Steel, *c92*, 112, 117, 177, *crt185*

U.S. Training and Industrial Schools, 104

Utah: Boulder Canyon Project Act, 234; water rights, 518; women's suffrage, 199

V

Valentino, Rudolph, 212

Valley Forge, 10

Vanderbilt, Cornelius, 131

Vanzetti, Bartolomeo, 225–26, 330

V-E (Victory in Europe) Day, *c280*, 310

Veiller, Lawrence, 132

Veracruz, 166

Vermonia School District* v. *Acton, 536

vernacular writing, 192

vertical integration, 111–12, *c150*

veterans: African American post-World War II, 370, 377; GI Bill, 370, *c372*, 377; Latinos and Mexican Americans, 492

Vichy, 284

Victory Bonds, 173, *g174*

victory gardens, 173, 303

"victory suits", 303

video cassette recorders (VCRs), 535

video games, 535

Vietcong: battle tactics of, 454–56, 458; South Vietnamese Communists, 448, 452–53; Tet Offensive, 460, 464

Vietminh, 448, 451, 452, 463

Vietnam: after the war, 470; becomes Socialist Republic of Vietnam, 449; Buddhism, 453; Dien Bien Phu, 452; division of, 452, 463; as French colony, 448; French leaving, 452; history of, 448; Ho Chi Minh, 448, 451, *p451*, *p453*; importance of, *m449*; under Japanese military, 448, 451; Paris Peace Accords, *c450*; U.S. combat troops in, *c450*, *g470*, *p470*; U.S. military aid and advisers in, *c450*, 452–53, *g452*; Vietminh, 448, 451–52

***Vietnam, A History* (Ronald J. Glasser)**, *q454*

Vietnamization, 351, 467

Vietnam Veterans Against the War, 468

Vietnam Veterans Memorial, 471, *p471*

Vietnam War: Agent Orange, 455; antiwar movement, 446, 448–49, *c450*, 457–62; bloody stalemate, 454; Calley, William, 467–68; Cambodia invasion, *c450*, 467, 468; Cold War and, 448; Cu Chi tunnels, 455; domino theory, 452; "Doves" versus "Hawks," 460; draft during, 446, 449, 458–60; Emergency Medical Technicians

(EMTs), 455; failure of, 449; Gulf of Tonkin Resolution, *c450*, 454, 457, 469; History of U.S. Decision-Making in Vietnam, 1945–68 (Daniel Ellsberg), 469; Ho Chi Minh Trail, 455–56, *m456*, 467; horrors of, 446; Huey helicopter, 455, *p455*; human toll of, 470–71; Johnson, Lyndon Baines, 454, 457, 460, 463, 464–65, *q465*; long-range radios, 455; malaria, jungle rot, dysentery, 446; Marines, *p445*; missing in action (MIA), 469, 471; My Lai massacre, 468; napalm, *p454*, 455; "National Teach-In," 458; nation's impact from, 471–72; Nixon and Kissinger's policy on, 351; Nixon's policies to end, 467; Operation Frequent Wind, 470, *p472*, *p474*; opposition to, 457–62, *g460*, *g475*; Paris Peace Accords, *c450*; Pentagon Papers, 469; prisoners of war (POWs), 469, 471; *Rumor of War, A* (Philip Caputo), *q454*; Saigon falling, 446, *c450*; search-and-destroy mission, 455; teach-ins, 458; Tet Offensive, *c450*, 460, 464; United States involvement ends, 469–70; U.S. combat troops in, *c450*, 454, *g470*, *p470*; Vietminh, 448, 452; *Vietnam, A History* (Ronald J. Glasser), *q454*; Vietnamization, 467; Vietnam Veterans Memorial, *p448*; war of attrition, 456; Westmoreland, William, 457–58, *p457*. *See also specific wars.*

Virginia: African American Loyalist militia, 10; Dunmore, governor of Virginia, 10; House of Burgesses, 8, 9; interracial marriage laws, 497; Loyalists in, 10; Virginia Resolves, 8

Virginia City, NV, 90, 93, *m94*

Virginia Plan, 22–23

VISTA program, 547

Vitale, William, 392

Vivian, C.T., *q430*

V-J (Victory Over Japan) Day, *c280*, 318

vocational education, 136

Voices of Freedom (John A. Stokes), *q415*

Voices of Freedom (Ruth Batson), *q439*

Volstead Act, 228

Volunteers in Service to America (VISTA), 388, 398

Volusia County, 2000 elections, 565

von Braun, Wernher, 371

von Steuben, Friedrich, 10, 11
voting rights. *See* suffrage.
Voting Rights Act of 1965, 200, *c410*, 427–28, *m428*, 607

W

Wabash, St. Louis & Pacific Railway Company v. *Illinois*, 115–16, 137
Wagner Act, 260
wagon trains, *m62*
Wald, Lillian, 120, 136, 198
Walk East on Beacon, 376
Walker, Aida Overton, 212
Walker, Alice, 192
Walker, Charles J., 116
Walker, Madam C. J., 116, *p116*
Walker, Quock, 12
Wallace, George, 424, 461, *m462*, 521
Wallace, Henry A., 379
Wall Street: explosions on, *p178*; stock market crash (1929), 237, *c238*, 240, 245, *p245*, 246, *p246*
Walmart, 535
Walton, Sam, 535
Wanamaker, John, 112
Wannsee Conference, 290
war bonds, 303
Ward, Lester Frank, 135, *p135*
War Industries Board (WIB), 173
War Labor Board (WLB), 303
Warner, Charles, 133
"War on Drugs", 536
War on Terror: Afghanistan, 560, 568, 569–70, 585; al-Qaeda, 560, 568, 569; anthrax attacks, 569; bin Laden, Osama, 560, 568; *Boumediene* v. *Bush*, 573; Guantánamo Bay, Cuba, 573; *Hamdan* v. *Rumsfeld*, 573; Iraq, 560, *c562*, 570–71, *p571*; Islamic State in Iraq and Syria (ISIS), 572; Military Commissions Act, 573; National Security Agency (NSA), 573–74; national security versus civil liberties, 573; Office of Homeland Security, 568; *Rasul* v. *Bush*, 573; Taliban, 560, 568, 569–70; USA PATRIOT Act, 568–69; wiretapping domestic calls, 573–74
War Powers Act, 471–72
War Production Board (WPB), 302
Warren, Earl, 386–87, 391, *p391*, *q394*, 418, 521
Warren Commission, 387
Warren Court, 386–87, 391–94, *p391*, 418

wars. *See specific* wars.
Warsaw ghetto, *p292*
Warsaw Pact, 338
Washington, Booker T., 136, 141, *141–q42*, 214, 409
Washington, George: Constitution, presenting, 34; at Constitutional Convention, 21–22; as Continental Army commander, 9; in French and Indian War, 7; House of Burgesses, 8; Valley Forge, 10
Washington Conference, 225
Washington Daily News (Evelyn Peyton Gordon), *q297*
Washington Post, 523
"The Watergate Committee," U.S. Senate: Select Committee on Presidential Campaign Activities, *q526*
Watergate scandal, 470, 518, 523–24, 525–30, *p525*, *crt529*, *c553*
water management projects, 255
Water Quality Act, 389
water rights, Colorado River, 518
Watkins, Gloria Jean, 485, *p485*, 506
Watts Riot, 435
Wayne, Anthony, 10
wealthy people. *See* upper-class people.
weapons of mass destruction (WMD), 570
Weaver, James B., 139
Weaver, Randy, 552
Weaver, Robert, 389
Webb, James E., 348
web URLs, HT12
Welch, Joseph, 375–76
Welfare Reform Act, 551
welfare system, 522
Wells, Ida B., 140, 141, 200, 213, 408–09, 429
West, Dorothy, 216
West Bank, 550
West Berlin: Berlin Airlift, *c332*, 338; France, Britain, and United States controlling, 330, 334, *m334*; Khrushchev demanding, 342; as part of West Germany, 338; reunification of, 357
Western Europe: Marshall Plan, 337–38, *g337*; Point Four Program, 337–38; post-war economy, 337–38; post-World War II, 337. *See also* Europe.
Western Hemisphere, HT26
West Germany: Berlin Airlift, *c332*; Federal Republic of Germany, 338; France, Britain, and United States controlling, 330, 334, *m334*; reunification of, *p327*,

c332, 357, 359, *p359*; Stasi, 357; united with East Germany, *c332*
Westinghouse, George, 110
Westinghouse Company, 209
Westmoreland, William, 457, *p457*
westward expansion: agriculture, 90; California Gold Rush, 90; cattle ranches, 90; mining impacting, 93, *m94*; Native Americans, 91; Oklahoma Land Rush, *c92*; in Oregon territory, 61–62; overlanders, *m62*; railroads impacting, 90, *m91*; reasons for, 61; slavery, 61; to Southwest, 96; into Texas territory, 62–63
Weyler, Valeriano, 159
Wharton, Edith, 211
What It Was Like To Go To War (Karl Marlantes), *q446*
"What We Want," *New York Review of Books*, *q437*
Wheat Belt, 98
Wheeler-Howard Act of 1934, 250
Whigs: Northern Whigs, 65; Southern Whigs, 65
"Whip Inflation Now", 390
whistleblower, 605
White, Walter, 214
White Citizens' Council of Mississippi, 419
white-collar jobs, 382
white flight, 439
The White House, "President Trump: 'We Have Rejected Globalism and Embraced Patriotism'", *q617*
White Pass Trail, 88
Whitewater Development, 552
Whitney, Eli, 111
"Why Veterans March Against the War" (Jan Berry), *q468*
"Why We the People? Citizens as Agents of Constitutional Change," *History Now* (Linda R. Monk), *q59*
Wilder, L. Douglas, 440
Wilderness Society, 578
Wiley, W.H., 201, 205
Wilkins, Roy, 422
Willamette Valley, 62
Williams, Robert F., 436
Williams, Daniel Hale, 141
Williams, Hosea, 427
Williams, William Carlos, 211
Wills, Helen, 212
Wilson, Darren, 587–88
Wilson, Pete, 539
Wilson, Woodrow: "America First," 597; Committee on Public Information (CPI), 180; economic regulation, 115; elections of

1912, 207; foreign policy, 165–66, 167; Fourteen Points, 176, *q181*; income taxes, 207; Mexico intervention, 155, 165–66; Progressive Era reforms, 207–08; Revenue Act of 1913, 207; Treaty of Versailles, 177; women backing re-election, 200; World War I, joining, 171; World War I neutrality, 168
Windows, 542
Windsor v. *United States*, 587
Winfrey, Oprah, 535
Winkel Tripel Projection, HT24, *mHT24*
Winnemem Wintu, 255
Winslow, Rose, 200
wireless digital technology, 542
Wisconsin, direct primary nomination, 194, 198
Wizard of Oz, The, 251
Wolfe, Thomas, 252
Woman's Peace Party, 169
women, employment of: during the 50s and 60s, 480, 483; African American, 506; in armed forces during World War II, 279, 301; Army Nurse Corps, 174, 279, 301; Bethune, Mary McLeod, 333; Brunauer, Esther, 375, *p375*; Chisholm, Shirley, 440, 478, *q486*; Civil Rights Act of 1964, 484; Equal Employment Opportunity Commission (EEOC), 484; Equal Pay Act, 386, 480, 484; Ferraro, Geraldine, 534; hooks, bell, 485, *p485*, 506; inequality for, 483–84; "Jane Crow," 485; Knights of Labor, 119; McCormick, Ruth Hanna, 201; organized labor, 120; Owen, Ruth Bryan, 201; percentage in the workforce, *g488*; in political office, 201; post-World War II, 378; "Rosie the Riveter," 302; Sandra Day O'Connor, first female Supreme Court justice, 516, *p517*, 534; Sanger, Margaret, 227; unions discriminating against, 119; Watkins, Gloria Jean, 485, *p485*; Women Airforce Service Pilots (WASPs), 301; Women's Army Auxiliary Corps (WAAC), 301; Women's Army Corps (WAC), 301; Women's Bureau, 201; working class during late 1800s, 132–33, *p132*; during World War I, 173; during World War II, 301, 302
women, role in society: in 1920s, 226–27; in Algonquian culture, 5; in armed forces during World War I, 174; Army Nurse Corps, 174; Black Panther

Party for Self Defense, 438; Civil Works Administration (CWA), 257; in early 1900s, *p191*, 195; in Iroquois culture, 5; jazz reflecting new roles, 216; in Mississippian cultures, 4; in Pentecostal movement, 228; post-World War II, 378; Prohibition, 195; during Revolutionary War, 12; social-welfare movement, 197; in Supreme Court, 516, *p517*, 534; in upper-class society, 131; Women's Club of Chicago, 131; during World War II, 279

Women Accepted for Volunteer Military Service (WAVES), 303

Women Airforce Service Pilots (WASPs), 301

Women's Army Auxiliary Corps (WAAC), 301

Women's Army Corps (WAC), 301

Women's Bureau, 201, 386

Women's Joint Congressional Committee (WJCC), 201

women's march, 605–06

Women's Political Council, 419

women's rights: abortion rights, *c482*, 487–88, 532, 549; Abzug, Bella, 478; African American, 506; American Birth Control League, 227; Belmont, Alva, *p480*; birth control, 227, 387, 484; Chisholm, Shirley, 440, 478, *q486*; Eastman, Crystal, 478; Educational Amendment, Title IX, 487, *p487*; education equality, 487; Equal Pay Act, 386, 480; Equal Rights Amendment (ERA), 478, *p479*, *p480*, *c482*, 484, 485–87, *m486*; Friedan, Betty, 478, *p483*, 484, *q484*; "Jane Crow," 485; marital privacy rights, 487; National Organization for Women (NOW), 478; origins of feminist movement, 483–85; Paul, Alice, 478; Presidential Commission on the Status of Women, 386, 484; reproductive rights, 399, 487–88; right to privacy, 487–88; *Roe* v. *Wade*, *c482*; Ruckelshaus, Jill, 478; Schlafly, Phyllis, 478; Steinem, Gloria, 478; Striebel, Charlotte, 487. *See also* **feminist movement, modern**.

women's suffrage, *m199*; Addams, Jane, 136, 169; Anthony, Susan B., 140, 199; Catt, Carrie Chapman, 169; in Colorado, 199; Connecticut Woman Suffrage Association, 70; *Declaration of Sentiments*, 199; Hooker, Isabella Beecher,

70; Howe, Julia Ward, 199; hunger strikes, 200; in Idaho, 199; National American Woman Suffrage Association, 145; National Association of Colored Women, 145; Nineteenth Amendment, *cHT4*, 51, 195, *c196*, 200–201; pickets and protests, 200; Progressive Era reforms, 198–201; "Progress of Colored Women, The" (Mary Church Terrell), 145; Seneca Falls convention, 199; Stanton, Elizabeth Cady, 199; Stone, Lucy, 199; by state governments, 199; in Utah, 199; in Wyoming, 199

Women's Trade-Union League (WTUL), 120

Wood, Grant, 252, *ptg252*

Woods, Granville T., 114

Woods, Rose Mary, 528

Woodson, Carter G., 222

Woodward, Bob, 523

Woolworth's, 112

Woolworth's sit-ins, 421

workers' rights: progressive ideals, 197; workers' "Magna Carta," 208

Work Experience Program, 388

workforce: industrial advantage of, 109; women during World War I, 173; during World War I, 173–74

working class: auto commuter, 209; computers impacting, 545; in early 1900s, 208; Fair Labor Standards Act, 263; living conditions of, 132–33, *p132*; Social Gospel movement, 135–36; standard of living, 208; Tenement House Act of 1901, 132; Tenement House Commission, 132; Tenement House Department, 132; working condition, 118–20. *See also* **unions**.

workplace segregation, 412

Works Progress Administration (WPA), 259–60, 263

World Bank, creation of, 333

world currency system, 333

World Health Organization, *m561*

World Health Organization (WHO), 609–10

world in spatial terms, *cHT21*

World Trade Center: September 11, 2001, *p557*; "Tribute in Light," *p557*

World Trade Organization (WTO), 540–41

World War I, *m170*; African American workers during, 174; aftermath of, 175–76; aircraft used in, 172; alliances,

167–68; Allies, countries of, 168; America enters, 171; American Expeditionary Force (AEF), 175; American interventionism, 155; American Jewish Joint Distribution Committee, 175; American neutrality debate, 168–69; American victory parade, *p179*; Armistice ending, *c156*, 175; armored tanks, 172; arms race before, 167; Army Nurse Corps, 174; Austria-Hungary, 175; Austria-Hungary/Serbia war, 168; beginning of, 168; Belgium, 168; blockades, 169; bombs, 172; Britain declaring war, 168; Cantigny, 175; Central Powers, countries of, 168; Château-Thierry, 175; Clemenceau, Georges, 176; Committee on Public Information (CPI), 174–75; Czechoslovakia, 175; elections of 1916, 168; ending of, 175–76; Espionage Act, 175, *crt184*; Food Administration, 173; Fuel Administration, 173; George, David Lloyd, 176; home front, 173–74; Hungary, 175; industry, 173–74; Jewish Welfare Board, 175; labor unions, 173; League of Nations, 176, 177, 181, 182; Liberty Bonds, 173, *g174*; *Lusitania* sinking, *c156*, 170; machine gun, 172; militarism, 167; National War Labor Board (NWLB), 173; Ottoman Empire, 175; paying for, 173–74, *g174*; poison chlorine gas (weaponized), 172; Poland, 175; propaganda, 169, 180; recruitment posters, *ptg151*; Russia leaving, 175; Russian Revolution, 175; Sedition Act, 175, *crt184*; *Sussex* sinking, 170; taxes during, 173; Treaty of Brest-Litovsk, 175; Treaty of Versailles, 176; trench warfare, *m170*, 171–72; U.S. economy during, 173–74; U.S. joins, *c156*; Victory Bonds, 173, *g174*; victory gardens, 173; War Industries Board (WIB), 173; women in armed forces during, 174; workforce, 173–74; zeppelin fleet, 172; Zimmermann, Arthur, 170

World War II: 761st Tank Battalion, 301; African American regiments in, 276; Afrika Korps, 305; Alien Registration Act of 1940, 304; Allies bombing Germany, 307; Allies invading Morocco and Algeria, 305; in America, 278–79, *p278*; American deaths in, 306;

American economy during, 301; amphibious invasion, 319, *m319*; amphtrac, 315; appeasement policy, 283; Army Nurse Corps, 279, 301; Atlantic Charter, 286; Axis Powers, 285; B-24 "Liberator" bombers, 302; B-29 Superfortress, 316, 317; Baker, Vernon, 276, *p277*; Battle of Iwo Jima, 313, 316–17, *p317*; Battle of Kasserine Pass, 305; Battle of Leyte Gulf, 316; Battle of Midway, 313–14, *m314*; Battle of the Atlantic, 306; Battle of the Bulge, 310; *blitzkrieg*, 284; bombing campaign, 307; Bracero program, 304, 387, 489–90; Bradley, Omar, 309; Bretton Woods System, 333; Britain and France defending Belgium, 284; Casablanca Conference, 307; code-breaking, 313; communism versus capitalism, 330–31; concentration camps, 290–91, *m290*; convoy system, 305; cost-plus system, 301; Davis, Benjamin O., 300–301; D-Day invasion, *c280*, 308–09, *p308*, 319–22, *m319*, *m324*; Declaration of Liberated Europe, 334; depth charges, 306; Destroyers-for-Bases, 285; "dollar-a-year men," 301; Doolittle Raid, 312–13; Dunkirk evacuations, 284, *p284*; *Einsatzgruppen*, 292; Eisenhower, Dwight D., 305; *Enterprise*, 314; European Recovery Program, 337; Executive Order 9066 (Japanese internment), 304, *p304*; extermination camps, 290, *m290*, 291–92; Fair Employment Practices Commission, 303; Filipinos during, 311–12, 312; Final Solution, 290–92; firebombing of Tokyo, 317; France and England declaring war, 278, 283–84; France falls, 284; German and Italian immigrants restricted, 304; Germany attacking Netherlands, Belgium, and Luxembourg, 284; Germany surrendering, 310; global scale of, *m279*; Goebbels, Joseph, 287; Guadalcanal, 316; Guam, 315; hemispheric defense zone, 286; Hirohito, emperor of Japan, 312, 317; Hispanics in, 301; Hitler, Adolf, 278, *c280*, 282; Hitler invading Poland, 278, 283–84; Hitler occupying

Austria and Czechoslovakia, 278, 283–84; Hitler's suicide, 310; Hitler underestimating U.S. strategy, 300; Hollandia, New Guinea, 316; Holocaust, the, 287–92, *m290*; *Hornet*, 314; industry, 301–02, *g302*; International Military Tribunal (IMT), 292; island hopping in the Pacific, 314, *m315*; Italy, *p276*; Italy and Germany declare war on U.S., 300; Italy and Sicily invasion, 307; Japanese Americans in military, 279, 301; Japanese internment, 304, *p304*; Japan invading Manchuria, 281; Japan invading Philippines, 311–12; kamikaze Japanese, 316; *Kristallnacht*, 287–88, *p288*; Kwajalein Atoll in the Marshall Islands, 315; *Lexington*, 313; Liberty ships, 302; London bombings, *p293*; Longest Day, 309; MacArthur recaptures Philippines, 316; Mariana Islands, 315; Marshall Islands, 315; Mexican people's migration during, 304; Midway Island, 312; minorities during, 303–04; "Miracle of Dunkirk," 284, *p284*; Morotai, 316; Munich Conference, 283, *p283*; Mussolini, Benito, 278, *c280*, 281–82, *p282*; napalm, 317; Native Americans in, 301; Navajo Code Talker, *p313*; Neutrality Act of 1935, 284–85, 294, *crt295*; Neutrality Act of 1936, 284–85, *crt295*; Neutrality Act of 1937, 285, *crt295*; Neutrality Act of 1939, 285, *crt295*; New Guinea, 314; Normandy, 308–09; Nuremberg Trials, 292; Nye Committee, 284, 294; Office of Economic Stabilization (OES), 303; Office of Price

Administration and Civilian Supply (OPACS), 303, Office of War Information (OWI), 303; Office of War Mobilization, 302; oil pipelines, 305; Okinawa, 317; Omaha beach, 309; Operation Overlord, 308–09; in the Pacific, 311–18; Paris liberated, 310; Patton, George, 305; Pearl Harbor, 278, *c280*, 299–300, *cHT4*; Potsdam Conference, 330; radar, 306; rationing coupons, 303; reparations, 334; *Reuben James*, 286; rise of dictators, 278; Rommel, Erwin (Desert Fox), 305; "Rosie the Riveter," 302; Saipan, 315; segregation in the workplace, 412; Solomon Islands, 314, 316; sonar, 306; Soviet Union deaths during, 306; Spanish Civil War, 285; Stalin, Joseph, 278, 282; strategies in Europe, 307–08; Suez Canal, 305; Tehran Declaration, *q307–q08*; time line of, *c323*; Tinian, 315; Tuskegee Airmen, 301, 417; unions during, 301, 303; United Nations created after, 333–34; U.S. foreign policy after, 331; U.S. military, building, 300–301, *g300*; U.S. neutrality, 278, 284–86, *crt285*, 293–98; V-E (Victory in Europe) Day, *c280*, 310; victory gardens, 303; "victory suits," 303; V-J (Victory Over Japan) Day, *c280*, 318; Wannsee Conference, 290; war bonds, 303; War Production Board (WPB), 302; women, role in society, 279, 301; Women Airforce Service Pilots (WASPs), 301; women in armed forces during, 279, 301; women in industry, 302; Women's Army Auxiliary Corps (WAAC), 301;

Women's Army Corps (WAC), 301; Yalta Conference, 328, *p329*; *Yorktown*, 313, 314

World War II: From the Battle Front to the Home Front (Luther D. Fletcher), 291

World Wide Web, 542

Wounded Knee, 101

Wounded Knee protest, 496

Wozniak, Stephen, 542

Wright brothers, Wilbur and Orville, 209

Wright, Moses, 420

writers and poets (1920s): Bentley, Gladys, 216; Cather, Willa, 211; Cullen, Countee, 216; Eliot, T. S., 211; Fitzgerald, F. Scott, 212; folklore, 192; Harlem Renaissance, 192, 216; Hemingway, Ernest, 211, *p211*, 212; Hughes, Langston, 216, 220, *ptg220*; Hurston, Zora Neale, 192, *p193*, 216, 252; Lewis, Sinclair, 211; Locke, Alain, 216; Lowell, Amy, 211; McKay, Claude, 216; Millay, Edna St. Vincent, 211; Nugent, Richard Bruce, 216; O'Neill, Eugene, 211; Pound, Ezra, 211; Sandburg, Carl, 211; West, Dorothy, 216; Wharton, Edith, 211; Williams, William Carlos, 211

writers and poets (Great Depression): Faulkner, William, 252; Federal Project Number One, 260; Hurston, Zora Neale, 252; Steinbeck, John, 252; Wolfe, Thomas, 252

writing about history: authorship, HT12; credentials, HT11; plagiarism, HT12; researching history, HT11–HT12; web URLs, HT12

writ of habeas corpus, Guantánamo Bay, Cuba, 573

WTBS, 535

Wuhan, China, 609

Wyoming: Boulder Canyon Project Act, 234; statehood of, 90; water rights, 518; women's suffrage, 199

Y

Yalta Conference, 328, *p329*, 334, *m334*

Yamamoto, 312, 313

Yannacone, Carol and Victor, 577

Yeager, Chuck, 371

Yekl, A Tale of the New York Ghetto (A. Cahan), *q128*

yellow journalism, 159

Yeltsin, Boris, 357, *p357*, 361

Yoffeh, Zalmen, 132

York, Alvin Cullum, 171, *p171*

Yorktown, 313, 314

Young, Andrew, 353, 440

Young Americans for Freedom (YAF), 532

Young Corn (Grant Wood), *ptg252*

Young Men's Christian Association (YMCA), 135

Yucatán Peninsula, Cortés conquering, 5

Yugoslavia, division of, 358

Yukon Territory: Dawson City, 88; Dyea, 88; Klondike Gold Rush, 88, *p89*; Skagway, 88

Z

zeppelin fleet, 172

Zimmerman, George, 587

Zimmermann, Arthur, 170

"zoot suit" riots, 303